THE MESSAGE
THREE-WAY
CONCORDANCE

THE MESSAGE THREE-WAY CONCORDANCE

WORD | PHRASE | SYNONYM

Eugene H. Peterson

NAVPRESS®

BRINGING TRUTH TO LIFE

OUR GUARANTEE TO YOU

We believe so strongly in the message of our books that we are making this quality guarantee to you. If for any reason you are disappointed with the content of this book, return the title page to us with your name and address and we will refund to you the list price of the book. To help us serve you better, please briefly describe why you were disappointed. Mail your refund request to: NavPress, P.O. Box 35002, Colorado Springs, Co 80935.

ISBN 1-57683-938-9

www.messagebible.com.

Library of Congress Cataloging-in-Publication Data

The message three-way concordance.
   p. cm.
   ISBN 1-57683-938-9
   1. Bible--Concordances, English--Message. I. NavPress (Firm) II. Bible. English. Message.
   BS425.M38 2006
   220.5'208--dc22

2005035691

Published in association with the literary agency of Alive Communications, Inc., 7680 Goddard St., Suite 200, Colorado Springs, CO 80920.

Printed in the United States of America

1 2 3 4 5 6 7 8 9 10 / 12 11 10 09 08 07 06

CONTENTS

THE MESSAGE THREE-WAY CONCORDANCE
INTRODUCTION

The Message has become one of the most popular reading Bibles in the United States. Eugene Peterson's unique Bible translation has opened the Scriptures in a fresh new way to millions of readers, helping them connect the truths of the Bible to their daily lives.

Readers of *The Message*, however, needed a companion tool to help them use this translation in personal Bible study. Words or phrases that opened up a passage for them were hard to find in other parts of Scripture. And when studying a theme based on words found in a traditional translation, it was difficult to find parallel themes in *The Message*.

The Message Three-Way Concordance gives readers of *The Message* three tools to mine the richness of Peterson's translation for their study of Scripture. Like *The Message* itself, this concordance is unique:

It's a word concordance that features the contemporary words unique to *The Message*. To ensure usability, not every word in *The Message* has been included. We've eliminated conjunctions (and, the), pronouns (he, she, they), minor biblical words, and other common biblical words that appear too often to be listed.

It's a synonym concordance that helps you bridge the gap between words you may be familiar with in a traditional translation (such as the NIV or KJV) and connect them with synonymous words used by Peterson in *The Message*.

It's a phrase concordance that lists entire phrases that are unique to the visual writing style Peterson employs in *The Message*. One of the features readers appreciate most about *The Message* is Eugene Peterson's ability to use not just individual words but entire phrases to communicate biblical concepts.

Now your favorite *reading* Bible can be a valuable tool in your personal *study* of the Scriptures as well!

CONCORDANCE

KEY WORDS AND THEIR REFERENCES
FOUND IN *THE MESSAGE BIBLE*

A

Abandon

Lev	21:12	neither **a** nor desecrate the Sanctuary
Dt	4:31	In the end he will not **a** you
	28:20	evil pursuits that led you to **a** me
	31:16	will **a** me and violate my Covenant
Jdg	5:2	The people volunteered with **a**
	5:9	Lift your hearts high . . . with **a**
	15:18	Are you going to **a** me to die
1Sa	15:30	I have sinned. But don't **a** me
2Sa	6:14	danced with great **a** before God
1Ki	22:36	**A** camp! Head for home
1Ch	28:9	if you **a** him, he'll leave you
2Ch	12:5	You abandoned me; now I **a** you
Ezr	9:9	even as slaves, our God didn't **a** us
Job	22:24	**a** your gold-plated luxury
Ps	27:9	Don't throw me out, don't **a** me
	89:33	never **a** or disown
	124:6	didn't **a** us defenseless
SS	4:8	**A** your wilderness seclusion
Isa	55:7	Let the wicked **a** their way of life
	65:11	But you who **a** me, your God
Jer	12:7	I will **a** the House of Israel
	14:21	Don't . . . **a** your glorious Temple
	29:11	take care of you, not **a** you
Eze	27:29	Sailors everywhere **a** ship
Joel	2:17	Don't **a** your heritage to contempt
Zec	9:7	**a** his vile ways
Mt	5:24	**a** your offering, leave immediately
Jn	8:29	He doesn't **a** me
Ac	6:2	**a** our responsibilities
	7:19	forcing us to **a** our newborn infants
	14:15	**a** these silly god-superstitions
Ro	3:3	God didn't **a** them
2Co	9:10	giving to the needy in reckless **a**

Abandoned

Nu	21:29	daughters **a** as captives
Dt	29:25	they **a** the Covenant of the God
	32:15	He **a** the God who made him
Jos	22:3	you have not **a** your brothers
Jdg	5:6	Public roads were **a**
	16:20	didn't realize that God had **a** him
1Ki	11:33	He faithlessly **a** me and went off
	19:10	people of Israel have **a** your covenant
	19:14	people of Israel have **a** your covenant
2Ki	7:10	tents **a** just as they were
	18:30	city will never be **a** to the king
1Ch	10:7	they **a** their cities and ran off
2Ch	12:1	had virtually **a** God and his ways
	12:5	You **a** me; now I abandon you
	21:10	Since Jehoram had **a** God
Ne	9:30	when they refused to listen you **a** them
	13:11	Why has The Temple of God been **a**?
Ps	37:25	not once have I seen an **a** believer
	71:11	God has **a** him. Pounce on him now
	78:60	He walked off and . . . **a** the shrine
	88:5	**A** as already dead
Isa	1:8	like a sinking ship **a** by the rats

	17:9	their fortress cities will be **a**
	31:6	the One you so cruelly **a**
	42:22	feeling ignored, **a**
	54:3	you're going to resettle **a** cities
	54:6	like an **a** wife, devastated with grief
Jer	4:7	your cities in rubble, **a**
	7:33	Corpses **a** in the open air
	9:13	Because they **a** my plain teaching
	49:25	bereft, **a**! The once famous city
	49:33	camps **a** to wind and sand
	50:6	They **a** them in the mountains
	50:7	They **a** the True Pasture
La	2:7	God **a** his altar
Eze	20:26	I **a** them. Filthy in the gutter
	21:12	my people—**a** to the sword!
Da	10:8	**a** by my friends, I went weak
Joel	1:17	Grain silos **a**. Who needs them?
Mic	1:6	leave her **a** foundations exposed
Mal	2:8	you priests have **a** the way of priests
Mt	27:46	My God, my God, why have you **a** me
Mk	15:34	My God, my God, why have you **a** me
Lk	10:40	my sister has **a** the kitchen to me
Jn	14:27	feeling **a**, bereft
	16:32	I'm not **a**. The Father is with me
Ro	3:3	**a** their post? God didn't abandon them

Abandoning

Dt	31:29	**a** the way I commanded
1Ki	11:9	furious with Solomon for **a** the God
2Ki	7:7	**a** tents, horses, donkeys
2Ch	21:10	God was **a** him
Ps	40:3	enter the mystery, **a** themselves to God
Eze	23:28	**a** you to those you hate
Mt	4:22	**a** boat and father
Jn	10:32	saving your own skins and **a** me
Jude	1:6	**a** it for other, darker missions

Abhor

Lev	26:30	I'll **a** you
	26:44	I won't reject or **a** or destroy them
Job	30:10	They **a** me, they abuse me
Pr	16:12	Good leaders **a** wrongdoing of all kinds

Abhorrent

Lev	18:22	That is **a**
	18:26	must not do any of these **a** things
	18:29	do any of these **a** things
	18:30	don't engage in any of the **a** acts
	20:13	both of them have done what is **a**
Pr	17:15	are equally **a** to God

Abhors

Job	19:19	Everyone I've ever been close to **a** me

Abide

Ps	119:168	I . . . **a** by your counsel

Abiding

Isa	58:2	right-living people — law-a
Lk	16:8	law-a citizens
Tit	3:1	respect the government and be law-a
1Jn	3:24	his deep and a presence in us

Ability

Ex	35:31	with skill, a, and know-how
	36:2	God had gifted with the a to work
1Ki	3:11	you have asked for the a to lead
Mt	13:54	How did he get so wise, get such a
Mk	6:2	all of a sudden, get such a
1Co	14:13	a to bring others into that intimacy

Able-bodied

2Sa	24:9	800,000 a fighting men in Israel
Mt	12:29	enter the house of an awake, a man
Mk	3:27	enter the house of an awake, a man

Abolish

Mic	5:12	I'll a your religious black markets
1Jn	3:8	to a the Devil's ways

Abolishing

Da	8:13	the a of daily worship
Hos	13:14	I'm a regret, banishing sorrow

Abominable

Dt	14:3	Don't eat anything a
	18:9	don't take on the a ways of life
	18:12	such a practices
2Ki	16:3	truly a act
2Ch	28:3	truly a thing
Isa	44:19	used the rest to make an a no-god

Abominate

Dt	7:26	Hate it. A it. Destroy it

Abomination

Dt	7:25	it's an a to God
	12:31	every imaginable a with their gods
	13:14	this a did in fact take place
	17:1	That's an a, an insult to God
	17:4	an a has been committed in Israel
	18:12	these things are an a to God
	22:5	an a to God
	23:18	both an a to God
	24:4	her remarriage would be an a
	25:16	Dishonest weights . . . are an a to God
	27:15	a god-image — an a to God
2Ki	23:13	the south slope of A Hill

Abominations

Dt	7:26	bring one of these a home
	20:18	practice the a that they engage in
2Ch	36:14	repeating the a of the pagans
Rev	17:5	mother of whores and a of the earth

About-face

Jos	8:21	toward the wilderness did an a
Pr	15:24	it's a clean a from descent into hell
Mk	4:12	making an a and getting forgiven

Absolution-offering

Ex	29:14	It is an A
	29:36	Offer a bull as an A for atonement
	30:10	the blood of the A of atonement
Lev	4:3	to God as an A for the sin
	4:8	the bull of the A
	4:14	a bull as an A
	4:20	as with the bull for the A
	4:21	It's the A for the congregation
	4:24	presence of God — it's an A
	4:25	the blood of the A
	4:29	lay his hand on the head of the A
	4:32	If he brings a lamb for an A
	4:33	lay his hand on the head of the A
	4:34	the blood of the A
	5:6	from the flock for an A
	5:7	one for the A
	5:8	first offer the one for the A
	5:9	the blood of the A
	5:11	fine flour for your A
	5:12	It's an A
	6:17	very holy, like the A
	6:25	for the A. Slaughter the A
	6:30	any A whose blood is brought
	7:7	Offering is the same as the A
	7:37	the Grain-Offering, the A
	8:2	the bull for the A
	8:14	the bull for the A
	9:2	bull-calf for your A
	9:3	male goat for an A
	9:7	sacrifice your A
	9:8	the calf as an A
	9:10	lobe of the liver from the A
	9:15	the A for the people
	9:22	the rituals of the A
	10:16	the goat of the A
	10:17	Why didn't you eat the A
	10:19	They sacrificed their A
	12:6	pigeon or dove for an A
	12:8	one for the A
	14:13	in the place where the A
	14:19	the priest will sacrifice the A
	14:22	one for an A
	14:31	one as an A
	15:15	offers one as an A
	15:30	priest will offer one for an A
	16:3	young bull for an A
	16:5	two male goats for an A

	16:6	bull for his own **A**
	16:9	the lot to God falls as an **A**
	16:11	his bull for an **A**
	16:15	goat designated as the **A**
	16:25	burn the fat of the **A**
	16:27	bull for the **A**
	23:19	one male goat for an **A**
Nu	6:11	offer one for the **A**
	6:14	healthy yearling ewe for an **A**
	6:16	offer up your **A**
	7:16	he-goat for an **A**
	7:22	he-goat for an **A**
	7:28	he-goat for an **A**
	7:34	he-goat for an **A**
	7:40	he-goat for an **A**
	7:46	he-goat for an **A**
	7:52	he-goat for an **A**
	7:58	he-goat for an **A**
	7:64	he-goat for an **A**
	7:70	he-goat for an **A**
	7:76	he-goat for an **A**
	7:82	he-goat for an **A**
	8:8	young bull for an **A**
	8:12	bulls, selecting one for the **A**
	15:24	he-goat as an **A**
	15:25	the Fire-Gift and **A**
	15:27	yearling she-goat as an **A**
	19:9	use in the Water-of-Cleansing, an **A**
	19:17	ashes from the burned **A**
	28:15	offered to God as an **A**
	28:22	goat as an **A**
	28:30	he-goat as an **A**
	29:5	he-goat as an **A**
	29:11	he-goat as an **A**
	29:16	he-goat as an **A**
	29:19	he-goat as an **A**
	29:22	he-goat as an **A**
	29:25	he-goat as an **A**
	29:28	he-goat as an **A**
	29:31	he-goat as an **A**
	29:34	he-goat as an **A**
	29:38	he-goat as an **A**
Dt	12:27	Sacrifice your **A**s
2Ch	29:21	he-goats to sacrifice as an **A**
	29:24	made an **A** with their blood
Ezr	6:17	as an **A** for all Israel
	8:35	he-goats as an **A**

Abstinence

Zec	7:3	day of mourning and **a** next August
1Co	7:6	commanding these periods of **a**

Absurd

1Co	1:23	miracle — and Greeks pass it off as **a**
	15:36	realize how **a** it is
Gal	5:11	is **a**. Why would I still be persecuted

Absurdity

1Sa	26:20	in life or death. The **a**!

Ecc	2:3	penetrate the **a** of life
Isa	57:12	expose the **a** of it all
1Co	1:25	next to the seeming **a** of God

Abuse

Ge	16:5	your fault that I'm suffering this **a**
	16:9	Put up with her **a**
Ex	22:21	Don't **a** or take advantage of strangers
Dt	24:14	Don't **a** a laborer who is destitute
Jdg	19:24	**A** them if you must, but don't
2Sa	14:7	rescue me from the **a** of the man
Ne	9:27	saved them from the cruel **a**
Job	17:5	leave a legacy of **a** to their children
	30:10	They abhor me, they **a** me
	31:38	furrows fill with tears from my **a**
Ps	10:14	the contempt, the **a**
	94:5	exploit and **a** your precious people
	105:14	permitted no one to **a** them
	107:39	**a** and evil and trouble declined
Pr	9:8	all you'll get for your pains is **a**
	10:6	wicked is a dark cave of **a**
	10:11	wicked is a dark cave of **a**
	11:29	Exploit or **a** your family
	12:10	bad people kick and **a** them
	15:28	the wicked are sewers of **a**
	28:16	leaders who lack insight, **a** abounds
Ecc	10:20	don't **a** your betters
Isa	9:4	The **a** of oppressors
	14:3	recover from the **a** and trouble
Jer	15:15	look at the **a** I'm taking
La	3:46	Our enemies shout **a**
Eze	35:12	all the vile **a** you've poured out
Mt	23:34	hounding them with **a**
1Co	6:9	use and **a** each other, use and **a** sex
	6:10	use and **a** the earth
2Co	12:10	cut me down to size — **a**
Eph	6:9	No **a**, please, and no threats
Heb	10:33	targets of every kind of **a**
	11:36	Others braved **a** and whips
	13:3	victims of **a**
	13:13	taking our share in the **a** of Jesus

Abused

Nu	20:15	viciously **a** both us and our ancestors
Dt	26:6	**a** and battered us
	28:29	**a** and robbed
	28:33	spend the rest of your lives **a**
1Sa	12:4	never **a** us
Job	5:4	out in the cold, **a** and exploited
	29:16	champion of **a** aliens
Ps	105:25	they **a** and cheated God's servants
Isa	14:2	ruling over those who had **a** them
Jer	12:14	bad neighbors who **a** the land
	51:51	humiliated, taunted and **a**
Eze	22:29	the poor and needy are **a**
Ro	1:27	they **a** and defiled one another
Jas	5:4	workers you used and **a**
1Pe	4:14	If you're **a** because of Christ

Abuser

Lk	13:34	**a** of the messengers of God

Abusers

Pr	29:13	The poor and their **a**
Isa	51:23	passed it over to your **a** to drink

Abuses

1Co	1:27	overlooks and exploits and **a**
Eph	5:29	No one **a** his own body

Abusing

2Ch	16:10	Asa started **a** some of the people
Job	19:3	have no conscience, **a** me like this
	19:22	Don't you ever tire of **a** me
Zec	11:16	using and **a** any and all
Mt	24:49	**a** the help
Ac	7:24	**a** one of them
1Th	4:5	not **a** it
Jas	2:6	you are **a** these same citizens

Abusive

Ge	16:6	Sarai was **a** to Hagar
Isa	10:20	fascinated by **a**, battering Assyria
Eze	22:7	insolent to parents, **a** to outsiders

Accountable

Ex	13:19	God will surely hold you **a**
Lev	24:15	Anyone who curses God will be held **a**
Job	13:26	hold me **a** for the sins of my youth
Pr	22:21	keep you **a** to those who sent you
Eze	20:4	Hold them **a**. Confront them
Jn	9:41	you're **a** for every fault

Accusation

Ge	26:21	he named it Sitnah (**A**
Dt	22:20	if it turns out that the **a** is true
Ezr	4:6	an **a** against those living in Judah
Ps	38:3	because of your **a**
Mt	26:60	making up one false **a** after another
	26:62	What do you have to say to the **a**
Mk	14:60	What do you have to say to the **a**
Ac	16:20	pulled them into a court with the **a**
	22:30	what was behind the Jewish **a**
Gal	2:17	are you ready to make the the **a**

Accusations

Ex	23:7	Stay clear of false **a**
Dt	1:16	Listen carefully to complaints and **a**
Job	27:5	no way I'll ever agree to your **a**
Mt	27:12	the **a** rained down hot and heavy
	27:13	long list of **a**
Mk	15:3	let loose a barrage of **a**
	15:4	That's quite a list of **a**

Lk	23:10	strident and shrill in their **a**
Ac	19:38	make all the **a** they want
	24:8	verify all these **a** when you examine
	25:7	hurling the most extreme **a**
	25:11	if there's nothing to their **a**
	25:15	brought a bunch of **a** against him
	25:19	**a** turned out to be nothing more than
	26:2	answering all these Jewish **a**

Accuse

Dt	19:16	hostile witness stands to **a** someone
1Sa	22:15	don't **a** me of any wrongdoing
Ne	6:13	good reputation so they could **a** me
Ps	109:6	Send the Evil One to **a**
Pr	30:10	They'll **a** you of being underhanded
Isa	59:12	our sins stand up and **a** us
Hos	2:2	Haul your mother into court. **A** her
Hab	2:11	your house will speak up and **a** you
Zec	3:1	the Accuser showed up to **a** him
Mt	26:65	Why do we need witnesses to **a** him
Lk	11:18	You **a** me of ganging up
Jn	5:45	don't think I'm going to **a** you
Ac	24:19	too cowardly to **a** me
	25:5	go back with me then and **a** him
	28:19	I did this not to **a** them
2Co	1:17	Are you now going to **a** me

Accused

Ge	42:30	spoke to us roughly and **a** us
	44:15	Joseph **a** them
Dt	22:17	now he has slanderously **a** her
1Ki	21:13	the two degenerates **a** him
Da	3:8	stepped up and **a** the Jews
Ac	25:16	Just because a man is **a**
Rev	12:10	who **a** them day and night

Accuser

Job	1:6	Satan, who was the Designated **A**
Isa	54:17	Any **a** who takes you to court
Zec	3:1	where the **A** showed up to accuse him
	3:2	said to the **A**, "I, God, rebuke you, **A**
Lk	12:58	settle up with your **a** on the way
Jn	5:45	whom you put so much stock, is your **a**
Rev	12:10	The **A** of our brothers and sisters

Accusers

Ps	7:7	My **a** have packed the courtroom
	35:11	Hostile **a** appear out of nowhere
	71:13	My **a**—make them lose face
	109:29	Dress my **a** in clothes dirty with shame
Isa	50:9	My **a** are a clothes bin of threadbare
Lk	21:15	reduce all your **a** to stammers
Ac	23:30	informing his **a**
	23:35	take up your case when your **a** show up
	24:15	my **a** are just as guilty as I
	25:16	face his **a** and defend himself
	25:18	**a** came at him from all sides

Accusing

2Ki	6:33	king showed up, a, "This trouble
Ps	109:6	Evil One to accuse my a judge
Jer	37:13	grabbed Jeremiah the prophet, a him
Mk	3:30	they were a him
Jn	3:17	point an a finger
1Jn	3:21	no longer a or condemning ourselves

Achieve

Pr	17:20	bad motive can't a a good end
Lk	1:15	He'll a great stature with God
Col	2:11	not something you figure out or a

Achievement

Isa	37:19	no great a since they were no-gods

Achievements

1Ki	22:45	Jehoshaphat's life, his a
2Ch	27:7	Jotham, including his wars and a
Job	21:28	the a of the wicked collapse
Isa	5:24	their a crumble into dust

Addicted

Pr	21:17	You're a to thrills
Jer	2:25	I'm a to alien gods
Eze	11:21	a to their rotten images
	20:7	vile things that you've become a to
	20:8	vile things they were a to
	20:24	remained a to the no god idols
Hos	4:17	Ephraim is a to idols
	11:12	no better, a to cheap gods
Am	6:6	those a to feeling good
Na	3:1	a to violence
Jn	3:20	a to denial and illusion
Eph	4:19	a to every sort of perversion
2Ti	3:4	a to lust
2Pe	2:10	a to a filthy existence
	2:13	despicable and a to pleasure
	2:19	they're a to corruption

Addictions

Gal	5:21	uncontrolled and uncontrollable a

Adopt

Eph	1:5	he decided to a us into his family

Adopted

Ex	2:10	Pharaoh's daughter who a him
2Ki	17:19	way of life that Israel had a
1Ch	22:10	He'll be my royal a son
	28:6	chosen him to be my royal a son
Est	2:7	Mordecai had a her
	2:15	a her as his daughter
Gal	4:6	now fully a as his own children

Adopting

Ge	48:5	I'm a your two sons

Adoration

Ps	139:14	I worship in a — what a creation
Mt	6:24	A of one feeds contempt for the other
Jn	4:24	spirits, their true selves, in a
1Co	11:13	angels, praying in a
1Pe	3:15	at attention, in a before Christ

Adore

Ps	22:23	give glory, you sons of Jacob; a him
	45:11	Since he's your lord, a him
Lk	16:13	a the first and despise the second

Adoring

Ps	2:11	Worship God in a embrace
Isa	57:8	a every curve of their naked bodies

Adorn

Hos	2:5	caress me, perfume and a me
Mt	13:43	lives will mature and a the kingdom

Adorned

Job	39:19	gave the horse his prowess and a him
Eze	16:11	I a you with jewelry
	23:42	They a the sisters with bracelets
Hos	2:8	wined and dined and a her
Rev	18:16	Dressed in the latest fashions, a

Adorning

Pr	20:15	better than a oneself with gold
Ecc	12:5	A a fragile . . . body

Adulterer

Lev	20:10	a and adulteress, must be put to death
Mt	5:32	automatically an a yourself

Adulterers

Ps	50:18	a are your friends of choice
Jer	23:10	A country teeming with a!
Hos	7:4	They're a bunch of overheated a
Mal	3:5	evidence against sorcerers, a
Lk	18:11	crooks, a

Adulteress

Lev	20:10	adulterer and a, must be put to death
Mt	5:32	responsible for making her an a
Ro	7:3	she's obviously an a

Adulteries

Jer	13:27	your god-a. Gods on the hills
Mt	15:19	vomit up evil arguments, murders, a
Mk	7:21	lusts, thefts, murders, a

Adulterous

Nu	5:19	have not had an a affair
Eze	16:38	the punishment for an a woman
Hos	4:14	the a wives of your sons

Adultery

Ex	20:14	No a
Lev	20:10	man commits a with another man's wife
Dt	5:18	No a
Job	31:12	A is a fire that burns the house down
Pr	6:32	A is a brainless act
Eze	23:37	a to murder. They committed a
	23:45	sentences for a and murder
Mt	14:4	his relationship with Herodias "a
	19:9	holding you liable for a
	19:18	Don't murder, don't commit a
Mk	6:18	his relationship with Herodias "a
	10:11	marry someone else commits a
	10:12	marry someone else commits a
	10:19	Don't murder, don't commit a
Lk	16:18	divorce as a cover for lust is a
Jn	8:3	caught in an act of a
	8:4	caught red-handed in the act of a
Ro	2:22	The same with a
Jas	2:11	God who said, "Don't commit a
2Pe	2:14	They're obsessed with a

Adversaries

Ps	68:1	A, run for the hills
Isa	9:11	God incited their a against them
	41:12	looking for your old a
Hab	3:7	Old wilderness a, Cushan and Midian

Adversary

1Ki	11:23	God incited another a against Solomon
Est	7:6	An enemy. An a. This evil Haman
Job	27:7	Let my a be proven guilty

Adversity

Pr	18:14	A healthy spirit conquers a
Lk	16:9	using every a to stimulate you

Advocate

1Sa	18:1	David's number-one a and friend
Pr	23:11	a powerful A who will go to bat
Jer	40:10	be your a before the Chaldeans

Affair

Nu	5:12	wife goes off and has an a

	5:19	you have not had an adulterous a
	5:20	if you have had an a while married
	5:29	woman goes off and has an a
	16:49	those who died in the a of Korah
1Ki	2:28	remained loyal in the Absalom a
Ps	51:1	the a with Bathsheba

Affection

Est	8:5	if he has any a for me at all
Ps	6:2	I'm so starved for a
2Co	6:13	plainly as I can and with great a
Gal	5:22	things like a for others

Afflict

1Sa	18:10	ugly mood was sent by God to a Saul
2Sa	7:10	Nor will evil men a you
2Ki	19:7	A him with self-doubt
1Ch	17:9	nor will evil nations a them
2Ch	21:14	God is going to a your people
Na	1:12	I've afflicted you . . . , but I won't a

Afflicted

Jdg	2:18	those who a and beat them
2Sa	12:15	God a the child that Uriah's wife
2Ki	5:1	a with a grievous skin disease
	15:5	a the king with a bad skin disease
Job	34:28	the cry of the a got God's attention
Ps	109:16	hounded the a and heartbroken
Isa	54:11	A city, storm-battered, unpitied
Na	1:12	I've a you . . . , but I won't afflict
Mt	8:16	demon-a people were brought to him
	12:22	poor demon-a wretch
	15:22	cruelly a by an evil spirit
Mk	1:32	brought sick and evil-a people to him
Lk	8:3	many demons a him
	8:43	been a with hemorrhages
	13:11	a with this for eighteen years

Affliction

Ex	3:7	the a of my people in Egypt
	3:17	get you out of the a of Egypt
	4:31	knew all about their a
Job	10:15	up to my ears in a swamp of a
	36:8	when a and suffering descend
Isa	48:10	like silver in the furnace of a
Mk	7:29	The demonic a is gone

Afflictions

Dt	7:15	all the evil a you experienced
Job	13:21	First, lay off the a
Lk	8:2	healed of various evil a and illnesses

Afraid

Ge	3:10	I was a because I was naked
	9:2	fall under your spell and be a of you
	15:1	Don't be a, Abram. I'm your shield

	18:15	because she was a
	19:30	he was a to stay in Zoar
	21:17	What's wrong, Hagar? Don't be a
	26:7	He was a to say "She's my wife."
	31:31	Jacob answered Laban, "I was a
	32:11	I'm a he'll come and attack us
	35:17	Don't be a — you have another boy
	42:4	a that something bad might happen
	46:3	Don't be a of going down to Egypt
	50:19	Joseph replied, "Don't be a
Ex	3:6	Moses hid his face, a to look at God
	14:10	They were totally a
	14:13	spoke to the people: "Don't be a
	20:18	were a — they pulled back
	20:20	Don't be a. God has come to test you
	34:30	a to get close to him
Nu	14:9	don't be a of those people
	21:34	Don't be a of him
Dt	1:21	promised it to you. Don't be a
	3:2	Don't be a of him
	3:22	Don't be a of them
	5:5	You were a, remember, of the fire
	7:18	I'm telling you, Don't be a
	7:19	these people you're now so a of
	20:8	wavering in resolve and a
	28:67	A, terrorized at what's coming
Jos	2:9	We're all a
Jdg	4:18	Stay here with me. Don't be a
	6:10	Don't for a minute be a of the gods
	6:27	he was a to do it openly
	7:3	Anyone a, anyone who has any qualms
	8:20	He was a — he was still just a boy
	9:21	he was a of his brother Abimelech
1Sa	4:20	midwife said, "Don't be a
	5:6	everyone was deathly a
	12:18	greatly a and in awe of God
	22:23	Stay here with me. Don't be a
2Sa	1:14	weren't a to up and kill
	10:19	Arameans were a to help
	12:18	servants were a to tell him
	13:28	kill him. And don't be a
	14:7	making my life miserable, and I'm a
1Ki	1:50	a for his life because of Solomon
2Ki	1:15	don't be a." Elijah got up
	25:24	Don't be a of the Babylonian
	25:26	a of what the Babylonians would do
1Ch	19:19	Arameans were a to help
2Ch	20:15	God's word: Don't be a
	20:17	Don't be a, don't waver
Ezr	3:3	they were a
Ne	4:14	Don't be a of them
Est	9:3	they were a of him
Job	13:11	Aren't you a to speak cheap lies
	31:34	I was a what people would say
Ps	23:4	I'm not a when you walk at my side
	27:1	I'm fearless, a of no one
	56:3	When I get really a I come to you
	118:6	God's now at my side and I'm not a
Pr	23:13	Don't be a to correct your young ones
Isa	7:4	Don't be a. And don't panic
	8:12	always a somebody is plotting
	12:2	I trust, I won't be a

	41:14	Jacob? Don't be a
	41:23	Do we need to be a
	43:1	Don't be a, I've redeemed you
	43:5	So don't be a
	44:2	Don't be a, dear servant Jacob
	44:8	Don't be a, and don't worry
	51:12	What are you a of — or who
	54:4	Don't be a
Jer	1:8	Don't be a of a soul
	26:21	Uriah, a for his life
	38:19	I'm a of the Judeans
	41:18	a of what the Chaldeans might do
Eze	2:6	don't be a of them, son of man
	3:9	Don't be a of them
Da	1:10	I'm a of what my master . . . will do
	10:12	Daniel, . . . 'don't be a
	10:19	Don't be a, friend. Peace
Hos	13:14	Who is a of you, Death
Zep	3:16	Don't be a. Dear Zion
Zec	8:13	good-news people. Don't be a
	8:15	Judah. Don't be a
Mt	2:22	he was a to go there
	14:5	a because so many people revered John
	14:27	Courage, it's me. Don't be a
	17:7	touched them. "Don't be a
	25:25	I was a I might disappoint you
Mk	6:50	Courage! It's me. Don't be a
	9:32	were a to ask him about it
	10:32	puzzled and not just a little a
	16:6	Don't be a
Lk	2:10	The angel said, "Don't be a
	12:32	Don't be a of missing out
	19:21	I was a little a
Jn	6:20	It's all right. Don't be a
	12:42	were a of getting kicked out
Ac	9:26	a of him. They didn't trust him
	23:10	a they would tear Paul apart
	27:29	A that we were about to run aground
1Co	15:55	Death, who's a of you now
2Co	11:3	a that exactly as the Snake seduced
Gal	4:11	a that all my hard work among you has
Heb	12:20	a to move

Agitated

Ne	2:2	That made me all the more a
Da	7:15	All these dream-visions had me a

Agitation

Gal	1:7	who are provoking this a among you

Agitators

Ac	16:20	dangerous Jewish a
Gal	5:12	these a, obsessive as they are

Agonizing

Mt	26:37	he plunged into an a sorrow
Ro	11:2	Elijah was a over this same Israel

Agony

Mk	14:33	a sinkhole of dreadful **a**
Lk	16:24	I'm in **a** in this fire
Ac	7:34	I've seen the **a** of my people

Agreement

Da	11:6	to cement the peace **a**
Ac	15:15	**a** with the words of the prophets
	21:25	we're not going back on our **a**
1Jn	5:8	the three in perfect **a**

Aid

2Sa	8:5	came to the **a** of Hadadezer
1Ch	18:5	came to the **a** of Hadadezer
2Ch	28:15	provided first **a** to the injured
Lk	10:34	He gave him first **a**
Ro	8:3	being used as a Band-**A** on sin
	12:8	give **a** to people in distress

Ailment

Mt	4:24	brought anybody with an **a**
Lk	4:40	anyone sick with some **a**

Ailments

Lk	5:15	listen and be healed of their **a**
	6:18	to be cured of their **a**

Aimless

Jer	17:6	lives rootless and **a**
	50:6	they wandered **a** through the hills
Mt	9:36	confused and **a** they were

Aimlessness

Job	7:3	months of **a**, nights of misery

Airhead

Ac	17:18	dismissed him with sarcasm: "What an **a**

Airheads

Pr	12:8	**a** are held in contempt
Jer	5:21	you scatterbrains, **a**

Alarm

Ex	1:9	spoke to his people in **a**
1Sa	13:3	raised the **a**
Ps	71:7	Many gasp in **a** when they see me
Jer	4:5	Sound the **a** in Judah
	6:17	to warn them, to set off the **a**
Eze	3:18	you don't sound the **a** warning them
	12:27	the **a** the prophet raises
	19:4	Nations sounded the **a**
	30:9	to sound the **a** among the easygoing

	33:5	He heard the **a**, he ignored it
Da	3:24	Nebuchadnezzar jumped up in **a**
Hos	8:1	Blow the trumpet! Sound the **a**
Joel	2:1	Trumpet the **a** on my holy mountain
Am	3:6	the **a** goes off in the city
Mic	1:11	In Alarmtown, the **a** is sounded

Alarmed

Jos	10:2	He and his people were **a**
1Sa	21:1	Ahimelech was **a** as he went
Ps	105:24	soon their numbers **a** their foes
Am	3:6	aren't people **a**
Jn	7:32	**a** at this seditious undertow
Ac	13:50	**A**, they turned on Paul
	17:8	crowd of people were totally **a**

Alarms

Pr	3:25	No need to panic over **a** or surprises
Eze	12:22	the prophetic warnings are false **a**
	12:24	False **a** and easygoing preaching

Alert

Dt	4:9	make sure you stay **a**
	4:23	So stay **a**
Jos	8:4	Get as close as you can. Stay **a**
	23:4	Stay **a**
Jdg	21:21	Stay **a**—when you see the Shiloh girls
2Sa	22:22	I've kept **a** to God's ways
1Ki	8:52	be **a** and attentive to the needy
	8:61	**a** and attentive
	20:22	On the **a** now—build up your army
2Ch	6:40	be **a** and attentive to prayer
	7:15	I'm **a** day and night to the prayers
	16:9	God is always on the **a**
	26:13	on constant **a**
Ne	4:18	trumpeter at my side to sound the **a**
Ps	18:21	Now I'm **a** to God's ways
	37:33	God, **a**, is also on watch
	103:21	armies of angels, **a** to respond
	105:4	be **a** for signs of his presence
	123:2	servants, **a** to their master's commands
Pr	8:34	**a** and responsive as I start
	15:3	he's **a** to good and evil alike
Ecc	10:9	Be **a**: Felling trees is hazardous
Isa	43:19	Be **a**, be present
Jer	9:25	Stay **a**! It won't be long now
	32:27	Stay **a**! I am God
	46:14	Tell Egypt, **a** Migdol
Zec	6:12	Be **a**
Mt	10:16	Stay **a**. This is hazardous work
	24:42	So stay awake, **a**
	25:13	So stay **a**
	26:41	Stay **a**; be in prayer
Mk	14:38	Stay **a**, be in prayer
Lk	16:8	on constant **a**, looking for angles
	17:3	Be **a**. If you see your friend
	23:52	He lived in **a** expectation
Ro	3:11	nobody **a** for God
	5:4	keeping us **a** for whatever God will do

	5:5	In a expectancy such as this
	11:22	stay a to these qualities
	12:11	Be a servants of the Master
	15:4	keeping us a for whatever he will do
	16:19	Stay a like this
1Co	9:27	I'm staying a and in top condition
Eph	4:3	a at noticing differences
Col	3:2	a to what is going on around Christ
	4:2	Pray diligently. Stay a
Heb	13:17	a to the condition of your lives
1Pe	5:8	Stay a. The Devil is poised
2Pe	1:6	a discipline, passionate patience
	1:13	keeping you a with frequent reminders

Aligns

Jn	5:24	a himself with the Father
	6:35	who a with me hungers no more
	6.40	a with him will enter real life

All-consuming-yet-never-satisfied

| Gal | 5:20 | a wants |

All-Debts-Are-Canceled

Dt	15:2	A — God says so
	15:9	the year of A
	31:10	every seven years, the Year-A

All-generous

| Ps | 100:5 | God is sheer beauty, a in love |

All-powerful

| Dt | 34:12 | that a hand of his |
| Job | 36:5 | God is a, but he doesn't bully |

All-purpose

| Col | 3:14 | love. It's your basic, a garment |

Allegiance

| Ps | 119:117 | total a to your definitions of life |

Allergic

| 2Ti | 3:4 | addicted to lust, and a to God |

Allowance

| Ne | 5:14 | used the governor's food a |
| | 5:18 | food a provided for the governor |

Allowances

Ne	12:47	a for the singers and security guards
Pr	6:34	wild for revenge, he won't make a
Mt	25:24	make no a for error

Alluring

| Isa | 47:1 | calling you 'charming' and 'a' anymore |

Ally

1Sa	29:6	you've been a trusty a
Mk	9:40	If he's not an enemy, he's an a
Lk	9:50	If he's not an enemy, he's an a

Almighty

Job	5:17	don't despise the discipline of A God
	6:4	The arrows of God A are in me
	6:14	desperate people give up on God A
	8:3	Does God A ever get things backward
	8:5	Get down on your knees before God A
	11:7	Do you think you can diagram God A
	13.3	taking my case straight to God A
	15:25	defying God A to his face
	21:15	Why should we have dealings with God A
	22:3	would God A even notice
	22:17	What good is God A to us
	22:23	Come back to God A
	22:25	God A will be your treasure
	23:16	God A gives me the shudders
	24:1	Judgment Day isn't hidden from the A
	27:2	God A! He's ruined my life
	27:10	interest have they ever shown in the A
	27:11	suppressed nothing regarding God A
	27:13	what evil people can expect from God A
	31:2	What do I deserve from God A
	31:35	let the A One answer
	32:8	breath of the A One
	33:4	the breath of God A gave me life
	34:37	piling up indictments against the A
	35:13	the A pays them no mind
2Th	2:4	set himself up . . . "God A

Alone

Ge	2:18	not good for the Man to be a
Ex	14:12	Leave us a here
	18:18	you can't do this a
	22:20	god other than God a
	23:11	leave it a and give it a rest
	32:10	Let me a now
Lev	13:46	unclean. That person must live a
Nu	11:17	carry the whole thing a
	15:31	ostracized, left a
Dt	11:12	he a keeps his eye on it
	29:14	Covenant and its oath with you a
	32:12	God a led him
Jos	22:34	God A Is God
Jdg	3:20	king was now quite a
1Sa	7:3	worship him and him a
	12:10	we'll worship you a
	17:7	spear tip a weighed
2Sa	18:25	If he's a, it must be good news
1Ki	3:18	We were a
	8:27	let a this Temple I've built
	11:29	a on that remote stretch of road

2Ki	4:21	man of God, shut him in **a**, and left
	4:27	Leave her **a**
2Ch	6:18	let **a** this Temple I've built
Ezr	4:3	We **a** will build for the God
	6:7	leaders of the Jews **a** so they can work
Ne	9:6	You're the one, God, you **a**
Est	9:12	palace complex **a** here
Job	7:16	Let me **a**!
	28:23	God **a** knows the way to Wisdom
Ps	25:16	I'm all **a** and in big trouble
	31:23	those arrogant enough to go it **a**
	33:16	No king succeeds with a big army **a**
	33:17	no one gets by on muscle **a**
	40:10	For myself **a**. I told it all
	142:4	bereft, left **a**
Pr	21:9	Better to live **a**
	25:24	Better to live **a**
Ecc	4:8	solitary person, completely **a**
	4:9	better to have a partner than go it **a**
	4:11	**A**, you shiver all night
Isa	2:11	God **a** at front-and-center
	2:17	God **a** at front-and-center
	22:4	Let me **a**. Let me grieve
	37:20	you and you **a** are God
	37:33	let **a** build a siege ramp against it
	63:3	I've been treading the winepress **a**
Jer	17:5	thinks he can make it on muscle **a**
Eze	9:8	I was left **a**
	20:7	I **a** am God, your God
Da	10:8	Left **a** after the appearance
Mt	2:3	not Herod **a**, but most of Jerusalem as well
	14:23	stayed there **a**, late into the night
	18:3	look at the kingdom, let **a** get in
	19:14	Let the children **a**, don't prevent them
Mk	4:34	**a** with his disciples
	11:6	the people let them **a**
	14:6	Let her **a**
Lk	9:36	they saw Jesus there **a**
	18:16	Let these children **a**
	23:15	let **a** anything deserving death
Jn	8:9	The woman was left **a**
	12:7	Jesus said, "Let her **a**
Ac	5:38	Hands off these men! Let them **a**
	10:43	But we're not **a** in this
	15:35	But they weren't **a**
	24:3	because of you and you **a** that we enjoy
	26:31	deserving prison, let **a** death
1Co	4:18	never listen to anyone, let **a** me
	8:3	recognize that God **a** knows it all
	9:6	have to go it **a** and pay our own way
	11:11	Neither man nor woman can go it **a**
2Co	5:11	God **a** knows how well we do
Col	2:1	You're not in this **a**
2Jn	1:1	not **a** — everyone who knows the Truth

Aloof

Job	9:23	**a** from the despair of the innocent
1Th	2:7	We weren't **a** with you

Amaze

Pr	30:18	Three things **a** me

Amazed

Ne	9:10	You **a** Pharaoh
Ps	106:46	while their captors looked on, **a**
Mt	9:8	**a** and pleased that God had authorized
Ac	12:12	**a**, he went to Mary's house

Amazing

Ge	45:7	an **a** act of deliverance
Ex	3:3	**A**! Why doesn't the bush burn up
Ne	9:19	You in your **a** compassion
Job	26:3	What **a** insights you've provided
Ps	106:8	he revealed his **a** power
Isa	9:6	A Counselor, Strong God
	45:14	**A**! God is with you
Jn	9:30	**a**! You claim to know nothing
Ro	5:11	this **a** friendship with God
2Co	13:14	**a** grace of the Master
Php	4:23	**a** grace of the Master
1Th	1:1	God's **a** grace be with you
	5:28	**a** grace of Jesus Christ

Ambition

Pr	11:23	wicked **a** ends in angry frustration
Ecc	4:4	work and **a** motivated by envy
Jer	51:58	Nothing comes of **a** like this
Jas	3:14	Mean-spirited **a** isn't wisdom

Ambitions

Pr	10:28	**a** of bad people crash
Hag	1:9	You've had great **a** for yourselves

Ammunition

1Co	9:15	**a** to discredit me

Amputated

Isa	59:1	God's arm is not **a**

Amputating

Jer	44:7	ruining your lives by **a** yourselves

Amuse

Isa	14:4	**a** yourselves by taking up this satire

Amused

Ps	2:4	he's **a** at their presumption
Ob	1:13	not have been **a** by their troubles

Amusements

Isa	33:15	reject violence, avoid evil **a**

Amusing

Zep	1:12	fat and lazy, **a** themselves

Anarchist

2Th	2:3	the **A**, a real dog of Satan
	2:6	the **A** is being held back
	2:8	the **A** will no longer be held back
	2:9	The **A**'s coming is all Satan's work

Anarchy

Isa	19:2	**a** and chaos and killing
	24:10	**A** reigns
Jer	40:15	plunge the land into **a**
Eze	22:11	Sex is now **a**
Hos	4:2	sheer **a**, one murder after another
Hab	1:3	**A** and violence break out
2Th	2:7	spirit of **a** is not now at work

Anchor

Job	41:2	snag him with an **a**
Ps	97:2	Right and justice **a** his rule
Ac	27:13	they weighed **a**

Angel-cherub

Eze	28:16	I threw you out — you, the anointed **a**

Angel-cherubim

Ge	3:24	stationed **a** and a revolving sword
Ex	26:1	material, with an **a** design
	26:31	design of **a** woven into it
	36:8	fabric with an **a** design
	36:35	wove a design of **a** into it
	37:7	sculpted two winged **a**
Nu	7:89	two **a** above the Atonement-Cover
Eze	41:18	**a** and palm trees were carved
	41:25	carved with **a** and palm trees

Angel-figures

Ex	25:22	between the **a** that are on it

Angel-like

1Ki	6:23	gigantic **a** figures
2Ch	3:10	gigantic **a** figures

Angel-Messenger

Zec	1:9	The **A** said, "Let me show you
	1:13	God reassured the **A**

Angel-prince

Da	10:13	the **a** of the kingdom of Persia
	10:20	fight against the **a** of Persia
	10:21	beings except Michael, your **a**
	12:1	Michael, the great **a**

Angel-princes

Da	10:14	Michael, one of the chief **a**

Angel-princess

SS	6:13	Shulammite, **A**! Dance

Angel-seraphs

Isa	6:2	**A** hovered above him
	6:6	one of the **a** flew to me

Angel-wing-shadowed

Heb	9:5	the **a** mercy seat

Angelic

Lk	2:13	huge **a** choir singing God's praises
Ro	8:38	living or dead, **a** or demonic
1Co	13:1	human eloquence and **a** ecstasy
Gal	3:19	arranged by **a** messengers

Anger

Ge	27:41	Esau seethed in **a**
	27:45	until his **a** subsides
	34:7	outraged, explosive with **a**
	49:7	curse on their uncontrolled **a**
Ex	11:8	Moses, seething with **a**, left
	15:7	You let loose your hot **a**
	22:24	I'll show my **a** and come raging
	32:10	give my **a** free reign
	32:12	Stop your **a**
	32:19	**a** flared. He threw down the tablets
Lev	26:28	in hot **a** will defy you
Nu	11:1	When he heard his **a** flared
	11:10	God's **a** blazed up
	11:33	God's **a** blazed out
	12:9	The **a** of God blazed out
	16:46	**A** is pouring out from God
	18:5	no more outbreaks of **a**
	22:22	God's **a** flared
	25:3	God was furious, his **a** blazing
	25:4	turn God's **a** away
	25:11	stopped my **a**
	32:13	God's **a** smoked against Israel
	32:14	already blazing **a** of God
Dt	1:34	he exploded in **a**
	1:37	Because of you God's **a** spilled over
	4:25	provoking his **a**
	6:15	igniting his hot **a**
	7:4	God would explode in **a**
	9:19	God's furious **a**, his blazing **a**

	11:17	God erupts in a
	13:17	God may turn from a to compassion
	29:20	God's a and jealousy will erupt
	29:27	God's a erupted against that land
	31:29	provoking his a by what you do
	32:22	My a started a fire
Jos	7:26	then did God turn from his hot a
	22:18	he'll vent his a on all of us
	22:20	a fall on the whole congregation
	23:16	God's a will blaze out
Jdg	2:14	God's a was hot against Israel
	2:20	God's a blazed against Israel
	3:8	God's hot a blazed against Israel
	10:7	God exploded in hot a at Israel
	14:19	smoking with a, he went home
1Sa	15:11	He prayed his a and disappointment
	20:30	Saul exploded in a at Jonathan
2Sa	6:7	God blazed in a against Uzzah
	11:20	if he flares in a
	12:5	David exploded in a
	22:16	let loose his hurricane a
	22:49	He rescued me from enemy a
	24:1	God's a blazed out against Israel
1Ki	8:46	in a you turn them over to the enemy
2Ki	3:27	furious a against Israel
	13:4	prayed for a softening of God's a
	22:13	God's a must be burning
	22:17	My a is raging white-hot
	23:26	God's hot a did not cool; the raging a
	24:20	God's a — God turned his back
1Ch	13:10	God erupted in a against Uzzah
	15:13	God exploded in a at us
	27:24	God's a broke out on Israel
2Ch	6:36	in a you turn them over to the enemy
	12:12	God's a was blunted
	25:15	That ignited God's a
	28:9	your a, uncalled for and irrational
	28:11	find out how real a God's a, works
	28:13	set off an explosion of divine a
	29:8	God's a flared up
	30:8	no longer be in danger of his hot a
	32:25	his a spilled over on Judah
	32:26	God withdrew his a
	34:21	God's a must be burning
	34:25	My a is raging white-hot
Ezr	10:14	hot a of our God
Ne	4:1	he exploded in a
Est	1:12	Seething with a over her insolence
	2:1	Xerxes' a had cooled
	7:10	the king's hot a cooled
Job	4:9	one blast of his a
	5:2	jealous a of a simpleton does her in
	9:13	God doesn't hold back on his a
	10:17	You compound your a
	14:13	out of the way until your a cools
	16:9	Your a tears at me
	20:23	God gives them a taste of his a
	32:2	blazed out in a against Job
	32:5	he exploded with pent-up a
Ps	2:12	His a is about to
	18:15	let loose your hurricane a
	18:48	He rescued me from enemy a

	37:8	Bridle your a, trash your wrath
	69:24	Blast them with your red-hot a
	74:1	how can you stomp off in a
	76:7	Who can stand up to your rising a
	78:21	his a flared against Jacob
	78:31	his a erupted
	78:38	he reined in his a
	78:49	His a flared, a wild firestorm
	78:58	pagan orgies provoked God's a
	85:3	you cooled your hot, righteous a
	88:7	pounded by your waves of a
	88:16	Your wildfire a has blazed
	90:7	Your a is far and away too much
	90:11	such a against the very ones who fear
	102:10	because of your furious a
	106:23	deflected God's a
	106:40	God was furious — a wildfire a
	119:53	I'm beside myself with a
	124:3	swallowed alive by their violent a
	145:8	mercy and grace — not quick to a
Pr	14:29	Slowness to a
	15:1	gentle response defuses a
	19:19	endure the backlash of their own a
	22:8	bullying a sputters into nothing
	27:4	blasted by and swamped by rage
Ecc	7:9	A boomerangs
Isa	5:25	God flamed out in a against his people
	10:5	weapon of my a
	10:25	my a against you will be spent
	12:1	your a wasn't forever
	13:9	day of wrath and a
	13:13	the Judgment Day of his raging a
	14:6	violent rule of a
	30:27	Smoking with a
	42:25	God's a that's behind all this
	48:9	tight rein on my a and hold my temper
	51:17	strong drink of his a
	51:20	strong drink of God's a
	51:22	drinking from that jug of my a
	54:8	In an outburst of a I turned
	54:9	I'm promising now no more a
	57:17	struck him hard and turned away in a
	63:6	I trampled the people in my a
	66:15	furious outburst of a
Jer	3:5	keep up your a nonstop?
	3:12	My a doesn't see the nonstop
	4:4	Prevent fire — the fire of my a
	4:8	God's sledgehammer a
	4:26	the blazing a of God
	7:20	My white-hot a is about to descend
	10:25	Vent your a on the godless nations
	11:17	goading me to a
	12:13	result of God's fierce a
	15:14	My a is blazing and fierce
	17:4	My a is hot and blazing
	18:20	trying to soften your a
	18:23	Strike while the iron of your a is hot
	21:5	holding nothing back. And in fierce a
	21:12	Prevent fire — the fire of my a
	23:20	God's raging a won't let up
	25:37	silenced by God's deadly a
	25:38	ripped and ravaged by his a

	30:24	God's raging **a** won't let up
	32:37	driven them in my **a** and rage
	33:5	killed because of my raging **a**
	42:18	with my **a** and wrath, I'll do the same
	44:6	So I let loose with my **a**
	49:37	my **a**-fueled doom
	50:13	Emptied of life by my holy **a**
	51:7	Filled with the wine of my **a**
	51:45	torched by God's raging **a**
	52:3	God's **a**. God turned his back
La	2:1	in his **a** treated his favorite
	2:3	His **a** blazing
	2:4	His **a**, like fire, burned
	4:11	God let all his **a** loose
Eze	5:13	calm down and let my **a** cool
	7:3	I've launched my **a** against you
	7:8	pay out my **a** against you
	9:8	pouring out of your **a** on Jerusalem
	13:13	torrent of my hailstone-**a**
	14:19	pouring out my lethal **a**
	16:42	By then my **a** will be played out
	20:8	inflicting my **a** on them in force
	20:13	unleashing my **a** on them
	20:21	dumping my **a** on them
	20:33	terrifying rush of **a**
	20:34	terrifying rush of **a**
	21:17	signal that my **a** is spent
	21:31	breathe hot **a** down your neck
	22:31	burn them to a crisp with my hot **a**
	24:13	until my **a** quiets down
	35:11	hate-bloated **a** and rage
	36:17	I poured out my **a** on them
	38:18	My raging **a** will erupt
	43:8	I destroyed them in **a**
Da	3:19	Nebuchadnezzar, his face purple with **a**
	11:30	he will be filled with **a**
Hos	5:10	of their bodies is going to feel my **a**
	8:5	seething with **a** against that rubbish
	11:9	not going to act on my **a**
	14:4	My **a** is played out
Am	1:11	Her **a** rampages day and night
Jnh	4:10	feelings from pleasure to **a**
	4:11	change . . . from **a** to pleasure
Mic	5:15	In raging **a**, I'll make a clean sweep
	7:18	You don't nurse your **a**
Na	1:6	Who can face such towering **a**
Zep	1:15	Judgment Day is payday — my **a** paid out
	2:2	God's Judgment-**a** sweeps down on you
	2:3	hidden on the Day of God's **a**
	3:8	let them feel the brunt of my **a**
Mk	14:5	They swelled up in **a**
Lk	4:28	seething with **a**
	6:11	beside themselves with **a**
Jn	11:33	**a** deep **a** welled up within him
	11:38	**a** again welling up within him
Eph	4:26	don't use your **a** as fuel
Col	3:6	God is about to explode in **a**
Jas	1:19	let a straggle along in the rear
	1:20	doesn't grow from human **a**
Rev	11:18	**a** taste of your **a**
	12:12	He's wild and raging with **a**

	14:10	unmixed in his chalice of **a**
	16:19	drink the wine of God's raging **a**

Angered

Dt	32:19	**a** and hurt by his sons and daughters
Jdg	2:12	how they **a** God
2Ki	23:19	shrines that had so **a** God
Ps	86:15	not easily **a**, immense in love
	103:8	not easily **a**, he's rich in love
	106:32	They **a** God again
Jnh	4:2	not easily **a**, rich in love

Angry

Ge	18:32	Don't get **a**, Master
	30:2	Jacob got **a** with Rachel
	31:36	Jacob's turn to get **a**
	32:11	my **a** brother
	41:10	Pharaoh got **a** with his servants
	44:18	Don't get **a**
Ex	4:14	God got **a** with Moses
	32:22	Master, don't be **a**
Lev	10:6	**a** with the whole congregation
	10:16	became **a** with Eleazar
Nu	14:18	God, slow to get **a**
	32:10	God got **a**—oh, did he get **a**
Dt	3:26	God was still **a** with me
	4:21	God was **a** with me
	9:7	how **a** you made God
	9:8	made God **a** at Horeb, made him so **a**
	9:18	evil in God's eyes and making him **a**
	29:24	What . . . could have made him this **a**
	29:28	God, furiously **a**, pulled them
	31:17	I'll get **a**, oh so **a**
Jos	7:1	God became **a** with the People of Israel
Jdg	9:30	son of Ebed was saying and got **a**
1Sa	15:11	Samuel was **a** when he heard this
	18:8	This made Saul — very **a**
	20:7	if he gets **a**, you'll know for sure
	20:34	stormed from the table, furiously **a**
	29:4	**A** with Achish
2Sa	6:8	**a** because of God's deadly outburst
	11:25	David got **a** at Joab
	17:8	brave and bitterly **a**
1Ki	14:9	you've made me mighty **a**
	14:15	they made God so **a** with Asherah
	14:22	wicked before God, making him very **a**
	15:30	making the God of Israel thoroughly **a**
	16:7	his making God so **a**
	16:13	making the God of Israel **a**
	16:26	making God **a**
	21:22	made me that **a** by making Israel sin
	22:53	God of Israel, **a**, oh, so **a**
2Ki	13:19	The Holy Man became **a** with him
	17:18	God was so thoroughly **a**
	21:6	career in evil. And God was **a**
	22:17	made me thoroughly **a**
1Ch	13:11	**a** because God exploded against Uzzah
2Ch	16:10	**A**, he put Hanani in the stocks
	19:2	God is good and **a** with you
	24:18	An **a** cloud hovered over Judah

	25:10	very **a** at losing their jobs
	25:13	**a** over their lost opportunity
	26:19	**a** words were exchanged
	28:9	**a** with Judah
	28:25	was God ever **a**
	29:10	God will no longer be **a** with us
	32:25	made God **a**, and his anger spilled over
	33:6	career in evil. And God was **a**
	34:25	they've made me thoroughly **a**
	36:16	God became more and more **a**
Ezr	5:12	made the God of the heavens really **a**
	9:14	**a** to the point of wiping us out
Ne	2:10	upset, **a** that anyone would come
	5:6	really **a** when I heard their protest
	13:8	I was **a**, really **a**
Est	1:18	**a** women who don't know their place
Job	19:11	He's **a** with me — oh, how he's **a**
	32:3	also **a** with the three friends
	35:15	waiting for him to get good and **a**
	36:13	**A** people without God
	36:33	roars in the thunder, **a** against evil
Ps	2:5	Then he gets good and **a**
	30:5	He gets **a** once in a while
	55:3	stockpile **a** slander
	56:7	Get **a**, God! Down with these people
	60:1	stalked off **a**. Come back
	78:62	**a**, he let them fend for themselves
	79:6	going to be **a**, be **a** with the pagans
	85:5	scowling and **a**, year after year
	89:43	**A**, you opposed him in battle
	106:29	so **a** that a plague spread
	138:7	keep me alive in the **a** turmoil
Pr	11:23	wicked ambition ends in **a** frustration
	14:35	shiftless work earns an **a** rebuke
	19:19	**a** people endure the backlash
	22:24	Don't hang out with **a** people
	29:22	**A** people stir up a lot of discord
Ecc	5:6	risk provoking God to **a** retaliation
Isa	5:25	he was still **a**
	8:21	When nothing works out they get **a**
	9:12	he was still **a**
	9:17	he was still **a**
	9:21	he was still **a**
	10:4	God is still **a**
	10:6	against the people I'm **a** with
	12:1	**a** but your anger wasn't forever
	13:3	carry out my **a** judgment
	27:4	I'm not **a**. I care
	30:30	Furiously **a**, showering sparks
	34:2	God is **a**, good and **a**
	57:16	I'm not going to be **a** forever
	57:17	I was **a**, good and **a**
	60:10	When I was **a** I hit you hard
	64:5	how **a** you've been with us
	64:9	Don't be too **a** with us, O God
Jer	7:29	generation that has made him so **a**
	10:10	When he's **a**, Earth shakes
	21:10	I'm that **a** with this place
	25:6	Don't make me **a**
	25:7	now I am really **a**
	32:30	making me **a** by the way they live
	32:31	This city has made me **a**

	32:32	deliberately making me **a**
	36:7	let them know how **a** he is
	44:3	making me **a**
	44:8	deliberately make me **a**
La	2:21	**A**, you killed them in cold blood
	3:66	Get good and **a**. Hunt them down
	5:22	You've been so very **a** with us
Eze	5:15	When I finish my **a** punishment
	6:12	I'm **a**, furiously **a**
	8:3	goddess that makes God so **a**
	8:5	Asherah, that makes God so **a**
	8:18	They have an **a** God
	16:43	when you were young but made me **a**
	22:24	during the time I was **a** with you
	36:6	I'm **a** — and I care
	36:18	I got thoroughly **a** with them
Da	9:16	stop being so **a** with Jerusalem
Hos	5:10	I'm **a**, good and **a**
Jnh	3:9	quit being **a** with us and let us live
	4:4	What do you have to be **a** about
	4:6	get him out of his **a** sulk
	4:9	What right do you have to get **a**
Mic	7:18	don't stay **a** long
Hab	3:8	**A** at old River?
	3:12	**A**, you stomped through Earth,
Zec	1:2	God was very **a** with your ancestors
	1:12	how long are you going to stay **a**
	1:15	thoroughly **a** with the godless nations
	7:12	God became **a**, really **a**
	8:2	I'm **a** about Zion — I'm involved
	8:14	your ancestors made me **a**
Mt	5:22	who is so much as **a** with a brother
	8:34	**a** about the drowned pigs
Mk	3:5	**a** now, furious at their hard-nosed
Lk	15:28	stalked off in an **a** sulk
Jn	3:36	an **a** darkness
Ro	1:18	God's **a** displeasure erupts
	9:22	to show his **a** displeasure
2Co	11:29	an **a** fire burns in my gut
	12:20	**a** words, vicious rumors
Eph	4:26	be **a**. You do well to be **a**
1Th	5:9	didn't set us up for an **a** rejection
1Ti	2:8	not shaking **a** fists at enemies
Rev	11:18	The **a** nations

Anguish

Ne	9:9	**a** of our parents
Job	3:24	leave the table and vomit my **a**
	6:26	treat my words of **a** as so much hot air
Isa	65:19	weeping in the city, no cries of **a**
Jer	15:8	Sudden **a** for the mothers
	49:21	cries of **a** heard at the distant
Eze	9:4	everyone who is in **a**
Zep	1:15	day of distress and **a**

Anguished

| Jer | 46:12 | world will hear your **a** cries |

Animosity

Eph	2:15	centuries of a and suspicion

Annihilate

Est	8:5	to a the Jews

Annihilating

Gal	5:15	you will be a each other

Annul

Gal	3:15	no one else can a it

Annulled

Nu	30:13	either affirmed or a by her husband
Gal	3:17	A will . . . ratified by God, is not a

Anoint

Ex	28:41	A, ordain, and consecrate them
	29:36	A and consecrate it
	30:26	Use it to a the Tent of Meeting
	30:30	a Aaron and his sons
	40:9	a The Dwelling and everything in it
	40:10	A the Altar of Whole-Burnt-Offering
	40:11	A the Washbasin and its base
	40:13	A him. Consecrate him to serve me
	40:15	A them
Jdg	9:8	trees set out one day to a a king
1Sa	9:16	You're to a him as prince
	15:1	God sent me to a you king
	16:0	I'll point out the one you are to a
1Ki	1:34	will a him king over Israel
	19:15	When you get there a Hazael
	19:16	Then a Jehu son of Nimshi
2Ki	9:3	God's word: I a you king over Israel
	9:12	God's word: I a you king of Israel
Ps	141:5	Don't let sin a my head
Isa	57:9	You a your king-god with ointments
Da	9:24	a The Holy of Holies
Mt	26:12	what she really did was a me
Jas	5:14	pray and a you with oil

Anointed

Ge	35:14	a it with oil
Ex	29:29	descendants so they can be a
	40:15	just as you a their father
Lev	4:3	the a priest who sins
	4:16	a priest will then bring
	6:20	present to God on the day he is a
	6:22	Aaron's son who is a to succeed him
	8:10	a The Dwelling
	16:32	priest who is a and ordained
Nu	3:3	a priests ordained to serve
	7:1	he a it and consecrated it
	7:10	When the Altar was a
	35:25	High Priest who was a

1Sa	2:10	set his a on top of the world
	2:35	in the service of my a one
	10:1	God has a you prince
	12:3	bring before God and his a
	12:5	his a is witness
	16:6	Here he is! God's a
	16:13	took his flask of oil and a him
	24:6	my master, God's a
	24:10	against my master — he's God's a
	26:9	lay a hand on God's a
	26:11	that I should lay a finger on God's a
	26:23	lift a finger against God's a
2Sa	1:14	weren't afraid to up and kill God's a
	1:16	you killed God's a king
	3:39	And I, though a king
	5:3	they a David king over Israel
	19:21	he cursed God's a
1Ki	1:39	a Solomon
	1:45	a him king at Gihon
2Ki	9:6	I've a you to be king
	11:12	As they a him, everyone applauded
	23:30	a and succeeded his father as king
1Ch	11:3	they a David king over Israel
	16:22	Don't you dare touch my a ones
2Ch	6:42	don't, God, back out on your a ones
	23:11	As Jehoiada and his sons a him
Ps	89:38	lost your temper with the one you a
	89:51	they dog the steps of your dear a
	105:15	Don't you dare lay a hand on my a
	132:10	don't disdain your a one
	132:17	I'll fill it with light for my a
Isa	45:1	God's Message to his a
	61:1	God a me. He sent me to preach
La	4:20	the a of God, was caught
Eze	16:9	a you with aromatic oils
	28:14	You were the a cherub
	28:16	you, the a angel-cherub
Da	9:25	until the coming of the A Leader
	9:26	the A Leader will be killed
Mt	26:7	a him
Mk	14:8	she pre-a my body for burial
Lk	7:38	his feet, kissed them, and a them
Jn	12:3	a and massaged Jesus' feet
Ac	10:38	a by God with the Holy Spirit
1Jn	2:20	The Holy One a you

Anointing

Ex	25:6	spices for a oils
	29:7	take the a oil and pour it
	29:21	mix it with some of the a oil
	30:25	Make these into a holy a oil
	30:31	This will be my holy a oil
	31:11	the a oil
	35:8	spices for a oils
	35:15	the a oil, the fragrant incense
	35:28	lamp oil, a oil, and incense
	37:29	holy a oil
	39:38	a oil fragrant incense screen
	40:9	take the a oil and anoint The Dwelling
	40:15	Their a will bring them
Lev	7:36	priests from the day of their a

	8:2	the garments, the **a** oil
	8:10	took the **a** oil and anointed
	8:11	**a** the Altar and all its utensils
	8:12	the **a** oil on Aaron's head, **a** him
	8:30	the **a** oil and some of the blood
	10:7	God's **a** oil is on you
	21:10	received the **a** oil poured on his head
	21:12	dedication of the **a** oil
Nu	4:16	Grain-Offering, and the **a** oil
	7:84	the **a** of the Altar
1Sa	10:1	sign will confirm God's **a** of you
	16:1	Fill your flask with **a** oil
1Ch	29:22	coronation, **a** David's son before God
Ezr	6:9	wheat, salt, wine, and **a** oil
Ps	84:9	shining with your gracious **a**
	133:2	It's like costly **a** oil
Jer	51:8	Get **a** balm for her wound
Mk	6:13	wellness to the sick, **a** their bodies
1Jn	2:27	Christ's **a**, no less!

Answers

Ge	24:14	who **a**, 'Drink, and let me also water
Jdg	5:29	**a** with calm, reassuring words
2Sa	20:18	If it's **a** you want, come
1Ki	18:24	The god who **a** with fire
Job	33:14	God always **a**, one way or another
	38:3	I want some straight **a**
	40:7	I want straight **a**
	42:4	me ask the questions. You give the **a**
Ps	3:4	His **a** thunder from the holy mountain
	4:1	give me **a**. God, take my side!
	143:1	Answer me—you're famous for your **a**
Pr	15:28	Prayerful **a** come from God
	18:23	the rich bark out **a**
Isa	16:4	Judah **a**, "the tyrant toppled
	19:3	go to their god-idols for **a**
Jer	23:38	don't pretend that you know all the **a**
Hos	4:12	expect **a** from a sturdy walking stick
	14:8	I'm the one who **a** and satisfies him
Mk	12:28	how sharp Jesus was in his **a**
Lk	2:47	the sharpness of his **a**
	11:7	The friend **a** from his bed

Ant

Pr	6:6	look at an **a** . . . let it teach you

Antagonism

Ac	23:6	exploit their **a**

Antagonists

Ps	119:157	My **a** are too many to count

Anti-god

Nu	27:3	part of Korah's rebel **a** gang

Anti-miracle

1Co	1:23	Jews treat this like an **a**

Anti-promise

Gal	3:21	an **a**, a negation of God's will

Anti-resurrection

1Co	15:33	poisoned by this **a** loose talk

Antichrist

1Jn	2:18	You heard that **A** is coming
	2:22	This is what makes an **a**: denying
	4:3	This is the spirit of **a**
2Jn	1:7	heir true title: Deceiver! **A**

Antichrists

1Jn	2:18	**a** everywhere you look

Ants

Pr	30:25	**a**—frail as they are, get plenty
Isa	40:22	people look like mere **a**
Eze	38:20	animals—even **a** and beetles

Anxieties

2Co	11:28	daily pressures and **a**

Anxious

Ge	43:18	became **a** when they were brought
Jos	22:24	We were **a** lest someday
Jdg	5:28	**a** weary, **a** watch
1Ch	28:20	Don't be **a** or get discouraged
Ezr	10:9	they were restless, uneasy, and **a**
Ps	34:4	he freed me from my **a** fears

Anxiously

Da	6:20	he called out **a**, "Daniel
Ro	3:28	not by proudly or **a** trying to run

Apologetically

Lk	19:8	He stammered **a**

Apologized

Ac	16:39	They hurried over and **a**

Apostasy

Job	34:28	**a** was announced by the cry of the poor
2Th	2:3	First, the **A**

Apostate

2Ch	21:13	step by step down the **a** path

Appetite

1Sa	1:7	reduced to tears and had no **a**
Job	33:20	have no **a** for their favorite
	38:39	satisfy the **a** of her cubs
Pr	13:25	An **a** for good brings much satisfaction
	16:26	**A** is an incentive to work
	23:3	don't stuff yourself; bridle your **a**
	27:20	Hell has a voracious **a**
Isa	5:14	Sheol developed a huge **a**
Eze	16:28	Your **a** was insatiable
	23:20	whetted her **a** for more virile
Mt	5:6	worked up a good **a** for God
	6:16	practice some **a**-denying discipline
Jn	6:54	brings a hearty **a** to this eating
Ac	27:21	**a** for both food and life long gone
2Co	5:5	Spirit of God whets our **a**
Heb	10:6	smoke from the altar that whet your **a**
	12:16	to satisfy a short-term **a**

Appetite-denying

Mt	6:16	practice some **a** discipline

Appetites

Pr	10:3	he frustrates the **a** of the wicked
Ecc	6:7	We work to feed our **a**
Isa	9:20	**A** insatiable
Php	3:19	all they can think of is their **a**
Tit	2:13	whetting our **a** for the glorious day

Applaud

Job	22:3	performance, do you think he'd **a**
Ps	100:1	On your feet now — **a** God
	117:1	Praise God, everybody! **A** God
	145:10	Creation and creatures **a** you, God
Na	3:19	whole world will **a** and cry "Encore!"

Applauded

2Sa	3:36	everything the king did was **a**
2Ki	11:12	everyone **a** and shouted
Ne	11:2	**a** those who voluntarily offered

Applauding

1Sa	19:5	were on your feet **a** with everyone
Eze	35:14	With the whole earth **a**
Mt	6:1	God who made you won't be **a**
	9:33	people were up on their feet **a**

Applauds

Mt	5:12	all heaven **a**
Lk	6:23	all heaven **a**

Applause

1Ch	16:33	trees in the forest will add their **a**
Ps	47:1	**A**, everyone.
	66:1	All together now — **a** for God
	96:11	a huge round of **a** from Sea
	98:7	sea and its fish give a round of **a**
Pr	8:30	with my joyful **a**
Isa	42:10	sea and its fish give a round of **a**
	55:12	exuberant with **a**
Na	1:12	all the **a** and all the votes
Mt	6:2	get **a**, true, but that's all they get
	7:28	crowd burst into **a**
Gal	1:10	curry favor with God? Or get popular **a**
2Ti	4:8	God's **a**! Depend on it

Appointment

1Sa	13:13	the **a** that your God commanded
	13:14	you didn't keep your **a** with God
	20:35	the **a** with David
1Ch	23:13	a permanent **a** for Aaron
Gal	1:1	nor does it come through the **a**
1Th	5:2	won't call ahead and make an **a**
Heb	4:8	wouldn't keep renewing the **a**

Appointments

Nu	17:4	where I keep **a** with you

Appoints

Heb	7:28	The law **a** as high priests

Appreciate

1Th	4:4	**a** and give dignity to your body
Heb	13:7	**A** your pastoral leaders

Appreciated

Ps	107:43	it's time you **a** God's deep love
Pr	28:23	reprimand is **a** far more

Appreciation

2Ch	17:5	showed their **a** by bringing gifts
Ro	15:9	show **a** to God
1Th	5:13	Overwhelm them with **a** and love

Appreciative

Ne	12:44	Judah was so **a** of the priests

Apprentice

Mt	10:42	giving or receiving makes you a true **a**
Lk	6:40	An **a** doesn't lecture the master
2Ti	3:10	You've been a good **a** to me

Approval

Ge	4:5	Cain and his offering didn't get his a
	32:5	my master, hoping for your a
	41:44	without your stamp of a
Dt	33:11	stamp your seal of a on what he does
2Ki	18:25	the express a of God
	20:3	lived for your a
Ne	2:6	the king gave his a to send me
Ps	37:6	stamp you with a at high noon
Pr	27:5	better than a that's never expressed
Lk	6:26	you live only for the a of others
Jn	5:41	I'm not interested in crowd a
	12:43	they cared more for human a
Ac	11:21	put his stamp of a on it
Ro	2:11	won't give you an automatic stamp of a
Gal	4:17	always depend on them for a
1Th	2:4	we're not after crowd a — only God a
1Pe	3:12	God looks on all this with a

Approve

La	3:36	Master does not a of such things
Ro	4:2	what he did for God, got God to a him

Approved

1Sa	18:5	a of and admired David's leadership
2Ch	30:4	revised date was a
Lk	6:26	scoundrel preachers were a
Heb	11:4	God noticed and a as righteous
1Pe	2:5	offering Christ-a lives up to God

Approves

Pr	16:7	When God a of your life

Aptitude

Ex	31:6	all who have an a for crafts
Mt	19:11	married life . . . requires a certain a

Arbitrate

Eze	44:24	the priests will a

Arbitrator

Job	9:33	wish we had an a to step in

Archangel

Ps	89:11	everything from atom to a
1Th	4:16	give the command. A thunder
Jude	1:9	The A Michael, who went to the mat

Archenemy

Est	3:10	to Haman . . . a of the Jews
	8:1	Haman, a of the Jews
	9:7	Haman . . . the a of the Jews
	9:24	the Agagite, the a of all Jews

Argue

Job	9:14	how could I ever a with him
	23:13	Who can a with him
Ecc	6:10	You can't a with fate
Isa	1:18	Let's a this out
Jer	12:1	you set things right. I can't a
Ac	6:9	trying to a him down
	9:15	But the Master said, "Don't a
	18:6	All they did was a contentiously
	22:21	Don't a. Go.

Arguing

Mk	9:34	they had been a with one another
Lk	9:46	They started a over which
Jn	6:41	the Jews started a over him
Ac	15:11	So what are we a about
	24:12	Nobody can say they saw me a

Argument

1Sa	30:23	David as he broke up the a
Job	15:3	nonsense in the middle of a serious a
Pr	25:9	In the heat of an a, don't betray
Jn	3:25	John's disciples got into an a
Ac	9:29	engaged in a running a with them
	23:7	going at each other in heated a
Ro	14:20	not going to permit an a

Argumentative

1Co	11:16	not going to be a about this
2Ti	2:24	God's servant must not be a

Arguments

Job	23:4	give him all my a firsthand
	32:5	exhausted their a
	32:11	listened carefully to your a
	32:14	I won't be using your a
	33:5	Lay out your a. Stand up
Isa	41:22	on behalf of your idols, offer a
	43:26	Make your a. Prove you're in the right
Mt	15:19	vomit up evil a
Ac	15:7	a went on and on
	25:19	a about their religion
Col	2:8	drag you off into endless a
2Th	3:12	to work immediately — no excuses, no a

Aristocracy

Ac	17:4	women from the a

Arithmetic

Ro	9:28	calls us by name. A is not his focus

Arm-twisting

2Co	9:7	protect you against sob stories and a

Aroma

Lev	26:31	hold my nose at the "pleasing **a**
2Co	2:15	an **a** redolent with life

Aromatic

Ex	30:35	to make an **a** incense
	31:11	the **a** incense for the Holy Place
	37:29	the pure **a** incense
Lev	16:12	finely ground **a** incense
2Ki	20:13	silver, gold, spices, **a** oils
2Ch	13:11	sacrificing . . . **a** incense to God
	16:14	crypt full of **a** oils and spices
Pr	7:17	My bed is **a** with spices
SS	1:3	headier than your **a** oils
	4:14	Mint and lavender, and all herbs **a**
	5:15	**a** man, **a** with wood and stone
Eze	16:9	anointed you with **a** oils
	16:18	perfumed them with my **a** oils
	23:41	sumptuous bed, **a** with incense
Jn	11:2	massaged the Lord's feet with **a** oils
	12:3	jar of very expensive **a** oils

Arouse

1Ki	1.2	in bed with you and **a** our master

Aroused

Nu	23:24	king-of-the-beasts, **a**, Unsleeping

Arousing

Ro	8:22	Spirit of God is **a** us within

Arrogance

2Ch	32:26	repented of his **a**
Ne	9:10	their bullying **a** against your people
	9:29	responded with haughty **a**
Ps	59:12	all their mean-mouthed **a**
	73:6	Pretentious with **a**, they wear
	101:5	I can't stand **a**
	139:21	how I loathe all this godless **a**
Pr	8:13	pride and **a** and crooked talk
	16:5	God can't stomach **a** or pretense
	21:4	A and pride
Isa	10:12	punish the bragging **a**
	37:29	your unbridled **a**
Jer	13:17	your stubborn **a**
	48:29	pride, the insufferable **a**
	48:42	his defiant **a** against me
Eze	30:10	I'll put a stop to Egypt's **a**
Hos	5:5	Bloated by **a**
	7:10	Bloated by **a**
Am	6:8	I hate the **a** of Jacob
	8:7	God swears against the **a** of Jacob
Mic	7:16	humiliated in their **a**
Mk	7:22	slander, **a**, foolishness
Ac	12:23	God had had enough of Herod's **a**

1Co	5:6	Your flip and callous **a**
1Ti	1:13	witch hunts and **a**

Arrogant

Dt	17:20	must not become proud and **a**
2Ch	26:16	A and proud, he fell
	28:19	A King Ahaz, acting as if
	32:25	made him **a**. This made God angry
Ne	9:16	they, our ancestors, were **a**
Job	40:11	Unleash your outrage. Target the **a**
	40:12	Target the **a**
Ps	13:2	my **a** enemies have looked down
	31:23	those **a** enough to go it alone
	49:6	demeaned by the **a** rich
	89:9	put the **a** ocean in its place
	94:2	throw the book at the **a**
	119:85	**a** godless try to throw me off track
	123:4	kicked when we're down by **a** brutes
Pr	6:17	eyes that are **a**
	9:7	If you reason with an **a** cynic
	13:10	A know-it-alls stir up discord
	15:25	God smashes the pretensions of the **a**
Isa	9:9	**a** proud and **a** bunch
	16:6	A, self-important, insufferable
	21:16	the **a** brutality of Kedar
Eze	30:18	put an end to her **a** oppression
	33:28	no more **a** bullying!
Da	5:22	you're as **a** as he ever was
Hab	2:5	The **a** rich don't last
Zep	3:11	gotten rid of your **a** leaders
Mal	4:1	the **a** people who do evil things
Mt	23:18	What **a** stupidity!
Jas	1:10	when the **a** rich are brought down
	5:1	**a** rich: Take some lessons in lament

Arrogantly

Ex	18:11	those who treated Israel **a**
Nu	14:44	recklessly and **a** they climbed
Job	35:12	People are **a** indifferent
Da	7:8	little horn, and **a** big mouth
	7:11	little horn was speaking **a**
	7:20	big mouth and spoke **a**
Mt	18:10	these childlike believers **a**
Ro	11:25	**a** assume that you're royalty

Art

Ex	30:35	the **a** of a perfumer
	37:29	the **a** of a perfumer
Jdg	3:2	experience, in the **a** of war
Ps	50:19	lying is a serious **a** form
Eze	31:9	work of **a** in limbs and leaves
Mt	19:6	no one should desecrate his **a**
Mk	10:9	no one should desecrate his **a**
Heb	6:1	grand work of **a**

Arthritis

Lk	13:11	twisted and bent over with **a**

Artisan

Ex	38:23	an a, designer, and embroiderer
2Ch	2:7	Send me a master a in gold
Ps	52:2	tongue cuts razor-sharp, a in lies
Isa	46:6	The a delivers the god

Artisans

Ex	36:4	a who were at work making
	36:8	the skilled a on The Dwelling
2Ki	24:14	all its craftsmen and a
	24:16	thousand or so craftsmen and a
1Ch	4:14	Ge Harashim (Colony of A
	22:15	masons, carpenters, a
	28:21	skillful craftsmen and a
	29:5	work by craftsmen and a
Ac	19:24	employing a number of a
	19:38	Demetrius and his guild of a
Rev	18:22	A of every kind — gone

Artist

1Ki	7:14	Hiram was a real a
SS	7:1	the work of a master a

Artists

2Ch	2:14	work out designs with your a
Jer	12:1	Why do con a make it big

Arts

2Ki	17:17	the black a of magic and sorcery
Rev	18:23	by black-magic a deceived the nations

Ascetic

Col	2:23	pious and humble and a

Ashamed

Ezr	9:6	I'm so totally a
Ps	69:7	an idiot, I walk around a
	71:24	slink off looking a
Isa	45:16	all those others will be a
	45:17	They won't be a
Jer	31:19	I was a of my past
	48:13	as a of god Chemosh as Israel was a
	48:39	Moab shamed and a to be seen
Eze	16:52	look righteous. Aren't you a
Zep	3:11	You'll no longer have to be a
Mk	14:29	Even if everyone else is a of you
2Ti	2:15	work you won't be a of
Rev	16:15	through the streets, naked and a

Assassinate

Est	6:2	who had conspired to a King Xerxes

Assassinated

2Ki	10:9	conspired against my master and a him
	12:20	formed a conspiracy and a Joash
	14:5	guard that had a his father
	15:10	a him in public view
	15:30	He a him and took over as king
	21:23	servants revolted and a him
2Ch	25:3	guard who had a his father
	33:24	Amon's servants revolted and a him

Assassination

1Ki	11:40	Solomon ordered the a of Jeroboam

Assassins

2Ki	12:21	son of Shomer were the a
	14:6	didn't kill the sons of the a
2Ch	25:4	didn't kill the sons of the a
	33:25	then killed the king's a
Ps	55:23	Cut the lifespan of a and traitors
Eze	28:9	protest to your a, "You can't do that

Assault

2Sa	11:25	Redouble your a on the city
Job	30:15	Terrors a me
Isa	51:19	A and battery, hunger and death
Mt	22:34	gathered their forces for an a
Lk	10:19	protection from every a of the Enemy

Assaulted

Jdg	9:52	got as far as the tower and a it
Zep	1:16	forts are a, as defenses are smashed

Assaulting

Hos	6:9	gangs of priests a worshipers

Assurance

Ro	9:11	special a from God

Astonish

Isa	29:14	shock them awake, a them

Astonished

2Ki	11:14	A, she saw the king standing
2Ch	23:13	A, she saw the young king
Isa	6:11	A, I said, "And Master, how long
La	2:15	A, passersby can't believe
Eze	8:27	When I looked, I was a
Mt	8:27	The men rubbed their eyes, a
	15:31	the blind looking around, they were a
Mk	16:5	completely taken aback, a
Ac	3:10	rubbed their eyes, a
Rev	17:6	A, I rubbed my eyes

Astonishing

Da	6:27	He performs a miracles
	12:6	How long is this a story to go on
2Co	9:8	pour on the blessings in a ways

Astray

Jer	50:6	Their shepherds led them a
2Ti	3:13	as deceived as the people they lead a
Rev	12:9	who led the whole earth a

Atheist

Ps	8:2	silence a babble

Athlete

Ps	19:5	sun an a racing to the tape
Ac	7:22	impressive as a thinker and an a
2Ti	2:5	a who refuses to play by the rules

Athletes

1Co	9:24	seen the a race
	9:25	All good a train hard

Athletic

Eph	6:12	This is no afternoon a contest

Atone

Nu	15:25	to a for the entire community
	15:28	to a for the person
	28:22	Absolution-Offering to a for you
	28:30	Absolution-Offering to a for you
	29:5	Absolution-Offering to a for you
	29:11	Absolution-Offering to a for you
2Ch	29:24	to a for the sin of all Israel
Ne	10:33	Absolution-Offerings to a for Israel

Atoned

Ex	29:33	A by these offerings
Nu	16:47	and a for the people

Atonement

Ex	25:17	for the Chest, an A-Cover
	25:18	gold for either end of the A-Cover
	25:19	one piece with the A-Cover
	25:20	hovering over the A-Cover
	25:21	Set the A-Cover as a lid
	25:22	from above the A-Cover
	26:34	place the A-Cover lid
	29:36	an Absolution-Offering for a each day
	29:37	Make a for the Altar
	30:6	in front of the A-Cover
	30:10	a, he is to make this a every
	30:12	all must pay an a-tax to God
	30:15	the a-tax for your lives
	30:16	the a-tax money from the Israelites
	31:7	Chest of The Testimony and its A-Cover
	35:12	the A-Cover and veiling curtain
	37:6	for the Chest, an A-Cover
	37:7	gold for the ends of the A-Cover
	37:8	of one piece with the A-Cover
	37:9	hover over the A-Cover
	39:35	Testimony with its poles and A-Cover
	40:20	placed the lid, the A-Cover
Lev	1:4	on your behalf to make a for you
	4:20	priest makes a for them
	4:26	priest makes a for him
	4:31	priest makes a for him
	4:35	priest makes a for him
	5:6	priest will make a for your sin
	5:10	priest will make a for your sin
	5:13	priest will make a for you
	5:16	the priest will make a for him
	5:18	priest will make a for him
	6:7	priest will make a for him
	6:30	to make a in the Sanctuary
	7:7	priest who makes a with it
	8:15	consecrated it so a could be made
	8:34	in order to make a for you
	9:7	Make a for yourself
	10:17	making a for them before God
	12:7	offer it to God and make a for her
	12:8	priest will make a for her
	14:18	man being cleansed and make a for him
	14:19	make a for the one to be cleansed
	14:20	made a for him
	14:21	Offering to make a for him
	14:29	making a for him before God
	14:31	priest will make a for the one
	14:53	He has made a for the house
	15:15	Offering and makes a for him
	15:30	priest will make a for her
	16:2	the A-Cover on the Chest
	16:6	make a for himself and his household
	16:10	to make a
	16:11	make a for himself and his household
	16:13	A-Cover which is over The Testimony
	16:14	the front of the A-Cover
	16:15	on and before the A-Cover
	16:16	make a for the Holy of Holies
	16:17	to make a in the Holy of Holies
	16:18	make a for it
	16:20	making a for the Holy of Holies
	16:24	making a for himself and the people
	16:27	into the Holy of Holies to make a
	16:30	on this day a will be made for you
	16:32	to make the a
	16:33	purges the Holy of Holies by making a
	16:34	Once a year a is to be made for all
	17:11	make a for your lives on the Altar
	19:22	perform the ritual of a for him
	23:27	is the Day of A
	23:28	it is a day of a to make a for you
	25:9	the Day of A
Nu	5:8	the ram by which a is made
	7:89	angel-cherubim above the A-Cover
	8:12	make a for the Levites

	8:19	Israel and to make a for them
	8:21	made a for them to purify them
	15:28	make a before God
	16:46	make a for them
	25:13	made a for the People of Israel
	31:50	to make a for our lives before God
1Ch	6:49	made a for Israel
Job	1:5	made a habit of this sacrificial a
Eze	16:63	when I make a for you
	45:15	the sacrifices for the people
	45:17	a for the people of Israel
	45:20	you make a for the Temple

Atonement-Cover

Ex	25:17	lid of pure gold for the Chest, an A
	25:18	gold for either end of the A
	25:19	Make them of one piece with the A
	25:20	wings spread, hovering over the A
	25:21	Set the A as a lid over the Chest
	25:22	speak with you from above the A
	26:34	place the A lid on the Chest
	30:6	in front of the A
	31:7	Chest of The Testimony and its A
	35:12	Chest with its poles, the A
	37:6	lid of pure gold for the Chest, an A
	37:7	gold for the ends of the A
	37:8	made them of one piece with the A
	37:9	appeared to hover over the A
	39:35	The Testimony with its poles and A
	40:20	placed the lid, the A, on it
Lev	16:2	curtain that's before the A
	16:13	the A which is over The Testimony
	16:14	on the front of the A
	16:15	on and before the A
Nu	7:89	two angel-cherubim above the A

Atonement-tax

Ex	30:12	all must pay an a to God
	30:15	the a for your lives
	30:16	a money from the Israelites

Atoning

| 1Ch | 28:11 | the place for a sacrifice |

Atrocities

Jer	19:8	a museum of a
	41:11	the a committed by Isahmael
Joel	3:19	the a and murders

Atrocity

| Jer | 19:5 | an a I never ordered |

Atrophy

| Isa | 5:24 | Their souls will a |

Attentive

Dt	29:4	perceptive eyes or a ears
1Ki	8:52	be alert and a to the needy prayers
	8:61	a to everything he has made plain
2Ch	6:40	be alert and a to prayer
	20:13	all present and a to God
1Th	5:14	a to individual needs
1Ti	3:4	a to his own children
	3:12	a to their own children

Attentively

1Ki	9:4	a obedient to my guidance
2Ch	7:17	a obedient to my guidance
Ps	119:15	I a watch how you've done it
Ac	22:22	crowd had listened a up to this point

Attitude

| Jdg | 4:9 | with an a like that |

Attorney

| Job | 16:19 | some A who can clear my name |

Attract

| Jn | 12:32 | a everyone to me and gather them |

Attracted

Dt	7:7	God wasn't a to you
1Ki	8:42	a here by your great reputation
2Ch	6:32	a here by your great reputation
Isa	14:1	Outsiders will be a
Eze	27:18	a by your vast array of products
Jn	6:2	a by the miracles they had seen

Attraction

| Ge | 34:3 | felt a strong a to Dinah |

Attractive

Dt	21:11	woman whom you find a
2Sa	13:1	sister who was very a
Pr	3:22	they'll keep you fit and a
Isa	53:2	There was nothing a about him
Eph	5:13	see how a they look in the light
Php	1:11	making Jesus Christ a to all

Attracts

| Pr | 19:4 | Wealth a friends as honey draws flies |
| Col | 3:5 | grabbing whatever a your fancy |

Audit

2Ch	24:11	brought the chest in for a royal a
Ps	10:13	cocksure they'll never come up for a
Lk	16:2	I want a complete a of your books

Authentic

Php	4:8	things true, noble, reputable, a

Authentically

Jn	7:24	to test what is a right

Author

Isa	29:16	Does a book say to its a
Ac	3:15	no sooner killed the A of Life

Authoritative

Lk	4:32	so confident, so a
Heb	8:1	priest: a right alongside God

Authorities

Mt	10:18	haul you before the civil a
Ro	13:3	Duly constituted a are only a threat
1Pe	2:13	Respect the a, whatever their level

Authority

Ge	41:35	stockpile the grain under Pharaoh's a
Ex	23:21	he's acting on my a
Nu	15:23	commanded you under the a of Moses
	27:20	Pass your magisterial a over
	36:13	commanded through the a of Moses
Dt	10:20	back up your promises with the a
1Ch	22:10	a of his kingdom over Israel lasts
	25:2	backed up by the king's a
2Ch	25:10	I have it on good a
	33:18	delivered by a of God
Ezr	5:1	in the a of the God of Israel
Est	9:29	using her full queenly a
Pr	8:16	all in legitimate a
	25:5	a will be credible and God-honoring
	29:14	Leadership gains a and respect
Isa	9:7	His ruling a will grow
	22:21	I'll give him your a
Jer	26:16	spoken to us with the a of our God
Da	7:27	the royal rule and the a
	11:20	reputation, and a already in shreds
Hag	2:23	my sovereign presence and a
Mt	23:9	Save that a for God
	26:63	by the a of the living God
Mk	3:15	give them a to banish demons
	6:7	gave them a and power
Lk	9:1	gave them a and power
	10:20	your a over evil, but in God's a over
	22:25	people in a like to give themselves
	22:29	the royal a my Father conferred
Jn	5:22	Father handed all a to judge over
	5:27	he has given him the a
	5:43	I came with the a of my Father
	10:18	received this a personally
	19:10	the a to pardon you, and the a to
	19:11	You haven't a shred of a over me
Ac	15:24	they had no a from us

	26:10	full a of the high priests
1Co	1:10	using the a of Jesus, our Master
	5:3	deal with it in the a of Jesus
	9:1	I have no a to write like this
	9:2	the a of my commission
	11:3	there is a from Christ to husband
	11:4	lack of respect for the a of Christ
	11:5	the a of her husband
2Co	3:1	asserting our a
	10:8	overstate the a he gave me
	13:10	The a the Master gave me
Gal	1:1	My a for writing to you
Col	2:15	their sham a
1Ti	1:9	the irresponsible, who defy all a
Heb	6:16	appeal to some a above them
	7:26	a extending as high as God's presence
2Pe	2:10	despise interference from true a
Rev	12:10	Kingdom of our God, a of his Messiah
	13:2	its throne and great a
	13:4	Dragon who gave the Beast a
	17:13	turn over their power and a
	18:1	His a was immense

Authorization

Ezr	6:14	a by Cyrus, Darius, and Artaxerxes
Lk	19:12	headquarters to get a for his rule
	19:15	bringing the a of his rule

Authorize

2Ki	22:6	a them to buy the lumber
Ezr	7:25	I a you, Ezra
Ne	2:7	the governors . . . that a my travel
Jer	23:36	Only the person I a speaks for me

Authorized

2Ch	22:7	whom God had already a to destroy
Ezr	3:7	shipment a by Cyrus the king
	7:15	You are also a to take the silver
	7:21	have formally a and ordered
	8:11	The king's order a the Jews
Jer	23:32	never a a single one of them
Jnh	3:7	proclamation . . . a by him
Mt	3:3	John and his message were a
	9:6	I'm the Son of Man and a to do
	9:8	pleased that God had a Jesus
	21:23	Who a you to teach here
	21:25	baptism of John — who a it
	28:18	God a and commanded me
Mk	2:10	I'm the Son of Man and a to do
	11:28	Who a you to speak and act like this
	11:30	baptism of John — who a it
Lk	5:24	I'm the Son of Man and a to do
	20:2	Who a you to speak and act like this
	20:4	baptism of John — who a it
Jn	1:33	The One who a me to baptize
	3:26	The one you a with your witness?
	10:25	has been a by my Father
Ro	1:1	a as an apostle to proclaim

Authorizes

2Co	3:6	letter a us to help carry out

Authorizing

2Sa	3:21	treaty with you, a you to rule them
Ezr	5:17	building permit a the rebuilding
Est	8:5	the bulletins a the plan of Haman
	8:13	a the Jews to be prepared on that day
Ac	22:5	a me to hunt down the Christians
	26:12	high priests a my action
1Co	16:3	write letters a whomever you delegate

Avenge

Ge	9:5	lifeblood I will a; I will a it
Nu	31:2	A the People of Israel
1Sa	18:24	A the king on his enemies
	24:12	God may a me
1Ki	2:44	God will now a that evil
Est	8:13	prepared on that day to a themselves
Jer	51:11	He's out to a his Temple
Rev	6:10	before you step in and a our murders

Avenged

Ge	4:24	If Cain is a seven times
Ex	21:20	slave must be a
	21:21	he's not to be a
Jdg	9:56	God a the evil Abimelech
	16:28	let me be a on the Philistines
Rev	19:2	He a on her the blood

Avenger

Nu	35:12	places of refuge from the a
	35:19	the a has a right to kill the murderer
	35:21	The a has a right to kill him
	35:24	judge between the killer and the a
	35:25	save the killer from the hand of the a
	35:27	the a finds him outside the borders
Dt	19:6	the a of blood racing
	19:12	hand him over to the a of blood
Jos	20:3	place of asylum from the a of blood
	20:5	If the a of blood chases after him
	20:9	not die by the hand of the a of blood
Jer	51:36	taking up your cause. I'm your A
Jas	5:4	the ears of the Master A

Avengers

Jer	51:53	I'd make sure my a would reach her

Avenges

Dt	32:43	He a the deaths of his servants
Na	1:2	He a his foes

Avenging

Lev	26:25	a your breaking of the covenant

Jdg	16:28	With one a blow let me be avenged
1Sa	25:26	God has kept you from this a murder
	25:31	guilt of an a murder
1Ki	2:32	God is a those bloody murders
2Ki	9:7	I am a the massacre of my servants
2Ch	24:25	a the murder of the son of Jehoiada
Ps	94:1	a God, show your colors
Jer	51:48	the a armies from the north
	51:56	The a destroyer is about to enter
Ac	7:24	a his underdog brother

Avoid

Lev	26:11	I won't a or shun you
Nu	18:32	you'll a guilt
1Sa	5:5	a stepping on the threshold
Job	24:13	those who a light at all costs
Ps	31:11	cross the street to a me
	38:11	old friends a me like the plague
	139:7	anyplace I can go to a your Spirit
Pr	4:24	a careless banter, white lies
	11:15	a rash bargains
	14:16	wise watch their steps and a evil
	15:12	they a the company of wise men
Isa	33:15	reject violence, a evil amusements
Mal	2:9	be disgusted with you and a you
Mk	4:12	Who a making an about-face
Jn	5:43	you either dismiss me or a me
Ac	15:29	a serving food offensive
	21:25	a serving food offensive
	27:17	only managed to a them
Ro	13:5	not just to a punishment
1Ti	6:20	A the talk-show religion

Avoidance

Pr	14:34	God-a leaves people weak
Ro	2:5	refusal and a of God

Avoided

Pr	19:4	poor people are a like a plague
Lk	10:32	he also a the injured man
Ac	27:21	We could have a all this trouble

Avoiding

Dt	2:8	a the Arabah Road
Ps	10:1	God, are you a me
	119:101	a the ditches and ruts of evil
Ro	15:3	a people's troubles
Heb	10:25	not a worshiping together

Avoids

Job	19:14	everyone who knows me a me
Pr	19:7	even your family a you
Jn	3:36	person who a and distrusts the Son
1Co	6:17	the kind of sex that a commitment

B

Award

| Pr | 16:31 | the **a** for a God-loyal life |

Awarded

| Mt | 20:21 | will be **a** the highest places |
| Mk | 10:37 | we will be **a** the highest places |

Awarding

| Mt | 20:23 | as to **a** places of honor |
| Mk | 10:40 | as to **a** places of honor |

Awesome

Ex	15:11	In **a** praises, wonder-working God
Dt	4:34	spectacle **a** and staggering
	7:21	God majestic, God **a**
	10:17	God immense and powerful and **a**
Ne	1:5	the great and **a** God
	4:14	the Master, great and **a**
Isa	35:2	**A** Carmel, stunning Sharon
Joel	2:31	the Day tremendous and **a**

Awestruck

Mt	9:8	The crowd was **a**, amazed
Lk	5:26	glory to God. **A**, they said
	24:5	The women were **a** and bowed down

B

Babies

Ge	3:16	give birth to your **b** in pain
	3:17	painful as having **b** is for your wife
	18:11	far past the age for having **b**
	20:17	they started having **b** again
	30:2	Am I the one who refused you **b**
Ex	1:17	they let the boy **b** live
	1:18	You've let those **b** live
	2:6	must be one of the Hebrew **b**
Nu	16:27	with their wives, children, and **b**
Dt	1:39	And your **b** of whom you said
	22:7	take the **b**, but let the mother go
	28:50	cruel to grandmothers and **b** alike
	28:53	you're going to eat your own **b**
	29:11	your **b**, your wives
	30:9	things go well for you: you'll have **b**
	32:25	breast-feeding **b**
2Ki	8:12	murder their youth, smash their **b**
	19:3	**B** poised to be born
Est	3:13	men, women and **b** — on a single day
Job	3:16	all the **b** who never saw light
	24:9	have their **b** snatched from them
Ps	17:14	crusts for their **b** to chew on
	22:31	**B** not yet conceived will hear
	105:24	God gave his people lots of **b**
	106:38	slit the throats of their **b**
	137:9	grabs your **b** and smashes their heads
Isa	13:16	**B** smashed on the rocks

	13:18	wantonly kick and kill even **b**
	28:9	We're not **b** in diapers
	33:11	you produce straw **b**
	59:4	pregnant with mischief and have sin-**b**
	65:20	No more **b** in the cradle
	66:8	barely in labor when she had her **b**
	66:9	I, the One who delivers **b**
Jer	7:31	altars for burning **b**
	30:6	Can men bear **b**?
	47:3	fear, won't even grab up their **b**
La	2:11	my people's fate. **B** and children
	2:20	women eat their own **b**
	4:3	Even wild jackals nurture their **b**
	4:4	**B** have nothing to drink
Hos	9:16	the dear **b** wouldn't live
	10:14	mothers and their **b** were smashed
	13:2	sacrifice live **b** to these dead gods
	13:16	**b** smashed on the rocks
Joel	2:16	even the nursing **b**
Na	3:10	**b** smashed to death in public view
Mt	21:16	From the mouths of children and **b**
Lk	18:15	People brought **b** to Jesus
	19:44	smash you and your **b** on the pavement
Ro	9:11	her **b** were still innocent in the womb

Baby

Ge	4:2	Then she had another **b**, Abel
	17:12	Every male **b** will be circumcised
	17:17	Sarah, at ninety years, have a **b**
	17:19	wife, Sarah, will have a **b**
	18:13	Have a **b**? An old woman like me
	18:14	Sarah will have a **b**
	21:7	Sarah would one day nurse a **b**
	21:8	The **b** grew up and was weaned
	47:12	right down to the smallest **b**
Ex	1:16	the **b**. If it's a boy, kill him
	1:19	they've already had the **b**
	2:4	**b**'s older sister found herself
	2:6	saw the child — a **b** crying
	2:7	she can nurse the **b** for you
	2:9	Take this **b** and nurse him for me
Nu	12:12	like a stillborn **b**
Ru	4:14	May this **b** grow up to be famous
	4:16	took the **b** and held him
	4:17	calling him "Naomi's **b** boy
1Sa	22:19	killing man and woman, child and **b**
1Ki	3:17	we were living together, I had a **b**
	3:18	this woman also had a **b**
	3:21	here was this dead **b**
	3:25	Cut the living **b** in two
	3:26	real mother of the living **b**
	3:27	Give the living **b** to the first
2Ki	5:14	like the skin of a little **b**
Job	38:8	gushed forth like a **b** from the womb
Ps	7:14	He's having the **b** — a Lie-**B**
	27:3	When besieged, I'm calm as a **b**
	48:6	pain like a woman having a **b**
	131:2	Like a **b** content in its mother's arms
Ecc	6:3	a stillborn **b** gets the better deal
Isa	8:4	Before that **b** says 'Daddy' or 'Mamma
	13:8	pain like a woman giving birth to a **b**

B

	21:3	pain like a woman having a **b**
	23:4	never had a **b**, never reared children
	26:17	Like a woman having a **b**
	26:18	writhed in labor but bore no **b**
	28:11	In **b** talk, one syllable at a time
	28:13	address them in **b** talk
	37:3	without even the strength to have a **b**
	42:14	like a woman who's having a **b**
	45:10	permission to use me to make a **b**
	49:15	walk away from the **b** she bore
	54:1	barren woman, who has never had a **b**
	66:7	had the **b**. Before the birth pangs
	66:9	open the womb and not deliver the **b**
Jer	13:21	pain of a woman having a **b**
	20:15	You've got a new **b**—a boy **b**
	20:17	rest of her life with a **b** dead in her
	44:7	man, woman, child, and **b**
	48:41	like a woman giving birth to a **b**
	49:22	like a woman giving birth to a **b**
	50:43	like a woman giving birth to a **b**
Eze	16:4	you weren't wrapped in a **b** blanket
Hos	11:4	lifted him, like a **b**, to my cheek
Mic	6:7	my precious **b**, to cancel my sin
Mt	1:25	she had the **b**. He named the **b** Jesus
Lk	1:41	the **b** in her womb leaped
	2:12	look for: a **b** wrapped in a blanket
	2:16	the **b** lying in the manger
	3:6	When you look at a **b**
	16:21	when the **b** is born, there is joy
Ac	7:20	Moses was born, a most beautiful **b**
	12:6	Peter slept like a **b**
Heb	5:12	**b**'s milk
Jas	1:15	Lust gets pregnant, and has a **b**: sin

Backsliders

| Ps | 125:5 | God will round up the **b** |

Backstabbing

Ro	1:29	grasping, vicious **b**
	8:35	not bullying threats, not **b**
1Ti	6:5	an epidemic of **b**

Bad-mouth

Ecc	10:20	Don't **b** your leaders
Lk	12:10	If you **b** the Son of Man
Jas	4:11	Don't **b** each other, friends

Bad-mouthing

Nu	16:11	have against Aaron that you're **b** him
2Ki	19:22	Who do you think you've been **b**
1Ti	6:4	envy, controversy, **b**

Bad-mouths

| Ps | 101:5 | gossip who **b** his neighbor |

Banish

Pr	30:8	**B** lies from my lips
Isa	25:7	God will **b** the pall of doom
	25:8	he'll **b** death forever
Jer	16:9	I'm about to **b** smiles and laughter
	25:10	I'll **b** every sound of joy
Eze	34:25	I'll **b** fierce animals
Da	9:27	he will **b** worship and prayers
Am	1:5	**b** the crime king
	1:8	**b** the crime king from Ashdod
Mk	3:15	give them authority to **b** demons
	5:10	begged Jesus not to **b** them

Banished

1Sa	26:19	let them be **b** from God's presence
1Ch	12:1	during the time he was **b** by Saul
Job	10:22	**b** for good to the land of the dead
	18:18	into darkness, **b** from the world
Pr	16:6	Guilt is **b** through love and truth
Isa	59:14	Righteousness is **b** to the sidelines
	65:16	troubles are . . . **b** far from my sight
Da	9:7	all the places we've been **b** to
	12:11	daily worship is **b** from the Temple
Mic	4:6	everyone I have bruised or **b**
2Th	2:12	**b** to their chosen world of lies

Bankrupt

Jdg	14:15	invited us here to **b** us
Ps	37:9	crooks will be **b**
	119:11	so I won't sin myself **b**
Pr	15:6	a misspent life is soon **b**
Isa	23:12	**b** and bereft Sidon
	42:17	invested in the no-gods are **b**
Eze	7:13	**b** because of its sins
Hos	9:3	going to end up **b** in Egypt
Mic	6:14	**b** lives, wasted souls
Zec	9:4	God will certainly **b** her
Lk	12:33	a bank that can't go **b**
Ac	16:19	business was suddenly **b**
1Co	13:3	I'm **b** without love
2Co	3:15	that old, **b** government

Banter

Ex	20:7	curses or silly **b**
Dt	5:11	curses or silly **b**
Pr	4:24	avoid careless **b**
Mt	7:6	**B** and silliness give no honor to God

Baptism

Mt	3:15	coming together right now in this **b**
	21:25	**b** of John—who authorized it
	28:19	marking them by **b**
Mk	1:4	preaching a **b** of life-change
	1:8	His **b**—a holy **b** by the Holy Spirit
	10:38	of being baptized in the **b**
	10:39	be baptized in my **b**
	11:30	**b** of John—who authorized it

Lk	3:3	preaching a **b** of life-change
	3:7	crowds of people came out for **b**
	7:30	have nothing to do with such a **b**
	20:4	**b** of John — who authorized it
Jn	3:5	a **b** into a new life
	3:25	the nature of **b**
Ac	18:25	went as far as the **b** of John
	19:3	In John's **b**
	19:4	preached a **b** of radical life-change
Ro	6:3	That is what happened in **b**
1Co	10:2	through the waters, in a **b** like ours
Gal	3:27	**b** in Christ was not just washing
Eph	4:5	one Master, one faith, one **b**
Col	2:12	by submitting to **b**
1Pe	3:21	The waters of **b** do that for you
1Jn	5:8	the Spirit, the **B**, the Crucifixion

Baptismal

1Jn	5:6	**b** birth of his ministry

Baptisms

Jn	4:1	keeping count of the **b**
1Co	1:14	not involved with any of your **b**
Jas	2:7	name — "Christian" — used in your **b**

Baptize

Mt	3:13	He wanted John to **b** him
Jn	1:25	nor the Prophet, why do you **b**
	1:26	I only **b** using water
	1.33	who authorized me to **b** with water

Baptized

Mt	3:6	were **b** into a changed life
	3:14	I'm the one who needs to be **b**
Mk	1:5	confessed their sins, were **b** by him
	1:9	was **b** by John in the Jordan
	10:38	being **b** in the baptism
	10:39	be **b** in my baptism
	16:16	Whoever believes and is **b** is saved
Lk	3:12	Tax men also came to be **b**
	3:21	the people were **b**, Jesus was **b**
	7:29	being **b** by him into the kingdom
Jn	10:40	place where John first **b**
Ac	1:5	**b** in water; you will be **b**
	1:22	Jesus was **b** by John
	2:38	Turn to God and be **b**
	2:41	took him at his word, were **b**
	8:12	forgot Simon and were **b**
	8:13	Simon himself believed and was **b**
	8:16	been **b** in the name of the Master
	8:36	Here's water. Why can't I be **b**
	8:38	Philip **b** him on the spot
	9:18	He got to his feet, was **b**
	10:48	ordered that they be **b**
	11:16	John **b** with water; you will be **b**
	16:15	After she was **b**
	16:33	couldn't wait till morning!—was **b**

	18:8	many Corinthians believed and were **b**
	19:3	How were you **b**, then
	19:4	If you've been **b** in John's baptism
	19:5	**b** in the name of the Master Jesus
	22:16	Get up and get yourself **b**
1Co	1:13	one of you **b** in Paul's name
	1:15	saying he was **b** in my name
	1:16	I also **b** Stephanas's family
	12:13	word and action when we were **b**
	15:29	people offer themselves to be **b**

Baptizing

Mt	3:11	I'm **b** you here in the river
Mk	1:8	I'm **b** you here in the river
Lk	3:16	I'm **b** you here in the river
Jn	1:28	where John was **b** at the time
	1:31	That is why I came here **b** with water
	3:22	He was also **b**
	3:23	John was **b** over at Aenon
	3:26	competing with us. He's **b**, too
	4:2	not Jesus, did the actual **b**
Ac	10:47	any objections to **b** these friends

Bar

Jos	7:21	fifty-shekel **b** of gold
	7:24	the gold **b**
Ne	7:3	shut and **b** the gates
Jer	51:55	taking his wrecking **b** to Babylon
Ac	13:7	wizard's name was **B**-Jesus
	25:10	before Caesar's **b** of justice

Barbarians

Dt	2:20	called them Zamzummites (**B**
2Ch	20:24	the horde of **b**
Ps	35:16	Like **b** desecrating a shrine
	74:10	How long, God, will **b** blaspheme
	79:1	**B** have broken into your home
	114:1	clan of Jacob left those **b** behind
	118:10	Hemmed in by **b**
	144:7	out of the grip of those **b**
	144:11	release me from the grip of those **b**
Isa	1:7	reduced to rubble by **b**
	56:9	Come, devour, beast **b**
Jer	12:12	The **b** will invade
	50:42	**b** they are, cruel and pitiless
Lk	21:24	Jerusalem under the boot of **b**

Barefaced

2Ki	19:10	That's a **b** lie
2Ch	32:15	don't let him get by with his **b** lies
Ps	59:12	every muttered curse — every **b** lie
	120:3	all you **b** liars
Jer	27:10	handing you a line of lies, **b** lies
1Co	15:15	a string of **b** lies about God

Bargain

Ge	38:23	I kept my part of the **b**

B

Pr	11:26	Curses on those who drive a hard **b**
	20:14	goes off boasting of the **b**
Mt	7:7	Don't **b** with God
Lk	11:10	Don't **b** with God
Heb	8:9	didn't keep their part of the **b**

Bargained

Jer	41:8	**b** with Isahmael, "Don't kill us
2Co	13:3	get more than you **b** for

Bargaining

Eze	7:7	no **b** for more time

Barren

Ge	11:30	Sarai was **b**; she had no children
	25:21	to God for his wife because she was **b**
	29:31	opened her womb. But Rachel was **b**
Ex	23:26	any miscarriages nor **b** women
Nu	13:20	soil: Is it fertile or **b**
Jdg	13:2	His wife was **b** and childless
	13:3	I know that you are **b**
1Sa	2:5	**b** woman has a houseful of children
2Sa	6:23	Michal, Saul's daughter, was **b**
Job	15:34	godless are fruitless — a **b** crew
Pr	30:16	a **b** womb, a parched land
Isa	35:7	**b** grasslands flourish richly
	41:18	rivers for them on the **b** hills
	54:11	Sing, **b** woman
Eze	36:13	eats people alive and makes women **b**
	36:14	nor make women **b**
	36:15	a land that makes women **b**
Hos	9:11	frigid and **b**
Joel	3:19	Edom turned into **b** badlands
Lk	1:36	Everyone called her **b**
Ro	8:23	sterile and **b** bodies of ours
Gal	4:27	Rejoice, **b** woman
Eph	5:11	the **b** pursuits of darkness
Heb	11:11	**b** Sarah was able
Jas	1:11	beautiful face is a **b** stem
	2:24	made right with God not by a **b** faith

Barriers

Jer	6:21	putting roadblocks and **b** on the road
Mt	16:19	no more **b** between heaven and earth
2Co	10:5	**b** erected against the truth of God

Battered

Dt	26:6	The Egyptians abused and **b** us
Jdg	10:8	bullied and **b** the People of Israel
2Ch	15:6	Nation **b** nation
Ezr	9:8	allowed us, this **b** band
Ps	9:9	God's a safe-house for the **b**
	88:7	I'm **b** senseless by your rage
Isa	42:22	a people **b** and cowed
	54:11	Afflicted city, storm-**b**, unpitied
	57:20	storm-**b** seas that can't quiet down
Jer	14:17	dear people are **b** and bruised

	51:42	**b** by waves of enemy soldiers
Eze	27:34	**b** to bits by the waves
Mic	4:7	I will transform the **b**
Mt	14:24	they were **b** by the waves
Lk	4:18	set the burdened and **b** free
2Co	4:8	surrounded and **b** by troubles

Beast

Job	3:8	Unleash the sea **b**, Leviathan
	40:15	the land **b**, Behemoth
	41:1	can you pull in the sea **b**, Leviathan
	41:12	Leviathan, the sea **b**
Isa	56:9	call to the savage **b**s: Come, **b**
Da	8:4	No **b** could stand up to him
Rev	11:7	**B** from the Abyss will emerge
	13:1	saw a **B** rising from the sea
	13:2	**B** I saw looked like a leopard
	13:3	One of the **B**'s heads looked as if
	13:4	**B** authority, and they worshiped the **B**
	13:5	The **B** had a loud mouth, boastful and
	13:8	Lab's Book of Life will worship the **B**
	13:11	another **B** rising out of the ground
	13:12	a puppet of the first **B**
	13:13	This second **B** worked magical signs
	13:14	magic it got from the **B** to dupe
	13:15	animate the image of the **B**
	13:17	name of the **B**
	13:18	number of the **B**
	14:9	If anyone worships the **B**
	14:11	those who worship the **B**
	15:2	God, triumphant over the **B**
	16:2	taken the mark of the **B**
	16:10	on the throne of the **B**
	16:13	mouths of the Dragon, the **B**
	17:3	**B**. Stuffed with blasphemies, the **B**
	17:7	woman and the **B** she rides, the **B**
	17:8	The **B** you saw once was, is no longer
	17:11	The **B** that once was and is no longer
	17:12	come to power with the Scarlet **B**
	17:13	power and authority to the **B**
	17:16	the **B**, will turn on the Whore
	17:17	turn over their rule to the **B**
	19:19	I saw the **B**
	19:20	The **B** was taken
	20:4	refused to worship either the **B**
	20:10	joining the **B** and False Prophet

Begged

Ge	27:36	**b**, "Haven't you kept back any blessing
Dt	3:23	I **b** God
1Sa	12:19	all the people **b** Samuel
Ps	116:1	listened as I **b** for mercy
Isa	26:16	O God, they **b** you for help
Mt	8:31	The evil spirits **b** Jesus
	15:25	went to her knees, and **b**
	18:26	at the king's feet and **b**
	18:29	threw himself down and **b**
	18:32	when you **b** me for mercy
Mk	5:10	desperately **b** Jesus not to banish
	5:12	The demons **b** him

	5:18	demon-delivered man **b** to go along
	5:23	beside himself as he **b**
	6:56	**b** him to let them touch
	8:22	sightless man and **b** Jesus
Lk	8:31	**b** Jesus desperately not to order
	8:32	demons **b** Jesus to order them
	8:41	fell at Jesus' feet and **b** him
Jn	9:8	the man we knew, who sat here and **b**
Ac	21:12	everyone there that day **b** Paul
2Co	12:8	**b** God to remove it
Heb	12:19	they **b** him to stop

Begging

Ge	42:21	when he was **b** us for mercy
Ex	11:8	**b** me to leave
1Sa	2.5	well-fed are out **b** in the streets
	2:36	will come to him **b** for handouts
2Sa	18:22	kept at it, **b** Joab
2Ch	28:19	now reduced to **b** for a handout
Est	8:3	**b** with tears to counter the evil
Job	20:10	children will go **b** on skid row
Ps	109:10	**b** street urchins, evicted
Jer	44:4	my servants, **b** you
Mt	17:14	fell to his knees **b**
Mk	1:40	came to him, **b** on his knees
	7:26	**b** for help. The woman
Jn	9:8	had seen him as a blind man **b**
Ac	3:10	one who sat **b** at the Temple's Gate
	13:11	**b** people to take his hand
Jude	1:3	insisting — **b**! — that you fight

Beginning

Ge	31:48	a witness, **b** now
Ex	12:18	**b** on the fourteenth day
Lev	19:25	**B** in the fifth year
	23:5	Passover, **b** at sundown
Dt	9:18	at the **b** of the forty days
Jdg	7:19	the **b** of the middle watch
	10:8	**b** that year, bullied
Ru	1:22	**b** of the barley harvest
2Sa	21:9	**b** of the barley harvest
	21:10	**b** of the harvest
Ezr	4:6	Xerxes, at the **b** of his reign
Job	26:14	this is only the **b**
	38:18	if you have even the **b** of an answer
Pr	20:21	A bonanza at the **b**
Isa	1:26	just like it was back in the **b**
	9:7	**b** now and lasting always
	44:7	From the **b**, who else
	46:10	From the very **b** telling you
	48:6	that was just the **b**
Jer	2:17	**b** to lead you in the right way
	26:1	**b** of the reign of Jehoiakim
Eze	21:19	signpost at the **b** of each road
	40:1	**b** of the year on the tenth
Joel	2:28	And that's just the **b**
Mic	6:13	**B** now, you're finished
Hag	2:9	a glorious **b**
Mt	4:23	**b** right now they were under God's
	23:35	**b** with the blood of that good man

Lk	1:3	starting from the story's **b**
	1:55	what he promised, **b** with Abraham
	3:15	all **b** to wonder
	24:27	started at the **b**
Jn	8:9	**b** with the oldest
Ac	11:4	Peter, starting from the **b**
	15:9	**b** at the very center of who they were
Ro	2:4	think this one through from the **b**
	8:29	very **b**. He decided from the outset
1Co	10:11	they at the **b**, we at the end
2Co	1:22	a sure **b** of what he is destined
Php	2:12	what you've done from the **b**
Col	1:18	was supreme in the **b**
Heb	1:2	created the world in the **b**
	7:3	no account of **b** or end
1Jn	2:24	what you heard from the **b**
	3:2	that's only the **b**
Rev	2:8	The **B** and Ending
	21:6	I'm the **B**, I'm the Conclusion
	22:13	First and the Final, **B** and Conclusion

Beginnings

Dt	3:24	you let me in on the **b**
Ecc	7.8	Endings are better than **b**
Zec	4:10	dare despise this day of small **b**

Behave

2Ki	16:2	didn't **b** in the eyes of his God
	17:34	what he says regarding how to **b**
	17:37	what to believe and how to **b**
Ecc	10:17	Where the princes **b** themselves

Behaved

2Ch	26:4	He **b** well in the eyes of God
	34:2	He **b** well before God

Behaving

1Sa	8:8	**b** like this, leaving me for other gods

Behavior

Lev	26:44	in spite of their **b**
Nu	25:6	flaunting his **b** in front of Moses
Dt	17:13	put an end to presumptuous **b**
2Sa	12:14	because of your blasphemous **b**
Job	31:11	For disgusting **b** like that
	35:8	God's not dependent on your **b**
Ps	38:4	I'm swamped by my bad **b**
Pr	9:7	confront bad **b**
	17:26	wrong to penalize good **b**
Jer	5:25	Your bad **b** blinds you to all this
	23:2	keeping track of your criminal **b**
	25:5	your evil way of life and bad **b**
	26:3	because of their evil **b**
	26:13	change your **b**
	44:22	he couldn't take your evil **b**
Eze	16:43	made me angry with all this **b**
Mt	7:12	simple, rule-of-thumb guide for **b**

B

	23:3	live it out in their **b**
Lk	6:31	simple rule of thumb for **b**
	16:9	just get by on good **b**
Ro	7:7	moral **b** would be mostly guesswork
	14:22	your **b** and your belief are coherent
1Co	5:11	treating it as acceptable **b**
Eph	5:1	like children who learn proper **b**
1Ti	6:1	blame God and our teaching for his **b**
Tit	2:5	because of their **b**
Heb	9:10	limited to matters of ritual and **b**
	9:13	matters of our religion and **b**
1Pe	2:20	treated badly for good **b**

Belief

Mt	6:22	eyes wide in wonder and **b**
	9:2	Jesus, impressed by their bold **b**
Mk	2:5	Impressed by their bold **b**
Lk	5:20	Impressed by their bold **b**
	11:34	wide-eyed in wonder and **b**
Jn	14:29	confirmation will deepen your **b**
Ro	11:20	no longer connected by **b**
	14:22	behavior and your **b** are coherent
	16:26	truth and be brought into obedient **b**
1Co	15:2	your **b** was the real thing and not
Gal	3:6	act of **b** was turned into a life
Heb	10:22	full of **b**, confident
	11:4	**b** continues to catch our notice

Believe

Ge	18:25	I can't **b** you'd do that
	45:3	couldn't **b** what they were hearing
	45:26	couldn't **b** his ears
Ex	3:3	I can't **b** this! Amazing!
	3:18	**B** me, they will listen
Dt	4:26	**B** me, you'll have a very short stay
	15:18	**B** me, God, your God, will bless
Jdg	6:16	**B** me, you'll defeat Midian
	15:13	**b** us, we won't kill you
1Sa	1:26	Would you **b** that I'm the very woman
	14:30	would have been a lot better, **b** me
	24:4	Can you **b** it? This is the day
	26:8	One hit will do it, **b** me
2Sa	17:12	**b** me, there won't be a single survivor
	20:20	**B** me, you've got me all wrong
2Ki	7:2	You expect us to **b** that
	7:19	You expect us to **b** that
	17:34	how to behave and what to **b**
	17:37	what to **b** and how to behave
	18:19	living in a world of make-**b**
	21:12	can't **b** it
	23:3	what to **b** and do
2Ch	7:16	**B** me, I've chosen and sanctified
	20:20	**B** firmly in God, your God
	34:31	what to **b** and do
Ne	4:2	Make building stones out of make-**b**
Job	2:12	couldn't **b** what they saw
	9:16	only then, would I **b** that he'd heard
	9:21	**B** me, I'm blameless
	17:8	can't **b** what they're seeing
	20:2	I can't **b** what I'm hearing!

	27:6	**b** me, I'll never regret it
	29:24	they could hardly **b** it
	33:9	**B** me, I'm clean
	36:4	giving you undiluted truth; **b** me
Ps	10:14	**b** that the luckless will get lucky
	62:4	far gone in make-**b**
	73:10	listen to them — can you **b** it?
	77:2	I didn't **b** a word they said
	78:22	they didn't **b** God
	78:32	can you **b** it
	106:24	didn't **b** a word of what God promised
	118:23	we can hardly **b** it
	126:2	couldn't **b** our good fortune
Pr	2:5	**B** me, before you know it
	4:8	**b** me, you won't regret it
	14:15	gullible **b** anything they're told
	16:5	**b** me, he'll put those upstarts
	22:21	**B** me — these are truths that work
	26:25	don't **b** him for a minute
Ecc	7:16	**B** me, you won't get anything
Isa	1:21	Can you **b** it?
	14:4	Can you **b** it?
	28:21	Hard to **b**, but true.
	59:16	couldn't **b** what he saw
	63:5	I couldn't **b** it — not one volunteer
Jer	7:4	Don't for a minute **b** the lies
	23:10	Can you **b** it?
	29:8	**B** it or not, this is the Message
	29:9	I never sent them, **b** me.
	40:14	Gedaliah son of Ahikam didn't **b**
	41:13	couldn't **b** their eyes
	49:20	**B** it or not, the young
	50:38	A land of make-**b** gods
	50:45	**B** it or not, the young
La	2:15	can't **b** what they see
	4:12	kings of the earth couldn't **b** it
Eze	3:23	couldn't **b** my eyes
	8:10	couldn't **b** my eyes
	14:22	**B** it or not, there'll be survivors
	16:27	can you **b** it?
	23:11	if you can **b** it
Hos	8:11	Can you **b** it?
	13:2	Can you **b** it? They sacrifice live
Hab	1:5	going to find it hard to **b**
Mt	9:28	Do you really **b** I can do this?
	9:29	Become what you **b**
	10:17	just because you **b** in me
	21:25	he'll ask us why we didn't **b** him
	21:42	we can hardly **b** it
Mk	1:15	Change your life and **b** the Message
	8:33	wondering what to **b**
	9:24	I **b**. Help me with my doubts
	10:24	disciples couldn't **b**
	11:31	he'll ask us why we didn't **b**
	12:11	we can hardly **b** it
	14:11	couldn't **b** their ears
	16:11	they didn't **b** her
	16:14	refusing to **b** those who had seen
Lk	1:18	Do you expect me to **b** this?
	1:20	because you won't **b** me
	8:12	so they won't **b** and be saved
	20:5	he'll ask us why we didn't **b**

	20:36	if you can **b** it
	22:5	couldn't **b** their good luck
	22:67	If I said yes, you wouldn't **b** me
	24:11	apostles didn't **b** a word of it
	24:25	Why can't you simply **b** all
	24:41	couldn't **b** what they were seeing
Jn	1:7	where to look, who to **b** in
	3:12	you don't **b** me
	3:14	see and then **b**
	3:18	failure to **b** in the one-of-a-kind Son
	4:21	**B** me, woman, the time is coming
	4:27	couldn't **b** he was talking
	4:48	you refuse to **b**
	5:46	you would **b** me
	6:36	you don't really **b** me
	6:42	expect anyone to **b** him
	7:5	they didn't **b** in him either
	8:24	If you won't **b** I am who I say
	8:30	many people decided to **b**
	8:31	who had claimed to **b** in him
	8:46	why don't you **b** me
	8:58	**B** me," said Jesus
	9:18	didn't **b** it, didn't **b** the man
	9:35	Do you **b** in the Son of Man
	9:36	so that I can **b** in him
	9:38	Master, I **b**
	10:25	I told you, but you don't **b**
	10:26	don't **b** because you're not my sheep
	10:37	well and good; don't **b** me
	11:26	Do you **b** this
	11:42	I've spoken so that they might **b**
	12:39	First they wouldn't **b**
	12:42	ranks of the leaders did **b**
	12:46	all who **b** in me won't have to stay
	13:19	**b** that I am who I say I am
	14:10	Don't you **b** that I am in the Father
	14:11	**B** me: I am in my Father
	16:9	refusal to **b** in me is their basic sin
	16:31	Do you finally **b**
	17:20	for those who will **b** in me
	17:21	might **b** that you, in fact, sent me
	19:35	truth so that you, also, will **b**
	20:25	hand in his side, I won't **b** it
	20:27	Don't be unbelieving. **B**
	20:29	you **b** because you've seen
	20:31	**b** that Jesus is the Messiah
Ac	10:45	couldn't **b** it, couldn't **b** that
	12:9	didn't **b** it was really an angel
	12:11	no dream. "I can't **b** it
	12:15	wouldn't **b** her, dismissing her
	13:39	He accomplishes, in those who **b**
	13:41	won't **b**
	13:48	could hardly **b** their good fortune
	14:9	ripe for God's work, ready to **b**
	14:22	they had begun to **b** and not quit
	15:11	Don't we **b** that we are saved
	16:15	**b** in the Master truly
	16:25	prisoners couldn't **b** their ears
	23:8	they don't **b** it. Pharisees **b** it all
	24:16	**B** me, I do my level best
	24:21	I **b** in the resurrection
	26:8	offense to **b** that God raises the dead

	26:27	You **b** the prophets, don't you
	27:25	**b** God will do exactly what he told me
	28:24	others refused to **b** a word of it
	28:28	**b** me, they're going to receive it
Ro	4:24	embrace and **b** the One
	6:6	What we **b** is this
	10:1	**B** me, friends, all I want for Israel
	14:23	inconsistent with what you **b**
1Co	6:5	I don't **b** it
	6:6	people who don't even **b** in God
	7:17	Live and obey and love and **b**
	9:14	those who **b** the Message
	11:18	I'm reluctant to **b** it
	11:21	I can't **b** it
	13:3	what I **b**, and what I do, I'm bankrupt
	14:21	they'll neither listen nor **b**
2Co	4:14	what we **b** is that the One
	10:7	**B** me, I am quite sure of my standing
	11:23	I can't **b** I'm saying these things.
Gal	1:6	I can't **b** your fickleness
	4:16	I can't **b** it
Col	2:5	**b** me, I'm on your side
2Th	1:10	celebrated by all who **b**
1Ti	5:8	worse than refusing to **b**
Tit	1:13	diseased talk of Jewish make-**b**
Heb	3:1	centerpiece of everything we **b**
	4:3	If we **b**, though, we'll experience
	10:31	getting by with anything, **b** me
	11:6	**b** both that he exists
Jas	2:19	professing to **b** in the one
	2:23	full meaning of "**b**"
1Jn	3:23	**b** in his personally named Son
	4:1	don't **b** everything you hear
	5:13	you who **b** in God's Son will know
2Jn	1:7	refuse to **b** that Jesus Christ

Believed

Ge	15:6	And he **b**! **B** God!
1Ki	10:7	wouldn't have **b** it if I hadn't seen
2Ch	9:6	wouldn't have **b** it if I hadn't seen
Ps	106:12	they **b** his words were true
Mt	8:13	What you **b** could happen has happened
	21:32	crooks and whores **b** him
Mk	16:13	but they weren't **b** either
Lk	1:45	who **b** what God said, **b** every word
Jn	1:12	who **b** he was who he claimed
	2:11	his disciples **b** in him
	2:22	**b** both what was written in Scripture
	4:50	**b** the bare word Jesus spoke
	4:53	Not only he but his entire household **b**
	5:46	If you **b**, really **b**, what Moses said
	7:39	the Spirit, whom those who **b** in him
	10:42	Many **b** in him then and there
	11:27	I have **b** that you are the Messiah
	11:40	If you **b**, you would see the glory
	11:45	saw what Jesus did, and **b** in him
	12:38	who **b** what we preached
	17:8	They **b** that you sent me
	20:8	look at the evidence, and **b**
Ac	4:4	had already **b** the Message
	8:13	Simon himself **b** and was baptized

	11:17	when we **b** in the Master Jesus
	11:21	**b** and turned to the Master
	15:9	as they trusted and **b** him
	16:14	a trusting heart—and she **b**
	18:8	His entire family **b** with him
	19:2	receive the Holy Spirit when you **b**
	19:18	who thus **b** came out of the closet
	22:19	hunting out those who **b** in you
	26:6	I **b** it and took it seriously
Ro	4:13	Abraham then entered when he **b**
	4:18	Abraham **b** anyway
	11:20	your graft "took" when you **b**
	13:12	work he began when we first **b**
1Co	11:22	never would have **b** you would stoop
2Co	4:13	I **b** it, so I said it
Gal	2:16	we **b** in Jesus as the Messiah
	3:6	Abraham? He **b** God
Eph	1:13	you heard the truth and **b** it
2Th	1:10	all because you **b** what we told you
1Ti	3:16	**b** in all over the world
2Ti	3:14	Stick with what you learned and **b**
	4:7	I've . . . **b** all the way
Heb	3:19	they never listened, never **b**
	11:4	what he **b**, not what he brought
	11:11	she **b** the One who made a promise
Jas	2:23	Abraham **b** God and was set right

Believer

Ps	37:25	not once have I seen an abandoned **b**
Pr	30:5	**b** replied, "Every promise of God
Mt	18:15	If a fellow **b** hurts you
Jn	1:50	You've become a **b** simply because
Ac	13:8	divert the governor from becoming a **b**
	13:12	he became a **b**
	26:19	became an obedient **b** on the spot
1Co	7:12	wife who is not a **b**
	7:13	husband who is not a **b**
	7:39	want to marry a **b**
1Ti	3:6	He must not be a new **b**
1Jn	5:16	see a Christian **b** sinning

Believers

Ps	66:16	All **b**, come here and listen
Mt	13:17	prophets and humble **b** among them
	16:8	Runt **b**
	18:10	these childlike **b**
	18:14	lose even one of these simple **b**
	27:42	We'll all become **b** then
	27:52	bodies of **b** asleep in their graves
Mk	9:23	There are no 'ifs' among **b**
	9:42	these simple, childlike **b**
	15:32	We'll all become **b** then
	16:17	signs that will accompany **b**
Ac	2:44	**b** lived in a wonderful harmony
	4:32	congregation of **b** was united
	6:1	Greek-speaking **b**
	8:1	**b** were all scattered
	8:12	becoming **b** right and left
	9:21	havoc in Jerusalem among the **b**
	9:32	met with the **b** there

	9:41	called in the **b** and widows
	15:5	They had become **b**, but continued
	15:10	loading these new **b** down with rules
	17:12	A lot of them became **b**
	18:27	help those who had become **b**
	21:20	God-fearing Jews have become **b**
	21:25	Gentiles who have become **b**
	26:10	I threw these **b**—I had no idea
Ro	14:1	Welcome with open arms fellow **b**
	15:26	the poor among the **b**
	16:4	non-Jewish gatherings of **b**
	16:7	They were **b** in Christ before I was
1Co	5:12	those within our community of **b**
	10:15	addressing **b** now who are mature
	14:22	It doesn't help **b**
	15:12	became **b** because you trusted
2Co	1:1	**b** all over Achaia province
Php	3:3	real **b** are the ones the Spirit
	4:22	**b** who work in the palace
1Th	1:7	**b** look up to you
	2:10	sensitivity to you as fellow **b**
	2:13	God himself at work in you **b**
2Th	3:2	not all "**b**" are **b**
1Ti	4:10	all men and women, especially **b**
	4:12	Teach **b** with your life
2Ti	2:18	throwing **b** off stride
Tit	1:6	Are his children **b**?
Phm	1:7	hospitality to fellow **b**
1Pe	4:6	those **b** who are now dead
1Jn	3:16	live sacrificially for our fellow **b**
Rev	3:9	who call themselves true **b**

Believes

Isa	53:1	Who **b** what we've heard and seen?
Mk	16:16	Whoever **b** and is baptized is saved
Jn	5:24	Anyone here who **b** what I am saying
	6:47	Whoever **b** in me has real life
	7:38	anyone who **b** in me this way
	11:25	one who **b** in me
	12:44	Whoever **b** in me, **b** not just in me
Ac	13:39	who **b** in this raised-up Jesus
Ro	3:22	for everyone who **b** in him
Gal	3:11	who **b** God, is set right by God
1Jn	5:1	who **b** that Jesus is
	5:5	the one who **b** Jesus is the Son of God
	5:10	Whoever **b** in the Son of God

Believing

1Ki	8:40	reverent and **b** obedience
2Ch	6:31	reverence and **b** obedience
Ps	36:2	smooth-talked himself into **b**
Jer	28:15	**b** a pack of lies
	29:31	seducing you into **b** lies
Hab	2:4	loyal and steady by **b**
Mt	18:7	these God-**b** children
	21:22	part of your **b** prayer
Lk	2:17	Seeing was **b**.
	19:6	hardly **b** his good luck
Jn	3:16	by **b** in him, anyone can have
	7:48	any of the leaders **b** in him

	11:15	new grounds for **b**
	11:26	lives **b** in me does not ultimately die
	11:48	soon everyone will be **b** in him
	12:11	Jews were going over and **b** in Jesus
	16:27	**b** I came directly from the Father
	20:31	**b**, have real and eternal life
Ac	3:10	scarcely **b** what they were seeing
	7:31	Moses, not **b** his eyes
	10:45	The **b** Jews who had come with Peter
	21:21	you advise **b** Jews
	24:24	a life of **b** in Jesus Christ
	26:18	begin real living by **b** in me
Ro	10:16	anyone listening and **b** a word of it
	15:13	**b** lives, filled with the life-giving
	15:18	triggered a **b** response
1Co	7:21	no roadblock to obeying and **b**
2Co	4.4	bother **b** a Truth they can't see
Gal	3:14	Spirit, in and with us by **b**
Php	1:5	**b** and proclaiming God's Message
Heb	11:7	rightness of the **b**
	11:13	promised, but still **b**
Jas	2:23	mesh of **b** and acting
	2:25	that seamless unity of **b** and doing
	5:15	**B**-prayer will heal you
1Pe	1:9	Because you kept on **b**
Rev	2:10	Stay there **b**.

Belly

Ge	3:14	Cursed to slink on your **b**
Lev	11:42	whether on their **b** or on all fours
Nu	5:21	your womb shrivel and your **b** swell
	5:22	your **b** swells and your womb shrivels
	5:27	**b** will swell and her womb shrivel
Jdg	3:21	plunged it into the king's big **b**
2Sa	2:23	Abner struck him in the **b**
	3:27	stabbed him in the **b**
	20:10	Joab stuck him in the **b**
Job	10:15	My **b** is full of bitterness
	40:16	the powerful muscles of his **b**
	41:30	His **b** is armor-plated
Pr	13:25	**b** of the wicked always wants more
	18:8	want junk like that in your **b**
	26:22	want junk like that in your **b**
Ecc	5:12	rich man's **b** gives him insomnia
Isa	45:10	Why have you cooped me up in this **b**
Jer	4:19	doubled up with cramps in my **b**
	20:9	words are fire in my **b**
Da	2:32	the **b** and hips were bronze
	7:5	Attack! Devour! Fill your **b**
Jnh	1:17	Jonah was in the fish's **b**
	2:1	prayed to his God from the **b**
	2:2	From the **b** of the grave I cried
Mt	12:40	days and nights in the fish's **b**
Ac	1:18	rupturing his **b** and spilling

Bellyachers

Jude	1:16	the "grumpers," the **b**

Beloved

Dt	33:12	God's **b**; God's permanent residence
2Sa	1:23	Saul and Jonathan — **b**, beautiful
	12:25	named Jedidiah (God's **B**
	22:51	God's chosen is **b**.
Ps	18:50	God's chosen is **b**.
	89:19	spoke to your faithful **b**
SS	1:14	My **b** is a bouquet of wildflowers
Jer	12:7	walk away from my **b** people
Mk	12:6	only one left: a **b** son
Lk	20:13	I'll send my **b** son
Ro	9:25	call the unloved and make them **b**
Eph	1:6	gift-giving by the hand of his **b** Son
1Jn	4:7	My **b** friends, let us continue
Rev	20:9	the **B** City

Bereft

1Sa	2:5	the mother of many is **b**
Job	21:25	Others die bitter and **b**
Ps	142:4	no exit — **b**, left alone
Isa	23:12	bankrupt and **b** Sidon
Jer	49:25	how lonely — **b**, abandoned
Jn	14:27	feeling abandoned, **b**

Best-dressed

Mt	6:29	ten **b** men and women in the country
Lk	12:27	ten **b** men and women in the country

Betray

1Ki	9:6	if you or your sons **b** me
1Ch	12:17	come to **b** me to my enemies
	12:19	they'll **b** us to their master
2Ch	7:19	But if you or your sons **b** me
Ne	1:8	If you **b** me, I'll scatter you
Job	17:5	Those who **b** their own friends
Pr	16:29	climbers **b** their very own friends
	25:9	don't **b** confidences
Isa	63:8	children who would never **b** me
Da	11:23	cease-fire, he'll **b** its terms
	11:30	all those who **b** the holy covenant
	11:32	those who **b** the holy covenant
Na	1:11	lies that seduce and **b**
Mk	14:10	high priests, determined to **b** him
Lk	22:4	how he might **b** Jesus to them
	22:6	looking for a way to **b** Jesus
	22:48	would **b** the Son of Man with a kiss
Jn	6:64	He knew also who would **b** him
	6:71	even then getting ready to **b** him
	12:4	even then getting ready to **b** him
	13:21	One of you is going to **b** me

Bible

Ps	50:5	swore on the **B** their loyalty
Mt	7:26	just use my words in **B** studies
	19:4	read in your **B** that the Creator
	23:16	if he swears with his hand on the **B**
	23:17	leather on the **B** carry more weight

B

Mk	12:26	don't you ever read the **B**?
Lk	6:49	just use my words in **B** studies

Bibles

Mt	21:42	read it for yourselves in your **B**
	22:29	You don't know your **B**
	22:31	don't you read your **B**
Mk	12:24	you don't know your **B**
Lk	24:45	showing them how to read their **B**
Jn	5:39	heads in your **B** constantly

Birthright

Ge	25:32	What good is a **b** if I'm dead
	27:36	first he took my **b** and now

Bitter

Ge	49:6	want no part in their **b** feuds
Ex	12:8	bread, made without yeast, and **b** herbs
	15:23	the water at Marah; it was **b**
Nu	5:18	the **b** water that delivers a curse
	5:19	this **b** water that delivers a curse
	5:23	wash the words off into the **b** water
	5:24	the **b** water that delivers a curse
	9:11	with unraised bread and **b** herbs
Dt	32:32	their grape-clusters **b**
Ru	1:13	a **b** pill for me to swallow — more **b**
	1:20	**B**. The Strong One has dealt me a **b**
1Sa	14:52	war, **b** and relentless
	30:6	**b** over the loss of their families
2Sa	13:20	**b** and desolate
Est	4:1	crying out in loud and **b** cries
Job	3:20	why bother keeping **b** people alive
	6:2	pile the whole **b** load on the scales
	7:11	my complaining to high heaven is **b**
	16:13	**b** bile poured from my gut
	21:25	Others die **b** and bereft
Ps	73:21	I was beleaguered and **b**
	75:8	drink it down to the last **b** drop
	95:8	as in the **B** Uprising
Pr	14:10	shuns the **b** moments of friends
	17:25	a **b** pill for a mother to swallow
Ecc	7:26	woman can be a **b** pill to swallow
Isa	5:4	why did I get **b** grapes
	5:20	substitute **b** for sweet and sweet for **b**
	33:7	Peacemaking diplomats are in **b** tears
Jer	2:19	what you've done and its **b** results
	4:18	The **b** taste is from your evil life
	13:17	**b**, **b** tears, Rivers of tears
	31:15	wild and **b** weeping
La	1:4	How **b** her fate
Eze	27:30	a choir of **b** lament over you
Zep	1:14	**B** and noisy cries on my Judgment Day
Heb	3:8	a deaf ear as in "the **b** uprising
	3:15	a deaf ear as in the **b** uprising
	12:15	weeds of **b** discontent
Rev	8:11	A third of the water turned **b**

Bitterly

Ge	27:34	sobbed violently and most **b**
2Sa	17:8	brave and **b** angry
2Ki	14:26	trouble in Israel, its **b** hard times
Jer	6:26	Weep most **b**, as for an only child
Eze	3:14	I went **b** and angrily
1Ti	6:10	live to regret it **b** ever after

Bitterness

2Sa	2:26	nothing but **b** will come from this
Job	9:18	piles **b** upon **b**
	10:1	all the **b** of my life
	10:15	My belly is full of **b**

Blacklisted

Ps	15:5	never get **b** if you live like this
Jer	2:37	I, God, have **b** those you trusted
	36:5	I'm **b**. I can't go into God's Temple

Blame

Ge	43:9	I'll take all the **b**
	45:5	don't **b** yourselves for selling me
Nu	24:11	You can **b** God
Jdg	21:22	you will incur **b**
1Sa	22:22	I'm to **b** for the death of everyone
	25:24	master, let me take the **b**
Ne	9:33	You are not to **b** for all that
Job	1:22	not once did he **b** God
	5:6	Don't **b** fate when things go wrong
	12:5	point their fingers in **b**
	36:17	obsessed with putting the **b** on God
Ps	15:3	don't **b** your neighbor
	69:9	They **b** me for everything they dislike
	79:8	**b** us for the sins of our parents
Hos	4:4	don't look for someone to **b**
Jnh	1:14	don't **b** us for his death
Mt	27:25	We'll take the **b**, we and our children
Jn	9:3	You're looking for someone to **b**
	15:24	they wouldn't be to **b**
Ac	5:28	**b** us for the death of this man
	7:60	Master, don't **b** them for this sin
Ro	3:7	why **b** me? I'm doing God a favor
	9:19	how can God **b** us for anything
1Ti	6:1	don't **b** God and our teaching
Jas	1:14	We have no one to **b**

Blamed

Jos	9:20	don't get **b** for breaking our promise
Pr	19:3	so why does God always get **b**
Ecc	10:5	can be **b** on whoever is in charge
Eze	14:9	I, God, get **b** for those lies
Mt	28:14	we will make sure you don't get **b**
2Co	6:8	when we're **b**; slandered, and honored

Blameless

Jdg	15:3	wreak havoc on the Philistines, I'm **b**

44

B

Job	9:20	**b** as I am
	9:21	Believe me, I'm **b**
Jn	9:41	you would be **b**, but since you claim

Blaspheme

Ps	74:10	How long, God, will barbarians **b**
Da	7:25	he will **b** the High God

Blasphemed

Lev	24:11	**b** the Name of God and cursed
1Ki	21:10	You **b** God and the king!
	21:13	He **b** God and the king!
Job	6:10	not having **b** the Holy God
Eze	20:14	honored and not **b** by the nations
	20:22	honored and not **b** by the nations
Mt	26:65	He **b**! Why do we need witnesses
Rev	13:6	against God, **b** his Name, **b** his Church

Blasphemer

Lev	24:14	Take the **b** outside the camp
	24:23	brought the **b** outside the camp
Pr	21:24	Brash, Impudent, **B**
Jn	10:36	why do you yell, '**B**! **B**!

Blasphemers

Job	12:6	insolent **b** live in luxury
Mic	4:12	**b** have no idea what God is thinking

Blasphemies

2Ki	19:6	these outrageous **b**
Hos	7:16	just deserts for their mocking **b**
2Pe	2:12	others with their ignorant **b**
Rev	13:6	It yelled **b** against God
	17:3	Stuffed with **b**, the Beast had

Blaspheming

Nu	15:30	deliberately **b** God
1Ti	1:20	taught a lesson or two about not **b**

Blasphemous

2Sa	12:14	because of your **b** behavior
2Ki	19:4	listening to the **b** speech
	19:28	your **b** foul temper
Isa	6:5	tainted — **b** even
	65:7	they've practiced their **b** worship
Eze	21:25	Zedekiah, **b** and evil prince
Lk	5:21	That's **b** talk!
Jude	1:9	level him with a **b** curse
Rev	13:1	each head inscribed with a **b** name
	13:5	loud mouth, boastful and **b**

Blasphemy

Lev	18:21	act of sheer **b** of your God
Eze	20:9	honor, not **b**

Mt	9:3	Why, that's **b**
	26:66	Are you going to stand for such **b**
Mk	2:7	He can't talk that way! That's **b**!
	14:64	You heard the **b**.
Jn	10:33	this **b** of calling yourself God

Bleed

Lev	17:13	must **b** it and cover the blood
Ps	72:14	when they **b**, he bleeds

Bleeding

Lev	12:4	purification from her **b**
	12:5	purification from her **b**
Ps	88:16	I'm **b**, black and blue
Jer	8:7	victims, **b** and moaning, lie all over
	48:37	Hands scratched and **b**
Ro	9:16	our **b** hearts or moral sweat

Blind

Ge	19:11	struck **b** the men who were trying
	27:1	old man and was nearly **b**
	48:10	he was nearly **b**
Ex	4:11	some sighted, some **b**
	23:8	Bribes **b** perfectly good eyes
Lev	19:14	stumbling block in front of the **b**
	21:18	anyone who is **b** or lame
	22:22	giving God an animal that is **b**
Dt	15:21	animal is defective, lame, say, or **b**
	27:18	anyone who misdirects a **b** man
	28:28	make you go crazy and **b**
	28:29	like a **b** person feeling his way
1Sa	4:15	ninety-eight years old then, and **b**
2Sa	5:6	Even the **b** and the lame
	5:8	lame and **b** bunch that David hates
1Ki	14:4	old man at this time, and **b**
2Ki	6:18	people **b**!" And God struck them **b**
Job	9:12	If he steals you **b**
	10:22	dead, **b** in the final dark
	28:7	Vultures are **b** to its riches
	29:15	I was eyes to the **b**
	30:12	come at me from my **b** side
Ps	6:7	my eyes are black holes; nearly **b**
	10:9	wait like a hunter in a **b**
	38:10	Cataracts **b** me to God and good
	69:23	Make them become **b** as bats
	70:2	send them down a **b** alley
	73:19	A **b** curve in the dark
	146:8	he gives sight to the **b**
Pr	4:12	don't want you ending up in **b** alleys
Isa	3:12	led them down a **b** alley
	9:16	led them down **b** alleys
	10:6	strip them clean, rob them **b**
	26:10	**b** to the splendor of God
	29:9	**B** yourselves so you see nothing
	29:18	the **b** will see
	35:5	**B** eyes will be opened
	42:7	opening **b** eyes
	42:18	Open your eyes! Are you **b**
	42:19	**b** as a bat — willfully **b**

B

	43:8	**b** and deaf out here and ready — the **b**
	56:10	Israel's watchmen are **b**
	59:10	Like the **b**, we inch along
Jer	6:10	**b** as a bat
	22:17	But you're **b** and brainless
	31:8	gather those who've gone **b**
La	2:11	My eyes are **b** with tears
Da	5:23	**b**, deaf, and imbecile gods
Hos	7:1	they steal you **b**
Ob	1:5	they'd rob you **b**
Mic	3:6	Therefore, you're going **b**
	7:18	Turning a **b** eye, a deaf ear
Zep	1:17	walk around groping like the **b**
Zec	11:17	Your right eye will go stone **b**
	12:4	make the enemy horses go **b**
Mal	1:8	**b** and sick and crippled animals
Mt	5:29	**b** your right eye
	9:27	followed by two **b** men crying out
	9:28	the **b** men went in with him
	9:32	as the **b** men were leaving
	11:5	The **b** see, The lame walk
	12:22	wretch, both **b** and deaf
	15:14	**b** men leading **b** men
	15:14	**b** man leads a **b** man
	15:30	the **b**, the maimed, the mute
	15:31	the **b** looking around
	20:30	two **b** men sitting alongside
	21:14	room for the **b** and crippled
Mk	10:46	**b** beggar by the name of Bartimaeus
	10:51	**b** man said, "Rabbi, I want to see
Lk	4:18	recovery of sight to the **b**
	6:39	Can a **b** man guide a **b** man?
	7:21	the **b** he gave the gift of sight
	7:22	The **b** see, The lame walk
	18:35	**b** man was sitting beside the road
Jn	5:3	**b**, crippled, paralyzed
	9:1	Jesus saw a man **b** from birth
	9:2	causing him to be born **b**
	9:6	rubbed the paste on the **b** man's eyes
	9:8	had seen him as a **b** man begging
	9:17	They came back at the **b** man
	9:18	didn't believe the man was **b**
	9:19	the one you say was born **b**
	9:20	we know he was born **b**
	9:24	the man who had been **b**
	9:25	I was **b** . . . I now see
	9:32	opened the eyes of a man born **b**
	9:39	will be exposed as **b**
	9:40	you're calling us **b**
	9:41	If you were really **b**
	10:21	Can a 'maniac' open **b** eyes
	11:37	opened the eyes of a **b** man
Ac	9:8	found himself stone **b**
	9:9	continued **b** for three days
	9:17	placed his hands on **b** Saul
	13:11	You're about to go **b**
	22:11	I was **b** as a bat
Ro	2:20	guide others through their **b** alleys
	2:21	are you going to rob people **b**
	3:12	they've all wandered down **b** alleys
	11:10	go **b** staring in their mirrors
2Co	4:4	They're stone-**b** to the dayspring

Heb	11:20	steal you **b**
	11:27	indifferent to the king's **b** rage
Jas	2:6	use the courts to rob you **b**
Rev	3:17	you're a pitiful, **b** beggar
	18:23	robbed the whole earth **b**

Blinded

2Ki	25:7	for they then **b** him
Ps	88:9	**b** by tears of pain and frustration
Jer	39:7	Nebuchadnezzar **b** him
	52:10	for they then **b** him
Eze	12:13	**B**, he'll never see that land
Jn	12:40	eyes are **b**, their hearts are hardened
1Jn	2:11	**b** by the darkness

Blockheads

Pr	8:5	You **b** — shape up
	19:10	**B** shouldn't live on easy street
Isa	6:10	Make these people **b**
Mt	13:15	The people are **b**!
Ac	28:27	These people are **b**

Bloodshed

Lev	17:4	guilty of **b**; he has shed blood
1Ch	22:8	too much killing, too much **b**
Eze	33:6	responsible for the **b** of any unwarned
	33:8	hold you responsible for their **b**
Heb	12:4	Jesus went through — all that **b**

Boast

Job	31:25	Did I **b** about my wealth
Ps	94:4	**b** and crow about their crimes
Eze	27:3	You **b**, Tyre
Da	11:36	brag and **b** in defiance of the God
2Co	10:12	**b** that they're our superiors
Gal	6:13	**b** of their success in recruiting you
	6:14	**b** about nothing but the Cross

Bold

Jdg	7:11	you'll be **b** and confident
1Sa	18:17	Be brave and **b** for my sake
2Sa	1:22	Jonathan's bow was **b**
1Ki	8:28	I'm **b** to ask: Pay attention
	8:54	these **b** and passionate prayers
	22:21	a **b** angel stepped out
2Ch	6:19	I'm **b** to ask: Pay attention
	18:20	a **b** angel stepped out
	19:11	Be **b** and diligent
Pr	22:18	you'll give it **b** expression
	28:1	confident, **b** as lions
Eze	16:23	built your **b** brothels in every town
	16:24	built your **b** brothels
	16:31	built your **b** brothels
	16:39	tear down your **b** brothels
	24:7	Blood runs **b** on the street stones
	29:21	**b** and confident words to speak
Hos	4:18	**B** and sordid debauchery

	7:1	written out in **b** print
Am	5:1	Message I'm sending in **b** print
Mt	9:2	impressed by their **b** belief
	14:28	Peter, suddenly **b**, said
Mk	2:5	Impressed by their **b** belief
Lk	5:20	Impressed by their **b** belief
Ac	2:14	spoke out with **b** urgency
	9:27	his **b** preaching in Jesus' name
Ro	15:15	my rather **b** and blunt language
Gal	6:11	**b** scrawls of my personal handwriting
Eph	3:12	**b** to go wherever we need to go
2Ti	1:7	shy with his gifts, but **b** and loving
Heb	3:6	firm grip on this **b** confidence
1Jn	3:21	we're **b** and free before God
	5:14	how **b** and free we then become
Rev	12:11	the **b** word of their witness

Boldly

Dt	28:26	birds and animals will **b** feast
2Ch	20:17	March out **b** tomorrow
Job	9:35	speak up and state my case **b**
	22:26	look to him joyfully, **b**
Ps	119:46	speak out **b** in public
Pr	7:13	kissed him, **b** took his arm
Heb	13:6	we can **b** quote, God is there
Jas	1:6	Ask **b**, believingly
Rev	2:13	you continue **b** in my Name

Bond

1Sa	18:1	immediate **b** was forged between them
	20:42	God will be the **b** between me and you
Pr	17:9	Overlook an offense and **b** a friendship
	18:19	nothing can untie that **b**
Eze	20:37	under the **b** of the covenant
Da	2:43	kingdom won't **b**, won't hold together
Mal	2:14	broken the faith-**b**
Col	1:23	steady in that **b** of trust
2Th	2:13	salvation by the **b** of faith

Boss

Ge	37:8	You're going to **b** us around?
Nu	16:13	you keep trying to **b** us around
Jdg	9:29	let's see who's **b** here
1Ki	18:8	Now go and tell your **b**
	21:7	Aren't you the **b**?
Pr	19:10	give orders to their **b**
	27:18	honor your **b**
	30:22	janitor becomes the **b**
Isa	1:3	The ox knows who's **b**
	37:29	I'll show you who's **b**.
	60:17	make Righteousness your **b**
Am	1:5	the vice **b** who gives orders
	1:8	the vice **b** from Ashkelon
Mt	10:24	doesn't make more money than his **b**

Boundaries

Ex	19:12	Post **b** for the people all around
	19:23	Post **b** around the mountain

Nu	11:1	burned the outer **b** of the camp
Dt	32:8	within **b** under the care of divine
Jos	19:49	inheritance and the setting of its **b**
Ne	9:22	establishing generous **b**
Ps	104:9	You set **b** between earth and sea
	145:3	There are no **b** to his greatness
Isa	10:13	wiped out the **b** of whole countries
Eze	47:13	the **b** by which you are to divide
	47:15	These are the **b** of the land
	48:10	north and south **b**

Boundary

Nu	22:36	right on the **b** of his land
Dt	3:16	whose middle was the **b**
	3:17	western **b** was the Jordan River
	19:14	Don't move your neighbor's **b** markers
	27:17	who moves his neighbor's **b** marker
Jos	13:23	The **b** for the Reubenites
	15:4	This is the southern **b**
	15:5	The eastern **b**: the Salt Sea
	15:12	the **b** around the people of Judah
	15:21	near the **b** of Edom
	16:5	The **b** of their inheritance
	17:7	The **b** of Manasseh
	17:9	The **b** continued south
	19:22	The **b** touched Tabor
	22:25	the Jordan a **b** between us and you
Job	14:5	you set the **b** and no one can cross it
	26:10	sets a **b** between light
Pr	8:29	When he drew a **b** for Sea
	22:28	stealthily move back the **b** lines
	23:10	stealthily move back the **b** lines
Eze	47:15	northern **b** runs from
	47:17	**b** runs from the Sea
	47:18	eastern **b** runs between
	47:19	southern **b** runs west from Tamar
	47:20	western **b** is formed by
	48:1	one portion, along the northern **b**
	48:23	from the eastern to the western **b**
	48:28	The southern **b** of Gad

Bounty

Ge	27:28	Earth's **b** of grain and wine
	27:39	live far from Earth's **b**
Dt	6:3	life of abundance and **b**
Ps	50:12	All creation and its **b** are mine
	85:12	land responds with **B** and Blessing
Ecc	5:19	**b** and the capacity to enjoy it
SS	8:11	pay anything to get in on that **b**
Isa	61:6	You'll feast on the **b** of nations
Jer	31:12	faces beaming because of God's **b**
Jn	1:16	We all live off his generous **b**
Php	1:21	dead, I'm his **b**

Brag

Ps	52:1	Why do you **b** of evil
	94:4	**b** and boast . . . about their crimes
Jer	9:23	**b** of their wisdom. Don't let heroes **b**
	9:24	If you **b**, **b** of this and this only

B

	49:4	**b** of your once-famous strength
Da	11:36	**b** and boast in defiance of the God
2Co	11:22	Do they **b** of being Hebrews
	11:30	to "**b**" about myself, I'll **b** about
	12:6	If I had a mind to **b** a little
Rev	3:17	You **b**, 'I'm rich

Brave

Jdg	5:13	down to greet the **b** ones
1Sa	10:26	some true and **b** men
	14:52	conscripted every strong and **b** man
	18:17	Be **b** and bold for my sake.
2Sa	17:8	**b** and bitterly angry
1Ki	1:42	A **b** and good man like you
1Ch	5:24	**b** warriors, famous
	7:40	**b** in battle — good leaders
	28:10	Be **b**, determined!
2Ch	26:17	eighty **b** priests of God
Job	10:16	try to **b** it out
	22:29	Chin up! Be **b**!
Ps	31:24	Be **b**. Be strong. Don't give up.
Isa	22:3	no **b** soldiers to honor
Jer	48:41	**B** warriors will double up in pain
	49:22	**B** warriors will double up in pain
	49:26	her **b** warriors silent as death
Ac	8:2	Good and **b** men buried Stephen

Breath

Ge	2:7	the **b** of life. The Man came alive
	7:15	anything that had the **b** of life
	25:8	Then he took his final **b**.
	35:18	With her last **b**
Ex	31:17	stopped and took a long, deep **b**
Jos	11:11	not a **b** of life left anywhere
2Sa	23:18	never named in the same **b**
1Ki	10:5	it took her **b** away
	17:21	put **b** back into this boy's body
	17:22	put **b** back into his body
2Ch	9:4	it all took her **b** away
	15:8	took a deep **b**
Ne	2:4	Praying under my **b**
Job	3:11	my first **b** out of the womb my last
	4:9	One **b** from God and they fall apart
	9:18	He won't even let me catch my **b**
	10:12	watched and guarded every **b**
	15:30	brought down by a puff of God's **b**
	26:13	With one **b** he clears the sky
	27:3	for as long as I draw **b**
	31:30	never cursed them, even under my **b**
	32:8	the **b** of the Almighty One
	33:4	the **b** of God Almighty gave me life
	33:22	next **b** may be their last
	34:14	If he decided to hold his **b**
	36:1	Here Elihu took a deep **b**
	37:1	I'm stunned, I can't catch my **b**
	37:10	**b** that forms the ice, it's God's **b**
Ps	10:3	the swindlers have foul **b**
	23:3	you let me catch my **b**
	34:18	he'll help you catch your **b**
	38:1	Take a deep **b**, God; calm down

	63:4	I bless you every time I take a **b**
	66:5	they'll take your **b** away
	76:8	holds her **b**
	83:15	Knock the **b** right out of them
	83:16	for **b**, gasping, "God
	123:2	holding our **b**, awaiting your word
Pr	9:9	Save your **b** for the wise
Ecc	10:20	not even under your **b**
SS	7:8	Your **b** clean and cool like fresh mint
Isa	11:4	mere **b** from his lips will topple
	30:33	God's **b**, like a river of burning pitch
	40:28	doesn't pause to catch his **b**
	45:19	mumble under my **b**
Jer	2:25	Slow down. Take a deep **b**
	4:31	gasping for **b**, reaching out for help
	15:9	gasping for **b**, Robbed of her children
	50:3	not a movement, not a **b**
	50:40	No one will again draw **b** in that land
La	4:20	Our king, our life's **b**
Eze	21:7	It'll knock the **b** out of everyone
	37:5	I'm bringing the **b** of life to you
	37:8	they had no **b** in them
	37:9	Prophesy to the **b**
	37:10	**b** entered them and they came alive
Hos	5:4	Every **b** they take is a whore's **b**
Joel	2:13	takes a deep **b**, puts up with a lot
Am	5:13	a waste of **b**
Mt	13:55	in the next **b** they were cutting
Mk	4:39	The wind ran out of **b**
	6:3	in the next **b** they were cutting
	9:39	in the next **b** cut me down
	15:37	Jesus . . . gave his last **b**
Jn	20:22	took a deep **b** and breathed into
Ac	13:16	paused and took a deep **b**
Ro	10:15	A sight to take your **b** away
	12:14	no cursing under your **b**
Eph	4:16	His very **b** and blood flow through us
Php	2:15	a **b** of fresh air in this squalid
Col	2:19	very **b** and blood flow through us
Rev	3:2	Take a deep **b**!
	14:1	it took my **b** away!
	14:14	I caught my **b**!

Bribe

Nu	35:31	Don't accept **b** money
	35:32	don't accept **b** money
Dt	16:19	Don't take a **b** — a **b** blinds
	27:25	curse on anyone who takes a **b** to kill
Jdg	16:18	They came, bringing the **b** money
1Sa	12:3	Have I ever taken a **b**
2Ki	16:8	to the king of Assyria as a **b**
Job	36:18	don't think you can **b** your way out
Ps	15:5	never take a **b**
	26:10	purses stuffed with **b**-money
Eze	16:33	You **b** men from all over
Mt	28:15	The soldiers took the **b**
Ac	1:18	he took the evil **b** money
	24:26	would offer him a substantial **b**

Bribes

Ex	23:8	Don't take **b**. **B** blind
Dt	10:17	doesn't play favorites, takes no **b**
1Sa	8:3	taking **b**, corrupting justice
Job	15:34	a life built on **b** goes up in smoke
Pr	6:35	neither **b** nor reason will satisfy
	17:23	The wicked take **b** under the table
Isa	5:23	line your pockets with **b**
	13:17	ruthless bunch indifferent to **b**
	30:6	loaded down with **b**
	33:15	refuse **b**, reject violence
Am	5:12	taking **b** right and left
Mic	7:3	Corrupt leaders demand **b**
Ac	8:21	striking bargains and offering **b**

Bride

Jdg	14:15	they said to Samson's **b**
	14:16	Samson's **b** turned on the tears
	14:20	Samson's **b** became the wife
	15:1	Samson visited his **b**
	15:6	took his **b** and gave her to his best
1Sa	17:25	offer his daughter as a **b**
2Sa	17:3	a **b** brought back to her husband
Ps	45:9	**B** glittering with golden jewelry
SS	4:8	Come with me from Lebanon, my **b**
Isa	49:18	to dress up like a **b**
	61:10	groom who puts on a tuxedo and a **b**
	62:5	young man marries his virgin **b**
Mal	2:14	marriage vows to your young **b**
Mt	10:35	**b** and mother-in-law
Mk	2:19	the **b** and groom are with you
Lk	5:34	the **b** and groom are with you
	12:53	Mother-in-law against **b**, and **b** against
Jn	3:29	The one who gets the **b**
Rev	18:23	never again laughter of **b**
	21:2	for God as a **b** for her husband
	21:9	the **B**, the Wife of the Lab
	22:17	Come!" say the Spirit and the **B**

Bridegroom

Ex	4:25	You're a **b** of blood to me
	4:26	**b** of blood
Isa	54:5	your Maker is your **b**
	61:10	as a **b** who puts on a tuxedo
	62:5	as a **b** is happy in his bride
Mt	25:1	went out to greet the **b**
	25:5	**b** didn't show up
	25:6	He's here! The **b**'s here
	25:10	the **b** arrived
Jn	2:9	he called out to the **b**
	3:29	**b**. And the **b**'s friend

Brimstone

Ge	19:24	God rained **b** and fire down
Dt	29:23	wasteland of **b** and salt flats
Ps	80:4	your people call for fire and **b**
Rev	9:17	breathing out fire and smoke and **b**
	9:18	fire and smoke and **b**

	14:10	torment from fire and **b**
	19:20	into Lake Fire and **B**
	20:10	hurled into Lake Fire and **B**
	21:8	for them it's Lake Fire and **B**

Brood

1Sa	25:22	cur in his misbegotten **b**
Ps	11:4	examining Adam's unruly **b**
	33:13	he sees all Adam's **b**
Ecc	5:20	useless to **b** over how long
Isa	34:15	carrion birds will breed and **b**
Mt	3:7	**B** of snakes!
Lk	3:7	**B** of snakes!
	13:34	like a hen, Her **b** safe under her

Brothels

Eze	16:16	using them as **b**
	16:17	images of them for your **b**
	16:23	built your bold **b** in every town square
	16:24	built your bold **b**
	16:31	built your bold **b**
	16:39	tear down your bold **b**

Build

Ge	6:14	**B** yourself a ship from teakwood
	6:16	**B** a roof for it
	11:4	**b** ourselves a city and a tower
	30:3	**b** a family
	35:1	**b** an altar to the God who revealed
	35:3	**b** an altar there to the God
Nu	23:1	**B** me seven altars here
	23:29	**B** seven altars for me here
	32:16	**b** corrals for our livestock
	32:24	**B** towns for your families
Dt	1:38	**B** up his courage
	6:10	bustling cities you didn't **b**
	8:12	**b** pleasant houses and settle in
	13:16	Don't **b** on that site again
	16:21	Altar of God, your God, that you **b**
	17:16	doesn't **b** up a war machine
	17:17	make sure he doesn't **b** up a harem
	19:3	**b** roads to the towns
	20:20	use the timbers to **b** siege engines
	22:8	When you **b** a new house
	25:9	who refuses to **b** up the family
	27:5	**B** an Altar of stones for God
	27:6	**b** the Altar to God
	28:30	you'll **b** a house and never live in it
Jos	22:26	Let's **b** an altar
	24:13	towns you did not **b**
Jdg	6:26	Then **b** an altar to God
2Sa	5:11	**b** a house for David
	7:5	You're going to **b** a 'house' for me
	7:11	God himself will **b** you a house
	7:13	He will **b** a house to honor me
	7:27	I will **b** you a house.
	24:18	**b** an altar on the threshing floor
	24:21	I can **b** an altar to God here
1Ki	2:36	**B** yourself a house in Jerusalem

B

	5:3	not able to **b** a temple in honor of God
	5:5	**B** a temple in honor of God
	6:38	took Solomon seven years to **b** it
	8:16	**b** a Temple to fix my Name there
	8:17	had it in his heart to **b** a Temple
	8:18	good that you wanted to **b** a Temple
	8:19	your son will **b** it to honor my Name
	9:15	Solomon raised to **b** The Temple of God
	11:7	**b** a sacred shrine to Chemosh
	11:38	I'll **b** you a kingdom as solid
	20:22	**b** up your army
2Ki	6:2	We'll **b** a roomier place
1Ch	14:1	**b** him a royal palace
	17:4	You will not **b** me a 'house'
	17:10	God himself will **b** you a house
	17:12	will **b** a house to honor me
	17:25	I will **b** you a house
	21:18	**b** an altar to God
	21:22	**b** an altar to God
	22:2	stone to **b** The Temple of God
	22:6	**b** a sanctuary for the God of Israel
	22:7	to **b** a sanctuary to honor my God
	22:10	will be the one to **b** a sanctuary
	22:11	**b** the sanctuary for your God
	22:19	**b** the sacred house of worship
	28:2	intended to **b** a permanent structure
	28:3	You may not **b** a house to honor me
	28:6	son Solomon will **b** my house
	28:10	chosen you to **b** his holy house
	29:12	**b** up and strengthen all
2Ch	2:4	**b** a house of worship in honor of God
	2:12	**b** a temple for God
	6:5	**b** a temple to honor my Name
	6:7	**b** a temple honoring the Name of God
	6:8	wanted to **b** a temple in my honor
	6:9	carry on your dynasty, will **b** it
	14:6	able to **b** up a good defense system
	14:7	let's **b** a solid defense system
	20:36	**b** ocean-going ships
	21:11	so far as to **b** pagan sacred shrines
	36:23	assigned me to **b** him a Temple
Ezr	1:2	assigned me to **b** him a Temple
	1:3	**b** The Temple of God
	1:5	**b** The Temple of God in Jerusalem
	4:2	We'll help you **b**. We worship your God
	6:14	leaders of the Jews continued to **b**
	9:9	the heart to **b** The Temple of our God
	9:12	**b** up a tidy estate to hand down
Ne	2:17	let's **b** the wall of Jerusalem
Est	5:14	**B** a gallows seventy-five feet high
Job	27:18	**b** elaborate houses that won't survive
	39:27	teach her to **b** her nest in the heights
Ps	4:5	**B** your case before God
	17:1	Listen while I **b** my case, God
	104:12	birds **b** nests
	104:17	Birds **b** their nests in those trees
	119:28	**b** me up again by your Word
Pr	6:27	Can you **b** a fire in your lap
	17:19	**b** a wall, invite a burglar
	24:3	It takes wisdom to **b** a house
	24:27	plant your fields; then **b** your barn
Isa	11:5	**b** righteousness and faithfulness

	26:6	outcast peoples **b** their lives
	29:3	**b** towers, bring in siege engines, **b**
	32:16	Right will **b** a home
	37:33	**b** a siege ramp against it
	45:13	He will **b** my city.
	57:14	**B**, **b**! Make a road!
	58:12	rubble of past lives to **b** anew
	62:10	**B** the highway
	65:21	They'll **b** houses and move in
	66:1	What sort of house could you **b** for me
Jer	6:6	**B** a siege ramp against Jerusalem
	7:18	fathers **b** fires
	22:14	**b** me an elaborate mansion
	24:6	**b** them up, not tear them down
	29:5	**B** houses and make yourselves at home
	29:28	**b** houses and make yourselves at home
	31:4	start over with you and **b** you up
	33:7	**b** everything back as good as new
	35:7	Neither shall you **b** houses
	35:9	We don't **b** houses
	42:10	I will **b** you up and not drag you down
Eze	4:2	**B** siege walls
	13:10	When people **b** a wall
	17:23	**b** nests in the shade of its branches
	26:8	**b** siege ramps against your walls
	28:26	They'll **b** houses
	34:4	You don't **b** up the weak ones
	34:16	I'll **b** up the weak ones
Da	11:15	he'll **b** siege works
Ob	1:4	if you **b** your nest in the stars
Mic	3:10	who **b** Zion by killing people
Zep	1:13	**b** a house and never move in
Zec	5:11	They will **b** a garage to house it
	6:12	**b** the Temple of God
	6:13	He'll **b** the Temple of God
Mt	7:24	words to **b** a life on
	13:32	eagles **b** nests in it
	23:29	**b** granite tombs for your prophets
Mk	9:5	Let's **b** three memorials
	14:58	**b** another without lifting a hand
Lk	6:47	foundation words, words to **b** a life on
	9:33	Let's **b** three memorials
	11:47	You **b** tombs for the prophets
	11:48	tombs you **b** are monuments
	12:18	tear down my barns and **b** bigger ones
	13:19	eagles **b** nests in it
	14:28	planning to **b** a new house
Jn	2:20	years to **b** this Temple
Ac	7:49	what kind of house will you **b** me
	15:41	to **b** up muscle and sinew
1Co	3:10	take care to **b** on the foundation
1Th	5:11	**B** up hope
1Ti	6:19	**b** a treasury that will last
Tit	2:15	**B** up their courage
Jas	3:13	**b** a reputation for wisdom
Jude	1:20	**b** yourselves up in this most holy

Builders

Ne	4:10	**b** are pooped, the rubbish piles up
Ps	127:1	the house, the **b** only build

Building

2Ch	2:6	who is capable of **b** such a structure
Ezr	4:3	**B** The Temple of our God is not

Bullheaded

2Ki	17:14	more **b** than their stubborn ancestors
Ne	9:16	**b**, they wouldn't obey your commands
Ps	78:8	like their parents, **b** and bad
Isa	1:5	you just keep to your **b** ways
Ac	7:51	And you continue, so **b**

Bullies

2Sa	22:49	You saved me from the **b**
Ps	17:7	running from the neighborhood **b**
	18:48	He saved me from the **b**
	27:2	Those **b** and toughs fall flat
	35:1	God, punch these **b** in the nose
	35:10	protect the unprotected from **b**
	36:11	Don't let the **b** kick me around
	37:14	**B** brandish their swords
	49:6	Shoved around by **b**
	62:3	How long will you run with the **b**?
	75:4	'That's enough,' to the **b**
	86:14	God, these **b** have reared their heads
	86:17	so the **b** who hate me will stand
Pr	13:2	**b** push and shove their way
Isa	25:5	shut the mouths of the big-mouthed **b**
Jer	22:13	who builds palaces but **b** people
Eze	18:12	**b** the weak, steals
Hos	2:18	Safe from beasts and **b**
Mic	5:6	Assyria and all other Nimrod-**b**
Mt	10:28	silence by the threats of **b**
Lk	12:4	the threats of religious **b**
Ro	1:30	**B**, swaggerers, insufferable windbags

Bully

Jdg	15:11	already **b** and lord it over us
1Ch	16:21	stood up for them against **b**-kings
Job	23:6	think he'd dismiss me or **b** me
	24:4	**b** the weak so that they fear
	36:5	he doesn't **b** innocent people
Ps	55:12	isn't the neighborhood **b** mocking
	71:4	from the clutch of Bad and **B**
	73:8	they **b** their way with words
Pr	3:31	Why be a **b**
Isa	3:12	Silly girls **b** them around
	14:5	power of the **b**-rulers
Jer	31:11	grip of the Babylonian **b**
Eze	18:7	doesn't **b** anyone
	18:16	doesn't **b** anyone
	34:4	You **b** and badger them
	45:8	princes will no longer **b** my people
Da	11:18	bullying ways. The **b** will be bullied
Am	5:12	You **b** right-living people
Mic	2:2	They **b** the neighbor and his family
Zec	10:11	**b** Egypt exposed as a fraud
Mt	10:31	intimidated by all this **b** talk

Lk	12:7	intimidated by all this **b** talk
Tit	1:7	not a drunk, not a **b**

Burden

2Sa	13:25	We'd just be a **b** to you
Pr	27:3	the **b** of putting up with a fool
Isa	28:12	the place to lay down your **b**
	53:11	carries the **b** of their sins
Ac	15:19	not going to unnecessarily **b**
	15:28	not be saddled with any crushing **b**
2Co	11:9	never to be a **b** to you
1Th	2:9	the **b** of supporting us

Burdens

Dt	1:12	carry . . . your troubles and **b**
2Sa	19:35	why add to the **b** of my master
Ezr	9:8	lighten our **b** as we serve
Isa	46:2	Dead weight, **b** who can't bear **b**
Zep	3:18	carried those **b** long enough
Gal	6:2	Share their **b**

Burial

Ge	23:4	sell me a **b** plot
	23:6	in the best of our **b** sites
	23:8	give my wife a proper **b**
	23:9	full price for a **b** plot
	23:20	possession as a **b** plot
	49:30	bought . . . for a **b** plot
	50:13	Abraham had bought as a **b** plot
Dt	21:23	Give him a decent **b**
	34:6	No one knows his **b** site
2Sa	2:4	given Saul a decent **b**
	21:14	given a decent **b** in the tomb
1Ki	13:29	own town to give it a decent **b**
	14:13	Everyone will come to his **b**
2Ki	9:10	No **b** for her
	9:34	give her a decent **b**
	11:26	buried Amon in his **b** plot
1Ch	10:12	a dignified **b** under the oak
2Ch	22:9	gave him a decent **b**
	26:23	disqualified him from **b**
	28:27	not honored with a **b** in the cemetery
Job	3:22	day of their death and **b** the happiest
Ps	22:15	laid me out for **b** in the dirt
	49:19	enter the family **b** plot
Ecc	8:10	wicked men given a solemn **b**
Isa	14:18	Other kings get a decent **b**
Eze	39:11	set aside a **b** ground for Gog
	39:14	cleanup **b** operation
	39:15	bury it in the mass **b** site
Am	6:10	prepare them for a decent **b**
Mt	14:12	gave it a reverent **b**
	26:12	really did was anoint me for **b**
	27:7	a **b** place for the homeless
Mk	6:29	gave it a decent **b**
	14:8	she pre-anointed my body for **b**
	15:47	Mary, mother of Joses, watched the **b**
Lk	7:12	son was being carried out for **b**
	23:56	prepare **b** spices and perfumes

B

	24:1	carrying the **b** spices
Jn	12:7	honoring the day of my **b**
	19:40	following the Jewish **b** custom
Ac	9:37	prepared her body for **b**
Ro	6:4	it is like the **b** of Jesus
	8:13	give it a decent **b**
Col	2:12	Going under the water was a **b**
Heb	11:22	made arrangements for his own **b**
Rev	11:9	prevented from getting a decent **b**

Burials

Jer	25:33	no **b** conducted
Eze	39:13	help with the **b**

Buried

Ge	3:19	dead and **b**; you started out as dirt
	25:8	was **b** with his family
	25:9	His sons Isaaac and Isahmael **b** him
	25:10	Abraham was **b** next to his wife
	25:17	he was **b** with his family
	35:4	Jacob **b** them under the oak tree
	35:8	She was **b** just below Bethel
	35:19	Rachel died and was **b** on the road
	35:29	He was **b** with his family
	49:31	Abraham and his wife Sarah were **b**
	50:13	took him on into Canaan and **b** him
Ex	2:12	killed the Egyptian and **b** him
Nu	11:34	they **b** the people who craved meat
	20:1	Miriam died there, and she was **b**
Dt	10:6	Aaron died there and was **b**
	31:16	die and be **b** with your ancestors
	34:6	God **b** him in the valley
Jos	7:21	**b** in my tent with the silver
	7:22	**b** in the tent with the silver
	24:30	**b** him in the land of his inheritance
	24:32	brought from Egypt, they **b** in Shechem
	24:33	They **b** him at Gibeah
Jdg	2:9	**b** him in his allotted inheritance
	2:10	entire generation died and was **b**
	8:32	**b** in the tomb of his father Joash
	10:2	died and was **b** at Shamir
	10:5	Jair died and was **b** in Kamon
	12:7	died and was **b** in his city
	12:10	Ibzan died and was **b** in Bethlehem
	12:12	Elon the Zebulunite died and was **b**
	12:15	Pirathonite died and was **b**
	16:31	**b** him in the tomb of Manoah
Ru	1:17	that's where I'll be **b**
1Sa	25:1	**b** in his hometown of Ramah
	28:3	mourned his death and **b** him in Ramah
	31:13	**b** the bones under the tamarisk tree
2Sa	2:32	brought Asahel and **b** him
	3:32	They **b** Abner in Hebron
	4:12	Isah-Bosheth's head they took and **b**
	7:12	When . . . you're **b** with your ancestors
	17:23	was **b** in the family tomb
	19:37	be **b** with my father and mother
1Ki	1:21	the moment you're **b** my son Solomon
	2:10	was **b** in the City of David
	2:34	**b** in his family plot out in the desert

	11:43	died and was **b** in the City of David
	13:22	not be **b** in your ancestral tomb
	13:31	same tomb where the holy man is **b**
	14:18	They **b** him and everyone mourned
	14:20	died and was **b** with his ancestors
	14:31	Rehoboam died and was **b**
	15:8	Abijah died and was **b**
	15:24	Then Asa died and was **b**
	16:6	Baasha died and was **b**
	16:28	Omri died and was **b**
	22:37	Samaria and there they **b** him
	22:40	**b** in the family cemetery
	22:50	Jehoshaphat died and was **b**
2Ki	8:24	Jehoram died and was **b**
	9:28	**b** him in the family plot
	10:35	Jehu died and was **b**
	12:21	Joash died and was **b**
	13:9	Jehoahaz died and was **b**
	13:13	Jehoash was **b** in Samaria
	13:20	Elisha died and they **b** him
	14:16	Jehoash died and was **b**
	14:20	**b** him in Jerusalem
	14:29	Jeroboam died and was **b**
	15:7	Azariah died and was **b**
	15:38	**b** him in the family cemetery
	16:20	Ahaz died and was **b**
	20:21	Hezekiah died and was **b**
	21:18	**b** in the palace garden
	21:26	They **b** Amon in his burial plot
	22:20	quiet death and be **b** in peace
	23:30	**b** him in his own tomb
	24:6	Jehoiakim died and was **b**
1Ch	17:11	life is complete and you're **b**
2Ch	9:31	Solomon died and was **b**
	12:16	Rehoboam died and was **b**
	14:1	Abijah died and was **b**
	16:14	They **b** him in a mausoleum
	21:1	Jehoshaphat died and was **b**
	21:20	**b** him in the City of David
	24:16	**b** him in the royal cemetery
	24:25	**b** him in the City of David
	25:28	**b** him in Jerusalem
	26:2	after his father was dead and **b**
	26:23	When Uzziah died, they **b** him
	27:9	Jotham died and was **b**
	28:27	When Ahaz died, they **b** him
	32:33	When Hezekiah died, they **b** him
	33:20	When Manasseh died, they **b** him
	34:28	quiet death and be **b** in peace
	35:24	**b** in the family cemetery
Ne	2:3	city where all my family is **b**
	2:5	city where my family is **b**
Job	3:5	day of my birth be **b** in deep darkness
	3:16	Why wasn't I stillborn and **b**
	10:19	a stillborn, **b** without ever
	10:21	Before I die and am **b**
	17:16	If hope and I are to be **b** together
	26:5	All the **b** dead are in torment
Ps	6:5	I can't sing . . . if I'm **b** in some tomb
	106:17	then **b** Abiram's gang
	115:17	word to be heard from those **b**
	143:3	**b** me like a corpse in that dungeon

Pr	21:7	wicked get **b** alive by their loot
Isa	14:9	All the **b** kings of the nations
	26:19	All you dead and **b**, wake up!
	38:18	Those **b** six feet under don't witness
	45:3	I'll lead you to **b** treasures
	53:9	They **b** him with the wicked
Jer	20:6	You'll die and be **b** there
	43:10	stones that I've had **b** here
Eze	26:20	in old ruins, with the **b** dead
	31:16	with all else that gets **b**
	31:18	uncircumcised who are dead and **b**
	32:18	the country of the dead and **b**
	32:21	the dead and **b** will greet them
	32:24	heathen grave with the dead and **b**
Da	12:2	long dead and **b** will wake up
Zec	1:5	your ancestors now? Dead and **b**
Mt	2:18	Her children gone, dead and **b**
	25:18	carefully **b** his master's money
Lk	9:34	found themselves **b** in the cloud
	16:22	rich man also died and was **b**
Jn	5:28	dead and **b** will hear his voice
	12:24	Unless a grain of wheat is **b**
Ac	2:29	David is dead and **b**
	5:6	carried him out and **b** him
	5:9	men who **b** your husband are at the door
	5:10	carried her out and **b** her
	7:16	**b** in the tomb for which Abraham paid
	8:2	Good and brave men **b** Stephen
	13:29	took him down from the cross and **b** him
1Co	15:4	that he was **b**; that he was raised
Php	2:10	even those long ago dead and **b**
1Th	4:13	those already dead and **b**
2Pe	3:4	Our ancestors are dead and **b**

Burnt-offering

Ex	18:12	brought a Whole-**B** and sacrifices
	29:18	a Whole-**B** to God
	29:25	on the Altar with the Whole-**B**
	29:42	your regular, daily Whole-**B**
	30:9	any unholy incense or Whole-**B**
	31:9	the Altar of Whole-**B**
	35:16	the Altar of Whole-**B**
	38:1	the Altar of Whole-**B**
	40:6	Place the Altar of Whole-**B**
	40:10	Anoint the Altar of Whole-**B**
	40:29	set the Altar of Whole-**B**
Lev	1:3	a Whole-**B** from the herd
	1:4	the head of the Whole-**B**
	1:6	Next, skin the Whole-**B**
	1:9	a Whole-**B**, a Fire-Gift
	1:10	If the Whole-**B** comes from the flock
	1:13	a Whole-**B**, a Fire-Gift
	1:14	presented to God for the Whole-**B**
	1:17	a Whole-**B**, a Fire-Gift
	3:5	along with the Whole-**B**
	4:7	the base of the Altar of Whole-**B**
	4:18	the base of the Altar of Whole-**B**
	4:24	where they slaughter the Whole-**B**
	4:25	the horns of the Altar of Whole-**B**
	4:29	at the place of the Whole-**B**
	4:30	the horns of the Altar of Whole-**B**

	4:33	place they slaughter the Whole-**B**
	4:34	horns of the Altar of **B**
	5:7	and the other for the Whole-**B**
	5:10	offer it as a Whole-**B**
	6:9	Whole-**B**. Leave the Whole-**B**
	6:10	ashes remaining from the Whole-**B**
	6:12	arrange the Whole-**B** on it
	6:25	where the Whole-**B** is slaughtered
	7:2	place that the Whole-**B** is slaughtered
	7:8	priest who presents a Whole-**B**
	7:37	instructions for the Whole-**B**
	8:18	ram for the Whole-**B**
	8:21	ram on the Altar. It was a Whole-**B**
	8:28	on top of the Whole-**B**
	9:2	a ram for your Whole-**B**
	9:3	without defect, for a Whole-**B**
	9:7	Absolution-Offering and your Whole-**B**
	9:12	slaughtered the Whole-**B**
	9:14	on top of the Whole-**B**
	9:16	presented the Whole-**B**
	9:17	along with the morning Whole-**B**
	9:22	Whole-**B**, and the Peace-Offering
	9:24	consumed the Whole-**B**
	10:19	Whole-**B** before God today
	12:6	lamb for a Whole-**B**
	12:8	one for the Whole-**B**
	14:13	Whole-**B** are slaughtered
	14:19	slaughter the Whole-**B**
	14:22	the other for a Whole-**B**
	14:31	the other as a Whole-**B**
	15:15	one as a Whole-**B**
	15:30	the other for a Whole-**B**
	16:3	a ram for a Whole-**B**
	16:5	Absolution-Offering and a Whole-**B**
	16:24	Whole-**B** for himself and the Whole-**B**
	17:8	a Whole-**B** or Peace-Offering
	22:18	presents a Whole-**B** to God
	23:12	for a Whole-**B** to God
	23:18	will be a Whole-**B** to God
Nu	6:11	one for the Whole-**B**
	6:14	lamb for the Whole-**B**
	6:16	Absolution-Offering and Whole-**B**
	7:15	yearling lamb for a Whole-**B**
	7:21	yearling lamb for a Whole-**B**
	7:27	yearling lamb for a Whole-**B**
	7:33	yearling lamb for a Whole-**B**
	7:39	yearling lamb for a Whole-**B**
	7:45	yearling lamb for a Whole-**B**
	7:51	yearling lamb for a Whole-**B**
	7:57	yearling lamb for a Whole-**B**
	7:63	yearling lamb for a Whole-**B**
	7:69	yearling lamb for a Whole-**B**
	7:75	yearling lamb for a Whole-**B**
	7:81	yearling lamb for a Whole-**B**
	7:87	animals used for the Whole-**B**
	8:12	another for the Whole-**B** to God
	15:3	Fire-Gift to God, a Whole-**B**
	15:5	lamb for the Whole-**B**
	15:8	young bull as a Whole-**B**
	15:24	young bull as a Whole-**B**
	23:3	watch here beside your Whole-**B**
	23:6	stationed beside his Whole-**B**

	23:15	here beside your Whole-**B**
	23:17	stationed beside his Whole-**B**
	28:3	each day as a regular Whole-**B**
	28:6	the standard Whole-**B**
	28:10	regular Sabbath Whole-**B**
	28:10	in addition to the regular Whole-**B**
	28:11	first of the month offer a Whole-**B**
	28:13	a Whole-**B**, a pleasing fragrance
	28:14	first of the month Whole-**B**
	28:15	In addition to the regular Whole-**B**
	28:19	a Fire-Gift to God, a Whole-**B**
	28:23	regular morning Whole-**B**
	28:24	in addition to the regular Whole-**B**
	28:27	Bring a Whole-**B**
	28:31	over and above the daily Whole-**B**
	29:2	Sacrifice a Whole-**B**
	29:8	Bring a Whole-**B**
	29:11	in addition to the regular Whole-**B**
	29:13	Bring a Whole-**B**, a Fire-Gift
	29:16	in addition to the regular Whole-**B**
	29:19	in addition to the regular Whole-**B**
	29:22	in addition to the regular Whole-**B**
	29:25	in addition to the regular Whole-**B**
	29:28	in addition to the regular Whole-**B**
	29:31	in addition to the regular Whole-**B**
	29:34	in addition to the regular Whole-**B**
	29:36	pleasing fragrance to God, a Whole-**B**
	29:38	in addition to the regular Whole-**B**
Jdg	6:26	bull and present it as a Whole-**B**
	13:16	prepare a Whole-**B** for God
	13:23	wouldn't have accepted our Whole-**B**
1Sa	7:9	offered it whole as a Whole-**B**
2Ch	7:1	struck the Whole-**B** and sacrifices
	29:18	including the Altar of Whole-**B**
	29:24	ordered that the Whole-**B**
	29:27	Whole-**B** was offered on the Altar
	29:28	sacrifice of the Whole-**B**
	35:12	set aside the Whole-**B**
	35:16	offering of the Whole-**B**

Burnt-offerings

Ge	8:20	offered them as **b** on the altar
Ex	20:24	Sacrifice your Whole-**B**
	24:5	offer Whole-**B**
	30:28	the Altar of Whole-**B**
	32:6	offered Whole-**B**
	40:29	offered up the Whole-**B**
Lev	23:37	Fire-Gifts to God: the Whole-**B**
Nu	10:10	blow the bugles over your Whole-**B**
	29:6	monthly and daily Whole-**B**
	29:39	your Whole-**B**, Grain-Offerings
Dt	27:6	offer your Whole-**B** on it to God
	33:10	the Whole-**B** on your Altar
Jos	8:31	offered to God Whole-**B**
	22:23	present on it Whole-**B**
	22:26	an altar—but not for Whole-**B**
	22:27	our Whole-**B** and our sacrifices
	22:28	It's not for Whole-**B**
	22:29	an altar for Whole-**B**
Jdg	20:26	sacrificed Whole-**B**
	21:4	sacrificed Whole-**B**

1Ki	3:4	sacrificed a thousand Whole-**B**
	3:15	worshiped by sacrificing Whole-**B**
	8:64	sacrificed the Whole-**B**
	9:25	sacrificing Whole-**B**
	10:5	worship extravagant with Whole-**B**
2Ki	16:13	Whole-**B** with billows of smoke
	16:15	morning Whole-**B**
1Ch	16:40	Whole-**B** offered on the Altar
	21:26	sacrificed Whole-**B**
	23:31	service of Whole-**B** to God
2Ch	1:6	sacrificed a thousand Whole-**B**
	2:4	Whole-**B** at morning and evening
	4:6	things used for the Whole-**B**
	7:7	sacrificed the Whole-**B**
	8:12	Solomon offered Whole-**B** to God
	9:4	worship extravagant with Whole-**B**
	13:11	sacrificing Whole-**B**
	23:18	offer the Whole-**B** of God
	24:14	daily worship, for the Whole-**B**
	29:31	generosity, even brought Whole-**B**
	29:32	all for Whole-**B** for God
	29:34	slaughter all the Whole-**B**
	29:35	overflow of Whole-**B**
	30:15	brought Whole-**B** to The Temple of God
	31:3	contribution for the Whole-**B**
Ezr	3:2	offer Whole-**B** on it
	3:3	Whole-**B** on it morning and evening
	3:4	the daily Whole-**B**
	3:5	the regular Whole-**B** for Sabbaths
	3:6	offering Whole-**B** to God
	6:9	Whole-**B** to the God-of-Heaven
	8:35	offered Whole-**B**
Ne	10:33	regular Whole-**B** for the Sabbaths

C

Cahoots

1Sa	20:30	you're in **c** with the son of Jesse
Isa	47:15	been in **c** with all your life

Calamities

Dt	31:17	**c** and disasters will devastate them
Jer	16:10	threatening us with all these **c**

Calamity

1Ki	8:37	**c** of any sort
2Ch	6:28	**c** of any sort
Job	5:19	he delivers you; no matter what the **c**
	9:23	When **c** hits and brings sudden death
	31:3	Isan't **c** reserved for the wicked?
Jer	26:19	bringing a terrible **c** upon ourselves
	35:17	I will bring **c** down on the heads

Calendar

Lev	23:44	**c** for the annual appointed feasts
Est	9:31	their assigned place on the **c**
Job	3:6	Rip the date off the **c**
Lk	17:20	counting the days on the **c**

Callous

Ps	39:12	open your ears. Don't be **c**
Lk	1:53	**c** rich were left out in the cold
1Co	5:6	Your flip and **c** arrogance
	10:32	don't be **c** in your exercise of freedom

Calm

Ex	32:11	Moses tried to **c** his God down
Jdg	5:29	answers with **c**, reassuring words
1Sa	16:23	That would **c** Saul down
1Ch	22:9	I will **c** his enemies down
Ps	27:3	When besieged, I'm **c** as a baby
	38:1	Take a deep breath, God; **c** down
	89:9	**c** its waves when they turn unruly
Pr	15:18	a **c**, cool spirit keeps the peace
	17:27	an understanding person remains **c**
	29:8	sages can **c** everyone down
Ecc	10:4	**c** disposition quiets intemperate rage
Isa	7:4	Listen, **c** down. Don't be afraid.
Jer	12:5	keep your wits during times of **c**
	17:8	Serene and **c** through droughts
Eze	5:13	**c** down and let my anger cool
Da	4:19	stay **c**. Don't let the dream
Zep	3:17	he'll **c** you with his love
1Th	4:11	Stay **c**; mind your own business

Calmed

Jdg	8:3	they **c** down and cooled off
Ne	8:11	The Levites **c** the people
Ps	94:19	you **c** me down and cheered me up
Ac	9:31	Things **c** down after that
	12:17	Peter put his hands up and **c** them

Calming

Est	9:30	**C** and reassuring letters

Campaign

Nu	31:3	Recruit men for a **c** against Midian
Jos	10:42	their lands in a single **c**
2Ch	34:6	The clean-up **c** ranged outward
Job	19:12	launched a major **c** against me
Mt	10:9	put on a fund-raising **c** before
Ac	14:2	a whispering **c** against Paul
	18:12	got up a **c** against Paul

Cancel

Dt	15:1	every seventh year, **c** all debts
Ne	10:31	**c** all debts
Isa	14:27	Who could ever **c** such plans?
	34:11	Chaos! He will **c** fertility
	58:6	free the oppressed, **c** debts
Joel	2:13	always ready to **c** catastrophe
Mic	6:7	my precious baby, to **c** my sin
Mt	15:6	You **c** God's command by your rules
Ro	3:31	we **c** out all our careful keeping
Jas	2:11	will **c** out your murder?

Canceled

Nu	30:12	Her husband has **c** them
Dt	15:2	All-Debts-Are-**C**—God says so
	15:9	the year of All-Debts-Are-**C**
	31:10	the Year-All-Debts-Are-**C**
Jos	2:20	oath you made us swear is **c**
2Ki	10:10	judgment on the family of Ahab is **c**
2Ch	29:7	**c** all the acts of worship
Ps	16:10	You **c** my ticket to hell
Eze	20:16	I **c** my promise because they despised
Lk	7:42	so the banker **c** both debts
Ro	3:27	claims and counterclaims? C? Yes, **c**
	3:29	having a corner on God? Also **c**
	11:29	warranty—never **c**, never rescinded
1Co	13:10	our incompletes will be **c**
2Co	1:18	careless yes **c** by an indifferent no
Col	2:14	old arrest warrant **c**
Heb	4:8	live promise. It wasn't **c**
Jude	1:11	they're **c** out in Korah's rebellion

Canceling

Job	33:24	**c** the death sentence
Jer	19:7	I'm **c** all the plans
Mk	14:56	they ended up **c** each other out
Heb	9:16	**c** the old obligations

Cancels

Nu	30:8	he **c** the vow or rash promise
	30:12	her husband **c** them
	30:15	**c** them sometime after he hears of them
Est	8:5	**c** the bulletins authorizing the plan
Mt	12:25	same person **c** himself out
Lk	11:18	If Satan **c** Satan
Ro	3:3	faithlessness **c** out his faithfulness

Cannibal

Dt	28:55	the **c** child-stew he is eating
Mic	3:3	throw it in a pot for **c** stew

Cannibalizing

Dt	28:53	end up **c** your own sons and daughters

Cannibals

Jer	19:9	The people will turn into **c**
Eze	5:10	turn families into **c**

Canopy

2Ch	5:8	formed a **c** over the Chest
SS	1:17	a **c** of cedars enclosed by cypresses
Isa	10:16	Under the **c** of God's bright glory
Jer	43:10	he'll spread out his **c** over them
Eze	41:25	**c** of wood in front of the vestibule

Capabilities

C

| 1Ki | 20:22 | build up your army, assess your c |

Capable

Ge	3:22	c of knowing everything
1Ki	3:9	who on their own is c of leading
2Ki	10:3	Pick the best and most c
2Ch	1:10	who on his own is c of leading
	2:6	who is c of building such a structure
	22:9	no one left . . . c of ruling
	25:5	judged c of military service
Ne	8:2	everyone c of understanding
Mt	19:12	c of growing into the largeness
	20:22	Are you c of drinking the cup
Mk	10:38	Are you c of drinking the cup
Jn	6:65	no one is c of coming to me on his own
Ro	15:14	quite c of guiding and advising
1Co	3:2	c of nothing much more than nursing
	10:11	just as c of messing it up

Capacity

1Ki	7:38	with a c of 230 gallons
2Ki	10:21	packed the temple of Baal to c
Ecc	5:19	and the c to enjoy it
Lk	5:6	fish, straining the nets past c
1Co	2:14	There's no c for them
1Ti	4:2	they've lost their c for truth

Captain

Ge	21:22	Abimelech and the c of his troops
	40:3	custody under the c of the guard
	40:4	c of the guard assigned Joseph
	41:10	house of the c of the guard
	41:12	belonged to the c of the guard
1Sa	17:18	the c of their division
	22:14	son-in-law and c of your bodyguard
2Sa	23:19	the Thirty and was their c
1Ki	16:9	c of half his chariot-force
2Ki	1:9	The king sent a c with fifty men
	1:10	Elijah answered the c
	1:11	sent another c with his fifty men
	1:12	incinerated the c and his fifty
	1:13	sent a third c with his fifty men
2Ch	17:14	cs of the military units
	17:15	his associate C Jehohanan
	26:11	Maaseiah the field c
Ne	7:2	Hananiah the c of the citadel
Isa	36:9	lowest-ranking c in my master's army
Jer	39:11	c of the king's bodyguard
	40:1	c of the bodyguard set him free
	40:2	c of the bodyguard singled out
	40:5	c of the bodyguard gave him food
	41:10	c of the bodyguard
	43:6	c of the bodyguard
Jnh	1:6	The c came to him and said
Mt	8:5	a Roman c came up in a panic
	8:8	Oh, no," said the c.
	8:13	Jesus turned to the c and said

	27:54	The c of the guard
Mk	15:39	Roman c standing guard
	15:44	called for the c to verify
	15:45	Assured by the c, he gave Joseph
Lk	7:2	A Roman c there
	7:6	c sent friends to tell him
	23:47	When the c there saw what happened
Ac	10:1	c of the Italian Guard
	10:22	C Cornelius, a God-fearing man
	21:31	c of the guard
	21:32	mob saw the c and his soldiers
	21:33	c came up and put Paul under arrest
	21:34	c ordered Paul taken
	21:37	Paul said to the c
	22:24	c intervened and ordered Paul taken
	22:26	he went directly to the c
	22:27	c came back and took charge
	22:28	c was impressed
	22:29	fear of God into the c
	22:30	c released Paul
	23:10	c was afraid they would tear Paul
	23:15	c to bring Paul back
	23:17	Take this young man to the c
	23:18	brought him to the c
	23:19	c took him by the arm
	23:22	c dismissed the nephew with a warning
	23:23	c called up two centurions
	24:22	When C Lysias comes down
	27:12	let the ship c and the shipowner talk
Jas	3:4	ship in the hands of a skilled c

Captive

Ge	34:29	took all the wives and children c
Nu	31:9	women and children c
Dt	32:42	Feasting on slain and c alike
1Ki	8:46	are taken c to the enemy's land
2Ki	15:29	took everyone c to Assyria
1Ch	3:17	born while he was c in Babylon
2Ch	6:36	taken off c to the enemy's land
	30:9	your c relatives and children
Ezr	2:1	had carried off c
Ne	7:6	had carried off c
Isa	52:2	get to your feet, c Jerusalem
Jer	34:3	be taken off with him, c
Eze	21:24	you'll be taken c
	32:9	when I take you off c
1Ti	2:6	exchange for everyone held c by sin
2Ti	2:26	caught and held c

Captives

Nu	21:29	daughters abandoned as c to the king
	31:12	c and booty and plunder
	31:19	Purify yourselves and your c
	31:26	count the c, people and animals
2Ch	28:11	return these c, every last one
	28:13	Don't bring the c here!
	28:14	turned over both the c and the plunder
	28:15	gathered the c together
	28:17	taking off a bunch of c
Ps	68:18	climbed to the High Place, c in tow

Isa	20:4	take the Egyptians as c
	61:1	Announce freedom to all c
Jer	40:1	all the other c from Jerusalem
	50:16	you c, while the destruction rages
Eze	12:11	will go into exile as c

Captivity

Dt	28:41	they'll go off to c
Jdg	18:30	the time of the land's c
1Ki	8:47	the country of their c
2Ch	6:37	the country of their c
Ezr	2:1	returned from the c
	3:8	back to Jerusalem from c
	8:35	exiles, now returned from c
	9:7	to killing, to c, to looting
Ne	7:6	returned from the c of the Exile
Ps	130:8	buy back Israel from c to sin
Isa	46:2	hauled off to c
La	1:14	harnessed me to c's yoke

Career

2Ki	21:6	a c in evil
2Ch	33:6	in God's view a c in evil
Pr	8:10	God-knowledge over a lucrative c
Gal	1:14	above my peers in my c
1Th	2:16	made a c of opposing God
Rev	2:21	a c in the god-business

Carefree

Pr	10:0	Honesty lives confident and c
Eze	38:11	unsuspecting, c people
Lk	12:24	c in the care of God
1Pe	5:7	Live c before God

Careless

2Ki	18:12	treated his covenant with c contempt
Pr	4:24	avoid c banter, white lies
	13:3	c talk may ruin everything
	14:11	Lives of c wrongdoing
	19:16	c living kills
	23:17	Don't for a minute envy c rebels
	26:19	c campers who walk away
Mt	6:26	c in the care of God
	12:36	Every one of these c words
	25:24	high standards and hate c ways
Lk	12:40	don't you be slovenly and c
2Co	1:18	c yes canceled by an indifferent no
Jas	3:6	c or wrongly placed word

Carelessly

Mt	5:22	C call a brother 'idiot!'
	23:23	you c take it or leave it
1Co	8:9	when you use your freedom c
Eph	5:17	Don't live c, unthinkingly

Carelessness

| Pr | 1:32 | C kills; complacency is murder |

Carousing

Mk	7:22	deceptive dealings, c, mean looks
2Pe	2:13	wild parties, c in broad daylight
Jude	1:12	c shamelessly, . . . c

Catastrophe

Dt	28:61	every disease and c imaginable
1Sa	6:9	this c is a divine judgment
1Ki	8:37	famine or c, crop failure or disease
2Ki	21:12	will visit c on Jerusalem
2Ch	6:28	famine or c, crop failure or disease
Est	8:6	see this c wipe out my people
Job	5:21	live fearless through any c
Ps	52:2	You scheme c
	52:7	made his living from c
Pr	1:27	What if c strikes
	6:15	C is just around the corner
Isa	31:2	He can call down c
	47:11	C, sudden and total
Jer	6:19	I'm visiting c on this people
	25:29	starting off the c in the city
	29:17	C is on the way
	32:42	will certainly bring this huge c
	36:3	finally understand the c
Eze	7:25	C descends
Da	9:13	c was total
Joel	2:13	always ready to cancel c
Am	6:3	C is just around the corner

Catastrophes

Dt	28:59	God will pound you with c
	32:23	I'll pile c on them
Job	27:22	C relentlessly pursue them

Catastrophic

1Sa	4:17	defeat was c, with enormous losses
Eze	14:21	I've sent my four c judgments
Da	9:12	You brought this c disaster on us
Zep	1:15	a day of c doom

Celebrate

Ex	12:14	c it as a festival to God
Lev	23:39	c the Feast of God for seven days
	23:40	c in the presence of your God
	23:41	seven full days c it
	23:44	feasts of God which Israel was to c
Nu	9:2	c Passover at the set time
	9:3	C it on schedule
	9:4	Israel to c the Passover
	9:6	some of them couldn't c the Passover
	9:10	you may still c God's Passover
	9:11	c it on the fourteenth day
	9:13	still fails to c the Passover

	9:14	wants to c God's Passover
	29:12	C a Festival to God
Dt	12:7	C everything that you
	12:12	C there in the Presence of God
	12:18	c in the Presence of God
	16:10	C the Feast-of-Weeks to God
	16:15	C the Feast to God
	26:11	C all the good things that God
	32:43	C, nations, join the praise
	33:18	C, Zebulun, as you go out
1Sa	29:5	David they c at their parties
1Ki	18:41	Eat and drink—c!
2Ki	23:21	C the Passover to God
2Ch	6:41	let your holy people c goodness
	30:1	c the Passover to Israel's God
	30:2	c Passover in the second month
	30:3	able to c it at the regular time
	30:5	c the Passover to Israel's God in
	30:13	c the Passover
Job	33:26	You'll see God's smile and c
Ps	2:11	C in trembling awe
	20:3	C your sacrifices
	32:11	C God. Sing together
	70:4	those on the hunt for you sing and c
	96:8	Bring gifts and c
	97:1	mainlands and islands — c
	106:5	c with your celebrating nation
	118:24	let's c and be festive
	149:2	all Israel c their Sovereign Creator
Pr	2:14	throw parties to c perversity
	21:15	Good people c when justice triumphs
SS	1:4	We'll c, we'll sing
	5:1	C with me, friends!
Isa	14:29	too soon to c the defeat
	25:1	God, you are my God. I c you
	25:9	Let's c, sing the joys of his salvation
	35:1	badlands will c and flower
	66:10	Jerusalem, and all who love her, c!
La	4:21	C while you can, O Edom
Joel	2:21	Fear not, earth! Be glad and c!
	2:23	Children of Zion, c
Na	1:15	A holiday, Judah! C!
Zep	3:14	Jerusalem, be happy! c
Zec	2:10	Shout and c, Daughter of Zion
	14:16	c the Feast of Booths
	14:18	c the Feast of Booths
	14:19	pilgrimage to c the Feast of Booths
Mt	26:18	c the Passover meal
Lk	15:6	C with me! I've found my lost sheep
	15:9	C with me! I found my lost coin
	15:32	we had to c
Ac	13:33	My very own Son! Today I c you
	20:7	worship and c the Master's Supper
Ro	15:11	People of all nations, c God!
2Co	13:9	we c them, and then go on to c
Php	4:4	C God all day, every day.
Heb	1:5	You're my Son; today I c you
	5:5	You're my Son; today I c you
Rev	18:20	O Heaven, c!
	19:7	Let us c, let us rejoice

Celebrating

Dt	16:1	c the Passover to God, your God
2Sa	6:12	to the City of David, c
1Ki	8:65	started out c for seven days
2Ch	7:9	started out c for seven days
	30:23	they just kept on c
Ps	13:5	I'm c your rescue
	35:9	c God's great work
	42:4	c, all of us, God's feast
	89:42	they're c for all they're worth
	106:5	celebrate with your c nation
Pr	8:31	happily c the human family
Jer	16:9	No more brides and bridegrooms c
Mt	9:15	When you're c a wedding
Mk	2:19	When you're c a wedding
Lk	5:34	When you're c a wedding
Jn	10:22	They were c Hanukkah
Jude	1:24	his bright presence, fresh and c

Celebration

Ge	31:27	sent you off with a great c
Ex	10:9	this is our worship-c of God
	12:14	fixed festival c to be observed always
	13:6	seventh day there is a festival c
Nu	10:10	at times of c, at the appointed feasts
Jdg	9:27	held a c in their god's temple
1Ki	8:65	Two solid weeks of c
1Ch	12:39	three days of feasting c
	29:9	people were full of a sense of c
2Ch	7:9	two solid weeks of c
	30:25	were all in on the joyous c
	35:7	everything needed for the Passover c
Ne	8:12	including the poor in a great c
	12:43	an exuberant c
Est	8:17	took to the streets in c
	9:19	fourteenth day of Adar for c
	9:21	annual c on the fourteenth
Job	22:19	call for a c
Ps	5:11	Stand guard over our c
Pr	10:28	aspirations of good people end in c
Isa	9:3	joy of a great c
	16:9	Instead of song and c, dead silence
	58:13	God's holy day as a c
	61:2	c of God's destruction of our enemies
	62:4	land will be like a wedding c
Jer	33:11	going to hear laughter and c
Zec	8:19	for Judah — c and holiday
Mt	14:6	at his birthday c, he got his chance
Ac	2:46	every meal a c, exuberant and joyful
	16:34	everyone in the house was in on the c
2Co	4:17	the lavish c prepared for us
Eph	1:6	c of his lavish gift-giving
Php	1:18	I'm going to keep that c going
1Pe	2:12	join in the c when he arrives
Rev	11:10	calling for a c

Celebrations

Pr	14:10	be an outsider at their c
Isa	22:2	the city noisy with c

C

Celibacy

1Co	7:7	c is not for everyone
	7:36	not even a "step down" from c

Ceremonial

Ne	12:45	ritual of c cleansing
Isa	66:20	offerings in a c vessel

Ceremonially

2Sa	6:14	David, c dressed in priest's linen
1Ki	9:24	Pharaoh's daughter c ascended
1Ch	29:22	they c reenacted Solomon's coronation
Ne	12:30	c purified themselves
	13:9	ordered that they c cleanse the room
	13:22	c cleanse themselves

Ceremony

Ex	29:1	c for consecrating them as priests
Jer	34:18	promised in the covenant c
Da	3:2	dedication c of the statue

Challenge

1Sa	17:10	I c the troops of Israel this day
	17:11	heard the Philistine's c
	17:23	gave his usual c
Job	37:20	think I'm dumb enough to c God
Da	8:11	dared to c the power of God
2Ti	4:2	C, warn, and urge your people
Jas	1:12	meets a testing c head-on

Challenged

2Sa	2:14	Abner c Joab
1Ki	18:21	Elijah c the people
2Ti	3:8	Jannes and Jambres, who c Moses

Challenges

Zec	9:1	God's Message c the country
Jas	1:2	c come at you from all sides

Challenging

1Sa	17:25	openly and defiantly c Israel
2Ki	14:8	c him to a fight
2Ch	25:17	c him to a fight
Mt	5:44	I'm c that

Chambers

Pr	7:3	etch it on the c of your heart
Isa	14:11	your underworld private c
Jer	36:12	c of the secretary of state
Eze	46:19	holy c assigned to the priests
Mt	26:3	c of the Chief Priest

Chaos

2Sa	22:18	that enemy c, the void
Ps	18:17	that enemy c, the void
	42:7	C calls to c
	51:10	Geesis week from the c of my life
Pr	28:2	When the country is in c
Isa	19:2	anarchy and c and killing
	24:18	C pours out of the skies
	34:11	C! He will cancel fertility
	51:9	dispatch the old c-dragon
	65:17	earlier troubles, c, and pain
Jer	4:23	back to pre-Geesis c and emptiness
	31:36	fell into c before me
	46:5	total c, total confusion
	51:42	Babylon drowned in c
Eze	22:5	notorious for c
Jas	3:6	turn harmony to c
2Pe	3:5	into existence out of watery c
	3:6	brought the c back in a flood

Character

1Sa	9:1	Aphiah — a Benjaminite of stalwart c
1Ch	7:40	excellent in c, and brave in battle
Job	13:27	brand me as a dangerous c
Pr	11:5	Moral c makes for smooth traveling
	11:6	Good c is the best insurance
	20:3	mark of good c to avert quarrels
Eze	36:22	to save my c, my holy name
Mt	3:11	main c in this drama
	7:15	look for c
	13:21	no soil of c
Mk	4:17	such shallow soil of c
Lk	3:16	main c in this drama
	23:50	man of good heart and good c
Jn	17:6	I spelled out your c in detail
Eph	4:24	God accurately reproduces his c in you
1Ti	4:16	firm grasp on both your c
Tit	2:10	good c will shine through
2Pe	1:5	good c, spiritual understanding

Charm

Ge	35:4	lucky-c earrings
Ps	58:5	Deaf to threats, deaf to c
Pr	31:30	C can mislead and beauty soon fades
Isa	47:11	you can't c it away

Charmed

Ps	10:6	They live (they think) a c life
	55:21	I've been c by his speech
Ecc	10:11	If the snake bites before it's been c
Jer	8:17	Snakes that can't be c

Charmer

Ecc	10:11	point in then sending for the c

Charming

Isa	47:1	Nobody will be calling you 'c'

Chatterboxes

Pr	10:21	c die of an empty heart

Chattering

Jdg	9:36	Gaal kept c away
Ecc	10:14	C stuff they know nothing about
Mt	24:51	cold shivering, teeth c

Chatty

Ro	15:18	a c account of my adventures

Cheat

Ge	29:25	Why did you c me
Lev	19:35	Don't c when measuring length
	25:14	your countrymen, don't c him
	25:17	Don't c each other
Jos	24:27	lest you c on your God
Ps	24:4	Men who won't c
Pr	23:10	c orphans out of their property
Ecc	5:9	good earth doesn't c anyone
Isa	65:20	anything less will seem like a c
Mal	2:15	Don't c on your spouse
	2:16	Don't let your guard down. Don't c
Mk	10:19	don't lie, don't c
Ac	13:10	schemes to c people out of God
2Co	12:17	Did I c or trick you

Cheated

Ge	31:7	your father has c me over and over
Ps	105:25	abused and c God's servants
Pr	6:34	jealousy detonates rage in a c husband
Isa	29:21	gone the people who c the poor
Mal	2:11	Judah has c on God
Jas	5:4	workers you've exploited and c

Cheating

Lev	6:2	robbing or c or threatening him
Job	24:2	stealing and lying and c
Ps	55:11	shopkeepers gouging and c
Pr	11:1	God hates c in the marketplace
	20:23	God hates c in the marketplace
	21:6	Make it to the top by lying and c
	28:8	rich as you want through c
Isa	33:18	that c moneychanger
Jer	9:4	like old c Jacob
	17:11	person who gets rich by c
Hos	3:1	your c wife
	5:10	rulers are crooks and thieves, c
Mic	6:10	wealth you've piled up by c
Lk	19:8	if I'm caught c, I pay four times
Ro	1:29	killing, bickering, and c
Jas	4:4	You're c on God

Cheats

Ps	11:5	if anyone c, God's outraged
	116:11	They're all liars and c
Jer	17:11	c by laying its eggs in another
	22:13	Who c his workers and won't pay

Cheerful

Pr	12:25	a c word picks us up
	15:13	A c heart brings a smile
	15:15	a c heart fills the day with song
	17:22	c disposition is good for your health
2Co	13:11	Be c. Keep things in good repair.
1Th	5:16	Be c no matter what

Cheerfully

2Ch	24:10	c brought their money
Ro	12:12	c expectant. Don't quit
2Co	5:9	C pleasing God is the main thing
Php	2:14	Do everything readily and c
1Pe	4:9	a bed to the homeless — c

Cherish

Ps	112:1	Who c and relish his commandments
	119:47	I c your commandments
Jude	1:3	a gift to guard and c

Cherished

Dt	7:6	a c, personal treasure
	14:2	his c personal treasure
	28:54	his c wife
	28:56	against her c husband

Cherishes

Eph	5:31	c his wife

Cherishing

Eph	5:23	not by domineering but by c

Childbearing

Isa	54:1	more children than all those c women
1Ti	2:15	her c brought about salvation

Childbirth

Ge	3:16	multiply your pains in c
Isa	54:1	who've never experienced c
Jer	22:23	pain worse than the pangs of c
	49:24	disabled, like a woman in c
Hos	9:11	neither conception nor c
Mic	4:10	like a woman in c
Gal	4:19	Like a mother in the pain of c
Rev	12:2	cried out in the pain of c
	12:4	crouched before the Woman in c

Childhood

Ps	71:5	my bedrock, God, since my c

Childless

Ge	15:2	use are your gifts as long as I'm c
Lev	20:20	held responsible and die c
	20:21	They will be c
Jdg	13:2	wife was barren and c
	13:3	I know that you are barren and c
1Sa	15:33	your sword made many a woman c
	15:33	so your mother will be c
Ps	113:9	He gives c couples a family
Jer	18:21	Let their wives be c and widowed
	22:30	Write this man off as if he were c
Mt	22:24	if a man dies c, his brother is
	22:26	second brother also left her c
Mk	12:20	first took a wife. He died c
Lk	1:7	c because Elizabeth could never
	20:29	first took a wife. He died c

Childlike

Jnh	4:11	c people who don't yet know right
Mt	18:5	receive the c on my account
	18:10	these c believers
Mk	9:42	these simple, c believers
Ro	8:15	greeting God with a c "What's next
1Co	14:20	c unfamiliarity with evil

Christ

Mt	1:1	The family tree of Jesus C
	1:16	the Jesus who was called C
	1:17	from the Babylonian exile to C
	16:16	You're the C, the Messiah
	22:42	the C? Whose son is he
	22:43	if the C is David's son
	23:10	one Life-Leader for you and them — C
	24:5	claiming, 'I am C, the Messiah.'
	27:17	Jesus the so-called C
	27:22	Jesus, the so-called C
Mk	1:1	The good news of Jesus C
	8:29	You are the C, the Messiah
Jn	1:41	the Messiah" (that is, "C
	17:3	Jesus C, whom you sent
Ac	2:38	in the name of Jesus C
	3:6	In the name of Jesus C
	4:10	By the name of Jesus C
	5:42	teaching and preaching C Jesus
	8:12	proclaiming the name of Jesus C
	9:34	Jesus C heals you
	10:36	through Jesus C everything is
	10:48	baptized in the name of Jesus C
	11:17	believed in the Master Jesus C
	15:26	sake of our Master Jesus C
	16:18	In the name of Jesus C, get out
	24:24	life of believing in Jesus C
	28:31	explained everything about Jesus C
Ro	1:1	devoted slave of Jesus C
	1:6	gift and call of Jesus C

	2:16	proclaim through Jesus C
	3:24	did it by means of Jesus C
	5:6	C arrives right on time
	5:15	gift poured through one man, Jesus C
	5:17	the one man Jesus C provides
	6:6	nailed to the Cross with C
	6:8	C's sin-conquering death
	7:4	When C died he took that entire
	7:25	Jesus C can and does
	8:1	C's being-here-for-us
	8:2	Spirit of life in C
	8:9	present God, the Spirit of C
	8:11	body will be as alive as C's
	8:17	exactly what C goes through
	8:35	drive a wedge between us and C's love
	9:2	C and the Holy Spirit are my witnesses
	9:5	produced the Messiah, the C
	10:17	unless C's Word is preached
	12:5	C's body of chosen people
	13:14	Dress yourselves in C
	14:3	guests at C's table
	14:15	persons for whom C died
	14:18	task is to single-mindedly serve C
	15:18	present words and deeds of C
	15:29	C's more extravagant blessings
	16:7	were believers in C before I was
	16:9	our companion in C's work
	16:10	veteran in following C
	16:12	dear friend and hard worker in C
	16:16	All the churches of C
	16:18	living for our Master C
	16:25	exactly as preached in Jesus C
1Co	1:3	the Master, Jesus C, be yours
	1:6	evidence of C has been clearly
	1:17	C on the Cross
	1:18	Message that points to C on the Cross
	1:23	we go right on proclaiming C
	1:24	C is God's ultimate miracle
	1:30	comes from God by way of Jesus C
	2:16	C knows, and we have C's Spirit
	3:1	like infants in relation to C
	3:11	the one already laid: Jesus C
	3:23	in union with C
	4:1	We are servants of C
	4:17	all the churches on the way of C
	7:22	if you were free when C called you
	8:11	C gave up his life for that person
	8:12	hurt your friend, you hurt C
	9:12	detract from the Message of C
	9:22	I kept my bearings in C
	10:4	And the Rock was C
	10:9	never try to get C to serve us
	10:16	the blood, the very life, of C
	10:17	C doesn't become fragmented in us
	11:3	authority from C to husband
	11:4	the authority of C, dishonors C
	12:12	exactly the same with C
	12:27	You are C's body
	12:29	C's church is a complete Body
	15:12	C is alive, risen from the dead
	15:13	no resurrection, there's no living C
	15:14	if there's no resurrection for C

	15:15	verifying that God raised up C
	15:16	C wasn't, because he was indeed dead
	15:17	if C wasn't raised
	15:18	hoping in C and resurrection
	15:19	all we get out of C
	15:20	C has been raised up
	15:22	everybody comes alive in C
	15:23	C is first, then those with him
	15:57	gift of our Master, Jesus C
2Co	1:2	the Master, Jesus C, be yours
	1:21	making us a sure thing in C
	2:10	as C is with us, guiding us
	2:14	In the Messiah, in C, God leads us
	2:15	Because of C, we give off a sweet
	2:17	stand in C's presence when we speak
	3:3	C himself wrote it
	3:4	written by C himself for God
	3:15	Only C can get rid of the veil
	4:4	Message that shines with C
	4:5	proclaiming Jesus C, the Master
	4:6	understood God in the face of C
	5:10	We will appear before C
	5:20	We're C's representatives
	5:21	How? you say. In C.
	6:15	Does C go strolling with the Devil
	8:9	generosity of our Master, Jesus C
	8:23	a real credit to C
	9:13	meaning of the Message of C
	10:1	gentle but firm spirit of C
	10:5	structure of life shaped by C
	10:7	example of someone on C's side
	10:14	the Message of C
	11:2	promised your hand in marriage to C
	11:3	simple purity of your love for C
	11:10	With C as my witness
	11:13	posing as C's agents but sham
	11:17	didn't learn this kind of talk from C
	11:23	Are they servants of C?
	12:2	seized by C and swept in ecstasy
	12:10	I just let C take over!
	12:19	God revealed in C
	13:3	proof that C speaks through me
	13:4	we'll be alive in C
	13:5	Jesus C is in you
	13:14	grace of the Master, Jesus C
Gal	1:4	Jesus C rescued us
	1:6	called you by the grace of C
	1:7	turning the Message of C on its head
	1:10	wouldn't bother being C's slave
	1:12	Message directly from Jesus C
	2:16	personal faith in Jesus C
	2:17	through C . . . to get things right
	2:20	C's life showed me how
	2:21	then C died unnecessarily
	3:7	who put their trust in C
	3:13	C redeemed us
	3:16	referring to C
	3:19	until C (the descendant) came
	3:26	By faith in C
	3:27	Your baptism in C
	3:28	In C's family there can be no division
	3:29	you are C's family

	4:19	until C's life becomes visible in your
	5:1	C has set us free
	5:2	C's hard-won gift of freedom
	5:3	free life in C
	5:4	you are cut off from C
	5:6	in C, neither our most conscientious
	5:24	those who belong to C
	6:2	and so complete C's law
	6:12	shares C's suffering and death
	6:14	Cross of our Master, Jesus C
	6:18	Master Jesus C gives freely
Eph	1:1	special agent of C Jesus
	1:2	our Master, Jesus C
	1:3	Father of our Master, Jesus C
	1:5	into his family through Jesus C
	1:9	set it all out before us in C
	1:11	in C that we find out who we are
	1:13	It's in C that you
	1:17	God of our Master, Jesus C
	1:20	All this energy issues from C
	1:22	C rules the church
	1:23	The church is C's body
	2:5	made us alive in C
	2:7	grace and kindness upon us in C Jesus
	2:10	creates each of us by C Jesus
	2:12	hadn't the faintest idea of C
	2:13	because of C—dying that death
	2:16	C brought us together
	2:17	C came and preached peace to you
	2:20	C Jesus as the cornerstone
	3:1	I, Paul, am in jail for C
	3:4	the mystery of C
	3:6	same promises in C Jesus
	3:11	then executed in C Jesus
	3:17	C will live in you
	4:7	the generosity of C
	4:13	fully alive like C
	4:15	in love—like C in everything
	4:20	You learned C
	4:25	In C's body we're all connected
	4:32	thoroughly as God in C forgave you
	5:2	Observe how C loved us.
	5:5	kingdom of C, the kingdom of God
	5:8	light of C makes your way plain
	5:10	Figure out what will please C
	5:13	they look in the light of C
	5:14	C will show you the light
	5:19	Sing songs from your heart to C
	5:20	in the name of our Master, Jesus C
	5:21	Out of respect for C, be courteous
	5:22	ways that show your support for C
	5:23	the way C does to his church
	5:24	just as the church submits to C
	5:25	exactly as C did for the church
	5:26	C's love makes the church whole
	5:29	how C treats us, the church
	5:32	the way C treats the church
	6:5	obeying the real master, C
	6:6	work heartily, as C's servants
	6:23	from the Master, Jesus C
	6:24	all who love our Master, Jesus C
Php	1:1	committed servants of C Jesus

C

	1:2 our Master, Jesus C	4:16	the dead in C will rise
	1:6 on the very day C Jesus appears	5:9	salvation by our Master, Jesus C
	1:8 feel as strongly about you as C does	5:18	you who belong to C Jesus to live
	1:11 making Jesus C attractive to all	5:23	the coming of our Master, Jesus C
	1:15 some here preach C	5:28	amazing grace of Jesus C
	1:18 C is proclaimed	2Th 1:12	Jesus C, giving himself freely
	1:19 response of the Spirit of Jesus C	2:1	our Master, Jesus C, will come back
	1:20 make C more accurately known	2:14	the glory of our Master, Jesus C
	1:21 Alive, I'm C's messenger	3:5	path of God's love and C's endurance
	1:23 be with C is powerful	3:18	grace of our Master, Jesus C
	1:26 We'll be praising C	1Ti 1:1	assignment for C, our living hope
	1:27 credit to the Message of C	1:2	best from our God and C be yours
	1:29 more to this life than trusting in C	1:12	I'm so grateful to C Jesus
	2:1 all out of following C	1:15	Jesus C came into the world to save
	2:5 the way C Jesus thought of himself	5:11	rather than serving C in this way
	2:10 bow in worship before this Jesus C	6:13	before C, who took his stand
	2:16 day that C returns	6:14	Our Master, Jesus C, is on his way
	2:17 faith that you make on C's altar	2Ti 1:1	on special assignment for C
	3:3 filling the air with C's praise	1:2	best from our God and C be yours
	3:7 And why? Because of C	1:13	faith and love rooted in C
	3:8 privilege of knowing C Jesus	2:1	throw yourself into this work for C
	3:9 comes from trusting C	2:10	the salvation of C
	3:10 so I could know C personally	3:12	who wants to live all out for C
	3:12 reaching out for C	3:15	salvation through faith in C Jesus
	3:18 They hate C's Cross	4:1	C himself is the Jdge
	3:20 the Savior, the Master, Jesus C	Tit 1:1	I, Paul, am God's slave and C's agent
	4:7 C displaces worry	2:13	God and Savior, Jesus C, appears
	4:23 grace of the Master, Jesus C	Phm 1:1	prisoner for the sake of C
Col	1:1 on special assignment by C	1:3	C's blessings on you
	1:2 stalwart followers of C	1:6	recognize C in all of it
	1:4 your steady faith in C, our Jesus	1:8	As C's ambassador
	1:7 reliable worker for C	1:20	You'll be doing it for C
	1:22 C brought you over to God's side	1:23	my cellmate in the cause of C
	1:24 the kind of suffering C takes on	1:25	best to you from the Master, Jesus C
	1:27 C is in you	Heb 3:6	C as Son is in charge of the house,
	1:28 We preach C	3:14	we're in this with C
	2:2 focused on C, God's great mystery	5:5	Neither did C presume to set himself
	2:5 solid substance of your faith in C	6:1	fingerpainting exercises on C
	2:6 You received C Jesus, the Master	9:14	blood of C cleans up our whole lives
	2:8 that's not the way of C	9:15	Through the Spirit, C offered himself
	2:9 realize the fullness of C	9:24	C didn't enter the earthly version
	2:11 what C has already gone through	9:28	C's death was also a one-time event
	2:12 from the dead as he did C	10:5	prophecy, put in the mouth of C
	2:13 alive — right along with C	10:12	C made a single sacrifice for sins
	2:14 canceled and nailed to C's Cross	10:26	we repudiate C's sacrifice
	2:17 the substance is C	13:9	grace of C is the only good ground
	2:19 the source of life, C	Jas 2:1	our glorious, C-originated faith
	2:20 So, then, if with C	2:16	Be clothed in C
	3:1 new resurrection life with C	1Pe 1:19	paid with C's sacred blood
	3:2 alert to what is going on around C	2:5	offering C-approved lives up to God
	3:3 is with C in God. He is your life	2:21	kind of life C lived
	3:4 C (your real life, remember)	3:15	in adoration before C, your Master
	3:11 by C, everyone is included in C	3:18	what C did definitively: suffered
	3:15 the peace of C	4:13	very thick of what C experienced
	3:16 the Word of C — the Message	4:14	abused because of C
	3:24 ultimate Master you're serving is C	5:1	in on C's sufferings as well
	4:3 telling the mystery of C	5:10	God who has great plans for us in C
	4:4 be able to make C plain as day	5:14	Peace to . . . all who walk in C's ways
1Th	1:3 following our Master, Jesus C	2Pe 1:1	servant and apostle of Jesus C
	2:6 some standing as C's apostles	1:11	our Master and Savior, Jesus C
	2:14 follow in the footsteps of Jesus C	1:16	return of our Master, Jesus C
	3:2 spreading the Message, preaching C	2:20	our Master and Savior, Jesus C

C

	3:18	our Master and Savior, Jesus C
1Jn	1:3	Father and his Son, Jesus C
	1:5	the message we heard from C
	2:1	Jesus C, righteous Jesus
	2:8	as it is in both C and you
	2:22	who denies that Jesus is the Divine C
	2:25	C promised: eternal life, real life
	2:27	C's anointing, no less
	2:28	stay with C. Live deeply in C
	3:2	when C is openly revealed, we'll see
	3:5	C showed up in order to get rid of sin
	3:6	one who lives deeply in C
	3:16	C sacrificed his life for us
	3:23	his personally named Son, Jesus C
	4:2	confesses openly his faith in Jesus C
	4:5	belong to the C-denying world
	4:17	standing . . . is identical with C's
	4:21	command we have from C is blunt
	5:6	Jesus — the Divine C
	5:20	Truth itself, in God's Son, Jesus C
2Jn	1:3	Jesus C, Son of the Father
	1:7	Jesus C was truly human
	1:9	walks out on the teaching of C
Jude	1:1	I, Jude, am a slave to Jesus C
	1:4	Jesus C, our one and only Master
	1:17	apostles of our Master, Jesus C
	1:21	the mercy of our Master, Jesus C
	1:25	our only Savior, through Jesus C
Rev	1:2	God's Word — the witness of Jesus C
	1:5	from Jesus C — Loyal Witness
	2:11	C-conquerors are safe from Devil-death
	12:11	were willing to die for C
	20:4	lived and reigned with C
	20:6	They're priests of God and C

Christian

Ac	19:9	the C way of life
	21:7	greeted our C friends there
	26:28	you'll make a C out of me
	28:14	We found C friends there
	28:22	only thing we know about this C sect
Ro	16:5	very first C in the province of Asia
1Co	5:11	one of your C companions
	7:12	C married to nonChristian
	8:9	a C still vulnerable to those old
Gal	1:22	unknown by face among the C churches
Eph	2:19	as much right to the name C as anyone
Php	4:21	Give our regards to every C you meet
Col	3:25	Being C doesn't cover up bad work
1Ti	3:16	This C life is a great mystery
	5:16	C woman who has widows in her family
Phm	1:16	a true C brother
Heb	3:1	dear C friends, companions
	12:23	C citizens
Jas	2:7	scorn the new name — "C"
1Pe	4:16	if it's because you're a C
1Jn	5:16	if we see a C believer sinning
3Jn	1:5	hospitality to C brothers and sisters

Christians

Ac	8:4	the C all became missionaries
	11:26	were for the first time called C
	11:29	fellow C in Judea to help out
	15:20	not serve food offensive to Jewish C
	15:29	food offensive to Jewish C
	18:22	greeted the assembly of C there
	18:23	time with the Antioch C
	21:25	food offensive to Jewish C
	22:5	hunt down the C there
Ro	1:1	letter to all the C in Rome
	12:13	Help needy C; be inventive
	14:2	assume all C should be vegetarians
	15:25	relief offering to the C
	15:31	offering to the Jerusalem C
	16:1	hospitality we C are famous for
	16:11	those C from the family
	16:15	all the C who live with them
1Co	1:2	C cleaned up by Jesus
	6:1	instead of a family of C
	6:2	a jury made up of C
	16:1	offering for poor C
	16:15	serving C ever since then
2Co	8:4	relief of poor C
	9:1	offering for the poor C
	9:12	meet the bare needs of poor C
	11:9	needs were always supplied by the C
Gal	2:4	spies pretending to be C
Eph	1:1	you faithful C in Ephesus
	1:15	outpouring of love to all the C
	1:18	glorious way of life he has for C
	3:8	any of the available C
	3:10	Through C like yourselves gathered
	3:18	take in with all C
	4:12	train C in skilled servant work
	5:4	C have better uses for language
Php	1:1	letter to all the C in Philippi
	1:14	most of the C here have become
	3:6	point of persecuting C
	4:22	All the C here
Col	1:2	I greet the C
	1:4	love you continuously extend to all C
	2:1	the C over at Laodicea
1Th	1:1	C assembled by God the Father
	5:26	Greet all the C there
2Th	1:1	church of the Thessalonian C
1Ti	4:3	with thanksgiving by C
	4:6	pass on this counsel to the C there
	5:10	tired C, the hurt and troubled
Phm	1:5	brims over to other C
Heb	6:10	shown him by helping needy C
1Pe	4:17	It's judgment time for C
	5:9	the same with C all over the world
3Jn	1:10	hospitality to traveling C
Rev	3:4	still have a few C in Sardis

Church

Mt	16:18	my c, a c so expansive with energy
	18:17	the c. If he won't listen to the c
	23:6	head table at c dinners

Mk	12:39	head table at every c function
Lk	11:43	head table at c dinners
	20:46	head table at every c function
Ac	5:11	By this time the whole c
	8:1	persecution of the c
	8:3	devastating the c
	9:31	c had smooth sailing for a while
	11:22	c in Jerusalem got wind of this
	11:26	meeting with the c and teaching
	12:1	to go after some of the c members
	12:5	c prayed for him
	12:25	offering to the c in Jerusalem
	14:23	handpicked leaders in each c
	14:27	got the c together and reported
	15:2	c decided to resolve the matter
	15:4	graciously received by the whole c
	15:22	carried considerable weight in the c
	15:24	men from our c went to you
	15:30	On arrival, they gathered the c
	21:18	All the c leaders were there
Ro	16:1	key representative of the c
	16:5	the c that meets in their house
	16:23	host here to both me and the whole c
1Co	1:2	letter to you in God's c
	5:1	scandalous sex within your c family
	11:22	stoop to desecrating God's c
	12:25	our lives together as a c
	12:28	parts that God has formed in his c
	12:29	Christ's c is a complete Body
	14:4	proclaiming God's truth to the c
	14:12	what helps everyone in the c
	14:19	when I'm in a c assembled for worship
	15:9	stamp God's c right out of existence
2Co	2:9	responsibility for the health of the c
	7:5	fights in the c
Gal	1:13	persecuting God's c
	2:2	those held in esteem by the c
	2:6	who were considered important in the c
	2:9	Peter, and John — the pillars of the c
	2:13	Antioch c joined in that hypocrisy
Eph	1:22	Christ rules the c
	1:23	The c, you see, is not peripheral
	3:21	Glory to God in the c!
	4:12	working within Christ's body, the c
	5:23	the way Christ does to his c
	5:24	just as the c submits to Christ
	5:25	as Christ did for the c
	5:26	Christ's love makes the c whole
	5:29	how Christ treats us, the c
	5:32	the way Christ treats the c
Php	4:15	not one c helped out
Col	1:18	c, he organizes and holds it together
	1:24	c's part of that suffering
	1:25	When I became a servant in this c
	4:15	the c that meets in her house
1Th	1:1	greetings to the c at Thessalonica
2Th	1:1	greet the c of the Thessalonian
1Ti	3:1	provide leadership in the c
	3:5	how can he take care of God's c
	3:8	who want to be servants in the c
	3:12	Servants in the c
	3:15	God's household, this God-alive c

	4:14	leaders of the c laid hands on you
	5:9	receive support from the c
	5:16	shouldn't be dumped on the c. The c
	5:22	appoint people to c leadership
Tit	1:7	a c leader, responsible for the affairs
Phm	1:2	the c that meets in your house
Jas	2:2	enters your c wearing an expensive
	5:14	Are you sick? Call the c leaders
1Pe	5:1	special concern for you c leaders
	5:13	The c in exile here with me
3Jn	1:6	made a full report back to the c
	1:9	wrote something . . . to the c
Rev	2:1	to the Angel of the c
	2:8	to the Angel of the c
	2:12	to the Angel of the c
	2:18	to the Angel of the c
	2:23	every c will know that appearances
	3:1	to the Angel of the c
	3:7	to the Angel of the c
	3:14	to the Angel of the c
	13:6	blasphemed his C

Churches

Ac	9:32	a mission to visit all the c
Ro	16:16	All the c of Christ send
1Co	4:17	instructions I . . . give all the c
	7:17	give this same counsel in all the c
	11:16	All God's c see it this way
	14:33	This goes for all the c
	16:1	same instructions I gave the c
	16:19	c here in western Asia send greetings
2Co	8:1	God is working in the c
	8:2	came down on the people of those c
	8:18	popular in the c for his preaching
	8:19	c handpicked him to go with us
	8:23	delegates from c
	8:24	love I've been talking up in the c
	11:8	other c paid my way
	11:28	anxieties of all the c
	12:13	than any of the other c
Gal	1:1	greetings to the Galatian c
	1:22	unknown by face among the Christian c
Eph	3:10	like yourselves gathered in c
1Th	2:14	footsteps of the c of God
2Th	1:4	tell everyone we meet in the c
Jude	1:19	the ones who split c
Rev	1:4	the seven c in Asia province
	1:11	Send it to the seven c
	1:20	the Angels of the seven c
	2:7	the Spirit blowing through the c
	2:11	the Spirit blowing through the c
	2:17	the Spirit blowing through the c
	2:29	the Spirit blowing through the c
	3:6	the Spirit blowing through the c
	3:13	the Spirit blowing through the c
	3:22	the Spirit blowing through the c
	22:16	testify to these things for the c

Circumcise

Ge	17:10	C every male

	17:11	C by cutting off the foreskin
	17:13	c both your own children
Lev	12:3	On the eighth day c the boy
Jos	5:2	c the People of Israel
Jer	4:4	c your lives for God's sake
Lk	1:59	they came to c the child
Jn	7:22	so you c a man
Ac	15:5	have to c the pagan converts
	21:21	don't need to c their children

Circumcised

Ge	17:12	Every male baby will be c
	17:23	c them, cutting off their foreskins
	17:24	ninety-nine years old when he was c
	17:25	thirteen years old when he was c
	17:26	were c the same day
	17:27	all were c with him
	21:4	c him just as God had commanded
	34:15	if all your men become c like us
	34:22	all our males become c
	34:24	every male was c
Ex	12:44	Any slave, if he's paid for and c
	12:48	every male in his family must be c
Jos	5:3	c the People of Israel
	5:5	had been c, but all those born
	5:7	Joshua c. They had never been c
Ac	15:1	everyone be c: "If you're not c
	16:3	took him aside and c him
Ro	2:25	it's worse than not being c
	2:27	law uncircumcised than break it c
	4:9	keep our religious ways and are c
Gal	2:3	was not required to be c
	6:13	want you to be c so they can boast
Php	3:5	legitimate birth, c on the eighth day
Col	2:11	not a matter of being c

Circumcision

Ge	34:25	Three days after the c
Ex	4:26	blood" because of the c
Jos	5:4	why Joshua conducted the c
Lk	2:21	eighth day arrived, the day of c
Jn	7:22	Moses prescribed c
Ac	7:8	signed it in Abraham's flesh by c
	11:2	old associates, concerned about c
Ro	2:25	C, the surgical ritual that marks you
	4:10	marked by the covenant rite of c
	4:11	c as evidence and confirmation
	4:12	c not just because of the ritual
Gal	2:12	pushing the old system of c
	5:2	submits to c or any other rule-keeping
	5:3	person who accepts the ways of c
	5:11	continue to preach the ways of c
	5:12	obsessive as they are about c
	6:12	force the ways of c on you
	6:15	submit to c, reject c

Citizen

Lev	16:29	both the c and the foreigner
2Ki	14:26	whether slave or c

Ps	135:21	God of Zion, First C of Jerusalem
Jer	47:2	washing away city and c
Lk	15:15	He signed on with a c there
Ac	21:39	a c still of that influential city
	22:25	torturing a Roman c
	22:26	This man is a Roman c
	22:27	You're a Roman c?
	22:29	had put a Roman c in chains
	23:27	learned that he was a Roman c
Ro	13:1	Be a good c
	13:7	Fulfill your obligations as a c

Citizens

Dt	13:13	together with some of the c
	13:15	execute the c of that town
Jos	8:33	foreigners and c alike
Jdg	19:16	all the local c were Benjaminites
1Sa	5:3	morning when the c of Ashdod got up
	5:6	God was hard on the c of Ashdod
2Sa	2:4	The c of Judah came to Hebron
	2:7	c of Judah have made me their king
2Ki	17:29	shrines that the c of Samaria
1Ch	8:13	drove out the c of Gath
	11:5	The c of Jebus told David
2Ch	19:10	involving any of your fellow c
	32:22	God saved Hezekiah and the c
	33:9	led Judah and the c of Jerusalem off
	33:25	c in their turn then killed
	34:9	the c of Jerusalem
	35:5	every grouping of your fellow c
	35:18	plus the c of Jerusalem
Ne	7:3	Appoint the guards from the c
Pr	17:26	good c pay for the crimes of others
Isa	8:14	preventing trespass to the c
	9:9	Ephraim and the c of Samaria
	30:19	people of Zion, c of Jerusalem
	37:27	leaving their c helpless
	48:2	claim to be c of the Holy City
Jer	11:2	c of Jerusalem
	11:9	c of Jerusalem
	13:13	c of Jerusalem
	17:25	c of Jerusalem
	18:11	c of Jerusalem my Message
	22:4	officials and the c of Judah
	25:2	c of Jerusalem
	35:13	c of Jerusalem
	42:18	swept the c of Jerusalem away
Eze	11:15	c of Jerusalem are saying
	33:2	take one of their c and make him
Da	9:7	c of Jerusalem
Mic	1:11	c of Exitburgh will never get out
Zec	11:16	disdains decent c
Lk	13:4	do you think they were worse c
	16:8	smarter . . . than law-abiding c
	19:14	But the c there hated him
Ac	13:27	The c and rulers in Jerusalem
	16:37	in jail, Roman c in good standing
	16:38	Paul and Silas were Roman c
	19:35	Fellow c, is there anyone anywhere
Ro	13:3	Decent c should have nothing to fear
1Co	6:10	don't qualify as c in God's kingdom

Php	3:20	We're c of high heaven!
Heb	12:23	Christian c
Jas	2:5	the kingdom's first c
	2:6	you are abusing these same c
1Pe	2:13	Master proud of you by being good c

Clamor

Ps	94:13	quiet within the c of evil
Eze	7:26	c for the prophet to tell them
Hos	9:11	dissipated in confusion and c
Mk	8:12	c for miraculous guarantees
1Co	1:22	c for miraculous demonstrations

Clap

Jer	11:16	only take a c of thunder
Eze	6:11	C your hands, stamp your feet
	21:14	C your hands. Get their attention
	21:17	I'll c my hands, a signal

Clapped

Eze	22:13	I've c my hands
	25:6	Because you c and cheered

Clarify

Job	4:3	spoken words that c
Gal	2:2	c with them what had been revealed

Cleanse

Lev	16:30	atonement will be made for you, to c
2Ch	34:3	set out to c the neighborhood
Ne	13:9	ceremonially c the room
	13:22	ceremonially c themselves
Da	11:35	testing will refine, c, and purify
Mk	1:40	If you want to, you can c me
Lk	5:12	If you want to, you can c me
Heb	13:12	brought to God's altar to c his people

Cleansed

Lev	14:4	brought for the one to be c
	14:7	sprinkle the person being c
	14:8	The c person
	14:14	right earlobe of the man being c
	14:17	right earlobe of the one being c
	14:18	head of the man being c
	14:19	atonement for the one to be c
	14:25	right ear of the one to be c
	14:28	right ear of the one to be c
	14:29	head of the one to be c
	14:31	atonement for the one to be c
	15:13	person with a discharge is c from it
	15:28	she is c from her discharge
Nu	19:13	doesn't get c desecrates
	19:19	is considered c. The c person must
Ne	13:30	I c them from everything foreign
Mt	8:4	Your c and grateful life
	11:5	Lepers are c

Lk	4:27	only one c was Naaman
	5:14	Your c and obedient life
	7:22	Lepers are c
Heb	12:29	won't quit until it's all c

Cleansing

Lev	14:2	infected person at the time of his c
	14:32	regular offerings for his c
	14:52	c the house with the blood
	15:13	seven days for his c
Nu	19:9	use in the Water-of-C
	19:12	purify himself with the Water-of-C
	19:13	Water-of-C has not been sprinkled
	19:20	not go through these c procedures
	19:21	man who sprinkles the Water-of-C
	31:23	washed in the Water-of-C
1Sa	7:6	before God in a ritual of c
Ne	12:45	ritual of ceremonial c
Mk	1:44	the offering for c

Clue

Job	12:25	grope in the dark without a c
	28:13	Mortals don't have a c
	38:17	Do you have one c regarding death
Ps	82:5	haven't a c to what's going on
Pr	5:6	She hasn't a c about Real Life
	24:7	serious discussion they haven't a c
Isa	3:7	I don't have a c
	6:10	won't have a c about what's going on
Eze	7:26	Priests don't have a c
Da	12:10	keep on being wicked, without a c
Zep	2:1	nation without a c about what it wants
Lk	21:7	What c will we get
Jn	4:45	not that they really had a c
	6:30	give us a c about who you are
	9:21	haven't a c about who opened his eyes
Ac	14:17	didn't leave them without a c
1Co	1:21	a c when it came to knowing God
	2:8	a c about what this eternal plan is
Eph	2:12	hadn't a c about what God was doing

Clueless

Hos	7:11	bird-brained, mindless, c
Mic	7:16	their arrogance, speechless and c

Code

Ro	7:5	old law c hemmed us in
	7:7	If the law c was as bad as all that
	7:8	law c started out as an excellent
	7:9	sin got its hands on the law c
	7:12	law c itself is God's good
	8:3	law c, weakened
	8:4	c asked for but we couldn't deliver
	10:5	using the law c to live right
	13:9	The law c—don't sleep with
	13:10	add up everything in the law c
1Co	15:56	law-c guilt that gave sin its leverage
Eph	2:15	repealed the law c

C

| 1Ti | 1:9 | law c isn't primarily for |
| Tit | 3:9 | fine print in the law c |

Comfort

Ge	24:67	found c after his mother's death
	37:35	tried to c him but he refused their c
Ex	16:3	Why didn't God let us die in c
1Ch	7:22	family gathered to give him c
Job	2:11	keep him company and c him
	16:5	I'd console and c
	17:13	only hope for c is a well-built coffin
	21:34	how do you expect me to get any c
Ps	119:77	Now c me so I can live
	119:82	how long must I wait for your c
Ecc	4:1	victims, no one to c them
Isa	40:1	C, oh c my people," says your God
	51:3	I, God, will c Zion, c all
	51:19	hunger and death — will anyone c
	57:18	heal him, lead him, and c
	61:2	to c all who mourn
	66:13	so I'll c you
Jer	31:13	lavishing c, invading their grief
La	2:13	give you c, dear Zion
Eze	16:54	some c to your two sisters
	32:31	take c in the company he'll keep
Hos	3:4	without religion and c
Zec	1:17	God will c Zion again
Mt	5:11	truth is too close for c
	14:27	Jesus was quick to c them
Mk	6:50	Jesus was quick to c them
Lk	6:22	truth is too close for c
Ac	4:36	Barnabas" (which means "Son of C
	24:25	getting a little too close for c
2Co	1:5	good times of his healing c
Rev	12:14	kept in safety and c for a time

Comfortable

Ge	43:24	made them c — gave them water
2Sa	7:2	c in a luxurious house of cedar
	19:18	to make the king c
1Ki	1:15	at his side making him c
1Ch	17:1	c in a luxurious palace of cedar
Isa	47:10	so confident and c in your evil life
Lk	10:34	led him to an inn, and made him c
1Co	7:37	c in his decision for a single life

Comfortably

Jdg	5:10	ride on prize donkeys c mounted
2Ki	25:30	everything he needed to live c
Jer	52:34	everything he needed to live c

Comforted

2Sa	12:24	David went and c his wife
Isa	12:1	moved in and c me
	49:13	God has c his people
	52:9	God has c his people
	66:13	You will be c in Jerusalem

Comforters

2Sa	10:3	honoring your father by sending you c
1Ch	19:3	honoring your father by sending you c
Job	6:2	What a bunch of miserable c

Comforting

Isa	51:12	I'm the One c you
Eze	13:6	fantasize c illusions and preach lying
Zec	1:13	good words, c words

Comforts

| Isa | 66:13 | As a mother c her child |
| Rev | 12:6 | all c provided her |

Commandment

Dt	5:31	tell you every c and all the rules
	6:1	This is the c
	6:25	do this entire c in the Presence
	8:1	Keep and live out the entire c
	11:8	in charge of keeping the entire c
	11:22	diligently keep all this c
	15:5	diligently observing every c
	27:1	Keep every c that I command you today
	30:11	This c that I'm commanding you today
Jos	22:5	Be vigilant in keeping the C
Ezr	10:3	those who honor God's c
Mt	5:27	You know the next c pretty well
Mk	12:31	no other c that ranks with these
Ro	7:13	hiding within God's good c
Eph	6:2	first c that has a promise attached
1Jn	2:7	the oldest c in the book
2Jn	1:5	this is not a new c
	1:6	his unifying c is that

Commandments

Ex	15:26	obeying his c and keeping all his laws
	20:6	thousands who love me and keep my c
	24:12	teachings and c that I've written
Lev	4:13	straying from one of the c of God
	4:27	straying from one of the c of God
	5:17	sins by breaking any of the c of God
	26:3	obediently keep my c
	26:14	won't observe my c
	27:34	the c that God gave to Moses
Nu	15:39	remember and keep all the c of God
	15:40	remembrance and observance of all my c
Dt	5:10	thousands who love me and keep my c
	6:6	Write these c that I've given you
	7:9	those who love him and observe his c
	8:2	whether you would keep his c or not
	8:6	paramount that you keep the c of God
	8:11	by not keeping his c
	10:13	obey the c and regulations of God
	11:1	obey his c for the rest of time
	11:13	listen obediently to the c
	11:27	listen obediently to the c of God
	11:28	if you don't pay attention to the c

	13:4	keep his c, listen obediently
	26:17	rules, regulations, and c; and listen
	26:18	entrusted with keeping his c
	27:10	Keep his c and regulations
	28:9	if you keep the c of God
	28:15	diligently keep all the c
	28:45	diligently keep his c
	30:8	keeping all his c
	30:10	keep the c and regulations written
	30:16	Walk in his ways. Keep his c
1Ch	28:8	study every last one of the c
2Ch	14:4	follow the c
	24:20	walked away from God's c
	31:21	carrying out of God's Law and C
Ezr	9:14	breaking your c by intermarrying
Ne	10:29	keep and carry out all the c of God
Ps	112:1	Who cherish and relish his c
	119:35	Guide me down the road of your c
	119:43	your c are what I depend on
	119:47	I cherish your c
	119:139	persistently ignored your c
Mk	10:19	You know the c: Don't murder
	12:28	most important of all the c
Lk	1:6	keeping to the ways of the c
	18:20	You know the c, don't you
Jn	14:21	who knows my c and keeps them
Heb	7:18	system of c that never worked out
1Jn	2:3	Keep his c
	2:4	doesn't keep his c
	5:3	comes when we keep his c
2Jn	1:6	Love means following his c

Commendable

1Ki	8:18	build a Temple in my honor — most c
2Ch	6:8	build a temple in my honor — most c
Mt	23:23	Careful bookkeeping is c
Lk	11:42	Careful bookkeeping is c

Commission

Nu	27:19	c him with everyone watching
Dt	1:13	I will c them as your leaders
	31:14	so that I can c him
Jos	18:4	men from each tribe so I can c them
Job	38:34	c a shower of rain
Ps	82:7	you've betrayed your c
Mt	28:18	commanded me to c you
Lk	19:14	sent a c with a signed petition
Ac	13:2	c them for the work I have called
1Co	9:2	admits the authority of my c

Commissioned

Ge	41:41	So Pharaoh c Joseph
Nu	27:23	laid his hands on him and c him
2Ch	33:7	that he had c in The Temple of God
Ps	82:6	I c you judges
Lk	9:2	He c them to preach the news
	9:6	C, they left
Ac	6:6	laid on hands and c them
	10:42	c us to announce this in public

	13:3	So they c them
1Co	9:1	Wasn't I c to this work
	15:7	those he c to represent him
Gal	1:1	raised him from the dead. I'm God-c

Commitment

Dt	33:11	God bless his c
Jos	24:14	Worship him in total c
2Ki	23:3	their c was unanimous
Isa	54:10	my covenant c of peace won't fall
	55:3	a lasting covenant c with you
Da	9:4	never waver in your covenant c
Mt	5:10	your c to God provokes persecution
	23:23	compassion and c — the absolute basics
Jn	6:29	That kind of a c gets you in
Ro	11:20	no longer connected by belief and c
	11:27	this is my c to my people
1Co	6:17	sex that avoids c and intimacy
2Co	8:12	the c is clear, you do what you can
	10:8	c is for the purpose of building
Php	3:15	something less than total c

Communion

1Co	2:14	God's Spirit and our spirits in open c
1Jn	1:3	experience of c with the Father

Communities

Ro	1:13	other non-Jewish towns and c

Community

Ge	6:9	a man of integrity in his c
	23:10	part of the local Hittite c
Ex	12:3	Address the whole c of Israel
	12:6	entire c of Israel will do this
	12:19	cut off from the c of Israel
	12:47	whole c of Israel is to be included
	34:31	Aaron and the leaders in the c
	35:20	everyone in the c of Israel left
	38:25	those in the c who were registered
Lev	10:17	taking away the guilt of the c
	16:5	from the Israelite c he will bring
	16:17	and the whole c of Israel
	20:2	The c must kill him by stoning
	20:14	purging the wickedness from the c
Nu	1:53	wrath will not fall on the c of Israel
	8:9	gather the entire c of Israel
	8:20	entire c of the People of Israel
	10:3	whole c will meet you at the entrance
	14:1	The whole c was in an uproar
	14:2	The entire c was in on it
	14:5	in front of the entire c
	14:10	c was talking of hurling stones
	14:27	this evil-infested c
	14:35	against this entire evil-infested c
	14:36	causing the entire c to grumble
	15:15	c has the same rules for you and
	15:25	atone for the entire c of the People
	15:26	The whole c of Israel including

C

	15:31	person must be kicked out of the c
	15:35	kill him, the whole c hurling stones
	15:36	whole c took him outside the camp
	16:3	This entire c is holy
	16:19	entire c could see the Glory of God
	16:22	take it out on the whole c
	16:24	Speak to the c. Tell them
	16:26	He then spoke to the c
	16:28	Moses continued to address the c
	16:33	the last the c heard of them
	16:41	the c of Israel, grumbling
	16:42	c got together against Moses
	19:20	must be excommunicated from the c
	20:2	no water there for the c
	20:8	Assemble the c, you and your brother
	26:2	Number the entire c of Israel
	26:9	c leaders from Korah's gang
	27:16	set a man over this c
	27:17	God's c will not be like sheep
	27:21	People of Israel, the entire c
	27:22	priest in front of the entire c
	31:26	family leaders in the c to count
	31:42	half-share for the Israelite c
	32:4	country that God laid low before the c
	35:12	he can appear before the c in court
	35:24	the c is to judge
	35:25	It's the task of the c to save
Dt	13:1	visionary gets up in your c
	13:9	everybody in the c getting in on it
	13:14	did in fact take place in your c
	17:7	the rest of the c joins in
2Ki	24:15	his chief officers, the c leaders
Job	30:5	Outcasts from the c, cursed
Pr	11:19	stand with God's loyal c and live
	15:27	greedy and grasping person destroys c
Isa	58:12	make the c livable again
Jer	30:20	being a c in which I take pride
	35:2	Go visit the Recabite c
	35:3	the whole c of the Recabites
	35:18	turning to the Recabite c
	36:3	the c of Judah will finally get it
Eze	18:18	what is dead wrong in the c
	22:7	c that's insolent to parents
Mal	2:12	no longer fit to be part of the c
Lk	7:3	sent leaders from the Jewish c
Ac	11:24	c grew large and strong in the Master
	17:1	Thessalonica, where there was a c
	17:10	they again met with the Jewish c
	17:12	Greeks who were prominent in the c
	20:32	this c of holy friends
	22:12	Jewish c in Damascus is unanimous
Ro	15:27	out of the Jerusalem c so generously
1Co	5:4	Assemble the c
	5:12	those within our c of believers
	6:7	an ugly blot on your c
Gal	5:21	ugly parodies of c
	6:10	closest to us in the c of faith
Php	2:1	being in a c of the Spirit
Jas	3:18	c that lives right with God

Compassion

Dt	13:17	God may turn from anger to c
	30:3	he'll have c on you
Jdg	2:18	God was moved to c
1Ki	8:50	captors to treat them with c
	12:7	their needs and respond with c
2Ch	10:7	their needs and respond with c
	36:15	Out of c for both his people and
Ne	9:19	You in your amazing c
	9:27	in keeping with your bottomless c
	9:28	in your great c you heard and helped
	9:31	because of your great c, you didn't
Ps	102:14	weep with c over its dust
Pr	14:21	c for the poor — what a blessing
Isa	14:1	God will have c on Jacob
	47:6	but you had no c
	54:7	with enormous c, I'm bringing
	54:10	The God who has c on you says so
	63:7	C lavished, love extravagant
	63:15	Your heartfelt pity, your c
Jer	13:14	Not an ounce of . . . c will slow me
	16:5	no more c
	42:10	feel deep c on account of the doom
Eze	9:5	Feel sorry for no one. Show no c
	24:14	I've run out of c
Da	9:9	C is our only hope, the c of you
	9:18	Our appeal is to your c
Mic	7:19	c is on its way to us
	7:20	continue the c you showed
Zec	1:16	back to Jerusalem, but with c
Mt	23:23	things like fairness and c
Ro	9:15	I'm in charge of c
	9:16	C doesn't originate in our bleeding
Gal	5:22	a sense of c in the heart
Col	3:12	c, kindness, humility

Compassionate

Ex	22:27	I'll step in — I'm c
Dt	4:31	your God, is above all a c God
Ne	9:17	forgiving God, gracious and c
Ps	78:38	And God? C! Forgave the sin!
	102:13	it's time for c help
	116:5	makes things right, our most c God
Isa	49:10	the C One guides them
Eze	39:25	I'll be c with all the people
Mic	6:8	be c and loyal in your love
Zec	7:9	Love your neighbors. Be c
Mt	6:2	acting c as long as someone
1Pe	3:8	be loving, be c, be humble

Compassionately

Dt	32:36	judge his people, but oh how c
1Ch	21:15	he c changed his mind
2Ch	30:9	children will be treated c
Jer	30:18	I'll c come in and rebuild homes

Compensation-offering

Lev	5:15	Sanctuary shekel for a C

	5:16	the ram of the C
	5:18	assessed at the value of the C
	5:19	It is a C; he was surely guilty
	6:5	on the same day he brings his C
	6:6	present to God as his C a ram
	6:17	Absolution-Offering and the C
	7:1	instructions for the C
	7:2	Slaughter the C in the same place
	7:5	a gift to God. It is a C
	7:7	C is the same as the Absolution
	7:37	Absolution-Offering, the C
	14:12	present it and the pint of oil as a C
	14:13	the C belongs to the priest
	14:14	take some of the blood of the C
	14:17	on top of the blood of the C
	14:21	one male lamb as a C
	14:24	the lamb for the C
	14:25	slaughter the lamb for the C
	14:28	same places he put the blood of the C
	19:21	must bring a C to God
Nu	6:12	yearling lamb for a C
Ezr	10:19	ram from the flock as a C

Compete

Ex	9:11	weren't able to c with Moses
1Ki	12:33	his own idea to c with the feast
Isa	59:7	They c in the race to do evil
Eze	22:6	c in crime
Mt	5:9	cooperate instead of c or fight
1Co	1:25	Human strength can't begin to c

Competent

Ex	18:21	keep a sharp eye out for c men
	18:25	Moses picked c men
2Ch	2:14	c to work out designs
Mt	23:2	c teachers in God's Law
2Co	2:16	Is anyone c to take it on
2Ti	2:2	leaders who are c to teach

Competing

2Ch	2:5	far better than c gods
Jn	3:26	now c with us. He's baptizing, too
1Co	4:7	point of all this comparing and c
	11:18	c with and criticizing each other
	12:31	some of you keep c
2Co	10:12	comparing and grading and c

Competition

Da	5:23	in c against the Master of heaven
Ro	5:20	c with the aggressive forgiveness
Gal	5:20	paranoid loneliness; cutthroat c
Php	1:17	They see me as their c

Complacency

Pr	1:32	Carelessness kills; c is murder

Complacent

Ps	123:4	Kicked in the teeth by c rich men

Complacently

Lk	16:9	not c just get by on good behavior
	18:9	who were c pleased with themselves
1Th	5:3	everybody's walking around c
Jas	2:19	c sitting back as if you had done

Complain

1Sa	29:3	nothing to c about
1Ki	12:10	These people who c
2Ch	10:10	These people who c
Job	33:13	then c that he won't answer
Ps	4:4	C if you must, but don't lash out
Isa	19:8	c that the fishing's been ruined
	40:27	Why would you ever c, O Jacob
	58:3	But they also c, 'Why do we fast
La	3:39	why would anyone gifted with life c
Mt	13:42	c to high heaven
Jas	5:9	Friends, don't c about each other

Complaining

Ex	16:7	You haven't been c against us
	16:8	c to us — you've been c to God
2Sa	19:9	populace was now c to its leaders
2Ki	4:19	c, "My head, my head!"
Job	7:11	my c to high heaven is bitter
	21:4	It's not you I'm c to — it's God
Jer	32:3	locked him up, c, "How dare you preach
Mt	13:50	a lot of desperate c
Lk	7:32	spoiled children c to their parents
Ro	9:14	grounds for c that God is unfair

Complaint

1Sa	12:3	any cs to bring before God
	29:8	Have you had a single cause for c
Job	23:2	My c is legitimate
	31:13	employees when they brought a c to me
Mic	6:1	If you have a c, tell the mountains
Hab	2:1	what God says, how he'll answer my c
Ac	19:38	guild of artisans have a c
1Ti	5:19	Don't listen to a c
Jas	5:9	greater c could be lodged against you

Conceive

Nu	11:11	Did I c them?
Ps	51:6	Enter me, then; c a new, true life
Jer	32:35	I can hardly c of such evil
Lk	1:7	Elizabeth could never c

Conceived

Ge	4:1	Eve his wife. She c and had Cain
	4:17	She c and had Enoch
Ru	4:13	By God's gracious gift she c

C

1Sa	1:20	Hannah had c and given birth
2Sa	12:24	they c a son
2Ki	4:17	The woman c.
1Ch	7:23	She c and produced a son.
Job	3:3	Blank out the night I was c
Ps	22:31	Babies not yet c will hear
Pr	21:30	Nothing clever, nothing c
Isa	8:3	She c and gave birth to a son.
Mt	1:20	Mary's pregnancy is Spirit-c.
	6:4	your God, who c you in love
	7:11	the God who c you in love
Lk	1:24	his wife, Elizabeth, c.
	1:36	your cousin Elizabeth c a son
	2:21	given by the angel before he was c
	11:13	the Father who c you in love
	23:29	Lucky the women who never c!
1Pe	1:23	a life c by God himself
1Jn	3:9	People c and brought into life by God
	5:1	surely love the child who was c

Conceives

Lev	12:2	woman who c and gives birth to a boy
1Jn	5:1	love the One who c the child

Concentrate

Ps	119:112	I c on doing exactly what you say
Pr	4:21	C! Learn it by heart
Mt	6:16	discipline to better c on God
Lk	16:9	c your attention
1Co	7:32	unmarried, you're free to c
	14:12	c on doing what helps everyone
2Ti	2:15	C on doing your best for God
Tit	3:8	c on the essentials that are good

Condemn

Job	34:17	you dare c the righteous, mighty God
Mt	12:41	evidence that will c this generation
	12:42	evidence that will c this generation
Lk	6:37	Don't c those who are down
	11:31	evidence that will c this generation
Jn	8:10	Does no one c you
Ro	2:1	criticize someone, you c yourself
Jas	5:6	what you've done is c and murder

Condemnation

2Co	3:9	If the Government of C was impressive

Condemned

Ge	44:32	I'll stand c before you, Father
Isa	24:10	Every house is boarded up, c
	33:18	inspector who c and confiscated
Mk	14:64	They c him, one and all.
Jn	5:24	no longer c to be an outsider
Ac	13:27	didn't recognize who he was and c him

Condescend

Job	39:9	Will the wild buffalo c to serve you
Ro	14:10	when you c to a sister

Conduct

Lev	13:8	who will c another examination
	14:39	come back and c another examination
	14:44	priest is to come and c an examination
Nu	30:16	c between a man and his wife
Dt	13:14	must c a careful examination
	19:18	judges must c a careful investigation
1Ki	20:34	I'll send you home under safe c
2Ki	17:32	to c a variety of rites
Job	11:4	doctrine is sound and my c impeccable
Isa	60:10	assist you in the c of worship
Eze	43:18	ordinances for c at the altar
Mal	1:9	in trouble. With this kind of c
Mt	5:23	how I want you to c yourself
Ac	18:14	If this was a matter of criminal c
	19:36	c unworthy of Artemis
	25:9	let me c your trial there
Ro	6:12	a vote in the way you c your lives
1Co	5:2	this person and his c be confronted
	5:5	man's c up to public scrutiny
Gal	4:3	no say in the c of our own lives
Eph	4:24	working itself into your c
Php	1:27	Let nothing in your c hang on whether
Col	2:5	orderly ways you c your affairs
2Jn	1:6	c your lives in love

Confer

Isa	56:5	I'll c permanent honors on them
	60:14	They'll c a title on you
Zec	7:3	to c with the priests of the Temple
	8:21	leaders will c with one another
Lk	22:29	Now I c on you the royal authority
Gal	1:17	without going up to Jerusalem to c

Confess

Lev	5:5	immediately c the sin
	16:21	c all the iniquities of the People
	26:40	if they c their sins
Nu	5:7	must c the sin
Job	27:4	refuse to c to any charge that's false
	34:31	why don't you simply c to God?
Eze	12:16	they can c among the foreign countries
Da	9:15	We c that we have sinned
Jnh	1:8	C. Why this disaster?
Mt	3:6	those who came to c their sins
Jas	5:16	C your sins to each other
1Jn	4:3	who refuses to c faith in Jesus

Confessed

1Sa	12:10	They c, 'We've sinned!
	15:24	Saul gave in and c, "I've sinned
	26:21	Saul c, "I've sinned
2Sa	12:13	David c to Nathan, "I've sinned

Ezr	10:1	As he prayed and c
Ne	9:2	c their sins and the iniquities
	9:3	they c and worshiped their God
Mk	1:5	they c their sins, were baptized

Confesses

1Jn	4:2	c openly his faith in Jesus Christ
	4:15	who c that Jesus is God's Son

Confessing

Ne	1:6	c the sins of the People of Israel

Confession

Jos	7:19	Make your c to him
Ezr	10:11	Now make your c to God
Hos	14:2	Prepare your c and come back to God

Confidence

2Sa	14:22	good graces and have your c
Ne	6:14	trying to undermine my c
Job	4:6	shouldn't your devout life give you c
Pr	11:13	integrity won't violate a c
	14:26	The Fear-of-God builds up c
Lk	11:22	arsenal that gave him such c
Jn	8:51	I say this with absolute c
Ac	4:29	give your servants fearless c
	4:31	speak God's Word with fearless c
	13:7	worked himself into the c
1Co	10:12	self-c; it's useless. Cultivate God-c
2Co	7:4	I have . . . the greatest c in you
Gal	5:10	Master has given me c
1Th	3:13	filled with c in the presence of God
	4:15	We can tell you with complete c
2Th	2:16	gifts of unending help and c
	3:4	we have great c in you
Heb	3:6	firm grip on this bold c

Confident

Nu	33:3	marched out heads high and c
Jos	10:25	Be strong! Be c!
Jdg	7:11	you'll be bold and c
Job	6:20	They arrive so c
	11:18	you'll relax, c again
Ps	7:8	I'm ready, c in your verdict
	86:7	I call on you, c that you'll answer
Pr	10:9	Honesty lives c and carefree
	28:1	Honest people are relaxed and c
Isa	41:16	you'll be c and exuberant
	47:10	c and comfortable in your evil life
	50:7	c that I'll never regret this
Eze	29:21	bold and c words to speak
Mk	1:22	his teaching — so forthright, so c
Lk	4:32	teaching was so forthright, so c
Jn	6:69	c that you are the Holy One of God
Ac	4:13	so c, so sure of themselves
	11:24	enthusiastic and c in the Holy Spirit
	16:15	c that I'm in this with you

1Co	10:12	Don't be so naive and self-c
	15:58	the work of the Master, c
2Co	1:15	C of your welcome
	7:16	I'm so c and proud of you
Col	2:2	minds c and at rest
	3:24	c that you'll get paid in full
	4:12	c in everything God wants you to do
Heb	10:22	full of belief, c
1Jn	5:15	we're c that he's listening

Confront

Ex	8:20	c Pharaoh as he goes down to the water
	9:13	c Pharaoh. Tell him
Dt	25:8	call for the brother and c him
1Sa	15:12	early in the morning to c Saul
2Sa	10:0	deployed them to c the Arameans
	10:10	deployed them to c the Ammonites
1Ki	21:18	go down and c Ahab of Samaria
1Ch	14:8	he marched out to c them
	19:10	deployed them to c the Arameans
Job	6:24	C me with the truth and I'll shut up
	21:31	ever c them with their crimes
	41:11	Who could c me and get by with it
Pr	9:7	c bad behavior and get a kick
Isa	14:22	I will c them
Eze	16:2	Son of man, c Jerusalem
	20:4	Hold them accountable. C them
	23:36	Son of man, will you c Oholah
	28:21	Son of man, c Sidon
	29:2	Son of man, c Pharaoh
	35:2	Son of man, c Mount Seir
	38:2	Son of man, c Gog
Da	11:40	king of the south will c him
Hos	8:10	gather them together and c them
Mic	3:8	c Jacob's crime and Israel's sin
Mt	18:17	c him with the need for repentance
Lk	12:51	I've come to disrupt and c

Confrontation

Jer	34:3	personal c with the king of Babylon
1Co	11:32	now than to face a fiery c later
Gal	2:11	face-to-face c with him

Conniving

Job	5:12	He aborts the schemes of c crooks
Pr	26:24	all the while c against you
Na	1:9	Why waste time c against God?
Ac	5:1	Sapphira, c in this with him
Jas	3:15	animal cunning, devilish c

Conscience

Job	19:3	Do you have no c, abusing me
	33:9	I'm clean — my c is clear
Ecc	7:14	On a bad day, examine your c
Jer	5:28	Worse, they have no c.
	36:24	showed the slightest twinge of c
Zep	3:5	without c and without shame
Lk	1:6	enjoying a clear c before God

C

Ac	23:1	lived with a clear c before God
	24:16	keep a clear c before God
Ro	7:3	free to marry another man in good c
	14:5	free to follow the convictions of c
1Co	8:7	c shaped under those conditions
	8:10	what his c tells him is wrong
2Co	1:12	come out of this with c and faith
Heb	9:9	can't assuage the c of the people
1Pe	3:16	Keep a clear c before God
	3:21	before God with a clear c
Rev	11:10	pricked the c of all the people

Consecrate

Ex	13:2	C every firstborn to me
	28:38	offerings that the Israelites c
	28:41	c them to serve me as priests
	29:27	C the Wave-Offering
	29:36	Anoint and c it
	29:37	atonement for the Altar and c it
	30:29	C them so they'll be soaked
	30:30	C them as priests to me
	40:9	c it and all its furnishings
	40:11	the Washbasin and its base: c it
	40:13	C him to serve me as priest
Lev	16:19	purify and c it from the uncleannesses
	22:2	offerings that the Israelites c to me
	22:3	offerings that the Israelites c to God
Nu	11:18	C yourselves. Get ready for tomorrow
Dt	15:19	C to God, your God, all the firstborn
1Ch	15:12	now c yourselves
2Ch	29:5	C yourselves and c The Temple
	29:17	to clean and c The Temple itself
	35:6	c yourselves and prepare the lambs
Jer	51:27	C the nations for holy work
	51:28	C the nations for holy work
Joel	2:16	Get everyone there. C the congregation

Consecrated

Ge	31:13	you c a pillar and made a vow to me
	49:26	the one c among his brothers
Ex	29:33	ordained and c by them
Lev	8:15	c it so atonement could be made
	12:4	may not touch anything c
Nu	3:13	I c for my own use every firstborn
	6:9	your c head is ritually defiled
	6:18	shave off the hair you c
	7:1	he anointed it and c it
	8:17	I c them for my holy uses
Dt	33:16	the c one among his brothers
Jdg	17:3	I had totally c this money to God
1Sa	16:5	be c, and join me in worship
	8:11	King David c these
1Ki	7:51	items c by his father David
	15:15	artifacts . . . c for holy use
1Ch	15:14	c themselves to bring up the Chest
	18:11	King David c these things
	26:26	valuables c by David the king
	28:16	the gold tables for c bread
2Ch	5:11	All the priests there were c
	15:18	artifacts . . . c for holy use

	23:6	permitted in because they've been c
	26:18	priests, especially c for the work
	29:15	c themselves, and set to work
	29:19	cleaned up and c all the vessels
	29:31	you're c to God
	29:33	animals c for sacrifice that day
	29:34	priests c themselves for the work
	30:8	c for all time. Serve God
	30:15	they c themselves
	30:17	properly c to God
	30:24	plenty of c priests
	35:3	they were especially c for this
	35:13	boiled the c offerings in pots
	36:14	Temple of God so recently c
Jer	31:40	will be c to me as a holy place
Eze	48:8	c area that you will set aside as holy
	48:9	c area reserved for God
	48:11	This is for the c priests
Jn	10:36	the unique One the Father c and sent
	17:17	Make them holy—c—with the truth
	17:19	they'll be truth-c in their mission

Consequences

Dt	31:29	inviting all kinds of evil c
1Ki	16:3	now the c—I will burn Baasha
Isa	65:7	let loose the c and pay them in full
Jer	40:3	now you're all suffering the c
Eze	17:19	I'll bring the c crashing down
	22:31	serve them with the c
Hos	4:9	take the c of the bad lives
	8:10	going to reap the c soon
Ac	7:42	the c, c described by the prophet
1Co	11:29	running the risk of serious c
Heb	9:27	die once, then face the c

Conspiracy

2Sa	15:12	c grew powerful
1Ki	16:20	along with his infamous c
2Ki	9:14	ignited the c of Jehu
	12:20	staff formed a c and assassinated
	15:15	account of the c are written
	15:25	were in on the c with him
	15:30	mounted a c against Pekah
2Ch	24:25	it was a palace c, avenging
Jer	11:9	a c among the people of Judah

Consult

Ex	28:3	C with the skilled craftsmen
Nu	27:21	He is to c with Eleazar the priest
Dt	17:9	C them and they will hand down
1Sa	28:8	I want you to c a ghost for me
	30:7	Bring me the Ephod so I can c God
1Ki	14:5	on her way to c with you
	22:7	prophet of God around here we can c
2Ki	1:2	messengers off to c Baal-Zebub
	1:3	running off to c Baal-Zebub
	1:6	running off to c Baal-Zebub
	1:16	messengers to c Baal-Zebub
	3:11	through whom we can c God

	3:13	Go c the puppet-prophets
2Ch	18:6	prophet of God around here we can c
Est	1:13	practice to c his expert advisors
Isa	8:19	C the spiritualists
Hag	2:11	C the priests for a ruling

Consultation

1Sa	6:2	experts on the supernatural for c
2Sa	21:2	called the Gibeonites together for c

Contempt

Lev	26:15	holding my laws in c
	26:43	treated my decrees with c
Nu	14:23	treated me with such repeated c
2Sa	12:9	treated the word of God with brazen c
	12:10	treated God with such c
1Ki	9:8	will become an object of c
2Ki	18:12	treated his covenant with careless c
	19:21	Zion holds you in utter c
1Ch	15:29	she was filled with c
2Ch	7:21	will become an object of c
Est	1:17	treating their husbands with c
Job	12:21	He dumps c on famous people
Ps	10:14	the c, the abuse
	39:8	save me from the c of dunces
	69:10	All it got me was more c
Pr	12:8	airheads are held in c
	17:23	show nothing but c for justice
	18:3	c for life is contemptible
Ecc	9:16	wise poor man was treated with c
Isa	37:22	for you, Sennacherib, nothing but c
	37:23	treating with such utter c
	60:14	who looked down at you in c
	61:7	more than your share of c
Jer	6:19	had nothing but c for my teaching
	20:8	my God-warnings are insults and c
	30:19	days of c will be over
	33:24	my people are treated with c
Eze	16:57	now you're the butt of c
	16:59	treated my oath with c
	22:8	treat my holy things with c
	25:6	venting all your malicious c
	28:26	have treated them with such c
	36:30	won't be able to hold you in c
Da	5:23	you treat with c the living God
Joel	2:17	Don't abandon your heritage to c
	2:19	won't expose you any longer to c
Am	6:8	nothing but c for his forts
Mt	6:24	Adoration of one feeds c for the other
	7:4	when your own face is distorted by c
Lk	6:42	when your own face is distorted by c
1Co	11:26	never let familiarity breed c

Content

Dt	4:28	your homemade gods to your hearts' c
	6:11	settle down, pleased and c
Jos	8:2	cattle to your heart's c
1Sa	14:34	feast to your heart's c
2Sa	2:21	be c with those spoils

1Ki	4:25	c with what they had
	11:37	Rule to your heart's c!
Job	20:20	God-denying people are never c
	21:3	mock me later to your heart's c
Ps	131:2	Like a baby c in its mother's arms
Isa	26:8	We're c to linger in the path
Jer	16:13	no-gods there to your heart's c
	50:19	He will eat to his heart's c
Eze	34:27	feel c and safe on their land
Zep	3:13	C with who they are and where
Mt	5:5	c with just who you are
	10:11	be c there until you leave
	10:25	Be c—pleased, even
	23:12	if you're c to simply be yourself
Mk	6:10	Get a modest place and be c there
Lk	3:14	be c with your rations
	9:4	get a modest place and be c there
	14:11	if you're c to be simply yourself
	18:14	if you're c to be simply yourself
Jn	14:8	show us the Father; then we'll be c
Ro	5:11	no longer c to simply say it
1Co	2:10	The Spirit, not c to flit around
	3:3	c only when everything's going
Php	4:11	be quite c whatever my circumstances
Col	3:4	be c with obscurity, like Christ
	3:13	even-tempered, c with second place
1Th	2:8	Not c to just pass on the Message
1Pe	2:23	c to let God set things right
	5:6	So be c with who you are

Contented

Pr	17:1	bread and water in c peace

Contribution-offering

Lev	7:14	a C to God; it goes to the priest
	7:32	as a C to the priest
	7:34	the thigh of the C to Aaron
	10:14	the C in a clean place
	10:15	the thigh of the C

Conversation

Ge	29:9	While Jacob was in c with them
	48:1	after this c, Joseph was told
1Sa	14:19	Saul was in c with the priest
Job	15:4	turn spiritual c into empty gossip
Ps	55:14	God a third party to our c
Pr	12:13	c of good people keeps them
	13:2	good acquire a taste for helpful c
	15:23	Congenial c—what a pleasure
	17:4	Evil people relish malicious c
	24:7	Wise c is way over the head of fools
Ecc	7:21	Don't eavesdrop on the c of others
Jer	38:24	Don't let anyone know of this c
	38:27	No one had overheard the c
Mt	10:13	be gentle in your c
	17:3	also there in deep c with him
Mk	9:4	in deep c with Jesus
	10:41	When the other ten heard of this c
Lk	24:14	They were deep in c

C

Jn	3:22	After this c, Jesus went on
Ac	22:9	but they didn't hear the c
Gal	4:7	privilege of intimate c with God
Col	4:6	bring out the best in others in a c
2Th	2:15	in personal c or by our letter

Conversations

Job	12:4	that's the man who had c with God
Jn	1:28	These c took place in Bethany
Ac	13:43	Barnabas, who urged them in long c
	17:18	pretty well through these c
	24:26	These c were repeated frequently

Convert

Jer	31:13	I'll c their weeping into laughter
Mt	10:5	some far-off place to c unbelievers
	23:15	halfway around the world to make a c
Ac	6:5	a c from Antioch

Converts

Est	9:27	their children, and all future c
Ac	13:43	a good many Jews and c to Judaism
	15:5	have to circumcise the pagan c
1Co	16:15	among the first c in Greece

Conviction

1Co	7:37	entirely his own c and not imposed
Gal	5:22	c that a basic holiness permeates

Convictions

Ps	110:6	handing out c wholesale
Ac	23:6	because of my Pharisee c
Ro	14:5	free to follow the c of conscience
1Co	16:13	hold tight to your c
1Th	1:5	The Holy Spirit put steel in your c

Cornerstone

Job	38:6	foundation poured, and who set the c
Zec	4:7	He'll proceed to set the C in place
Mt	21:42	the masons threw out is now the c
Mk	12:10	the masons threw out is now the c
Lk	20:17	It's now the c
Ac	4:11	which is now the c
Eph	2:20	with Christ Jesus as the c
1Pe	2:6	in Zion, a c in the place of honor

Coronation

1Ki	1:9	Adonijah held a c feast
	1:19	has thrown a huge c feast
	1:25	He's thrown a huge c feast
	1:41	finishing their "c" feast
1Ch	29:22	ceremonially reenacted Solomon's c
Ps	2:6	A c banquet Is spread for him

Correct

Job	36:23	tell him what to do, or c him
Ps	94:10	think the trainer of nations doesn't c
	141:5	may the Kind One c me
Pr	9:8	if you c those who care about life
	13:24	A refusal to c is a refusal to love
	23:13	Don't be afraid to c your young ones
Isa	59:16	soul around to c this awful situation
Jer	10:24	So c us, God, as you see best.
Mt	7:21	Knowing the c password
Lk	17:3	see your friend going wrong, c him
Rev	3:19	prod and c and guide

Correction

Pr	3:11	don't sulk under his loving c
	10:17	ignore c and you're lost for good
	12:1	how shortsighted to refuse c
	13:18	embrace c and live an honored life
	15:5	welcoming c is a mark of good sense
	19:20	Take good counsel and accept c
Jer	5:3	disciplined them, but they refused c
Zep	3:2	wouldn't accept c, Wouldn't trust God
	3:7	accept my discipline and c

Corrupt

Ge	6:12	c and corrupting — life itself c
Ex	23:1	give c testimony
Dt	4:16	don't turn c and make a form
	4:25	become c and make any carved images
1Sa	2:23	your c and evil carrying on
Job	34:18	exposing c rulers as scoundrels
Pr	2:22	The c will lose their lives
	12:5	the plots of degenerates c
Ecc	3:16	The very place of judgment — c
	3:17	The place of righteousness — c!
Isa	6:5	words that c and desecrate
Eze	20:44	the c history you've compiled
	28:18	your c ways of doing business
Da	11:24	in c and lavish luxury
Mic	7:3	C leaders demand bribes
Zec	11:8	I got rid of the c shepherds
Lk	18:6	that judge, c as he is, is saying
2Co	10:4	that entire massively c culture
Jas	5:2	money is c and your fine clothes stink

Corrupted

2Ki	3:3	ones that had c Israel for so long
Ps	82:2	You've c justice long enough
Isa	29:21	Gone the people who c the courts
Eze	28:17	You c wisdom by using it
Zep	1:18	fire to burn up the c world
Mal	2:8	c the covenant of priest Levi
Mt	5:28	Your heart can be c by lust
2Pe	1:4	turned your back on a world c by lust
Rev	19:2	Whore who c the earth with her lust

Corruption

Dt	25:16	all this c in business deals
2Ki	21:2	moral rot and spiritual c
	23:9	part of the general priestly c
2Ch	27:2	pushed right on in their lives of c
	33:2	moral rot and spiritual c
Pr	28:16	one who hates c, the future is bright
	28:28	When c takes over, good people go
Eze	24:11	the c is burned off
Lk	11:44	rot and c that is six feet under
2Co	6:17	leave the c and compromise
Jas	1:27	guard against c from the godless world
2Pe	2:19	they themselves are slaves of c

Cosmos

1Ki	8:27	the c itself isn't large enough
1Ch	16:26	God made the c
2Ch	2:6	entire c! — can't begin to contain him
	6:18	the c itself isn't large enough
Job	25:2	everything in the c fits and works
Ps	50:6	whole c attests to the fairness
	89:2	you built the c and guaranteed
	89:5	Let the c praise your wonderful ways
	89:11	You own the c
	97:9	You, God, are High God of the c
	136:5	The God whose skill formed the c
Isa	42:5	the God who created the c
Jer	10:12	who crafted the c
	31:36	If this ordered c ever fell to pieces
	51:15	He crafted the c
Am	5:8	a c star-flung with constellations

Counsel

Ex	18:24	Moses listened to the c
1Sa	28:7	seek c from those spirits
2Sa	14:22	king is taking the c of his servant
	15:31	turn Ahithophel's c to foolishness
	15:34	confuse Ahithophel's c for me
	16:20	Are you ready to give c?
	16:23	The c that Ahithophel gave
	17:7	The c that Ahithophel has given
	17:14	the c of Hushai the Arkite
	17:21	Ahithophel has given c against you
	17:23	realized that his c was not followed
1Ki	12:6	What's your c?
	12:8	rejected the c of the elders
	12:13	spurned the c of the elders
1Ch	29:19	live by your directions and c
2Ch	10:6	What's your c?
	10:8	rejected the c of the elders
	10:13	spurned the c of the elders
Job	29:23	welcomed my c like spring rain
Ps	16:7	wise c God gives when I'm awake
	78:3	c we learned at our mother's knee
	107:11	turning your back on the High God's c
	119:6	comparing my life with your c
	119:13	all the c that comes from your mouth
	119:23	absorbed in pondering your wise c
	119:40	how hungry I am for your c

	119:48	relishing every fragment of your c
	119:56	I live by your Word and c
	119:64	Train me to live by your c
	119:78	I kept my mind fixed on your c
	119:87	I haven't relaxed my grip on your c
	119:99	I've pondered and absorbed your c
	119:168	abide by your c
	119:173	I've chosen to live by your c
Pr	1:9	Wear their c like flowers
	1:25	laugh at my c
	4:2	I'm giving you good c
	8:14	Good c and common sense
	11:14	the more wise c you follow, the better
	13:10	listen to each other's c
	15:22	take good c and watch them succeed
	19:20	Take good c and accept correction
	20:18	Form your purpose by asking for c
	24:6	to win, you need a lot of good c
Isa	30:15	Holy of Israel, has this solemn c
	44:26	confirms the c of his messengers
Jer	10:21	never asked God for c
Mt	5:33	c is embedded deep in our traditions
Ro	7:12	each command sane and holy c
	15:4	personal c in Scripture
	16:17	One final word of c, friends
1Co	7:6	providing my best c
	7:17	give this same c in all the churches
	7:25	you can trust my c
	12:8	wise c clear understanding
2Co	1:3	God of all healing c
	2:8	My c now is to pour on the love
Gal	5:16	My c is this: Live freely
Col	2:6	My c for you is simple
1Th	5:14	Our c is that you warn the freeloaders
1Ti	1:8	moral guidance and c need to be given
.	4:6	pass on this c to the Christians
	4:13	giving c, teaching
Heb	13:17	Listen to their c
Jas	1:25	the revealed c of God
3Jn	1:9	loves being in charge, denigrates my c

Counselor

1Ch	26:14	his son Zechariah, a shrewd c
	27:32	a wise and literate c
	27:33	Ahithophel was the king's c
Isa	9:6	Amazing C, Strong God, Eternal Father
1Co	4:21	good friend and c who wants to share

Counselors

2Ki	25:19	five of the king's c
Est	1:13	the king called in his c
Isa	1:26	set honest judges and wise c among you
Jer	18:18	wise c to give us advice
	52:25	seven of the king's c
Da	3:27	government leaders and king's c

Courage

Dt	1:38	Build up his c.
	3:28	Give him c. Give him strength

C

	31:6	Be strong. Take c.
	31:7	Be strong. Take c.
	31:23	Be strong. Take c.
Jos	1:6	Strength! C! You are going to lead
	1:9	Strength! C! Don't be timid
	1:18	Strength! C
	5:1	the c drained out of them
1Sa	4:9	On your feet, Philistines! C!
2Sa	7:27	able to find the c to pray
	10:12	C! We'll fight with might and main
	13:28	C! You can do it
1Ch	17:25	able to find the c to pray
	19:13	C! We'll fight might and main
	22:13	C! Take charge! Don't be timid
2Ch	32:7	Be strong! Take c!
Ps	60:4	an unfurled flag to look to for c
Isa	35:4	C! Take heart! God is here
Da	10:19	Take c. Be strong.
Mt	9:21	C, daughter. You took a risk of faith
	14:27	C, it's me. Don't be afraid
Mk	6:50	C! It's me. Don't be afraid
	15:43	Working up his c, he went to Pilate
Lk	9:51	gathered his c and steeled himself
Ac	15:32	with many words of c and hope
Gal	6:12	lacking the c to live by a faith
Eph	6:19	have the c to say it at the right time
Php	1:28	Your c and unity will show them
Tit	2:15	Build up their c, and discipline them
Rev	2:3	your persistence, your c in my cause

Courageous

Ru	3:11	knows what a c woman you are
1Sa	16:18	excellent musician. He's also c
2Ch	14:8	They were all c warriors
Ps	46:2	c in seastorm and earthquake
Zec	10:5	C and vigorous because God is with

Courteous

Mt	10:12	be c in your greeting
Ro	14:21	be sensitive and c to the others
1Co	11:33	be reverent and c with one another
	14:40	Be c and considerate in everything
1Th	2:10	how discreet and c we were
Tit	3:2	be bighearted and c

Courteously

2Ki	25:28	The king treated him most c
Jer	52:32	The king treated him most c
Eph	5:21	be c reverent to one another

Courtesy

1Ti	6:11	faith, love, steadiness, c
1Pe	3:15	always with the utmost c

Covet

Jos	6:18	don't c anything in it

Mic	2:2	They c fields and grab them
Ro	7:7	You shall not c

Coward

Pr	29:24	if you're a c to their cause

Cowardly

Dt	20:8	his timidity and c spirit
Ac	24:19	too c to accuse me in front of you

Cowards

Est	9:2	fear made c of them all
Ps	6:10	C, my enemies disappear.
	78:10	They were c to God's Covenant
Isa	22:3	Your leaders were all c
Jer	46:21	they'll run off, c every one
	50:36	her soldiers, c to a man
	51:30	C who've given up without a fight
Mt	8:26	Why are you such c, such faint-hearts
Mk	4:40	Why are you such c?
Ac	24:19	They're c, too cowardly to accuse me

Craving

Nu	11:4	riff-raff among the people had a c
	11:34	Kibroth Hattaavah (Graves-of-the-C)
Dt	9:22	Kibroth Hattaavah (Graves-of-the-C)
	12:20	you happen to be c meat at the time
2Sa	23:15	David had a sudden c
1Ch	11:17	David had a sudden c

Crazed

Ps	4:2	How long will you live c by illusion
Isa	49:26	your enemies, c and desperate
Am	4:8	c for water and never quenching
Zec	12:4	all the war horses into a c panic
Mt	8:32	C, the pigs stampeded over a cliff
Mk	5:13	C, they stampeded over a cliff
Lk	8:29	c and driven wild by the demon
	8:33	C, they stampeded over a cliff

Craziness

Ecc	7:25	stupidity, foolishness and c
Gal	3:3	Are you going to continue this c
2Pe	2:16	prevented the prophet's c

Crazy

Dt	28:28	He'll make you go c and blind
	28:34	What you see will drive you c
	32:6	This is c; don't you have any sense
1Sa	21:13	he pretended to go c
	21:14	Can't you see he's c?
	21:15	I have enough c people to put up with
2Ki	9:11	What did that c fool want with you?
	9:20	driving of Jehu son of Nimshi — c
Ecc	9:3	people go c right and left

C

Isa	44:20	and say, "This is c
Jer	29:26	locking up any c fellow
	50:38	land of make-believe gods gone c
	51:7	drank the wine and they've all gone c
Eze	23:12	went c with lust for Assyrians
Hos	9:7	The prophet is c!
Mt	11:18	fasting and they called him c
	15:23	She's driving us c
Lk	7:33	fasting and you called him c
Jn	7:20	You're c! Who's trying to kill you?
	8:48	said you were c — demon-possessed
	8:49	I'm not c. I simply honor my Father
	8:52	Now we know you're c. Abraham died
	10:20	He's c, a maniac — out of his head
	10:21	These aren't the words of a c man
Ac	12:15	You're c," they said.
	26:24	Paul, you're c!
	26:25	Your Honor, I'm not c.
	26:26	nothing of what I've said sounds c
2Co	5:13	If I acted c, I did it for God
	11:23	It's c to talk this way!
Gal	3:1	You c Galatians!
	3:3	only c people would think they could

Create

Ex	31:4	to c designs and work in gold
Ne	4:8	c as much trouble as they could
Job	39:20	Did you c him to prance proudly
Ps	89:47	Did you c men and women for nothing
Isa	45:7	c darkness, I make harmonies and c
	54:16	I c the blacksmith
	65:18	c Jerusalem as sheer joy, c my
Jer	31:22	God will c a new thing in this land
Mt	13:13	tell stories: to c readiness
Gal	3:21	had power to c life in us

Created

Ge	1:1	God c the Heavens and Earth
	1:21	God c the huge whales
	1:27	God c human beings; he c them godlike
	2:4	of Heaven and Earth when they were c
	5:1	When God c the human race
	5:2	He c both male and female
Ex	34:10	wonders that have never been c
Dt	4:32	God c man and woman on this Earth
	32:6	your father who c you
1Ki	4:32	He c three thousand proverbs
	12:32	he c a holy New Year festival
Job	38:4	Where were you when I c the earth
	39:17	She wasn't c very smart
	40:15	I c him as well as you
Ps	106:22	Who c a world of wonders
Isa	41:20	It's c and signed by The Holy
	42:5	the God who c the cosmos
	43:7	Whom I c for my glory
	45:12	I made earth, and I c man and woman
	57:16	These souls I c would tire out
Jer	15:8	I c more widows among you
	32:17	my Master, you c earth and sky
La	3:23	They're c new every morning

Eze	28:13	for you the same day you were c
Mal	2:10	Aren't we all c by the same God?
Mt	5:45	your true selves, your God-c selves
	5:48	Live out your God-c identity
	19:6	c this organic union of the two sexes
Mk	10:9	c this organic union of the two sexes
Lk	6:35	Live out this God-c identity
Jn	1:3	Everything was c through him
Ac	17:13	and c a mob scene there, too
	17:28	We're the God-c
	17:29	if we are the God-c
Ro	1:20	look at what God has c
	8:19	The c world itself can hardly wait
1Co	6:15	bodies are c with the same dignity
	11:11	Man was c first
2Co	5:17	gets a fresh start, is c new
Eph	2:15	he c a new kind of human being
	3:9	God, who c all this in the first place
Php	2:10	all c beings in heaven and on earth
Col	1:15	God's original purpose in everything c
1Ti	4:3	good food God c to be eaten heartily
	4:4	Everything God c is good
Heb	1:2	By his Son, God c the world
	9:11	c world and went straight into heaven
	11:3	what we see c by what we don't see
Rev	4:11	You c it all; It was c because
	10:6	who c Heaven and everything in it
	21:1	I saw Heaven and earth new-c
	21:2	I saw Holy Jerusalem, new-c

Creation

Ge	6:7	I'll get rid of my ruined c
Job	35:11	the entire c as a science classroom
Ps	50:12	All c and its bounty are mine
	65:9	C was made for this
	104:31	Let God enjoy his c
	139:14	I worship in adoration — what a c
	145:10	C and creatures applaud you, God
Ecc	7:13	simplify and reduce C's curves
Isa	34:11	God will reverse c. Chaos!
	43:4	trade the c just for you
Eze	28:15	From the day of your c you were
Mt	19:28	followed me. In the re-c of the world
Mk	10:6	original c, God made male and female
Jn	3:5	person submits to this original c
Ac	14:17	for he made a good c
Ro	2:15	woven into the very fabric of our c
	8:20	Everything in c is . . . held back
	8:21	c and all the creatures are ready
	8:22	All around us we observe a pregnant c
1Ti	4:5	prayers make every item in c holy
2Pe	3:4	as it has from the first day of c
Rev	3:14	Accurate Witness, the First of God's c

Creator

Ge	14:19	The High God, C of Heaven and Earth
	14:22	The High God, C of Heaven and Earth
Job	4:17	can humans be purer than their C
Ps	149:2	celebrate their Sovereign C
Pr	17:5	mocks poor people, insults their C

C

Ecc	12:1	Honor and enjoy your **C**
Isa	40:28	He's **C** of all you can see or imagine
	43:15	your Holy One, **C** of Israel
	45:18	God, **C** of the heavens
Mt	19:4	**C** originally made man and woman
Col	3:10	way of life is custom-made by the **C**

Creature

Ge	2:19	each living **c**, that was its name
	6:19	take two of each living **c**
	7:16	male and female of every **c** came
	7:22	Every living, breathing **c**
	8:19	every **c** on the face of
	9:2	Every living **c** — birds, animals, fish
	9:16	every last living **c** on Earth
Lev	11:44	unclean by any **c** that crawls
	22:5	contaminated by touching a crawling **c**
	22:20	slipping in some **c** that has a defect
2Sa	22:11	rode a winged **c**, swift on wind-wings
Job	12:10	every breathing **c**
	14:15	longing for the **c** you made
	41:9	What hope would you have with such a **c**
	41:33	not an ounce of fear in that **c**
Ps	18:10	a winged **c**, swift on wind-wings
	50:10	Every **c** in the forest is mine
	150:6	every living, breathing **c** praise God
Eze	1:11	touching the **c** on either side
	1:12	Each **c** went straight ahead
Col	1:23	**c** under heaven gets this same Message
Rev	5:13	every **c** in Heaven and earth

Credit

Dt	32:27	chance to take **c** for all of it
Jdg	7:2	they'll take all the **c**
1Sa	18:8	They **c** David with 'ten thousands
2Sa	12:28	I'll capture it and get all the **c**
	23:18	got **c** for killing three hundred
2Ki	3:2	to his **c** he destroyed the obscene
1Ch	11:22	many exploits to his **c**
Est	2:22	giving **c** to Mordecai
Ps	30:1	I give you all the **c**, God
	35:18	give you full **c** when everyone gathers
	87:7	Singers and dancers give **c** to Zion
	106:31	This was counted to his **c**
Eze	18:20	live upright and well, you get the **c**
Jn	9:24	Give **c** to God.
Ac	12:23	Herod had given God no **c**
Ro	4:2	could certainly have taken **c** for it
1Co	4:7	that you could take **c** for
2Co	8:23	churches, a real **c** to Christ
	10:16	what others have done and taking **c**
	10:17	to claim **c**, claim it for God
Php	1:27	you are a **c** to the Message of Christ
	3:7	everything else I used to take **c** for
1Ti	3:13	a real **c** to this Jesus-faith
1Pe	4:11	he'll get all the **c** as the One
Rev	2:6	You do have this to your **c**

Creed

Da	3:4	Every race, color, and **c**, listen
	3:7	every race, color, and **c**
	3:29	anywhere, of any race, color, or **c**
	4:1	every race, color, and **c**
	5:19	whatever their race, color, and **c**
	6:25	every race, color, and **c** on earth
	7:14	Everyone — race, color, and **c**

Criminal

2Sa	3:39	God, requite the **c** for his crime
Pr	14:21	It's **c** to ignore a neighbor in need
Jer	23:2	keeping track of your **c** behavior
Mt	25:26	It's **c** to live cautiously like that
	26:8	they were furious. "That's **c**
	26:55	as if I were a dangerous **c**
	27:37	posted the **c** charge against him
Mk	14:4	That's **c**! A sheer waste
	14:48	as if I were a dangerous **c**
Lk	22:52	as if I were a dangerous **c**
Ac	18:14	If this was a matter of **c** conduct
	23:29	nothing remotely **c**
	24:21	sound to you like grounds for a **c** case
	26:8	I can't see why it's a **c** offense

Crippled

Lev	21:19	**c** in foot or hand
	22:22	giving God an animal that is blind, **c**
Mal	1:8	blind and sick and **c** animals
Mt	12:10	a man there with a **c** hand
	21:14	room for the blind and **c** to get in
Mk	3:1	where he found a man with a **c** hand
	3:3	He said to the man with the **c** hand
Lk	6:6	a man there with a **c** right hand
	6:8	spoke to the man with the **c** hand
Jn	5:3	Hundreds of sick people — blind, **c**
Ac	3:2	a man **c** from birth being carried
	14:8	**c** since the day of his birth

Crippling

2Sa	3:29	forever be victims of **c** diseases
1Jn	4:18	love banishes fear. Since fear is **c**

Crisis

Pr	24:10	If you fall to pieces in a **c**
Isa	37:3	We're in **c**
Jer	11:14	single syllable of their **c**-prayers
	14:9	who doesn't know what to do in a **c**
Jn	3:19	This is the **c** we're in
	12:31	this moment the world is in **c**

Crisis-prayers

Jer	11:14	a single syllable of their **c**

Criticism

Jos	10:21	no c that day from the People
Ro	2:1	Judgmental c of others
	15:15	blunt language as c. It's not c
1Jn	3:20	shut down debilitating self-c

Criticize

Mt	7:1	jump on their failures, c their faults
Lk	6:37	jump on their failures, c their faults
Ro	2:1	you c someone, you condemn yourself
	14:10	when you c a brother

Critics

Ps	92:11	The sight of my c going down
	119:39	Deflect the harsh words of my c
Lk	13:17	his c were left looking quite silly
Ro	2:29	comes from God, not legalistic c
1Co	2:15	can't be judged by unspiritual c
	9:3	not shy in standing up to my c
1Ti	5:14	not give c any foothold
	5:23	worry too much about what the c will

Crooks

Job	5:12	aborts the schemes of conniving c
	12:6	C reside safely
Ps	26:9	sweep me out with the quacks and c
	28:3	same jail cell with those c
	37:9	Before long the c will be bankrupt
	140:5	c invent traps to catch me
Pr	11:3	deviousness of c brings them to ruin
	11:6	c get trapped in their sinful lust
	28:28	when the c are thrown out, it's safe
Isa	1:23	turncoats who keep company with c
	32:5	nor c be rewarded with fame
	32:7	the c? Underhanded sneaks
Eze	30:12	sell off the land to a bunch of c
Hos	5:10	Israel's rulers are c and thieves
Mt	9:11	acting cozy with c and riff-raff
	21:31	c and whores are going to precede you
	21:32	the c and whores believed him
Lk	5:30	eating and drinking with c
	18:11	not like other people — robbers, c
1Co	5:10	outsiders of that sort. Or with c

Cross-examine

Job	23:10	He can c me all he wants
Ps	139:23	C and test me, get a clear picture
Jer	11:20	You examine and c human actions
1Co	10:27	c your host on the ethical purity

Crucified

Mt	27:38	they also c two criminals
	27:44	two criminals c next to him joined
Mk	15:27	they c two criminals
	15:32	Even the men c alongside him joined
Lk	23:23	demanding that he be c

	23:33	they c him, along with the criminals
	24:20	sentenced to death, and c him
Jn	19:16	turned him over to be c
	19:18	they c him, and with him two others
	19:20	place where Jesus was c
	19:23	When they c him, the Roman soldiers
	19:32	legs of the first man c with Jesus
	19:41	garden near the place he was c
1Co	1:13	Was Paul c for you?
	1:23	go right on proclaiming Christ, the C
	2:2	Jesus and what he did — Jesus c
Gal	2:20	Indeed, I have been c with Christ
	3:1	have the c Jesus in clear focus
	5:24	killed off for good — c
	6.14	have been c in relation to the world
Heb	6:6	re-c Jesus! They've repudiated him
	13:12	was c outside the city gates
Rev	11:8	same City where their Master was c

Crucifixion

Mt	20:19	for mockery and torture and c
	26:2	betrayed and handed over for c
	27:26	then handed over for c
	27:31	they proceeded out to the c
Mk	15:15	turned Jesus over for whipping and c
Php	2:8	worst kind of death at that: a c
1Jn	5:6	God's presence at Jesus' baptism and c
	5:8	the Spirit, the Baptism, the C

Crucify

Lk	23:21	kept shouting back, "C! C him
Jn	19:6	shouted in a frenzy, "C! C!"
	19:10	the authority to c you
	19:15	C him!" Pilate said, "I am to c

Cruel

Ex	1:14	crushing them under the c workload
	6:6	out from under the c hard labor
	6:7	out from under the c hard labor
Dt	26:6	in a c and savage slavery
	26:7	our trouble, our c plight
	28:50	c to grandmothers and babies alike
Ne	9:27	who saved them from the c abuse
Ps	72:4	come down hard on the c tyrants
	105:18	put c chains on his ankles
Pr	11:17	when you're c to others, you hurt
	30:14	merciless and c as wolves
Ecc	9:12	Like fish caught in a c net
Isa	13:9	C it is, a day of wrath and anger
	14:6	relentless rain of c outrage
	14:29	defeat of your c oppressor
	19:4	over to a tyrant most c
	47:6	old men and women to c, hard labor
Jer	2:6	a c, inhospitable land
	48:39	Moab a c joke!
	50:42	barbarians they are, c and pitiless
La	1:14	I'm goaded by c taskmasters
	4:3	have turned c to their babies
Eze	21:28	against their c taunts

C

	23:29	exposed in the c glare of the sun
Am	4:1	c to the down-and-out
Na	3:19	Your c evil has seeped into every
Zep	2:8	The c talk they've used
Ac	7:19	to the elements to die a c death
Ro	1:31	Stupid, slimy, c, cold-blooded
Heb	11:38	on the c edges of the world

Culture

Jer	1:18	one-man defense system against this c
	23:14	Subsidizing a c of wickedness
Ac	2:40	get out of this sick and stupid c
Ro	12:2	become so well-adjusted to your c
1Co	1:27	men and women that the c overlooks
	4:13	potato peelings from the c's kitchen
2Co	10:4	that entire massively corrupt c

Curiosity

1Sa	6:19	out of c, irreverently peeked into
Mt	12:39	something to titillate your c
Mk	1:27	incredulous, buzzing with c
Lk	11:29	something to titillate your c
Ac	19:17	C about Paul developed into reverence
Php	1:13	piqued their c

Curious

Dt	12:30	don't get c about them after
Da	7:19	I was c about the fourth animal
Mt	8:18	a c crowd was growing by the minute
Lk	8:35	they were more reverent than c
	9:9	C, he looked for a chance to see him
Jn	11:56	They were c about Jesus
Rev	11:9	stared at by the c from all over

Curse

Ge	8:21	never again c the ground
	12:3	those who c you I'll c
	27:12	bring down a c on myself
	27:13	I'll take the c on myself
	27:29	Those who c you will be cursed
	49:7	A c on their uncontrolled anger
Ex	22:28	Don't c God
Lev	19:14	Don't c the deaf
Nu	5:18	bitter water that delivers a c
	5:19	bitter water that delivers a c
	5:21	priest puts the woman under this c
	5:21	may God cause your people to c
	5:22	water that delivers a c
	5:24	bitter water that delivers a c
	5:27	the water that delivers a c
	22:6	Come and c them for me
	22:11	Come and c them for me
	22:12	don't c the others
	22:17	only come and c this people
	23:7	Go, c Jacob for me
	23:8	How can I c whom God has not cursed
	23:11	brought you here to c my enemies
	23:13	c them for my sake

	23:25	if you can't c them, at least don't
	23:27	you'll be able to c them for me
	24:10	I got you in here to c my enemies
Dt	11:26	the crossroads of Blessing and C
	11:28	The C: if you don't pay attention
	11:29	the C from Mount Ebal
	23:4	Pethor in Mesopotamia to c you
	23:5	turned the c into a blessing
	27:13	will stand on Mount Ebal for the c
	27:15	God's c on anyone who carves
	27:16	God's c on anyone who demeans
	27:17	God's c on anyone who moves
	27:18	God's c on anyone who misdirects
	27:19	God's c on anyone who interferes
	27:20	God's c on anyone who has sex
	27:21	God's c on anyone who has sex
	27:22	God's c on anyone who has sex
	27:23	God's c on anyone who has sex-
	27:24	God's c on anyone who kills
	27:25	God's c on anyone who takes
	27:26	God's c on whoever does not give
	28:16	c in the city, God's c in the country
	28:17	God's c on your basket
	28:18	God's c on your children
	28:19	c in your coming in, God's c
	28:20	God will send The C
	30:19	Life and Death, Blessing and C
Jos	2:10	whom you put under a holy c
	6:17	is under a holy c
	6:18	in the city under holy c
	6:21	in the city under the holy c
	7:1	Israel violated the holy c
	8:34	the Blessing and the C
	10:1	it and its king under a holy c
	10:28	He carried out the holy c
	10:32	He carried out the holy c
	10:35	carrying out the holy c
	10:37	carried out the holy c
	10:39	everything under the holy c
	10:40	carried out the holy c on everything
	11:11	carrying out the holy c
	11:12	the holy c commanded by Moses
	11:20	under the holy c without mercy
	11:21	carried out the holy c on them
	22:20	violated the holy c
	24:9	son of Beor to come and c you
Jdg	1:17	the holy c and named the city C-town
	5:23	C Meroz," . . . "C, double c
	9:57	the c of Jotham son of Jerub-Baal
	17:2	when you pronounced your c
1Sa	14:24	c on the man who eats anything before
	14:26	the soldiers to a man feared the c
	14:28	c on the man who eats anything before
	17:45	Israel's troops, whom you c and mock
2Sa	3:29	be under the c of this bloodguilt
	16:10	God told him, 'C David.'
	16:11	let him c; he's preaching God's word
Ne	13:2	God turned the c into a blessing
Job	1:11	He'd c you right to your face
	2:5	c you to your face
	2:9	C God and be done with it
	3:8	who are good at cursing c that day

	31:40	c it with thistles instead of wheat
Ps	59:12	every muttered c
	62:4	every "blessing" breathes a c
	74:10	enemies c and get by with it
	102:8	taunt me, while others just c
	109:28	Let them c all they want
Pr	3:33	God's c blights the house
	26:2	an undeserved c
	27:14	more like a c than a blessing
	30:11	Don't c your father
Isa	24:6	a c, like a cancer, ravages the earth
Jer	20:14	C the day I was born!
	20:15	c the man who delivered the news
	23:10	They're a c on the land
	24:9	their names used as c words
	29:22	use it as a c
Da	9:11	solemn c written out plainly
Zec	11:17	c on your arm! A c on your right eye
Mal	1:14	c on the person who makes a big show
	2:2	I'll put you under a c
	2:3	the c will extend to your children
	2:12	God's c on those who do this!
	3:9	now you're under a c
	4:6	put the land under a c
Php	4:8	things to praise, not things to c
Jas	3:9	with the same tongues we c
Jude	1:9	level him with a blasphemous c

Cursed

Ge	3:14	you're c, c beyond all cattle
	3:17	very ground is c because of you
	5:29	farming the ground that God c
	9.25	C be Canaan! A slave of slaves
	27:29	Those who curse you will be c
Lev	24:11	blasphemed the Name of God and c
Nu	5:27	She will be c among her people
	22:6	those you curse stay c
	23:8	How can I curse whom God has not c
	24:9	whoever curses you is c
Jos	6:18	take something that's c
	6:26	C before God is the man who sets
	7:1	took some of the c things
	7:12	rid yourselves of the c things
	7:13	There are c things in the camp
	7:15	found with the c things will be burned
	9:23	For that you are c
Jdg	21:18	C is anyone who provides a wife
1Sa	17:43	he c him by his gods
2Sa	19:21	he c God's anointed
1Ki	2:8	the one who c me so viciously
2Ki	2:24	c them in the name of God
Job	5:3	suddenly, their houses are c
	24:18	useless, c junk, good for nothing
	30:5	c as dangerous delinquents
	31:30	never c them, even under my breath
Ps	120:5	c with a home in Kedar
Jer	11:3	the terms of this covenant is c
	17:5	C is the strong one who depends
	42:18	You'll end up being c
	44:12	You'll end up c
	48:10	Sloppy work in God's name is c, and c

Mal	1:4	the God-c tribe
Mk	11:21	fig tree you c is shriveled up
Lk	23:39	criminals hanging alongside c him
Ro	9:3	any way I could be c by the Messiah
Gal	1:8	let him be c
	1:9	let him be c
	3:10	Utterly c is every person who fails
	3:13	that self-defeating, c life
Rev	16:9	they c God's Name
	16:11	c the God of Heaven for their torment
	16:21	they c God for the hail
	22:3	Never again will anything be c

Curses

Ge	4:11	get nothing but c from this ground
Ex	20:7	No using the name of God . . . in c
	21:17	If someone c father or mother
Lev	20:9	every person who c his father
	24:15	who c God will be held accountable
Nu	5:23	priest is to write these c on a scroll
	24:9	whoever c you is cursed
Dt	5:11	No using the name of God . . . in c
	28:15	these c will come down hard
	28:45	these c are going to come on you
	28:46	The c will serve as signposts
	29:20	c written in this book will bury him
	29:21	c of the Covenant written in this Book
	29:27	all the c written in this book
	30:1	blessings and c come in
	30:7	will put these c on your enemies
2Sa	16:7	accompaniment of c he shouted
	16:12	exchange the c for something good
Ps	109:17	let c rain down
	109:18	He dressed up in c
	109:19	costume of c; he can wear c every day
Pr	11:26	C on those who drive a hard bargain
	20:20	Anyone who c father and mother
	28:27	run a gauntlet of c
	29:24	you'll be included in their c
Isa	9:4	their whips and cudgels and c
Jer	44:8	an example used in c
Mal	2:2	blessings for c. In fact, the c
Ac	22:23	filled the air with c
Jas	3:10	C and blessings out of the same mouth

Cursing

Lev	20:9	By c his father or mother
Nu	22:7	the fee for the c tucked safely
2Sa	16:10	If he's c, it's because God told him
	16:13	c, throwing stones down on them
Ne	13:2	work against them by c them
Job	3:8	who are good at c curse that day
Ps	109:17	Since he loved c so much
Isa	8:21	they get angry, c first this god
Ac	6:11	We heard him c Moses and God
	26:11	bullying them into c Jesus
Ro	12:14	no c under your breath

D

Custom

Jdg	11:39	It became a **c** in Israel
2Ki	4:8	then it became his **c**
	17:29	a local **c**-made god for each people
Pr	25:11	like a **c**-made piece of jewelry
Isa	43:21	a people **c**-made to praise me
Eze	6:6	all your **c**-made sun-god pillars
Mt	27:15	an old **c** during the Feast
Mk	15:6	**c** at the Feast to release a prisoner
Jn	18:39	**c** that I pardon one prisoner
	19:40	following the Jewish burial **c**
Ac	17:24	doesn't live in **c**-made shrines
Col	3:10	way of life is **c**-made by the Creator

Customs

1Sa	2:13	the **c** of priests among the people
Est	3:8	Their **c** and ways are different
Ac	6:14	throw out all the **c** Moses gave us
	28:17	against Jewish laws or Jewish **c**
1Co	11:6	origin of these **c** we have
	14:35	guides our manners and **c** here
Gal	2:14	conform to Jewish **c**

Cynical

Isa	29:20	**C** scoffers will be an extinct species
Mt	12:24	when they heard the report, were **c**
Lk	11:15	some from the crowd were **c**
2Ti	3:3	impulsively wild, savage, **c**

Cynics

Pr	1:22	**C**! . . . you feed your cynicism
	14:6	**C** look high and low for wisdom
	24:9	**c** desecrate beauty
	29:8	A gang of **c** can upset a whole city
Ac	13:41	Watch out, **c**; Look hard

D

Damage

Ex	21:23	if there is further **d**
Ezr	4:22	done enough **d** to kings
Pr	8:36	**d** your very soul when you reject me
Isa	27:3	watch over it so that no one can **d**
1Jn	4:10	clear away our sins and the **d**

Damaged

Lev	21:20	running sores or **d** testicles
2Ch	32:5	part of the city wall that was **d**
Isa	56:3	I'm **d** goods. I don't really belong
Ac	27:18	badly **d** now by the storm
Phm	1:18	If he **d** anything or owes you

Damages

Ex	22:6	started the fire must pay for the **d**
	22:11	no **d** are assessed

	22:13	no **d** have to be paid
Lk	19:8	cheating, I pay four times the **d**

Damn

Ex	22:28	don't **d** your leaders
Nu	23:7	go, **d** Israel
	23:8	How can I **d** whom God has not damned
La	3:65	**D** their eyes
Mic	3:5	God bless you' turns into 'God **d** you

Damnation

Na	2:10	Doom! **D**! Desolation!
Mt	12:37	Words can also be your **d**
1Co	5:5	devastation and embarrassment than **d**

Damned

Nu	23:8	How can I damn whom God has not **d**
2Ki	9:34	Take care of that **d** woman
1Ch	11:19	rather be **d** by God than drink this
Ps	55:15	every desolate detail of a **d** life
Jer	8:14	we're **d** if we do and **d** if we don't —
Mt	23:15	a replica of yourselves, double-**d**
Mk	16:16	whoever refuses to believe is **d**
Jn	7:49	that is taken in by him — and **d**
1Co	12:3	prompt anyone to say "Jesus be **d**

Dance

Jdg	21:21	girls come out to **d** the dances
	21:23	carried off girls from the **d**
2Sa	6:21	In God's presence I'll **d** all I want
1Ch	13:8	worshiped exuberantly in song and **d**
Job	41:22	To meet him is to **d** with death
Ps	2:9	command them all to **d** for you
	29:9	trees dancing A wild **d**
	30:11	changed wild lament into whirling **d**
	45:8	makes you want to **d**
	48:11	**D**, Judah's daughters!
	65:9	ask her to join the **d**
	89:16	Delighted, they **d** all day long
	90:14	skip and **d** all the day long
	96:12	Animals, come **d**
	119:70	I **d** to the tune of your revelation
	119:77	your revelation is the tune I **d** to
	149:3	Let them praise his name in **d**
	149:6	in the wild sword-**d**
	150:4	Praise him with castanets and **d**
Pr	23:16	My heart will **d** and sing
Ecc	7:5	Than from the song and **d** of fools
SS	6:13	**D**, **d**, dear Shulammite . . . **D**
Isa	34:14	demons and devils **d** through the night
Jer	31:4	joining the **d**
	31:13	Young women will **d** and be happy
Jn	5:35	glad enough to **d** for an hour or so
1Co	10:7	partied, then they threw a **d**
1Th	4:1	a living, spirited **d**

Danced

2Sa	6:14	**d** with great abandon before God
Eze	35:15	Since you **d** in the streets
Mk	6:22	**d** for the guests
Lk	10:17	even the demons **d** to your tune

Dancing

Ex	15:20	followed her with tambourines, **d**
	32:19	saw the calf and the people **d**
Jdg	11:34	welcome him home — **d** to tambourines
1Sa	2:1	I'm **d** my salvation
	18:6	villages of Israel singing and **d**
2Sa	6:16	David leaping and **d** before God
1Ch	15:29	saw King David **d** ecstatically
Job	21:12	have good times singing and **d**
Ps	26:6	**d** around your altar, God
	29:9	oak trees **d** A wild dance
	51:8	set these once-broken bones to **d**
	65:12	Set the hills to **d**
Pr	5:5	**d** down the primrose path to Death
Isa	22:13	drinking and **d** in the streets
	29:19	laughing and **d** in God
Mt	14:6	**d** for the guests
Lk	1:47	I'm **d** the song of my Savior God
	15:25	he heard the music and **d**
Ac	3:8	**d** and praising God

Danger

Ex	23:33	Beware. That's a huge **d**
Lev	19:16	your neighbor's life is in **d**
Ru	2:2	no **d** now of being raped
2Ch	30:8	no longer be in **d** of his hot anger
Job	36:16	God's wooing you from the jaws of **d**
	39:22	He laughs at **d**, fearless
Ps	2:12	Your very lives are in **d**
	19:11	God's Word warns us of **d**
	32:7	keeps **d** far from the shore
	55:18	secure in the middle of **d**
	142:3	Know the **d** I'm in
Pr	2:11	Good Sense will scout ahead for **d**
SS	8:6	Love is invincible facing **d**
Isa	24:1	**D** ahead! God's about to ravish
	48:19	no **d** of losing touch with me
Jer	4:21	listen to the siren of **d**
	6:25	Death is on the prowl. **D** everywhere
	18:11	**D**! I'm shaping doom against you
	19:15	**D**! I'm bringing down on this city
	20:3	not Pashur but **D**-Everywhere
	20:4	You're a **d** to yourself and everyone
	20:10	There goes old 'D-Everywhere.'
	46:5	total confusion, **d** everywhere
	49:29	Death! Doom! **D** everywhere
Zec	13:3	lies about God put everyone in **d**
Mt	26:41	without even knowing you're in **d**
Mk	14:38	so you don't enter the **d** zone
Ac	19:27	business in **d** of falling apart
	19:40	putting our city in serious **d**
1Co	8:10	great **d** if someone still struggling
	10:11	These are all warning markers — **d**

2Co	12:7	No **d** then of walking around high
Gal	3:24	protect them from **d** or distraction
1Pe	2:15	fools who think you're a **d** to society

Dangerous

Est	8:17	now it was **d** not to be a Jew
Job	13:27	brand me as a **d** character
	30:5	cursed as **d** delinquents
Pr	22:5	The perverse travel a **d** road
	26:13	It's **d** out there!
Ecc	10:9	Quarrying stones is **d**
Isa	30:6	A most **d**, treacherous route
	35:9	no **d** wild animals
Jer	9:10	wastelands too **d** for travelers
	25:6	making and selling gods — a **d** business
Zec	8:10	the streets were **d**
Mt	26:55	as if I were a **d** criminal
Mk	14:48	as if I were a **d** criminal
Lk	22:52	as if I were a **d** criminal
	23:5	He's a **d** man, endangering the peace
Ac	16:20	**d** Jewish agitators
	27:9	too **d** for sailing
Ro	7:13	Is good just as **d** as evil?
	10:7	no **d** descent into hell
1Co	15:30	risking my neck in this **d** work
2Pe	2:18	full of hot air, but still they're **d**

Dare

Ge	18:27	**d** open my mouth again to my Master
Dt	7:26	**d** bring one of these abominations
	13:11	will **d** to do an evil thing like this
	18:10	Don't you **d** sacrifice your son
1Sa	2:3	Don't **d** talk pretentiously
	26:9	Don't you **d** hurt him!
2Ki	14:8	Come and meet with me — I **d** you
1Ch	16:22	Don't you **d** touch my anointed ones
2Ch	17:10	didn't **d** go to war
	25:17	Come and meet with me, I **d** you
Job	20:3	How **d** you insult my intelligence
	22:13	Yet you **d** raise questions
	30:10	How **d** those scoundrels — they spit
	33:13	how **d** you haul him into court
	34:17	Do you **d** condemn the righteous
	39:11	would you **d** turn the job over to him
	41:14	who would **d** knock at the door
Ps	10:14	I **d** to believe that the luckless
	66:7	Rebels don't **d** raise a finger
	105:15	**d** lay a hand on my anointed
	118:6	who would **d** lay a hand on me
Isa	19:11	could any of you **d** tell Pharaoh
	50:9	Who would **d** call me guilty?
Jer	2:23	How **d** you tell me, 'I'm not stained
	6:25	Don't **d** go outdoors!
	26:9	**d** you preach — and using God's name
	30:21	**d** to do that on his own
	32:3	How **d** you preach
Eze	33:28	No one will **d** pass through them
Da	11:36	even **d** to brag and boast
Zec	4:10	**d** despise this day of small beginnings
Mt	4:7	Don't you **d** test the Lord your God

D

	22:12	**d** you come in here looking like that
Mk	6:19	wanted to kill him, but didn't **d**
Lk	4:12	Don't you **d** tempt the Lord your God
Jn	9:34	How **d** you take that tone
	18:22	How **d** you speak to the Chief Priest
Ac	4:17	so they won't **d** to use Jesus' name
	23:4	**d** you talk to God's Chief Priest
Ro	8:33	who would **d** tangle with God
	8:34	would **d** even to point a finger
	14:16	Don't you **d** let a piece of God-blessed
1Co	6:1	how **d** you take each other to court
2Co	10:12	We wouldn't **d** do that
Rev	13:4	would **d** go to war with the Beast

Dared

2Sa	14:7	I've **d** come to the king
Ps	80:16	those who **d** to set it on fire
Da	8:11	**d** to challenge the power of God
Mk	12:34	no one else **d** ask a question
Lk	20:40	no one **d** put questions to him
Jn	21:12	Not one of the disciples **d** ask
Ac	7:52	**d** talk about the coming of the Just
Ro	4:17	he **d** to trust God to do
	10:20	**d** to speak out these words of God
Jude	1:9	wouldn't have **d** level him

Dares

Ge	49:9	who **d** mess with him
Nu	24:9	who **d** disturb him
2Sa	16:10	who **d** raise questions
Ezr	6:12	people who **d** to defy this decree
Ecc	8:4	Who **d** say to him
Isa	50:8	Who **d** bring suit against me?
Eze	14:15	wilderness and no one **d** enter it
Zec	13:3	anyone **d** persist in spreading

Daybreak

Ge	32:24	wrestled with him until **d**
	32:26	man said, "Let me go; it's **d**."
Ex	19:16	On the third day at **d**
	22:3	happens after **d**, there is bloodguilt
Nu	9:15	until **d** it was over The Dwelling
	9:21	sunset to **d** and then lifted at **d**
	22:41	At **d** Balak took Balaam
Dt	16:7	Then, at **d**, turn around and go home
1Sa	29:11	by **d** they were on their way
2Sa	23:4	first light at **d** without a cloud
Ps	88:13	on my knees each **d**
	90:14	Surprise us with love at **d**
	92:2	announce your love each **d**, sing
Isa	21:11	How long till **d**?
Da	6:19	At **d** the king got up
Ac	5:21	entered the Temple at **d**
	12:18	At **d** the jail was in an uproar
	16:35	At **d**, the court judges sent
	27:39	At **d**, no one recognized the land
2Pe	1:19	wait for **d** and the rising

Dead-end

Job	11:20	headed down a **d** road
Ps	1:1	don't slink along **D** Road
	37:38	insolent souls are on a **d** street
Pr	15:10	**d** street for those who hate God
	24:20	headed down a **d** street
Isa	1:8	tumbledown shack on a **d** street
Jer	2:31	Am I nothing but a **d** street?
Hos	2:6	lose her in a **d** alley
Am	2:4	got their ancestors onto **d** roads
Jn	8:34	trapped in a **d** life
Ac	24:14	which they malign as a **d** street
Ro	5:15	**d** abyss of separation from God
Php	3:19	easy street is a **d** street
Col	1:13	rescued us from **d** alleys
Heb	9:15	freeing us from all those **d** efforts
1Pe	1:18	**d**, empty-headed life you grew up in

Deadly

Ex	9:15	you and your people with **d** disease
Lev	26:25	I'll send a **d** epidemic
2Sa	6:8	God's **d** outburst against Uzzah
Job	20:16	a **d** diet
Ps	41:8	got some dirty, **d** disease
	91:3	shields you from **d** hazards
Isa	30:6	menaced by lions and **d** snakes
Jer	9:8	**D** lies stream from their mouths
	25:37	silenced by God's **d** anger
	50:42	Flourishing **d** weapons
Eze	9:1	bring your **d** weapons with you
	12:16	killing, starvation, and **d** sickness
	14:19	visit a **d** disease on that country
Joel	2:25	Locusts savage, locusts **d**

Deaf

Ex	4:11	who makes some mute, some **d**
Lev	19:14	Don't curse the **d**
Nu	14:22	turning a **d** ear to me
1Ki	12:15	turned a **d** ear to the people
2Ch	10:15	turned a **d** ear to the people
Ne	9:17	turned a **d** ear
Ps	28:1	Don't turn a **d** ear when I call you
	38:13	But I'm **d** and mute to it all
	58:5	**D** to threats, **d** to charm
	66:20	God: he didn't turn a **d** ear
	88:14	Why, God, do you turn a **d** ear?
	95:8	Don't turn a **d** ear
	106:25	turned a **d** ear to God's voice
	109:1	God, don't turn a **d** ear
Pr	1:24	you've turned a **d** ear
Isa	29:18	**d** will hear word-for-word
	35:5	**d** ears unstopped
	42:18	Pay attention! Are you **d**?
	43:8	Get the blind and **d** out here
Jer	3:13	While turning a **d** ear to me
	6:10	**d** as a post, blind as a bat
	35:15	what do I get from you? **D** ears
	35:17	turned a **d** ear when I spoke
Da	5:23	blind, **d**, and imbecile gods

	9:6	turned a **d** ear to your servants
Mic	7:18	Turning a blind eye, a **d** ear
Mt	11:5	The **d** hear
	12:22	wretch, both blind and **d**
Mk	7:37	gives hearing to the **d**
	9:25	Dumb and **d** spirit, I command you
Lk	7:22	The **d** hear
Heb	3:8	don't turn a **d** ear
	3:15	don't turn a **d** ear
	3:16	people who turned a **d** ear
	3:17	those who turned a **d** ear
	3:18	the ones who turned a **d** ear
	4:7	don't turn a **d** ear
	12:25	don't turn a **d** ear

Death

Ge	15:15	die a good and peaceful **d**
	20:7	certain **d** both for you and everyone
	24:67	comfort after his mother's **d**
	25:11	After Abraham's **d**, God blessed
	26:18	after Abraham's **d**
	27:41	mourning my father's **d**
	27:46	I'm sick to **d** of these Hittite
	42:2	survive and not starve to **d**
	43:8	we're all going to starve to **d**
	47:19	starve to **d** right in front of you
	50:16	Before his **d**, your father gave
Ex	5:3	strike us with either disease or **d**
	9:7	not one **d**
	10:17	get **d** out of here
	12:27	he hit Egypt with **d** but rescued us
	16:3	starve us to **d**, the whole company
	18:4	saved me from **d** by Pharaoh
	19:12	dies — a certain **d**
	19:13	shot with arrows, shot to **d**
	21:12	**d** results, the penalty is **d**
	21:14	if it's from my Altar, to be put to **d**
	21:15	father or mother, the penalty is **d**
	21:16	kidnaps a person, the penalty is **d**
	21:17	father or mother, the penalty is **d**
	21:28	ox gores a man or a woman to **d**
	21:29	the owner given the **d** penalty
	21:30	ransom is agreed upon instead of **d**
	22:19	sex with an animal gets the **d** penalty
	22:20	other than God alone must be put to **d**
	23:7	**d** of innocent and good people
	31:14	will most certainly be put to **d**
	31:15	will most certainly be put to **d**
	35:2	works on this day must be put to **d**
Lev	16:1	After the **d** of Aaron's two sons
	19:20	they aren't to be put to **d**
	20:2	god Molech must be put to **d**
	20:9	put to **d**. By cursing his father
	20:10	adulteress, must be put to **d**
	20:11	man and woman must be put to **d**
	20:12	both of them must be put to **d**
	20:13	They must be put to **d**
	20:15	with an animal, he must be put to **d**
	20:16	They must be put to **d**
	20:27	sorcerer among you must be put to **d**
	24:16	the Name of God must be put to **d**

	24:17	kills a fellow human must be put to **d**
	24:21	kills a fellow human will be put to **d**
	27:29	He must be put to **d**
Nu	1:51	who even goes near it will be put to **d**
	3:10	elbow his way in will be put to **d**
	3:38	perform these duties was to be put to **d**
	15:35	Give the man the **d** penalty
	16:29	If these men die a natural **d**
	17:12	This is our **d** sentence
	18:3	things of the Altar under penalty of **d**
	18:22	for their sin and the penalty is **d**
	19:18	was killed or died a natural **d**
	35:16	murderer and must be put to **d**
	35:17	he's a murderer and must be put to **d**
	35:18	he's a murderer and must be put to **d**
	35:21	that's murder — he must be put to **d**
	35:25	until the **d** of the High Priest
	35:28	until the **d** of the High Priest
	35:31	deserves the **d** penalty. Put him to **d**
	35:32	before the **d** of the High Priest
Dt	1:27	a **d** sentence for sure
	7:10	pays them the wages of **d**
	13:5	visionary must be put to **d**
	17:6	witnesses may a person be put to **d**
	17:6	No one may be put to **d**
	21:22	been given the **d** sentence
	22:8	become responsible for the **d**
	22:21	stone her to **d**
	24:16	not be put to **d** for their children
	30:15	Life and Good **D** and Evil
	30:19	I place before you Life and **D**
	32:39	I bring **d** and I give life
	33:1	this blessing before his **d**
Jos	1:1	**d** of Moses the servant of God
	1:10	will be put to **d**
	2:13	Save our souls from **d**
	8:25	The **d** toll that day
	13:21	whom Moses put to **d**
	13:22	the soothsayer, was put to **d**
	20:6	**d** of the current high priest
Jdg	1:1	after the **d** of Joshua
	5:18	risked life and limb, defied **d**
	13:7	moment of birth to the day of his **d**
	15:6	burned both her and her father to **d**
	16:30	killed more people in his **d**
	20:13	put them to **d** and burn the evil out
	21:5	at Mizpah had to be put to **d**
Ru	1:17	not even **d** itself is going to come
	2:11	after the **d** of her husband
1Sa	2:6	God brings **d** and God brings life
	2:25	fed up with them, decreed their **d**
	5:11	We're threatened with mass **d**!"
	5:11	everyone was scared to **d**
	13:7	still with him but scared to **d**
	14:42	**d** to the one God points to
	22:16	The king said, "**D**, Ahimelech!"
	22:22	blame for the **d** of everyone
	25:1	Everyone grieved over his **d**
	26:20	not separate me from God in life or **d**
	28:3	All Israel had mourned his **d**
	28:5	shook in his boots, scared to **d**
2Sa	1:12	grieving the **d** of Saul

	1:16	sealed your **d** sentence
	1:23	Together in life, together in **d**
	1:26	Jonathan, I'm crushed by your **d**
	3:37	nothing to do with the **d** of Abner
	3:37	David mourned the **d** of his son
	3:39	come to terms with Amnon's **d**
	4:32	guilty, then he can put me to **d**
	5:21	whether it means life or **d**
	8:33	my **d** and not yours, O Absalom
	21:4	put anyone in Israel to **d**
	22:5	The waves of **d** crashed over me
	22:6	**d** traps barred every exit
	24:16	angel who was spreading **d**
1Ki	1:47	On his **d** bed the king worshiped
	2:8	I won't put you to **d**
	2:26	You deserve **d** but I'm not
	2:37	decreed your own **d** sentence
	2:42	decreed your own **d** sentence
	12:2	report of Solomon's **d**
	14:13	come to his burial, mourning his **d**
	14:18	everyone mourned his **d**
	19:17	Anyone who escapes **d** by Hazael
	21:10	throw him out and stone him to **d**
	21:14	Naboth had been stoned to **d**
2Ki	4:40	**D** in the pot, O man of God! **D**
	5:7	god with the power to bring **d**
	7:3	sitting here at **d**'s door
	7:17	trampling him to **d**
	7:20	trampled the man to **d**
	14:17	years after the **d** of Jehoash
	14:22	Following his father's **d**
	15:5	skin disease until the day of his **d**
	22:20	You'll have a quiet **d**
	23:29	Josiah's **d** came about
1Ch	2:24	After the **d** of Hezron
	19:2	condolences about his father's **d**
	21:15	ordered the **d** angel, "Enough
2Ch	10:2	report of Solomon's **d**
	22:4	After the **d** of his father
	24:17	But after the **d** of Jehoiada
	25:25	years after the **d** of Jehoash
	34:28	you'll have a quiet **d**
Ezr	7:26	**d**, banishment, a fine
Est	4:11	without being invited: **d**
	8:11	defend themselves to the **d**
Job	3:21	can't imagine anything better than **d**
	3:22	day of their **d** and burial the happiest
	3:26	**d** has invaded life
	4:14	I was scared to **d**
	9:23	calamity hits and brings sudden **d**
	9:34	To break God's **d** grip on me
	15:30	**d** — don't think they'll escape that
	18:13	a treat for ravenous **D**
	18:14	marched straight to the **d** house
	33:22	hang on the cliff-edge of **d**
	33:24	canceling the **d** sentence
	33:28	saved me from certain **d**
	38:17	Do you know the first thing about **d**?
	38:17	Do you have one clue regarding **d**
	41:22	To meet him is to dance with **d**
Ps	9:13	pulled me back from the gates of **d**
	18:5	**d** traps barred every exit

	23:4	the way goes through **D** Valley
	49:14	**D** herds them like sheep
	49:15	snatches me from the clutch of **d**
	51:14	Commute my **d** sentence, God
	55:4	specters of **d** have me down
	56:13	pulled me from the brink of **d**
	63:9	marked for **d**, bound for hell
	68:20	God knows all **d**'s ins and outs
	77:16	Deep Ocean was scared to **d**
	79:11	pardon those on **d** row
	89:48	We'll see **d** soon enough
	102:20	opened the doors of their **d** cells
	105:38	they were scared to **d**
	107:20	pulled you back from the brink of **d**
	116:3	**D** stared me in the face
	116:8	Soul, you've been rescued from **d**
	116:15	When they arrive at the gates of **d**
	118:18	he didn't hand me over to **D**
	143:7	That would be certain **d**
Pr	5:5	down the primrose path to **D**
	5:23	**D** is the reward of an undisciplined
	7:26	she's the **d** of many a poor man
	8:36	you're flirting with **d**
	13:14	no more drinking from **d**-tainted wells
	21:6	a promotion — to **d**
	23:14	something worse than **d**
	31:7	for whom life is a living **d**
Ecc	3:2	time for birth and another for **d**
	7:1	**d** date tells more than your birth date
	8:8	say-so regarding the day of **d**
	9:3	Life leads to **d**
SS	8:6	Love is invincible facing danger and **d**
Isa	5:13	big men" will starve to **d**
	14:10	royal invitations to **d**
	14:17	his prisoners to a living **d**
	14:29	From the **d** throes of that snake
	25:8	Yes, he'll banish **d** forever
	28:18	careful precautions against **d**
	37:7	Killed — a violent **d**
	38:10	spent in **d**'s waiting room
	51:19	battery, hunger and **d**
	53:12	looked **d** in the face
	57:7	your foul sex-and-**d** religion
	65:12	your destiny, **D**
	65:15	I, God, will put you to **d**
	66:16	a **d** sentence on the human race
Jer	2:6	parched deserts and **d** valleys
	6:24	Terror has a **d** grip on our throats
	6:25	**D** is on the prowl
	9:16	I'll send **D** in pursuit
	9:21	**D** has climbed in through the window
	14:19	beaten us nearly to **d**
	15:3	**d** in battle, the corpses dropped
	16:3	**d** warrant on all the children
	16:4	epidemic of **d**. **D** unlamented
	20:16	haunted to his **d** with the bad news
	21:8	I'm giving you a choice: life or **d**
	25:31	verdict is clear-cut: **d** by the sword
	25:37	sheepfolds will be silent with **d**
	26:8	**D**! You're going to die for this
	26:11	**D** to this man! He deserves
	26:16	No **d** sentence for this man

	27:13	get killed or starve to **d**		8:34	Those tending the pigs, scared to **d**
	30:6	Faces contorted, pale as **d**		9:60	Your business is life, not **d**
	31:40	a **d** valley if there ever was one		15:17	here I am starving to **d**
	34:5	You'll die a peaceful **d**		20:36	nor, of course, with **d**
	38:2	killed or starve to **d**		23:15	let alone anything deserving **d**
	42:22	you'll starve to **d**		23:22	found nothing in him deserving **d**
	43:11	his assigned fate: **d**, exile		24:20	got him sentenced to **d**
	44:12	killed or starve to **d**		24:37	were scared half to **d**
	44:22	a wasteland, a **d** valley	Jn	3:18	under the **d** sentence without knowing
	49:26	brave warriors silent as **d**		4:47	on the brink of **d**
	49:29	Terror! **D**! Doom!		4:49	It's life or **d** for my son
	50:13	a desert of **d** and emptiness		8:51	never have to look **d** in the face
	50:36	War to the **d** on her boasting		8:52	never have to face **d**
	50:37	War to the **d** on her hired killers		11:13	Jesus was talking about **d**
	50:38	War to the **d** on her water supply		12:33	show how he was going to be put to **d**
	50:39	land will reek with the stench of **d**		19:31	logs be broken to speed **d**
	51:1	A **d**-dealing hurricane		21:19	**d** by which Peter would glorify God
	51:50	escaped a Babylonian **d**	Ac	1:3	After his **d**, he presented himself
	51:55	**D** throes like the crashing of waves		2:24	the **d** ropes and raised him up. **D**
La	2:19	children who are starving to **d**		2:27	never even smell the stench of **d**
	4:9	slowly starve to **d**		2:31	no stench of **d**
Eze	3:18	it's a matter of life or **d**		5:28	blame us for the **d** of this man
	5:17	disease, unrestrained murder, **d**		7:4	After the **d** of his father
	6:12	**d** everywhere you look		7:19	to the elements to die a cruel **d**
	18:23	take any pleasure in the **d**		11:19	persecution triggered by Stephen's **d**
	18:32	take no pleasure in anyone's **d**		13:27	who he was and condemned him to **d**
	19:13	a bare stick in a desert of **d**		13:30	And then God raised him from **d**
	26:21	introduce you to the terrors of **d**		13:35	never let your Holy One see **d**'s rot
	30:4	**D** will rain down on Egypt		15:26	looked **d** in the face
	31:14	They're all slated for **d**		17:3	Messiah absolutely had to be put to **d**
	32:16	for the **d** of its pomp		25:11	committed a crime and deserve **d**
	33:8	you're on the fast track to **d**		25:15	wanted me to sentence him to **d**
	33:11	take no pleasure in the **d**		26:31	deserving prison, let alone **d**
Da	2:13	When the **d** warrant was issued	Ru	5:6	himself for this sacrificial **d**
	5:23	your entire life from birth to **d**		5:8	offering his Son in sacrificial **d**
Hos	13:14	snatch them from a certain **d**		5:9	by means of this sacrificial **d**
	13:14	Who is afraid of you, **D**?		5:10	sacrificial **d** of his Son
Joel	2:3	**D** Valley. Nothing escapes unscathed		5:12	first sin, then **d**
Ob	1:16	they'll drink themselves to **d**		5:13	**d**, this huge abyss separating us
Jnh	1:14	don't blame us for his **d**		5:15	parallel to the **d**-dealing sin
Na	3:10	babies smashed to **d** in public view		5:16	comparison between that **d**-dealing
Hab	1:9	**D** is on their minds		5:17	If **d** got the upper hand
	2:5	Like **d**, they always want more		5:18	all this trouble with sin and **d**
Zec	13:3	stab him to **d** in the very act		5:21	All sin can do is threaten us with **d**
Mt	2:15	lived in Egypt until Herod's **d**		6:8	included in Christ's sin-conquering **d**
	4:16	dark, dark country of **d**		6:9	**d**-as-the-end. Never again will **d**
	8:22	Your business is life, not **d**		6:23	your pension is **d**
	8:33	Scared to **d**, the swineherds bolted		8:2	tyranny at the hands of sin and **d**
	17:6	fell flat on their faces, scared to **d**		14:8	all the way from life to **d**
	20:18	They will sentence him to **d**		14:9	the entire range of life and **d**
	23:32	daily add to the **d** count	1Co	2:3	I was scared to **d**
	26:59	in order to sentence him to **d**		3:22	the world, life, **d**
	26:66	**D**! That seals his **d** sentence		10:2	from enslaving **d** to salvation
	27:24	responsibility for this man's **d**		11:26	reenact . . . the **d** of the Master
	27:54	were scared to **d**		11:27	jeered and spit on him at his **d**
	28:4	guards at the tomb were scared to **d**		15:4	raised from **d** on the third day
Mk	5:14	Those tending the pigs, scared to **d**		15:21	**D** initially came by a man
	5:23	dear daughter is at **d**'s door		15:26	the very last enemy is **d**
	10:33	They will sentence him to **d**		15:31	I look **d** in the face
	14:55	they could sentence him to **d**		15:52	beyond the reach of **d**
	14:64	The sentence: **d**		15:54	**D** swallowed by triumphant Life
Lk	1:79	those sitting in the shadow of **d**		15:55	**D**? Oh, **D**, who's afraid of you now

	15:56	sin that made **d** so frightening
	15:57	sin, guilt, **d** — are gone
2Co	1:9	like we'd been sent to **d** row
	3:7	The Government of **D**
	5:15	He included everyone in his **d**
	11:23	at **d**'s door time after time
Gal	6:12	shares Christ's suffering and **d**
Eph	1:20	God raised him from **d**
	2:13	Christ — dying that **d**
	2:16	through his **d** on the Cross
	6:12	a life-or-**d** fight to the finish
Php	2:8	died a selfless, obedient **d**
	2:27	His **d** would have been one huge grief
	3:10	go all the way with him to **d** itself
Col	1:20	all because of his **d**
	3:5	connected with that way of **d**
1Th	5:10	a **d** that triggered life
1Ti	6:16	He's the only one **d** can't touch
2Ti	1:10	**d** defeated, life vindicated
Heb	2:9	through the experience of **d**
	2:14	rescue them by his **d**. By embracing **d**
	2:15	scared to **d** of **d**
	5:7	lived on earth, anticipating **d**
	9:16	Jesus' **d**. His **d** marked the transition
	9:18	required a **d** to set it in motion
	9:22	a will hinges on a **d**
	9:23	prominence of blood and **d**
	9:28	Christ's **d** was also a one-time event
	10:28	physical **d**
	11:5	Enoch skipped **d** completely
1Pe	3:18	was put to **d** and then made alive
1Jn	3:14	transferred from **d** to life
	4:18	fear of **d**, fear of judgment
	5:6	life-giving birth and a **d**-killing **d**
	5:16	leading to eternal **d**
Rev	1:18	They open and lock **D**'s doors
	2:11	safe from Devil-**d**
	6:8	Its rider was **D**
	9:6	prefer **d** to torture
	11:11	spectators will be scared to **d**
	18:8	disasters will crush her — **d**
	20:6	No second **d** for them!
	20:13	**D** and Hell turned in their dead
	20:14	**D** and Hell were hurled into Lake Fire
	21:4	**D** is gone for good
	21:8	Fire and Brimstone. Second **d**

Debt

2Sa	16:4	I'll be forever in your **d**
2Ki	4:1	man to whom he was in **d**
Ne	5:8	brothers back into **d** slavery
Mt	18:24	a **d** of a hundred thousand dollars
	18:27	let him off, erasing the **d**
	18:30	in jail until the **d** was paid
	18:32	I forgave your entire **d**
	18:34	until he paid back his entire **d**
Lk	7:41	Two men were in **d** to a banker
	16:5	who were in **d** to his master
Ro	13:8	the huge **d** of love you owe

Debts

Dt	15:1	every seventh year, cancel all **d**
	15:2	All-**D**-Are-Canceled — God says so
	15:9	the year of All-**D**-Are-Canceled
	31:10	the Year-All-**D**-Are-Canceled
2Ki	4:7	make good on your **d**
Ne	10:31	leave the land fallow and cancel all **d**
Isa	58:6	free the oppressed, cancel **d**
Eze	18:7	doesn't pile up bad **d**
	18:12	piles up bad **d**, admires idols
Lk	7:42	so the banker canceled both **d**
Ro	13:8	Don't run up **d**

Decay

Jer	51:43	Her towns stink with **d** and rot
Ac	13:34	no going back to that rot and **d**
	13:35	Holy One see death's rot and **d**

Deceit

Job	15:35	Their lives are wombs for breeding **d**
	31:5	or hung out in the company of **d**
Pr	12:17	liars lay down a smoke screen of **d**
Jer	17:11	the eggs hatch, the **d** is exposed
Hos	12:12	made it big through treachery and **d**
Mt	27:64	final **d** surpassing the first

Deceitful

Ps	119:128	I despise every **d** detour
Jer	17:9	The heart is hopelessly dark and **d**
1Ti	3:8	servants in the church: serious, not **d**
Jas	1:17	There is nothing **d** in God

Deceive

Lev	19:11	Don't **d** anyone
1Sa	15:29	Israel's God-of-Glory doesn't **d**
Isa	37:10	God, on whom you so naively lean, **d**
Mt	24:5	They will **d** a lot of people
	24:11	preachers will . . . **d** a lot of people
Mk	13:6	They will **d** a lot of people
1Jn	2:26	those who are trying to **d** you
Rev	19:20	used signs to dazzle and **d**

Deceived

Job	12:16	both **d** and deceiver must answer
	21:27	I'm not **d**
Eze	14:9	If a prophet is **d**
Gal	6:3	you are badly **d**
1Ti	2:14	woman was **d** first
2Ti	3:13	as **d** as the people they lead astray
Jas	1:26	self-**d**. This kind of religion
Rev	18:23	by black-magic arts **d** the nations
	20:10	The Devil who **d** them

Deceiver

Job	12:16	both deceived and **d** must answer

2Jn 1:7 true title: **D!** Antichrist

Deceivers

Pr	11:20	God can't stand **d**
Mt	24:4	Watch out for doomsday **d**
Mk	13:5	Watch out for doomsday **d**
Lk	21:8	Watch out for the doomsday **d**

Deceives

Hab	2:5	Money **d**. The arrogant rich don't last
Rev	21:27	no one who defiles or **d**

Deceiving

Lev	6:2	betraying trust with God by **d**
Tit	1:10	loose, confusing, and **d** talk
Rev	20:3	**d** the nations
	20:8	old work of **d** the nations

Deception

1Ki	14:6	But why the **d**?
Pr	22:12	he'll have nothing to do with **d**
1Jn	4:6	Spirit of Truth from the spirit of **d**

Decision

Ge	24:52	Abraham's servant heard their **d**
Dt	17:9	will hand down the **d** for you
	17:12	override or twist the **d**
2Sa	15:2	case to bring to the king for a **d**
	19:29	Here's my **d**: You and Ziba divide
1Ki	3:27	**d**: "Give the living baby
Pr	18:18	draw straws when faced with a tough **d**
Da	1:13	**d** on the basis of what you see
Joel	3:14	mob uproar—in D Valley
Lk	12:59	kind of **d** I'm asking you to make
Jn	5:23	Father's **d** to put the Son in the place
	5:30	You can trust my **d**
Ac	15:19	So here is my **d**
Ro	2:16	God makes his final **d** about every man
	4:13	based on God's **d**
	8:30	**d** of what his children should be like
	9:11	a sure thing determined by his **d**
1Co	7:4	Marriage is a **d** to serve the other
	7:37	his **d** for a single life
	9:12	Our **d** all along has been
	9:13	not use our **d** to take advantage
2Co	5:16	Because of this **d** we don't evaluate

Decisions

1Ch	16:14	you come on his judgments and **d**
	28:7	carrying out my **d** as he is doing
Ne	1:7	haven't respected the **d** you gave
	10:29	all his **d** and standards
Ps	19:9	The **d** of God are accurate
	119:62	your **d** are so right, so true
	119:75	see now, God, that your **d** are right
	119:120	your **d** leave me speechless
	119:137	God; your **d** are right on target
	119:160	Your righteous **d** are eternal
Pr	5:23	foolish **d** trap you in a dead end
Isa	7:15	twelve years old, able to make moral **d**
	11:4	render **d** on earth's poor with justice
	26:8	path sign-posted with your **d**
	26:9	your **d** are on public display
	32:4	The impulsive will make sound **d**
	33:22	For God makes all the **d** here
	51:4	My **d** light up the world
Zec	3:7	you'll make the **d** around here
Jn	8:50	making the **d** that will bring it about
Ro	7:20	My **d**, such as they are
	9:19	If the big **d** are already made
1Co	6:5	can make fair **d** when disagreements

Dedicate

Ex	22:29	**D** your firstborn sons to me
Lev	27:26	**d** the firstborn of an animal
Eze	43:26	purifying it. This is how you **d** it

Dedicated

Ge	35:15	Jacob **d** the place where God had spoken
Dt	20:5	built a new house but hasn't yet **d** it
1Sa	1:28	have **d** him to God. He's **d** to God
	2:20	this child you have **d** to God
1Ki	8:63	**d** The Temple of God
2Ki	12:18	gifts **d** for holy use by his ancestors
	21:4	Temple **d** exclusively by God's decree
1Ch	26:27	**d** the plunder
	26:28	everything that had been **d** by Samuel
2Ch	30:26	Israel had built and **d** The Temple
	31:6	owned that had been **d** to God
	33:5	Temple **d** exclusively by God's decree
Ne	12:47	set aside what was **d** to the Levites
Pr	31:2	The son I **d** to God
Eze	48:20	**d** area, set apart for holy purposes

Dedication

Lev	21:12	**d** of the anointing oil
Nu	7:10	brought their offerings for its **d**
	7:11	offering for the **d** of the Altar
	7:84	**d** offerings of the leaders of Israel
2Ch	7:5	at the **d** of The Temple
	29:31	**d** is complete—you're consecrated
	31:18	ardent **d** they showed
Ezr	6:16	celebrated the **d** of The Temple
	6:17	At the **d** of this Temple of God
Ne	10:33	appointed feasts **D**-Offerings
	12:27	time for the **d** of the wall
Ps	132:7	Let's go to the shrine **d**!
Eze	43:27	After these seven days of **d**
Da	3:2	the **d** ceremony of the statue
	3:3	all came for the **d**

Defeat

Ge	22:17	your descendants will **d** their enemies
Ex	32:18	those aren't songs of **d**

Lev	26:7	chase out your enemies and **d** them
	26:17	stand by while your enemies **d** you
Dt	1:44	to Hormah, a stinging **d**
	28:7	God will **d** your enemies
	28:25	God will **d** you by enemy attack
Jos	7:3	men are enough to **d** Ai
	7:4	fled in **d** before the men of Ai
Jdg	6:16	you'll **d** Midian as one man
	20:34	were about to go down in **d**
1Sa	4:17	**d** was catastrophic
1Ki	20:21	an enormous **d** for Aram
2Ki	13:19	you'll **d** him three times only
	14:12	all their soldiers ran home in **d**
2Ch	13:18	flat on its face — a humiliating **d**
	13:20	never did recover from his **d**
	25:20	decided to let Jehoash **d** him
	25:22	all the soldiers straggled home in **d**
Isa	14:29	too soon to celebrate the **d**
	36:22	tearing their clothes in **d**
Php	1:28	**d** for them, victory for you
Rev	17:14	the Lab will **d** them

Defeated

Ge	14:5	**d** the Rephaim in Ashteroth
	36:35	the king who **d** the Midianites
Ex	17:13	Josua **d** Amalek and its army
Dt	1:4	after he had **d** Sihon
Jos	10:13	Until he **d** his enemies
	12:1	kings that the People of Israel **d**
	12:6	People of Israel **d** them
	12:7	People of Israel **d**
	13:12	Moses had **d** them
Jdg	1:4	They **d** them at Bezek
	11:21	Israel **d** them. Israel took all
2Sa	8:2	He also fought and **d** Moab
	8:3	David next **d** Hadadezer
	8:13	fought and **d** the Edomites
2Ki	13:25	three times and **d** him each time
	14:7	Amaziah roundly **d** Edom
	14:10	because you've **d** Edom in battle
1Ch	1:46	who **d** Midian in the country of Moab
	5:10	fought and **d** the Hagrites
	18:2	He also fought and **d** Moab
	18:3	David **d** Hadadezer
	18:12	fought and **d** the Edomites
2Ch	14:12	God **d** the Ethiopians
	25:19	because you've **d** Edom in battle
	28:23	just been **d** by Damascus
Jer	37:10	even if you **d** the entire
	46:2	Egypt at the time it was **d**
	48:1	Kiriathaim demeaned and **d**
1Co	9:22	the **d**, the demoralized
	10:5	**d** by temptation during the hard times
2Ti	1:10	death **d**, life vindicated
Rev	12:11	**d** him through the blood of the Lab

Defend

Jdg	6:31	**d** his own altar
Est	8:11	arm and **d** themselves to the death
Job	13:8	needs a lawyer to **d** himself

	13:15	I'd **d** my innocence
	34:6	When I **d** myself, I'm called a liar
Ps	59:1	**d** me from these mutineers
	82:3	You're here to **d** the defenseless
Jer	46:21	soldiers are stationed to **d** her
Zec	9:8	country and **d** it against invaders
Mal	3:11	I will **d** you against marauders
Lk	12:9	think I'll **d** you before God's angels
Ac	18:14	as Paul was about to **d** himself
	25:16	face his accusers and **d** himself
1Co	5:5	Let him **d** it if he can

Defending

2Ki	9:14	**d** Ramoth Gilead against Hazael
Isa	49:25	on your side, **d** your cause
Jer	15:20	at your side, **d** and delivering
Lk	12:11	don't worry about **d** yourselves
Ac	24:10	fortunate to be **d** myself
Php	1:16	I am here **d** the Message

Defenseless

Dt	31:17	devastate them because they are **d**
Job	24:14	kills the poor and robs the **d**
Ps	82:3	You're here to defend the **d**
	124:6	He didn't abandon us **d**
Isa	1:17	Go to bat for the **d**
	1:23	never stick up for the **d**
	10:2	Exploiting **d** widows
	22:8	God has left Judah exposed and **d**
Jer	49:32	these **d** nomads on the fringes
Ob	1:13	they were knocked flat, **d**
Mic	2:8	like soldiers who plunder the **d**

Defiance

Lev	26:23	continue your **d**
	26:40	treacherous betrayal, the **d**
	26:41	my **d** that sent them off
Dt	31:29	willful in **d** in **d** of God
1Ki	15:5	willful **d** of God's clear directions
	21:25	in open **d** of God
Ne	9:29	They set their jaws in **d**
Jer	3:13	Admit your God-**d**.
Da	11:36	boast in **d** of the God of gods
Zec	7:11	they set their jaws in **d**

Defiantly

Nu	15:30	who sins **d**, deliberately blaspheming
1Sa	17:25	openly and **d** challenging Israel
Job	34:37	**D** shaking your fist at God
Da	9:14	we persistently and **d** ignored you

Defied

Jdg	5:18	Zebulun risked life and limb, **d** death
1Ki	11:6	Solomon openly **d** God
Ps	106:7	when they **d** the High God
	106:33	Because they **d** God yet again
Jer	2:8	The rulers **d** me.

Da	9:11	We **d** your instructions
Hos	7:13	They've **d** me
	8:1	broken my covenant and **d** my revelation

Defile

Lev	21:15	He must not **d** his descendants
Nu	5:3	so that they won't **d** their camp
	6:7	must not ritually **d** yourself
Dt	24:4	**d** the land with sin
2Ki	23:9	did not **d** the Altar in The Temple
Isa	56:2	keep Sabbath and don't **d** it
	56:6	keep Sabbath and don't **d** it
Da	1:8	would not **d** himself by eating
Ac	24:6	trying to **d** our holy Temple

Defiled

Ge	49:4	mounting that couch, and you **d** it
Lev	7:18	it has become **d** meat
	11:43	unclean or be **d** by them
	22:4	touches anything **d** by a corpse
Nu	5:13	even though she has **d** herself
	5:20	**d** yourself by sleeping with a man
	5:27	has **d** herself in being unfaithful
	5:28	if she has not **d** herself
	6:9	consecrated head is ritually **d**
	6:12	your consecration was ritually **d**
2Ch	29:5	give this much-**d** place a good
Ne	13:29	how they **d** the priesthood
Jer	2:7	trashed and **d** my dear land
Eze	22:16	You will be **d**
	23:38	They've **d** my holy Sanctuary
	23:39	walked into my Sanctuary and **d** it
	28:18	you **d** your holy places of worship
Ac	21:28	He's . . . **d** this holy place
Ro	1:27	they abused and **d** one another
Rev	21:27	Nothing dirty or **d** will get into

Defined

2Ch	7:14	my people, my God-**d** people
Lk	12:15	Life is not **d** by what you have
	13:14	Six days have been **d** as work days
Jn	17:16	no more **d** by the world Than I am **d**
Ro	9:7	Your family will be **d** by Isaaac
Col	3:11	everyone is **d** by Christ

Defy

Lev	26:21	If you **d** me and refuse to listen
	26:24	it will be my turn to **d** you
	26:27	still won't listen, still **d** me
	26:28	in hot anger will **d** you
Nu	22:18	**d** the orders of my God
Dt	33:11	Disable the loins of those who **d** him
Jer	6:12	people who dares to **d** this decree
Th	2:4	He'll **d** and then take over
Ti	1:9	who **d** all authority

Degenerate

Pr	14:2	a **d** life is a slap in his face
Isa	2:9	A **d** race, facedown in the gutter
	3:9	flout their sins like **d** Sodom

Degenerates

1Ki	21:13	the two **d** accused him
Ps	43:1	away from these lying **d**
Pr	12:5	the plots of **d** corrupt
	29:16	When **d** take charge, crime runs wild
Jer	9:2	a congregation of **d**
	23:14	the **d** of old Gomorrah
Rev	21:8	faithless, **d** and murderers

Delight

1Sa	12:22	God took **d** in making you
Ne	1:11	servants who **d** in honoring you
Job	22:26	take **d** in God, the Mighty One
	33:26	pray — to God's **d**
Ps	5:12	decking us out in **d**
	51:18	Make Zion the place you **d** in
	119:14	I **d** far more in what you tell me
	119:24	sayings on life are what give me **d**
	119:143	your commands always gave me **d**
Pr	3:12	a father's **d** is behind all this
	5:19	ever quit taking **d** in her body
	11:27	The one who seeks good finds **d**
	12:2	A good person basks in the **d** of God
	22:11	leaders also in their friendship
	25:2	God **d** in concealing things
	27:9	lotions and fragrance give sensual **d**
	29:3	love wisdom, you'll **d** your parents
Ecc	11:8	Take **d** in each light-filled hour
Isa	11:3	Fear-of-God will be all his joy and **d**
	62:4	be called Hephzibah (My **D**)
	65:18	create my people as pure **d**
	65:19	take **d** in my people
	66:3	you **d** in self-centered worship
	66:11	**d** yourselves and drink your fill
Jer	9:24	**d** in those who do the same things
	15:16	What **d** I took in being yours, O God
	32:41	how I'll **d** in doing good things
Eze	24:16	take from you the **d** of your life
	24:21	the **d** of your life
	24:25	the **d** of their life
	43:27	accept you with pleasure, with **d**
Hos	7:3	**d** the princes with their acrobatic
Zep	3:17	**d** you with his songs
Mt	3:17	marked by my love, **d** of my life
	12:18	take such **d** in him
	16:2	Red sky at night, sailor's **d**
	17:5	marked by my love, focus of my **d**
Lk	1:14	many will **d** in his birth
Ac	21:20	listened with **d** and gave God the glory
Ro	6:22	**d** of listening to God telling you
	7:22	I truly **d** in God's commands
	7:23	not all of me joins in that **d**
1Co	1:21	God in his wisdom took **d** in using
Eph	1:9	plans he took such **d** in making

D

Jas	1:25	**d** and affirmation in the action
1Pe	3:7	Honor them, **d** in them
	5:5	takes **d** in just plain people
2Pe	1:17	marked by my love, focus of all my **d**

Deliverance

Ge	45:7	an amazing act of **d**
Ex	3:7	cries for **d** from their slave masters
Jdg	13:5	**d** from Philistine oppression
2Ki	13:17	The arrow of **d** from Aram
Est	4:14	help and **d** will arrive for the Jews
Isa	9:4	**d** as surprising and sudden as
	46:13	**D** is not a long-range plan
	51:5	My **d** arrives on the run
Jer	32:21	signs and wonders — a powerful **d**
Eze	29:21	the dawn of **d**
Lk	1:71	**D** from our enemies
Ac	7:17	God promised Abraham for **d**
Ro	8:23	yearning for full **d**
2Co	1:11	lifted in praise for God's **d** of us

Demand

1Sa	2:16	servant would **d**, "No, I want it now
	8:6	When Samuel heard their **d**
Pr	22:29	skilled workers are always in **d**
Eze	20:40	I'll **d** your best gifts
Am	4:1	you **d** of your husbands
Mic	7:3	Corrupt leaders **d** bribes
Mt	25:24	**d** the best and make no allowances
Jn	19:16	Pilate caved in to their **d**
1Co	9:12	Others **d** plenty from you

Demanded

Jdg	6:30	men of the town **d** of Joash
1Sa	5:11	**d**, "Get it out of here, this Chest
2Sa	14:7	family ganged up against me and **d**
2Ki	18:14	king of Assyria **d** tribute
	23:33	**d** that Judah pay tribute
	23:35	the silver and gold **d** by Pharaoh
Ps	137:3	our captors **d** songs
Da	2:10	has ever **d** anything like this
Mt	8:34	**d** that Jesus get out
	18:28	He seized him by the throat and **d**
	21:23	**d**, "Show us your credentials
Mk	5:17	**d** that Jesus leave and not come back
	11:28	**d**, "Show us your credentials
Lk	20:2	**d**, "Show us your credentials
Jn	7:45	**d**, "Why didn't you bring him
Ac	13:28	**d** that Pilate execute him anyway
	25:21	Paul refused and **d** a hearing
1Co	9:12	who have never **d** deserve even more

Demean

1Sa	2:30	those who scorn me I **d**
Isa	29:20	never missed a chance to hurt or **d**

Demeaned

Ps	49:6	**d** by the arrogant rich
Jer	48:1	Kiriathaim **d** and defeated

Demolish

Dt	12:2	Ruthlessly **d** all the sacred shrines
Jdg	8:9	I'll **d** this tower
Jer	1:10	take apart and **d**
Eze	6:14	**d** the country wherever they live
	30:14	I'll **d** Pathros, burn Zoan
	35:14	I'll **d** you
Mic	5:10	**d** your chariots
Mt	5:17	have come to **d** the Scriptures

Demolished

Lev	14:45	The house has to be **d**
Jdg	8:17	he **d** the tower of Peniel
2Ki	14:13	He **d** the wall of Jerusalem
	23:10	Josiah **d** the Topheth
2Ch	25:23	He **d** the Wall of Jerusalem
	34:7	he **d** the altars and Asherah groves
Jer	31:28	took apart and **d**
	33:4	kings that have been **d**
Eze	6:6	pagan shrines **d**
	30:4	their foundations **d**
	35:15	Israel's inheritance was **d**
Am	3:15	luxury homes will be **d**
Na	2:6	The palace is **d**

Demon

2Ch	11:15	had installed goat and calf **d**-idols
Ps	106:37	at the altars of **d** gods
Mt	8:16	**d**-afflicted people were brought to him
	12:22	poor **d**-afflicted wretch
	17:18	He ordered the afflicting **d** out
Mk	5:16	**d**-possessed man and the pigs
	5:18	the **d**-delivered man begged to go
	9:17	made speechless by a **d**
	9:20	When the **d** saw Jesus, it threw
	9:28	Why couldn't we throw the **d** out
	9:29	no way to get rid of this kind of **d**
Lk	8:29	the **d** threw the man into convulsions
	9:42	**d** slammed him to the ground
	11:14	Jesus delivered a man from a **d**
Jn	7:20	You're **d**-possessed
	8:48	you were crazy — **d**-possessed
1Co	10:20	worse than nothing, a minus, a **d**
Rev	16:14	**d** spirits performing signs

Demon-afflicted

Mt	8:16	**d** people were brought to him
	12:22	poor **d** wretch, both blind and deaf

Demon-delivered

Mk	5:18	the **d** man begged to go along

Demon-possessed

Mk	5:16	the **d** man and the pigs
Jn	7:20	Who's trying to kill you? You're **d**
	8:48	said you were crazy — **d**

Demonic

Ps	141:9	all their **d** subterfuge
Mk	1:27	shuts up defiling, **d** spirits
	7:29	The **d** affliction is gone
Lk	4:35	The **d** spirit threw the man down
	4:36	orders **d** spirits to get out
Ro	8:38	living or dead, angelic or **d**
1Ti	4:1	chase after **d** illusions

Demons

Lev	17:7	offer their sacrifices to goat-**d**
Dt	32:17	They sacrificed to no-god **d**
Ps	58:2	you make deals with **d**
Isa	34:14	**d** and devils dance through the night
Mt	7:22	we bashed the **d**
	8:28	two madmen, victims of **d**
	10:8	Kick out the **d**
Mk	1:34	**d** knew his true identity
	1:39	preaching and throwing out the **d**
	3:15	give them authority to banish **d**
	5:12	**d** begged him, "Send us to the pigs
	6:13	they sent the **d** packing
	9:38	saw a man using your name to expel **d**
	16:9	whom he had delivered from seven **d**
	16:17	They will throw out **d** in my name
Lk	4:41	**D** left in droves, screaming
	8:2	from whom seven **d** had gone out
	8:27	he was a victim of **d**
	8:30	many **d** afflicted him
	8:32	**d** begged Jesus to order them into
	8:35	man from whom the **d** had been sent
	8:38	man whom he had delivered from the **d**
	9:1	power to deal with all the **d**
	9:49	saw a man using your name to expel **d**
	10:17	even the **d** danced to your tune
	11:18	the prince of **d**, to cast out **d**
	11:20	sends the **d** on their way
	13:32	busy clearing out the **d**
1Co	10:21	slumming with **d** the next
Jas	2:19	**D** do that, but what good does
Rev	9:20	didn't quit worshiping **d**
	16:13	saw three foul **d** crawl out
	16:16	frog-**d** gathered the kings together
	18:2	ghost town for **d** is all that's left

Demoralized

Nu	32:9	completely **d** the People of Israel
2Sa	19:3	straggled back to the city that day **d**
2Ch	32:18	scare them into **d** submission
1Co	9:22	the defeated, the **d**
2Co	4:8	but we're not **d**

Dependable

1Sa	25:28	a rule solid and **d**
2Ch	19:9	be **d** and honest in your duties
Ps	40:10	how **d** you are, how thorough
	59:10	God in **d** love shows up on time
	59:17	always count on you — God, my **d** love
	89:37	**D** as the phases of the moon
	119:91	Your Word and truth are **d** as ever
Isa	46:7	a **d** god, always right
Lk	12:42	Who is the **d** manager
Eph	6:21	a **d** servant of the Master
1Th	5:24	One who called you is completely **d**
1Ti	3:11	serious, **d**, not sharp-tongued
1Pe	5:12	Silas, a most **d** brother
Rev	21:5	each word **d** and accurate
	22:6	These are **d** and accurate words

Dependence

Isa	30:15	settling down in complete **d** on me
Mic	3:11	posturing and pretending **d** on God

Depravity

2Ch	28:19	unleashed an epidemic of **d**
Pr	28:4	you're free to embrace **d**
Isa	3:9	Brazen in their **d**
Mk	7:22	greed, **d**, deceptive dealings

Depressed

Ne	2:2	not sick, are you? Or are you **d**
	2:3	why shouldn't I be **d** when
Isa	19:10	**d** in their forced idleness
Jer	12:4	the country **d**, the farms in ruin
Ro	12:8	irritated with them or **d** by them
2Ti	3:6	**d** by their sinfulness

Depression

1Sa	16:15	awful tormenting **d** from God
	16:23	bad **d** from God tormented Saul
Jer	30:19	**D** days are over

Desecrate

Lev	21:12	neither abandon nor **d** the Sanctuary
	21:23	It would **d** my Sanctuary
	22:2	so they won't **d** my holy name
	22:16	they **d** themselves
	22:32	Don't **d** my holy name
Nu	18:32	you won't **d** the holy offerings
	35:34	Don't **d** the land in which you live
Dt	21:23	don't **d** your God-given land
2Ch	27:2	he didn't **d** The Temple of God
Pr	24:9	Fools incubate sin; cynics **d** beauty
Isa	6:5	words that corrupt and **d**
	14:21	**d** the face of the world
Jer	17:21	not to **d** the Sabbath
Eze	7:22	walk in and **d** place and people
	9:7	**D** the Temple. Fill it with corpses

	22:8	**d** my Sabbaths
	24:21	I will **d** my Sanctuary
Da	11:31	march in and **d** the Sanctuary
Zep	3:4	Her priests **d** the Sanctuary
Mal	2:10	we **d** the covenant of our ancestors
Mt	19:6	no one should **d** his art
Mk	10:9	no one should **d** his art
Rev	11:2	They'll **d** the Holy City

Desecrated

Lev	20:3	**d** my holy name
Nu	19:20	he has **d** the Sanctuary of God
Isa	14:19	Your dead body **d**, mutilated
Jer	51:51	God's house, **d** by strangers
Eze	20:13	they totally **d** my holy Sabbaths
	20:16	**d** my holy Sabbaths
	20:21	they **d** my Sabbaths
	20:24	They **d** my Sabbaths
	22:26	violated my law and **d** my holy things
	23:38	**d** my holy Sabbaths
	25:3	cheered when my Sanctuary was **d**
Da	8:11	**d** the Sanctuary
Am	6:10	must not be mentioned in this **d** place
Mal	2:11	has **d** the holiness of God

Desire

2Sa	23:5	My entire salvation, my every **d**
1Ki	10:13	queen of Sheba all her heart's **d**
2Ch	9:12	queen of Sheba all her heart's **d**
Est	5:3	what's your **d**, Queen Esther
	5:8	pleased to do what I **d** and ask
Pr	10:24	what the good people **d**, they get
SS	7:5	**d**, longings for the heights
Isa	60:10	It's my **d** now to be tender
Eze	24:21	delight of your life, your heart's **d**
Php	1:23	**d** to . . . be with Christ

Desires

Dt	18:6	free to move wherever he **d**
2Ch	30:19	everyone who sincerely **d** God
Ps	20:4	Give you what your heart **d**
Pr	11:23	**d** of good people lead straight
1Co	7:9	they can't manage their **d**

Desolate

Dt	8:15	those **d**, arid badlands
2Sa	13:20	bitter and **d**
2Ch	36:21	**d** land put to an extended sabbath
Ps	55:15	every **d** detail of a damned life
	69:25	Leave them **d** with nobody at home
Isa	1:9	we'd be as **d** as Sodom
	17:9	the country will be empty, **d**
Jer	32:43	is going to end up **d**
	33:10	empty and **d** towns of Judah
Eze	29:10	reduce Egypt to an empty, **d** wasteland
	29:12	Egypt the most **d** of all desolations
	30:7	Egypt, most **d** of the **d**
	33:28	mountains will become dangerously **d**

Mt	23:38	so **d**, nothing but a ghost town
Ac	8:26	walk over to that **d** road

Despair

Ge	37:29	ripped his clothes in **d**
	44:13	ripped their clothes in **d**
Ex	23:28	I'll send **D** on ahead of you
1Sa	23:17	Don't **d**. My father, Saul, can't
2Ki	18:37	ripped their robes in **d**
Ezr	9:4	sat there in **d**, waiting
Job	9:23	aloof from the **d** of the innocent
	15:22	They **d** of things ever getting better
Ps	126:5	those who planted their crops in **d**
	142:3	I sink in **d**, my spirit ebbing away
	143:4	I sat there in **d**, my spirit draining
Isa	36:22	tearing their clothes in defeat and **d**
Jer	30:10	Don't **d**, Israel. Look up!
La	1:4	her priests in **d**
Eze	7:27	The king holds his head in **d**
Joel	1:11	Dirt farmers, **d**!
Mic	7:1	sunk in a swamp of **d**
Zep	3:16	Dear Zion, don't **d**

Desperate

1Ki	8:33	prayers **d** and devout
	8:49	prayers **d** and devout
	18:26	**D**, they jumped and stomped
2Ch	6:24	prayers **d** and devout
	6:39	prayers **d** and devout
	28:21	**D**, Ahaz ransacked The Temple
Job	6:14	**d** people give up on God Almighty
Ps	31:14	**D**, I throw myself on you
	34:6	When I was **d**, I called out
	54:2	Listen, God — I'm **d**
	55:8	**d** for a change from rage
	107:6	in your **d** condition, you called out
	107:13	called out to God in your **d** condition
	107:19	called out to God in your **d** condition
	107:28	called out to God in your **d** condition
	120:1	I cry to God, **d** for an answer
Pr	6:3	Go, put on a long face; act **d**
Isa	19:3	hold seances, **d** for answers
	41:17	poor and homeless are **d** for water
	49:26	enemies, crazed and **d**
La	1:11	**d** for food, so **d** to stay alive
Eze	22:25	leaders among you became **d**
Na	1:8	No matter how **d** the trouble
Mt	13:50	a lot of **d** complaining
Eph	5:16	These are **d** times
Rev	3:2	Your condition is **d**

Desperately

1Sa	1:16	I'm so **d** unhappy and in such pain
2Sa	12:16	David prayed **d** to God
2Ch	13:14	They prayed **d** to God
Ps	102:2	just when I need you so **d**
SS	3:1	I wanted him **d**
Jer	22:27	**d** homesick, but you'll never get home
Mk	5:10	**d** begged Jesus not to banish them

Lk	8:31	begged Jesus **d** not to order them
	17:22	you are going to be **d** homesick
	19:3	He wanted **d** to see Jesus
1Co	7:15	You don't have to hold on **d**
2Co	8:2	incredibly happy, though **d** poor

Desperation

1Sa	8:18	will cry in **d** because of this king
Jnh	1:5	called out in **d** to their gods
2Co	11:29	I feel the **d** in my bones

Despicable

Jos	7:15	did this **d** thing in Israel
Jdg	11:35	I'm dirt. I'm **d**
Ps	15:4	despise the **d**
Jer	40:17	Stinking, **d** trash
2Pe	2:13	so **d** and addicted to pleasure

Despise

Job	5:17	don't **d** the discipline of Almighty God
	19:18	Even street urchins **d** me
Ps	15:4	**d** the despicable
	119:128	I **d** every deceitful detour
Pr	13:19	fools bent on evil **d** matters of soul
Isa	33:15	speak the truth, **d** exploitation
La	1:8	All who admired her **d** her now
Zec	4:10	dare **d** this day of small beginnings
Mal	1:6	You priests **d** me
Lk	16:13	adore the first and **d** the second
Ro	7:15	doing things I absolutely **d**
2Pe	2:10	**d** interference from true authority

Despised

Nu	15:31	He has **d** God's word
2Ch	36:16	**d** the message itself
Ne	4:4	We're so **d**: Boomerang their ridicule
Isa	49:7	says to the **d** one
	60:15	Not long ago you were **d** refuse
Eze	16:57	**d** by the Edomite women
	17:19	king **d** my oath and broke my covenant
	20:13	**d** my laws for living well
	20:16	**d** my laws for living obediently
	21:10	you've **d** the scepter of Judah
	21:13	Why have you **d** discipline
Joel	2:26	Never again will my people be **d**
	2:27	Never again will my people be **d**
Ob	1:2	runt of the godless nations, **d**

Destiny

Ecc	6:10	Its **d** is fixed
Isa	65:12	Fate it will be: your **d**, Death
Jas	4:12	God is in charge of deciding human **d**

Destitute

Dt	24:12	if he is **d**, don't use his cloak
	24:14	Don't abuse a laborer who is **d**

Ps	72:12	**d** who have run out of luck
Pr	31:9	Stand up for the poor and **d**
Isa	10:2	rob my **d** people of dignity
1Ti	5:3	Take care of widows who are **d**

Destroyer

Ex	12:23	he won't let the **d** enter your house
Isa	14:31	the wake of a brutal, disciplined **d**
	33:1	Doom to you, D, not yet destroyed
	54:16	I also create the **d**
Jer	48:18	The **d** of Moab will come against you
	51:25	I'm your enemy, Babylon, Mount D
	51:56	avenging **d** is about to enter Babylon
Jn	10:28	protected from the D for good
	10:29	so much greater than the D and Thief
Hob	11.28	**d** of the firstborn wouldn't touch
Rev	9:11	Abaddon, in Greek, Apollyon — "D

Determined

Ex	3:17	**d** to get you out of the affliction
	14:8	stubborn, **d** to chase the Israelites
Dt	31:29	**d** to do evil in defiance of God
1Sa	20:1	makes him so **d** to kill me
	20:3	he's **d** to kill me
	23:15	Saul was **d** to hunt him down
2Sa	17:14	God had **d** to discredit the counsel
1Ch	12:38	united and **d** to make David king
	28:10	Be brave, **d**! And do it
2Ch	11:16	who **d** to seek the God of Israel
	24:4	Joash **d** to renovate The Temple of God
	27:6	steady and **d** life of obedience to God
	32:1	cities under siege, **d** to take them
Job	30:13	**d** to ruin me
	30:23	I know you're **d** to kill me
Ps	17:11	**d** to bring me down
	39:1	I'm **d** to watch steps and tongue
	59:4	they're after me, **d** to get me
	140:5	**d** to bring me down
Ecc	8:16	When I **d** to load up on wisdom
Jer	18:23	they're **d** to kill me
	21:10	I'm **d** to see this city destroyed
	26:21	they **d** to kill him
	32:19	**d** in purpose and relentless
	42:15	If you have **d** to go to Egypt
	42:17	who is **d** to go to Egypt
	42:22	where you've **d** to go and live
Eze	20:25	they were **d** to live bad lives
Da	1:8	**d** that he would not defile himself
	9:17	this **d** prayer of your servant
Hos	5:11	**d** to do it his own worthless way
Joel	2:7	so disciplined, so **d**
Mt	1:19	chagrined but noble, **d** to take care
	2:16	**d** that age from information
Mk	14:10	**d** to betray him
Ac	22:30	**d** to get to the root of the trouble
	27:43	the centurion, **d** to save Paul
Ro	1:13	**d** to get some personal enjoyment
	9:8	identity was never racially **d**
	9:11	a sure thing **d** by his decision
1Co	2:7	what God **d** as the way

Gal	2:5	**d** to preserve the truth
1Th	1:6	**d** to live that way yourselves
2Th	1:4	so steady and **d** in your faith
1Pe	1:2	has **d** by the work of the Spirit

D

Detest

Lev	11:10	creatures in the deeps, you are to **d**
	11:11	**d** them. Don't eat their meat
	11:11	Don't eat their meat; **d** their carcass
	11:13	birds you are to **d**. Don't eat them
	11:23	insects . . . you are to **d**

Detestable

Lev	11:12	doesn't have fins and scales is **d**
	11:13	Don't eat them. They are **d**
	11:20	insects that . . . are **d** to you
	11:41	crawl on the ground are **d**
	11:42	or on many feet — they are **d**

Devastate

Dt	31:17	calamities and disasters will **d** them
Isa	37:26	using you to **d** strong cities
Eze	33:29	I am God when I **d** the country
Hos	5:7	locusts will **d** their violated land
	13:15	**d** the country, leaving a trail of ruin
Ac	11:28	famine was about to **d** the country

Devastated

Ge	41:36	country won't be **d** by the famine
	47:13	alike were **d** by the famine
Jdg	6:5	marched in and **d** the country
	20:21	**d** twenty-two Israelite divisions
	20:25	**d** another eighteen Israelite divisions
1Sa	5:6	**d** them by hitting them with tumors
1Ki	11:15	when David **d** Edom
2Ki	19:11	country after country laid waste, **d**
2Ch	14:14	**d** all the towns around Gerar
Isa	37:11	one country after another **d**
	37:18	have **d** all the nations
	49:19	Your **d**, decimated land
	54:6	abandoned wife, **d** with grief
Eze	6:9	how **d** I was by their betrayals
	7:27	the prince is **d**
	25:3	land of Judah was **d**
Hos	11:8	**d** like luckless Zeboim
Am	4:11	left you **d** like Sodom and Gomorrah
Zec	13:8	two-thirds will be **d**
Lk	4:25	drought when famine **d** the land
	21:20	know that she is about to be **d**

Devastating

1Sa	6:5	rats that are **d** the country
2Ki	15:16	**d** both the town and its suburbs
Eze	38:8	has recovered from a **d** war
Da	8:13	this **d** judgment against sin
Ac	8:3	Saul just went wild, **d** the church
1Co	5:5	It will be totally **d** to him

Rev	16:18	a huge and **d** earthquake

Devastation

Nu	21:30	**D** as far off as Nophah
Dt	29:22	see the widespread **d**
Jos	8:24	returned to Ai and completed the **d**
	10:20	finished them off, total **d**
1Ki	9:9	what's behind this God-visited **d**
2Ch	7:22	what's behind this God-visited **d**
Ezr	9:5	picked myself up from my utter **d**
Isa	6:13	the **d** will start up again
Jer	48:5	cries of loss and **d**
Joel	2:25	the great locust **d**
1Co	5:5	better **d** and embarrassment

Deviate

2Ki	13:11	He didn't **d** one bit from the sins
	15:28	he didn't **d** so much as a hair's
Pr	4:5	Don't **d** an inch

Devil

2Sa	22:5	**d** waters rushed over me
	23:6	**d**'s henchmen are like thorns culled
Job	3:6	the **d** take it
Ps	6:8	Get out of here, you **D**'s crew
	18:4	**d** waters rushed over me
	28:4	moonlight for the **D**
	55:12	isn't a foreign **d** spitting invective
	140:11	let the **D** hunt them down
Zec	11:6	the **d** take the hindmost
Mt	4:1	The **D** was ready to give it
	4:3	the **D** took advantage of
	4:5	second test the **D** took him
	4:6	The **D** goaded him by quoting Psalm
	4:8	third test, the **D** took him
	4:11	The Test was over. The **D** left
	6:13	Keep us safe from ourselves and the **D**
	9:34	He's probably made a pact with the **d**
	12:24	Some **d** trick he's pulled
	12:27	slinging **d** mud at me, calling me a **d**
	13:38	thistles are subjects of the **d**
	13:39	the enemy who sows them is the **D**
Mk	3:22	using **d** tricks to impress them
	3:23	send a **d** to catch a **d**
Lk	4:2	he was tested by the **D**
	4:3	The **D**, playing on his hunger
	4:6	the **D** said, "They're yours
	4:9	third test the **D** took him
	4:13	The **D** retreated temporarily
	8:12	the **D** snatches it from them
	11:4	Keep us safe from ourselves and the **d**
	11:15	Some **d** trick he's pulled
	11:18	accuse me of ganging up with the **D**
	11:19	slinging **d** mud at me, calling me a **d**
Jn	6:70	Still, one of you is a **d**
	8:44	You're from your father, the **D**
	13:2	The **D** by now had Judas
Ac	10:38	everyone who was beaten down by the **D**
	13:10	You bag of wind, you parody of a **d**

2Co	6:15	Does Christ go strolling with the **D**
Eph	4:27	Don't give the **D** that kind of foothold
	6:11	everything the **D** throws your way
	6:12	fight to the finish against the **D**
1Ti	3:6	the **D** trip him up
	3:7	**D** will figure out a way to lure him
2Ti	2:26	escape the **D**'s trap
Heb	2:14	he destroyed the **D**'s hold on death
Jas	4:7	Yell a loud no to the **D**
1Pe	5:8	The **D** is poised to pounce
1Jn	3:8	sin are straight from the **D**
	3:10	God's children and the **D**'s children
Jude	1:9	went to the mat with the **D**
Rev	2:10	The **D** is about to throw you in jail
	2:11	Christ-conquerors are safe from **D**
	2:24	scorn this playing around with the **D**
	12:9	the one called **D** and Satan
	12:12	**D**'s come down on you
	20:2	the very **D**, Satan himself
	20:10	**D** who deceived them will be hurled

Devils

Ps	18:44	The foreign **d** gave up
Isa	34:14	demons and **d** dance through the night
Jer	30:23	heads of the wicked like dust **d**
Mt	12:27	calling me a devil kicking out **d**
	12:45	now all the **d** are moving back in
Lk	11:19	calling me a devil who kicks out **d**

Devoted

Lev	27:28	Everything **d** is holy
	27:29	human who has been **d** to destruction
Nu	18:14	You get every Totally-**D** gift
Dt	13:17	plunder **d** to holy destruction
1Ki	8:58	May he keep us centered and **d** to him
2Ki	4:1	what a good man he was, **d** to God
2Ch	25:2	wasn't wholeheartedly **d** to God
Ne	13:14	forget the **d** work I have done
Job	1:1	totally **d** to God and hated evil
	1:8	totally **d** to God and hating evil
	2:3	totally **d** to God and hating evil
Pr	11:28	life **d** to things is a dead life
Jer	23:11	Prophets and priests **d** to desecration
Ro	1:1	I, Paul, am a **d** slave of Jesus Christ
2Co	8:16	giving Tit the same **d** concern
Php	2:22	He's been a **d** son to me

Devotion

2Sa	16:17	Is this the way you show **d**
Pr	14:34	God-**d** makes a country strong
Jer	8:2	in doglike **d**

Devour

Ex	10:5	They'll **d** everything left over
Dt	5:25	huge fire will **d** us
	28:38	the grasshoppers will **d** it
	28:39	the worms will **d** them
Ps	22:20	don't let those mongrels **d** me

Isa	56:9	Come, **d**, beast barbarians
Da	7:5	Attack! **D**! Fill your belly
Am	3:4	if there's no carcass to **d**

Devout

1Ki	8:28	my prayers, energetic and **d**
	8:33	prayers desperate and **d**
	8:49	prayers desperate and **d**
	18:3	Obadiah feared God — he was very **d**
2Ch	6:19	my prayers, energetic and **d**
	6:24	prayers desperate and **d**
	6:39	prayers desperate and **d**
	35:26	Josiah, his exemplary and **d** life
Job	4:6	your **d** life give you confidence
Mt	2:7	Pretending to be as **d** as they
Lk	1:17	kindle **d** understanding
Ac	2:5	**d** pilgrims from all over the world
	10:7	one particularly **d** soldier
	16:1	Timothy, son of a **d** Jewish mother
Php	3:5	strict and **d** adherent to God's law
1Ti	6:6	A **d** life does bring wealth

Diameter

1Ki	7:23	basin of cast metal fifteen feet in **d**
	7:32	wheels were twenty-seven inches in **d**
	7:38	washbasins, each six feet in **d**
2Ch	4:2	basin of cast metal fifteen feet in **d**

Difficulties

Jn	16:33	will continue to experience **d**
1Co	7:9	The **d** of marriage are preferable

Difficulty

Mt	13:21	emotions wear off and some **d** arrives
Mk	4:17	emotions wear off and some **d** arrives
Ac	27:7	After much **d**, we finally made it

Dignity

Dt	33:26	his **d** haloed by clouds
1Sa	2:8	Restoring **d** and respect
Job	30:15	my **d** in shreds
Isa	10:2	rob my destitute people of **d**
	57:2	They lived well and with **d**
1Co	6:15	bodies are created with the same **d**
	12:23	You give it **d** and honor
2Co	7:16	**d** and sensitivity of your hospitality
1Th	4:4	appreciate and give **d** to your body
Tit	2:2	lives of temperance, **d**, and wisdom
Jas	3:18	treating each other with **d** and honor
1Pe	2:17	Treat everyone you meet with **d**

Diligence

Pr	10:4	Sloth makes you poor; **d** brings wealth
	13:11	steady **d** pays off

D

D

2Th	3:9	wanted to provide an example of **d**
1Pe	5:2	all the **d** of a shepherd

Diligent

Dt	16:12	be **d** in observing these regulations
2Ch	19:5	**d** in appointing judges in the land
	19:11	Be bold and **d**. And God be with you
	34:12	The workmen were honest and **d**
Pr	12:24	The **d** find freedom in their work
	14:35	**D** work gets a warm commendation
	15:19	the **d** walk down a smooth road
	20:9	trusted to be always **d** and honest
	31:19	**d** in homemaking
Ro	16:12	such **d** women in serving the Master
1Ti	3:12	**d** in looking after their own affairs
2Ti	2:6	the **d** farmer who gets the produce
Tit	3:14	have to learn to be **d** in their work
2Jn	1:4	**d** in living out the Truth

Disadvantaged

Ro	12:8	if you work with the **d**, don't let

Disagreements

1Co	6:4	As these **d** and wrongs surface
	6:5	fair decisions when **d** and disputes

Disappointment

1Sa	15:11	prayed his anger and **d**
Job	6:20	arrive so confident — but what a **d**
Pr	13:12	Unrelenting **d** leaves you heartsick

Disapproval

Ro	7:3	good conscience, with no one's **d**

Disbelief

2Ki	21:12	they'll shake their heads in **d**
Jer	2:12	Throw up your hands in **d**
	18:16	will shake their heads in **d**

Discern

Job	6:30	trust me to **d** good from evil
Eze	44:23	how to **d** between unclean and clean
Jn	7:24	head — and heart! — to **d** what is right

Discerning

2Sa	14:7	like an angel of God in **d** good
1Ki	3:9	**d** the difference between good and evil
Isa	29:10	put the **d** prophets to sleep
Eph	1:17	intelligent and **d** in knowing him

Discernment

1Ch	22:12	God also give you **d** and understanding
Da	2:21	he provides both intelligence and **d**

Discipline

Lev	26:18	**d** you seven times over for your sins
	26:23	refuse my **d** and continue your defiance
Dt	4:36	his voice out of Heaven to **d** you
	11:2	didn't experience the **d**
	21:18	though they **d** him he still won't obey
Jos	22:31	saved the People . . . from God's **d**
1Sa	1:11	set him apart for a life of holy **d**
2Sa	7:14	I'll **d** him in the usual ways
	13:22	but he didn't **d** Amnon
Job	5:17	don't despise the **d** of Almighty God
	34:37	rebelling against God's **d**
	37:13	for **d** or grace or extravagant love
Pr	3:11	don't, dear friend, resent God's **d**
	6:23	moral **d** is a life path
	8:33	Mark a life of **d** and live wisely
	12:1	you love the **d** that goes with it
	13:18	Refuse **d** and end up homeless
	19:18	**D** your children while you still
	22:15	cure comes through tough-minded **d**
	29:1	people who hate **d**
	29:15	Wise **d** imparts wisdom
	29:17	**D** your children; you'll be glad
Isa	26:16	your **d** was so heavy
Jer	2:30	paid no attention to me, ignored my **d**
	7:28	wouldn't obey God, that refused all **d**
Eze	21:13	Why have you despised **d**
Hab	1:12	God, you gave them the job of **d**
Zep	3:7	accept my **d** and correction
Mt	6:16	practice some appetite-denying **d**
	9:14	rigorously **d** body and spirit
Mk	2:18	take on the **d** of fasting
Ac	2:46	followed a daily **d** of worship
	24:25	life of moral **d**
Eph	4:2	do this with humility and **d**
Col	3:12	humility, quiet strength, **d**
Tit	2:15	**d** them if they get out of line
Heb	12:5	don't shrug off God's **d**
	12:11	At the time, **d** isn't much fun
2Pe	1:6	alert **d**, passionate patience

Disciplined

Ps	69:26	gossiped about the one you **d**
Pr	5:12	Why did I reject a **d** life
	10:17	The road to life is a **d** life
	23:12	Give yourselves to **d** instruction
Isa	14:31	wake of a brutal, **d** destroyer
Jer	5:3	**d** them, but they refused correction
Joel	2:7	does what he's told, so **d**
Zep	2:3	Seek God, all you quietly **d** people
1Ti	4:8	a **d** life in God is far more so
Tit	2:6	guide the young men to live **d** lives

Disciplines

Dt	8:5	God **d** you in the same ways a father
Pr	8:10	Prefer my life-**d** over chasing
Ro	4:9	never brought up in the **d** of God
Heb	12:6	It's the child he loves that he **d**

Disciplining

Job	21:9	never experience God's **d** rod
	22:4	he's **d** you, putting you on the spot
Pr	13:24	love your children by **d** them

Discontent

1Co	10:10	We must be careful not to stir up **d**
	10:10	**d** destroyed them
Heb	12:15	weeds of bitter **d**

Discord

Pr	13:10	Arrogant know-it-alls stir up **d**
	29:22	Angry people stir up a lot of **d**

Discouraged

Jos	1:9	Don't be timid; don't get **d**
	14:8	went with me **d** the people
1Ch	28:20	Don't be anxious or get **d**
Ps	69:6	Be **d** by what happens to me
1Th	3:2	wouldn't be **d** by these hard times

Discredit

2Sa	17:14	God had determined to **d** the counsel
Isa	43:28	repudiate Jacob and **d** Israel
Jer	18:18	let's **d** him so we don't have to
Mt	5:11	speak lies about you to **d** me
Lk	6:22	blackens your name to **d** me
1Co	9:15	give anyone ammunition to **d** me

Discredited

Job	8:22	With your enemies thoroughly **d**
Mic	7:10	be **d** — yes, disgraced
Ac	19:26	barged in and **d** what we're doing

Disease

Ex	5:3	strike us with either **d** or death
	9:3	striking them with a severe **d**
	9:15	you and your people with deadly **d**
Lev	13:2	a serious skin **d** on the body
	13:3	a serious skin **d** and infectious
	13:8	a serious skin **d** and infectious
	13:9	a serious and infectious skin **d**
	13:11	it is a chronic skin **d**
	13:12	serious **d** breaks out that covers all
	13:13	if the **d** covers his entire body
	13:15	evidence of a serious skin **d**
	13:20	a serious skin **d**
	13:25	a serious skin **d**
	13:27	a serious skin **d** and infectious
	13:30	an infectious skin **d**
	13:42	serious skin **d** is breaking out
	13:43	sore of a serious skin **d**
	13:44	has a serious skin **d** and is unclean
	13:45	a serious skin **d**
	14:3	healed of the serious skin **d**

	14:7	cleansed from the serious skin **d**
	14:32	anyone who has a serious skin **d**
	14:54	every kind of serious skin **d**
	22:4	an infectious skin **d**
	26:16	debilitating **d**, high fevers
Nu	5:2	anyone who has an infectious skin **d**
Dt	24:8	If a serious skin **d** breaks out
	28:21	God will infect you with The **D**
	28:61	every **d** and catastrophe imaginable
	32:24	blistering heat, killing **d**
1Ki	8:37	catastrophe, crop failure or **d**
2Ki	5:1	afflicted with a grievous skin **d**
	5:3	would be healed of his skin **d**
	5:6	heal him of his skin **d**
	5:7	orders to heal this man from his **d**
	5:11	get rid of the **d**
	5:27	Naaman's skin **d** will now infect you
	15:5	afflicted the king with a bad skin **d**
2Ch	6:28	catastrophe, crop failure or **d**
	20:9	war or flood or **d** or famine
	21:15	a terrible **d** of the colon
	21:18	terrible and fatal **d** in his colon
	26:19	a skin **d** appeared on his forehead
	26:20	God then and there had given him the **d**
	26:21	skin **d** for the rest of his life
	26:23	His skin **d** disqualified him
Ps	41:8	He's got some dirty, deadly **d**
	78:49	advance guard of **d**-carrying angels
	91:6	**d** that prowls through the darkness
Isa	10:16	will send a debilitating **d**
	10:18	like a **d**-ridden invalid
Jer	14:12	with war and famine and **d**
	21:7	who haven't died from **d**
	21:9	in battle or by starvation or **d**
	24:10	war, starvation, **d**, whatever
	27:8	war and starvation and **d**
	29:17	on the way: war, hunger, **d**
	29:18	war and hunger and **d**
	32:24	Killing and starvation and **d**
	32:36	killing and starvation and **d**
	34:17	killed in war or by **d**
	44:13	massacre, starvation, and **d**
Eze	5:12	will die of either **d** or hunger
	5:17	Epidemic **d**, unrestrained murder
	6:11	dying of hunger, dying of **d**
	7:15	go home and die of hunger and **d**
	14:19	visit a deadly **d** on that country
	14:21	war, famine, wild animals, **d**
	28:23	I'll order an epidemic of **d**
	33:27	forts and caves will die of **d**
	38:22	judgment: **d** and massacre
Am	4:9	I hit your crops with **d**
Rev	6:8	fourth of the earth by war, famine, **d**

Diseased

2Ki	5:11	wave his hand over the **d** spot
Zec	13:2	polluted the air with their **d** words
	13:3	spreading **d**, polluting words
Mt	7:16	**d** trees with their bad apples
	9:35	healed their **d** bodies
	12:33	If you grow a **d** tree

D

Lk	6:43	nor good apples off a **d** tree
Tit	1:13	Stop that **d** talk

Diseases

Ex	15:26	won't strike you with all the **d**
Lev	14:57	infectious skin **d** and mildew
2Sa	3:29	forever be victims of crippling **d**
Ps	103:3	He heals your **d** — every one
Mt	4:23	He also healed people of their **d**
	8:17	He carried our **d**
Lk	7:21	Jesus healed many from **d**
	9:1	deal with all the demons and cure **d**

Disgrace

Lev	20:17	and they have sex, that's a **d**
2Sa	13:13	you'll be out on the street in **d**
2Ch	26:18	you are unfaithful and a **d**
	32:21	forced to return home in **d**
Ne	2:17	not live with this **d** any longer
Pr	19:26	parents are an embarrassment and **d**
Isa	25:8	He'll remove every sign of **d**
Jer	23:40	going down in history as a **d**
Hos	5:5	they're a public **d**
	7:10	Israel's a public **d**
Mic	7:4	Look at them slinking away in **d**
Hab	2:16	It's a time of **d**

Disgraced

Ge	34:14	uncircumcised. Why, we'd be **d**
2Sa	16:21	you have openly **d** your father
Ps	6:10	my enemies disappear. **D**, they turn
	40:14	will be heckled and **d**
	44:9	you've **d** us and won't fight for us
Isa	22:18	You've **d** your master's house
	24:23	red-faced sun will skulk, **d**
	45:24	**d** by their unbelief
	50:7	so I'm not **d**
Jer	17:18	Let them be **d**, not me.
	22:22	**d** by your evil life
Eze	28:16	threw you, **d**, off the mountain of God
Mic	7:10	be discredited — yes, **d**
Mt	1:19	quietly so Mary would not be **d**

Disgust

Ezr	8:22	turns away in **d** from those who leave
Job	20:7	Acquaintances look at them with **d**
Ps	5:6	Blood-Thirsty and Truth-Bender **d** you
Jer	33:5	have turned my stomach in **d**
Eze	23:22	lovers you got tired of and left in **d**

Disgusted

1Ch	21:6	Joab, **d** by the command
Isa	47:6	thoroughly **d** with my progeny
Jer	31:37	I turn my back on Israel, **d**
Eze	6:9	They'll be **d** with their evil ways
	36:31	be thoroughly **d** with yourselves

Mal	2:9	Everyone will be **d** with you
Mt	20:24	thoroughly **d** with the two brothers

Disgusting

Job	31:11	For **d** behavior like that, I'd deserve
Isa	66:3	self-centered worship — **d**
Jer	24:9	whole world will look on as **d**
	44:22	evil behavior and your **d** acts
Eze	5:9	Because of your **d** no-god idols
	5:11	obscenities and **d** no-god idols
	6:9	**d** to God in the way they've lived
	7:3	make you pay for your **d** obscenities
	7:4	Your **d** obscenities will boomerang
	7:8	make you pay for your **d** obscenities
	7:9	Your **d** obscenities will boomerang
	12:16	**d** obscenities they've been involved in

Dishonest

Dt	25:16	**D** weights and measures
Pr	2:22	the **d** will be gone for good
Jer	6:13	Everyone's after the **d** dollar
	8:10	Everyone's after the **d** dollar

Dishonestly

Lev	27:10	**d** substitute one animal for another
	27:33	If he **d** makes a substitution

Dishonesty

2Ch	19:7	God hates **d**, partiality, and bribery

Dishonor

Pr	30:9	might steal and **d** the name of my God
Jer	3:25	tangled up in the dirty sheets of **d**
Jn	8:49	honor my Father, while you **d** me

Dismay

2Ki	11:14	ripped her robes in **d**
	22:11	ripped his robes in **d**
	22:19	tearing your robe in **d**
2Ch	23:13	ripped her robes in **d**
	34:19	ripped his robes in **d**
	34:27	tearing your robe in **d**

Disobedience

Lev	26:15	holding my laws in contempt by your **d**
1Sa	2:25	far gone in **d** and refused to listen
1Ch	10:13	Saul died in **d**, disobedient to God
Jer	43:7	in total **d** of God's Message
Eph	2:2	unbelief, and then exhaled **d**
Heb	4:11	not drop out through some sort of **d**

Disobedient

1Ch	9:1	their unbelieving and **d** lives
	10:13	Saul died in disobedience, **d** to God

Tit	1:16	real creeps, **d** good-for-nothings
Heb	4:6	because they were **d**

Disobey

Ex	16:28	How long are you going to **d**
Job	36:12	if they **d**, they'll be cut down

Disobeyed

Jos	5:6	had **d** the call of God
1Ki	11:10	Solomon faithlessly **d** God's orders
	13:21	You **d** God's command
	13:26	holy man who **d** God's strict orders
Jer	11:10	their ancestors — the ones who **d** me

Disorder

1Co	7:2	life in a world of sexual **d**
2Co	12:21	evil, sexual **d**, and indecency

Disordered

Ro	8:3	**d** mess of struggling humanity

Disorderly

1Th	4:7	us into a **d**, unkempt life

Dispute

Ex	23:3	don't show favoritism in a **d**
	23:6	a **d** concerning your poor
Dt	25:1	When men have a legal **d**
Pr	20.21	A quarrelsome person in a **d**

Disputes

Dt	17:8	homicides, legal **d**, fights
	21:5	settling legal **d**
Mic	4:3	settle **d** in faraway places
1Co	6:5	when disagreements and **d** come up
Gal	6:17	bothered anymore by these **d**

Disregard

Est	3:8	Worse, they **d** the king's laws
Isa	42:3	won't **d** the small and insignificant
Eze	17:20	trial because of his total **d** for me
Gal	5:6	**d** of religion amounts to anything
1Th	4:8	If you **d** this advice, you're not

Disreputable

Mt	9:10	**d** characters came and joined them
Mk	2:15	a collection of **d** guests
Lk	5:29	tax men and other **d** characters
	7:29	ordinary and **d** people who heard John

Distress

Ge	41:55	people called out in **d** to Pharaoh

2Ki	4:27	can't you see that she's in **d**
Isa	26:17	woman having a baby, writhing in **d**
Zep	1:15	a day of **d** and anguish
Lk	7:21	healed many from diseases, **d**
Ro	12:8	give aid to people in **d**
2Co	7:9	let the **d** bring you to God
	7:10	**D** that drives us to God
	7:11	this **d** has goaded you closer to God

Divorce

Dt	22:19	his wife and can never **d** her
	22:29	he can never **d** her
	24:1	he may give her **d** papers
	24:3	husband also gives her **d** papers
Ezr	10:19	They all promised to **d** their wives
Isa	50:1	produce your mother's **d** papers
Mal	2:16	I hate **d**," says the God of Israel
Mt	5:32	If you **d** your wife, you're responsible
	19:3	Is it legal for a man to **d** his wife
	19:7	**d** papers and **d** procedures
	19:8	Moses provided for **d** as a concession
	19:9	**d** your faithful wife and then marry
Mk	10:2	Is it legal for a man to **d** his wife
	10:4	a certificate of dismissal and **d** her
Lk	16:18	Using the legalities of **d** as a cover

Divorced

Lev	21:7	prostitute or a **d** woman
	22:13	widowed or **d** and without children
Nu	30:9	pledge taken by a widow or **d** woman
Dt	24:4	who **d** her can't marry her again
1Ch	8:8	had children after he **d** his wives
Mt	5:32	if you marry such a **d** adulteress

Divorcee

Lev	21:14	not a widow, not a **d**

Divorcees

Eze	44:22	Priests are not to marry widows or **d**

Divorces

Mt	5:31	**d** his wife, let him do it legally
Mk	10:11	**d** his wife so he can marry someone
	10:12	**d** her husband so she can marry

Doctrine

Job	11:4	**d** is sound and my conduct impeccable
Gal	3:9	lived by faith—this is no new **d**
Tit	2:1	things that make for solid **d**

Dog-eat-dog

2Ch	15:5	it was a **d** world
Zec	11:6	It's **d**, survival of the fittest
Mt	24:10	it will be **d**
Mk	13:9	will go from bad to worse, **d**

D

Lk	21:12	will go from bad to worse, **d**
2Co	10:3	It's **d** out there
2Ti	3:3	**d**, unbending, slanderers

Dollar

Jer	6:13	Everyone's after the dishonest **d**
	8:10	Everyone's after the dishonest **d**
Mt	20:2	agreed on a wage of a **d** a day
	20:9	were each given a **d**
	20:10	got the same, each of them one **d**
	20:11	Taking the **d**, they groused angrily
	20:13	agreed on the wage of a **d**, didn't we

Dollars

Mt	18:24	a debt of a hundred thousand **d**
	18:28	fellow servants who owed him ten **d**
	25:15	To one he gave five thousand **d**
	25:20	The one given five thousand **d** showed

Doom

Nu	21:29	**D**, Moab!
	24:23	**D**! Who stands a chance when God
Dt	8:20	You'll go to your **d**
	32:35	day of their **d** is just around
1Ki	3:11	**d** of your enemies
	14:10	I'm bringing **d** on the household
	21:21	will most certainly bring **d** upon you
	21:29	not bring the **d** during his lifetime
	22:8	only **d**, **d**, **d**
	22:18	word for me from God, only **d**
	22:23	God has pronounced your **d**
2Ki	9:25	That's when God pronounced this **d**
	21:12	a **d** so terrible
	21:13	a rerun of Ahab's **d**
	22:16	on my way to bring the **d** of judgment
	22:19	took seriously the **d** of judgment
	22:20	You won't be around to see the **d**
	24:20	The source of all this **d**
1Ch	2:7	who brought **d** on Israel
2Ch	1:11	and the **d** of your enemies
	18:7	only **d**, **d**, **d**
	18:17	word for me from God, only **d**
	18:22	God has pronounced your **d**
	22:4	graduated with a degree in **d**
	22:8	executing **d** on the dynasty of Ahab
	34:24	on my way to bring the **d** of judgment
	34:27	took seriously the **d** of judgment
	34:28	You won't be around to see the **d**
Job	22:16	sweeping them off to their **d**
	34:20	wicked rulers tumble to their **d**
Ps	46:2	fearless at the cliff-edge of **d**
	56:13	my feet from the cliff-edge of **d**
	60:3	made your people look **d** in the face
	63:9	marked for **d**, marked for death
	79:11	pardon those on death row from their **d**
	81:10	the very God who rescued you from **d**
Pr	17:22	gloom and **d** leave you bone-tired
Isa	3:9	**D** to their eternal souls
	3:11	But **d** to the wicked!

	5:8	**D** to you who buy up all the houses
	5:11	**D** to those who get up early
	5:18	**D** to you who use lies to sell evil
	5:20	**D** to you who call evil good
	5:21	**D** to you who think you're so smart
	6:5	I said, "**D**! It's Doomsday!
	10:1	**D** to you who legislate evil
	10:5	**D** to Assyria
	18:1	**D** to the land of flies
	24:16	all I can see is **d**, **d**, and more **d**
	25:7	banish the pall of **d** hanging over all
	28:1	**D** to the pretentious drunks
	29:1	**D**, Ariel, Ariel, the city
	29:15	**D** to you! You pretend to have
	30:1	**D**, rebel children!
	31:1	**D** to those who go off to Egypt
	33:1	**D** to you, Destroyer
	45:9	**d** to you who fight your Maker
	57:6	Your worship will be your **d**
	61:3	Messages of joy instead of news of **d**
Jer	6:1	**D** pours out of the north
	11:11	I'm about to visit **d** on you
	11:15	pious programs will save you from **d**
	11:17	yes, I have pronounced **d** on you
	11:23	visiting the men of Anathoth with **d**
	17:18	Bring down upon them the day of **d**
	18:11	I'm shaping **d** against you
	18:12	the way we've always lived, **d** or no **d**
	18:17	On their day of **d**, they'll stare
	19:3	I'm about to bring **d** crashing down
	19:4	**D** — because they've walked off
	19:5	**D** — because they've built altars
	19:15	the **d** that I have pronounced
	22:13	**D** to him who builds palaces
	22:18	**D** to this man!
	23:1	**D** to the shepherd-leaders who butcher
	23:12	It will be the Year of **D**
	25:7	businesses of yours are your **d**
	40:2	Your God pronounced **d** on this place
	42:10	the **d** I have visited on you
	42:17	No one will escape the **d**
	44:2	terrible **d** that I brought down
	44:11	I've decided to bring **d** on you
	44:23	This **d** has come upon you because
	44:27	I've targeted each one of you for **d**
	44:29	decrees of **d** against you are the real
	44:30	Watch for this sign of **d**
	46:25	when I visit **d** on the god Amon
	48:1	**D** to Nebo! Leveled to the ground
	48:2	Conspirators plot Heshbon's **d**
	48:3	Disaster — **d** and more **d**
	48:16	Moab's **d** is on countdown
	49:8	I'm bringing **d** to Esau
	49:29	Terror! Death! **D**! Danger everywhere
	49:37	bring **d** on them, my anger-fueled **d**
	50:18	I'm bringing **d** on the king of Babylon
	50:21	Go after Pekod, country of **d**
	50:27	Send them to their **d**! **D** to them
	51:44	I'll bring **d** on the glutton god-Bel
	51:52	I will bring **d** on her no-god idols
	52:3	source of all this **d**
Eze	2:10	lamentations and mourning and **d**

	13:3	God, the Master, pronounces **d**
	13:18	Say '**D**' to the women who sew magic
	16:23	**D**! **D** to you, says God, the Master
	24:6	**D** to the city of murder
	24:9	**D** to the city of murder
	34:2	**D** to you shepherds of Israel
Hos	7:13	**D**! They've run away from home
	9:7	**D**'s at the doorstep. It's payday
Joel	2:25	locusts of **d**
Am	5:16	malls and shops with cries of **d**
Mic	2:1	**D** to those who plot evil
Na	2:10	**D**! Damnation! Desolation!
	3:1	**D** to Murder City
Zep	1:15	a day of catastrophic **d**
	2:5	**D** to the seaside people
	3:1	**D** to the rebellious city
Zec	11:17	**D** to you, useless shepherd
Mt	11:21	**D** to you, Chorazin! **D**, Bethsaida
	18:7	**D** to the world
	25:46	herded to their eternal **d**
Lk	4:29	throw him to his **d**
	10:13	**D**, Chorazin! **D**, Bethsaida!
	21:26	the threat of **d**
Ac	28:20	hostage here for hope, not **d**
2Co	1:10	rescued us from certain **d**
1Th	1:10	Jesus, who rescued us from certain **d**
Rev	8:13	**D**! **D**! **D** to everyone left on earth
	9:12	first **d** is past. Two **d**s yet to come
	11:14	second **d** is past, the third **d** coming
	12:12	**d** to earth and sea
	18:4	don't get caught in her **d**
	18:10	cry their lament: **D**, **d**
	18:16	**D**, **d**, the great city doomed!
	18:19	**D**, **d**, the great city doomed!

Doomed

Nu	17:13	Are we all **d**
2Sa	19:28	Wasn't everyone in my father's house **d**
2Ki	8:10	God showed me — that he's **d** to die
	9:8	The entire line of Ahab is **d**
Est	7:7	finished with him and that he was **d**
Job	10:15	If I'm truly guilty, I'm **d**
Ps	102:20	He listened to the groans of the **d**
	120:5	I'm **d** to live in Meshech
Pr	2:18	Her whole way of life is **d**
	28:17	A murderer haunted by guilt is **d**
	28:18	a devious life is a **d** life
Isa	1:9	**d** just like Gomorrah
	13:22	Babylon is **d**
	22:4	These people are **d**
	38:14	I squawk like a **d** hen
Jer	18:11	Turn back from your **d** way of life
La	4:18	our days numbered. We were **d**
Eze	30:9	Egypt's **d**! Judgment's coming
Da	2:9	can't tell me my dream, you're **d**
Hos	9:17	They're **d** to be wanderers
Na	2:7	Nineveh stripped, Nineveh **d**
Mt	27:3	realized that Jesus was **d**
Ac	27:22	the ship itself is **d**
1Co	9:16	compelled to do it, and **d** if I don't
Gal	3:10	independent of God, is **d** to failure

Col	1:14	sins we were **d** to keep repeating
Rev	18:10	Doom, doom, the great city **d**!
	18:16	Doom, doom, the great city **d**!
	18:19	Doom, doom, the great city **d**!

Doomsday

2Sa	2:26	keep killing each other till **d**
1Ki	14:14	**d** for Jeroboam
2Ki	19:3	black day, a terrible day — **d**
	19:25	Using you as a **d** weapon
Job	15:23	every day is **d**
Ps	64:1	obsessed with feelings of **d**
Pr	3:25	**d**'s just around the corner
Isa	6:5	Doom! It's **D**! I'm as good as dead!
	10:3	on Judgment Day, when **D** arrives
Jer	11:23	men of Anathoth with doom. **D**
	17:16	wasn't my idea to call for **D**
	25:32	Prepare for the worst! **D**!
	36:31	**d** disaster of which I warned them
	39:17	I'll deliver you on that **d**
	47:4	it will be **d** for Philistines
	48:44	This is my agenda for Moab on **d**
	50:27	Doom to them! Yes, **D**!
	50:31	That's right: It's **d**
	51:2	A total and final **d**
Eze	30:3	**D**!' Time's up! God's big day
Joel	1:15	**D**! God's Judgment Day has come
	2:2	A black day! A **D**!
Mic	2:3	It's **d** for you
	4:9	So why the **d** hysterics?
Hab	3:16	wait for **D** to descend on our attackers
Mt	13:13	stare till **d** and not see it
	18:7	it's **d** to you if you do
	24:4	Watch out for **d** deceivers
Mk	13:5	Watch out for **d** deceivers
Lk	21:8	Watch out for the **d** deceivers
	22:22	traitor to the Son of Man, this is **d**

Double-talk

Job	6:29	Think it over — no **d**!
Pr	17:20	**d** brings you double trouble
Col	2:8	big words and intellectual **d**

Double-tongued

| Hos | 7:1 | Two-faced and **d**, they steal |

Doubt

1Sa	24:20	know now beyond **d** that you will rule
1Ki	20:13	know, beyond the shadow of a **d**
2Ki	5:15	now know beyond a shadow of a **d**
	19:7	Afflict him with self-**d**.
Ps	73:1	No **d** about it! God is good
	130:8	No **d** about it — he'll redeem Israel
Jer	14:7	No **d** about it — we've sinned
	32:28	No **d** about it, I'm handing
Mt	21:21	don't **d** God
Lk	1:4	know beyond the shadow of a **d**
Jn	17:7	know now, beyond the shadow of a **d**

D

D

Ac	2:36	There's no longer room for **d**
Ro	3:9	Scripture leaves no **d** about it
2Co	1:7	going to make it, no **d** about it
Php	1:6	never been the slightest **d** in my mind
Heb	4:12	**d** or defense, laying us open
1Jn	5:13	know beyond the shadow of a **d**

Down-and-out

Ex	22:25	any of the **d** among you
2Sa	22:28	You take the side of the **d**
Job	5:11	He raises up the **d**
Ps	18:27	You take the side of the **d**
	30:3	chance at life when I was **d**
	35:10	You put the **d** on their feet
	72:13	opens a place in his heart for the **d**
Isa	1:17	Work for justice. Help the **d**
	5:15	**d** on a par with the high-and-mighty
	58:10	giving yourselves to the **d**
Jer	22:16	He stuck up for the **d**
Eze	33:15	being generous to the **d**
Da	4:27	look after the needs of the **d**
Am	4:1	Mean to the poor, cruel to the **d**
Ob	1:12	your brother when he was **d**
Jas	2:5	**d** as the kingdom's first citizens

Downfall

Ne	13:26	foreign women were his **d**
Ps	35:4	those who are plotting my **d**
	70:2	Those who relish my **d**

Drained

Jos	5:1	hearts sank; the courage **d** out
Jdg	16:19	His strength **d** from him
Est	7:8	blood **d** from Haman's face
Ps	75:8	it's **d** to the dregs
Jer	50:38	her water supply — **d** dry
La	1:6	beauty has **d** from Daughter Zion
Da	5:9	All the blood **d** from his face
	10:8	the blood **d** from my face

Dream

Ge	20:3	came to Abimelech in a **d**
	20:6	God said to him in the **d**
	31:10	I had a **d** and saw the billy goats
	31:11	In the **d** an angel of God called out
	31:24	God came to Laban the Aramean in a **d**
	37:5	Joseph had a **d**
	37:6	Listen to this **d** I had
	37:9	another **d** and told this one also
	40:5	had a **d** on the same night, each **d**
	40:9	told his **d** to Joseph: "In my **d**
	40:16	My **d** went like this: I saw
	41:1	Pharaoh had a **d**
	41:7	Pharaoh woke up — another **d**
	41:11	on the same night, each **d** with its
	41:15	I dreamed a **d**," Pharaoh told Joseph
	41:17	In my **d** I was standing on the bank
	41:22	In my second **d** I saw seven ears

	41:26	seven years — they're the same **d**
	41:32	Pharaoh dreamed the same **d** twice
Jdg	7:13	**d**. He said, "I had this **d**
	7:15	the **d** and its interpretation
1Sa	28:6	God didn't answer — neither by **d**
	28:15	either by prophet or by **d**
1Ki	3:5	God appeared to Solomon in a **d**
	3:15	Solomon woke up — what a **d**!
Job	4:13	came in a scary **d** one night
	20:8	like a **d** that can't be remembered
	33:15	**d**, for instance, a vision at night
	37:18	could you even **d** of making a dent
	41:13	Who would even **d** of piercing
Ps	90:5	no more to you than a wispy **d**
	126:1	It seemed like a **d**, too good
	141:4	Don't let me so much as **d** of evil
Isa	29:7	will turn out to be a bad **d**
	48:7	something you'd never guess or **d** up
Jer	23:25	I had this **d**! I had this **d**
	23:28	prophets who do nothing but **d**
	23:32	who preach the lies they **d** up
Da	2:3	a **d** that I can't get out of my mind
	2:4	Tell us the **d** and we will interpret
	2:5	tell me both the **d** itself
	2:6	both the **d** and its interpretation
	2:7	tell us the **d**. We'll give
	2:9	can't tell me my **d**, you're doomed
	2:16	so that he could interpret the **d**
	2:24	I'll interpret his **d**
	2:25	who can interpret the king's **d**
	2:26	tell me the **d** I had and interpret it
	2:28	This is the **d** you had
	2:36	This was your **d**
	2:45	accurate telling of the **d**
	4:5	I had a **d** that scared me
	4:6	interpret the **d** for me
	4:7	I told them the **d**
	4:8	divine Holy Spirit. I told him my **d**
	4:9	Listen to this **d** that I had
	4:19	Don't let the **d** and its interpretation
	7:1	Daniel had a **d**
	7:2	**d** that night I saw the four winds
	7:7	a fourth animal appeared in my **d**
	7:13	My **d** continued
	7:15	All these **d**-visions had me agitated
	7:16	told me, interpreting the **d** for me
Joel	2:28	Your old men will **d**
Mt	1:20	had a **d**. God's angel spoke in the **d**
	1:24	God's angel commanded in the **d**
	2:12	In a **d**, they were warned
	2:13	angel showed up again in Joseph's **d**
	2:19	angel appeared in a **d** to Joseph
	2:22	Joseph was directed in a **d**
	27:19	troubled night because of a **d**
Ac	2:17	your old men **d** dreams
	9:12	He has just had a **d**
	12:11	Peter realized it was no **d**
	16:9	That night Paul had a **d**
	16:10	The **d** gave Paul his map
	18:9	Master spoke to Paul in a **d**

Dreamed

Ge	28:12	he **d**: A stairway was set
	37:9	I **d** another dream
	40:8	We **d** dreams and there's no one
	41:5	**d** a second time: Seven ears
	41:15	I **d** a dream," Pharaoh told Joseph
	41:32	Pharaoh **d** the same dream twice
	42:9	remembering the dreams he had **d**
Jos	22:29	never **d** of building an altar
Ps	84:2	**d** of a room in your house
Ecc	6:2	all they ever wanted or **d** of
Da	2:30	you will understand what you **d**
	4:18	what I, King Nebuchadnezzar, **d**
Lk	19:26	get more than you ever **d** of
Jn	10:10	better life than they ever **d** of
1Co	4:5	things we never even **d** of
	7:22	freedom you would never have **d** of

Dreams

Ge	37:8	hated him . . . because of his **d**
	37:20	We'll see what his **d** amount to
	40:8	**d** and there's no one to interpret
	41:8	told them his **d**, but they couldn't
	41:11	both had **d** on the same night
	41:12	told him our **d** and he interpreted
	41:25	Pharaoh's two **d** both mean the same
	42:9	remembering the **d** he had dreamed
Nu	12:6	I speak to him in **d**
Ps	14:6	mess with the **d** of the poor
	112:10	nothing to the **d** of the wicked
Ecc	9:6	even their **d**, are long gone
SS	5:2	but in my **d** I was wide awake
	6:4	Lovely as Jerusalem, city of **d**
Jer	2:8	empty god-**d** and silly god-schemes
	2:11	traded my Glory for empty god-**d**
	23:27	They swap **d** with one another
	23:28	go ahead and tell your silly **d**
	49:4	**d** of glory days and vainly thinks
Da	1:17	all sorts of visions and **d**
	2:1	**d** that disturbed him deeply
	2:2	interpret his **d** for him
	5:12	He could do anything — interpret **d**
	5:16	heard that you interpret **d**
	11:14	own people, drunk on **d**, will join
Mal	3:10	blessings beyond your wildest **d**
Mt	13:8	a harvest beyond his wildest **d**
	13:23	a harvest beyond his wildest **d**
Mk	4:8	harvest exceeding his wildest **d**
	4:20	a harvest beyond their wildest **d**
Ac	2:17	your old men dream **d**
Eph	3:20	or request in your wildest **d**

Drinking

Ge	4:22	When the camels had finished **d**
	43:34	feasted with Joseph, **d** freely
Jdg	7:5	**d** with his face to the water
	9:27	a feast, eating and **d**
Ru	3:7	eating and **d** his fill
1Sa	1:15	I haven't been **d**

	30:16	eating and **d**, gorging themselves
2Sa	16:2	the wine is for **d**
1Ki	1:25	eating and **d** and shouting
	16:9	**d** himself drunk
	20:12	he was into some heavy **d**
	20:16	serious **d** in the field shelters
2Ki	18:27	**d** their own pee
1Ch	11:19	like **d** the lifeblood of these men
	29:22	eating and **d** before God
Ne	8:12	off to feast, eating and **d**
Est	5:6	As they were **d** the wine
	7:2	while they were **d** wine
Job	29:23	counsel like spring rain, **d** it all in
Ps	11:6	**D** from a canteen filled with hot
	63:2	**d** in your strength and glory
	69:12	Make up **d** songs about me
Pr	13:14	no more **d** from death-tainted wells
	14:27	won't go off **d** from poisoned wells
	20:15	**D** from the . . . chalice of knowledge
	23:30	for whom **d** is serious business
Isa	5:11	start **d** booze before breakfast
	5:22	All you're good at is **d**
	21:5	luxurious ease, Eating and **d**
	22:13	Eating and **d** and dancing
	29:8	dreaming she's **d** iced tea
	36:12	**d** their own urine
	43:20	**D** water for the people I chose
	51:21	hangovers that didn't come from **d**
	51:22	No more **d** from that jug of my anger
Eze	25:4	off your tables and **d** your milk
Da	1:8	eating the king's food or **d** his wine
Am	2:8	sit around **d** wine they've conned
Ob	1:7	**d** buddies will stab you in the back
Hab	2:16	**d**, you were **d** from the cup of God
Hag	1:6	You keep **d** and **d** and **d**
Mt	20:22	**d** the cup that I'm about to drink
	26:29	I'll not be **d** wine from this cup again
	26:42	**d** this cup to the dregs, I'm ready
Mk	10:38	Are you capable of **d** the cup I drink
	14:25	not be **d** wine again until the new day
Lk	5:30	eating and **d** with crooks
	21:34	parties and **d** and shopping
Jn	6:54	this eating and **d** has eternal life
	6:56	By eating my flesh and **d** my blood
1Co	11:34	an eating and **d** binge
Eph	5:19	Sing hymns instead of **d** songs

Dropouts

Pr	15:5	Moral **d** won't listen to their elders
Isa	1:4	Shame! Misguided God-**d**
	40:29	gives fresh strength to **d**

Drought

Dt	28:48	Life will be famine and **d**
1Ki	17:1	total **d** — not a drop of dew or rain
	17:7	brook dried up because of the **d**
	17:14	rain on the land and ends this **d**
	18:1	The **d** was now in its third year
	18:2	the **d** in Samaria at the time
Job	12:15	If he holds back the rain, there's a **d**

D

Ps	126:4	bring rains to our **d**-stricken lives
Jer	14:1	came to Jeremiah regarding the **d**
Hag	1:11	decreeing a season of **d**
	2:17	I hit you with **d** and blight and hail
Lk	4:25	three and a half years of **d**

Drunk

Ge	9:21	got **d** and passed out
	19:32	Let's get our father **d** with wine
	19:33	got their father **d** with wine
	19:34	We'll get him **d** again
	19:35	got their father **d** again
	24:19	until they've **d** their fill
Lev	11:34	that could be **d** from it is unclean
Nu	23:24	it's eaten and **d** its fill
Dt	21:20	He's a glutton and a **d**
	32:42	I'll make my arrows **d** with blood
1Sa	1:13	the conclusion that she was **d**
	1:14	You're **d**! How long do you plan
	25:36	high spirits — and very, very **d**
	30:12	hadn't eaten or **d** a thing
2Sa	11:13	David got him **d**
1Ki	16:9	drinking himself **d**
2Ki	19:24	**d** their exotic waters
Ps	107:27	you reeled like a **d**
Pr	20:1	a staggering **d** is not much fun
	23:20	Don't drink too much wine and get **d**
	23:34	Reeling and seasick, **d** as a sailor
	26:9	a scalpel in the hands of a **d**
	26:10	Hire a fool or a **d** and you shoot
Isa	19:14	falling-down-in-his-own-vomit **d**
	24:20	Earth staggers like a **d**
	29:9	Get **d**, but not on wine
	51:17	You've **d** the cup God handed you
	56:12	Let's go out and get **d**!
Jer	13:13	wine that will make them **d**
	23:9	I'm staggering like a **d**
	25:16	They'll drink it and get **d**
	25:27	Drink and get **d** and vomit
	48:26	**d** on the wine of my wrath
	51:7	my anger to make the whole world **d**
	51:39	falling-down **d**. Dead **d**, they'll sleep
	51:57	get them **d**, the whole lot of them
La	4:21	Get **d** on God's wrath
Eze	23:33	You'll be falling-down-**d**
	39:19	drink blood till you're **d**
Da	11:14	people, **d** on dreams, will join them
Hos	4:12	**D** on sex, they can't find their way
	7:5	princes get **d** on wine
Lk	12:45	parties for his friends, and gets **d**
Ac	2:13	They're **d** on cheap wine
	2:15	aren't **d** as some of you suspect
1Co	5:11	gets **d** or becomes greedy
	11:21	carried out, too **d** to walk
1Th	5:7	sleep at night and get **d** at night
Tit	1:7	not a **d**, not a bully
Rev	14:8	**d** on the wine of her whoring
	17:2	earth dwellers **d** on her whorish lust
	17:6	**d**, **d** on the blood of God's holy people

Drunks

Job	12:25	lurching and staggering like **d**
Ps	69:12	**d** and gluttons Make up drinking songs
Pr	23:21	**D** and gluttons will end up on skid row
Isa	5:14	to say nothing of all the **d**
	28:1	Doom to the pretentious **d**
	28:7	falling-down **d**, Besotted with wine
Joel	1:5	Sober up, you **d**!
Na	3:11	staggering like a bunch of **d**
Tit	2:3	end up as neither gossips nor **d**

Dumb

Ex	15:16	they were struck **d** like a stone
Job	37:20	think I'm **d** enough to challenge God
Ps	73:22	a **d** ox in your very presence
Pr	30:32	If you're **d** enough to call attention
Jer	47:5	Ashkelon struck **d** as a post
Hab	2:19	to a **d** stone, 'Get up'
Mk	9:25	**D** and deaf spirit, I command you
Lk	6:49	like a **d** carpenter who built a house
1Co	1:21	what the world considered **d**
2Pe	2:16	**d** animal spoke in a human voice
Rev	18:22	a millstone grinding falls **d**

Duties

Ge	41:45	Joseph took up his **d**
Ex	31:10	in their priestly **d**
Nu	3:8	come to perform their **d**
	3:38	who tried to perform these **d**
	18:2	assist you and your sons in your **d**
	18:3	their **d** related to the Tent
Dt	24:5	given any business or work **d**
1Sa	3:15	rose early and went about his **d**
	29:4	Let him stick to his normal **d**
2Sa	8:15	evenhanded in all his **d**
1Ki	8:11	couldn't carry out their priestly **d**
1Ch	9:34	they were exempt from all other **d**
	12:32	both the times and Israel's **d**
	18:14	evenhanded in all his **d**
2Ch	5:14	couldn't carry out their **d**
	19:9	be dependable and honest in your **d**
Mt	12:5	priests carrying out their Temple **d**
Lk	1:8	carrying out his priestly **d**
Ac	25:1	to take up his **d** as governor
Heb	9:6	priests went about their **d**

Duty

Ge	38:8	it's the **d** of a brother-in-law
Nu	4:31	This is their assigned **d**
	10:8	their assigned **d**
	32:22	fulfilled your **d** to God and Israel
Dt	10:8	to be on **d** in the Presence of God
	25:5	do the brother-in-law's **d** by her
	25:7	do the brother-in-law's **d** by me
1Sa	1:9	Eli was on **d** at the entrance
	8:2	were assigned in Beersheba
2Sa	13:34	sentry on **d** looked up and saw
2Ki	4:13	gone far beyond the call of **d**

	9:17	sentry standing **d** on the watchtower
	11:5	come on **d** on the Sabbath and guard
	11:9	those who came on **d** on the Sabbath
1Ch	9:33	were on twenty-four-hour **d**
	23:31	were on regular **d** to serve God
	26:15	sons pulled **d** at the storehouse
	27:1	were on **d** a month at a time
2Ch	7:6	The priests were all on **d**
	8:14	guards to be on **d** at each gate
	23:4	who come on **d** on the Sabbath
	23:8	those who came on **d** on the Sabbath
	35:15	guards were on **d** at each gate
Ezr	4:13	pay a penny of tribute, tax, or **d**
	4:20	exacted taxes, tribute, and **d**
	7:24	tribute, tax, or **d** on any priest
Ne	7:3	while the guards are still on **d**
Ps	56:2	make it their **d** to beat me up
	135:2	you priests on **d** in God's temple
Mt	28:14	hears about your sleeping on **d**
Ac	26:9	was my **d** to oppose this Jesus
Ro	15:27	it was also their **d**
2Th	3:13	don't slack off in doing your **d**
2Ti	2:4	A soldier on **d** doesn't get caught

Dying

Ge	35:18	for she was now **d**, she named him
1Ki	18:5	keep our horses and mules from **d**
Job	24:12	People are **d** right and left
	29:13	The **d** blessed me
Isa	24:6	They dwindle away, **d** out one by one
	32:6	ignoring those **d** of thirst
	65:20	No more babies **d** in the cradle
Jer	4:31	I'm **d**! The killers are on me
	6:4	Day is **d**? Evening shadows are upon us
	12:4	Even animals and birds are **d** off
La	2:12	fainting like **d** soldiers
Eze	6:11	**d** of hunger, **d** of disease
	6:12	people far away **d**, people nearby **d**
Joel	1:20	Wild animals, **d** of thirst
Zec	14:12	people will be **d** on their feet
Lk	8:42	daughter, his only child, was **d**
Jn	11:37	do something to keep him from **d**
	16:19	Jesus knew they were **d** to ask
Ac	20:28	thought they were worth **d** for
Ro	5:7	**d** for a person worth **d** for
Eph	2:13	**d** that death, shedding that blood
Col	1:22	actually **d** for you, Christ brought you
Heb	11:22	Joseph, while **d**, prophesied

E

Eager

Ex	36:2	The men were **e** to get started
1Ch	12:8	they were seasoned and **e** fighters
	28:9	with a whole heart and **e** mind
Job	39:21	paws . . . fiercely, **e** and spirited
Ps	36:1	all ears, **e** to sin
	36:7	How **e** we are to run under your wings
	42:4	**e** to arrive and worship
Pr	15:14	always **e** to take in more truth

	31:17	**e** to get started
Hos	6:3	**e** for God-knowledge
Zec	6:7	**e** to patrol through the earth
Mt	26:41	**e**, ready for anything in God
Mk	14:38	**e**, ready for anything in God
Jn	9:27	so **e** to become his disciples
Ac	12:14	**e** to tell everyone Peter was there
Ro	15:32	with a light and **e** heart
1Co	14:12	**e** to participate in what God is doing
Gal	2:10	I was already **e** to do that
2Ti	4:8	everyone **e** for his coming
Heb	9:28	those **e** to greet him
2Pe	1:15	**e** that you have all this down
	3:12	Day of God, **e** for its arrival

Eagerness

| 2Co | 8:17 | his **e** to go to you and help out |

Earthly

Ecc	2:19	the **e** results of my intense thinking
	8:15	best possible. The only **e** good
Eph	6:5	respectfully obey your **e** masters
Col	3:22	do what you're told by your **e** masters
Heb	9:24	the **e** version of the Holy Place
	12:25	those who ignored **e** warnings
Rev	1:5	Ruler of all **e** kings

Earthy

1Co	15:48	people since then are **e**
	15:49	worked from our **e** origins
	15:50	our natural, **e** lives
Php	3:21	transform our **e** bodies

Easygoing

Eze	12:24	False alarms and **e** preaching
	30:9	alarm among the **e** Ethiopians
Mt	7:13	**e** formulas for a successful life

Ecstasy

SS	6:4	the ravishing visions of my **e**
1Co	13:1	human eloquence and angelic **e**
2Co	12:2	seized by Christ and swept in **e**

Ecstatic

Ps	119:162	I'm **e** over what you say
Pr	7:18	spend the night in **e** lovemaking
Mt	13:44	The finder is **e**
Lk	8:56	Her parents were **e**, but Jesus warned
Ac	2:26	I'm glad from the inside out, **e**
	3:11	arms around Peter and John, **e**

Educated

Da	1:4	handsome, intelligent and well-**e**
Ac	7:22	Moses was **e** in the best schools
	18:25	well-**e** in the way of the Master

| | 22:3 | e here in Jerusalem |
| 1Co | 1:20 | truly wise, truly e, truly intelligent |

| Lk | 23:11 | dressed him up in an e king costume |
| 2Co | 12:16 | behind which I worked an e scam |

Effective

Ecc	9:17	words of the wise are more e
Ac	18:28	particularly e in public debate
Heb	9:13	rituals of purification were e

Effectively

| 1Co | 14:17 | you have very e cut that person out |

Effort

Isa	64:7	makes the e to reach out to you
Mk	12:6	In a last-ditch e, he sent him
1Co	4:15	time and e to help you grow up
	15:58	do for him is a waste of time or e
Gal	3:10	who tries to live by his own e

Efforts

Isa	30:15	silly e to save yourselves
	64:6	Our best e are grease-stained rags
Hag	2:16	halfhearted e at rebuilding
Ac	18:8	Paul's e with the Jews
Ro	8:4	instead of redoubling our own e
1Co	10:24	foremost e should be to help others
Gal	3:3	complete by their own e
	3:21	getting by our own e
Php	2:12	redouble your e. Be energetic
	3:3	couldn't carry this off by our own e
Heb	9:15	e to make ourselves respectable

Ego

Pr	16:18	bigger the e, the harder the fall
Am	5:23	your noisy e-music
Gal	2:20	My e is no longer central
1Pe	2:11	Don't indulge your e

Egomaniacs

| 2Co | 11:21 | admire the e of the pulpit |

Egos

| Isa | 2:11 | pretentious e brought down a peg |
| | 2:17 | pretentious e brought down to earth |

Elaborate

1Ki	7:17	an e filigree of seven braided chains
	10:5	e worship extravagant with Whole-Burnt
2Ch	3:16	an e filigree of chains
	9:4	e worship extravagant with Whole-Burnt
Job	27:18	build e houses that won't survive
Pr	16:1	Mortals make e plans
Jer	22:14	build me an e mansion
Eze	23:15	e turbans on their heads
	27:24	dyed textiles, and e carpets

Elder

| Lev | 19:32 | honor the presence of an e |
| Joel | 1:2 | Attention, e statesmen! |

Elderly

| 2Ch | 36:17 | the e and weak |
| Job | 12:12 | think the e have a corner on wisdom |

Elders

Ex	12:21	Moses assembled all the e of Israel
	17:5	some of the e of Israel
	17:6	with the e of Israel right there
	18:12	along with all the e of Israel
	19:7	Moses . . . called the e of Israel
	24:1	seventy of the e of Israel
	24:9	seventy of the e of Israel
	24:14	He told the e of Israel
Lev	4:15	The e of the congregation
Dt	19:12	The e of his own city
Jos	8:33	e, officers, and judges
	23:2	e, chiefs, judges, and officers
	24:1	e, chiefs, judges, and officers
	24:31	the e who outlived him
Jdg	11:5	the e of Gilead went to get
	11:7	Jephthah said to the e of Gilead
	11:8	The e of Gilead replied
	11:9	addressed the e of Gilead
	11:11	went along with the e of Gilead
	21:16	e of the congregation said
Ru	4:2	gathered ten of the town e
	4:4	here and before the town e
	4:9	Boaz then addressed the e
	4:11	backing up the e
1Sa	4:3	Israel's e said, "Why
	8:4	e of Israel got together
	30:26	plunder to the e of Judah
	30:27	sent them to the e in Bethel
2Sa	3:17	Abner got the e of Israel together
	12:17	e in his family came in
	17:4	all the e of Israel agreed
	17:15	advised Absalom and the e
	19:11	Ask the e of Judah
	24:16	David and the e bowed in prayer
1Ki	12:6	talked it over with the e
	12:8	rejected the counsel of the e
	12:13	spurned the counsel of the e
	20:7	meeting of all his tribal e
	20:8	The e, backed by the people, said
	21:8	sent them to the e in Naboth's
	21:11	the e and civic leaders
2Ki	6:32	the e sitting with him
	10:1	the city e, and those in charge
	10:5	mayor of the city, the e
	23:1	assembling all the e of Judah
1Ch	11:3	e of Israel came to the king
	15:25	the e of Israel

	21:16	David and the e bowed in prayer
2Ch	10:6	talked it over with the e
	10:8	rejected the counsel of the e
	10:13	spurned the counsel of the e
	34:29	assembling all the e of Judah
Ezr	10:8	ruling of the leaders and e
	10:14	accompanied by the e and judges
Job	12:20	deprives e of their good sense
Ps	107:32	shout Hallelujah when the e meet
Pr	15:5	won't listen to their e
Isa	9:15	The big-head e were the head
Jer	29:1	what was left of the e
La	2:10	The e of Daughter Zion sit silent
	4:16	he cares nothing for the e
	5:12	dishonored our e
	5:14	city gate is empty of wise e
Eze	7:26	the e don't know what to say
	8:12	do you see what the e are doing
Joel	2:16	Make sure the e come
Mk	8:31	tried and found guilty by the e
Rev	4:4	with Twenty-four E seated
	4:10	E would fall prostrate before the One
	5:5	One of the E said, "Don't weep
	5:6	surrounded by Throne, Animals, and E
	5:8	E fell down and worshiped the Lab
	5:11	the Throne, the Animals, and the E
	5:14	E fell to their knees and worshiped
	7:11	E, Animals — fell on their faces
	7:13	one of the E addressed me
	11:16	Twenty-four E seated before God
	14:3	Throne and the Four Animals and the E
	19:4	Twenty-four E and the Four Animals

Elected

1Ch	12:31	e to come and make David king

Elegance

1Ki	10:7	Such wisdom and e
2Ch	9:6	Such wisdom and e
SS	1:10	earrings line the e of your cheeks
Isa	60:13	give a splendid e to my Sanctuary

Elegant

2Sa	1:24	spared no expense in making you e
1Ch	15:27	all dressed in e linen
Pr	31:25	Her clothes are well-made and e
SS	1:5	I am weathered but still e
	4:3	your mouth e and inviting
	7:1	Your limbs are lithe and e
Isa	2:16	e three-masted schooners
Eze	16:13	exquisite clothes and e food
	27:24	bringing e clothes, dyed textiles
1Co	12:15	I'm not e like Hand

Elite

Ex	15:4	The e of his officers he drowned
2Sa	23:9	the next of the e Three
Jer	10:7	Look far and wide among the e

Eze	17:21	All his e soldiers
	23:7	a whore to the Assyrian e
	23:12	the Assyrian e
	23:23	ambassadors and governors, e officers
	27:10	E troops in uniformed splendor
Mic	4:7	battered into a company of the e
Ac	27:1	Julius, a member of an e guard
Php	3:5	Israelite from the e tribe

Eloquence

Pr	17:7	We don't expect e from fools
Isa	32:4	the tongue-tied will speak with e
1Co	13:1	If I speak with human e and angelic
2Co	11:6	haven't mastered that smooth e
1Ti	1:7	holding forth with such imposing e

Eloquent

Ac	18:24	e and powerful in his preaching
Ro	2:23	e talk about God and his law

Embalm

Ge	50:2	to e his father
Mk	16:1	bought spices so they could e him

Embalmed

Ge	50:2	The physicians e Israel
	50:26	They e him and placed him in a coffin

Embarrass

Ps	25:3	You won't e me, will you?
	31:17	Don't e me by not showing up
Pr	15:20	lazy students e their parents
	28:7	e your family
	29:15	spoiled adolescents e their parents

Embarrassed

1Sa	18:18	David, e, answered
2Ch	30:15	e in their laziness
Ezr	8:22	I was e to ask the king
Ps	40:14	will be e and lose face
Isa	54:4	you're not going to be e
Jer	6:15	suppose they are e over this outrage
	8:12	suppose they are e over this outrage
	10:14	god-makers e by their handmade gods
	51:17	god-makers e by their handmade gods
Mk	8:38	e over me and the way I'm leading you
Lk	7:6	I'd be e for you to come to my house
	7:7	even e to come to you in person
	9:26	e with me and the way I'm leading you
	9:45	were e to ask him what he meant
1Co	15:34	e that you've let this kind of thing
Php	1:20	don't expect to be e in the least
2Ti	1:8	don't be e to speak up for our Master
	1:16	wasn't e a bit that I was in jail

E

Embarrassing

Isa	30:5	All show, no substance, an e farce
Jer	48:20	Moab will be an e memory
1Co	5:5	devastating to him … and e to you

Embarrassingly

2Co	2:2	put you in an e painful position

Embarrassment

Pr	19:26	against their parents are an e
Da	9:16	now we're an e to everyone around us
Mk	8:38	even greater e to the Son of Man
1Co	5:5	better devastation and e than

Embrace

Jos	22:5	do what he's commanded, e him
2Sa	5:10	a larger e since the God
2Ki	4:36	Elisha said, "E your son
1Ch	11:9	stride became longer, his e larger
Ps	2:11	Worship God in adoring e
	34:14	do something good. E peace
	85:10	Right Living and Whole Living e
	119:119	I lovingly e everything you say
Pr	3:18	very Tree of Life to those who e her
	8:32	who e these my ways are most blessed
	13:18	e correction and live an honored life
	28:4	free to e depravity
Ecc	3:5	A right time to e and another to part
Isa	56:2	you men and women who e them
Jer	31:22	will e the transforming God
Eze	14:4	e the wickedness that will ruin them
	14:7	turn their backs on me and e idols
Zec	8:19	E truth! Love peace
Mt	16:24	Don't run from suffering; e it
	21:21	if you e this kingdom life
	23:37	often I've ached to e your children
Mk	4:20	those who hear the Word, e it
	8:34	Don't run from suffering; e it
	11:22	E this God-life. Really e it
	11:24	as you e this God-life
Lk	9:23	Don't run from suffering; e it
Ac	14:15	e God himself, the living God
	15:7	Message of this good news and e it
	19:2	did you also e him with your heart
	24:14	e everything written in all
Ro	2:10	if you e the way God does things
	4:12	people who e what God does for them
	4:24	when we e and believe the One
	8:4	e what the Spirit is doing in us
	10:10	With your whole being you e God
	11:28	e the good news of the Message
1Co	15:49	let's e our heavenly ends
2Co	13:12	Greet one another with a holy e
Eph	2:16	The Cross got us to e
Php	2:29	a grand welcome, a joyful e
	3:8	so that I could e Christ
1Th	1:9	so you could e and serve God
	5:26	all the Christians there with a holy e

Heb	12:9	why not e God's training
1Pe	3:10	wants to e life and see the day fill
	5:12	This is God's generous truth; e it
1Jn	2:23	affirming the Son is an e

Embraced

Ge	29:13	e and kissed him and brought him home
	33:4	e him, held him tight and kissed him
	48:10	Old Israel kissed and e them
Ru	1:14	Ruth e her and held on
2Ki	4:37	she e her son
Ps	135:4	God chose Jacob, e Israel
Isa	53:12	he e the company of the lowest
Jer	13:25	you forgot me and e the Big Lie
Eze	14:3	e the wickedness that will ruin them
Mt	5:4	Only then can you be e by the One
	28:9	e his feet, and worshiped him
Lk	1:54	He e his chosen child, Israel
	15:20	ran out, e him, and kissed him
Ro	4:11	God he had e with his whole life
	8:39	way that Jesus our Master has e us
	9:30	actually e what God was doing
Eph	2:5	he e us. He took our sin-dead lives
Php	3:9	be e by him
1Ti	6:12	the life you so fervently e

Embraces

Ge	2:24	e his wife. They become one flesh
Mk	9:37	e one of these children as I do e
Ac	15:33	with laughter and e all around
Ro	16:16	Holy e all around!
1Co	16:20	Pass the greetings around with holy e
Heb	12:6	the child he e, he also corrects
1Pe	5:14	Give holy e all around!

Embracing

Dt	30:20	obediently to him, firmly e him
Ro	4:9	e what God did for him
	4:16	simply e him and what he does
	8:32	e our condition and exposing himself
	10:9	e, body and soul, God's work
	12:1	E what God does for you is the best
Gal	1:6	e a variant message
	3:11	does it by e what God arranges
Heb	2:14	By e death, taking it into himself

Emmanuel

Mt	1:23	name him E (Hebrew for "God is with us

Emotion

1Ki	3:26	was overcome with e for her son
Ac	28:15	e-packed meetings
2Co	10:5	every loose thought and e and impulse

Emotional

Mt	4:24	ailment, whether mental, e

| 1Co | 2:5 | fancy mental or e footwork |
| Gal | 5:19 | accumulation of mental and e garbage |

Emotions

Job	15:12	Why do you let your e take over
Pr	14:30	runaway e corrode the bones
	30:33	riled e turn into fist fights
Mt	7:16	leader will never exploit your e
	13:21	e wear off and some difficulty arrives
Mk	4:17	e wear off and some difficulty arrives
Ro	2:20	confused e to God
1Co	7:9	they can't manage their desires and e
1Ti	5:6	widow who exploits people's e

Employ

| Ge | 50:2 | the physicians in his e |

Employed

2Ch	2:17	census-taking method e by his father
Ac	19:25	workers and others similarly e
1Co	9:7	Are soldiers self-e?

Employee

| Pr | 10:26 | lazy e will give you nothing |
| Jn | 13:16 | e doesn't give orders |

Employees

| Job | 31:13 | Have I ever been unfair to my e |
| Ps | 28:3 | those who are full-time e of evil |

Employer

| Jn | 13:16 | employee doesn't give orders to the e |

Employing

| Ac | 19:24 | e a number of artisans |

Empowered

| 1Co | 4:20 | it's an e life |
| Gal | 4:29 | the child who came — e by the Spirit |

Empowering

| 1Sa | 16:13 | God vitally e him |

Empty-headed

1Ki	16:26	such an e, empty-hearted life
Job	2:10	You're talking like an e fool
Pr	9:13	brazen, e, frivolous
	15:21	The e treat life as a plaything
Eze	13:3	doom on the e prophets
Hos	12:11	teeming with e religion
Mal	1:10	this silly, e worship

| Eph | 4:17 | the e, mindless crowd |
| 1Pe | 1:18 | dead-end, e life you grew up in |

Enchanter

| Da | 2:10 | any magician, e, or fortuneteller |
| | 2:27 | no wise man, e, magician, diviner |

Enchanters

Da	1:20	better than all the magicians and e
	2:2	e, sorcerers, and fortunetellers
	4:7	all assembled — magicians, e
	5:7	He yelled out for the e
	5:11	head of all the magicians, e
	5:15	The wise men and e were brought

Encourage

2Sa	11:25	destroy it.' E Joab
Pr	29:10	moral folks e them
Isa	50:4	I know how to e tired people
Jer	29:6	E your children to marry
Col	4:8	he could e you in your faith
1Th	5:14	Getly e the stragglers

Encouraged

1Sa	23:16	visited David . . . and e him in God
2Ch	35:2	e them in the work of leading worship
Job	4:3	e those who were about to quit
Ac	16:40	e them in the faith
	20:1	e them to keep up the good work

Encouragement

Ac	13:15	A word of e, perhaps
	20:2	he gave constant e
	20:20	Every truth and e that could
1Th	2:12	holding your hand, whispering e

Encouraging

Ro	12:8	if you give e guidance
	14:19	Help others with e words
1Co	7:38	pastoral reasons for e singleness
2Co	1:6	given a helping hand and e word
1Th	5:11	So speak e words to one another
Heb	10:24	how inventive we can be in e love

End

| Eze | 7:6 | E — the e comes. The e is ripe |

Endorse

Est	9:30	to e and ratify what he wrote
Isa	42:8	don't e the no-god idols
Ro	16:1	I heartily e both her and her work

Endurance

2Th	3:5	path of God's love and Christ's **e**
Tit	2:2	healthy faith, love, and **e**

Endure

Pr	19:19	Let angry people **e** the backlash
Isa	14:3	harsh servitude that you had to **e**
2Co	1:7	just as willing to **e** the hard times

Energetic

1Ki	8:28	my prayers, **e** and devout
2Ch	6:19	my prayers, **e** and devout
Pr	13:4	the **e** have something to show
Isa	23:7	city you remember as **e** and alive
Ro	10:2	impressively **e** regarding God
Php	2:12	Be **e** in your life of salvation
Tit	2:14	he can be proud of, **e** in goodness
1Pe	1:15	a life **e** and blazing with holiness

Energetically

Jn	9:4	be **e** at work for the One
2Co	8:22	as **e** as the day he started

Enjoy

Ge	29:27	E your week of honeymoon
Lev	26:34	get a break and **e** its Sabbath years
	26:43	**e** its Sabbaths while they're gone
Nu	14:31	to **e** the land you rejected
Dt	30:9	**e** an all-around good life
Jdg	9:19	**e** Abimelech and let him **e** you
	19:9	stay another night and **e** yourself
1Sa	2:32	no one in your family will live to **e**
2Sa	11:11	eat and drink and **e** my wife
2Ki	20:19	I'll **e** peace and security
2Ch	6:41	**e** your new place of quiet repose
Ne	9:36	eat well and **e** a good life
Est	5:13	But I can't **e** any of it
Job	20:18	unable to relax and **e** anything
	21:8	watch and **e** their grandchildren
Ps	67:3	God! Let people thank and **e** you
	67:3	Let all people thank and **e** you
	67:5	God! Let people thank and **e** you
	67:5	Let all people thank and **e** you
	68:4	E God, cheer when you see him
	68:10	For your people to camp in and **e**
	104:31	Let God **e** his creation
	106:4	God, when you **e** your people
	128:2	E the blessing! Revel in the goodness
	128:5	E the good life in Jerusalem
	128:6	And **e** your grandchildren
	132:8	Up, God, **e** your new place
Pr	3:24	you'll **e** a good night's sleep
	5:18	E the wife you married as a young man
	27:18	orchard, you'll **e** its fruit
Ecc	5:19	the bounty and the capacity to **e** it
	6:2	God doesn't let them **e** it
	6:3	long life but never **e** themselves

	6:6	didn't **e** anything, what's the point
	7:14	On a good day, **e** yourself
	12:1	Honor and **e** your Creator
SS	1:17	We **e** a canopy of cedars
Isa	32:20	But you will **e** a blessed life
	39:8	I'll **e** peace and stability
	58:14	Then you'll be free to **e** God!
	65:20	people who don't **e** a full lifetime
Jer	16:8	don't go . . . to **e** the festivities
	31:5	sit back and **e** the fruit
	31:5	oh, how you'll **e** those
Am	6:14	E it while you can, you Israelites
Ac	24:3	because of you . . . we **e** all this peace
	27:3	**e** the hospitality of his friends
Ro	15:24	stop off on the way to **e** a good visit
	16:20	E the best of Jesus
1Co	10:27	go ahead and **e** yourself
	14:7	catch the melody and **e** the music
	14:18	wonderful intimacies we **e** with him
2Co	1:7	hard times as to **e** the good times
Jas	3:18	lives right with God and **e** its results
1Jn	1:4	We want you to **e** this, too
Rev	11:10	impossible for them to **e** their sins

Enjoyed

Dt	20:6	hasn't yet **e** the grapes
	28:63	Just as God once **e** you
	30:9	as he **e** doing it for your ancestors
1Ki	22:1	They **e** three years of peace
2Ch	14:7	they built and **e** prosperity
Isa	44:19	**e** a good meal
Jnh	4:6	Jonah was pleased and **e** the shade

Enjoying

Dt	30:9	God will start **e** you again
Jdg	19:22	They were relaxed and **e** themselves
Ne	9:35	**e** your generous goodness
Ps	66:4	can't stop **e** your name and fame
Pr	8:30	always **e** his company
Lk	1:6	**e** a clear conscience before God
Php	1:26	praising Christ, **e** each other

Enjoyment

Ps	111:2	A lifetime of study — endless **e**
Ro	1:13	get some personal **e** out of God's work

Enormity

2Ki	24:3	**e** of the sins of Manasseh
Jer	30:14	Because of the **e** of your guilt
	30:15	Because of the **e** of your guilt
Am	5:12	the **e** of your sins

Enormous

Ex	32:30	You have sinned an **e** sin!
	32:31	it's an **e** sin
Dt	9:26	redeemed, using your **e** strength
1Sa	4:17	defeat was catastrophic, with **e** losses

1Ki	20:21	an **e** defeat for Aram
2Ki	25:16	for The Temple of God was **e**
Job	41:12	Leviathan, the sea beast, his **e** bulk
Ps	8:3	your macro-skies, dark and **e**
Isa	54:7	with **e** compassion, I'm bringing you
Jer	52:20	for the Temple of God was **e**
Eze	9:9	guilt of Israel and Judah is **e**
Da	8:8	the billy goat swelled to an **e** size
	8:9	then grew to an **e** size
Ro	9:2	It's an **e** pain deep within me
1Co	12:19	An **e** eye or a gigantic hand wouldn't
Rev	21:10	He took me . . . to an **e**, high mountain

Enslave

Ex	6:5	whom the Egyptians continue to **e**
Dt	24.7	to **e** or sell him
Eze	23:25	They'll **e** your children

Enslaved

Ge	15:13	they'll be **e** and beaten down
Ac	7:6	alien country where they would be **e**
Gal	4:8	you were **e** to so-called gods
2Pe	2:19	to corruption . . . they're **e**

Entertain

Job	11:14	refuse to **e** evil in your home
Ps	41:6	to **e** the street-corner crowd
Ecc	2:8	singers to **e** me with song
Hos	7:3	**e** the king with their evil circus

Entertainment

Eze	33:32	To them you're merely **e**
Mt	14:6	Herodias's daughter provided the **e**

Enthroned

1Sa	4:4	the Cherubim-E-God
2Sa	6:2	God-of-the-Angel-Armies, who was **e**
1Ki	22:19	I saw God **e**
2Ch	18:18	I saw God **e**
Ps	113:5	God, our God, so majestically **e**
Isa	37:16	God-of-the-Angel-Armies, **e**
Rev	14:15	shouting to the Cloud-E
	14:16	The Cloud-E gave a mighty sweep
	17:1	Whore who sits **e** over many waters
	17:15	on which the Whore was **e**
	20:11	Great White Throne and the One **E**
	21:5	The **E** continued, "Look!

Enthusiasm

Ex	32:4	The people responded with **e**
Mt	13:20	hears and instantly responds with **e**
	14:7	In his drunken **e**, he promised her
Mk	4:16	they respond with great **e**
Lk	8:13	hear with **e**, but the **e** doesn't go
Jn	6:15	in their **e**, they were about to grab
Ac	13:12	became a believer, full of **e**

	17:11	received Paul's message with **e**
	18:25	fiery in his **e**
2Co	8:8	the Macedonians' **e** as a stimulus
	9:2	Your **e** by now has spread

Enthusiastic

Lk	19:37	disciples burst into **e** praise
Ac	11:24	**e** and confident in the Holy Spirit
Gal	1:14	**e** about the traditions of my ancestors

Enthusiastically

Ezr	1:6	neighbors rallied behind them **e**

Entrust

Jn	2:24	Jesus didn't **e** his life to them
1Co	3:5	**e** your lives to our mutual Master
	6:4	why would you ever **e** them

Entrusted

Lev	6:2	regarding something **e** to him
	6:4	restore what was **e** to him
Dt	26:18	people **e** with keeping his commandments
Jer	41:10	king's daughters **e** to the care
Jn	2:23	straight to God, **e** their lives to him
	4:41	more people **e** their lives to him
Ac	14:23	Master to whom they had **e** their lives
1Co	9:17	something solemnly **e** to me
	15:11	you **e** your lives
Gal	2:7	God had **e** me with the same message
Tit	1:3	I've been **e** to proclaim this Message
Jude	1:3	this faith **e** to us as a gift

Envy

Ge	26:14	the Philistines began to **e** him
Ps	73:21	totally consumed by **e**
Pr	23:17	Don't . . . **e** careless rebels
	24:1	Don't **e** bad people
Ecc	4:4	work and ambition motivated by **e**
Eze	31:9	The **e** of every tree in Eden
Ro	1:29	their **e**, wanton killing, bickering
1Ti	6:4	who infect the air with germs of **e**
1Pe	2:1	pretense, **e** and hurtful talk

Epidemic

Lev	26:25	I'll send a deadly **e** on you
2Sa	24:13	an **e** on the country
	24.15	God let loose an **e**
1Ch	21:12	an **e** unleashed on the country
	21:14	God unleashed an **e** in Israel
2Ch	28:19	unleashed an **e** of depravity
	36:14	kicked off an **e** of evil
Jer	16:4	an **e** of death
	21:6	in a raging **e**
Eze	5:17	**E** disease, unrestrained murder
	22:29	Extortion is rife, robbery is **e**
	28:23	I'll order an **e** of disease there

E

Am	5:13	Justice is a lost cause. Evil is e
1Co	10:9	God launched an e of poisonous snakes
1Ti	6:5	an e of backstabbing
Jas	5:20	an e of wandering away from God

Equal

Ge	39:9	He treats me as an e
	48:5	they have e status with Reuben
Ex	30:34	Mix the spices in e proportions
Dt	18:8	he will get an e share to eat
1Sa	30:24	the one who fights — e shares
2Sa	15:5	treat him like an e
Eze	48:13	e in size to that of the priests
Mt	20:12	you just made them e to us
Gal	3:28	Among us you are all e
Php	2:6	He had e status with God
Rev	21:16	length, width, and height all e

Equally

Lev	7:10	belongs e to all the sons of Aaron
Job	34:19	Isan't he e responsible to everybody
Pr	17:15	are e abhorrent to God
Eze	14:10	They'll be e guilty
	47:14	It is to be divided up e
Jn	5:23	Son will be honored e with the Father
Ac	7:22	e impressive as a thinker and
	20:21	e radical trust in our Master Jesus
Ro	4:24	when the conditions were e hopeless

Equals

Job	3:19	The small and the great are e
	9:32	God and I are not e
	31:15	the same stuff, e before God
	42:15	treated them as e with their brothers
Pr	22:2	rich and the poor shake hands as e
Eph	2:18	treated us as e, and so made us e
Heb	7:5	they are all more or less e
1Pe	3:7	you're e. Treat your wives, then, as e

Erase

Ex	32:32	if not, e me out of the book
	32:33	I'll only e from my book those who sin
Job	3:4	E it from the books
Zec	13:2	e their names from memory

Erratic

Ecc	1:6	the whirling, e wind
Gal	5:18	escape the e compulsions

Error

Lev	5:18	make atonement for him for his e
Nu	15:26	everyone was involved in the e
Ecc	10:5	e that can be blamed on whoever
Mt	25:24	make no allowances for e
Jn	16:8	expose the e of the godless world

1Th	2:4	both we and the Message are free of e
Jude	1:11	sucked into Balaam's e by greed

Essentials

Lk	16:9	concentrate . . . on the bare e
2Ti	2:14	Repeat these basic e over and over
Tit	3:8	concentrate on the e that are good
Heb	12:27	so that the unshakable e stand clear

Establish

Ge	6:18	I'm going to e a covenant with you
	17:19	I'll e my covenant with him
	17:21	I'll e my covenant with Isaaac
1Sa	2:35	I'll e for myself a true priest
2Sa	7:12	I'll firmly e his rule
1Ki	8:26	confirm and e it
1Ch	17:11	I'll firmly e his rule
2Ch	1:9	E, God, the words you spoke
	6:17	confirm and e it
Isa	14:1	He'll e them in their own country
	34:14	will e permanent quarters
	61:8	e my eternal covenant with you
Jer	23:5	I'll e a truly righteous David-Branch
	30:9	the David-King I'll e for them
Eze	16:62	I'll firmly e my covenant with you
Mic	4:3	He'll e justice in the rabble

Established

Ex	6:4	I also e my covenant with them
	15:17	sanctuary . . . that you e
Lev	26:46	instructions that God e
Nu	13:29	Canaanites are e on the Mediterranean
	14:25	so well e in the valleys
2Sa	7:24	You e for yourself a people
1Ch	17:22	You e for yourself a people
2Ch	13:5	God of Israel, e David
	29:36	God had a firm foundation
Ps	105:10	The very statute he e with Jacob
Isa	14:6	E a violent rule of anger
	14:32	God has e Zion
	16:5	government of love will be e
	30:4	officials strategically e in Zoan
	44:28	to the Temple, "Be e
Eze	17:6	the roots became e
	37:28	when my holy place of worship is e
	38:14	When my people Israel are e securely
Jn	8:35	The Son, though, has an e position
Ro	8:30	after getting them e, he stayed
Heb	9:22	the covenant God has e with you
Rev	12:10	Salvation and power are e

Eternal

Ge	9:16	remember the e covenant between God
	21:33	praying to the E God
	49:26	the delights of the e hills
Nu	18:19	e and unchangeable before God
	25:13	a covenant of e priesthood
1Ch	16:17	this e covenant with Israel

Ps	75:9	telling the story of God E
	92:8	You, God, are High and E
	93:2	Your throne ever firm — you're E
	103:5	He wraps you in goodness — beauty e
	105:10	the e Covenant with Israel
	117:2	God's faithful ways are e
	119:160	Your righteous decisions are e
	133:3	commands the blessing, ordains e life
	135:13	God, your name is e
	138:8	Your love is e
	139:24	guide me on the road to e life
	145:13	Your kingdom is a kingdom e
Ecc	12:5	well on your way to e rest
Isa	3:9	Doom to their e souls!
	9:6	Strong God, E Father
	24:5	violated the sacred and e covenant
	45:17	saved with an e salvation
	51:11	Joy e wreathing their heads
	60:19	God will be your e light
	60:20	I will be your e light
	61:8	establish my e covenant with you
Jer	10:10	the living God, the e King
	50:5	bound in a covenant e
	51:62	wastelands, an e nothing
La	5:19	your throne intact and e
Da	2:44	through it all standing strong and e
	12:2	some to e life, others to e shame
	12:7	solemnly swear by the E One
Mt	18:8	godless in a furnace of e fire
	18:18	What you say to one another is e
	19:16	what . . . must I do to get e life
	19:29	the considerable bonus of e life
	26:46	herded to their e doom
Mk	9:43	godless in a furnace of e fire
	9:50	protected from the e flames
	10:17	what must I do to get e life
	10:30	the bonus of e life
Lk	10:25	what do I need to do to get e life
	18:18	what must I do to deserve e life
	18:30	the bonus of e life
Jn	3:15	will gain a real life, e life
	3:27	I'm talking about e success
	4:36	grain that's ripe for e life
	5:39	you'll find e life there
	6:40	will enter real life, e life
	6:47	has real life, e life
	6:54	has e life and will be fit and ready
	6:68	the words of real life, e life
	10:10	so they can have real and e life
	10:28	I give them real and e life
	12:25	have it forever, real and e
	12:50	his command produces: real and e life
	17:2	give real and e life to all
	17:3	this is the real and e life
	20:31	have real and e life
Ac	13:46	no taste or inclination for e life
Ro	1:20	e power
	6:23	God's gift is real life, e life
1Co	2:8	a clue about what this e plan is
	8:11	risking his e ruin
2Co	1:22	he has stamped us with his e pledge
	11:31	The e and blessed God and Father

Gal	6:8	harvests a crop of real life, e life
2Th	1:9	E exile from the presence
1Ti	6:12	Seize the e life
	6:16	Honor to him, and e rule!
Heb	5:10	source of e salvation to all
	6:2	e judgment
	9:16	heirs to receive the e inheritance
	11:10	unseen city with real, e foundations
	13:20	blood that sealed the e covenant
1Pe	5:10	e and glorious plans they are
2Pe	1:11	the e kingdom of our Master
1Jn	2:25	exactly what Christ promised: e life
	3:15	e life and murder don't go together
	5:11	God gave us e life
	5:13	you have e life
	5:16	leading to e death
Rev	14:6	He had an E Message to preach

Eternally

Ps	89:28	I'll preserve him e in my love
	103:17	God's love . . . is . . . e present
	119:142	Your righteousness is e right
Da	6:26	His rule continues e
1Co	9:25	You're after one that's gold e
Heb	7:28	the Son, who is absolutely, e perfect

Eternity

Ex	15:18	Let God rule forever, for e
Job	10:5	You have all e to work things out
Ps	145:1	I'll bless your name into e
	145:2	keep it up from now to e
	145:21	bless his holy name from now to e
	148:6	set them in place from all time to e
Isa	57:15	God, who lives in E
	63:16	our Redeemer, famous from e
Mic	4:7	I rule from Mount Zion, from here to e
Hab	1:12	God, you're from e, aren't you?
2Co	3:11	government installed for e
Php	4:20	glory that just pours out into e
Tit	3:7	more life to come — an e of life
Heb	7:24	He's there from now to e
1Jn	2:17	does what God wants is set for e

Evenhanded

2Sa	8:15	fair and e in all his duties
1Ch	18:14	He ruled well, fair and e

Everlasting

Dt	33:15	the best from the e hills
	33:27	home on a foundation of e arms
1Ch	16:36	Blessed be God . . . from e to e
Eze	37:26	an e covenant

Evicted

Ps	109:10	street urchins, e from their homes

E

Evicting

Isa	5:8	E the old owners, posting
Jer	10:18	I'm e Everyone who lives here

Evidence

Ge	31:37	Let's see it — display the e
	37:26	concealing the e
Ex	22:13	animal must be brought in as e
Lev	13:15	e of a serious skin disease
Nu	16:38	e of what happened this day
Dt	17:4	look at the e and investigate
	22:20	no e of the girl's virginity
Jos	9:14	looked them over and accepted the e
1Sa	18:24	bring e of your vengeance
	18:26	brought their e back in a sack
	24:11	Look at the e! I'm not against you
2Ch	21:10	The e accumulated
	31:10	just look at the e
Job	27:12	The e is right before you
	34:23	God doesn't need to gather any more e
Ps	119:79	turn to me for e of your wise guidance
	119:152	the e of your words
Pr	30:3	I see no e of a holy God
Isa	27:9	e that his sin is removed will be
	41:20	e That I, God, personally did this
	41:21	Bring your e," says the King
	43:12	you're my witnesses, you're the e
	45:21	Look at the e
	48:6	e confirmed by your own eyes and ears
	55:13	living and lasting e of God
Jer	17:2	The e against them is plain to see
	26:11	heard the e with your own ears
	44:29	this will be the e
La	3:36	Tampering with e
Da	6:4	could find no e of negligence
Hab	2:11	woodwork will step forward with e
Zep	3:8	I'll be there to bring e
Mal	3:5	compelling e against sorcerers
Mt	12:38	Give us some hard e that God is
	12:39	the absence of proof: Jonah-e
	12:41	e that will condemn this generation
	12:42	e that will condemn this generation
Mk	14:55	high and low for e against Jesus
	16:20	the Message with indisputable e
Lk	7:29	are the clearest e
	11:31	e that will condemn this generation
	11:32	e that condemns this generation
	22:71	Why do we need any more e?
Jn	3:11	instead of facing the e and accepting
	3:32	e of what he saw and heard in heaven
	3:33	anyone who examines this e will come
	7:31	better or more convincing e than this
	7:53	Examine the e
	10:38	just take the e of the actions
	15:27	your side must give your confirming e
	17:23	e That you've sent me and loved them
	20:8	took one look at the e, and believed
Ac	14:3	presented the clear e of God's gifts
	14:17	e of good beyond your doing
	24:13	backed up with e or witnesses

Ro	4:11	underwent circumcision as e
1Co	1:6	e of Christ has been clearly verified
	4:5	before all the e is in
	7:18	Don't try to remove the e
2Co	12:12	mark a true apostle were in e
	12:16	an elaborate scam? Where's the e
	13:1	two or three witnesses give e
	13:5	need firsthand e, not mere hearsay
1Th	4:10	province of Macedonia are the e
1Ti	1:16	e of his endless patience
Heb	9:22	blood, the e of death
1Pe	1:7	on display as e of his victory

Evil

Ge	2:9	the Tree-of-Knowledge-of-Good-and-E
	2:17	the Tree-of-Knowledge-of-Good-and-E
	3:5	ranging all the way from good to e
	3:22	everything, ranging from good to e
	6:5	saw that human e was out of control
	8:21	they have this bent toward e
	13:13	The people of Sodom were e
	44:4	Why did you pay me back e for good
	48:16	Angel who delivered me from every e
	50:20	you planned e against me
Ex	23:2	along with the crowd in doing e
	32:12	Think twice about bringing e against
	32:14	not to do the e he had threatened
	32:22	how set on e they are
Nu	14:27	this e-infested community
	14:35	this entire e-infested community
	32:13	entire generation that acted out e
Dt	1:35	single person of this e generation
	4:25	doing what is sheer e in God's eyes
	6:22	e-visitations on Egypt, on Pharaoh
	7:15	all the e afflictions you experienced
	9:4	all the e these nations have done
	9:18	doing what is e in God's eyes
	9:27	this people, their e and their sin
	13:5	Purge the e from your company
	13:11	No one will dare to do an e thing
	13:13	e men have gotten together
	17:5	who did this e thing outside
	17:7	purge the e from your community
	17:12	root him out, rid Israel of the e
	19:19	Clean the polluting e
	19:20	put a stop to this kind of e
	21:21	will have purged the e pollution
	22:21	Purge the e from among you
	22:22	Purge that e from Israel
	22:24	You must purge the e from among you
	24:7	Purge that e from among you
	28:20	because of your e pursuits
	28:54	his eye e, against his own brother
	28:56	will turn hard, her eye e
	30:15	Life and Good Death and E
	31:17	all this e has come upon us
	31:18	because of all their e
	31:29	inviting all kinds of e consequences
Jdg	2:11	Israel did e in God's sight
	2:15	but for e, just as God had said
	2:19	didn't drop a single e practice

	3:7	Israel did **e** in God's sight	1Ch	4:10	don't let **e** hurt me
	3:12	went back to doing **e** in God's sight		17:9	nor will **e** nations afflict them
	4:1	kept right on doing **e** in God's sight	2Ch	19:2	You have no business helping **e**
	6:1	went back to doing **e** in God's sight		21:6	God considered him an **e** man
	9:56	avenged the **e** Abimelech had done		22:3	his mother training him in **e** ways
	9:57	all the **e** that they had done		22:4	God also considered him **e**
	10:6	went back to doing **e** in God's sight		33:2	a bad king — an **e** king
	11:27	this is an **e** thing that you are doing		33:6	Much **e** - . . . a career in **e**
	13:1	doing what was **e** in God's sight		33:9	**e** exceeding even the **e** of the pagan
	20:3	How did this outrageous **e** happen		33:22	In God's opinion he lived an **e** life
	20:10	this outrageous and vile **e**		36:5	In God's opinion he was an **e** king
	20:13	burn the **e** out of Israel		36:9	In God's opinion he was an **e** king
1Sa	2:23	your corrupt and **e** carrying on		36:12	he was just one more **e** king
	3:14	The **e** of Eli's family		36:14	The **e** mindset spread to the leaders
	15:19	you brazenly carry out this **e**	Ezr	4:12	that rebellious and **e** city
	24:13	**E** deeds come from **e** people		9:13	suffered because of our **e** ways
	24:17	I've dumped **e** on you	Ne	9:28	right back at it — more **e**
	25:28	no **e** will stick to you		9:35	turn their backs on the practice of **e**
	25:39	kept me from an **e** act		13:17	What's going on here? This **e**
	25:39	let Nabal's **e** boomerang		13:27	engaging in this extensive **e**
2Sa	4:11	**e** men who killed an innocent man	Est	7:6	An adversary. This **e** Haman
	7:10	Nor will **e** men afflict you		8:3	counter the **e** of Haman
	12:9	brazen contempt, doing this great **e**		9:25	the **e** scheme that Haman had worked
	13:16	an even worse **e** than what you just did	Job	1:1	hated **e** with a passion
	14:7	discerning good and **e**		1:8	totally devoted to God and hating **e**
1Ki	1:52	if there is **e** in him, he'll die		2:3	totally devoted to God and hating **e**
	2:44	you know all the **e** that you did		4:8	who plow **e** and sow trouble reap **e**
	3:9	difference between good and **e**		5:19	the **e** can't touch you
	13:33	Jeroboam kept right on doing **e**		6:30	trust me to discern good from **e**
	14:9	set a new record in works of **e**		11:11	spots **e** a long way off
	15:26	He was openly **e** before God		11:14	refuse to entertain **e** in your home
	15:34	He was openly **e** before God		15:16	we humans, . . . who lap up **e** like water
	16:7	his life of open **e** before God		15:35	have sex with sin and give birth to **e**
	16:19	living a flagrantly **e** life before God		20:6	The **e** might become world famous
	16:25	lived an **e** life — set new records in **e**		20:12	They savor **e** as a delicacy
	16:30	did even more open **e** before God		20:13	real gourmets of **e**
	21:20	you've bought into the business of **e**		20:16	They gorge on **e**
	21:25	making big business of **e**		21:20	experience the effects of their **e**
	22:52	he lived an **e** life		21:30	**e** men and women who got off scot-free
2Ki	8:18	an **e** man living an **e** life		22:23	Clean house of everything **e**
	8:27	the same **e**-in-God's-sight line of sin		24:20	nothing that is **e** lasts
	13:2	He lived an **e** life before God		27:13	this is what **e** people can expect
	13:11	In God's eyes he lived an **e** life		28:28	Insight means shunning **e**
	14:24	he lived an **e** life		30:26	I expected good but **e** showed up
	15:18	he lived an **e** life		34:10	impossible for God to do anything **e**
	15:24	In God's eyes he lived an **e** life		34:22	to hide those who do **e**
	15:28	In God's view he lived an **e** life		34:32	Whatever **e** I've done
	17:11	a long list of **e** actions		36:21	don't make things worse with more **e**
	17:13	Turn away from your **e** way of life		36:33	roars in the thunder, angry against **e**
	17:17	every kind of **e** available to them	Ps	5:4	don't . . . invite **E** over
	21:2	he was a bad king — an **e** king		7:9	Close the book on **E**, God
	21:6	Much **e** - . . . a career in **e**		7:14	he's pregnant with **e**
	21:9	**e** even exceeding the **e** of the pagan		10:15	break all the **e** left arms
	21:11	setting new records in **e**		11:2	the **e** bows are bent
	21:15	I won't put up with their **e** any longer		21:11	All their **e** schemes
	21:20	In God's opinion he lived an **e** life		28:3	full-time employees of **e**
	23:16	desacralizing the **e** altars		36:2	That his **e** will never be noticed
	23:32	In God's opinion, he was an **e** king		36:4	he fathers another **e** plot
	23:37	In God's opinion he was an **e** king		37:27	Turn your back on **e**
	24:9	he also was an **e** king		37:40	we're delivered from **e**
	24:19	Zedekiah was just one more **e** king		38:20	I give out good and get back **e**
	25:27	**E**-Merodach became king in Babylon		51:4	seen the full extent of my **e**

E

E

52:1	Why do you brag of *e*	29:6	E people fall into their own traps
52:3	You love *e* more than good	29:12	all the workers get infected with *e*
54:5	E is looping back on my enemies	29:27	can't stand the sight of deliberate *e*
55:3	quail before the *e* eye	Ecc 7:15	living a long life of sheer *e*
56:7	Pay them back in *e*!	7:25	wanted to identify *e* and stupidity
58:2	you brew cauldrons of *e*	8:8	No one who does *e* can be saved by *e*
64:5	calisthenics of *e* purpose	8:11	sentence against *e* deeds
66:18	If I had been cozy with *e*	8:13	*e* person will not experience a "good"
90:15	seen enough *e* to last a lifetime	9:3	people are obsessed with *e*
91:10	E can't get close to you	9:12	caught By accidents *e* and sudden
92:7	*e* men and women took over	10:13	ends up spouting insanity and *e*
92:9	all those hirelings of *e*	12:14	intent, whether it's good or *e*
94:1	God, put an end to *e*	Isa 5:18	Doom to you who use lies to sell *e*
94:13	quiet within the clamor of *e*	5:20	who call *e* good and good *e*
94:16	Who took my side against *e* workers	9:17	All of them were godless and *e*
94:23	their *e* back on them: for their *e*	10:1	Doom to you who legislate *e*
97:10	God loves all who hate *e*	13:11	I'll put a full stop to the *e* on earth
101:4	shake hands with those who plan *e*	14:20	The progeny of your *e* life
101:8	all who make a business of *e*	33:15	reject violence, avoid *e* amusements
106:32	Moses got mixed up in their *e*	34:14	dance through the night. The night—*e*
107:34	because of the *e* of the people	34:15	infestations of ominous *e*
107:39	abuse and *e* and trouble declined	34:16	this breeding, brooding *e*
109:5	They return my good with *e*	47:10	comfortable in your *e* life
109:6	Send the E One to accuse	55:7	and the *e* their way of thinking
119:101	avoiding the ditches and ruts of *e*	56:2	don't do anything *e*
121:7	God guards you from every *e*	59:7	race to do *e*
129:4	ripped the harnesses of the *e* plowmen	59:15	Anyone renouncing *e* is beaten
140:1	get me out of here, away from this *e*	65:12	did the very things I exposed as *e*
141:4	Don't let me so much as dream of *e*	66:4	did the very things I exposed as *e*
141:5	I'm praying hard against their *e* ways	Jer 2:19	*e* ways will get you a sound thrashing
141:9	Protect me from their *e* scheming	2:33	taught graduate courses in *e*
Pr 2:14	losers who make a game of *e*	3:17	stuck in the ruts of their *e* ways
3:7	Run to God! Run from *e*	4:14	Scrub the *e* from your lives
4:16	E people are restless	4:18	bitter taste is from your *e* life
4:27	leave *e* in the dust	4:22	Experts at the *e* but klutzes at good
6:18	heart that hatches *e* plots	6:29	Nothing can refine *e* out of them
8:7	I can't stand the taste of *e*	7:12	because of the *e* ways of my people
8:13	The Fear-of-God means hating E	7:24	indulged any and every *e* whim
10:16	*e* person ends up with nothing but sin	7:30	people of Judah have lived *e* lives
11:5	an *e* life is a hard life	8:3	all from this *e* generation
11:11	*e* talk turns it into a ghost town	9:3	They advance from one *e* to the next
11:19	chase after phantoms of *e* and die	10:5	useless for either good or *e*
11:27	the student of *e* becomes *e*	11:18	opened my eyes to their *e* scheming
12:20	E scheming distorts the schemer	13:23	you who are so long-practiced in *e*
12:21	No *e* can overwhelm a good person	14:16	get the full brunt of all their *e*
13:19	fools bent on *e* despise	18:20	Should I get paid *e* for good
14:16	watch their steps and avoid *e*	21:12	Your *e* regime is fuel for my anger
14:19	*e* will pay tribute to good	21:14	I'll punish your *e* regime
14:32	The *e* of bad people leaves them out	22:22	disgraced by your *e* life
15:3	he's alert to good and *e* alike	23:22	gotten them out of their *e* ruts
15:26	God can't stand *e* scheming	25:5	your *e* way of life and bad behavior
16:6	Fear-of-God deflects *e*	26:3	because of their *e* behavior
16:17	road of right living bypasses *e*	32:35	I can hardly conceive of such *e*
16:30	shifty eye betrays an *e* intention	33:5	the *e* actions in this city
17:4	E people relish malicious conversation	35:15	make a clean break with your *e* past
17:13	*e* for good will meet their own *e*	44:3	because they took up with *e* ways
20:30	A good thrashing purges *e*	44:5	or repented of *e*
21:12	undo the *e* they've planned	44:9	*e* lives of your ancestors, the *e*
21:15	for the workers of *e* it's a bad day	44:22	he couldn't take your *e* behavior
24:8	person who's always cooking up some *e*	51:24	all the *e* they did in Zion
26:23	Smooth talk from an *e* heart	52:2	Zedekiah was just one more *e* king
26:26	eventually his *e* will be exposed	52:31	E-Merodach became king

La	1:22	Take a good look at their e ways
	4:6	e guilt of my dear people was worse
	4:13	the e of her priests
	4:22	He'll punish your e life
Eze	3:20	take up with e when I step in
	6:9	disgusted with their e ways
	6:11	all the e obscenities rife in Israel
	7:11	brandishing the e scepter
	11:2	who think up new programs for e
	13:22	easy for others to persist in e
	16:23	to top off all your e acts
	16:57	before your e ways were exposed
	20:44	what I feel about the e lives
	21:25	blasphemous and e prince
	28:15	imperfection — e! — was detected
	31:11	to call its e to account
	33:11	Reverse your e ways!
	33:13	their good deeds and turn to e
	36:31	your terrible lives — the e
	38:10	cook up an e plot
Da	9:5	We've done e things
	11:27	two kings, each with e designs
Hos	4:8	can't wait for the latest in e
	5:4	Their e life is a bad habit
	7:3	entertain the king with their e circus
	7:15	how am I repaid? With e scheming
	9:15	All their e came out into the open
	10:13	reaped a crop of e
	10:15	because of your off-the-charts e
Joel	3:13	full, overflowing with vintage e
Am	5:13	E is epidemic
	5:14	Seek good and not e — and live!
	5:15	Hate e and love good
Jnh	0:0	turn back from an e life
	3:10	turned away from their e lives
Mic	2:1	Doom to those who plot e
	2:3	because of this interbreeding e
	3:2	Haters of good, lovers of e
	3:4	because of their history of e
	7:3	They've all become experts in e
Na	1:11	Nineveh's an anthill of e plots
	3:4	ruin with your e spells
	3:19	cruel e has seeped into every nook
Hab	1:3	Why do you force me to look at e
	1:13	You can't condone e!
	1:15	this e Babylonian arrives
Zep	3:5	in her midst, untouched by the e
	3:15	nothing to fear from e ever again
Zec	1:4	Leave your e life. Quit your e
	7:10	scheme against one another — that's e
Mal	1:4	Land of E!
	4:1	people who do e things will be burned
Mt	8:31	The e spirits begged Jesus
	9:32	struck speechless by an e spirit
	9:33	Jesus threw the e tormenting spirit
	10:1	power to kick out the e spirits
	12:28	I am sending the e spirits packing
	12:35	An e person is a blight
	12:43	When a defiling spirit is expelled
	12:45	other spirits more e than itself
	13:19	the E One comes along and plucks it
	15:19	we vomit up e arguments

	15:22	cruelly afflicted by an e spirit
	16:4	An e and wanton generation
	18:32	You e servant!
	24:12	spread of e will do them in
Mk	1:32	brought sick and e-afflicted people
	3:4	Doing good or doing e?
	3:11	E spirits, when they recognized him
	3:30	accusing him of being in league with E
	5:8	commanded the tormenting e spirit
	6:7	power to deal with the e opposition
Lk	3:20	capped his long string of e deeds
	6:9	Doing good or doing e?
	6:18	Those disturbed by e spirits
	7:21	diseases, distress, and e spirits
	8:2	healed of various e afflictions
	10:20	not in your authority over e
	11:39	maggoty with greed and secret e
Jn	3:20	makes a practice of doing e
	7:7	I expose the e behind its pretensions
	17:15	you guard them from the E One
	18:30	If he hadn't been doing something e
Ac	1:18	he took the e bribe money
	3:26	turn, one by one, from your e ways
	8:7	The e spirits protested loudly
	19:9	began spreading e rumors
	19:13	Jesus over victims of e spirits
	19:15	when the e spirit talked back
Ro	1:29	all hell broke loose: rampant e
	3:8	The more e we do, the more good
	7:13	Is good just as dangerous as e?
	12:9	Run for dear life from e
	12:21	Don't let e get the best of you
	16:19	gullible in regard to smooth-talking e
1Co	5:8	bread swollen with the yeast of e
	14:20	have a childlike unfamiliarity with e
2Co	12:21	turn away from the pigsty of e
Gal	1:4	Christ rescued us from this e world
1Th	5:22	Throw out anything tainted with e
2Th	2:10	e sleight of hand
	2:11	they're so obsessed with e
	3:3	He'll . . . protect you from e
2Ti	2:19	Spurn e, all you who name God
Heb	3:12	Make sure there's no e unbelief
	11:7	e of the unbelieving world
Jas	1:13	anyone under pressure to give in to e
	1:14	temptation to give in to e
	1:21	throw . . . cancerous e in the garbage
	4:16	vaunting self-importance is e
	4:17	that, for you, is e
1Pe	1:14	slip back into those old grooves of e
	3:10	Say nothing e or hurtful
	3:11	Snub e and cultivate good
	3:12	turns his back on those who do e
2Pe	2:9	rescue the godly from e trials
	2:10	don't hesitate to speak e
	2:13	Their e will boomerang on them
	2:15	a connoisseur of e
1Jn	2:13	won a big victory over the E One
	2:14	gain a victory over the E One
	3:12	Cain, who joined the E One
	5:18	The E One can't lay a hand on them
	5:19	who continue in the grip of the E One

E

2Jn	1:11	a platform to perpetuate his e ways
3Jn	1:11	Friend, don't go along with e
Rev	2:2	I know you can't stomach e
	18:5	God has remembered every e she's done

Evildoers

Ps	119:115	Get out of my life, e
Isa	31:2	stands up against interfering e
Rev	22:11	Let e do their worst

Exaggerate

| 1Ki | 10:7 | they didn't e! Such wisdom |
| 2Ch | 9:6 | they didn't e! Such wisdom |

Exaggerated

| 2Co | 7:14 | I hadn't e one bit |

Exaggerating

| Ro | 9:2 | I'm not e — Christ |

Exalted

Ne	9:5	your glorious name, e above all
Isa	6:1	Master sitting on a throne — high, e
	52:13	E, tall, head and shoulders above
Jer	17:12	a throne of glory, e
2Th	1:10	he will be e by his followers

Examination

Lev	13:8	who will conduct another e
	13:13	priest will make a thorough e
	13:20	for an e. If it looks like it
	13:21	if the e shows that there is no white
	13:26	if on e there is no white hair
	13:39	the priest is to make an e
	13:55	another e after it has been washed
	13:56	when the priest makes his e
	14:3	outside the camp and make an e
	14:39	come back and conduct another e
	14:44	priest is to come and conduct an e
	14:48	priest comes and conducts his e
Dt	13:14	you must conduct a careful e
	22:17	before the leaders for their e
Pr	18:17	until the cross-e starts

Examine

Lev	13:3	The priest will e the sore
	13:5	the priest will e it again
	13:6	priest will e him a second time
	13:10	The priest will e him
	13:15	The priest will e the open sores
	13:25	the priest is to e it
	13:43	The priest is to e it
	13:50	The priest will e the spot
	14:36	until he can come to e the fungus
Job	23:10	He can cross-e me all he wants

Ps	17:3	Go ahead, e me from inside out
	26:2	E me, God, from head to foot
	139:23	Cross-e and test me
Ecc	7:14	On a bad day, e your conscience
	8:16	load up on wisdom and e everything
Jer	11:20	You e and cross-e human actions
	17:10	search the heart and e the mind
Da	3:27	gathered around to e them
Jn	7:53	E the evidence.
	20:27	Take your finger and e my hands
Ac	24:8	accusations when you e him yourself
1Co	10:27	bad spirituality to cross-e your host
	11:28	E your motives, test your heart
2Th	3:17	e my signature as proof
1Jn	4:1	weigh and e what people tell you

Examined

Lev	13:3	After the priest has e it
Ecc	12:9	e, and arranged many proverbs
Lk	23:14	I e him in front of all of you

Examiner

| Jer | 6:27 | I have made you the e of my people |

Examines

Lev	13:31	But if when he e the itch
	13:53	when the priest e it
	14:37	the priest comes and e the house
1Ch	28:9	God e every heart and sees
Job	31:14	When God e my books, what can I say
Pr	21:2	God e our motives
Eze	21:21	he e a goat liver
Jn	3:33	anyone who e this evidence will come

Examining

Ps	11:4	e Adam's unruly brood inside and out
Pr	20:27	watching and e us inside and out
Mk	9:14	religion scholars cross-e them
Ac	17:11	met with him daily, e the Scriptures

Exasperate

| Eph | 6:4 | Fathers, don't e your children |

Exasperated

2Ki	13:3	E, God was furious with Israel
Ps	95:11	E, I exploded
	106:26	E, God swore that he'd lay them low
Jn	1:22	E, they said, "Who, then?
Ac	18:6	Totally e, Paul had finally had it
	22:24	By now the captain was thoroughly e
1Co	14:20	e with your infantile thinking
Heb	3:11	E, I vowed
	4:3	E, I vowed

Excite

SS	2:7	Don't e love, don't stir it up
	3:5	Don't e love, don't stir it up
	8:4	Don't e love, don't stir it up
2Co	3:12	With that kind of hope to e us

Excited

Ecc	1:10	Don't get e — it's the same old story
SS	5:4	the more e I became
Isa	8:6	gotten all e over Rezin
	14:9	the underworld dead are all e
Mk	6:25	E, she ran back to the king
Ac	8:18	he pulled out his money, e
	12:14	so e and eager to tell everyone
2Th	2:2	get you e over some breathless report

Excitement

Job	39:24	He quivers with e
	39:25	smelling the e of battle
Ecc	4:16	the e died quickly
Mk	7:37	beside themselves with e
	9:15	admiring e stirred them

Excommunicated

Ex	30:38	copies it for personal use will be e
	31:14	Whoever works on it will be e
Nu	19:13	is to be e
	19:20	he must be e from the community

Excuse

1Sa	1:26	Hannah said, "E me, sir
2Sa	1:20	one more e for a drunken party
Job	32:13	don't e yourselves by saying
Ps	9:16	They have no e
Pr	6:30	Hunger is no e for a thief to steal
Jer	2:21	a poor e for a vine
Am	7:2	God, my Master! E me, but what
Mt	8:21	Master, e me for a couple of days
Mk	14:40	they didn't have a plausible e
Lk	9:59	first e me for a couple of days
	9:61	first e me while I get things
Jn	15:22	As it is, they have no e
Ac	19:40	no e for what's happened today
Ro	1:20	So nobody has a good e
1Co	6:13	that's no e for stuffing your body
Gal	5:13	don't use this freedom as an e
Eph	4:22	we do not have the e of ignorance
	5:20	any e for a song to God the Father

Excuses

Dt	13:8	don't make e for him
Pr	6:29	you'll pay for it. No e
	24:12	Someone not impressed with weak e
Mic	3:7	lame e to cover up their God-ignorance
Lk	14:18	one after another making e

2Th	3:12	no e, no arguments
1Jn	2:28	guilt or lame e when he arrives

Execute

Nu	25:5	Each of you must e the men
Dt	13:15	must e the citizens of that town
	32:41	my lightning sword and e judgment
Eze	39:21	they'll all see the judgment I e
Ac	13:28	demanded that Pilate e him anyway

Executed

Nu	18.7	who invades the Sanctuary will be e
	35:30	Anyone who kills another may be e
Dt	21:22	death sentence, e and hung
1Sa	11:13	Nobody is going to be e this day
2Sa	8:2	chose . . . randomly and e them
	21:6	sons be handed over to us to be e
	21:9	when they were e
2Ki	14:5	he e the palace guard
	14:6	e for their children's sins
	25:7	sons were e right before his eyes
2Ch	25:3	he e the palace guard
	25:4	e for their childrens' sins
Eph	3:11	then e in Christ Jesus
Php	2:17	Even if I am e here and now

Execution

Nu	15:36	an e commanded by God
Dt	17:7	throw the first stones in the e
	19:12	over to the avenger of blood for e
2Ki	10:17	a mass e, just as God had told
Jer	29:22	take what they see at the e
Da	2:13	They also were marked for e
	2:14	making arrangements for the e
	2:24	the e. He said, "Call off the e
Mt	27:20	pardon of Barabbas and the e of Jesus
Lk	23:32	were taken along with him for e
Ac	12:19	he ordered their e
	25:24	most vehement in demanding his e
	26:10	I voted for their e

Exemplary

1Ki	15:5	David had lived an e life before God
2Ch	32:1	after this e track record, this
	35:26	Josiah, his e and devout life
Job	4:6	Shouldn't your e life give you hope
Da	6:4	He was totally e and trustworthy
Php	1:10	a lover's life, circumspect and e
Heb	11:39	though their lives of faith were e
1Pe	2:12	Live an e life among the natives

Exhausted

1Sa	14:31	the soldiers ended up totally e
	30:4	wept until they were e with weeping
2Sa	16:14	all the men of the company were e
	17:29	army must be starved and e
	21:15	David became e

E

	23:10	right and left until he was **e**
1Ki	19:5	**E**, he fell asleep under the lone
Job	32:5	other men had **e** their arguments
Isa	47:13	you're **e** trying out remedies
Ro	13:11	don't get so absorbed and **e**
1Th	5:14	reach out for the **e**, pulling them

Exhaustion

Jdg	4:21	while he was fast asleep from **e**
Ps	107:5	stumbling, on the brink of **e**
La	1:6	like deer . . . chased to **e** by hunters

Existence

2Ki	11:3	Athaliah, oblivious to his **e**, ruled
2Ch	22:12	Athaliah, oblivious to his **e**, ruled
Isa	14:23	I'll bulldoze it out of **e**
Eze	22:4	forced a premature end to your **e**
	36:36	nations around you that are still in **e**
Jn	1:4	What came into **e** was Life
1Co	8:4	idols have no actual **e**
	15:9	stamp God's church right out of **e**
Gal	5:18	compulsions of a law-dominated **e**
Col	1:17	there before any of it came into **e**
Heb	11:1	The fundamental fact of **e**
	11:3	the world called into **e** by God's word
2Pe	2:10	addicted to a filthy **e**
	3:5	brought into **e** out of watery chaos

Exorcists

Mt	12:27	same mud stick to your own **e**
Lk	11:19	same mud stick to your own **e**
Ac	19:13	Some itinerant Jewish **e**
	19:16	jumped the **e**, beat them up

Expectancy

Lk	2:25	prayerful **e** of help for Israel
Ro	5:5	In alert **e** such as this
	8:25	the more joyful our **e**

Expectant

Ps	14:2	God-**e**, just one God-ready
	53:2	God-**e**, just one God-ready
	145:15	All eyes are on you, **e**
SS	5:5	Desiring and **e** as I turned
Jn	3:15	looks up to him, trusting and **e**
Ro	8:15	It's adventurously **e**, greeting God
	12:12	cheerfully. Don't quit
2Co	1:24	working alongside you, joyfully **e**

Expectantly

Job	29:21	hung **e** on my every word
Ps	104:27	All the creatures look **e** to you
	119:166	I wait **e** for your salvation
Isa	42:4	islands wait **e** for his teaching
Mk	15:43	He was one who lived **e**
Lk	2:38	waiting **e** for the freeing of Jerusalem

1Co	1:7	wait **e** for our Master Jesus to arrive
Gal	5:5	**e** wait for a satisfying relationship
1Th	1:10	how **e** you await the arrival of his Son

Expectation

Lk	19:11	**e** was building that God's kingdom
	21:34	sharp edge of your **e** get dulled
	23:52	lived in alert **e** of the kingdom of God

Expert

Ge	25:27	Esau became an **e** hunter
2Ch	2:14	he is also an **e** engraver
Ezr	7:11	**e** in matters involving the truths
Job	12:3	doesn't take an **e** to know these things
Isa	40:14	What **e** would he have gone to
	43:9	Let them present their **e** witnesses
Jn	5:33	he gave **e** and reliable testimony
	9:17	You're the **e**. He opened your eyes
Php	3:13	By no means do I count myself an **e**

Expertise

Ex	31:3	skill and know-how and **e** in every

Experts

1Sa	6:2	priests, and **e** on the supernatural
Est	1:13	counselors, all **e** in legal matters
Job	12:2	I'm sure you speak for all the **e**
	12:17	strips **e** of their vaunted credentials
	32:9	**e** have no corner on wisdom
Ps	146:3	**e** who know nothing of life
Isa	28:15	We're advised by the **e**
	44:25	He makes the **e** look trivial
	47:14	Your '**e**' are in it and won't get out
Jer	2:8	The religion **e** knew nothing of me
	4:22	**E** at evil but klutzes at good
	8:8	religion **e** have taken you for a ride
	46:9	Soldiers . . . **e** with bow and arrow
Mic	3:7	**e** will be all mixed up
	7:3	They've all become **e** in evil
Zec	10:2	Religious **e** spout rubbish
Mt	23:9	set people up as **e** over your life
1Co	1:19	expose so-called **e** as crackpots
	2:6	fashionable wisdom of high-priced **e**
	2:8	The **e** of our day haven't a clue
1Ti	1:7	set themselves up as **e** on religious
	6:20	practiced confusion of the so-called **e**
2Pe	2:14	is greed, and they're **e** at it

Exploit

Lev	19:13	Don't **e** your friend or rob him
2Ki	17:20	permitted anyone with a mind to **e** them
Job	24:3	rip off the poor and **e** the unfortunate
Ps	82:4	prosecute all those who **e** them
	94:5	**e** and abuse your precious people
Pr	11:29	**E** or abuse your family
	14:31	you **e** the powerless
	15:27	who refuse to **e** live and let live

	16:10	doesn't mislead, doesn't e
	22:16	E the poor or glad-hand the rich
Jer	5:28	e the poor
Eze	18:8	doesn't e the poor
	18:17	doesn't e the poor
Am	8:6	You e the poor, using them
Mal	3:5	liars, those who e workers
Mt	7:16	leader will never e your emotions
Ac	20:35	on behalf of the weak and not e them
	23:6	decided to e their antagonism
2Ti	3:13	con men will continue to e the faith
Jas	2:6	the high and mighty who e you
2Pe	2:3	anything, that sounds good to e you

Exploitation

Ecc	5.8	E filters down from one petty official
Isa	33:15	speak the truth, despise e
	58:6	get rid of e in the workplace
Heb	13:10	not for e by insiders

Exploited

1Sa	12:3	ever taken advantage of you or e you
Job	5:4	children . . . abused and e
	20:19	Because they e the poor
	22:6	e their helplessness
Pr	5:10	Why be e by those who care nothing
Isa	26:6	All the e and outcast peoples
La	4:13	Who e good and trusting people
Eze	34:16	so they're not e
	34:28	No longer will they be e by outsiders
Hos	5:1	E people at Mizpah
Ac	7:19	He e our race mercilessly
2Co	7:2	never e or taken advantage of anyone
2Ti	3:7	They get e every time
Jas	5:4	All the workers you've e and cheated

Exploiters

er	21:12	Rescue victims from their e
	22:3	Rescue victims from their e

Exposure-offering

Nu	5:18	place the e in her hands
	5:26	the Grain-Offering, using it as an e

Extinct

a	29:20	Cynical scoffers will be an e species
Mic	7:2	Right-living humans are e

Extinction

lg	21:17	can prevent an entire tribe from e

Extortion

	28:8	through cheating and e
e	22:12	e is commonplace
	22:29	E is rife, robbery is epidemic

Hab	2:6	getting rich by stealing and e
Lk	3:13	No more e — collect only

Extravagant

1Ki	10:5	worship e with Whole-Burnt-Offerings
2Ch	9:4	worship e with Whole-Burnt-Offerings
Job	28:17	e jewelry can't touch it
	37:13	discipline or grace or e love
Isa	5:9	Those e estates will be deserted
	7:11	Ask anything. Be e
	63:7	Compassion lavished, love e
Joel	2:13	This most patient God, e in love
Ac	20:24	this incredibly e generosity of God
Ro	5:17	this wildly e life-gift
	11:33	this e generosity of God
	15:29	one of Christ's more e blessings
2Co	9:10	is more than e with you
	13:14	the e love of God
Eph	3:18	the e dimensions of Christ's love
	5:2	His love was not cautious but e

Eyewitness

Jn	12:17	was there giving e accounts
	19:35	The e to these things has presented
	21:24	This is the same disciple who was e

Eyewitnesses

Nu	35:30	executed only on the testimony of e
Dt	7:19	great contests to which you were e
	29:3	massive trials to which you were e
Isa	44:8	You're my e: Have you ever
Lk	1:2	the original e who served this Word

F

Fads

Pr	15:14	fools feed on fast-food f and fancies
	22:15	prone to foolishness and f
Jer	25:6	Don't follow the god-f of the day
Mk	7:8	taking up the latest f
2Ti	4:10	Demas, chasing f, went off

Failures

Ps	32:5	make a clean breast of my f to God
Isa	53:4	God was punishing him for his own f
Mt	7:1	Don't pick on people, jump on their f
Lk	6:37	Don't pick on people, jump on their f

Faith

Dt	32:51	This is because you broke f with me
Jdg	8:35	didn't keep f with the family
1Ki	11:11	no intention of keeping f with me
	15:19	I'm showing my good f with this gift
2Ch	16:3	I'm showing my good f with this gift
Ps	19:6	warming hearts to f
	61:7	Steady Love and Good F as lookouts

F

F

Isa	7:9	If you don't take your stand in f		4:5	one Master, one f, one baptism
	19:18	learn to speak the language of f		6:16	f, and salvation are more
Jer	14:21	Don't break f with us		6:22	cheer you on in your f
Hos	6:7	You broke f with me — ungrateful		6:23	Love mixed with f be yours from God
Mal	2:14	broken the f-bond	Php	1:14	more sure of themselves in the f
Mt	8:12	grew up 'in the f' but had no f		2:17	element in the offering of your f
	9:21	You took a risk of f	Col	1:4	reports on your steady f in Christ
	15:28	Oh, woman, your f is something else		2:5	solid substance of your f in Christ
	17:20	if you had a mere kernel of f		2:7	You know your way around the f
Mk	4:40	Don't you have any f at all		4:8	so he could encourage you in your f
	5:34	Daughter, you took a risk of f	1Th	1:3	call to mind your work of f
	10:52	Your f has saved and healed you		1:8	The news of your f in God is out
Lk	7:50	Your f has saved you		3:2	a brother and companion in the f
	17:5	said to the Master, "Give us more f		3:5	how you were doing in the f
	17:6	don't need more f		3:6	terrific report on your f and love
	17:6	There is no 'more' or 'less' in f		3:8	Knowing that your f is alive
	17:19	Your f has healed and saved you		3:10	help when your f falters
	18:8	that kind of persistent f		5:8	dressed up in f, love, and the hope
	18:42	Your f has saved and healed you	2Th	1:3	Your f is growing phenomenally
Jn	6:6	said this to stretch Philip's f		1:4	steady and determined in your f
	7:31	committed themselves in f to him		1:11	good ideas and acts of f
	8:56	with jubilant f		2:13	plan of salvation by the bond of f
Ac	3:16	F in Jesus' name put this man	1Ti	1:2	Timothy, my son in the f
	6:5	Stephen, a man full of f		1:4	deepening f and obedience
	6:7	priests submitted themselves to the f		1:5	self-interest and counterfeit f
	14:27	throw the door of f wide open		1:14	Grace mixed with f and love
	16:5	congregations became stronger in f		1:19	keeping a firm grip on your f
	16:40	encouraged them in the f		2:7	explaining how it works by simple f
	20:11	telling stories of the f until dawn		2:15	comes to those who continue in f
Ro	1:8	telling me about your lives of f		3:9	reverent before the mystery of the f
	1:17	right shows up in the acts of f		3.13	a real credit to this Jesus-f
	3:25	Having f in him sets us in the clear		4:1	some are going to give up on the f
	4:1	Abraham, our first father in the f		4:6	raised on the Message of the f
	4:12	risky f-embrace of God's action		4:12	by love, by f, by integrity
	4:16	He is our f father		5:8	in need repudiates the f
	5:1	entering through f into what God		6:10	some lose their footing in the f
	7:4	bear "offspring" of f for God		6:11	a life of wonder, f, love, steadiness
	14:1	weak in the f department		6:12	Run hard and fast in the f
	15:1	strong and able in the f		6:21	miss the whole point of f
1Co	2:5	life of f is a response to God's power	2Ti	1:5	honest f — and what a rich f it is
	13:2	if I have f that says to a mountain		1:13	this f and love rooted in Christ
2Co	1:12	with conscience and f intact		2:14	nitpicking, which chips away at the f
	1:24	in charge of how you live out the f		2:22	mature righteousness — f, love, peace
	10:15	as your lives grow in f		3:8	They were rejects from the f
	13:5	make sure you are solid in the f		3:10	direction, f, steadiness, love
Gal	1:1	I, Paul, and my companions in f here		3:13	will continue to exploit the f
	2:16	through personal f in Jesus Christ		3:15	salvation through f in Christ Jesus
	2:20	lived by f in the Son of God	Tit	1:1	Christ's agent for promoting the f
	3:7	like Abraham: children of f		1:4	Dear Tit, legitimate son in the f
	3:8	set things right with non-Jews by f		1:14	so they can recover a robust f
	3:9	who live by f are blessed		2:2	into healthy f, love, and endurance
	3:12	naturally evolve into living by f		3:15	Say hello to our friends in the f
	3:20	direct blessing of God, received by f	Phm	1:5	love and f you have for the Master
	3:21	can only get by waiting in f for God		1:6	this f we hold in common
	3:23	respond freely in f to the living God	Heb	4:2	didn't receive the promises with f
	3:26	By f in Christ you are in direct		4:3	But not if we don't have f
	3:27	dressing you in an adult f wardrobe		6:12	stay the course with committed f
	5:6	f expressed in love		11:1	this trust in God, this f
	6:10	closest to us in the community of f		11:2	The act of f is what distinguished
	6:12	a f that shares Christ's suffering		11:3	By f, we see the world called
	6:17	the serious living of this f		11:4	By an act of f, Abel brought
Eph	2:19	kingdom of f is now your home country		11:5	By an act of f, Enoch skipped

	11:6	impossible to please God apart from f
	11:7	By f, Noah built a ship
	11:8	By an act of f, Abraham said yes
	11:9	By an act of f he lived,
	11:11	By f, barren Sarah was able
	11:13	people of f died not yet having
	11:17	By f, Abraham
	11:20	By an act of f, Isaaac reached
	11:21	By an act of f, Jacob
	11:22	By an act of f, Joseph
	11:23	By an act of f, Moses' parents
	11:24	By f, Moses, when grown, refused
	11:27	By an act of f, he turned
	11:28	By an act of f, he kept
	11:29	By an act of f, Israel walked
	11:30	By f, the Israelites marched
	11:31	By an act of f, Rahab
	11:33	Through acts of f, they toppled
	11:39	lives of f were exemplary
	11:40	their f and our f would come together
	12:3	find yourselves flagging in your f
Jas	1:3	your f-life is forced into the open
	2:1	glorious, Christ-originated f
	2:14	Does merely talking about f indicate
	2:18	You take care of the f department
	2:20	cut f and works in two
	2:22	f and works are yoked partners
	2:24	not by a barren f but by f fruitful
	2:26	Separate f and works and you get
1Pe	1:7	genuine f put through this suffering
	5:9	keep a firm grip on the f
2Pe	1:5	complementing your basic f
1Jn	4:2	confesses openly his f in Jesus Christ
	4:3	refuses to confess f in Jesus
	5:4	brings the world to its knees is our f
3Jn	1:5	you make the f visible
Jude	1:3	f entrusted to us as a gift to guard
	1:20	build yourselves up in . . . holy f
	1:22	Go easy on those who hesitate in the f
Rev	2:19	The love and the f
	6:11	companions and friends in the f

Faithful

1Sa	2:9	protectively cares for his f friends
1Ch	5:25	not f to the God of their ancestors
2Ch	31:15	F support out in the priestly cities
Ne	1:5	f to those who love him and obey
Ps	52:9	in company with your f friends
	73:26	God is rock-firm and f
	88:11	Is your f presence noticed
	89:1	telling everyone how f you are
	89:5	angels sing anthems to your f ways
	89:8	powerful and f from every angle
	89:19	you spoke to your f beloved
	92:2	sing your f presence all through
	115:1	do it on account of your f ways
	116:10	I stayed f, though bedeviled
	116:16	your servant, your f servant
	117:2	God's f ways are eternal
	119:138	how to live ever f to you
Pr	30:23	when a "girlfriend" replaces a f wife

Isa	38:18	don't witness to your f ways
	38:19	full reports on your f ways
	65:16	use my f name for the blessing
Jer	35:15	settle down and be f in this country
	42:5	a true and f witness against us
Hos	4:1	No one is f. No one loves.
	12:13	served as f pastors
Mt	19:9	if you divorce your f wife
Gal	4:29	from the f promise
Eph	1:1	you f Christians in Ephesus
Php	1:19	Through your f prayers
Heb	3:2	f in everything God gave him to do
2Jn	1:9	stays f to both the Father and the Son
Rev	2:13	witness who stayed f to me
	3:14	God's Yes, the F and Accurate Witness
	14:12	staying f to Jesus
	17:14	will be the called, chosen, and f
	19:11	The Rider, named F and True, judges

Faithfully

Ge	24:40	God before whom I've walked f
1Sa	12:2	I've led you f from my youth
1Ki	3:6	he lived f in your presence
Ps	89:28	I'll f do all I so solemnly promised
Isa	38:3	I've lived f in your presence
	49:7	God, who has f kept his word
Jer	23:28	message from me — tell it truly and f
Eze	18:9	f honors and obeys my laws
	44:15	Zadok, who f took care of my Sanctuary
Am	5:25	worship me f for forty years
Mal	1:5	you'll see how f I've loved you
Ac	7:8	each f passing on the covenant sign
	18:11	f teaching the Word of God
Rev	13:10	passionately and f stand their ground

Faithfulness

Ps	57:10	every cloud is a flag to your f
	71:22	thank you to the tune of your f, God
	108:4	every cloud's a flag to your f
	138:2	thank you for your f
Isa	11:5	build righteousness and f in the land
La	3:23	How great your f
Ro	3:3	their faithlessness cancels out his f
Heb	13:7	let their f instruct you

Faithless

Ne	13:27	evil, showing yourselves f to God
Ps	78:8	A fickle and f bunch
Pr	2:17	f to the husband she married
Jer	9:2	They're a f, feckless bunch
	23:10	f, promiscuous idolater-adulterers
Eze	15:8	because they've been f
Gal	4:29	the child who came from f connivance
Rev	21:8	feckless and f, degenerates

Fame

Dt	26:19	high in praise, f, and honor
2Ki	10:34	his accomplishments and f

2Ch	1:11	didn't grasp for money, wealth, f
	1:12	money, wealth, and f beyond anything
Ps	7:17	I'm singing the f of heaven-high God
	9:6	names erased from the halls of f
	49:16	get rich and pile up f and fortune
	49:17	f and fortune all get left behind
	66:4	can't stop enjoying your name and f
	72:17	his f shine on like sunshine
	78:4	God's f and fortune
	145:7	The f of your goodness spreads
Pr	27:21	tested by giving them a little f
Isa	24:15	broadcast God's f, the f of the God
	32:5	nor crooks be rewarded with f
Eze	28:17	by using it to get worldly f
Da	5:20	stripped him of his f
Hos	14:7	f as the vintage children of God

Fantasies

Ex	5:9	their whining, their god-f
2Ki	4:16	teasing me with such f
Jer	29:8	Don't pay any attention to the f
Hos	12:1	Ephraim, obsessed with god-f

Fantasize

Pr	6:25	Don't lustfully f on her beauty
	26:16	Dreamers f their self-importance
Eze	7:13	don't f an upturn in the market
	13:6	All they do is f comforting illusions

Fantasized

Ps	131:1	no business or f grandiose plans
Eze	13:7	Haven't you f sheer nonsense

Fantasy

2Ki	18:19	a world of make-believe, of pious f
Ecc	5:7	against all illusion and f
Jer	42:20	you are living out a f
Am	5:20	we face hard reality, not f
1Ti	1:4	introducing f stories and fanciful

Fashion

Ps	119:90	Your truth never goes out of f
Zec	6:11	f crowns. Place one on the head
Mt	6:25	clothes in your closet are in f
	6:28	time and money wasted on f
	23:5	Their lives are perpetual f shows
Lk	12:22	clothes in your closet are in f
Ac	15:1	not circumcised in the Mosaic f
	20:33	had any taste for wealth or f

Fashions

Job	27:16	resplendent in the latest f
Ps	73:6	wear the latest f in violence
Isa	3:22	the latest f in hats
La	4:5	People used to the latest in f
Hos	2:8	dressed her up in the big-city f

Mic	6:16	you've slavishly followed their f
Zec	14:14	gold, silver, the latest f
Mt	6:28	Instead of looking at the f
Mk	7:9	in following the religious f
Lk	16:19	expensively dressed in the latest f
Col	3:10	All the old f are now obsolete
1Ti	2:9	chasing the latest f
Rev	18:16	Dressed in the latest f

Fast-food

Ps	14:4	Treating people like a f meal
	53:4	Treating people like a f meal
Pr	15:14	fools feed on f fads and fancies

Fasted

Jdg	20:26	That day they f until evening
1Sa	7:6	They f all day and prayed
	31:13	f in mourning for seven days
2Sa	1:12	wept and f the rest of the day
	12:16	He f, wouldn't go out
	12:21	you f and wept and stayed up all night
	12:22	While the child was alive, I f
1Ki	21:27	in penitential rough burlap, and f
Ezr	8:23	we f and prayed about these concerns

Fasting

Ezr	10:6	still f from food and drink
Ne	1:4	mourned for days, f and praying
Est	4:3	f, weeping, wailing
	9:31	regarding their f and mourning
Ps	69:10	I poured myself out in prayer and f
Isa	58:4	The food of f you do won't get
	58:5	Do you call that f
Jer	36:6	Wait for a day of f when everyone
Da	6:18	couldn't sleep. He spent the night f
	9:3	praying earnestly, f from meals
Joel	2:12	Come f and weeping, sorry
Zec	7:5	f every fifth and seventh month
Mt	4:2	Jesus prepared for the Test by f
	9:14	discipline body and spirit by f
	11:18	John came f and they called him crazy
Mk	2:18	Pharisees made a practice of f
Lk	5:35	the groom is gone, the f can begin
	7:33	John the Baptizer came f
Ac	13:2	also f as they waited for guidance
	13:3	obedience, of f and praying
	14:23	their prayers intensified by f
1Co	7:5	for the purposes of prayer and f

Fastings

Lk	2:37	worshiping . . . with her f and prayers

Fate

1Sa	11:7	let this be the f of his oxen
1Ki	16:3	identical f of Jeroboam
	21:22	I'll bring down on you the same f
2Ki	9:9	experiences the same f as the family

	21:13	I'll visit the f of Samaria
2Ch	22:7	The f of Ahaziah
Ne	9:28	left them again to their f
Est	4:11	a single f for every man or woman
Job	5:6	Don't blame f when things go wrong
	8:14	hitch their f to a spider web
	18:20	Westerners are aghast at their f
Ecc	2:14	One f for all — and that's it
	2:15	my f's the same as the fool's
	2:24	that's it — divine f
	6:10	You can't argue with f
	9:2	It's one f for everybody
	9:3	everyone's lumped together in one f
Isa	17:14	this is the f of those out to get us
	22:24	not only the f of Davidic descendants
	24:13	This is the f of all nations
	34:17	decreed their f in detail
	36:12	It's their f that's at stake
	47:15	the f of your friends in sorcery
	57:6	You've chosen your f
	65:11	throw cocktail parties for Sir f
	65:12	F it will be: your destiny, Death
Jer	39:5	Nebuchadnezzar decided his f
	43:11	sending each to his assigned f
	44:12	same f will fall upon both
	51:9	Give her up to her f
La	1:4	How bitter her f
	2:11	turned to jelly over my people's f
Eze	7:7	your f, you who live in this land
	7:10	F has caught up with you
Da	6:17	fixing Daniel's f
Am	6:5	indifferent to the f of others
Na	3:15	as if by locusts — a fitting f
	3:19	When the story of your f gets out
Hab	6:2	going to rule on the world's f

Fatigue

2Sa	16:2	overcome by f in the wilderness
La	4:14	wasted lives, shuffling from f

Fatigued

1Sa	30:10	too f to cross the Brook Besor
Isa	44:12	works away, f with hunger and thirst
Gal	6:9	let's not allow ourselves to get f

Fault

Ge	16:5	Sarai told Abram, "It's all your f
	31:39	made me pay whether it was my f or not
Ex	5:16	being beaten. And it's not our f
Nu	32:15	disaster will be all your f
Dt	19:6	didn't deserve it. It wasn't his f
Jos	2:19	his own f — we aren't responsible
1Ch	21:17	I'm the one at f
Job	19:28	his trouble is all his own f
Ps	50:8	don't find f with your acts of worship
	106:25	They found f with the life they had
	145:16	Generous to a f, you lavish
Jer	2:5	did your ancestors find f with in me
Eze	3:18	they will die and it will be your f

	33:4	it's his own f
	33:5	he ignored it — it's his own f
Da	9:16	it's our f that this has happened
Jnh	1:12	It's all my f. I'm the cause
Mk	8:16	were finding f with each other
	14:27	falling apart and that it's my f
Jn	9:41	accountable for every f and failure
	19:11	has committed a far greater f
Ro	14:20	don't drag them down by finding f
2Co	7:3	Don't think I'm finding f with you
	12:11	it's not all my f
1Ti	5:14	any foothold for finding f

Faults

1Sa	12:5	nothing against me — no f
Mt	7:1	their failures, criticize their f
Lk	6:37	their failures, criticize their f

Favoritism

Ex	23:3	don't show f in a dispute
Lev	19:15	Don't show f to either
1Ti	5:21	Carry them out without f

Fear

Ge	20:11	no f of God in this place
	22:12	Now I know how fearlessly you f God
	26:24	don't f a thing because I'm with you
	31:42	God of Abraham and the F of Isaaac
	31:53	Jacob promised, swearing by the F
	35:5	A paralyzing f descended on all
	50:21	you have nothing to f
Ex	18:21	men who f God, men of integrity
	19:16	Everyone in the camp shuddered in f
Lev	19:14	f your God. I am God
	19:32	f your God. I am God
	25:17	F your God. I am God, your God
	25:43	f your God
	26:6	sleep at night without f
Dt	4:10	learn to f me in holy f
	11:25	God-sent f and trembling will precede
	17:19	learn what it means to f his God
	20:1	do not recoil in f of them
	20:3	Don't f. Don't hesitate
Jos	24:14	So now: F God. Worship him
1Sa	12:14	If you f God, worship and obey him
	12:24	f God and worship him honestly
	18:28	his f of David increased
	20:21	as God lives, not a thing to f
	23:3	We live in f of our lives
	28:13	You have nothing to f
2Ki	17:36	Reverence and f him. Worship him.
1Ch	10:4	restrained by both reverence and f
	14:17	God put the f of God into the godless
2Ch	14:14	paralyzed by the f of God
	17:10	strong sense of the f of God
	19:7	Live in the f of God
	19:9	Do your work in the f of God
	20:29	the f of God descended on them
Ezr	9:4	Many were in f and trembling

Ne	5:9	Is there no f of God left in you?
	5:15	out of f of God I did none of that
Est	9:2	f made cowards of them all
Job	6:21	you shrink in f
	21:9	homes are peaceful and free from f
	22:10	trapped in terror, paralyzed by f
	24:4	they f for their lives
	28:28	F-of-the-Lord — that's Wisdom
	31:23	f of God has kept me from these things
	41:33	not an ounce of f in that creature
Ps	49:5	So why should I f in bad times
	55:5	I shake with f, I shudder
	77:16	God, saw you and trembled with f
	78:53	they had nothing to f
	85:9	salvation is to those who f him
	86:11	I'll worship in joyful f
	90:11	against the very ones who f you
	91:5	F nothing
	97:4	Earth, wide-eyed, trembles in f
	103:11	strong is his love to those who f him
	103:13	God feels for those who f him
	103:17	eternally present to all who f him
	111:5	He gave food to those who f him
	111:10	The good life begins in the f of God
	112:1	Blessed man, blessed woman, who f God
	115:11	You who f God, trust in God
	115:13	let God bless all who f God
	118:4	you who f God, join in
	119:38	promises made to all who f you
	119:63	friend and companion of all who f you
	119:74	those who f you will take heart
	119:79	Let those who f you turn to me
	128:1	you who f God, how blessed you are
	135:20	You who f God, bless God
	145:19	does what's best for those who f him
	147:11	Those who f God get God's attention
Pr	24:21	F God, dear child
	26:2	little to f from an undeserved curse
	29:25	The f of human opinion disables
Ecc	3:14	simply worship in holy f
	5:7	this rock foundation: F God
	8:13	because he doesn't f God
	12:13	F God. Do what he tells you
Isa	8:12	Don't f what they f
	8:13	F God-of-the-Angel-Armies
	14:31	Fall prostrate in f, Philistia
	19:17	f of the God-of-the-Angel-Armies
	41:10	no need to f for I'm your God
	49:9	those huddled in f, 'It's all right
	54:14	far from any trouble — nothing to f
	59:19	In the west they'll f the name of God
Jer	6:24	We're paralyzed with f
	23:4	won't live in f or panic anymore
	30:10	So f no more, Jacob, dear servant
	39:17	men whom you have good reason to f
	40:9	nothing to f from the Chaldean
	42:11	don't have to f the king of Babylon
	42:16	the very wars you f will catch up
	46:27	my servant, you have nothing to f
	46:28	my servant, you have nothing to f
	47:3	Fathers, paralyzed by f
	49:23	Their hearts will melt in f

	49:37	live in constant f and terror
Eze	7:27	Gripped by f, they can't move
	11:8	You f war, but war is what you're
	12:18	drink your water trembling with f
	30:13	in his place I'll put f — f throughout
Da	10:7	were overcome with f and ran off
Joel	2:21	F not, earth! Be glad and celebrate
	2:22	F not, wild animals
Mic	7:17	Fill them with holy f and trembling
Na	1:5	Earth shakes in f of God
Zep	3:15	nothing to f from evil ever again
Mt	10:28	Save your f for God
	28:5	There is nothing to f here
Mk	5:33	stepped up in f and trembling
Lk	1:12	Zachariah was paralyzed in f
	1:13	reassured him, "Don't f, Zachariah
	1:30	Mary, you have nothing to f
	1:65	A deep, reverential f settled
	5:10	There is nothing to f
	12:5	Save your f for God
	23:40	Have you no f of God?
Jn	12:15	No f, Daughter Zion
Ac	5:5	put the f of God into everyone
	22:29	put the f of God into the captain
Ro	13:3	should have nothing to f
1Jn	4:18	no room in love for f
	4:18	Well-formed love banishes f
Rev	1:17	Don't f: I am First, I am Last
	2:10	F nothing
	11:18	Reward small and great who f your Name
	14:7	F God and give him glory!
	15:4	Who can fail to f you, God
	18:10	for f they'll get burned
	18:15	kept their distance for f
	19:5	All you who f him, small and great

Fear-of-God

2Sa	23:3	who rules in the f
Pr	1:29	had nothing to do with the f
	2:5	F will be yours
	8:13	The F means hating Evil
	9:10	Skilled living gets its start in the F
	10:27	The F expands your life
	14:26	The F builds up confidence
	14:27	The F is a spring of living water
	15:16	A simple life in the F is better
	15:33	F is a school in skilled living
	16:6	F deflects evil
	19:23	F is life itself, a full life
	22:4	payoff for meekness and F is plenty
	23:17	soak yourself in the f
	31:30	woman who lives in the f
Isa	11:2	Spirit that instills knowledge and f
	11:3	F will be all his joy and delight
	33:6	best of all, Zion's treasure, f

Fear-of-the-Lord

Job	28:28	F — that's Wisdom

Feared

Dt	32:27	I f the enemy would grab the chance
1Sa	14:26	the soldiers to a man f the curse
	18:12	Now Saul f David
1Ki	18:3	Obadiah f God — he was very devout
Ne	7:2	he was an honest man and f God
Da	6:26	Daniel's God shall be worshiped and f

Fearful

Lev	26:36	give them over to f timidity
1Sa	7:2	a widespread, f movement toward God
	12:20	Samuel said to them, "Don't be f
	18:15	he himself grew more f
2Sa	6:9	David became f of God that day
1Ki	1:51	Adonijah, f of King Solomon
Isa	35:4	Tell f souls, "Courage! Take heart
Lk	22:2	f of the people
Jn	20:19	f of the Jews, had locked
Ac	5:26	f that the people would riot
Gal	2:12	f he was of the conservative Jewish
1Jn	4:18	fear is crippling, a f life

Fearing

Ge	42:18	I'm a God-f man
1Sa	21:12	he panicked, f the worst from Achish
Job	31:34	f the gossip of the neighbors
Isa	57:1	God-f people are carted off
Da	10:7	ran off and hid, f the worst
Jn	3:20	f a painful exposure
Ac	10:22	God-f man well-known for his fair play
	16:14	known to be a God-f woman
	17:4	among them a great many God-f Greeks
	18:7	Titius Justus, a God-f man
	21:20	thousands of God-f Jews
	26:23	people both godless and God-f

Fearless

2Sa	1:22	Saul's sword was f
Job	5:21	live f through any catastrophe
	11:15	firm grip on life, guiltless and f
	39:22	He laughs at danger, f
Ps	3:6	F before the enemy mobs
	27:1	with him on my side I'm f
	46:2	We stand f at the cliff-edge of doom
	56:4	f now, I trust in God
	56:11	F now, I trust in God
Eze	34:28	live safe and sound, f and free
Joel	2:8	Undaunted and f, unswerving
Na	2:11	Cozy with their cubs, fierce and f
Ac	4:29	give your servants f confidence
	4:31	speak God's Word with f confidence
1Ti	1:18	do this well, f in your struggle
Heb	13:6	God is there, ready to help; I'm f

Fearlessly

Ge	22:12	Now I know how f you fear God

Job	5:22	stroll f among wild animals
Php	1:14	speaking out f about God

Fears

Dt	1:29	I tried to relieve your f
Job	3:25	The worst of my f has come true
Ps	34:4	he freed me from my anxious f
	128:4	how he blesses the one who f God
Ecc	7:18	person who f God deals responsibly
	8:12	reserved for the person who f God
Isa	50:10	Who out there f God, actually listens
	66:4	let you realize your worst f
Jer	42:11	Your f are for nothing
2Co	7:5	the f in our hearts kept us
	12:20	f that when I come you'll disappoint

Fearsome

Dt	8:15	through that huge and f wilderness
2Sa	7:23	performing great and f acts
1Ch	17:21	performing great and f acts
Job	25:2	God is sovereign, God is f
Ps	76:7	Fierce you are, and f!

Feast-of-Booths

Dt	16:13	Observe the F for seven days
	16:16	Feast-of-Weeks, and at the F

Feast-of-Unraised-Bread

Dt	16:16	at the F (Passover)

Feast-of-Weeks

Nu	28:26	offering of new grain to God on your F
Dt	16:10	Celebrate the F to God, your God
	16:16	at the F, and at the Feast-of-Booths

Feeble

Ge	30:42	That way the f animals

Feebler

Ge	30:42	before the f animals

Feeling

Ge	40:6	he noticed that they were f low
Dt	28:29	like a blind person f his way
Jos	20:5	there was no history of ill-f
Jdg	16:25	Everyone was f high
	21:6	were f sorry for Benjamin
2Sa	13:28	well into the sauce and f no pain
Job	3:13	asleep forever, f no pain
Ps	7:10	And I'm f so fit, so safe
	38:6	f sorry for myself morning to night
	107:17	your bodies f the effects of your sin
	119:25	I'm f terrible — I couldn't feel worse
	142:3	spirit ebbing away, you know how I'm f

Isa	9:17	had no f for their orphans and widows
	42:22	f ignored, abandoned
La	3:20	the f of hitting the bottom
Eze	9:10	I'm not f sorry for any of them
Am	6:6	Woe to those addicted to f good
Jn	11:12	get a good rest and wake up f fine
	14:27	f abandoned, bereft
	18:37	who has any f for the truth
Ro	2:17	f smug because you're an insider
	5:5	we're never left f shortchanged
	8:22	We're also f the birth pangs
	11:23	don't get to f superior
Eph	4:19	F no pain, they let themselves go

Feelings

Nu	5:14	f of jealousy come over the husband
	5:30	tormented with f of jealousy
	35:22	there is no history of hard f
Ps	34:5	Never hide your f from him
	64:1	obsessed with f of doomsday
SS	7:5	f I get when I see the high mountain
Jnh	4:10	change your f from pleasure to anger
Mt	12:20	He won't walk over anyone's f
Ac	6:1	hard f developed
1Co	10:33	considerate of everyone's f
Php	1:9	use your head and test your f
Col	3:5	life shaped by things and f
2Pe	3:3	the level of their puny f

Fellowship

1Jn	2:14	Your f with God enables you to gain

Fermented

Ex	13:7	not to be a trace of anything f
	34:25	my sacrifices with anything f

Ferocious

Hab	1:6	Babylonians, fierce and f

Fertility

Ex	34:13	chop down their f poles
Dt	16:21	Don't plant f Asherah trees
Jdg	6:25	chop down the Asherah f pole
1Sa	7:3	foreign gods and f goddesses
	12:10	left God and worshiped the f gods
2Ki	12:3	get rid of the sacred f shrines
	17:32	rites at the local f shrines
	18:4	got rid of the local f shrines
SS	7:13	f surrounds, suffuses us
Isa	17:10	to honor and influence your f gods
	34:11	Chaos! He will cancel f
Eze	6:13	in the lush f groves
	8:14	Tammuz, the Babylonian f god
Mic	1:7	All her sacred f groves burned

Fickle

Job	6:15	my brothers are f as a gulch
Ps	78:8	A f and faithless bunch
Isa	48:8	sorry track record of f attachments
Jer	3:6	how f Israel has visited every hill
	3:8	because of f Israel's loose morals
	3:11	F Israel was a good sight better
	3:12	Turn back, f Israel
	31:22	before you make up your f mind
Hos	9:11	Ephraim is f and scattered
Mk	8:38	your f and unfocused friends
Ac	14:19	turned the f crowd against them
Jas	1:17	nothing two-faced, nothing f

Fickleness

Gal	1:6	I can't believe your f

Fidelity

Ps	89:2	your f has been the roof

Filth

Ps	50:19	Your mouth drools f
	74:23	Don't tune out their malicious f
Isa	9:17	godless and evil, talking f and folly
Eze	20:39	quit throwing f and mud on me
	22:5	infamous in f, notorious for chaos
	23:7	compounded her f with the idols
	24:6	thick with a f that can't be scoured
	24:12	The f is too thick
	24:13	Your encrusted f is your filthy sex
Hos	9:10	took to sin like a pig to f
Ro	1:24	smeared with f, filthy inside and out
2Pe	2:7	the sexual f and perversity
Jude	1:15	have spewed of their pious f

Filthy

Eze	14:11	make themselves f in their rebellions
	16:6	you, lying there helpless and f
	20:7	Don't make yourselves f
	20:18	Don't make yourselves f
	20:26	I abandoned them. F in the gutter
	20:30	You're making your lives f
	20:31	become as f as your no-god idols
	20:43	you've lived that has made you so f
	22:3	no-god idols, making yourself f
	22:4	idol-making, you've become f
	22:15	put a full stop to your f living
	23:13	she also had become incredibly f
	23:30	f with their no-god idols
	24:13	encrusted filth is your f sex
	36:33	scrub you clean from all your f living
Zec	3:4	Get him out of those f clothes
	3:9	I'll strip this land of its f sin
Ro	1:24	smeared with filth, f inside and out
Eph	5:3	promiscuity, f practices, or bullying
Col	3:9	like a f set of ill-fitting clothes

2Pe	2:10	addicted to a f existence
Rev	22:15	outside for good are the f curs

Finance

Est	3:9	royal bank to f the operation
	4:7	royal bank to f the massacre

Finances

1Ch	26:22	supervised the f of the sanctuary
Ac	8:27	minister in charge of all the f

Financial

1Ch	26:20	f affairs of The Temple of God
	26:24	Gershom . . . was the chief f officer
2Ch	8:15	f stewards were kept right

Fire-Gift

Lev	1:9	a Whole-Burnt-Offering, a F
	1:13	a Whole-Burnt-Offering, a F
	1:17	a Whole-Burnt-Offering, a F
	2:2	a F, a pleasing fragrance to God
	2:9	a F, a pleasing fragrance to God
	2:11	never burn any yeast or honey as a F
	2:16	incense as a memorial — a F to God
	3:3	a F to God from the Peace-Offering
	3:5	a F, a pleasing fragrance to God
	3:9	a F to God from the Peace-Offering
	3:11	a meal, a F to God
	3:14	a F to God
	3:16	a meal, a F, a pleasing fragrance
	23:13	a F to God, a pleasing fragrance
	23:25	Offer a F to God
	23:27	fast, and offer a F to God
Nu	15:3	sacrifice a F to God
	15:10	a F, a pleasing fragrance to God
	15:13	a F as a pleasing fragrance to God
	15:14	a F as a pleasing fragrance to God
	15:25	offered to God the F
	18:17	a F, a pleasing fragrance to God
	28:3	the F that you are to present to God
	28:6	a pleasing fragrance, a F to God
	28:8	a F of pleasing fragrance for God
	28:13	a pleasing fragrance, a F to God
	28:19	Bring a F to God
	28:24	Prepare the food this way for the F
	29:6	a pleasing fragrance, a F to God
	29:13	a F of pleasing fragrance to God
	29:36	a F of pleasing fragrance to God
Dt	18:1	They get the F-Offerings of God
Jos	13:14	The F offerings to God

Fire-Gift-Offerings

Dt	18:1	They get the F of God

Firstfruits

Ex	23:16	the f of all your work in the fields

	34:26	Bring the finest of the f
Lev	2:12	an offering of f but not on the Altar
	2:14	a Grain-Offering of f to God
Nu	18:12	offered to God as the f
	18:13	all the f they offer to God
	28:26	Day of F when you bring an offering
Dt	18:4	give them the f of your grain
	26:2	some of all the f of what you grow
	26:10	I've brought the f of what I've grown
2Ch	31:5	f of the grain harvest
Ne	10:35	annually to The Temple of God the f
	12:44	offerings, the f, and the tithes
	13:31	at the appointed times and for the f
Rev	14:4	f of the harvest for God and the Lab

Flatter

Job	41:3	f you with flowery speech
Eze	33:31	They f you with compliments
Zep	3:13	won't use words to f or seduce
Gal	4:17	teachers go to great lengths to f you

Flatterers

Pr	26:28	f sabotage trust

Flatteries

Ac	12:22	shouted f: "The voice of God!

Flattering

Pr	29:5	A f neighbor is up to no good

Flatters

Lk	6:26	saying what f them

Flattery

Pr	28:23	far more than bootlicking f
Mt	23:7	preening in the radiance of public f
Mk	12:38	preening in the radiance of public f
Lk	11:43	yourselves in the radiance of public f
	20:46	preen in the radiance of public f

Flawless

1Sa	3:19	Samuel's prophetic record was f
Ps	51:16	a f performance is nothing to you
SS	4:7	beautiful beyond compare, absolutely f
Mt	13:46	Finding one that is f

Flirt

Hos	3:1	even as they f and party with every god

Flirting

Pr	8:36	you reject me, you're f with death
Jas	4:4	f with the world every chance you get

Focused

1Ch	29:19	an uncluttered and f heart
Job	28:27	He f on Wisdom
Jn	20:27	he f his attention on Thomas
Ro	11:13	f on the so-called outsiders
	15:15	this highly f assignment God gave me
	16:27	All our praise is f through Jesus
2Co	1:12	God who kept us f on him
Eph	1:18	your eyes f and clear
Php	3:15	So let's keep f on that goal
Col	2:2	confident and at rest, f on Christ

Focusing

Ro	8:7	F on the self is the opposite
	8:7	the opposite of f on God
2Pe	1:19	You'll do well to keep f on it

Folly

Pr	17:12	a fool hellbent on f
Isa	9:17	godless and evil, talking filth and f

Fondled

Eze	23:3	Their breasts were f
	23:21	breasts were caressed and f

Fondles

Jer	49:4	f his trophies and dreams of glory

Fondling

Ge	26:8	saw Isaaac f his wife Rebekah

Fool

Dt	6:14	Don't f around with other gods
Jdg	8:6	why should we help you on a f's errand
	8:15	saying that we were on a f's errand
Ru	3:18	that man isn't going to f around
1Sa	13:13	That was a f thing to do
	25:3	The man's name was Nabal (F)
	25:25	the meaning of his name: Nabal, F
	26:21	I've acted the f—a moral dunce
2Sa	6:22	I'll gladly look like a f
1Ki	1:10	not to f around with other gods
2Ki	9:11	What did that crazy f want
	18:29	Don't let Hezekiah f you
2Ch	17:3	didn't f around with the popular Baal
	32:15	Don't let Hezekiah f you
Job	2:10	talking like an empty-headed f
	5:2	temper of a f eventually kills him
Ps	10:10	hapless f is kicked to the ground
	19:12	Or know when we play the f
Pr	6:6	You lazy f, look at an ant
	7:25	Don't f around with a woman like that
	14:1	Sir F comes along and tears it down
	17:10	more than a whack on the head of a f
	17:12	a f hellbent on folly

	17:21	Having a f for a child is misery
	18:6	The words of a f start fights
	26:4	Don't respond to the stupidity of a f
	26:5	Answer a f in simple terms
	26:6	when you send a message by a f
	26:8	Putting a f in a place of honor
	26:10	Hire a f or a drunk
	26:12	far more from a f than from him
	27:3	burden of putting up with a f
	27:22	Pound on a f all you like
	28:26	you're a f for sure
	29:9	trying to work things out with a f
	29:11	A f lets it all hang out
	30:22	when a f gets rich
Ecc	2:15	my fate's the same as the f's
	4:5	The f sits back and takes it easy
	5:3	Over-talk shows you up as a f
	6:8	what advantage has a sage over a f
	7:9	spot a f by the lumps on his head
	10:12	talk of a f self-destructs
Isa	19:15	a senile, doddering old f
	41:24	sham gods, no-gods, f-making gods
Jer	17:11	What a f he'll look like then
	18:16	a f's memorial to be spit on
	44:4	don't f around in this loathsome
Hos	10:6	Ephraim makes a f of himself
Am	5:5	Don't f around at those shrines
Lk	12:20	F! Tonight you die
	19:22	you've acted the f
1Co	3:18	Don't f yourself
	3:19	Be God's f—that's the path
	15:33	But don't f yourselves
2Co	11:19	afford to humor an occasional f
	11:21	your old friend, the f, talking
	12:6	anything other than the f
	12:11	I've made a complete f of myself
Gal	6:7	No one makes a f of God
Jas	1:22	Don't f yourself

Fool-making

Isa	41:24	sham gods, no-gods, f gods

Fooled

Ac	15:8	God, who can't be f by any pretense
	25:11	We've f around here long enough
Ro	7:9	I was f, and fell for it

Fooling

Dt	31:20	f around with other gods
Jos	24:19	won't put up with your f around
1Sa	15:23	far worse than f around in the occult
Isa	1:29	All that f around in god and goddess
1Jn	1:8	we're only f ourselves

Foolish

Nu	12:11	this f and thoughtless sin
1Sa	14:24	Saul did something really f that day
2Ch	16:9	You were f to go for human help

Ps	35:4	make them look f
Pr	5:23	your f decisions trap you
	13:1	f children do their own thing
	14:18	F dreamers live in a world of illusion
	26:4	you'll only look f yourself
Ecc	4:13	f king who doesn't know which end
	5:4	God takes no pleasure in f gabble
Isa	1:29	will leave you looking mighty f
Jer	10:14	Stick-god worshipers looking mighty f
	51:17	Stick-god worshipers look mighty f
Lk	14:29	you're going to look pretty f
2Co	11:1	Will you put up with a little f aside
	11:16	if I continue to sound a little f

Foolishness

1Sa	25:25	Nabal, Fool. F oozes from him
2Sa	15:31	turn Ahithophel's counsel to f
Pr	14:8	the f of fools lands them in the ditch
	22:15	Young people are prone to f and fads
	27:22	you can't pound out f
Ecc	7:25	identify evil and stupidity, f
	10:1	a little f decomposes much wisdom
Mk	7:22	mean looks, slander, arrogance, f

Fools

Job	5:3	f putting down roots
	12:17	exposes judges as witless f
Ps	44:20	made f of ourselves
	49:10	wiped out right along with f
	85:8	they'll never again live like f
	92:6	f never do get it
	94:8	think again, you idiots, f
Pr	1:7	f thumb their noses at such wisdom
	10:18	f openly spread slander
	12:15	F are headstrong
	12:16	F have short fuses and explode
	12.23	talkative f broadcast their silliness
	13:16	f litter the country with silliness
	13:19	f bent on evil despise matters of soul
	13:20	hang out with f and watch your life
	14:7	Escape quickly from the company of f
	14:8	foolishness of f lands them in
	14:16	f are headstrong and reckless
	14:24	f get stupider by the day
	14:33	f never even get to say hello
	15:2	f are leaky faucets, dripping nonsense
	15:7	f are hollow
	15:14	f feed on fast-food fads
	16:22	f sweat it out the hard way
	17:7	don't expect eloquence from f
	17:16	F out shopping for wisdom
	17:24	f look for it everywhere
	18:2	F care nothing for thoughtful
	18:7	F are undone by their big mouths
	19:29	slap in the face brings f to attention
	20:3	f love to pick fights
	21:20	f put it all out for yard sales
	23:9	Don't bother talking sense to f
	24:7	way over the head of f
	24:9	F incubate sin

	26:1	We no more give honors to f
	26:3	a stick for the back of f
	26:7	A proverb quoted by f is limp
	26:11	f recycle silliness
	31:4	can't afford to make f of themselves
Ecc	7:4	F waste their lives in fun
	7:5	the song and dance of f
	7:6	giggles of f are like
	9:17	the ranting of a king of f
	10:3	F on the road have no sense
	10:14	F talk way too much
	10:15	A decent day's work so fatigues f
Isa	19:11	The princes of Zoan are f
	19:13	the princes of Zoan are all f
	29:14	will be exposed as f
	32:5	No more will f become celebrities
	32:6	For f are f and that's that
	35:8	Not even f can get lost on it
Jer	4:22	What f my people are!
	17:13	All who leave you end up as f
	20:12	God-of-the-Angel-Armies, no one f you
	23:13	I saw prophets acting like silly f
	50:36	boasting pretenders, f one and all
Lk	19:21	don't suffer f gladly
	19:22	I don't suffer f gladly
1Pe	2:15	f who think you're a danger

Forbid

1Sa	24:6	God f that I should have done this
	26:11	God f that I should lay a finger
Ps	78:8	f they should be like their parents
Jer	40:16	Don't do it. I f it
Lk	18:11	heaven f, like this tax man

Forbidden

Dt	7:26	No: It is f! Hate it.
Jos	7:11	they've taken f plunder
1Ki	12:31	Jeroboam built f shrines
	13:33	recruiting priests for the f shrines
2Ki	12:7	You are f to take any more money
Est	4:16	go to the king, even though it's f
Isa	65:4	Eat f foods and drink a witch's brew
Eze	4:14	I've never eaten anything f by law
Ro	7:8	making a piece of "f fruit" out of it
1Co	9:7	Are gardeners f to eat vegetables
2Co	12:3	was f to tell what he heard

Forbidding

Da	6:12	decree f anyone to pray to any god
Mk	3:12	f them to identify him in public
Lk	23:2	f taxes to be paid to Caesar

Forecast

Mic	5:7	Not mentioned in the weather f
Mt	13:14	don't want Isaiah's f repeated
	16:3	find it easy enough to f the weather

Foreclose

Ps	109:11	May the bank f and wipe him out
Pr	13:23	Banks f on the farms of the poor

Forgave

Ps	78:38	God? Compassionate! F the sin!
Mt	18:32	I f your entire debt when you begged
Eph	4:32	thoroughly as God in Christ f you
Col	3:13	completely as the Master f you

Forgive

Ge	50:17	Tell Joseph, 'F your brothers' sin
Ex	32:32	if you will only f their sin
	34:9	F our iniquity and sin
Nu	14:19	f the wrongdoing of this people
	14:20	God said, "I f them
1Sa	25:28	F my presumption
2Sa	24:10	now God f my guilt
1Ki	8:30	and when you hear, f
	8:34	f the sin of your people Israel
	8:36	f the sins of your servants
	8:50	F your people who have sinned
2Ki	5:18	see to it that God f me for this
1Ch	21:8	f my sin — I've been really stupid
2Ch	6:21	and when you hear, f
	6:25	f the sin of your people Israel
	6:27	f the sins of your servants
	6:30	f and reward us
	6:39	F your people who have sinned
	7:14	I'll listen from heaven, f their sins
	30:18	May God who is all good, pardon and f
Ne	4:5	don't f their iniquity
	5:11	f your claims on their money
Job	7:21	Why don't you just f my sins
	42:6	I'm sorry — f me
Ps	25:11	God; F my bad life
	79:9	out of this mess, f us our sins
Pr	19:11	their grandeur is to f and forget
Jer	5:1	I want to f that person
	33:8	f everything they've done wrong, f
	36:3	let me f their perversity and sin
Da	9:19	Master, f us!
Joel	3:21	I haven't already forgiven, I'll f
Mt	9:2	Cheer up, son. I f your sins
	9:5	I f your sins
	12:32	the Holy Spirit can f you
	18:21	how many times do I f
	18:35	f unconditionally anyone who asks
Mk	2:5	Son, I f your sins
	2:7	God and only God can f sins
	2:9	I f your sins
	11:25	against someone, f
Lk	5:20	Friend, I f your sins
	5:21	God and only God can f sins
	5:23	I f your sins
	7:48	I f your sins
	17:3	If he responds, f him
	17:4	sorry, I won't do it again,' f him
	18:13	God, give mercy. F me, a sinner

	23:34	Jesus prayed, "Father, f them
Jn	20:23	If you f someone's sins
Ac	8:22	Ask the Master to f you
2Co	2:7	Now is the time to f this man
	2:10	So if you f him, I f him
	12:13	I'm sorry. F me for depriving you
Eph	4:32	F one another as quickly
Col	3:13	quick to f an offense. F as quickly
Tit	2:11	God's readiness to give and f
1Jn	1:9	He'll f our sins and purge us

Forgiven

Lev	4:20	atonement for them and they are f
	4:26	on account of his sin and he's f
	4:31	atonement for him and he's f
	4:35	on account of his sin and he's f
	5:10	atonement for your sin and you're f
	5:13	sins you've committed and you're f
	5:16	Compensation-Offering and he's f
	5:18	that he was unaware of and he's f
	6:7	he's f of any of the things
	19:22	stand f of the sin he committed
Nu	15:25	they will stand f
Isa	40:2	her sin is taken care of — f
La	3:42	you haven't f
Joel	3:21	The sins I haven't already f
Mt	6:12	Keep us f with you
	12:31	nothing done or said that can't be f
Mk	3:28	nothing done or said that can't be f
	4:12	about-face and getting f
Lk	7:43	the one who was f the most
	7:47	She was f many, many sins
	11:4	Keep us f with you
Ac	2:38	so your sins are f
	5:31	gift of a changed life and sins f
	26:18	to present my offer of sins f
1Co	5:5	on his feet and f before the Master
Col	2:13	Think of it! All sins f
Heb	8:12	get to know me by being kindly f
Jas	5:15	if you've sinned, you'll be f
1Jn	2:12	Your sins are f in Jesus' name

Forgiveness

Ps	130:4	f is your habit
Isa	55:7	our God, who is lavish with f
Hos	1:6	run out of mercy. There's no more f
Jnh	4:2	punishment into a program of f
Mt	6:14	You can't get f from God
	26:28	for many people for the f of sins
Mk	1:4	life-change that leads to f of sins
Lk	1:77	the f of their sins
	3:3	life-change leading to f of sins
	7:47	f is minimal, the gratitude is minimal
	24:47	life-change through the f of sins
Ac	10:43	he is the means to f of sins
	13:38	f of your sins can be promised
Ro	5:20	the aggressive f we call grace
2Co	2:10	joining in with your f
	5:19	fresh start by offering f of sins

Gal	6:1	might be needing f
Heb	9:22	especially regarding f of sins

Forgives

2Sa	12:13	God f your sin
Ps	103:3	He f your sins — every one
Mt	12:31	repudiating the very One who f
	12:32	connection with the One who f
Mk	3:29	repudiating the very One who f
Jn	1:30	He f the sins of the world!

Forgiving

Ex	34:7	f iniquity, rebellion, and sin
Nu	14:18	f iniquity and rebellion and sin
	14:19	you have been f this people
Ne	9:17	you, a f God, gracious
Ps	86:5	You're well-known as good and f
Isa	2:9	They're not worth f
Mt	6:12	Keep us forgiven with you and f others
	6:14	without also f others
	18:17	offer again God's f love
Lk	7:49	Who does he think he is, f sins
	11:4	Keep us forgiven with you and f others
Ro	6:1	Keep on sinning so God can keep on f

Forgivingly

Gal	6:1	someone falls into sin, f restore him

Fornicate

Isa	57:5	f at whim
Eze	16:28	You went on to f with the Assyrians

Fornicated

Eze	16:26	You f with the Egyptians
	23:17	f with her, made her dirty

Fornicating

Eze	22:9	sex shrines and f unrestrained

Fornication

Eze	23:18	Then she went public with her f

Fornications

Mt	15:19	adulteries, f, thefts, lies
Rev	17:4	defiling obscenities, her foul f

Fornicators

Rev	22:15	filthy curs: sorcerers, f, murderers

Forsake

Jos	24:16	answered, "We'd never f God

Forsaken

Isa	62:12	God-Redeemed, Sought-Out, City-Not-F
Eze	8:12	God has f the country
	9:9	God has f the country

Fortune

Ge	35:18	named him Ben-jamin (Son-of-Good-F
Jdg	17:8	seeking his f
1Ch	29:3	turning over my personal f
Job	42:10	God restored his f
Ps	49:16	get rich and pile up fame and f
	49:17	fame and f all get left behind
	78:4	God's fame and f
	126:2	we couldn't believe our good f
Mk	6:37	You want us to go spend a f on food
Ac	13:48	could hardly believe their good f
3Jn	1:2	I pray for good f in everything you do

Fortune-hunting

Pr	31:3	f women, promiscuous women

Fortunes

Job	8:6	reestablish your f
Eze	16:53	reverse their f, the f of Sodom

Fortunetellers

Isa	8:19	Try out the f
	44:25	turns f into jokes
Jer	27:9	prophets and spiritualists and f
Da	2:2	f to interpret his dreams for him
	2:4	f, speaking in the Aramaic language
	2:5	The king answered the f
	2:10	f said, "Nobody anywhere can do
	3:8	Babylonian f stepped up and accused
	4:7	magicians, enchanters, f, witches
	5:7	enchanters, the f, and the diviners
	5:11	magicians, enchanters, f, and diviners

Fortunetelling

Dt	18:10	Don't practice divination, sorcery, f
2Ki	21:6	He practiced black magic and f
2Ch	33:6	He practiced witchcraft and f
Da	1:4	the lore of magic and f
Ac	16:16	with her f, made a lot of money

Fragile

2Ki	19:26	Useless as weeds, f as grass
Job	4:19	bodies composed of mud, f as moths
	14:3	occupy your time with such f wisps
Ecc	12:5	f and impotent matchstick body
Isa	40:6	their love f as wildflowers
	41:14	Feel like a f insect, Israel
Eze	16:7	naked and vulnerable, f and exposed
Rev	2:27	their resistance f as clay pots

F

Fragrance

Ge	8:21	God smelled the sweet **f**
Ex	29:18	Offering to God, a pleasant **f**
	29:25	a pleasing **f** before God
	29:41	a pleasing **f**, a gift to God
Lev	1:9	a Fire-Gift, a pleasing **f** to God
	1:13	a Fire-Gift, a pleasing **f** to God
	1:17	a Fire-Gift, a pleasing **f** to God
	2:2	a Fire-Gift, a pleasing **f** to God
	2:9	a Fire-Gift, a pleasing **f** to God
	2:12	not on the Altar as a pleasing **f**
	3:5	a Fire-Gift, a pleasing **f** to God
	3:16	a Fire-Gift, a pleasing **f**
	4:31	on the Altar for a pleasing **f** to God
	6:15	on the Altar, a pleasing **f** to God
	6:21	as a pleasing **f** to God
	8:21	a pleasing **f** — a gift to God
	8:28	a pleasing **f** to God
	17:6	a pleasing **f** to God
	23:13	a Fire-Gift to God, a pleasing **f**
	23:18	Fire-Gifts, a pleasing **f** to God
Nu	15:3	as a pleasing **f** for God
	15:7	Present it as a pleasing **f** to God
	15:10	a Fire-Gift, a pleasing **f** to God
	15:13	a Fire-Gift as a pleasing **f** to God
	15:14	a Fire-Gift as a pleasing **f** to God
	15:24	Offering, a pleasing **f** to God
	18:17	a Fire-Gift, a pleasing **f** to God
	28:2	my Fire-Gifts of pleasing **f**
	28:6	a pleasing **f**, a Fire-Gift to God
	28:8	a Fire-Gift of pleasing **f** for God
	28:13	a pleasing **f**, a Fire-Gift to God
	28:24	the Fire-Gift, a pleasing **f** to God
	28:27	lambs as a pleasing **f** to God
	29:2	a pleasing **f** to God
	29:6	a pleasing **f**, a Fire-Gift to God
	29:8	Offering to God as a pleasing **f**
	29:13	a Fire-Gift of pleasing **f** to God
	29:36	a Fire-Gift of pleasing **f** to God
Ps	66:15	Even the **f** of roasted lamb
Pr	27:9	lotions and **f** give sensual delight
SS	1:12	my **f** filled the room
	4:10	your **f** more exotic than select spices
	4:16	fill the air with spice **f**
	5:1	breathed the sweet **f**
	7:13	Love-apples drench us with **f**,
Hos	14:6	his **f** like a grove of cedars
Jn	12:3	The **f** of the oils filled the house
2Co	2:14	people breathe in the exquisite **f**
Php	4:18	filling the air with **f**, pleasing God
Heb	10:6	It's not **f** and smoke from the altar

Fragrances

Pr	7:17	aromatic with spices and exotic **f**

Fragrant

Ex	25:6	for anointing oils and for **f** incense
	30:7	Aaron will burn **f** incense
	30:23	**f** cinnamon
	30:34	Take **f** spices — gum resin
	35:8	for anointing oils and for **f** incense
	35:15	the anointing oil, the **f** incense
	39:38	anointing oil **f** incense screen
	40:27	burned **f** incense on it
Lev	4:7	the Altar of **F** Incense before God
Nu	4:16	the **f** incense
1Ki	10:11	loads of **f** sandalwood
2Ch	9:10	**f** sandalwood and expensive gems
Ps	45:7	God, poured **f** oil on your head
	45:8	garments are **f** with mountain breeze
SS	1:17	enclosed by cypresses, **f** and green
	2:13	cherry trees **f** with blossoms
	4:6	The sweet, **f** curves of your body
Eze	8:11	incense rising in a **f** cloud
Heb	1:9	God, poured **f** oil on your head

Frail

Ge	33:13	can see that the children are **f**
Pr	30:25	**f** as they are, get plenty of food

Frailties

1Co	4:10	we live in the midst of **f**

Frantic

Da	12:4	a lot of **f** running around

Frantically

1Ki	22:25	when you're **f** and futilely looking
2Ch	18:24	when you're **f** and futilely looking

Fraud

Job	15:5	You chose an education in **f**
Jer	3:24	The **F** picked us clean
	50:2	god-Marduk exposed as a **f**
	51:47	the whole country as a sickening **f**
Hos	12:7	businessmen engage in wholesale **f**
	12:8	not a hint of **f**, not a sign of sin
Mic	6:10	piled up by cheating and **f**
Zec	10:11	bully Egypt exposed as a **f**

Frauds

Job	32:15	You're total **f**
Ps	119:78	tricksters be exposed as **f**
Jer	10:14	Their gods are **f** — dead sticks
	50:2	all her play-gods exposed as cheap **f**
	51:17	Their gods are **f**, dead sticks
Jnh	2:8	worship hollow gods, god-**f**
Mt	15:7	**F**! Isaiah's prophecy of you
	23:13	religion scholars, you Pharisees! **F**
	23:15	religion scholars and Pharisees! **F**
	23:23	religion scholars and Pharisees! **F**
	23:25	religion scholars and Pharisees! **F**
	23:27	religion scholars and Pharisees! **F**
	23:28	beneath the skin you're total **f**
	23:29	religion scholars and Pharisees! **F**

F

Mk	7:6	Isaiah was right about f like you
Lk	11:42	You're hopeless, you Pharisees! F
	11:43	You're hopeless, you Pharisees! F
	11:44	F! You're just like unmarked graves
	12:56	F! You know how to tell a change
	13:15	You f! Each Sabbath every one of you
Eph	5:13	Rip the cover off those f
2Ti	3:8	old Egyptian f Jannes and Jambres

Freedom

Ge	49:15	gave up his f and went to work
Ex	21:5	I don't want my f
Lev	19:20	not yet been ransomed or given her f
	25:10	Proclaim f all over the land
Ps	34:22	God pays for each slave's f
	68:6	leads prisoners to f
Pr	12:24	The diligent find f in their work
Isa	61:1	Announce f to all captives
Jer	34:8	people of Jerusalem to decree f
	34:15	decreeing f for your brothers
Jn	18:40	Barabbas was a Jewish f fighter
Ro	6:14	You're living in the f of God
	6:15	we're free in the f of God
	6:16	acts of so-called f that destroy f
	6:18	free to live openly in his f
	6:19	I'm using this f language
	7:6	a new life in the f of God
1Co	7:21	If you have a chance at f, go ahead
	7:22	experience a marvelous f
	8:9	when you use your f carelessly
	8:10	flaunt your f
	10:32	don't be callous in your exercise of f
2Co	11:20	impostors who rob your f
Gal	5:2	Christ's hard-won gift of f
	5:13	don't use this f as an excuse
	5:14	That's an act of true f
	5:15	where will your precious f be then
	5:21	If you use your f this way
1Pe	2:16	Exercise your f by serving God
2Pe	2:19	They promise these newcomers f

Freeing

Dt	30:6	f you to love God, your God
1Sa	14:48	f Israel from the savagery and looting
Est	9:16	f themselves from oppression
Ps	18:46	my free and f God
Lk	2:38	for the f of Jerusalem
Ro	8:2	f you from a fated lifetime
Heb	9:15	f us from all those dead-end efforts

Freeloaders

1Th	2:10	God knows we weren't f
	5:14	warn the f to get a move on

Freeloading

2Th	3:14	refuse to subsidize his f

Freewill

Ex	36:3	bringing in their f offerings
Lev	7:16	a Votive-Offering or a F-Offering
	22:18	or as a F-Offering
	22:21	or as a F-Offering
	22:23	deformed or stunted as a F-Offering
	23:38	F-Offerings you give to God
Nu	15:3	or F-Offering at one
	29:39	Vow-Offerings and F-Offerings
Dt	12:6	Vow-Offerings, your F-Offerings
	12:17	nor your F-Offerings
	16:10	F-Offering — give as generously
2Ki	12:4	mandatory offerings and f offerings
2Ch	31:14	in charge of the F-Offerings of God
Ezr	1:4	F-Offerings for The Temple of God
	1:6	over and above these, F-Offerings
	2:68	F-Offerings toward the rebuilding
	3:5	F-Offerings for God
	8:28	F-Offerings to the God
Eze	46:12	prince brings a f offering to God
Am	4:5	announce f offerings

Frenzy

Isa	1:11	Why this f of sacrifices?
	49:26	a f of self-destruction
Hos	7:5	the f of the mocking mob
Jn	19:6	they shouted in a f, "Crucify
Ac	19:28	That set them off in a f

Fret

Php	4:6	Don't f or worry

Fretting

Da	12:13	Go about your business without f

Friend

Ge	38:12	Judah with his f Hirah
	38:20	by his f from Adullam
Ex	32:27	Kill brother, f, neighbor
Lev	19:13	Don't exploit your f or rob him
Dt	13:6	even your dear wife or lifelong f
Jdg	7:13	hear a man tell his f a dream
	7:14	His f said, "This has to be the sword
Ru	4:1	"Step aside, old f," said Boaz
1Sa	18:1	David's number-one advocate and f
	20:14	continue to be my covenant f
	20:41	wept, f over f
2Sa	13:3	Amnon had a good f, Jonadab
	15:37	Hushai, David's f, arrived
	16:16	Hushai the Arkite, David's f
	16:17	show devotion to your good f
	16:17	Why didn't you go with your f
1Ki	4:5	priest and f to the king
	9:13	What kind of reward is this, my f
1Ch	27:33	Hushai the Arkite was the king's f
2Ch	20:7	the descendants of Abraham your f
Job	1:8	Have you noticed my f Job

F

	2:3	Have you noticed my f Job
	16:20	My Champion, my F
	42:8	go to my f Job
Ps	15:3	Don't hurt your f
	35:14	like I'd lost my best f
	41:9	my best f, the one I always told
	55:13	You! My best f
	55:20	my best f, betrayed his best friends
	88:18	only f I have left is Darkness
	119:63	f and companion of all who fear you
Pr	1:8	Pay close attention, f
	1:10	Dear f, if bad companions tempt you
	1:15	Oh, f, don't give them a second look
	2:1	f, take to heart what I'm telling
	2:10	Lady Wisdom will be your close f
	3:1	Good f, don't forget all I've taught
	3:11	don't, dear f, resent God's discipline
	3:21	Dear f, guard Clear Thinking
	4:10	Dear f, take my advice
	4:20	Dear f, listen well
	5:1	Dear f, pay close attention
	5:7	So, my f, listen closely
	6:1	Dear f, if you've gone into hock
	6:3	F, don't waste a minute
	6:20	f, follow your father's good advice
	7:1	Dear f, do what I tell you
	18:19	Do a favor and win a f forever
	18:24	a true f sticks by you like family
	19:6	everyone's a f to the philanthropist
	25:12	a wise f's timely reprimand
	25:17	when you find a f, don't outwear
	25:25	a letter from a long-lost f
	26:24	greets you like an old f
	27:14	wake your f in the early morning
	27:17	one f sharpens another
	28:8	some f of the poor is going to give
Ecc	4:12	With a f you can face the worst
	12:12	anything beyond this, dear f, go easy
SS	1:15	Oh, my dear f! You're so beautiful
	2:2	that's my dear f among the girls
	2:10	my dear f, fair and beautiful lover
	2:13	dear f, my fair and beautiful lover
	4:9	You've captured my heart, dear f
	4:10	How beautiful your love, dear, dear f
	4:12	Dear lover and f
	5:1	dear f, best lover
	5:2	dear companion, dearest f
	6:4	Dear, dear f and lover
Isa	41:8	descendants of my good f Abraham
Jer	9:4	F against f spreads malicious gossip
Da	10:19	Don't be afraid, f. Peace
Am	5:14	being your best f
Mic	7:5	don't confide in your f
Zec	13:6	I ran into a door at a f's house
Mt	5:23	a grudge a f has against you
	5:24	go to this f and make things right
	5:43	old written law, 'Love your f,'
	11:19	a f of the riff-raff
	18:15	If he listens, you've made a f
	20:13	F, I haven't been unfair
	22:12	F, how dare you come in here
	26:50	F, why this charade?

Lk	5:20	F, I forgive your sins
	11:5	went to a f in the middle of the night
	11:6	f traveling through just showed up
	11:7	f answers from his bed, 'Don't bother
	11:8	won't get up because he's a f
	14:10	F, come up to the front
	17:3	If you see your f going wrong, correct
	24:17	like they had lost their best f
Jn	3:29	the bridegroom's f, his 'best man'
	11:11	Our f Lazarus has fallen asleep
	14:16	he'll provide you another F
	14:17	This F is the Spirit of Truth
	14:26	The F, the Holy Spirit
	15:26	the F I plan to send you
	16:7	If I don't leave, the F won't come
	16:13	the F comes, the Spirit of the Truth
	19:12	you're no f of Caesar's
Ro	16:1	welcome our f Phoebe
	16:5	Hello to my dear f Epenetus
	16:8	my good f in the family of God
	16:9	my good f Stachys
	16:12	a dear f and hard worker in Christ
	16:23	our good f Quartus
1Co	1:1	along with my f Sosthenes
	4:21	as a good f and counselor
	7:36	a woman f to whom he is loyal
	8:11	if you hurt your f terribly
	8:12	When you hurt your f, you hurt Christ
	16:12	About our f Apollos
2Co	5:20	God; he's already a f
	8:22	sending another trusted f along
	11:21	this is your old f, the fool, talking
Eph	6:21	Tychicus, my good f here
Php	2:25	my good f and companion in my work
Col	1:1	Together with my f Timothy
	1:7	you learned it from our f
	4:7	My good f Tychicus will tell you
	4:14	Luke, good f and physician
Phm	1:1	my good f and companion in this work
	1:7	F, you have no idea how good your love
	1:20	Do me this big favor, f
Jas	2:15	come upon an old f dressed in rags
	2:16	Good morning, f! Be clothed in Christ
	2:23	got Abraham named "God's f
1Jn	2:1	we have a Priest-F . . .: Jesus
3Jn	1:1	my good f Gaius: How truly I love
	1:5	Dear f, when you extend hospitality
	1:11	F, don't go along with evil

Friendless

| Am | 7:17 | You will die homeless and f |
| Heb | 11:37 | homeless, f, powerless |

Friendliness

| 2Pe | 1:7 | warm f, and generous love |

Friendly

| Ge | 26:29 | that we maintain f relations |
| Dt | 2:26 | They carried a f message |

2Sa	3:25	This was no **f** visit
Ps	69:20	looked in vain for one **f** face
	122:7	**F** insiders, get along!
Zec	3:10	**f** visits across the fence, **f**
Mt	9:15	throws cold water on a **f** bonfire
Mk	2:19	throws cold water on a **f** bonfire
Lk	5:35	throws cold water on a **f** bonfire
Ac	19:31	who had become **f** to Paul
	28:2	went out of their way to be **f** to us
Ro	5:10	we were put on **f** terms with God

Friends

Ge	19:2	Please, my **f**, come to my house
	26:31	they parted as **f**
	29:4	Hello **f**. Where are you from?
	34:21	they are our **f**
Jos	22:8	Share the wealth with your **f**
Jdg	11:37	I will never marry, I and my dear **f**
	14:11	arranged for thirty **f** to mingle
1Sa	2:9	protectively cares for his faithful **f**
	8:14	hand them over to his special **f**
	20:3	knows that we are the best of **f**
2Sa	3:8	all his family and **f**
1Ki	16:11	so many stray dogs — relatives and **f**
2Ki	9:37	Old **f** and lovers will say
	10:11	leaders, **f**, priests
Est	5:10	He got his **f** together with his wife
	5:14	His wife Zeresh and all his **f** said
	6:13	telling . . . all his **f** everything
Job	2:11	Job's **f** heard of all the trouble
	5:23	wild animals will become your good **f**
	6:14	give up on God Almighty, their **f**
	6:21	you, my so-called **f**
	6:27	Are **f** just items of profit and loss
	7:10	never again will **f** drop in
	12:4	I'm ridiculed by my **f**
	17:5	Those who betray their own **f**
	18:3	treat your **f** like slow-witted animals
	19:14	My relatives and **f** have all left
	19:21	Oh, **f**, dear **f**, take pity on me
	29:7	sat with my **f** in the public square
	32:1	Job's three **f** now fell silent
	32:3	angry with the three **f**
	34:2	So, my fine **f** — listen to me
	35:4	neither you nor your **f**
	35:8	your family and **f** and neighbors
	42:7	I've had it with you and your two **f**
	42:10	After Job had interceded for his **f**
	42:11	his brothers and sisters and **f** came
Ps	7:4	betrayed my **f**, ripped off my enemies
	12:1	All the **f** I depended on gone
	16:3	what splendid **f** they make
	22:22	Here's the story I'll tell my **f**
	31:11	My **f** are horrified
	34:15	God keeps an eye on his **f**
	36:10	Keep on loving your **f**
	37:28	never turns away from his **f**
	38:11	old **f** avoid me like the plague
	41:7	These "**f**" who hate me whisper slanders
	50:11	scampering field mice are my **f**
	50:16	talking like we are good **f**

	50:18	adulterers are your **f** of choice
	52:9	in company with your faithful **f**
	55:20	betrayed his best **f**
	58:10	righteous will call up their **f**
	63:11	his true **f** spread the joy
	69:22	May their best **f** be trappers
	77:2	**f** said, "Everything will turn out
	78:1	Listen, dear **f**, to God's truth
	80:6	You make us look ridiculous to our **f**
	88:8	You turned my **f** against me
	122:8	For the sake of my family and **f**
	148:14	intimate **f** of God
Pr	2:16	Wise **f** will rescue you
	3:13	when you make **f** with Madame Insight
	4:1	Listen, **f**, to some fatherly advice
	7:24	So, **f**, listen to me
	8:32	So, my dear **f**, listen carefully
	14:10	who shuns the bitter moments of **f**
	16:29	betray their very own **f**
	17:17	**F** love through all kinds of weather
	18:24	**F** come and **f** go, but a true friend
	19:4	Wealth attracts **f** as honey draws flies
	19:7	even your best **f** wish you'd get lost
	21:10	feel nothing for **f** and neighbors
	25:13	Reliable **f** who do what they say
	27:10	Don't leave your **f** or your parents' **f**
Ecc	4:8	no children, no family, no **f**
	12:5	your **f** make plans for your funeral
SS	5:1	Celebrate with me, **f**!
	6:9	the neighbors and **f**, blessed
	8:13	my **f** are with me listening
Isa	26:19	But **f**, your dead will live
	28:22	Sober up, **f**, and don't scoff
	38:11	no more rubbing shoulders with **f**
	47:15	That's the fate of your **f** in sorcery
	51:18	no one among your **f** or children
Jer	6:21	parents and children, neighbors and **f**
	9:20	your **f** the songs of heartbreak
	12:2	talk as if they're old **f** with you
	18:21	their **f** die
	19:9	eat one another, family and **f** alike
	20:4	All your **f** are going to get killed
	20:10	Old **f** watch, hoping I'll fall flat
	22:22	all your **f** end up in exile
	26:19	**F**, we're at the brink
	30:14	fair-weather **f** have skipped town
	38:22	those so-called **f** of yours
	48:17	Weep for Moab, **f** and neighbors
La	1:2	Her **f** have all dumped her
	1:19	I called to my **f**; they betrayed me
	2:22	You invited, like **f** to a party
Da	10:8	abandoned by my **f**, I went weak
Hos	9:10	in the mud with their newfound **f**
Ob	1:7	Your old **f** will lie to your face
Mic	7:12	old **f** and family from faraway places
Na	3:9	Put and Libya, strong **f**
Zec	3:8	both you and your **f** sitting here
	3:8	with you, for your **f**
Mt	24:49	throwing drunken parties for his **f**
Mk	3:21	His **f** heard what was going on
	8:38	your fickle and unfocused **f**
Lk	7:6	the captain sent **f** to tell him

F

	12:4	I'm speaking to you as dear f		28:23	home with a number of their f
	12:32	You're my dearest f!	Ro	1:1	all the Christians in Rome, God's f
	12:45	throws parties for his f		1:13	my failure to visit you, f
	14:12	don't just invite your f and family		7:1	any trouble understanding this, f
	15:2	treating them like old f		7:4	So, my f, this is something
	15:6	call in your f and neighbors		10:1	Believe me, f, all I want for Israel
	15:9	she'll call her f and neighbors		11:25	on the table as clearly as I can, f
	15:29	thrown a party for me and my f		11:28	they remain God's oldest f
	16:21	His best f were the dogs		12:10	Be good f who love deeply
	21:16	brothers, relatives, and f		12:15	Laugh with your happy f
	24:24	Some of our f went off to the tomb		12:16	Make f with nobodies
	24:33	the Eleven and their f gathered		15:15	So, my dear f, don't take my
Jn	11:31	Jewish f saw Mary run off		15:30	one request, dear f: Pray for me
	15:13	Put your life on the line for your f		16:17	One final word of counsel, f
	15:14	You are my f when you do the things	1Co	1:10	concern to bring up with you, my f
	15:15	named you f because I've let you		1:26	Take a good look, f, at who you were
Ac	1:16	F, long ago the Holy Spirit spoke		2:1	remember, f, that when I first came
	2:29	Dear f, let me be completely frank		3:1	now, f, I'm completely frustrated
	3:17	f, I know you had no idea		4:6	All I'm doing right now, f, is showing
	4:23	they went to their f and told them		5:11	flip with God or rude to f
	6:3	So, f, choose seven men		7:24	F, stay where you were called to be
	7:2	F, fathers, and brothers		7:29	f, . . . time is of the essence
	7:26	F, you are brothers, why are		10:1	Remember our history, f, and be warned
	9:30	When his f learned of the plot		10:14	So, my very dear f, when you see
	9:37	Her f prepared her body for burial		11:33	So, my f, when you come together
	9:39	Her old f, most of them widows		14:6	Think, f: If I come to you
	10:24	relatives and close f waiting with him		15:1	F, let me go over the Message
	10:47	baptizing these f with water		15:50	f, . . . our natural, earthy lives
	11:1	leaders and f back in Jerusalem heard		15:58	my dear, dear f, stand your ground
	11:12	went with them, I and six f		16:11	him, and any f he has with him
	12:12	house was packed with praying f		16:15	Would you do me a favor, f
	13:15	F, do you have anything you want		16:20	All the f here say hello
	13:16	Fellow Israelites and f of God	2Co	1:8	We don't want you in the dark, f
	13:26	children of Abraham, and f of God		2:3	disappointing the very f I had
	13:38	I want you to know, my very dear f		5:20	Become f with God
	15:7	F, you well know that from early on		6:14	Is light best f with dark
	15:13	F, listen		7:1	promises . . . to pull us on, dear f
	15:23	your f, to our f in Antioch		8:1	Now, f, I want to report
	15:25	our good f Barnabas and Paul		11:26	struggle with f, struggle with foes
	15:32	strengthened their new f		13:11	f. Be cheerful
	15:33	sent off by their new f	Gal	1:11	I am most emphatic here, f
	15:36	go back and visit all our f		2:12	himself and his non-Jewish f
	15:40	offered up by their f to the grace		3:15	F, let me give you an example
	16:2	F in Lystra and Iconium all said		4:12	My dear f, what I would really like
	16:40	saw their f again		4:28	Isn't it clear, f, that you
	17:6	collared Jason and his f instead		6:1	Live creatively, f
	17:9	made Jason and his f post heavy bail		6:18	be deeply and personally yours, my f
	17:10	their f got Paul and Silas out	Eph	6:23	Good-bye, f. Love mixed with faith
	17:14	With the help of his f, Paul	Php	1:12	report to you, f, that my imprisonment
	18:18	time to take leave of his f		2:2	love each other, be deep-spirited f
	18:27	his Ephesian f gave their blessing		2:12	f, . . . you should simply keep on
	20:32	this community of holy f		3:1	f. Be glad in God!
	21:7	greeted our Christian f there		3:13	F, don't get me wrong
	21:17	In Jerusalem, our f, glad to see us		3:17	Stick with me, f
	23:1	F, I've lived with a clear conscience		4:1	My dear, dear f! I love you so much
	23:6	F, I am a stalwart Pharisee		4:8	f, I'd say you'll do best by
	24:23	not prevent his f from helping him		4:21	Our f here say hello
	27:3	enjoy the hospitality of his f	Col	4:15	Say hello to our f in Laodicea
	27:21	F, you really should have listened	1Th	1:4	clear to us, f, that God not only
	27:25	So, dear f, take heart		2:1	So, f, it's obvious that our visit
	28:14	We found Christian f there		2:9	remember us in those days, f
	28:15	F in Rome heard we were on the way		2:14	F, do you realize that you followed

	2:17	homesick we became for you, dear f
	4:1	One final word, f
	4:10	your f all over the province
	4:12	not lying around sponging off your f
	4:13	question, f, that has come up
	5:1	don't think, f, that I need to deal
	5:4	But f, you're not in the dark
	5:12	And now, f, we ask you to honor
	5:25	F, keep up your prayers for us
2Th	1:3	know, f, that thanking God over
	2:1	f, read these next words carefully
	2:13	thanking God for you, our good f
	2:15	So, f, take a firm stand
	3:1	One more thing, f: Pray for us
	3:13	F, don't slack off in doing your duty
2Ti	4:21	all your f here send greetings
Tit	3:15	Say hello to our f in the faith
Heb	2:12	tell my good f . . . all I know
	3:1	So, my dear Christian f, companions
	3:12	So watch your step, f
	6:9	that won't happen to you, f
	10:33	days it was you, other days your f
	10:34	f went to prison, you stuck by them
	13:22	F, please take what I've written
Jas	1:2	Consider it a sheer gift, f
	1:16	f, don't get thrown off course
	1:19	dear f: Lead with your ears
	2:1	f, don't let public opinion influence
	2:5	Listen, dear f. Isn't it clear by now
	2:14	f, do you think you'll get anywhere
	3:1	any rush to become a teacher, my f
	3:10	My f, this can't go on
	4:11	Don't bad-mouth each other, f
	5:7	f, wait patiently for the Master
	5:9	F, don't complain about each other
	5:19	f, if you know people
1Pe	2:11	F, this world is not your home don't
	4:4	your old f don't understand
	4:12	F, when life gets really difficult
2Pe	1:10	f, confirm God's invitation to you
	3:1	f, this is now the second time
	3:8	Don't overlook the obvious here, f
	3:14	f, since this is what you have
	3:17	But you, f, are well-warned
1Jn	2:7	f, I'm not writing anything new here
	3:2	f, that's exactly who we are
	3:13	don't be surprised, f
	3:21	f, once that's taken care of
	4:1	f, don't believe everything you hear
	4:7	f, let us continue to love each other
	4:11	dear f, if God loved us like this
2Jn	1:5	permit me a reminder, f
3Jn	1:2	We're the best of f
	1:3	happy when some f arrived
	1:14	The f here say hello. Greet our f
Jude	1:3	f, I've dropped everything to write
	1:17	remember, dear f, that the apostles
	1:20	f, carefully build yourselves up
Rev	6:11	servant companions and f in the faith

Friendship

1Sa	20:15	keep the covenant f with my family
	20:17	pledge of love and f for David
	20:42	two of us have vowed f in God's name
2Sa	1:26	Your f was a miracle-wonder
Job	29:4	years when God's f graced my home
Ps	25:14	God-f is for God-worshipers
Pr	3:14	her f is better than a big salary
	17:9	Overlook an offense and bond a f
	22:11	good leaders also delight in their f
	27:9	a sweet f refreshes the soul
Ro	5:11	received this amazing f with God
2Co	13:14	intimate f of the Holy Spirit

Friendships

Pr	16:28	gossips break up f

Fright

Isa	10:29	Ramah trembles with f

Frighten

Job	7:14	scare me with nightmares and f me

Frightened

Ge	42:28	They were puzzled — and f
1Sa	7:7	Israel got the report and became f
	17:24	moment they saw the giant — totally f
2Sa	9:7	Don't be f," said David
2Ki	19:7	f for his life, retreat
Ps	17:7	take in your f children
Da	5:9	now the king was really f
Hos	11:10	My f children will come running
	11:11	Like f birds they'll come
Am	3:8	The lion has roared — who isn't f
Jnh	1:10	the men were f, really f
Mt	28:4	so f, they couldn't move
	28:10	Don't be f like that
Ac	7:32	F nearly out of his skin, Moses
Rev	11:13	f to the core of their being, f

Frightening

Dt	1:19	huge and f wilderness
1Co	15:56	sin that made death so f

Frivolity

Isa	22:14	his verdict on this f
Ro	13:13	daylight hours in f and indulgence

Frivolous

Pr	9:13	brazen, empty-headed, f
	14:3	F talk provokes a derisive smile
Gal	2:17	The accusation is f

F

Fruit-bearing

Ge	1:11	Every sort of f tree
	1:12	f trees of all sorts
	1:29	every kind of f tree
Pr	11:30	A good life is a f tree

Fruitful

| Jas | 2:24 | but by faith f in works |

Fruitless

| Job | 15:34 | The godless are f |

Frustrate

| Ps | 35:4 | F all those who are plotting |
| 2Co | 6:3 | don't f God's work by showing up late |

Frustrated

Ne	4:15	their plan and that God had f it
Isa	8:21	F and famished, they try one thing
1Co	3:1	I'm completely f by your unspiritual

Frustrates

| Pr | 10:3 | he f the appetites of the wicked |

Frustration

Ps	88:9	blinded by tears of pain and f
Pr	11:23	wicked ambition ends in angry f
2Co	5:2	we cry out in f
	12:20	in f with each other
Gal	4:20	language out of sheer f

Fugitive

| Ge | 14:13 | A f came and reported to Abram |
| Jdg | 12:5 | an Ephraimite f said, "Let me cross |

Fugitives

Nu	21:29	Sons turned out as f
Isa	15:9	a lion to finish off the f
	21:14	greet f with bread
Jer	44:14	except maybe a few f

Fulfill

Lev	22:18	to f a vow or as a Freewill-Offering
	22:21	to f a vow or as a Freewill-Offering
Mt	26:56	confirm and f the prophetic writings
Ac	3:18	used it to f his plans
Ro	13:7	F your obligations as a citizen

Fulfilled

| Nu | 32:22 | have f your duty to God and Israel |
| Jdg | 11:39 | He f the vow with her |

1Ki	17:16	God's promise f to the letter
2Ki	23:17	altar at Bethel that you have just f
2Ch	36:22	this f the message of God
Ezr	1:1	this f the Message of God
Isa	42:9	predictions of judgment have been f
Mt	2:15	exile f what Hosea had preached
	2:17	Jeremiah's sermon was f
	8:17	He f Isaiah's well-known sermon
	13:35	His storytelling f the prophecy
Lk	24:44	in the Psalms have to be f
Ac	1:16	That Scripture had to be f
Heb	4:6	So this promise has not yet been f
1Pe	1:12	the Message of those prophecies f

Fulfilling

Ge	26:3	f the oath that I swore to your father
Lev	22:23	it is not acceptable in f a vow
1Ki	2:27	f God's word at Shiloh
1Co	7:2	a balanced and f sexual life

Fulfillment

2Ki	23:16	This was a f of the word of God
Mt	2:23	a f of the prophetic words
Jn	12:16	didn't notice the f of many Scriptures
	13:18	not to interfere with the f
Ro	4:16	the f of God's promise depends
Gal	3:27	the f of God's original promise

Fulfills

| Jn | 8:17 | f the conditions set down in God's Law |

Full-bodied

Ge	41:5	Seven ears of grain, f and lush
	41:22	seven ears of grain, f and lush
Ps	92:3	the f music of strings
Pr	23:31	its bouquet, or its f flavor
1Co	12:24	prefer good digestion to f hair
Heb	6:11	same intensity toward a f hope

Fullness

Eph	3:19	Live full lives, full in the f of God
Col	2:9	realize the f of Christ
	2:10	that f comes together for you
	2:11	this f is not something you figure out

Fury

Est	3:6	hated to waste his f on just one
Ps	7:6	pit your holy f against my furious
Isa	59:18	f for his foes, just deserts for
Na	1:6	his f shatters boulders

Fuss

Mt	6:25	don't f about what's on the table
	6:32	f over these things
Lk	12:22	Don't f about what's on the table

	12:26	why **f** at all
	12:27	don't **f** with their appearance
	12:30	**f** over these things

Fussing

Mt	6:27	Has anyone by **f** in front of the mirror
Mk	8:17	Why are you **f** because you forgot bread
Lk	10:41	Martha, you're **f** far too much
	12:25	Has anyone by **f** before the mirror
	12:26	If **f** can't even do that, why fuss

Futile

Mic	6:16	lives will be derided as **f** and fake

Futilely

1Ki	22:25	frantically and **f** looking for a place
2Ch	18:24	frantically and **f** looking for a place
Job	39:13	The ostrich flaps her wings **f**

Futility

Gal	3:21	**f** of devising some religious system

Future

Ge	18:19	train his children and **f** family
Ex	16:32	an omer, for **f** generations
	16:33	keeping it safe for **f** generations
Nu	15:14	In **f** generations, when a foreigner
	15:15	the regular rule for **f** generations
	15:21	**f** generations make this offering
Dt	4:30	in **f** days you will come back to God
	20:19	Those trees are your **f** food
Jos	22:27	say to our children in the **f**
	22:28	to our children in the **f**
Ru	1:11	who can become your **f** husbands
1Sa	2:31	both your family and your **f** family
	9:20	Israel's **f** is in your hands
	20:31	your **f** in this kingdom is at risk
	22:7	have any **f** with the son of Jesse
2Sa	7:19	my family far into the **f**
	20:1	no **f** for us with the son of Jesse
1Ch	17:17	my family far into the **f**
	28:8	insuring a good **f**
Est	9:27	their children, and all **f** converts
Job	6:11	What **f** do I have to keep me going
Ps	37:37	There's a **f** in strenuous wholeness
Pr	23:18	That's where your **f** lies
	24:14	Get that and your **f**'s secured
	24:20	Those people have no **f** at all
	28:16	who hates corruption, the **f** is bright
Isa	29:15	Plotting the **f** as if you knew
	41:23	tell us what will happen in the **f**
Jer	27:9	who claim to know the **f**
	29:11	plans to give you the **f** you hope for
Eze	12:27	preaching about the far-off **f**
	17:14	so that it would have a **f**
	38:8	In the distant **f** you'll arrive
Da	8:26	It refers to the far **f**

Mt	24:34	not just saying this for some **f**
Mk	13:30	not just saying this for some **f**
Lk	21:32	not just saying this for some **f**
1Co	3:22	the present, the **f**—all of it
Col	1:5	tied as they are to your **f** in heaven
Heb	11:20	Isaaac reached into the **f**
1Pe	1:4	a **f** in heaven—and the **f** starts now
	1:5	watch over us and the **f**
	1:21	you have a **f** in God

G

Gain

2Sa	3:6	to **g** power for himself
Job	20:10	have to give back their ill-gotten **g**
Pr	10:2	Ill-gotten **g** gets you nowhere
Jer	5:27	stuffed with ill-gotten **g**
Hab	3:19	I take heart and **g** strength
Jn	3:15	will **g** a real life, eternal life
Ac	19:33	to the front to try to **g** control
	21:30	couldn't get back in and **g** sanctuary
	24:3	**g** daily profit from your reforms
2Co	7:9	result was all **g**, no loss
1Jn	2:14	God enables you to **g** a victory

Game

Ge	25:28	loved his **g**, but Rebekah loved Jacob
	27:3	out in the country and hunt me some **g**
	27:5	off to the country to hunt **g**
	27:7	some **g** and fix me a hearty meal
	27:19	sit up and eat of my **g**
	27:25	so I can eat of my son's **g**
	27:31	get up and eat of his son's **g**
	27:33	who hunted **g** and brought it to me
1Sa	31:4	make a **g** out of killing me
Ps	9:5	throw dirty players out of the **g**
	50:21	you thought I went along with your **g**
Pr	2:14	losers who make a **g** of evil
Jer	50:7	no qualms: 'Fair **g**' they said
Eze	22:11	Sex is now anarchy. Anyone is fair **g**
Mt	7:8	a cat-and-mouse, hide-and-seek **g**
Lk	11:10	a cat-and-mouse, hide-and-seek **g**
	11:22	beaten at his own **g**
	23:36	poked fun at him, making a **g** of it
Ac	13:11	against God himself, and your **g** is up
	19:13	what they assumed to be Paul's "**g**."
Jas	1:26	talking a good **g** is self-deceived

Games

Ge	27:12	He'll think I'm playing **g** with him
Ex	8:29	don't play **g** with us
Nu	22:29	you've been playing **g** with me
Jdg	16:13	You're still playing **g** with me
2Ki	4:16	don't play **g** with me
Job	18:2	monotonous these word **g** are getting
Ps	140:2	spend their days plotting war **g**
Ecc	7:4	Fools waste their lives in fun and **g**
Isa	1:13	can't stand your trivial religious **g**
Jer	6:19	result of the **g** they've been playing

	9:21	men and women collapse at their **g**
Hos	5:3	played your sex-and-religion **g** long
Mt	22:18	Why are you playing these **g** with me
	26:25	Don't play **g** with me
Mk	12:15	Why are you playing these **g** with me
Lk	6:25	if you think life's all fun and **g**
2Co	4:2	refuse to wear masks and play **g**
Jas	4:9	The fun and **g** are over
Rev	2:22	play their sex-and-religion **g**

Gatekeeper

Mk	13:34	commanding the **g** to stand watch
Jn	10:3	The **g** opens the gate to him

Gatekeepers

2Ki	7:11	**g** got the word to the royal palace

Gateposts

Jdg	16:3	doors of the city gate and the two **g**
Eze	40:21	Its **g** and porch were the same
	40:24	He measured its **g** and its porch
	40:26	palm trees decorating its **g**
	40:48	measured the **g** of the porch
	40:49	Columns flanked the **g**
	46:2	stand at the **g** as the priests present

Gateway

Eze	26:2	The **g** city is smashed!
	27:3	Tyre, **g** to the sea
	40:19	from the front of the entrance **g**
	40:22	identical to the east **g**

Gateways

Eze	40:18	the same length as the **g**

Genealogical

Ne	7:5	**g** record of those who were in
Heb	7:16	not by **g** descent but by

Genealogies

Tit	3:9	pointless quarreling over **g**

Generate

Ge	1:24	God spoke: "Earth, **g** life!
Isa	45:8	I, God, **g** all this

Generated

Ex	1:5	Seventy persons in all **g** by Jacob's

Generation

Ge	7:1	in this **g**, you're the righteous one
	15:16	Not until the fourth **g** will your

	17:9	you and your descendants, **g** after **g**
	17:12	circumcised . . . , **g** after **g**
	50:23	Ephraim's sons into the third **g**
Ex	1:6	all his brothers—that whole **g**
	20:5	the fourth **g** of those who hate me
	29:42	Offering before God, **g** after **g**
	30:8	incense burning before God, **g** after **g**
	31:13	sign between me and you, **g** after **g**
Lev	21:17	None of your descendants, in any **g**
Nu	14:18	into the third, even the fourth **g**
	14:29	this whole **g** of grumblers
	14:33	until the last of your **g** lies a corpse
	32:13	entire **g** that acted out evil
Dt	1:35	Not a single person of this evil **g**
	2:14	how long it took for the entire **g**
	5:9	even to the fourth **g**
	23:2	even to the tenth **g**
	23:3	even to the tenth **g**
	23:8	congregation of God in the third **g**
	29:22	next **g**, your children who come after
	32:20	a turned-around, upside-down **g**
Jdg	2:10	entire **g** died and was buried
1Ch	3:10	In the next **g** Solomon had Rehoboam
Est	9:28	remembered and kept by every single **g**
Ps	48:13	tell the next **g** . . . the story of God
	78:4	passing it along to the next **g**
	78:6	So the next **g** would know
	102:18	Write this down for the next **g**
	145:4	**G** after **g** stands in awe of your work
Ecc	1:4	One **g** goes its way
Isa	13:20	**g** after **g** a ghost town
	30:9	a rebel **g**, a people who lie
	34:10	**G** after **g** of wasteland
	34:17	This is permanent — **g** after **g**
	57:4	A race of rebels, a **g** of liars
Jer	2:31	What a **g** you turned out to be!
	7:29	God has rejected and left this **g**
	8:3	all from this evil **g** unlucky enough
Mt	11:16	How can I account for this **g**?
	12:41	evidence that will condemn this **g**
	12:42	evidence that will condemn this **g**
	12:45	That's what this **g** is like
	16:4	An evil and wanton **g**
	17:17	What a **g**! No sense of God!
	23:34	scholars **g** after **g** — and **g** after
	23:36	coming down on you, on your **g**
	24:34	not just saying this for some future **g**
Mk	8:12	Why does this **g** clamor for miraculous
	9:19	What a **g**! No sense of God!
	13:30	not just saying this for some future **g**
Lk	7:31	can I account for the people of this **g**
	9:41	What a **g**! No sense of God!
	11:31	evidence that will condemn this **g**
	11:32	evidence that condemns this **g**
	11:51	the bill of this **g** and this **g** will pay
	21:32	not just saying this for some future **g**

Generations

Ex	12:14	festival to God down through the **g**
	12:17	Honor the day down through your **g**
	12:42	all **g** will honor God by keeping watch

	16:32	an omer, for future **g** so they can see
	16:33	keeping it safe for future **g**
	27:21	permanent practice down through the **g**
	30:10	every year down through the **g**
	30:21	down through the **g**
	30:31	anointing oil throughout your **g**
	31:16	Sabbath-keeping down through the **g**
	34:7	loyal in love for a thousand **g**
	40:15	priesthood, down through the **g**
Lev	3:17	fixed rule down through the **g**
	6:18	God's gifts, stretching down the **g**
	7:36	fixed rule down through the **g**
	10:9	fixed rule down through the **g**
	17:7	perpetual decree down through the **g**
	23:14	perpetual decree for all your **g**
	23:21	wherever you live down through your **g**
	23:31	perpetual decree for all the **g**
	24:3	extravagantly **g** in love with David
Nu	10:8	assigned duty down through the **g**
	15:14	In future **g**, when a foreigner
	15:15	regular rule for future **g**
	15:21	future **g** make this offering to God
Dt	7:9	his commandments for a thousand **g**
2Ki	10:30	throne of Israel for four **g**
	15:12	**g** your sons will sit on the throne
1Ch	16:15	commitments across thousands of **g**
Job	42:16	four **g** of them
Ps	45:17	I'll make you famous for **g**
	78:6	would know, and all the **g** to come
	105:8	for a thousand **g** he's been as good
Isa	30:8	be there to instruct the coming **g**
Mt	1:17	fourteen **g** from Abraham to David
Ac	14:16	In the **g** before us, God let all
Eph	3:21	Glory down all the **g**!
1Pe	3:19	God's salvation to earlier **g**

Generosity

Dt	9:26	in your immense **g**, you redeemed
2Ch	29:31	overflowing with **g**
	29:32	**g** expressed in seventy bulls
Est	2:18	handed out gifts with royal **g**
Job	36:31	symbols of . . . his **g**, his loving care
Ps	111:3	His **g** never gives out
	112:3	a **g** that never runs dry
	112:9	A **g** that goes on, and on
Pr	25:22	Your **g** will surprise him
Mk	4:25	G begets **g**
Lk	6:38	G begets **g**
	8:18	G begets **g**
Jn	4:10	If you knew the **g** of God
Ac	15:11	out of sheer **g** moved to save us
	18:27	believers through God's immense **g**
	20:24	Incredibly extravagant **g** of God
Ro	1:7	all the **g** of God our Father
	3:24	God did it for us. Out of sheer **g**
	11:33	this extravagant **g** of God
	12:20	Your **g** will surprise him
1Co	10:23	Because of God's immense **g** and grace
2Co	8:9	familiar with the **g** of our Master
Gal	1:15	chose and called me out of sheer **g**
Eph	3:8	inexhaustible riches and **g** of Christ

	4:7	Out of the **g** of Christ, each of us
Php	4:17	the blessing that issues from **g**
	4:19	his **g** exceeding even yours
Heb	12:15	no one gets left out of God's **g**

Generous

Ge	24:27	How **g** and true you've been
	24:49	plan to respond with a **g** yes
	33:15	Your **g** welcome is all I need
Dt	15:11	Always be **g**, open purse and hands
Ru	2:12	with a **g** bonus besides from God
1Sa	1:5	especially **g** helping to Hannah
	1:24	makings of a **g** sacrificial meal
	25:8	be **g** with my men
2Sa	2:6	matching your **g** act of goodness
1Ki	2:7	be **g** to the sons of Barzillai
	3:6	extravagantly **g** in love with David
1Ch	29:14	been given from your **g** hand
	29:18	keep this **g** spirit alive forever
2Ch	1:8	extravagantly **g** with David
Ezr	7:9	under the **g** guidance of his God
	8:18	the **g** hand of our God was on us
Ne	2:8	The **g** hand of my God was with me
	9:22	establishing **g** boundaries
	9:35	enjoying your **g** goodness
Est	1:7	wine flowed freely—a **g** king
Job	42:11	brought **g** housewarming gifts
Ps	37:22	G gets it all in the end
	51:1	G in love—God, give grace!
	52:8	trusted in the **g** mercy of God
	57:3	God delivers **g** love
	63:3	In your **g** love I am really living
	84:11	God, **g** in gifts and glory
	100:5	God is sheer beauty, all-**g** in love
	112:5	good person is **g** and lends lavishly
	119:17	Be **g** with me and I'll live a full life
	127:3	the fruit of the womb his **g** legacy
	130:7	with God's arrival comes **g** redemption
	145:16	G to a fault, you lavish your favor
Pr	11:24	world of the **g** gets larger
	19:6	people flock around a **g** person
	22:9	G hands are blessed hands
	28:27	Be **g** to the poor
Ecc	11:1	Be **g**: Invest in acts of charity
SS	4:2	Your smile is **g** and full
	6:6	Your smile is **g** and full
Isa	43:24	You've been plenty **g** with them
	58:10	**g** with the hungry and start giving
	63:7	All the **g** bounties of God
Jer	36:32	There were also **g** additions
Eze	33:15	being **g** to the down-and-out
Mt	5:16	Keep open house; be **g** with your lives
	20:15	get stingy because I am **g**
Lk	12:33	Be **g**. Give to the poor
Jn	1:14	like Father, like Son, G inside
	1:16	We all live off his **g** bounty
Ro	1:5	**g** gift of his life and the urgent task
	5:16	this **g**, life-giving gift
	10:12	same incredibly **g** way to everyone
	16:1	all the **g** hospitality
1Co	15:10	God was so gracious, so very **g**

G

	16:2	Be as **g** as you can
2Co	8:1	**g** ways in which God is working
	8:2	outpouring of pure and **g** gifts
	9:10	This most **g** God who gives seed
	9:11	so that you can be **g** in every way
	9:13	show . . . through your **g** offerings
Gal	6:6	enter into a **g** common life
Php	1:7	experienced . . . **g** help from God
	1:19	the **g** response of the Spirit
1Ti	6:18	helping others, to be extravagantly **g**
1Pe	4:10	**g** with . . . things God gave you
	5:10	this **g** God who has great plans
	5:12	This is God's **g** truth
2Pe	1:7	warm friendliness, and **g** love

Generously

Ge	18:19	live kindly and **g** and fairly
Dt	13:17	**g** making you prosper
	16:10	give as **g** as God
	16:17	giving **g** in response
1Sa	24:18	treated me **g**
1Ki	9:25	he did **g** and well
	10:13	what he had already so **g** given her
2Ch	31:5	the Israelites responded **g**
Ezr	7:16	the **g** donated offerings all over
Pr	31:12	she treats him **g** all her life long
Isa	19:25	will **g** bless them all
Mt	5:42	No more tit-for-tat stuff. Live **g**
	5:48	Live **g** and graciously toward others
	10:8	You have been treated **g**, so live **g**
Lk	6:30	No more tit-for-tat stuff. Live **g**
	6:35	way our Father lives toward us, **g**
	11:41	give **g** to the poor
Ro	5:5	everything God **g** pours into our lives
	15:27	the Jerusalem community so **g**
2Co	4:1	Since God has so **g** let us in
Col	1:29	the energy God so **g** gives me
Tit	3:6	Savior Jesus poured out new life so **g**

Genitals

Lev	15:2	When a man has a discharge from his **g**
Dt	25:11	grabs the **g** of the man hitting him
Isa	7:20	shave the hair off your heads and **g**
Hos	2:10	I'll expose her **g** to the public
	4:12	replaced their God with their **g**

Genius

| Lk | 12:57 | don't have to be a **g** to understand |

Gentle

Dt	28:54	most **g** and caring man among you
	28:56	most **g** and caring woman among you
	32:2	My teaching, let it fall like a **g** rain
1Ki	19:12	after the fire a **g** and quiet whisper
Job	20:17	picnics for them beside **g** streams
Ps	18:35	caress me with your **g** ways
	81:5	**g** whisper from One I never guessed
Pr	11:16	A woman of **g** grace gets respect

	15:1	A **g** response defuses anger
	25:15	**g** speech breaks down rigid defenses
Zec	9:16	become like sheep, **g** and soft
Mt	10:13	be **g** in your conversation
Ac	24:2	your wise and **g** rule
	27:13	When a **g** southerly breeze came up
Ro	11:22	**g** kindness and ruthless severity
2Co	10:1	in the **g** but firm spirit of Christ
Eph	4:32	Be **g** with one another, sensitive
1Ti	3:3	not pushy but **g**
2Ti	2:24	a **g** listener and a teacher
Jas	3:17	It is **g** and reasonable
1Pe	3:4	inner beauty, the **g**, gracious kind

Gentleness

Ecc	8:1	gives **g** to words and manners
Ro	11:22	But don't presume on this **g**
2Co	6:6	**g**, holiness, and honest love

Gently

2Sa	18:5	Deal **g** for my sake with the young man
Job	15:11	spoken so **g** and tenderly
	21:33	**G** lowered into expensive graves
Ps	86:17	As you, God, **g** and powerfully put me
Isa	8:6	turned its back on the **g** flowing
Ac	5:26	they handled them **g**
Ro	14:1	Treat them **g**
Eph	3:20	his Spirit deeply and **g** within us
1Th	5:14	**G** encourage the stragglers
Heb	5:2	deal **g** with their failings

Genuine

Pr	15:8	delights in **g** prayers
Mt	7:16	A **g** leader will never exploit
1Co	5:8	simple, **g**, unpretentious
2Th	3:17	proof that the letter is **g**
1Pe	1:7	**g** faith put through this suffering
1Jn	4:2	test for the **g** Spirit of God

Genuinely

Job	4:7	Do **g** upright people ever lose
Jn	3:29	**g** happy. How could he be jealous
Php	2:20	loyal, and **g** concerned for you

Get-rich-quick

| Pr | 28:20 | **g** schemes are ripoffs |

Ghost

Lev	26:22	think you are living in a **g** town
1Sa	12:21	Don't chase after **g**-gods
	12:22	They're nothing but **g**-gods
	28:8	I want you to consult a **g** for me
Job	15:28	end up living in a **g** town
Ps	78:33	nothing to show . . . but a **g** town
	102:4	I'm a **g** of my former self
Pr	11:11	evil talk turns it into a **g** town

Isa	13:20	generation after generation a **g** town
	29:4	like the muttering of a **g**
	64:10	all **g** towns: Zion's a **g** town
Jer	4:26	All the towns were **g** towns
	6:8	being turned into a **g** town
	22:6	wasteland, as empty as a **g** town
	34:22	I'll turn them into **g** towns
	44:2	Look at what's left: **g** towns
	44:22	a horror story, a **g** town
	48:9	Her towns will all be **g** towns
	50:43	He goes white as a **g**
	51:37	a godforsaken **g** town
Eze	26:19	city empty of people, a **g** town
	35:9	all your towns will be **g** towns
Da	5:6	he went white as a **g**
	7:28	like a man who had seen a **g**
Zep	2:9	Ammon a **g** town like Gomorrah
	2:14	The **g** town of a city
Mal	1:3	whole country into a **g** town
Mt	14:26	"A **g**!" they said
	23:38	nothing but a **g** town
Mk	6:49	thought it was a **g** and screamed
Lk	24:37	thought they were seeing a **g**
	24:39	A **g** doesn't have muscle and bone
Ro	9:29	would have ended up like **g** towns
Rev	18:2	Great Babylon, ruined! A **g** town

Ghost-gods

1Sa	12:21	Don't chase after **g**
	12:22	They're nothing but **g**!

Ghostly

Isa	14:9	ready to greet you are the **g** dead

Ghosts

Dt	2:11	lumped in with the Rephaites (**G**)
Job	7:14	frighten me with **g**
Ps	88:10	Do **g** ever join the choirs
Pr	21:16	ends up in a congregation of **g**
Isa	19:3	they'll conjure **g** and hold séances
	26:14	The dead don't talk, **g** don't walk
Da	5:10	Don't sit around looking like **g**
Hos	12:1	chases **g** and phantoms

Gift

Ge	23:11	The field is yours — a **g**
	30:20	God has given me a great **g**
	32:18	They are a **g** to my master Esau
Ex	29:25	fragrance before God, a **g** to God
	29:41	a pleasing fragrance, a **g** to God
	30:20	offer **g** offerings to God
	35:24	silver or bronze as a **g** to God
Lev	1:9	a Fire-**G**, a pleasing fragrance
	1:13	a Fire-**G**, a pleasing fragrance
	1:17	a Fire-**G**, a pleasing fragrance
	2:2	a Fire-**G**, a pleasing fragrance
	2:9	a Fire-**G**, a pleasing fragrance
	2:11	as a Fire-**G** to God

	2:16	a memorial — a Fire-**G** to God
	3:3	Fire-**G** to God from the Peace-Offering
	3:5	a Fire-**G**, a pleasing fragrance
	3:9	a Fire-**G** to God from the Peace-Offering
	3:11	a meal, a Fire-**G** to God
	3:14	As a Fire-**G** to God
	3:16	a Fire-**G**, a pleasing fragrance
	7:5	burns them on the Altar as a **g** to God
	7:25	a **g** has been presented to God
	7:30	**g** to God in your own hands
	8:21	a pleasing fragrance — a **g** to God
	8:28	pleasing fragrance to God, a **g** to God
	22:22	on the Altar as a **g** to God
	22:27	acceptable as an offering, a **g** to God
	23:13	a Fire-**G** to God, a pleasing fragrance
	23:25	Offer a Fire-**G** to God
	23:27	offer a Fire-**G** to God
	24:7	as a memorial; it is a **g** to God
Nu	6:25	God smile on you and **g** you
	15:3	sacrifice a Fire-**G** to God
	15:10	a Fire-**G**, a pleasing fragrance to God
	15:13	Fire-**G** as a pleasing fragrance to God
	15:14	Fire-**G** as a pleasing fragrance to God
	15:25	offered to God the Fire-**G**
	18:6	to you as a **g**, a **g** of God
	18:7	priesthood is my exclusive **g** to you
	18:11	your sons and daughters as a **g**
	18:14	You get every Totally-Devoted **g**
	18:17	a Fire-**G**, a pleasing fragrance to God
	28:3	Fire-**G** that you are to present to God
	28:6	a pleasing fragrance, a Fire-**G** to God
	28:8	Fire-**G** of pleasing fragrance for God
	28:13	a pleasing fragrance, a Fire-**G** to God
	28:19	Bring a Fire-**G** to God
	28:24	Fire-**G**, a pleasing fragrance to God
	29:6	pleasing fragrance, a Fire-**G** to God
	29:13	Fire-**G** of pleasing fragrance to God
	29:36	Fire-**G** of pleasing fragrance to God
	31:52	offered as a **g** to God weighed about
Dt	1:21	placed this land as a **g** before you
	18:1	They get the Fire-**G**-Offerings of God
Jos	13:14	The Fire-**G** offerings to God
	15:19	Give me a marriage **g**
Jdg	1:15	Give me a marriage **g**
	6:18	until I come back and bring you my **g**
Ru	4:13	By God's gracious **g** she conceived
1Sa	9:7	nothing to bring as a **g**
	25:27	take this **g** that I, your servant
	25:35	David accepted the **g** she brought him
	30:26	A **g** from the plunder of God's enemies
1Ki	9:11	rewarded Hiram king of Tyre with a **g**
	13:7	I have a **g** for you
	15:19	this **g** of silver and gold
	22:12	An easy victory! God's **g** to the king
	22:15	An easy victory. God's **g** to the king
2Ki	5:15	In gratitude let me give you a **g**
	5:22	Supply their needs with a **g**
	8:8	Take a **g** with you and go meet
	20:12	sent a get-well card and a **g**
2Ch	16:3	showing my good faith with this **g**
	18:11	An easy victory! God's **g** to the king
	18:14	an easy victory! God's **g** to the king

Ne	7:70	governor made a **g** to the treasury
Ps	44:3	we didn't work for it — it was a **g**
	60:6	I hand out Succoth Valley as a **g**
	72:1	Give the **g** of wise rule to the king
	100:2	Bring a **g** of laughter
	105:44	a **g** of the country they entered
	108:7	I hand out Succoth Valley as a **g**
	109:19	give him a **g** — a costume of curses
	111:6	the nations on a platter — a **g**
	119:111	it's mine forever — what a **g**
	127:3	children are God's best **g**
	135:12	a **g** of good land to his people
Pr	17:8	Receiving a **g** is like getting
	18:16	A **g** gets attention
	21:14	A quietly given **g** soothes
	29:13	their sight, God's **g**
Ecc	3:13	your job. It's God's **g**
	5:19	the work. It's God's **g**
	9:9	Each day is God's **g**
Isa	9:6	the **g** of a son — for us
	16:1	Dispatch a **g** of lambs
	29:23	his children, my personal **g** to him
	35:2	Mountain glories of Lebanon — a **g**
	39:1	greetings and a **g** to Hezekiah
Jer	7:14	this place I gave as a **g**
	17:4	You'll lose your **g** of land
	40:5	food for the journey and a parting **g**
Eze	46:16	deeds a **g** from his inheritance
	46:17	deeds a **g** from his inheritance
	48:12	special **g**, a **g** from the land itself
Hos	10:6	present it as a **g** to the great king
Joel	2:19	I'm sending a **g**: Grain and wine
Mt	13:11	Not everybody has this **g**
	16:27	coming to you, a personal **g**
Mk	7:11	**G**! What I owed you I've given as a **g**
Lk	7:21	the blind he gave the **g** of sight
Jn	1:16	generous bounty, **g** after **g** after **g**
	6:65	get to me only as a **g** from the Father
	14:27	That's my parting **g** to you
	17:11	you conferred as a **g** through me
Ac	2:38	Receive the **g** of the Holy Spirit
	5:31	give Israel the **g** of a changed life
	7:53	handed to you by angels — **g**-wrapped
	8:20	unthinkable — trying to buy God's **g**
	10:45	the **g** of the Holy Spirit
	11:17	God gave the same exact **g** to them
Ro	1:5	both the generous **g** of his life
	1:6	You are who you are through this **g**
	1:11	deliver God's **g** in person
	3:24	A pure **g**. He got us out of the mess
	4:4	we don't call your wages a **g**
	4:5	right with God, by God. Sheer **g**
	4:16	God's promise arrives as pure **g**
	5:15	the rescuing **g** is not exactly parallel
	5:16	this generous, life-giving **g**
	5:17	this wildly extravagant life-**g**
	6:23	God's **g** is real life, eternal life
1Co	3:10	**g** God gave me as a good architect
	3:21	Everything is already yours as a **g**
	7:7	**g** of the single life to some, the **g**
	14:18	grateful to God for the **g** of praying
	15:57	the **g** of our Master, Jesus Christ

	16:3	to Jerusalem to deliver your **g**
2Co	9:15	Thank God for this **g**, his **g**
	12:7	I was given the **g** of a handicap
	12:8	I didn't think of it as a **g**
Gal	5:2	Christ's hard-won **g** of freedom
Eph	1:6	celebration of his lavish **g**-giving
	2:8	It's God's **g** from start to finish
	3:7	It came as a sheer **g** to me
	4:7	each of us is given his own **g**
	4:29	Say only what helps, each word a **g**
	4:30	Don't take such a **g** for granted
Php	1:29	the suffering is as much a **g** as
Col	1:23	don't walk away from a **g** like that
	1:25	suffering as a sheer **g**, God's way
1Th	4:8	making you a **g** of his Holy Spirit
2Th	3:16	**g** of getting along with each other
1Ti	4:14	special **g** of ministry you were given
2Ti	1:6	special **g** of ministry you received
	1:9	a **g** prepared for us in Jesus
	2:21	every kind of **g** to his guests
Tit	3:7	God's **g** has restored
Heb	12:16	trading away God's lifelong **g**
	13:10	God gives us the **g** of himself
Jas	1:2	Consider it a sheer **g**, friends
	1:17	Every . . . **g** comes out of heaven
	5:11	What a **g** life is to those who
1Pe	1:10	this **g** of life God was preparing
	1:13	ready to receive the **g** that's coming
1Jn	5:20	the truth of God — what a **g**!
Jude	1:3	faith entrusted to us as a **g**
Rev	2:27	the **g** my Father gave me
	3:3	the **g** you once had . . ., the Message
	3:21	That's my **g** to the conquerors

Gift-giving

Eph	1:6	**g** by the hand of his beloved Son

Gift-wrapped

Ac	7:53	God's Law handed to you by angels — **g**

Gifted

Ex	28:3	those whom I have **g** in this work
	35:26	women who were **g** in spinning
	35:35	He's **g** them with the know-how
	36:2	all whom God had **g** with the ability
1Ch	15:22	a very **g** musician
La	3:39	why would anyone **g** with life complain
Da	1:17	Daniel was **g** in understanding

Gifts

Ge	15:2	Master, what use are your **g**
	24:10	loaded with **g** from his master
	24:22	the man brought out **g**
	24:53	he brought out **g** of silver and gold
	25:6	he gave **g** to the sons he had
	30:20	my husband will honor me with **g**
	32:20	soften him up with the succession of **g**
	32:21	So his **g** went before him

	33:10	welcome me, accept these **g**		66:3	presentation of memorial **g**
	33:11	Accept the **g** I have brought for you	Eze	16:19	herbs and spices, which were my **g**
	43:11	take them to the man as **g**		16:32	accept **g** from their lovers
	43:15	men took the **g**, double the money		20:40	I'll demand your best **g** and offerings
	43:25	The brothers spread out their **g**		44:30	special **g**, comes to the priests
	43:26	presented him with the **g**	Da	2:6	I'll lavish you with **g** and honors
	45:23	sent his father these **g**		2:48	lavished him with **g**
Lev	2:3	most holy part of the Fire-**G** to God		5:17	You can keep your **g**, or give them
	2:10	most holy part of the **g** to God	Hos	3:5	reverence before God and his good **g**
	4:35	on the Altar on top of the **g** to God	Mic	1:14	give your good-bye **g**
	5:12	on the Altar with the **g** for God	Mt	2:11	presented **g**: gold, frankincense, myrrh
	6:17	share of the **g** presented to me	Lk	12:48	Great **g** mean great responsibilities
	6:18	a fixed rule regarding God's **g**		21:5	its stonework and memorial **g**
	7:35	these allotments from the **g** of God	Jn	3:35	a lavish distribution of **g**
	10:12	the Fire-**G** for God	Ac	14:3	clear evidence of God's **g**
	10:13	from the Fire-**G** for God	Ro	11:29	God's **g** and God's call
	10:15	pieces of the Fire-**G** and lift them up		15:27	they got in on all the spiritual **g**
	21:6	their job is to present the **g** of God	1Co	1:3	all the **g**... that come from God
	21:21	any defect is to offer **g** to God		1:7	All God's **g** are right in front of you
	23:8	Offer Fire-**G** to God for seven days		2:12	the **g** of life and salvation
	23:18	Fire-**G**, a pleasing fragrance to God		2:14	can't receive the **g** of God's Spirit
	23:36	Offer Fire-**G** to God for seven days		4:7	everything you are sheer **g** from God
	23:37	presenting Fire-**G** to God		12:4	God's various **g** are handed out
	23:38	in addition to other **g**		12:11	All these **g** have a common origin
	24:9	holy share from the **g** to God		14:1	Give yourselves to the **g** God gives you
Nu	18:8	all the holy **g** I get	2Co	1:2	all the **g**... that come from God
	18:27	same as other people's **g** of grain		8:2	outpouring of pure and generous **g**
	28:2	my Fire-**G** of pleasing fragrance		8:19	sharing God's **g** to honor God
Dt	33:16	The best of Earth's exuberant **g**	Gal	5:22	He brings **g** into our lives
1Sa	18:4	He formalized it with solemn **g**	Eph	4:8	handed it all out in **g** to the people
2Sa	8:10	brought with him **g** of silver, gold		4:10	He handed out **g** above and below
1Ki	10:25	everyone who came brought **g**		4:11	filled earth with his **g**
2Ki	5:23	servants to carry the **g** back		4:11	He handed out **g** of apostle
	5:24	Gehazi took the **g** from the servants	Php	4:18	The **g** you sent with Epaphroditus
	5:26	lining your pockets with **g**	2Th	2:16	surprised you with **g** of unending help
	12:18	**g** dedicated for holy use	2Ti	1:7	doesn't want us to be shy with his **g**
2Ch	9:24	Everyone who came brought **g**	Heb	2:4	with **g** through the Holy Spirit
	17:5	appreciation by bringing **g**		8:3	priest is to offer both **g**
	17:11	Some Philistines even brought **g**		8:4	priests who offer the **g**
	21:3	father had lavished them with **g**		9:9	**g** and sacrifices can't really get
	31:8	saw the extent of the mounds of **g**	Jas	1:17	**g** are rivers of light cascading down
	31:10	huge outpouring of **g** to The Temple			
	31:12	offerings of tithes and sacred **g**			
	31:14	the offerings and sacred **g**	**Girlfriend**		
	31:18	bringing themselves and their **g**	Pr	30:23	a "**g**" replaces a faithful wife
Ezr	1:6	pack animals, expensive **g**			
Ne	7:71	heads of the families made **g**	**Girlfriends**		
	7:72	**G** from the rest of the people	Jdg	11:38	She and her dear **g** went
Est	2:18	handed out **g** with royal generosity			
	9:19	parties and the exchange of **g**	**Glad-hand**		
	9:22	and of giving **g** to the poor	Pr	22:16	Exploit the poor or **g** the rich
Job	42:11	brought generous housewarming **g**			
Ps	21:3	You filled his arms with **g**	**Gladly**		
	45:12	Wedding **g** pour in from Tyre	1Sa	26:19	I **g** offer my life as a sacrifice
	68:29	kings bring **g** to you	2Sa	6:22	I'll **g** look like a fool
	84:11	God, generous in **g** and glory		12:8	I'd have **g** thrown in much more
	96:8	Bring **g** and celebrate	Job	40:14	I'll **g** step aside and hand things over
	112:9	They lavish **g** on the poor	Lk	19:21	don't suffer fools **g**
Isa	9:3	sharing rich **g** and warm greetings		19:22	I don't suffer fools **g**
	35:2	**g**. God's resplendent glory			
	35:10	Welcomed home with **g** of joy			
	60:7	Welcome **g** for worship at my altar			

G

Ac	18:14	I would **g** hear you out
Ro	8:32	anything else he wouldn't **g** . . . do
1Jn	5:16	ask for God's help and he **g** gives it

Gladness

Isa	35:10	Welcomed home with gifts of joy and **g**
Jn	16:20	your sadness will develop into **g**

Glamour

Jer	10:2	Don't be impressed by their **g**

G

Gloat

Job	31:29	Or **g** over my rival's bad luck
Ps	30:1	you didn't let my foes **g**
Eze	28:17	let them **g** over your demise

Gloated

Ob	1:12	shouldn't have **g** over your brother
Rev	18:7	she **g**, "I'm queen over all

Gloating

Pr	17:5	**g** over misfortune is a punishable
Rev	11:11	all those **g** spectators will be scared

Gloom

Ex	33:4	they were plunged into **g**
Pr	17:22	**g** and doom leave you bone-tired

Glories

Ps	145:11	the **g** of your rule
Isa	35:2	Mountain **g** of Lebanon

Glorified

Jn	7:39	because Jesus had not yet been **g**
	12:16	after Jesus was **g**, they remembered
	12:23	come for the Son of Man to be **g**
	12:28	I have **g** it, and I'll glorify it again
	13:32	In glorifying him, he himself is **g**
	17:4	I **g** you on earth
Ac	3:13	has **g** his Son Jesus
1Pe	1:21	God then raised from the dead and **g**

Glorify

Jn	12:28	have glorified it, and I'll **g** it again
	17:5	**g** me with your very own splendor
	21:19	death by which Peter would **g** God

Glorifying

Da	4:34	thanking and **g** God
Lk	2:20	**g** and praising God for everything
	17:15	shouting his gratitude, **g** God
	18:43	then followed Jesus, **g** God

Jn	11:4	show God's glory by **g** God's Son
	13:32	In **g** him, he himself is glorified

Glorious

Dt	28:58	This Name **g** and terrible, God
2Sa	23:7	They'll make a **g** bonfire
1Ki	3:9	capable of leading your **g** people
2Ch	1:10	leading these, your **g** people
	30:22	that **g** seven days of worship
Ne	9:5	Blessed be your **g** name
Ps	97:6	everyone will see it happen — **g**
Pr	4:8	she'll make your life **g**
	21:21	finds life itself — **g** life
Isa	4:5	his **g** presence, his immense
	9:1	he'll make that whole area **g**
	11:10	His headquarters will be **g**
	13:19	Babylon, most **g** of all kingdoms
	24:23	Splendid and **g** before all his leaders
	60:7	I bathe my **g** Temple in splendor
	60:13	as I make my footstool **g**
Jer	11:16	A mighty oak tree, majestic and **g**
	14:21	abandon your **g** Temple
La	2:1	dashed Israel's **g** city to earth
Da	5:18	great kingdom and a **g** reputation
Hag	2:3	Temple the way it used to be, all **g**
	2:9	**g** beginning but an even more **g**
Zec	12:8	weakest person will be as **g** as David
Mt	4:8	earth's kingdoms, how **g** they all were
	25:31	take his place on his **g** throne
Lk	9:31	what a **g** appearance they made
	21:27	welcomed in grand style—a **g** welcome
Ac	19:27	her **g** reputation fades to nothing
	19:35	protector of **g** Artemis
Ro	3:23	living the **g** lives God wills
	8:21	be released . . . into the **g** times ahead
	9:23	crafted to show his **g** goodness
1Co	15:43	when it's raised, it's **g**
Eph	1:11	had designs on us for **g** living
	1:14	a praising and **g** life
	1:18	**g** way of life he has for Christians
	3:16	a **g** inner strength
Php	2:11	to the **g** honor of God the Father
	3:21	into **g** bodies like his own
Col	1:27	know this rich and **g** secret
	3:4	the real you, the **g** you
Tit	2:13	**g** day when our great God and Savior
Jas	2:1	our **g**, Christ-originated faith
1Pe	5:10	eternal and **g** plans they are

Gloriously

Ps	90:6	springs up **g** with the rising sun
	104:1	beautifully, **g** robed
Mt	19:28	when the Son of Man will rule **g**
Jn	8:50	God intends something **g** grand
Ro	3:7	show off God's truth all the more **g**
	8:30	**g** completing what he had begun
2Co	1:20	God's Yes and our Yes together, **g**

Glory

Ex	14:4	put my **G** on display
	14:18	put my **G** on display
	16:7	you will see the **G** of God
	16:10	the **G** of God visible in the Cloud
	24:16	The **G** of God settled over Mount Sinai
	24:17	**G** of God looked like a raging fire
	28:2	to symbolize **g** and beauty
	28:40	to express **g** and beauty
	29:43	the place made holy by my **G**
	33:18	Please. Let me see your **G**
	33:22	When my **G** passes by
	40:34	the **G** of God filled The Dwelling
	40:35	the **G** of God filled The Dwelling
Lev	9:6	the Shining **G** of God will appear
	9:23	the **G** of God appeared to all
	10:3	I will show my **g**
Nu	14:10	the bright **G** of God appeared
	14:21	as the **G** of God fills the whole Earth
	14:22	saw my **G**, saw the miracle signs
	16:19	community could see the **G** of God
	16:42	the **G** of God for all to see
	20:6	they saw the **G** of God
Dt	5:24	God has revealed to us his **g**
Jos	7:19	My son, give **g** to God
Jdg	4:9	there'll be no **g** in it for you
	9:9	That gives **g** to gods and men
	13:6	terror laced with **g**
1Sa	4:21	named the boy Ichabod (**G**'s-Gone
	4:22	**G** is exiled from Israel
	6:5	offering to the **g** of the God of Israel
	15:20	Israel's God-of-**G** doesn't deceive
2Sa	6:21	I'll dance to God's **g**
1Ki	3:13	the wealth and **g** you didn't ask for
	8:11	the **g** of God filled The Temple of God
1Ch	16:24	Publish his **g** among the godless
	16:28	in awe of the **G**
	29:11	the **g**, the victory, the majesty
	29:12	Riches and **g** come from you
	29:28	full of days, wealth, and **g**
2Ch	5:14	the cloud — the **g** of God!
	7:1	the **G** of God filled The Temple
	7:2	The **G** was so dense
	7:3	saw . . . the **G** of God fill The Temple
Job	29:20	My soul suffused with **g**
Ps	18:28	I'm blazing with **g**, God's **g**
	19:1	God's **g** is on tour in the skies
	22:23	you God-worshipers; give **g**
	24:7	King-**G** is ready to enter
	24:8	Who is this King-**G**
	24:9	King-**G** is ready to enter
	24:10	Who is this King-**G**? God
	26:8	your house glows with your **g**
	29:2	In awe before the **g**
	29:9	we call out, "**G**
	57:5	Cover the whole earth with your **g**
	57:11	Cover the whole earth with your **g**
	61:8	I'll be the poet who sings your **g**
	62:7	My help and **g** are in God
	63:2	drinking in your strength and **g**
	66:2	songs to the tune of his **g**, set **g**

	72:19	blazing **g**! All earth brims with his **g**
	84:11	God, generous in gifts and **g**
	85:9	Our country is home base for **G**
	96:3	Take the news of his **g** to the lost
	102:15	see your **g**, worship your name
	102:16	when he shows up in all his **g**
	104:31	The **g** of God — let it last forever
	106:20	traded the **G** for a cheap
	106:47	join in the **g** when you are praised
	108:5	Cover the whole earth with your **g**
	115:1	for your name's sake, show your **g**
	138:5	How great the **g** of God
Pr	8:18	Wealth and **G** accompany me
	15:33	humility, then you experience **g**
	25:27	nor is **g** piled on **g** good for you
Isa	6:3	His bright **g** fills the whole earth
	10:16	Under the canopy of God's bright **g**
	24:15	from the east God's **g** will ascend
	26:15	the more **g** you display
	35:2	God's resplendent **g**, fully on display
	40:5	Then God's bright **g** will shine
	42:8	I don't franchise my **g**
	42:12	Make God's **g** resound
	43:7	Whom I created for my **g**
	44:23	God's **g** is on display in Israel
	46:13	and **g** in Israel
	58:8	The God of **g** will secure your passage
	59:19	they'll fear the **g** of God
	60:1	God's bright **g** has risen for you
	60:2	his sunrise **g** breaks over you
	60:21	with my own hands to display my **g**
	61:3	planted by God to display his **g**
	61:6	you'll bask in their **g**
	62:2	world leaders your **g**
	66:5	Let us see God's **g**!
	66:12	the **g** of nations like a river
	66:18	They'll come and see my **g**
	66:19	preach my **g** among the nations
Jer	2:11	my people have traded my **G**
	17:12	set high, a throne of **g**, exalted
	33:9	a center of joy and praise and **g**
	48:2	Moab's **g** — dust and ashes.
	49:4	dreams of **g** days and vainly thinks
La	5:16	crown of **g** has toppled
Eze	1:28	It turned out to be the **G** of God
	3:12	Blessed be the **G** of God
	3:23	the **G** of God! Right there!
	8:4	Right before me was the **G** of the God
	9:3	The **G** of the God of Israel ascended
	10:4	the **G** of God ascended
	10:18	the **G** of God left the Temple entrance
	10:19	The **G** of the God of Israel
	11:22	the **G** of the God of Israel hovering
	11:23	The **G** of God ascended from within
	39:21	I'll put my **g** on display
	43:2	The bright **G** of the God of Israel
	43:4	The bright **G** of God poured into
	43:5	the bright **G** of God filled the Temple
	44:4	the bright **G** of God filling the Temple
Da	2:37	rule, power, strength, and **g**
	4:30	adequate to display my honor and **g**
	7:14	all the **g** of royalty

G

G

	7:27	g of all the kingdoms under heaven
Hos	4:7	They traded in their g for shame
Mic	1:15	Glorytown has seen its last of g
	4:8	The g that once was will be again
Hab	2:14	fills up with awareness of God's g
Zec	2:8	the One of G who sent me
	12:7	the g of David's family
Mt	16:28	see the Son of Man in kingdom g
	17:1	three of them saw that g
Mk	10:37	places of honor in your g
Lk	2:9	God's g blazed around them
	2:14	G to God in the heavenly heights
	2:32	g for your people Israel
	5:25	giving g to God all the way
	5:26	also gave g to God
	9:32	they saw Jesus in his g
	13:13	straight and tall, giving g to God
	17:18	come back and give g to God
	19:38	G in the high places
	24:26	only then enter into his g
Jn	1:14	We saw the g with our own eyes
	2:11	Jesus gave, the first glimpse of his g
	11:4	show God's g by glorifying God's Son
	11:40	if you believed, you would see the g
	12:28	Father, put your g on display
	12:43	for human approval than for God's g
	13:32	God's g will be on display
	17:22	The same g you gave me, I gave them
	17:24	So they can see my g
Ac	7:2	the God of g appeared
	7:55	whom he saw in all his g with Jesus
	21:20	delight and gave God the g
Ro	1:23	They traded the g of God
	5:2	wide open spaces of God's grace and g
	9:4	family, g, covenants, revelation
	11:36	Always g! Always praise!
	14:6	eat it to the g of God
	15:7	welcome one another to God's g
1Co	10:31	you're eating to God's g
	15:40	the diversity of resurrection g
2Co	3:13	notice that the g was fading away
	4:15	to your advantage and to God's g
Gal	1:5	G to God forever!
Eph	1:17	Jesus Christ, the God of g
	3:21	G to God in the church!
	3:21	G to God in the Messiah, in Jesus! G
Php	1:11	involved in the g and praise of God
	4:19	the g that pours from Jesus
	4:20	Our God and Father abounds in g
Col	1:11	the g-strength God gives
	1:27	look forward to sharing in God's g
2Th	2:14	you get in on the g of our Master
1Ti	1:17	Deep honor and bright g to the King
	3:16	taken up into heavenly g
2Ti	2:10	the salvation of Christ in all its g
Heb	2:9	a g "bright with Eden's dawn light."
	2:10	he leads all these people to g
	13:21	All g to Jesus forever and always!
1Pe	1:11	suffering, followed by g
	4:13	g just around the corner
	4:14	the Spirit of God and his g in you
	5:1	sufferings as well as the coming g

2Pe	1:17	the voice of Majestic G spoke
	1:19	God's g, God's voice
	3:18	G to the Master, now and forever!
Jude	1:8	g dragged in the mud
	1:25	our Master, be g, majesty, strength
Rev	1:5	G and strength to Christ
	4:9	Animals gave g and honor and thanks
	4:11	Take the g! the honor! the power!
	5:12	Take the honor, the g, the blessing
	5:13	blessing, the honor, the g
	7:12	blessing and g and wisdom
	14:7	Fear God and give him g!
	15:4	God, give g to your Name
	15:8	God's g and power poured out
	18:1	his g flooded earth with brightness
	19:1	salvation and g and power are God's
	19:7	let us give him the g!
	21:11	resplendent in the bright g of God
	21:18	the color of G
	21:23	God's G is its light
	21:26	bring the g and honor of the nations

Glutton

Dt	21:20	He's a g and a drunk
Jer	51:44	I'll bring doom on the g god-Bel

Gluttonous

Jer	51:34	a huge g belch
Eze	16:49	proud, g, and lazy

Gluttons

Ps	69:12	drunks and g Make up drinking songs
Pr	23:21	Drunks and g will end up on skid row

Gluttony

Mt	23:25	maggoty with your greed and g

Goal

Dt	12:9	you haven't arrived at the g
Jn	14:28	the Father is the g and purpose
	17:21	g is for all of them to become one
Gal	1:10	If my g was popularity
Php	3:13	I've got my eye on the g
	3:15	let's keep focused on that g
	3:17	headed for this same g
Col	4:6	g is to bring out the best in others
Heb	4:1	pulls us on to God's g for us

Goals

Am	5:22	your pretentious slogans and g
Php	3:18	other paths, choosing other g

Gobble

Job	18:12	hungry grave is ready to g them up
Pr	23:2	Don't g your food

God-acts

| Jas | 2:17 | God-talk without **G** is outrageous |

God-adulteries

| Jer | 13:27 | your goddess affairs, your **g** |

God-affirmers

| Ps | 32:10 | **G** find themselves loved |

God-alive

Ge	16:14	got named "G-Sees-Me Spring."
1Sa	17:26	taunting the armies of **G**
	17:36	taunting the troops of **G**
Job	27:2	**G**! He's denied me justice!
Ps	42:2	I'm thirsty for **G**
	84:2	I could sing for joy to **G**
Isa	11:9	knowing **G**, a living knowledge of God
1Ti	3:15	this **G** church, bastion of truth

God-alive-sees-me

| Ge | 16·14 | desert spring got named "G Spring." |

God-avoidance

| Pr | 14:34 | **G** leaves people weak |

God-aware

| Isa | - 23:18 | put to the use of **G**, God-Serving |

God-bashers

| Ro | 1:30 | fork-tongued **G** |

God-begotten

Jn	1:13	These are the **G**, not blood-begotten
1Jn	3:9	not in the nature of the **G**
	5:1	Jesus is, in fact, the Messiah, is **G**
	5:4	Every **G** person conquers
	5:18	none of the **G** makes a practice of sin

God-believing

| Mt | 18:7 | giving these **G** children a hard time |

God-blessed

Isa	65:23	children and grandchildren likewise **G**
Jer	3:24	**G** flocks and God-given children
Mt	13:16	**G** eyes — eyes that see! And **G**
	24:46	A **G** man or woman, I tell you
Ro	14:16	Don't you dare let a piece of **G** food

God-breathed

| Ti | 3:16 | Scripture is **G** and useful |

God-business

| Rev | 2:21 | giving up a career in the **g** |

God-businesses

| Jer | 25:6 | Don't make me angry with your **g** |

God-created

Mt	5:45	your true selves, your **G** selves
	5:48	Live out your **G** identity
Lk	6:35	Live out this **G** identity
Ac	17:28	We're the **G**
	17:29	if we are the **G**

God-deniers

| Ps | 2:2 | The **G**, the Messiah-defiers |
| Ac | 4:26 | The **G**, the Messiah-defiers |

God-designed

| 1Co | 2:8 | killed the Master of the **G** life |

God-direction

| 2Sa | 22:31 | Every **G** is road-tested |
| Ps | 18:30 | Every **G** is road-tested |

God-dreams

| Jer | 2:8 | chased empty **g** and silly god-schemes |
| | 2:11 | traded my Glory for empty **g** |

God-expectant

| Ps | 14:2 | someone not stupid — one man, even, **G** |
| | 53:2 | someone not stupid — one man, even, **G** |

God-expression

| Jn | 1:18 | This one-of-a-kind **G**, who exists |

God-fearers

| Mal | 3:16 | with the names of the **G** written down |

God-fearing

Ge	42:18	Do this and you'll live. I'm a **G** man
Isa	57:1	**G** people are carted off
Ac	10:22	a **G** man well-known for his fair play
	16:14	known to be a **G** woman
	17:4	among them a great many **G** Greeks
	18:7	Titius Justus, a **G** man
	21:20	**G** Jews have become believers
	26:23	people both godless and **G**

God-filled

| 1Co | 1:2 | set apart for a **G** life |
| Tit | 2:12 | how to take on a **G**, God-honoring life |

God-for-us

| Ps | 68:20 | He's **G**, he's God-who-saves-us |

God-frauds

| Jnh | 2:8 | Those who worship hollow gods, **g** |

God-friendship

| Ps | 25:14 | **G** is for God-worshipers |

God-haters

2Ch	19:2	cozying up to **G**
Ps	38:20	**G** who can't stand a God-lover
	81:15	I'll send the **G** cringing like dogs
	83:2	the **G** are living it up

God-honored

| 1Sa | 25:29 | Your **G** life is tightly bound |

God-honoring

1Ki	3:3	live in the **G** ways of David
Pr	25:5	authority will be credible and **G**
Isa	58:2	right-living people — law-abiding, **G**
Tit	2:12	how to take on a God-filled, **G** life

God-ignorant

| Job | 18:21 | This is how the **G** end up |
| 1Pe | 4:3 | your time in that **G** way of life |

God-image

| Dt | 27:15 | anyone who carves or casts a **g** |

God-images

Dt	7:5	set fire to their carved **g**
Isa	30:22	scrap your expensive and fashionable **g**
Jer	7:30	their obscene **g** in the very Temple
Hos	10:2	pulverize their **g**
	13:2	manufacturing **g** they can use

God-imitations

| Ps | 139:20 | infatuated with cheap **g** |

God-initiative

| Mt | 6:33 | Steep your life in God-reality, **G** |
| Lk | 12:31 | Steep yourself in God-reality, **G** |

God-inspired

| Hos | 9:6 | What use will all your **g** silver be |

God-junk

| Jer | 16:18 | piles of stinking **g** all over |

God-knowledge

| Pr | 8:10 | **G** over a lucrative career |
| Hos | 6:3 | ready to study God, eager for **G** |

God-life

| Mk | 11:22 | Embrace this **G**. Really embrace it |
| | 11:24 | embrace this **G**, and you'll get God's |

God-light

Jn	3:19	**G** streamed into the world
	3:20	hates **G** and won't come near it
	3:21	welcomes **G** so the work can be seen

God-lover

| Ps | 38:20 | God-haters who can't stand a **G** |

God-loyal

Pr	13:6	A **G** life keeps you on track
	13:21	**G** people get a good life
	14:19	the wicked will respect **G** people
	15:6	The lives of **G** people flourish
	15:28	Prayerful answers come from **G** people
	15:29	attends to the prayers of **G** people
	16:31	the award for a **G** life
	20:7	**G** people, living honest lives
	21:12	A **G** person will see right through
	21:26	the **G** are always giving
	24:16	**G** people don't stay down long

God-maker

| Hab | 2:18 | sense does it make to be a pious **g** |

God-makers

| Jer | 10:14 | **g** embarrassed by their handmade gods |
| | 51:17 | **g** embarrassed by their handmade gods |

God-making

2Ki	22:17	angry by setting up their **g** businesses
2Ch	34:25	angry by setting up their **g** businesses
Jer	25:7	**g** businesses of yours are your doom

God-news

| 1Sa | 2:1 | I'm bursting with **G**! |
| Lk | 1:46 | I'm bursting with **G** |

God-planted

Ro   11:16   a holy, G, God-tended root

God-pleasing

1Ki   10:9   nurture a G people
2Ch   9:8   nurture a G people

God-protected

1Sa   25:29   bound in the bundle of G life
1Jn   5:18   The God-begotten are also the G

God-provisions

Mt   6:33   life in God-reality, God-initiative, G
Lk   12:31   in God-reality, God-initiative, G

God-questers

Ps   24:6   what happens to God-seekers, G

God-reality

Isa   44:11   Make them face G
Mt   6:33   Steep your life in G, God-initiative
Lk   12:31   Steep yourself in G, God-initiative

God-rebel

Ps   36:1   The G tunes in to sedition

God-redeemed

Isa   62:12   Holy People, G, Sought-Out

God-rejecting

Jn   17:9   not praying for the G world

God-revealed

Hos   12:5   God-of-the-Angel-Armies, G, God-Known
Am   5:8   God, G, does all this
Mic   5:4   centered in the majesty of G

God-revealer

Jn   1:31   ready to recognize him as the G

God-revealing

Lk   2:32   A G light to the non-Jewish nations
Jn   3:2   all the God-pointing, G acts you do
      9:16   can a bad man do miraculous, G things
      20:30   Jesus provided far more G signs

God-saved

Co   9:22   lead those I meet into a G life

God-saves

Nu   13:16   a new name — Joshua (G

God-seekers

1Ch   16:10   Revel in his holy Name, G, be jubilant
Ps   5:12   You are famous, God, for welcoming G
      24:6   This, Jacob, is what happens to G
      34:10   G are full of God
      69:32   Oh, you G, take heart

God-shaped

Pr   11:28   a G life is a flourishing tree

God-stories

Ps   26:7   telling G

God-story

Ro   4:2   the story we're given is a G

God-strong

Ps   37:17   the righteous are G
Zec   10:12   I'll make them strong, G

God-talk

Jas   2:17   G without God-acts is outrageous

God-taught

1Th   4:9   You're G in these matters

God-tended

Ro   11:16   a holy, God-planted, G root

God-thoughts

Ps   40:5   stockpile of God-wonders and G

God-visited

1Ki   9:9   what's behind this G devastation
2Ch   7:22   what's behind this G devastation

God-who-puts-everything-right

Jer   23:6   This is the name they'll give him: 'G

God-willed

Pr   15:32   an obedient, G life is spacious
Eze   36:26   a heart that's G, not self-willed

G

God-with-us

| Isa | 7:14 | a son and name him Immanuel (G |
| | 8:10 | the last word is Immanuel — G |

God-wrestler

| Ge | 32:28 | From now on it's Israel (G) |
| | 35:10 | From now on your name is Israel (G |

Godforsaken

Nu	21:5	out of Egypt to die in this g country
Ps	10:12	The luckless think they're G
Jer	8:3	still be alive in whatever g place
	51:37	a g ghost town
Ac	13:18	forty years in that g wilderness

Godless

1Ch	14:17	fear of God into the g nations
	16:24	Publish his glory among the g nations
	16:35	get us out of these g places
Job	8:19	The sooner the g are gone, the better
	15:34	The g are fruitless
	20:5	g joy is only momentary
Ps	9:5	You blow the whistle on g nations
	9:15	They're trapped, those g countries
	44:2	weeded out the g from the fields
	44:14	You made us a joke among the g
	46:6	G nations rant and rave
	47:8	God is Lord of g nations
	59:8	treat the g nations like jokes
	66:7	keeps his eye on the g nations
	67:2	all the g nations see how you save
	72:11	g nations sign up to serve him
	72:17	May all g people enter his circle
	79:10	Go public and show the g world
	102:15	g nations will sit up and take notice
	104:35	no more g men and women
	106:34	didn't wipe out those g cultures
	119:69	The g spread lies about me
	119:85	arrogant g try to throw me off track
	119:122	don't let the g take advantage of me
	135:15	gods of the g nations are mere
	139:21	I loathe all this g arrogance
Pr	11:9	tongue of the g spreads destruction
Isa	9:17	All of them were g and evil
	10:6	I send him against a g nation
	33:14	the g are at their wit's end
Jer	3:17	All the g nations, no longer stuck
	3:19	land that the g nations would die for
	4:2	g nations will get caught up
	9:16	scatter them . . . among g peoples
	10:2	the g nations as your models
	10:10	the g nations quake
	10:25	Vent your anger on the g nations
	14:22	the no-gods of the g nations
	16:19	The g nations will come
	18:13	Ask around. Survey the g nations
	25:13	preached against all the g nations
	25:31	makes his case against the g nations

	30:11	I'll finish off all the g nations
	46:1	Jeremiah regarding the g nations
	46:28	I'll finish off all the g nations
	51:20	I'll use you to smash g nations
Eze	7:21	the g spit on it and make jokes
Hos	3:4	without religion and comfort, g
	9:17	vagabonds among the g nations
Joel	3:2	I'll assemble all the g nations
	3:9	Announce this to the g nations
Ob	1:1	messenger sent out to the g nations
	1:2	the runt of the g nations
	1:11	G foreigners invaded and pillaged
	1:15	Judgment Day is near for all the g
	1:16	g nations will drink God's wrath
Mic	4:11	ganged up against you, many g peoples
	4:13	God's juggernaut to crush the g
	5:15	I'll make a clean sweep of g nations
	7:16	the g nations: Put them in their place
Hab	1:5	Look around at the g nations
	3:12	Furious, you crushed the g nations
Zep	3:6	So I cut off the g nations
Hag	2:7	I'll shake down all the g nations
Zec	1:15	angry with the g nations
	1:21	They'll dehorn the g nations
	2:8	the g nations who stripped you
	2:11	g nations will be linked up with God
	12:9	clean sweep of all the g nations
	14:2	bringing all the g nations to war
	14:3	God will march out against the g
	14:16	All the survivors from the g nations
Mt	18:8	g in a furnace of eternal fire
	20:25	g rulers throw their weight around
Mk	9:43	g in a furnace of eternal fire
	10:42	g rulers throw their weight around
Jn	14:17	The g world can't take him in
	14:30	this g world is about to attack
	15:18	you find the g world is hating you
	16:8	error of the g world's view of sin
	16:11	this g world is brought to trial
	16:20	while the g world throws a party
	16:33	In this g world you will continue
	17:14	The g world hated them because of it
	17:23	give the g world evidence
Ac	21:11	hand him over to g unbelievers
	26:23	people both g and God-fearing
Ro	1:27	g and loveless wretches
Tit	2:12	turn our backs on a g, indulgent life
Jas	1:27	guard against corruption from the g

Godlessness

| Ps | 10:16 | God's grace and order wins; g loses |
| Jer | 23:15 | cause of the g polluting this country |

Godlike

Ge	1:27	human beings; he created them g
	5:1	human race, he made it g
Zec	12:8	family of David itself will be g

Godliness

Mt	5:13	how will people taste **g**

Godly

Nu	24:16	the man who hears **g** speech
2Sa	9:3	to whom I can show some **g** kindness
2Ch	26:5	Uzziah lived a **g** life
Pr	11:9	common sense of the **g** preserves them
1Ti	6:3	this **g** instruction
2Ti	2:16	If they're not backed by a **g** life
2Pe	2:9	God knows how to rescue the **g**

Going-to-work

Ro	12:1	your sleeping, eating, **g** . . . life

Good-for-nothing

2Sa	20:1	Just then a **g** named Sheba
Jer	30:17	dismissed you as hopeless — that **g**

Good-for-nothings

Am	6:7	a rag-tag bunch of **g**
2Th	3:11	a bunch of lazy **g**
Tit	1:16	real creeps, disobedient **g**

Good-hearted

Job	17:8	the **g** wake up and insist
Ps	64:10	**G** people, make praise your habit
	73:1	good to good people, good to the **g**
Pr	12:10	the "**g**" bad people kick and abuse
	29:7	**g** understand what it's like

Good-looking

Dt	21:11	a **g** woman whom you find attractive
1Sa	16:12	picture of health — bright-eyed, **g**
	16:18	courageous, of age, well-spoken, and **g**
	25:3	The woman was intelligent and **g**
1Ki	1:6	he was very **g** and the next in line
Est	1:11	She was extremely **g**
Eze	23:6	**g** young men mounted on fine horses
	23:23	**g** young men, ambassadors and governors

Goodness

Ex	33:19	make my **G** pass right in front of you
Dt	28:47	out of the joy and **g** of your heart
1Sa	25:30	completes all the **g** he has promised
2Sa	2:6	matching your generous act of **g**
1Ch	17:19	O God, out of the **g** of your heart
2Ch	6:41	let your holy people celebrate **g**
Ne	9:25	reveled in your bountiful **g**
	9:35	enjoying your generous **g**
Job	1:9	out of the sheer **g** of his heart
	7:7	have had their last look at **g**
Ps	18:25	The good people taste your **g**
	27:13	see God's **g** in the exuberant earth

	34:9	worship opens doors to all his **g**
	45:1	spilling beauty and **g**
	48:10	your arms are heaped with **g**-in-action
	73:2	nearly missed it, missed seeing his **g**
	85:12	God gives **G** and Beauty
	103:5	He wraps you in **g** — beauty eternal
	119:68	train me in your **g**
	128:2	Enjoy the blessing! Revel in the **g**
	145:7	The fame of your **g** spreads
Pr	25:22	generosity will surprise him with **g**
	29:27	can't stand the sight of well-chosen **g**
Isa	42:21	intended, out of the **g** of his heart
	45:8	pour out buckets of my **g**
	48:9	out of the sheer **g** of my heart
	63:7	God, his great **g** to the family
Eze	20:25	statutes that could not produce **g**
Ru	9:23	crafted to show his glorious **g**
	12:3	people who are bringing this **g** to God
	12:20	generosity will surprise him with **g**
	14:17	put in your stomach, for **g**' sake
Tit	2:3	nor drunks, but models of **g**
	2:14	he can be proud of, energetic in **g**
Heb	6:5	experienced the sheer **g** of God's Word

Gorging

1Sa	30:16	**g** themselves on all the loot
Isa	9:20	stuffing and **g** themselves

Gossip

Ex	23:1	Don't pass on malicious **g**
Lev	19:16	Don't spread **g** and rumors
Job	5:21	You'll be protected from vicious **g**
	15:4	spiritual conversation into empty **g**
	31:34	fearing the **g** of the neighbors
Ps	31:13	street-talk **g** has me "criminal
	31:20	you silence the poisonous **g**
	35:20	spend all their time cooking up **g**
	41:6	gathering **g** about me to entertain
	44:16	**G** and ridicule fill the air
	52:4	You love malicious **g**
	71:11	The **g** is: "God has abandoned him
	101:5	the **g** who bad-mouths his neighbor
	112:7	Unfazed by rumor and **g**
	119:23	bad neighbors maliciously **g** about me
Pr	4:24	careless banter, white lies, and **g**
	11:13	A gadabout **g** can't be trusted
	12:13	**g** of bad people gets them in trouble
	16:27	Mean people spread mean **g**
	17:4	ears of liars itch for dirty **g**
	18:8	Listening to **g** is like eating cheap
	24:28	no slander or **g**, please
	26:20	when the **g** ends, the quarrel dies
	26:22	Listening to **g** is like eating cheap
	29:12	When a leader listens to malicious **g**
Ecc	7:21	What if the **g**'s about you
	10:20	birds drop the crumbs of your **g**
Jer	9:4	spreads malicious **g**
	48:27	didn't you cluck and **g** and snicker
La	3:61	You heard, God, their vicious **g**
Eze	36:3	you've become the butt of cheap **g**

G

Mic	1:10	Don't g about this in Telltown
Mk	5:39	Why all this busybody grief and g
Ac	17:21	Athens was a great place for g
2Co	12:16	keep coming across these whiffs of g
Eph	5:4	some tongues just love the taste of g
1Ti	1:6	wander off into cul-de-sacs of g
	5:13	their days on empty talk, g

Gossips

Ps	63:11	small-minded g are gagged for good
	70:3	those g off clucking their tongues
Pr	16:28	g break up friendships
	20:19	G can't keep secrets
Mt	9:23	pushed their way through the g
Mk	5:38	pushed their way through the g
Tit	2:3	end up as neither g nor drunks

Gossipy

Pr	25:23	a g tongue stormy looks
Mt	9:4	Why this g whispering
Lk	5:22	Why all this g whispering

Govern

Lev	26:17	People who hate you will g you
1Ki	3:11	the ability to lead and g well
2Ch	1:11	so you could g well my people
Pr	8:16	With my help, governors g

Government

2Sa	8:6	David set up a puppet g
	8:14	David set up a puppet g
1Ki	4:2	These were the leaders in his g
	9:22	g leaders and commanders
	13:34	root sin of Jeroboam's g
	18:18	your g — you've dumped God's ways
2Ki	15:5	his son Jotham ran the g
	24:12	advisors, and g leaders, surrendered
1Ch	18:6	David set up a puppet g
	18:13	He set up a puppet g
2Ch	8:9	g leaders and commanders
	21:4	some of the g officials
	26:21	took over the g of the country
Est	3:1	highest-ranking official in the g
	5:11	to the highest position in the g
	9:3	the g officials, satraps, governors
Isa	7:2	When the Davidic g learned
	7:13	listen to this, g of David
	7:17	on you and your people and your g
	16:5	A new g of love will be established
	17:3	not a trace of g left in Damascus
	22:21	father-leader to Jerusalem and the g
Jer	29:2	the queen mother, the g leaders
	36:12	g officials were holding a meeting
	36:19	The g officials told Baruch
	36:31	his g for their blatant sin
	38:25	If the g officials get wind
	44:17	kings and g leaders in the cities
	44:21	your kings, your g officials

Da	1:4	leadership positions in the g
	3:27	the g leaders and king's counselors
Mt	4:23	under God's g, a good g
Ro	13:3	want to be on good terms with the g
	13:4	g working to your advantage
2Co	3:7	The G of Death
	3:8	the G of Living Spirit
	3:9	the G of Condemnation was impressive
	3:10	Bright as that old g was
	3:11	shining g installed for eternity
	3:15	that old, bankrupt g
Tit	3:1	respect the g and be law-abiding
1Pe	2:17	Revere God. Respect the g

Governmental

1Ch	28:1	heads of various g operations

Governments

1Sa	10:18	g that made your life miserable
Jer	1:10	a job to do among nations and g
Hag	2:22	overthrow g, destroy foreign powers
Ro	13:1	All g are under God
Eph	1:21	everything from galaxies to g
1Ti	2:2	Pray especially for rulers and their g

Governs

2Sa	23:3	Whoever g fairly and well

Grace

Ge	43:14	may The Strong God give you g
Ex	34:6	God, a God of mercy and g
Jdg	5:30	to g the neck of the plunderer
Ru	2:13	such g, such kindness
2Sa	15:20	God's g and truth go with you
Ne	9:31	you are a God of g and compassion
Job	22:30	escape through God's g in your life
	37:13	discipline or g or extravagant love
Ps	4:1	Now I'm in trouble again: g me!
	10:16	God's g and order wins
	17:7	Paint g-graffiti on the fences
	41:10	God, give g, get me up on my feet
	45:2	every word from your lips is sheer g
	51:1	Generous in love — God, give g!
	67:1	God, mark us with g and blessing!
	103:8	God is sheer mercy and g
	111:4	This God of G, this God of Love
	112:4	God's g and mercy and justice
	119:29	g me with your clear revelation
	145:8	God is all mercy and g
	145:9	everything he does is suffused with g
Pr	4:9	She'll garland your life with g
	11:16	A woman of gentle g gets respect
	14:14	a gracious person in g
	15:26	puts words of g and beauty on display
Ecc	9:11	Nor g to the learned
SS	6:13	we'll feast our eyes on your g
Isa	26:10	If the wicked are shown g
	30:19	you'll find it's g and more g

	61:2	announce the year of his g
Jer	31:2	They found g out in the desert
Da	1:9	by God's g, liked Daniel
Jnh	4:2	knew you were sheer g and mercy
Zec	12:10	pour a spirit of g and prayer over
Mal	3:12	what it's like to be a country of g
Mt	6:6	you will begin to sense his g
	8:12	outsiders to g and wondering
	11:29	Learn the unforced rhythms of g
	19:11	requires a certain aptitude and g
Lk	2:40	the g of God was on him
	13:28	strangers to g
Ac	4:33	g was on all of them
	6:8	brimming with God's g and energy
	13:43	this living in and by God's g
	14:26	God's g and now safely home by God's g
	15:40	offered up by their friends to the g
Ro	5:2	wide open spaces of God's g
	5:20	aggressive forgiveness we call g
	5:21	G, because God is putting everything
	6:3	entered into the new country of g
	6:5	our new g-sovereign country
	11:6	convinced of God's g and purpose
	12:3	as every one of you does, in pure g
1Co	10:5	experiencing God's wonder and g
	10:23	God's immense generosity and g
	15:10	not about to let his g go to waste
2Co	4:15	to God's glory: more and more g
	4:16	not . . . without his unfolding g
	12:9	My g is enough; it's all you need
	13:14	amazing g of the Master, Jesus Christ
Gal	1:3	the great words, g and peace
	1:6	who called you by the g of Christ
	2:21	refuse to . . . repudiate God's g
	4:17	out of the free world of God's g
	5:4	you fall out of g
Eph	1:2	greet you with the g and peace
	2:7	shower g and kindness upon us
	6:24	Pure g and nothing but g be with all
Php	1:2	the g and peace that comes from God
	4:23	experience the amazing g of the Master
Col	4:18	G be with you
1Th	1:1	God's amazing g be with you!
	5:28	amazing g of Jesus Christ be with you
2Th	1:12	G is behind and through all of this
	3:18	incredible g of our Master
1Ti	1:14	G mixed with faith and love poured
	6:21	Overwhelming g keep you
2Ti	4:22	God be with you. G be with you
Tit	3:15	G to all of you
Heb	2:9	by God's g, he fully experienced death
	12:24	became a proclamation of g
	13:9	g of Christ is the only good ground
	13:25	G be with you, every one
Jas	4:6	God gives g to the willing humble
1Pe	3:7	new life of God's g, you're equals
2Pe	1:2	G and peace to you many times
	3:18	Grow in g and understanding
2Jn	1:3	Let g, mercy, and peace be with us
Jude	1:4	replace the sheer g of our God
Rev	22:21	The g of the Master Jesus be with all

Graceful

SS	2:9	My lover is like a gazelle, g
	7:1	Shapely and g your sandaled feet
Eph	4:13	g in response to God's Son

Graces

2Sa	14:22	know that I'm still in your good g
	15:25	If I get back in God's good g
Ezr	9:9	put us in the good g of the kings

Gracious

Ge	43:29	God be g to you, my son
Ru	4:13	By God's g gift she conceived
2Sa	7:16	I'll never remove my g love from him
2Ki	13:23	God was g and showed mercy to them
1Ch	17:13	never remove my g love from him
2Ch	30:9	Your God is g and kind
Ne	9:17	forgiving God, g and compassionate
Ps	41:4	God, be g! Put me together again
	84:9	shining with your g anointing
	116:5	God is g
	119:58	be g to me just as you promised
	145:13	God . . . is g in everything he does
Pr	13:15	Sound thinking makes for g living
	14:14	a g person in grace
	16:21	g words add to one's reputation
	16:24	G speech is like clover honey
	22:1	a g spirit is better than money
Ecc	10:12	The words of a wise person are g
Isa	30:18	waiting around to be g to you
	63:7	make a list of God's g dealings
Da	4:2	g miracles that the High God has done
Am	5:15	will notice your remnant and be g
Mal	1:9	pray that I will be g to you
Ac	20:32	marvelous God whose g Word can make
1Co	15:10	God was so g, so very generous
Php	4:8	authentic, compelling, g
Col	4:6	Be g in your speech
Heb	10:29	insult this most g Spirit
	12:25	don't turn a deaf ear to these g words
1Pe	3:4	inner beauty, the gentle, g kind

Graciously

Ge	24:14	you're working g behind the scenes
Ru	1:8	may God treat you as g
1Ki	15:4	his God g gave him a lamp
Mt	5:48	Live generously and g toward others
Lk	6:35	toward us, generously and g
	9:11	Jesus g welcomed them
Ac	15:4	were g received by the whole church

Graduate

Jer	2:33	taught g courses in evil

Graduated

2Ch	22:4	g with a degree in doom

Graduates

Jer	2:34	**g**, resplendent in cap and gown

Graft

Ro	11:20	your **g** "took" when you believed
	11:24	if he could **g** you

Grafted

Ro	11:17	wild olive shoots were **g** in
	11:19	pruned so that I could be **g** in
	11:22	gentle with the **g** shoot
	11:23	could very well get **g** back in

Grafting

Ro	11:24	**g** branches back into the tree

Grafts

Ro	11:23	He can perform miracle **g**

Grateful

Ge	47:25	Master, we're **g** and glad to be slaves
2Ch	32:25	instead of making Hezekiah **g**
Job	29:18	**g** for a long and full life
Ps	63:6	spend the hours in **g** reflection
Mt	8:4	Your cleansed and **g** life
Lk	7:16	then noisily, **g**, calling out
	7:42	Which of the two would be more **g**
	7:47	so she is very, very **g**
	17:16	He kneeled at Jesus' feet, so **g**
Jn	11:41	Father, I'm **g** that you have listened
Ac	24:2	we are most **g** in all times and places
Ro	16:4	I'm not the only one **g** to them
1Co	10:30	**g** to God for what is on the table
	14:18	I'm **g** to God for the gift of praying
1Ti	1:12	I'm so **g** to Christ Jesus

Gratifying

Pr	18:20	good talk is as **g** as a good harvest
Eze	6:9	**g** themselves in their idolatries
1Th	3:6	especially **g** to know

Grating

Ex	38:5	the bronze **g** to hold the poles
	38:30	Bronze Altar with its bronze **g**

Gratitude

Ge	47:31	bowed his head in submission and **g**
1Ki	8:66	exuberant with heartfelt **g**
2Ki	5:15	In **g** let me give you a gift
Isa	29:24	complainers and whiners learn **g**
Lk	7:47	the **g** is minimal
	17:15	shouting his **g**, glorifying God
Ro	12:3	deep **g** for all that God has given me

2Co	9:13	live at your very best, showing your **g**
Col	4:2	your eyes wide open in **g**
1Ti	5:4	pay back with **g** some of what

Greed

Job	20:20	their **g** drives them relentlessly
Ps	78:30	But their **g** knew no bounds
Eze	18:8	doesn't live by impulse and **g**
	18:17	doesn't live by impulse and **g**
	22:13	attention to your rapacious **g**
	34:10	I'll rescue my sheep from their **g**
Mt	6:23	live squinty-eyed in **g** and distrust
	21:38	they rubbed their hands in **g**
	23:25	maggoty with your **g** and gluttony
Mk	7:22	**g**, depravity, deceptive dealings,
	12:7	rubbed their hands together in **g**
Lk	11:34	live squinty-eyed in **g** and distrust
	11:39	maggoty with **g** and secret evil
	12:15	against the least bit of **g**
Eph	5:3	filthy practices, or bullying **g**
2Pe	2:14	Their specialty is **g**
Jude	1:11	sucked into Balaam's error by **g**

Greedy

Dt	7:25	Don't get **g** for the veneer of silver
Pr	15:27	**g** and grasping person destroys
	30:14	Don't be **g**, merciless and cruel
Ecc	4:8	compulsively **g** for more and more
SS	8:12	Solomon, you and your **g** guests
1Co	5:11	becomes **g** and predatory
Php	1:17	merely **g**, hoping to get something
Jas	5:3	**g** luxuries are a cancer in your gut

Greeting

Ru	2:4	**g** his harvesters, "God be with you!"
2Ki	10:15	G him, he said, "Are we together
Isa	51:16	**g** Zion: 'Welcome, my people
Mt	10:12	be courteous in your **g**
	23:34	**g** them with lynch mobs
Lk	1:29	what was behind a **g** like that
	1:41	When Elizabeth heard Mary's **g**
	1:44	moment the sound of your **g** entered
	7:45	You gave me no **g**
	10:6	If your **g** is received
Jn	20:21	Jesus repeated his **g**: "Peace to you
Ac	10:25	Cornelius was up on his feet **g** him
	21:19	After a time of **g** and small talk
Ro	8:15	adventurously expectant, **g** God
1Co	1:2	**g** all who call out to Jesus
2Co	1:2	joins me in this **g**
Heb	11:13	waved their **g**

Greetings

Isa	9:3	sharing rich gifts and warm **g**
	39:1	messengers with **g** and a gift
Ac	23:26	Honorable Governor Felix: G
Ro	16:16	send their warmest **g**
	16:21	some more **g** from our end

	16:22	send you my personal g
	16:23	good friend Quartus send their g
1Co	16:19	churches here in western Asia send g
	16:20	Pass the g around with holy embraces
Gal	1:1	send g to the Galatian churches
Col	4:10	in jail here with me, sends g
	4:14	physician, and Demas both send g
1Th	1:1	g to the church at Thessalonica
2Ti	4:21	all your friends here send g
2Jn	1:13	your sister congregation sends g

Grief

Ge	37:34	Jacob tore his clothes in g
	44:31	He'll die of g
	44:34	watch my father die in g
	50:10	letting their g out in loud
	50:11	saw the g being poured out
Job	2:12	as a sign of their g
	5:11	firm footing to those sinking in g
	10:17	pile on the g and pain
Pr	21:23	you'll save yourself a lot of g
Ecc	2:23	Pain and g from dawn to dusk
Isa	15:3	Everyone in tears, everyone in g
	15:4	Moab sobs, shaking in g
	17:11	you'll get nothing but g and pain
	54:6	an abandoned wife, devastated with g
Jer	8:18	I drown in g. I'm heartsick
	8:21	I weep, seized by g
	31:13	invading their g with joy
	31:16	Collect wages from your g work
Eze	24:17	Keep your g to yourself
	27:30	cry out in g, a choir of bitter lament
Hos	4:3	everything in it is g-stricken
Mk	5:39	Why all this busybody g and gossip
Lk	15:29	never giving you one moment of g
	22:45	found them asleep, drugged by g
	23:48	overcome with g and headed home
1Co	7:30	g, joy, whatever
Php	2:27	His death would have been one huge g
2Ti	3:11	suffering along with me in all the g

Grief-stricken

Hos	4:3	everything in it is g

Grievance

Job	36:13	people without God pile g upon g

Grieve

Isa	15:5	Oh, how I g for Moab!
	22:4	Let me g by myself
	32:15	g until the Spirit is poured down
Zec	12:12	Everyone will weep and g
Eph	4:30	Don't g God. Don't break his heart

Grieved

1Sa	15:35	he g long and deeply over him
	25:1	Everyone g over his death

2Sa	11:26	she g for her husband
1Ch	7:22	Ephraim g a long time
Isa	63:10	they g his Holy Spirit
2Co	7:7	how much you cared, how much you g

Grieves

Joel	1:10	The very ground g

Grieving

Ge	44:29	put my old gray, g head in the grave
2Sa	1:12	g the death of Saul and his son
	14:2	you'll look like you've been g
	19:2	David is g over his son
Ecc	7:4	Sages invest themselves in hurt and g
Isa	60:20	Your days of g are over
Zec	12:10	mourning as of a parent g the loss

Groan

Ps	12:5	dark streets where the homeless g
	31:10	My life leaks away, g by g
	34:15	his ears pick up every moan and g
Jer	51:52	all over this land her wounded will g
Eze	21:6	So, son of man, g!
	24:23	you'll g among yourselves
	30:24	g like one who is mortally wounded
Joel	1:18	farm animals g — oh, how they g

Groaned

Ex	2:23	Israelites g under their slavery
La	1:11	people g, so desperate for food
Mt	27:46	Jesus g out of the depths
Mk	7:34	Jesus looked up in prayer, g mightily
	15:34	Jesus g out of the depths

Groaning

Jdg	2:18	compassion when he heard their g
Job	24:12	dying right and left, g in torment
Ps	79:11	Give g prisoners a hearing
Isa	21:2	put an end to all the moaning and g
	29:2	The moaning and g will continue
	59:11	We're no better off than bears, g
La	1:22	G in pain, body and soul
	2:5	left Daughter Judah moaning and g
Eze	21:7	Why all this g, this carrying on
Am	2:13	overloaded, creaking and g

Groanings

Ex	2:24	God listened to their g
	6:5	heard the g of the Israelites

Groans

Job	3:24	Instead of bread I get g for my supper
Ps	5:2	my g and cries? King-God, I need you
	32:3	my words became daylong g
	38:8	my life is a vomit of g

	38:9	my **g** an old story to you
	102:20	listened to the **g** of the doomed
Pr	29:2	when the ruler is bad, everyone **g**
Isa	51:11	not a sign of moans or **g**
La	1:8	Miserable, she **g** and turns away
	1:21	listen to my **g**. No one listens
Eze	26:15	at the **g** of your wounded
Ac	7:34	people in Egypt. I've heard their **g**
Ro	8:26	our wordless sighs, our aching **g**
Jas	5:4	**g** of the workers you used and abused

Groom

Mk	2:19	As long as the bride and **g** are with
Lk	5:34	As long as the bride and **g** are with
	5:35	When the **g** is gone, the fasting
Rev	18:23	never again laughter of bride and **g**

Grounded

Isa	54:14	built solid, **g** in righteousness
Col	1:23	**g** and steady in that bond of trust

Groundless

Nu	5:14	his jealousy and suspicions are **g**

Grovel

Ps	129:5	who hate Zion **g** in humiliation
Jer	25:34	**G** in the dirt, you masters of flocks
Mic	4:11	want to see Zion **g** in the dirt
1Co	13:6	Doesn't revel when others **g**

Groveling

Jos	7:10	Get up. Why are you **g**
Est	7:8	Haman was **g** at the couch

Grow

Ge	1:11	Earth, green up! **G** all varieties
	2:9	God made all kinds of trees **g**
	48:16	may they **g** covering the Earth
Ex	23:29	lest the land **g** up in weeds
Lev	13:37	black hair has begun to **g** in it
	26:9	make sure you **g** in numbers
Dt	26:2	firstfruits of what you **g** in the land
	30:9	have babies, get calves, **g** crops
Jdg	16:19	Immediately he began to **g** weak
	16:22	hair, though cut off, began to **g** again
Ru	4:14	May this baby **g** up to be famous
2Sa	10:5	Stay in Jericho until your beards **g**
1Ch	19:5	Stay in Jericho until your beards **g**
Job	5:25	You'll see your children **g** up
	8:11	pine trees **g** tall without soil
	8:19	good plants can **g** in their place
	12:12	**g** old before you understand life
Ps	38:5	flesh stink and **g** maggots
	92:12	**G** tall like Lebanon cedars
	92:13	**g** tall in the presence of God
	104:14	You make grass **g** for the livestock

	119:82	My eyes **g** heavy watching for some sign
	139:16	you watched me **g** from conception
Pr	13:13	honor God's commands and **g** rich
	19:8	**G** a wise heart
Isa	9:7	His ruling authority will **g**
	11:7	calves and cubs **g** up together
	17:11	even though you make them **g** so well
	27:6	blossom and **g** fresh branches
	29:22	no longer **g** gaunt and pale
	32:13	farms that **g** nothing but thistles
	44:14	lets it **g** strong in the forest
	55:10	work of making things **g**
	62:9	farmers who **g** the food will eat
	65:21	plant fields and eat what they **g**
Jer	48:11	Never had to **g** up
Eze	16:7	**G** up like a plant in the field
	17:23	It will **g**, putting out branches
	36:29	telling them to **g** bumper crops
	47:12	will **g** fruit trees of all kinds
Da	11:5	king of the south will **g** strong
Zec	8:4	a good city to **g** old in
	8:5	a good city to **g** up in
	8:12	Vines will **g** grapes
Mt	5:48	**G** up. You're kingdom subjects
	12:33	If you **g** a healthy tree
	13:30	Let them **g** together until harvest
Ac	26:5	who watched me **g** up
Ro	1:11	watch you **g** stronger
1Co	3:6	but God made you **g**
	3:7	God, who makes things **g**
	4:14	I love you and want you to **g** up well
	4:15	time and effort to help you **g** up
	14:3	truth so that they can **g** and be strong
	14:20	How long before you **g** up
2Co	8:10	not let those good intentions **g** stale
	10:15	as your lives **g** in faith
Eph	4:15	God wants us to **g** up
	4:16	we will **g** up healthy in God
Col	1:5	purpose in your lives never **g** slack
	2:19	We can **g** up healthy in God
Heb	6:1	**G** up in Christ
Jas	1:20	doesn't **g** from human anger
1Pe	2:3	you'll **g** up mature and whole in God
2Pe	1:8	no grass will **g**
	3:18	**G** in grace and understanding

Growing

Ge	41:22	**g** out of a single stalk
Dt	29:23	nothing planted, nothing **g**
Jos	17:14	There are a lot of us, and **g**
1Sa	2:26	very much alive, **g** up, blessed by God
1Ch	5:9	**g** herds of livestock spilled out
2Ch	26:10	he loved **g** things
Ps	52:8	an olive tree, **g** green in God's house
Isa	18:5	hack off all the **g** branches
	54:3	elbow room for your **g** family
Eze	31:8	oaks looked like bushes **g** alongside
Mt	8:18	a curious crowd was **g** by the minute
	19:12	**g** into the largeness of marriage
Lk	2:52	**g** up in both body and spirit
Ro	15:12	**g** tree tall

2Co	12:19	get in the way of your **g** up
2Th	1:3	Your faith is **g** phenomenally
Jas	5:18	everything started **g** again
2Pe	1:8	qualities active and **g** in your lives

Grown

Ge	38:14	even though Shelah was **g** up
Dt	26:10	what I've **g** on this ground you gave me
Jos	5:12	eating food **g** in the land
Ru	1:13	satisfied to wait until they were **g**
2Sa	14:26	it had **g** so heavy
1Ki	12:8	young men he'd **g** up with
	12:10	The young turks he'd **g** up with
2Ch	10:8	young men he'd **g** up with
	10:10	The young turks he'd **g** up with
Eot	9:4	reputation had **g** in all the provinces
Job	38:21	**g** up in the same neighborhood
	41:32	Ocean had **g** a gray beard
Isa	23:3	wheat from Shihor, **g** along the Nile
Jer	46:19	a vacant lot **g** over with weeds
Eze	44:30	The best of everything **g**
Da	4:22	You have **g** great and strong
Jn	3:4	who has already been born and **g** up
	6:17	It had **g** quite dark
	9:21	a **g** man and can speak for himself
	9:23	Ask him. He's a **g** man
1Co	15:44	the seed **g** is supernatural
Heb	11:24	By faith, Moses, when **g**, refused

Grows

Ge	1:30	whatever **g** out of the ground for food
	38:11	until my son Shelah **g** up
Lev	25:5	Don't reap what **g** of itself
Nu	13:20	sample of the produce that **g** there
Dt	11:17	no rain and nothing **g** in the fields
	14:22	produce which **g** in your fields
1Ki	4:33	cedar that **g** in Lebanon
2Ki	2:19	water is polluted and nothing **g**
Job	14:9	comes to life, buds and **g**
Pr	23:22	when your mother **g** old, don't neglect
Isa	15:6	grass brown, buds stunted, nothing **g**
	30:23	The grain that **g** will be abundant
	32:15	badlands desert **g** crops
	42:5	the earth and all that **g** from it
Jer	17:6	aimless in a land where nothing **g**
	29:5	eat what **g** in that country
	48:9	Make sure nothing ever **g** here again
Eze	36:10	your population **g** all over Israel
Mt	13:32	it **g** into a huge pine tree
Mk	4:27	The seed sprouts and **g**
	4:32	it **g** into a huge pine tree
Lk	13:19	It **g** into a huge pine tree
1Co	15:38	What we plant in the soil and what **g**
2Co	9:10	**g** into full-formed lives
Gal	5:13	that's how freedom **g**
Jas	1:15	Sin **g** up to adulthood

Growth

Ps	115:14	giving **g** to you, **g** to your children

Jer	2:21	a tangle of rancid **g**
	5:10	That **g** didn't come from God
Eze	36:8	Israel, will burst with new **g**
1Co	14:4	brings the whole church into **g**
Gal	6:8	letting God's Spirit do the **g** work
Php	1:25	**g** and joy in this life of trusting God

Grudge

Ge	50:15	What if Joseph is carrying a **g**
Lev	19:18	Don't seek revenge or carry a **g**
Ps	85:4	don't hold a **g** against us forever
	89:46	Will you hold this **g** forever
Eze	35:5	kept this age-old **g** going
Mt	5:23	remember a **g** a friend has against you

Grudges

Ps	103:9	nag and scold, nor hold **g** forever
2Co	2:10	a list of personal **g**
Php	4:2	doesn't want his children holding **g**

Grumble

Nu	14:36	entire community to **g** against Moses

Grumbled

Nu	14:2	Israel **g** against Moses and Aaron

Grumblers

Nu	14:29	whole generation of **g** and grousers

Grumbling

Nu	11:1	fell to **g** over their hard life
	14:27	all this **g** against me
	16:41	G broke out the next day
	17:5	put a stop to this endless **g**
	17:10	put a stop to the **g** against me
Lk	15:3	Their **g** triggered this story

Guarantee

Jos	2:12	give me some tangible proof, a **g**
	9:15	a covenant to **g** their lives
2Sa	7:13	**g** his kingdom's rule permanently
	7:25	**g** it permanently! Do exactly
1Ki	8:59	to **g** justice for his people
	9:5	same **g** I gave David your father
	9:7	then the **g** is off
2Ki	18:31	**g** everyone your own plot of ground
1Ch	17:12	**g** his kingdom's rule forever
	17:23	**g** it forever! Do exactly
	28:7	will **g** that his kingdom will last
2Ch	7:18	same covenant **g** I gave to David
	7:20	then the **g** is off
Job	32:9	getting old doesn't **g** good sense
Ps	19:9	a lifetime **g**. The decisions of God
	49:8	even then it doesn't **g**
	89:29	I'll **g** his family tree

G

Pr	20:21	no **g** of blessing at the end
Heb	6:16	promises, they **g** them by appeal
	6:17	When God wanted to **g** his promises
	7:22	makes Jesus the **g** of a far better way

Guaranteed

2Sa	23:5	God **g** his covenant with me
Ps	89:2	you built the cosmos and **g** everything
	89:4	Everyone descending from you is **g** life
	111:7	All his products are **g** to last
Jn	6:27	He and what he does are **g** by God
Ac	13:34	give to all of you David's **g** blessings
1Co	15:31	as **g** by the resurrected Messiah Jesus
1Th	2:4	**g** that both we and the Message
1Ti	6:15	his arrival **g** by the Blessed

Guarantees

Mk	8:12	clamor for miraculous **g**

Guard

Ge	40:3	in custody under the captain of the **g**
	40:4	captain of the **g** assigned Joseph
	41:10	house of the captain of the **g**
	41:12	he belonged to the captain of the **g**
Ex	21:29	did nothing to **g** against it
	21:36	did nothing to **g** against it
	23:20	to **g** you in your travels
	34:12	Don't let down your **g**
Nu	10:25	the rear **g** of all the camps
Dt	4:15	Carefully **g** yourselves
	4:19	carefully **g** yourselves
	11:1	**g** well his rules and regulations
	29:18	Don't let down your **g** lest even now
Jos	6:7	**g** march before the Chest of God
	6:9	The armed **g** marched ahead
	6:13	**g** marching before and the rear **g**
	23:11	vigilantly **g** your souls: Love God
Jdg	18:16	stood **g** at the entrance to the gate
1Sa	25:13	stayed behind to **g** the camp
	26:15	Why weren't you standing **g**
2Sa	20:3	placed them in seclusion, under **g**
1Ki	13:25	with the lion standing **g** beside it
	20:39	**G** this man with your life
2Ki	11:5	duty on the Sabbath and **g** the palace
	14:5	palace **g** that had assassinated
1Ch	9:18	security **g** at the King's Gate
	9:21	security **g** at the entrance of the Tent
	16:42	formed the security **g**
2Ch	23:5	another third will **g** the palace
	25:3	palace **g** who had assassinated
	31:14	security **g** of the East Gate
Ezr	2:42	Security **g** families
	7:24	temple security **g**, temple servant
	8:29	**G** them with your lives
Ne	3:25	near the Court of the **G**
	4:9	set a round-the-clock **g** against them
	4:16	other half stood **g** with lances
	7:45	Security **g** families
Ps	5:11	Stand **g** over our celebration

	34:13	**G** your tongue from profanity
	78:49	advance **g** of disease-carrying angels
	91:11	ordered his angels to **g** you
	119:44	**g** with my life what you've revealed
	127:1	If God doesn't **g** the city
	141:3	Post a **g** at my mouth, God
Pr	2:1	collect my counsels and **g** them
	3:21	**g** Clear Thinking and Common Sense
	4:13	**G** it well — your life is at stake
	6:22	whenever you rest, they'll **g** you
	7:2	as precious as your eyesight — **g** it
SS	4:8	lions and panthers **g** your safety
Isa	28:6	prowess to those who **g** and protect
	52:12	God of Israel is also your rear **g**
	56:1	**G** my common good: Do what's right
Jer	37:13	the officer on **g** there
	38:6	the courtyard of the palace **g**
	38:13	the courtyard of the palace **g**
Eze	44:11	work in the Sanctuary: **g** the gates
Na	3:9	Ethiopia stood **g** to the south
Zec	8:10	you could never let down your **g**
Mal	2:15	So **g** the spirit of marriage
	2:16	Don't let your **g** down
Mt	27:54	captain of the **g** and those with him
	27:65	You will have a **g**
Mk	15:39	captain standing **g** in front
Lk	8:29	had been placed under constant **g**
	11:21	stands **g** in his front yard
	11:28	God's Word and **g** it with their lives
	20:26	His answer caught them off **g**
	21:34	But be on your **g**
Jn	17:11	**g** them as they pursue this life
	17:15	you **g** them from the Evil One
Ac	9:21	They were caught off **g** by this
	10:1	captain of the Italian **G** stationed
	10:7	particularly devout soldier from the **g**
	12:4	four soldiers each to **g** him
	12:5	Peter was under heavy **g**
	12:10	Past the first **g** and then the second
	15:20	**g** the morality of sex and marriage
	15:29	**g** the morality of sex and marriage
	16:23	put them under heavy **g**
	20:28	to **g** and protect them
	20:31	So stay awake and keep up your **g**
	21:25	**g** the morality of sex and marriage
	21:31	word came to the captain of the **g**
	23:32	sending Paul on to Caesarea under **g**
	27:1	Julius, a member of an elite **g**
	28:16	soldier who had been assigned to **g** him
1Co	10:6	We must be on **g** so that we never
2Co	8:5	caught us completely off **g**
1Th	5:4	how could you be taken off **g**
1Ti	6:20	**g** the treasure you were given! **G** it
2Ti	1:14	**G** this precious thing
Heb	13:4	**g** the sacredness of sexual intimacy
Jas	1:27	**g** against corruption from the godless
1Pe	5:9	Keep your **g** up
2Pe	3:17	Be on **g** lest you lose your footing
1Jn	5:21	on **g** against all clever facsimiles
Jude	1:3	faith entrusted to us as a gift to **g**
Rev	2:10	stay on **g**! Fear nothing!
	17:9	But don't drop your **g**

Guarded

Dt	2:7	He has **g** you in your travels
2Ki	12:9	priests who **g** the entrance
1Ch	9:19	as their ancestors had **g** the entrance
Est	2:21	eunuchs who **g** the entrance
	6:2	eunuchs who **g** the entrance
Job	10:12	You watched and **g** every breath
SS	3:7	carried and **g** by sixty soldiers
Jn	7:13	talk went on in **g** whispers
	17:12	As long as I was with them, I **g** them

Guardian

Ps	121:3	your **G** God won't fall asleep
	121:4	Israel's **G** will never doze or sleep
	121:5	God's your **G**, right at your side

Guardians

Dt	32:8	under the care of divine **g**
2Ki	10:5	the elders, and the **g** to Jehu
Ps	136:9	Moon and stars as **g** of the night

Guarding

Ge	3:24	**g** the path to the Tree-of-Life
Dt	32:10	**g** him as the apple of his eye
	33:9	he was **g** your sayings and watching
1Sa	25:21	**g** everything this man had
2Sa	4:6	maid **g** the bedroom had fallen asleep
1Ch	9:23	**g** the gates of God's house
SS	5:7	who were supposed to be **g** the city

Guardroom

1Ki	14:28	always returned them to the **g**
2Ch	12:11	always returned them to the **g**

Guessing

Jdg	5:15	there was much second-**g**
Job	42:3	second-**g** my purposes
Jn	4:22	You worship **g** in the dark
	10:24	How long are you going to keep us **g**
Php	2:14	no bickering, no second-**g** allowed

Guesswork

Ro	7:7	moral behavior would be mostly **g**

Guidance

1Sa	22:10	pray with him for God's **g**
	22:13	praying with him for God's **g**
	22:15	prayed with him for God's **g**
1Ki	9:4	obedient to my **g** and judgments
	9:6	ignoring my **g** and judgments
	22:5	before you do anything, ask God for **g**
1Ch	10:13	he went to a witch to seek **g**
2Ch	7:17	obedient to my **g** and judgments
	7:19	ignoring my **g** and judgments

	18:4	before you do anything, ask God for **g**
Ezr	7:9	under the generous **g** of his God
	8:21	pray for wise **g** for our journey
Ps	119:79	turn to me for evidence of your wise **g**
Eze	5:6	refused my **g**, ignored my directions
	5:7	refusing my **g**, ignoring my directions
	20:1	came to ask for **g** from God
Mal	2:7	supposed to look to them for **g**
Ac	13:2	fasting as they waited for **g**
Ro	12:8	if you give encouraging **g**, be careful
1Ti	1:8	moral **g** and counsel need to be given

Guide

Ex	13:21	Cloud during the day to **g** them
Jdg	16:26	man who was acting as his **g**
Ps	31:3	be my true mountain **g**
	61:2	**G** me up High Rock Mountain
	119:35	**G** me down the road
	139:24	**g** me on the road to eternal life
Pr	6:22	Wherever you walk, they'll **g** you
Isa	28:6	insights of justice to those who **g**
	42:16	I'll be a personal **g** to them
Mt	7:12	simple, rule-of-thumb **g** for behavior
Lk	6:39	Can a blind man **g** a blind man?
Jn	16:13	**g** you into all the truth there is
Ac	1:16	the **g** to those who arrested Jesus
Ro	2:20	qualified to **g** others
	2:21	who is going to **g** you
	7:8	law code, instead of being used to **g**
	7:10	command that was supposed to **g** me
1Co	4:2	The requirements for a good **g**
	4:4	disqualify me from being a good **g**
Tit	2:2	**G** older men into lives of temperance
	2:3	**G** older women into lives of reverence
	2:6	**g** the young men to live disciplined
	2:9	**G** slaves into being loyal workers
1Jn	2:1	to **g** you out of sin
Rev	3:19	**g** so that they'll live at their best

Guided

Ex	15:13	You **g** them under your protection
2Ki	20:13	a **g** tour of all his prized possessions
Ps	78:72	he **g** the people wisely and well
Jer	17:23	refusing to be **g** or instructed by me

Guiding

2Ch	35:3	in charge of teaching and **g** Israel
Ro	2:21	While you are **g** others
	15:14	quite capable of **g** and advising
2Co	2:10	Christ is with us, **g** us
1Th	5:12	**g** you along in your obedience

Guilt

Ge	26:10	responsible for bringing **g** down on us
Ex	28:38	take on any **g** involved
	28:43	so that they won't incur **g** and die
Lev	4:3	priest who sins and so brings **g**
	5:17	the moment he does realize his **g**

	6:7	things that one does that bring **g**
	10:17	for taking away the **g** of the community
	19:17	you are an accomplice in his **g**
Nu	5:15	bringing the **g** out into the open
	18:32	you'll avoid **g**, you won't desecrate
	30:15	he takes her **g** on himself
Dt	21:8	Clear your people Israel from any **g**
1Sa	25:31	the **g** of an avenging murder
2Sa	24:10	David was overwhelmed with **g**
1Ki	2:31	the **g** from Joab's senseless murders
2Ch	28:13	are about to compound our sin and **g**
Ezr	9:6	our **g** touches the skies
	9:7	been stuck in a muck of **g**
	9:13	our evil ways and accumulated **g**
	10:10	You've piled **g** on Israel
	10:19	For their **g** they brought a ram
Job	13:16	If I were **g**-stricken do you think
	15:6	Your own words have exposed your **g**
	31:33	conceal my **g** behind closed doors
	32:1	wouldn't admit to an ounce of **g**
	36:17	laden with the **g** of the wicked
Ps	5:10	Pile on the **g**, God!
	32:5	my **g** dissolved, my sin disappeared
	38:4	collapsed under gunnysacks of **g**
	40:12	so swamped by **g** I couldn't see my way
	40:12	couldn't see my way clear. More **g**
	51:2	Scrub away my **g**, soak out my sins
	55:3	they pile on the **g**
	65:2	loaded with **g**
	69:27	Pile on the **g**, Don't let them off
	85:2	You lifted the cloud of **g**
Pr	16:6	**G** is banished through love and truth
	28:1	The wicked are edgy with **g**
	28:17	A murderer haunted by **g** is doomed
Isa	1:4	staggering under their **g**-baggage
	6:7	Gone your **g**, your sins wiped out
	27:9	Jacob's **g** was taken away
	33:24	they'll all live **g**-free
	59:3	your fingers dripping with **g**
Jer	3:13	Just admit your **g**
	13:22	hugely guilty. Your **g** has
	14:10	note their **g** and punish their sins
	30:14	the enormity of your **g**
	30:15	the enormity of your **g**
	50:20	a sign of Israel's **g** — nothing
La	4:6	The evil **g** of my dear people
Eze	9:9	The **g** of Israel and Judah is enormous
	18:19	child not share the **g** of the parent
	18:20	does not share the **g** of the parent
	18:20	nor the parent the **g** of the child
	21:23	he will remind them of their **g**
	22:4	you've piled up **g**
	40:39	sin offerings, and **g** offerings
	42:13	sin offerings, and **g** offerings
	44:29	sin offerings, and the **g** offerings
	46:20	priests will cook the **g** offering
Da	9:7	all we have to show for our lives is **g**
Hos	8:13	I'll keep remembering their **g**
	9:7	Because of your great **g**
	9:9	God's keeping track of their **g**
Mic	7:18	wiping the slate clean of **g**
Mk	6:20	he was miserable with **g**

Jn	7:51	Does our Law decide about a man's **g**
1Co	15:56	law-code **g** that gave sin its leverage
	15:57	all three — sin, **g**, death — are gone
2Co	2:7	If all you do is pour on the **g**
Heb	10:3	actually heightened awareness and **g**
1Jn	2:28	no cause for red-faced **g**

Guilt-baggage

Isa	1:4	staggering under their **g**

Guilt-free

Isa	33:24	Best of all, they'll all live **g**

Guilt-stricken

Job	13:16	If I were **g** do you think I'd

Guiltless

Job	11:15	keep a firm grip on life, **g**
	25:4	person pretend to be **g**

Guilty

Ge	43:9	I'm the **g** one
	44:16	We stand **g** before you
Ex	22:9	The one the judges pronounce **g**
Lev	4:13	they become **g** even though no one
	4:22	must not be broken, he is **g**
	4:27	must not be broken, he is **g**
	5:2	you're contaminated and you're **g**
	5:3	later you realize it and you're **g**
	5:4	come to realize it and you're **g**
	5:5	When you are **g**, immediately confess
	5:19	he was surely **g** before God
	6:4	when he sins and is found **g**
	17:4	man is considered **g** of bloodshed
	22:9	lest they become **g** and die
	22:16	make themselves **g** when they eat
Nu	5:6	has broken trust with God, is **g**
	35:27	he's not considered **g** of murder
	35:31	He's **g** and deserves the death penalty
Dt	23:21	if you don't you're **g**
	25:1	one innocent and the other **g**
	25:2	If the **g** one deserves punishment
1Sa	24:5	Immediately, he felt **g**
2Sa	4:11	Don't think I won't find you **g**
	14:32	If he finds me **g**, then he can
2Ch	19:10	you'll end up being as **g** as they are
	28:13	We're **g** enough as it is
Ezr	9:15	standing here, **g** before you
Job	9:29	already been handed down — '**G**!
	10:2	Don't, God, bring in a verdict of **g**
	10:7	You know good and well I'm not **g**
	10:15	If I'm truly **g**, I'm doomed
	22:30	even the **g** will escape
	27:7	Let my adversary be proven **g**
Ps	109:7	let the verdict be, "**G**,"
Pr	18:5	not right to go easy on the **g**
	30:10	then you'll be the **g** one

Isa	5:23	bribes from the **g**
	50:9	Who would dare call me **g**
Jer	13:22	answer's simple: You're **g**, hugely **g**
	14:7	We know we're **g**. We've lived bad lives
Eze	14:10	They'll be equally **g**
	18:20	you're **g** as charged
Hos	5:5	weaving down their **g** streets
	10:2	They're **g** as sin
	12:12	He ran off **g** to Aram
Mt	5:22	angry with a brother or sister is **g**
Mk	8:31	tried and found **g** by the elders
Lk	9:22	tried and found **g**
Jn	19:4	I do not find him **g** of any crime
Ac	24:15	my accusers are just as **g** as I am
1Co	15:15	**g** of telling a string of . . . lies

Gullibility

1Co	14:20	save you from falling into **g**

Gullible

Pr	14:15	The **g** believe anything they're told
Ro	16:19	Don't be **g** in regard to . . . evil
1Th	5:21	don't be **g**. Check out everything

H

Habit

Lev	17:5	they're in the **h** of sacrificing
Job	1:5	a **h** of this sacrificial atonement
Ps	64:10	make praise your **h**
	106:3	when you form the **h** of justice
	130:4	forgiveness is your **h**
Hos	5:4	Their evil life is a bad **h**
Mt	3:4	John dressed in a camel-hair **h**
Mk	1:6	John wore a camel-hair **h**
Ac	8:23	this is an old **h** with you
	10:2	had the **h** of prayer
1Co	7:23	don't, out of old **h**, slip back
2Co	11:18	it's a bad **h** I picked up
Gal	5:21	vicious **h** of depersonalizing everyone
Heb	5:11	this bad **h** of not listening
Jas	4:15	a **h** to say, "If the Master wills it
1Pe	4:1	weaning from that old sinful **h**

Habits

Pr	18:9	Slack **h** and sloppy work are as bad

Halfhearted

Dt	30:10	Nothing **h** here; you must return to God

Happiness

Ge	30:13	women will congratulate me in my **h**
Job	21:25	bereft, never getting a taste of **h**
Ps	67:4	people become happy and shout their **h**
Ecc	2:2	the pursuit of **h**? Who needs it
Gal	5:19	frenzied and joyless grabs for **h**

Happy

Ge	25:8	He died **h** at a ripe old age
	30:13	A **h** day! The women will congratulate
	34:16	become one big, **h** family
Dt	24:5	be at home making his wife **h**
Ru	3:1	so you can have a **h** life
2Sa	19:6	be dead — would that make you **h**
1Ki	4:20	they ate and drank and were **h**
2Ch	11:23	kept them **h** with much food
Ne	12:43	raised their **h** voices
Est	5:9	left the palace that day **h**
Ps	16:9	I'm **h** from the inside out
	32:1	how **h** you must be
	34:2	hear this and be **h**
	37:23	his path blazed by God, he's **h**
	40:16	let them sing and be **h**
	67:4	become **h** and shout their happiness
	86:4	Give your servant a **h** life
	92:4	You made me so **h**, God
	104:15	people **h**, Their faces glowing
	105:3	Live a **h** life
	106:3	**h** man when you do what's right, one **h**
	119:111	how **h** it makes me
	126:3	we are one **h** people
	137:3	Sing us a **h** Zion song
Pr	23:15	become wise, I'll be one **h** parent
	23:25	So make your father **h**
	27:11	Become wise, dear child, and make me **h**
Isa	14:8	Ponderosa pine trees are **h**
	32:13	Cry . . . for the **h** homes no longer **h**
	62:5	as a bridegroom is **h** in his bride
	62:5	so your God is **h**
	66:5	If God's so great, why aren't you **h**?
	66:10	join in the **h** singing
Jer	20:15	How **h** it made him
	31:13	Young women will dance and be **h**
	41:13	They were so **h**
	49:25	the once **h** city
Da	6:23	king heard these words, he was **h**
Hos	13:11	but I wasn't **h** about it
Hab	1:15	a good day of fishing! He's **h**
Zep	3:14	Daughter Jerusalem, be **h**!
	3:17	**H** to have you back, he'll calm you
Jn	3:29	genuinely **h**. How could he be jealous
Ac	8:39	down the road as **h** as he could be
	13:52	two **h** disciples
	14:17	bellies were full and your hearts **h**
Ro	12:15	with your **h** friends when they're **h**
	15:27	They were **h** to do this
2Co	8:2	incredibly **h**, though desperately poor
	12:15	I'd be most **h** to empty my pockets
Php	3:2	knife-**h** circumcisers
	4:10	**h** that you're again showing
	4:12	I'm just as **h** with little
Heb	10:38	if he cuts and runs, I won't be very **h**
2Jn	1:4	how **h** I am to learn that many
3Jn	1:3	**h** when some friends arrived

Harass

Ex	10:7	are you going to let this man **h** us

Nu	24:24	will **h** Asshur and Eber
Ru	2:9	orders to my servants not to **h** you
Ps	35:1	**H** these hecklers, God
	119:86	they **h** me with lies
	143:12	make a clean sweep of those who **h** me
Jer	17:18	Let those who **h** me be harassed

Harassed

Ps	42:9	in tears, **h** by enemies
Jer	17:18	Let those who harass me be **h**
Gal	4:29	**h** the child who came

Harassing

2Sa	14:10	Bring the man who has been **h** you
Ezr	4:4	**h** them as they built

Harassment

Gal	4:29	the **h** you are now experiencing

Hardened

Ex	9:12	God **h** Pharaoh in his stubbornness
Eze	2:4	**h** in their sin
	2:7	They're **h** rebels
	3:7	a hard case, **h** in their sin
Mk	4:15	seed that falls on the **h** soil
Lk	1:17	devout understanding among **h** skeptics
Jn	12:40	their hearts are **h**

Harm

Nu	5:19	water that delivers a curse not **h** you
1Sa	25:26	all who seek my master's **h**
Ps	20:1	God-of-Jacob put you out of **h**'s reach
	91:4	his arms fend off all **h**
	91:7	no **h** will even graze you
	91:10	**h** can't get through the door
Pr	28:21	great **h** in seemingly harmless ways
Ecc	5:1	Doing more **h** than good
Isa	7:5	have plotted to do you **h**
Da	6:22	I've done nothing to **h** you
Ac	19:37	done nothing to **h** either our temple

Harmed

1Sa	14:45	hair on his head is going to be **h**
Jer	15:10	I've never hurt or **h** a soul

Harmless

Lev	13:6	it is a **h** rash
Nu	20:19	We're **h** — just . . . footsore travelers
Ps	37:14	They're out to beat up on the **h**
Pr	14:12	a way of life that looks **h** enough
	16:25	There's a way that looks **h** enough
	28:21	can do great harm in seemingly **h** ways
Lk	23:4	He seems **h** enough to me

Harmlessly

Job	41:26	Javelins bounce **h** off his hide

Harmony

1Ch	15:21	with harps filling in the **h**
2Ch	5:13	in perfect **h** singing and playing
Zec	6:13	king and priest can coexist in **h**
	11:7	named one Lovely and the other **H**
	11:14	I broke the other staff, **H**
Ac	2:44	believers lived in a wonderful **h**
	4:24	voices in a wonderful **h** in prayer
	5:12	met regularly and in remarkable **h**
Ro	15:6	singing in **h** in a stunning anthem
1Co	14:33	he brings us into **h**
2Co	13:11	Think in **h**. Be agreeable
Jas	3:6	ruin the world, turn **h** to chaos

Hate

Ge	26:27	You **h** me; you threw me out
	37:4	they grew to **h** him
	49:23	shooting their **h**-tipped arrows
Ex	20:5	fourth generation of those who **h** me
Lev	19:17	Don't secretly **h** your neighbor
	26:17	People who **h** you will govern you
Nu	10:35	Chase those who **h** you to the hills
Dt	7:10	he also pays back those who **h** him
	7:15	not on you but on those who **h** you
	7:26	**H** it. Abominate it. Destroy it
	24:3	he also comes to **h** her
	32:41	pay back those who **h** me
	33:11	heard the last from those who **h** him
Jdg	11:7	But you **h** me. You kicked me out
	14:16	You **h** me. You don't love me
1Sa	18:28	settled into **h**. Saul hated David
2Sa	19:6	loving those who **h** you
	22:18	that ocean of **h**, that enemy chaos
1Ki	22:8	But I **h** him. He never preaches
2Ch	18:7	But I **h** him. He never preaches
Job	7:16	I **h** this life!
	9:21	I **h** my life
	10:1	I can't stand my life — I **h** it!
	34:30	those who **h** God won't take over
Ps	18:16	he pulled me out Of that ocean of **h**
	25:19	How viciously they **h** me
	26:5	I **h** that pack of gangsters
	31:6	I **h** all this silly religion
	35:19	Those who **h** me for no reason
	41:7	"friends" who **h** me whisper slanders
	44:7	you made those who **h** us lose face
	44:10	those whom **h** us have cleaned us out
	45:7	You love the right and **h** the wrong
	86:17	bullies who **h** me will stand there
	89:23	I'll clean out all who **h** him
	97:10	God loves all who **h** evil
	109:3	barking their **h**, nipping my heels
	109:5	they return my love with **h**
	119:104	that's why I **h** false propaganda
	119:113	I **h** the two-faced
	119:163	I **h** lies — can't stand them

	129:5	let all those who **h** Zion grovel
	139:21	See how I **h** those who **h** you, God
	139:22	**h** it with pure, unadulterated hatred
	140:3	practice the sharp rhetoric of **h**
	144:7	pull me out of the ocean of **h**
Pr	8:13	Evil, whose ways I **h** with a passion
	15:10	for those who **h** God's rules
	15:17	a slab of prime rib served in **h**
	26:28	Liars **h** their victims
	29:1	people who **h** discipline
	29:10	Murderers **h** honest people
Ecc	2:17	I **h** life
	3:8	time to love and another to **h**
	9:1	whether it's love or **h**
Isa	1:14	meetings for that. I **h** them!
	61:8	love fair dealing and **h** thievery
	65:12	you chose what I **h**
	66:4	you chose what I **h**
	66:5	own families **h** you and turn you out
Jer	32:30	doing what I **h**, making me angry
	44:4	gods that I **h** with a passion
Eze	23:28	abandoning you to those you **h**
	35:11	I'll turn your **h**-bloated anger
Am	5:10	People **h** this kind of talk
	5:15	**H** evil and love good
	6:8	I **h** the arrogance of Jacob
Zec	8:17	I **h** all that stuff
Mal	2:16	I **h** divorce," says the God of Israel
Mt	5:43	unwritten companion, 'H your enemy
	10:22	experiencing so much **h**
	25:24	high standards and **h** careless ways
Mk	6:19	Herodias, smoldering with **h**
	13:13	no telling who will **h** you
Lk	16:13	either **h** the first and love the second
	19:21	high standards and **h** sloppiness
	21:17	no telling who will **h** you
Jn	15:19	the world is going to **h** you
	15:23	**H** me, **h** my Father
Ro	8:36	'They kill us . . . because they **h** you
Php	3:18	They **h** Christ's Cross
2Th	2:10	those who **h** the truth
Heb	1:9	you **h** it when things are wrong
Rev	2:6	**h** the Nicolaitan business. I **h** it, too
	17:16	they'll **h** her, violate her

Hated

Ge	37:5	his brothers, they **h** him even more
	37:8	they **h** him more than ever
Lev	20:23	I **h** every minute of it
Dt	21:15	two wives, one loved and the other **h**
	21:16	cutting out the son of the **h** wife
	21:17	real firstborn, the son of the **h** wife
	30:7	curses on your enemies who **h** you
Jdg	15:2	by now you **h** her with a passion
1Sa	18:28	Saul **h** David
2Sa	13:15	he **h** her — an immense hatred
	13:22	he **h** him for violating his sister
1Ki	11:25	king over Aram, and he **h** Israel
Est	3:6	Haman **h** to waste his fury
	9:1	Jews overpowered those who **h** them
	9:5	as they pleased to those who **h** them

	9:16	killed 75,000 of those who **h** them
Job	1:1	devoted to God and **h** evil
Ps	106:41	people who **h** them ruled them
Pr	1:29	Because you **h** Knowledge
Ecc	2:18	I **h** everything I'd accomplished
Hos	9:8	He's **h** right in God's house
	9:15	how I **h** them there!
Zep	3:19	countries where they were **h**
Mal	1:3	**h** Esau
Lk	19:14	citizens there **h** him
Jn	15:24	they saw the God-signs and **h** anyway
	15:25	They **h** me for no good reason
	17:14	godless world **h** them because of it
Ac	23:6	how they **h** each other
Ro	9:13	I loved Jacob; I **h** Esau
Tit	3:3	**h** and hating back

Haters

2Sa	22:41	I wiped out the **h**
2Ch	19:2	cozying up to God-**h**
Ps	18:40	I wiped out the **h**
	21:8	a fistful of **h** in the other
	38:20	get back evil from God-**h**
	81:15	send the God-**h** cringing like dogs
	83:2	the God-**h** are living it up
Mic	3:2	**H** of good, lovers of evil

Hates

Ex	23:5	see the donkey of someone who **h** you
Dt	1:27	God **h** us
	7:25	God **h** it
	12:31	God **h** it all with a passion
	16:22	God, your God, **h** them
2Sa	5:8	lame and blind bunch that David **h**
2Ch	19:7	God **h** dishonesty, partiality
Job	34:17	Can someone who **h** order, keep order
Pr	6:16	Here are six things God **h**
	11:1	God **h** cheating in the marketplace
	13:5	A good person **h** false talk
	20:10	two things God **h**
	20:23	God **h** cheating in the marketplace
	28:16	for one who **h** corruption
Ecc	9:6	Their loves, their **h**
Jn	3:20	**h** God-light and won't come near it
1Jn	2:9	claims to live in God's light and **h**
	2:11	whoever **h** is still in the dark
	3:13	when the world **h** you
	3:15	Anyone who **h** a brother or sister

Hating

Dt	9:28	He ended up **h** them
2Sa	19:6	and **h** those who love you
Job	1:8	totally devoted to God and **h** evil
	2:3	totally devoted to God and **h** evil
Ps	34:21	they waste their lives **h** the good
Pr	8:13	Fear-of-God means **h** Evil
Mt	6:24	you'll end up **h** the other
	24:9	everyone **h** you because you carry
	24:10	everyone **h** each other

H

Jn	15:18	If you find the godless world is **h** you
	15:18	remember it got its start **h**
Tit	3:3	hated and **h** back
1Jn	4:20	goes right on **h** his brother or sister

Hatred

Nu	35:20	if out of sheer **h** a man pushes another
Dt	19:6	no history of **h** between them
	19:11	if a man with a history of **h**
2Sa	13:15	immense **h**. The **h** that he felt for her
Ps	139:22	I hate it with pure, unadulterated **h**
Pr	10:12	**H** starts fights
	10:18	Liars secretly hoard **h**
Ro	8:35	not hard times, not **h**, not hunger

Haunt

Ps	46:4	this sacred **h** of the Most High
Isa	13:21	unspeakable night hags will **h** it
Zep	2:14	the **h** of wild animals
Mt	12:36	going to come back to **h** you
	12:44	I'll go back to my old **h**
Lk	11:24	I'll go back to my old **h**

Haunted

Pr	28:17	A murderer **h** by guilt is doomed
Jer	20:16	**h** to his death with the bad news
	50:39	place will be **h** with jackals
Ac	1:20	Let his farm become **h**

Hazardous

Ecc	10:9	Be alert: Felling trees is **h**
Mt	10:16	This is **h** work I'm assigning you
Lk	10:3	be careful — this is **h** work

Heal

Nu	12:13	Please, God, **h** her, please **h** her
Dt	32:39	I wound and I **h**
2Ki	5:6	**h** him of his skin disease
	5:7	orders to **h** this man from his disease
	20:5	I'm going to **h** you
Ps	12:5	**h** the ache in the heart
	60:2	**H** the breaks
	77:2	an open wound that wouldn't **h**
Pr	15:4	Kind words **h** and help
Ecc	3:3	time to kill and another to **h**
Isa	19:22	wound Egypt, first hit and then **h**
	57:18	I decided to **h** him, lead him
	57:19	yes, I will **h** them
	61:1	**h** the heartbroken
Jer	3:22	I can **h** your wanderlust
Eze	30:21	so the bones can knit and **h**
	34:4	don't **h** the sick
Hos	5:13	But he can't **h** you
	6:1	He hurt us, but he'll **h** us
	14:4	I will **h** their waywardness
Zep	3:19	I'll **h** the maimed
Mt	8:2	Master, if you want to, you can **h**

	8:7	Jesus said, "I'll come and **h** him
	12:10	Is it legal to **h** on the Sabbath
	13:15	let me **h** them
Mk	3:2	to see if he would **h** him
Lk	4:23	Doctor, go **h** yourself
	6:7	to see if he would **h** the man
	7:3	asking him to come and **h** his servant
	9:2	news of God's kingdom and **h** the sick
	10:9	**h** anyone who is sick
	14:3	Is it permitted to **h** on the Sabbath
Jn	4:47	asked that he come down and **h** his son
	12:40	turn to me, God, so I could **h** them
Ac	28:27	let me **h** them
Jas	5:15	Believing-prayer will **h** you

Healed

Ge	20:17	God **h** Abimelech, his wife
Lev	13:37	the itch is **h**. The person is clean
	14:3	has been **h** of the serious skin disease
Jos	5:8	in camp until they were **h**
1Sa	6:3	Pay compensation. Then you will be **h**
1Ki	13:6	the king's arm was **h**
2Ki	2:21	God's word: I've **h** this water
	2:22	sure enough, the water was **h**
	5:3	he would be **h** of his skin disease
	5:10	Your skin will be **h**
	5:14	His skin was **h**
2Ch	30:20	God responded . . . and **h** the people
Job	33:25	you're **h**, the very picture of health
Ps	107:20	He spoke the word that **h** you
Isa	53:5	Through his bruises we get **h**
Mt	4:23	He also **h** people of their diseases
	4:24	Jesus **h** them, one and all
	8:4	present your **h** body to the priest
	9:35	**h** their diseased bodies, **h** their
	12:13	He held it out and it was **h**
	12:15	he **h** them all
	12:22	Jesus **h** him, gave him his sight
	14:14	overcome with pity and **h** their sick
	14:36	whoever touched him was **h**
	15:30	what he would do with them. He **h** them
	19:2	he **h** them
	21:14	They came to Jesus and he **h** them
Mk	3:10	He had **h** many people
	5:34	now you're **h** and whole
	6:5	a few sick people and **h** them
	10:52	Your faith has saved and **h** you
Lk	4:40	placed his hands on them and **h** them
	5:14	present your **h** self to the priest
	5:15	to listen and be **h** of their ailments
	6:18	Those disturbed by evil spirits were **h**
	6:19	so many people **h**
	7:21	Jesus **h** many from diseases
	8:2	had been **h** of various evil afflictions
	8:47	at that same moment she was **h**
	8:48	now you're **h** and whole
	9:11	Those who needed healing, he **h**
	9:42	the vile spirit gone, **h** the boy
	13:14	because Jesus had **h** on the Sabbath
	14:4	he took the man, **h** him
	17:15	he realized that he was **h**

	17:17	Jesus said, "Were not ten **h**
	17:19	Your faith has **h** and saved you
	18:42	Your faith has saved and **h** you
	22:51	touching the servant's ear, he **h** him
Jn	5:9	The man was **h** on the spot
	5:10	The Jews stopped the **h** man and said
	5:13	But the **h** man didn't know
	9:14	Jesus . . . and **h** his blindness
Ac	3:16	nothing but faith put this man **h**
	4:14	standing there so upright — so **h**
	4:22	man who had been miraculously **h**
	5:16	they all were **h**
	8:7	could neither stand nor walk were **h**
	19:12	The touch did it —they were **h**
	28:8	hands on him and prayed, the man was **h**
	28:9	who was sick came and got **h**
Ro	6:19	your lives **h** and expansive in holiness
	6:22	A whole, **h**, put-together life
Jas	5:15	you'll be forgiven — **h** inside and out
	5:16	you can live together whole and **h**
1Pe	1:5	have it all — life **h** and whole
Rev	13:3	struck a deathblow, and then **h**
	13:12	had been **h** of its deathblow

Healer

Ex	15:26	I am God your **h**
1Co	12:30	not all **H**, not all Prayer in Tongues

Healers

1Co	12:28	teachers miracle workers **h** helpers

Healing

Dt	28:35	no **h** or relief from head to foot
1Ki	13:6	Pray to your God for the **h** of my arm
2Ki	20:8	sign is there that God is **h** me
Ps	69:29	Give me space for **h**
Pr	12:18	there is **h** in the words of the wise
	13:17	a reliable reporter is a **h** presence
Jer	8:15	We were waiting around for **h**
	8:22	Are there no **h** ointments in Gilead
	14:19	We looked for **h** — and got kicked
	15:18	ever worsening wound and no **h** in sight
	30:17	I'll come with **h**, curing the incurable
	33:6	working a true **h** inside and out
	46:11	mountains of Gilead, get **h** balm
Eze	47:12	for food and their leaves for **h**
Mic	1:9	wounded with no **h** in sight
Mal	4:2	**h** radiating from its wings
Mk	1:44	will validate your **h** to the people
	6:13	**h** their spirits
	7:32	asked Jesus to lay a **h** hand on him
	8:22	begged Jesus to give him a **h** touch
Lk	5:17	The **h** power of God was on him
	9:11	Those who needed **h**, he healed
	13:32	clearing out the demons and **h** the sick
	18:43	The **h** was instant
Ac	4:9	investigation regarding this **h**
	10:38	**h** everyone who was beaten down
	28:9	Word of the **h** got around fast

Ro	8:3	on sin instead of a deep **h** of it
1Co	12:9	simple trust **h** the sick
	12:26	involved in the hurt, and in the **h**
2Co	1:3	God of all **h** counsel
	1:5	the good times of his **h** comfort
	1:6	works out for your **h** and salvation
1Pe	2:24	His wounds became your **h**
Rev	22:2	leaves of the Tree are for **h**

Healings

Ac	4:30	your hand to us in **h** and miracles

Heals

Lev	13:18	a person has a boil and it **h**
Job	5:18	the same hand that hurts you, **h** you
Ps	103:3	He **h** your diseases — every one
	147:3	He **h** the heartbroken
Isa	30:26	on the Day God **h** his people
Ac	9:34	Jesus Christ **h** you

Health

Ge	41:2	out of the Nile, all shimmering with **h**
	41:18	Seven cows, shimmering with **h**
1Sa	16:12	the very picture of **h** — bright-eyed
2Ch	7:14	restore their land to **h**
Job	2:5	reached down and took away his **h**
	15:27	the picture of **h**, trim and fit
	33:25	you're healed, the very picture of **h**
Ps	18:25	The whole people taste your **h**
	41:3	nurses us back to **h**
	51:9	give me a clean bill of **h**
	104:15	happy, Their faces glowing with **h**
Pr	3:8	Your body will glow with **h**
	4:22	body and soul, they're bursting with **h**
	17:22	is good for your **h**
SS	5:10	My dear lover glows with **h**
La	4:7	sacred nobles once glowed with **h**
Mt	10:8	Bring **h** to the sick. Raise the dead
Lk	6:44	**h** of the apple tells the **h** of the tree
	23:15	sent . . . with a clean bill of **h**
2Co	2:9	responsibility for the **h** of the church
3Jn	1:2	and for your good **h**

Healthy

Ge	32:16	keep a **h** space between each herd
	41:4	skinny cows ate the seven **h** cows
	41:7	swallowed up the full, **h** ears
	41:20	ate up the first seven **h** cows
	41:26	The seven **h** cows are seven years
Ex	4:7	took it back out — as **h** as before
	12:5	Your lamb must be a **h** male
	29:1	rams, **h** and without defects
Nu	6:14	offerings to God: a **h** yearling
	19:2	a red cow, a **h** specimen
	28:3	present to God: two **h** yearling
	28:9	sacrifice two **h** yearling lambs
	28:11	male yearling lambs — all **h**
	28:19	male yearling lambs — all **h**

H

H

	28:31	Remember, the animals must be **h**
	29:2	male yearling lambs — all **h**
	29:8	yearling male lambs — all **h**
	29:13	yearling male lambs — all **h**
	29:17	yearling male lambs— all **h**
	29:20	male yearling lambs —all **h**
	29:23	male yearling lambs — all **h**
	29:26	male yearling lambs — all **h**
	29:29	male yearling lambs — all **h**
	29:32	male yearling lambs — all **h**
	29:36	male yearling lambs — all **h**
1Ki	5:12	**h** peace between Hiram and Solomon
Ps	37:29	good land and put down **h** roots
	37:37	Keep your eye on the **h** soul
Pr	18:14	A **h** spirit conquers adversity
Da	1:4	young men who were **h** and handsome
	1:10	sees that you are not as **h** as the rest
Hos	7:15	gave them good minds and **h** bodies
Mt	9:12	Who needs a doctor: the **h** or the sick
	12:33	grow a **h** tree, you'll pick **h** fruit
	15:31	mutes speaking, the maimed **h**
Mk	1:42	his skin smooth and **h**
	2:17	Who needs a doctor: the **h** or the sick
Lk	1:80	The child grew up, **h** and spirited
	5:31	Who needs a doctor: the **h** or the sick
	6:43	don't get wormy apples off a **h** tree
Ac	4:10	stands before you **h** and whole
	5:11	had a **h** respect for God
Eph	4:16	we will grow up **h** in God
Col	2:19	grow up **h** in God only as he nourishes
Tit	2:2	into **h** faith, love, and endurance
Jas	3:18	develop a **h**, robust community

Heart

Ge	6:6	it broke his **h**
	33:10	find it in your **h** to welcome me
	50:21	speaking with them **h**-to-**h**
Ex	2:6	Her **h** went out to him
	9:35	Pharaoh's **h** turned rock-hard
	14:4	I'll make Pharaoh's **h** stubborn again
	15:1	I'm singing my **h** out to God
	20:17	Don't set your **h** on anything
	28:29	Breastpiece of Judgment over his **h**
	28:30	over Aaron's **h** when he enters
	35:21	every one whose **h** was roused
	35:29	whose **h** moved them freely to bring
Dt	1:21	Don't be afraid. Don't lose **h**
	1:36	all for following God, **h** and soul
	2:30	his spirit mean and his **h** hard
	4:9	Don't let your **h** wander off
	4:11	into the very **h** of Heaven
	4:29	looking for him with your whole **h**
	4:39	Take it to **h** right now
	6:5	Love God, your God, with your whole **h**
	8:5	learned deep in your **h** that God
	10:16	away the thick calluses from your **h**
	15:10	Don't have a stingy **h**
	28:47	the joy and goodness of your **h**
	28:65	God will give you a restless **h**
	29:4	God didn't give you an understanding **h**
	30:2	obey him with your whole **h** and soul

	30:6	away the thick calluses on your **h**
	30:14	as near as the **h** in your chest
	30:17	If you have a change of **h**
	31:19	to sing it by **h**
	32:46	Take to **h** all these words
Jos	1:7	everything you have, **h** and soul
	7:5	The **h** of the people sank
	8:2	plunder . . . to your **h**'s content
	23:14	Know this with all your **h**
Jdg	10:16	God took Israel's troubles to **h**
	11:35	My **h** is torn to shreds
	20:23	The army took **h**
Ru	1:18	Ruth had her **h** set on going
	2:13	You've touched my **h**
1Sa	1:13	Hannah was praying in her **h**, silently
	1:15	my **h**, pouring it out to God
	12:20	Worship and serve him **h** and soul
	14:34	you can feast to your **h**'s content
	16:7	God looks into the **h**
	25:8	Give whatever your **h** tells you
	25:31	this dead weight in his **h**
	25:37	he had a **h** attack
2Sa	1:18	everyone in Judah learn it by **h**
	4:1	His **h** sank
	6:16	her **h** filled with scorn
	7:3	Whatever is on your **h**, go and do it
	7:21	who you are — out of your very **h**
	18:14	stabbed Absalom in the **h**
	19:7	put some **h** into your servants
	22:25	I opened the book of my **h** to his eyes
1Ki	2:4	staying true to me **h** and soul
	2:44	Deep in your **h** you know all the evil
	3:6	were just and his **h** right
	3:9	Give me a God-listening **h**
	3:12	I'm giving you a wise and mature **h**
	8:17	had it in his **h** to build a Temple
	8:48	turn back to you **h** and soul
	8:51	rescued from the **h** of that iron
	9:1	projects he had set his **h** on
	9:3	eyes are on it and my **h** in it
	9:4	pure in **h** and action
	10:2	emptying her **h** to him
	10:13	Sheba all her **h**'s desire
	11:37	Rule to your **h**'s content
	14:8	lived from his undivided **h**
	15:14	his **h** was in the right place
	19:10	I've been working my **h** out
	19:14	I've been working my **h** out for God
2Ki	8:11	stared hard at Hazael, reading his **h**
	9:24	went right through his **h**
	10:31	God of Israel from an undivided **h**
	20:3	My **h**'s been true and steady
	23:3	follow his instructions, **h** and soul
	23:25	obedience to God, **h** and mind
1Ch	17:2	Whatever is on your **h**, go and do it
	17:19	God, out of the goodness of your **h**
	22:19	give yourselves, **h** and soul
	28:9	serve him with a whole **h**
	28:20	Take charge! Take **h**
	29:3	because my **h** is in this
	29:17	I have given from the **h**
	29:19	an uncluttered and focused **h**

2Ch	1:11	This is what has come out of your **h**
	6:38	they turn back to you **h** and soul
	7:11	projects he had set his **h** on doing
	7:16	my eyes are on it and my **h** in it
	7:17	pure in **h** and action
	9:1	She emptied her **h** to Solomon
	9:12	Sheba all her **h**'s desire
	12:14	his **h** neither cared for nor sought
	15:7	Be strong. Take **h**
	15:15	their promise joyfully from the **h**
	15:17	his **h** was in the right place
	32:31	he wanted to test his **h**
	34:31	follow his instructions, **h** and soul
Ezr	9:9	given us the **h** to build The Temple
Ne	2:12	what my God had put in my **h** to do
	4:6	the people had a **h** for the work
	7:5	God put it in my **h** to gather,
	9:8	found his **h** to be steady and true
Job	1:9	out of the sheer goodness of his **h**
	5:27	Take it to **h** and you won't go wrong
	11:13	set your **h** on God and reach out to him
	21:3	mock me later to your **h**'s content
	22:22	take his words to **h**
	23:16	God makes my **h** sink
	31:24	set my **h** on making big money
	32:20	I have to say what's on my **h**
	33:3	I'm speaking honestly from my **h**
	37:1	Whenever this happens, my **h** stops
Ps	4:4	let your **h** do the talking
	9:1	thanking you, God, from a full **h**
	11:2	every **h** open to God
	12:5	heal the ache in the **h** of the wretched
	16:7	confirmed by my sleeping **h**
	17:2	I'm innocent — in your **h** you know I am
	18:24	opened the book of my **h** to his eyes
	20:4	Give you what your **h** desires
	22:14	My **h** is a blob of melted wax
	25:17	My **h** and kidneys are fighting
	27:8	When my **h** whispered, "Seek God,"
	27:14	Stay with God! Take **h**. Don't quit
	34:18	If your **h** is broken, you'll find God
	37:31	His **h** pumps God's Word like blood
	38:10	My **h**'s about to break
	40:12	More guilt in my **h** than hair on my
	45:1	My **h** bursts its banks
	49:3	my **h**-seasoned understandings of life
	51:17	**H**-shattered lives ready for love
	55:21	turned to daggers in my **h**
	56:12	thanking you with all my **h**
	64:6	mystery in the dark of the cellar **h**
	69:32	you God-seekers, take **h**
	72:13	a place in his **h** for the down-and-out
	78:58	obscene idolatries broke his **h**
	78:72	His good **h** made him a good shepherd
	86:11	Put me together, one **h** and mind
	86:12	From the bottom of my **h** I thank you
	94:15	every good **h** put right
	97:8	Zion, you listen and take **h**
	97:11	Joy-seeds are planted in good **h**-soil
	101:4	crooked in **h** keep their distance
	106:15	along with it they got an empty **h**
	112:7	**H** ready, trusting in God

	119:7	speaking straight from your **h**
	119:11	promises in the vault of my **h**
	119:58	beg you from the bottom of my **h**
	119:74	those who fear you will take **h**
	122:1	my **h** leaped for joy
	131:2	I've cultivated a quiet **h**
	143:4	spirit draining away, my **h** heavy
Pr	2:1	take to **h** what I'm telling you
	2:2	set your **h** on a life of Understanding
	3:1	take to **h** my commands
	3:3	carve their initials on your **h**
	3:5	Trust God from the bottom of your **h**
	4:4	Take this to **h**. Do what I tell you
	4:21	Concentrate! Learn it by **h**
	4:23	Keep vigilant watch over your **h**
	5:4	a wound in your **h**
	6:18	**h** that hatches evil plots
	7:3	etch it on the chambers of your **h**
	10:8	A wise **h** takes orders
	10:21	chatterboxes die of an empty **h**
	14:33	Wisdom is . . . in an understanding **h**
	15:13	A cheerful **h** brings a smile
	15:15	A miserable **h** means a miserable life
	15:30	twinkle in the eye means joy in the **h**
	19:8	Grow a wise **h**
	20:5	right is like deep water in the **h**
	22:17	take to **h** what I can teach you
	23:16	My **h** will dance and sing
	26:23	Smooth talk from an evil **h**
	27:19	so your face mirrors your **h**
Ecc	7:3	blotches the face but it scours the **h**
	7:7	destroys the strongest **h**
	9:7	Drink wine with a robust **h**
	11:9	Follow the impulses of your **h**
SS	3:11	garlanded for his wedding, his **h** full
	4:9	You've captured my **h**, dear friend
	6:12	my **h** was raptured
Isa	15:8	**h**-racking sobs all the way
	35:4	Courage! Take **h**! God is here
	38:3	a **h** that was totally yours
	41:1	Say what's on your **h**
	42:21	out of the goodness of his **h**
	42:25	they don't take it to **h**
	46:8	Take it to **h**
	47:7	took nothing to **h**
	48:9	out of the sheer goodness of my **h**
	57:16	Otherwise, people would lose **h**
	60:5	Your **h** will swell and, yes, burst
	61:3	praising **h** instead of a languid spirit
Jer	4:9	King and princes will lose **h**
	4:18	That's what's piercing your **h**
	12:15	take them tenderly to my **h**
	16:13	no-gods there to your **h**'s content
	17:9	**h** is hopelessly dark and deceitful
	17:10	I, God, search the **h**
	24:7	I'll give them a **h** to know me, God
	31:20	my **h** bursts with longing for him
	32:39	I'll make them of one mind and **h**
	32:41	**H** and soul, I'll plant them
	48:36	My **h** moans for Moab
	50:19	He will eat to his **h**'s content
La	1:20	my **h** wrecked by a life of rebellion

H

H

	2:18	Give out **h**-cries to the Master
	2:19	Pour your **h** out face to face
	3:51	the pain breaks my **h**
Eze	11:19	I'll give you a new **h**! Get a new spirit!
	18:31	Get a new **h**! Get a new spirit!
	24:21	your **h**'s desire. The children
	28:2	Your **h** is proud
	36:26	I'll give you a new **h**
	44:7	uncircumcised in **h** and flesh
	44:9	uncircumcised in **h** or flesh
Da	7:4	a human **h** was placed in it
	9:4	poured out my **h**, baring my soul to God
	9:20	pouring out my **h**, baring my sins
Am	1:11	She has no pity, she has no **h**
Hab	3:19	I take **h** and gain strength
Mt	5:8	your mind and **h**—put right
	5:28	Your **h** can be corrupted by lust
	9:36	his **h** broke. So confused and aimless
	12:7	I prefer a flexible **h**
	12:34	so foul-minded? It's your **h**
	13:12	Whenever someone has a ready **h**
	13:19	plucks it right out of that person's **h**
	14:31	Faint-**h**, what got into you
	15:8	but their **h** isn't in it
	15:10	Listen, and take this to **h**
	15:18	gets its start in the **h**
	15:19	from the **h** that we vomit up evil
Mk	6:34	At the sight of them, his **h** broke
	7:6	but their **h** isn't in it
	7:14	all of you—take this to **h**
	7:19	doesn't enter your **h** but your stomach
	7:23	all these are vomit from the **h**
	8:2	This crowd is breaking my **h**
	9:22	Have a **h** and help us
	10:22	he walked off with a heavy **h**
	13:11	say what's on your **h**
Lk	1:66	who heard about it took it to **h**
	3:18	words that put **h** in them
	7:13	When Jesus saw her, his **h** broke
	10:33	his **h** went out to him
	15:20	His **h** pounding, he ran out
	23:50	man of good **h** and good character
Jn	1:18	who exists at the very **h** of the Father
	7:24	use your head—and **h**!—to discern
	10:30	I and the Father are one **h** and mind
	16:33	take **h**! I've conquered the world
	17:11	So they can be one **h** and mind
	17:12	As we are one **h** and mind
	17:21	all of them to become one **h** and mind
Ac	4:32	united as one—one **h**, one mind
	10:33	whatever the Master put in your **h**
	13:22	man whose **h** beats to my **h**
	16:14	Master gave her a trusting **h**
	18:23	putting fresh **h** into the disciples
	19:2	did you also embrace him with your **h**
	20:31	pouring my **h** out with you
	26:7	committed myself **h** and soul
	27:25	So, dear friends, take **h**
Ro	2:29	It's the mark of God on your **h**
	7:25	want to serve God with all my **h**
	10:1	want it with all my **h** and pray
	10:8	as close as the **h** in your chest

	10:11	trusts God like this—**h** and soul
	15:32	way to you with a light and eager **h**
1Co	4:7	really knows you, knows your **h**
	4:21	who wants to share **h**-to-**h** with you
	11:28	Examine your motives, test your **h**
	14:22	goes straight to the **h** of believers
	14:29	listening and taking it to **h**
	14:39	speak forth God's truth, speak your **h**
2Co	6:6	pure **h**, clear head, steady hand
	7:11	come out of this with purity of **h**
	8:11	Your **h**'s been in the right place
	8:12	The **h** regulates the hands
Gal	5:22	a sense of compassion in the **h**
Eph	4:30	Don't grieve God. Don't break his **h**
	5:19	Sing songs from your **h** to Christ
Php	1:4	praying for you with a glad **h**
	1:15	others do it with the best **h**
	2:1	if you have a **h**, if you care
	2:19	how that will do my **h** good
Col	3:23	Work from the **h** for your real Master
1Th	2:13	took it to **h** as God's true word
2Th	2:17	put a fresh **h** in you
1Ti	1:15	Here's a word you can take to **h**
	4:9	can count on this. Take it to **h**
2Ti	2:25	change of **h** and a turning to the truth
Phm	1:20	but it will also do my **h** good
Heb	9:9	can't really get to the **h**
1Pe	3:13	If with **h** and soul you're doing good
2Pe	1:21	concocted in the human **h**
2Jn	1:12	in person and have a **h**-to-**h** talk
3Jn	1:14	in person and have a **h**-to-**h** talk
Rev	9:21	wasn't a sign of a change of **h**

Hearts

Lev	26:41	soften their hard **h** and make amends
Nu	32:11	their **h** weren't in it
	32:12	they followed me—their **h** were in it
Dt	4:28	homemade gods to your **h**' content
	6:6	I've given you today on your **h**
	11:18	Place these words on your **h**
	30:6	on your heart and your children's **h**
Jos	2:11	We heard it and our **h** sank
	5:1	their **h** sank; the courage drained
Jdg	5:9	Lift your **h** high, O Israel
2Sa	15:6	stole the **h** of everyone in Israel
	17:10	are valiant with **h** of lions
	19:14	captured the **h** of everyone
1Ki	4:29	the largest of **h**
	8:38	**h** penetrated by the disaster
	8:47	pray with changed **h** in their exile
1Ch	29:18	keep their **h** set firmly in you
2Ch	6:29	their **h** penetrated by disaster
	6:37	pray with changed **h** in their exile
Ezr	10:1	weeping as if their **h** would break
Job	35:10	God puts spontaneous songs in their **h**
Ps	10:17	the **h** of the hopeless pump red blood
	17:10	Their **h** are hard as nails
	19:6	warming **h** to faith
	30:4	you saints! Sing your **h** out to God
	32:11	All you honest **h**, raise the roof
	33:21	our **h** brim with joy

	36:10	do your work in welcoming **h**
	44:18	our **h** were never false
	45:5	shoot sharp arrows Into enemy **h**
	97:8	Zion, sing your **h** out
	105:43	people marched, singing their **h** out
	107:12	A hard sentence, and your **h** so heavy
	107:26	your **h** were stuck in your throats
	125:4	God, to those whose **h** are right
	126:6	those who went off with heavy **h**
	132:16	holy people will sing their **h** out
	144:5	volcanoes in the **h** of the mountains
Pr	13:19	Souls who follow their **h** thrive
	15:11	do you think he can't read human **h**
	27:21	purity of human **h** is tested
Isa	12:6	Sing your **h** out, O Zion
	29:13	but their **h** aren't in it
	30:29	Your **h** will burst with song
	65:14	My servants will laugh from full **h**
Jer	4:4	Plow your unplowed **h**, all you
	17:1	engraved on their granite **h**
	24:7	returned to me with all their **h**
	31:33	write it on their **h**
	32:40	I'll fill their **h** with a deep respect
	49:23	Their **h** will melt in fear
La	3:41	lift our **h** and hands
	3:65	Break their miserable **h**!
	5:15	All the joy is gone from our **h**
Eze	14:3	have installed idols in their **h**
	14:4	who install idols in their **h**
	14:5	work on the **h** of the house of Israel
	21:7	**H** will stop cold
Joel	1:12	joy is dried up and withered in the **h**
Mic	6:14	hollow stomachs, empty **h**
Na	2:10	**H** sink, knees fold, stomachs retch
Mt	8:26	are you such cowards, such faint-**h**
	23:3	don't take it into their **h**
Mk	6:52	had yet penetrated their **h**
Lk	1:17	soften the **h** of parents to children
	8:15	the good-**h** who seize the Word
	11:41	Turn both your pockets and your **h**
Jn	12:40	their **h** are hardened
Ac	7:51	Calluses on your **h**, flaps on your ears
	14:17	bellies were full and your **h** happy
Ro	9:16	doesn't originate in our bleeding **h**
1Co	5:2	Shouldn't this break your **h**
	8:2	our humble **h** can help us more
	14:25	probe their **h**
2Co	5:5	puts a little of heaven in our **h**
	7:5	fears in our **h** kept us
	7:6	lifted our heads and our **h**
Gal	5:25	in our heads or a sentiment in our **h**
Col	3:16	sing your **h** out to God
1Th	2:8	we wanted to give you our **h**
	2:17	separated from you, not our **h**
Heb	8:10	carving it on the lining of their **h**
	10:16	carving it on the lining of their **h**
1Pe	3:15	keep your **h** at attention
2Pe	1:19	rising of the Morning Star in your **h**
1Jn	3:20	God is greater than our worried **h**
Jude	1:2	open your **h**, love is on the way

Hero

2Sa	3:38	today a prince and **h** fell victim
1Ch	1:10	Nimrod, the first great **h** on earth
2Ch	28:7	Zicri, an Ephraimite **h**
Ps	89:19	I've crowned a **h**, I chose the best

Heroes

Ne	3:16	far as the Pool and the House of **H**
Isa	22:3	no combat **h** to be proud of
Jer	9:23	Don't let **h** brag of their exploits
Eze	32:27	segregated from the **h**
	39:18	eat off the bodics of great **h**
	39:20	**h** and fighters of every kind
Da	8:24	knocking off **h** and holy ones
Ob	1:9	Your great **h** will desert you

Heroic

| 2Ki | 5:13 | asked you to do something hard and **h** |
| 1Co | 15:32 | just trying to act **h** when I fought |

Hoard

Pr	10:18	Liars secretly **h** hatred
Ecc	11:2	Don't **h** your goods
Mt	6:19	Don't **h** treasure down here
1Co	14:13	don't **h** the experience for yourself

Hoards

| Ecc | 5:13 | **h** far more wealth than is good for him |

Holiday

Ex	5:4	suggest the people be given a **h**
Dt	16:8	Set aside the seventh day as a **h**
Jdg	19:6	Stay the night — make it a **h**
1Sa	20:24	On the **h** of the New Moon
	20:27	day two of the **h**
Ne	8:10	prepare a feast, **h** food and drink
Est	2:18	proclaimed a **h** for all the provinces
	9:18	made the fifteenth their **h**
	9:22	mourning somersaulted into a **h**
Ps	89:42	declared a **h** for all his enemies
Isa	66:1	What **h** spot reserve for me
Jer	7:34	No wedding songs, no **h** sounds
Hos	7:5	On the royal **h** the princes get drunk
Na	1:15	peace! A **h**, Judah! Celebrate!
Zec	8:19	celebration and **h**. Embrace truth

Holidays

| Hos | 2:11 | her wild weekends and unholy **h** |

Holier

| Isa | 65:5 | Don't touch me. I'm **h** than thou |

Holier-than-thou

Mt	7:5	playing a h-than-thou part
Lk	6:42	playing a h-than-thou part

Holies

Ex	26:33	Holy Place from the Holy-of-H
	26:34	The Testimony in the Holy-of-H
Lev	16:2	not to enter into the Holy of H
	16:16	make atonement for the Holy of H
	16:17	make atonement in the Holy of H
	16:20	making atonement for the Holy of H
	16:23	dressed to enter the Holy of H
	16:27	has been taken into the Holy of H
	16:33	purges the Holy of H by making
1Ki	6:16	the Holy of H
	7:50	Inner Sanctuary, the Holy of H
	8:6	Inner Sanctuary, the Holy of H
1Ch	6:49	work surrounding the Holy of H
	23:13	ordained to work in the Holy of H
2Ch	3:8	He made the Holy of H a cube
	3:10	angel-like figures, for the Holy of H
	4:20	Inner Sanctuary, the Holy of H
	4:22	doors to the Holy of H
	5:7	Inner Sanctuary, the Holy of H
Eze	41:4	This is The Holy of H
	45:3	Sanctuary with its Holy of H
Da	9:24	anoint The Holy of H
Heb	9:3	This was called "the Holy of H."

Holiest

Ex	30:36	will be for you the h of holy places
Nu	18:29	God's portion is the best and h

Holiness

Ex	29:37	Altar will become soaked in h
	30:29	so they'll be soaked in h
Dt	7:26	Destroy it and preserve God's h
1Ch	16:29	resplendent in his robes of h
Ps	51:11	or fail to breathe h in me
Eze	28:25	put my h on display among them
	36:23	I am God, when I show my h through you
	38:16	I am putting my h on display
	39:27	use them to demonstrate my h
Am	2:11	best youth for training in h
	4:2	I, God, have sworn by my h!
Hag	2:9	I will hand out wholeness and h
Zec	8:3	God-of-the-Angel-Armies, and Mount H
Mal	2:11	has desecrated the h of God
Lk	5:8	a sinner and can't handle this h
Jn	13:10	My concern . . . is h, not hygiene
Ro	6:19	lives healed and expansive in h
1Co	7:14	shares . . . in the h of his wife
	15:34	Awaken to the h of life
2Co	6:6	in gentleness, h, and honest love
Gal	5:22	a basic h permeates things and people
Eph	5:27	dazzling white silk, radiant with h
1Ti	2:15	continue in faith, love, and h

1Pe	1:15	life energetic and blazing with h
Rev	22:11	the holy continue on in h

Homage

1Sa	25:23	her face to the ground in h
2Sa	14:4	bowed deeply before him in h
	19:18	bowed deeply in h to the king
Ps	72:10	Kings remote and legendary will pay h
Isa	49:7	fall on their faces in h
Mt	2:2	find and pay h to the newborn King

Honest

Ge	42:11	we're h men
	42:19	If you're as h as you say you are
	42:31	We are h men and in no way spies
	42:34	you're h men and not spies
Lev	19:36	Use h scales and weights and measures
Dt	25:15	Use only . . . a true and h weight
Jos	14:7	brought back an h and accurate report
Jdg	9:19	think that this is an h day's work
2Ki	12:15	they were h men
	20:3	I've lived an h life before you
	22:7	they're all h men
2Ch	19:9	be dependable and h in your duties
	34:12	The workmen were h and diligent
Ne	7:2	he was an h man and feared God
Job	1:1	He was h inside and out
	1:8	h and true to his word
	2:3	h and true to his word
	6:25	H words never hurt anyone
	7:11	to high heaven is bitter, but h
	31:6	Weigh me on a set of h scales
	42:7	haven't been h either with me
	42:8	for not being h with me
Ps	15:5	make an h living, never take a bribe
	17:1	most h prayer you'll ever hear
	26:1	I've kept an h shop
	32:11	All you h hearts, raise the roof
	58:1	Is there an h politician in the house
	111:8	All that he makes and does is h
Pr	10:2	an h life is immortal
	10:3	God won't starve an h soul
	10:6	Blessings accrue on a good and h life
	10:7	good and h life is a blessed memorial
	11:3	integrity of the h keeps them on track
	14:2	An h life shows respect for God
	16:13	Good leaders cultivate h speech
	19:1	Better to be poor and h than
	20:7	God-loyal people, living h lives
	20:9	be always diligent and h
	21:29	h people are sure of their steps
	24:26	An h answer is like a warm hug
	28:1	H people are relaxed and confident
	29:10	Murderers hate h people
Ecc	5:12	h work earns a good night's sleep
Isa	1:26	h judges and wise counselors among
	8:2	I got two h men
	32:12	Shed h tears for the lost harvest
Eze	45:10	h scales — h weights and h measures
	45:12	your coins must be h

Am	8:5	never do an **h** day's work
Zec	8:17	Keep your lives simple and **h**
Mal	3:8	Begin by being **h**. Do **h** people rob God
Mt	18:16	witnesses will keep things **h**
Lk	16:10	**h** in small things, you'll be **h** in
	16:12	If you're not **h** in small jobs
	20:20	spies who posed as **h** inquirers
	20:21	Teacher, we know that you're **h**
Jn	1:19	John who he was, he was completely **h**
Ro	14:11	**h** truth that I and only I am God
2Co	6:6	gentleness, holiness, and **h** love
	11:12	keep things open and **h** between us
	12:18	just as aboveboard, just as **h**
Eph	4:28	Get an **h** job
2Ti	1:5	your **h** faith
	2:22	those who are in **h** and serious prayer
	4:8	Depend on it, he's an **h** judge

Honestly

Ge	44:20	answered **h**, 'We have a father
Dt	16:18	judge the people fairly and **h**
1Sa	12:24	fear God and worship him **h**
1Ch	29:17	given from the heart, **h** and happily
Job	33:3	I'm speaking **h** from my heart
Pr	2:8	He keeps his eye on all who live **h**
Ecc	5:9	even a bad king is **h** served
Jer	33:15	will run this country **h** and fairly
Mt	6:6	be there as simply and **h** as you can
	22:17	tell us **h**: Is it right to pay taxes
Jn	4:23	those who are simply and **h** themselves
2Co	2:17	say it as **h** as we can

Honesty

Ge	30:33	you can check on my **h** when you assess
Ne	13:13	had a reputation for **h** and hard work
Pr	10:9	**H** lives confident and carefree
	16:11	God cares about **h** in the workplace
Isa	59:14	**H** is nowhere to be found
Lk	2:35	the rejection will force **h**
Ro	16:19	never been any question about your **h**

Honeymoon

Ge	29:27	Enjoy your week of **h**, and then
	29:28	When he'd completed the **h** week
Ps	19:5	husband leaping from his **h** bed
Joel	2:16	men and women on their **h**—interrupt
Lk	12:36	master to come back from his **h**

Honorable

Jdg	9:16	think you did a right and **h** thing
1Sa	22:14	None more **h** either
Ezr	4:10	the great and **h** Ashurbanipal deported
Ps	72:2	be **h** to your meek and lowly
Lk	1:3	most **h** Theophilus
Ac	23:26	to the Most **H** Governor Felix
	24:2	Most **H** Felix, we are most grateful

Honored

Ex	1:21	the midwives **h** God
	20:24	place where I cause my name to be **h**
Nu	9:19	they **h** God's command
1Sa	25:29	Your God-**h** life is tightly bound
	26:21	You've **h** me this day
	26:24	Just as I **h** your life today
2Sa	6:22	I'll be **h** no end
1Ki	1:47	name even more **h** than yours
	8:29	My Name will be **h** there
2Ki	2:15	They welcomed and **h** him
	17:25	they neither **h** nor worshiped him
	17:32	They **h** and worshiped God
	17:33	They **h** and worshiped God
1Ch	11:21	He was highly **h** by the Thirty
	11:25	was highly **h** among the Thirty
2Ch	17:5	ended up very rich and much **h**
	18:1	was very rich and much **h**
	24:25	was not **h** with a grave
	28:27	was not **h** with a burial
	32:27	ended up very wealthy and much **h**
Est	5:11	all the times the king had **h** him
	8:16	they celebrated, they were **h**
Job	6:8	a last request to be **h**
	22:8	strong and **h** by everyone
	29:8	I was **h** by everyone in town
Ps	84:10	**h** as a guest in the palace of sin
	92:10	you've **h** me with a festive parade
	112:9	An **h** life! A beautiful life
	113:8	Seats them among the **h** guests
Pr	12:8	A person who talks sense is **h**
	13:18	embrace correction and live an **h** life
	15:31	an **h** guest among wise men
	17:2	is **h** as one of the family
	27:18	if you honor your boss, you'll be **h**
Isa	14:18	**h** with eulogies and placed in a tomb
	19:13	The **h** pillars of your society
	19:18	cities will be **h** with the title
	55:5	The Holy of Israel has **h** you
	56:5	I'll provide them an **h** place
	61:6	**h** as ministers of our God
Jer	34:5	funeral rites as they **h** your ancestors
	35:14	They **h** and obeyed their ancestor
Eze	20:14	might be **h** and not blasphemed
	20:22	might be **h** and not blasphemed
	44:24	appointed feasts are **h**
Zep	3:20	You'll be famous and **h** all over
Hag	1:12	In listening to Haggai, they **h** God
Mal	1:11	I am **h** all over the world
	1:14	God-of-the-Angel-Armies, **h** far
	2:5	kept my covenant with him, and he **h** me
	3:16	those whose lives **h** God
Lk	23:47	saw what happened, he **h** God
Jn	5:23	Son will be **h** equally with the Father
Ac	5:34	God's Law who was **h** by everyone
	13:48	**h** God's Word by receiving that life
	14:18	sacrifice that would have **h** them
	15:21	wisdom from Moses, preached and **h**
1Co	6:14	God **h** the Master's body by raising it
2Co	6:8	we're blamed; slandered, and **h**
Php	2:9	God lifted him high and **h** him

H

Heb	1:6	presents his **h** Son to the world
	5:4	No one elects himself to this **h**
	5:7	Because he **h** God, God answered him

Honoring

Ge	33:3	bowed seven times, **h** his brother
Nu	14:20	I forgive them, **h** your words
Dt	33:3	sit at your feet, **h** your teaching
Jdg	8:35	**h** all the good he had done
2Sa	2:5	bless you for this — for **h** your master
	9:6	abasing himself, **h** David
	10:3	suppose that David is **h** your father
	24:20	bowing deeply, **h** the king
1Ki	1:16	As Bathsheba bowed low, **h** the king
	1:23	came before the king, **h** him
	1:53	came and bowed down, **h** the king
	3:3	live in the God-**h** ways of David
	8:17	build a Temple **h** the Name of God
2Ki	23:11	horse statues **h** the sun god
1Ch	17:18	to your **h** your servant
	19:3	suppose that David is **h** your father
	21:21	bowed deeply before David, **h** the king
	29:16	worship for you, **h** your Holy Name
2Ch	6:6	Jerusalem for **h** my Name
	6:7	build a temple **h** the Name of God
Ne	1:11	servants who delight in **h** you
Est	6:6	must be talking about **h** me
Pr	25:5	authority will be credible and God-**h**
Isa	58:2	law-abiding, God-**h**
	66:3	no different from **h** a no-god idol
Jer	32:39	one mind and heart, always **h** me
Mic	4:5	we live **h** God
Mal	1:12	Instead of **h** me, you profane me
	2:2	you're not serious about **h** me
Jn	12:7	**h** the day of my burial
Tit	2:12	take on a God-filled, God-**h** life
Jas	4:11	You're supposed to be **h** the Message
	5:10	never once quit, all the time **h** God

Honors

Job	23:10	I'll pass the test with **h**
	36:7	he **h** them lavishly
Ps	12:8	collect **h** For their wonderful lies
	50:23	It's the praising life that **h** me
	71:21	streaming with **h**; turn to me
Pr	26:1	We no more give **h** to fools
	29:23	humility prepares you for **h**
Isa	53:12	best of everything, the highest **h**
	56:5	I'll confer permanent **h** on them
Eze	18:9	faithfully **h** and obeys my laws
Da	2:6	I'll lavish you with gifts and **h**
Ob	1:21	a rule that **h** God's kingdom
Mal	1:6	a son **h** his father
	3:17	parents give the child who **h** them
1Co	6:13	the Master **h** you with a body
2Th	1:12	If your life **h** the name of Jesus

Hope

Ge	49:18	wait in **h** for your salvation, God

Ru	1:12	There's still **h**!
1Sa	2:8	burned-out lives with fresh **h**
	17:11	were terrified and lost all **h**
	17:32	said David, "don't give up **h**
2Sa	1:26	anything I've known — or ever **h**
2Ki	10:4	what **h** do we have
	14:26	no **h** of help anywhere
Ezr	10:2	there is still **h** for Israel
Job	4:4	put fresh **h** in people
	4:6	your exemplary life give you **h**
	5:16	the poor continue to **h**
	6:19	tourists from Sheba **h** for a cool drink
	7:2	nothing to **h** for but payday
	11:18	Full of **h**, you'll relax
	14:7	For a tree there is always **h**
	14:19	you relentlessly grind down our **h**
	17:12	**h** that night would turn into day, my **h**
	17:13	only **h** for comfort is a . . . coffin
	17:15	Do you call that **h**?
	17:15	Who on earth could find any **h**
	17:16	If **h** and I are to be buried together
	19:10	he yanked out **h** by the roots
	27:8	What **h** do people without God have
	41:9	What **h** would you have
Ps	52:9	your good name my **h**
	62:5	Everything I **h** for comes from him
	69:6	those who look to you in **h**
	119:81	waiting for your word of **h**
	131:3	Wait with **h**. **H** now; **h** always
	142:5	my last chance, my only **h** for life
	143:9	God — you're my only **h**
	146:5	put your **h** in God
Pr	11:7	the story's over, end of **h**
	24:14	your **h** is on solid rock
Ecc	9:4	anyone selected out for life has **h**
Isa	8:17	while I wait and **h** for him
	8:18	I stand my ground and **h**
	20:5	Everyone who has put **h** in Ethiopia
	20:6	we thought they were our best **h**
	33:2	treat us kindly. You're our only **h**
	51:5	take **h** in my saving power
	64:5	Is there any **h** for us?
Jer	6:15	There's no **h** for them
	8:12	There's no **h** for them
	13:27	sordid life! Is there any **h** for you
	14:8	**H** of Israel! Our only **h**!
	17:13	O God, you're the **h** of Israel
	29:11	give you the future you **h** for
	31:17	There's **h** for your children
	47:4	no **h** of help for Tyre and Sidon
	50:7	True Pasture, the **h** of their parents
	51:46	Don't lose **h**. Don't ever give up
La	3:21	remembering, I keep a grip on **h**
	3:26	quietly **h**, quietly **h** for help from God
	3:29	Wait for **h** to appear
Eze	19:5	that her **h** for that cub was gone
	29:21	I'll stir up fresh **h** in Israel
	37:11	Our bones are dried up, our **h** is gone
Da	9:9	Compassion is our only **h**
	9:18	This prayer is our last and only **h**
Hos	2:15	turn Heartbreak Valley into Acres of **H**
	14:3	You're our last **h**

H

Zec	1:21	no one had any **h** left
	9:12	Come home, **h**-filled prisoners
Mt	12:21	mere sound of his name will signal **h**
	19:13	brought to Jesus in the **h** that he
	24:20	**H** and pray this won't happen
Mk	13:18	**H** and pray this won't happen
Lk	6:34	give for what you **h** to get out of it
Ac	2:26	pitched my tent in the land of **h**
	15:32	many words of courage and **h**
	20:2	charging them with fresh **h**
	23:6	the **h** and resurrection of the dead
	26:7	my ancestors — the identical **h**
	27:20	we lost all **h** of rescue
	28:20	I'm a hostage here for **h**
Ro	6:2	I should **h** not!
	11:9	I **h** they get sick eating
	11:10	I **h** they go blind staring
	11:24	**h** for the best for the others
	15:12	everyone everywhere to see and take **h**
	15:13	May the God of green **h** fill you up
	15:29	My **h** is that my visit with you
1Co	5:3	**h** it goes away on its own
	6:15	I should **h** not
	10:33	I **h** you will be, too
	11:16	**h** you're not going to be argumentative
	13:13	Trust steadily in God, **h** unswervingly
2Co	3:12	With that kind of **h** to excite us
	5:11	**h** you realize how much . . . we care
	12:19	**h** you don't think that all along
	13:6	**h** the test won't show
Php	3:1	**h** you don't mind hearing it again
Col	1:5	kept taut by **h**
1Th	1:3	patience of **h** in following our Master
	5:8	faith, love, and the **h** of salvation
	5:11	Build up **h** so you'll all be together
1Ti	1:1	Christ, our living **h**
	3:14	I **h** to visit you soon
	5:5	she has put all her **h** in God
Heb	6:11	intensity toward a full-bodied **h**
	6:18	grab the promised **h** with both hands
2Jn	1:12	I **h** to be there soon in person
3Jn	1:14	I **h** to be there soon in person

Hoped

2Ki	18:24	these **h**-for Egyptian chariots
Ecc	2:20	could be **h** for on this earth
Isa	21:4	I had **h** for a relaxed evening
Jer	8:15	**h** things would turn out for the best
	14:19	We **h** for peace — nothing good came
Mt	22:35	question they **h** would show him up
Lk	23:8	**h** to see him do something spectacular
Ro	5:2	where we always **h** we might stand

Hopeless

Jos	2:9	Everyone in the country feels **h**
Ps	10:17	hearts of the **h** pump red blood
	88:4	one more statistic, a **h** case
Isa	19:15	Egypt's **h**, past helping
Jer	6:10	It's **h**! Their ears are stuffed
	30:13	given up on you. You're **h**

	30:17	gave up on you and dismissed you as **h**
Eze	24:12	But it's **h**. It's too far gone
Zec	9:11	prisoners from their **h** cells
Mt	23:13	You're **h**, you religion scholars
	23:15	You're **h**, you religion scholars
	23:16	You're **h**! What arrogant stupidity
	23:23	You're **h**, you religion scholars
	23:25	You're **h**, you religion scholars
	23:27	You're **h**, you religion scholars
	23:29	You're **h**, you religion scholars
Lk	11:42	You're **h**, you Pharisees! Frauds
	11:43	You're **h**, you Pharisees! Frauds
	11:46	You're **h**, you religion scholars
	11:47	You're **h**! You build tombs
	11:52	You're **h**, you religion scholars
Ro	4:18	When everything was **h**, Abraham
	4:19	It's **h**. This hundred-year-old body
	4:24	the conditions were equally **h**

Hopelessly

SS	4:9	One look my way and I was **h** in love
Jer	10:19	**H** wounded, I said
	14:17	bruised, **h** and cruelly wounded
	17:9	The heart is **h** dark and deceitful
Lk	16:14	dismissing him as **h** out of touch

Hopes

2Ki	4:28	Don't tease me with false **h**
Job	6:11	Where's the strength to keep my **h** up
	8:13	all their **h** come to nothing
	17:11	all my **h** are snuffed out
Ps	119:116	Don't disappoint all my grand **h**
Isa	49.23	No one who **h** in me regrets it
Lk	24:21	we had our **h** up that he was the One
Eph	1:11	heard of Christ and got our **h** up
Php	1:7	prayers and **h** have deep roots
Tit	1:2	raise **h** by pointing the way to life

Hoping

Ge	32:5	my master, **h** for your approval
	33:8	I was **h** that they would pave the way
1Sa	17:28	see the sights, **h** for a ringside seat
Job	13:15	even if he killed me, I'd keep on **h**
	14:14	through these difficult days I keep **h**
Ps	39:7	**H**, that's what I'm doing
	119:147	for help, **h** for a word from you
Pr	7:15	**h** to catch sight of your face
Jer	20:10	Old friends watch, **h** I'll fall flat
Am	8:12	**h** to hear God's Word
Hab	3:7	terrified, **h** he wouldn't notice them
Mt	6:5	their prayers, **h** for stardom
Mk	3:2	**h** to catch him in a Sabbath infraction
	9:18	**h** they could deliver him
	10:13	to Jesus, **h** he might touch them
	12:13	**h** to catch him saying something
Lk	6:7	**h** to catch him in a Sabbath infraction
	18:15	to Jesus, **h** he might touch them
	20:20	**h** to trick him into saying something
Ac	5:15	**h** they would be touched

H

	24:26	secretly **h** that Paul would offer
Ro	11:14	**h** they'll realize what they're missing
1Co	15:18	who died **h** in Christ and resurrection
	15:32	**h** it wouldn't be the end of me
2Co	1:13	plain, unembellished truth, **h** that
	7:12	what I was **h** for in the first place
	8:8	**h** to bring the best out of you
	10:15	What we're **h** for
Php	1:17	**h** to get something out of it
	2:24	**h** and praying to be right on his heels
2Th	3:9	**h** it would prove contagious

Horror

Dt	28:25	Earth will see you as a **h**
	28:37	treated as a lesson or a proverb — a **h**
Ps	55:15	let them experience the **h**
Isa	21:4	Absolutely stunned, **h**-stricken
Jer	25:9	a **h** to top all the horrors
	25:18	a vast wasteland, a **h** to look at
	34:17	I'll make you a spectacle of **h**
	44:22	a **h** story, a ghost town
	48:39	The stark **h** of Moab
Eze	5:15	turned into a **h** story
	20:26	The very **h** should have shocked them
	27:36	This **h** can't happen
Da	7:7	This one was a grisly **h** — hideous

Horrors

Job	20:25	They're trapped in a house of **h**
Isa	21:15	refugees escaping the **h** of war
Jer	25:9	a horror to top all the **h** in history

Hospitable

Mt	12:45	you weren't **h** to my kingdom message
Ac	17:26	made the earth **h**
1Ti	3:2	accessible, and **h**. He must know

Hospitality

Dt	23:4	nations didn't treat you with **h**
1Ki	2:7	extend every **h** to them
Isa	21:14	Show your desert **h**
Lk	7:22	God's salvation **h** extended to them
	9:52	to make arrangements for his **h**
	9:53	they refused **h**
Ac	16:15	she said in a surge of **h**
	27:3	enjoy the **h** of his friends there
Ro	12:13	be inventive in **h**
	16:1	generous **h** we Christians are famous
2Co	7:15	dignity and sensitivity of your **h**
Phm	1:7	your **h** to fellow believers
Heb	13:2	some have extended **h** to angels
3Jn	1:5	**h** to Christian brothers and sisters
	1:6	**h** worthy of God himself
	1:10	not only refuses **h** to traveling

Host

Jer	50:9	rallying a **h** of nations against

Lk	14:8	might have been invited by the **h**
	14:10	when the **h** comes he may very well say
	14:12	Then he turned to the **h**
Jn	2:8	take them to the **h**," Jesus said
	2:9	When the **h** tasted the water
Ro	16:23	Gaius, who is **h** here to both me
1Co	10:27	cross-examine your **h** on the ethical

Hostage

Mt	20:28	exchange for the many who are held **h**
Mk	10:45	exchange for many who are held **h**
Ac	28:20	I'm a **h** here for hope, not doom
1Co	7:23	once held **h** in a sinful society

Hostages

Ge	42:37	my two sons in your hands as **h**
1Ki	20:18	take them alive as **h**
2Ki	14:14	for good measure, he took **h**
2Ch	25:24	for good measure, he took **h**

Hostile

Dt	19:16	a **h** witness stands to accuse someone
2Sa	22:7	A **h** world! I called to God
1Ki	11:14	into **h** actions against Solomon
Ps	18:6	A **h** world! I call to God
	35:11	**H** accusers appear out of nowhere
	47:3	He crushes **h** people
	122:7	**H** outsiders, keep your distance
Isa	11:13	Judah no longer the **h** rival
Mt	13:58	because of their **h** indifference

Hostility

Isa	11:13	the **h** of Judah will vanish
Eph	2:16	that was the end of the **h**
Heb	12:3	long litany of **h** he plowed through

Hosting

Job	1:4	take turns **h** parties in their homes

Humiliate

1Sa	11:2	I'll **h** every last man and woman
2Ki	19:4	to **h** the living God
	19:23	to **h** the Master
Ps	119:22	Don't let them mock and **h** me
Mic	5:1	They **h** Israel's king

Humiliated

Dt	21:14	use her as a slave since you've **h** her
2Sa	10:5	they were seriously **h**
1Ch	19:5	they were seriously **h**
2Ch	28:20	came instead and **h** Ahaz even more
Ps	25:3	It's the traitors who should be **h**
	89:44	**h** this warrior
Isa	24:23	Shamefaced moon will cower, **h**
	44:11	Watch the no-god makers slink off **h**

	45:16	**H**, all those others will be ashamed
Jer	31:19	**H**, I beat on my chest
	51:51	we've been **h**, taunted and abused
Eze	36:6	you've been **h** among the nations
	36:7	It's their turn to be **h**
Da	5:19	He promoted or **h** people capriciously
Mic	7:16	**h** in their arrogance
Zec	13:4	will be publicly exposed and **h**
2Co	13:4	when we were **h** among you

Humility

Pr	15:33	skilled living — first you learn **h**
	18:12	**h** is precursor to honor
	29:23	**h** prepares you for honors
Isa	58:5	a day to show off **h**?
Eph	4:2	do this with **h** and discipline
Col	3:12	compassion, kindness, **h**
1Ti	2:9	with the men in **h** before God
Jas	1:21	In simple **h**, let our gardener, God

Hurt

Ge	31:7	God never let him really **h** me
	31:52	I won't cross this line to **h** you
	37:22	but don't **h** him
	42:22	Don't **h** the boy
Ex	9:32	the wheat and spelt weren't **h**
	21:22	miscarries but is not otherwise **h**
	24:11	He didn't **h** these pillar-leaders
Lev	24:20	What he did to **h** that person
Nu	16:15	haven't **h** a single hair
Dt	32:19	angered and **h** by his sons
Jdg	15:12	Just promise not to **h** me
1Sa	26:9	Don't you dare **h** him!
	26:21	I won't **h** you anymore
2Sa	13:12	No, brother!" she said, "Don't **h** me
	20:6	going to **h** us even worse than Absalom
	20:20	I'm not here to **h** anyone
1Ki	1:52	not a hair of his head will be **h**
1Ch	4:10	don't let evil **h** me
2Ch	25:8	God only has the power to help or **h**
Ne	6:2	knew they were scheming to **h** me
Job	1:12	Just don't **h** him
	6:25	Honest words never **h** anyone
	7:20	I'd sinned — how would that **h** you
	14:21	if they do badly, we're spared the **h**
	16:17	I've never **h** a soul
Ps	15:3	Don't **h** your friend
	37:33	Wicked won't **h** a hair of his head
	69:29	I'm **h** and in pain
	105:15	lay a hand on my anointed, don't **h**
	106:6	We've fallen short, **h** a lot of people
	140:3	sharp rhetoric of hate and **h**
Pr	11:17	cruel to others, you **h** yourself
	23:35	but it didn't **h**; they beat
	31:5	the people who depend on them are **h**
Ecc	1:18	The more you know, the more you **h**
	7:4	Sages invest themselves in **h**
	8:5	Carrying out orders won't **h** you
	8:9	have the power to **h** each other
Isa	11:9	Neither animal nor human will **h**

	29:20	never missed a chance to **h**
	41:23	Can you **h** us or help us
	42:3	won't brush aside the . . . **h**
	53:9	Even though he'd never **h** a soul
	54:17	no weapon that can **h** you has ever
	65:25	Neither animal nor human will **h**
Jer	2:34	You cut and **h** a lot of people
	7:18	gods they come across, just to **h** me
	15:10	I've never **h** or harmed a soul
	30:16	Everyone who **h** you will be **h**
Eze	33:15	ways that don't **h** others
Da	6:22	lions so that they would not **h** me
Hos	6:1	He **h** us, but he'll heal us
Am	9:4	made up my mind to **h** them
Mic	4:6	round up all the **h** and homeless
Zec	9:8	Nobody is going to **h** my people
Mt	9:35	healed their bruised and **h** lives
	10:1	care for the bruised and **h** lives
	15:32	I **h** for these people
Mk	16:18	will drink poison and not be **h**
Lk	2:48	they were upset and **h**
	4:35	The demon didn't **h** him
	15:14	he began to **h**
Ac	18:10	no one is going to be able to **h** you
1Co	6:8	more injustice, bringing more **h**
	8:11	if you **h** your friend terribly
	8:12	When you **h** your friend, you **h** Christ
	12:26	If one part **h**s, every other part
2Co	7:2	We've never **h** a soul
1Ti	5:10	tired Christians, the **h** and troubled
Rev	7:3	Don't **h** the earth! Don't **h** the sea
	7:3	Don't so much as **h** a tree
	9:4	Don't **h** the grass
	9:4	don't **h** anything green
	11:5	If anyone tries to **h** them

Hysteria

1Sa	5:9	It was mass **h**
Da	5:10	**h** among the king and his nobles
Zec	14:13	Mass **h** when that happens — total panic
Ac	21:34	one word from another in the mob **h**

Hysterical

Isa	13:7	Everyone paralyzed in the panic, **h**
	19:16	will be like **h** schoolgirls
Jer	49:24	**H**, she'll fall to pieces

Hysterically

Isa	31:9	their leaders scatter **h**
Ac	17:6	before the city fathers, yelling **h**

Hysterics

Jer	49:3	Go into **h**, run around in circles!
Mic	4:9	So why the doomsday **h**?

H

I

I-Am

| Ex | 3:14 | God said to Moses, "I-WHO-I |
| | 6:3 | by my name God (I-Present) |

Idiot

Ps	69:7	Because of you I look like an i
	74:18	each i desecration
Mt	5:22	Carelessly call a brother 'i!'

Idiots

2Ch	36:16	treated the prophets like i
Ps	71:13	make them look Like i
	94:8	think again, you i, fools
Pr	1:22	I! How long will you refuse to learn
	1:32	simpletons, you i? Carelessness kills
	8:5	Listen, you i — learn good sense

Idolaters

Eze	14:9	tells these i the lies they want
Rev	21:8	sorcerers, i and all liars
	22:15	i — all who love and live lies

Idolatrous

1Ki	22:43	pray and worship at these i shrines
2Ch	20:33	pray and worship at these i god shops
	33:19	i images that he worshiped previous

Idolatry

Ps	119:118	their casual i is lethal
Ro	2:22	The same with i
1Co	10:25	don't have to run an "i test"
Eph	5:5	the usual variations on i

Ignite

1Ki	18:23	an altar on firewood — but don't i it
Ps	144:5	God; i volcanoes in the hearts
Mt	3:11	will i the kingdom life within you
Lk	3:16	will i the kingdom life, a fire

Ignorance

Pr	1:22	How long will you wallow in i?
Mic	3:7	lame excuses to cover up their God-i
Mt	23:17	What i! Does the leather on the Bible
Lk	12:10	out of misunderstanding or i
	12:48	if he does a poor job through i
1Co	15:34	I of God is a luxury you can't afford
Eph	4:22	we do not have the excuse of i
1Pe	2:15	cure the i of the fools
1Jn	1:10	only shows off our i of God

Ignorant

Job	18:21	This is how the God-i end up
Ps	73:22	I was totally i, a dumb ox
	82:5	I judges! Head-in-the-sand judges
	119:85	i as they are of God and his ways
Pr	19:2	I zeal is worthless; haste makes waste
Jer	9:3	from one evil to the next, i of me
Mt	6:7	prayer warriors who are prayer-i
Jn	7:49	this crowd, i of God's Law
1Ti	6:4	i windbags who infect the air
1Pe	4:3	your time in that God-i way of life
2Pe	2:12	with their i blasphemies

Ignore

Ex	34:7	he doesn't i sin
Ps	40:4	i what the world worships
	79:6	your rival kingdoms who i you
	119:53	I see the wicked i your directions
	143:7	Don't turn away; don't i me!
Pr	4:25	i all sideshow distractions
	10:17	i correction and you're lost for good
	13:13	I the Word and suffer
	14:21	criminal to i a neighbor in need
Am	4:6	You continued to i me
	4:9	you continued to i me
	4:10	You continued to i me
	4:11	You continued to i me
Jnh	1:2	I can't i it any longer
	3:2	I can't i it any longer
Hag	2:17	You continued to i me
Jas	2:3	either i the street person or say

Ignored

Jdg	12:2	did call to you for help but you i me
2Ch	33:10	they i him
Ne	9:34	They i your commands
Job	19:7	I shout 'Murder!' and I'm i
	31:16	Have I i the needs of the poor
Ps	13:1	God — you've i me long enough
	119:139	persistently i your commandments
Pr	1:24	reached out to you, but you've i me
Isa	42:22	Victims . . . feeling i, abandoned
	60:15	out-of-the-way, unvisited, i
	65:1	to a nation that i me
	65:12	when I invited you, you i me
	66:4	when I invited you, you i me
Jer	2:30	no attention to me, i my discipline
	6:19	They've i everything I've said
	11:8	despite all my warnings, they had i
	16:11	i me and wouldn't do a thing I told
	34:14	your ancestors totally i me
	35:14	get your attention, and you've i me
	44:23	i the covenant conditions
Eze	5:6	refused my guidance, i my directions
	16:49	i the oppressed and the poor
	33:5	He heard the alarm, he i it
	34:8	you shepherds i them and only fed
Da	3:28	They i the king's orders
	9:11	All of us in Israel i what you said

	9:14	persistently and defiantly i you
Am	4:8	never got thirsty for me. You i me
Zec	1:4	they i everything I said to them
Mt	15:23	Jesus i her
	25:40	someone overlooked or i, that was me
	25:45	someone who was being overlooked or i
Lk	7:50	He i them and said to the woman
Ro	8:8	God isn't pleased at being i
2Co	6:9	i by the world, but recognized by God
Heb	12:25	those who i earthly warnings didn't

Ignores

Job	19:16	he i me, i me even though I plead
Isa	40:23	He i what all the princes say and do
Jer	35:16	this people i me
Eze	33:4	hears the sound of the trumpet and i
Da	6:13	one of the Jewish exiles, i you
Zec	11:16	who i the lost, abandons the injured
Lk	12:47	knows what his master wants and i it
Ro	8:7	completely absorbed in self i God

Ignoring

1Sa	2:29	get fat on these offerings, and i me
	17:30	I his brother, he turned to someone
1Ki	9:6	betray me, i my guidance
2Ch	7:19	betray me, i my guidance
Est	5:9	at the King's Gate i him
Ps	119:21	i everything you tell them
Isa	32:6	i those dying of thirst
	48:8	You have a history of i me
Eze	5:7	refusing my guidance, i my directions
Da	3:12	These men are i you, O king
Hos	7:10	despite all the signs, i God
Mal	3.7	a long history of i my commands
Jn	5:44	ranking your rivals and i God
Ac	7:51	Deliberately i the Holy Spirit
	24:27	playing up to the Jews and i justice
Ro	6:20	did what you felt like doing, i God
Gal	6:7	i the needs of others — i God
Jas	2:10	things in God's law and i others

Ill

Ge	48:1	Joseph was told, "Your father is i
Jos	20:5	there was no history of i
Pr	10:2	I-gotten gain gets you nowhere
	13:22	i-gotten wealth ends up with good
	31:7	terminally i, for whom life is
Isa	58:7	clothes on the shivering i-clad
Jer	5:27	stuffed with i-gotten gain
Eze	18:7	doesn't refuse clothing to the i-clad
	18:16	give clothes to the i-clad
Mt	8:16	He cured the bodily i
	11:29	won't lay anything heavy or i-fitting
Ro	9:18	we play our part for good or i
Col	3:9	filthy set of i-fitting clothes

Illnesses

| Dt | 28:59 | hideous interminable i |

Mt	8:17	He took our i
Lk	8:2	various evil afflictions and i

Illusion

Job	20:8	like a shadowy i that vanishes
	24:23	They may have an i of security
Ps	4:2	How long will you live crazed by i
Pr	14:18	Foolish dreamers live in a world of i
Ecc	5:7	against all i and fantasy
Isa	59:4	They trust in i, they tell lies
Jer	8:8	where it's gotten you — stuck in i
	14:14	sheer i, tissues of lies
Jn	3:20	addicted to denial and i
Col	2:23	give the i of being pious
1Jn	5:13	the reality and not the i

Illusions

Isa	28:18	a pack of i and lies
Jer	8:5	stubbornly hold on to their i
	16:19	lies, useless i, all smoke
	48:12	That will smash his i
La	2:14	wishful thinking, deceptive i
Eze	13:6	fantasize comforting i
	13.8	prophets who substitute i for visions
Mt	13:22	weeds of worry and i
2Th	2:12	their chosen world of lies and i
1Ti	4:1	chase after demonic i

Imagine

Dt	4:32	as far back as you can i
	4:32	as far away as you can i
Ru	1:13	can you i being satisfied to wait
Job	3:21	can't i anything better than death
	11:8	God is far higher than you can i
	22:25	more wealth than you can i
	36:26	greater than anything you could ever i
	38:30	don't for a minute i these marvels
	39:10	i hitching your plow to a buffalo
Pr	18:11	they i themselves safe behind it
	30:12	Don't i yourself to be
SS	8:3	I! His left hand cradling my head
Isa	40:28	Creator of all you can see or i
Eze	18:5	I a person who lives well
Mk	10:24	You can't i how difficult
Lk	11:5	I what would happen if you went
	14:31	i a king going into battle
	15:8	i a woman who has ten coins
	23:31	i what they'll do with deadwood
Jn	21:25	can't i a world big enough to hold
Ac	28:15	as you can well i
Ro	5:17	i the breathtaking recovery life makes
	11:12	i the effect of their coming back
1Co	4:1	Don't i us leaders to be something
	12:21	Can you i Eye telling Hand, "Get lost
	14:36	i that you're a sacred oracle
	15:41	i what the resurrection "plants
Eph	3:20	far more than you could ever i
1Th	2:18	You can't i how much we missed you

Imagined

Ge	6:5	thought evil, i evil
1Ki	10:7	far more than I could ever have i
2Ch	9:6	far more than I could ever have i
Isa	64:4	no one has ever i, No ear heard
Jer	3:19	I i that you would say, 'Dear father
1Co	2:9	Never so much as i anything quite like

Immortal

Ps	49:12	We aren't i. We don't last long
	49:20	We aren't i. We don't last long
Pr	10:2	an honest life is i
1Co	15:53	this mortal replaced by the i
1Ti	1:17	One God, I, Invisible

Impostors

Ps	14:4	Don't they know anything, all these i
	53:4	Don't they know anything, all these i
Jer	29:23	sex predators and prophet-i
2Co	11:20	tolerance for i who rob your freedom
Eph	4:14	children who are an easy mark for i
2Ti	3:9	nothing will come of these latest i

Impotence

Ro	4:19	Abraham didn't focus on his own i
Gal	5:20	an i to love or be loved

Impotent

Ps	76:5	warriors were . . . left there i
	89:45	left him an i, ruined husk
Ecc	12:5	a fragile and i matchstick body
Jer	11:13	sacrifices to that i sex god
Hos	4:19	sex-worship leaves them finally i
1Co	1:25	Human wisdom is so tinny, so i

Impugn

Mt	10:17	Some people will i your motives
1Co	9:15	discredit me or i my motives

Impulse

Ecc	2:10	I gave in to every i
Eze	18:8	doesn't live by i and greed
	18:17	doesn't live by i and greed
2Co	10:5	every loose thought and emotion and i

Impure

Nu	5:14	suspects that his wife is i
	5:19	had an adulterous affair and become i

Impurity

Lev	15:19	the i of her menstrual period
Nu	5:28	is innocent of i
Col	3:5	sexual promiscuity, i, lust

Incinerate

Ex	32:10	burst into flames and i them
Hos	7:7	they i their rulers
Lk	9:54	lightning down out of the sky and i
Rev	11:5	fire from their mouths will i them

Incriminating

Mk	12:13	to catch him saying something i
Lk	20:26	trap him into saying anything i
Jn	8:6	trap him into saying something i

Incurable

Dt	28:27	hemorrhoids, scabs, and an i itch
Jer	30:17	I'll come with healing, curing the i

Independent

Pr	30:9	If I'm too full, I might get i
Jn	5:32	an i witness confirms me
Gal	3:10	to live by his own effort, i of God

Independently

Jn	5:19	The Son can't i do a thing
1Co	12:13	each used to i call our own shots

Indicting

Isa	30:27	searing, i words
Jer	15:10	unhappy job of i the whole country
Mal	2:4	I'm i you in order to put new life

Indictment

Job	31:35	I want to see my i in writing
Mal	2:1	now this i, you priests
Ro	10:21	capped it with a damning i

Indifferent

Job	35:12	People are arrogantly i to God
Ps	10:11	sure that God is i to his plight
	22:3	Are you i, above it all
Isa	13:17	ruthless bunch i to bribes
Am	6:5	i to the fate of others
Zec	11:16	a shepherd i to victims
Mt	22:16	i to popular opinion
Mk	12:14	you are i to public opinion
1Co	10:28	may be i as to where it came from
2Co	1:18	a careless yes canceled by an i no
	1:23	I was being considerate of you, not i
Php	1:18	motives, whether mixed, bad, or i
Heb	11:27	i to the king's blind rage
	12:28	God is not an i bystander
1Pe	3:1	i as they are to any words about God

Indigent

Lev	25:35	If one of your brothers becomes i

Job	25:39	If one of your brothers becomes **i**
	31:16	turned my back on the **i**
Pr	10:15	the poverty of the **i** is their ruin
Isa	14:19	murdered and **i** corpses

Indignant

Jdg	8:1	They were **i** and let him know it
Lk	19:7	Everyone who saw the incident was **i**
Jn	2:20	They were **i**: "It took forty-six years
	8:39	They were **i**. "Our father is Abraham
Ac	4:2	**i** that these upstart apostles

Indignation

Jer	15:17	You'd filled me with **i**
	32:37	my anger and rage and **i**
Mk	14:5	nearly bursting with **i**

Indolent

Isa	32:9	Take your stand, **i** women
	32:11	Oh tremble, you **i** women
Am	4:1	**I** and pampered

Indulge

Eze	18:6	doesn't **i** in casual sex
	33:26	you **i** in sex at random
1Pe	2:11	Don't **i** your ego at the expense
2Pe	2:10	preferring to **i** in self-rule
	2:13	they **i** in wild parties
1Jn	3:4	All who **i** in a sinful life
Rev	2:14	why do you **i** that Balaam crowd

Indulgence

Hos	2:13	pay for her **i** in promiscuous religion
Ac	24:4	beg your kind **i** in listening to me
Ro	13:13	daylight hours in frivolity and **i**
2Ti	2:22	Run away from infantile **i**

Indulgent

Isa	32:9	I, indolent women, listen closely
Jer	3:9	religion as . . . an **i** recreation
Tit	2:12	turn our backs on a godless, **i** life

Inexperienced

Sa	17:33	You're too young and **i**
Job	30:2	considered their fathers mere **i** pups
r	1:4	To teach the **i** the ropes
Heb	5:13	Milk is for beginners, **i** in God's ways

Infamous

Ki	16:20	along with his **i** conspiracy
Ch	28:26	The rest of Ahaz's **i** life
ze	22:5	deride you as **i** in filth, notorious
t	27:16	had the **i** Jesus Barabbas in prison
:	27:14	a gale-force wind, the **i** nor'easter

Infantile

1Co	3:4	aren't you being totally **i**
	14:20	exasperated with your **i** thinking
Col	2:20	pretentious and **i** religion behind you
2Ti	2:22	Run away from **i** indulgence

Infidelities

Nu	15:39	that seduces you into **i**
Hos	13:12	I have a detailed record of your **i**

Infinite

Job	36:26	See how great he is — **i**
1Jn	1:2	The **i** Life of God himself took shape

Influence

1Ki	1:9	everyone . . . who had position and **i**
Job	9:14	construct a defense that would **i** God
	31:21	used my strength and **i** to take
Ps	54:1	Use your **i** to clear me
Isa	17:10	to honor and **i** your fertility gods
Eze	13:21	deliver my people from your **i**
Da	11:6	her **i** will weaken
Ac	17:12	in the community, women and men of **i**
Ro	7:25	pulled by the **i** of sin
Jas	2:1	public opinion **i** how you live

Influential

1Sa	22:7	give you all **i** jobs
2Ch	23:1	certain **i** officers in the army
Ezr	7:28	all his advisors and **i** officials
Job	1:3	the most **i** man in all the East
Pr	23:1	go out to dinner with an **i** person
Ac	21:39	a citizen still of that **i** city
1Co	1:26	not many **i**, not many

Informed

Isa	44:8	Haven't I always kept you **i**
Da	6:24	conspirators who had **i** on Daniel
Ro	2:18	**i** on the latest doctrines
1Co	12:1	I want you to be **i** and knowledgeable

Inhospitable

Jer	2:6	a cruel, **i** land
Mal	3:5	those who are **i** to the homeless

Iniquities

Lev	16:21	confess all the **i** of the People
	16:22	The goat will carry all their **i**
	18:25	I punished it for its **i**
Ezr	9:6	our **i** are piled up so high
Ne	9:2	confessed their sins and the **i**

Iniquity

Ex	34:7	forgiving i, rebellion, and sin
	34:9	Forgive our i and sin
Lev	7:18	must take responsibility for his i
Nu	14:18	forgiving i and rebellion and sin
Ne	4:5	don't forgive their i

Initiation

Isa	66:17	i in those unholy rituals
Col	2:11	not through some secretive i rite
	2:12	If it's an i ritual you're after

Initiative

Mt	6:33	Steep your life in God-reality, God-i
	7:12	grab the i and do it for them
Lk	6:31	grab the i and do it for them
	12:31	Steep yourself in God-reality, God-i
	18:28	Peter tried to regain some i
Ro	9:11	decision, flowing steadily from his i

Injured

Ex	21:18	i one doesn't die but is
	22:10	dies or is i or lost
	22:14	it gets i or dies
Dt	22:4	donkey or ox i along the road
2Ki	1:2	and was i
2Ch	28:15	provided first aid to the i
Eze	34:4	don't doctor the i
	34:16	I'll doctor the i
Zec	11:16	ignores the lost, abandons the i
Lk	10:32	he also avoided the i man
2Co	2:5	I am not the one i in this

Injustice

Job	5:16	while i is bound and gagged
Pr	24:23	very wrong, to go along with i
Isa	30:12	Preferring to live by i
	58:6	break the chains of i
Eze	9:9	The city is bloated with i
1Co	6:8	fuel for more wrong, more i

Innocence

Ge	44:16	How can we prove our i?
Job	13:15	I'd defend my i to the very end
Ac	26:31	quickly agreed on Paul's i

Innocent

Ge	20:4	Master, would you kill an i man
Ex	23:7	Don't contribute to the death of i
Nu	5:14	Even if she is i
	5:28	is i of impurity
Dt	19:10	no chance of i blood being spilled
	25:1	declaring one i and the other guilty
	27:25	takes a bribe to kill an i person
1Sa	19:5	sinning against an i person

2Sa	3:28	are totally i of this murder
	4:11	evil men who killed an i man
2Ki	21:16	with the i blood of his victims
	24:4	streets flow with the i blood
1Ch	12:17	i as I am
Job	4:7	Has a truly i person ever ended up
	8:6	If you're as i and upright as you say
	9:15	Even though I'm i I could never prove
	9:20	though i, anything I say incriminates
	9:23	aloof from the despair of the i
	10:15	But if I'm i, it's no better
	35:2	I'm perfectly i before God
	36:5	he doesn't bully i people
Ps	1:5	unfit company for i people
	7:8	confident in your verdict: "I
	17:2	Show the world I'm i
	94:21	plotted behind the backs of the i
Pr	6:17	hands that murder the i
	18:5	or come down hard on the i
SS	6:9	Pure and i as the day she was born
Isa	5:23	violate the rights of the i
	9:5	shirts soaked with i blood
	29:21	the people who victimized the i
Jer	5:26	Their victims are i men and women
	7:6	no longer taking advantage of i people
	19:4	they have massacred i people
	26:15	kill me, you're killing an i man
Eze	13:22	unsuspecting and i people
Da	6:22	I've been found i before God
Jnh	4:11	to say nothing of all the i animals
Mt	27:4	I've betrayed an i man
Lk	10:21	showed them to these i newcomers
	23:47	This man was i! A good man
Ac	3:13	The very One that Pilate called i
	22:14	actually seen the Righteous I
	22:18	saw God's Righteous I
Ro	9:11	her babies were still i in the womb

Insane

Ps	31:13	gossip has me "criminally i"
Ecc	2:2	the fun-filled life? I! Inane!

Insatiable

Job	5:5	i for everything they have
Ps	119:20	i for your nourishing commands
Isa	9:20	Appetites i, stuffing and gorging
Jer	2:24	i, indiscriminate, promiscuous
Eze	16:28	Your appetite was i

Insider

Am	7:10	he's doing it as an i
Ro	2:17	you're an i to God's revelation
	3:27	our proud Jewish i claims
	3:29	outsider non-Jews as well as i Jews
	11:25	hardness on the part of i Israel
Col	3:11	i and outsider
Heb	13:14	This "i world" is not our home

Insiders

Ps	122:7	Friendly i, get along!
Isa	33:23	weak and strong, i and outsiders
	56:7	welcome to worship the same as the 'i
Mt	9:13	invite outsiders, not coddle i
Lk	5:32	inviting outsiders, not i
Ro	3:9	all of us, whether i or outsiders
	11:14	Israelite kin, the so-called i
	15:8	special way to the Jewish i
	15:10	Outsiders and i, rejoice together
Eph	2:14	non-Jewish outsiders and Jewish i
	2:17	you outsiders and peace to us i
	3:6	I've been calling outsiders and i
Col	2:11	No, you're already in — i
Heb	13:10	exploitation by i who grab and loot
	13:13	not trying to be privileged i

Insight

Job	28:12	find Wisdom? Where does I hide
	28:20	where does I live
	28:28	Wisdom, and I means shunning evil
	32:8	One, that makes wise human i possible
Ps	119:34	Give me i so I can do what you tell me
	119:169	provide me with the i that comes only
Pr	2:3	make I your priority
	2:11	I will keep an eye out for you
	3:13	make friends with Madame I
	3:19	with Madame I, he raised Heaven
	7:4	Treat I as your companion
	8:1	Can you hear Madame I
	8:14	I am both I and the Virtue to live it
	9:10	i into life from knowing a Holy God
	10:13	wisdom on the lips of a person of i
	16:16	choose i over income every time
	16:21	A wise person gets known for i
	23:23	buy wisdom, buy education, buy i
	28:16	Among leaders who lack i, abuse
Mt	13:11	been given i into God's kingdom
	13:13	nudge the people toward receptive i
Mk	4:11	been given i into God's kingdom
Lk	8:10	been given i into God's kingdom
Ac	21:4	from i given by the Spirit
Co	12:3	without the i of the Holy Spirit
	14:6	don't address you plainly with some i
	14:13	Pray for the i and ability
	14:26	lead a prayer, provide an i

Insightful

Mk	12:34	Jesus realized how i he was
Co	8:7	you're articulate, you're i

Insights

Job	15:9	What i do you have that we've missed
	26:3	What amazing i you've provided
Pr	18:15	always listening for fresh i
Isa	28:6	i of justice to those who guide
	13:12	i and understandings flow freely

Insignificant

1Sa	9:21	the most i clan in the tribe
Isa	42:3	won't disregard the small and i
Gal	5:9	don't toss this off as i
Php	3:8	had going for me is i — dog dung

Insist

Ge	19:21	If you i. I'll let you have your way
	23:15	If you i, master
Lev	22:32	I i on being treated with holy
Dt	20:12	don't settle for peace and i on war
Jos	7:7	Why did you i on bringing this people
2Sa	19:22	Why do you i on being so contentious
1Ki	22:17	All right," said Micaiah, "since you i
2Ch	18:16	All right," said Micaiah, "since you i
Job	15:25	i on shaking their fists at God
	17:8	wake up and i I've given up on God
	19:5	Why do you i on putting me down
Isa	65:2	who i on doing things their own way
Mt	10:11	don't i on staying in a luxury inn
Jn	4:20	i that Jerusalem is the only place
Ac	24:25	i on right relations with God
	26:14	you i on going against the grain
Ro	2:8	those who i on getting their own way
	12:19	Don't i on getting even
	14:7	None of us are permitted to i
Eph	4:17	so I i — and God backs me up

Insistent

2Sa	13:27	But Absalom was so i
Ps	106:14	provoked God with their i demands

Insisting

Ac	12:15	She stuck by her story, i
	15:1	i that everyone be circumcised
Ro	4:6	without i on having a say in it
	10:3	i instead on making their own deals
2Co	3:1	i on our credentials
Col	2:18	i that you join their obsession
Jude	1:3	I have to write i — begging!

Insolence

Est	1:12	Seething with anger over her i
	1:18	get wind of the queen's i
Job	17:2	have to put up with their i
Isa	33:19	Their i nothing now but a fading stain
Jer	50:29	brazen i is an outrage against God
Eze	36:5	orgy of violence and shameless i

Insolent

Nu	16:30	these men have been i with God
Job	12:6	i blasphemers live in luxury
Ps	36:1	he stands i before him
	37:38	i souls are on a dead-end street
	119:51	The i ridicule me without mercy
Pr	19:25	Punish the i

Eze	22:7	community that's i to parents,
2Pe	2:10	indulge in self-rule. I egotists

Insolently

Jer	44:20	people who had answered so i
Eze	35:13	i pitting yourselves against me
Lk	12:47	i does whatever he pleases

Inspection

Ge	44:11	opening them up for i
Ne	2:15	continuing my i of the wall
	3:31	up to the I Gate
1Co	3:13	Eventually there is going to be an i
	3:14	If your work passes i, fine

Inspiration

Mt	22:43	David, under i, named Christ
1Co	15:19	get out of Christ is a little i

Inspired

Job	26:4	How did you become so i
Hos	9:6	What use will all your god-i silver be
Mk	12:36	David, i by the Holy Spirit, said, God
Jn	10:34	I'm only quoting your i Scriptures
1Co	13:8	I speech will be over some day
	14:37	God . . . has i you to do something

Instinct

Ro	2:14	follow it more or less by i
Jude	1:10	living by animal i only

Instruct

Ex	24:12	commandments that I've written to i
1Sa	10:25	Samuel went on to i the people
2Ki	17:27	i the people in what the god of
Job	8:10	i you in what they knew
Ps	94:12	the woman you i in your Word
	105:22	i his princes and train his advisors
	119:138	i us in how to live ever faithful
Isa	30:8	be there to i the coming generations
La	2:9	no one left to i or lead
Mt	13:30	I'll i the harvesters to pull up
	28:20	i them in the practice of all I have
Col	3:16	I and direct one another
Heb	13:7	let their faithfulness i you

Instructed

Ge	32:4	He i them: "Tell my master Esau this
	32:17	Then he i the first one out
	49:29	Then he i them
	50:2	Joseph then i the physicians
Ex	8:27	sacrifice to our God, just as he i us
	16:9	Moses i Aaron: "Tell the whole
Lev	9:7	Moses i Aaron, "Approach the Altar
	10:8	God i Aaron

Nu	3:16	as he was i by the mouth of God
	7:11	because God had i Moses
	8:3	as God had i Moses
	16:40	as God had i him by Moses
	23:3	Balaam i Balak: "Stand watch
	29:40	Moses i the People of Israel
	31:47	just as God had i him
Dt	2:1	as God had i me
Jos	3:6	Josua i the priests
	4:8	just as God had i Josua
	4:10	everything God had i Josua to tell
	7:2	He i them, "Go up and spy out
	8:33	as Moses the servant of God had i
	20:2	as I i you through Moses
1Sa	11:9	Saul i the messengers
2Sa	11:19	He i the messenger
	13:28	he i his servants, "Look sharp
	14:2	wise woman who lived there and i her
1Ki	17:9	I've i a woman who lives thereto
2Ki	12:4	Joash i the priests: "Take the money
1Ch	15:15	exactly as Moses, i by God, commanded
2Ch	35:10	at their posts as i by the king
Ne	4:22	I also i the people
Jer	17:23	refusing to be guided or i by me
	38:27	responded as the king had i
Mt	2:9	I by the king, they set off
	20:8	owner of the vineyard i his foreman
Mk	11:6	exactly as Jesus had i them
Lk	5:14	Jesus i him, "Don't talk about this
	19:13	gave them each a sum of money, and i
Ac	22:3	i in our religious traditions
Ro	15:14	well-motivated and well-i
Eph	4:21	well i in the truth

Instructing

Ge	49:33	Jacob finished i his sons
2Ki	22:8	i us in God's ways
2Ch	34:15	i us in God's way
Mt	22:4	servants, i them to tell the guests
Ac	4:2	upstart apostles were i the people

Instruction

Nu	33:2	Under God's i Moses kept a log
Ne	9:14	you decreed commands, rules, and i
Ps	119:104	With your i, I understand life
Pr	23:12	Give yourselves to disciplined i
1Ti	6:3	our Master Jesus and this godly i

Instructions

Ge	32:19	gave the same i to the second servant
	50:12	continued to carry out his i
Ex	5:10	to the people with their new i
	13:10	Follow these i at the set time
	16:10	gave out the i to the whole company
	16:16	these are God's i
	16:28	commands and not follow my i
	18:16	teach them God's laws and i
	18:20	teach them the rules and i
Lev	6:9	i for the Whole-Burnt-Offering

	6:14	i for the Grain-Offering
	6:25	i for the Absolution-Offering
	7:1	i for the Compensation-Offering
	7:11	i for the Peace-Offering
	7:37	i for the Whole-Burnt-Offering
	11:46	i on animals, birds, fish
	12:7	i for a woman who gives birth
	13:59	i regarding a spot of serious fungus
	14:2	i for the infected person
	14:32	i to be followed for anyone
	22:9	priests must observe my i
	26:46	laws, and i that God established
Nu	6:13	i for the time set when your special
	6:21	i for Nazirites as they bring
	8:24	i regarding the Levites of
	31:41	following God's i to Moses
Dt	17:11	Follow their i precisely
Jos	4:12	obedient to Moses' i
	8:27	God's i to Josua allowed for that
	8:31	built it following the i of Moses
	11:9	treated them following God's i
Jdg	21:11	These are your i
1Sa	15:24	over God's Word and your i
	25.5	of his young men off with these i
	28:21	carried out your i to the letter
1Ki	6:12	following my i carefully
	21:11	followed Jezebel's i
2Ki	6:33	While he was giving his i
	9:26	God's i carried out to the letter
	11:5	commanded them, "These are your i
	17:15	They were contemptuous of his i
	21:8	everything I've commanded in the i
	22:3	to The Temple of God with i
	22:13	followed none of the i directed to us
	23:3	to follow his i, heart and soul
	23:25	i revealed to and written by Moses
1Ch	6:32	followed the i given to them
	6:49	made atonement . . . following the i
	15:13	make proper preparation and follow i
2Ch	29:25	following the original i of David
	33:8	everything I've commanded in the i
	34:21	followed none of the i directed to us
	34:31	follow his i, heart and soul
	35:2	gave the priests detailed i
	35:4	following the i left by David king
	35:12	offer it to God following the i
	35:13	Passover lamb according to the i
	35:15	in their places following the i
Ne	9:13	You gave them i on how to live well
Est	4:8	i to go to the king and intercede
	4:17	and carried out Esther's i
Ps	45:4	Your i are glow-in-the-dark
	105:45	could follow his i to the letter
	119:54	I set your i to music and sing them
	119:83	keep a steady gaze on the i you post
	119:125	the inner meaning of your i
	119:146	so I can carry out all your i
	119:167	My soul guards and keeps all your i
Pr	7:1	treasure my careful i
Isa	37:9	with i to deliver this message
Jer	35:18	followed through on his i
	44:10	following my i that I've set out

Eze	44:5	way all the laws work, i regarding it
Da	9:11	defied your i and did what we pleased
Mt	19:7	why did Moses give i for divorce
	21:2	these i: "Go over to the village
	26:19	followed Jesus' i to the letter
Mk	6:8	He sent them off with these i
	11:1	sent off two of the disciples with i
Lk	19:29	he sent off two of the disciples with i
Jn	14:31	I am carrying out my Father's i
Ac	16:35	with the i, "Release these men
1Co	4:17	i I regularly give all the churches
	11:23	received my i from the Master
	16:1	the same i I gave the churches
Gal	3:18	addendum, with its i and regulations
	4:3	slaves ordered around by simple i
1Ti	5:21	angels all back me up in these i
Tit	1:5	in every town according to my i
Heb	6:2	baptismal i; laying on of hands

Instrument

1Ch	15:28	brass and percussion and string i
Ac	7:25	even see him as an i of God

Instruments

1Ch	13:8	a marching band of all kinds of i
	16:5	Jeiel, who played the musical i
	16:42	other i for accompanying sacred songs
	23:5	praising God with i
2Ch	20:28	all the i of the band playing
	29:25	Temple of God with their musical i
Ne	12:35	playing the musical i of David
Ps	147:7	play music on your i to God
Da	3:7	all the musical i of Babylon
Zec	10:4	Use them as tools and i
1Co	7:34	becoming whole and holy i of God
	14:7	If musical i . . . aren't played
1Pe	2:9	God's i to do his work

Insufferable

Isa	16:6	Arrogant, self-important, i
Jer	48:29	puffed-up pride, the i arrogance
Ro	1:30	Bullies, swaggerers, i windbags

Insult

Dt	17:1	an abomination, an i to God
	21:23	a hanged man is an i to God
1Sa	18:8	He took it as a personal i
2Sa	16:9	This mangy dog can't i my master
2Ki	17:4	adding i to injury, Hoshea was
	19:16	a brazen i to the living God
2Ch	28:18	Adding i to injury the Philistines
Job	20:3	How dare you i my intelligence
Pr	14:31	You i your Maker when you exploit
Jer	7:30	In deliberate i to me
Heb	10:29	i this most gracious Spirit

I

Insulted

2Sa	21:21	He i Israel, and Jonathan
2Ki	19:22	Who do you think it is you've i
Ezr	4:14	sit idly by while our king is being i
Ne	4:5	they've i the builders
Est	1:16	not only the king Queen Vashti has i
Eze	20:27	parents further i me by betraying
Hos	12:14	continually and inexcusably i God

Insulting

2Ch	32:17	letters i the God of Israel
Zec	11:12	They paid me an i sum
Lk	11:45	in saying these things you're i us

Insults

1Sa	25:14	he tore into them with i
	25:21	now he rewards me with i
	25:39	stood up for me against Nabal's i
2Sa	16:5	As he followed along he shouted i
Ps	35:15	riffraff . . . came chanting i about me
Pr	12:16	the prudent quietly shrug off i
	17:5	mocks poor people, i their Creator
Isa	50:6	Didn't dodge their i
	51:7	Pay no attention to i
	51:8	Those i and mockeries are moth-eaten
Jer	20:8	all I get for my God-warnings are i
Tit	3:2	No i, no fights

Insurance

Ps	37:3	Get i with God and do a good deed
	49:9	Life forever, or i against
Pr	11:6	Good character is the best i
Isa	28:15	We've taken out good life i
	28:18	life i policy wasn't worth

Integrity

Ge	6:9	a man of i in his community
Ex	18:21	men who fear God, men of i
Job	2:3	still has a firm grip on his i
	2:9	Still holding on to your precious i
	6:29	my i is on the line
	27:5	not deny my i even if it costs me
	27:6	I'm holding fast to my i
	31:6	God has proof of my i
Pr	2:21	the women with i who will last here
	11:3	i of the honest keeps them on track
	11:13	one of i won't violate a confidence
	11:20	how he relishes i
	14:32	i of good people creates a safe place
	20:28	leadership is founded on loving i
Mt	22:16	Teacher, we know you have i
Mk	12:14	Teacher, we know you have i
1Ti	4:12	by love, by faith, by i
2Ti	3:14	sure of the i of your teachers

Intellectual

Da	5:11	well known for his i brilliance
Col	2:8	big words and i double-talk

Intelligence

2Ch	20:2	Jehoshaphat received this i report
Job	20:3	How dare you insult my i like this
Pr	16:22	True i is a spring of fresh water
	24:5	i outranks muscle any day
	30:2	so-called human i escapes me
Isa	37:9	king received an i report
Jer	3:15	who rule you with i and wisdom
Eze	28:4	Your sharp i made you world-wealthy
Da	2:21	he provides both i and discernment
	6:3	Daniel, brimming with spirit and i
Mt	22:37	all your passion and prayer and i
Mk	12:30	all your passion and prayer and i
	12:33	all passion and i and energy
Lk	10:27	prayer and muscle and i
1Co	12:2	God wants us to use our i
	14:14	all that i is wasted
	14:20	well-exercised i can save you

Intelligent

1Sa	25:3	woman was i and good-looking
Pr	13:1	I children listen to their parents
	15:14	i person is always eager
	15:20	I children make their parents proud
Da	1:4	handsome, i and well-educated
Ac	13:7	an i man not easily taken in
1Co	1:20	truly wise, truly educated, truly i
Eph	1:17	i and discerning in knowing him
Php	1:10	so that your love is sincere and i

Intemperate

Pr	16:14	An i leader wreaks havoc in lives
	21:24	i hotheads, every one
	29:22	the i stir up trouble
Ecc	10:4	A calm disposition quiets i rage

Intercede

Ge	23:8	i for me with Ephron
1Ch	16:4	to i, give thanks, and praise the God
Est	4:8	to the king and i and plead with him
Joel	2:17	Let them i: "Have mercy, God

Interceding

1Sa	7:9	prayed fervently to God, i for Israel
Da	9:20	i for the holy mountain of my God

Intercession

Ne	1:6	praying . . . in i for your servants
2Co	9:14	praying for you in passionate i

Intercessory

1Ki	8:28	my prayers, both i and personal
2Ch	6:19	my prayers, both i and personal

Intercourse

Jdg	21:11	man and woman who has had sexual i
	21:12	never had sexual i with a man

Interfere

2Ki	15:35	didn't i with the traffic
2Ch	35:21	you'll only i with God
Pr	24:15	Don't i with good people's lives
Jn	13:18	not to i with the fulfillment
Ro	14:21	i with the free exchange of love

Interfering

2Sa	16:10	Why are you . . . always i
Isa	31:2	stands up against i evildoers
Ro	14:4	i with God's welcome
2Co	10:15	i with their ministries

Intermarry

Ge	34:9	I with us. Give your daughters to us
Jos	23:12	i, say, and have other dealings

Interpretation

Ge	40:16	saw how well Joseph's i turned out
	40:18	Joseph said, "This is the i
Jdg	7:15	the telling of the dream and its i
2Ch	19:10	like matters of i of the law
Da	2:5	both the dream itself and its i
	2:6	both the dream and its i
	2:7	tell us the dream. We'll give the i
	2:9	you're on the up and up with the i
	2:30	But the i is given through me
	2:45	the i is also accurate
	4:19	Don't let the dream and its i scare
1Co	12:10	spirits tongues i of tongues

Intimacies

Pr	5:20	trade enduring i for cheap thrills
Mt	11:27	Father and Son i and knowledge
	22:30	ecstasies and i then will be with God
Mk	12:25	ecstasies and i then will be with God
Lk	20:36	ecstasies and i then will be with God
1Co	14:2	sharing i just between you and him
	14:5	develop i with God in prayer
	14:18	wonderful i we enjoy with him

Intimacy

1Co	6:17	sex that avoids commitment and i
	14:13	ability to bring others into that i
Heb	13:4	sacredness of sexual i

Intimate

Dt	4:7	gods that are i with them the way God
Ps	148:14	Israel's children, i friends of God
Jn	15:5	the relation i and organic
2Co	13:14	the i friendship of the Holy Spirit
Gal	4:7	privilege of i conversation with God
Eph	4:30	the most i part of your life
Heb	11:7	Noah became i with God
1Jn	2:6	Anyone who claims to be i with God
	4:15	an i relationship with God

Intimately

Nu	12:8	I speak to him i, in person
Mt	10:40	are i linked in this harvest work
Jn	15:10	you'll remain i at home in my love
2Pe	1:3	know, personally and i, the One

Intimidate

Ne	6:9	trying to i us into quitting
	6:19	Tobiah would send letters to i me
Eze	3:9	Don't let them i you
Ac	18:9	don't let anyone i or silence you

Intimidated

Dt	7:21	So don't be i by them
	31:6	Take courage. Don't be i
	31:8	he won't leave you. Don't be i
2Ch	14:11	aren't impressed by numbers or i
	32:7	Don't be i by the king of Assyria
Da	5:19	were totally i by him
Mt	10:26	Don't be i. Eventually everything
	10:31	don't be i by all this bully talk
	21:46	i by public opinion, they held back
Mk	12:12	i by public opinion, held back
Lk	12:7	don't be i by all this bully talk
	20:19	i by public opinion
Jn	9:22	i by the Jewish leaders
	19:38	because he was i by the Jews
Gal	4:10	i into scrupulously observing

Invalid

Isa	10:18	like a disease-ridden i
Jn	5:5	One man had been an i there

Invest

Ecc	7.4	Sages i themselves in hurt
	11:1	Be generous: I in acts of charity
Mt	25:27	would have been to i the sum
Lk	19:23	Why didn't you at least i the money

Invested

Isa	42:17	who i in the no-gods are bankrupt
Ro	11:2	has too much i

Investigate

Dt	13:14	Ask questions, i
	17:4	look at the evidence and i carefully
Ps	139:1	God, i my life
	139:23	I my life, O God
Jer	26:10	came to God's Temple to i
Ac	23:15	i the charges in more detail
	23:20	pretext that they want to i

Investigated

Est	2:22	the thing was i and confirmed as true
Lk	1:3	i all the reports in close detail
Ac	17:9	let them go while they i the charges
	28:18	the Romans i the charges

Investigation

Lev	19:20	there must be an i
Dt	19:18	The judges must conduct a careful i
Ezr	7:14	advisors to carry out an i of Judah
Ac	4:9	put under i regarding this healing

Investment

Job	15:32	before the due date. Some i
Mt	25:16	doubled his master's i
	25:20	how he had doubled his i
	25:22	also had doubled his master's i

Invincible

1Sa	14:48	He became i! He smashed Amalek
Job	41:15	His pride is i
SS	8:6	Love is i facing danger and death
Da	8:25	He'll think he's i
Joel	1:6	country's being invaded by an army i
	2:5	like an i army shouting for blood
Mic	4:13	remaking you into a people i
Na	3:8	proudly i on the River Nile

Invulnerable

Job	39:28	i on pinnacle and crag
	41:24	tough inside as out, rock-hard, i

Irresponsible

2Sa	19:19	Overlook my i outburst
Pr	13:17	I talk makes a real mess of things
Ro	13:2	you're i to the state, then you're i
1Ti	1:9	the i, who defy all authority
Heb	12:8	Only i parents leave children
2Pe	3:16	I people who don't know what they are

Irreverence

Lev	22:9	die by treating the offerings with i
	22:15	not treat with i the holy offerings

Irreverent

Dt	5:11	the i use of his name
Pr	19:29	The i have to learn reverence
Eze	44:7	dragging i and unrepentant outsiders
	44:9	No i and unrepentant aliens

Irreverently

1Sa	6:19	i peeked into the Chest of God
1Co	11:27	drinks the cup of the Master i

Irritable

Nu	21:4	became i and cross as they traveled
Pr	21:14	quietly given gift soothes an i person

Irritated

Ge	18:30	Master, don't be i with me
Ro	12:8	don't let yourself get i with them
1Co	9:8	not just sounding off because I'm i

J

Jealous

Ge	30:1	she became j of her sister
	37:11	Now his brothers were really j
Ex	20:5	I'm a most j God
	34:14	his name is The-J-One — is a j God
Nu	11:29	Moses said, "Are you j for me
Dt	4:24	he's a consuming fire, a j God
	5:9	I'm a most j God
	6:15	God, who is alive among you is a j God
	32:16	j with their foreign newfangled gods
Jos	24:19	He is a holy God. He is a j God
Job	5:2	the j anger of a simpleton does her in
Ps	106:16	One day in camp some grew j of Moses
Eze	5:13	I'm a j God and not to be trifled with
Jn	3:29	How could he be j when he knows
Ro	10:19	you'll become insanely j
Jas	4:5	he's a fiercely j lover

Jealousy

Nu	5:14	feelings of j come over the husband
	5:15	a Grain-Offering for j
	5:18	the Grain-Offering for j
	5:25	a handful of the Grain-Offering for j
	5:29	This is the law of j
	5:30	tormented with feelings of j
Dt	29:20	God's anger and j will erupt
Pr	6:34	j detonates rage in a cheated husband
	27:4	but who can survive j
Isa	11:13	The j of Ephraim will dissolve
Eze	16:42	My j will subside
	38:19	Fueled by blazing j
Ac	7:9	burning up with j, sent Joseph off
	13:45	went wild with j and tore into Paul
	17:5	Mad with j, they rounded up a bunch
2Co	12:20	quarrels, j, flaring tempers

Jeering

Ps	79:12	j neighbors what they've got coming
Isa	37:23	Who do you think you've been j
Lk	23:11	soldiers joined in, taunting and j

Jeers

Ps	31:18	who heckle me . . . with j and catcalls
Isa	20:4	exposed to mockery and j

Jobs

1Sa	22:7	give you all influential j
2Ch	24:13	workers kept at their j steadily
	25:10	very angry at losing their j
Ne	13:11	put them back on their j
Job	12:19	fires high officials from their j
Ps	104:23	go out to work, busy at their j
Lk	16:12	If you're not honest in small j
1Co	3:8	menial servant j at minimum wages
	4:12	we pick up odd j anywhere we can

Jockeying

Jn	5:44	spend all your time j for position

Joke

Ge	19:14	would-be husbands treated it as a j
1Ki	9:7	Israel will become nothing but a bad j
2Ch	7:20	Israel will be nothing but a bad j
	30:10	treated them as a j
Job	41:29	treats a brandished harpoon as a j
Ps	37:13	they're a j with no punch line
	44:14	a j among the godless, a cheap j
	79:4	nothing but a j to our neighbors
	89:41	a j to all the neighbors
	109:25	j in poor taste to those who see me
Pr	1:25	make a j of my advice
	1:26	j about your troubles
Jer	20:7	now I'm a public j
	26:6	make this city nothing but a bad j
	48:26	Moab a falling-down drunk, a j
	48:39	Moab a cruel j!
La	3:14	Everyone took me for a j
Eze	22:4	the world's worst j
Mic	6:16	will be laughed at, a tasteless j
Hab	1:4	Justice is a j
Jude	1:18	They'll treat them like a j

Joked

Ob	1:12	shouldn't have laughed and j at Judah
Mt	27:49	others j, "Don't be in such a hurry
Ac	2:13	Others j, "They're drunk on cheap wine

Jokes

Job	30:1	Now I'm the butt of their j
Ps	59:8	you treat the godless nations like j
	89:50	the butt of the j of all nations

	89:51	The taunting j of your enemies
Isa	44:25	turns fortunetellers into j
Jer	10:15	deadwood gods, tasteless j
	48:27	Moab, who made crude j over Israel
	51:17	deadwood gods, tasteless j
Eze	5:14	Nations who walk by will make coarse j
	7:21	the godless spit on it and make j
	36:3	the butt of cheap gossip and j
	36:4	turned into j by all
Ac	17:32	laughed at him and walked off making j

Jonah-evidence

Mt	12:39	looks like the absence of proof: J

Jonah-proof

Lk	11:29	proof you're going to get is the J

Jostling

Isa	22:5	J and stampeding in the Valley
Eze	23:42	The crowd gathered, j and pushing
Mk	5:24	tagging along, pushing and j him
	5:31	With this crowd pushing and j you
Lk	8:42	through the pushing, j crowd

Journey

Ge	28:20	stands by me and protects me on this j
	30:36	put a three-day j between himself
	45:23	provisions for his father's j back
	45:24	Take it easy on the j
	46:1	set out on the j with everything
Ex	3:18	a three-day j into the wilderness
	4:24	On the j back, as they camped
	5:3	a three-day j into the wilderness
	8:27	three days' j into the wilderness
	12:39	hadn't time to fix food for the j
	18:8	trouble they had experienced on the j
	33:3	lest I destroy you on the j
	33:14	I'll see the j to the end
Nu	33:1	These are the camping sites in the j
Dt	10:11	Lead your people as they resume the j
Jos	5:4	died in the wilderness on the j out
	8:35	who had been with them on the j
	19:27	opened the door to continue his j
1Ki	19:4	into the desert another day's j
	19:7	you've got a long j ahead of you
Ezr	8:21	pray for wise guidance for our j
Jer	40:5	gave him food for the j
Zec	5:6	This is a bushel basket on a j
Lk	0:51	steeled himself for the J to Jerusalem
Ac	15:4	reported on their recent j
	18:22	on to Antioch, completing the j
	20:4	His companions for the j were
	22:21	I'm sending you on a long j
	28:10	outfitted us for the rest of the j
Gal	4:13	prevented from continuing my j
Heb	4:10	end of the j we'll . . . rest with God
1Pe	1:17	Your life is a j you must travel

J

Joy

Dt	28:47	didn't serve God . . . out of the j
2Ki	11:14	everybody beside themselves with j
1Ch	12:40	j in Israel
	16:27	strength and j fill his place
	29:17	giving freely, willingly—what a j
	29:22	drinking before God, exuberant with j
2Ch	23:13	everybody beside themselves with j
	29:30	sang their praises with j
	30:26	Jerusalem was bursting with j
Ezr	3:12	many were noisily shouting with j
	6:22	With great j they celebrated
Ne	8:10	The j of God is your strength
	8:17	a terrific day! Great j
	12:43	God had filled them with great j
Est	8:15	city of Susa exploded with j
	9:22	their sorrow turned to j
Job	8:21	raise the roof with shouts of j
	20:5	godless j is only momentary
Ps	4:7	More j in one ordinary day
	9:2	laughing, and jumping for j
	19:8	showing the way to j
	28:7	Now I'm jumping for j
	33:21	our hearts brim with j
	45:15	A procession of j and laughter
	46:4	River fountains splash j
	48:2	in its heights—earth's j
	60:6	Bursting with j, I make a present
	63:11	his true friends spread the j
	68:3	they'll laugh and sing for j
	78:61	let his pride and j go to the dogs
	84:2	could sing for j to God-alive
	92:4	saw your work and I shouted for j
	97:11	J-seeds are planted in good heart-soil
	105:43	led his people out singing for j
	106:5	Hallelujahs of your pride and j
	108:7	Brimming over with j, I make a present
	113:9	j as the parents of children
	122:1	my heart leaped for j
Pr	4:3	the pride and j of my mother
	12:20	peace-planning brings j to the planner
	15:30	twinkle in the eye means j
Ecc	2:26	give wisdom and knowledge and j
	5:20	God deals out j in the present
SS	3:11	his heart full, bursting with j
	6:9	cradled in j by her mother
Isa	9:3	you expanded its j
	11:3	Fear-of-God will be all his j
	13:19	the pride and j of Chaldeans
	24:11	no more j for this old world
	35:10	unfading halos of j encircling
	51:11	J eternal wreathing their heads
	55:12	you'll go out in j
	56:7	give them j in my house of prayer
	58:13	treat the Sabbath as a day of j
	60:15	towering and grand forever, a j
	61:3	Messages of j instead of news of doom
	61:7	your j go on forever
	61:10	I will sing for j in God
	65:18	Look ahead with j
	65:19	I'll take j in Jerusalem

	66:14	You'll see all this and burst with j
Jer	25:10	I'll banish every sound of j
	31:7	God says so: "Shout for j
	31:9	They'll come weeping for j
	31:12	climb up Zion's slopes shouting with j
	31:13	invading their grief with j
	33:9	Jerusalem will be a center of j
La	2:4	our young men, our pride and j
	5:15	All the j is gone from our hearts
Eze	24:25	the people's refuge, their great j
Joel	1:12	j is dried up and withered
	1:16	j and singing from God's Sanctuary
Zec	10:7	their lives brimming with j
Mt	28:8	deep in wonder and full of j
Mk	5:42	all beside themselves with j
Lk	1:14	going to leap like a gazelle for j
	1:44	skipped like a lamb for sheer j
	6:21	J comes with the morning
	15:7	there's more j in heaven
	18:16	children are the kingdom's pride and j
	24:52	returned to Jerusalem bursting with j
Jn	8:29	sees how much j I take in pleasing him
	15:11	my j might be your j, and your j
	16:21	there is j in the birth
	16:22	the coming j is also similar
	16:24	Your j will be a river overflowing
	17:13	experience My j completed in them
Ac	2:28	your face shining sun-j all around
	8:8	what j in the city
	13:52	brimming with j and the Holy Spirit
Ro	14:17	completes it with j
	15:13	God of green hope fill you up with j
1Co	7:30	grief, j, whatever.
2Co	6:10	yet always filled with deep j
	7:4	overwhelmed with j
	7:13	our j doubled
Php	1:25	growth and j in this life of trusting
	4:1	You make me feel such j
Col	1:11	spills over into j
1Th	1:6	take great j from the Holy Spirit
	2:20	You're our pride and j
	3:9	all the j we experience before him
2Ti	1:4	look forward to a j-packed reunion
Heb	13:17	the j of their leadership
1Jn	1:4	Your j will double our j

Joyful

1Ch	15:16	fill the air with j sound
2Ch	15:14	a j sound accompanied with blasts
	20:27	God had given them j relief
Ps	86:11	I'll worship in j fear
Pr	8:30	I was there, with my j applause
Isa	16:9	The j shouting at harvest is gone
	52:8	shouting in j unison
Hab	3:18	I'm singing j praise to God
Mk	6:12	preached with j urgency
Lk	2:10	here to announce a great and j event
Ac	2:46	meal a celebration, exuberant and j
Ro	8:21	the j anticipation deepens
	8:25	the more j our expectancy
Php	2:29	Give him a grand welcome, a j embrace

Joyfully

2Ch	15:15	given their promise j from the heart
	30:23	as j as they began
Job	22:26	look to him j, boldly
Isa	12:3	J you'll pull up buckets of water
2Co	1:24	working alongside you, j expectant
Gal	1:16	j tell non-Jews about him

Joyless

Gal	5:19	frenzied and j grabs for happiness

Joyous

2Ch	30:25	all in on the j celebration

Joyously

Isa	35:1	Wilderness and desert will sing j

Jubilant

1Sa	6:13	saw the Chest. J, they ran to meet it
1Ch	16:10	holy Name, God-seekers, be j
	16:31	let heaven rejoice, let earth be j
Jn	8:56	Abraham — your 'father' — with j faith

Jubilee

Lev	25:10	a J for you
	25:11	fiftieth year is your J year
	25:12	it's the J and a holy year for you
	25:13	year of J everyone returns home
	25:15	number of years since the J
	25:28	J. In the J it will be returned
	25:30	It is not returned in the J
	25:31	have to be returned at the J
	25:33	reverts to them in the J
	25:40	He will work for you until the J
	25:50	he sold himself to the year of J
	25:51	If many years remain before the J
	25:52	if only a few years remain until the J
	25:54	he goes free in the year of J
	27:17	the year of J, the set value stays
	27:18	if he dedicates it after the J
	27:21	When the field is released in the J
	27:23	in relation to the next year of J
	27:24	In the year of J it goes back
Nu	36:4	when the Year of J comes
Eze	46:17	the year of liberation (the J year)

Judge

Ge	18:25	J of all the Earth j with justice
Ex	5:21	God see what you've done and j you
	18:13	Moses took his place to j the people
	18:16	I j between a man and his neighbor
Lev	19:15	J on the basis of what is right
Nu	35:24	j between the killer and the avenger
Dt	17:9	priests and the j who is in office
	17:12	handed down by the priest or j

	25:2	the j will have him prostrate
	32:36	God will j his people
Jdg	2:19	j died, the people went right back
	4:4	She was j over Israel at that time
	11:27	Today God the J will decide
1Sa	3:17	as God is your j!
	24:15	God is our j
2Sa	15:4	Why doesn't someone make me a j
1Ki	3:28	wisdom that enabled him to j truly
	8:32	J your servants, making the offender
1Ch	5:12	Janai, the j in Bashan
2Ch	6:23	j your servants, making the offender
Job	9:15	can only throw myself on the J's mercy
	22:13	how can he j
	23:7	my J would acquit me for good
Ps	50:6	here God is j
	55:19	from his j's bench puts them
	67:4	You j them fair and square
	72:2	May he j your people rightly
	94:2	J of the earth, take your stand
	109:6	accuse my accusing j; dispatch Satan
	109:31	rescue a life from the unjust j
Pr	23:31	Don't j wine by its label
	23:32	J it rather by the hangover
Ecc	3:17	God will j righteous and wicked
	12:14	j it according to its hidden intent
Isa	3:13	place at the bench to j his people
	11:3	He won't j by appearances
	11:4	He'll j the needy by what is right
Jer	11:20	God . . . you're a fair j
Eze	7:27	j them on their terms
	18:30	I'll j each of you according
	21:30	I'll j you in your home country
	22:2	Son of man, are you going to j
Joel	3:2	j them one and all
	3:12	place at the bench and j all
Mal	2:17	Judgment? God's too nice to j
Mt	12:25	j who gives opposite verdicts
	27:24	You're j and jury
Lk	12:14	business to be a j or mediator for you
	12:58	if the case went to the j
	18:2	a j in some city who never gave God
	18:6	hear what that j, corrupt as he is
Jn	5:22	authority to j over to the Son
	18:31	You take him. J him by your law
Ac	10:42	destined as J of the living and dead
	23:3	sit there and j me by the Law
1Co	6:3	we're even going to j angels
2Co	4:2	j for themselves in the presence
2Ti	4:1	Christ himself is the J
	4:8	he's an honest j. He'll do right
Heb	10:30	God will j his people
	12:23	the city where God is J
Jas	5:9	J is standing just around the corner
Rev	11:18	time has come to j the dead

Judged

Jdg	10:2	He j Israel for twenty-three years
	10:3	He j Israel for twenty-two years
	12:7	Jephthah j Israel six years
	12:8	Ibzan of Bethlehem j Israel

	12:10	He j Israel seven years
	12:11	j Israel. He j Israel ten years
	12:13	Abdon . . . j Israel
	12:14	He j Israel eight years
	15:20	Samson j Israel for twenty years
	16:31	He j Israel for twenty years
2Ki	23:22	the days that the judges j Israel
2Ch	25:5	300,000 j capable of military service
Ps	109:7	When he's j, let the verdict be
Ac	17:31	when the entire human race will be j
1Co	2:15	can't be j by unspiritual critics
Jas	2:12	expecting to be j by the Rule
Rev	18:20	God has j her; every wrong
	19:2	He j the great Whore who corrupted
	20:12	dead were j by what was written
	20:13	was j by the way he or she had lived

Judges

Ex	18:22	in the routine cases they'll be the j
	18:26	in the routine cases they were the j
	22:9	before the j. The one the j pronounce
Nu	25:5	Moses issued orders to the j of Israel
Dt	1:16	I gave orders to your j
	16:18	Appoint j and officers
	19:17	priests and j who are in office
	19:18	j must conduct a careful investigation
	21:2	your leaders and j are to go out
	21:3	The leaders and j of the city
	25:1	the j will decide between them
Jos	8:33	with their elders, officers, and j
	23:2	elders, chiefs, j, and officers
	24:1	called in the elders, chiefs, j
Jdg	2:16	God raised up j who saved them
	2:17	wouldn't listen to their j
	2:18	When God was setting up j for them
Ru	1:1	back in the days when j led Israel
1Sa	8:1	set his sons up as j in Israel
	16:7	God j persons differently
2Sa	7:11	I set j over my people Israel
2Ki	23:22	days that the j judged Israel
1Ch	17:10	I set j over my people Israel
	23:4	6,000 are officials and j
	26:29	j responsible for affairs outside
2Ch	1:2	captains, the j, every leader
	19:5	diligent in appointing j in the land
	19:6	He charged the j: "This is serious
Ezr	4:9	the j and officials over the people
	7:25	j so they can administer justice
	10:14	accompanied by the elders and j
Job	9:24	j who can't tell right from wrong
	12:17	exposes j as witless fools
Ps	2:10	Upstart-j, learn your lesson
	82:1	God calls the j into his courtroom
	82:5	Ignorant j! Head-in-the-sand j!
	82:6	commissioned you j, each one of you
Isa	1:26	set honest j and wise counselors
	3:2	withdrawing police and protection, j
Mic	3:11	J sell verdicts to the highest bidder
Zep	3:3	Her j are rapacious timber wolves
Lk	12:11	into police courts and before j
Ac	13:20	God provided j to lead them

	16:22	The j went along with the mob
	16:35	court j sent officers
	16:36	The j sent word that you're free to go
	16:38	officers reported this, the j panicked
Jas	2:4	you are j who can't be trusted
Rev	18:8	God, the Strong God who j her
	19:11	The Rider, named Faithful and True, j

Judging

Ex	18:22	everyday work of j among the people
	18:26	everyday work of j among the people
2Ch	19:6	not merely j between men and women
Eze	34:17	I'm stepping in and j between one
Mt	27:19	Don't get mixed up in j this noble man
Ac	24:10	fair-minded you've been in j us
Ro	12:19	"I'll do the j," says God

Judgment

Ex	6:6	intervening with great acts of j
	7:4	from Egypt by mighty acts of j
	12:12	bring j on all the gods of Egypt
	21:31	daughter is gored, the same j holds
	28:15	Now make a Breastpiece of J
	28:29	the Breastpiece of J over his heart
	28:30	in the Breastpiece of J
Lev	13:5	if, in his j, the sore is the same
Dt	1:17	This is God's j you're dealing with
	32:41	execute j, I take vengeance
1Sa	3:13	I'm bringing j on his family
	6:9	this catastrophe is a divine j
	28:18	refused to carry out his seething j
1Ki	3:28	Israel heard of the king's j
2Ki	10:10	God spoke in j on the family of Ahab
	21:2	In God's j he was a bad king
	21:6	in God's j, a career in evil
	21:12	this is my j, God's verdict
	22:16	bring the doom of j on this place
	22:19	the doom of J I spoke
	23:27	God, not swerving in his j
	24:3	it was God's j as he turned his back
	24:20	turned his back on them as an act of j
1Ch	12:17	see through you and bring j on you
2Ch	22:7	was God's j on him
	24:19	warning of j
	24:24	implemented God's j against Joash
	34:24	the doom of j on this place
	34:27	the doom of j I spoke
Job	19:29	God's coming j, for j is most
	24:1	J Day isn't hidden from the Almighty
	34:25	j is signed, sealed, and delivered
Ps	7:7	packed the courtroom; it's j time
	76:8	From heaven you thunder j
	110:6	Bringing j on the nations
	122:5	Thrones for righteous j are set there
	149:9	j on them carried out to the letter
Pr	16:4	wicked are included — but for j
	29:4	A leader of good j gives stability
Ecc	3:16	The very place of j — corrupt
Isa	4:4	purge the place with a firestorm of j
	7:17	a j worse than anything since

	10:3	What will you have to say on J Day
	13:3	passion to carry out my angry j
	13:6	God's Day of J is near
	13:9	Watch now. God's J Day comes
	13:13	the J Day of his raging anger
	42:9	predictions of j have been fulfilled
	59:17	Put on J like an overcoat
	66:6	God's voice, handing out j
	66:16	it's by fire that God brings j
	66:19	I'll send the survivors of j all over
Jer	1:16	pronounce my j on the people of Judah
	2:35	Don't look now, but j's on the way
	4:12	pronouncing my hurricane j
	6:9	Harvest the grapes for j
	10:15	When the fires of j come
	12:12	The j sword of God will take its toll
	15:14	burning in hot j against you
	16:16	pull them in for j
	25:33	those killed in God's j that day
	28:8	preached j against many countries
	48:21	My j will come to the plateau cities
	51:9	The j on her will be vast
	52:3	turned his back on them as an act of j
La	1:21	Bring on J Day!
Eze	6:10	my j against them was no empty threat
	7:10	J Day! Fate has caught up with you
	7:12	J wrath has turned the world
	7:19	either want or need on J Day
	11:10	I'll carry out j on you at the borders
	11:11	carry out j on you at the borders
	13:5	help Israel stand on God's Day of J
	14:22	this severe j I brought on Jerusalem
	16:41	A massive j—with all the women
	20:35	you'll be face to face with j
	20:36	I faced your parents with j
	23:10	name became Shame—history's j on her
	23:24	I'll turn over the task of j to them
	23:45	Righteous men will pronounce j on them
	28:26	I'll bring j on all the neighbors
	30:3	God's big day of j is near
	30:9	Egypt's doomed! J's coming
	35:11	when I bring j on you
	38:22	I'll deluge Gog with j
	39:21	they'll all see the j I execute
Da	8:12	As j against their sin
	8:13	this devastating j against sin
	8:19	as the j days of wrath wind down
	11:36	time of wrathful j is completed
Hos	6:5	wake you up to my j blazing
Joel	1:15	Doomsday! God's J Day has come
	2:1	God's J's on its way
	2:11	God's J Day—great and terrible
	2:31	Before the J Day of God
	3:2	I'll lead them down into J Valley
	3:12	pagan nations set out for J Valley
	3:14	God's J Day has arrived
Am	4:2	Be well warned: J Day is coming
	5:18	Woe to all of you who want God's J Day
	8:9	On J Day, watch out!
	8:10	That's a hint of J Day
	8:11	J Day is coming!
	8:13	On J Day, lovely young girls

	9:11	on that J Day I will restore
	9:12	everyone else under my sovereign j
Ob	1:15	God's J Day is near
Mic	1:9	J has marched through the city gates
	1:12	Harsh j has come from God
Hab	1:12	chose Babylonians for your j work
	3:2	as you bring j, as you surely must
Zep	1:7	Time's up. My J Day is near
	1:8	On the Holy Day, God's J Day
	1:10	J Day!" God's Decree!
	1:12	On J Day, I'll search
	1:14	The Great J Day of God is almost here
	1:15	J Day is payday—my anger paid out
	1:18	the Day of God's J—my wrath
	2:2	God's J-anger sweeps down on you
	3:20	On J Day I'll bring you back home
Zec	14:1	God's J Day is on the way
Mal	2:17	J? God's too nice to judge
	3:5	I'm on my way to visit you with J
	4:5	Big Day of God—the decisive J Day
Mt	7:22	at the Final J thousands strutting
	10:15	on J Day they'll be mighty sorry
	11:22	At J Day they'll get off easy
	11:24	At J Day they'll get off easy
	12:41	On J Day, the Ninevites will stand up
	12:42	On J Day, the Queen of Sheba
Lk	3:7	going to deflect God's j
	10:12	Sodom will have it better on J Day
	10:14	have it easy on J Day compared to you
	11:31	On J Day the Ninevites will stand
	11:32	On J Day the Queen of Sheba
Jn	5:27	decide and carry out matters of J
	5:29	into a resurrection J
	8:16	my j would be true
	16:8	view of sin, righteousness, and j
	16:11	j takes place as the ruler
	19:13	sat down at the j seat
Ac	24:25	moral discipline and the coming J
Ro	2:5	God's fiery and righteous j
	14:10	in the place of j, facing God
1Co	4:4	The Master makes that j
	5:5	before the Master on the Day of J
	6:4	the j of people you don't trust
	5:11	one day stand in that place of J
	11:19	sit there in the j seat observing
2Co	12:1	I do it against my better j
Gal	5:10	whoever he is, will bear the divine j
Heb	6:2	resurrection of the dead; eternal j
	10:27	face the J—and a mighty fierce j
Jas	2:13	Kind mercy wins over harsh j
	5:3	What you've piled up is j
	5:4	cry out for j
1Pe	3:19	who ended up in the prison of j
	4:17	It's j time for Christians
2Pe	2:4	jailed them in hell till J Day
	2:9	wicked to the fire until J Day
	3:7	signal for the j and destruction
	3:10	when the Day of God's J does come
1Jn	4:17	so that we're free of worry on J Day
	4:18	fear of death, fear of j
Jude	1:6	jailed . . . until the great J Day
	1:15	to bring j against them all

J

Rev	14:7	His hour of j has come!
	17:1	I'll show you the j of the great Whore
	17:2	show you the j on earth dwellers
	18:10	In one hour it's over, your j come
	20:4	Those put in charge of j sat

Judgmental

| Ro | 2:1 | J criticism of others is |

Judgments

Nu	35:29	These are the procedures for making j
1Ki	9:4	obedient to my guidance and j
	9:6	ignoring my guidance and j
1Ch	16:12	the miracles and j that came out
	16:14	wherever you go you come on his j
2Ch	7:17	obedient to my guidance and j
	7:19	ignoring my guidance and j
	19:6	these are God's j
Ps	119:151	all your j true
Eze	14:21	four catastrophic j on Jerusalem
	44:24	decide on the basis of my j, laws
Zep	3:15	God has reversed his j against you
Jn	8:15	I don't make j like that
	8:26	j to make that affect you
1Co	4:5	jump to conclusions with your j
	4:6	not rush into making j
Heb	12:23	God is Jdge, with j that make us just
Rev	15:4	they see your j are right
	16:5	your j are righteous, The Isa, The Was
	16:7	Your j are true and just
	19:2	his j true, his j just

Jump

Job	19:3	time after time you j all over me
	30:12	j on me while I'm down
Ps	29:6	high ridges j like wild kid goats
Pr	25:8	Don't j to conclusions
Hos	13:8	I'll j them like a sow grizzly robbed
Mic	3:5	pay up and j on their bandwagon
Zec	14:14	then Judah will j into the fray
Mt	4:6	Since you are God's Son, j
	7:1	pick on people, j on their failures
	21:21	Go j in the lake,' and it will j
Mk	11:23	Just say, 'Go j in the lake'
Lk	4:9	If you are God's Son, j
	6:37	pick on people, j on their failures
	17:6	Go j in the lake,' and it would do it
Ac	22:1	before you j to conclusions about me
	27:30	Some of the sailors tried to j ship
Ro	14:1	don't j all over them every time
1Co	4:5	don't . . . j to conclusions
	13:2	faith that says to a mountain, "J
1Th	4:15	will not get a j on the dead
1Pe	4:12	don't j to the conclusion

Jumped

| Ex | 4:3 | It became a snake; Moses j back |
| Jdg | 4:15 | Sisera j out of his chariot |

	7:21	whole Midianite camp j to its feet
	13:10	She j to her feet and ran
	18:20	The priest j at the chance
1Sa	1:13	j to the conclusion that she was drunk
2Sa	13:29	j on their mules, and rode off
1Ki	12:18	King Rehoboam j in his chariot
	18:26	they j and stomped on the altar
2Ki	5:21	j down from his chariot to greet him
2Ch	10:18	King Rehoboam j in his chariot
Ne	4:3	Tobiah the Ammonite j in and said
Jer	41:2	j to their feet and knocked Gedaliah
Da	3:24	Nebuchadnezzar j up in alarm
Lk	24:12	j to his feet and ran to the tomb
Jn	6:34	They j at that
	9:28	With that they j all over him
	11:29	she j up and ran out to him
Ac	3:8	He j to his feet and walked
	9:34	he did it — j right out of bed
	14:10	up in a flash — j up and walked around
	15:38	j ship on them in Pamphylia
	19:16	went berserk — j the exorcists
	28:4	natives j to the conclusion
	28:6	j to the conclusion that he was a god

Jumping

1Sa	5:6	J from ships there, rats swarmed
Ps	9:2	whistling, laughing, and j for joy
	28:7	Now I'm j for joy
Mt	14:29	J out of the boat, Peter walked
Lk	22:52	j me with swords and clubs as if
2Th	2:1	don't go j to conclusions

Jumps

Dt	19:11	waits in ambush, then j him
2Sa	17:9	If he j your men from ambush
1Co	13:2	says to a mountain, "Jump," and it j

Jungle

Jer	12:8	like a snarling lion in the j
	49:19	lion coming up from the thick j
	50:44	lion coming up from the thick j
Zec	11:3	The mighty j of the Jordan

Junk

Dt	29:17	silver and gold j-gods
2Ch	29:16	accumulation of defiling j
Job	24:18	useless, cursed j, good for nothing
Pr	18:8	really want j like that in your belly
	20:14	That's j — I'll take it off your hands
	26:22	want j like that in your belly
Isa	1:25	purge the j from your life
	5:2	for all his pains he got j grapes
	55:2	Why do you spend your money on j food
Jer	12:11	leave them littered with j
	16:18	piles of stinking god-j all over
La	2:1	treated his favorite as throwaway j
Eze	7:21	I'll give away their religious j
Hos	8:8	Among the pagans they're a piece of j

Mt	12:45	think you have cleaned out the j
2Ti	4:3	fill up on spiritual j food
Heb	12:27	the historical and religious j

Jurisdiction

Nu	25:5	execute the men under your j
Lk	23:7	he properly came under Herod's j
Ac	23:30	he's now under your j
	25:4	Caesarea was the proper j for Paul

Jury

Ge	31:37	Our two families can be the j
Job	13:9	Your lies might convince a j
Ps	50:4	He summons heaven and earth as a j
Isa	1:2	Heaven and earth, you're the J
Mic	2:5	speak for you before God and his j
	6:2	hear God's case; listen, J Earth
Mt	27:24	You're judge and j
1Co	6:2	stand before a j made up of Christians
2Co	12:19	making our defense before you, the J
	12:19	You're not the J; God is the j

Justice

Ge	18:25	Jdge of all the Earth judge with j
	49:16	Da will handle matters of j
Ex	23:6	don't tamper with the j due them
Lev	19:15	Don't pervert j
Dt	17:8	When matters of j come up
	27:19	curse on anyone who interferes with j
Jdg	4:5	went to her in matters of j
13a	8:3	taking bribes, corrupting j
1Ki	7:7	built a court room, the Hall of J
	8:59	guarantee j for his people Israel
Ezr	7:25	so they can administer j
Job	9:19	If it's a question of j, who'll serve
	27:2	God-Alive! He's denied me j!
	34:12	for the Mighty One to subvert j
	36:3	everything I know about j I owe
	37:23	Unsurpassable in power and j!
Ps	82:2	You've corrupted j long enough
	89:14	Right and J are the roots of your rule
	94:15	Rest assured that j is on its way
	97:2	Right and j anchor his rule
	99:4	Strong King, lover of j
	101:1	My theme song is God's love and j
	106:3	happy . . . when you form the habit of j
	111:7	He manufactures truth and j
	112:4	God's grace and mercy and j
	119:121	I stood up for j and the right
	119:149	in your j, God, keep me alive
	132:9	Get your priests all dressed up in j
	143:11	In your j, get me out of this trouble
Pr	8:20	at the intersection of J Avenue
	12:5	principled people makes for j
	17:23	show nothing but contempt for j
	19:28	An unprincipled witness desecrates j
	21:3	Clean living before God and j
	21:15	Good people celebrate when j triumphs
	28:5	J makes no sense to the evilminded

	29:26	only God will give us j
	31:9	Speak out for j
Ecc	5:8	j and right violated all over
Isa	1:17	Learn to do good. Work for j
	1:21	She was once all j
	5:7	looked for a crop of j and saw
	5:16	by working j, God-of-the-Angel-Armies
	11:4	decisions on earth's poor with j
	16:5	A Ruler passionate for j
	28:6	insights of j to those who guide
	28:17	I'll make j the measuring stick
	32:1	his leaders will carry out j
	32:16	J will move into the badlands
	40:14	school would he attend to learn j
	51:5	I'll bring j to the peoples
	53:8	J miscarried, and he was led off
	59:8	less than nothing about j
	59:11	We look for j — not a sign of it
	59:14	J is beaten back
	59:15	so much evil and no sign of J
Jer	21:12	Start each day by dealing with j
	22:3	Attend to matters of j
	23:5	He'll make sure of j
La	3:35	j to victims in the court of High God
Eze	22:29	no access to j
Hos	5:1	You're in charge of j around here
	12:6	Commit yourself in love, in j
Am	5:7	Woe to you who turn j to vinegar
	5:13	J is a lost cause. Evil is epidemic
	5:24	I want j — oceans of it
	6:12	you've made a shambles of j
Mic	3:1	Don't you know anything of j
	3:2	Isan't j in your job description?
	3:8	filled with God's Spirit of j
	3:9	Leaders contemptuous of j
	4:3	He'll establish j in the rabble
Hab	1:4	order fall to pieces. J is a joke
Zep	2:3	live by God's j. Seek God's right ways
	3:5	meting out j. At evening
Mt	12:18	he'll decree j to the nations
	12:20	his j will triumph
Lk	11:42	basic matters of j and God's love
	18:5	see that she gets j
	18:7	you think God won't step in and work j
Ac	24:27	playing up to the Jews and ignoring j
	25:10	before Caesar's bar of j
1Co	6:6	How can they render j if they don't
2Th	1:6	j is on the way
Heb	11:33	toppled kingdoms, made j work

Justify

Pr	21:2	We j our actions by appearances
Jn	2:18	What credentials can you present to j

Justly

Ge	31:16	from our father is j ours
Jer	23:5	ruler who knows how to rule j
Ob	1:21	And rule j and fairly
Zec	7:9	Treat one another j

J

K

Key

Jdg	3:25	they got a k and unlocked them
2Ki	3:19	level the k villages
1Ch	9:27	had the k to open the doors
Pr	24:6	Strategic planning is the k to warfare
Isa	22:22	give him the k of the Davidic heritage
Da	11:39	he will attack the k fortresses
	12:4	Put the book under lock and k
	12:9	confidential and under lock and k
Lk	11:52	You took the k of knowledge
Ac	22:15	be a k witness to everyone you meet
Ro	16:1	She's a k representative of the church
Rev	3:7	David's k in his hand, opening doors
	9:1	The Star was handed a k to the Well
	20:1	He carried the k to the Abyss

Kick

2Ch	20:11	k us out of the country you gave us
Job	13:25	Why k me around like an old tin can
Ps	5:10	K them out! They've had their chance
	36:11	Don't let the bullies k me around
	40:14	gets a k out of making me miserable
	57:3	humiliates those who k me around
	69:19	You know how they k me around
	91:13	k young lions and serpents
Pr	9:7	get a k in the shins
	12:10	bad people k and abuse them
	22:10	K out the troublemakers
Isa	13:18	wantonly k and kill even babies
	37:25	with one k of my foot
	45:2	k down barred entrances
	51:13	thinks he can k down the world
Jer	49:2	Israel will k out the invaders
Hos	9:15	I'll k them off my land
Am	4:3	And k you to kingdom come
Mic	4:11	K her when she's down!
Mt	8:31	If you k us out of these men
	10:1	power to k out the evil spirits
	10:8	K out the demons

Kicking

2Sa	16:13	stones down on them, and k up dirt
Da	8:13	the k around of God's holy people
Am	5:12	k the poor when they're down
Mt	12:27	calling me a devil k out devils

Kidnapped

Ge	40:15	I was k from the land of the Hebrews
2Ki	11:2	took Ahaziah's son Joash and k him
2Ch	22:11	took Ahaziah's son Joash, and k him
Job	24:9	infants of the poor are k and sold
Gal	4:4	us who have been k by the law

Kidnapper

Dt	24:7	the k must die

Kidnapping

Dt	24:7	man is caught k one of his kinsmen

Killer

Ex	21:13	place to which the k can flee
	21:14	then drag the k away
Nu	35:16	if the k has used an iron object
	35:24	judge between the k and the avenger
	35:25	save the k from the . . . avenger
Jos	21:21	asylum-city for the unconvicted k
	21:27	asylum-city for the unconvicted k
	21:32	asylum-city for the unconvicted k
	21:38	asylum-city for the unconvicted k
2Ki	9:31	you dashing king-k
	24:3	Manasseh, the k-king
Jer	15:3	corpses dropped off by k dogs
Eze	21:11	ready to be brandished by the k
Mt	23:37	K of the ones who brought you
Lk	13:34	k of prophets
Jn	8:44	He was a k from the very start
Jas	1:15	becomes a real k
	3:8	The tongue runs wild, a wanton k

Kindly

Ge	18:19	live k and generously and fairly
	26:29	we treated you k and let you leave
	50:5	If you have reason to think k of me
Ru	2:2	some harvester who will treat me k
	2:10	pick me out and treat me so k
2Sa	10:2	as k as his father treated me
1Ch	19:2	as k as his father treated me
Ps	119:132	Turn my way, look k on me
Pr	31:26	she always says it k
Isa	33:2	God, treat us k
La	4:10	k women boiled their own children
Lk	10:37	The one who treated him k
Ac	19:40	Rome . . . does not look k on rioters
Heb	8:12	know me by being k forgiven
Jas	2:13	if you refuse to act k

Kindness

Ge	39:21	reached out in k to him
Ru	2:13	such grace, such k—I don't deserve
1Sa	15:6	showed real k to the Israelites
2Sa	9:1	show him some k in honor of
	9:3	to whom I can show some godly k
	10:2	I'd like to show some k to Hanun
	16:4	may you always look on me with such k
1Ch	19:2	I'd like to show some k to Hanun
Ps	86:16	look me in the eye and show k
	90:13	treat your servants with k
Mal	3:17	with the same consideration and k
Mt	12:12	Surely k to people is as legal as k
Ro	2:4	In k he takes us firmly by the hand

	11:22	gentle k and ruthless severity
Eph	2:7	grace and k upon us in Christ Jesus
Col	3:12	compassion, k, humility
1Pe	2:3	drink deep of God's pure k

King-glory

Ps	24:7	K is ready to enter
	24:8	Who is this K? God
	24:9	K is ready to enter
	24:10	Who is this K? God

King-god

| Ps | 5:2 | K, I need your help |
| Isa | 57:9 | You anoint your k with ointments |

King-lover

SS	1:4	An elopement with my K!
	1:12	When my K lay down beside me
	3:11	My K, dressed and garlanded

King-maker

| Ps | 110:7 | The K put his King on the throne |

King-of-the-beasts

| Nu | 23:24 | like a lion, a k, aroused |
| | 24:9 | k—who dares disturb him? |

Kingdom

Ge	10:10	His k got its start with Babel
	20:9	bring on me and my k this huge offense
Ex	19:6	a k of priests, a holy nation
Nu	24:7	their k surpassingly majestic
	32:33	the k of Sihon
Dt	3:4	Og's k in Bashan
	3:10	Og's k
	3:13	Og's k—all the region of Argob
	17:18	sits down on the throne of his k
Jos	13:12	the whole k of Og in Bashan
	13:21	the whole k of Sihon
	13:27	the rest of the k of Sihon
	13:30	entire k of Og king of Bashan
1Sa	10:25	rules and regulations involved in a k
	15:28	God has just now torn the k from you
	18:8	they'll be giving him the k
	20:31	your future in this k is at risk
	24:20	k of Israel is already in your grasp
	28:17	ripped the k right out of your hands
2Sa	3:9	transfer the k from the house of Saul
	3:28	I and my k are totally innocent
	7:13	guarantee his k's rule permanently
	7:16	and your k are permanently secured
	16:3	restore my grandfather's k to me
	16:8	stealing his k. God has given the k
1Ki	1:46	seated on the throne of the k
	2:12	he had a firm grip on the k
	2:15	I had the k right in my hands

	2:22	hand over the whole k to him
	2:24	has put me in charge of the k
	2:33	his descendants, his family and k
	2:46	k was now securely in Solomon's grasp
	3:7	ruler of the k in place of David
	11:11	rip the k from you and hand it over
	11:31	ripping the k out of Solomon's hands
	11:34	I won't take the whole k away
	11:35	I'll remove the k from his son
	11:38	k as solid as the one I built
	12:21	recover the k for Rehoboam
	12:26	won't be long before the k is reunited
	14:8	ripped the k from the hands of David
	18:10	there isn't a country or k where
2Ki	14:5	had the affairs of the k well in hand
	20:13	wasn't a thing in his palace or k
1Ch	10:14	turned the k over to David
	12:23	to hand over Saul's k
	14:2	reputation that God was giving his k
	16:20	camped out in one k after another
	17:12	I will guarantee his k's rule forever
	17:14	set him over my house and my k forever
	22:10	authority of his k over Israel lasts
	28:1	held responsible positions in the k
	28:7	guarantee that his k will last
	29:11	the k all yours!
2Ch	1:1	firm grip on the reins of his k
	9:19	no throne like it in any other k
	11:1	war against Israel and recover the k
	11:17	tremendous boost to the k of Judah
	12:1	Rehoboam had secured his k
	13:5	God's k ruled by God's king
	14:5	his k was at peace
	15:15	a most peaceable k
	17:5	God secured the k under his rule
	21:3	gave him the k of Judah
	21:4	Jehoram had taken over his father's k
	22:9	capable of ruling the k
	25:3	had the affairs of the k well in hand
	32:15	No god of any country or k ever
	36:20	until the k of Persia took over
	36:22	announcement throughout his k
Ezr	1:1	announcement throughout his k
	7:13	people of Israel living in my k
Ne	9:35	Even when they had their own k
Est	1:20	public knowledge throughout the k
	1:22	bulletins to every part of the k
	2:3	officials in every province of his k
	3:6	throughout the whole k of Xerxes
	3:8	provinces of your k who don't fit in
	5:3	it's yours—even if it's half my k
	5:6	Half of my k isn't too much to ask
	7:2	Half of my k! Just ask and it's yours
	9:30	the 127 provinces of Xerxes' k
Job	27:23	blown wild to k come by the storm
Ps	89:40	blasted his home to k come
	90:2	from "once upon a time" to "k come
	145:12	the lavish splendor of your k
	145:13	Your k is a k eternal
Isa	7:17	since the time the k split
	9:7	promised k. He'll put that k on a firm
	19:2	City fight city, k fight k

K

	34:12	They'll name it No K There		12:28	God's k is here for sure
	39:2	nothing in his house or k		12:45	you weren't hospitable to my k message
	60:12	Any nation or k that doesn't deliver		13:11	been given insight into God's k
Jer	7:15	that former k to the north		13:19	When anyone hears news of the k
	27:8	any nation or k that won't submit		13:22	person who hears the k news
	48:45	from the capital of Sihon's k		13:24	God's k is like a farmer
Eze	17:14	make sure that this k stayed weak		13:31	God's k is like a pine nut
Da	1:20	magicians and enchanters in his k		13:33	God's k is like yeast
	2:39	will be taken over by another k		13:38	pure seeds are subjects of the k
	2:40	and after that by a fourth k		13:41	weed out the thistles from his k
	2:41	deteriorate into a mongrel k		13:43	holy lives will mature and adorn the k
	2:43	That k won't bond, won't hold together		13:44	God's k is like a treasure hidden
	2:48	Daniel to a high position in the k		13:45	God's k is like a jewel merchant
	4:3	His k lasts and lasts		13:47	God's k is like a fishnet cast
	4:17	He arranges k affairs however he		13:52	every student well-trained in God's k
	4:25	he arranges all k		16:19	complete and free access to God's k
	4:26	your k will still be there for you		16:28	see the Son of Man in k glory
	4:31	Your k is taken from you		18:1	gets the highest rank in God's k
	4:34	his k never declines and falls		18:3	not even going to get a look at the k
	4:36	making my k shine		18:4	will rank high in God's k
	5:7	be third-in-command in the k		18:23	The k of God is like a king
	5:11	in your k who is full of the divine		19:12	not to get married for k reasons
	5:16	and third-in-command in the k		19:14	God's k is made up of people like
	5:18	Nebuchadnezzar a great k		19:23	for the rich to enter God's k
	5:28	Your k has been divided up		19:24	for the rich to enter God's k
	5:29	third-in-charge in the k		20:1	God's k is like an estate manager
	6:1	Darius reorganized his k		20:21	highest places of honor in your k
	6:3	put him in charge of the whole k		21:21	embrace this k life and don't doubt
	6:26	feared in all parts of my k		21:31	precede you into God's k
	7:18	the High God will be given the k		21:43	God's k will be taken back from you
	7:22	God's holy people took over the k		22:2	God's k," he said, "is like a king
	7:23	The fourth animal is a fourth k		23:13	Your lives are roadblocks to God's k
	7:24	that will come from this k		24:14	good news — the Message of the k
	8:21	goat stands for the k of the Greeks		25:1	God's k is like ten young virgins
	10:13	angel-prince of the k of Persia		25:34	Take what's coming to you in this k
	10:14	the prince of the k of Persia		26:29	drink with you in the k of my Father
	11:2	war against the entire k of Greece	Mk	1:8	turning your old life in for a k life
	11:4	his k will split into four parts		1:15	Time's up! God's k is here
	11:21	out of nowhere, and will seize the k		2:19	This is K Come
Hos	1:4	calling it quits on the k of Israel		4:11	been given insight into God's k
	10:15	find Israel, king and k, a blank		4:18	the ones who hear the k news
Am	4:3	And kick you to k come		4:26	God's k is like seed thrown
	9:8	have my eye on the K of Sin		4:30	How can we picture God's k?
Ob	1:21	a rule that honors God's k		6:23	I'll split my k with you if you say so
Mic	4:8	daughter will be the k center		9:1	see the k of God arrive in full force
Zec	9:3	put together quite a k for herself		10:14	at the very center of life in the k
Mt	3:2	Change your life. God's k is here		10:15	Unless you accept God's k
	3:11	turning your old life in for a k life		10:23	who 'have it all' to enter God's k
	4:17	Change your life. God's k is here		10:25	for the rich to get into God's k
	4:23	God's k was his theme		11:10	Blessed the coming k of our father
	5:10	drives you even deeper into God's k		12:34	right on the border of God's k
	5:19	you will find honor in the k		14:25	when I drink it in the k of God
	5:20	first thing about entering the k		15:43	on the lookout for the k of God
	5:48	You're k subjects. Now live like it	Lk	1:33	no end, ever, to his k
	8:11	sitting down at God's k banquet		3:16	will ignite the k life
	9:15	his is K Come		4:43	have to tell the Message of God's k
	9:35	reported k news, and healed		5:35	This is K Come
	10:7	Tell them that the k is here		6:20	God's k is there for the finding
	10:18	a platform for preaching the k news		7:28	in the k he prepared you for
	11:11	in the k he prepared you for		7:29	baptized by him into the k
	11:12	to force themselves into God's k		8:1	preaching God's k
	11:13	the way for the Messiah of the k		8:10	been given insight into God's k

	9:2	preach the news of God's k
	9:11	talked to them about the k of God
	9:27	see with their own eyes the k of God
	9:60	life is urgent: Announce God's k
	9:62	can't put God's k off till tomorrow
	10:9	God's k is right on your doorstep
	10:11	God's k was right on your doorstep
	11:20	God's k is here for sure
	12:32	wants to give you the very k itself
	13:18	How can I picture God's k for you
	13:20	How can I picture God's k
	13:28	the prophets march into God's k
	13:29	sit down at the table of God's k
	14:15	who gets to eat dinner in God's k
	16:16	Now it's all k of God
	17:20	when the k of God would come
	17:21	Because God's k is already among you
	18:16	children are the k's pride and joy
	18:17	Unless you accept God's k
	18:24	who have it all to enter God's k
	18:25	get a rich person into God's k
	19:11	that God's k would appear any minute
	21:31	you know God's k is about here
	22:16	eat it together in the k of God
	22:18	until the k of God arrives
	22:30	eat and drink at my table in my k
	23:42	remember me when you enter your k
	23:52	alert expectation of the k of God
Jn	3:3	see what I'm pointing to — to God's k
	3:5	it's not possible to enter God's k
	18:36	My k," said Jesus, "doesn't consist
Ac	1:3	things concerning the k of God
	1:6	Master, are you going to restore the k
	2:30	descendant of his would rule his k
	8:12	announcing the news of God's k
	14:22	Anyone signing up for the k of God
	19:8	make the things of the k of God real
	20:25	the news of God's inaugurated k
	28:23	everything involved in the k of God
	28:31	all matters of the k of God
Ro	11:12	non-Jewish outsiders to God's k
	14:17	God's k isn't a matter of what
1Co	6:9	will not be joining in his k
	6:10	don't qualify as citizens in God's k
	15:24	hands over his k to God the Father
	15:50	lead us . . . into the k of God
Gal	5:21	you will not inherit God's k
Eph	2:19	This k of faith is now your home
	5:5	near the k of Christ, the k of God
Col	1:13	set us up in the k of the Son
	4:11	stuck with me in working for God's k
1Th	2:12	God, who called us into his own k
2Th	1:5	decided to make you fit for the k
2Ti	4:18	keeping me safe in the k of heaven
Heb	12:28	An unshakable k!
Jas	1:1	tribes scattered to K Come
	2:5	down-and-out as the k's first citizens
2Pe	1:11	the way wide open into the eternal k
Rev	1:6	made us a K, Priests for his Father
	1:9	the trial and the K and the passion
	5:10	made them a K, Priests for our God
	11:15	k of the world is now the K of our

	12:10	K of our God, authority of his Messiah
	16:10	Its k fell into sudden eclipse

Kingdoms

Dt	3:21	same thing to all the k over there
	28:25	All the k of Earth will see you
Jos	11:10	had been head of all these k
1Sa	14:47	capturing neighboring k
1Ki	4:21	Solomon was sovereign over all the k
	10:20	like it in any of the surrounding k
2Ki	19:15	one and only God, sovereign over all k
	19:17	laid waste countries and k
	19:19	Make all the k on earth know
1Ch	29:30	Israel and the surrounding k passed
2Ch	17:10	fear of God in all the k
	20:6	God in heaven above and ruler of all k
	20:29	surrounding k got word that God
	36:23	has given me all the k of the earth
Ezr	1:2	has given me all the k of the earth
Ne	9:22	You gave them k and peoples
Ps	46:6	kings and k threaten
	79:6	your rival k who ignore you
	136:17	Smashed huge k right and left
Ecc	2:8	loot from kings and k
Isa	10:10	eliminated k full of gods
	13:4	Thunder of k in an uproar
	13:19	Babylon, most glorious of all k
	14:16	Who terrorized earth and its k
	23:11	threw the sea k into turmoil
	23:17	promiscuous with all the k of earth
	37:16	God of all k on earth
	37:20	Let all the k of earth know
	47:5	called 'First Lady of the K
Jer	25:26	All the k on planet Earth
	28:8	judgment against many countries and k
	51:20	use you to knock k to bits
	51:27	Call k into service against her
Eze	37:22	divided into two nations, two k
Da	2:40	it will bust up the previous k
	2:44	throughout the history of these k
	4:17	the High God rules human k
	4:25	the High God rules over human k
	4:32	the High God rules human k
	5:21	the High God rules human k
	7:17	four k will appear on earth
	7:23	different from the first three k
	7:27	glory of all the k under heaven
	8:23	k cool down and rebellions heat up
Zep	3:8	round up all the k
Mt	4:8	earth's k, how glorious they all were
Lk	4:5	all the k of the earth on display
Heb	11:33	they toppled k, made justice work

Kiss

Ge	27:26	Come close, son, and k me
	31:28	wouldn't permit me so much as a k
2Sa	20:9	in his right hand as if to k him
1Ki	19:20	Let me k my father and mother
Ps	2:12	K Messiah! Your very lives are
	85:10	Whole Living embrace and k

K

SS	1:2	**K** me — full on the mouth
	8:2	drink my wine and **k** my cheeks
Hos	13:2	kill living babies and **k** golden calves
Mt	26:48	The one I **k**, that's the one
Mk	14:44	The one I **k**, that's the one
Lk	14:33	**k** it good-bye, you can't be
	22:47	came right up to Jesus to **k** him
	22:48	betray the Son of Man with a **k**

Kissed

Ge	27:27	He came close and **k** him
	29:11	he **k** Rachel and broke into tears
	29:13	**k** him and brought him home
	31:55	**k** his grandchildren and his daughters
	33:4	held him tight and **k** him
	45:15	**k** all his brothers and wept.
	48:10	Old Israel **k** and embraced them
	50:1	wept over him, and **k** him
Ex	4:27	at the mountain of God and **k** him
	18:7	bowed to him and **k** him
Ru	1:9	She **k** them and they cried openly
	1:14	Orpah **k** her mother-in-law good-bye
1Sa	10:1	poured it on Saul's head, and **k** him
	20:41	then they **k** one another and wept
2Sa	14:33	the king **k** Absalom
	19:39	The king **k** and blessed Barzillai
1Ki	19:18	mouths that haven't **k** his image
Pr	7:13	threw her arms around him and **k** him
Mt	26:49	How are you, Rabbi?" and **k** him
Mk	14:45	said, "Rabbi!" and **k** him
Lk	7:38	she dried his feet, **k** them
	15:20	embraced him, and **k** him

Kisses

Pr	27:6	**k** from an enemy do you in
SS	4:11	The **k** of your lips are honey
	5:16	His words are **k**, his **k** words.
	7:9	my love's **k** flow from his lips to mine

Know-it-alls

Job	5:13	catches the **k** in their conspiracies
Pr	10:14	**k** talk too much — a sheer waste
	13:10	Arrogant **k** stir up discord
	15:12	**K** don't like being told what to do
Jer	8:9	Your **k** will be unmasked
	8:10	here's what will happen to the **k**
	29:8	so-called preachers and **k**
Mt	11:25	your ways from sophisticates and **k**
Lk	10:21	hid these things from the **k**
1Co	3:20	through the smoke screens of the **k**
	8:7	**k** who treat others as know-nothings

Knowledge

Ge	2:9	the Tree-of-**K**-of-Good-and-Evil
	2:17	the Tree-of-**K**-of-Good-and-Evil
Ex	31:13	keep the **k** alive that I am the God
2Ch	1:10	give me wisdom and **k** as I come and go
	1:11	asked for wisdom and **k**

	1:12	what you asked for — wisdom and **k**
	6:30	the only one with such inside **k**
Est	1:20	ruling becomes public **k** throughout
Pr	1:29	you hated **K** and had nothing to do
	2:5	you'll have come upon the **K** of God
	2:6	plainspoken in **K** and Understanding
	2:10	Brother **K** your pleasant companion
	8:10	God-**k** over a lucrative career
	8:12	**K** and Discretion live just down
	10:14	The wise accumulate **k**
	12:23	Prudent people don't flaunt their **k**
	15:2	**K** flows . . . from the wise
	15:7	Perceptive words spread **k**
	20:15	Drinking from the . . . chalice of **k**
	22:12	God guards **k** with a passion
	23:12	open your ears to tested **k**
	24:4	It takes **k** to furnish its rooms
	24:14	**k**, and wisdom for your soul
Ecc	1:16	I've stockpiled wisdom and **k**
	1:17	wisdom and **k** are mindless and witless
	2:26	God may give wisdom and **k** and joy
	12:9	the Quester also taught others **k**
Isa	11:2	Spirit that instills **k** and Fear-of-God
	11:9	a living **k** of God ocean-deep
	33:6	salvation, wisdom, and **k** in surplus
	44:25	their latest **k** look silly
Da	1:17	gave these four young men **k** and skill
Hos	4:6	you've turned your back on **k**
	6:3	ready to study God, eager for God-**k**
Mt	11:27	Father and Son intimacies and **k**
Lk	11:52	You took the key of **k**
Ac	2:22	God did through him are common **k**
Ro	2:16	will become public **k** on the day God
1Co	1:5	it's beyond speech, beyond **k**
	4:2	reliability and accurate **k**
	8:7	Real **k** isn't that insensitive
	14:5	access to the **k** and love of God
2Co	2:14	he brings **k** of Christ
Col	2:3	treasures of wisdom and **k**
Tit	1:9	spur people on in **k**
Jas	4:6	common **k** that "God goes against
1Pe	1:20	become public **k**, God always knew

L

Labor

Ge	35:16	Rachel went into **l** — hard, hard **l**
	35:17	When her **l** pains were at their worst
Ex	1:11	put them to hard **l** under gang-foremen
	1:13	crushing them with slave **l**
	1:14	made them miserable with hard **l**
	2:11	saw all that hard **l**
	2:23	cries for relief from their hard **l**
	6:6	under the cruel hard **l** of Egypt
	6:7	under the cruel hard **l** of Egypt
	14:5	letting Israel, our slave **l**, go free
Jos	9:23	From now on it's menial **l** for you
	16:10	they are made to do forced **l**
	17:13	put the Canaanites to forced **l**
Jdg	1:28	put the Canaanites to forced **l**
	1:30	they were put to forced **l**

	1:33	put them to forced l
	1:35	they were put to forced l
1Sa	4:19	to give birth, going into hard l
	8:12	put some to forced l on his farms
2Sa	12:31	put them to slave l
1Ki	4:6	manager of the slave l
	9:15	the work record of the l force
	9:21	by Solomon for his gangs of slave l
1Ch	20:3	put the people to hard l
2Ch	8:8	by Solomon for his gangs of slave l
Job	7:1	It's a life sentence to hard l
	24:11	No matter how back-breaking their l
Ps	25:18	look at my life of hard l
	81:6	freed you from a life of hard l
Ecc	2:22	what do you get from a life of hard l
	2:26	sinners are assigned a life of hard l
SS	8:5	mother went into l under that tree
Isa	23:4	I've never had l pains
	24:22	then sentenced and put to hard l
	26:18	We writhed in l but bore no baby
	47:6	put old men and women to cruel, hard l
	49:7	slave l to the ruling class
	66:7	Before she went into l, she had
	66:8	barely in l when she had her babies
Jer	4:31	The cry of a woman in l
	30:6	holding their bellies like women in l
	30:8	No more slave l to foreigners
	48:12	I'll put him to work at hard l
La	1:3	After years of pain and hard l
Mic	4:9	panicked like a woman in l
Mk	14:58	this Temple, built by hard l
2Co	11:27	I've known drudgery and hard l
1Th	1:3	your work of faith, your l of love

2Sa	1:11	In l, David ripped his clothes
	1:17	David sang this l over Saul
	3:31	Abner's funeral procession with loud l
	3:32	The king's voice was loud in l
	15:23	whole country was weeping in loud l
2Ch	35:25	Jeremiah composed an anthem of l
Est	4:3	there was loud l among the Jews
Job	2:12	They cried out in l
Ps	30:11	changed wild l into whirling dance
Ecc	3:4	right time to l and another to cheer
Isa	15:2	goes up to l. Moab weeps and wails
	16:7	So now let Moab l for a change
Jer	4:28	earth will mourn and the skies l
	7:29	Go bald to the hills and l
	9:18	help us express our loss and l
	12:11	a ruined land, a land in l
	48:2	Dungface Dimon will loudly l
	48:17	all who know how famous he's been. L
Eze	27:30	a choir of bitter l over you
	32:2	sing a funeral l over Pharaoh
	32:18	l over Egypt's pompous ways
Joel	1:11	L the loss of wheat and barley
	1:13	lead people in worship, lead them in l
Am	5:16	Go out into the streets and l loudly
Mic	1:8	This is why I l and mourn
	1:11	L, Last-Stand City: There's nothing
Mt	2:18	heard in Ramah, weeping and much l
	24:30	will raise a huge l as they watch
	27:39	shaking their heads in mock l
Mk	15:29	shaking their heads in mock l
Jas	5:1	Take some lessons in l
Rev	1:7	will tear their clothes in l
	18:10	they'll cry their l: Doom, doom
	18:18	cried their l when they saw the smoke

Laborer

Dt	24:14	Don't abuse a l who is destitute
Mt	10:24	A l doesn't make more money than

Laborers

Dt	20:11	conscripted as forced l and work
2Ch	2:2	Solomon assigned 70,000 common l
	2:18	assigned 70,000 of them as common l
	34:13	in charge of the common l
Ne	4:17	The common l held a tool in one hand
Jer	24:1	the craftsmen, and the skilled l
	29:2	all the skilled l and craftsmen

Laggard

1Sa	11:7	one and all, not a l among them
2Sa	19:11	Why are you so l in bringing the king

Lament

Ge	50:10	grief out in loud and lengthy l
	50:11	the name Abel Mizraim (Egyptian L
Ex	11:6	l such as has never been
	12:30	what wild wailing and l in Egypt
Jdg	11:37	through the hills and l my virginity
1Sa	5:12	cries of pain and l filled the air

Lamentation

Jdg	21:2	cried loudly; there was widespread l
Jer	48:38	in Moab there'll be loud l
Zec	12:11	The l in Jerusalem that day

Lamenting

Jdg	11:38	l that she would never marry
2Sa	19:1	David was weeping and l over Absalom
Jer	3:21	Israel l the wasted years
	9:10	l the loss of the mountain pastures

Laments

2Sa	13:36	loud l and weeping
2Ch	35:25	The anthem is written in the L
Job	30:31	my mouth harp wails l
Isa	16:7	antiphonal mock-l from the neighbors
Jer	31:15	L coming out of Ramah, wild and bitter

Land-inheritance

Nu	18:24	are to receive no l among the People
	34:29	hand out the assignments of l
Dt	18:1	don't get any l with the rest
	18:2	don't get l like the rest

L

Laugh

Ge	18:13	Sarah l saying, 'Me? Have a baby?
	18:15	Sarah lied. She said, "I didn't l
	21:6	all who get the news will l
Job	8:21	God will let you l again
Ps	13:4	or l when I fall on my face
	38:16	I wait and pray so they won't l me off
	52:6	They'll l in relief
	68:3	they'll l, they'll sing, they'll l
	85:6	your people will l and sing
Pr	1:25	you l at my counsel and make a joke
	24:17	Don't l when your enemy falls
Ecc	3:4	A right time to cry and another to l
Isa	36:6	Egypt? Don't make me l
	65:14	My servants will l from full hearts
Ro	12:15	L with your happy friends

Laughed

Ge	17:17	then he l, thinking, "Can a hundred
	18:12	Sarah l within herself
	18:15	Yes you did; you l
Ne	2:19	they l at us, mocking
Ps	126:2	We l, we sang
La	1:7	Enemies looked on and l
	1:7	l at her helpless silence
Ob	1:12	shouldn't have l and joked at Judah
Mic	6:16	Your way of life will be l at
Lk	8:53	They l at him. They knew she was dead
Ac	17:32	Some l at him and walked off

Laughing

1Sa	2:1	I'm l at my rivals
Est	9:18	their holiday for l and feasting
Job	39:18	oh, how she runs, l
Ps	2:4	Heaven-throned God breaks out l
	9:2	whistling, l, and jumping for joy
	35:10	Every bone in my body l, singing
	59:8	But you, God, break out l
	126:6	heavy hearts will come home l
Ecc	7:3	Crying is better than l
Isa	13:22	curdle your blood with their l
	29:19	The castoffs of society will be l
Zec	8:5	fill the public parks, l and playing

Laughs

Job	39:7	He l at his city cousins
	39:22	He l at danger, fearless
SS	8:6	Passion l at the terrors of hell

Laughter

Ge	17:19	Name him Isaaac (L).
	21:6	God has blessed me with l
Est	8:16	For Jews it was all sunshine and l
	9:17	celebrated with much food and l
	9:22	holiday for parties and fun and l
Ps	14:7	turned-around Israel sings l
	30:5	give way to days of l

	45:15	A procession of joy and l
	53:6	turned-around Israel sings l
	100:2	Bring a gift of l, sing
Pr	14:13	all that l will end in heartbreak
Ecc	10:19	L and bread go together
Isa	16:10	No more boisterous l in the orchards
	24:8	The l of castanets is gone, the shouts of
	51:3	A place filled with exuberance and l
Jer	7:34	I'll empty both smiles and l
	15:17	never joined the party crowd in their l
	16:9	about to banish smiles and l
	25:10	banish every sound of joy—singing, l
	30:19	l will spill through the doors
	31:13	I'll convert their weeping into l
	33:11	hear l and celebration
	48:33	Lush Moab stripped of song and l
Ac	15:33	sent off by their new friends with l
1Pe	1:8	yet you trust him—with l and singing
Rev	18:23	never again l of bride and groom

Laundry

2Ki	18:17	on the road to the l commons
Job	20:27	hang their dirty l out for all to see
Ps	51:2	soak out my sins in your l
	51:7	Soak me in your l
Isa	7:3	on the road to the public l
	36:2	on the road to the public l
	49:23	scrub your floors, do your l
Mal	3:2	like the strongest lye soap at the l

Lavish

Ge	9:7	reproduce, l life on the Earth
Ex	13:5	a land l with milk and honey
Dt	28:11	God will l you with good things
1Sa	15:22	not staging a l religious production
1Ki	10:5	l crystal, and the elaborate worship
2Ch	29:35	l libations that went with the Whole
Ps	112:9	They l gifts on the poor
	145:12	the l splendor of your kingdom
	145:16	you l your favor on all creatures
Isa	25:6	a feast l with gourmet desserts
	42:21	to be l in his revelation
	55:7	God, who is l with forgiveness
	57:9	l perfumes on yourselves
Eze	34:29	rich gardens, l in vegetables
Da	2:6	I'll l you with gifts and honors
	11:24	living . . . in corrupt and l luxury
	11:38	a l show of silver and gold
Hos	10:1	The more l the harvest, the more
Jn	3:35	a l distribution of gifts
2Co	4:17	the l celebration prepared for us
	9:6	a l planter gets a l crop
Eph	1:6	celebration of his l gift-giving

Lavished

Ge	27:37	and l grain and wine on him
Dt	32:10	l attention on him, guarding him
2Ch	21:3	Their father had l them with gifts

| Isa | 63:7 | Compassion l, love extravagant |
| Da | 2:48 | l him with gifts |

Lavishly

Nu	22:17	I will honor and reward you l
Dt	15:4	God is going to bless you l
Job	36:7	the righteous; he honors them l
Ps	112:5	good person is generous and lends l
Hos	14:4	I will love them l
Gal	3:5	God who l provides you
1Pe	5:4	commend you l

Law-abiding

Isa	58:2	right-living people — l, God-honoring
Lk	16:8	smarter in this regard than l citizens
Tit	3:1	respect the government and be l

Lawful

Eze	18:19	careful to do what is l and right
Mk	12:14	Is it l to pay taxes to Caesar
Lk	20:22	Is it l to pay taxes to Caesar

Lawless

| 2Pe | 3:17 | these l and loose-talking teachers |
| 1Jn | 3:4 | sinful life are dangerously l |

Lawyer

Job	13:8	think he needs a l to defend himself
Ac	24:1	along with Tertullus, a trial l
Ro	4:15	contract drawn up by a hard-nosed l
Tit	3:13	Zenas the l and Apollos a hearty

Layperson

Lev	22:10	No l may eat anything set apart
	22:12	If a priest's daughter marries a l
	22:13	But no l may eat of it

Lazy

Ex	5:8	They're getting l
	5:17	L! That's what you are! L!
Pr	6:6	You l fool, look at an ant
	10:26	A l employee will give you nothing
	12:24	the l are oppressed by work
	12:27	A l life is an empty life
	15:19	The path of l people is overgrown
	15:20	l students embarrass their parents
	19:24	too l to raise it to their mouth
	20:4	A farmer too l to plant in the spring
	21:25	L people finally die of hunger
	26:15	too l to lift it to his mouth
Ecc	10:18	l woman ends up with a leaky roof
Isa	32:10	you'll be shaken out of your l lives
	56:10	l dogs, dreaming in the sun
Jer	48:11	l as a dog in the sun
Eze	16:49	proud, gluttonous, and l

Zep	1:12	sitting it out, fat and l
Mt	26:41	l as an old dog sleeping by the fire
Mk	14:38	l as an old dog sleeping by the fire
2Th	3:6	who are l and refuse to work
	3:11	bunch of l good-for-nothings
Tit	1:12	barking dogs, l bellies

Lazybones

Pr	19:15	l go hungry
	24:30	walked by the field of an old l
	26:14	so a l turns back over in bed

Leader

Nu	7:3	an ox from each l
	7:11	one l is to present his offering
	7:18	the l of Isasachar
	7:24	the l of the people of Zebulun
	7:30	the l of the people of Reuben
	7:36	the l of the people of Simeon
	7:42	the l of the people of Gad
	7:48	the l of the people of Ephraim
	7:54	the l of the people of Manasseh
	7:60	the l of the people of Benjamin
	7:66	the l of the people of Da
	7:72	the l of the people of Asher
	7:78	the l of the people of Naphtali
	13:2	tried-and-true l in the tribe
	14:4	Let's pick a new l
	17:2	one from the l of each ... tribe
	17:3	staff for the l of each ancestral
	17:9	Each l took the staff with his name
	25:18	Cozbi, daughter of a Midianite l
	34:18	Assign one l from each tribe to help
	34:22	l from the tribe of Da
	34:23	l from the tribe of Manasseh
	34:24	l from the tribe of Ephraim
	34:25	l from the tribe of Zebulun
	34:26	l from the tribe of Isasachar
	34:27	l from the tribe of Asher
	34:28	l from the tribe of Naphtali
Jdg	4:7	Sisera, the l of Jabin's army
1Sa	13:14	he'll appoint him l of his people
	22:2	David became their l
2Sa	22:44	you made me a l of nations
1Ki	11:24	band of outlaws and became their l
	14:7	made you the l of my people Israel
	16:2	set you up as the l of my people
1Ch	2:10	prominent l in the Judah family
	11:2	you were the real l of Israel
	12:4	a l of the Thirty
	12:27	Jehoiada l of the family of Aaron
	27:4	Mikloth was the l of his division
	29:22	David's son before God as their l
2Ch	1:2	every l, and all the heads of families
	6:5	chosen one person to be the l
	11:22	the "first son" and l of the brothers
	13:12	God is on our side; he's our l
	19:11	the l of the tribe of Judah
Job	29:25	I was their l, establishing
Ps	9:14	I'll be the song l

	18:43	you made me a l of nations
	28:8	ample refuge for his chosen l
	31:3	my safe l, be my true mountain guide
	78:67	He disqualified Joseph as l
	89:3	joined forces with my chosen l
Pr	14:28	mark of a good l is loyal followers
	16:10	A good l motivates, doesn't mislead
	16:14	An intemperate l wreaks havoc
	20:26	a wise l makes a clean sweep of rebels
	20:28	Love and truth form a good l
	25:3	understanding of a good l is broad
	28:2	takes a l of real understanding
	29:4	A l of good judgment gives stability
	29:12	When a l listens to malicious gossip
	29:26	Everyone tries to get help from the l
Isa	22:21	He'll be a father-l to Jerusalem
	55:4	made him a prince and l of the nations
Jer	30:21	One of their own . . . shall be their l
Eze	31:11	turned it over to a world-famous l
Da	9:25	until the coming of the Anointed L
	9:26	the Anointed L will be killed
Hos	1:11	They'll choose a single l
Mic	5:2	l who will shepherd-rule Israel
Mal	3:1	the L you've been looking for
Mt	2:6	From you will come the l who will
	7:16	A genuine l will never exploit
	23:10	only one Life-L for you and them
Mk	5:35	came from the l's house and told him
	5:36	said to the l, "Don't listen to them
	5:38	They entered the l's house
Lk	8:49	someone from the l's house came up
	22:26	let the l act the part of the servant
Jn	3:1	a prominent l among the Jews
1Ti	3:2	A l must be well-thought-of
	5:19	a complaint against a l that isn't
Tit	1:7	church l, responsible for the affairs
1Pe	5:1	I know what it's like to be a l

Leaders

Ge	19:11	down the door, both l and followers
Ex	3:16	Gather the l of Israel
	3:18	you and the l of Israel will go
	4:29	round up all the l of Israel
	16:22	the l of the company came to Moses
	18:21	appoint them as l over groups
	18:25	set them as l over the people
	22:28	Don't curse God; and don't damn your l
	24:11	He didn't hurt these pillar-l
	34:31	Aaron and the l in the community came
	35:27	The l brought onyx and other
Lev	9:1	Aaron and his sons and the l of Israel
Nu	1:16	l of their ancestral tribes
	1:44	the l of Israel, twelve men
	3:32	supervised the l of the Levites
	4:34	the l of the congregation counted
	4:46	l of Israel counted all the Levites
	7:2	l of Israel, the heads
	7:3	a wagon from each pair of l
	7:10	the l brought their offerings
	7:84	dedication offerings of the l
	10:4	the l, the heads of the clans

	11:16	men from among the l of Israel
	11:24	called together seventy of the l
	11:25	put it on the seventy l
	11:26	were listed as l but they didn't leave
	11:30	l of Israel went back to the camp
	13:3	All of them were l in Israel
	16:2	with him 250 l of the congregation
	16:25	The l of Israel followed him
	17:6	Their l handed over twelve staffs
	21:18	Dug out by the peoples' l
	22:4	Moab spoke to the l of Midian
	22:7	The l of Moab and Midian were
	25:4	Take all the l of Israel and kill them
	26:9	community l from Korah's gang
	27:2	before the l and the congregation
	31:13	all the l of the congregation went
	31:26	family l in the community
	32:2	the l of the congregation
	36:1	l who were heads of the families
Dt	1:13	I will commission them as your l
	1:15	made them your l—l of thousands
	5:23	heads of your tribes and your l
	21:2	l and judges are to go out and measure
	21:3	l and judges of the city
	21:4	The l will take the heifer
	21:6	all the l of that town that is nearest
	21:19	before the l at the city gate
	22:15	proof of her virginity to the town l
	22:16	The father is to tell the l
	22:17	before the l for their examination
	22:18	town l then are to take the husband
	25:7	she is to go to the l
	25:8	the l will call for the brother
	27:1	Moses commanded the l of Israel
	29:10	the heads of your tribes, your l
	31:9	and to all the l of Israel
	31:28	gather the l of the tribes
	33:5	the l and tribes of Israel gathered
Jos	1:10	gave orders to the people's l
	3:2	three days, l went through the camp
	7:6	l throwing dirt on their heads
	8:10	the l of Israel led the troops
	9:11	Our l and everybody else
	9:15	The l of the congregation swore
	9:18	l of the congregation had given
	9:19	The l were united in their response
	9:21	the l continued, "We'll let them live
	17:4	and the l and said, "God commanded
	19:51	ancestral l assigned by lot
	20:4	before the city's l. The l must then
	24:11	The Jericho l ganged up on you
Jdg	2:7	the l who survived him, l who
	5:8	God chose new l, who then fought
	5:14	from Zebulun high-ranking l came
	8:6	But the l in Succoth said
	8:14	the officials and l of Succoth
	8:16	seventy-seven l of Succoth
	9:3	the proposal to the l of Shechem
	9:6	Then all the l of Shechem
	9:7	Listen to me, l of Shechem
	9:18	king over Shechem's l
	9:20	burn up the l of Shechem

	9:23	between Abimelech and Shechem's l		8:9	government l and commanders
	9:24	loose among Abimelech and Shechem's l		12:5	accompanied by the l of Judah
	9:25	Shechem's l put men in ambush		12:6	The l of Israel . . . were repentant
	9:26	The l of Shechem trusted him		24:10	people and their l were glad to do it
	9:39	backed by the l of Shechem		24:17	l of Judah made a formal presentation
	9:46	l connected with Shechem's Tower		24:23	massacred the l
	9:51	the city's l had fled there		26:12	The roster of family l
	10:18	The l in Gilead said		28:12	Some of their Ephraimite l
	20:2	l of all the people, representing		28:14	plunder to the l and the people
1Sa	5:7	the l of Ashdod saw what was going on		29:20	got all the l of the city together
	5:8	called together all the Philistine l		29:30	l told the Levites to finish things
	5:11	called the Philistine l together		30:6	invitations from the king and his l
	6:2	Philistine l called together		31:8	l came and saw the extent
	6:4	l . . . all of you—l and people		32:3	talked to his advisors and military l
	6:12	The Philistine l followed them		33:11	God directed the l of the troops
	6:16	five Philistine l saw what they came		35:8	l in The Temple of God
	6:18	ruled by the five l		36:14	evil mindset spread to the l
	7:7	Philistine l went on the offensive	Ezr	5:5	God had his eye on the l of the Jews
	11:3	The town l of Jabesh said		5:9	asked the l, "Who issued you
	12:6	God who made Moses and Aaron your l		6:7	Leave the governor and l of the Jews
	15:30	your presence before the l		6:8	how you are to help the l of the Jews
2Sa	5:3	the l of Israel met with King David		6:14	the l of the Jews continued to build
	7:7	did I ever say to any of the l		7:28	organized all the l of Israel to go
	10:3	the Ammonite l warned Hanun		8:16	So I sent for the l
	19:9	populace was now complaining to its l		9:1	the l came to me and said
	21:12	from the l at Jabesh Gilead		9:2	l have led the way in this betrayal
1Ki	4:2	These were the l in his government		10:5	the l of the priests
	8:1	Solomon called in the l of Israel		10:8	compliance with the ruling of the l
	8:3	With all Israel's l present		10:14	Let our l act on behalf of the whole
	9:22	government l and commanders	Ne	11:1	l of the people were already living
	21:8	city and to the civic l		11:3	l in the province who resided
	21:11	the elders and civic l		11:16	two of the l of the Levites
2Ki	10:6	l of the city had taken responsibility		12:31	had the l of Judah come up on the wall
	10:11	Ahab's family in Jezreel—l, friends		12:32	half the l of Judah followed them
	24:12	and government l, surrendered		13:17	confronted the l of Judah
	24:14	all its l and soldiers	Est	1:16	it's all of us, l and people alike
	24:15	his chief officers, the community l	Job	12:24	He robs world l of their reason
	25:26	all took off for Egypt, l and people	Ps	2:2	Earth-l push for position
1Ch	4:38	these were the l in their families		83:11	Cut down their l as you did
	7:40	brave in battle—good l		141:6	let their l be pushed off a high
	12:19	Philistine l, after talking it over		148:11	all races, l and important people
	12:20	all l among the families of Manasseh		149:8	their l behind bars for good
	12:21	good l among his raiders	Pr	8:15	With my help, l rule
	12:28	twenty-two l from his family		16:12	Good l abhor wrongdoing of all kinds
	12:32	200 l with their families		16:13	Good l cultivate honest speech
	13:1	David consulted with all of his l		16:15	Good-tempered l invigorate lives
	17:6	did I ever say to any of the l		17:7	nor do we expect lies from our l
	19:3	the Ammonite l warned Hanun		19:12	Mean-tempered l are like mad dogs
	22:17	David gave orders to all of Israel's l		20:2	Quick-tempered l are like mad dogs
	23:2	brought together all the l of Israel		20:8	L who know their business and care
	24:4	more l in Eleazar's family than in		22:11	good l also delight in their
	24:5	They assigned the l by lot		24:21	respect your l; don't be defiant
	24:6	the l of the priestly . . . families		28:16	l who lack insight, abuse abounds
	24:31	the l of the priestly . . . families		31:3	promiscuous women who shipwreck l
	25:1	David and the worship l selected		31:4	L can't afford to make fools of
	26:12	guards, supervised by their l	Ecc	10:20	Don't bad-mouth your l
	28:1	David called together all the l	Isa	1:10	you Sodom-schooled l
	28:21	Both l and people are ready		1:23	Your l are turncoats
	29:6	heads of families, l of the tribes		3:12	l are taking you down a blind alley
	29:24	All the l of the people		3:14	l of his people into the dock
2Ch	5:2	Solomon got all the l together		9:16	who followed the l ended up lost
	5:4	When all the l of Israel were ready		16:1	a gift . . . to the l in Jerusalem

L

	22:3	Your l were all cowards
	24:23	glorious before all his l
	30:10	They tell their spiritual l
	31:9	their l scatter hysterically
	32:1	his l will carry out justice
	34:12	L will have no one to lead
	43:28	had to disqualify the Temple l
	62:2	and world l your glory
Jer	1:18	against the priests and local l
	7:8	l are handing you a pack of lies
	10:21	It's because our l are stupid
	19:1	get a few l from the people
	22:22	All your l will be blown away
	23:1	Doom to the shepherd-l who butcher
	23:2	shepherd-l who misled my people
	23:4	set shepherd-l over them
	24:1	along with the l of Judah
	24:8	how I'll treat him and his l
	25:18	along with their kings and l
	25:19	with his attendants and l
	26:17	some of the respected l stood up
	27:20	exile along with all the l of Judah
	29:2	the queen mother, the government l
	32:32	kings and l and priests and preachers
	34:10	All the l and people who had signed
	34:19	l of Judah and Jerusalem
	40:7	When the army l and their men
	44:17	government l in the cities of Judah
	50:35	war against people, l, and
	51:28	king of the Medes, his l and people
La	1:19	betrayed me. My priests and my l
Eze	8:1	meeting with the l of Judah
	8:11	seventy of the l of Israel
	9:6	started with the l in front
	11:1	I recognized the l
	14:1	Some of the l of Israel approached me
	17:12	took its king and its l back
	17:13	took all the top l into exile
	20:1	l of Israel came to ask for guidance
	20:3	Son of man, talk with the l of Israel
	21:23	l, who themselves have sworn oaths
	22:6	Your l, the princes of Israel
	22:25	The l among you became desperate
	34:2	against the shepherd-l of Israel
Da	3:2	all the important l in the province
	3:27	important people, the government l
	4:17	makes l out of losers
	4:36	All the l and important people came
	9:6	preached your Word to our kings and l
	9:8	shame, all of us—our kings, l
Hos	9:15	l are a bunch of rebellious
	13:10	Where are all the local l you wanted
Joel	1:14	get the l together
Jnh	3:5	famous and obscure, l and followers
	3:7	authorized by him and his l
Mic	3:1	Listen, l of Jacob, l of Israel
	3:4	these same l will cry out for help
	3:9	l of Jacob and the l of Israel are L
	3:10	L who build Zion by killing people
	7:3	Corrupt l demand bribes
Na	3:10	Her prize l auctioned off
	3:18	shepherd-l, in charge of caring

Zep	1:8	I will punish the l and the royal sons
	3:3	Her very own l are rapacious lions
	3:11	gotten rid of your arrogant l
Zec	8:20	People and their l will come from all
	8:21	The l will confer with one another
	12:5	our l are strong and able
	12:7	glory of David's family and the l
	13:1	family of David and all the l
Mt	16:21	at the hands of the religious l
	20:18	will be betrayed to the religious l
	21:15	religious l saw the outrageous things
	21:23	The high priests and l of the people
	21:45	When the religious l heard this story
	24:5	Many l are going to show up
	26:3	high priests and religious l
	26:47	high priests and religious l
	26:57	religion scholars and l had assembled
	27:1	high priests and religious l met
	27:12	high priests and religious l
	27:20	religious l had talked the crowd
	27:41	religion scholars and l, were
	28:12	meeting of the religious l
Mk	5:22	One of the meeting-place l
	10:33	betrayed to the religious l
	11:27	religion scholars, and l came
	13:6	Many l are going to show up
	14:43	religion scholars, and l
	14:53	religious l, and scholars had gathered
	15:1	with the religious l and scholars
Lk	7:3	sent l from the Jewish community
	9:22	found guilty by the religious l
	14:1	Sabbath meal with one of the top l
	19:47	l of the people were trying their best
	20:1	religion scholars, and l confronted
	21:8	Many l are going to show up
	22:52	Temple police, religion l
	22:66	religious l of the people and
	24:20	high priests and l betrayed him
Jn	7:13	because of the intimidating Jewish l
	7:48	don't see any of the l believing
	9:22	intimidated by the Jewish l
	12:42	from the ranks of the l did believe
Ac	3:17	killed Jesus, and neither did your l
	4:5	rulers, religious l
	4:8	Rulers and l of the people
	4:21	religious l renewed their threats
	4:23	high priests and religious l had said
	4:26	Earth's l push for position
	6:12	stirred up the people, the religious l
	11:1	l and friends back in Jerusalem heard
	11:30	deliver the collection to the l
	14:5	organized by their l to beat them up
	14:23	handpicked l in each church
	15:2	put it before the apostles and l
	15:4	including the apostles and l
	15:6	apostles and l called a special
	15:22	Everyone agreed: apostles, l
	15:23	the apostles and l, your friends
	16:4	guidelines the . . . l had come up with
	19:31	Prominent religious l in the city
	20:17	sent to Ephesus for the l
	21:18	All the church l were there

L

	23:14	high priests and religious l
	24:1	arrived with a contingent of l
	25:2	high priests and top l renewed
	25:15	high priests and Jewish l brought
	28:17	Paul called the Jewish l together
Ro	13:7	pay your bills, respect your l
	16:7	Both of them are outstanding l
1Co	4:1	Don't imagine us l to be something
Gal	2:2	I did this in private with the l
	2:6	these l were able to add nothing
1Th	5:12	honor those l who work so hard
1Ti	4:14	l of the church laid hands on you
	5:17	Give a bonus to l who do a good job
	6:3	have l there who teach otherwise
	6:9	if it's only money these l are after
2Ti	2:2	reliable l who are competent to teach
Tit	1:5	Appoint l in every town
Heb	13:7	Appreciate your pastoral l
	13:17	Be responsive to your pastoral l
	13:24	Say hello to your pastoral l
Jas	5:14	Call the church l together to pray
1Pe	5:1	special concern for you church l
	5:5	you who are younger must follow your l
	5:5	all of you, l and followers

Leadership

Jdg	10:3	Jair the Gileadite stepped into l
1Sa	7:15	Samuel gave solid l to Israel
	7:16	gave l to Israel in each
	18:5	approved of and admired David's l
1Ki	20:24	Remove each sheik from his place of l
2Ki	6:1	where we're living under your l
1Ch	26:6	provided outstanding l in the family
Pr	14:20	l is nothing without a following
	16:12	sound l has a moral foundation
	20:28	sound l is founded on loving integrity
	21:1	Good l is . . . controlled by God
	25:5	Remove the wicked from l
	29:14	L gains authority and respect
Da	1:4	good prospects for l positions
Ac	1:25	take the place in this ministry and l
Eph	5:23	The husband provides l to his wife
	5:24	Christ as he exercises such l
1Ti	3:1	If anyone wants to provide l
	5:22	appoint people to church l positions
Heb	13:17	Contribute to the joy of their l

Leading

Ex	14:19	angel of God that had been l the camp
Nu	10:35	With the Chest l the way, Moses
	32:17	l the People of Israel into their place
Dt	1:30	God, your God, is l the way
Jos	1:14	in battle formation, l your brothers
	6:6	ram's horn trumpets l God's Chest
	6:8	They blew the trumpets, l God's Chest
Jdg	9:2	Ask all the l men of Shechem
1Sa	12:2	Your king among you, l you
1Ki	3:9	who on their own is capable of l
	10:5	at the steps l up to The Temple of God
	10:19	The throne had six steps l up to it

	12:33	Jeroboam himself l the worship
2Ki	4:8	A l lady of the town talked
1Ch	12:34	l 37,000 men heavily armed
	25:3	l the thanks and praise to God
	25:6	in charge of l the singing
	28:13	their work of l and ordering worship
2Ch	1:10	who on his own is capable of l these
	9:18	The throne had six steps l up to it
	21:13	l Judah and Jerusalem away from God
	23:13	choir and orchestra l the praise
	29:11	serve in conducting and l worship
	35:2	work of l worship in The Temple of God
Ezr	8:24	I picked twelve of the l priests
Ps	42:4	right out in front, L them all
	68:27	Benjamin's out front and l Princes
Isa	40:11	l the nursing ewes to good pasture
	52:12	God is l you out of here
Jer	19:1	a few of the l priests
Eze	40:14	the porch l into the courtyard
	40:30	the gate complexes l to the inside
	42:11	from the east l to the hallway
	47:3	l me through water that was ankle-deep
	47:4	l me through water that was knee-deep
Da	6:7	governors, and all your l officials
Mic	2:13	I will be out in front l them
Zec	12:8	like the Angel of God l the people
Mt	15:14	They are blind men l blind men
	26:32	will go ahead of you, l the way
Mk	8:38	embarrassed over me and the way I'm l
	14:28	I will go ahead of you, l the way
Lk	3:3	life-change l to forgiveness of sins
	9:26	embarrassed with me and the way I'm l
Ac	13:50	most respected women and l men
	20:12	l the boy off alive
1Co	7:34	l to so many more demands
Col	1:18	l the resurrection parade
	2:4	l you off on some wild-goose chase
1Jn	5:16	l to eternal death

Lecture

Mt	13:54	gave a l in the meetinghouse
Mk	6:2	he gave a l in the meeting place
Lk	6:40	An apprentice doesn't l the master

Leftovers

Ex	12:10	if there are l, burn them
	16:23	set aside the l until morning
	34:25	Don't leave l from the Passover Feast
Lev	8:32	Burn up the l from the meat and bread
	10:12	Take the l of the Grain-Offering
	22:30	don't leave any l until morning
Nu	18:9	the l from Grain-Offerings
Ru	2:18	also gave her the l from her lunch
2Ki	4:44	they not only ate, but had l
Jer	42:19	plainly told you, you l from Judah
Da	7:19	trampling the l into the dirt
Mt	14:20	They gathered twelve baskets of l
	15:37	seven large baskets to collect the l
	16:10	how many baskets of l you collected
Mk	6:43	gathered twelve baskets of l

	8:8	Seven sacks of l were collected
	8:19	How many baskets of l did you pick up
	8:20	how many bags full of l did you get
Lk	9:17	twelve baskets of l were gathered
Jn	6:12	Gather the l so nothing is wasted
	6:13	filled twelve large baskets with l

Legacy

2Sa	20:19	would you want to mess with God's l
	21:3	bless God's l of land and people
Job	17:5	leave a l of abuse
Ps	127:3	fruit of the womb his generous l
Isa	14:20	left a l of massacre
	65:15	Your l to my chosen
Ro	9:29	provided us a l of living children
1Co	15:20	the first in a long l of those

Legal

Dt	17:8	cases regarding homicides, l disputes
	21:5	settling l disputes
	25:1	When men have a l dispute
Jdg	11:2	l wife had given him other sons
Est	1:13	all experts in l matters
	1:15	what l recourse they had against Queen
Jer	32:7	You have the l right to buy it
	32:8	you have the l right to keep it
	32:16	handed over the l documents
Mt	5:32	righteous just because you are 'l.'
	12:10	Is it l to heal on the Sabbath?
	12:12	as l as kindness to animals
	19:3	Is it l for a man to divorce his wife
Mk	10:2	Is it l for a man to divorce his wife
Ac	22:25	Is this l: torturing a Roman citizen
1Co	6:12	because something is technically l
2Co	3:6	pages of l footnotes
Gal	3:16	careful language of a l document

Legally

Jer	32:44	people will buy farms again, and l
Mt	5:31	divorces his wife, let him do it l
Ro	7:2	a wife is l tied to her husband
Gal	4:1	l he owns the entire inheritance

Legislate

Pr	8:15	leaders rule, and lawmakers l fairly
Isa	10:1	Doom to you who l evil

Leisure

Ps	55:14	Those long hours of l as we walked
	56:13	Now I stroll at l with God
Eze	34:14	graze at l, feed in the rich pastures

Leisurely

Ac	14:28	a long, l visit with the disciples
1Co	16:7	want a good, long, l visit

Lend

Ge	33:15	Let me at least l you some of my men
Ex	22:25	If you l money to my people
Dt	15:6	will l to many nations but won't
	15:8	l whatever and as much as he needs
	28:12	You will l to many nations
	28:44	He'll l to you; you won't l to him
Mt	25:8	l us some of your oil
Lk	10:40	Tell her to l me a hand
	11:5	Friend, l me three loaves of bread
Ro	15:1	step in and l a hand to those
Php	2:4	l a helping hand
Tit	3:1	always ready to l a helping hand

Lent

Dt	15:2	l money to a neighbor writes it off
	15:3	whatever you have l to your fellow

Lesson

Dt	28:37	you'll be treated as a l or a proverb
1Sa	7:13	learned their l and stayed home
	23:2	Philistines and teach them a l
2Ch	28:22	King Ahaz didn't learn his l
	29:8	a moral history l
Job	15:31	There's a l here
	37:19	give us a l in how to address God
Ps	2:10	Upstart-judges, learn your l
	34:11	I'll give you a l in God worship
Pr	19:25	Somebody might learn a good l
Jer	35:13	Why won't you learn your l
Eze	14:8	make an example of them — a warning l
Da	5:21	learned his l: that the High God rules
Hos	10:10	I'll come to teach them a l
Mt	24:32	Take a l from the fig tree
Mk	13:28	Take a l from the fig tree
1Co	14:26	Sing a hymn, teach a l
1Ti	1:20	a l or two about not blaspheming

Lessons

Ps	119:33	God, teach me l for living
Heb	8:11	a book called God in Five Easy L
Jas	5:1	Take some l in lament

Lethal

Ge	49:17	a l serpent in ambush by the road
Dt	32:33	mixed with l cobra poison
Ps	7:13	L weapons in hand, each arrow
	58:4	Poison, l rattlesnake poison
	119:118	their casual idolatry is l
Eze	5:16	When I shoot my l famine arrows
	9:2	each carrying his l weapon
	14:19	pouring out my l anger
Na	2:3	brandished spears, l on the horizon

Liable

Jer	26:15	city and the people in it will be l

Mt	19:9	holding you l for adultery
1Ti	5:12	they're l to go from bad to worse

Liar

Job	24:25	You're free to try to prove me a l
	34:6	I'm called a l to my face
Pr	19:5	Would you let a l go free
	19:22	better to be poor than a l
Isa	54:17	will be dismissed as a l
Jer	43:2	L! Our God never sent you with this
Zec	5:4	the house of every thief and every l
Mt	27:63	that l announced while he was still
Jn	8:44	When the L speaks, he makes it up
	8:55	I would be as much of a l as you are
1Jn	1:10	make a l out of him
	2:4	he's obviously a l
	4:20	he is a l
	5:10	in effect calls God a l

Liars

Ps	27:12	those l who are out to get me
	31:18	Gag those loudmouthed l who heckle me
	35:19	Don't let these l, my enemies
	69:4	Sneaks and l are out to knife me
	101:7	I have no patience with l
	109:2	L are pouring out invective on me
	116:11	They're all l and cheats
	120:2	Deliver me from the l, God!
	120:3	what's coming, all you barefaced l
Pr	10:18	L secretly hoard hatred
	12:17	l lay down a smoke screen of deceit
	12:22	God can't stomach l
	13:15	l walk a rough road
	17:4	the ears of l itch for dirty gossip
	26:28	L hate their victims
	30:8	Banish . . . l from my presence
Isa	57:4	A race of rebels, a generation of l
Jer	5:2	they're nothing but a bunch of l
	9:3	mighty army of l, the sworn enemies
	14:14	God said, "These preachers are l
	29:9	They're a bunch of l preaching lies
Zec	5:3	worldwide against thieves and l
Mal	3:5	sorcerers, adulterers, l
1Ti	4:1	illusions put forth by professional l
	4:2	These l have lied so well
Tit	1:12	The Cretans are l from the womb
Rev	21:8	sorcerers, idolaters and all l

License

Jer	7:10	the place itself gives you a l
Ac	9:14	give him l to do the same to us
1Co	14:35	no l to use the time of worship
Jude	1:4	sheer grace of our God with sheer l

Life-change

Mk	1:4	l that leads to forgiveness of sins
Lk	3:3	l leading to forgiveness of sins
	24:47	l through the forgiveness of sins

Ac	10:37	John preached a total l
	13:24	preparing them for a total l
	17:30	calling for a radical l
	19:4	preached a baptism of radical l
	20:21	alike to a radical l before God
	26:20	this l — this radical turn to God
Ro	2:4	leads us into a radical l

Life-giving

Ps	51:14	I'll sing anthems to your l ways
Pr	10:11	a good person is a deep, l well
Isa	11:2	The l Spirit of God will hover
	55:3	my l, life-nourishing words
Lk	6:44	must begin with your own l lives
Ac	7:38	took the l words given to him
Ro	5:16	this generous, l gift
	15:13	the l energy of the Holy Spirit
1Co	15:45	the Last Adam is a l Spirit
1Ti	6:13	before the l God and before Christ
1Jn	5:6	a l birth and a death-killing death

Life-light

Jn	1:5	The L blazed out of the darkness
	1:7	point out the way to the L
	1:9	The L was the real thing

Lifeblood

Ge	9:4	Except for meat with its l still in it
	9:5	your own l I will avenge
1Ch	11:19	like drinking the l of these men
Isa	63:6	soaked the earth with their l

Lifeless

Lev	26:32	I'll turn your land into a l moonscape
Isa	24:4	silent and sad, sky and land l
Jer	51:29	a l moonscape — a wasteland
Hos	4:3	fish in the sea are listless, l
	5:9	will be left wasted, a l moonscape
Joel	1:10	The wheat fields are l
Ro	7:8	sin looked pretty dull and l

Lifeline

Isa	38:17	you held tight to my l
Jer	51:13	your life is over, your l cut
Heb	6:19	It's an unbreakable spiritual l

Light-bearers

Mt	5:15	If I make you l

Light-filled

Job	24:13	who scorn the l path
Ecc	11:8	Take delight in each l hour
Ro	6:5	raised into a l world by our Father
Rev	21:11	like a precious gem, l, pulsing light

L

Light-giving

Nu	4:9	cover the l Lapstand and the lamps
Php	2:15	Carry the l Message into the night

Light-radiant

Mt	17:5	a l cloud enveloped them
Mk	9:7	a l cloud enveloped them
Lk	9:34	a l cloud enveloped them

Limit

Ge	34:12	the sky's the l!
2Ki	21:15	They pushed me to my l
Ezr	7:22	There is no l on the salt
Ps	66:11	pushed us to our very l
	78:41	they pushed him to the l
Jer	6:8	You've pushed me to the l
	10:18	I'm going to press them to the l
Hab	1:15	He catches his l and fills his creel
Mal	3:15	They push God to the l
1Co	10:13	never let you be pushed past your l
	13:8	understanding will reach its l
	14:27	two or three's the l
2Co	8:2	pushing them to the very l

Limitations

Ro	8:10	you still experience all the l of sin
2Co	12:7	keep me in constant touch with my l
	12:10	Now I take l in stride
	13:9	our l; we celebrate them

Limited

Job	14:5	Mortals have a l life span
Da	7:12	other animals lived on for a l time
Heb	8:4	If he were l to earth
	9:10	l to matters of ritual and behavior

Limits

Dt	8:2	pushing you to your l, testing you
Job	6:10	before being pressed past the l
Ps	119:96	I see the l to everything human
Isa	9:7	no l to the wholeness he brings
	33:21	off-l to predatory pirates
La	1:10	this assembly off-l
2Co	10:13	the l of what God has set for us
	10:16	still be within the l God sets

Limp

2Ki	19:26	slumped shoulders, l souls
Ps	37:36	a punctured bladder, vapid and l
Pr	26:7	A proverb quoted by fools is l
Isa	35:3	Energize the l hands
Jer	6:24	we're as l as wet dishrags
	23:9	My head is reeling, my limbs are l
	50:43	white as a ghost, l as a dishrag
Eze	7:17	Every hand hangs l

	30:25	the arms of Pharaoh shall go l
Da	5:6	legs went l and his knees knocked
Zec	11:17	Your arm will hang l and useless

Limping

Ge	32:31	l because of his hip
Jer	31:8	those who are lame and l

Linger

1Sa	25:42	Abigail didn't l
Isa	26:8	content to l in the path sign-posted
Jer	51:6	Don't l and lose your lives
Ro	13:14	Don't loiter and l

Listener

2Ti	2:24	a gentle l and a teacher
Jas	1:22	thinking that you are a l

Listeners

Isa	48:8	You've never been good l to me
Ac	10:44	the Holy Spirit came on the l
	17:32	the l split: Some laughed at him

Listless

Hos	4:3	even the fish in the sea are l
1Co	11:30	many of you even now are l and sick

Liturgical

2Ki	12:13	used for l "extras" (silver chalices
	25:14	bronze-crafted l accessories
1Ch	28:13	caring for the l furnishings
2Ch	24:14	other gold and silver l artifacts
Jer	52:18	bronze-crafted l accessories

Loan

Dt	23:19	interest to your kinsmen on any l
	24:6	millstone as collateral for a l
	24:10	When you make a l of any kind
	24:17	cloak of a widow as security for a l
	28:12	yourself won't have to take out a l
Pr	19:17	Mercy to the needy is a l to God
	20:16	collateral on any l to a stranger
	27:13	collateral on any l to a stranger
Eze	18:16	doesn't refuse to l money
Mt	21:12	kicked over the tables of l sharks
Jn	2:14	The l sharks were also there
	2:15	upending the tables of the l sharks

Loathe

Ps	139:21	I l all this godless arrogance
Eze	20:43	you'll l yourselves

Loathsome

Jer	44:4	this l gutter of gods that I hate
Rev	16:2	L, stinking sores erupted on all
	18:2	garrison of l, carrion birds

Lofty

2Sa	22:4	I sing to God the Praise-L
Ps	18:3	I sing to God, the Praise-L
	75:10	righteous are l green branches
SS	6:12	raptured, carried away by l thoughts

Lonely

Ps	7:15	man-trap down that l stretch of road
Jer	49:25	now how l — bereft, abandoned
1Co	6:17	leaving us more l than ever
2Co	11:27	many a long and l night without sleep

Long-lost

Ps	22:27	L families are falling on their faces
Pr	25:25	a letter from a l friend
Isa	66:20	all your l brothers and sisters

Longing

Dt	28:65	restless heart, l eyes, a homesick
Job	7:2	field hands l for quitting time
	14:15	Homesick with l
Ps	119:81	I'm homesick — l for your salvation
Jer	31:20	my heart bursts with l for him

Longings

Ps	38:9	Lord, my l are sitting in plain sight
SS	7:5	stirrings of desire, l for the heights

Love

Ge	22:2	your dear son Isaaac whom you l
	29:32	a sign that now my husband will l me
	30:15	in exchange for your son's l-apples
	32:10	don't deserve all the l and loyalty
	34:3	fell in l with her and wooed her
	34:8	in l with your daughter
	39:14	He tried to make l to me
Ex	15:13	you led in merciful l
	20:6	who l me and keep my commandments
	21:5	I l my master and my wife
	34:6	so much l, so deeply true
	34:7	loyal in l for a thousand generations
Lev	19:18	L your neighbor as yourself
	19:34	L him like one of your own
Nu	14:18	huge in loyal l
	14:19	the extravagance of your loyal l
Dt	5:10	who l me and keep my commandments
	6:5	L God, your God, with your whole heart
	7:8	He did it out of sheer l
	7:9	loyal l with those who l him
	7:12	keep the covenant of loyal l

	7:13	He will l you, he will bless you
	10:12	l him, serve God, your God
	10:15	ancestors that God fell in l with
	11:1	So l God, your God; guard well his rules
	11:13	l God, your God, and serve him
	11:22	l God, your God, do what he tells you
	13:3	if you totally l him with everything
	19:9	l God, your God, and do what he tells
	30:6	freeing you to l God, your God
	30:16	L God, your God. Walk in his ways
	30:20	l God, your God, listening obediently
	33:3	how you l the people
Jos	22:5	L God, your God, walk in all his ways
	23:11	L God, your God
Jdg	14:16	You hate me. You don't l me
	16:4	fell in l with a woman in the Valley
	16:15	How can you say 'I l you'
Ru	3:10	What a splendid expression of l
1Sa	18:3	out of his deep l for David
	18:20	Michal was in l with David
	20:17	pledge of l and friendship for David
2Sa	1:26	a miracle-wonder, l far exceeding
	7:15	never remove my gracious l from him
	12:24	God had a special l for him
	13:1	Amnon, also David's son, was in l
	13:4	I'm in l with her
	13:15	greater than the l he'd had for her
	19:6	hating those who l you
1Ki	3:6	extravagantly generous in l with David
	10:9	God's l for Israel is behind this
	11:2	Solomon fell in l with them anyway
1Ch	16:34	he is good and his l never quits
	16:41	thanks to God, for his l never quits
	17:13	never remove my gracious l from him
2Ch	5:13	His loyal l goes on forever
	6:42	the l promised to David
	7:3	God is good! His l never quits
	7:6	anthems to the praise and l of God
	9:8	God's l for Israel is behind this
	20:21	thanks to God, His l never quits
Ne	1:5	faithful to those who l him
	9:17	Incredibly patient, with tons of l
	9:32	loyal in covenant and l
	13:22	your great and steadfast l
Est	2:17	The king fell in l with Esther
Job	10:12	gave me life itself, and incredible l
	37:13	discipline or grace or extravagant l
Ps	6:4	if you l me at all, get me out
	18:1	I l you, God — you make me strong
	23:6	Your beauty and l chase after me
	25:6	your mercy and l, God
	25:7	Mark me with your sign of l
	26:3	So I never lose sight of your l
	26:8	God, I l living with you
	30:5	across a lifetime there is only l
	31:7	singing in the circle of your l
	31:16	save me because you l me
	31:21	His l is the wonder of the world
	31:23	L God, all you saints
	33:18	the ones who are looking for his l
	33:22	L us, God, with all you've got
	36:5	God's l is meteoric

L

36:7	How exquisite your l, O God
40:10	didn't hold back pieces of l and truth
40:11	Your l and truth are all that keep
42:8	God promises to l me all day
44:26	If you l us so much, Help us
45:7	You l the right and hate the wrong
48:9	We pondered your l-in-action, God
51:1	Generous in l — God, give grace!
51:17	Heart-shattered lives ready for l
52:3	You l evil more than good
52:4	l malicious gossip, you foul-mouth
57:3	God delivers generous l
57:10	deeper your l, the higher it goes
59:10	God in dependable l shows up on time
59:17	count on you — God, my dependable l
60:5	the one you l best is saved
61:5	welcome among those who know and l you
61:7	Steady L and Good Faith as lookouts
62:12	L to you, Lord God!
63:3	In your generous l I am really living
66:20	he stayed with me, loyal in his l
69:9	I l you more than I can say
69:13	God, answer in l!
69:16	answer me, God, because you l me
70:4	Let all who l your saving way say
77:8	Is his l worn threadbare?
79:13	the ones you l and care for
85:7	Show us how much you l us, God!
85:10	L and Truth meet in the street
86:13	what l! You snatched me from the brink
86:15	not easily angered, immense in l
86:17	Make a show of how much you l me
88:11	Does your l make any difference
89:1	Your l, God, is my song
89:2	telling the story of your l
89:14	L and Truth are its fruits
89:24	I'll l him forever
89:28	I'll preserve him eternally in my l
89:49	where is the l you're so famous for
90:14	Surprise us with l at daybreak
92:2	announce your l each daybreak
94:18	your l, God, took hold and held me
97:10	God loves . . . And those who l
98:3	He remembered to l us
100:5	all-generous in l, loyal always
101:1	My theme song is God's l and justice
102:14	your servants l this city's rubble
103:4	He crowns you with l and mercy
103:8	not easily angered, he's rich in l
103:11	strong is his l
103:17	God's l, though, is ever and always
106:1	because his l lasts
106:7	your great and wonderful l
106:45	immense with l, took them by the hand
107:1	His l never runs out
107:8	thank God for his marvelous l
107:15	thank God for his marvelous l
107:21	thank God for his marvelous l
107:31	thank God for his marvelous l
107:43	time you appreciated God's deep l
108:4	The deeper your l, the higher it goes
108:6	the sake of the one you l so much

109:5	they return my l with hate
109:21	your l is so great
109:26	save me through your wonderful l
111:4	This God of Grace, this God of L
115:1	Do it on account of your merciful l
116:1	I l God because he listened to me
116:15	God welcomes those who l him
117:2	His l has taken over our lives
118:1	because his l never quits
118:2	His l never quits
118:3	His l never quits
118:4	His l never quits
118:29	His l never quits
119:35	I l traveling this freeway
119:41	Let your l, God, shape my life
119:47	your commandments — oh, how I l them
119:64	Your l, God, fills the earth!
119:76	Oh, l me — and right now!
119:88	In your great l revive me
119:97	how I l all you've revealed
119:113	I l your clear-cut revelation
119:124	Let your l dictate how you deal
119:127	I l what you command, I l it better
119:132	to those who personally l you
119:140	I, your servant, l it dearly
119:149	In your l, listen to me
119:159	how I l what you tell me
119:163	I l what you have revealed
119:165	those who l what you reveal
119:167	how much I l them
119:174	I l it when you show yourself
130:7	with God's arrival comes l
136:1	His l never quits
136:2	His l never quits
136:3	His l never quits
136:4	His l never quits
136:5	His l never quits
136:6	His l never quits
136:7	His l never quits
136:8	His l never quits
136:9	His l never quits
136:10	His l never quits
136:11	His l never quits
136:12	His l never quits
136:13	His l never quits
136:14	His l never quits
136:15	His l never quits
136:16	His l never quits
136:17	His l never quits
136:18	His l never quits
136:19	His l never quits
136:20	His l never quits
136:21	His l never quits
136:22	His l never quits
136:23	His l never quits
136:24	His l never quits
136:25	His l never quits
136:26	His l never quits
138:2	Thank you for your l
138:8	Your l is eternal
143:12	In your great l, vanquish my enemies
145:8	not quick to anger, is rich in l

L

	145:17	the trademark on all his works is l
	145:20	God sticks by all who l him
	148:14	Praise from all who l God
	149:1	in the company of all who l him
	149:9	all who l God in the seat of honor
Pr	3:3	Don't lose your grip on L and Loyalty
	4:6	Wisdom — she guards your life; l her
	7:18	Come, let's make l all night
	8:17	I l those who l me
	8:21	Handing out life to those who l me
	9:8	they'll l you for it
	10:12	l pulls a quilt over the bickering
	12:1	l learning, you l the discipline
	13:24	refusal to correct is a refusal to l
	13:24	l your children by disciplining
	14:22	the thoughtful win l and trust
	15:17	Better a bread crust shared in l
	16:6	Guilt is banished through l and truth
	16:13	l advisors who tell them the truth
	17:17	Friends l through all kinds of weather
	20:3	fools l to pick fights
	20:28	L and truth form a good leader
	21:10	Wicked souls l to make trouble
	23:23	don't sell it for l or money
	28:4	if you l God's law, you fight for it
	29:3	l wisdom, you'll delight your parents
Ecc	3:5	A right time to make l and another
	3:8	A right time to l and another to hate
	9:1	whether it's l or hate they're dealing
	9:9	Relish life with the spouse you l
SS	1:2	your l is better than wine
	1:7	I l you so much
	2:5	I'm about to faint with l
	2:7	Don't excite l, don't stir it up
	3:3	Have you seen my dear lost l
	3:4	found my dear lost l
	3:5	Don't excite l, don't stir it up
	4:7	beautiful from head to toe, my dear l
	4:9	You looked at me, and I fell in l
	4:10	How beautiful your l, dear
	4:11	your lips are honey, my l
	6:1	where has this l of yours gone
	6:13	victory dances of l and peace
	7:9	my l's kisses flow from his lips
	7:12	give myself to you, my l to your l
	7:13	L-apples drench us with fragrance
	8:4	Don't excite l, don't stir it up
	8:6	L is invincible facing danger
	8:7	Flood waters can't drown l
sa	5:1	ballad to the one I l, a l ballad
	16:5	new government of l will be
	26:11	your zealous l for your people
	40:6	their l fragile as wildflowers
	43:4	That's how much I l you!
	48:14	I, God, l this man Cyrus
	54:8	lasting l that I'm tenderly caring
	54:10	My l won't walk away from you
	55:3	sure, solid, enduring l
	58:2	busy at worship, and l studying
	61:8	I, God, l fair dealing
	63:7	Compassion lavished, l extravagant
	63:9	Out of his own l and pity he redeemed

	66:10	all who l her, celebrate
Jer	2:2	our l as newlyweds
	3:12	I'm committed in l to you
	5:31	And my people l it
	9:24	I'm God, and I act in loyal l
	11:15	What business do the ones I l have
	12:7	I will turn over those I most l
	16:5	No more loyal l on my part
	31:3	Expect l, l, and more l
	32:18	You're loyal in your steadfast l
	33:11	His l never quits
La	3:22	God's loyal l couldn't have run out
	3:32	His stockpiles of loyal l are immense
Eze	13:19	people who l listening to lies
	16:8	you were ready for l and a lover
	33:32	sad l songs, playing a guitar. They l
Da	9:4	never give up on those who l you
Hos	2:19	in l and tenderness
	3:1	Start all over: L your wife again
	3:5	the End of the story of his l
	4:18	sordid debauchery — how they l it
	6:4	declarations of l last no longer than
	6:6	I'm after l that lasts
	9:15	I'm wasting no more l on them
	10:12	Sow righteousness, reap l
	12:6	Commit yourself in l, in justice!
	12:7	They l to rip people off
	14:4	I will l them lavishly
Joel	2:13	most patient God, extravagant in l
Am	4:5	show you Israelites just l
	5:15	Hate evil and l good
Jnh	2:8	walk away from their only true l
	4:2	not easily angered, rich in l
Mic	6:8	be compassionate and loyal in your l
	7:18	That's what you l most
Zep	3:17	calm you with his l and delight you
Zec	7:9	L your neighbors. Be compassionate
	8:19	Embrace truth! L peace
Mal	1:2	God said, "I l you."
	2:11	the holiness of God by falling in l
Mt	3:17	my Son, chosen and marked by my l
	5:43	old written law, 'L your friend,'
	5:44	I'm telling you to l your enemies
	5:46	If all you do is l the lovable
	6:4	God, who conceived you in l
	7:11	God who conceived you in l
	10:22	proclaiming so much l
	12:18	my handpicked servant; I l him so much
	17:5	This is my Son, marked by my l
	18:17	offer again God's forgiving l
	19:19	l your neighbor as you do yourself
	22:37	L the Lord your God
	22:39	L others as well as you l yourself
	23:6	They l to sit at the head table
	24:12	nothing left of their l but . . . ashes
Mk	1:11	my Son, chosen and marked by my l
	9:7	This is my Son, marked by my l
	12:30	l the Lord God with all your passion
	12:31	L others as well as you l yourself
	12:33	loving others as well as you l
	12:38	l to walk around in academic gowns
Lk	3:22	my Son, chosen and marked by my l

	6:27	L your enemies		2:8	My counsel now is to pour on the l
	6:32	If you only l the lovable		6:6	gentleness, holiness, and honest l
	6:35	I tell you, l your enemies		8:7	you're passionate, you l us
	10:27	l the Lord your God		8:8	enthusiasm as a stimulus to your l
	11:13	Father who conceived you in l		8:24	the l I've been talking up
	11:42	matters of justice and God's l		11:3	simple purity of your l for Christ
	11:43	You l sitting at the head table		11:11	It's not that I don't l you
	16:13	hate the first and l the second		12:15	the more I l you, the less I'm loved
	20:46	l to walk around in academic gowns		13:11	God of l and peace will be with you
Jn	5:42	know that I, especially God's l		13:14	the extravagant l of God
	8:42	you would l me, for I came from God	Gal	5:6	faith expressed in l
	11:3	the one you l so very much is sick		5:13	serve one another in l
	12:25	let it go, reckless in your l		5:14	L others as you l yourself
	13:34	a new command: L one another		5:20	impotence to l or be loved
	13:35	see the l you have for each other	Eph	1:4	settled on us as the focus of his l
	14:15	If you l me, show it		1:15	Jesus and your outpouring of l to all
	14:31	how thoroughly I l the Father		2:4	mercy and with an incredible l
	15:9	Make yourselves at home in my l		3:17	both feet planted firmly on l
	15:10	intimately at home in my l		3:18	extravagant dimensions of Christ's l
	15:12	L one another the way I loved you		4:2	out for each other in acts of l
	15:13	This is the very best way to l		4:15	know the whole truth and tell it in l
	15:17	the root command: L one another		4:16	grow up healthy in God, robust in l
	15:19	would l you as one of its own		5:2	Mostly what God does is l you
	16:27	committed yourselves to l and trust		5:3	Don't allow l to turn into lust
	17:26	your l for me Might be in them		5:4	tongues just l the taste of gossip
	21:15	do you l me more than these		5:25	go all out in your l for your wives
	21:16	Simon, son of John, do you l me		5:26	Christ's l makes the church whole
	21:16	Yes, Master, you know I l you		5:28	how husbands ought to l their wives
	21:17	Simon, son of John, do you l me		6:23	L mixed with faith be yours from God
Ro	1:9	God, whom I so l to worship and serve		6:24	grace be with all who l our Master
	1:27	all lust, no l	Php	1:8	He knows how much I l and miss you
	5:8	God put his l on the line for us		1:9	my prayer: that your l will flourish
	8:28	our lives of l for God		1:10	your l is sincere and intelligent
	8:29	shape the lives of those who l him		1:16	One group is motivated by pure l
	8:35	wedge between us and Christ's l for us		2:1	if his l has made any difference
	8:39	nothing can get between us and God's l		2:2	Agree with each other, l each other
	12:9	L from the center of who you are		4:1	I l you so much
	12:10	Be good friends who l deeply	Col	1:4	l you continuously extend to all
	13:8	huge debt of l you owe each other		1:8	l had been worked into your lives
	13:9	L other people as well as		2:2	want you woven into a tapestry of l
	13:10	can't go wrong when you l others		3:12	chosen by God for this new life of l
	14:15	no longer a companion with them in l		3:14	wear l
	14:21	interfere with the free exchange of l		3:19	go all out in l for your wives
	15:30	through the l of the Spirit	1Th	1:3	your work of faith, your labor of l
1Co	2:9	God has arranged for those who l him		3:6	report on your faith and l
	4:14	I l you and want you to grow up well		3:12	may the Master pour on the l
	6:18	God-given and God-modeled l		4:9	Just l one another
	7:17	Live and obey and l and believe		5:8	faith, l, and the hope of salvation
	11:34	a spiritual meal — a l feast		5:13	Overwhelm them with appreciation and l
	13:1	but don't l, I'm nothing	2Th	1:3	your l for each other is developing
	13:2	but I don't l, I'm nothing		2:16	God our Father, who reached out in l
	13:3	but I don't l, I've gotten nowhere		3:5	path of God's l and Christ's endurance
	13:4	L never gives up.	1Ti	1:5	l — uncontaminated by self-interest
	13:4	L cares more for others than for self		1:14	Grace mixed with faith and l
	13:8	L never dies.		2:15	continue in faith, l, and holiness
	13:13	hope unswervingly, l extravagantly		4:12	by demeanor, by l, by faith
	14:1	Go after a life of l		6:11	life of wonder, faith, l, steadiness
	14:5	access to the knowledge and l of God	2Ti	1:2	Timothy, the son I l so much
	16:14	l without stopping		1:13	this faith and l rooted in Christ
	16:22	If anyone won't l the Master		2:22	mature righteousness — faith, l, peace
	16:24	I l all of you in the Messiah		3:10	faith, steadiness, l, patience
2Co	2:4	more than care — l you	Tit	2:2	healthy faith, l, and endurance

	2:4	will know how to l their husbands		25:28	Isaaac l Esau because he l his game
Phm	1:5	l and faith you have for the Master		25:28	but Rebekah l Jacob
	1:7	how good your l makes me feel		27:14	the kind his father l so much
Heb	1:9	You l it when things are right		29:18	And it was Rachel that Jacob l
	6:10	all the l you've shown him		29:20	he l her so much
	10:24	inventive we can be in encouraging l		29:30	And he l Rachel more than Leah
	13:1	held together by l		37:3	Israel l Joseph more than any
Jas	1:12	persons loyally in l with God		37:4	realized that their father l him more
	2:8	L others as you l yourself	Dt	4:37	He l your ancestors and chose
	4:6	what he gives in l is far better		21:15	two wives, one l and the other hated
1Pe	1:8	You never saw him, yet you l him		21:16	must not treat the son of the l wife
	1:22	following the truth, l one another	1Sa	1:5	Hannah because he l her so much
	2:17	L your spiritual family.		18:16	everyone else . . . l David
	4:8	Most of all, l each other		18:16	They l watching him
2Pc	1:7	warm friendliness, and generous l		18:28	his own daughter, Michal, l him
	1:17	This is my Son, marked by my l		20:17	He l David more than his own soul
1Jn	2:5	in whom we see God's mature l	2Sa	14:2	grieving over a dead l one
	2:15	Don't l the world's ways		22:20	saved — surprised to be l
	2:15	Don't l the world's goods. L of the world	1Ki	3:3	Solomon l God
	2:15	L of the world		5:1	Hiram had l David his whole life
	3:1	What marvelous l the Father has		11:1	many foreign women he l
	3:10	one who won't l brother or sister	2Ch	11:21	favorite wife; he l her more
	3:11	We should l each other		26:10	he l growing things
	3:14	l our brothers and sisters	Ne	13:26	God l him and made him king
	3:16	come to understand and experience l	Job	19:19	my dearest l ones reject me
	3:17	what happens to God's l?	Ps	18:19	saved — surprised to be l
	3:18	let's not just talk about l		32:10	God-affirmers find themselves l
	3:18	let's practice real l		109:4	l l them and now they slander me
	3:23	He told us to l each other		109:17	Since he l cursing so much
	4:7	l each other since l comes from God	SS	5:6	My l one had tired of waiting
	4:8	person who refuses to l doesn't know	Isa	40:10	reward those who have l him
	4:9	This is how God showed his l for us		57:8	whores and l every minute of it
	4:10	the kind of l we are talking about	Jer	6:12	all they own, even their l ones
	4:12	if we l one another, God dwells deeply		14:10	Since they l to wander this way
	4:17	This way, l has the run of the house	La	2:22	The children l l and reared
	4:18	no room in l for fear	Eze	16:37	ones you l and the ones you loathed
	4:18	Well-formed l banishes		35:6	Since you l blood so much
	4:19	are going to l — l and be loved	Da	9:23	You are much l!
	4:20	If anyone boasts, "I l God,"	Hus	10:11	a trained heifer that l to thresh
	4:21	You've got to l both		11:1	When Israel was only a child, I l him
	5:1	we l the One who conceives the child	Mal	1:2	"Really? How have you l us?"
	5:2	whether or not we l God's children		1:5	how faithfully I've l you
	5:3	The proof that we l God comes	Mk	10:21	looked him hard in the eye — and l him
2Jn	1:1	I, your pastor, l you in very truth	Jn	3:16	This is how much God l the world
	1:3	in truth and l from God the Father		11:5	Jesus l Martha and her sister
	1:5	basic charter: that we l each other		11:36	Look how deeply he l him
	1:6	L means following his commandments		11:37	if he l him so much, why didn't he
3Jn	1:1	How truly I l you		13:1	Having l his dear companions
	1:6	a message about your l		13:23	the one Jesus l dearly
Jude	1:2	open your hearts, l is on the way		13:34	In the same way I l you, you love
	1:12	are warts on your l feasts		14:21	who loves me will be l by my Father
	1:21	at the center of God's l		14:28	If you l me, you would be glad
Rev	2:4	you walked away from your first l		15:9	I've l you the way my Father has l me
	2:5	Recover your dear early l		15:12	Love one another the way I l you
	2:19	Impressive! The l and the faith		17:23	l them In the same way you've l me
	3:19	The people I l, I call to account		17:24	Having l me Long before
	12:11	They weren't in l with themselves		19:26	the disciple he l standing near her
	22:15	all who l and live lies		20:2	the other disciple, the one Jesus l
				21:7	the disciple Jesus l said to Peter
Loved				21:20	the disciple Jesus l following
e	24:67	she became his wife and he l her	Ro	9:13	I l Jacob; I hated Esau
			2Co	12:15	the more I love you, the less I'm l

Gal	2:20	Son of God, who l me and gave himself
	5:20	impotence to love or be l
Eph	5:2	Observe how Christ l us
1Th	2:8	We l you dearly
2Th	2:13	so l by God! God picked you out
Heb	11:35	their l ones back from the dead
1Jn	4:10	not that we once upon a time l God
	4:10	but that he l us and sent
	4:11	if God l us like this
	4:19	are going to love — love and be l
	4:19	First we were l, now we love
Jude	1:1	writing to those l by God the Father
Rev	3:9	to acknowledge it's you that I've l

Loveless

Jn	14:23	a l world," said Jesus

Lover

Ps	38:20	God-haters who can't stand a God-l
	88:18	made l and neighbor alike dump me
	99:4	Strong King, l of justice
Pr	27:6	The wounds from a l are worth it
SS	1:4	An elopement with my King-L!
	1:12	When my King-L lay down beside me
	1:13	head of my l was a sachet
	1:16	my dear l — you're so handsome
	2:3	my l stands above the young men
	2:8	Look! Listen! There's my l!
	2:9	My l is like a gazelle, graceful
	2:10	My l has arrived and he's speaking
	2:13	my fair and beautiful l
	2:16	My l is mine, and I am his
	2:17	Turn to me, dear l
	3:1	I longed for my l
	3:2	I wanted my l in the worst way
	3:11	My King-L, dressed and garlanded
	4:12	l and friend, you're a secret garden
	4:16	let my l enter his garden
	5:1	went to my garden, dear friend, best l
	5:2	It's the sound of my l knocking
	5:4	my l wouldn't take no for an answer
	5:5	I got up to open the door to my l
	5:8	if you find my l, Please tell him
	5:9	What's so great about your l
	5:10	My dear l glows with health
	5:16	That's my l, that's my man
	6:2	My l is already on his way
	6:3	I am my l's and my l is mine
	6:4	friend and l, you're as beautiful
	7:6	absolute, dear l, close companion
	7:10	I am my l's. I'm all he wants
	7:11	Come, dear l — let's tramp
	8:5	arm in arm with her l
	8:10	when my l sees me, he knows
	8:14	Run to me, dear l
Isa	44:20	This l of emptiness, of nothing
Jer	3:2	You've solicited many l-gods
Eze	16:8	you were ready for love and a l
	16:36	stripped down for every l

Php	1:10	Live a l's life
Jas	4:5	he's a fiercely jealous l

Lovers

Jdg	5:31	while his l be like the unclouded sun
2Ki	9:37	Old friends and l will say
Ps	69:36	The l of his name will live in it
	122:6	Prosperity to all you Jerusalem-l
·	149:5	Let true l break out in praise
La	1:2	No one's left among her l
Eze	16:32	husbands accept gifts from their l
	16:33	But you pay your l!
	16:37	going to get all your l together
	16:39	I'll gather all your l around you
	16:41	no more paying l to come to your bed
	23:5	lusted after Assyrians as l
	23:9	left her to her Assyrian l
	23:20	virile, vulgar, and violent l
	23:22	I will incite your old l against you
	23:22	l you got tired of
Hos	2:5	I'm off to see my l!
	2:7	on the hunt for her l
	2:10	her fly-by-night l will be helpless
	2:13	stalking her l, dressed to kill
	8:9	goes out and pays to get l
Mic	3:2	Haters of good, l of evil

Loves

Ge	27:9	meal, the kind that your father l
	44:20	his father l him more than anything
Dt ·	15:16	your slave, because he l you
	23:5	how God, your God, l you
Ru	2:20	He still l us, in bad times
	4:15	brought him into the world and l you
1Sa	18:22	everyone at court l you
1Ki	8:23	relentlessly l them
2Ch	2:11	It's plain that God l his people
	6:14	unfailingly l them
Ps	11:7	he l getting the lines straight
	21:7	Is it any wonder the king l God
	33:5	He l it when everything fits
	37:28	God l this kind of thing
	78:68	Mount Zion, which he l so much
	85:8	The holy people he l so much
	87:2	God l his home! L it far better
	97:10	God l all who hate evil
	107:8	his miracle mercy to the children he l
	107:15	his miracle mercy to the children he l
	107:21	his miracle mercy to the children he l
	107:31	his miracle mercy to the children he l
	127:2	he enjoys giving rest to those he l
	146:8	God l good people
Pr	3:12	It's the child he l that God corrects
	11:1	he l it when business is aboveboard
	12:22	he l the company of those who keep
	14:20	everyone l a winner
	15:9	he l those who run straight
	22:11	God l the pure-hearted and well-spoken
Ecc	5:10	who l money is never satisfied
	9:6	Their l, their hates

SS	1:3	everyone l to say your name
	1:4	Everyone l you — of course
Hos	4:1	No one is faithful. No one l
Mal	2:17	God l sinners and sin alike. God l all
Lk	7:5	He l our people
Jn	3:35	The Father l the Son extravagantly
	5:20	The Father l the Son
	10:17	This is why the Father l me
	14:21	who l me. And the person who l me
	14:23	If anyone l me, he will carefully
	16:27	the Father l you directly
Ro	8:37	because Jesus l us
2Co	9:7	God l it when the giver delights
Col	1:13	kingdom of the Son he l so much
1Th	1:4	God not only l you very much
Heb	12:6	the child he l that he disciplines
Jas	1:5	pray to the Father. He l to help
	2:5	is promised to anyone who l God
1Jn	2:10	the person who l brother and sister
	4:7	Everyone who l is born of God
2Jn	1:2	permanent residence in us l you
3Jn	1:9	Diotrephes, who l being in charge
Rev	1:5	Glory and strength to Christ, who l us

Lowly

Ps	72:2	be honorable to your meek and l
Isa	35:7	Even l jackals will have water
	41:14	Do you feel like a l worm, Jacob
Da	10:17	How can I, a l servant, speak to you

Loyalty

Ge	32:10	don't deserve all the love and l
1Ch	29:24	as their king and promised their l
Ps	36:5	love is meteoric, his l astronomic
	50:5	who swore on the Bible their l to me
Pr	3:3	Don't lose your grip on Love and L
Jer	2:2	I remember your youthful l
Eze	17:13	making him swear his l
	17:16	king who broke his pledge of l

Luck

1Sa	9:4	they went over to Shaalim — no l
	22:2	all who were down on their l came
2Ki	14:10	Why press your l?
1Ch	7:23	because of the bad l
2Ch	25:19	Why press your l?
Est	6:13	your bad l has only begun
Job	21:18	How often are they blown away by bad l
	29:12	for those who were down on their l
	31:29	Or gloat over my rival's bad l
Ps	25:22	a break From this run of bad l
	41:1	those who are down on their l
	72:12	destitute who have run out of l
	73:14	A long run of bad l
	77:10	Just my l," I said
	90:10	with l we might make it to eighty
	116:10	despite a ton of bad l
	145:14	a hand to those down on their l
Pr	3:34	if you're down on your l

	19:7	When you're down on your l
Ecc	5:13	Here's a piece of bad l I've seen
	5:16	This is bad l, for sure
	7:17	don't press your l by being bad
	9:11	Sooner or later bad l hits us all
Isa	13:15	But tough l to stragglers
	65:11	hold dinners for Lady L
Jer	3:20	But no l. Like a false-hearted woman
	44:17	standard of living, and no bad l
	46:17	nickname Pharaoh 'Big-Talk-Bad-L
Lk	19:6	hardly believing his good l
	22:5	couldn't believe their good l
Ac	18:6	But no such l

Lust

Ps	4:2	How long will you l after lies
	34:12	Who out there has a l for life
	68:30	Rapacious in her l for silver
Pr	11:6	crooks get trapped in their sinful l
	27:20	l just never quits
Isa	57:5	You satisfy your l any place
Eze	6:9	voracious l for gratifying themselves
	23:7	Her l was unrestrained
	23:8	spent their l on her
	23:9	she was so obsessed with l
	23:11	even worse than her sister in l
	23:12	went crazy with l for Assyrians
	23:16	she went wild with l
	23:20	stallions obsessive in their l
	23:29	Your sluttish l
	23:30	Your l has brought you to this
Hos	7:6	red-hot with l
Mt	5:28	heart can be corrupted by l
	12:39	satisfy your l for miracles
Lk	11:29	satisfy your l for miracles
	16:18	divorce as a cover for l is adultery
Ac	8:23	you reek with money-l
Ro	1:27	all l, no love
Eph	5:3	Don't allow love to turn into l
Col	3:5	promiscuity, impurity, l
1Ti	6:10	L for money brings trouble
2Ti	3:4	addicted to l, and allergic to God
Jas	1:14	seducing flare-up of our own l
	1:15	L gets pregnant, and has a baby: sin
	4:2	You l for what you don't have
2Pe	1:4	on a world corrupted by l
	2:10	these "teachers" who live by l
Rev	17:2	earth dwellers drunk on her whorish l
	19:2	corrupted the earth with her l

Lying

Ge	4:7	sin is l in wait for you
Ex	23:5	l helpless under its load
Dt	21:1	has given you, l out in the open
Ru	3:7	l down at the end of a stack of barley
2Sa	20:12	Amasa was l in a pool of blood
1Ki	13:18	But the man was l
2Ki	10:19	Jehu was l, of course
2Ch	32:11	he's l — you're all going to
Job	13:7	are you going to keep on l

L

	24:2	stealing and l and cheating
Ps	34:13	no more l through your teeth
	43:1	away from these l degenerates
	50:19	l is a serious art form with you
	109:2	Their l tongues are like a pack
Pr	7:10	she'd been l in wait for him
	21:6	Make it to the top by l and cheating
	21:28	A l witness is unconvincing
Isa	9:15	the l prophets were the tail
Jer	23:10	what God says regarding the l prophets
	27:15	both you and the l prophets
	48:15	young soldiers are l dead right now
Eze	13:6	preach l sermons
	16:6	l there helpless and filthy
Da	2:28	dream you had when you were l
Hos	4:2	All this cussing and l and killing
Zec	13:4	l prophets will be publicly exposed
Mt	24:11	l preachers will come forward
	24:24	Fake Messiahs and l preachers
Mk	13:22	Fake Messiahs and l preachers
Lk	2:12	wrapped in a blanket and l in a manger
	2:16	the baby l in the manger
	4:13	l in wait for another opportunity
	18:20	no stealing, no l
Jn	8:44	makes it up out of his l nature
	20:5	pieces of linen cloth l there
	20:6	observed the linen cloths l there
	20:7	not l with the linen cloths
Ac	23:21	forty men l in ambush for him
Ro	1:18	wrongdoing and l accumulate
	3:4	whole world is l through its teeth
	8:1	continuous, low-l black cloud
1Co	2:7	don't find it l around on the surface
2Co	11:13	pseudo-apostles, l preachers
	11:31	Master Jesus knows I'm not l
Eph	4:25	you end up l to yourself
1Th	4:12	not l around sponging off your friends
Heb	3:12	no evil unbelief l around
2Pe	2:1	there were also l prophets
1Jn	1:6	obviously l through our teeth
	2:22	So who is l here?
	4:1	There are a lot of l preachers loose

M

Mad

1Sa	13:4	stirred up and **m** as hornets
2Ki	5:12	He stomped off, **m** as a hornet
Job	16:14	charging me like a **m** bull
Pr	19:12	Mean-tempered leaders are like **m** dogs
	20:2	Quick-tempered leaders are like **m** dogs
	26:17	You grab a **m** dog by the ears
Da	8:7	**m** with rage, it charged the ram
Hab	3:8	God, is it River you're **m** at
Ac	17:5	**M** with jealousy, they rounded up
Rev	16:10	**M** with pain, men and women bit

Magic

Nu	23:23	No **m** spells can bind Jacob
2Ki	17:17	black arts of **m** and sorcery

	21:6	practiced black **m** and fortunetelling
Eze	13:18	women who sew **m** bracelets
	13:21	I'll rip your **m** bracelets and scarves
Da	1:4	lore of **m** and fortunetelling
Mic	5:12	underworld traffic in black **m**
Mt	12:24	"Black **m**," they said.
Mk	3:22	rumors that he was working black **m**
Lk	11:15	"Black **m**," they said
Ac	8:9	had practiced **m** in the city
Gal	5:20	trinket gods; **m**-show religion
Rev	13:14	used the **m** it got from the Beast
	18:23	by black-**m** arts deceived the nations

Magician

Isa	47:15	your **m** buddies you've been in cahoots
Da	2:10	demanded anything like this from any **m**
	2:27	no wise man, enchanter, **m**, diviner

Magicians

Ge	41:8	sent for all the **m** and sages of Egypt
	41:24	told all this to the **m** but they can't
Ex	7:11	The **m** of Egypt did the same thing
	7:22	the **m** of Egypt did the same thing
	8:7	again the **m** did the same thing
	8:18	The **m** tried to produce gnats
	8:19	**m** said . . . "This is God's doing
	9:11	**m** weren't able to compete with Moses
Isa	44:25	makes the **m** look ridiculous
Da	1:20	ten times better than all the **m**
	2:2	called in all the Babylonian **m**
	4:7	all assembled — **m**, enchanters
	4:9	Belteshazzar,' I said, 'chief of the **m**
	5:11	head of all the **m**, enchanters

Maimed

2Sa	4:4	son who was **m** in both feet
Ps	9:16	made by the wicked has **m** their own
Zep	3:19	I'll heal the **m**
Mt	15:30	the blind, the **m**, the mute
	15:31	saw the mutes speaking, the **m** healthy
	18:8	better off **m** or lame and alive
Mk	9:43	better off **m** or lame and alive

Majestic

Ex	15:10	like a lead weight in the **m** waters
Nu	24:7	their kingdom surpassingly **m**
Dt	7:21	God **m**, God awesome
Ne	9:32	the great God, God **m** and terrible
Job	37:4	echoes his voice, powerful and **m**
Ps	48:1	God **m**, praise abounds in our God-city
	99:2	God looms **m** in Zion
Isa	33:21	God **m**, God himself the place
	35:2	on display. God awesome, God **m**
Jer	11:16	mighty oak tree, **m** and glorious
Eze	17:23	a **m** cedar
2Pe	1:17	God the Father as the voice of **M** Glory
Rev	21:12	a wall **m** and high with twelve gates

Majestically

Ps	45:3	Ride **m**! Ride triumphantly
	113:5	God, our God, so **m** enthroned

Majesty

Ex	15:7	In your mighty **m** you smash
	15:11	compares with you in power, in holy **m**
2Ki	6:26	A woman cried out, "Help! Your **m**
	19:15	seated in **m** on the cherubim-throne
1Ch	16:27	Splendor and **m** flow out of him
	29:11	the victory, the **m**, the splendor
Isa	24:14	they'll shout of God's **m**
Eze	31:7	stunning in its **m**
Da	2:7	please your **m**, tell us the dream
	4.22	Your royal **m** reaches sky-high
	4:36	given back my **m** and splendor
Mic	5:4	centered in the **m** of God-Revealed
Ac	25:21	demanded a hearing before His **M**
Jude	1:25	our Master, be glory, **m**, strength

Maker

2Ki	19:15	**M** of heaven, **m** of earth
Job	32:22	my **M** would make short work of me
	36:3	justice I owe to my **M** himself
Ps	5:5	shake your head over Mischief-**M**
	65:6	Mountain-**M**, Hill-Dresser
	94:9	Do you think Ear-**M** doesn't hear
	110:7	The King-**M** put his King on the throne
Pr	14:31	You insult your **M** when you exploit
Isa	45:9	doom to you who fight your **M**
	45:11	God, The Holy of Israel, Israel's **M**
	45:18	he is, remember, God. **M** of earth
	54:5	For your **M** is your bridegroom
Hos	8:14	Israel has forgotten his **M**
Am	4:13	Mountain-Shaper! Wind-**M**! He laid out
Hab	2:18	pious god-**m** who makes gods that can't
Zec	10:1	Spring thunderstorm **m**, **m** of
Rev	14:7	Worship the **M** of Heaven and earth

Makers

Isa	44:11	the no-god **m** slink off humiliated
	45:16	the **m** of no-god idols won't know
Jer	10:14	god-**m** embarrassed by their handmade
	51:17	god-**m** embarrassed by their handmade

Malice

Ge	49:23	The archers with **m** attacked
Ps	49:5	bad times, hemmed in by enemy **m**
Pr	19:28	the mouths of the wicked spew **m**
	26:26	how cunningly he conceals his **m**
	26:27	**M** backfires; spite boomerangs
Isa	59:13	pregnant with lies, muttering **m**
La	3:62	dreaming up mischief, hatching out **m**
Eze	25:15	all those centuries of stored-up **m**
1Pe	2:1	Make a clean sweep of **m** and pretense

Malicious

Ex	23:1	Don't pass on **m** gossip
Ps	52:4	You love **m** gossip, you foul-mouth
	74:23	Don't tune out their **m** filth
	92:11	the rout of my **m** detractors
Pr	17:4	Evil people relish **m** conversation
	29:12	When a leader listens to **m** gossip
Jer	9:4	Friend against friend spreads **m** gossip
Eze	25:6	venting all your **m** contempt

Maliciously

2Sa	18:32	all who **m** rose against you end up
Ps	119:23	bad neighbors **m** gossip about me

Manage

Dt	16:17	must bring as much as he can **m**
Jdg	1:18	But Judah didn't **m** to capture Gaza
2Ch	2:2	foremen to **m** the workforce
	2:18	foremen to **m** the work crews
Ps	12:4	Our lips **m** the world
Pr	23:35	When I'm sober enough to **m** it
	30:26	**m** to arrange for rock-solid homes
Mt	6:6	simply and honestly as you can **m**
Lk	11:42	**m** to find loopholes for getting around
1Co	7:9	if they can't **m** their desires
Gal	2:12	as much distance as he could **m**
1Ti	5:14	have children, **m** their homes
	6:17	all the riches we could ever **m**

Managed

Jdg	1:27	Manasseh never **m** to drive out
	9:5	**m** to hide, the only survivor
2Sa	15:12	he **m** also to involve Ahithophel
1Ki	4:19	he **m** the whole district by himself
2Ch	26:21	Jotham, who **m** the royal palace
	34:12	these **m** the project
Jer	44:14	None of those who **m** to get out
Ac	27:16	**m** to get a lifeboat ready
	27:17	only **m** to avoid them by throwing

Manager

Ge	37:36	**m** of his household affairs
	39:1	the **m** of his household
1Ki	4:6	Ahishar — **m** of the palace
	16:9	the house of Arza the palace **m**
Mt	20:1	God's kingdom is like an estate **m**
	20:3	**m** saw some other men hanging around
	20:11	they groused angrily to the **m**
Lk	8:3	Joanna, wife of Chuza, Herod's **m**
	12:42	Who is the dependable **m**
	16:1	was once a rich man who had a **m**
	16:1	He got reports that the **m** had
	16:3	The **m** said to himself
	16:6	**m** said, 'Here, take your bill
	16:8	The master praised the crooked **m**!

M

Managers

Ge	41:34	Pharaoh needs to appoint **m**
1Ki	4:5	in charge of the regional **m**
	4:7	Solomon had twelve regional **m**
	4:27	The district **m**, each according
	9:23	were also the project **m** responsible
2Ki	12:11	the **m** of The Temple project
2Ch	8:10	were also the project **m** responsible
	24:12	the **m** of The Temple project
	31:13	were project **m** under the direction
	34:13	served as accountants, **m**
	34:17	handed it over to the **m** and workers
Jer	48:7	hauled off, his priests and **m** with him
	49:3	all his priests and **m** right with him

Manages

Am	3:12	**M** to recover just a pair of legs
Jas	1:12	challenge head-on and **m** to stick it

Managing

Ge	39:22	ended up **m** the whole operation
1Ki	5:16	foremen **m** the project
2Ki	22:5	foremen who are **m** the work
2Ch	34:10	foremen **m** the work on The Temple

Manger

Lk	2:7	and laid him in a **m**
	2:12	wrapped in a blanket and lying in a **m**
	2:16	and the baby lying in the **m**

Manipulate

Mt	5:37	you **m** words to get your own way
Ro	12:8	if you're put in charge, don't **m**
2Co	4:2	don't maneuver and **m** behind the scenes
Gal	1:10	speak this strongly . . . to **m** crowds

Manipulation

2Co	10:4	aren't for marketing or **m**

Manipulative

2Co	1:23	not indifferent, not **m**

Manners

Ps	77:9	Has God forgotten his **m**?
Pr	23:1	mind your **m**
Ecc	8:1	gives gentleness to words and **m**
Ro	14:4	If there are . . . or **m** to be learned
1Co	10:27	both bad **m** and bad spirituality
	14:35	God's Book of the law guides our **m**
	15:33	Bad company ruins good **m**

Marauders

2Sa	22:30	I smash the bands of **m**

Ps	18:29	I smash the bands of **m**
Mal	3:11	I will defend you against **m**

Marble

Est	1:6	silver rings on **m** columns
Pr	26:8	like setting a mud brick on a **m** column
Mt	23:29	**m** monuments for your saints
Rev	18:12	precious woods, bronze, iron, and **m**

Marketplace

Pr	11:1	God hates cheating in the **m**
	20:23	God hates cheating in the **m**
SS	8:7	it's not to be found in the **m**
Mk	6:56	brought their sick to the **m**
2Ti	2:4	caught up in making deals at the **m**

Marriage

Ge	29:21	I'm ready to consummate my **m**
	29:23	Leah and brought her to the **m** bed
	29:25	There was Leah in the **m** bed
	34:6	went . . . to work out **m** arrangements
	34:16	freely exchange daughters in **m**
	34:21	even exchange our daughters in **m**
	46:20	from his **m** to Asenath
	49:4	climbed into your father's **m** bed
Ex	22:16	he must pay the **m** price and marry
	22:17	must still pay the **m** price for virgins
Lev	21:4	only related to him by **m**
Jos	15:19	She said, "Give me a **m** gift
Jdg	1:15	She said, "Give me a **m** gift
	3:6	their own daughters to their sons in **m**
	12:9	gave his daughters in **m** outside
	21:1	daughter to a Benjaminite in **m**
	21:7	give any of our daughters to them in **m**
Ru	2:1	Naomi had a relative by **m**
	3:4	you are available to him for **m**
	3:7	signal her availability for **m**
1Sa	18:26	Michal his daughter to David in **m**
1Ki	3:1	Solomon arranged a **m** contract
	11:19	his wife, Queen Tahpenes, in **m**
2Ki	8:27	related by both **m** and sin to the Ahab
	14:9	Give your daughter to my son in **m**
2Ch	18:1	made a **m** alliance with Ahab
	22:4	related by both **m** and sin to the Ahab
	25:18	Give your daughter to my son in **m**
Ezr	9:2	given some of their daughters in **m**
	9:12	don't give your daughters in **m**
Jer	25:10	singing, laughter, **m** festivities
	33:11	celebration, **m** festivities
Eze	16:8	entered the covenant of **m** with you
Da	11:17	give his daughter in **m** to the king
Mal	2:14	witness when you spoke your **m** vows
	2:15	God, not you, made **m**
	2:16	dismembering of the 'one flesh' of **m**
Mt	1:18	Before they came to the **m** bed
	1:25	did not consummate the **m** until she had
	19:10	If those are the terms of **m**
	19:11	**M** isn't for everyone
	19:12	never give **m** a thought

	22:30	At the resurrection we're beyond **m**
Mk	10:7	leaves father and mother, and in **m**
	12:25	we're past the **m** business
Lk	16:18	legalities of **m** as a cover for lust
	20:34	**M** is a major preoccupation here
	20:35	will no longer be concerned with **m**
Jn	3:29	the **m** is off to a good start
Ac	15:20	guard the morality of sex and **m**
	15:29	guard the morality of sex and **m**
	21:25	guard the morality of sex and **m**
1Co	7:2	**m** is strong enough to contain them
	7:3	**m** bed must be a place of mutuality
	7:4	**M** is not a place to "stand up for
	7:7	not for everyone any more than **m** is
	7:9	difficulties of **m** are preferable
	7:29	Keep it simple — in **m**
	7:33	**M** involves you in all the
	7:38	**M** is spiritually and morally right
	11:3	a **m** relationship, there is authority
2Co	11:2	promised your hand in **m** to Christ
Eph	5:28	they're already "one" in **m**
Heb	13:4	Honor **m**, and guard the sacredness
Rev	19:7	The **M** of the Lab has come

Marriages

1Co	7:12	rest of you who are in mixed **m**

Martyr

1Co	13:3	to the stake to be burned as a **m**
Rev	6:11	each **m** was given a white robe

Martyred

Rev	2:13	when they **m** Antipas
	18:24	prophets, the murdered and the **m**

Martyrs

Ps	44:22	No, you decided to make us **m**
Rev	6:11	the full number of **m** was filled
	17:6	drunk on the blood of the **m** of Jesus

Marvelous

Ps	78:4	the **m** things he has done
	88:12	Are your **m** wonders ever seen
	107:8	So thank God for his **m** love
	107:15	So thank God for his **m** love
	107:21	So thank God for his **m** love
	107:31	So thank God for his **m** love
	145:6	Your **m** doings are headline news
Jer	33:3	I'll tell you **m** and wondrous things
Ac	2:20	the Day tremendous and **m**
	20:32	God, our **m** God whose gracious Word
1Co	7:22	going to experience a **m** freedom
2Co	6:1	don't squander one bit of this **m** life
1Jn	3:1	What **m** love the Father has extended
Rev	15:3	Mighty your acts and **m**, O God

Marvelously

Ps	139:14	Body and soul, I am **m** made!
Ro	12:5	**m** functioning parts

Massacre

Jos	8:22	a real **m**
	10:28	a **m** that included the king
Jdg	11:33	twenty cities! A **m**!
1Sa	22:18	You do it — **m** the priests!
	22:19	He then carried the **m** into Nob
1Ki	19:1	including the **m** of the prophets
2Ki	3:23	fought each other — a bloody **m**
	6:21	Father, shall I **m** the lot
	9:7	avenging the **m** of my servants
	25:25	Mizpah — a bloody **m**
2Ch	14:13	a **m** before God and his troops
	36:17	it was a ruthless **m**
Est	3:13	provinces with orders to **m**, kill
	4:7	to finance the **m** of the Jews
	4:8	posted in Susa ordering the **m**
	8:6	watch the **m** of my own relatives
Isa	13:18	They **m** the young, wantonly
	14:20	left a legacy of **m**
Jer	19:6	but **M** Meadows
	25:27	You're slated for a **m**
	41:8	talked their way out of the **m**
	44:13	**m**, starvation, and disease
	44:27	Judeans in Egypt will die off by **m**
Eze	7:23	A bloody **m**, as crime and violence
	9:8	While the **m** went forward
	21:14	a sword for a **m**
	26:8	He'll **m** your surrounding villages
	26:15	at your mayhem and **m**
	38:22	judgment: disease and **m**
Hos	1:4	make the people . . . pay for the **m**
Heb	7:1	returning from "the royal **m**

Massacred

Jos	10:30	captured city and king and **m** the lot
	11:12	captured and **m** all the royal towns
Jdg	9:18	You **m** his sons
	9:45	captured the city and **m** everyone
	18:27	They **m** the people and burned
	20:37	ambush spread out and **m** the city
2Sa	21:1	from the time he **m** the Gibeonites
1Ki	11:15	**m** all the men of Edom
	18:40	they **m** the lot
2Ki	10:14	taken and then **m** at the well
	10:17	Jehu **m** everyone left in Samaria
	19:35	angel of God came and **m**
2Ch	20:23	those from Mount Seir and **m** them
	24:23	and Jerusalem, **m** the leaders
Est	7:4	sold to be **m**, eliminated
	9:6	the Jews **m** five hundred men
Job	1:17	and **m** the camel drivers
Ps	78:64	Their priests were **m**
Jer	18:21	Let them be **m** in battle!
	19:4	they have **m** innocent people
Eze	35:8	**M** bodies will cover your hills

M

Massacres

Jer	44:18	had nothing but **m** and starvation
La	1:20	**M** in the streets, starvation
Hab	2:8	payback for all your murders and **m**
	2:17	Hung over from animal **m**

Mature

1Ki	3:12	giving you a wise and **m** heart
Ecc	10:17	Lucky the land whose king is **m**
Mt	13:43	holy lives will **m** and adorn
	19:11	**m** enough to live a married life
Jn	15:8	when you **m** as my disciples
	15:11	and your joy wholly **m**
	17:23	they'll be **m** in this oneness
1Co	8:10	looks up to you as knowledgeable and **m**
	10:15	believers now who are **m**
	14:20	Only **m** and well-exercised intelligence
Gal	3:23	**m** enough to respond freely
Eph	4:13	fully **m** adults, fully developed
Col	1:28	To be **m** is to be basic
	4:12	stand firm, **m** and confident
1Ti	4:15	will all see you **m**
2Ti	2:22	Run after **m** righteousness
Heb	5:14	solid food is for the **m**
	12:11	**m** in their relationship with God
Jas	5:7	waiting for their valuable crops to **m**
1Pe	2:3	you'll grow up **m** and whole in God
2Pe	1:8	**m** in your experience of our Master
1Jn	2:5	person in whom we see God's **m** love
	4:17	at home and **m** in us

Matured

Eze	16:7	grew tall and **m** as a woman
Lk	2:52	Jesus **m**, growing up

Maturing

Isa	18:5	blossom has turned into a **m** grape

Maturity

Eze	19:3	She reared one of her cubs to **m**
Mk	4:33	stories to their experience and **m**
Ro	15:5	God develop **m** in you
2Co	10:6	building lives of obedience into **m**
Gal	6:6	trained to a self-sufficient **m**
Col	1:28	bring each person to **m**
1Ti	2:15	gathering it all into **m**
Heb	5:9	full stature of his **m**
	7:19	the law brought nothing to **m**

Medicine

Dt	19:19	same **m** he intended for the other party
Ps	70:3	Give them a taste of their own **m**
Jer	44:13	the same **m** I gave those in Jerusalem
	50:15	Give her a good dose of her own **m**
	50:29	a dose of her own **m**
Hos	5:11	a taste of his own **m**

Hab	2:8	get a taste of your own **m**
1Ti	5:23	good **m** for what ails you
Rev	3:18	buy **m** for your eyes from me

Medicines

Jer	46:11	You will vainly collect **m**

Meditate

Jos	1:8	Ponder and **m** on it day and night
Ps	119:55	I **m** on your name all night, God

Meditating

Ge	24:63	while **m** he looked up and saw camels
1Ki	18:27	Maybe he's off **m** somewhere
Da	9:2	I, Daniel, was **m** on the Scriptures
Php	4:8	and **m** on things true

Mediums

Lev	19:31	traffic with **m**; you'll pollute
	20:6	traffic with **m**, prostituting
1Sa	28:9	swept the country clean of **m**
2Ki	23:24	trashed spirit-**m**, sorcerers

Meek

Ps	45:4	Ride for the righteous **m**
	72:2	be honorable to your **m** and lowly

Meekness

Pr	22:4	payoff for **m** and Fear-of-God is plenty

Menial

Jos	9:23	From now on it's **m** labor for you
Eze	44:11	do only the **m** work in the Sanctuary
1Co	3:8	**m** servant jobs at minimum wages

Menstrual

Lev	15:19	impurity of her **m** period
	15:24	and her **m** blood gets on him
	15:33	for a woman in her **m** period
	18:19	during the time of her **m** period

Menstruation

Lev	12:2	seven days, the same as during her **m**
	12:5	the same as during her **m**

Mental

Mt	4:24	ailment, whether **m**, emotional
1Co	2:5	some fancy **m** or emotional footwork
Gal	5:19	**m** and emotional garbage

M

Mentality

Mt	7:5	traveling road-show **m** all over again
Lk	6:42	this I-know-better-than-you **m**

Mercies

Ps	119:156	Your **m**, God, run into the billions
Lk	1:54	he remembered and piled on the **m**
	1:78	Through the heartfelt **m** of our God

Merciful

Ge	19:16	God was so **m** to them!
Ex	15:13	people you redeemed, you led in **m** love
Ps	115:1	Do it on account of your **m** love
Ion	55:7	Let them come back to God, who is **m**
La	3:22	his **m** love couldn't have dried up
Joel	2:13	God is kind and **m**
Mt	18:33	be **m** to your fellow servant

Mercifully

Job	33:24	messenger who would **m** intervene
1Ti	1:13	I was treated **m** because I didn't know

Merciless

Ex	5:13	The slave-drivers were **m**
Job	16:13	**M**, they shot me full of arrows
Pr	30:14	Don't be greedy, **m** and cruel as wolves
Isa	18:2	this people mighty and **m**
	18:7	this people once mighty and **m**
	19:4	under the rule of a mean, **m** king
	27:1	his **m**, massive, mighty sword

Mercilessly

Dt	25:18	**m** cut off your stragglers
Jdg	10:8	battered the People of Israel **m**
1Sa	4:10	They thrashed Israel so **m**
1Ki	21:13	stoned him **m**, and he died
Ac	7:19	He exploited our race **m**

Mercy

Ge	42:21	when he was begging us for **m**
Ex	34:6	God, a God of **m** and grace
Jos	2:12	I showed you **m**; now show my family **m**
	2:14	we'll do right by you in loyal **m**
	9:25	We're at your **m**
	11:20	under the holy curse without **m**
2Sa	12:22	thinking God might have **m** on me
	24:14	punished by God, whose **m** is great
2Ki	7:4	throw ourselves on their **m**
	13:23	God was gracious and showed **m** to them
1Ch	21:13	punished by God whose **m** is great
Ne	13:22	my God. Treat me with **m**
Job	5:8	throw myself on the **m** of God
	9:15	throw myself on the Jdge's **m**
	12:4	Ridiculed without **m**
	41:3	Will he beg you over and over for **m**

Ps	25:6	Mark the milestones of your **m** and love
	35:12	They pay me back misery for **m**
	40:15	booed and jeered without **m**
	51:1	God, give grace! Huge in **m**
	52:1	God's **m** carries the day
	52:8	trusted in the generous **m** of God
	69:16	Let me see your great **m** full-face
	78:34	they turned and pled for **m**
	86:3	You're my God; have **m** on me
	103:4	He crowns you with love and **m**
	103:8	God is sheer **m** and grace
	106:46	He poured out his **m** on them
	107:8	his miracle **m** to the children he loves
	107:15	his miracle **m** to the children he loves
	107:21	his miracle **m** to the children he loves
	107:31	his miracle **m** to the children he loves
	112:4	God's grace and **m** and justice
	116:1	listened as I begged for **m**
	119:51	insolent ridicule me without **m**
	119:121	leave me to the **m** of my oppressors
	123:2	awaiting your word of **m**
	123:3	**M**, God, **m**!
	130:2	Listen to my cries for **m**
	140:6	Listen, God! **M**
	142:1	loudly I plead with God for **m**
	145:8	God is all **m** and grace
Pr	19:17	**M** to the needy is a loan to God
	28:13	you find **m** by admitting and leaving
Isa	30:18	gathering strength to show **m** to you
Jer	13:14	Not an ounce of pity or **m**
	21:7	kill them ruthlessly, showing no **m**
	26:14	I'm at your **m**
	26:19	honor him and pray for **m** from God
	33:26	I will have **m** on them
	42:12	I'll pour **m** on you
La	2:21	cut them down without **m**
	3:43	chased us and cut us down without **m**
Eze	8:18	From now on, no **m**
Da	2:18	pray to the God of heaven for **m**
	9:17	Have **m** on your ruined Sanctuary
Hos	1:6	Name this one No-**M**
	1:7	I'll continue having **m** on them
	1:8	After Gomer had weaned No-**M**
	2:1	Rename your sisters 'All **M**
	2:23	I'll have **m** on No-**M**
	14:3	in you the orphan finds **m**
Joel	2:17	Have **m**, God, on your people!
Jnh	4:2	I knew you were sheer grace and **m**
Mic	7:18	**m** is your specialty
Hab	3:2	as you surely must, remember **m**
Mt	9:13	I'm after **m**, not religion
	9:27	**M**, Son of David! **M** on us
	15:22	**M**, Master, Son of David!
	17:15	Master, have **m** on my son
	18:32	entire debt when you begged me for **m**
	18:33	your fellow servant who asked for **m**
	18:35	unconditionally anyone who asks for **m**
	20:30	Master, have **m** on us! **M**, Son of David
	20:31	Master, have **m** on us! **M**, Son of David
Mk	5:19	what the Master did, how he had **m**
	10:47	Jesus! **M**, have **m** on me
	10:48	Son of David! **M**, have **m** on me

M

Lk	1:50	His **m** flows in wave after wave
	1:58	God had overwhelmed her with **m**
	1:72	**M** to our fathers
	10:13	repenting and crying for **m**
	16:24	Father Abraham, **m**! Have **m**!
	17:13	Jesus, Master, have **m** on us
	18:13	God, give **m**. Forgive me, a sinner
	18:38	Son of David! **M**, have **m** on me
	18:39	Son of David! **M**, have **m** on me
Ro	9:15	God told Moses, "I'm in charge of **m**
	9:16	but in God's **m**
	15:9	able to experience **m**
1Co	7:25	experienced in the **m** of the Master
2Co	1:3	Father of all **m**! God of all
Gal	6:16	Peace and **m** on them
Eph	2:4	immense in **m**
Php	2:27	but God had **m** on him
1Ti	1:16	never have made it apart from sheer **m**
Heb	4:16	Take the **m**, accept the help
	9:5	the angel-wing-shadowed **m** seat
Jas	2:13	Kind **m** wins over harsh judgment
	3:17	overflowing with **m** and blessings
2Jn	1:3	Let grace, **m**, and peace be with us
Jude	1:21	ready for the **m** of our Master

Merrily

Heb	10:2	would have gone **m** on their way

Merry

Isa	32:13	the **m** city no longer **m**
Rev	9:20	went on their **m** way

Meticulous

Mt	23:23	Frauds! You keep **m** account books
Lk	11:42	Frauds! You keep **m** account books
1Co	9:21	**m** moralists, loose-living immoralists
Php	3:6	a **m** observer of everything set down

Midnight

Ex	11:4	At **m** I will go through Egypt
	12:29	At **m** God struck every firstborn
Jdg	16:3	was in bed with the woman until **m**
Ps	63:6	If I'm sleepless at **m**
Mk	13:35	evening, **m**, cockcrow, or morning
Ac	16:25	Along about **m**, Paul and Silas
	20:7	Paul talked on, way past **m**
	27:27	at about **m** the sailors sensed

Midwife

Ge	35:17	the **m** said to her, "Don't be afraid
	38:28	the **m** tied a red thread on his hand
Ex	1:19	Before the **m** can get there
1Sa	4:20	her **m** said, "Don't be afraid
Ps	22:9	you were **m** at my birth

Midwives

Ex	1:15	had a talk with the two Hebrew **m**
	1:17	the **m** had far too much respect for God
	1:18	The king of Egypt called in the **m**
	1:19	The **m** answered Pharaoh
	1:20	God was pleased with the **m**
	1:21	because the **m** honored God, God gave

Mighty

Ge	6:4	These were the **m** men of ancient lore
	33:20	**M** Is the God of Israel
Ex	7:4	from Egypt by **m** acts of judgment
	15:7	In your **m** majesty you smash
Dt	7:19	signs, the wonders, God's **m** hand
	26:5	became a great nation, **m** and many
Jdg	5:13	people of God joined the **m** ones
	6:12	God is with you, O **m** warrior
2Sa	1:19	the **m** warriors — fallen, fallen
	1:25	The **m** warriors — fallen, fallen
	1:27	The **m** warriors — fallen, fallen
1Ki	14:9	you've made me **m** angry
2Ki	7:6	a **m** army on the march. They told one
1Ch	11:10	the chiefs of David's **M** Men
	11:11	The list of David's **M** Men
	11:12	one of the Big Three of the **M** Men
	11:19	the Big Three of the **M** Men did
	11:22	was a **M** Man from Kabzeel
	11:26	The **M** Men of the military
	12:1	they were among the **M** Men
	12:4	a **M** Man among the Thirty
	27:6	was a **M** Man among the Thirty
2Ch	6:41	you and your **m** covenant Chest
Job	4:10	The **m** lion, king of the beasts
	8:11	Can **m** pine trees grow tall without
	12:21	disarms the strong and **m**
	22:26	take delight in God, the **M** One
	29:5	When the **M** One was still by my side
	34:10	no way can the **M** One do wrong
	34:12	for the **M** One to subvert justice
	34:17	dare condemn the righteous, **m** God
	34:24	deposes the so-called high and **m**
	37:5	**m** acts staggering our understanding
	37:23	**M** God! Far beyond our reach!
	40:2	haul me, the **M** One, into court
	41:34	He surveys all the high and **m**
Ps	35:26	who made themselves so high and **m**
	68:15	**m** mountains, dragon mountains
	70:4	God is **m**
	75:1	your **m** works are all we talk about
	78:25	They ate the bread of the **m** angels
	93:4	**M** God rules from High Heaven
	106:2	declaim God's **m** acts
	132:8	you and your **m** covenant ark
	135:10	he slew **m** kings
	145:4	tells stories of your **m** acts
Isa	1:29	will leave you looking **m** foolish
	5:9	Those **m** houses will end up empty
	5:15	on a par with the high-and-**m**
	10:12	his high and **m** posturing
	18:2	this people **m** and merciless

	18:7	this people once **m** and merciless
	25:12	those **m** walls reduced to dust
	26:5	Those who lived high and **m** he knocked
	27:1	his merciless, massive, **m** sword
	33:10	Now see how **m** I am
	49:26	I, the **M** One of Jacob
	63:1	I speak what is right, I, **m** to save
	63:15	your famous **m** acts
Jer	6:22	a **m** power on the move
	9:3	A **m** army of liars
	10:14	Stick-god worshipers looking **m** foolish
	11:16	A **m** oak tree, majestic and glorious
	46:10	country, along the **m** Euphrates
	48:1	The **m** fortress reduced to a molehill
	48:17	His **m** scepter snapped in two
	51:17	Stick-god worshipers look **m** foolish
Eze	7:24	strutting of the high-and-**m**
	16:52	look **m** good compared with you
	16:56	acting so high and **m**
	20:33	With a **m** show of strength
	20:34	with a **m** show of strength
	31:6	All the **m** nations lived in its shade
	31:8	**M** oaks looked like bushes
	32:19	You think you're so high and **m**
Zec	11:3	The **m** jungle of the Jordan is wasted
Mt	10:15	on Judgment Day they'll be **m** sorry
	26:64	at the right hand of the **M** One
Mk	14:62	At the right hand of the **M** One
Lk	19:37	praise over all the **m** works
2Co	12:7	walking around high and **m**
	13:4	he's alive now — in the **m** power of God
1Th	2:16	have gotten **m** good at it
Heb	10:27	a **m** fierce judgment it will be
Jas	1:12	manages to stick it out is **m** fortunate
	2:6	the high and **m** who exploit you
1Pe	4:11	credit as the One **m** in everything
Rev	14:16	The Cloud-Enthroned gave a **m** sweep
	15:3	**M** your acts and marvelous, O God
	19:6	the sound of a **m** cataract

Mind

Ge	31:29	If I had a **m** to, I could destroy you
	41:16	God will set Pharaoh's **m** at ease
Ex	8:29	change your **m** about releasing us
Lev	27:13	If the owner changes his **m**
Nu	23:19	not a son of man changing his **m**
Dt	9:7	Keep in **m** . . . how angry you
Jos	1:8	Book of The Revelation be out of **m**
Jdg	13:14	Keep in **m** everything I told the woman
1Sa	9:19	all about what's on your **m**
	14:6	saving when he sets his **m** to it
	20:4	Tell me what you have in **m**
	20:7	made up his **m** to kill me
2Sa	24:13	Think it over and make up your **m**
1Ki	3:20	I was sound asleep, **m** you!
	12:16	David, **m** your own business
	19:20	**m** you, don't forget what I've just
2Ki	10:15	together and of one **m** in this
	17:20	permitted anyone with a **m** to exploit them
	23:25	obedience to God, heart and **m**
1Ch	12:38	was of the same **m**

	13:3	out of sight, out of **m**
	21:12	Think it over and make up your **m**
	21:15	compassionately changed his **m**
	28:9	with a whole heart and eager **m**
	28:12	God's Spirit had brought to his **m**
2Ch	6:42	keep in **m** the love promised to David
	10:16	David, **m** your own business
	20:15	don't pay any **m** to this vandal horde
	25:16	God has made up his **m** to throw you out
	36:13	repentance never entered his **m**
Ezr	6:22	changed the **m** of the king
	7:27	put it in the **m** of the king
Ne	13:16	in Jerusalem, **m** you!
	13:25	gave them a piece of my **m**
Job	2:6	But **m** you, don't kill him
	4:2	Would you **m** if I said something
	5:17	**M** you, don't despise the discipline
	11:5	God would give you a piece of his **m**
	20:3	here's a piece of my **m**
	34:10	certainly we're of one **m** on this
	35:13	the Almighty pays them no **m**
	37:16	miracle-wonders of a perfect **M**
	37:21	No one in his right **m** stares straight
Ps	31:22	Out of sight, out of **m**
	35:20	against those who **m** their own business
	45:16	Set your **m** now on sons
	55:19	they pay him no **m**
	86:11	Put me together, one heart and **m**
	103:14	keeps in **m** that we're made of mud
	119:78	I kept my **m** fixed on your counsel
Pr	14:30	A sound **m** makes for a robust body
	18:20	Words satisfy the **m**
	19:7	out of sight, out of **m**
	23:1	**m** your manners
Ecc	3:22	made up my **m** that
SS	6:2	Never **m**. My lover is already
Isa	5:12	pay no **m** to what he is doing
	9:13	people paid no **m** to him who hit them
	10:7	he has something else in **m**
	19:12	what God-of-the-Angel-Armies has in **m**
	33:18	In your **m** you'll go over the old
	53:10	it's what God had in **m** all along
	64:9	Keep in **m**, please, we are your people
Jer	1:5	nations — that's what I had in **m** for you
	2:35	God doesn't **m**. He hasn't punished me
	4:28	I've decided and won't change my **m**
	17:10	search the heart and examine the **m**
	23:11	My very own Temple, **m** you
	31:22	make up your fickle **m**
	32:39	I'll make them of one **m** and heart
	38:22	Picture this in your **m**
	43:10	my servant, **m** you!
Eze	24:14	I'm not changing my **m**
Da	2:3	a dream that I can't get out of my **m**
	2:9	confuse the issue until I change my **m**
	2:28	the vision that filled your **m**
	4:16	lose his **m** and get an animal's **m**
	4:19	thoughts that came swarming into his **m**
	4:34	I was given my **m** back
	4:36	I was given back my **m**
	5:14	you've got a brilliant **m**
	5:21	lost his **m**, and lived like a wild

M

	11:28	m will be set on destroying the holy
Hos	7:2	never crosses their m that I keep
	7:12	I'll teach them to m me
Am	9:4	I've made up my m to hurt them
Jnh	3:9	change his m about us
	3:10	He did change his m about them
Zec	13:3	his own parents, m you
Mt	5:8	your inside world — your m and heart
	17:15	goes out of his m and suffers terribly
Lk	13:24	Put your m on your life with God
	21:14	Make up your m right now
Jn	10:30	I and the Father are one heart and m
	17:11	So they can be one heart and m
	17:12	As we are one heart and m
	17:21	all of them to become one heart and m
Ac	4:32	united as one — one heart, one m
	8:39	But he didn't m
	12:3	all this during Passover Week, m you
	15:24	M you, they had no authority
	19:2	Did you take God into your m only
	26:7	the identical hope, m you
Ro	2:11	He makes up his own m
	6:15	we do anything that comes to m
	7:25	serve God with all my heart and m
1Co	7:36	his m, deciding he should marry
	14:14	my spirit prays but my m lies fallow
	15:42	keep in m that when we're raised
2Co	9:7	make up your own m what you will give
	12:6	If I had a m to brag a little
Eph	1:4	he had us in m
	6:7	always keeping in m that no matter
Php	1:3	Every time you cross my m
	1:6	never been the slightest doubt in my m
	3:1	don't m repeating what I have written
	3:15	If any of you have something else in m
Col	3:24	Keep in m always that the ultimate
1Th	1:3	as we call to m your work of faith
	4:11	Stay calm; m your own business
1Ti	1:3	I haven't changed my m
2Ti	2:8	Fix this picture firmly in your m
Heb	6:9	I have better things in m for you
1Pe	1:13	put your m in gear
2Pe	1:20	main thing to keep in m here
	2:7	driven nearly out of his m
	3:2	Keep in m what the holy prophets said

Mindful

1Co	14:15	also be thoughtful and m as I pray

Minds

Ex	13:17	they'll change their m and go back
	14:5	he and his servants changed their m
Jos	22:29	last thing on our m right now
Jdg	5:16	divisions couldn't make up their m
	20:7	So, Israelites, make up your m
1Ki	18:21	Make up your m!
Ne	4:14	Put your m on the Master
Ps	95:10	Can't they keep their m on God
Pr	6:14	perverse m are always cooking up

	8:9	open m; truth-ready m will see
Isa	26:3	People with their m set on you
	46:8	Wrap your m around it
Jer	23:13	messing with the m of my people
Eze	13:17	make up stuff out of their own m
Hos	7:15	I'm the one who gave them good m
Hab	1:9	Death is on their m
Zec	6:15	put your m to a life of responsive
Mt	12:34	You have m like a snake pit!
Lk	2:48	half out of our m looking for you
	22:71	they had made up their m
Jn	16:20	fix this firmly in your m
Ac	14:2	sowing mistrust and suspicion in the m
1Co	8:2	help us more than our proud m
Php	4:8	your m and meditating on things true
Col	1:9	asking God to give you wise m
	2:2	will have m confident and at rest
Heb	3:10	They'll never keep their m on God
2Pe	3:1	your m in . . . undistracted attention

Miracle

Ex	7:9	Prove yourselves. Perform a m
Nu	14:22	saw the m signs I did in Egypt
Dt	6:22	God delivered m-signs, great wonders
	7:19	you were eyewitnesses: the m-signs
	11:2	displayed his power in the m-signs
	13:1	gives out a m-sign or wonder
	13:2	the m-sign or wonder that he gave out
	26:8	with signs and m-wonders
	29:3	the great signs and m-wonders
	34:11	the signs and m-wonders that God sent
Jos	3:5	God will work m-wonders among you
Jdg	6:13	Where are all the m-wonders
2Sa	1:26	Your friendship was a m-wonder
Ne	9:10	with wonders and m-signs
Job	9:10	his m-surprises can't be counted
	10:11	What a m of skin and bone
	37:14	Take in God's m-wonders
	37:16	all these m-wonders of a perfect Mind
Ps	107:8	his m mercy to the children he loves
	107:15	his m mercy to the children he loves
	107:21	his m mercy to the children he loves
	107:31	his m mercy to the children he loves
	109:21	work a m for me — you can do it
	119:18	what you show me of your m-wonders
	119:27	so I can ponder your m-wonders
	119:129	Every word you give me is a m word
	136:4	Thank the m-working God
Isa	25:1	You've done your share of m-wonders
Hos	9:16	if by some m they had children
Mic	7:15	Reproduce the m-wonders of our exodus
Mt	12:38	How about a m
Lk	11:16	prove himself with a spectacular m
Jn	4:48	Unless you people are dazzled by a m
Ac	4:16	it's known . . . that a m has occurred
Ro	11:23	He can perform m grafts
1Co	1:23	Jews treat this like an anti-m
	1:24	Christ is God's ultimate m and wisdom
	12:28	prophets teachers m workers healers
	12:29	not all M Worker

Miracles

Ex	3:20	my **m** will send them reeling
Dt	4:34	using trials, **m**, and war
1Ch	16:12	wonders he performed, the **m**
Ne	9:17	they refused to remember the **m**
Ps	78:12	He performed **m** in plain sight
	78:43	When he did **m** in Egypt
	88:10	a live audience for your **m**
	105:5	world of wonders he has made, his **m**
	105:27	marvels in that spiritual wasteland, **m**
	111:4	His **m** are his memorial
	135:9	Pharaoh and his servants with **m**
Jer	21:2	intervene with one of his famous **m**
Da	4:2	gracious **m** that the High God has done
	4:3	His **m** are staggering
	6:27	He performs astonishing **m** in heaven
Mt	11:21	half of the powerful **m** you have seen
	12:39	satisfy your lust for **m**
	13:58	He didn't do many **m** there
	14:2	That's why he's able to work **m**
Mk	6:14	that's why he's able to work **m**
Lk	11:29	satisfy your lust for **m**
Jn	6:2	attracted by the **m** they had seen him
	10:41	John did no **m**
Ac	2:22	**m** and wonders and signs that God did
	4:30	healings and **m** and wonders done
	8:6	the **m**, the clear signs of God's action
	8:13	all the God-signs and **m**
	14:3	corroborating their work with **m**
	15:12	the **m** and wonders God had done
2Th	2:9	All his power and signs and **m** are fake
Heb	2:4	all sorts of signs and **m**

Miraculous

Mk	8:12	clamor for **m** guarantees
Jn	7:21	I did one **m** thing a few months ago
	9:16	How can a bad man do **m**
1Co	1:22	While Jews clamor for **m** demonstrations
	12:10	**m** acts proclamation distinguishing

Miraculously

Ac	4:22	man who had been **m** healed
1Co	10:1	taken **m** through the Sea
2Pe	1:3	life of pleasing God has been **m** given

Mischief

Ne	6:14	get by with all the **m** they've done
Ps	5:5	you shake your head over M-Maker
	7:16	**m** backfires; violence boomerangs
Pr	10:23	An empty-head thinks **m** is fun
Isa	32:6	thinking up new ways to do **m**
	59:4	pregnant with **m** and have sin-babies
La	3:62	dreaming up **m**, hatching out malice
Ro	7:13	sin did far more **m** than it
2Co	2:11	give Satan an opening for yet more **m**

Miserable

Ex	1:14	made them **m** with hard labor
Nu	20:5	dragging us into this **m** country
1Sa	10:18	governments that made your life **m**
	16:15	making your life **m**
2Sa	14:7	They're making my life **m**
Ne	4:2	What are these **m** Jews doing?
Job	3:20	does God bother giving light to the **m**
	16:2	What a bunch of **m** comforters
Ps	40:14	who gets a kick out of making me **m**
	86:1	I'm one **m** wretch
	107:18	so **m** you thought you'd be better off
Pr	4:16	they've made life **m** for somebody
	15:15	A **m** heart means a **m** life
Ecc	5:17	All for a **m** life spent in the dark
Isa	64:12	Haven't you made us **m** long enough
La	1:8	**M**, she groans and turns away
	3:65	Break their **m** hearts!
Eze	16:6	I saw you all **m** and bloody
Zep	3:19	those who've made your life **m**
Mk	6:20	he was **m** with guilt
Ro	6:6	a decisive end to that sin-**m** life
2Co	2:3	have to spend a **m** time disappointing

Misfits

1Sa	22:2	losers and vagrants and **m** of all sorts
Lk	14:13	**m** from the wrong side of the tracks
	14:21	all the **m** and homeless and wretched
1Co	4:10	We're the Messiah's **m**

Misfortune

Pr	12:26	A good person survives **m**
	17:5	gloating over **m** is a punishable crime
Ecc	9:12	No one can predict **m**

Mislead

Job	36:18	Don't let your great riches **m** you
Pr	16:10	A good leader motivates, doesn't **m**
	31:30	Charm can **m** and beauty soon fades
Isa	36:18	Don't let Hezekiah **m** you with his lies
Rev	2:20	**m** my dear servants into Cross-denying

Misleading

Jn	8:46	single **m** word, a single sinful act

Misled

Jer	23:2	shepherd-leaders who **m** my people
Gal	6:7	Don't be **m**: No one makes a fool of God

Mission

Jdg	18:5	whether our **m** will be a success
1Sa	18:26	**m** completed!
	21:2	The king sent me on a **m**
	21:5	do it this way when I'm on a **m**
	21:8	The king's **m** was urgent

M

2Ch	17:7	Micaiah on a teaching **m**
Zec	2:8	the One of Glory who sent me on my **m**
	2:9	God . . . sent me on this **m**
	2:11	God . . . sent me on this **m**
Jn	17:18	a **m** in the world, I give them a **m**
	17:19	be truth-consecrated in their **m**
	17:25	you sent me on this **m**
Ac	9:32	Peter went off on a **m**
	16:3	wanted to recruit him for their **m**
2Co	1:1	sent on a special **m** by the Messiah

Missionaries

Isa	66:19	send them out as **m** to preach my glory
Ac	8:4	Christians all became **m**

Missionary

1Co	9:4	We who are on **m** assignments for God

Missions

Jude	1:6	abandoning it for other, darker **m**

Mist

Dt	5:22	from the fire and cloud and dark **m**
Ecc	6:4	It gets its start in a **m**
Hos	6:4	last no longer than morning **m**
Ac	13:11	plunged immediately into a shadowy **m**
1Co	13:12	in a fog, peering through a **m**

Mistress

Ge	16:4	she looked down on her **m**
	16:8	I'm running away from Sarai my **m**
	16:9	Go back to your **m**
Dt	28:30	another man will take her for his **m**
2Ki	5:3	One day she said to her **m**

Mistrust

Ac	14:2	sowing **m** and suspicion in the minds
Ro	1:18	acts of human **m** and wrongdoing
2Co	6:15	Do trust and **m** hold hands

Misunderstanding

Mt	12:32	reject the Son of Man out of some **m**
Lk	12:10	bad-mouth the Son of Man out of **m**

Misunderstood

Lk	2:34	A figure **m** and contradicted
1Co	12:1	This is complex and often **m**

Moaning

Isa	21:2	put an end to all the **m** and groaning
	29:2	The **m** and groaning will continue
	59:11	no worse off than doves, **m**
Jer	6:7	Victims, bleeding and **m**, lie

	14:2	people fall to the ground, **m**
La	2:5	left Daughter Judah **m** and groaning
Eze	7:16	Each one **m** for his own sins
Na	2:7	Maids and slaves **m** like doves

Moans

Isa	5:7	heard only the **m** of victims
	51:11	not a sign of **m** or groans
Jer	48:36	My heart **m** for Moab

Mock

1Sa	17:45	whom you curse and **m**
Job	11:3	let you rail and **m** and not step in
	21:3	then you can **m** me later
Ps	119:22	Don't let them **m** and humiliate me
Pr	9:12	**m** life and life will **m** you
Isa	16:7	**m**-laments from the neighbors
	37:4	king of Assyria to **m** the living God
	37:6	of the Assyrian king have used to **m** me
	37:17	that he sent to **m** the living God
	37:24	used your servants to **m** the Master
La	3:63	they **m** me with vulgar doggerel
Hab	1:10	They **m** kings, poke fun at generals
Mt	27:39	shaking their heads in **m** lament
Mk	10:34	who will **m** and spit on him
	15:19	knelt down in **m** worship
	15:29	shaking their heads in **m** lament
2Pe	3:4	they'll **m**, "So what's happened

Mocked

Dt	32:15	he **m** the Rock of his salvation
1Ch	20:7	When he **m** Israel
Isa	51:7	when **m** don't let it get you down
Jer	42:18	cursed, reviled, ridiculed, and **m**
	44:12	cursed, reviled, ridiculed, and **m**
Ac	8:33	He was **m** and put down
Rev	1:7	those who **m** and killed him

Mockers

Job	17:2	See how these **m** close in on me
2Pe	3:3	**m** are going to have a heyday

Mockery

Ps	3:2	all around me, roaring their **m**
	119:42	I'll be able to stand up to **m**
Isa	20:4	exposed to **m** and jeers
Jer	34:16	making a **m** of both me and the covenant
Eze	5:15	an object of ridicule and **m**
Mt	20:19	hand him over . . . for **m** and torture
	27:44	crucified next to him joined in the **m**
Mk	15:18	their **m**: "Bravo, King of the Jews
	15:32	alongside him joined in the **m**
2Co	4:10	trial and torture, **m** and murder

Mocking

Ne	2:19	laughed at us, **m**, "Ha!

Job	30:9	mistreating me, taunting and **m**
Ps	31:20	slam the door on those oily, **m** faces
	35:21	open their mouths in ugly grins, **M**
	55:12	This isn't the neighborhood bully **m** me
	137:3	demanded songs, sarcastic and **m**
Isa	37:23	Who do you think you've been **m**
	59:13	**M** and denying God
	65:7	**m** me at their hillside shrines
Hos	7:5	the frenzy of the **m** mob
	7:16	just deserts for their **m** blasphemies
Mic	2:4	**M** ballads will be sung of you
Mt	27:29	knelt before him in **m** reverence

Mocks

Pr	17:5	Whoever **m** poor people, insults

Modest

SS	2:14	Come, my shy and **m** dove
Mt	10:11	Get a **m** place with some **m** people
Mk	6:10	Get a **m** place and be content there
Lk	9:4	get a **m** place and be content there

Modesty

Jn	8:55	If I, in false **m**, said I didn't know

Money

Ge	23:13	take my **m** so that I can go ahead
	31:15	All he wanted was the **m**
	42:25	their **m** be put back in each sack
	42:27	at the mouth of his bag was his **m**
	42:28	My **m** has been returned
	42:35	purse of **m**. On seeing their **m**
	43:12	take plenty of **m** — pay back double
	43:15	took the gifts, double the **m**
	43:18	the **m**; he thinks we ran off with the **m**
	43:21	found our **m** at the mouth of the bag
	43:22	have no idea who put the **m** in our bags
	44:1	replace each one's **m** at the top
	44:2	along with the **m** for his food
	44:8	the **m** we found in our bags earlier
	47:14	Joseph collected all the **m** that was
	47:15	**m** from Egypt and Canaan had run out
	47:16	since your **m**'s run out
	47:18	our **m**'s gone
Ex	22:7	gives a neighbor **m** or things
	22:25	If you lend **m** to my people
	30:16	Take the atonement-tax **m**
Lev	25:16	The more years left, the more **m**
	25:28	get together enough **m** to repay him
	25:49	gets the **m** together, he can redeem
Nu	3:48	Give that **m** to Aaron and his sons
	3:49	Moses collected the redemption **m**
	3:51	Moses turned over the redemption **m**
	35:31	Don't accept bribe **m**
	35:32	don't accept bribe **m** for anyone
Dt	8:13	more and more **m** come in
	14:25	exchange your tithe for **m**
	14:25	take the **m** to the place God

	14:26	Use the **m** to buy anything you want
	15:2	Everyone who has lent **m** to a neighbor
	18:8	even though he has **m**
	23:19	not for **m** or food or clothing
Jdg	9:4	With the **m** he hired some reckless
	16:18	They came, bringing the bribe **m**
	17:2	I have the **m**; I stole it
	17:3	consecrated this **m** to God
1Sa	18:24	king isn't expecting any **m** from you
2Sa	21:4	We don't want any **m** from Saul
1Ki	21:2	if you'd prefer I'll pay you **m** for it
2Ki	5:23	He tied up the **m** in two sacks
	12:4	Take the **m** that is brought in
	12:7	to take any more **m** for Temple
	12:8	agreed not to take any more **m**
	12:10	large sum of **m** had accumulated
	12:11	They would give the **m** accounted for
	12:13	But none of the **m** brought in
	12:15	handled the **m** given for the project
	15:20	He raised the **m** by making every
	22:4	count the **m** that has been brought
	22:7	don't need to get a receipt for the **m**
	22:9	**m** that has been collected
	23:35	scraped up the **m** by gouging the people
2Ch	1:11	You didn't grasp for **m**, wealth
	1:12	a bonus — **m**, wealth, and fame
	13:9	enough **m** to pay for it can be a priest
	24:5	collect **m** from the people to repair
	24:10	cheerfully brought their **m** until
	24:11	collected a lot of **m**
	24:12	gave the **m** to the managers
	24:14	returned the surplus **m** to the king
	25:9	what about all this **m**
	34:9	the high priest all the **m** collected
	34:14	**m** that had been given for The Temple
	34:17	took all the **m** that was collected
Ezr	3:7	gave **m** to hire masons and carpenters
	7:17	Use this **m** carefully to buy bulls
	9:12	so you can make a lot of **m**
Ne	5:4	borrow **m** to pay the royal tax
	5:10	have also loaned them **m**
	5:11	forgive your claims on their **m**
Est	3:11	It's your **m** — do whatever you want
	4:7	told him the exact amount of **m**
	5:11	bragging about how much **m** he had
Job	22:24	Relax your grip on your **m**
	27:16	Even if they make a lot of **m**
	27:17	the decent who will divide up the **m**
	31:24	Did I set my heart on making big **m**
Ps	26:10	purses stuffed with bribe-**m**
	52:7	trusted in big **m**
Pr	3:14	She's worth far more than **m**
	3:20	the **m**'s right there in your pocket
	8:10	life-disciplines over chasing after **m**
	16:16	Get wisdom — it's worth more than **m**
	22:1	a gracious spirit is better than **m**
	23:23	truth — don't sell it for love or **m**
	31:16	with **m** she's put aside
Ecc	5:10	who loves **m** is never satisfied with **m**
	6:2	on whom God showers everything — **m**
	7:11	better when it's paired with **m**
	10:19	it's **m** that makes the world go around

M

Isa	10:3	What good will your m do you
	23:3	Making m on wheat from Shihor
	23:18	all the m she takes in
	46:6	People with a lot of m hire craftsmen
	55:1	Buy without m — everything's free
	55:2	Why do you spend your m on junk food
	58:13	business as usual,' making m
Jer	32:10	weighed out the m on the scales
	48:7	You trusted in thick walls and big m
	51:13	you have more m than you need
Eze	7:19	They throw their m into the gutters
	18:16	doesn't refuse to loan m
	18:24	like m in the bank he can draw on
	28:5	made a lot of m. But the m has gone
	33:31	all they care about is making m
Hos	3:2	I paid good m to get her back
	10:1	The more m they got, the more
Am	2:6	ways of making m
Mic	2:11	anything you want from God: More m
Hab	2:5	M deceives.
Zep	1:11	The god M is
	1:13	lose everything they have, m and house
	1:18	Your m is worthless for this
Hag	1:6	You have spent a lot of m
Zec	11:5	butcher them for quick and easy m
	11:7	crass, m-grubbing owners
	11:11	The m-hungry owners saw me do it
Mt	6:24	You can't worship God and M both
	6:28	time and m wasted on fashion
	10:24	doesn't make more m than his boss
	13:44	raise m and buy that field
	20:15	Can't I do what I want with my own m
	25:18	carefully buried his master's m
	25:25	your m. Here it is, safe and sound
	26:9	m handed out to the poor
	28:12	took a large sum of m and gave it
Mk	5:26	taking all her m
	12:41	crowd tossed m in for the collection
Lk	8:14	making m, and having fun
	14:29	foundation laid and then run out of m
	15:14	After he had gone through all his m
	15:30	has thrown away your m on whores
	16:14	Pharisees, a m-obsessed bunch
	19:13	gave them each a sum of m
	19:15	servants to whom he had given the m
	19:16	first said, 'Master, I doubled your m
	19:18	made a fifty percent profit on your m
	19:20	here's your m safe and sound
	19:23	Why didn't you at least invest the m
	19:24	Take the m from him and give it
Jn	10:13	He's only in it for the m
	12:5	sold and the m given to the poor
Ac	1:18	took the evil bribe m
	4:37	brought the m, and made an offering
	5:4	the m was yours to do with as
	8:18	he pulled out his m, excited
	8:20	To hell with your m!
	8:22	trying to use God to make m
	8:23	you reek with m-lust
	16:16	fortunetelling, made a lot of m
	21:23	have no m to pay the expenses
2Co	8:20	one penny of this m for ourselves

	11:12	I'd die before taking your m
1Ti	3:3	not m-hungry
	6:9	if it's only m these leaders are after
	6:10	Lust for m brings trouble
	6:17	obsessed with m
2Ti	3:2	self-absorbed, m-hungry
Tit	1:7	not a bully, not m-hungry
Jas	4:13	a business and make a lot of m
	5:2	Your m is corrupt

Monster

Ps	31:11	To my enemies I'm a m
Da	7:7	this one was a real m
	7:11	the m was killed and its body cremated
	7:19	hideous m with the iron teeth
	7:23	a m kingdom that will chew up everyone
Mt	24:15	see the m of desecration set up
Mk	13:14	see the m of desecration set up
1Co	12:19	wouldn't be a body, but a m

Monsters

Dt	2:10	The Emites (M) used to live there
Job	9:13	even dragon-bred m cringe before him
	26:12	by his wisdom he tames sea m
Eze	8:10	pictures of reptiles and animals and m

Mood

1Sa	16:14	a black m sent by God settled on him
	16:16	When the black m from God moves in
	18:10	ugly m was sent by God to afflict Saul
	19:9	a black m from God settled over Saul
1Ki	20:43	arrived in Samaria in a very bad m
	21:4	Ahab went home in a black m
Job	29:25	establishing the m and setting
Lk	11:29	The m of this age is all wrong

Moral

1Sa	26:21	acted the fool — a m dunce
2Ki	21:2	reintroduced all the m rot
2Ch	29:8	a m history lesson
	33:2	reintroduced all the m rot
Ezr	9:11	filled it with their m rot
Job	22:5	you're a first-class m failure
Ps	36:11	the m midgets slap me down
	37:15	slapstick figures in a m circus
	37:17	For the wicked are m weaklings
Pr	6:23	m discipline is a life path
	11:5	M character makes for smooth traveling
	14:9	a m life is a favored life
	15:5	M dropouts won't listen
	16:12	sound leadership has a m foundation
	29:10	m folks encourage them
Isa	7:15	able to make m decisions
Da	7:25	rid of sacred worship and m practice
Mt	5:22	simple m fact is that words kill
	5:32	legal cover to mask a m failure
Lk	18:9	themselves over their m performance
Ac	24:25	a life of m discipline

M

Ro	7:7	**m** behavior would be mostly guesswork
	8:5	measuring their own **m** muscle
	9:16	our bleeding hearts or **m** sweat
Gal	3:5	your strenuous **m** striving
	3:11	carrying out such a **m** program
1Ti	1:8	**m** guidance . . . to be given
2Pe	2:8	Surrounded by **m** rot day after day

Morale

2Sa	16:21	the **m** of everyone on your side
2Ch	32:8	**M** surged
Ezr	4:4	beating down the **m** of the people
Jer	21:4	**m** and weapons flushed down the drain

Mortal

Ge	18:27	a mere **m** made from a handful of dirt
Jdg	16:13	would be as helpless as any other **m**
	16:17	would be as helpless as any other **m**
2Sa	7:14	pitfalls and obstacles of this **m** life
Job	15:14	mere **m** to be sinless in God's sight
	25:4	can a mere **m** . . . stand up to God
Ps	17:9	from **m** enemies closing in
Isa	31:3	Egyptians are **m**, not God
	31:8	a sword not swung by a **m**
Jer	49:18	no **m** soul move in there
	49:33	no **m** soul move in there
Eze	28:2	You, a mere **m**, not even close
	28:9	To them you're a mere **m**
Da	6:7	pray to any god or **m** except you
1Co	15:53	this **m** replaced by the immortal
1Pe	1:23	Your old birth came from **m** sperm

Motion

Nu	11:31	A wind set in **m** by God
Ps	59:11	Bring them down in slow **m**
Isa	34:16	His Spirit set it in **m**
Ac	4:28	the plans you long ago set in **m**
Heb	9:18	required a death to set it in **m**

Motioned

Jdg	16:19	she **m** to a man to cut off
Jn	13:24	Peter **m** to him to ask who Jesus
Ac	24:10	The governor **m** to Paul

Motions

Ps	51:16	Going through the **m** doesn't please you
Pr	16:33	Make your **m** and cast your votes
Mk	7:3	going through the **m** of a ritual

Motivated

Ecc	4:4	work and ambition **m** by envy
Ro	15:14	to be well-**m** and well-instructed
Gal	5:16	animated and **m** by God's Spirit
Php	1:16	One group is **m** by pure love

Motivates

Pr	16:10	A good leader **m**, doesn't mislead

Motive

1Ch	28:9	sees through every **m**
Pr	17:20	A bad **m** can't achieve a good end
Gal	2:4	Their ulterior **m** was to reduce
	6:12	only one **m**: They want an easy way
1Jn	1:4	Our **m** for writing is simply this
Rev	2:23	I x-ray every **m** and make sure

Motives

Job	33:3	I have no ulterior **m** in this
Pr	20:11	if their **m** are on the up and up
	21:2	God examines our **m**
	21:8	Mixed **m** twist life . . .; pure **m**
Jer	11:20	cross-examine human actions and **m**
Mt	10:17	Some people will impugn your **m**
1Co	4:5	inner **m** and purposes and prayers
	9:15	discredit me or impugn my **m**
	11:28	Examine your **m**, test your heart
Gal	4:17	their **m** are rotten
Php	1:17	Their **m** are bad
	1:18	don't care about their **m**
1Th	2:4	free of error, mixed **m**, or hidden

Mourn

Jdg	11:40	went out to **m** for the daughter
Isa	61:2	to comfort all who **m**
	61:3	To care for the needs of all who **m**
Jer	4:28	The earth will **m** and the skies lament
	9:17	singers who can help us **m** our loss
	14:2	Judah weeps, her cities **m**
	34:5	They will properly **m** your death
	48:31	I will **m** for the people of Moab
Mic	1:8	This is why I lament and **m**
Zec	11:2	**M**, you sister cedars!

Mourned

Ge	23:2	Abraham **m** for Sarah
	37:34	**m** his son a long, long time
Nu	14:39	they **m** long and hard
1Sa	28:3	All Israel had **m** his death
2Sa	13:37	David **m** the death of his son
1Ki	13:30	The people **m**, saying, "A sad day
	14:18	buried him and everyone **m** his death
1Ch	10:12	**m** their deaths for seven days
Ne	1:4	I **m** for days, fasting and praying

Mourners

Isa	57:18	a new language of praise for the **m**

Mournful

Ps	102:7	**m** as a sparrow in the gutter
Mic	1:8	moan like a **m** owl in the night

M

Mourning

Ge	23:3	Abraham got up from **m** his dead wife
	27:41	The time for **m** my father's death
	37:35	I'll go to the grave **m** my son
	38:12	When the time of **m** was over
	50:3	There was public **m** by the Egyptians
	50:4	When the period of **m** was completed
	50:10	they stopped for a period of **m**
	50:11	Look how deeply the Egyptians are **m**
Lev	10:6	No **m** rituals for you
Nu	20:29	went into thirty days of **m** for him
Dt	21:13	a full month, **m** her father and mother
	26:14	eaten from the sacred share while **m**
	34:8	**m** for Moses came to an end
1Sa	6:19	The whole town was in **m**
	31:13	fasted in **m** for seven days
2Sa	1:2	Disheveled and obviously in **m**
	3:31	Wear **m** clothes!
	11:27	When the time of **m** was over
	14:2	Pretend you are in **m**
	19:2	victory turned into a day of **m**
1Ki	14:13	come to his burial, in **m** his death
Ezr	10:6	continuing his **m** over the betrayal
Est	9:22	**m** somersaulted into a holiday
	9:31	regarding their fasting and **m**
Ps	30:11	You ripped off my black **m** band
Isa	3:26	clotted with people **m** their dead
	22:12	dress in somber clothes of **m**
Jer	9:20	**M** women! Oh, listen to God's Message
	16:5	Don't enter a house where there's **m**
	48:37	signs of **m**: heads shaved, beards cut
	49:3	Dress in **m**, weep buckets of tears
Eze	2:10	lamentations and **m** and doom
	24:17	grief to yourself. No public **m**
	31:15	I threw the great deep into **m**
Da	10:2	I, Daniel, went into **m** over Jerusalem
Joel	1:8	dressed in black, **m** the loss
Am	9:5	The whole world goes into **m**
Mic	1:16	Shave your heads in **m** over the loss
Zec	7:3	plan for a day of **m** and abstinence
	8:19	The days of **m** set for the fourth
	12:10	Deep **m** as of a parent grieving
Jn	16:20	You're going to be in deep **m**
Ac	9:39	widows, were in the room **m**

Mourns

Isa	33:9	The very ground under our feet **m**

Mouth

Ge	18:27	dare open my **m** again to my Master
	24:15	words were barely out of his **m**
	27:40	live by your sword, hand-to-**m**
	29:2	stone over the **m** of the well was huge
	29:10	rolled the stone from the **m**
	42:27	at the **m** of his bag was his money
	43:21	found our money at the **m** of the bag
	45:12	my own **m**, telling you all this
Ex	4:11	who do you think made the human **m**
	4:12	right there with you — with your **m**

	4:16	He'll act as your **m**
	13:9	the teaching of God in your **m**
Nu	3:16	as he was instructed by the **m** of God
	16:31	The words were hardly out of his **m**
	16:32	Earth opened its **m** and in one gulp
Dt	8:3	every word that comes from God's **m**
	24:15	he's living from hand to **m**
	30:14	as near as the tongue in your **m**
	32:1	I've got a **m** full of words
Jos	10:18	stones against the **m** of the cave
	10:22	Open the **m** of the cave
	10:27	large stones at the **m** of the cave
	15:5	Salt Sea up to the **m** of the Jordan
Jdg	9:38	Where is that big **m** of yours now
1Sa	21:13	foaming at the **m**
	24:8	David stood at the **m** of the cave
2Sa	14:19	put these very words in my **m**
	22:9	his **m** spit fire
1Ki	19:13	went to the **m** of the cave
2Ki	4:34	covered him with his body, **m** on **m**
	19:28	and my bit in your **m**
1Ch	16:12	judgments that came out of his **m**
Est	7:8	When that word left the king's **m**
Job	15:13	words like this come out of your **m**
	30:31	my **m** harp wails laments
	40:4	should never have opened my **m**
	41:14	dare knock at the door of his **m**
	41:19	Comets pour out of his **m**
	41:21	flames of fire stream from his **m**
Ps	1:1	you don't go to Smart-**M** College
	4:4	Keep your **m** shut
	18:8	his **m** spits fire
	19:14	These are the words in my **m**
	34:8	Open your **m** and taste
	36:3	Words gutter from his **m**
	38:13	ears shut, **m** shut
	39:9	I'll shut my **m**
	50:19	Your **m** drools filth
	52:4	love malicious gossip, you foul-**m**
	66:17	I called out to him with my **m**
	71:8	my **m** brims with praise
	109:30	My **m**'s full of great praise for God
	119:13	all the counsel that comes from your **m**
	119:72	Truth from your **m** means more
	119:131	**M** open and panting, I wanted
	141:3	Post a guard at my **m**, God
	145:21	My **m** is filled with God's praise
Pr	4:24	Don't talk out of both sides of your **m**
	5:4	long after she's gravel in your **m**
	6:19	**m** that lies under oath
	8:7	**m** chews and savors and relishes truth
	8:8	hear true and right words from my **m**
	10:6	**m** of the wicked is a dark cave
	10:11	**m** of a good person is . . . life-giving
	10:26	it's vinegar in the **m**
	10:31	good person's **m** is a clear fountain
	18:2	all they do is run off at the **m**
	19:24	too lazy to raise it to their **m**
	20:17	soon your **m** is full of gravel
	22:14	The **m** of a whore is a bottomless pit
	23:2	don't talk with your **m** full
	24:13	delicacies that melt in your **m**

M

	26:15	too lazy to lift it to his **m**
Ecc	5:2	Don't shoot off your **m**
	5:6	Don't let your **m** make a total sinner
	10:20	Don't bad-**m** your leaders
SS	1:2	Kiss me—full on the **m**
	4:3	your **m** elegant and inviting
Isa	6:7	He touched my **m** with the coal
	30:27	Words steaming from his **m**
	37:29	my bit in your **m**
	45:23	Every word out of my **m** does what
	55:11	words that come out of my **m** not
	62:1	I can't keep my **m** shut
	62:2	name straight from the **m** of God
Jer	1:9	God reached out, touched my **m**
	5:14	my words as fire in your **m**
	20:8	Every time I open my **m** I'm shouting
	36:18	Every word right from his own **m**
Eze	2:8	Open your **m** and eat what I give you
	3:2	I opened my **m**, he gave me the scroll
	3:26	tongue stick to the roof of your **m**
Da	4:31	words were no sooner out of his **m**
	7:8	big **m** speaking arrogantly
	7:20	big **m** and spoke arrogantly
	10:16	opened my **m** and started talking
Hos	2:17	I'll wash your **m** out with soap
Mal	3:1	Message from the **m** of God
Mt	4:4	steady stream of words from God's **m**
	13:35	I will open my **m** and tell stories
	15:18	what comes out of the **m** gets its start
	17:27	Open its **m** and you'll find a coin
	26:47	The words were barely out of his **m**
	27:14	not a word from his **m**
Mk	9:18	He foams at the **m**
	9:20	foam at the **m**
	9:24	No sooner were the words out of his **m**
	14:43	No sooner were the words out of his **m**
Lk	1:64	Zachariah's **m** was now open
	9:39	convulsions, his **m** foaming
	11:54	trap him in something from his own **m**
	12:10	If you bad-**m** the Son of Man
	22:47	No sooner were the words out of his **m**
Jn	19:29	wine on a javelin and lifted it to his **m**
Ac	4:25	spoke through the **m** of your servant
	5:10	No sooner were the words out of his **m**
	9:18	No sooner were the words out of his **m**
	10:44	these words out of Peter's **m**
	15:7	firsthand, straight from my **m**
	19:34	the moment he opened his **m**
Ro	10:8	as near as the tongue in your **m**
1Co	14:9	what's the point of opening your **m**
2Co	1:17	I talk out of both sides of my **m**
	11:6	when I do open my **m**, I at least know
Eph	4:29	foul or dirty come out of your **m**
Php	1:18	opens his **m**, Christ is proclaimed
Col	4:4	Pray that every time I open my **m**
Heb	10:5	put in the **m** of Christ
Jas	3:3	A bit in the **m** of a horse
	3:5	A word out of your **m** may seem
	3:6	wrongly placed word out of your **m**
	3:10	Curses and blessings out of the same **m**
	4:11	Don't bad-**m** each other, friends
Rev	1:16	His **m** a sharp-biting sword

	2:12	sword draws from the sheath of his **m**
	10:10	it was sweet honey in my **m**
	12:16	the Dragon spewed from its **m**
	13:2	leopard with bear paws and a lion's **m**
	13:5	The Beast had a loud **m**
	19:15	A sharp sword comes out of his **m**
	19:21	the sword that comes from his **m**

Mouths

Ex	14:14	You keep your **m** shut
1Ki	19:18	the **m** that haven't kissed his image
	22:23	filled the **m** of your puppet prophets
2Ch	18:22	filled the **m** of your puppet prophets
Job	13:5	I wish you'd shut your **m**
Ps	12:3	Pull the braggart tongues from their **m**
	17:10	their **m** blast hot air
	35:21	They open their **m** in ugly grins
	41:6	he **m** empty platitudes
	78:30	they stuffed their **m** with more
	101:5	gag on the gossip who bad-**m**
	115:5	Carved **m** that can't talk
	135:16	Chiseled **m** that can't talk
Pr	6:12	talk out of both sides of their **m**
	17:28	as long as they keep their **m** shut
	18:7	Fools are undone by their big **m**
	19:28	the **m** of the wicked spew malice
Isa	25:5	shut the **m** of the big-mouthed bullies
	59:21	your **m** nor the **m** of your children
Jer	7:28	not a trace of it left in your **m**
	9:8	Deadly lies stream from their **m**
La	3:46	their **m** full of derision
	4:4	tongues stick to the roofs of their **m**
Eze	34:2	feeding your own **m**!
Da	6:22	angel, who closed the **m** of the lions
Am	5:11	take the bread right out of their **m**
Na	3:12	they fall straight into hungry **m**
Zec	14:12	and their tongues in their **m**
Mt	15:26	take bread out of children's **m**
	21:16	From the **m** of children and babies
Mk	12:17	Their **m** hung open, speechless
Ro	3:8	trying to put such words in our **m**
	3:14	open their **m** and pollute the air
1Co	14:21	from the **m** of strangers I will preach
Jas	3:2	wrong nearly every time we open our **m**
Rev	9:19	The horses killed with their **m**
	11:5	a blast of fire from their **m**
	14:5	Not a false word in their **m**
	16:13	From the **m** of the Dragon, the Beast

Muck

Ezr	9:7	We've been stuck in a **m** of guilt
Job	30:19	facedown in the **m**, I'm a muddy mess
Rev	3:4	in the **m** of the world's ways

Mud

Ex	14:25	they were stuck in the **m**
Dt	32:5	throw **m** at him but none of it sticks
2Sa	1:21	shields were dragged through the **m**
Job	4:19	these bodies composed of **m**

M

	10:9	Will you reduce me now to a **m** pie
	33:6	we're both made of the same kind of **m**
Ps	35:6	Make their road lightless and **m**-slick
	36:12	flat on their faces in the **m**
	40:2	pulled me from deep **m**
	89:39	you stomped his crown in the **m**
	90:3	So don't return us to **m**
	103:14	keeps in mind that we're made of **m**
	104:29	revert to original **m**
	107:33	springs of water into sunbaked **m**
Pr	17:15	throwing **m** on good people
	22:5	dangerous road, potholed and **m**-slick
	26:8	setting a **m** brick on a marble column
Isa	10:6	push their faces in the **m**
	14:12	on your face in the underworld **m**
	41:25	He'll stomp the rulers into the **m**
	57:20	The waves stir up garbage and **m**
Jer	23:11	**m**-spattered with their crimes
	38:6	only **m**. Jeremiah sank into the **m**
	38:22	stuck, about knee-deep in **m**
Eze	20:39	quit throwing filth and **m** on me
	22:16	defiled, spattered with your own **m**
	39:7	let my holy name be dragged in the **m**
	43:7	drag my holy name through the **m**
	43:8	dragged my holy name through the **m**
Hos	6:10	Israel in the **m** right there with him
	7:2	They're **m**-spattered head to toe
	9:10	in the **m** with their newfound friends
Am	5:7	stomp righteousness into the **m**
	8:8	recedes, leaving behind a sea of **m**
Ob	1:12	when they were facedown in the **m**
Na	1:5	hills dissolve into **m** flats
Zec	10:5	striding through swamps and **m**
Mt	12:27	you're slinging devil **m** at me
Lk	1:52	pulled victims out of the **m**
	10:15	You're on a **m** slide to hell
	11:19	you're slinging devil **m** at me
Ro	3:13	their tongues slick as **m** slides
Jas	3:6	throw **m** on a reputation
	3:12	dip into a polluted **m** hole
1Pe	3:16	when people throw **m** at you
2Pe	2:22	A scrubbed-up pig heads for the **m**
Jude	1:8	glory dragged in the **m**

Mule

2Sa	18:9	riding his **m**, when the **m** ran under
1Ki	1:33	mount my son Solomon on my royal **m**
	1:38	mounted Solomon on King David's **m**
	1:44	mounted Solomon on the royal **m**
Ps	32:9	Don't be ornery like a horse or **m**
Isa	1:3	the **m** knows the hand that feeds him
Hos	4:16	Israel is stubborn as a **m**

Mules

Dt	9:6	You're stubborn as **m**
Jdg	2:19	Stubborn as **m**, they didn't drop
2Sa	13:29	jumped on their **m**, and rode off
1Ki	10:25	exotic spices, and horses and **m**
	18:5	keep our horses and **m** from dying
1Ch	12:40	arrived with donkeys, camels, **m**

2Ch	9:24	exotic spices, horses, and **m**
Ezr	2:66	they had 736 horses, 245 **m**
Ne	7:68	there were 736 horses, 245 **m**
Job	11:12	about the same time **m** learn to talk
Isa	46:1	no-god hunks of wood are loaded on **m**
	66:20	on **m** and camels, straight to my holy
Jer	7:26	Stubborn as **m** and worse than
Eze	27:14	traded . . . **m** for your products
Zec	14:15	will also hit the animals — horses, **m**
Ac	23:24	you'll need a couple of **m** for Paul

Mumble

| Isa | 29:4 | you'll **m** words from the dirt |
| | 45:19 | I don't just . . . **m** under my breath |

Mumbles

| 2Co | 10:10 | he's a weakling and **m** when he talks |

Murder

Ge	37:22	No **m**. Go ahead and throw him
	42:22	now we're paying for his **m**
Ex	20:13	No **m**
	21:14	if the **m** was premeditated
Nu	35:16	that's just plain **m**
	35:17	and the man dies, that's **m**
	35:18	and the man dies, that's **m**
	35:21	and kills him, that's **m**
	35:33	**M** pollutes the land
Dt	4:42	If the **m** was unintentional
	5:17	No **m**
	19:13	Clean out the pollution of wrongful **m**
	21:8	Israel from any guilt in this **m**
	21:9	absolved yourselves of . . . the **m**
1Sa	25:26	kept you from this avenging **m**
	25:31	the guilt of an avenging **m**
	25:33	Bless you for keeping me from **m**
2Sa	3:27	for the **m** of his brother
	3:28	totally innocent of this **m** of Abner
	4:11	find you guilty of **m**
	12:10	killing and **m** will continually plague
1Ki	21:19	First **m**, then theft?
2Ki	8:12	**m** their youth
	15:25	After the **m** he became the next king
	25:7	the summary **m** of his sons
2Ch	19:10	it seems large (like **m**)
	24:25	avenging the **m** of the son of Jehoiada
Job	19:7	I shout 'M!' and I'm ignored
	24:2	people out there getting by with **m**
Ps	82:2	let the wicked get away with **m**
	94:3	God, the wicked get away with **m**
Pr	1:32	Carelessness kills; complacency is **m**
	6:17	hands that **m** the innocent
Ecc	8:11	think they can get by with **m**
Isa	59:7	run to be the first to **m**
Jer	7:9	Do you think you can rob and **m**
	7:32	call the place what it is: M Meadow
	11:21	who are trying to **m** you
	20:8	I'm shouting, "M!" or "Rape!"
	41:4	after the **m** of Gedaliah

M

	41:9	cover up the earlier **m** of Gedaliah
	41:16	after the **m** of Gedaliah
	41:18	**m** of Gedaliah
	52:10	The summary **m** of his sons
Eze	5:17	disease, unrestrained **m**, death
	9:9	The land is swollen with **m**
	22:12	**M** is for hire
	23:37	obscenities ranging from adultery to **m**
	23:45	sentences for adultery and **m**
	24:6	Doom to the city of **m**
	24:9	Doom to the city of **m**
	28:23	**m** and mayhem in the streets
	33:25	worship no-god idols, you **m** at will
Hos	4:2	anarchy, one **m** after another
	11:6	the **m** rate skyrockets
Am	1:11	hunts down her brother to **m** him
Na	3:1	Doom to **M** City
Hab	1:2	do I have to yell, "Help! **M**!
	2:12	building a town by **m**
	2:17	hung over from **m** and mayhem
Mt	2:16	commanded the **m** of every little boy
	2:20	those out to **m** the child are dead
	5:21	command to the ancients, 'Do not **m**
	5:22	brother or sister is guilty of **m**
	17:23	They will **m** him
	19:18	Jesus said, "Don't **m**
	27:6	give this—a payment for **m**
	27:8	field got called "**M** Meadow,"
Mk	9:31	will **m** him. Three days after his **m**
	10:19	the commandments: Don't **m**
	15:7	committed **m** during the uprising
Lk	23:19	starting a riot in the city and for **m**
	23:25	thrown in prison for rioting and **m**
Ac	1:19	they call the place **M** Meadow
	9:29	who plotted his **m**
	23:13	bound themselves to this **m** pact
	23:21	so they can **m** him
	23:30	they had cooked up a plot to **m** him
2Co	4:10	trial and torture, mockery and **m**
Heb	12:24	The **m** of Jesus
Jas	2:11	also said, "Don't **m**."
	5:6	condemn and **m** perfectly good persons

Murdered

Ge	4:11	receive the blood of your **m** brother
	34:25	**m** every man there
Jdg	20:4	the husband of the **m** woman
1Sa	22:21	Saul had **m** the priests of God
2Sa	3:30	Joab and his brother, Abishai, **m** Abner
	12:9	You **m** Uriah the Hittite
	14:7	for the life of the brother he **m**
1Ki	2:5	He **m** them in cold blood
	2:32	men he **m**, men better by far than he
	19:10	**m** your prophets
	19:14	**m** your prophets
2Ki	9:26	I saw the blood of **m** Naboth
	19:37	sons Adrammelech and Sharezer **m** him
2Ch	24:21	they **m** him, pelting him with rocks
	24:22	He **m** Jehoiada's son
Ps	106:38	**m** their infant girls and boys
Isa	14:19	rotting bodies, **m** and indigent corpses

	26:21	show where the **m** have been hidden
	37:38	was **m** by his sons
La	2:20	Should priests and prophets be **m**
Eze	7:15	get **m** out in the country or die
	11:6	You've **m** a lot of people
Da	5:30	Babylonian king Belshazzar was **m**
Hos	7:16	Their rulers will be cut down, **m**
Am	8:10	your only son, say, **m**
Mt	21:35	The next one they **m**
	23:35	whom you **m** at his prayers
Lk	11:48	more than to the **m** prophets
	13:2	**m** Galileans were worse sinners
Ac	12:2	He **m** James, John's brother
	22:20	when your witness Stephen was **m**
Ro	11:3	God, they **m** your prophets
Heb	11:37	sawed in two, **m** in cold blood
Rev	18:24	the **m** and the martyred

Murderer

Nu	35:12	so that the alleged **m** won't be killed
	35:16	obviously a **m** and must be put to death
	35:17	he's a **m** and must be put to death
	35:18	he's a **m** and must be put to death
	35:19	avenger has a right to kill the **m**
	35:26	if the **m** leaves the asylum-city
	35:27	avenger has a right to kill the **m**
	35:31	money in exchange for the life of a **m**
	35:33	except through the blood of the **m**
Dt	4:42	the **m** could flee to one of these cities
	19:4	**m** who flees there to take refuge
2Sa	14:7	Hand over this **m** so we can kill him
2Ki	6:32	this **m** has just now sent a man
	21:16	he was an indiscriminate **m**
Job	24:14	the sun goes down, the **m** gets up
Pr	28:17	A **m** haunted by guilt is doomed
Eze	16:21	And now you're a **m**
Mt	23:37	Jerusalem! **M** of prophets!
Ac	3:14	asked for a **m** in his place
	28:4	was a **m** getting his just deserts
Jas	2:11	No, you're a **m**, period
1Jn	3:15	who hates a brother or sister is a **m**

Murderers

Ps	139:19	And you **m**—out of here
Pr	29:10	**M** hate honest people
Mt	23:31	cut from the same cloth as those **m**
Ac	7:52	traitors and **m**, all of you
	22:20	holding the coats of the **m**
Rev	21:8	degenerates and **m**, sex peddlers
	22:15	fornicators, **m**, idolaters

Murmur

SS	1:3	your name **m** like a meadow brook
Lk	11:27	above the **m** of the crowd

Murmured

2Ki	17:22	never **m** so much as a word of protest

Music

Ge	31:27	celebration — m, timbrels, flutes
Jdg	5:3	Make m to God
1Sa	16:16	play his m and you'll feel better
	19:9	while David was playing m
2Sa	19:35	Can't taste food; can't hear m
1Ch	6:32	ministers of m in the place of worship
	15:22	Kenaniah, the Levite in charge of m
	15:27	Kenaniah who was directing the m
	25:1	special service in preaching and m
	25:7	well-trained in the sacred m
2Ch	8:14	lead the sacred m for praising God
Job	21:12	They make m with fiddles and flutes
	21:31	Did they ever have to face the m
Ps	27:6	I'm making m to God
	45:8	Chamber m — from the throne room
	55:21	His words, which were m to my ears
	66:17	my tongue shaped the sounds of m
	71:22	I'll make m for you on a harp
	81:2	m from the band, sweet sounds
	89:32	make them face the m
	92:3	the full-bodied m of strings
	105:2	translate his wonders into m
	119:54	I set your instructions to m
	141:6	make them face the m
	147:7	play m on your instruments to God
	149:3	strike up the band and make great m
SS	1:4	we'll sing, we'll make great m
Isa	14:11	where your pomp and fine m led you
	30:29	make m like the sound of flutes
	30:32	in time to the m of drums and pipes
Jer	9:18	make tearful m of our crying
	32:4	forced to face the m
La	5:14	M from the young is heard no more
Am	5:23	all I can take of your noisy ego-m
Lk	15:25	he heard the m and dancing
Rev	14:2	then I heard m, harp m
	18:22	Silent the m of harpists and singers

Musical

1Ch	16:5	who played the m instruments
	25:6	m accompaniment in the work of worship
2Ch	29:25	their m instruments — cymbals, harps
Ne	12:35	playing the m instruments of David
Da	3:7	all the m instruments of Babylon
1Co	14:7	m instruments — flutes, say, or harps

Musician

1Sa	16:18	an excellent m
1Ch	15:22	a very gifted m

Musicians

1Ki	10:12	making harps and dulcimers for the m
1Ch	9:33	And then there were the m
2Ch	5:12	all the Levites who were m were there
	9:11	making harps and dulcimers for the m
	34:12	Levites — they were all skilled m

Mute

Ex	4:11	who makes some m, some deaf
Job	16:8	a m witness to your treatment of me
Ps	38:13	But I'm deaf and m to it all
Mt	15:30	the blind, the maimed, the m
Mk	9:17	Teacher, I brought my m son

Mutilate

Dt	14:1	don't m your bodies
Eze	23:25	They'll m you

Mutilated

Ex	22:31	Don't eat m flesh you find
Lev	22:22	an animal that is blind, crippled, m
Isa	14:19	Your dead body desecrated, m
	56:3	make sure no physically m person
	56:4	To the m who keep my Sabbaths

Muzzle

Dt	25:4	Don't m an ox while it is threshing
Job	7:12	Are you going to put a m on me
Ps	68:22	put a m on the Deep Blue Sea
	107:29	put a m on all the big waves
1Co	9:9	Don't m an ox to keep it from eating
1Ti	5:18	Don't m a working ox

Myrrh

Ex	30:23	liquid m; half that much
Est	2:12	treatment with oil of m
SS	1:13	my lover was a sachet of sweet m
Mt	2:11	gifts: gold, frankincense, m
	27:34	a mixture of wine and m
Mk	15:23	painkiller (wine mixed with m)
Jn	19:39	a mixture of m and aloes
Rev	18:13	incense, m, and frankincense

Myrtle

Ne	8:15	pine branches, m branches
Isa	41:19	also acacia, m, and olive

Mysteries

Job	38:17	one clue regarding death's dark m
Da	2:28	a God in heaven who solves m
	2:29	The Revealer of M showed you
	2:47	he solves all m, I know
	5:12	interpret dreams, solve m
	5:16	interpret dreams and solve m
Mt	7:6	Don't reduce holy m to slogans
1Co	13:2	revealing all his m
Col	2:4	after other so-called m

Mysterious

Isa	29:15	acting m, never showing your hand

1Co	2:7	God's wisdom is something **m**
	14:5	God's presence in a **m** prayer language

Mysteriously

Ac	1:11	come as certainly — and **m** — as he left

Mystery

Job	11:7	think you can explain the **m** of God
Ps	40:3	enter the **m**, abandoning themselves
	64:6	**m** in the dark of the cellar heart
Ecc	11:5	you'll never understand the **m** of life
SS	7:4	eyes are wells of light, deep with **m**
Da	2:18	mercy in solving this **m**
	2:19	answer to the **m** was given to Daniel
	2:23	You've solved the king's **m**
	2:27	No mere human can solve the king's **m**
	2:47	because you've solved this **m**
	4:9	there is no **m** that you can't solve
Lk	7:16	were in a place of holy **m**
Ro	1:20	the **m** of his divine being
	16:25	Christ, precisely as revealed in the **m**
1Co	6:16	Sex is as much spiritual **m**
	15:42	the **m** of the resurrection body
	15:51	a **m** I'll probably never fully
Eph	3:4	into the **m** of Christ
	3:6	The **m** is that people who have never
	5:32	This is a huge **m**
	6:19	telling the **m** to one and all
Col	1:26	**m** has been kept in the dark
	1:27	The **m** in a nutshell is just this
	2:2	Christ, God's great **m**
	2:3	embedded in that **m** and nowhere else
	4:3	open doors for telling the **m** of Christ
1Ti	3:9	reverent before the **m** of the faith
	3:16	This Christian life is a great **m**
Rev	10:7	the **M** of God, all the plans

N

Nagging

Jdg	14:17	worn out by her **n**, he told her
	16:16	She kept . . . **n** and tormenting him
Pr	19:13	a **n** spouse is a leaky faucet
	21:9	than share a mansion with a **n** spouse
	25:24	than share a mansion with a **n** spouse
	27:15	A **n** spouse is like the drip
Mk	6:17	sent him to prison at the **n** of

Naive

Jer	11:19	**n** as a lamb being led to slaughter
Mt	10:17	Don't be **n**
Mk	14:38	Don't be **n**. Part of you is eager
1Co	10:12	Don't be so **n** and self-confident
2Ti	3:1	Don't be **n**. There are difficult times

Naively

Job	21:28	**N** you claim that the castles
Isa	37:10	God, on whom you so **n** lean

Naked

Ge	2:25	the Man and his Wife, were **n**
	3:7	saw themselves **n**!
	3:10	I was afraid because I was **n**
	3:11	Who told you you were **n**?
	9:21	passed out, **n** in his tent
	9:22	saw that his father was **n**
1Sa	19:24	a day and a night, stretched out **n**
2Ch	28:15	dressed the ones who were **n**
Job	1:21	**N** I came from my mother's womb
	1:21	**n** I'll return to the womb of the earth
Ecc	5:15	arrived **n** from the womb of his mother
	5:16	**n** he came, **n** he went
Isa	20:2	going about **n** and barefooted
	20:3	walked around town **n** and barefooted
	20:4	march them out of there **n**
	20:6	**N** and barefooted, shuffling off
	57:8	adoring every curve of their **n** bodies
Ja	4:21	wake up with nothing, stripped **n**
Eze	16:7	you were **n** and vulnerable
	16:22	when you were **n** and exposed
	16:37	I'll strip you **n** before them
	16:39	leave you **n** and exposed
	23:29	leave you publicly **n**
Hos	2:3	expose her, **n** as a newborn
Am	2:16	run off for dear life, stripped **n**
Hab	3:13	Stripped him **n** from head to toe
Mk	14:52	he got away, running off **n**
Ac	19:16	tore off their clothes. **N** and bloody
2Co	11:27	blasted by the cold, **n** to the weather
Col	2:15	marched them **n** through the streets
Rev	3:18	gone around half-**n** long enough
	16:15	through the streets, **n** and ashamed
	17:16	violate her, strip her **n**

Nakedness

Ge	9:23	covered their father's **n**
Ex	20:26	that will expose your **n**
	28:42	cover their **n** from waist to thigh

Nature

Ge	1:26	make them reflecting our **n**
	1:27	godlike, Reflecting God's **n**
	5:1	godlike, with a **n** akin to God
	9:6	in his image reflecting God's very **n**
Jer	10:7	It's your very **n** to be worshiped
Jn	3:25	over the **n** of baptism
	8:44	makes it up out of his lying **n**
Ac	25:26	something in the **n** of a charge
Ro	8:3	as it always was by fractured human **n**
1Co	2:14	unspiritual self, just as it is by **n**
	15:50	lead us by their very **n**
1Jn	3:9	not in the **n** of the God-begotten

N

Needle

Mt	19:24	gallop a camel through a **n**'s eye
Mk	10:25	a camel to go through a **n**'s eye
Lk	18:25	thread a camel through a **n**'s eye

Needles

Job	7:6	swifter than the click of knitting **n**
2Co	7:5	fears . . . kept us on pins and **n**

Needs

Ge	40:4	assigned Joseph to see to their **n**
	41:33	Pharaoh **n** to look for a wise . . . man
	41:34	Pharaoh **n** to appoint managers
	45:11	make sure all your **n** are taken care of
Dt	15:7	someone who's in trouble or **n** help
	15:8	lend whatever and as much as he **n**
	24:15	living from hand to mouth and **n** it now
2Sa	10:12	God will do whatever he sees **n** doing
	19:32	He had supplied the king's **n**
	20:3	He provided for their **n**
1Ki	4:20	All their **n** were met
	12:7	be considerate of their **n**
	18:27	**n** to be waked up
2Ki	5:22	Supply their **n** with a gift
1Ch	16:37	responsible for the **n** of worship
	19:13	God will do whatever he sees **n** doing
2Ch	10:7	be considerate of their **n**
Ezr	4:13	The king **n** to know that once
Job	7:16	Who **n** any more of this?
	13:8	Do you think he **n** a lawyer
	31:16	Have I ignored the **n** of the poor
	31:17	Taken care of my own **n**
Ps	32:6	Every one of us **n** to pray
	32:9	mule that **n** bit and bridle to stay
	37:5	he'll do whatever **n** to be done
Pr	10:13	shortsighted **n** a slap in the face
	28:27	shut your eyes to their **n**
	30:9	God? Who **n** him?
Ecc	2:2	pursuit of happiness? Who **n** it
Isa	61:3	To care for the **n** of all who mourn
Jer	5:7	I satisfied their deepest **n**
	40:15	No one **n** to know about it
Da	4:27	look after the **n** of the down-and-out
Hos	10:3	Who **n** a king? We couldn't care less
	13:6	took care of all your **n**
Joel	1:17	Grain silos abandoned. Who **n** them?
Zec	10:6	I'll do what **n** to be done for them
Mt	3:14	I'm the one who **n** to be baptized
	4:11	Angels came and took care of Jesus' **n**
	9:12	Who **n** a doctor
	21:3	The Master **n** them!
Mk	2:17	Who **n** a doctor
	11:3	The Master **n** him
Lk	5:31	Who **n** a doctor
	7:16	looking to the **n** of his people
	19:31	His Master **n** him
	19:34	His Master **n** him
Ac	20:34	took care of my own basic **n**
	28:10	took care of all our **n**

Ro	9:22	If God **n** one style of pottery
	15:2	one of us **n** to look after the good
	15:16	spiritual **n** of the non-Jewish
2Co	9:8	ready to do what **n** to be done
	9:12	the bare **n** of poor Christians
	11:9	My **n** were always supplied
Gal	6:7	ignoring the **n** of others
Eph	3:12	free to say whatever **n** to be said
1Th	5:14	attentive to individual **n**
1Ti	5:5	praying to him . . . for the **n** of others
Heb	7:26	priest who perfectly fits our **n**
	12:29	torching all that **n** to burn
1Pe	3:1	your husbands, responsive to their **n**
Rev	22:5	the Master, is all the light anyone **n**

Needy

Dt	15:9	turn aside and leave your **n** neighbor
	15:11	always going to be poor and **n** people
	24:14	laborer who is destitute and **n**
1Ki	8:52	attentive to the **n** prayers of me
Job	29:16	Father to the **n**
Ps	72:4	help the children of the **n**
	109:31	at hand to take the side of the **n**
Pr	19:17	Mercy to the **n** is a loan to God
	30:14	shredding the **n** to pieces only
Isa	11:4	He'll judge the **n** by what is right
	14:30	The **n** will escape the terror
Eze	22:29	the poor and **n** are abused
Ac	4:34	not a person among them was **n**
Ro	12:13	Help **n** Christians; be inventive
2Co	9:9	giving to the **n** in reckless abandon
	9:13	offerings to your **n** brothers
2Ti	3:6	unstable and **n** women
Tit	3:14	are met (especially among the **n**)
Heb	6:10	by helping **n** Christians

Neglect

Dt	12:19	you never, never **n** the Levite
Ne	10:39	We will not **n** The Temple of our God
Pr	23:22	when your mother grows old, don't **n** her

Neglected

Dt	33:9	and **n** his children
Est	9:28	days of Purim must never be **n**
Eze	36:34	The **n** land will be worked again

Neglecting

1Sa	1:11	If you'll quit **n** me
Heb	2:3	risk **n** this latest message

Negotiating

Jdg	12:2	our hands full **n** with the Ammonites
Da	11:23	After **n** a cease-fire, he'll betray

Neighbor

Ex	2:13	Why are you hitting your **n**

N

	3:22	will ask her **n** and any guests
	11:2	from his **n** and each woman from her **n**
	12:4	lamb, then share it with a close **n**
	18:16	I judge between a man and his **n**
	20:16	No lies about your **n**
	20:17	No lusting after your **n**'s house
	21:35	If someone's ox injures a **n**'s ox
	22:7	gives a **n** money or things
	22:8	the one who took the **n**'s goods
	22:14	If someone borrows an animal from a **n**
	22:26	If you take your **n**'s coat as security
	22:27	it may be your **n**'s only covering
	32:27	Kill brother, friend, **n**
Lev	6:2	deceiving his **n** regarding something
	18:20	Don't have sex with your **n**'s wife
	19:16	when your **n**'s life is in danger
	19:17	Don't secretly hate your **n**
	19:18	Love your **n** as yourself
	20:10	the wife, say, of his **n**
	24:19	Anyone who injures his **n** will get back
Dt	5:20	No lies about your **n**
	5:21	No coveting your **n**'s wife
	15:2	has lent money to a **n** writes it off
	15:9	leave your needy **n** in the lurch
	19:4	killed his **n** without premeditation
	19:5	a man goes with his **n** into the woods
	19:11	history of hatred toward his **n**
	19:14	Don't move your **n**'s boundary markers
	22:24	violating the fiancée of his **n**
	22:26	comes across his **n** out in the country
	23:24	When you enter your **n**'s vineyard
	23:25	walk through the ripe grain of your **n**
	24:10	you make a loan of any kind to your **n**
	27:17	who moves his **n**'s boundary marker
	27:24	anyone who kills his **n** in secret
1Sa	15:28	handed it over to your **n**, a better man
	28:16	is now on the side of your **n**
	28:17	given it to your **n**
2Sa	12:11	I'll give them to some **n**
1Ki	8:31	When someone hurts a **n** and promises
2Ch	6:22	When someone hurts a **n** and promises
Job	16:21	as a **n** stands up for a **n**
Ps	15:3	hurt your friend, don't blame your **n**
	22:11	I need a **n**
	88:18	You made lover and **n** alike dump me
	101:5	gossip who bad-mouths his **n**
Pr	3:28	Don't tell your **n**, "Maybe some other
	3:29	ways of taking advantage of your **n**
	6:1	if you've gone into hock with your **n**
	6:29	when you have sex with your **n**'s wife
	14:21	It's criminal to ignore a **n** in need
	29:5	A flattering **n** is up to no good
Isa	3:5	**N** against **n**, young against old
	19:2	brother fight brother, **n** fight **n**
	66:3	no different from murdering the **n**
Jer	5:8	pawing and snorting for his **n**'s wife
	9:8	**N** greets **n** with a smile
Eze	18:6	doesn't seduce a **n**'s spouse
	18:11	seduces his **n**'s spouse
	18:15	doesn't seduce his **n**'s spouse
	22:11	Anyone is fair game: **n**, daughter
Am	5:19	and is raped by a **n**

Mic	2:2	They bully the **n** and his family
	6:8	Do what is fair and just to your **n**
	7:5	Don't trust your **n**, don't confide
Mt	7:3	easy to see a smudge on your **n**'s face
	7:5	fit to offer a washcloth to your **n**
	19:19	love your **n** as you do yourself
Lk	6:41	easy to see a smudge on your **n**'s face
	6:42	fit to offer a washcloth to your **n**
	10:27	love your **n** as well as you do yourself
	10:29	just how would you define '**n**
	10:36	a **n** to the man attacked by robbers
Ac	10:3	angel . . . as real as his next-door **n**
	11:13	real as his next-door **n**
Eph	4:25	Tell your **n** the truth

Neighbors

Ex	33:11	as **n** speak to one another
Dt	6:14	other gods, the gods of your **n**
	15:11	give to your **n** in trouble
Jos	9:16	learned that they were next-door **n**
	9:22	when you're our next-door **n**
	10:1	were living as **n**
Jdg	18:22	before Micah and his **n** got organized
1Sa	30:26	to the elders of Judah, his **n**
2Ki	4:3	borrow jugs and bowls from all your **n**
1Ch	5:11	The family of Gad were their **n**
	12:40	N ranging from as far north
Ezr	1:6	Their **n** rallied behind them
	3:3	what their non-Israelite **n** might do
Ne	4:12	Jews who were their **n** kept reporting
	10:28	separated themselves from the foreign **n**
	10:30	our daughters to our foreign **n**
	10:31	foreign **n** bring goods or grain to sell
Job	31:34	fearing the gossip of the **n** so much
	35:8	your family and friends and **n**
Ps	31:11	I'm ridiculed by the **n**
	38:11	my **n** stab me in the back
	79:4	We're nothing but a joke to our **n**
	79:12	Give our jeering in what they've got
	89:41	a joke to all the **n**
	119:23	bad **n** maliciously gossip about me
	119:24	I listen to them as to good **n**
	120:6	camping among quarreling **n**
	129:8	Before the **n** have a chance to call out
Pr	21:3	justice with our **n** mean far more
	21:10	feel nothing for friends and **n**
	24:28	Don't talk about your **n** behind
	25:18	Anyone who tells lies against the **n**
SS	1:8	Stay with your shepherd **n**
	6:9	**n** and friends, blessed and praised
Isa	1:21	everyone living as good **n**
	16:7	antiphonal mock laments from the **n**
	38:11	No more meetings with my **n**
Jer	6:21	parents and children, **n** and friends
	7:5	the way you live and treat your **n**
	9:4	Be wary of even longtime **n**
	9:5	**N** gyp **n**, never telling the truth
	12:14	all the bad **n** who abused the land
	12:15	Once I've pulled the bad **n** out
	29:23	their **n**' wives, no less
	48:17	Weep for Moab, friends and **n**

N

	49:10	children and relatives and **n**
	49:18	their **n** in the sewers of history
	50:40	their **n**, the cities I did away with
Eze	28:24	put up with their thistle-and-thorn **n**
	28:26	I'll bring judgment on all the **n**
Joel	3:8	sell your children as slaves to your **n**
Hab	2:15	inviting your **n** to your drunken
Zec	7:9	Love your **n**. Be compassionate
Mt	9:23	and the **n** bringing in casseroles
Mk	5:38	and **n** bringing in casseroles
Lk	1:58	Her **n** and relatives
	2:44	looking for him among relatives and **n**
	11:8	knocking and waking all the **n**
	14:12	friends and family and rich **n**
	15:6	call in your friends and **n**
	15:9	she'll call her friends and **n**
Ac	24:16	clear conscience before God and my **n**
2Co	11:10	protect you from what the **n** will think
1Th	4:8	you're not offending your **n**

Nerve

Ne	6:16	our enemies totally lost their **n**
Isa	13:2	Direct them to the **n** center of power
Jer	3:4	Then you have the **n** to call out
	36:29	burn this scroll and then the **n** to say
Mt	7:4	Do you have the **n** to say
	14:30	he lost his **n** and started to sink
	18:21	Peter got up the **n** to ask
Lk	6:42	Do you have the **n** to say

Nerves

Job	6:12	Do you think I have **n** of steel
Ps	7:11	his **n** are sandpapered raw
Isa	65:3	They get on my **n**, are rude to my face
1Th	5:15	when you get on each other's **n**

Newborn

Dt	28:57	even the afterbirth of her **n** infants
Pr	8:25	I was already there, **n**
Eze	16:5	dirty and unwashed — a **n** nobody wanted
	16:22	naked and exposed, a blood-smeared **n**
Hos	2:3	expose her, naked as a **n**
Mt	2:2	pay homage to the **n** King of the Jews
Ac	7:19	forcing us to abandon our **n** infants

Newcomers

Job	8:9	we're **n** at this, with a lot to learn
Lk	10:21	showed them to these innocent **n**
2Pe	2:19	They promise these **n** freedom
1Jn	2:13	you **n** have won a big victory
	2:14	you **n** — such vitality and strength

News

Ge	21:6	all who get the **n** will laugh with me
	22:20	Abraham got the **n**
	26:32	came to him with **n** about the well
	29:13	When Laban heard the **n**

	31:22	Laban got the **n**: "Jacob's run off
	45:2	**n** was soon reported to Pharaoh
	45:16	It was good **n** to Pharaoh
Ex	15:2	I'm spreading the **n** far and wide
	18:1	the **n** that God had delivered Israel
Nu	20:29	the **n** that Aaron had died
Jos	9:1	Jebusites — got the **n**
Jdg	16:2	The **n** got around: "Samson's here."
1Sa	2:1	I'm bursting with God-**n**!
	4:13	into town to tell the bad **n**
	13:3	When the Philistines heard the **n**
	31:9	spread the good **n** all through
2Sa	1:4	said David. "What's the **n**?"
	1:20	don't post the **n** in the streets
	4:10	Good **n**! Saul is dead!
	11:7	David asked him for **n** from the front
	17:10	they'll fall apart at such **n**
	18:19	the good **n** that God has delivered him
	18:20	not the one to deliver the good **n**
	18:25	If he's alone, it must be good **n**
	18:26	This also must be good **n**
	18:27	He's bringing good **n** for sure
	18:31	Good **n**, my master and king!
1Ki	1:42	good man like you must have good **n**
	2:28	When this **n** reached Joab
	14:6	I've got bad **n** for you
2Ki	3:10	Bad **n**! God has gotten us three kings
	7:9	This is a day of good **n**
	9:15	sneak out of the city and blab the **n**
1Ch	10:9	reporting the victory **n** to their idols
	16:23	Get out his salvation **n** every day
Ne	6:16	all our enemies heard the **n**
Est	2:11	get **n** of what she was doing
	3:15	the city of Susa reeled from the **n**
Ps	21:13	We are out singing the good **n**
	22:31	good **n** — that God does what he says
	34:3	Join me in spreading the **n**
	39:4	Give me the bad **n**
	40:10	didn't keep the **n** of your ways
	68:11	thousands called out the good **n**
	71:18	the **n** Of your strong right arm
	96:2	Shout the **n** of his victory
	96:3	Take the **n** of his glory to the lost
	96:3	**N** of his wonders to one and all
	132:6	Remember how we got the **n**
	145:6	Your marvelous doings are headline **n**
Pr	15:30	good **n** makes you feel fit
Isa	12:4	spread the **n** of his great reputation
	21:3	Because of this **n** I'm doubled up in pain
	21:9	I heard them call out the war **n**
	21:10	The good **n** I get from God-of-the-Angel
	27:9	good **n** is that through this experience
	37:7	he'll get a rumor of bad **n** back home
	37:26	**n** that I've been behind this all along
	40:9	You're the preacher of good **n**
	41:27	I gave Jerusalem a preacher of good **n**
	48:14	Who among the gods has delivered the **n**
	48:20	Shout the **n**. Broadcast it
	52:7	bringing good **n**, Breaking the **n**
	61:1	preach good **n** to the poor
	61:3	Messages of joy instead of **n** of doom
Jer	4:5	broadcast the **n** in Jerusalem

	4:15	Bad **n** from Ephraim's hills
	4:16	Broadcast the **n** to Jerusalem
	6:24	We've heard the **n**, and we're as limp
	15:8	get the **n** of their sons killed
	20:15	curse the man who delivered the **n**
	20:16	haunted … with the bad **n** he brought
	31:7	Announce the good **n**
	32:24	is coming to pass — it's daily **n**
	39:16	to this city — bad **n**, not good **n**
	48:20	Tell the bad **n** along the Arnon
	49:23	shock when they hear the bad **n**
	50:28	reporting the **n** of God's vengeance
	50:46	**n** will be heard all over the world
	51:10	Let's tell the good **n** Back home
Eze	21:7	Because of the **n** that's coming
	26:2	cheered when they got the **n**
	33:30	Let's go hear the latest **n** from God
Da	10:11	I've been sent to bring you **n**
Am	5:18	it will be bad **n** before it's good **n**
Ob	1:1	We got the **n** straight from God
Na	1:15	bringing the latest good **n**: peace
Zep	2:5	The Word of God is bad **n** for you
Zec	8:13	a reputation as a bad-**n** people
Mt	9:26	The **n** was soon out
	9:35	reported kingdom **n**
	10:18	platform for preaching the kingdom **n**
	13:19	When anyone hears **n** of the kingdom
	13:22	person who hears the kingdom **n**
	13:23	person who hears and takes in the **N**
	14:13	When Jesus got the **n**, he slipped away
	23:37	the ones who brought you God's **n**
	24:14	good **n** — the Message of the kingdom
Mk	1:1	The good **n** of Jesus Christ
	1:28	**N** of this traveled fast
	1:45	spreading the **n** all over town
	4:18	the ones who hear the kingdom **n**
	16:15	announce the Message of God's good **n**
Lk	1:19	especially to bring you this glad **n**
	1:40	I'm bursting with God-**n**
	4:14	**N** that he was back spread
	4:18	preach the Message of good **n**
	7:17	The **n** of Jesus spread all through
	7:18	disciples reported back to him the **n**
	9:2	preach the **n** of God's kingdom
	9:6	telling the latest **n** of God
	16:16	the glad **n** and compelling invitation
	24:9	broke the **n** of all this to the Eleven
Jn	20:18	telling the **n** to the disciples
Ac	8:12	announcing the **n** of God's kingdom
	10:34	Peter fairly exploded with his good **n**
	11:1	The **n** traveled fast
	13:32	we're here today bringing you good **n**
	15:3	the **n** cheered — it was terrific **n**
	15:7	hear the Message of this good **n**
	16:10	God had called us to preach the good **n**
	19:17	It was soon **n** all over Ephesus
	20:25	the **n** of God's inaugurated kingdom
Ro	1:9	spreading the good **n** of his Son
	1:15	preaching this wonderful good **n** of God
	1:16	It's **n** I'm most proud to proclaim
	11:28	embrace the good **n** of the Message
2Co	2:13	for me with **n** of your condition

Php	1:27	trust in the Message, the good **n**
	2:19	all the **n** of you he can gather
1Th	1:8	The **n** of your faith in God is out
1Ti	2:6	Eventually the **n** is going to get out
	2:7	my appointed work: getting this **n**
3Jn	1:3	the **n** that you persist in following

Noble

Jdg	9:28	bear the **n** name of Shechem
Ne	10:29	all joined their **n** kinsmen
Est	6:9	one of the king's most **n** princes
Isa	32:8	those who are **n** make **n** plans
	32:8	and stand for what is **n**
Eze	17:8	became a **n** vine
Mt	1:19	Joseph, chagrined but **n**
	27:19	mixed up in judging this **n** man
Ro	5:7	someone good and **n** could inspire us
Php	4:8	meditating on things true, **n**

Noblemen

| Nu | 22:21| went off with the **n** from Moab |

Nobles

Nu	22:8	The Moabite **n** stayed with him
	22:13	told Balak's **n**, "Go back home
	22:14	So the Moabite **n** left
	22:15	Balak sent another group of **n**
	22:35	Balaam continued to go with Balak's **n**
	22:40	Balaam and the **n** who were with him
	23:6	with him all the **n** of Moab
	23:17	and the **n** of Moab with him
2Ch	23:20	got everyone together — officers, **n**
Ne	2:16	priests, **n**, local officials
	3:5	**n**, who wouldn't work with their master
	4:14	spoke to the **n**, officials, and
	4:19	I spoke to the **n** and officials
	5:7	I called the **n** and officials
	6:17	between the **n** of Judah and Tobiah
	6:18	Many of the **n** had ties to him
	7:5	God put it in my heart to gather the **n**
Est	2:18	great banquet for all his **n**
Jer	39:6	then killed all the **n** of Judah
La	4:7	splendid and sacred **n** once glowed
Da	5:1	great feast for his one thousand **n**
	5:2	he and his **n**, his wives and concubines
	5:3	king and his **n**, his wives
	5:9	The **n** were in a panic
	5:10	hysteria among the king and his **n**
	5:23	party so that you and your **n**
	6:17	and the signet rings of all his **n**

Nobodies

1Sa	18:18	I'm from a family of **n**!
Job	20:9	now they're **n**, unnoticed
Isa	24:2	celebrities and **n** alike
Hos	1:9	You've become **n** to me
Ro	9:25	I'll call **n** and make them somebodies

N

| | 12:16 | don't be stuck-up. Make friends with **n** |
| 1Co | 1:28 | chose these "**n**" to expose |

Nomads

Isa	42:11	calling the Kedar **n** to join in
	60:6	young camels of **n** in Midian
	60:7	roundup of flocks from the **n**
Jer	25:23	**n** on the fringe of the desert
	35:7	Live in tents as **n**
	35:10	We live in tents as **n**
	49:28	Plunder the Bedouin **n** from the east
	49:30	run for your lives, You **n** from Hazor
	49:31	Go after these relaxed **n** who live free
	49:32	defenseless **n** on the fringes

Noose

Job	18:9	caught, their necks in a **n**
	30:18	tied hand and foot, my neck in a **n**
Ps	18:4	hangman's **n** was tight at my throat
Jer	18:22	The **n** is practically around my neck
	50:29	Tighten the **n**! Leave no loopholes!

Nothingness

Ge	1:2	Earth was a soup of **n**
Job	3:7	turn that night into pure **n**
Ecc	4:7	wisp of smoke on its way to **n**
Isa	45:19	Seek me in emptiness, in dark **n**
Jer	48:30	the sheer **n** of Moab

Nourish

| Joel | 2:23 | words to refresh and **n** your soul |
| Mt | 5:45 | sun to warm and the rain to **n** |

Nourished

1Ki	19:8	**N** by that meal, he walked forty days
Isa	44:14	in the forest, **n** by the rain
Eze	31:14	No more trees **n** from the great deep

Nourishes

| Jn | 6:27 | food that **n** your lasting life |
| Col | 2:19 | grow up healthy in God only as he **n** us |

Nourishing

2Sa	13:6	come and make some **n** dumplings here
	13:10	took the **n** dumplings she had prepared
Ps	119:20	insatiable for your **n** commands
Isa	33:16	A **n**, satisfying way to live
	55:3	my life-giving, life-**n** words
Eze	33:15	cultivating life-**n** ways
Eph	4:16	**n** us so that we will grow up healthy

Nurse

| Ge | 21:7 | Sarah would one day **n** a baby |
| | 24:59 | their sister Rebekah with her **n** |

	35:8	when Rebekah's **n**, Deborah, died
Ex	2:7	so she can **n** the baby for you
	2:9	Take this baby and **n** him for me
2Sa	4:4	His **n** picked him up and ran
1Ki	3:21	got up in the morning to **n** my son
2Ki	11:2	She hid him and his **n**
2Ch	22:11	She hid him and his **n**
Ps	41:3	God becomes our **n**, nurses us
Isa	66:12	You'll **n** at her breasts
Mic	7:18	You don't **n** your anger
1Co	3:2	**n** you since you don't seem capable

Nursed

Ex	2:9	woman took the child and **n** him
1Sa	1:23	She stayed home and **n** her son
Isa	49:13	tenderly **n** his . . . people
Lk	11:27	and the breasts at which you **n**

Nursing

Ge	32:15	camels with their **n** young
	33:13	the flocks and herds are **n**
Ex	2:7	go and get a **n** mother from the Hebrews
Nu	11:12	carry them around like a **n** mother
2Ki	4:16	you're going to be **n** an infant son
Job	24:9	**N** mothers have their babies snatched
Ps	8:2	**N** infants gurgle choruses about you
Isa	11:8	**n** child will crawl over rattlesnake
	40:11	leading the **n** ewes to good pasture
	51:21	You who are **n** the hangovers
Joel	2:16	the children, too, even the **n** babies
Mt	24:19	**n** mothers will have it especially hard
Mk	13:17	**n** mothers will have it especially hard
Lk	21:23	**n** mothers will have it especially hard
1Co	3:2	nothing much more than **n** at the breast

O

Obedience

Dt	11:9	Your **o** will give you a long life
	17:19	in reverent **o** before these rules
Jos	19:50	In **o** to God's word
Jdg	2:17	the road of **o** to God's commands
1Ki	8:23	sincerely live in **o** to your way
	8:40	lifelong reverent and believing **o**
2Ki	23:24	in **o** to the words of God's Revelation
	23:25	in total and repentant **o** to God
1Ch	21:19	in **o** to God's command
	22:12	will rule in reverent **o** under God's
2Ch	6:14	sincerely live in **o** to your way
	6:31	lifelong reverence and believing **o**
	6:33	live in reverent **o** before you
	26:5	live in reverent **o** before God
	27:6	steady and determined life of **o** to God
Ne	13:27	Do you call this **o**
Ps	65:1	Zion-dwelling God, And also **o**
Ecc	8:2	you gave a sacred oath of **o**
Jer	11:4	Your **o** will close the deal
	31:19	After you trained me to to **o**
Zec	6:15	a life of responsive **o**

0

Mt	7:21	What is required is serious o
	12:50	O is thicker than blood
Mk	3:35	O is thicker than blood
Lk	8:21	O is thicker than blood
Ac	13:3	that circle of intensity and o
Ro	2:14	they confirm its truth by their o
2Co	7:15	the story of your prompt o
	10:6	building lives of o into maturity
Gal	5:7	from the true course of o
Php	2:9	Because of that o, God lifted him high
	2:12	you lived in responsive o
1Th	5:12	urging and guiding you along in your o
1Ti	1:4	deepening faith and o
Heb	5:8	learned trusting-o by what he suffered

Obedient

Nu	9:20	stayed in camp, o to God's command
Jos	4:12	o to Moses' instructions
1Ki	8:61	your lives must be totally o to God
	9:4	o to my guidance and judgments
	17:1	before whom I stand in o service
2Ki	14:6	He was o to what God commanded
2Ch	7:17	o to my guidance and judgments
	17:4	God of his father and was o to him
Ps	119:34	my whole life one long, o response
Pr	15:32	an o, God-willed life is spacious
Jer	31:18	put me, trained and o, to use
Zech	3:7	remain o in my service
Lk	5:14	Your cleansed and o life
Ac	5:21	Promptly o, they entered the Temple
	26:19	became an o believer on the spot
Ro	1:5	entering into o trust in Jesus
	16:26	be brought into o belief
2Co	9:13	o to the plain meaning of the Message
Php	2:8	he lived a selfless, o life
	2:8	and then died a selfless, o
1Ti	2:12	study to be quiet and o
1Pe	1:2	work of the Spirit to keep you o
	1:15	As o children, let yourselves be

Obediently

Ex	15:26	listen o to how God tells you to live
	19:5	listen o to what I say
Lev	26:3	my decrees and o keep my
Nu	9:23	They lived o by God's orders
	14:43	you have left off o following God
	27:20	will listen o to him
Dt	4:30	listen o to what he says
	4:40	O live by his rules and commands
	5:1	Listen o to the rules and regulations
	6:3	Listen o, Israel. Do what you're told
	11:13	if you listen o to the commandments
	11:27	listen o to the commandments of God
	12:28	listen o to these words that I command
	13:4	listen o to what he says, serve him
	13:18	O listen to God, your God
	15:5	listen o to the Voice of God
	18:15	a prophet like me. Listen o to him
	26:14	I have listened o to the Voice of God
	26:17	and commandments; and listen o to him

	27:9	Listen o, Israel
	28:13	o listen to and diligently keep
	28:15	what will happen if you don't o listen
	28:45	didn't o listen to the Voice of God
	28:62	didn't listen o to the Voice of God
	30:8	make a new start, listening o to God
	30:10	But only if you listen o to God
	30:17	refuse to listen o, and willfully
	30:20	your God, listening o to him
	34:9	People of Israel listened o to him
Jos	22:2	o done everything I have commanded
	23:6	O do everything written in the Book
1Ki	6:12	following my instructions . . . o
	8:25	as careful to live o in my presence
2Ki	23:3	to follow God believingly and o
2Ch	6:16	as careful to live o in my presence
	34:31	to follow God believingly and o
	34:33	o following God
Jer	26:13	Listen o to the Message of your God
Eze	3:10	Listen to them o. Make them your own
	20:11	how to live well and o before me
	20:13	my laws for living well and o
	20:16	despised my laws for living o
Mal	2:2	If you refuse to o listen
Lk	2:51	and lived o with them

Obey

Ge	49:10	ruler comes and the nations o him
Ex	1:18	Why didn't you o my orders?
	23:21	Pay close attention to him. O him
	23:22	o him and do everything I tell you
	24:7	God said, we'll do. Yes, we'll o
Lev	18:4	O my laws and live by my decrees
	26:14	But if you refuse to o me
Dt	7:12	When you, on your part, will o
	8:20	doom because you wouldn't o
	9:23	Refused to trust him. Wouldn't o him
	10:13	o the commandments and regulations
	11:1	regulations; o his commandments
	11:22	commandment that I command you to o
	21:18	discipline him he still won't o
	30:2	o him with your whole heart and soul
Jos	1:17	We obeyed Moses . . . ; we'll also o
	1:18	refuses to o whatever you command
Jdg	3:4	whether they would o God's commands
1Sa	12:14	If you fear God, worship and o him
	12:15	But if you don't o him and rebel
	15:19	So why did you not o God?
	15:20	I did o God. I did the job God set
	28:18	It's because you did not o God
1Ki	11:34	follow my directions and o my orders
	20:36	Because you wouldn't o God's orders
1Ch	10:13	He didn't o God's words
	28:8	as God's people, o and study
	29:19	so that he can o what you command
Ezr	7:26	Anyone who does not o the Teaching
Ne	1:5	who love him and o his commands
	9:16	they wouldn't o your commands
Job	36:11	If they o and serve him
Ps	119:88	so I can alertly o your every word
	119:129	miracle word—how could I help but o

O

Isa	1:19	If you'll willingly o, you'll feast
	65:8	preserve those in Israel who o me
Jer	7:23	O me. Do what I say
	7:28	the nation that wouldn't o God
	11:4	O what I tell you
	11:7	I warned them . . . : "O me or else
	11:8	But they didn't o
	13:10	wicked bunch of people who won't o me
	22:4	If you o these commands
	22:5	But if you don't o these commands
	42:6	We'll o whatever our God tells us
	42:13	refusing to o the command of your God
Eze	11:20	o my statutes and be careful to o my
Da	7:27	other rulers will serve and o them
Joel	2:11	the strength of those who o him
Ac	5:29	necessary to o God rather than men
	5:32	whom God gives to those who o him
1Co	7:17	Live and o and love and believe
Eph	6:5	respectfully o your earthly masters
2Th	1:8	refuse to o the Message
	3:14	anyone refuses to o our clear command
2Ti	2:25	patiently with those who refuse to o
Heb	4:12	laying us open to listen and o
	5:10	salvation to all who believingly o him

Obeyed

Ge	22:18	your descendants because you o me
	26:5	Because Abraham o my summons
	28:7	Jacob had o his parents
Nu	20:27	Moses o God's command
Jos	1:17	We o Moses to the letter
Jdg	2:2	But you haven't o me!
1Ki	11:33	hasn't followed directions or o orders
	17:5	Elijah o God's orders
2Ki	11:9	captains o the orders of Jehoiada
	18:6	o to the letter everything God had
	22:13	ancestors haven't o a thing written
1Ch	29:23	all Israel o him
2Ch	23:8	o the orders of Jehoiada the priest
	34:21	ancestors haven't o a thing written
Job	23:12	I've o every word he's spoken
Jer	34:17	You have not o me and set your
	35:14	honored and o their ancestor's command
	35:18	o his commands and followed through
	42:21	you haven't o a word of it
Mt	2:14	Joseph o.
	2:21	Joseph o.

Obeying

Ex	15:26	in his presence, o his commandments
Nu	26:3	O God's command
Dt	2:37	land you didn't take, o God's command
	20:17	o the command of God, your God
1Ki	11:38	following directions and o orders
Est	1:15	Vashti for not o King Xerxes' summons
Ps	148:8	hurricanes o his orders
Jnh	3:3	o God's orders to the letter
1Co	7:19	really important thing is o God's call
	7:21	Slavery is no roadblock to o
Eph	6:5	with an eye to o the real master

Obeys

Lev	18:5	The person who o them lives by them
Ecc	8:5	wise person o promptly and accurately
Eze	18:9	faithfully honors and o my laws
Mt	12:50	person who o my heavenly Father's will
Mk	3:35	person who o God's will is my brother

Oblivion

Ge	19:13	sent to blast this place into o
Ps	88:5	I'm a black hole in o
	109:15	but they themselves sunk in o
Isa	14:20	your evil life will never be named. O
Jer	13:19	the whole country dragged to o
Eze	36:35	the ruined cities, smashed into o
Da	2:35	by the wind, scattered to o

Oblivious

Ge	19:33	He was o, knowing nothing
	19:35	Again he was o, knowing nothing
2Ki	11:3	Athaliah, o to his existence, ruled
2Ch	22:12	Athaliah, o to his existence, ruled
Est	5:9	ignoring him, o to him
Job	28:8	Wild animals are o to it
	39:7	He's o to the cries of teamsters
Isa	30:24	O to war and earthquake
Da	9:13	o to your clear warning
Hos	7:10	Israel lumbers along o to God
	10:5	are o to the sham, the shame
Mt	7:3	be o to the ugly sneer on your own
Lk	6:41	be o to the ugly sneer on your own
Ro	13:11	doze off, o to God
2Co	2:11	we're not o to his sly ways
2Pe	1:9	o that your old sinful life has been
Rev	3:3	sleep on, o to God
	3:17	o that in fact you're a pitiful

Obscene

Lev	7:21	animal uncleanness or an o object
Jdg	19:23	Don't be o — this man is my guest
1Ki	15:13	shockingly o memorial to the whore
2Ki	3:2	he destroyed the o Baal stone
	23:6	took the o phallic Asherah pole
	23:13	the o Sidonian sex goddess Ashtoreth
	23:24	foul and o relics and images
2Ch	15:8	cleaned out the o and polluting
	15:16	shockingly o image of the sex goddess
Ezr	9:11	polluted with the o vulgarities
Ps	78:58	their o idolatries broke his heart
Isa	66:17	climaxed in that foul and o meal
Jer	7:30	set up their o god-images
	16:18	lives with their o no-gods
	32:34	set up o god and goddess statues
Eze	8:17	provoke me . . . with their o gestures
	11:18	all the rotten images and o idols
	11:21	their rotten images and o idols
	16:50	They put on airs and lived o lives
	16:58	the shame of your o and vile life
	43:8	their o and vile worship

	44:13	the shame of their vile and o lives
Da	11:31	set up in its place the o sacrilege
	12:11	o desecration is set up in its place
Mic	6:10	Do you expect me to overlook o wealth

Obscenities

Dt	29:17	an eyeful of their o
	32:16	with o they vexed him no end
1Ki	21:26	indulged in outrageous o
Ezr	9:1	with all their vulgar o
	9:14	people who practice all these o
Ps	42:10	these tormentors with their o
	74:22	saying about you, all the vile o
Isa	59:3	tongue swollen from muttering o
Eze	5:11	your o and disgusting no-god idols
	6:11	all the evil o rife in Israel
	7:3	make you pay for your disgusting o
	7:4	Your disgusting o will boomerang
	7:8	make you pay for your disgusting o
	7:9	Your disgusting o will boomerang
	7:20	make those god-o a stench
	8:6	see what they're doing? Outrageous o
	8:9	look at the o they're engaging in
	8:17	Judah engages in these outrageous o
	9:4	anguish over the outrageous o
	12:16	disgusting o they've been involved in
	14:6	Turn your backs on all your . . . o
	16:22	years of outrageous o and whorings
	16:43	compound your outrageous o
	16:47	you engaged in outrageous o
	16:51	committed far more o than she ever did
	18:12	admires idols, commits outrageous o
	18:24	vile o that the wicked person
	20:4	the outrageous o of their parents
	22:2	Face her with all her outrageous o
	23:36	Make them face their outrageous o
	23:37	o ranging from adultery to murder
	33:26	you engage in o
	33:29	because of all the o they've practiced
	36:31	all those o you've carried out
	37:23	all those vile o and rebellions
	44:6	No more of these vile o, Israel
	44:7	With all your vile o
Mk	7:21	o, lusts, thefts, murders
Rev	17:4	brimming with defiling o

Obscenity

Jer	49:13	a stinking garbage dump, an o
Na	9:27	a desecrating o will be set up

Observance

Ex	13:9	The day of o will be like a sign
	13:16	The o functions like a sign
Nu	15:40	tassels will signal remembrance and o

Observation

Job	4:8	It's my o that those who plow evil

Observe

Ge	18:19	to o God's way of life
Ex	13:5	you are to o this service
	20:8	O the Sabbath day, to keep it holy
	31:16	keep the Sabbath, o Sabbath-keeping
Lev	22:9	The priests must o my instructions
	23:32	total rest, a fast day. O your Sabbath
	25:2	the land will o a Sabbath to God
	25:18	Keep my decrees and o my laws
	26:14	won't o my commandments
Nu	13:19	O the land: Is it pleasant or harsh?
Dt	5:15	commands you to o the day of Sabbath
	7:9	who love him and o his commandments
	11:32	O all the regulations and rules
	12:1	regulations that you must diligently o
	16:1	O the month of Abib by celebrating
	16:13	O the Feast-of-Booths for seven days
Jdg	13:14	She's to o everything I commanded
1Sa	23:22	Learn his routines. O his movements
Pr	22:29	O people who are good at their work
	29:16	will eventually o their collapse
	29:20	O the people who always talk
Jer	36:9	there in Jerusalem to o a fast to God
Eze	45:21	you will o the Passover
Ro	8:22	All around us we o a pregnant creation
Gal	3:16	You will o that Scripture
	6:13	selective in the laws they do o
Eph	5:2	O how Christ loved us
Jas	2:19	then o you complacently sitting back

Observed

Ex	12:14	festival celebration to be o always
	12:17	fixed festival to be o always
1Ki	11:28	Solomon o what a good worker he was
2Ki	20:5	I've o your tears
Ecc	4:4	I o all the work and ambition
	8:9	All this I o as I tried my best
Eze	41:8	I o that the Temple had
	46:21	In each corner I o another court
Mt	2:2	We o a star in the eastern sky
	20:25	You've o how godless rulers throw
Mk	10:42	You've o how godless rulers throw
Jn	7:2	Tabernacles, a feast o annually
	20:6	o the linen cloths lying there
Ro	15:17	accomplished and what I have o
Gal	2:14	not being o by the watchdogs
	3:12	a fact o in Scripture

Observer

Php	3:6	o of everything set down in God's law

Observing

Dt	6:2	o all his rules and regulations
	15:5	diligently o every commandment
	16:12	be diligent in o these regulations
Job	31:4	Isn't God looking, o how I live?
Ecc	9:13	I was o how wisdom fares on this earth
Mk	12:41	he was o how the crowd tossed money in

Ac	21:20	more zealous than ever in o the laws
	22:12	sterling reputation in o our laws
2Co	11:19	you sit there in the judgment seat o
Gal	4:10	scrupulously o all the traditions

Obsessed

1Sa	26:20	king of Israel o with a single flea
2Sa	13:2	Amnon was o with his sister Tamar
1Ki	11:1	King Solomon was o with women
Job	36:17	o with putting the blame on God
Ps	37:12	o with doing them in
	64:1	o with feelings of doomsday
Ecc	9:3	so many people are o with evil
Eze	22:3	a city o with no-god idols
	23:9	for whom she was so o with lust
Hos	12:1	Ephraim, o with god-fantasies
Am	6:6	those o with looking good
Lk	16:14	the Pharisees, a money-o bunch
Ac	22:19	how o I was with hunting out those
	26:11	a one-man terror o with obliterating
Ro	8:5	o with measuring their own moral
Php	2:4	o with getting your own advantage
2Th	2:11	they're so o with evil
1Ti	5:11	o with wanting to get a husband
	6:17	quit being . . . so o with money
Heb	13:5	o with getting more material things
2Pe	2:14	They're o with adultery

Obsession

Ro	8:6	O with self in these matters
Eph	4:19	let themselves go in sexual o
Col	2:18	their o with angels

Obsessions

Jer	13:27	Your o with gods, gods, and more gods

Obsessive

Eze	23:20	stallions o in their lust
	23:49	pay the price for all your o sex
Gal	5:12	o as they are about circumcision

Obsessively

Ecc	4:8	working o late into the night

Obsolete

Ps	111:8	Never out-of-date, never o
	119:98	my enemies; they never become o
Isa	30:11	Don't bore us with o religion
	51:6	setting-things-right will never be o
2Co	3:17	legislation is recognized as o
Col	3:10	All the old fashions are now o

Occult

Lev	19:31	Don't dabble in the o
	20:6	reject persons who dabble in the o

1Sa	15:23	worse than fooling around in the o
Rev	9:21	o, promiscuous, and thieving ways

Odd

Est	3:8	There is an o set of people scattered
Eze	3:25	And then something o: "Son of man
1Co	4:12	we pick up o jobs anywhere we can

Offend

Ac	16:3	circumcised him so he wouldn't o

Offended

Ge	38:7	grievously o God and God took his life
	38:10	God was much o by what he did
1Ki	8:32	setting the o free of any charges
1Ch	21:7	God, o by the whole thing, punished
2Ch	6:23	set the o free, dismissing all charges
Lk	5:30	came to his disciples greatly o
	11:38	Pharisee was shocked and somewhat o
	23:11	Mightily o, Herod turned on Jesus
Gal	5:11	no one would be o if I mentioned

Offender

1Ki	8:32	making the o pay for his offense
2Ch	6:23	making the o pay for the offense
2Co	2:9	wasn't on punishing the o

Offending

Pr	30:32	call attention to yourself by o people
1Th	4:8	you're not o your neighbors

Offense

Ge	20:9	bring on me and my kingdom this huge
Ex	8:26	our God would give great o
1Ki	8:32	making the offender pay for his o
2Ch	6:23	making the offender pay for the o
Pr	17:9	Overlook an o and bond a friendship
Mal	2:13	a second o: You fill the place
Ac	26:8	why it's a criminal o to believe
Col	3:13	quick to forgive an o

Offensive

Ex	8:26	sacrifice what is so deeply o
Dt	23:14	don't permit anything indecent or o
1Sa	7:7	Philistine leaders went on the o
2Ki	16:18	were o to the king of Assyria
	17:9	things o to their God
Ac	15:20	not serve food o to Jewish Christians
	15:29	food o to Jewish Christians
	21:25	food o to Jewish Christians
1Th	2:15	They make themselves o to God

Opening

Ge	18:10	Sarah was listening at the tent o

	44:11	and o them up for inspection
Ex	28:32	with an o for the head
	39:23	The o of the robe at the center
1Sa	3:15	duties, o the doors of the sanctuary
2Ki	7:2	Trapdoors o in the sky and food
	7:19	Trapdoors o in the sky and food
	25:4	escaped through an o in the wall
Isa	42:7	o blind eyes, releasing prisoners
Jer	52:7	army fled through an o in the wall
Da	6:17	slab was placed over the o of the den
Mt	5:16	By o up to others, you'll prompt
Mk	14:3	O the bottle, she poured it on
	15:46	rolled a large stone across the o
1Co	14:9	what's the point of o your mouth
2Co	2:11	give Satan an o for yet more mischief
Rev	3:7	o doors no one can lock

Opinion

2Ki	18:3	In God's o he was a good king
	21:20	In God's o he lived an evil life
	23:32	In God's o, he was an evil king
	23:37	In God's o he was an evil king
	24:9	In God's o he also was an evil king
2Ch	18:6	Let's get a second o
	25:16	Did I ask for your o? Shut up
	29:2	In God's o he was a good king
	33:2	In God's o he was a bad king
	33:22	In God's o he lived an evil life
	36:5	In God's o he was an evil king
	36:9	In God's o he was an evil king
Ezr	9:12	Don't cultivate their good o
Pr	29:25	The fear of human o disables
Isa	5:21	hold such a high o of yourselves
Eze	44:24	When there's a difference of o
Hos	7:16	Ridicule in the court of world o
Mt	10:32	Stand up for me against world o
	11:19	O polls don't count for much
	21:46	intimidated by public o
	22:16	indifferent to popular o
Mk	12:12	intimidated by public o, held back
	12:14	you are indifferent to public o
Lk	7:35	O polls don't count for much
	20:19	were intimidated by public o
Ac	14:4	there was a split in public o
1Co	4:3	even less where I rank in popular o
	7:40	The Master, in my o, thinks so, too
Gal	2:20	or have your good o
1Th	2:13	pass it off as just one more human o
Jas	2:1	don't let public o influence how you
2Pe	1:20	Scripture is a matter of private o

Opinions

Ro	14:1	strong on o but weak in the faith
	14:23	trying to impose your o on others
1Co	2:13	rely on the world's guesses and o
2Ti	4:3	spiritual junk food — catchy o

Oppress

| Pr | 28:3 | The wicked who o the poor |

Oppressed

Jdg	4:3	because he had cruelly o them
	10:12	o you and you cried out to me for help
Ne	5:15	o the people by taxing them
Pr	12:24	the lazy are o by work
Isa	52:4	At the other end, Assyria o them
	58:6	free the o, cancel debts
Eze	16:49	They ignored the o and the poor
Hos	8:10	feel what it's like to be o
Gal	6:2	reach out to those who are o

Oppressing

| Eze | 18:18 | o the weak, robbing brothers |

Oppression

Ex	14:30	delivered Israel that day from the o
	18:9	delivering them from Egyptian o
	18:10	delivered his people from the o
Jdg	2:18	save them from their enemies' o
	13:5	deliverance from Philistine o
1Sa	7:3	he'll save you from Philistine o
	9:16	free my people from Philistine o
	10:18	I delivered you from Egyptian o
2Sa	3:18	save my people Israel from the o
2Ki	13:5	brought them out from under Aram's o
	13:7	Jehoahaz's army after Hazael's o
	17:7	brutal o of Pharaoh king of Egypt
	17:39	who will save you from enemy o
Est	9:16	freeing themselves from o
Ps	106:10	He saved them from a life of o
	107:2	Tell how he freed you from o
	136:11	rescued Israel from Egypt's o
Isa	14:25	lift the weight of o from all
Eze	30:18	put an end to her arrogant o

Oppressive

| Eze | 22:7 | o against orphans and widows |
| Ro | 7:6 | all those o regulations |

Oppressor

Jdg	6:9	every o; I pushed them out of your way
Isa	14:29	celebrate the defeat of your cruel o
	60:14	descendants of your o will come bowing
Da	12:7	o of the holy people was brought down

Oppressors

Ps	106:11	the waters flowed back on their o
	119:121	don't leave me to the mercy of my o
Ecc	4:1	the iron grip of o, no one to rescue
Isa	1:24	I'll get my o off my back
	8:9	But face the facts, all you o
	9:4	abuse of o and cruelty of tyrants
	19:20	cry out in prayer to God because of o
	25:3	brutal o bow in worshipful reverence
	25:4	Brutal o are like a winter blizzard
	28:12	he'll do it through foreign o

O

Jer	50:33	Their o have them in a grip of steel
Zep	3:1	the rebellious city, the home of o
Heb	11:25	soft life of sin with the o

Oracle

Nu	23:7	Balaam spoke his message-o
	23:18	Balaam spoke his message-o
	24:3	and he spoke his o-message
	24:15	Then he spoke his o-message
	24:20	Balaam . . . delivered an o-message
	24:21	delivered his o-message to them
	24:23	Balaam spoke his final o-message
	27:21	the priest who, using the o-Urim
Jdg	9:37	coming straight from the O Oak
1Co	14:36	imagine that you're a sacred o
Rev	1:3	hearers and keepers of these o words

Ordeal

Mt	16:21	submit to an o of suffering
Mk	8:31	proceed to an o of suffering
Lk	9:22	proceed to an o of suffering

Ordinance

Lev	16:29	practice for you, a perpetual o
	16:31	You must fast. It is a perpetual o
	16:34	This is a perpetual o for you

Ordinances

Eze	5:6	rebelled against my laws and o
	11:12	haven't followed my statutes and o
	43:18	These are the o for conduct
	44:5	the o of this Temple of God

O

Orgies

Dt	4:3	who joined in the Baal Peor o
Ps	78:58	Their pagan o provoked God's anger
Jer	5:7	left me for o in sex shrines
Eze	16:26	seeking them out in their sex o
Hos	2:8	that she wasted on wild Baal-o
	7:14	bloody in their sex-and-religion o
	9:1	Don't waste your life in wild o
Hab	2:15	roping them into your sexual o

Orgy

| Lev | 17:7 | a kind of religious o |
| Eze | 36:5 | against Edom, who in an o of violence |

Orphan

Dt	14:29	the foreigner, the o, and the widow
	16:11	the foreigner, the o and widow
	24:19	the foreigner, the o, and the widow
	24:20	the foreigner, the o, and the widow
	24:21	the foreigner, the o, and the widow
	26:12	the foreigner, the o, and the widow
	26:13	given it to the Levite, foreigner, o

| | 27:19 | justice due the foreigner, o, or widow |
| Hos | 14:3 | in you the o finds mercy |

Orphaned

2Ki	25:21	Judah went into exile, o from her land
Jer	52:27	Judah went into exile, o from her land
Jn	14:18	I will not leave you o

Orphans

Ex	22:22	Don't mistreat widows or o
	22:24	end up widows and your children o
Dt	10:18	o and widows are treated fairly
	16:14	and the o and widows who live
	24:17	foreigners and o get their just rights
Job	22:9	heartless, you crushed o
Ps	10:14	o won't be o forever
	10:18	O get parents, the homeless get homes
	68:5	Father of o, champion of widows
	109:9	Make o of his children
	109:12	no one willing to give his o a break
	146:9	takes the side of o and widows
Pr	23:10	cheat o out of their property
Isa	9:17	no feeling for their o and widows
Jer	5:28	throw o to the wolves
	7:6	exploiting . . . o and widows
	22:3	take advantage of the homeless, the o
	49:11	I'll take care of your o
La	5:3	O we are, not a father in sight
Eze	22:7	oppressive against o and widows
Zec	7:10	Don't take advantage of widows, o
Mal	3:5	who take advantage of widows and o

Outlaw

1Sa	22:8	has taken the side of this, this... o
	22:13	setting him up as an o
	22:15	trying to get at with this 'o' talk
Pr	29:24	Befriend an o and become an enemy
Eze	13:9	o them from the land of Israel

Outlawed

| 2Ch | 28:3 | the o burning of incense |

Outlaws

| 1Ki | 11:24 | collected a band of o |
| Ps | 54:3 | O are out to get me |

Outrage

Jdg	19:23	man is my guest. Don't commit this o
	20:12	What's the meaning of this o
2Sa	13:32	This happened because of Absalom's o
Job	40:11	Unleash your o. Target the arrogant
Pr	20:23	rigged scales are an o
Isa	14:6	A relentless rain of cruel o
	22:14	You'll pay for this o
Jer	6:15	embarrassed over this o?
	8:12	embarrassed over this o?

	50:29	brazen insolence is an o against God
Hab	1:13	o! Evil men swallow up the righteous
Zec	11:3	Do you hear the o of the lions
Lk	3:20	this o: He put John in jail
Rev	2:24	who have nothing to do with this o

Outraged

Ge	34:7	They were o, explosive with anger
Est	3:5	kneel before him, he was o
Ps	11:5	if anyone cheats, God's o
Mt	18:31	servants saw this . . ., they were o
	22:7	king was o and sent his soldiers
Lk	14:21	He was o and told the servant
Ac	22:24	that provoked this o violence

Outrageous

Ge	44:5	uses it for divination. This is o
Jdg	20:3	How did this o evil happen
	20:6	vile and o crime was committed
	20:10	accounts for this o and vile evil
1Ki	20:7	Look at this — o!
	21:26	He indulged in o obscenities
2Ki	16:3	indulged in the o practice of
	19:6	these o blasphemies
	21:11	has committed these o sins
2Ch	28:3	indulged in the o practice of
	36:8	the o sacrilege he committed
Ps	43:2	wringing my hands over these o people
Ecc	4:1	attention to all the o violence
	9:3	I find this o — the worst thing
Jer	7:10	go on with all this o sacrilege
	32:34	an o desecration
Eze	8:6	see what they're doing? O obscenities
	8:17	Judah engages in these o obscenities
	9:4	anguish over the o obscenities
	14:6	backs on all your o obscenities
	16:2	Jerusalem with her o violations
	16:22	years of o obscenities and whorings
	16:43	compound your o obscenities
	16:47	Haven't you engaged in o obscenities
	18:12	commits o obscenities
	20:4	the o obscenities of their parents
	22:2	Face her with all her o obscenities
	23:36	Make them face their o obscenities
Mt	21:15	leaders saw the o things he was doing
2Co	10:13	We aren't making o claims here
Jas	2:17	God-talk without God-acts is o

Outstanding

Jos	17:1	he was an o fighter
1Ch	26:6	sons who provided o leadership
	26:8	all of them o and strong
	26:9	sons and relatives who were o
	26:31	o men were found at Jazer
Ro	16:7	Both of them are o leaders

Oversee

Ge	1:18	o Day and Night, to separate light

Eze	34:16	I'll . . . o the strong ones
Zec	3:7	decisions around here and o my affairs
	10:4	use them to o his work

Overseeing

Mt	24:45	qualifies for the job of o the kitchen

Overseen

Est	2:14	return to a second harem o by

Overseer

Est	2:8	Hegai who was o of the women

Oversees

Est	2:3	the king's eunuch who o the women

Owe

Job	36:3	justice I o to my Maker himself
Ps	89:18	All we are and have we o to God
Lk	16:5	How much do you o my master
	16:7	you, what do you o?
Ro	8:12	don't o this old do-it-yourself life
	13:8	huge debt of love you o each other
	16:4	believers also o them plenty
Phm	1:19	you o your very life to me

Owed

Mt	15:5	What I o to you I've given to God
	18:28	servants who o him ten dollars
Mk	7:11	What I o you I've given as a gift
Lk	7:41	One o five hundred silver pieces

Owes

Phm	1:18	damaged anything or o you anything

P

P

Pain

Ge	3:16	multiply your ps in childbirth
	21:11	The matter gave great p to Abraham
	35:18	named him Ben-oni (Son-of-My-P)
Ex	3:7	I know all about their p
Nu	5:24	enter her body and cause acute p
	5:27	enter her body and cause acute p
1Sa	1:11	take a good, hard look at my p
	1:16	desperately unhappy and in such p
	5:12	cries of p and lament filled the air
2Sa	13:28	well into the sauce and feeling no p
	24:16	God felt the p of the terror
1Ki	11:39	I am bringing p and trouble
1Ch	4:9	named him Jabez (Oh, the p!)
2Ch	20:9	pray out our p and trouble
	21:18	died writhing in p
Job	3:13	asleep forever, feeling no p

	10:17	pile on the grief and **p**
	14:22	a lifetime of **p**, a lifetime of sorrow
	30:17	the **p** never lets up
	33:19	might get their attention through **p**
Ps	13:2	lived with a stomach full of **p**
	22:2	Doubled up with **p**, I call to God
	31:7	you saw my **p**
	38:17	the **p** in my gut keeps burning
	48:6	doubled up in **p**
	64:7	They double up in **p**
	69:29	I'm hurt and in **p**
	81:7	You called to me in your **p**
	88:9	tears of **p** and frustration
	102:1	listen to the **p** in my cries
Pr	5:4	a **p** in your gut, a wound in your heart
	17:25	A surly, stupid child is sheer **p**
	31:6	to kill the **p** and dull the ache
Ecc	2:23	**P** and grief from dawn to dusk
Isa	13:8	Doubled up in **p**
	17:11	get nothing but grief and **p**, **p**, **p**
	21:3	doubled up in **p**, writhing in **p**
	26:17	screaming her **p** as the baby is
	53:3	who knew **p** firsthand
	53:10	to crush him with **p**
	65:17	earlier troubles, chaos, and **p**
Jer	13:21	The **p** of a woman having a baby
	13:22	your guilt has you writhing in **p**
	15:18	why this chronic **p**
	22:23	doubled up in **p**, **p** worse than
	45:3	God is piling on the **p**
	48:41	warriors will double up in **p**
	49:22	warriors will double up in **p**
	50:43	Terror-stricken, he doubles up in **p**
	51:29	trembles in terror, writhes in **p**
La	1:3	After years of **p** and hard labor
	1:9	Look at my **p**, O God!
	1:12	Ever seen **p** like my **p**
	1:22	Groaning in **p**, body and soul
	3:51	the **p** breaks my heart
Eze	21:6	son of man, groan! Double up in **p**
	30:16	Pelusium will writhe in **p**
	36:21	much **p** over my holy reputation
Am	6:6	feeling good — life without **p**!
Hab	3:10	They twisted in **p**
Zec	10:6	I know their **p**
Mt	8:6	He can't walk. He's in terrible **p**
Lk	2:35	the **p** of a sword-thrust through you
Jn	16:21	wipes out memory of the **p**
	16:22	right now is similar to that **p**
Ac	20:38	The **p** cut deep
Ro	8:22	times of **p** throughout the world
	9:2	an enormous **p** deep within me
2Co	1:23	was to spare you **p**
	2:4	there was **p** enough just in writing
	2:5	who caused all this **p**
	7:10	We never regret that kind of **p**
Gal	4:19	Like a mother in the **p** of childbirth
Eph	4:19	Feeling no **p**, they let themselves go
Heb	2:18	all the **p**, all the testing
	5:7	Jesus cried out in **p** and wept
Rev	2:9	I can see your **p** and poverty
	2:9	constant **p**, dire

	9:5	the **p** like a scorpion sting
	12:2	cried out in the **p** of childbirth
	16:10	Mad with **p**, men and women bit
	21:4	tears gone, crying gone, **p** gone

Painful

Ge	3:17	getting food . . . Will be as **p**
Dt	28:35	God will hit you with **p** boils
1Ch	4:9	A **p** birth! I bore him in great pain
2Ch	21:15	disease of the colon, **p**
SS	3:1	His absence was **p**
Isa	38:3	Hezekiah wept as he prayed — **p** tears
Zep	3:20	**p** partings turned into reunions
Jn	3:20	fearing a **p** exposure
2Co	2:1	visit that could only be **p** to both
	2:2	in an embarrassingly **p** position
Gal	3:4	through this whole **p** learning process

Pampered

Ps	73:7	**P** and overfed, decked out
Isa	32:11	Get serious, you **p** dolls
	47:7	I'll always be the **p** darling
Jer	48:18	**p** beauty of Dibon
	48:19	Stand on the roadside, **p** women
Am	4:1	Indolent and **p**, you demand

Panic

Ex	14:24	army and threw them into a **p**
	23:27	peoples you're approaching into a **p**
Lev	26:36	will throw them into a **p**
Nu	22:3	people of Moab were in a total **p**
Dt	2:25	they'll totally **p**
	7:23	throw them into a huge **p**
	20:3	Don't fear. Don't hesitate. Don't **p**
Jos	2:24	Everybody there is in a state of **p**
Jdg	6:23	God reassured him, "Easy now. Don't **p**
1Sa	14:15	**p** like you've never seen before
Est	9:24	throw them into a **p** and destroy
Job	35:13	nothing behind such prayers except **p**
Pr	3:25	No need to **p** over alarms
Ecc	10:4	don't **p**; A calm disposition quiets
Isa	7:4	don't **p** over these two burnt-out cases
	10:31	The people of Gebim flee in **p**
	13:7	Everyone paralyzed in the **p**
	19:1	Egyptians paralyzed by **p**
	19:17	Say "Judah" to an Egyptian and see **p**
	41:5	Far-flung ocean islands see it and **p**
	41:10	Don't **p**. I'm with you
	41:13	Don't **p**. I'm right here to help you
Jer	18:22	Let cries of **p** sound
	23:4	They won't live in fear or **p** anymore
	30:5	Cries of **p** are being heard
	46:5	Their soldiers **p**
Da	5:9	The nobles were in a **p**
	11:44	will throw him into a **p**
Joel	2:6	sight of this army, the people **p**
Na	1:5	fear of God. The whole world's in a **p**
Hab	3:7	I saw everyone worried, in a **p**
Zep	1:10	Cries of **p** from the city

P

Zec	9:5	Ashkelon will see it and **p**
	12:4	war horses into a crazed **p**
	14:13	hysteria when that happens — total **p**
Mt	8:5	a Roman captain came up in a **p**
	24:6	keep your head and don't **p**
Mk	13:7	keep your head and don't **p**
Lk	21:9	keep your head and don't **p**
	21:26	everyone all over the world in a **p**

Paradise

Ps	103:4	love and mercy — a **p** crown
SS	4:13	Body and soul, you are **p**
Am	1:5	who gives orders from **P** Palace
Lk	23:43	I will. Today you will join me in **p**
2Co	12:3	this man was hijacked into **p**

Paralyzed

1Ki	13:4	his arm was **p** and hung useless
2Ch	14:14	helpless, **p** by the fear of God
Job	22:10	trapped in terror, **p** by fear
Isa	13:7	Everyone **p** in the panic, hysterical
	19:1	Egyptians **p** by panic
Jer	6:24	We're **p** with fear
	47:3	Fathers, **p** by fear, won't even
Eze	7:14	My wrath has them **p**
	7:27	The common people are **p**
Da	10:17	I'm **p**. I can hardly breathe
Lk	1:12	Zachariah was **p** in fear
Jn	5:3	sick people — blind, crippled, **p**
Ac	9:33	had been in bed eight years **p**

Paraplegic

Mt	9:2	some men carried a **p** on a stretcher
	9:6	he turned to the **p** and said, "Get up
	15:30	bringing along the **p**, the blind
Mk	2:3	They brought a **p** to him
	2:4	lowered the **p** on his stretcher
	2:5	Jesus said to the **p**, "Son, I forgive
	2:9	Which is simpler: to say to the **p**
	2:10	he looked now at the **p**
Lk	5:18	Some men arrived carrying a **p**
	5:24	spoke directly to the **p**: "Get up

Pardon

1Sa	9:18	**P** me, but can you tell me where
2Ki	5:18	thing for which I need God's **p**
2Ch	30:18	May God who is all good, **p** and forgive
Ps	79:11	**p** those on death row
Isa	61:1	**p** all prisoners
Mt	27:15	to **p** a single prisoner
	27:17	Which prisoner do you want me to **p**
	27:20	asking for the **p** of Barabbas
	27:21	Which of the two do you want me to **p**
Lk	4:18	Sent me to announce **p** to prisoners
Jn	18:39	custom that I **p** one prisoner
	19:10	I have the authority to **p** you
	19:12	Pilate tried his best to **p** him

Parent

Dt	27:16	God's curse on anyone who demeans a **p**
Ps	22:30	word is passed along from **p** to child
Pr	17:21	it's no fun being the **p** of a dolt
	19:13	**p** is worn . . . by a stupid child
	23:15	become wise, I'll be one happy **p**
Eze	18:4	belongs to me, **p** and child alike
	18:11	even though the **p** has done none
	18:14	sees all the sins done by his **p**
	18:18	**p** will die for what the **p** did
	18:19	child not share the guilt of the **p**
	18:20	does not share the guilt of the **p**
	18:20	nor the **p** the guilt of the child
Zec	12:10	mourning as of a **p** grieving
Mt	15:6	can hardly be called respecting a **p**

Parents

Ge	24:47	whose **p** were Naor and Milcah
	28:7	Jacob had obeyed his **p** and gone
	32:9	Go back to your **p**' homeland
	46:34	can remember — we and our **p** also
Ex	20:5	children for any sins their **p** pass on
Nu	14:18	extending the fallout of **p**' sins
Dt	1:35	land that I promised to give to your **p**
	5:3	this covenant with our **p**; he made
	5:9	I hold **p** responsible for any sins
	8:3	neither you nor your **p** knew anything
	18:8	the sale of his **p**' possessions
	22:21	whore while still in her **p**' home
	24:16	**P** shall not be put to death for
	28:64	gods neither you nor your **p** ever heard
	32:7	Ask your **p** what it was like
Jdg	2:12	deserted God, the God of their **p**
	2:17	leaving the road walked by their **p**
	2:19	even worse than their **p**
	2:20	covenant that I commanded their **p**
	2:22	walk down it as their **p** did
	3:4	commands that were given to their **p**
	6:13	miracle-wonders our **p** . . . told us
	14:3	**p** said to him, "Isan't there a woman
	14:6	didn't tell his **p** what he had done
	14:16	I haven't told my own **p**
1Sa	22:4	David left his **p** in the care
2Ki	14:6	**p** shouldn't be executed for
2Ch	25:4	**p** shouldn't be executed for
Ne	9:2	the iniquities of their **p**
	9:9	saw the anguish of our **p** in Egypt
Est	2:7	After her **p** died, Mordecai had
Job	15:19	By their **p**, back in the days
Ps	10:18	Orphans get **p**, the homeless get homes
	22:4	We know you were there for our **p**
	78:5	commanded our **p** to teach it
	78:8	forbid they should be like their **p**
	78:12	miracles in plain sight of their **p**
	78:57	worse . . . than their **p**: traitors
	79:8	Don't blame us for the sins of our **p**
	103:13	As **p** feel for their children
	106:6	sinned a lot, both we and our **p**
	106:7	After our **p** left Egypt
	113:9	gives them joy as the **p** of children

P

	127:5	Oh, how blessed are you **p**
Pr	13:1	Intelligent children listen to their **p**
	15:20	Intelligent children make their **p**
	17:6	children take pride in their **p**
	19:14	House and land are handed down from **p**
	19:26	Kids who lash out against their **p**
	23:24	**P** rejoice when their children
	27:10	your friends or your **p**' friends
	29:3	love wisdom, you'll delight your **p**
	29:15	spoiled adolescents embarrass their **p**
Isa	38:19	**P** give their children full reports
	65:7	the sins of their **p** lumped in
Jer	6:21	send you sprawling, **p** and children
	9:14	following the example of their **p**
	9:16	nor their **p** have ever heard of
	19:4	never heard of by them, their **p**
	31:29	**P** ate the green apples
	32:18	the fallout from their **p**' sins
	44:10	so plainly before you and your **p**
	44:21	sacrifices that you and your **p**
	50:7	True Pasture, the hope of their **p**
La	5:7	Our **p** sinned and are no more
Eze	5:10	**p** eating children
	18:2	The **p** ate green apples
	20:4	outrageous obscenities of their **p**
	20:18	Don't do what your **p** did
	20:24	the no-god idols of their **p**
	20:27	your **p** further insulted me
	20:30	filthy by copying the ways of your **p**
	20:36	As I faced your **p** with judgment
	20:42	upraised arm to give to your **p**
	22:7	a community that's insolent to **p**
Da	9:6	Word to our kings and leaders, our **p**
	9:8	shame, all of us — our . . . **p**
	9:16	because of our sins and our **p**' sins
Hos	9:12	I'd declare them unfit **p**
Zec	1:4	Don't be like your **p**
	13:3	his very own **p** will step in
Mal	3:17	kindness that **p** give the child
	4:6	convince **p** to look after their
Mt	11:16	spoiled children whining to their **p**
Mk	13:12	children killing **p**
Lk	1:17	soften the hearts of **p** to children
	2:27	As the **p** of the child Jesus brought
	2:41	Jesus' **p** traveled to Jerusalem
	2:43	in Jerusalem, but his **p** didn't know it
	2:48	But his **p** were not impressed
	7:32	children complaining to their **p**
	8:51	John, James, and the child's **p**
	8:56	Her **p** were ecstatic, but Jesus
	18:29	brothers and sisters, **p**, children
	21:16	You'll even be turned in by **p**
Jn	9:2	who sinned: this man or his **p**
	9:18	the **p** of the man now bright-eyed
	9:20	His **p** said, "We know he is our son
	9:22	His **p** were talking like this
	9:23	That's why his **p** said, "Ask him
Ro	1:30	They ditch their **p**
	2:9	what your **p** taught you
2Co	12:14	shouldn't have to look out for their **p**
	12:14	**p** look out for the children
Eph	5:1	learn proper behavior from their **p**

	6:1	Children, do what your **p** tell you
Col	3:20	Children, do what your **p** tell you
	3:21	**P**, don't come down too hard
2Ti	3:2	profane, contemptuous of **p**, crude
Heb	11:23	Moses' **p** hid him away for three months
	12:5	forgotten how good **p** treat children
	12:8	irresponsible **p** leave children to fend
	12:9	We respect our own **p** for training
	12:10	our **p** did what seemed best to them

Partner

2Ch	20:36	went in as **p** with him to build
Ecc	4:9	better to have a **p** than go it alone
Mt	25:21	did your job well. From now on be my **p**
	25:23	did your job well. From now on be my **p**
Ro	16:21	Timothy, my **p** in this work
Php	3:10	be a **p** in his suffering
2Jn	1:11	his evil ways, making you his **p**

Partners

Jer	3:13	promiscuous life with casual **p**
Ob	1:7	old **p** will drive you to the edge
Lk	5:7	waved to their **p** in the other boat
2Co	1:24	We're **p**, working alongside you
	6:14	Don't become **p** with those who reject
Jas	2:22	faith and works are yoked **p**
Rev	2:22	lay her low, along with her **p**

Passionate

1Ki	8:54	all these bold and **p** prayers
	9:3	your ever-so-**p** prayers
Isa	16:5	A Ruler **p** for justice
Ro	5:3	troubles can develop **p** patience
2Co	7:11	more human, more **p**, more responsible
	8:7	you're insightful, you're **p**
	9:14	praying for you in **p** intercession
2Pe	1:6	**p** patience, reverent wonder
Rev	3:10	you kept my Word in **p** patience

Passionately

Nu	14:24	a different spirit; he follows me **p**
Ps	37:34	Wait **p** for God, don't leave the path
La	3:25	to the man who **p** waits
Ac	22:3	I've always been **p** on God's side
Rev	13:10	holy people **p** and faithfully stand
	14:12	the saints stand **p** patient

Pastor

1Ch	21:9	speaking to Gad, David's **p**
2Ch	26:5	well trained by his **p** and teacher
Eph	4:11	prophet, evangelist, and **p**-teacher
2Jn	1:1	I, your **p**, love you in very truth
3Jn	1:1	The **P**, to my good friend Gaius

Pastors

| Isa | 3:2 | judges and courts, **p** and teachers |

P

Hos	12:13	served as faithful p
Php	1:1	all the Christians in Philippi, p

Patience

Ge	18:31	I know I'm trying your p, Master
Ps	50:21	I kept a quiet p while you
	78:40	tried his p in those wilderness years
	90:4	P! You've got all the time
	95:10	over and over they tried my p
	101:7	I have no p with liars
Ro	5:3	troubles can develop passionate p
	5:4	that p in turn forges
1Th	1:3	your labor of love, and your p of hope
1Ti	1:16	evidence of his endless p
2Ti	3:10	faith, steadiness, love, p
Heb	3:9	over and over they tried my p
2Pe	1:6	passionate p, reverent wonder
Rev	1:9	the passion of p in Jesus
	3:10	you kept my Word in passionate p

Patient

Ex	34:6	God of mercy and grace, endlessly p
Ne	9:17	Incredibly p, with tons of love
Pr	25:15	P persistence pierces through
Joel	2:13	This most p God, extravagant in love
Na	1:3	He's powerful, but it's a p power
1Th	5:14	Be p with each person, attentive
Jas	5:8	Be p like that. Stay steady and strong
2Pe	3:15	Interpret our Master's p restraint
Rev	14:12	saints stand passionately p

Peace

Ge	26:29	let you leave us in p
Ex	4:18	Go. And p be with you
	20:24	your P-Offerings, your sheep
	24:5	sacrifice P-Offerings of bulls
	29:28	regularly from their P-Offerings
	32:6	brought P-Offerings
Lev	3:1	If your offering is a P-Offering
	3:3	Fire-Gift to God from the P-Offering
	3:6	If your P-Offering to God comes
	3:9	Fire-Gift to God from the P-Offering
	4:10	from the bull of the P-Offering
	4:26	as with the fat of the P-Offering
	4:31	same as with the P-Offering
	4:35	as for the lamb of the P-Offering
	6:12	burn the fat of the P-Offering
	7:11	instructions for the P-Offering
	7:13	with the P-Offering of thanksgiving
	7:14	the blood of the P-Offering
	7:15	Eat the meat from the P-Offering
	7:18	any of the meat from the P-Offering
	7:20	eat meat from the P-Offering for God
	7:21	eat from a P-Offering for God
	7:29	When you present a P-Offering to God
	7:32	the right thigh from your P-Offerings
	7:33	blood and fat of the P-Offering
	7:34	From the P-Offerings of Israel
	7:37	and the P-Offering

	9:4	a bull and a ram for a P-Offering
	9:18	the people's P-Offerings
	9:22	and the P-Offering
	10:14	from the P-Offerings
	17:5	sacrifice them as P-Offerings to God
	17:8	who offers a . . . P-Offering
	19:5	When you sacrifice a P-Offering to God
	22:21	as a P-Offering to God
	23:19	yearling lambs for a P-Offering
	26:6	I'll make the country a place of p
Nu	6:14	a healthy ram for a P-Offering
	6:17	ram as a P-Offering to God
	6:18	burning under the P-Offering
	7:17	sacrificed as a P-Offering
	7:23	sacrificed as a P-Offering
	7:29	sacrificed as a P-Offering
	7:35	sacrificed as a P-Offering
	7:41	sacrificed as a P-Offering
	7:47	sacrificed as a P-Offering
	7:53	sacrificed as a P-Offering
	7:59	sacrificed as a P-Offering
	7:65	sacrificed as a P-Offering
	7:71	sacrificed as a P-Offering
	7:77	sacrificed as a P-Offering
	7:83	sacrificed as a P-Offering
	7:88	sacrifice of the P-Offering
	10:10	Whole-Burnt-Offerings and P-Offerings
	15:8	for a special vow or a P-Offering
	25:12	I am making a Covenant-of-P with him
	29:39	Drink-Offerings, and P-Offerings
Dt	20:10	a city to attack it, call out, "P
	20:11	answer, "Yes, p!" and open the city
	20:12	if they don't settle for p
	27:7	When you sacrifice your P-Offerings
Jos	8:31	sacrificed P-Offerings
	9:15	Josua made p with them
	11:19	Not one town made p with the People
	22:23	enact there sacrificial P-Offerings
	22:27	sacrifices and our P-Offerings
Jdg	6:24	named it "God's P."
	20:26	P-Offerings before God
	21:4	sacrificed . . . P-Offerings
	21:13	at the Rimmon Rock and offered them p
1Sa	1:17	Eli answered her, "Go in p
	7:14	there was p between Israel and
	10:8	burnt offerings and p offerings
	11:15	worshiped, sacrificing p offerings
	12:11	and you lived in p
	13:9	"Bring me the . . . p offerings!"
	20:42	Jonathan said, "Go in p!
	25:5	Greet him in my name, 'P
	25:6	Life and p to you
	25:6	P to your household, p to everyone
	25:35	Return home in p
2Sa	6:17	burnt offerings and p offerings
	6:18	sacrifices of burnt and p offerings
	7:1	God gave him p from all his enemies
	7:11	give you p from all your enemies
	10:19	made p and became Israel's vassals
	17:3	everyone will be together in p
	18:28	said to the king, "P!"
	24:25	burnt offerings and p offerings

P

1Ki	2:13	Do you come in p?" He said, "In p		57:19	P to the far-off, p to the near
	2:33	the final verdict is God's p		57:21	no p," God says, "for the wicked
	3:15	sacrificing . . . P-Offerings		59:8	They know nothing about p
	4:24	P reigned everywhere		60:17	I'll install P to run your country
	5:4	now God has provided p all around		62:7	no p until he does what he said
	5:12	just as he had promised. The healthy p	Jer	4:19	never a moment's p
	8:56	Blessed be God, who has given p		14:19	We hoped for p—nothing good came
	8:63	Solomon offered P-Offerings		30:5	The p has been shattered
	8:64	and fat from the P-Offerings		32:37	let them live here in p
	9:25	sacrificing . . . P-Offerings	Eze	7:25	They look for p, but there's no p
	20:18	If they've come in p, take them alive		19:9	voice be heard disturbing the p
	22:1	They enjoyed three years of p		34:25	I'll make a covenant of p with them
2Ki	5:19	Everything will be all right. Go in p		37:26	I'll make a covenant of p with them
	13:5	able to live at p in their own homes		43:27	and your p offerings
	16:13	blood from the P-Offerings		45:15	p offerings for making the atonement
	20:19	I'll enjoy p and security as long		45:17	p offerings for making atonement
	22:20	quiet death and be buried in p		46:2	p offerings while he worships
1Ch	12:17	If you have come in p		46:12	a burnt offering or a p offering
	16:1	p offerings to God	Da	4:1	P and prosperity to all
	19:19	made p with David and served him		6:25	P to you! Abundant p
	21:26	sacrificed . . . P-Offerings		10:19	Don't be afraid, friend. P.
2Ch	7:7	and fat from the P-Offerings		11:6	to cement the p agreement
	14:1	into Asa's reign the country was at p		11:17	He'll cook up a p treaty
	14:5	his kingdom was at p	Hos	2:18	I'll make a p treaty between you
	14:6	God kept the p	Mic	1:12	wait in vain for sweet p
	15:15	God gave them p within and without		3:5	Isan't life wonderful! P to all!
	20:30	Jehoshaphat reigned, p reigned	Na	1:15	good news: p! A holiday, Judah!
	29:35	choice pieces for the P-Offerings	Zep	3:13	unanxious, they'll live at p
	33:16	sacrificing P-Offerings	Zec	8:19	Embrace truth! Love p
	34:28	quiet death and be buried in p		9:10	He will offer p to the nations
Ezr	4:17	P be with you	Mal	2:5	covenant . . . was to give life and p
	5:7	To Darius the king. P and blessing		2:6	walked with me in p and uprightness
	7:12	Teaching of the God-of-Heaven. P	Mk	9:50	Preserve the p
Est	10:3	cared for the p and prosperity	Lk	1:79	down the path of p
Job	3:13	could be resting in p right now		2:14	P to all men and women on earth
	3:26	repose is shattered, my p destroyed		2:29	release me in p as you promised
	7:19	Can't you even let me spit in p		7:50	Your faith has saved you. Go in p
Ps	28:4	They talk a good line of "p," then		10:5	enter a home, greet the family, 'P
	29:11	God gives his people p		23:5	disturbing the p everywhere
	34:14	Embrace p—don't let it get away		23:14	this man to me as a disturber of the p
	55:7	I want some p and quiet		24:36	Jesus . . . said, "P be with you
	72:7	p abound until the moon fades	Jn	14:27	That's my parting gift to you. P.
	73:9	loudmouths disturbing the p		16:33	unshakable and assured, deeply at p
	120:7	I'm all for p, but		20:19	stood among them, and said, "P to you
	122:6	Pray for Jerusalem's p!		20:21	Jesus repeated his greeting: "P to you
	122:8	I say it again: live in p		20:26	stood among them, and said, "P to you
	125:5	P over Israel	Ac	16:20	These men are disturbing the p
	128:6	enjoy your grandchildren. P to Israel		16:36	Congratulations! Go in p
	147:14	He keeps the p at your borders		24:3	that we enjoy all this p and gain
Pr	10:10	face-to-face meeting results in p		24:5	time and again disturbing the p
	12:20	p-planning brings joy to the planner	Ro	13:1	there is p and order, it's God's order
	15:18	a calm, cool spirit keeps the p		15:13	fill you up with p
	17:1	bread and water in contented p		15:33	God's p be with all of you
Ecc	3:8	time to wage war and another to make p		16:20	the God of p will come down on Satan
SS	6:13	her victory dances of love and p	2Co	13:11	the God of love and p will be with you
Isa	32:17	where there's Right, there'll be P	Gal	1:3	with the great words, grace and p
	33:8	The p treaty is broken		6:16	chosen people. P and mercy on them
	36:16	Make p with me. Come and join me	Eph	1:2	grace and p poured into our lives
	39:8	I'll enjoy p and stability as long as		2:17	p to you outsiders and p to us
	48:22	no p," says God, "for the wicked		6:15	p, faith, and salvation
	54:10	my covenant commitment of p	Php	1:2	grace and p that comes from God
	57:2	now they're finally at p	Col	3:15	Let the p of Christ keep you

1Th	1:1	grace be with you! God's robust **p**
2Th	3:16	May the Master of **P** himself give you
2Ti	2:22	mature righteousness — faith, love, **p**
Heb	7:2	"Salem" means "**P**."
	7:2	So, he is also "King of **P**
1Pe	3:11	run after **p** for all you're worth
	4:15	broke the law or disturbed the **p**
	5:14	**P** to you — to all who walk in Christ
2Pe	1:2	Grace and **p** to you many times over
	3:14	living at your best, in purity and **p**
2Jn	1:3	Let grace, mercy, and **p** be with us
3Jn	1:14	**P** to you
Rev	6:4	rider was off to take **p** from the earth

Peaceful

Ge	15:15	full life and die a good and **p** death
2Sa	20:19	We're a **p** people here
1Ch	4:40	lots of elbow room, **p** and quiet
	22:9	he will be a quiet and **p** man
	22:18	given you **p** relations with everyone
2Ch	14:7	have this **p** land because we sought God
Job	21:9	Their homes are **p** and free from fear
Ecc	4:6	One handful of **p** repose
Isa	26:12	God, order a **p** and whole life for us
	32:18	people will live in a **p** neighborhood
Jer	25:37	**p** sheepfolds will be silent with death
	34:5	You'll die a **p** death
	42:14	Egypt, where things are **p**
Zec	9:10	a **p** rule worldwide

Penalty

Ex	21:12	and death results, the **p** is death
	21:15	hits father or mother, the **p** is death
	21:16	kidnaps a person, the **p** is death
	21:17	curses father . . . , the **p** is death
	21:29	and the owner given the death **p**
	22:19	sex with an animal gets the death **p**
Lev	5:6	as your **p** to God for the sin
	5:7	bring as your **p** to God for the sin
	5:15	he is to bring as his **p** to God
Nu	15:35	Give the man the death **p**
	18:3	the Altar under **p** of death
	18:22	penalized . . . and the **p** is death
	35:31	He's guilty and deserves the death **p**
Heb	10:28	the **p** for breaking the law of Moses

Perfect

Lev	22:21	it has to be **p**, without defect
Dt	32:4	His works are **p**
2Ch	5:13	choir in **p** harmony singing
Job	22:3	Even if you gave a **p** performance
	25:5	even the stars aren't **p** in God's eyes
	37:16	these miracle-wonders of a **p** Mind
Ps	27:5	The **p** getaway, far from the buzz
	64:6	no one can detect our **p** crime
Eze	27:3	I'm the **p** ship — stately, handsome
	27:11	a final, **p** touch to your beauty
Da	1:4	**p** specimens!
	9:14	You, our God, had a **p** right to do this

Mk	8:25	realized that he had recovered **p** sight
Ac	15:15	in **p** agreement with the words of
	25:10	where I have a **p** right to stand
Ro	9:21	potter has a **p** right to shape
1Co	1:18	it makes **p** sense
	9:12	what we've always had a **p** right to
	15:28	absolutely comprehensive — a **p** ending
Gal	2:17	noticed that we are not yet **p**
	3:3	how do you suppose you could **p** it
Heb	2:10	making the Salvation Pioneer **p**
	7:11	could really make people **p**
	7:15	story provides a **p** analogy
	7:28	Son, who is absolutely, eternally **p**
	10:14	a **p** sacrifice by a **p** person
	10:14	to **p** some very imperfect
Jas	3:2	none of us is **p**ly qualified
1Jn	4:12	love becomes complete in us — **p** love
	5:8	the three in **p** agreement
Rev	14:5	A **p** offering
	21:16	The City was laid out in a **p** square

Perfection

SS	6:9	My dove is **p**, Pure and innocent
Eze	16:14	legendary beauty brought to **p**
	27:4	a real beauty, crafted to **p**
	28:15	you were sheer **p**

Persecuted

Da	7:25	God's holy people will be **p** by him
Gal	1:23	man who once **p** us is now preaching
	5:11	Why would I still be **p**

Persecuting

Gal	1:13	I went all out in **p** God's church
Php	3:6	even to the point of **p** Christians

Persecution

Isa	14:6	rule of anger rife with torture and **p**
Mt	5:10	your commitment to God provokes **p**
	5:10	The **p** drives you even deeper
Ac	8:1	set off a terrific **p** of the church
	11:19	Those who had been scattered by the **p**

P

Perverse

Lev	18:23	sex with an animal. That is **p**
	20:12	What they have done is **p**
Job	18:21	this is what happens to **p** people
Pr	6:14	Their **p** minds are always cooking
	22:5	The **p** travel a dangerous road
Isa	30:13	This **p** way of life will be like
Jer	51:1	against all who live in that **p** land
Ro	3:7	It's simply **p** to say

Perversity

Pr	2:14	throw parties to celebrate **p**
	4:17	**P** is their food and drink

Jer	36:3	let me forgive their **p** and sin
Mt	12:32	severing by your own **p** all connection
Mk	3:29	severing by your own **p** all connection
2Pe	2:7	the sexual filth and **p**

Pervert

Lev	19:15	Don't **p** justice. Don't show favoritism
Eze	16:34	You even **p** whoredom
Ro	7:8	sin found a way to **p** the command

Petition

Jer	11:14	Not a word of **p**
Mk	15:8	its **p** for him to release a prisoner
Lk	19:14	a signed **p** to oppose his rule

Petitioned

Ge	50:4	Joseph **p** Pharaoh's court
1Sa	11:1	The men of Jabesh **p** Naash
	22:3	He **p** the king of Moab
Lk	19:27	enemies of mine who **p** against my rule
Jn	19:31	**p** Pilate that their legs be broken
	19:38	**p** Pilate to take the body of Jesus
Ac	25:24	A bunch of Jews **p** me first

Pious

2Ki	18:19	a world of make-believe, of **p** fantasy
Job	6:25	the point of all this **p** bluster
Ps	40:6	Being religious, acting **p**
Pr	15:8	God can't stand **p** poses
Isa	7:13	your **p**, timid hypocrisies
	36:15	**p** sermons telling you to lean on God
	58:5	put on a **p** long face and parade
Jer	11:15	think . . . **p** programs will save
Hab	2:18	sense does it make to be a **p** god-maker
Zep	3:11	No more **p** strutting on my holy hill
Mt	5:34	lay down a smoke screen of **p** talk
Ro	16:18	using **p** sweet talk to dupe
Col	2:23	give the illusion of being **p**
2Ti	2:14	Warn them . . . against **p** nitpicking
	2:16	Stay clear of **p** talk that is only talk
Jude	1:4	who beneath their **p** skin are shameless
	1:15	have spewed of their **p** filth

Pity

Dt	25:12	cut off her hand. Show no **p**
Job	19:21	dear friends, take **p** on me
Pr	23:29	Who do you know who reeks of self-**p**
	24:18	then take **p** on his plight
Isa	63:9	Out of his own love and **p** he redeemed
	63:15	Your heartfelt **p**, your compassion
Jer	13:14	Not an ounce of **p** or mercy
	30:15	So why all this self-**p**
Eze	5:11	Not an ounce of **p** will I show you
Joel	2:14	maybe he'll turn around and show **p**
	2:18	He took **p** on his people
Am	1:11	She has no **p**, she has no heart
Mt	14:14	he was overcome with **p** and healed

Pleasure

Ge	19:8	you can take your **p** with them
Dt	28:63	took **p** in making life good for you
Job	3:7	no sounds of **p** from that night
Pr	8:35	to say nothing of God's good **p**
	15:23	Congenial conversation — what a **p**
	21:17	The pursuit of **p** is never satisfied
Ecc	2:1	experiment with **p**, have a good time
	2:10	sucked the marrow of **p** out
	5:4	God takes no **p** in foolish gabble
	8:3	You're serving his **p**, not yours
	9:7	God takes **p** in your **p**
Jer	6:20	sacrifices in worship give me no **p**
	31:20	my child in whom I take **p**
La	3:33	He takes no **p** in making life hard
Eze	16:37	those you've used for your own **p**
	18:23	Do you think I take any **p** in the death
	18:32	I take no **p** in anyone's death
	33:11	take no **p** from the death of the wicked
	43:27	I'll accept you with **p**
Am	3:4	Does a young lion growl with **p**
Jnh	4:10	change your feelings from **p** to anger
	4:11	what I feel . . . from anger to **p**
Mt	23:4	take **p** in watching you stagger
Lk	4:6	all their splendor to serve your **p**
	4:15	places to everyone's acclaim and **p**
1Co	9:18	the **p** of proclaiming the Message
	13:6	Takes **p** in the flowering of truth
Eph	1:5	What **p** he took in planning this
Php	2:13	what will give him the most **p**
2Th	1:3	not only a **p**; it's a must
Heb	13:16	God takes particular **p** in acts
	13:21	Make us into what gives him most **p**
2Pe	2:13	despicable and addicted to **p**

Poison

Dt	32:32	Their grapes are **p** grapes
	32:33	mixed with lethal cobra **p**
2Ki	2:21	no longer kill you or **p** your land
Job	6:4	arrows of God . . . are in me, **p** arrows
	20:16	gorge on evil, make a diet of that **p**
Ps	5:9	their lungs breathe out **p** gas
	14:1	Their words are **p** gas
	53:1	**p** gas — they foul themselves, they **p**
	58:4	**P**, lethal rattlesnake **p**, drips
	64:3	**p** words, **p**-tipped arrow-words
	69:21	They put **p** in my soup
	140:9	drown in their own verbal **p**
Pr	18:21	words give life; they're either **p**
Jer	9:8	Their tongues are **p** arrows
	9:15	I'll give them **p** to drink
La	3:19	taste of ashes, the **p** I've swallowed
Mk	16:18	they will drink **p** and not be hurt
Ro	3:13	Every word they speak is tinged with **p**
2Ti	2:17	they accumulate as **p** in the soul

Poisoned

Job	6:4	poison arrows — and I'm **p** all through
Pr	14:27	won't go off drinking from **p** wells

Isa	34:9	the soil sterile, **p** with waste
1Co	15:33	Don't let yourselves be **p** by this
Rev	8:11	many people died from the **p** water

Police

Isa	3:2	He's withdrawing **p** and protection
	34:11	Vultures and skunks will **p** the streets
Jer	37:14	arrested him and took him to the **p**
	37:15	The **p** were furious with Jeremiah
Eze	27:11	Your city **p** were imported
Hab	1:2	I have to yell, "Help! Murder! **P**!"
Lk	12:11	into **p** courts and before judges
	22:52	priests, Temple **p**, religion leaders
Jn	7:32	sent their **p** to arrest him
	7:45	the Temple **p** reported back
	7:46	The **p** answered, "Have you heard
	18:3	**p** sent by the high priests
	18:12	commander, joined by the Jewish **p**
	18:18	The servants and **p** had made a fire
	19:6	When the high priests and **p** saw him
Ac	4:1	priests, the chief of the Temple **p**
	5:22	**p** got there, they couldn't find
	5:24	**p** and the high priests were puzzled
	5:26	chief and his **p** went and got them
	16:19	Then the **p** arrested them
Ro	13:4	**p** aren't there just to be admired

Policemen

Jn	18:22	the **p** standing there slapped Jesus

Political

2Ki	25:28	experienced by the other **p** prisoners
Pr	16:32	self-control better than **p** power
Jer	52:32	experienced by the **p** prisoners

Politicians

Ps	119:161	slandered unmercifully by the **p**
Eze	22:27	Your **p** are like wolves prowling
	22:28	Your preachers cover up for the **p**

Pollute

Lev	18:24	Don't **p** yourself in any of these ways
	18:28	if you **p** it, the land will vomit you
	18:30	Don't **p** yourselves with them
	19:31	you'll **p** your souls
	20:25	Don't **p** yourselves with any animal
Nu	35:33	Don't **p** the land in which you live
Dt	19:10	don't want to **p** it with innocent blood
2Ki	9:22	your mother Jezebel **p** the country
Pr	10:32	the words of the wicked **p** it
Eze	37:23	Never again will they **p** their lives
Ro	3:14	They open their mouths and **p** the air
2Co	6:17	with those who will **p** you

Polluted

Lev	18:24	This is how the nations became **p**

	18:25	Even the land itself became **p**
	18:27	did all these things and **p** the land
	19:7	it is **p** meat and not acceptable
	20:3	he has **p** my Sanctuary and desecrated
1Ki	11:8	who then **p** the countryside
2Ki	2:19	the water is **p** and nothing grows
Ezr	9:11	a **p** land, **p** with the obscene
Pr	5:16	barrel empty and your well **p**
	25:26	a muddied spring, a **p** well
Isa	24:5	Earth is **p** by its very own people
Jer	2:7	you barged in and **p** my land
Eze	5:11	**p** my Sanctuary with your obscenities
	36:17	they **p** it by the way they lived
	39:24	their **p** and sin-sated lives deserved
Hos	5:3	All Israel is thoroughly **p**
	9:4	your souls **p** by the spirit-dirty air
Mic	2.10	You've **p** this place, and now you're **p**
Zec	13:2	prophets who **p** the air
Eph	2:2	filled your lungs with **p** unbelief
Php	2:15	this squalid and **p** society
Jas	3:12	not going to dip into a **p** mud hole

Pollutes

Nu	35:33	Murder **p** the land
Mt	15:11	not what you swallow that **p** your life
	15:20	That's what **p**. Eating or not eating
Mk	7:15	not what you swallow that **p** your life
	7:20	It's what comes out of a person that **p**

Polluting

Dt	19:19	Clean the **p** evil from your company
1Ki	14:24	male sacred prostitutes, **p** the country
2Ki	23:5	clean of the **p** stench
2Ch	15:8	obscene and **p** sacred shrines
	19:3	the **p** sex-and-religion shrines
	36:14	and **p** The Temple of God so recently
Jer	23:15	the godlessness **p** this country
Eze	36:18	**p** the country with their wanton
Zec	13:3	spreading diseased, **p** words

Pollution

Dt	19:13	Clean out the **p** of wrongful murder
	21:21	purged the evil **p** from among you
2Ch	34:33	cleaning up the **p** that had spread
Isa	34:9	flow sluggish, thick with **p**
Eze	36:29	I'll pull you out of that stinking **p**
Mk	7:15	what you vomit—that's the real **p**
	7:23	There is the source of your **p**
Rev	22:11	the dirty-minded go all out in **p**

Pomposity

Eze	32:12	puncture that hot-air **p**
Ac	12:21	Herod, robed in **p**, took his place

Pompous

Job	13:4	You're a bunch of **p** quacks
Eze	31:2	king of Egypt, that **p** old goat

P

	31:18	This means Pharaoh, the **p** old goat
	32:18	lament over Egypt's **p** ways
	32:25	Elam into a resort for the **p** dead
	32:31	**p** old goat that he is

Poor

Ge	48:10	eyesight was **p** from old age
Ex	23:3	just because someone is **p**, don't
	23:6	a dispute concerning your **p**
	23:11	rest so that your **p** may eat from it
	30:15	rich are not to pay more nor the **p**
Lev	14:21	If he is **p** and cannot afford
	19:10	Leave them for the **p** and the foreigner
	19:15	Don't show favoritism to either the **p**
	23:22	Leave them for the **p** and the foreigner
	25:25	If one of your brothers becomes **p**
	25:47	brothers becomes **p** and sells himself
	27:8	If anyone is too **p** to pay
Nu	22:32	Why have you beaten your **p** donkey
Dt	15:4	There must be no **p** people among you
	15:11	going to be **p** . . . people among you
1Sa	2:8	He puts **p** people on their feet
2Sa	12:3	The **p** man had nothing but one little
	12:4	he took the **p** man's lamb
1Ki	22:17	These **p** people have no one
2Ki	24:14	only ones he left were the very **p**
	25:12	He left a few **p** dirt farmers behind
2Ch	18:16	These **p** people have no one
	32:10	**p** people — do you think you're safe
Ne	8:12	including the **p** in a great celebration
Est	9:22	and of giving gifts to the **p**
Job	5:16	so the **p** continue to hope
	20:19	Because they exploited the **p**
	22:9	You turned out widows away
	24:3	They rip off the **p** and exploit
	24:5	**p**, like stray dogs and cats, scavenge
	24:9	infants of the **p** are kidnapped
	24:14	kills the **p** and robs the defenseless
	27:19	go to bed wealthy and wake up **p**
	30:25	heartsick over the lot of the **p**
	31:16	Have I ignored the needs of the **p**
	31:19	Have I ever left a **p** family shivering
	31:20	Didn't the **p** bless me
	34:19	rich and famous and slight the **p**
	34:28	announced by the cry of the **p**
Ps	9:18	No longer will the **p** be nameless
	10:2	wicked are hot on the trail of the **p**
	10:9	When the **p** wretch wanders too close
	12:5	Into the hovels of the **p**
	14:6	the dreams of the **p**
	22:29	the **p** and powerless, too — worshiping
	69:32	The **p** in spirit see and are glad
	69:33	For God listens to the **p**
	72:4	Please stand up for the **p**
	72:12	rescues the **p** at the first
	107:40	gave the **p** a safe place to live
	109:25	I'm a joke in **p** taste
	112:9	They lavish gifts on the **p**
	113:7	He picks up the **p** from out of the dirt
	140:12	you care for the rights of the **p**
Pr	6:11	You can look forward to a dirt-**p** life

	7:26	she's the death of many a **p** man
	10:4	Sloth makes you **p**
	13:8	the **p** are free of such threats
	13:23	Banks foreclose on the farms of the **p**
	13:23	the **p** lose their shirts
	14:21	compassion for the **p** — what a blessing
	14:31	you're kind to the **p**, you honor God
	16:8	Far better to be right and **p** than
	16:19	better to live humbly among the **p**
	17:5	mocks **p** people, insults their Creator
	18:23	The **p** speak in soft supplications
	19:1	Better to be **p** and honest than
	19:4	**p** people are avoided like a plague
	19:22	better to be **p** than a liar
	21:13	stop your ears to the cries of the **p**
	22:2	rich and the **p** shake hands as equals
	22:7	**p** are always ruled over by the rich
	22:9	they give bread to the **p**
	22:16	Exploit the **p** or glad-hand the rich
	22:22	Don't walk on the **p**
	22:22	just because they're **p**
	24:34	You can look forward to a dirt-**p** life
	28:3	The wicked who oppress the **p**
	28:6	better to be **p** and direct than
	28:8	some friend of the **p** is going to give
	28:11	the **p** can see right through them
	28:15	the wicked lord it over the **p**
	28:27	Be generous to the **p**
	29:7	understand what it's like to be **p**
	29:13	The **p** and their abusers have
	29:14	the voiceless **p** are treated fairly
	30:9	If I'm **p**, I might steal
	30:14	Tearing into the **p** and feasting
	31:9	Stand up for the **p** and destitute
	31:20	reaches out to help the **p**
Ecc	4:13	**p** youngster with some wisdom is better
	5:8	upset when you see the **p** kicked
	6:8	some **p** wretch who barely gets by
	9:15	a **p** but wise man in that town
	9:16	wise **p** man was treated with contempt
Isa	3:14	with what you've stolen from the **p**
	3:15	grinding the faces of the **p** into
	10:2	Laws that make misery for the **p**
	11:4	decisions on earth's **p** with justice
	14:30	The **p** won't have to worry
	25:4	see that you take care of the **p**
	25:4	that you take care of **p** people
	29:21	gone the people who cheated the **p**
	32:7	Exploiting the **p** with scams
	41:17	The **p** and homeless are desperate
	46:1	wearing out the **p** mules
	51:12	Some **p** wretch destined for dust
	58:7	inviting the homeless **p** into your
	61:1	sent me to preach good news to the **p**
Jer	2:21	a **p** excuse for a vine
	5:4	these are just **p** people
	5:28	exploit the **p**
	22:18	P, **p** brother!' Nobody will shed tears
	39:10	didn't bother taking the few **p** people
	40:7	children of the poorest of the **p**
	52:16	He left a few **p** dirt farmers behind
Eze	16:49	ignored the oppressed and the **p**

P

	18:8	doesn't exploit the **p**
	18:13	exploits the **p**
	18:17	doesn't exploit the **p**
	22:29	the **p** and needy are abused
Am	2:6	sell a **p** man for a pair of shoes
	2:8	Stuff they've extorted from the **p**
	4:1	Mean to the **p**, cruel to the down
	5:11	you run roughshod over the **p**
	5:12	kicking the **p** when they're down
	8:4	treat **p** people as less than nothing
	8:6	You exploit the **p**, using them
Jnh	3:5	Everyone did it — rich and **p**
Zep	3:12	people among you who are **p** in spirit
Zec	7:10	orphans, visitors, and the **p**
	10:2	**p** lost sheep without a shepherd
	11:13	Throw it in the **p** box
Mt	12:22	Next a **p** demon-afflicted wretch
	18:26	The **p** wretch threw himself
	18:29	The **p** wretch threw himself down
	19:21	give everything to the **p**
	26:9	a lot and the money handed out to the **p**
	26:11	You will have the **p** with you
Mk	10:21	whatever you own and give it to the **p**
	12:42	One **p** widow came up and put in two
	12:43	this **p** widow gave more
	14:5	wages and handed out to the **p**
	14:7	You will have the **p** with you every day
Lk	1:53	The starving **p** sat down to a banquet
	4:18	Message of good news to the **p**
	11:41	give generously to the **p**
	12:33	Be generous. Give to the **p**
	12:48	if he does a **p** job through ignorance
	16:20	A **p** man named Lazarus
	16:22	Then he died, this **p** man
	18:22	give it away to the **p**
	19:8	I give away half my income to the **p**
	21:2	saw a **p** widow put in two pennies
Jn	12:5	sold and the money given to the **p**
	12:6	cared two cents about the **p**
	12:8	You always have the **p** with you
	13:29	should give something to the **p**
Ac	6:2	God to help with the care of the **p**
	12:16	All this time **p** Peter was standing
	24:17	I took up a collection for the **p**
Ro	15:26	take up a collection for the **p**
1Co	11:22	Why would you actually shame God's **p**
	13:3	If I give everything I own to the **p**
	16:1	relief offering for **p** Christians
2Co	8:2	happy, though desperately **p**
	8:4	the relief of **p** Christians
	8:9	he became **p** and we became rich
	9:1	relief offering for the **p** Christians
	9:12	meet the bare needs of **p** Christians
Gal	2:10	asked was that we remember the **p**
Rev	13:16	small and great, rich and **p**

Popularity

Lk	6:26	**P** contests are not truth contests
Ac	12:3	raised his **p** ratings with the Jews
2Co	8:19	there's far more to him than **p**
Gal	1:10	If my goal was **p**, I wouldn't bother

Pornographic

| Eze | 16:17 | made **p** images of them |
| | 16:36 | because of your **p** idols |

Possessed

Ge	25:5	Abraham gave everything he **p** to Isaaac
Dt	3:12	Of the land that we **p** at that time
	30:5	the land your ancestors once **p**
Mk	5:16	what had happened to the demon-**p** man
Jn	7:20	trying to kill you? You're demon-**p**
	8:48	said you were crazy — demon-**p**
Ac	16:18	commanded the spirit that **p** her
	19:16	Then the **p** man went berserk

Poverty

Jdg	6:6	reduced to grinding **p** by Midian
1Sa	2:7	God brings **p** and God brings wealth
Pr	6:11	**p** your permanent houseguest
	10:15	the **p** of the indigent is their ruin
	24:34	**p** as your permanent houseguest
Ro	15:27	do what they can to relieve their **p**
Rev	2:9	pain and **p** — constant pain, dire **p**

Praise

Ge	29:35	She said, "This time I'll **p** God."
	29:35	So she named him Judah (**P**-God
	49:8	your brothers will **p** you
Lev	19:24	an offering of **p** to God
Dt	10:21	He's your **p**! He's your God!
	26:19	high in **p**, fame, and honor
	32:43	join the **p** of his people
2Sa	22:4	I sing to God the **P**-Lofty
1Ch	16:4	give thanks, and **p** the God of Israel
	16:7	regular worship of **p** to God
	16:35	bask in your life of **p**
	23:5	instruments that I have provided for **p**
	25:3	leading the thanks and **p** to God
2Ch	5:13	one voice of **p** and thanks to God
	7:6	anthems to the **p** and love of God
	20:19	stood to their feet to **p** God
	23:13	choir and orchestra leading the **p**
	23:18	with **p** and song as directed by David
	29:30	anthems of **p** to God
	31:2	sure that thanks and **p** took place
Ezr	3:10	**p** God in the tradition of David
	3:11	sang antiphonally **p** and thanksgiving
Ne	9:5	exalted above all blessing and **p**
	12:8	was in charge of songs of **p**
	12:46	songs of **p** and thanksgiving to God
Job	36:24	Remember, then, to **p** his workmanship
	38:7	all the angels shouted **p**
Ps	18:3	I sing to God, the **P**-Lofty
	22:3	on the cushions of Israel's **p**
	22:25	I have discovered this **p**-life
	33:2	Play his **p** on a grand piano
	34:1	my lungs expand with his **p**
	40:3	God-song, a **p**-song to our God
	44:8	All day we parade God's **p**

P

	45:3	Accept **p**! Accept due honor!		150:5	**P** him with cymbals and a big bass drum

45:3 Accept **p**! Accept due honor!
47:6 Sing to our King, sing **p**
48:1 **p** abounds in our God-city!
49:18 folks **p** them because they've made good
50:14 Spread for me a banquet of **p**
51:15 I'll let loose with your **p**
56:4 I'm proud to **p** God; fearless now
56:10 I'm proud to **p** God, proud to **p** God
63:4 My arms wave like banners of **p** to you
64:10 Good-hearted people, make **p** your habit
65:1 Silence is **p** to you
66:2 set glory to the rhythms of his **p**
68:26 Like a fountain of **p**
69:34 You heavens, **p** him; **p** him, earth
71:6 I'll never run out of **p**
71:8 my mouth brims with **p**
71:14 reaching for you, and daily add **p** to **p**
71:23 I let out lungsful of **p**
72:16 Cornucopias of **p**, praises springing
76:10 Instead of smoldering rage — God-**p**!
88:10 ghosts ever join the choirs that **p** you
89:5 Let the cosmos **p** your wonderful ways
89:15 people who know the passwords of **p**
97:12 God's people, shout **p** to God
99:3 let everyone **p** you!
100:4 Make yourselves at home, talking **p**
102:18 people not yet born will **p** God
102:21 God's **p** will be sung in Jerusalem
106:12 broke out in songs of **p**
109:30 My mouth's full of great **p** for God
113:1 You who serve God, **p** God!
113:1 Just to speak his name is **p**
115:17 Dead people can't **p** God
117:1 **P** God, everybody! Applaud God
118:20 so the victors can enter and **p**
118:28 O my God, I lift high your **p**
119:171 Let **p** cascade off my lips
119:175 Invigorate my soul so I can **p** you well
135:1 **P** the name of God, **p** the works of God
145:1 David's **p** I lift you high in **p**, my God
145:21 My mouth is filled with God's **p**
146:1 Hallelujah! O my soul, **p** God
146:2 All my life long I'll **p** God
147:1 sing **p** to our God; **p** is beautiful, **p**
147:12 Zion, **p** your God
148:1 **P** God from heaven, **p** him from
148:2 **P** him, all you his angels, **p** him
148:3 **P** him, sun and moon, **p** him
148:4 **P** him, high heaven, **p** him
148:5 **P**, oh let them **p** the name of God
148:7 **P** God from earth, you sea dragons
148:13 Let them **p** the name of God
148:14 **P** from all who love God!
149:1 Sing to God a brand-new song, **p** him
149:3 Let them **p** his name in dance
149:5 Let true lovers break out in **p**
150:1 **P** God in his holy house of worship
150:2 **P** him for his acts of power, **p** him
150:3 **P** with a blast on the trumpet
150:3 **p** by strumming soft strings
150:4 **P** him with castanets and dance
150:4 **p** him with banjo and flute

Pr	
Isa	

150:5 **P** him with cymbals and a big bass drum
150:6 every living, breathing creature **p** God
Pr 31:28 her husband joins in with words of **p**
Isa 12:5 Sing **p**-songs to God
24:16 All **p** to the Righteous One!
25:1 I celebrate you. I **p** you.
29:19 down-and-outs shouting **p** to The Holy
43:21 a people custom-made to **p** me
57:18 a new language of **p** for the mourners
60:18 install **P** Park at the center of town
61:10 explode in **p** from deep in my soul
61:11 puts **p** on display before the nations
62:7 Jerusalem famous as the City of **P**
62:9 eat the food and **p** God for it
Jer 17:14 You are my **p**
20:13 Sing to God! All **p** to God!
33:9 a center of joy and **p** and glory
Da 2:23 all thanks! all **p**!
Hab 3:18 I'm singing joyful **p** to God
Mt 21:16 I'll furnish a place of **p**
Lk 2:38 broke into an anthem of **p** to God
18:43 joined in, shouting **p** to God
19:37 disciples burst into enthusiastic **p**
19:40 do it for them, shouting **p**
Ac 28:15 Paul, brimming over with **p**
Ro 5:2 standing tall and shouting our **p**
5:3 We continue to shout our **p**
11:36 Always glory! Always **p**!
15:11 All colors and races, give hearty **p**
16:25 All of our **p** rises to the One
16:27 All our **p** is focused through Jesus
1Co 14:2 If you **p** him in the private language
2Co 1:3 All **p** to the God and Father
1:11 lifted in **p** for God's deliverance
4:15 more and more **p**
9:11 producing with us great **p** to God
9:15 No language can **p** it enough
Php 1:11 involved in the glory and **p** of God
2:11 call out in **p** that he is the Master
3:3 filling the air with Christ's **p**
3:19 belches are their **p**
4:8 things to **p**, not things to curse
2Ti 4:18 All **p** to him, **p** forever!
Heb 2:12 I'll join them in worship and **p** to you
Rev 19:5 **P** our God, all you his servants

Praised

Ge 24:48 bowed in worship to God. I **p** God
2Ch 20:19 they **p** at the top of their lungs
30:21 priests **p** God day after day
31:8 they **p** God and commended God's people
Ne 5:13 Yes, we'll do it!" and **p** God
8:6 Then Ezra **p** God, the great God
Ps 106:47 join in the glory when you are **p**
145:3 God . . . can never be **p** enough
Pr 31:30 woman to be admired and **p** is
SS 6:9 blessed and **p** her
Da 5:4 drunkenly **p** their gods made of gold
Mk 2:12 incredulous — and then **p** God
Lk 16:8 The master **p** the crooked manager!
Ac 2:47 as they **p** God

2Co	6:8	when we're **p**, and when we're blamed

Praises

Ex	15:11	In awesome **p**, wonder-working God
Nu	23:21	with him, shouting **p** to their King
2Ch	29:30	sang their **p** with joy and reverence
Job	33:27	sing God's **p** to everyone you meet
Ps	42:4	Shouting **p**, singing thanksgiving
	57:9	singing your **p** in town and country
	63:3	My lips brim **p** like fountains
	63:5	It's time to shout **p**
	68:32	Sing **p** to the Lord
	72:16	Cornucopias of praise, **p** springing
	74:21	make them a choir that sings your **p**
	75:9	singing the **p** of Jacob's God
	95:1	Come, let's shout **p** to God
	95:2	march into his presence singing **p**
	98:4	Shout your **p** to God, everybody
	98:6	Fill the air with **p** to King God
	106:2	God's mighty acts, broadcast all his **p**
	107:32	Lift high your **p**
	108:3	singing your **p** in town and country
	113:3	keep lifting all your **p** to God
	119:164	each day I stop and shout **p**
	149:6	Shout the high **p** of God
Pr	31:31	Festoon her life with **p**
Isa	38:18	choirs don't sing **p** from the morgue
	42:10	sing his **p** all over the world
	42:12	echo his **p** from coast to coast
	60:6	preaching the **p** of God
	64:11	our ancestors filled with your **p**
Jer	31:7	Raise cheers! Sing **p**
Joel	2:26	You'll be full of **p** to your God
Hab	1:16	He **p** his rod and reel
	3:3	his **p** sounding through the earth
Lk	2:13	a huge angelic choir singing God's **p**
Ro	5:11	shout our **p** to God through Jesus
Eph	5:20	Sing **p** over everything
Php	4:6	Let petitions and **p** shape your worries
Heb	13:15	sacrificial **p** from our lips to God

Pray

Ge	20:7	will **p** for you — **p** for your life
Ex	8:8	P to God to rid us of these frogs
	8:28	Only don't go too far. Now **p** for me
	8:29	will **p** to God that tomorrow the flies
	9:28	P to God. We've had enough
	10:17	P to your God to get me out of this
Nu	21:7	P to God; ask him to take these snakes
Jos	1:17	**p** that God, your God, will be with you
	23:7	don't worship or **p** to them
1Sa	1:18	Think well of me — and **p** for me
	7:5	I'll **p** for you
	7:8	P with all your might
	12:17	But I'm going to **p** to God
	12:19	P to your God for us, your servants. P
	22:10	**p** with him for God's guidance
2Sa	7:27	find the courage to **p** this prayer
1Ki	8:30	prayers that I **p** at this place
	8:35	then they **p** at this place

	8:42	who come to **p** at this Temple
	8:44	**p** to God toward the city you chose
	8:45	Listen from heaven to what they **p**
	8:47	**p** with changed hearts in their exile
	8:48	**p** to you toward their homeland
	13:6	Help me! P to your God for the healing
	18:24	you **p** to your gods and I'll **p** to God
	18:25	**p** to your god, but don't light
	22:43	continued to **p** and worship at these
2Ki	1:16	no God in Israel to whom you could **p**
	22:13	Go and **p** to God for me
1Ch	17:25	find the courage to **p** this prayer
	21:30	wouldn't go there to **p** to God anymore
2Ch	1:5	the congregation gathered to **p**
	6:20	listen to the prayers that I **p**
	6:21	listen . . . when they **p** at this place
	6:26	then they **p** at this place
	6:32	who come to **p** to this Temple
	6:34	they **p** to God toward the city you chose
	6:35	Listen from heaven to what they **p**
	6:37	**p** with changed hearts in their exile
	6:38	**p** to you toward their homeland
	20:4	all the cities of Judah to **p** to God
	20:9	**p** out our pain and trouble
	20:33	continued to **p** and worship at these
	25:15	Why . . . would you **p** to inferior gods
	34:21	Go and **p** to God for me
Ezr	6:10	**p** for the life of the king
	8:21	**p** for wise guidance for our journey
Job	22:27	You'll **p** to him and he'll listen
	27:10	Have they ever been known to **p** before
	33:26	you may fall on your knees and **p**
	42:8	My friend Job will **p** for you
Ps	14:4	meal over which they're too busy to **p**
	19:14	these are what I chew on and **p**
	32:6	Every one of us needs to **p**
	34:7	protection around us while we **p**
	38:12	devoutly they **p** for my ruin
	38:16	wait and **p** so they won't laugh me off
	40:15	those who **p** for my ruin will be booed
	44:20	If we had forgotten to **p** to our God
	53:4	meal over which they're too busy to **p**
	69:13	I **p**. God, it's time for a break!
	105:1	Thank God! P to him by name!
	116:13	I'll **p** in the name of God
	116:17	sacrifice and **p** in the name of God
	122:6	P for Jerusalem's peace!
	130:5	I **p** to God — my life a prayer
	145:18	God's there, listening for all who **p**
	145:18	for all who **p** and mean it
Pr	26:1	than **p** for snow in summer
Isa	16:12	When Moab trudges to the shrine to **p**
	37:4	P for us, Isaiah. P for those of us
	48:1	**p** to the God of Israel
	55:6	**p** to him while he's close at hand
	58:9	when you **p**, God will answer
Jer	10:25	the people who won't **p** to you
	12:16	living my way and **p** to me
	14:11	Don't **p** that everything will turn out
	14:12	skip their meals in order to **p**
	21:2	P to God for us. Ask him for help
	26:19	**p** for mercy from God

P

	29:7	**P** for Babylon's well-being
	29:12	when you come and **p** to me, I'll listen
	37:3	**P** for us — **p** hard! — to the Master
	42:2	Please listen. **P** to your God for us
	42:3	**P** that your God will tell us
	42:4	I will **p** to your God as you have asked
	42:20	**P** for us to our God
Da	2:18	asked them to **p** to the God of heaven
	6:7	no one is to **p** to any god or mortal
	6:10	continued to **p** just as he had always
	6:12	forbidding anyone to **p** to any god
Hos	11:7	They **p** to god Baal for help
	14:2	come back to God. **P** to him
Joel	1:19	God! I **p**, I cry out to you!
Jnh	1:6	Get up! **P** to your god!
Zec	7:2	to **p** for God's blessing
	8:21	**P** to God-of-the-Angel-Armies
	10:1	**P** to God for rain
	13:9	**p** to me by name and I'll answer
Mal	1:9	**p** that I will be gracious to you
Mt	5:34	saying, 'I'll **p** for you
	6:9	you can **p** very simply
	9:38	On your knees and **p** for harvest
	14:23	so he could be by himself and **p**
	19:13	lay hands on them and **p** over them
	24:20	Hope and **p** this won't happen
	26:36	Stay here while I go over there and **p**
	26:44	went back a third time to **p**
Mk	6:46	he climbed a mountain to **p**
	11:24	**p** for absolutely everything
	13:18	Hope and **p** this won't happen
	14:32	Sit here while I **p**
Lk	6:12	he climbed a mountain to **p**
	9:28	he climbed the mountain to **p**
	11:2	When you **p**, say, Father, Reveal
	18:1	necessary for them to **p** consistently
	18:10	Two men went up to the Temple to **p**
	21:36	**P** constantly that you will have
	22:40	**P** that you don't give in to temptation
	22:46	**P** so you won't give in to temptation
Jn	17:9	I **p** for them
Ac	7:33	God said, 'Kneel and **p**
	8:15	**p** for them to receive the Holy Spirit
	8:24	**p** for me! **P** to the Master
	10:9	Peter went out on the balcony to **p**
Ro	8:26	If we don't know how or what to **p**
	10:1	**p** to God for it all the time
	12:12	Don't quit in hard times; **p** all
	15:30	**P** for me. **P** strenuously
	15:31	**P** also that my relief offering
1Co	12:28	those who **p** in tongues
	14:6	and all I do is **p** privately to God
	14:13	**p** in your private prayer language
	14:14	If I **p** in tongues, my spirit prays
	14:15	spiritually free and expressive as I **p**
	14:39	how they should or shouldn't **p**
2Co	1:20	this is what we preach and **p**
	13:9	triumph of the truth in you. We **p** hard
Eph	6:19	don't forget to **p** for me. **P**
Php	4:6	Instead of worrying, **p**
Col	1:10	We **p** that you'll live well
	1:11	We **p** that you'll have the strength

	4:2	**P** diligently. Stay alert
	4:3	Don't forget to **p** for us
	4:4	**P** that every time I open my mouth
	4:18	Remember to **p** for me in this jail
1Th	5:17	**p** all the time
2Th	1:11	we **p** for you all the time — **p** that
	3:1	**P** for us. **P** that the Master's Word
	3:2	**p** that we'll be rescued
1Ti	2:1	first thing I want you to do is **p**
	2:1	**P** every way you know how
	2:2	**P** especially for rulers
Heb	13:18	**P** for us. We have no doubts
	13:19	**P** that we may be together soon
Jas	1:5	**p** to the Father. He loves to help
	5:13	Are you hurting? **P**.
	5:14	Call the church leaders together to **p**
	5:16	Confess your sins to each other and **p**
1Jn	5:16	I'm not urging you to **p** about that
3Jn	1:2	I **p** for good fortune in everything

Prayed

Ge	12:8	built an altar there and **p** to God
	13:4	Abram **p** there to God
	20:17	Then Abraham **p** to God
	24:12	He **p**, "O God, God of my master
	24:27	and **p**, "Blessed be God
	24:42	I **p**, 'God, God of my master
	25:21	Isaaac **p** hard to God for his wife
	26:25	Isaaac built an altar there and **p**
	32:9	Jacob **p**, "God of my father Abraham
Ex	8:12	Moses **p** to God about the frogs
	8:30	Moses left Pharaoh and **p** to God
	10:18	Moses left Pharaoh and **p** to God
Nu	11:2	Moses **p** to God and the fire died
	12:13	Moses **p** to God: Please, God, heal her
	21:7	Moses **p** for the people
Dt	9:20	I **p** also for Aaron at that same time
	9:26	I **p** to God for you
Jdg	13:8	Manoah **p** to God: "Master
1Sa	1:10	Hannah **p** to God and cried
	1:27	I **p** for this child, and God gave me
	2:1	Hannah **p**: I'm bursting with God-news!
	7:6	They fasted all day and **p**
	7:9	He **p** fervently to God, interceding
	8:6	How awful! Samuel **p** to God
	12:18	Samuel **p** to God
	14:37	So Saul **p** to God
	14:41	Then Saul **p** to God
	15:11	Samuel . . . **p** his anger
	22:15	I **p** with him for God's guidance
	23:10	David **p** to God: "God of Israel
	28:6	Saul **p** to God, but God didn't answer
	30:8	Then David **p** to God
2Sa	2:1	After all this, David **p**
	5:19	Then David **p** to God
	5:23	David again **p** to God
	7:18	took his place before God, and **p**
	12:16	David **p** desperately to God
	15:31	He **p**, "Oh, God — turn Ahithophel
	22:1	David **p** to God the words of this song
	24:10	David **p** to God, "I have sinned badly

	24:17	he **p**, "Please! I'm the one who sinned
1Ki	1:48	**p**, 'Blessed be God, Israel's God
	8:23	**p**, O God, God of Israel
	8:38	prayer that's **p** from anyone at all
	8:59	words that I've **p** in the presence
	13:6	The holy man **p** for him
	17:20	**p**, "O God, my God, why
	18:26	**p** to Baal. They **p** all morning
	18:28	They **p** louder and louder
	18:36	Elijah the prophet came up and **p**
2Ki	4:33	in the room — and **p** to God
	6:17	Elisha **p**, "O God, open his eyes
	6:18	Elisha **p** to God, "Strike these people
	6:20	Elisha **p**, "O God, open their eyes
	13:4	**p** for a softening of God's anger
	19:15	Hezekiah **p** — oh, how he **p**!
	19:20	You've **p** to me regarding
1Ch	4.10	Jabez **p** to the God of Israel
	14:10	David **p** to God
	14:14	David again **p** to God
	17:16	took his place before God, and **p**
	21:8	David **p**, "I have sinned badly
	21:17	**p**, "Please! I'm the one who sinned
2Ch	6:14	**p**: God, O God of Israel
	6:29	prayer that's **p** from anyone at all
	13:14	They **p** desperately to God
	14:11	Then Asa **p** to God
	20:3	Shaken, Jehoshaphat **p**
	30:18	Hezekiah **p** for these
	32:24	Hezekiah became deathly sick. He **p**
	33:13	As he **p**, God was touched
Ezr	8:23	we fasted and **p** about these concerns
	9:6	I **p**: "My dear God, I'm so . . . ashamed
	10:1	As he **p** and confessed
Ne	4:4	Nehemiah **p**, "Oh listen to us
	6:9	I **p**, "Give me strength
Job	10:2	Job **p**: "Here's what I want to say
Ps	35:13	instead of eating, I **p**
	99:6	Samuel among those who **p** to him
	99:6	They **p** to God and he
	102:24	I **p**, "please don't let me die
	105:40	They **p** and he brought quail
	140:6	I **p**, "God, you're my God!
Pr	30:7	he **p**, "God, I'm asking for two things
Isa	37:15	Hezekiah **p** to God
	38:2	facing the wall, **p** to God
	38:3	Hezekiah wept as he **p**
Jer	15:11	**p** for them and against their enemies
	32:16	I **p** to God
Eze	11:13	**p** loudly, "O Master, God!
Hos	12:4	Jacob wept and **p**
Jnh	1:14	**p** to God, "O God, Don't let us drown
	2:1	Jonah **p** to his God from the belly
	2:2	He **p**: "In trouble, deep trouble, I **p**
	4:8	He **p** to die: "I'm better off dead
Mt	10:1	no sooner **p** than it was answered
	26:42	Again he **p**, "My Father
Mk	1:35	went out to a secluded spot and **p**
	14:35	fell to the ground and **p** for a way out
	14:39	went back and **p** the same prayer
Lk	18:11	The Pharisee posed and **p** like this
	22:32	Simon, I've **p** for you in particular

	22:41	knelt down, and **p**
	22:44	He **p** on all the harder
	23:34	Jesus **p**, "Father, forgive them
Jn	11:41	Jesus raised his eyes to heaven and **p**
	18:1	Jesus, having **p** this prayer, left
Ac	1:24	they **p**, "You, O God, know every
	7:59	Stephen **p**, "Master Jesus, take my life
	9:40	He knelt and **p**
	12:5	the church **p** for him most strenuously
	20:36	all of them kneeling with him, and **p**
	21:5	kneeled together on the beach and **p**
	27:29	threw out four anchors and **p**
	28:8	when he laid hands on him and **p**
Eph	1:16	every time I **p**, I'd think of you
1Ti	4:14	laid hands on you and **p**
2Ti	1:6	when I laid hands on you and **p**
Jas	5:17	**p** hard that it wouldn't rain
	5:18	Then he **p** that it would rain

Prayer

Ge	17:20	Isahmael? Yes, I heard your **p** for him
	24:45	barely finished offering this **p**
	25:21	God answered his **p** and Rebekah
Ex	8:13	God responded to Moses' **p**
	15:25	So Moses cried out in **p** to God
	17:4	Moses cried out in **p** to God
Nu	21:3	God listened to Israel's **p**
Jdg	7:15	went to his knees before God in **p**
1Sa	1:12	as she continued in **p** before God
	23:2	David went in **p** to God
	23:4	So David went back to God in **p**
2Sa	7:27	the courage to pray this **p** to you
	24:16	David and the elders bowed in **p**
1Ki	8:38	**p** that's prayed from anyone at all
	17:22	God listened to Elijah's **p**
	18:42	top of Carmel, bowed deeply in **p**
2Ki	19:20	I've heard your **p**
	20:5	I've listened to your **p**
	20:11	Isaiah called out in **p** to God
1Ch	15:27	David also wore a linen **p** shawl
	17:25	the courage to pray this **p** to you
	21:16	David and the elders bowed in **p**
2Ch	6:29	**p** that's prayed from anyone at all
	6:40	be alert and attentive to **p**, all **p**
	7:12	I accept your **p**
	30:20	God responded to Hezekiah's **p**
	33:12	went to his knees in **p** asking for help
	33:18	his **p** to his God
	33:19	His **p** and how God was touched by his **p**
Ne	1:6	Pay attention to this **p**
	1:11	listen to your servant's **p**
	4:9	We countered with **p** to our God
	11:17	who led in thanksgiving and **p**
Job	6:8	All I want is an answer to one **p**
	42:8	I will accept his **p**
	42:9	God accepted Job's **p**
Ps	17:1	A David **p** Listen while I build
	39:12	Ah, God, listen to my **p**, my cry
	42:8	My life is God's **p**
	55:1	Open your ears, God, to my **p**
	61:1	bend an ear to my **p**

P

	65:2	You hear the **p** in it all
	66:19	he came . . . when he heard my **p**
	69:10	poured myself out in **p** and fasting
	69:30	tell his greatness in a **p** of thanks
	70:1	A David **p** God! Please hurry
	86:6	Pay attention, God, to my **p**
	88:1	A Korah **p** of Heman
	89:1	An Ethan **p** Your love, God
	90:1	A **p** of Moses, man of God
	102:1	A **p** of one whose life is falling
	102:17	he attends to the **p** of the wretched
	108:1	A David **p** I'm ready, God
	109:1	A David **p** My God, don't turn
	109:4	treat my **p** like a crime
	109:7	when he prays, let his **p** turn to sin
	110:1	A David **p** The word of God to my Lord
	130:5	I pray to God — my life a **p**
	132:9	prompt your worshipers to sing this **p**
	141:2	Treat my **p** as sweet incense rising
	142:1	A David **p** — when he was in the cave
	143:1	A David psalm Listen to this **p**
Isa	1:15	you put on your next **p**-performance
	19:20	When they cry out in **p** to God
	26:16	so heavy they could barely whisper a **p**
	31:1	not so much as a **p** to God
	37:21	Sennacherib of Assyria to me in **p**
	38:5	heard your **p**. I have seen your tears
	56:7	give them joy in my house of **p**
Jer	5:4	never went to **p** meetings
	27:18	to God-of-the-Angel-Armies in **p**
	42:9	you sent me to present your **p**
La	2:19	get up and cry out in **p**
	3:29	Bow in **p**. Don't ask questions
Eze	9:8	I fell on my face in **p**
Da	6:10	Three times a day he knelt there in **p**
	9:17	listen, God, to this determined **p**
	9:18	This **p** is our last and only hope
	9:23	started your **p** when the answer
	10:12	your **p** was heard
Hos	6:6	know God, not go to more **p** meetings
	7:14	crying out to me in heartfelt **p**
Joel	1:14	God's Sanctuary for serious **p** to God
Jnh	2:7	my **p** got through to you
Hab	3:1	A **p** of the prophet Habakkuk
Zep	1:6	a thought or offering a **p**
Zec	12:10	pour a spirit of grace and **p** over them
Mt	5:44	respond with the energies of **p**
	6:2	treating **p** meeting and street
	6:7	**p** warriors who are **p**-ignorant
	6:14	In **p** there is a connection
	10:1	**p** was no sooner prayed than it was
	11:25	Abruptly Jesus broke into **p**
	14:19	lifted his face to heaven in **p**
	18:19	anything . . . make a **p** of it
	21:13	was designated a house of **p**
	21:22	make it a part of your believing **p**
	22:37	your passion and **p** and intelligence
	23:5	embroidered **p** shawls one day
	26:41	be in **p** so you don't wander
Mk	6:41	lifted his face to heaven in **p**
	7:34	Then Jesus looked up in **p**
	9:29	rid of this kind of demon except by **p**

	11:17	was designated a house of **p**
	11:25	when you assume the posture of **p**
	12:30	your passion and **p** and intelligence
	14:38	Stay alert, be in **p**
	14:39	went back and prayed the same **p**
Lk	1:13	Zachariah. Your **p** has been heard
	5:12	fell down before him in **p** and said
	5:16	out-of-the-way places for **p**
	6:12	was there all night in **p** before God
	6:28	respond with the energies of **p**
	9:16	lifted his face to heaven in **p**
	9:29	While he was in **p**, the appearance
	10:27	your passion and **p** and muscle
	19:46	My house is a house of **p**
	22:45	He got up from **p**, went back
Jn	17:1	in **p**, he said: Father, it's time
	18:1	Jesus, having prayed this **p**
	18:9	This validated the words in his **p**
Ac	1:14	completely together in **p**
	3:1	into the Temple for **p** meeting
	4:24	voices in a wonderful harmony in **p**
	6:4	tasks of **p** and speaking God's Word
	10:2	had the habit of **p**
	13:35	So also the psalmist's **p**
	16:13	heard there was to be a **p** meeting
	16:16	on our way to the place of **p**
	16:25	Paul and Silas were at **p**
Ro	8:26	making **p** out of our wordless sighs
	11:2	cried out in **p**
1Co	7:5	if it's for the purposes of **p**
	12:30	not all Healer, not all **P** in Tongues
	14:4	who prays using a private "**p** language"
	14:5	develop intimacies with God in **p**
	14:13	pray in your private **p** language
	14:16	blessing using your private **p** language
	14:26	lead a **p**, provide an insight
Eph	6:18	**p** is essential in this ongoing warfare
Php	1:4	Each exclamation is a trigger to **p**
	1:9	my **p**: that your love will flourish
1Ti	2:8	**p** is at the bottom of all this
2Ti	1:3	Every time I say your name in **p**
	2:22	in honest and serious **p** before God
Jas	5:15	Believing-**p** will heal you
	5:16	**p** of a person living right with God
1Pe	4:7	Stay wide-awake in **p**

Prayerful

2Ch	31:21	did well in a spirit of **p** worship
Ps	37:7	Quiet down before God, be **p**
Pr	15:28	**P** answers come from God-loyal people
Lk	2:25	lived in the **p** expectancy of help

Prayers

2Sa	21:14	God responded to Israel's **p**
	24:25	God was moved by the **p**
1Ki	8:28	Pay attention to these my **p**
	8:30	listen to the **p** that I pray
	8:33	acknowledge your rule in **p** desperate
	8:49	to their **p** desperate and devout
	8:52	attentive to the needy **p** of me

P

	8:54	all these bold and passionate **p**
	9:3	all your **p**, your ever-so-passionate **p**
2Ki	19:4	**p** for what's left of these people
1Ch	5:20	God answered their **p**
	23:30	to be present for morning **p**
2Ch	6:19	Pay attention to these my **p**
	6:20	listen to the **p** that I pray
	6:24	**p** desperate and devout in this Temple
	6:33	honor the **p** of the foreigner
	6:39	their **p** desperate and devout
	7:15	alert . . . to the **p** offered at this
	13:11	at the daily morning and evening **p**
	30:27	their **p** entered his holy heaven
Job	16:17	never hurt a soul and my **p** are sincere
	35:13	nothing behind such **p** except panic
Ps	6:9	my **p** are answered
	13:6	I'm so full of answered **p**
	35:14	My **p** were like lead in my gut
	72:15	Offer **p** unceasing to him
	88:13	at my **p** every morning
	141:2	my raised hands are my evening **p**
Pr	15:8	he delights in genuine **p**
	15:29	attends to the **p** of God-loyal people
	28:9	no use for the **p** of the people
Isa	19:22	God will listen to their **p** and heal
	58:4	won't get your **p** off the ground
Jer	11:14	a single syllable of their crisis-**p**
	14:12	When they redouble their **p**
	36:7	God will hear their **p**
La	3:44	clouds so no **p** could get through
Eze	14:3	Why should I even bother with their **p**
Da	9:27	he will banish worship and **p**
Hos	14:2	Receive as restitution our repentant **p**
Joel	1:13	no offerings, no **p**—nothing
Zep	1:9	introduce pagan **p** and practices
Mt	6:5	making a regular show out of their **p**
	23:5	flowery **p** the next
	23:35	whom you murdered at his **p**
Mk	12:40	The longer their **p**, the worse they get
Lk	2:37	night and day with her fastings and **p**
	5:33	known for keeping fasts and saying **p**
	20:47	The longer their **p**, the worse they get
Ac	2:42	the common meal, and the **p**
	10:4	**p** and neighborly acts have brought
	10:31	your daily **p** and neighborly acts
	14:23	their **p** intensified by fasting
	24:18	found me quietly at my **p** in the Temple
	28:15	led us in **p** of thanksgiving
Ro	1:10	in my **p**, which is practically all
1Co	4:5	inner motives and purposes and **p**
	14:27	If **p** are offered in tongues
2Co	1:11	**p** are part of the rescue operation
Php	1:7	**p** and hopes have deep roots in reality
	1:19	Through your faithful **p**
	4:6	shape your worries into **p**
Col	1:3	Our **p** for you are always spilling
	4:12	tireless in his **p** for you
1Th	1:2	Day and night you're in our **p**
	5:25	Friends, keep up your **p** for us
1Ti	1:18	All those **p** are coming together
	4:5	God's Word and our **p** make every item
Phm	1:4	Every time your name comes up in my **p**

	1:22	Because of your **p**, I fully expect
Heb	5:7	offered up priestly **p** to God
	13:18	it's hard going and we need your **p**
Jas	1:6	People who "worry their **p**" are like
1Pe	3:7	your wives, then, as equals so your **p**
Rev	5:8	the **p** of God's holy people
	6:10	cried out in loud **p**, "How long
	8:3	offer up the **p** of all the holy people
	8:4	incense-laced **p** of the holy ones

Praying

Ge	4:26	**p** and worshiping in the name of God
	16:13	**p** to the God who spoke to her
	21:33	**p** to the Eternal God
	30:24	**p**, "May God add yet another son
1Sa	1:13	Hannah was **p** in her heart, silently
	1:26	at this very spot, **p** to God
	12:23	right here at my post **p** for you
	22:13	even **p** with him for God's guidance
1Ki	8:54	Having finished **p** to God
	17:21	**p** with all his might, "God, my God
2Ki	20:2	turned from Isaiah and faced God, **p**
1Ch	10:13	Instead of **p**, he went to a witch
	22:19	heart and soul, to **p** to your God
2Ch	7:1	When Solomon finished **p**
	7:14	humbling themselves, **p**
	32:20	responded by **p**, calling up to heaven
Ne	1:4	fasting and **p** before the God-of-Heaven
	1:6	I'm **p** day and night in intercession
	2:4	**P** under my breath to the God-of-Heaven
Ps	28:6	Blessed be God—he heard me **p**
	84:8	God of Jacob, open your ears—I'm **p**
	141:5	I'm **p** hard against their evil ways
Isa	10:12	**p** for relief is useless
	44:19	Here I am **p** to a stick of wood
	45:14	in reverence, **p** before you
	45:20	**p** for help to a dead stick
	62:6	they keep at it, **p**, calling out
Jer	7:16	waste your time **p** for this people
	11:12	Jerusalem will start **p** to the gods
	11:14	I don't want you **p** for this people
	36:7	they'll start **p** and God will hear
La	3:41	**p** to God in heaven
Da	6:11	conspirators came and found him **p**
	9:3	asking for an answer—**p** earnestly
	9:20	**p** my life out before my God
	9:21	while I was absorbed in this **p**
Zep	3:10	**p**—All my scattered, exiled people
Mt	8:2	knees before Jesus, **p**, "Master
	26:39	**p**, "My Father, if there is any way
Lk	1:10	gathered and **p** outside the Temple
	2:38	At the very time Simeon was **p**
	3:21	As he was **p**, the sky opened up
	9:18	Jesus was off **p** by himself
	11:1	One day he was **p** in a certain place
Jn	17:9	I'm not **p** for the God-rejecting world
	17:20	I'm **p** not only for them But also
Ac	4:31	While they were **p**, the place
	6:6	**P**, the apostles laid on hands
	7:60	**p** loud enough for everyone to hear
	9:11	His name is Saul. He's there **p**

P

	10:30	midafternoon, I was home **p**
	11:5	was in the town of Joppa **p**
	12:12	house was packed with **p** friends
	13:3	obedience, of fasting and **p**
	14:23	After **p** — their prayers intensified
	22:17	**p** one day in the Temple
	26:29	That's what I'm **p** for, whether now
Ro	8:26	He does our **p** in and for us
1Co	11:13	**p** in adoration
	13:8	**p** in tongues will end
	14:18	the gift of **p** in tongues
	14:23	as you're all **p** in tongues
	14:39	when they're **p** in tongues
2Co	9:14	respond by **p** for you
Php	1:4	**p** for you with a glad heart
	2:24	hoping and **p** to be right on his heels
	4:10	Not that you ever quit **p**
Col	1:9	we haven't stopped **p** for you
	4:12	**p** that you'll stand firm
1Th	3:10	We do what we can, **p** away
	5:5	hope in God, **p** to him constantly
Phm	1:6	**p** that this faith we hold in common
Jude	1:20	by **p** in the Holy Spirit
Rev	1:10	I was in the Spirit, **p**

	3:2	big city of Nineveh! **P** to them
Mic	2:6	Don't **p**," say the preachers. "Don't **p**
	2:11	I'll **p** sermons that will tell you
	3:11	prophets **p** for high fees
Mt	11:1	on to teach and **p** in their villages
Mk	1:38	villages so I can **p** there also
	5:20	began to **p** in the Ten Towns area
Lk	4:18	Spirit is on me; he's chosen me to **p**
	9:2	He commissioned them to **p** the news
	12:3	thing in private and **p** the opposite
Ac	13:5	was **p** God's Word
	13:42	were invited back to **p** again
	16:10	God had called us to **p** the good news
	18:19	go to the meeting place and **p**
Ro	12:6	If you **p**, just **p** God's Message
1Co	1:17	to **p** the Message of what he has done
	14:21	from the mouths of strangers I will **p**
2Co	1:20	In him, this is what we **p** and pray
Gal	1:8	**p** something other than what
	4:13	the reason I ended up **p**ing to you
	5:11	continue to **p** the ways of circumcision
Php	1:15	some here **p** Christ because
Col	1:28	We **p** Christ, warning people not to add
Rev	14:6	He had an Eternal Message to **p** to all

Preach

Isa	61:1	God anointed me. He sent me to **p**
	66:19	send them out as missionaries to **p**
Jer	3:12	Go and **p** this message
	5:31	Prophets **p** lies and priests hire on
	7:2	God's Temple and **p** this Message
	11:2	**P** to the people of Judah
	11:6	God continued: "**P** all this
	11:21	Don't **p** to us in God's name
	14:15	All the preachers who **p** using my name
	19:2	Gate, and **p** there what I tell you
	19:14	where God had sent him to **p** the sermon
	20:1	He heard Jeremiah **p** this sermon
	23:17	**p** their 'Everything Will Turn Out Fine
	23:25	all these prophets who **p** lies using me
	23:26	as they **p** their lies
	23:32	prophets who **p** the lies they dream up
	25:30	**P** it all . . . **P** the entire Message
	26:2	in the court of God's Temple and **p**
	26:9	How dare you **p** — and using God's name
	26:12	God sent me to **p** against both
	32:3	How dare you **p**, saying, 'God says
	50:2	Get the word out to the nations! **P** it
Eze	4:7	**p** against her
	6:2	**p** against them
	11:4	Oppose them . . . **P** against them
	13:2	Son of man, **p** against the prophets
	13:6	illusions and **p** lying sermons
	25:2	face Ammon and **p** against the people
	28:21	confront Sidon. **P** against it
	29:2	**P** against him and all the Egyptians
	30:2	**p**. Give them the Message of God
	36:6	**p** to the mountains and hills
Am	7:15	Go **p** to my people Israel
	7:16	You tell me, 'Don't **p** to Israel
Jnh	1:2	big city of Nineveh! **P** to them

Preached

Dt	1:1	the sermons Moses **p** to all Israel
1Ki	13:2	**p** (these were God's orders)
	13:4	the holy man **p** against the Altar
	13:32	**p** by God's command against the Altar
1Ch	25:3	who **p** and accompanied himself
2Ch	20:37	**p** against Jehoshaphat's venture
	24:27	the many sermons **p** to Joash
	36:12	when the prophet Jeremiah **p** God's word
	36:21	message of God that Jeremiah had **p**
	36:22	the message of God **p** by Jeremiah
Ezr	1:1	the Message of God **p** by Jeremiah
Ps	40:9	I've **p** you to the whole congregation
Pr	24:32	the fields **p** me a sermon
Jer	2:8	The prophets **p** god Baal
	20:6	your cronies to whom you **p** your lies
	23:13	**p** using that no-god Baal for a text
	23:21	I never spoke to them, but they **p** away
	23:22	they'd have **p** my Message to my people
	25:13	**p** against all the godless nations
	26:11	He has **p** against this city
	26:18	**p** to the people of Judah this sermon
	26:20	had **p** similarly in the name of God
	28:8	old prophets . . . **p** judgment
	29:23	**p** lies claiming it was my Message
	29:32	he has **p** rebellion against me
	37:19	your prophets who **p** all those sermons
Eze	13:16	prophets of Israel who **p** to Jerusalem
	24:18	I **p** to the people in the morning
Da	9:6	servants the prophets, who **p** your Word
Jnh	3:4	went one day's walk and **p**
Hag	1:13	God's messenger, **p** God's Message
Zec	1:5	And the prophets who **p** to them?
	7:12	sermons **p** by the earlier prophets
Mt	2:15	exile fulfilled what Hosea had **p**
	7:22	Master, we **p** the Message

P

	12:41	when Jonah **p** to them they changed
	24:14	the Message . . . will be **p** all over
	26:13	in the whole world the Message is **p**
Mk	1:7	As he **p** he said
	6:12	They **p** with joyful urgency
	13:10	The Message has to be **p** all across
	14:9	in the whole world the Message is **p**
Lk	8:39	went back and **p** all over town
	11:31	when Jonah **p** to them they changed
Jn	1:23	I'm doing what the prophet Isaiah **p**
	1:45	the Law, the One **p** by the prophets
	12:38	God, who believed what we **p**?
Ac	8:4	they **p** the Message about Jesus
	8:35	he **p** Jesus to him
	9:28	as he **p** in the Master's name
	10:37	after John **p** a total life-change
	14:25	and **p** in Perga
	15:21	basic wisdom from Moses, **p** and honored
	15:36	where we **p** the Word of God
	17:2	three Sabbaths running he **p**
	18:26	He **p** with power in the meeting place
	19:4	**p** a baptism of radical life-change
	19:13	I command you by the Jesus **p** by Paul
Ro	10:17	unless Christ's Word is **p**
	16:25	exactly as **p** in Jesus Christ
2Co	11:4	quite another Jesus than we **p**
Gal	1:8	other than what we **p** originally
Eph	2:17	Christ came and **p** peace
1Th	1:5	When the Message we **p** came to you
	2:13	When you got the Message of God we **p**
1Pe	4:6	**p** to those believers who are now dead
Rev	14:7	He **p** in a loud voice, "Fear God

Preacher

Isa	40:9	You're the **p** of good news
	41:27	I gave Jerusalem a **p** of good news
Jer	11:19	Let's get rid of the **p**
Am	7:14	I never set up to be a **p**
Mic	2:11	you'd hire him on the spot as your **p**
Mt	12:41	A far greater **p** than Jonah is here
Mk	1:2	I'm sending my **p** ahead of you
Lk	11:31	A far greater **p** than Jonah is here
Eph	6:20	jailbird **p** that I am
2Ti	1:11	I've been set apart to proclaim as **p**

Preachers

Isa	30:10	tell their **p**, "Don't waste our time
Jer	14:13	Their **p** have been telling them
	14:14	These **p** are liars, and they use my
	14:15	All the **p** who preach using my name
	14:18	I watch the **p** and priests
	20:8	Don't let all those so-called **p**
	32:32	kings and leaders and priests and **p**
Eze	22:28	Your **p** cover up for the politicians
Mic	2:6	Don't preach," say the **p**
	3:5	the **p** who lie to my people
Mt	7:15	Be wary of false **p** who smile a lot
	7:16	Who **p** are is the main thing
	24:11	lying **p** will come forward and deceive
	24:24	Fake Messiahs and lying **p**

Mk	13:22	Fake Messiahs and lying **p**
Lk	6:23	my **p** . . . have always been treated
	6:26	how many scoundrel **p** were approved
Ac	13:1	blessed with a number of prophet-**p**
	15:32	Judas and Silas, good **p** both of them
	15:35	number of teachers and **p** at that time
Ro	10:18	**P**' voices have gone 'round the world
2Co	11:12	in with those money-grubbing "**p**,"
	11:13	pseudo-apostles, lying **p**
	11:18	three-ring **p** that are so popular
1Jn	4:1	lot of lying **p** loose in the world

Predators

Job	24:15	Sexual **p** can't wait for nightfall
Jer	29:23	sex **p** and prophet-impostors
2Pe	2:12	born in the wild, **p** on the prowl

Pregnancy

Ge	16:11	From this **p**, you'll get a son
Mt	1:20	Mary's **p** is Spirit-conceived
Lk	1:24	five months, relishing her **p**
	1:26	In the sixth month of Elizabeth's **p**
	1:57	When Elizabeth was full-term in her **p**

Pregnant

Ge	16:4	she got **p**. When she learned she was **p**
	16:5	the minute she knows she's **p**
	18:12	An old woman like me? Get **p**?
	19:31	by whom we can get **p**
	19:36	daughters became **p** by their father
	21:2	Sarah became **p** and gave Abraham a son
	26:21	Rebekah became **p**
	29:32	Leah became **p** and had a son
	29:33	became **p** again and had another son
	29:34	became **p** yet again — another son
	29:35	became **p** a final time and had a fourth
	30:5	Bilhah became **p** and gave Jacob a son
	30:7	Rachel's maid Bilhah became **p** again
	30:17	became **p** and gave Jacob a fifth son
	30:19	Leah became **p** yet again
	30:23	became **p** and had a son
	38:3	became **p** and had a son
	38:4	got **p** again and had a son
	38:18	slept with her. And she got **p**
	38:24	now she's a **p** whore
	38:25	I'm **p** by the man who owns these things
Ex	2:2	The woman became **p** and had a son
	21:22	**p** woman is hit so that she miscarries
Jdg	13:3	going to become **p** and bear a son
	13:5	You are, in fact, **p** right now
	13:7	but he told me, 'You're **p**
1Sa	4:19	was **p** and ready to deliver
2Sa	11:5	Before long she realized she was **p**
2Ki	8:12	rip open their **p** women
	15:16	ripped open all the **p** women
Job	39:2	Do you know how many months she is **p**?
Ps	7:14	had sex with sin, he's **p** with evil
Ecc	11:5	mystery of life forming in a **p** woman
Isa	4:1	Just give us a child. Make us **p**

P

	7:14	a virgin will get **p**
	26:18	We were **p** full-term
	33:11	**P** with chaff, you produce straw babies
	37:3	like **p** women without even the strength
	59:4	**p** with mischief and have sin-babies
	59:13	**p** with lies, muttering malice
Jer	20:17	My mother **p** for the rest of her life
	31:8	gather **p** women
Hos	1:3	She got **p** and gave him a son
	1:6	Gomer got **p** again
	1:8	she got **p** yet again and had a son
	13:16	**p** women ripped open
Am	1:13	ripped open **p** women in Gilead
Mt	1:18	Joseph discovered she was **p**
	1:20	God's Holy Spirit has made her **p**
	1:23	a virgin will get **p** and bear a son
	24:19	**P** and nursing mothers will have it
Mk	13:17	**P** and nursing mothers will have it
Lk	1:31	will become **p** and give birth to a son
	1:36	here she is six months' **p**
	2:5	Mary, his fiancée, who was **p**
	21:23	**P** and nursing mothers will have it
Ro	8:22	All around us we observe a **p** creation
	8:24	than waiting diminishes a **p** mother
	8:27	knows our **p** condition
	9:10	became **p** by our one-of-a-kind ancestor
1Th	5:3	as birth pangs to a **p** woman
Heb	11:11	barren Sarah was able to become **p**
Jas	1:15	Lust gets **p**, and has a baby: sin

President

Lk	8:41	He was **p** of the meeting place
	13:14	The meeting-place **p**, furious
Ac	13:15	the **p** of the meeting asked them
	18:8	Crispus, the meeting-place **p**
	18:17	Sosthenes, the new meeting-place **p**

Pretense

Ps	33:10	God takes the wind out of Babel **p**
Pr	16:5	God can't stomach arrogance or **p**
Jn	9:39	who have made a great **p** of seeing
Ac	15:8	God, who can't be fooled by any **p**
Eph	4:25	no more lies, no more **p**
1Pe	2:1	Make a clean sweep of malice and **p**

Pretensions

Job	11:11	He sees through vain **p**
Ps	9:19	Expose these grand **p**
Pr	15:25	God smashes the **p** of the arrogant
Eze	28:7	puncture the balloon of your god-**p**
Jn	7:7	expose the evil behind its **p**
1Co	1:28	expose the hollow **p** of the "somebodies
Rev	3:9	watch as I strip off their **p**

Pretentious

Ps	37:35	like a toad, croaking **p** nonsense
	73:6	**P** with arrogance, they wear

Pr	13:7	A **p**, showy life is an empty life
Isa	2:11	**p** egos brought down a peg
	2:17	the **p** egos brought down to earth
	27:10	nothing left of that **p** grandeur
	28:1	Doom to the **p** drunks of Ephraim
	37:28	I know all about your **p** poses
Jer	5:27	**P** and powerful and rich
Eze	7:10	The scepter outsized and **p**
	7:20	Proud and **p** with their jewels
Am	3:15	demolished, all those **p** houses
	5:22	your **p** slogans and goals
Mal	1:3	I reduced **p** Esau to a molehill
1Co	1:20	God exposed it all as **p** nonsense
Col	2:20	put all that **p** . . . religion behind

Pride

Lev	26:19	I'll break your strong **p**
1Ch	26:31	Jeriah held **p** of place
Job	36:9	their **p** has caused their trouble
	41:15	His **p** is invincible
Ps	51:17	God-worship when my **p** was shattered
	57:4	I find myself in a **p** of lions
	78:61	let his **p** and joy go to the dogs
	106:5	join the Hallelujahs of your **p** and joy
Pr	4:3	the **p** and joy of my mother
	8:13	whose ways I hate with a passion — **p**
	16:18	First **p**, then the crash
	17:6	children take **p** in their parents
	18:12	**P** first, then the crash
	21:4	Arrogance and **p** — distinguishing marks
	29:23	**P** lands you flat on your face
Isa	5:29	Roaring like a **p** of lions
	13:3	bursting with **p** and passion
	13:19	the **p** and joy of Chaldeans
	16:6	Moab's **p**, world-famous for **p**
	23:9	show the sordid backside of **p**
	25:11	Their **p** will pull them under
	32:19	forest of your **p** will be clear-cut
Jer	13:9	ruin the **p** of Judah and the great **p**
	30:20	a community in which I take **p**
	48:29	heard of Moab's **p**, that legendary **p**
	48:30	his rooster-crowing **p**
	50:31	get it, Mister **P**? I'm your enemy
	50:32	Mister **P** will fall flat
	51:41	**p** of the whole earth is flat
La	2:4	our young men, our **p** and joy
Eze	7:10	**p** bursting all bounds
	19:2	crouched in a **p** of young lions
	32:12	swords of champions to lay your **p** low
	32:24	Elam is there in all her **p**
	32:26	Meshech-tubal is there in all her **p**
Na	2:2	the **P** of Jacob, the **P** of Israel
Zep	2:10	what they get for their bloated **p**
Mt	6:30	take **p** in you, do his best for you
Mk	1:11	my Son, . . . **p** of my life
Lk	3:22	my Son, . . . **p** of my life
	12:28	take **p** in you, do his best for you
	18:16	children are the kingdom's **p** and joy
Php	4:1	fill me with such **p**. Don't waver
1Th	2:20	You're our **p** and joy

P

Priority

Pr	2:3	if you make Insight your **p**
Mal	1:7	worship of God is no longer a **p**
Ro	9:10	promise . . . that took **p** over genetics
1Co	11:11	can go it alone or claim **p**

Privilege

Da	4:2	It is my **p** to report to you
Jn	11:48	what little power and **p** we still have
2Co	8:4	pleading for the **p** of helping out
Gal	4:7	**p** of intimate conversation with God
Php	3:8	the high **p** of knowing Christ Jesus

Privileged

Isa	45:4	given you this **p** work
1Co	3:23	you are **p** to be in union with Christ
Heb	13:13	not trying to be **p** insiders

Privileges

Php	2:7	set aside the **p** of deity
	2:8	He didn't claim special **p**
Heb	11:24	Moses, when grown, refused the **p**
Jas	2:5	citizens, with full rights and **p**

Problem

1Sa	12:14	you and your king follow God, no **p**
Job	16:3	What's your **p** that you go on
Eze	13:10	lied to my people. They've said, 'No **p**
Na	1:1	A report on the **p** of Nineveh
Hab	1:1	The **p** as God gave Habakkuk to see it
Mt	16:11	bread isn't the **p**? The **p** is yeast
	27:4	What do we care? That's your **p**
Ac	21:20	a **p** because they are more zealous
Ro	2:24	an old **p** that isn't going to go away
	8:3	didn't deal with the **p** as something
	9:6	The **p** goes back a long way
2Th	3:15	talk about the **p** as someone who cares
Heb	10:11	never makes a dent in the sin **p**
1Jn	2:2	he solved the sin **p** for good

Problems

Ex	24:14	if there are any **p**, go to them
Job	35:15	do something about the world's **p**
Zec	8:6	the **p** of returning and rebuilding

Procrastinate

Pr	6:4	Don't **p** — there's no time to lose
Hag	11:2	The people **p**
Jn	3:11	you **p** with questions

Procrastination

Ps	31:2	please — no **p**!
Lk	9:62	No **p**. No backward looks

Productive

Pr	31:27	keeps them all busy and **p**
Isa	36:17	more than enough fertile and **p** land

Profane

Ex	20:25	use a chisel on the stones you'll **p**
Lev	21:4	related to him by marriage and thus **p**
	21:6	must not **p** the name of their God
Mal	1:12	you **p** me. You **p** me when you say
Eph	4:31	break with all . . . **p** talk
2Ti	3:2	stuck-up, **p**, contemptuous of parents

Profaned

2Sa	6:7	because he had **p** the Chest
Eze	13:19	You have **p** me among my people

Profanity

Ps	34:13	Guard your tongue from **p**
Col	3:8	meanness, **p**, dirty talk

Professionals

1Sa	6:2	called together their religious **p**
Hos	13:2	customized to taste. **P** see to it

Profit

Lev	25:37	don't give him food for **p**
1Ki	10:15	beyond the taxes and **p** on trade
2Ch	9:14	beyond the taxes and **p** on trade
Job	6:27	Are friends just items of **p** and loss
	31:39	raped the earth for my own **p**
Ps	30:9	Can you sell me for a **p** when I'm dead
Pr	9:9	they'll **p** from it
	27:26	sell your goats for a **p**
Isa	23:4	dead numbers, **p** and loss
Lk	19:18	I made a fifty percent **p** on your money
Ac	24:3	gain daily **p** from your reforms

Profiteer

2Pe	2:15	the prophet who turned **p**

Profits

2Ki	8:6	all **p** from the farm
Ecc	5:10	one who loves wealth with big **p**
Isa	23:18	**p** will be put to the use of God-Aware
Mt	21:34	servants back to collect his **p**
	21:41	hand over the **p** when it's time
Mk	12:2	to the farmhands to collect his **p**
Lk	20:10	to the farmhands to collect the **p**

Prolific

Ex	1:7	kept on reproducing. They were very **p**
1Ch	4:27	his brothers were not nearly as **p**

P

Prominence

2Sa	5:12	giving his kingship world **p**
1Ch	26:13	regardless of the **p** of their families
Pr	25:6	push your way into the place of **p**
Ecc	10:6	Immaturity is given a place of **p**
Heb	9:23	the **p** of blood and death in all these

Promiscuity

Eze	16:36	you've been unrestrained in your **p**
Mt	5:32	already made herself that by sexual **p**
Eph	5:3	a downhill slide into sexual **p**
Col	3:5	that way of death: sexual **p**, impurity
1Th	4:3	Keep yourselves from sexual **p**

Promiscuous

2Ki	9:22	**p** whoring and sorceries of your mother
Pr	5:20	for dalliance with a **p** stranger
	31:3	**p** women who shipwreck leaders
Isa	23:17	**p** with all the kingdoms of earth
Jer	2:24	insatiable, indiscriminate, **p**
	3:13	your **p** life with casual partners
	23:10	faithless, **p** idolater-adulterers
Eze	16:26	more **p** you became, the angrier I got
	23:49	pay in full for your **p** affairs
Hos	2:13	pay for her indulgence in **p** religion
	10:1	the more **p** the worship
1Co	5:9	at home among the sexually **p**
	5:11	one of your Christian companions is **p**
	10:8	We must not be sexually **p**
Rev	9:21	occult, **p**, and thieving ways

Promise

Ge	24:7	spoke to me in solemn **p**
	24:37	My master made me **p**
	47:31	Israel said, "**P** me." Joseph promised
	50:6	as he made you **p** under oath
	50:25	made the sons of Israel **p** under oath
Nu	23:19	Does he **p** and not come through
	30:6	has made some rash **p** or pledge
	30:8	cancels the vow or rash **p** that binds
Dt	7:8	the **p** he made to your ancestors
	32:40	By that very life I **p**
Jos	2:12	Now **p** me by God
	9:20	get blamed for breaking our **p**
	9:21	the leaders' **p** was kept
Jdg	15:12	Just **p** not to hurt me
	15:13	We **p**," they said
1Sa	24:21	Now **p** me under God that you will not
	30:15	"**P** me by God," he said
2Sa	21:7	the **p** David and Jonathan had spoken
1Ki	1:13	Didn't you, my master the king, **p** me
	2:42	Didn't I make you **p** me under God
	2:43	why didn't you keep your sacred **p**
	5:5	following the **p** that God gave to David
	6:12	complete in you the **p** I made to David
	8:15	Now he has kept the **p** he made
	17:16	God's **p** fulfilled to the letter
	22:16	How many times have I made you **p**

2Ch	6:10	And now you see the **p** completed
	6:15	your word to David my father, your **p**
	15:14	shouted out their **p** to God
	15:15	felt good about the covenant **p**
	15:15	they had given their **p** joyfully
	18:15	How many times have I made you **p**
Ne	5:12	made them **p** to keep their word
	5:13	everyone who doesn't keep this **p**
Job	42:6	I'll never do that again, I **p**
Ps	77:8	Has his salvation **p** burned out
	89:34	Do you think I'd withdraw my holy **p**
	89:39	tore up the **p** you made to your servant
	89:49	What happened to your **p** to David
	92:11	ears are filled with the sounds of **p**
	105:19	God confirmed his **p**
	105:42	his Covenant, his **p** to Abraham
	111:5	He remembered to keep his ancient **p**
	119:57	God, I **p** to do everything you say
	119:82	watching for some sign of your **p**
	119:123	waiting for you to keep your **p**
	119:133	Steady my steps with your Word of **p**
	119:140	Your **p** has been tested through
	119:148	prayerfully pondering your **p**
	119:170	rescue me on the terms of your **p**
	132:11	he won't back out on this **p**
Pr	30:5	Every **p** of God proves true
Isa	19:18	speak the language of faith and **p**
	45:23	I **p** in my own name
Jer	32:42	life of prosperity. I **p**
	33:14	when I will keep the **p** I made
	34:5	This is a solemn **p**
	34:11	reneged on the covenant, broke their **p**
Eze	17:18	even though he gave his solemn **p**
	20:15	oath there in the desert and **p** them
	20:16	I canceled my **p** because they despised
Zep	3:20	reunions!" God's **p**
Mt	16:20	made them **p** they would tell no one
	23:16	makes a **p** with his fingers crossed
	23:18	shake hands on a **p**, that's nothing
	23:20	A **p** is a **p**
Lk	6:35	You'll never—I **p**—regret it
Ac	1:4	what the Father promised: the **p**
	2:33	receiving the **p** of the Holy Spirit
	2:39	The **p** is targeted to you
	7:5	He did **p** to give the country to him
Ro	4:13	That famous **p** God gave Abraham
	4:14	turns the **p** into an ironclad contract
	4:15	simply a **p**—and God's **p** at that
	4:16	God's **p** depends entirely on trusting
	4:20	He didn't tiptoe around God's **p**
	9:7	God's **p**. Remember how it was put
	9:8	it was God-determined by **p**
	9:9	Remember that **p**
	9:10	To Rebecca, also, a **p** was made
Gal	3:8	anticipated this in the **p** to Abraham
	3:17	thereby negating the **p** of the will
	3:20	the original **p** is the direct blessing
	3:21	an anti-**p**, a negation of God's will
	3:27	the fulfillment of God's original **p**
	4:23	was born by God's **p**
	4:28	you, like Isaaac, are children of **p**
	4:29	from the faithful **p** (Isaaac)

P

Eph	6:2	commandment that has a **p** attached
Heb	4:1	that **p** of resting in him
	4:6	this **p** has not yet been fulfilled
	4:7	God keeps renewing the **p**
	4:8	this is still a live **p**
	4:9	The **p** of "arrival" and "rest"
	6:13	When God made his **p** to Abraham
	6:14	He said, "I **p** that I'll bless you
	6:18	the **p** is likewise unchangeable
	7:21	priesthood into being with an added **p**
	11:11	believed the One who made a **p** would do
2Pe	2:19	They **p** these newcomers freedom
	3:4	what's happened to the **p** of his Coming
	3:9	God isn't late with his **p**

Promised

Ge	18:19	complete in Abraham what he **p** him
	21:1	God did to Sarah what he **p**
	28:15	until I've done everything I **p** you
	31:53	Jacob **p**, swearing by the Fear
	45:21	the wagons that Pharaoh had **p**
	47:31	Israel said, "Promise me." Joseph **p**
	50:24	the land he so solemnly **p** to Abraham
Ex	6:8	the land that I **p** to give Abraham
	12:25	land which God will give you as he **p**
	13:5	which he **p** to your fathers to give you
	13:11	as he **p** you and your fathers
	33:1	the land which I **p** to Abraham
Nu	10:29	God **p**, 'I'll give it to you.'
	11:12	the land you **p** to their ancestors
	14:16	the land which he had **p** to give them
	14:23	land I so solemnly **p** to their
	14:30	the firmly and solemnly **p** land
	14:40	attack the land that God **p** us
	16:14	haven't given us the **p** inheritance
	32:11	the land that I **p** to Abraham
Dt	1:8	the land God **p** to give your ancestors
	1:11	bless you just as he **p**
	1:21	the God-of-Your-Fathers, **p** it to you
	1:35	land that I **p** to give to your parents
	6:3	abundance and bounty, just as God **p**
	6:10	the land he **p** through your ancestors
	6:18	land that God so solemnly **p**
	6:23	land he so solemnly **p** to our ancestors
	8:1	land that God **p** to your ancestors
	8:18	covenant that he **p** to your ancestors
	9:3	just as God **p** you would
	9:5	so that he can keep his **p** word
	9:28	take them to the land he **p** them
	10:9	inheritance, as God, your God, **p** them
	10:11	the land that I **p** their ancestors
	11:9	the soil that God **p** to give
	11:21	the soil that God **p** to give
	11:25	will precede you, just as he **p**
	12:20	expands your territory as he **p**
	13:17	prosper, just as he **p** your ancestors
	15:6	God, will bless you just as he **p**
	19:8	extending its borders as he solemnly **p**
	23:23	vowed to God, your God. You **p** it
	26:3	the land that God **p** our ancestors
	26:15	the ground you gave us, just as you **p**

	26:18	dearly held treasure just as he **p**
	26:19	your God. That's what he has **p**
	27:3	God, the God-of-Your-Fathers, **p** you
	28:9	he **p** you, if you keep the commandments
	28:11	the land that God **p** your ancestors
	28:68	by a road I **p** you'd never see again
	29:13	he is God, your God, just as he **p** you
	30:20	the soil that God, your God, **p** to give
	31:7	this land that God **p** their ancestors
	31:20	the land that I **p** to their ancestors
	31:21	this land I **p** them
	31:23	the land I **p** to give them
	34:4	This is the land I **p** to your ancestors
Jos	1:3	just as I **p** Moses
	1:6	inherit the land that I **p** to give
	5:6	the land God had solemnly **p**
	6:22	just as you **p** her
	9:19	We **p** them in the presence of the God
	14:9	the day that Moses solemnly **p**
	14:10	God has kept me alive, as he **p**
	14:12	this hill country that God **p** me
	22:4	rest to your brothers just as he **p**
	23:5	just as God, your God, **p** you
	23:10	he fights for you, just as he **p** you
	23:14	good things God, your God, **p** you
	23:15	God, your God, has **p** has come true
Jdg	2:1	I led you to the land that I **p**
1Sa	24:22	David **p** Saul
	25:30	completes all the goodness he has **p**
2Sa	3:9	What God **p** David, I'll help
	7:25	Do exactly what you've **p**
	23:5	kept every **p** word
1Ki	1:17	you **p** me in God's name
	1:29	king solemnly **p**, "As God lives
	1:30	I'll do exactly what I **p** in God's name
	2:4	God will confirm what he **p** me
	2:8	I **p** him under God
	2:24	in charge of the kingdom just as he **p**
	5:12	gave Solomon wisdom, just as he had **p**
	8:20	ruled over Israel just as God **p**
	8:24	You did exactly what you **p**
2Ki	8:19	**p** to keep a lamp burning
1Ch	17:23	Do exactly what you've **p**
	27:23	because God had **p** to give Israel
	29:24	and **p** their loyalty
2Ch	2:15	wine you **p** for my work crews
	6:4	Now he has done what he **p**
	6:15	You did exactly what you **p**
	6:20	this place you **p** to dignify
	6:42	the love you **p** to David your servant
	21:7	**p** to keep a light burning
	23:3	going to rule just as God **p**
	33:8	He had **p**, "Never again
Ezr	10:19	They all **p** to divorce their wives
Ne	5:13	the people did what they **p**
	9:15	the land, which you **p** to give them
	9:23	the land that you **p** their ancestors
Est	4:7	money that Haman had **p** to deposit
Job	22:27	he'll help you do what you've **p**
Ps	22:25	I'll do what I **p** right here
	56:12	God, you did everything you **p**
	89:28	faithfully do all I so solemnly **p**

P

	106:24	didn't believe a word of what God p
	116:14	complete what I p God I'd do
	116:18	complete what I p God I'd do
	119:25	Get me on my feet again. You p
	119:41	salvation, exactly as you p
	119:58	be gracious to me just as you p
	119:76	hold me tight! just the way you p
	119:116	Take my side as you p
	119:154	give me back my life, just as you p
	132:2	remember how he p God, made a vow
Pr	6:2	impulsively p the shirt off your back
Isa	9:7	David throne over that p kingdom
	38:7	I, God, will do exactly what I have p
	54:9	I p then that the waters of Noah
	62:11	prepared to complete what he p
Jer	11:5	I will be able to do what I p
	29:10	take care of you as I p
	32:22	gave them this land and solemnly p
	34:18	who didn't do what was solemnly p
	40:9	p them and their men
Eze	16:8	I p you my love
	20:6	in the solemn oath, I p them
	20:28	into that land that I had solemnly p
	20:42	the land that I solemnly p . . . to give
Da	5:29	Belshazzar did what he had p
Am	7:4	Then it burned up the P Land
Jnh	2:9	I'll do what I p I'd do!
Mic	7:20	Everything you p our ancestors
Zec	7:14	Their 'p land' became a vacant lot
Mt	14:7	he p her on oath anything she wanted
Mk	14:11	p to pay him well
Lk	1:55	It's exactly what he p
	1:70	Just as he p long ago
	2:29	release me in peace as you p
	24:49	I am sending what my Father p to you
Ac	1:4	must wait for what the Father p
	7:17	the time God p Abraham for deliverance
	13:23	Jesus, exactly as he p
	13:32	Message that what God p the fathers
	13:38	the forgiveness of your sins can be p
	18:21	he p, "I'll be back, God willing."
	26:7	to what God p my ancestors
	26:22	God has stood by me, just as he p
2Co	1:20	Whatever God has p gets stamped
	9:5	get you and your p offering all ready
	11:2	I p your hand in marriage to Christ
Gal	3:18	nothing to do with the p inheritance
Tit	1:2	This is the life God p long ago
Heb	6:12	then get everything p to them
	6:15	got everything that had been p to him
	6:18	every reason to grab the p hope
	9:16	eternal inheritance that was p them
	10:36	be there for the p completion
	11:9	he lived in the country p him
	11:13	not yet having in hand what was p
	11:17	ready to return the p son
	11:39	got their hands on what was p
Jas	2:5	kingdom is p to anyone who loves God
2Pe	3:13	p new heavens and the p new earth
1Jn	2:25	exactly what Christ p: eternal life

Promises

Dt	6:13	Back up your p with his name only
	10:20	back up your p with . . . his name
1Ki	1:51	Solomon p that he won't kill me
	8:25	Continue to keep the p you made
	8:31	hurts a neighbor and p to make things
2Ch	6:16	Continue to keep the p you made
	6:22	hurts a neighbor and p to make things
Job	15:11	Are God's p not enough for you
Ps	42:8	Then God p to love me all day
	50:14	serve High God a feast of kept p
	74:20	Remember your p
	119:11	banked your p in the vault of my heart
	119:38	Affirm your p to me — p made to all
	119:50	your p rejuvenate me
	119:158	walked away from your p so casually
	119:172	let your p ring from my tongue
	147:15	He launches his p earthward
Pr	2:17	second thought to her p before God
Isa	48:1	use God's name to back up your p
Jer	11:15	Do you think making p . . . will save
Na	3:17	at your service, full of smiles and p
Ro	9:4	covenants, revelation, worship, p
	15:8	the old ancestral p would come true
2Co	1:17	accuse me of being flip with my p
	7:1	With p like this to pull us on
Gal	3:16	the p were made to Abraham
	3:18	original covenant p made to Abraham
	3:19	inheriting the p and distributing them
	3:29	heirs according to the covenant p
Eph	2:12	rich history of God's covenants and p
	3:6	same help, same p in Christ Jesus
Tit	1:2	he doesn't break p
Heb	4:2	We received the same p as those people
	6:16	When people make p, they guarantee
	6:17	When God wanted to guarantee his p
	7:6	the one to whom the p had been given
	10:23	firm grip on the p that keep us going
	11:33	took the p for themselves
2Pe	1:4	terrific p to pass on to you

Proof

Ge	21:30	take it as p that I dug this well
	49:3	my strength, first p of my manhood
Ex	3:12	the p that I am the one who sent you
Dt	21:17	son is the first p of his virility
	22:15	take her with the p of her virginity
	22:17	the p of my daughter's virginity
Jos	2:12	give me some tangible p, a guarantee
1Sa	2:34	the p: Both will die the same day
1Ki	8:24	The p is before us today
	13:3	This is the p God gives
2Ch	6:15	The p is before us today
Job	31:6	so God has p of my integrity
Ps	111:8	never obsolete, rust-p
Mt	11:19	The p of the pudding is in the eating
	12:39	Jesus said, "You're looking for p
Lk	7:35	The p of the pudding is in the eating
	11:29	Everybody's looking for p
Ac	18:28	brought out p after convincing p

1Co	9:1	Aren't you . . . **p** of the good work
	9:2	living **p** of my authority
2Co	13:3	**p** that Christ speaks through me
Php	2:16	You'll be living **p**
2Th	3:17	examine my signature as **p**
1Ti	1:15	I'm **p**— Public Sinner Number One
1Jn	5:3	The **p** that we love God comes when
Rev	17:14	**p** that he is Lord over all lords

Propaganda

2Ch	32:18	shouting their **p** in Hebrew
Ps	119:104	that's why I hate false **p**
Eze	21:29	Despite false sword **p** circulated

Prophecies

1Pe	1:12	the Message of those **p** fulfilled

Prophecy

1Ki	22:10	prophets were staging a **p**-performance
2Ch	9:29	the **p** of Ahijah of Shiloh
	15:8	Asa heard the **p** of Azariah
	18:9	prophets were staging a **p**-performance
Ne	6:12	The so-called **p** he spoke to me
Eze	36:3	here is a **p** in the name of God
Mt	2:8	told them the **p** about Bethlehem
	3:3	authorized by Isaiah's **p**
	13:35	His storytelling fulfilled the **p**
	15:7	Isaiah's **p** of you hit the bull's-eye
Heb	10:5	That is what is meant by this **p**
2Pe	1:20	no **p** of Scripture is . . . private
	1:21	**P** resulted when the Holy Spirit
Rev	19:10	witness of Jesus is the spirit of **p**
	22:7	keeps the words of the **p** of this book
	22:10	Don't seal the words of the **p**
	22:18	all who hear the words of the **p**
	22:19	the words of the book of this **p**

Prophesied

Nu	11:25	When the Spirit rested on them they **p**
	11:26	they **p** in the camp
1Ki	15:29	as God's servant Ahijah . . . had **p**
Eze	37:7	I **p** just as I'd been commanded
	37:10	So I **p**, just as he commanded me
	38:17	**p** that I would bring you against them
Mt	4:17	This Isaiah-**p** sermon came to life
Lk	1:67	was filled with the Holy Spirit and **p**
Jn	11:51	**p** that Jesus was about to die
Ac	21:9	Philip had four virgin daughters who **p**
Heb	11:22	Joseph, while dying, **p** the exodus
Jude	1:14	Enoch, the seventh after Adam, **p**

Prophesy

Eze	20:46	**P** against the wilderness forest
	21:2	**P** against the land of Israel
	21:9	Son of man, **p**. Tell them
	21:14	So, **p**, son of man! Clap your hands
	21:28	son of man, your job is to **p**

	34:2	**p** against the shepherd-leaders
	35:2	confront Mount Seir. **P** against it
	36:1	**p** to the mountains of Israel
	36:6	Therefore **p** over the land of Israel
	37:4	He said to me, "**P** over these bones
	37:9	**P** to the breath. **P**, son of man
	37:12	**p**. Tell them, 'God, the Master, says
	38:2	**P** against him
	38:14	Therefore, son of man, **p**! Tell Gog
	39:1	Son of man, **p** against Gog
Joel	2:28	Your sons will **p**, also your daughters
Am	2:12	told the young prophets, 'Don't **p**
Mt	26:68	**P**, Messiah: Who hit you that time
Mk	14:65	saying, "Who hit you? **P**!"
Ac	2:17	Your sons will **p**, also your daughters
	2:18	men and women both, and they'll **p**
Rev	10:11	You must go back and **p** again
	11:3	Dressed in sackcloth, they'll **p**

Prophesying

Nu	11:27	Eldad and Medad are **p** in the camp
1Sa	10:5	And they'll be **p**
	10:6	you'll be **p** right along with them
	10:10	he was **p** right along with them
	10:11	saw him **p** with the prophets
	10:13	When Saul was done **p**, he returned home
	19:20	saw a band of prophets **p** with Samuel
	19:21	They, too, were soon **p**
Eze	13:2	their own heads and calling it '**p**
Zec	13:3	in the very act of **p** lies about God
Rev	11:6	doesn't rain for the time of their **p**

Prophetic

1Sa	3:19	Samuel's **p** record was flawless
Eze	12:22	all the **p** warnings are false alarms
Mt	2:23	a fulfillment of the **p** words
	26:56	confirm and fulfill the **p** writings
Mk	14:49	confirm the **p** writings
Lk	1:80	until the day he made his **p** debut
Ro	16:26	an open book through the **p** Scriptures
1Ti	1:18	The **p** word that was directed to you
2Pe	1:19	The **p** Word was confirmed to us

Prosperity

Ge	41:52	named his second son Ephraim (Double **P**
2Ch	14:7	So they built and enjoyed **p**
	17:12	an age of **p** for Judah
Est	10:3	cared for the peace and **p** of his race
Ps	122:6	**P** to all you Jerusalem-lovers
Jer	32:42	usher in a wonderful life of **p**
Da	4:1	Peace and **p** to all
Jas	1:10	**P** is as short-lived as a wildflower

Prosperous

Ge	48:4	going to make you **p** and numerous
1Sa	25:2	He was very **p**
Ps	25:13	Their kids inherit a **p** farm
Jas	1:11	a picture of the "**p** life."

P

Prostitute

Ge	38:15	assumed she was a **p**
	38:21	Where's the **p** that used to sit
	38:22	there never has been a **p** there
Lev	21:7	harlot or a cult **p** or a divorced woman
	21:14	not a cult **p**—he is only to marry
Dt	23:17	is to become a sacred **p**
Jdg	16:1	Samson went to Gaza and saw a **p**
Pr	30:20	Here's how a **p** operates

Prostituted

Jdg	2:17	they **p** themselves to other gods
	8:27	All Israel **p** itself there
2Ki	17:17	**p** themselves to every kind of evil

Prostitutes

1Ki	3:16	two **p** showed up before the king
	14:24	they had male sacred **p**
	15:12	He got rid of the sacred **p**
	22:46	he got rid of the sacred **p**
2Ki	23:7	the rooms of the male sacred **p**

Prostrate

Dt	9:25	When I was on my face, **p** before God
	25:2	will have him **p** himself before him
Jos	7:6	leaders . . . **p** until evening
Ezr	10:1	Ezra wept, **p** in front of The Temple
Ps	5:7	here I am, **p** in your inner sanctum
Isa	14:31	Fall **p** in fear, Philistia!
Eze	3:23	I fell to the ground, **p**
Rev	4:10	would fall **p** before the One Seated

Protect

Ge	4:15	God put a mark on Cain to **p** him
	28:15	I'll **p** you wherever you go
Nu	4:19	**P** them so they will live and not die
1Sa	22:23	Stick with me. I'll **p** you
2Sa	18:12	For my sake, **p** the young man Absalom
	22:36	You **p** me with salvation-armor
Ezr	8:22	bodyguard to **p** us from bandits
Job	12:6	paid for a god who'll **p** them
Ps	18:35	You **p** me with salvation-armor
	35:10	**p** the unprotected from bullies
	80:12	why do you no longer **p** your vine
	91:4	His huge outstretched arms **p** you
	121:5	Guardian, right at your side to **p** you
	140:1	**p** me from these vicious people
	140:4	**p** me from these vicious people
	140:7	**p** me when the fighting breaks out
	141:9	**P** me from their evil scheming
	144:14	**P** us from invasion and exile
Pr	6:24	They'll **p** you from wanton women
SS	2:15	you must **p** me from the foxes
	8:9	virgin and vulnerable, and we'll **p** her
Isa	16:3	help us out! **P** us, hide us
	28:6	prowess to those who guard and **p**
	31:5	Jerusalem. I'll **p** and rescue it

	49:2	He kept his hand on me to **p** me
Jer	13:11	Just as shorts clothe and **p**
Eze	22:30	stand in the gap to **p** this land
Mic	3:11	He'll **p** us from disaster
Zec	9:15	God-of-the-Angel-Armies will **p** them
Mal	3:11	**p** your wheat fields and vegetable
Lk	4:10	in the care of angels to **p** you
	12:15	Take care! **P** yourself
	18:3	My rights are being violated. **P** me
Ac	20:28	God's people they are — to guard and **p**
1Co	4:1	security guards posted to **p** them
2Co	9:7	That will **p** you against sob stories
	11:10	to keep it quiet just to **p** you
Gal	3:24	escort children . . . and **p** them
2Th	3:3	He'll stick by you and **p** you from evil

Protected

1Sa	25:29	bound in the bundle of God-**p** life
2Sa	21:2	**p** by a treaty with Israel
Job	5:21	You'll be **p** from vicious gossip
Ps	37:39	life is from God, it's also **p** and safe
Eze	16:8	dressed you and **p** you
Na	3:8	**P** by the great River
Mk	9:50	preserved, **p** from the eternal flames
Jn	10:28	They are **p** from the Destroyer
Gal	3:23	surrounded and **p** by the Mosaic law
Heb	11:33	They were **p** from lions
1Jn	5:18	The God-begotten are also the God-**p**

Protection

Ex	15:13	You guided them under your **p**
Lev	26:25	when you huddle in your cities for **p**
Nu	14:9	They have no **p** and God is on our side
Ru	2:12	God, to whom you've come seeking **p**
1Ch	4:10	provide your personal **p**
Ps	34:7	God's angel sets up a circle of **p**
Pr	18:10	God's name is a place of **p**
Ecc	7:12	Double **p**: wisdom and wealth
Isa	3:2	He's withdrawing police and **p**
	30:2	Running off to Pharaoh for **p**
	30:3	Well, some **p** Pharaoh will be!
	30:6	Thinking you can buy **p**
La	4:20	king under whose **p** . . . we'd live
Hos	3:4	stripped of security and **p**
Lk	10:19	**p** from every assault of the Enemy
Ac	27:4	under the **p** of the northeast shore

Protective

Dt	23:16	within the **p** gates of your city
Isa	4:5	his immense, **p** presence

Protects

Ge	28:20	stands by me and **p** me on this journey
Ps	46:3	God of angel armies **p** us
	46:7	God of angel armies **p** us
	46:11	God of angel armies **p** us
	146:9	**p** strangers, takes the side of orphans
Pr	18:11	The rich think their wealth **p** them

P

	29:25	trusting in God **p** you
	30:5	he **p** everyone who runs to him for help
Isa	31:5	God-of-the-Angel-Armies **p** Jerusalem

Proud

Ge	47:11	made them **p** owners of choice land
Dt	17:20	must not become **p** and arrogant
	28:52	They'll knock those high, **p** walls flat
	31:7	You will make them the **p** possessors
	32:42	the **p** and vain enemy corpses
2Sa	1:23	stronger than **p** lions
2Ki	14:10	Go ahead and be **p**, but stay home
	19:25	reducing **p** cities to piles of rubble
2Ch	25:19	Go ahead and be **p**, but stay home
	26:16	Arrogant and **p**, he fell
	30:11	weren't too **p** to accept the invitation
No	12:45	made David and his son Solomon **p**
Job	41:16	Nothing can get through that **p** skin
Ps	37:26	his children making him **p**
	56:4	I'm **p** to praise God
	56:10	I'm **p** to praise God, **p** to praise God
	69:35	The **p** owners of the land
	97:7	were so **p** of their ragamuffin gods
Pr	3:34	He gives **p** skeptics a cold shoulder
	15:20	children make their parents **p**
	23:24	wise children become **p** parents
	23:25	Make your mother **p**
	30:31	rooster, **p** and strutting
Isa	2:15	against all **p** obelisks and statues
	4:2	survivors something to be **p** of again
	5:2	a vineyard to be **p** of
	5:7	the garden he was so **p** of
	9:9	they were a **p** and arrogant bunch
	13:12	**P** humanity will disappear
	14:31	Wail and howl, **p** city!
	22:3	no combat heroes to be **p** of
	23:12	nothing left here to be **p** of
	28:1	parodies of a **p** and handsome past
	44:5	be **p** to be called Israel
Jer	8:8	We're the **p** owners of God's revelation
	13:11	I could show off . . . and be **p** of
	18:21	their **p** young men be killed
	50:12	your mother would hardly be **p** of you
Eze	7:20	**P** and pretentious with their jewels
	16:49	**p**, gluttonous, and lazy
	24:21	my Sanctuary, your **p** impregnable fort
	28:2	Your heart is **p**
	30:6	her **p** strength will collapse
	30:15	knock Thebes off its **p** pedestal
	31:10	swaggering and **p** of its stature
	32:18	Dispatch Egypt and her **p** daughter
	32:20	Drag her off in all her **p** pomp
Da	4:37	turn a **p** person into a humble man
Am	1:2	shrivels Mount Carmel's **p** peak
Zec	9:6	I'll take **p** Philistia down a peg
	10:3	make them **p** to be on God's side
	10:5	They'll be a workforce to be **p** of
	11:1	Open your borders . . . **p** Lebanon
Mt	5:5	you find yourselves **p** owners
	18:8	lame and alive than the **p** owners
Mk	9:43	lame and alive than the **p** owner

Lk	16:3	I'm too **p** to beg
Ro	1:16	It's news I'm most **p** to proclaim
	3:27	our **p** Jewish insider claims
	3:29	our **p** Jewish claim
	6:21	Nothing you're **p** of now
	15:17	context of Jesus, I'd even say **p**
	16:19	I couldn't be more **p** of you
1Co	8:2	help us more than our **p** minds
	16:18	Be **p** that you have people like this
2Co	1:14	We want you to be as **p** of us
	5:12	would make you feel good, **p** even
	7:4	If only you knew how **p** I am of you
	7:16	I'm so confident and **p** of you
Eph	3:13	Be **p**
Php	1:10	a life Jesus will be **p** of
	2:16	have good cause to be **p** of you
Col	1:10	for the Master, making him **p** of you
1Th	2:19	do you think we're going to be **p** of
2Th	1:4	We're so **p** of you
Tit	2:14	making us a people he can be **p** of
Heb	11:16	see why God is so **p** of them
Jas	4:6	God goes against the willful **p**
1Pe	2:7	he's a Stone to be **p** of
	2:13	Make the Master **p** of you
	4:16	Be **p** of the distinguished status
	5:5	God has had it with the **p**

Provocative

2Ki	21:7	flagrant and **p** violation
2Ch	33:7	flagrant and **p** violation
Eze	23:40	put on makeup and **p** lingerie

Provoke

Dt	6:15	Don't **p** him, igniting his hot anger
Jdg	18:25	you just might **p** some fierce
Eze	8:17	**p** me even further with their obscene
	24:8	to **p** my wrath, to trigger my vengeance

Provoked

Ps	78:41	**p** Israel's Holy God
	78:58	Their pagan orgies **p** God's anger
	85:3	You took back your sin-**p** threats
	95:10	I was **p** — oh, was I **p**!
	106:14	**p** God with their insistent demands
Pr	24:18	God might see, and become very **p**
Jer	32:29	who knows how many other gods **p** me
	32:30	were the first time they had **p** me
Ml	14:4	John had **p** Herod by naming
Mk	5:40	**P** to sarcasm, they told him
	6:18	For John had **p** Herod
	8:12	**p**, he said, "Why does this generation
Jn	7:28	That **p** Jesus, who was teaching
Ac	5:17	**P** mightily by all this, the Chief
	22:24	had done that **p** this outraged violence
Heb	3:10	And I was **p**, oh, so **p**!
	3:17	who was God **p** with for forty years

P

Provokes

Pr	14:3	Frivolous talk p a derisive smile
Mt	5:10	your commitment to God p persecution

Prudent

Pr	12:16	the p quietly shrug off insults
	12:23	P people don't flaunt their knowledge
	14:15	the p sift and weigh every word
	22:3	p person sees trouble coming
	27:12	p person sees trouble coming

Prune

Lev	25:3	Sow your fields, p your vineyards
	25:4	you will not . . . p your vineyards
Dt	28:39	You'll plant and hoe and p vineyards
Job	16:8	You've shriveled me like a dried p
Isa	18:5	He'll step in and p back the new shoots
Jer	5:10	Leave a few. P back those vines

Pruned

Am	7:14	I raised cattle and I p trees
Jn	15:3	You are already p back by the message
Ro	11:17	Some of the tree's branches were p
	11:18	no cause to crow over the p branches
	11:19	p so that I could be grafted in
	11:20	they were p because they were
	11:23	feeling superior to those p branches

Punish

Ge	15:14	Then I'll p their slave masters
Lev	26:24	will p you for your sins
2Sa	24:17	P me and my family, not them
1Ch	21:17	P me, not them, me and my family
2Ch	28:9	used you to p them
Pr	19:25	P the insolent
Isa	10:12	I'll p the bragging arrogance
	26:21	p the wrong of the people on earth
	27:1	He'll p the serpent Leviathan
Jer	3:12	I'm not just hanging back to p you
	14:10	note their guilt and p their sins
	21:14	I'll p your evil regime
	23:34	I'll p him and his family
	25:12	I'll p the king of Babylon
	27:8	I'll p that nation with war
	29:32	I will p Shemaiah the Neelamite
	30:11	I'll p you, but fairly
	30:20	I'll p anyone who hurts them
	36:31	I will p him and his children
	46:28	I'll p you, but fairly
Eze	5:8	p you in full sight of the nations
	23:24	p you according to their rules
	25:11	I'll p Moab severely
	30:14	burn Zoan to the ground, and p Thebes
	30:19	That's how I'll p Egypt
	44:12	I've taken an oath to p them
Hos	5:2	I'm going to p the lot of you
	8:13	I'll p their sins and send them back

Hab	1:6	raise up Babylonians to p you
Zep	1:8	p the leaders and the royal sons
	1:9	p all who import pagan superstitions
	1:12	p those who are sitting it out
Zec	8:14	the same way that I decided to p you

Punished

Lev	18:25	I p it for its iniquities — the land
2Sa	24:14	rather be p by God, whose mercy
2Ki	7:9	we'll get caught and p
1Ch	21:7	offended by the whole thing, p Israel
	21:13	rather be p by God whose mercy
Ezr	9:13	God, p us far less than we deserved
Job	8:4	why would God have p them
	34:6	I've done nothing wrong, and I get p
Ps	107:11	P for defying God's Word
Isa	40:2	forgiven! She's been p enough
Jer	2:35	God doesn't mind. He hasn't p me
La	3:39	complain when p for sin
Hos	12:2	hauled into court to be p
Zec	14:19	celebrate the Feast of Booths gets p
1Pe	3:17	than to be p for doing bad

Punishment

Ge	4:13	Cain said to God, "My p is too much
	19:15	you're caught in the p of the city
Lev	26:21	your p will be seven times more
Nu	14:34	your p will be a year for each day
Dt	25:2	If the guilty one deserves p
	29:21	the tribes of Israel for special p
1Ki	15:30	p for Jeroboam's sins
2Ch	24:24	their p for deserting God
Job	21:19	saving up the p for their children
	31:11	I'd deserve the worst p you could
Ps	149:7	a signal that p's coming
Pr	20:30	p goes deep within us
Isa	30:26	bruises from the time of p
	53:5	He took the p, and that made us whole
Jer	15:3	I've arranged for four kinds of p
	15:13	In p for your sins, I'm giving
	30:14	a p you will never forget
	44:29	I will bring p right here
La	4:22	for you, Zion. The p's complete
Eze	5:10	children eating parents! P indeed
	5:15	When I finish my angry p
	12:19	land is . . . stripped bare as p
	16:38	the p for an adulterous woman
	21:25	Time's up. It's "p payday
	21:29	for whom it's p payday
	22:3	just asking for p
	35:5	looking their final p in the face
Jnh	4:2	turn your plans of p into
Zep	3:7	find relief from the p I'm bringing
Ro	13:5	live responsibly — not just to avoid p
2Co	2:6	agreed to as p is p enough
Heb	12:7	This trouble you're in isn't p
1Pe	2:20	no particular virtue in accepting p

P

Punishments

1Ch	21:10	You have your choice of three **p**
Job	31:28	I would deserve the worst of **p**
Jer	11:8	ordered the **p** set out in the covenant
Eze	25:17	Huge acts of vengeance, massive **p**
Eph	1:7	free people — free of penalties and **p**

Pure

Ge	20:6	I know your intentions were **p**
	24:16	stunningly beautiful, a **p** virgin
Ex	15:3	God is a fighter, **p** God
	24:10	like sapphires — **p**, clear sky-blue
	25:11	Cover it with a veneer of **p** gold
	25:17	a lid of **p** gold for the Chest
	25:24	Cover it with a veneer of **p** gold
	25:29	Make them of **p** gold
	25:31	Make a Lapstand of **p** hammered gold
	25:36	one piece of hammered **p** gold
	25:38	trays out of **p** gold
	25:39	brick of **p** gold to make the Lapstand
	27:20	bring you **p**, clear olive oil for light
	28:14	two chains of **p** gold and braid them
	28:22	make braided chains of **p** gold
	28:36	Make a plate of **p** gold
	30:3	Cover it with a veneer of **p** gold
	30:34	add **p** frankincense
	30:35	art of a perfumer, salted and **p**
	31:8	the **p** Lapstand and all its implements
	31:15	seventh day is Sabbath, **p** rest
	37:2	a veneer of **p** gold
	37:6	a lid of **p** gold for the Chest
	37:11	covered it with a veneer of **p** gold
	37:16	Out of **p** gold he made the utensils
	37:17	a Lapstand of **p** hammered gold
	37:22	one piece of hammered **p** gold
	37:23	candle snuffers, all out of **p** gold
	37:24	brick of **p** gold to make the Lapstand
	37:26	covered it with a veneer of **p** gold
	37:29	oil and the **p** aromatic incense
	39:15	chains of **p** gold for the Breastpiece
	39:25	They also made bells of **p** gold
	39:30	the sacred crown, of **p** gold
	39:37	Lapstand of **p** gold
Lev	24:4	the Lapstand of **p** gold before God
	24:6	the Table of **p** gold before God
	24:7	Along each row spread **p** incense
1Ki	6:21	Everywhere you looked there was **p** gold
	7:49	the **p** gold candelabras
	7:50	the **p** gold dishes
	9:4	**p** in heart and action
	10:21	House . . . were **p** gold
2Ch	4:20	the Lapstands of **p** gold
	7:17	**p** in heart and action
	9:20	House . . . were **p** gold
Job	3:7	turn that night into **p** nothingness
	17:9	their clean, **p** hands will get stronger
	33:9	I'm **p** — I've done nothing wrong
Ps	12:6	God's words are **p** words, **P** silver
	24:4	only the **p**-hearted
	81:16	with butter and rock-**p** honey

	139:22	I hate it with **p**, unadulterated hatred
Pr	21:8	**p** motives take you straight
	22:11	God loves the **p**-hearted
Ecc	7:20	Not one who is truly **p** and sinless
SS	4:12	a private and **p** fountain
	5:11	My golden one, **p** and untarnished
	6:9	My dove is perfection, **P** and innocent
Isa	65:18	create my people as **p** delight
Eze	36:25	I'll pour **p** water over you
Da	2:32	The head of the statue was **p** gold
	10:5	a belt of **p** gold around his waist
Am	4:5	Burn **p** sacrifices
Mt	5:29	If you want to live a morally **p** life
	13:37	farmer who sows the **p** seed is the Son
	13:38	**p** seeds are subjects of the kingdom
Ro	3:8	That's **p** slander
	3:24	right standing with himself. A **p** gift
	4:16	God's promise arrives as **p** gift
	12:3	as every one of you does, in **p** grace
2Co	6:6	with **p** heart, clear head
	8:2	outpouring of **p** and generous gifts
	11:2	as a **p** virgin to her husband
	11:22	the **p** race of Abraham
Eph	6:24	**P** grace and nothing but grace
Php	1:16	One group is motivated by **p** love
1Th	4:3	God wants you to live a **p** life
Tit	2:5	be virtuous and **p**
	2:14	into this good, **p** life
1Pe	1:7	**P** gold put in the fire comes out
	2:3	drink deep of God's **p** kindness
1Jn	1:5	God is light, **p** light
Rev	19:11	makes war in **p** righteousness
	21:18	the City was **p** gold
	21:21	main street of the City was **p** gold

Pure-hearted

Ps	24:4	Only the clean-handed, only the **p**
Pr	22:11	God loves the **p** and well-spoken

Purification

Lev	12:4	for **p** from her bleeding
	12:5	for **p** from her bleeding
	12:6	the days for her **p** . . . are complete
2Sa	11:4	time of "**p**" following her period
Lk	2:22	days stipulated by Moses for **p**
Ac	21:23	taken a vow involving ritual **p**
	21:27	seven days of their **p** were nearly up
Heb	9:13	other rituals of **p** were effective

Purified

Lev	8:15	slaughtered the bull and **p** the Altar
Nu	8:7	they will have **p** themselves
	8:15	After you have **p** the Levites
	8:21	The Levites **p** themselves
	31:23	then it will be ritually **p**
Ezr	6:20	priests and Levites had **p** themselves
Ne	12:30	ceremonially **p** themselves
Eze	43:22	Purify the altar the same as you **p** it
	43:23	when you have **p** it, offer a bull
	44:26	after he has been **p**, he must wait

P

Purify

Ex	30:10	Once a year Aaron is to **p** the Altar
Lev	14:49	He then is to **p** the house
	16:19	to **p** and consecrate it
Nu	8:6	**p** them for doing God's work
	8:21	made atonement for them to **p** them
	19:12	**p** himself with the Water-of-Cleansing
	31:19	**P** yourselves and your captives
	31:20	**P** every piece of clothing
Dt	21:8	**P** your people Israel whom you redeemed
Jos	7:13	So get started. **P** the people
Isa	52:11	**P** yourselves in the process of worship
Eze	43:20	That's to **p** the altar and make it fit
	43:22	for a sin offering. **P** the altar
	45:18	calf and **p** the Sanctuary
Da	11:35	testing will refine, cleanse, and **p**
Zep	3:8	zeal is a fire that will purge and **p**
Jas	4:8	**P** your inner life

Purifying

Nu	6:9	shave your head on the day of your **p**
	6:11	**p** you from the ritual contamination
Jos	7:13	Get ready for tomorrow by **p** yourselves
Eze	43:26	get the altar ready for its work, **p** it
Heb	10:14	who takes part in the **p** process

Purity

Job	22:4	because he cares about your **p**
Pr	27:21	The **p** of silver and gold is tested
Zec	13:9	test them for **p** as gold is tested
1Co	10:27	the ethical **p** of each course
2Co	7:11	come out of this with **p** of heart
	11:3	simple **p** of your love for Christ
Php	3:6	defender of the **p** of my religion
1Th	3:13	May you be infused with strength and **p**
2Pe	3:14	living at your best, in **p** and peace
1Jn	3:3	the . . . **p** of Jesus' life as a model

Q

Quake

Ps	18:7	huge mountains . . . **Q** like aspen leaves
Isa	13:13	earth **q** to its roots
Jer	10:10	the godless nations **q**
Eze	31:16	I made the whole world **q**
Joel	3:16	Earth and sky **q** in terror
Na	1:5	Mountains **q** in their roots

Qualities

Ro	11:22	alert to these **q** of gentle kindness
2Pe	1:8	With these **q** active and growing
	1:9	Without these **q** you can't see

Quarantine

Lev	13:4	will **q** the person for seven days
	13:5	in **q** for another seven days

	13:11	he doesn't need to **q** him
	13:21	will put him in **q** for seven day
	13:26	will put him in **q** for seven days
	13:31	put the person in **q** for seven days
	13:33	back to **q** for another seven days
Nu	12:14	**Q** her outside the camp for seven days
	12:15	So Miriam was in **q** outside the camp
2Ch	26:21	had to live in **q**

Quarrel

Ex	21:18	If a **q** breaks out and one hits
Dt	19:17	both parties involved in the **q**
Pr	17:14	start of a **q** is like a leak in a dam
	26:17	a **q** that's none of your business
	26:20	when the gossip ends, the **q** dies down
Ac	23:9	a huge and noisy **q** broke out
	23:10	**q** flamed up and became so violent

Quarreled

Ge	26:20	shepherds of Gerar **q** with

Quarrels

Ge	13:7	**q** broke out between Abram's shepherds
Dt	1:12	your troubles and burdens and **q**
Pr	17:1	better than a banquet spiced with **q**
	20:3	mark of good character to avert **q**
Hab	1:3	violence break out, **q** and fights
Ac	18:15	hairsplitting **q** over religion
	26:3	Jewish ways and all our family **q**
2Co	12:20	**q**, jealousy, flaring tempers
Jas	4:1	these appalling wars and **q** come from

Quarrelsome

Pr	20:1	Wine makes you mean, beer makes you **q**
	26:21	**q** person in a dispute is like kerosene
Ro	11:8	their **q**, self-centered ways
Tit	3:10	Warn a **q** person once or twice

Quibbling

Mk	1:22	not **q** and quoting like
	7:19	That took care of dietary **q**
Lk	4:32	the **q** and quoting they were used to

Quietly

Nu	12:3	Moses was a **q** humble man
Ru	3:7	Ruth **q** followed; she lay down
1Sa	1:9	slipped away **q**
Job	9:11	**q** but surely he's active
Pr	12:16	the prudent **q** shrug off insults
	21:14	A **q** given gift soothes an irritable
	29:11	a sage **q** mulls it over
Isa	14:7	the whole earth **q** at rest
La	3:26	**q** hope, **q** hope for help from God
Da	2:15	**q** asked what was going on
	11:20	He'll slip out of history **q**
Zep	2:3	Seek God, all you **q** disciplined people

Mt	1:19	determined to take care of things **q**
	6:4	Just do it — **q** and unobtrusively
	8:4	**q** present your healed body
	10:14	If they don't welcome you, **q** withdraw
Mk	6:11	**q** withdraw. Don't make a scene
Lk	5:14	**q** present your healed self
	7:16	They were **q** worshipful
	23:56	They rested **q** on the Sabbath
Ac	24:18	found me **q** at my prayers in the Temple
1Ti	2:2	we can be **q** about our business

Quiver

Ge	27:3	Get your **q** of arrows and your bow
1Sa	20:40	Jonathan gave his **q** and bow
Job	39:23	clanging of **q** and lance don't faze him
Isa	49:2	his straight arrow and hid me in his **q**

R

Rabble

1Sa	30:22	marched with David, the **r** element
Ps	4:2	You **r** — how long do I put up with
	44:14	a cheap joke among the **r**
Eze	23:42	jostling and pushing, a drunken **r**
Mic	4:3	establish justice in the **r** of nations
Jn	7:47	carried away like the rest of the **r**
Ac	18:17	Now the street turned on Sosthenes
Ro	11:25	you're royalty and they're just **r**

Race

Ge	5.1	the family tree of the human **r**
	5:2	blessed them, the whole human **r**
	6:1	When the human **r** began to increase
	6:6	sorry that he had made the human **r**
	6:13	It's the end of the human **r**
	10:25	in his days the human **r** divided
Jdg	9:28	We belong to the **r** of Hamor
Est	2:20	kept her . . . **r** a secret
	10:3	for the peace and prosperity of his **r**
Job	28:28	Then he addressed the human **r**
Ps	116:11	Despite giving up on the human **r**
Pr	6:18	feet that **r** down a wicked track
Ecc	3:18	human **r**, "God's testing the lot of us
	9:11	The **r** is not always to the swift
Isa	2:9	degenerate **r**, facedown in the gutter
	57:4	A **r** of rebels, a generation of liars
	59:7	They compete in the **r** to do evil
	66:16	a death sentence on the human **r**
Jer	12:5	wornout in this foot**r** with men
	25:31	about to put the human **r** on trial
Joa	3:4	Every **r**, color, and creed, listen
	3:7	everyone — every **r**, color, and creed
	3:29	Anyone anywhere, of any **r**, color
	4:1	every **r**, color, and creed
	5:19	whatever their **r**, color, and creed
	6:25	to every **r**, color, and creed
	7:14	Everyone — **r**, color, and creed

Am	6:12	hold a horse **r** in a field of rocks
Ac	7:19	He exploited our **r** mercilessly
	10:28	relax with people of another **r**
	10:28	God has just shown me that no **r**
	17:25	need the human **r** to run errands
	17:26	he made the entire human **r**
	17:31	the entire human **r** will be judged
Ro	3:15	**r** for the honor of sinner-of-the-year
	9:5	the **r** that produced the Messiah
1Co	9:24	seen the athletes **r**
2Co	11:22	the pure **r** of Abraham
Gal	5:8	the One who called you into the **r**
2Th	3:1	Word will simply take off and **r**
2Ti	4:7	This is the only **r** worth running
Heb	12:2	who both began and finished this **r**
Rev	9:10	ordered to torture the human **r**
	9:15	to kill a third of the human **r**
	9:18	killed a third of the human **r**

Racial

Est	2:10	about her family and **r** background
Ac	15:14	sure that **r** outsiders were included
Ro	4:16	He is not our **r** father

Racially

Ro	9:8	identity was never **r** determined

Radiance

Dt	33:14	The best **r** streaming from the sun
Ps	148:13	His **r** exceeds anything
Mt	23:7	preening in the **r** of public flattery
Mk	12:38	preening in the **r** of public flattery
Lk	11:43	in the **r** of public flattery
	20:46	preen in the **r** of public flattery

Radiant

Ex	34:30	saw Moses, saw his **r** face
1Sa	1:18	she ate heartily, her face **r**
Ps	16:11	all **r** from the shining of your face
	132:17	I'll make the place **r** for David
SS	4:3	your veiled cheeks soft and **r**
	5:10	glows with health — red-blooded, **r**
	6:7	Your veiled cheeks are soft and **r**
	6:10	dawn-fresh, moon-lovely, sun-**r**
Da	10:6	his face **r**, his eyes bright
Zec	2:5	a **r** presence within
Mt	17:5	a light-**r** cloud enveloped them
Mk	9:7	a light-**r** cloud enveloped them
Lk	9:34	a light-**r** cloud enveloped them
Eph	5:27	white silk, **r** with holiness
Rev	10:1	his face was sun-**r**

Radical

Ac	17:30	he's calling for a **r** life-change
	19:4	preached a baptism of **r** life-change
	20:21	to a **r** life-change before God
	26:20	this **r** turn to God

Ro	2:4	leads us into a r life-change
Heb	7:12	brought with it a r new kind of law

Rage

Dt	29:23	which God overthrew in fiery r
1Sa	11:6	he flew into a r
2Sa	22:8	Quaked . . . because of his r
Ps	18:7	Quake . . . because of his r
	55:8	desperate for a change from r
	76:10	Instead of smoldering r — God-praise
	76:10	All that sputtering r
	78:50	let the plague r through their lives
	79:5	Will your smoldering r never cool
	88:7	I'm battered senseless by your r
	90:11	Who can make sense of such r
	124:4	Swept away by the flood of r
Pr	6:34	detonates r in a cheated husband
	27:4	blasted by anger and swamped by r
Ecc	10:4	calm disposition quiets intemperate r
Isa	51:20	God's anger, the r of your God
	63:5	fed and fueled by my r
Jer	21:14	a fire that will r unchecked
	25:32	storm is about to r all across planet
	32:37	driven them in my anger and r
La	1:12	what God did to me in his r
Eze	19:12	it was ripped up in a r
	35:11	turn your . . . r right back on you
	36:5	r against the rest of the nations
Da	8:7	mad with r, it charged the ram
	9:26	War will r right up to the end
	11:44	Towering in r, he'll rush to
Joel	1:19	forest and prairie fires r unchecked
Mic	7:9	I can take God's punishing r
Na	1:6	Who can stand up to this fierce r
Mt	2:16	flew into a r
Lk	11:53	scholars and Pharisees went into a r
	21:23	Incredible misery! Torrential r
Heb	11:27	indifferent to the king's blind r
Rev'	12:17	Helpless with r, the Dragon raged

Raged

Isa	9:18	lives r like an out-of-control fire
	45:24	who have r against him will be brought
Da	3:23	while the fire r around Shadrach
Rev	12:17	the Dragon r at the Woman

Rages

Job	40:23	when the river r he doesn't budge
Ps	112:10	Someone wicked takes one look and r
Jer	50:16	while the destruction r, get out
	51:32	Wildfire r through the swamp grass

Raging

Ex	22:24	show my anger and come r among you
	24:17	Glory of God looked like a r fire
1Sa	14:16	confusion and turmoil r in the camp
2Ki	22:17	My anger is r white-hot against this
	23:26	the r anger ignited by Manasseh

2Ch	34:25	My anger is r white-hot against this
Est	7:7	The king, r, left his wine
Ps	22:12	the r bulls stampede
	124:5	lost our lives in the wild, r water
Isa	8:8	A huge wingspan of a r river
	13:13	the Judgment Day of his r anger
	28:21	God will rise to full stature, r
	37:29	all your wild r against me
	47:14	A fire that is even now r
	63:3	r, I trampled the people
Jer	7:20	a r wildfire that no one can put out
	21:6	alike, in a r epidemic
	23:20	God's r anger won't let up
	30:24	God's r anger won't let up
	33:5	killed because of my r anger
	48:45	firestorm r from the capital
	51:45	this place torched by God's r anger
La	2:2	R, he smashed Judah's defenses
	4:11	He poured out his r wrath
Eze	38:18	My r anger will erupt
Jnh	1:13	worse and worse, wild and r
Mic	5:15	In r anger, I'll make a clean sweep
Na	1:2	against his enemies, fierce and r
Hab	3:8	Were you r at Sea when you rode
Zep	3:8	my anger, my r wrath
Mal	4:1	day is coming, r like a forest fire
Rev	12:12	He's wild and r with anger
	16:19	drink the wine of God's r anger
	19:15	winepress of the r wrath of God

Rainbow

Ge	9:13	I'm putting my r in the clouds
	9:14	the r appears in the cloud
	9:16	When the r appears in the cloud
Ps	21:5	dressed him in r colors
Pr	22:26	pot of gold at the end of the r
Eze	1:28	The way a r springs out of the sky
Rev	10:1	There was a r over his head

Rampage

Da	11:12	will go on a bloodletting r

Rampaged

2Ch	25:13	r through the towns of Judah
Eze	19:7	He r through their defenses

Rampages

Am	1:11	Her anger r day and night

Rampaging

Nu	23:22	out of Egypt, r like a wild ox
	24:8	out of Egypt, r like a wild ox

Ransom

Ex	21:30	If a r is agreed upon
Job	33:24	I've come up with the r

R

Ps	111:9	He paid the **r** for his people
Jer	31:11	I, God, will pay a stiff **r** price
1Co	7:23	a huge sum was paid out for your **r**

Ransomed

Lev	19:20	not yet been **r** or given her freedom
Isa	35:10	The people God has **r** will come back
	51:11	In the same way God's **r** will come back

Rant

Ps	46:6	Godless nations **r** and rave
2Co	11:16	let me **r** on a little

Ranting

1Sa	19:20	they were **r** and raving right along
Ecc	9:17	more effective Than the **r** of a king

Rapacious

Ps	68:30	**R** in her lust for silver
Isa	9:20	safe from their **r** hunger
	34:14	night-demon Lilith, evil and **r**
Eze	22:13	**r** greed and your bloody brutalities
Zep	3:3	leaders are **r** lions
	3:3	Her judges are **r** timber

Rapaciously

Eze	22:27	**r** taking whatever they want

Rapacity

Eze	16:27	over to the **r** of your enemies

Rape

Ge	34:7	Shechem's **r** of Jacob's daughter
	34:27	in retaliation for Dinah's **r**
Jer	6:7	streets echo the cries: 'Violence! R!'
	20:8	shouting, "Murder!" or "R!"
Da	11:24	in his **r** of the country

Raped

Ge	34:2	saw her and **r** her
	34:5	Shechem had **r** his daughter Dinah
	34:13	Their sister, after all, had been **r**
Dt	22:24	the man because he **r** her
	22:25	engaged girl and grabbed and **r** her
	22:29	the man who **r** her has to give
Jdg	19:25	They **r** her repeatedly
	20:5	They gang-**r** my concubine
Ru	2:22	no danger now of being **r**
2Sa	13:14	much stronger than she, he **r** her
	13:15	No sooner had Amnon **r** her than
Job	31:39	ever **r** the earth for my own profit
Isa	13:16	Houses looted, wives **r**
Jer	46:24	**r** by vandals from the north
La	5:11	Our wives were **r** in the streets

Eze	30:16	Thebes blown away, Memphis **r**
Am	5:19	is **r** by a neighbor
Zec	14:2	Houses plundered, women **r**

Ratified

2Ch	13:5	**r** by a 'covenant of salt'
Gal	3:15	Once a person's will has been **r**
	3:17	A will, earlier **r** by God

Ratify

Est	9:30	to endorse and **r** what he wrote

Ravage

Dt	28:51	They'll **r** the young of your animals
2Ki	3:19	You will **r** the country
Jer	25:36	God is about to **r** their fine pastures
	50:16	**r** her fields, empty her barns
Gal	5:15	If you bite and **r** each other

Ravaged

Jdg	16:24	The one who **r** our country
1Ch	20:1	led the army out and **r** the Ammonites
2Ch	32:14	that either I or my ancestors have **r**
Jer	25:38	ripped and **r** by his anger
Eze	34:28	**r** by fierce beasts
Jn	10:12	leaving the sheep to be **r**

Reality

Job	18:4	Should **r** be suspended to accommodate
Pr	1:4	give our young people a grasp on **r**
Ecc	7:18	God deals responsibly with all of **r**
Isa	44:11	Make them face God-**r**
	44:20	so out of touch with **r**
Jer	49:7	no one with a sense of **r**?
Joel	1:5	Get in touch with **r** — and weep
Am	5:20	At God's coming we face hard **r**
Mt	6:33	Steep your life in God-**r**
Lk	12:31	Steep yourself in God-**r**
Jn	3:21	truth and **r** welcomes God-light
	7:18	doesn't tamper with **r**
Ro	1:19	the basic **r** of God is plain enough
Eph	4:18	not only with God but with **r** itself
Php	1:7	hopes have deep roots in **r**
Heb	4:15	priest who is out of touch with our **r**
1Jn	3:19	living truly, living in God's **r**
	5:2	**r** test on whether . . . we love God's
	5:6	the **r** of God's presence
	5:13	life, the **r** and not the illusion

Reap

Lev	23:10	**r** its harvest, bring to the priest
	23:22	**r** the harvest of your land, don't **r**
	25:5	Don't **r** what grows of itself
	25:11	don't **r** what volunteers itself
Job	4:8	plow evil and sow trouble **r** evil
Ecc	3:2	time to plant and another to **r**

R

Jer	12:13	They will plant wheat and r weeds
Hos	8:10	going to r the consequences soon
	10:12	Sow righteousness, r love
Rev	14:15	Swing your sickle and r

Reaped

Ps	107:37	they r a bountiful harvest
Hos	10:13	plowed wicked ways, r a crop of evil

Reapers

Jer	9:22	wheat cut down by r and left to rot

Reaping

Isa	37:30	regular sowing and r
Rev	14:15	Earth's harvest is ripe for r

Reassure

Ps	35:3	R me; let me hear you say
Isa	3:10	R the righteous
	41:14	I, God, want to r you
Php	2:26	r you that he is just fine
1Th	4:18	r one another with these words

Reassured

Ge	50:21	He r them, speaking with them
Jdg	6:23	But God r him, "Easy now
2Sa	14:22	blessed the king. "I'm r to know
Zec	1:13	God r the Angel-Messenger
Mt	9:21	he r her: "Courage, daughter
Lk	1:13	the angel r him, "Don't fear
Jn	6:20	he r them, "It's me. It's all right
1Jn	5:9	be r when God gives testimony
Rev	1:17	his voice r me: "Don't fear

Reassures

Ro	10:11	Scripture r us

Reassuring

Ex	6:2	God continued speaking to Moses, r him
Jdg	5:29	answers with calm, r words
2Ch	32:24	prayed to God and was given a r sign
Est	9:30	Calming and r letters went out
Ps	139:5	you're there, too — your r presence
SS	5:13	His voice, his words, warm and r
Jer	37:9	Don't kid yourselves, r one another
2Co	2:13	looking for Tit and a r word

Rebel

Nu	14:9	Just don't r against God!
	27:3	wasn't part of Korah's r anti-God gang
Dt	17:3	any r sky-gods
	21:18	a stubborn son, a real r
	21:20	son of ours is a stubborn r
Jos	22:18	If you r against God today

	22:19	don't r against God
	22:19	And don't r against us
1Sa	12:14	don't r against what he tells you
	12:15	r against what he tells you
	24:11	I'm not against you. I'm no r
Ne	6:6	you and the Jews are planning to r
Ps	2:10	r-kings, use your heads
	36:1	The God-r tunes in to sedition
	39:8	You'll save me from a r life
	78:17	r in the desert against the High God
	106:18	Fire flared against that r crew
Isa	24:21	r powers in the skies and R kings
	30:1	Doom, r children!
	30:9	this is a r generation
Eze	2:8	don't r like these rebels
	33:12	won't save him when he decides to r
Jn	17:12	Except for the r bent on destruction
Ro	7:23	Parts of me covertly r
2Pe	2:4	God didn't let the r angels off

Rebellion

Ex	34:7	forgiving iniquity, r, and sin
Lev	16:16	the Israelites, their acts of r
	16:21	all their acts of r, all their sins
Nu	14:18	forgiving iniquity and r and sin
	26:9	in the Korah R against God
Jos	22:16	a blatant act of r against God
	22:23	an altar in r against God
1Ki	12:19	in r against the Davidic regime
2Ch	10:19	in r against the Davidic dynasty
Ezr	4:19	r is an old story there
Ps	89:32	rub their faces in the dirt of their r
Jer	29:32	he has preached r against me
La	1:20	my heart wrecked by a life of r
Eze	2:3	fomented r right up to the present
	33:12	prevent him from repenting of his r
Da	9:9	in our r we've forfeited our rights
	9:24	throttle r, stop sin
Zep	3:11	ashamed of all those acts of r
2Ti	3:16	showing us truth, exposing our r
Jude	1:11	canceled out in Korah's r

Rebellious

Dt	31:27	you're r against God
Jos	22:22	if this is a r betrayal of God
Ezr	4:12	rebuilding that r and evil city
	4:15	that city is a r city
Isa	35:8	No one rude or r is permitted
Eze	2:3	a r nation if there ever was one
	12:2	living with a bunch of r people
	18:30	Turn your backs on your r living
Hos	9:15	leaders are a bunch of r adolescents
Zep	3:1	Doom to the r city
Ro	5:6	death when we were far too weak and r
	7:5	this made us all the more r
Col	1:21	thinking r thoughts of him
Tit	2:14	free us from a dark, r life
	3:11	out of line, r against God

Rebels

Nu	17:10	Keep it there as a sign to r
	20:10	Moses spoke: "Listen, r!
Dt	9:7	you got to this place, r all the way
	9:13	hardheaded, hardhearted r
	9:24	You've been r against God
	31:27	I know what r you are
Ps	34:16	God won't put up with r
	51:13	Give me a job teaching r your ways
	66:7	R don't dare raise a finger
	68:6	leaves r to rot in hell
	68:18	your arms full of booty from r
Pr	20:26	wise leader makes a clean sweep of r
	23:17	Don't for a minute envy careless r
Isa	1:28	it's curtains for r and God-traitors
	46:8	This is serious business, r
	48:8	r from the womb
	57:4	A race of r, a generation of liars
Jer	3:25	we've been r, disobeying . . . our God
	5:5	they were no better! R all!
	50:21	Attack Merathaim, land of r!
Eze	2:6	They're a bunch of r
	2:7	They're hardened r
	2:8	don't rebel like these r
	3:9	they're a bunch of r
	3:26	they are a bunch of r
	3:27	They are a bunch of r
	12:2	They're r all
	12:3	r though they are
	12:9	Israel, that bunch of r
	12:25	I'll do — and soon, you r
	17:12	Tell this house of r
	20:38	I'll cull out the r and traitors
	24:3	Tell this company of r a story
	44:6	Tell this bunch of r
Tit	1:10	there are a lot of r out there

Rebuke

Ps	38:2	sharp-pointed arrows of r draw blood
	68:30	R that old crocodile, Egypt
Pr	14:35	shiftless work earns an angry r
	17:10	A quiet r to a person of good sense
Ecc	7:5	You'll get more from the r of a sage
Isa	66:15	a r fierce and fiery
Am	5:13	Protest and r are useless
Zec	3:2	I, God, r you, Accuser! I r you
Mt	4:10	He backed his r with a third quotation
Lk	3:19	stung by John's r in the matter

Reckless

Jdg	9:4	hired some r riff-raff soldiers
Job	33:17	from some r choice
Pr	14:16	fools are headstrong and r
Ecc	7:17	don't be r. Why die needlessly
Jer	23:32	their cheap and r lies
Jn	12:25	if you let it go, r in your love
2Co	9:9	giving to the needy in r abandon

Recklessly

Nu	14:44	r and arrogantly they climbed
2Sa	6:22	more r even than this
Hab	2:9	r grabbing and looting

Recognition

Pr	3:16	with the other she confers r
Isa	30:14	smashed beyond r or repair
	52:14	a ruined face, disfigured past r
Jer	50:23	Babylon pummeled beyond r
Ro	2:29	r comes from God, not legalistic
1Co	16:15	special r to the family of Stephanas

Red-faced

Isa	24:23	r sun will skulk, disgraced
Lk	13:17	left looking quite silly and r
	14:9	R, you'll have to make your way
2Co	9:4	we'd all be pretty r
1Jn	2:28	no cause for r guilt or lame excuses

Redeem

Ex	6:6	I will r you
	13:13	can r every first birth of a donkey
	13:15	r every firstborn son
	34:20	R your firstborn donkey
Lev	25:26	If a man has no one to r it but
	25:29	during that year he can r it
	25:49	family may r him
	27:13	changes his mind and wants to r it
	27:20	if he doesn't r it or sells the field
	27:27	If he doesn't r it, it is to be sold
Nu	3:46	R the 273 firstborn Israelites
	18:17	don't r a firstborn ox, sheep, or goat
2Sa	7:23	whom God set out to r for himself
1Ch	17:21	whom God set out to r as his own
Ps	130:8	he'll r Israel, buy back Israel
Mic	4:10	He'll r you from your enemies
Gal	4:4	r those of us who have been kidnapped

Redeemed

Ex	15:13	you r, you led in merciful love
Lev	25:30	if it is not r before the full year
	25:31	They can be r and have to be returned
	25:54	If he is not r in any of these ways
	27:29	devoted to destruction can be r
	27:33	cannot be r
Nu	3:49	exceeded the number r by the Levites
	18:16	must be r at the redemption price
Dt	9:26	in your immense generosity, you r
	13:5	who r you from a world of slavery
	15:15	your God, r you from that slave world
	21:8	Purify your people Israel whom you r
Ne	1:10	you so powerfully and impressively r
Isa	29:22	the same God who r Abraham
	35:9	Only the r will walk on it
	43:1	Don't be afraid, I've r you
	44:22	Come back to me, come back. I've r you
	44:23	God has r Jacob

	48:20	God r his dear servant Jacob
	51:10	a road for the r to walk across
	52:9	He's r Jerusalem
	62:12	Holy People, God-R, Sought-Out
	63:9	Out of his own love and pity he r them
Gal	3:13	Christ r us from that self-defeating

Redeemer

Ru	3:13	as the closest covenant r, he'll have
	4:4	You have first r rights
	4:5	along with the r responsibility
	4:8	Boaz's "r" relative said
Ps	78:35	High God was their r
Isa	43:14	God, your R, The Holy of Israel
	44:6	God, King of Israel, your R
	44:24	God, your R, who shaped your life
	47:4	Our R speaks, named God
	48:17	this Message from God, your R
	49:7	God, R of Israel, The Holy of Israel
	54:5	Your R is The Holy of Israel
	54:7	Your R God says: "I left you, but only
	59:20	I'll arrive in Zion as R, to those
	60:16	I, God, am your Savior, your R
	63:16	you're our living Father, our R
Ac	7:35	sent back as ruler and r

Redeemers

| Ru | 2:20 | one of our circle of covenant r |
| | 3:9 | in the circle of covenant r |

Redemption

Ex	21:30	pay it in full as a r for his life
Lev	25:24	right of r for any of the land
	25:26	prospers and earns enough for its r
	25:32	are always subject to r
	25:48	he still has the right of r
	25:52	calculate his r price accordingly
Nu	3:48	for the r of the excess number
	3:49	Moses collected the r money
	3:51	Moses turned over the r money
	18:15	but its r price; firstborn humans
	18:16	must be redeemed at the r price
Ps	130:7	with God's arrival comes generous r
Isa	63:4	The time for r had arrived

Refine

Jer	6:29	Nothing can r evil out of them
Da	11:35	testing will r, cleanse, and purify
Zec	13:9	I'll r them as silver is

Reflected

| Hag | 2:16 | r in a sluggish, halfway return on |
| 1Pe | 4:16 | distinguished status r in that name |

Reflecting

| Ge | 1:26 | make them r our nature |
| | 1:27 | created them godlike, R God's nature |

| | 9:6 | made humans in his image r God's |
| 2Ki | 3:22 | the water r the sun looked red |

Reflection

| Ps | 63:6 | I spend the hours in grateful r |
| 1Co | 11:11 | a beautiful shining r of God |

Refresh

Ge	18:5	I'll get some food to r you on your way
Ps	74:2	R your memory of us
Jer	31:25	I'll r tired bodies
Joel	2:23	words to r and nourish your soul
Ac	3:19	showers of blessing to r you
1Co	4:17	will r your memory on the instructions
2Co	2:2	then be free to cheer and r me

Refuge

Ex	21:13	to which the killer can flee for r
Nu	35:12	places of r from the avenger
Dt	4:42	a person could flee and find r
	19:4	murderer who flees there to take r
	23:15	he's come to you for r
	32:37	the rock in which they sought r
Jos	20:4	escape for r to one of these cities
1Sa	23:6	After Abiathar took r with David
	24:22	went up to their wilderness r
2Sa	22:3	the granite hideout; My mountaintop r
1Ki	2:28	he took r in the sanctuary of God
1Ch	6:57	was also given the cities of r
	6:67	cities of r: Shechem
Ps	28:8	ample r for his chosen leader
	91:2	God, you're my r. I trust in you
	91:9	because God's your r
	118:8	better to take r in God than trust
	118:9	better to take r in God than trust
Isa	14:32	Those in need and in trouble find r
	17:10	not remembered your Rock-of-R
	23:13	a r for wild dogs and stray cats
Eze	24:25	The day I take away the people's r
Rev	6:16	calling out to mountains and rocks, "R

Regret

Job	27:6	I'll never r it
Ps	2:12	make a run for God — you won't r it
	71:1	I'll never live to r it
Pr	4:8	you won't r it
	14:17	hotheaded do things they'll later r
	31:11	never has reason to r it
Isa	50:7	confident that I'll never r this
Jer	8:6	No one expressed one word of r
Hos	13:14	I'm abolishing r, banishing sorrow
Lk	6:35	You'll never — I promise — r it
	18:29	said Jesus, "and you won't r it
Ro	10:11	heart and soul — will ever r it
2Co	7:10	We never r that kind of pain
1Ti	6:10	live to r it bitterly ever after
1Pe	2:6	will never have cause to r it

R

Reject

Lev	20:3	I will resolutely r that man
	20:5	I will resolutely r that man
	20:6	I will resolutely r persons
	26:44	I won't r or abhor or destroy them
Job	8:20	no way that God will r a good person
	19:19	my dearest loved ones r me
Ps	101:3	I r made-in-Canaan gods
	106:24	They went on to r the Blessed Land
	119:119	You r earth's wicked
Pr	5:12	Why did I r a disciplined life
	8:36	damage your very soul; when you r me
Isa	33:15	refuse bribes, r violence
Da	11:21	His place will be taken by a r
Mt	12:32	If you r the Son of Man
Jn	12:47	I don't r him. I didn't come to r
2Co	6:14	partners with those who r God
Gal	6:15	submit to circumcision, r circumcision

Rejection

Lk	2:35	the r will force honesty
Jn	12:48	willfully choosing r
Ro	3:4	R doesn't faze you
1Th	5:9	God didn't set us up for an angry r

Rejoice

Dt	16:11	R in the Presence of God, your God,
	16:14	R at your festival: you, your son
	26:11	r! Celebrate all the good things
1Ch	16:31	let heaven r, let earth be jubilant
Pr	23:24	r when their children turn out well
Isa	65:13	My servants will r
	66:10	R, Jerusalem, and all who love her
Jer	32:41	Oh how I'll r in them!
Ro	15:10	Outsiders and insiders, r together
Gal	4:27	R, barren woman who bears no children
Php	2:17	r in being an element in the offering
	2:28	how you'll r and how relieved
Rev	12:12	r, O Heavens, and all who live there
	19:7	Let us celebrate, let us r

Rejoicing

Dt	27:7	r in the Presence of God, your God
1Ch	15:25	they went r
2Ch	7:10	They left r, exuberant over all
Lk	10:20	that's the agenda for r
	15:5	put it across your shoulders, r
Php	2:17	on Christ's altar, a part of your r
	2:18	you must join me in my r

Relationship

Est	8:1	Esther had explained their r
Mt	14:4	naming his r with Herodias "adultery
Mk	6:18	naming his r with Herodias "adultery
Ro	14:22	Cultivate your own r with God
1Co	11:3	In a marriage r, there is authority
2Co	5:18	God who settled the r between us

Gal	2:21	personal and free in my r with God
	3:11	can sustain a r with God that way
	3:21	out of right r with God
	3:26	you are in direct r with God
	3:28	all in a common r with Jesus Christ
	4:24	two ways of being in r with God
	5:5	a satisfying r with the Spirit
Tit	3:7	God's gift has restored our r with him
Heb	12:11	mature in their r with God
1Jn	4:7	experiences a r with God
	4:10	damage they've done to our r with God
	4:15	in an intimate r with God

Relationships

2Sa	8:15	evenhanded in all his duties and r
1Ki	3:6	his r were just and his heart right
1Ch	18:14	evenhanded in all his duties and r
Eze	18:5	treating others fairly, keeping good r
2Co	5:18	to settle our r with each other

Relax

Ru	3:18	Sit back and r, my dear daughter
Job	11:18	Full of hope, you'll r, confident
	20:18	unable to r and enjoy anything
	22:24	R your grip on your money
Ps	9:10	The moment you arrive, you r
	116:7	R and rest. God has showered you
Pr	1:33	First pay attention to me, and then r
	4:13	Hold tight to good advice; don't r
Isa	7:16	the threat of war will be over. R
Da	10:12	R, Daniel,' he continued
	12:13	without fretting or worrying. R
Mt	6:31	trying to . . . get you to r
Lk	12:29	trying to . . . get you to r
Ac	7:49	Where I can get away and r
	10:28	r with people of another race
2Co	2:13	I couldn't r. Worried about you
	7:5	on pins and needles. We couldn't r
Jude	1:2	R, everything's going to be all right

Relaxed

Jdg	19:22	They were r and enjoying themselves
Ps	112:8	Ever blessed, r among enemies
	119:87	I haven't r my grip on your counsel
Pr	28:1	Honest people are r and confident
Isa	21:4	I had hoped for a r evening
Jer	49:31	Go after these r nomads who live free
Mk	7:30	found her daughter r on the bed
Jn	3:22	into the Judean countryside and r
Heb	13:5	Be r with what you have

Reliability

Lk	1:4	the r of what you were taught
1Co	4:2	requirements for a good guide are r

Reliable

2Sa	20:19	We're a peaceful people here, and r

R

2Ki	2:16	We have fifty r men here		3:9	took up cheap sex-and-r as a sideline
Pr	13:17	a r reporter is a healing presence		3:13	into the sex-and-r groves
	25:13	R friends who do what they say		3:23	All that popular r was a cheap lie
Jer	2:21	planted you from completely r stock		8:8	r experts have taken you for a ride
Jn	5:32	me, the most r Witness of all		9:26	nations are big on performance r
	5:33	gave expert and r testimony about me		10:3	The r of these peoples is nothing
	21:24	his . . . account is r and accurate		17:2	sex-and-r altars
Col	1:7	He is one r worker for Christ	Eze	6:13	their ruined sex-and-r shrines
2Ti	2:2	r leaders who are competent to teach		20:28	a hill with a sex-and-r shrine
Heb	11:5	know on the basis of r testimony	Hos	2:13	her indulgence in promiscuous r
				3:4	without r and comfort

Religion

				4:13	make a picnic out of r
Ex	34:15	take up with their sex-and-r life		5:3	played your sex-and-r games long
Lev	26:30	I'll smash your sex-and-r shrines		6:6	I'm after love that lasts, not more r
Nu	25:2	to their sex-and-r worship		7:14	in their sex-and-r orgies
Dt	7:5	chop down their sex-and-r Asherah		9:1	every sex-and-r party on the street
	12:3	Burn their sex-and-r Asherah shrines		11:2	he played at r with toy gods
1Ki	13:32	against all the sex-and-r shrines		12:11	teeming with empty-headed r
	14:15	angry with Asherah sex-and-r shrines	Am	13:2	R customized to taste
	14:23	built Asherah sex-and-r shrines		5:22	want nothing to do with your r
	15:14	rid of the local sex-and-r shrines		7:9	sex-and-r shrines will be smashed
	22:43	the neighborhood sex-and-r shrines	Mic	1:5	all the sex-and-r shrines in Judah
2Ki	13:6	including the sex-and-r shrines	Zep	1:4	the sex-and-r Baal shrines
	14:4	the local sex-and-r shrines continued	Zec	7:6	You're interested in r
	15:4	rid of the local sex-and-r shrines	Mal	1:10	play at r with this silly . . . worship
	15:35	the neighborhood sex-and-r shrines	Mt	2:4	all the high priests and r scholars
	16:4	the neighborhood sex-and-r shrines		7:29	quite a contrast to their r teachers
	17:9	built local sex-and-r shrines		8:19	a r scholar asked if he could go along
	17:10	set up their sex-and-r symbols		9:3	Some r scholars whispered
	17:16	frequented the sex-and-r shrines		9:13	I'm after mercy, not r
	17:29	the neighborhood sex-and-r shrines		11:28	Burned out on r? Come to me
	18:4	cut down the sex-and-r Asherah groves		12:6	far more at stake here than r
	21:3	rebuilt all the sex-and-r shrines		12:38	a few r scholars and Pharisees got
	23:5	supervise the local sex-and-r shrines		15:1	Pharisees and r scholars came to Jesus
	23:8	smashed the sex-and-r shrines		17:10	Why do the r scholars say that Elijah
	23:9	sex-and-r priests did not defile		22:35	One of their r scholars spoke for them
	23:13	all the sex-and-r shrines		23:2	The r scholars . . . are competent
	23:19	built neighborhood sex-and-r shrines		23:13	You're hopeless, you r scholars
2Ch	14:3	chopped down the sex-and-r groves		23:15	You're hopeless, you r scholars
	15:17	rid of the local sex-and-r shrines		23:23	You're hopeless, you r scholars
	17:3	fool around with the popular Baal r		23:25	You're hopeless, you r scholars
	17:6	got rid of the local sex-and-r shrines		23:27	You're hopeless, you r scholars
	19:3	polluting sex-and-r shrines		23:29	You're hopeless, you r scholars
	20:33	the neighborhood sex-and-r shrines		26:57	where the r scholars . . . had assembled
	28:4	the neighborhood sex-and-r shrines		27:41	along with the r scholars and leaders
	33:3	rebuilt the sex-and-r shrines	Mk	1:22	quoting like the r scholars
	34:3	cleanse the neighborhood of sex-and-r		2:6	Some r scholars sitting there started
Job	15:4	You trivialize r		2:16	The r scholars and Pharisees saw him
Ps	31:6	I hate all this silly r		3:5	furious at their hard-nosed r
Isa	1:14	I'm sick of your r, r, r		3:22	The r scholars from Jerusalem came
	2:6	their world is full of hokey r		7:1	with some r scholars who had come
	17:8	their homemade, handmade r		7:5	The Pharisees and r scholars asked
	27:9	clean out all the sex-and-r shrines		8:31	elders, high priests, and r scholars
	30:11	Don't bore us with obsolete r		9:11	Why do the r scholars say that Elijah
	57:6	set up your sex-and-r shrines		9:14	r scholars cross-examining them
	57:7	practice your foul sex-and-death r		11:18	high priests and r scholars heard
	57:9	search out the latest in r		11:27	the high priests, r scholars
	57:12	all your 'righteous' attempts at r		12:28	One of the r scholars came up
	65:3	Make up their own kitchen r		12:32	r scholar said, "A wonderful answer
Jer	2:8	The r experts knew nothing of me		12:35	r scholars say that the Messiah
	2:20	Visiting every sex-and-r shrine		12:38	Watch out for the r scholars
				14:1	r scholars were looking for a way

	14:43	sent by the high priests, r scholars
	15:31	priests, along with the r scholars
Lk	5:17	Pharisees and r teachers were sitting
	5:21	set the r scholars . . . buzzing
	5:30	their r scholars came to his disciples
	6:7	The r scholars . . . had their eye on
	9:22	and r scholars, be killed
	10:25	a r scholar stood up with a question
	10:37	the r scholar responded. Jesus said
	11:45	One of the r scholars spoke up
	11:46	You're hopeless, you r scholars!
	11:52	You're hopeless, you r scholars!
	11:53	r scholars . . . went into a rage
	14:3	Jesus asked the r scholars
	15:2	The . . . r scholars were not pleased
	19:47	high priests, r scholars
	20:1	r scholars, and leaders confronted
	20:19	r scholars and high priests wanted
	20:39	Some of the r scholars said
	20:46	Watch out for the r scholars
	22:2	r scholars were looking for a way
	22:52	priests, Temple police, r leaders
	23:10	r scholars were right there
Jn	8:3	r scholars . . . led in a woman
Ac	4:5	rulers, religious leaders, r scholars
	6:12	religious leaders, and r scholars
	17:22	you Athenians take your r seriously
	18:15	endless hairsplitting quarrels over r
	21:28	telling lies against us and our r
	23:9	the r scholars . . . side shouted
	25:8	nothing wrong against the Jewish r
	25:19	arguments about their r and a dead man
	26:5	the most demanding branch of our r
Ro	2:17	lean back in the arms of your r
	3:30	who have never heard of our r
1Co	10:7	must not turn our r into a circus
Gal	2:21	old rule-keeping, peer-pleasing r
	5:6	conscientious r nor disregard of r
	5:20	trinket gods; magic-show r
Eph	5:5	using people or r or things just for
Php	3:6	fiery defender of the purity of my r
Col	2:20	put all that pretentious . . . r behind
1Ti	4:7	silly stories that get dressed up as r
	5:4	r begins at their own doorstep
	6:5	think r is a way to make a fast buck
	6:20	Avoid the talk-show r
2Ti	3:5	They'll make a show of r
Heb	9:13	cleaning up certain matters of our r
Jas	1:26	This kind of r is hot air
	1:27	Real r, the kind that passes muster
Jude	1:18	make a r of their own whims and lusts
Rev	2:20	Cross-denying, self-indulging r
	2:22	as they play their sex-and-r games

Remember

Ge	9:15	I'll r my covenant between me and you
	9:16	see it and r the eternal covenant
	40:14	Only r me when things are going well
	46:34	kept livestock for as long as we can r
Ex	13:3	Always r this day
	22:21	you, r, were once strangers in Egypt

Lev	19:34	R that you were once foreigners
	20:24	told you, r, that you will possess
	26:42	I'll r my covenant with Jacob, I'll r
	26:45	For their sake I will r the covenant
Nu	3:41	r, I am God
	15:39	r and keep all the commandments
	28:31	R, the animals must be healthy
Dt	4:15	from out of the fire. R that
	5:5	You were afraid, r, of the fire
	7:18	R, yes, r in detail what God
	7:19	R the great contests to which you
	8:2	R every road that God led you on
	8:18	R that God, your God, gave you
	9:27	R your servants Abraham
	10:19	r, you were once foreigners
Jos	1:13	R what Moses . . . commanded
	14:6	r what God said to Moses
Jdg	9:2	r that I am your own flesh and blood
	17:2	He said to his mother, "R
	21:18	R, the Israelites had taken the oath
1Sa	2:30	God's word, r!
	20:8	a covenant of God with me, r
	20:23	r that God's in on this with us
	25:31	for good for my master, r me
2Sa	11:25	Didn't you r how Abimelech
	12:11	This is God speaking, r!
1Ki	22:28	r where you heard it
2Ki	9:25	R when you and I were driving
	20:3	R, O God, who I am, what I've done
1Ch	16:12	R all the wonders he performed
Ne	1:8	r the warning you posted
	5:19	R in my favor, O my God
	9:17	refused to r the miracles you had done
	13:14	R me, O my God, for this
	13:22	R me also for this, my God
	13:29	R them, O my God, how they defiled
	13:31	R me, O my God, for good
Est	9:19	r the fourteenth day of Adar
	9:27	r these two days every year
Job	10:9	r how beautifully you worked my clay
	36:24	R, then, to praise his workmanship
Ps	36:3	Can't r when he did anything decent
	74:18	Mark and r, God, all the enemy taunts
	74:20	R your promises; the city is
	77:3	I r God — and shake my head
	80:8	R how you brought a young vine
	88:15	For as long as I r I've been hurting
	89:47	R my sorrow and how short life is
	90:9	All we can r is that frown
	103:18	r to do whatever he said
	105:5	R the world of wonders he has made
	105:43	R this! He led his people out singing
	106:4	R me, God, when you enjoy your people
	113:2	Just to r God is a blessing
	115:12	O God, r us and bless us
	119:25	You promised, r
	119:49	R what you said to me, your servant
	132:1	O God, r David, r all his troubles
	132:2	r how he promised God, made a vow
	132:6	R how we got the news in Ephrathah
	137:6	turn black if I fail to r you
	137:7	God, r those Edomites, and r the ruin

R

Ecc	1:11	Nobody rs what happened yesterday
	10:10	R: The duller the ax the harder
Isa	23:7	Is this the city you r as energetic
	38:3	R how I've lived my life
	44:21	R these things, O Jacob
	45:18	he is, r, God
	46:9	R your history, your long and
	62:6	reminding God to r
Jer	2:2	I r your youthful loyalty
	3:16	R the Ark of the Covenant
	14:21	R your covenant
	15:6	You left me, r?
	15:15	R what I'm doing here!
	18:20	R all the times I stood up for them
	50:6	couldn't r where they came from
	51:50	R God in your long and distant exile
La	3:20	I r it all — oh, how well I r
	3:21	there's one other thing I r
	5:1	R, God, all we've been through
Eze	6:9	they'll r me
	13:8	the Message of God, the Master, r
	16:22	did you r your infancy
	16:43	r what happened when you were young
	16:56	R . . . when you were putting on airs
	16:60	I'll r the covenant I made with you
	16:61	You'll r your sorry past
	16:63	You'll r your past life
	20:43	you'll r all that you've done
Da	6:15	R, O king, it's the law of the Medes
Mic	6:5	R what Balak king of Moab tried
Hab	3:2	as you surely must, r mercy
Zep	3:8	r I'll be there to bring evidence
Zec	10:9	they'll r me in the faraway places
Mal	4:4	R and keep the revelation I gave
Mt	5:23	r a grudge a friend has against you
	5:31	R the Scripture that says
	16:9	Don't you r the five loaves of bread
Mk	8:19	R the five loaves I broke
	11:25	prayer, r that it's not all asking
Lk	16:25	r that in your lifetime you got
	17:32	R what happened to Lot's wife
	18:21	kept them all for as long as I can r
	23:42	r me when you enter your kingdom
	24:6	but raised up. R how he told you
Jn	15:16	You didn't choose me, r; I chose you
	15:17	r the root command: Love one another
	15:18	r it got its start hating me
	15:20	When that happens, r this
Ac	16:34	It was a night to r
	19:40	Rome, r, does not look kindly
	20:31	R those three years I kept at it
Ro	6:13	r, you've been raised from the dead
	7:8	Don't you r how it was?
	9:7	R how it was put
	9:9	R that promise, "When I come back
	11:1	R that I, the one writing these things
	11:2	Do you r that time Elijah was
	11:4	And do you r God's answer?
	11:18	R, you aren't feeding the root
	14:1	R, they have their own history
	14:15	r, are persons for whom Christ died
1Co	2:1	You'll r . . . that when I first came

	3:11	R, there is only one foundation
	3:17	and you, r, are the temple
	6:15	r that your bodies are created with
	10:1	R our history, friends, and be warned
	10:8	they paid for that, r
	10:13	r is that God will never let you down
	11:24	Do this to r me
	11:25	Each time you drink this cup, r me
	12:2	R . . . when you didn't know God
2Co	4:5	R, our Message is not about ourselves
	9:6	R: A stingy planter gets a stingy crop
	11:21	r, this is your old friend, the fool
	11:32	R the time I was in Damascus
	13:1	R the Scripture that says
Gal	2:10	asked was that we r the poor
	3:13	Do you r the Scripture that says
	4:14	r that even though taking in a sick
	4:22	Abraham, r, had two sons
	4:27	R what Isaiah wrote: Rejoice
Php	2:30	R the ministry to me that you started
	4:3	R, their names are also in the book
Col	3:4	Christ (your real life, r) shows up
	4:18	R to pray for me in this jail
1Th	2:9	You r us in those days, friends
2Th	2:5	Don't you r me going over all this
	2:6	r that I told you the Anarchist is
	3:10	r the rule we had when we lived
2Ti	1:4	when I r that last tearful good-bye
Heb	4:3	if we don't have faith. R that God
	10:32	R those early days after you first saw
Jas	3:5	a spark, r, to set off a . . . fire
Jude	1:17	But r . . . that the apostles
Rev	2:14	r that Balaam was an enemy agent

Remembrance

Ex	28:29	into the presence of God for r
Nu	15:40	tassels will signal r and observance
1Co	11:27	Is that the kind of "r" you want

Remnant

Ge	45:7	make sure there was a r in the land
Jdg	5:13	r went down to greet the brave ones
2Ki	19:30	A r of the family of Judah
	19:31	The r will come from Jerusalem
Isa	7:3	Shear-jashub (A-R-Will-Return)
	10:21	The ragtag r — what's left of Jacob
Am	5:15	will notice your r and be gracious
Ob	1:21	The r of the saved in Mount Zion

Render

Isa	11:4	r decisions on earth's poor
Eze	7:8	R my verdict on the way you've lived
1Co	6:6	How can they r justice if they don't

Renovate

2Ki	12:5	use them to r The Temple
2Ch	24:4	determined to r The Temple of God
	34:8	to r The Temple of God
Isa	58:12	restore old ruins, rebuild and r

Repair

1Sa	13:20	sickles — sharp and in good **r**
2Ki	12:12	**r** and renovation of The Temple of God
2Ch	24:5	collect money . . . to **r** The Temple
	24:12	paid . . . for the **r** work on The Temple
Ps	51:18	**r** Jerusalem's broken-down walls
Pr	6:15	their lives ruined beyond **r**
Isa	22:9	places in the city walls that needed **r**
	30:14	smashed beyond recognition or **r**
Eze	13:5	to **r** the defenses of the city
	22:30	to **r** the defenses of the city
Am	9:11	I'll **r** the holes in the roof
2Co	13:11	Keep things in good **r**

Repaired

2Ch	29:3	having first **r** the doors of The Temple
	29:19	we have **r** them
Ne	3:1	they **r** it and hung its doors
	3:3	they **r** it, hung its doors
	3:6	they **r** it, hung its doors
	3:13	they **r** it, hung its doors
	3:14	he **r** it, hung its doors
	3:15	he **r** it, roofed it, hung its doors
	3:31	**r** the wall as far as the house

Repairing

2Ki	12:14	to pay for their **r** God's Temple
	22:5	pay the workers who are **r** God's Temple
2Ch	32:5	work **r** every part of the city wall
	34:11	on to the workers **r** God's Temple
Ne	3:28	each priest **r** the wall in front
	4:6	kept at it, **r** and rebuilding the wall

Repent

1Ki	8:47	**r** in the country of their captivity
2Ch	6:37	**r** in the country of their captivity
	33:23	he never did **r** to God
Job	36:10	they must **r** of their bad life
Isa	31:6	**R**, return, dear Israel, to the One
Jer	7:13	when I called you to **r**
	18:8	if they **r** of their wicked lives
La	2:14	with your sin so that you could **r**
Eze	14:6	God, the Master, says, **R**!
Rev	16:9	refused to **r**, refused to honor God
	16:11	refused to **r** and change their ways

Repentance

1Ki	18:37	people another chance at **r**
	21:29	Because of his **r** I'll not bring
2Ki	22:19	because you responded in humble **r**
2Ch	33:12	total **r** before the God of
	34:27	because you responded in humble **r**
	36:13	**r** never entered his mind
Ne	9:1	faces smudged with dirt as signs of **r**
Joel	2:15	Declare a day of **r**, a holy fast day
	2:17	God's servants, weep tears of **r**
Jnh	3:5	dressed in burlap to show their **r**

Mt	18:17	confront him with the need for **r**

Repentant

2Ki	23:25	turned in total and **r** obedience to God
2Ch	12:6	leaders of Israel and the king were **r**
	12:7	When God saw that they were humbly **r**
	12:12	was **r**, God's anger was blunted
Isa	22:12	Called for a day of **r** tears
La	2:18	heart-cries to the Master, dear **r** Zion
Hos	14:2	Receive as restitution our **r** prayers

Repented

2Ch	32:26	**r** of his arrogance
	33:23	repent to God as Manasseh **r**
Jer	31:19	I **r**. After you trained me to obedience
	44:5	paid the least bit of attention or **r**

Reprimand

Job	13:10	He'd **r** you on the spot
Pr	25:12	a wise friend's timely **r**
	27:5	A spoken **r** is better than
	28:23	serious **r** is appreciated far more

Reprimanded

Ge	37:10	his father **r** him
Mt	8:26	Jesus **r** them
Mk	4:40	Jesus **r** the disciples
1Co	8:8	nor **r** when we just can't stomach it

Reproach

Jos	5:9	I have rolled away the **r** of Egypt
1Sa	29:6	beyond **r** in the ways you have

Reproduce

Ge	1:22	**R**! Fill Ocean! Birds, **r** on Earth
	1:28	Prosper! **R**! Fill Earth!
	8:17	they can **r** and flourish on the Earth
	9:1	Prosper! **R**! Fill the Earth
	9:7	here to bear fruit, **r**, lavish life
Mic	7:15	**R** the miracle-wonders of our exodus

Repudiate

1Ki	9:7	**r** this Temple I've just sanctified
2Ch	7:20	**r** this Temple I've just sanctified
Isa	43:28	**r** Jacob and discredit Israel
Gal	2:21	I refuse to do that, to **r** God's grace
Heb	10:26	we **r** Christ's sacrifice

Repudiated

Ac	3:13	One that Pilate called innocent, you **r**
	3:14	You **r** the Holy One, the Just One
Heb	6:6	re-crucified Jesus! They've **r** him

R

Repudiates

1Ti	5:8	**r** the faith. That's worse than

Repudiating

Mt	12:31	you are **r** the very One who forgives
Mk	3:29	you are **r** the very One who forgives
2Pe	2:21	**r** the experience and the holy command

Repudiation

Ro	11:2	we're not talking about **r**

Repugnant

1Sa	27:12	He's made himself so **r** to his people
Jer	24:9	disgusting — **r** outcasts

Reputation

Ex	9:16	my **r** spreads in all the Earth
Nu	22:6	You have a **r**: Those you bless
Jos	7:9	how will you keep up your **r**
Ru	4:10	The memory and **r** of the deceased
2Sa	7:26	your **r** will flourish always
	14:9	to compromise the king and his **r**
	16:23	That was the **r** of Ahithophel's counsel
1Ki	4:34	who had heard of his **r**
	8:41	a far country because of your **r**
	8:42	attracted here by your great **r**
	10:1	came to put his **r** to the test
	10:6	**r** for accomplishment and wisdom
1Ch	14:2	**r** that God was giving his kingdom
	17:24	your **r** will be confirmed and flourish
2Ch	6:32	a far country because of your **r**
	9:1	queen of Sheba heard of Solomon's **r**
	9:5	**r** for accomplishment and wisdom
	26:8	his **r** extending all the way to Egypt
Ne	6:13	ruining my good **r**
	13:13	had a **r** for honesty and hard work
Est	9:4	his **r** had grown in all the provinces
Job	19:9	He destroyed my **r**, robbed me
	29:11	my **r** went ahead of me
Ps	9:6	their **r** trashed, their names erased
	19:9	God's **r** is twenty-four-carat gold
	25:11	Keep up your **r**, God; Forgive
	35:16	they destroyed my **r**
	56:5	they smear my **r** and huddle to plot
	79:9	Your **r** is on the line
	112:6	a sterling and solid and lasting **r**
	143:11	Keep up your **r**, God — give me life
Pr	3:4	Earn a **r** for living well in God's eyes
	6:33	a **r** ruined for good
	16:21	gracious words add to one's **r**
	16:23	whenever they speak, their **r** increases
	22:1	A sterling **r** is better than
	24:8	soon gets a **r** as prince of rogues
	28:7	get a **r** for wisdom
Ecc	6:2	property, **r** — all they ever wanted
	7:1	good **r** is better than a fat bank
Isa	12:4	spread the news of his great **r**

	48:11	I have my **r** to keep up
	52:5	incessantly, my **r** blackened
	66:22	So will your children and your **r** stand
Jer	14:21	Your **r** is at stake!
	32:20	You've made a **r** for yourself
Eze	16:52	What a **r** to carry into history
	28:7	hash of your **r** for knowing it all
	36:13	a **r** of being a land that eats people
	36:21	I suffered much pain over my holy **r**
Da	5:18	a great kingdom and a glorious **r**
	11:20	**r**, and authority already in shreds
Zec	8:13	gotten a **r** as a bad-news people
Mt	10:17	others will smear your **r**
Lk	15:1	men and women of doubtful **r**
Ac	19:27	as her glorious **r** fades to nothing
	22:12	a sterling **r** in observing our laws
2Co	8:21	in our **r** with the public as in our **r**
Gal	1:9	anyone, regardless of **r** or credentials
	2:6	their **r** doesn't concern me
1Ti	5:10	a **r** for helping out with children
Heb	6:13	putting his own **r** on the line
Jas	3:6	throw mud on a **r**
	3:13	to build a **r** for wisdom
Rev	3:1	You have a **r** for vigor and zest

Reputations

Isa	23:9	puncture the inflated **r**
Mic	3:7	They'll hide behind their **r**
1Co	4:6	inflating or deflating **r** based on

Respect

Ex	1:17	midwives had far too much **r** for God
	9:20	servants who had **r** for God's word
	9:30	and your servants have no **r** for God
	19:23	**R** the holy mountain
Lev	19:3	must **r** his mother and father
	19:32	Show **r** to the aged
Nu	12:8	why did you show no reverence or **r**
Dt	5:16	**R** your father and mother
	6:13	Deeply **r** God, your God
	8:6	reverently **r** him
	10:20	Reverently **r** God, your God
1Sa	2:8	Restoring dignity and **r** to their lives
2Sa	1:2	fell to his knees in **r** before David
	23:23	held in greatest **r** among the Thirty
1Ki	11:12	out of **r** for your father David
	11:13	out of **r** for my chosen city
	11:32	out of **r** for Jerusalem
	15:4	out of **r** for David, his God
2Ki	1:13	O Holy Man, have **r** for my life
	1:14	please, I beg you, **r** my life
	3:14	the **r** I have for Jehoshaphat
	13:23	out of **r** for his covenant with Abraham
	25:24	**r** the king of Babylon
2Ch	22:9	Out of **r** for his grandfather
Est	1:20	show proper **r** to her husband
Job	19:9	robbed me of all self-**r**
	29:8	Young and old greeted me with **r**
Ps	33:18	God's eye is on those who **r** him
	111:9	holy, worthy of our **r**

R

Pr	3:32	It's the straightforward who get his r
	11:16	A woman of gentle grace gets r
	14:2	An honest life shows r for God
	14:3	wise speech evokes nothing but r
	14:19	the wicked will r God-loyal people
	23:22	r to the father who raised you
	24:21	Fear God . . . r your leaders
	29:14	Leadership gains authority and r
	31:28	Her children r and bless her
Isa	18:2	This people held in r everywhere
	18:7	people once held in r everywhere
Jer	32:40	fill their hearts with a deep r for me
Eze	45:8	r the land as it has been allotted
Da	3:12	They don't r your gods
	3:14	you don't r my gods
	11:37	no r for the gods of his ancestors
Mic	5:4	whole world will hold him in r
	6:6	show proper r to the high God
Mal	1:6	If I'm your Master, where's the r
Mt	15:4	R your father and mother
	21:37	they will r my son
Mk	7:10	R your father and mother
	12:6	Surely they will r my son
Lk	20:13	They're bound to r my son
Ac	5:11	had a healthy r for God
	26:25	With all r, Festus, Your Honor
Ro	13:7	pay your bills, r your leaders
1Co	11:4	lack of r for the authority of Christ
	11:5	lack of r for . . . her husband
Eph	5:21	Out of r for Christ, be
1Th	4:12	command the r of outsiders
1Ti	3:4	his own children and having their r
	6:1	giving r to his master
Tit	1:6	Do they r him and stay out of trouble
	3:1	Remind the people to r the government
Heb	12:9	We r our own parents
1Pe	2:13	R the authorities
	2:17	Revere God. R the government

Respectable

Heb	9:15	efforts to make ourselves r

Respected

Ex	11:3	a r public figure
Nu	11:16	whom you know to be r and responsible
2Sa	23:19	He was the most r of the Thirty
Ne	1:7	haven't r the decisions you gave
Est	10:3	greatly r by them
Pr	21:28	a person who speaks truth is r
	31:23	Her husband is greatly r
Isa	3:5	the no-account against the well-r
Jer	26:17	some of the r leaders stood up
Mk	15:43	highly r member of the Jewish Council
Jn	3:10	You're a r teacher of Israel
	4:44	a prophet is not r in the place
Ac	13:50	convinced the most r women
1Ti	3:13	servant work will come to be highly r

Respectful

Dt	28:10	Name of God and hold you in r awe
Lk	23:49	stood at a r distance and kept vigil

Respectfully

Ge	23:7	bowed r to the people of the land
	23:12	bowed r before the assembled council
	43:26	bowed r before him
	43:28	they again bowed r before him
	48:12	bowed r, his face to the ground
1Ki	2:19	welcomed her, bowing r
Ne	8:7	while people stood, listening r
Eph	6:5	Servants, r obey your earthly masters

Respecting

Mt	15:6	That can hardly be called r a parent

Restitution

Ex	22:3	A thief must make full r
	22:5	r must be made from the best
Hos	14:2	Receive as r our repentant prayers

Restore

Lev	6:4	r what was entrusted to him
Nu	21:27	rebuild the city, r Sihon's town
Dt	30:3	God, your God, will r everything
2Sa	8:3	his way to r his sovereignty
	16:3	going to r my grandfather's kingdom
2Ki	14:25	he did r the borders of Israel
1Ch	18:3	his way to r his sovereignty
2Ch	7:14	r their land to health
Ezr	5:3	rebuild this Temple and r it to use
	5:9	rebuild this Temple and r it to use
	9:9	The Temple of our God, r its ruins
Isa	1:27	God's right actions will r her
	58:12	who can fix anything, r old ruins
Jer	31:25	I'll r tired souls
	32:44	I will r everything that was lost
	33:7	I'll r everything that was lost
	33:11	I'll r everything that was lost.
Am	9:11	I will r David's house
Lk	19:10	Son of Man came to find and r the lost
Ac	1:6	Master, are you going to r the kingdom
Gal	6:1	falls into sin, forgivingly r him

Restored

Ge	40:21	Then he r the head cupbearer
1Sa	7:14	had taken from Israel were r
1Ki	11:27	had r the fortifications
2Ki	14:22	he rebuilt and r Elath to Judah
2Ch	33:16	back in working order and r worship
Ezr	4:16	city gets rebuilt and its walls r
Job	42:10	God r his fortune
Eze	33:22	had been on me and r my speech
Na	2:2	God has r the Pride of Jacob
Ac	3:21	until everything is r to order again

R

Ro	3:24	r us to where he always wanted us
	8:29	first in the line of humanity he r
Tit	3:7	God's gift has r our relationship

Restores

Ps	72:13	he r the wretched of the earth

Restoring

1Sa	2:8	R dignity and respect to their lives
2Ch	28:15	r them to their families
Eze	33:15	r what he had stolen
Zec	12:7	I, God, will begin by r the common

Resurrection

Job	14:14	waiting for the final change — for r
Ps	85:6	make a fresh start — a r life
Mt	22:23	denies any possibility of r
	22:28	At the r, whose wife is she?
	22:30	At the r we're beyond marriage
	27:53	After Jesus' r, they left the tombs
Mk	12:18	denies any possibility of r
	12:23	at the r, whose wife is she?
Lk	14:14	at the r of God's people
	20:27	denies any possibility of r
	20:33	in the r whose wife is she?
	20:35	who are included in the r of the dead
	20:37	Even Moses exclaimed about r
Jn	5:29	will walk out into a r Life
	11:24	he will be raised up in the r
	11:25	I am, right now, R and Life
Ac	1:22	as a witness to his r
	2:31	he talked of the r of the Messiah
	4:2	r . . . had taken place in Jesus
	4:33	witness to the r of the Master
	17:18	go on about Jesus and the r
	23:6	the hope and r of the dead
	23:8	nothing to do with a r or angels
	24:21	I believe in the r
Ro	5:10	by means of his r life
	6:4	it is like the r of Jesus
	6:8	included in his life-saving r
	7:4	free to "marry" a r life
	8:15	This r life you received from God
1Co	6:14	treat yours with the same r power
	12:13	Each of us is now a part of his r body
	15:12	say that there is no such thing as a r
	15:13	no r, there's no living Christ
	15:14	if there's no r for Christ
	15:15	sheer fabrications, if there's no r
	15:18	those who died hoping in Christ and r
	15:21	r from death came by a man
	15:29	If there's no chance of r for a corpse
	15:31	convinced of your r and mine
	15:32	It's r, r, always r
	15:33	poisoned by this anti-r loose talk
	15:34	playing fast and loose with r facts
	15:35	Show me how r works
	15:38	the r body that comes from it
	15:40	hint at the diversity of r glory

	15:41	only looking at pre-r "seeds"
	15:42	the mystery of the r body
	15:53	In the r scheme of things
2Co	5:1	they will be replaced by r bodies
	5:2	our true home, our r bodies
	5:15	a r life, a far better life
Php	3:10	experience his r power
	3:11	get in on the r from the dead
Col	1:18	leading the r parade
	2:12	coming up out of it was a r
	3:1	living this new r life with Christ
2Ti	2:18	saying the r is over and done with
Heb	6:2	r of the dead; eternal judgment
	7:16	by the sheer force of r life
	11:35	preferring something better: r
1Pe	3:21	through Jesus' r before God
Rev	20:5	This is the first r

Revenge

Lev	19:18	Don't seek r or carry a grudge
Pr	6:34	a cheated husband; wild for r
Jer	51:36	I'm your Avenger. You'll get your r
Eze	25:12	in spiteful r
Eph	4:26	don't use your anger as fuel for r

Reverence

Lev	9:24	fell down, bowing in r
	22:2	consecrate to me with r
	22:32	I insist on being treated with holy r
	25:36	out of r for your God help
	26:2	treat my Sanctuary with r. I am God
Nu	12:8	why did you show no r or respect
	20:12	didn't treat me with holy r
	27:14	didn't honor me in holy r
Dt	6:2	live in deep r before God lifelong
	10:12	Live in his presence in holy r
	13:4	God, your God, hold him in deep r
	14:23	learn to live in deep r before God
	32:6	don't you have any sense of r?
Jos	4:24	hold God in solemn r always
1Sa	24:8	David fell to his knees and bowed in r
2Sa	14:22	Joab bowed deeply in r
	14:33	bowed deeply in r before him
1Ki	1:31	Kneeling in r before the king
	18:7	fell on his knees, bowing in r
2Ki	16:12	saw the altar he approached it with r
	17:36	R and fear him. Worship him
1Ch	10:4	restrained by both r and fear
2Ch	6:31	in lifelong r and believing obedience
	29:30	sang their praises with joy and r
Job	37:24	So bow to him in deep r
Ps	119:120	leave me speechless with r
Pr	19:29	have to learn r the hard way
Isa	25:3	oppressors bow in worshipful r
	45:14	Hands folded in r, praying
Jer	44:10	trace of remorse, not a sign of r
Hos	3:5	come back chastened to r before God
Mt	27:29	knelt before him in mocking r
Mk	10:17	greeted him with great r
Jn	9:31	anyone who lives in r and does

R

Ac	9:31	a deep sense of r for God
	19:17	developed into r for the Master Jesus
	21:24	scrupulous in your r for the laws
1Co	11:13	his head bared in r, praying
Tit	2:3	Guide older women into lives of r

Revive

1Sa	30:12	Life began to r in him
Ps	23:5	You r my drooping head
	119:88	In your great love r me
	119:156	following your guidelines, r me
Zec	10:3	He'll r their spirits

Revived

Ge	45:27	their father Jacob's spirit r
Jdg	15:19	His spirit r—he was alive again
2Sa	16:14	There they rested and were r
Ac	25:3	r their old plot to set an ambush
2Co	7:13	how r and refreshed he was

Reward

Ge	15:1	Your r will be grand
	31:9	used your father's livestock to r me
Ex	5:5	now you want to r them with time off
Nu	22:17	I will honor and r you lavishly
Ru	2:12	God r you well for what you've done
1Sa	17:25	The king will give him a huge r
1Ki	9:13	What kind of r is this
2Ki	10:30	As r, your sons will occupy the throne
2Ch	6:30	forgive and r us: r each life
Ps	58:10	see the wicked get their r
	120:4	burning coals will be your r
	137:8	A r to whoever gets back at you
	137:9	a r to the one who grabs your babies
Pr	5:23	the r of an undisciplined life
	12:14	well-done work has its own r
Ecc	2:10	my r to myself for a hard day's work
Isa	40:10	r those who have loved him
	53:12	I'll r him extravagantly
Da	12:13	on your feet to receive your r
Mt	6:18	he'll r you well
	25:46	the 'sheep' to their eternal r
Jn	12:26	The Father will honor and r anyone
Jas	1:12	the r is life and more life
2Pe	1:8	no day will pass without its r
2Jn	1:8	get every r you have coming to you
Rev	2:26	the r I have for every conqueror
	11:18	to judge the dead, to r your servants

Rich

Ge	13:2	By now Abram was very r
	13:5	Abram, was also r in sheep
	14:23	I made Abram r
	31:1	make himself r at our father's expense
	49:20	Asher will become famous for r foods
Ex	30:15	The r are not to pay more
Lev	25:47	resident among you becomes r
Dt	8:17	I'm r. It's all mine

Jos	22:8	You're going home r—great herds
Ru	2:1	a man prominent and r
2Sa	12:2	The r man had huge flocks of sheep
	12:4	traveler dropped in on the r man
2Ch	17:5	Jehoshaphat ended up very r
	18:1	even though Jehoshaphat was very r
	32:29	saw to it that he was extravagantly r
Job	20:15	They gag on all that r food
	21:7	live to a ripe old age and get r
	24:6	sort through the garbage of the r
	34:19	Does he play favorites with the r
Ps	45:12	r guests shower you with presents
	49:6	demeaned by the arrogant r
	49:16	impressed with those who get r
	72:10	kings r and resplendent will turn
	103:8	not easily angered, he's r in love
	119:72	striking it r in a gold mine
	119:162	like one who strikes it r
	123:4	Kicked . . . by complacent r men
	145:8	not quick to anger, is r in love
Pr	2:7	He's a r mine of Common Sense
	10:15	wealth of the r is their bastion
	10:21	talk of a good person is r fare
	10:22	God's blessing makes life r
	13:8	The r can be sued for everything
	13:13	honor God's commands and grow r
	15:16	a r life with a ton of headaches
	16:8	than to be wrong and r
	16:19	live it up among the r and famous
	18:11	The r think their wealth protects them
	18:23	the r bark out answers
	19:1	than a r person no one can trust
	22:1	better than striking it r
	22:2	r and the poor shake hands as equals
	22:7	poor are always ruled over by the r
	22:16	Exploit the poor or glad-hand the r
	23:4	wear yourself out trying to get r
	28:6	than r and crooked
	28:8	Get as r as you want through cheating
	28:11	The r think they know it all
	28:20	get-r-quick schemes are ripoffs
	28:22	A miser in a hurry to get r
	30:22	when a fool gets r
Ecc	5:12	a r man's belly gives him insomnia
Isa	9:3	sharing r gifts and warm greetings
	16:8	the r Sibmah vineyards withered
	34:6	the suet-r kidneys of rams
	43:3	with r Cush and Seba thrown in
	46:9	your long and r history
	53:9	threw him in a grave with a r man
	60:5	a r harvest of exiles gathered in
	60:13	r woods of Lebanon will be delivered
Jer	5:27	Pretentious and powerful and r
	9:23	Don't let the r brag of their riches
	14:3	The r people sent their servants
	17:11	the person who gets r by cheating
Eze	13:18	use living souls to make yourselves r
	27:27	Everything sinks—your r goods
	27:33	trade made earth's kings r
	34:14	the r pastures on the mountains
	34:29	I'll give them r gardens
	38:13	brought in your troops to get r quick

R

Da	5:7	what it means will be famous and **r**
	5:16	you'll be **r** and famous
Hos	12:8	Ephraim boasted, "Look, I'm **r**!
Jnh	3:5	Everyone did it — **r** and poor
	4:2	not easily angered, **r** in love
Mic	6:12	violent **r** bullying their way
	7:3	powerful **r** make sure they get
Hab	2:5	The arrogant **r** don't last
	2:6	getting **r** by stealing and extortion
Mt	19:23	for the **r** to enter God's kingdom
	19:24	than for the **r** to enter God's kingdom
Mk	10:25	for the **r** to get into God's kingdom
	12:41	the **r** were making large contributions
Lk	1:53	the callous **r** were left out
	8:8	Other seed fell in **r** earth
	12:16	The farm of a certain **r** man
	14:12	friends and family and **r** neighbors
	16:1	once a **r** man who had a manager
	16:19	There once was a **r** man
	16:21	scraps off the **r** man's table
	16:22	The **r** man also died and was buried
	16:27	The **r** man said, 'Then let me ask
	18:23	was very **r** and became terribly sad
	18:25	than get a **r** person into God's kingdom
	19:2	the head tax man and quite **r**
	21:1	saw the **r** people dropping offerings
Ro	11:17	now fed by that **r** and holy root
2Co	8:9	**R** as he was, he gave it all away
Eph	2:12	that **r** history of God's covenants
Col	1:27	know this **r** and glorious secret
1Ti	6:6	the **r** simplicity of being yourself
	6:17	Tell those **r** in this world's wealth
	6:18	to be **r** in helping others
2Ti	1:5	what a **r** faith it is
Jas	1:10	arrogant **r** are brought down to size
	5:1	**r**: Take some lessons in lament
Rev	3:17	You brag, 'I'm **r**, I've got it made
	3:18	Then you'll be **r**
	6:15	princes, generals, **r** and strong
	13:16	people, small and great, **r** and poor
	18:19	Got **r** on her getting and spending

Riches

Dt	33:19	hauled **r** in from the sea
1Ki	3:11	long life, or **r**
1Ch	29:12	**R** and glory come from you
Job	28:7	Vultures are blind to its **r**
	36:18	Don't let your great **r** mislead you
Ps	68:10	they went from rags to **r**
	73:12	they have it made, piling up **r**
	119:14	than in gathering a pile of **r**
Pr	23:5	**R** disappear in the blink of an eye
Ecc	4:14	go from rags to **r**
	9:11	Nor **r** to the smart
Isa	8:4	and the **r** of Samaria
	60:9	loaded with **r**, with silver and gold
Jer	9:23	Don't let the rich brag of their **r**
Lk	18:22	You will have **r** in heaven
Eph	3:8	**r** and generosity of Christ
1Ti	6:17	God, who piles on all the **r**

Riddle

Jdg	14:12	Let me put a **r** to you
	14:13	Put your **r**. Let's hear it
	14:16	You've told a **r** to my people
	14:19	clothing to those who had solved the **r**
Ps	49:4	I solve life's **r** with the help
Eze	17:2	make a **r** for the house of Israel
Rev	13:18	Solve a **r**: Put your heads together
	17:5	A **r**-name was branded on her forehead
	17:7	the **r** of the woman and the Beast

Ridicule

Ne	4:4	Boomerang their **r** on their heads
Ps	44:16	Gossip and **r** fill the air
	119:51	The insolent **r** me without mercy
Pr	14:9	The stupid **r** right and wrong
Jer	44:8	an object of **r** among all the nations
Eze	5:15	reduced to an object of **r**
Hos	7:16	**R** in the court of world opinion

Right-living

Nu	23:10	want to die like these **r** people
Ps	33:1	**R** people sound best when praising
Pr	4:18	The ways of **r** people glow with light
	11:11	When **r** people bless the city
Isa	26:7	The path of **r** people is level
	57:1	Meanwhile, **r** people die
	58:2	they're a nation of **r** people
Hos	14:9	**R** people walk them easily
Am	5:12	You bully **r** people
Mic	7:2	**R** humans are extinct
2Co	9:9	His **r**, right-giving ways never run out

Righteous

Ge	7:1	you're the **r** one
Dt	24:13	will be viewed as a **r** act
1Sa	12:7	all the **r** ways in which God has worked
2Ki	10:9	participants in God's **r** workings
Ezr	9:15	You are the **r** God of Israel
Ne	9:8	kept your word because you are **r**
Job	4:17	can mere mortals be more **r** than God
	22:3	So what if you were **r**
	34:17	dare condemn the **r**, mighty God
	36:7	He never takes his eyes off the **r**
Ps	37:16	One **r** will outclass fifty wicked
	37:17	the **r** are God-strong
	37:21	**R** gives and gives
	37:30	**R** chews on wisdom like a dog on a bone
	37:32	Wicked sets a watch for **R**
	45:4	Ride for the **r** meek!
	58:10	The **r** will call up their friends
	68:3	When the **r** see God in action
	69:28	honor for them among the **r**
	71:19	Your famous and **r** ways, O God
	71:24	you and your **r** ways
	75:10	arms of the **r** are lofty green branches
	85:3	you cooled your hot, **r** anger
	88:12	your **r** ways noticed in the Land

R

	118:19	the city gates — the r gates
	119:7	I learn the pattern of your r ways
	119:40	preserve my life through your r ways
	119:106	living by your r order
	119:160	Your r decisions are eternal
	122:5	Thrones for r judgment are set there
	125:3	never violate What is due the r
	140:13	the r personally thank you
Pr	3:33	he blesses the home of the r
	4:11	I'm drawing a map to R Road
	8:20	You can find me on R Road
	12:12	the roots of the r give life
	29:16	the r will eventually observe
Ecc	9:2	one fate for everybody — r and wicked
Isa	3:10	Reassure the r that their good
	24:16	All praise to the R One!
	53:11	what he experienced, my r one
	57:12	all your 'r' attempts at religion
Jer	23:5	establish a truly r David-Branch
Eze	3:20	r turn back from living righteously
	3:21	if you warn these r people not to sin
	16:52	actually made them look r
	18:21	living a just and r life
	21:3	killing both the wicked and the r
	23:45	R men will pronounce judgment
	33:14	starts living a r and just life
	33:19	starts living a just and r life
Hab	1:4	The wicked have the r hamstrung
	1:13	Evil men swallow up the r
Zep	3:5	Yet God remains r in her midst
Mt	5:32	pretending to be r
	23:35	Every drop of r blood ever spilled
Lk	11:50	every drop of r blood ever spilled
Jn	17:25	R Father, the world has never known
Ac	22:14	You've actually seen the R Innocent
	22:18	I saw him, saw God's R Innocent
Ro	2:5	God's fiery and r judgment
Gal	2:20	no longer important that I appear r
1Ti	6:11	Pursue a r life — a life of wonder
Heb	11:4	what God noticed and approved as r
1Pe	3:18	the R One for the unrighteous ones
2Pe	2:8	that r man was in constant torment
1Jn	2:1	Jesus Christ, r Jesus
	2:29	convinced that he is right and r
	3:7	see it lived out in our r Messiah
	3:10	The one who won't practice r ways
	3:12	the acts of his brother were r
Rev	15:3	R your ways and true
	16:5	R you are, and your judgments
	22:11	let the r maintain a straight course

Righteousness

Job	32:2	for pitting his r against God's
Ps	71:15	I'll write the book on your r
	72:7	Let r burst into blossom
	119:142	Your r is eternally right
	145:7	your r is on everyone's lips
Ecc	3:17	The place of r — corrupt!
Isa	5:7	He looked for a harvest of r
	5:16	By working r, Holy God will show
	10:22	brimming over with r

	11:5	build r and faithfulness in the land
	28:17	r the plumb line for the building
	54:14	built solid, grounded in r
	58:8	Your r will pave your way
	59:14	R is banished to the sidelines
	59:16	fueled by his own R
	59:17	dressed in R . . . like a suit of armor
	60:17	make R your boss
	61:3	Rename them "Oaks of R" planted by God
	61:10	he outfitted me in a robe of r
	61:11	God, brings r into full bloom
	62:1	Until her r blazes down like the sun
	62:2	Foreign countries will see your r
Eze	14:14	r would only save their own lives
	14:20	delivered because of their r
Hos	10:12	Sow r, reap love
Am	5:7	stomp r into the mud
	6:12	a bloated corpse of r
Mal	3:3	fit to present offerings of r
	4:2	The sun of r will dawn on those
Jn	16:8	godless world's view of sin, r
	16:10	that r comes from above
Eph	6:14	Truth, r
Php	3:9	some petty, inferior brand of r
2Ti	2:22	Run after mature r — faith, love
Heb	7:2	"Melchizedek" means "King of R."
Jas	1:20	God's r doesn't grow from human anger
2Pe	2:5	Noah, the sole voice of r
	3:13	earth, all landscaped with r
1Jn	2:29	who practice r are God's true children
Rev	19:8	The linen is the r of the saints
	19:11	judges and makes war in pure r

Rights

Ge	25:31	my stew for your r as the firstborn
	25:33	traded away his r as the firstborn
	25:34	shrugged off his r as the firstborn
Ex	21:10	she retains all her full r to meals
Dt	21:17	inheritance r of the real firstborn
	22:30	that would violate his father's r
	24:17	orphans get their just r
Jos	14:4	with pasture r for their flocks
Ru	3:13	wants to exercise his customary r
	4:4	You have first redeemer r
	4:6	you can have my r — I can't do it
1Ch	5:1	his r as the firstborn were passed
	5:2	the firstborn r stayed with Joseph
Job	36:6	champions the r of their victims
Ps	140:12	you care for the r of the poor
Pr	31:8	the r of all the down-and-outers
Isa	5:23	you violate the r of the innocent
Da	9:9	in our rebellion we've forfeited our r
Mt	5:31	divorce papers and her legal r
Lk	18:3	My r are being violated
1Co	7:4	stand up for your r
Jas	2:5	citizens, with full r and privileges

Risk

Dt	5:25	But why r it further
Jdg	11:25	Did he r war

R

1Sa	20:31	your future in this kingdom is at **r**
1Ch	21:3	why **r** getting Israel into trouble
Ezr	7:23	**r** stirring up his wrath
Ecc	5:6	Why **r** provoking God
La	5:9	We **r** our lives to gather food
Mt	9:21	You took a **r** of faith
	22:46	Unwilling to **r** losing face again
Mk	5:34	Daughter, you took a **r** of faith
Lk	8:48	Daughter, you took a **r** trusting me
	19:26	**R** your life and get more
Jn	6:64	weren't going to **r** themselves
Ro	14:15	Would you **r** sending them to hell
1Co	11:29	running the **r** of serious consequences
	11:34	by no means **r** turning this Meal into
2Co	4:11	at constant **r** for Jesus' sake
	11:26	at **r** in the city, at **r** in the country
Heb	2:3	**r** neglecting this latest message
Jas	4:2	**r** violence to get your hands on it

Ritual

Lev	19:22	priest will perform the **r** of atonement
	22:3	a state of **r** uncleanness
Nu	6:11	purifying you from the **r** contamination
1Sa	7:6	before God in a **r** of cleansing
1Ki	18:28	a **r** common to them
Ne	12:45	the **r** of ceremonial cleansing
Eze	45:20	Repeat this **r** on the seventh day
	46:15	offering are a regular daily **r**
Mt	12:7	a flexible heart to an inflexible **r**
Mk	7:2	careful with **r** washings before meals
	7:3	the motions of a **r** hand-washing
Jn	2:6	used by the Jews for **r** washings
Ac	14:13	ready for the **r** of sacrifice
	21:23	a vow involving **r** purification
Ro	2:25	surgical **r** that marks you as a Jew
	4:12	not just because of the **r**
Col	2:12	If it's an initiation **r** you're after
Heb	9:10	limited to matters of **r** and behavior
	9:19	in a solemn **r**, sprinkled the document

Rituals

Lev	9:22	the **r** of the Absolution-Offering
	10:6	No mourning **r** for you
	20:5	in the **r** of the god Molech
Nu	3:38	the **r** of worship
1Sa	15:22	sacrifices — empty **r** just for show
Isa	17:8	altars and monuments and **r**
	66:17	initiation in those unholy **r**
Jer	6:20	Your religious **r** mean nothing to me
Eze	24:17	none of the usual funeral **r**
	24:22	none of the usual funeral **r**
Lk	2:27	to carry out the **r** of the Law
Heb	9:13	the other **r** of purification

Rooted

Dt	32:32	who they are is **r** in Gomorrah
2Ch	27:6	strength was **r** in his steady . . . life
Job	29:19	A life deep-**r** and well-watered
Pr	12:3	life **r** in God stands firm

SS	5:15	like a cedar, strong and deep-**r**
Isa	40:24	Like seeds barely **r**, just sprouted
Col	2:7	You're deeply **r** in him
2Ti	1:13	this faith and love **r** in Christ

Roughshod

1Sa	15:24	I've trampled **r** over God's Word
Isa	41:2	so he could run **r** over kings
Eze	45:8	bully my people, running **r** over them
Am	5:11	you run **r** over the poor
1Th	4:6	Don't run **r** over the concerns of
1Ti	1:9	defy all authority, riding **r** over God

Rumor

2Sa	13:30	a **r** came to the king
2Ki	19:7	He's going to hear a **r**
Job	42:6	crusts of hearsay, crumbs of **r**
Ps	41:8	The **r** goes out, "He's got some
	112:7	Unfazed by **r** and gossip
Isa	21:7	note every whisper, every **r**
	37:7	he'll get a **r** of bad news back home
Jer	40:16	spreading a false **r** about Isahmael
Eze	7:26	one **r** after another
Jn	21:23	the **r** got out among the brothers
Gal	5:11	the **r** that I continue to preach

Rumors

Lev	19:16	Don't spread gossip and **r**
Nu	13:32	spread scary **r** among the People
	14:36	returned to circulate false **r**
	14:37	Having spread false **r** of the land
Dt	2:25	**R** of you are going to spread
Job	28:22	We've only heard **r** of it
	42:5	I once lived by **r** of you
Pr	19:9	the person who spreads **r** is ruined
Isa	59:13	Spreading false **r**, inciting sedition
Jer	33:24	**r** afoot that there's nothing to them
	51:46	Don't ever give up when the **r** pour in
Mk	3:22	**r** that he was working black magic
Ac	19:9	some of them began spreading evil **r**
	21:24	nothing to the **r** going around
1Co	4:13	When they spread **r** about us
2Co	12:20	angry words, vicious **r**
1Ti	6:4	bad-mouthing, suspicious **r**
3Jn	1:10	spreading vicious **r** about us

Runt

Jdg	6:15	I'm the **r** of the litter
1Sa	16:11	Well, yes, there's the **r**
Isa	60:22	The **r** will become a great tribe
Ob	1:2	the **r** of the godless nations
Mic	5:2	David's country, the **r** of the litter
Mt	16:8	**R** believers

Ruthless

2Sa	22:3	he saves me from **r** men
2Ch	36:17	it was a **r** massacre

R

Isa	13:17	A **r** bunch indifferent to bribes
Jer	15:21	get you out of the clutch of the **r**
Ro	11:22	gentle kindness and **r** severity
2Ti	3:4	treacherous, **r**, bloated windbags

Ruthlessly

Dt	12:2	**R** demolish all the sacred shrines
Isa	18:5	**r** hack off all the growing branches
Jer	21:7	He'll kill them **r**, showing no mercy

S

Sacrilege

2Ch	36:8	the outrageous **s** he committed
Isa	24:6	Its people pay the price of their **s**
Jer	7:10	go on with all this outrageous **s**
Da	11:31	set up in its place the obscene **s**
Am	2:7	a **s** against my Holy Name
Mt	7:6	you're only being cute and inviting **s**
Jude	1:15	every defiling act of shameless **s**

Sage

Pr	21:22	**s** entered a whole city of armed
	29:9	A **s** trying to work things out
	29:11	a **s** quietly mulls it over
Ecc	6:8	what advantage has a **s** over a fool
	7:5	get more from the rebuke of a **s**
SS	5:13	his beard smells like **s**

Sages

Ge	41:8	sent for all the magicians and **s**
Job	12:20	He forces trusted **s** to keep silence
Ps	119:100	I've become wiser than the wise old **s**
Pr	29:8	a group of **s** can calm everyone down
Ecc	7:4	**S** invest themselves in hurt
Jer	51:57	drunk . . . princes, **s**, governors
Ob	1:8	when I wipe out all **s** from Edom

Saint

Dt	33:8	and Urim belong to your loyal **s**
Job	40:8	calling me a sinner so you can be a **s**
Mt	6:16	celebrity but it won't make you a **s**
Ro	4:17	attention by living like a **s**

Saints

Ps	30:4	All you **s**! Sing your hearts out to God
	31:23	Love God, all you **s**
	50:5	Round up my **s** who swore on the Bible
Mt	23:28	People . . . think you're **s**
	23:29	marble monuments for your **s**
Rev	11:18	all prophets and **s**, Reward
	14:12	the **s** stand passionately patient
	16:6	poured out the blood of **s** and prophets
	18:20	join in, **s**, apostles, and prophets
	18:24	the blood of **s** and prophets
	19:8	the righteousness of the **s**

Salary

Ge	47:22	received a fixed **s** from Pharaoh
Pr	3:14	friendship is better than a big **s**
	8:19	more than a big **s**, even a very big **s**
Ecc	5:16	working for a **s** of smoke

Salvation

Ge	49:18	I wait in hope for your **s**, God
Ex	14:13	watch God do his work of **s** for you
	15:2	God is my **s**
Nu	13:16	Moses gave Hoshea (**S**) son of Nun
Dt	32:15	he mocked the Rock of his **s**
1Sa	2:1	I'm dancing my **s**
	14:45	this stunning **s** victory for Israel
2Sa	22:36	You protect me with **s**-armor
	22:47	Blessing to my Rock, my towering **S**-God
	23:5	My entire **s**, my every desire
2Ki	13:17	The arrow of God's **s**
1Ch	16:23	Get out his **s** news every day
2Ch	6:41	Dress your priests up in **s** clothes
Job	13:16	work out for the best — my **s**
	30:15	dignity in shreds, **s** up in smoke
Ps	9:14	we'll fill the air with **s** songs
	18:35	You protect me with **s**-armor
	50:23	I'll show you my **s**
	51:14	God, my **s** God
	65:5	All your **s** wonders are on display
	69:13	Answer with your sure **s**
	71:2	give me space for **s**
	71:3	You're my **s**
	71:15	talk up your **s** the livelong day
	74:12	he works **s** in the womb of the earth
	77:8	Has his **s** promise burned out
	80:3	blessing smile: That will be our **s**
	80:7	blessing smile: That will be our **s**
	80:19	blessing smile: That will be our **s**
	85:7	Give us the **s** we need
	85:9	See how close his **s** is
	88:2	Put me on your **s** agenda
	89:26	my God, my Rock of **S**
	91:16	give you a long drink of **s**
	98:2	God made history with **s**
	98:3	Look — God's work of **s**
	116:13	I'll lift high the cup of **s**
	118:14	he's also my song, and now he's my **s**
	118:21	you've truly become my **s**
	118:25	**S** now, God. **S** now!
	119:41	God, shape my life with **s**
	119:81	longing for your **s**
	119:155	**S**" is only gibberish to the wicked
	119:166	I wait expectantly for your **s**
	119:174	I'm homesick, God, for your **s**
	132:16	I'll dress my priests in **s** clothes
	146:3	know nothing of life, of **s** life
	149:4	festoons plain folk with **s** garlands
Isa	12:2	Yes, indeed — God is my **s**
	12:3	buckets of water from the wells of **s**
	17:10	you have forgotten God-Your-**S**
	25:9	sing the joys of his **s**
	26:1	We have a strong city, **S** City

S

	30:15	s requires you to turn back to me
	33:6	s, wisdom, and knowledge in surplus
	42:9	I'm announcing the new s work
	45:8	Loosen up, earth, and bloom s
	45:17	by you, God, saved with an eternal s
	45:24	S and strength are in God!
	46:13	S isn't on hold. I'm putting s
	49:6	my s becomes global
	51:5	my s right on time
	51:6	But my s will last forever
	51:8	my s goes on and on and on
	52:7	proclaiming good times, announcing s
	52:10	sees him at work, doing his s work
	56:1	s is just around the corner
	59:11	for s — not so much as a hint
	59:16	took on the work of S
	59:17	with S on his head like a helmet
	60:18	You'll name your main street S Way
	61:10	He dressed me up in a suit of s
	62:1	her s flames up like a torch
Jer	3:23	our true God, the s of Israel
	4:14	so you'll be fit for s
Eze	14:22	their s is right in your face
Jnh	2:9	S belongs to God
Mic	6:5	Keep all God's s stories fresh
Hab	3:3	retracing the old s route
	3:8	rode horse and chariot through to s
Mt	12:37	Words can be your s
Lk	1:69	He set the power of s in the center
	1:77	Present the offer of s to his people
	2:30	With my own eyes I've seen your s
	3:6	see The parade of God's s
	7.22	wretched of the earth have God's s
	13:24	sit down to God's s banquet
	19:9	Today is s day in this home
Jn	4:22	God's way of s is made available
Ac	4:12	S comes no other way
	8:25	spread the Message of God's s
	13:26	s has been precisely targeted
	13:47	proclaim s to the four winds
	13:49	Message of s spread like wildfire
	16:17	laying out the road of s for you
Ro	9:17	player in this drama of my s power
	9:27	s comes by personal selection
	10:1	best for Israel: s, nothing less
	10:3	s is God's business
	10:9	trusting him . . . . That's s
	13:12	s work he began when we first believed
1Co	1:18	for those on the way of s
	1:21	those who trust him into the way of s
	2:12	gifts of life and s that he is giving
	10:2	from enslaving death to s life
2Co	1:6	works out for your healing and s
	2:15	recognized by those on the way of s
	7:10	It gets us back in the way of s
Gal	3:19	keep a sinful people in the way of s
Eph	1:13	believed it (this Message of your s)
	6:17	and s are more than words
Php	2:12	Be energetic in your life of s
1Th	5:8	faith, love, and the hope of s
	5:9	but for s by our Master, Jesus Christ
2Th	2:13	included in God's original plan of s

1Ti	2:15	her childbearing brought about s
	4:16	those who hear you will experience s
2Ti	2:10	the s of Christ in all its glory
	3:15	the way to s through faith in Christ
Tit	2:11	S's available for everyone
Heb	1:14	those lined up to receive s
	2:3	latest message, this magnificent s
	2:5	in charge of this business of s
	2:10	making the S Pioneer perfect
	5:10	became the source of eternal s
	6:1	turning your back on "s by self-help"
	6:9	better things in mind for you — s things
	9:28	eager to greet him is, precisely, s
Jas	1:21	making a s-garden of your life
1Pe	1:9	looking forward to: total s
	3:19	proclaimed God's s to earlier
2Pe	3:15	patient restraint for what it is: s
Jude	1:3	this life of s that we have
Rev	7:10	S to our God on his Throne! S to
	12:10	S and power are established
	19:1	The s and glory and power are God's

Sanctify

Lev	25:10	S the fiftieth year
Jos	3:5	S yourselves. Tomorrow God will work

Sanctity

Ne	13:22	keep the s of the Sabbath day
Jer	3:9	flouting sanity and s alike

Sane

Ac	26:25	both accurate and s in what I'm saying
Ro	7:12	each command s and holy counsel
Tit	2:8	your words solid and s

Sanity

Pr	8:12	Lady Wisdom, and I live next to S
Jer	3:9	flouting s and sanctity alike

Sarcasm

Pr	29:9	gets only scorn and s for his trouble
Mk	5:40	Provoked to s, they told him
Ac	17:18	Some of them dismissed him with s
1Pe	3:9	No retaliation. No sharp-tongued s

Sarcastic

2Ki	7:19	attendant's s reply to the Holy Man
Ps	137:3	demanded songs, s and mocking

Satisfaction

2Ch	7:11	Everything was done — success! S
Job	6:10	have the s of not having blasphemed
Ps	33:5	drenched in God's affectionate s
Pr	12:14	Well-spoken words bring s
	13:25	An appetite for good brings much s

S

Ecc	9:11	Nor s to the wise
Isa	65:22	my chosen ones will have s in their work
Hos	4:10	have sex and get no s
Gal	4:15	What has happened to the s you felt

Satisfied

Ge	24:19	When he had s his thirst she said
Dt	8:10	After a meal, s, bless God
	8:12	when you eat and are s
Jos	22:30	They were s
Jdg	11:24	Why don't you just be s with what
Ru	1:13	being s to wait until they were grown
1Ki	10:13	S, she returned home
2Ki	4:13	I'm secure and s in my family
	15:20	That s the king of Assyria
2Ch	9:12	S, she returned home
Ps	119:57	Because you have s me, God
Pr	16:2	Humans are s with whatever looks good
	21:17	The pursuit of pleasure is never s
	30:15	Three things are never s
Ecc	5:10	who loves money is never s with money
SS	8:10	he knows he'll soon be s
Isa	44:16	eats his fill and sits back s
Jer	5:7	I s their deepest needs
Eze	16:28	But still you weren't s
	16:29	and still you weren't s
	27:33	you s many peoples
	34:18	Aren't you s to feed in good pasture
Lk	6:25	trouble ahead if you're s
Ro	15:14	completely s with who you are
Gal	5:20	all-consuming-yet-never-s wants

Satisfy

Job	38:39	s the appetite of her cubs
Pr	6:35	neither bribes nor reason will s him
	18:20	Words s the mind
Isa	57:5	You s your lust any place
	66:11	You newborns can s yourselves
Mt	12:39	s your lust for miracles
Lk	6:25	self will not s you for long
	11:29	s your lust for miracles
1Co	7:3	husband seeking to s his wife
	7:3	the wife seeking to s
Heb	12:16	to s a short-term appetite

Satisfying

Pr	22:4	plenty and honor and a s life
Isa	33:16	A nourishing, s way to live
Jer	31:26	what a pleasant and s sleep
Gal	5:5	a s relationship with the Spirit
2Jn	1:12	far more s to both you and me

Savage

Dt	26:6	a cruel and s slavery
Isa	56:9	A call to the s beasts
Jer	19:8	speechless by the s brutality
Joel	2:25	Locusts s, locusts deadly
2Ti	3:3	impulsively wild, s, cynical

Savior

Jdg	3:9	God raised up a s who rescued them
	3:15	God raised up for them a s
1Sa	14:39	As God lives, Israel's S God
2Ki	13:5	God provided a s for Israel
1Ch	16:35	Save us, S God
Ps	25:5	You are my S, aren't you
	68:20	He's our S, our God
	106:21	They forgot God, their very own S
	140:7	God, my Lord, Strong S, protect me
Isa	19:20	a s who will keep them safe
	43:3	God, The Holy of Israel, your S
	43:11	I, am God. I'm the only S there is
	45:15	God of Israel, S God
	60:16	I, God, am your S, your Redeemer
	62:11	Your S comes, Ready to do
	63:8	So he became their S
Da	6:27	He is a s and rescuer
Hab	3:18	cartwheels of joy to my S God
Lk	1:47	dancing the song of my S God
	2:11	A S has just been born
Jn	4:42	He's the S of the world
Ac	5:31	on high at his side, Prince and S
	13:23	God produced a S for Israel, Jesus
Php	3:20	waiting the arrival of the S
1Ti	1:1	Under God our S's command
	2:3	the way our S God wants us to live
	4:10	living God, S of all men and women
2Ti	1:10	Since the appearance of our S
Tit	1:3	Message by order of our S, God himself
	1:4	God our Father and Jesus our S
	2:10	the teaching of our S God
	2:13	when our great God and S, . . . appears
	3:4	God, our kind and loving S God
	3:6	Our S Jesus poured out new life
Heb	2:14	the S took on flesh and blood
2Pe	1:1	intervention of our God and S
	1:11	our Master and S, Jesus Christ
	2:20	our Master and S, Jesus Christ
	3:2	the command of our Master and S
	3:18	understanding of our Master and S
1Jn	4:14	sent his Son as S of the world
Jude	1:25	our one God, our only S

Scandal

Isa	32:7	inventive in sin and s
Da	6:4	old s or skeleton in Daniel's life
Hos	12:11	Gilead rampant with religious s
2Co	8:20	taking every precaution against s
Eph	5:12	It's a s when people waste their lives

Scandalized

Ac	23:4	The aides were s: "How dare you

Scandalous

1Co	5:1	s sex within your church family

S

Scare

2Ch	32:18	trying to **s** them into . . . submission
Ne	6:13	He had been hired to **s** me off
Job	7:14	You come and so **s** me with nightmares
Da	4:19	the dream and its interpretation **s** you
Hos	5:8	S the daylights out of Benjamin
Mt	7:10	do you **s** him with a live snake
Lk	11:11	do you **s** him with a live snake

Scared

Ge	15:11	Abram **s** them off
	32:7	Jacob was **s**. Very **s**. Panicked
Ex	15:14	When people heard, they were **s**
Lev	26:17	You'll run **s** even when there's no one
1Sa	5:11	everyone was **s** to death when the Chest
	13:7	soldiers still with him but **s** to death
	28:5	he shook in his boots, **s** to death
Job	4:14	I was **s** to death — I shook from head
	23:15	I get **s** all over again
Ps	77:16	Deep Ocean was **s** to death
	105:38	they were **s** to death of them
Jer	46:5	They're **s** out of their wits!
Da	4:5	I had a dream that **s** me
	5:6	**s** out of his wits
Hos	11:11	from Assyria like **s** doves
Mt	8:33	S to death, the swineherds bolted
	14:26	They were **s** out of their wits
	17:6	fell flat on their faces, **s** to death
	27:54	were **s** to death
	28:4	guards at the tomb were **s** to death
Mk	5:14	Those tending the pigs, **s** to death
	6:49	screamed, **s** out of their wits
Lk	8:34	Those tending the pigs, **s** to death
	8:37	and they were **s**
	24:37	were **s** half to death
Jn	6:19	They were **s** senseless
	19:8	he became even more **s**
1Co	2:3	I was **s** to death
2Ti	4:16	They all ran like **s** rabbits
Heb	2:15	cower through life, **s** to death of death
Rev	11:11	gloating spectators will be **s** to death

Scheme

Est	9:25	the evil **s** that Haman had worked out
Ps	52:2	You **s** catastrophe
Da	8:25	plot and **s** to make crime flourish
Zec	7:10	Don't plot and **s** against one another
1Co	15:53	In the resurrection **s** of things

Schemed

2Sa	21:5	who **s** to wipe us off the map
Est	9:24	had **s** to destroy all Jews

Schemer

Pr	12:20	Evil scheming distorts the **s**

Schemers

Pr	12:2	wants nothing to do with devious **s**

Schemes

Job	5:12	He aborts the **s** of conniving crooks
Ps	21:11	All their evil **s** . . . have fizzled
	33:10	shoots down the world's power-**s**
Pr	28:20	get-rich-quick **s** are ripoffs
Jer	2:8	empty god-dreams and silly god-**s**
	2:11	empty god-dreams and silly god-**s**
	9:4	Brother **s** against brother
La	3:60	you saw their mean-minded **s**
Am	5:22	sick of your fund-raising **s**
Ac	13:10	inventing **s** to cheat people out of God

Scheming

Dt	31:21	what they are already **s** to do
Ne	6:2	I knew they were **s** to hurt me
Ps	141:9	Protect me from their evil **s**
Pr	12:20	Evil **s** distorts the schemer
	15:26	God can't stand evil **s**
Ecc	7:26	full of seductive **s** and grasping
Jer	9:8	while **s** to do away with him
	11:18	opened my eyes to their evil **s**
Hos	7:15	how am I repaid? With evil **s**
Mic	6:11	tolerate shady deals and shifty **s**
Na	1:9	He's putting an end to all such **s**
Ac	20:19	putting up with no end of **s**

Scholar

Ezr	7:6	a **s** well-practiced in the Revelation
	7:11	Ezra, priest and **s**, expert
	7:12	Ezra the priest, a **s** of the Teaching
	7:21	Ezra the priest, **s** of the Teaching
Ne	8:1	asked the **s** Ezra to bring the Book
	8:4	The **s** Ezra stood on a wooden platform
	8:9	along with Ezra the priest and **s**
	8:13	gathered around Ezra the **s**
	12:26	and of Ezra the priest and **s**
	12:36	Ezra the **s** led them
Mt	8:19	religion **s** asked if he could go along
Mk	12:32	religion **s** said, "A wonderful answer
Lk	10:25	a religion **s** stood up with a question
	10:37	kindly," the religion **s** responded

Scholars

Mt	2:1	a band of **s** arrived in Jerusalem
	2:4	high priests and religion **s**
	2:7	secret meeting with the **s**
	2:13	After the **s** were gone
	2:16	realized that the **s** had tricked him
	9:3	Some religion **s** whispered
	12:38	religion **s** and Pharisees got on him
	15:1	religion **s** came to Jesus
	17:10	Why do the religion **s** say that Elijah
	20:18	betrayed to the religious . . . **s**

S

	22:35	One of their religion s spoke for them
	23:2	religion s and Pharisees are competent
	23:13	You're hopeless, you religion s
	23:15	You're hopeless, you religion s
	23:23	You're hopeless, you religion s
	23:25	You're hopeless, you religion s
	23:27	You're hopeless, you religion s
	23:29	You're hopeless, you religion s
	23:34	prophets and wise guides and s
	26:57	religion s and leaders had assembled
	27:41	along with the religion s and leaders
Mk	1:22	quoting like the religion s
	2:6	Some religion s . . . started whispering
	2:16	The religion s and Pharisees saw him
	3:22	The religion s from Jerusalem came
	7:1	with some religion s who had come
	7:5	The Pharisees and religion s asked
	8:31	priests, and religion s, be killed
	9:11	Why do the religion s say that Elijah
	9:14	religion s cross-examining them
	10:33	betrayed to the religious . . . s
	11:18	high priests and religion s heard
	11:27	religion s, and leaders came up
	12:28	One of the religion s came up
	12:35	religion s say that the Messiah is
	12:38	Watch out for the religion s
	14:1	religion s were looking for a way
	14:43	sent by the high priests, religion s
	14:53	religious leaders, and s had gathered
	15:1	with the religious leaders and s
	15:31	priests, along with the religion s
Lk	5:21	set the religion s . . . buzzing
	5:30	religion s came to his disciples
	6:7	religion s . . . had their eye on Jesus
	9:22	priests, and religion s, be killed
	11:45	One of the religion s spoke up
	11:46	You're hopeless, you religion s
	11:52	You're hopeless, you religion s
	11:53	religion s . . . went into a rage
	14:3	So Jesus asked the religion s
	15:2	religion s were not pleased
	19:47	religion s, and the leaders
	20:1	religion s, and leaders confronted
	20:19	religion s . . . wanted to lynch him
	20:39	Some of the religion s said
	20:46	Watch out for the religion s
	22:2	religion s were looking for a way
	22:66	high priests and s all got together
	23:10	religion s were right there
Jn	8:3	religion s . . . led in a woman
Ac	4:5	religious leaders, religion s
	6:12	religious leaders, and religion s
	23:9	religion s on the Pharisee side

Scorn

1Sa	2:30	those who s me I demean
2Sa	6:16	- her heart filled with s
Job	12:5	to pour s on the strugglers
	24:13	who s the light-filled path
Ps	4:2	how long do I put up with your s
	10:13	why the wicked s God and get away

	107:40	he heaped s on princes and sent them
Pr	29:9	only s and sarcasm for his trouble
Isa	30:12	Because you s this Message
Jas	2:7	ones who s the new name — "Christian"
Rev	2:24	s this playing around with the Devil

Scoundrel

| Ps | 89:22 | no s will do him in |
| Lk | 6:26 | many s preachers were approved |

Scoundrels

Job	30:10	How dare those s — they spit
	34:18	rulers as s and criminals
2Th	3:2	we'll be rescued from these s
Jude	1:4	beneath . . . are shameless s

Scrawny

Ge	41:27	the seven s ears of grain dried out
1Sa	17:28	tending that s flock of sheep
Isa	53:2	grew up before God — a s seedling

Scream

| Jer | 47:2 | Men and women will s in terror |
| Mic | 4:10 | twist and s, Daughter Jerusalem |

Screamed

Ge	39:18	When I yelled and s, he left his coat
Dt	9:7	You've kicked and s against God
Mt	8:29	Seeing Jesus, the madmen s out
Mk	6:49	thought it was a ghost and s
Lk	4:33	a man demonically disturbed. He s
	8:28	When he saw Jesus he s

Screaming

Ge	39:15	With all my yelling and s, he left
Job	6:3	I'm s like a caged cat
Isa	19:16	like hysterical schoolgirls, s
	26:17	s her pain as the baby is being born
Zep	1:14	even strong men s for help
Mk	5:5	s out and slashing himself
	9:26	S, and with much thrashing about
Lk	4:41	Demons left in droves, s, "Son of God
	9:39	he's s, thrown into convulsions

Screams

| Jer | 4:31 | the s of a mother giving birth |

Scriptural

| 1Co | 9:8 | This is all written in the s law |

Scripture

| Ps | 1:2 | you chew on S day and night |
| Mt | 5:31 | Remember the S that says |

S

	9:13	Go figure out what this S means
	12:7	had any idea what this S meant
	26:31	S that says, I'll strike the shepherd
Mk	9:12	who will, according to S, suffer
	12:10	Read it for yourselves in S
	14:27	S that says, I will strike
Lk	1:1	the wonderful harvest of S
	4:21	You've just heard S make history
	19:46	It's written in S, My house is
	22:37	What was written in S
Jn	2:17	when his disciples remembered the S
	2:22	believed both what was written in S
	6:32	The real significance of that S
	7:38	this way, just as the S says
	10:35	and S doesn't lie
	12:14	just as the S has it
	13:18	the fulfillment of this S
	17:12	exception that proved the rule of S
	19:24	confirmed the S that said
	19:28	so that the S record might also be
	19:36	things that happened confirmed the S
	19:37	other S that reads, "They will stare
	20:9	No one yet knew from the S that
Ac	1:16	That S had to be fulfilled
	4:13	laymen with no training in S
	23:5	S does say, 'Don't speak abusively
Ro	1:17	confirming what S has said all along
	2:24	The line from S, "It's because of you
	3:4	S says the same: Your words stand fast
	3:9	S leaves no doubt
	4:3	What we read in S Is
	4:17	what we've always read in S
	8:35	not even the worst sins listed in S
	10:11	S reassures us
	10:15	That's why S exclaims
	14:11	Read it for yourself in S
	15:3	is the way S puts it
	15:4	it was written in S long ago
1Co	2:9	That's why we have this S text
	3:19	It's written in S, He exposes
	6:16	As written in S, "The two become one
	14:21	It's written in S that God said
	15:3	died for our sins, exactly as S tells
	15:4	third day, again exactly as S says
	15:27	When S says that "he walked all over
	15:45	We follow this sequence in S
2Co	13:1	Remember the S that says
Gal	3:8	all laid out beforehand in S
	3:10	S backs this up: "Utterly cursed
	3:12	a fact observed in S
	3:13	remember the S that says, "Cursed
	3:16	S, in the careful language of a legal
	4:30	a S that tells us what to do
1Ti	4:13	Stay at your post reading S
	5:18	S tells us, "Don't muzzle a working ox
2Ti	3:16	Every part of S is God-breathed
Heb	2:6	It says in S, What is man and woman
	7:8	a priest who, the S says, "lives
Jas	2:23	meaning of "believe" in the S sentence
2Pe	1:20	no prophecy of S is . . . opinion

Scriptures

Isa	8:20	we're going to study the S
Da	9:2	I, Daniel, was meditating on the S
Mt	5:17	I have come to demolish the S
	26:24	treachery well-marked by the S
	26:54	how would the S come true
Mk	14:21	treachery well-marked by the S
Lk	24:27	everything in the S that referred
	24:32	as he opened up the S for us
Jn	5:39	These S are all about me
	6:31	It says so in the S
	7:42	S tell us that the Messiah comes
	10:34	only quoting your inspired S
	12:16	fulfillment of many S at the time
	15:25	verified the truth of their own S
	19:24	The soldiers validated the S
Ac	13:15	the reading of the S—God's Law
	17:2	running he preached to them from the S
	17:11	examining the S to see if they
	18:24	powerful in his preaching of the S
	18:28	convincing proof from the S
	24:14	embrace everything . . . in all our S
Ro	3:2	God's revelation, these Holy S
	3:19	whatever is written in these S
	12:20	Our S tell us that if you see
	15:9	all the S that will come true
	16:26	open book through the prophetic S
2Ti	3:15	you took in the sacred S with
Jas	2:8	complete the Royal Rule of the S
1Pe	2:6	The S provide precedent
2Pe	3:16	They do it to the rest of the S
Jude	1:4	our S warned us this would happen

Secluded

1Sa	23:15	the wilderness of Ziph, s at Horesh
Mt	6:6	Find a quiet, s place
Mk	1:35	went out to a s spot and prayed
Jn	11:54	s himself there with his disciples

Seclusion

2Sa	20:3	placed them in s, under guard
SS	2:14	leave your s, come out in the open
	4:8	Abandon your wilderness s
Isa	26:20	Go into s for a while

Secrecy

2Ki	11:4	swore them to s
Mt	16:20	He swore the disciples to s
	17:9	Jesus swore them to s
Mk	9:9	Jesus swore them to s

Secret

Ge	47:18	it's no s to you that we're broke
Dt	13:6	friend, comes to you in s and whispers
	27:15	sets it up in s
	27:24	anyone who kills his neighbor in s
	28:57	she plans to eat them in s

S

Jdg	16:6	the **s** of your great strength
	16:9	The **s** of his strength was still a **s**
	16:15	tell me the **s** of your great strength
	16:18	he had told her his **s**
1Sa	21:2	This is top **s**
2Sa	12:12	You did your deed in **s**
	22:16	The **s** sources of ocean were exposed
Est	2:20	her family background and race a **s**
Job	4:12	A word came to me in **s**
Ps	18:15	The **s** sources of ocean are exposed
	40:10	didn't keep the news . . . a **s**
	86:12	never kept **s** what you're up to
Pr	11:13	gossip can't be trusted with a **s**
SS	4:12	you're a **s** garden
Isa	45:3	treasures, **s** caches of valuables
Jer	38:16	swore . . . but in **s**
Da	12:4	Keep it **s**
Mt	2:7	Herod then arranged a **s** meeting
	5:14	God is not a **s** to be kept
	16:17	in on this **s** of who I really am
Lk	11:39	maggoty with greed and **s** evil
Jn	18:20	I've said nothing in **s**
Ac	6:11	in **s** they bribed men to lie
	8:19	Sell me your **s**! Show me how
	19:18	a clean break with their **s** sorceries
Ro	16:25	the mystery kept **s** for so long
Eph	3:9	has been doing in **s**
Col	1:27	to know this rich and glorious **s**
	2:4	other so-called mysteries, or "the **S**
Rev	2:17	your new name, your **s** new name

Secretive

Col	2:11	not through some **s** initiation rite

Secretly

Lev	19:17	Don't **s** hate your neighbor
Jos	2:1	**s** sent out . . . two men as spies
Jdg	9:31	**S** he sent messengers to Abimelech
Ne	6:10	Then I met **s** with Shemaiah
Ps	64:5	keep lists of the traps they've **s** set
Pr	10:18	Liars **s** hoard hatred
Eze	20:32	What you're **s** thinking is never
Jn	19:38	he was a disciple of Jesus, but **s**
Ac	5:2	**s** kept part of the price for himself
	5:3	**s** keep back part of the price
	24:26	he was **s** hoping that Paul would offer
2Th	2:7	It is, **s** and underground

Secrets

Job	28:11	bring earth's **s** to light
Pr	15:11	Even hell holds no **s** from God
	20:19	Gossips can't keep **s**
Isa	48:16	I've never kept **s** from you
Da	2:22	He opens up the depths, tells **s**
Mk	4:22	We're not keeping **s**, we're telling
Lk	8:17	We're not keeping **s**; we're telling
1Co	4:1	guides into God's most sublime **s**

Secure

Ex	28:28	it rests **s** on the decorated band
	39:21	it rested **s** on the decorated band
Lev	25:18	observe my laws and you will live **s**
	25:19	will live safe and **s**
	26:5	will live safe and **s**
Nu	24:21	Your home is in a nice **s** place
	32:17	our families . . . **s** in fortified towns
	32:22	when the land is **s** you will have
	32:29	then after the land is **s**
Jdg	5:17	safe and **s** in his harbors
1Sa	2:35	I'll make his position **s**
	6:8	**S** the gold replicas
1Ki	15:4	follow him and keep Jerusalem **s**
2Ki	4:13	I'm **s** and satisfied in my family
2Ch	11:12	Judah and Benjamin were **s**
Ezr	8:20	weigh them out in a **s** place
Ps	23:4	shepherd's crook makes me feel **s**
	27:5	only quiet, **s** place in a noisy world
	55:18	**s** in the middle of danger
	140:13	good people are **s** in your presence
	147:13	He made your city **s**
Isa	22:23	He'll **s** the Davidic tradition
	33:6	God keeps your days stable and **s**
	58:8	God of glory will **s** your passage
Jer	21:13	got it made, all snug and **s**
	23:6	In his time Judah will be **s** again
	30:10	find life good, safe and **s**
	33:16	when Judah will be **s**
	46:27	for Jacob, safe and **s**
	48:18	He'll wreck your safe, **s** houses
Eze	37:26	I'll make them **s**
	38:8	now live safe and **s**
	39:6	where people are so seemingly **s**
Na	3.8	walled in by the River, **s**
Zec	6:8	sense of my Spirit, serene and **s**
Mt	27:65	Go ahead and **s** it the best you can

Secured

Jdg	3:28	**s** the fords of the Jordan against
2Sa	7:16	and your kingdom are permanently **s**
1Ki	8:21	I've **s** a place for the Chest
2Ch	6:11	and have **s** a place for the Chest
	12:1	By the time Rehoboam had **s** his kingdom
	17:5	God **s** the kingdom under his rule
	21:4	and had **s** his position
Pr	24:14	Get that and your future's **s**
Isa	22:9	You **s** the water supply
Mt	25:25	good hiding place and **s** your money
	27:66	So they went out and **s** the tomb

Securely

Dt	33:28	Israel lived **s**
1Ki	2:46	kingdom was now **s** in Solomon's grasp
2Ki	25:7	**S** handcuffed, he was hauled off
Jer	52:11	**S** handcuffed, Zedekiah was hauled
Eze	38:14	my people Israel are established **s**
	39:26	when they lived **s** in their own land
Mk	15:1	After tying Jesus **s**, they took him out

S

Security

Ex	22:26	If you take your neighbor's coat as **s**
Nu	1:53	responsible for the **s** of The Dwelling
Dt	24:17	cloak of a widow as **s** for a loan
1Ki	7:21	pillar to the south he named **S**
2Ki	11:4	bodyguards and the Palace **S** Force
	11:19	the bodyguard and the palace **s**
	20:19	I'll enjoy peace and **s**
1Ch	9:17	The **s** guards were Shallum
	9:18	**s** guard at the King's Gate
	9:20	in charge of the **s** guards
	9:21	was the **s** guard at the entrance
	9:22	chosen to be **s** guards
	9:24	the main **s** guards were posted
	9:25	four main **s** guards were responsible
	9:26	responsible for the **s** of all supplies
	15:18	as **s** guards
	16:38	in charge of the **s** guards
	16:42	sons of Jeduthun formed the **s** guard
	23:5	4,000 are **s** guards
	26:1	**s** guards were from the family of Korah
	26:12	teams of **s** guards, supervised
	26:19	teams of **s** guards from
2Ch	3:17	right pillar he named Jakin (**S**)
	8:14	assigned **s** guards to be on duty
	23:4	posted as **s** guards at the gates
	23:19	**s** guards at the gates of God's Temple
	31:14	**s** guard of the East Gate
	34:9	money collected by the . . . **s** guards
	34:13	accountants, managers, and **s** guards
	35:15	**s** guards were on duty at each gate
Ezr	2:42	**S** guard families: Shallum, Ater
	2:70	**s** guards, and temple support staff
	7:7	temple **s** guards, and temple slaves
	7:24	temple **s** guard, temple servant
	10:24	From the temple **s** guards
Ne	7:1	installed the doors, and the **s** guards
	7:45	**S** guard families: Shallum, Ater
	7:73	priests, Levites, **s** guards, singers
	10:28	priests, Levites, **s** guards, singers
	10:39	priests who serve, the **s** guards
	11:19	From the **s** guards: Akkub, Talmon
	12:25	The **s** guards included
	12:45	along with the singers and **s** guards
	12:47	allowances for the . . . **s** guards
	13:5	oil for the . . . **s** guards
Job	12:6	Crooks reside safely in high-**s** houses
	24:23	They may have an illusion of **s**
Hos	3:4	stripped of **s** and protection
Ac	16:24	threw them into the maximum **s** cell
1Co	4:1	not **s** guards posted to protect them

Seduce

Ge	39:14	he's trying to **s** us
Jdg	16:5	approached her and said, "**S** him
1Ki	11:2	**s** you into infatuations with their
	11:3	they did **s** him away from God
	22:20	How can we **s** Ahab into attacking'
	22:21	and said, 'I'll **s** him.'
	22:22	said God. 'On your way — **s** him

2Ch	18:19	How can we **s** Ahab into attacking
	18:20	and said, "I'll **s** him."
	18:21	said God; "On your way — **s** him
Ps	24:4	Men who won't cheat, women who won't **s**
Pr	7:10	dressed to **s** him
Jer	4:30	You're not going to **s** anyone
Eze	18:6	doesn't **s** a neighbor's spouse
	18:15	doesn't **s** his neighbor's spouse
Na	1:11	think tank for lies that **s** and betray
Zep	3:13	won't use words to flatter or **s**
Ac	20:30	twisting words so as to **s** disciples
Ro	7:8	was used to **s** me

Seduced

Ge	3:13	"The serpent **s** me," she said
Nu	25:18	your enemies when they **s** you
	31:16	**s** the People of Israel away from God
Dt	4:19	be **s** into worshiping and serving them
	11:16	be vigilant, lest you be **s** away
Jdg	8:27	his family, too, were **s** by it
1Ch	21:1	**s** David into taking a census of Israel
Job	31:9	If I've let myself be **s** by a woman
	31:27	That I let myself become **s** by them
2Co	11:3	exactly as the Snake **s** Eve

Seduces

Ex	22:16	If a man **s** a virgin who is not engaged
Nu	15:39	that **s** you into infidelities
Eze	18:11	**s** his neighbor's spouse

Seducing

2Ch	21:11	away from God, **s** the whole country
Jer	29:31	He is **s** you into believing lies
Ac	18:13	man is **s** people into acts of worship
Jas	1:14	leering, **s** flare-up of our own lust
2Pe	2:14	**s** every vulnerable soul they come upon
Rev	2:14	an enemy agent, **s** Balak

Seduction

Na	3:4	Witch of **S**, luring nations
2Pe	2:18	most susceptible to their brand of **s**

Seductive

1Ki	22:23	your puppet prophets with **s** lies
2Ch	18:22	your puppet prophets with **s** lies
Pr	5:3	The lips of a **s** woman
	6:24	from the **s** talk of some temptress
Ecc	7:26	full of **s** scheming and grasping
Isa	3:24	Instead of wearing **s** scents
Da	11:32	corrupting them . . . with his **s** talk
Na	3:4	Whore City, Fatally **s**
	3:5	I'll strip you of your **s** silk robes

Sermon

Pr	24:32	the fields preached me a **s**
Jer	19:14	where God had sent him to preach the **s**

	20:1	heard Jeremiah preach this **s**
	23:17	'Everything Will Turn Out Fine' **s**
	23:31	then pretend it's a real **s**
	26:8	When Jeremiah had finished his **s**
	26:18	preached to the people of Judah this **s**
	26:19	kill Micah . . . because of that **s**
	26:21	heard his **s**, they determined to kill
Mt	1:22	prophet's embryonic **s** to full term
	2:17	when Jeremiah's **s** was fulfilled
	4:14	This move completed Isaiah's **s**
	4:17	This Isaiah-prophesied **s** came to life
	8:17	He fulfilled Isaiah's well-known **s**
Ac	13:40	don't want the prophet's **s** to describe

Sermons

Dt	1:1	These are the **s** Moses preached
2Ch	24:27	the many **s** preached to Joash
	33:18	**s** the prophets personally delivered
Isa	36:15	Hezekiah's pious **s** telling you
Jer	11:19	That will stop the **s**!
	14:14	The **s** they've been handing out
	23:16	Don't listen to the **s** of the prophets
	23:30	who get all their **s** secondhand
	37:19	all those **s** saying that the king
La	2:14	Their **s** were all wishful thinking
Eze	13:6	illusions and preach lying **s**
	13:7	Aren't your **s** tissues of lies
	13:8	use **s** to tell lies
Mic	2:11	I'll preach **s** that will tell you
Zec	7:12	Spirit-filled **s** preached by

Serpent

Ge	3:1	The **s** was clever
	3:2	The Woman said to the **s**, "Not at all
	3:4	The **s** told the Woman, "You won't die
	3:13	"The **s** seduced me," she said
	3:14	God told the **s**: "Because you've done
	49:17	a lethal **s** in ambush by the road
2Ki	18:4	pulverized the ancient bronze **s**
Job	26:13	with one finger he crushes the sea **s**
Isa	11:8	stick his hand down the hole of a **s**
	27:1	the **s** Leviathan as it flees, the **s**
Jn	3:14	Moses lifted the **s** in the desert
Rev	12:9	The great Dragon — ancient **S**
	12:14	safe and sound from the **S**
	12:15	The **S** vomited a river of water

Sex

Ex	1:16	look at the **s** of the baby
	22:19	Anyone who has **s** with an animal
	34:15	take up with their **s**-and-religion life
Lev	18:6	Don't have **s** with a close relative
	18:7	having **s** with your mother
	18:8	Don't have **s** with your father's wife
	18:9	Don't have **s** with your sister
	18:10	Don't have **s** with your son's daughter
	18:11	Don't have **s** with the daughter
	18:12	Don't have **s** with your father's sister
	18:13	Don't have **s** with your mother's sister

	18:14	by having **s** with his wife
	18:15	Don't have **s** with your daughter-in-law
	18:16	Don't have **s** with your brother's wife
	18:17	Don't have **s** with both a woman and
	18:18	have **s** with her while your wife is
	18:19	Don't have **s** with a woman during
	18:20	Don't have **s** with your neighbor's wife
	18:22	Don't have **s** with a man as one does
	18:23	Don't have **s** with an animal
	19:20	If a man has **s** with a slave girl
	19:29	a brothel, filled with sordid **s**
	20:11	If a man has **s** with his father's wife
	20:12	man has **s** with his daughter-in-law
	20:13	If a man has **s** with a man as one does
	20:15	If a man has **s** with an animal
	20:16	If a woman has **s** with an animal
	20:17	father or mother, and they have **s**
	20:18	during her period and has **s** with her
	20:19	Don't have **s** with your aunt
	20:20	If a man has **s** with his aunt
	26:30	smash your **s**-and-religion shrines
Nu	25:1	began to have **s** with the Moabite women
	25:2	to their **s**-and-religion worship
Dt	7:5	chop down their **s**-and-religion Asherah
	12:3	Burn their **s**-and-religion Asherah
	16:22	Don't set up phallic **s** pillars
	27:20	who has **s** with his father's wife
	27:21	who has **s** with an animal
	27:22	who has **s** with his sister
	27:23	who has **s** with his mother-in-law
Jdg	19:22	We want to have **s** with him
1Sa	21:5	My men abstain from **s**
1Ki	1:4	king did not have **s** with her
	13:32	against all the **s**-and-religion shrines
	14:15	Asherah **s**-and-religion shrines
	14:23	built Asherah **s**-and-religion shrines
	15:14	the local **s**-and-religion shrines
	22:43	neighborhood **s**-and-religion shrines
2Ki	13:6	including the **s**-and-religion shrines
	14:4	local **s**-and-religion shrines continued
	15:4	the local **s**-and-religion shrines
	15:35	neighborhood **s**-and-religion shrines
	16:4	neighborhood **s**-and-religion shrines
	17:9	built local **s**-and-religion shrines
	17:10	set up their **s**-and-religion symbols
	17:16	frequented the **s**-and-religion shrines
	17:29	neighborhood **s**-and-religion shrines
	18:4	the **s**-and-religion Asherah groves
	21:3	rebuilt all the **s**-and-religion shrines
	21:7	image of the **s** goddess Asherah
	23:5	the local **s**-and-religion shrines
	23:8	smashed the **s**-and-religion shrines
	23:9	**s**-and-religion priests did not defile
	23:13	all the **s**-and-religion shrines
	23:19	neighborhood **s**-and-religion shrines
2Ch	14:3	chopped down the **s**-and-religion groves
	15:16	image of the **s** goddess Asherah
	15:17	the local **s**-and-religion shrines
	17:6	the local **s**-and-religion shrines
	19:3	the polluting **s**-and-religion shrines
	20:33	neighborhood **s**-and-religion shrines
	24:18	took up with the cult of **s** goddesses

S

	28:4	neighborhood s-and-religion shrines
	33:3	rebuilt the s-and-religion shrines
	33:7	image of the s goddess Asherah
	33:19	the s-goddess Asherah sites
	34:3	neighborhood of s-and-religion shrines
Job	15:35	have s with sin and give birth to evil
Ps	7:14	s with sin, he's pregnant with evil
Pr	6:29	s with your neighbor's wife
	30:20	she has s with her client
Isa	27:9	all the s-and-religion shrines
	57:6	set up your s-and-religion shrines
	57:7	your foul s-and-death religion
Jer	2:20	Visiting every s-and-religion shrine
	2:23	never chased after the Baal s gods
	2:24	wind for the slightest scent of s
	3:2	Where have you not had s?
	3:9	She took up cheap s-and-religion
	3:13	into the s-and-religion groves
	5:7	left me for orgies in s shrines
	7:9	have s with the neighborhood wives
	11:13	that impotent s god Baal
	17:2	s-and-religion altars and sacred s
	23:14	s-driven, living a lie
	29:23	s predators and prophet-impostors
Eze	6:13	ruined s-and-religion shrines
	8:3	image of the s goddess
	8:5	altar of the s goddess, Asherah
	16:24	exposed your sluttish s
	16:26	seeking them out in their s orgies
	16:34	regular whores who get paid for s
	16:36	flaunting your s
	16:39	your bold brothels and s shrines
	18:6	doesn't indulge in casual s
	20:28	a hill with a s-and-religion shrine
	22:9	flocking to the hills to the s shrines
	22:11	S is now anarchy
	23:18	She exhibited her s to the world
	23:27	put a stop to your sluttish s
	23:35	pay for your sluttish s
	23:43	She's burned out on s
	23:48	put an end to sluttish s
	23:49	pay the price for all your obsessive s
	24:13	Your encrusted filth is your filthy s
	33:26	you indulge in s at random
Hos	2:13	all the promiscuous s that went
	4:2	theft and loose s, sheer anarchy
	4:10	have s and get no satisfaction
	4:12	Drunk on s, they can't find their way
	4:15	Don't go to the s shrine at Gilgal
	4:18	it's s, s, and more s
	4:19	s-worship leaves them finally impotent
	5:3	played your s-and-religion games
	7:14	their s-and-religion orgies
	9:1	at every s-and-religion party
	11:2	worshiped the popular s gods
	13:1	in the lewd s-worship of Baal
Am	7:9	Isaaac's s-and-religion shrines
	8:14	oaths at the Samaria Sin-and-S Center
Mic	1:5	all the s-and-religion shrines
	5:14	your sacred s-and-power centers
Zep	1:4	s-and-religion Baal shrines
Lk	18:20	No illicit s, no killing

Jn	1:13	not flesh-begotten, not s-begotten
Ac	7:43	shrines to war gods, to s goddesses
	15:20	guard the morality of s and marriage
	15:29	guard the morality of s and marriage
	21:25	guard the morality of s and marriage
1Co	5:1	scandalous s within your church
	6:9	use and abuse s
	6:13	indulging it with s
	6:16	more to s than mere skin on skin. S is
	6:17	kind of s that avoids commitment
	7:5	Abstaining from s is permissible
Gal	5:19	repetitive, loveless, cheap s
1Ti	1:10	s, truth, whatever
Jude	1:8	dirty s, rule and rulers thrown out
Rev	2:22	play their s-and-religion games
	21:8	s peddlers and sorcerers

Sexual

Jdg	21:11	has had s intercourse you must kill
	21:12	never had s intercourse with a man
Job	24:15	S predators can't wait for nightfall
	36:14	Living it up in s excesses
Eze	23:21	longed for the s prowess of her youth
Hab	2:15	roping them into your s orgies
Mt	5:32	made herself by that by s promiscuity
Ro	9:8	never . . . determined by s transmission
1Co	6:18	s sins are different from all others
	7:1	Is it a good thing to have s relations
	7:2	S drives are strong, but marriage
2Co	12:21	pigsty of evil, s disorder
Eph	4:19	let themselves go in s obsession
	5:3	downhill slide into s promiscuity
Col	3:5	s promiscuity, impurity, lust
1Th	4:3	Keep yourselves from s promiscuity
Heb	13:4	s intimacy between wife and husband
2Pe	2:7	out of his mind by the s filth
Jude	1:7	went to s rack and ruin

Sexually

Ro	1:27	S confused, they abused and defiled
1Co	5:9	at home among the s promiscuous
	7:9	preferable by far to a s tortured life
	10:8	We must not be s promiscuous

Shame

Ge	2:25	naked, but they felt no s
Ezr	9:7	to looting, and to public s
Ps	44:15	my nose rubbed in my s
	109:29	accusers in clothes dirty with s
Pr	18:3	wickedness arrives, s's not far behind
Isa	1:4	S! Misguided God-dropouts
	16:7	What a s! How terrible!
	23:4	Hang your head in s, Sidon
	26:11	your people. S them.
	29:22	No longer . . . hang his head in s
	44:11	hide their faces in s
Jer	6:15	No, they have no s
	8:12	They have no s
	13:26	expose and s you

S

	50:2	god-Bel hanging his head in **s**
La	1:8	she groans and turns away in **s**
Eze	16:54	going to have to live with your **s**
	16:54	by facing and accepting your **s**
	16:58	have to face it, to accept the **s**
	16:63	your past life and face the **s** of it
	23:10	Among women her name became S
	32:24	They carry their **s** with them
	32:25	they carry their **s** down
	32:26	they carry their **s** down
	32:30	who carry their **s** to their graves
	36:31	your terrible lives — the evil, the **s**
	36:32	S on you. What a mess you made
	39:26	memory of their **s** over their betrayals
	44:13	carry the **s** of their vile
Da	9:7	show for our lives is guilt and **s**
	9:8	we've been exposed in our **s**
	12:2	others to eternal **s**
Hos	4:7	They traded in their glory for **s**
	10:5	are oblivious to the sham, the **s**
Zep	3:5	without conscience and without **s**
1Co	11:22	Why would you actually **s** God's poor?
Heb	12:2	cross, **s**, whatever
Jude	1:13	on the beach but the foam of their **s**

Shamed

Lev	20:21	He has **s** his brother
Isa	7:20	leaving you **s**, exposed, and denuded
	66:5	the ones who are going to end up **s**
Jer	9:19	we're a **s** people
	48:39	Moab **s** and ashamed to be seen

Shepherd

Ge	29:9	She was the **s**
	46:34	look down on anyone who is a **s**
	48:15	The God who has been my **s**
	49:24	the S, the Rock of Israel
Lev	27:32	animal that passes under the **s**'s rod
Nu	27:17	not be like sheep without a **s**
1Sa	17:34	David said, "I've been a **s**
	17:40	Then David took his **s**'s staff
2Sa	5:2	You will **s** my people Israel
	7:7	the leaders I commanded to **s** Israel
	24:17	I, the **s**, did the wrong
1Ki	22:17	sheep with no **s**
1Ch	11:2	You will **s** my people Israel
	17:6	the leaders I commanded to **s** Israel
2Ch	18:16	sheep with no **s**
Ps	23:1	God, my **s**! I don't need a thing
	23:4	Your trusty **s**'s crook makes me feel
	28:9	carry them like a good **s**
	78:72	His good heart made him a good **s**
	80:1	Listen, S, Israel's S
Ecc	12:11	They are given by God, the one S
SS	1:8	Stay with your **s** neighbors
Isa	13:14	like lost sheep with no **s**
	40:11	Like a **s**, he will care for his flock
	44:28	My **s** — everything I want, you'll do it
Jer	3:15	I'll give you good **s**-rulers
	23:1	Doom to the **s**-leaders who butcher

	23:2	the **s**-leaders who misled my people
	23:4	I'll set **s**-leaders over them
	31:10	like a **s** with his flock
	43:12	Like a **s** who picks lice from his robes
	51:23	use you to smash **s** and sheep
Eze	34:2	prophesy against the **s**-leaders
	34:5	because there was no **s**
	34:11	From now on, I myself am the **s**
	34:15	I myself will be the **s** of my sheep
	34:23	I'll appoint one **s** over them all
	37:24	They'll all be under one **s**
Am	3:12	a **s** trying to save a lamb
Mic	5:2	the leader who will **s**-rule Israel
	5:4	in his **s**-rule by God's strength
	5:6	S-rule will extend as far as needed
	7:14	S, O God, your people with your staff
Na	3:18	Your **s**-leaders, in charge of caring
Zec	10:2	poor lost sheep without a **s**
	11:7	sed the sheep marked for slaughter
	11:15	Dress up like a stupid **s**
	11:16	a **s** in this land — a **s** indifferent
	11:17	Doom to you, useless **s**
	13:7	Sword, get moving against my **s**
Mt	2:6	the leader who will **s**-rule my people
	9:36	like sheep with no **s**
	25:32	as a **s** sorts out sheep and goats
	26:31	I'll strike the **s**
	26:32	I, your S, will go ahead of you
Mk	6:34	like sheep with no **s** they were
	14:27	I will strike the **s**
Jn	10:2	The **s** walks right up to the gate
	10:11	I am the Good S. The Good S puts
	10:12	A hired man is not a real **s**
	10:14	I am the Good S. I know my own sheep
	10:16	Then it will be one flock, one S
	21:16	Jesus said, "S my sheep
Heb	13:20	Who led Jesus, our Great S
1Pe	2:25	kept for good by the S of your souls
	5:2	with all the diligence of a **s**
	5:4	God, who is the best **s** of all
Rev	2:27	S-King rule as firm as an iron staff
	7:17	The Lab on the Throne will **s** them
	12:5	a Son who will **s** all nations

Shepherds

Ge	13:7	between Abram's **s** and Lot's **s**
	13:8	between us, between your **s** and my **s**
	26:20	**s** of Gerar quarreled with Isaaac's
	29:3	**s** would roll the stone from the well
	29:8	Not until all the **s** get here
	46:32	The men are **s**
	47:3	Your servants are **s**
Ex	2:17	some **s** came and chased the girls off
	2:19	rescued us from a bunch of **s**
Nu	14:33	children of yours will live as **s**
1Sa	21:7	He was chief of Saul's **s**
	25:7	When your **s** were camped near us
	25:14	one of the young **s** told Abigail
2Ki	10:12	Beth Eked (Binding House) of the S
Job	1:16	lightning struck the sheep and the **s**
Isa	13:20	S will give it a wide berth

S

	31:4	s who arrive to chase it off
	56:11	these are Israel's s!
	63:11	who brought the s of his flock up
Jer	6:3	's' from the north have discovered
	12:10	Foreign, scavenging s will loot
	25:34	Wail, s! Cry out for help!
	25:35	no escape for those s
	25:36	s of the flock wailing
	33:12	become a pasture for s who care
	33:13	s who keep track of each sheep
	49:19	The s of Edom are helpless
	50:6	Their s led them astray
	50:44	the so-called s are helpless
Eze	34:2	Yes, prophesy! Tell those s
	34:7	s, listen to the Message of God
	34:8	you s ignored them and only fed
	34:10	I'm coming down on the s
	34:12	As s go after their flocks
Am	1:1	Am, one of the s of Tekoa
	1:2	withers the pastures tended by s
Zep	2:6	A country for s and sheep
Zec	10:3	I'm furious with the so-called s
	11:3	Do you hear the wailing of s?
	11:5	They have s who couldn't care less
	11:8	I got rid of the corrupt s

Shield

Ge	15:1	Don't be afraid, Abram. I'm your s
Dt	33:29	God! The S who defends you
Jdg	5:8	not a s or spear to be seen
1Sa	17.7	His s bearer walked ahead of him
	17:41	his s bearer in front of him
2Ki	19:32	Won't brandish a s, won't even begin
	19:34	I'll s this city, I'll save this city
	20:6	I'm covering this city with my s
1Ch	5:18	skilled in handling s, sword
	12:8	knew how to handle s and spear
	12:24	from Judah, carrying s and spear
2Ch	17:17	fully equipped with bow and s
Ps	3:3	But you, God, s me on all sides
Isa	37:33	Won't brandish so much as one s

Shields

2Sa	1:21	s were dragged through the mud
	8:7	David plundered the gold s
1Ki	10:16	body-length s of hammered gold
	10:17	smaller s about half that size
	14:26	even the gold s that Solomon had made
	14:27	replaced them with bronze s
	14:28	carried the s but always returned
2Ki	11:10	armed the officers with spears and s
1Ch	18:7	David plundered the gold s
2Ch	9:15	body-length s of hammered gold
	9:16	small s about half that size
	11:12	He installed arms — large s and spears
	12:9	took the gold s that Solomon had made
	12:10	replaced the gold s with bronze s
	12:11	guards went with him carrying the s
	14:8	Judeans, equipped with s and spears
	23:9	with spears and the large and small s

	26:14	well-armed with s, spears, helmets
	32:5	store of armaments — spears and s
	32:27	spices, s, and valuables
Ne	4:16	stood guard with lances, s, bows
Ps	84:9	Look at our s, glistening in the sun
	91:3	s you from deadly hazards
Jer	46:9	from Cush and Put with your s
Eze	26:8	A forest of s will advance against you
	27:11	hung their s from the city walls
	32:27	their s covering their bones
	38:4	full armor — all those s and bucklers
	39:9	piling on s large and small

Shiver

Job	24:7	Homeless, they s through cold nights
Ps	119:120	I s in awe before you
Ecc	4:11	Alone, you s all night

Shivering

Job	31:19	Have I ever left a poor family s
Pr	6:2	find yourself s out in the cold
SS	5:2	drenched with dew, s and cold
Isa	58:7	putting clothes on the s ill-clad
Mt	24:51	out in the cold s, teeth chattering
	25:36	I was s and you gave me clothes
	25:43	I was s and you gave me no clothes
	25:44	homeless or s or sick

Shivers

| Isa | 13:22 | howling of coyotes will give you the s |

Shock

1Sa	28:21	realizing that he was in deep s
Job	21:6	When I look back, I go into s
Isa	29:14	I'm going to step in and s them awake
	64:3	To s your enemies into facing you
Jer	2:12	Stand in s, heavens, at what you see
	15:4	a sight to s the whole world
	49:20	the flock in s, helpless to help
	49:23	in s when they hear the bad news
	50:45	the flock in s, helpless to help
La	4:12	World rulers were in s
Eze	26:10	a city in s
	32:10	I'll s people with you
Da	7:28	I, Daniel, was in s
	11:15	their famous commando s troops
Hab	1:5	Brace yourself for a s

Shocked

Ge	20:8	the whole story. They were s
Lev	26:32	will be s at what they see
Jdg	6:28	s to find Baal's altar torn down
1Sa	5:3	s to find Dagon toppled from his place
Isa	52:15	kings s into silence when they see
Jer	14:18	s by the killing fields strewn
	19:8	will be s speechless
Eze	16:27	were s at your sluttish life

S

	20:26	should have s them into recognizing
Lk	11:38	Pharisee s and somewhat offended
Jn	4:27	his disciples came back. They were s

Shocking

Jer	7:31	a s perversion of all that I am
	23:13	prophets acting like silly fools — s
Hos	6:10	I saw a s thing in the country
	10:9	that ancient, unspeakable, s sin

Shrewd

1Sa	23:22	He's very s, you know
2Sa	20:16	a s woman called out from the city
1Ch	26:14	Zechariah, a s counselor
2Ch	2:12	a son so wise, so knowledgeable and s
	11:23	He was s in deploying his sons in all the
Mk	4:24	be wary of the s advice that tells

Shudder

Ps	55:2	I really need you. I s
	55:5	with fear, I s from head to foot
Isa	19:1	The god-idols of Egypt s and shake
	64:1	make the mountains s at your presence
	64:3	made the mountains s at your presence
Jer	34:17	world will take one look at you and s
	49:21	The very earth will s
	50:46	very earth will s at the sound
Eze	32:10	Kings will take one look and s

Shunned

Pr	14:20	An unlucky loser is s by all
Eze	23:32	You'll be s and taunted

Shunning

Job	28:28	Insight means s evil

Shuns

Pr	14:10	who s the bitter moments of friends

Shy

Job	39:22	doesn't s away from the sword
Ps	50:3	he's not s in his coming
SS	2:14	Come, my s and modest dove
1Co	9:3	not s in standing up to my critics
2Ti	1:7	doesn't want us to be s with his gifts

Siok

Ge	12:17	everybody . . . got seriously s
	27:46	I'm s to death of these Hittite women
	41:27	The seven s and ugly cows
Nu	11:20	going to be so s of meat
Dt	29:22	how God made the whole land s
1Sa	19:14	He's s in bed
	30:13	left me when I got s

2Sa	5:8	he was so s and tired of it
	12:15	and he came down s
	13:2	making himself s over her
	13:5	Go to bed and pretend you're s
	13:6	Amnon took to his bed and acted s
1Ki	14:1	Abijah came down s
	14:5	consult with you regarding her s son
	17:17	Later on the woman's son became s
2Ki	8:7	king of Aram, was s at the time
	13:14	Elisha came down s
	20:1	Hezekiah became deathly s
	20:12	heard that the king was s
2Ch	32:24	Hezekiah became deathly s
Ne	2:2	You're not s are you?
Job	6:7	repulsed by it — it makes me s
Ps	35:13	When they were s, I dressed in black
	41:3	Whenever we're s and in bed
	107:17	s because you'd lived a bad life
Pr	25:16	you'll make yourself s
Isa	1:14	I'm s of your religion
	33:24	No one in Zion will say, "I'm s."
	38:1	At that time, Hezekiah got s
	38:9	after he'd been s and then recovered
	39:1	Hezekiah had been s and was now well
Jer	27:13	or get s and die
	31:30	you're the one who gets s
	38:2	or get s and die
	42:17	or get s and die
	42:22	you'll get s and die
La	1:13	left me s, and s of living
Eze	16:30	What a s soul!
	34:4	don't heal the s
Hos	5:13	When Ephraim saw he was s
Am	5:22	I'm s of your fund-raising schemes
Mal	1:8	blind and s and crippled animals
Mt	8:6	Master, my servant is s
	8:14	found Peter's mother-in-law s in bed
	9:12	needs a doctor: the healthy or the s
	10:8	Bring health to the s
	14:14	overcome with pity and healed their s
	14:35	rounded up all the s
	25:36	I was s and you stopped to visit
	25:38	did we ever see you s or in prison
	25:43	S and in prison, and you never visited
	25:44	or s or in prison
Mk	1:30	Simon's mother-in-law was s in bed
	1:32	brought s and evil-afflicted people
	1:34	cured their s bodies
	2:17	needs a doctor: the healthy or the s
	2:17	I'm here inviting the sin-s, not
	6:5	laid hands on a few s people
	6:13	brought wellness to the s
	6:55	bringing their s on stretchers
	6:56	brought their s to the marketplace
	16:18	lay hands on the s and make them well
Lk	4:40	anyone s with some ailment
	5:31	needs a doctor: the healthy or the s
	9:2	news of God's kingdom and heal the s
	10:9	heal anyone who is s
	13:32	out the demons and healing the s
Jn	4:46	the king's court whose son was s
	5:3	Hundreds of s people

S

	5:7	The s man said
	6:2	had seen him do among the s
	11:1	A man was s, Lazarus of Bethany
	11:2	her brother Lazarus who was s
	11:3	one you love so very much is s
	11:6	he heard that Lazarus was s
Ac	2:40	get out of this s and stupid culture
	4:9	trial today for helping a s man
	5:15	carried the s out into the streets
	5:16	bringing the s and bedeviled
	9:37	she became s and died
	19:12	then touching the s with them
	28:8	Publius's father was s at the time
	28:9	everyone … who was s … got healed
Ro	11:9	get s eating self-serving meals
1Co	11:30	you even now are listless and s
	12:9	simple trust healing the s
Gal	4:14	a s guest was most troublesome
2Ti	4:20	had to leave Trophimus s in Miletus
Jas	5:14	Are you s? Call the church leaders

Silence

	13:30	called for s before Moses
Nu	13:30	
Job	12:20	He forces trusted sages to keep s
	13:5	s is your only claim to wisdom
	21:4	I'm getting fed up with his s
Ps	8:2	and s atheist babble
	19:4	their s fills the earth
	28:1	all I get from you is deafening s
	31:20	you s the poisonous gossip
	39:2	longer I kept s The worse it got
	65:1	S is praise to you, Zion-dwelling God
Isa	16:9	Instead of song … dead s
	16:10	s — deathly and deadening s
	17:13	God will s them with a word
	52:15	kings shocked into s when they see him
	53:7	he took it all in s
Jer	7:34	no holiday sounds. Dead s
La	1:7	laughed at her helpless s
	3:28	go off by yourself. Enter the s
Eze	24:27	You'll break your s
Hab	2:20	Quiet everyone — a holy s
Zep	1:7	Reverent s before me, God, the Master
Zec	2:13	Quiet, everyone! Shh! S before God
Mt	8:26	the sea to quiet down: "S!"
	10:28	Don't be bluffed into s
	27:14	Jesus kept s — not a word
Mk	9:34	The s was deafening
Lk	8:24	he told the wind, "S!"
	12:4	Don't be bluffed into s or insincerity
Ac	4:17	let's s them with threats
	15:12	There was dead s
	15:13	The s deepened
	18:9	don't let anyone intimidate or s you
1Pe	2:23	He suffered in s
Rev	8:1	complete s for about half an hour
	10:4	Seal with s the Seven Thunders

Silent

| Ge | 24:21 | man watched, s. Was this God's answer? |

	30:14	if her husband is s and doesn't speak
Nu	30:14	
2Ki	18:36	The people were s
Est	4:14	If you persist in staying s
Job	13:24	Why do you stay hidden and s?
	32:1	Job's three friends now fell s
	34:29	If God is s, what's that to you?
Ps	83:1	don't give me the s treatment
Isa	18:4	s as dew during harvest
	24:4	the world s and sad
	36:21	The three men were s
Jer	25:37	sheepfolds will be s with death
	49:26	her brave warriors s as death
	50:30	her soldiers dead, s forever
La	2:10	elders of Daughter Zion sit s
Hab	1:13	Why are you s now?
Mt	8:26	he stood up and told the wind to be s
	26:63	Jesus kept s
Mk	14:61	Jesus was s. He said nothing
Lk	14:4	They were s. So he took the man
Ac	8:32	He was s, saying nothing
Rev	18:22	S the music of harpists and singers

Silliness

Ps	73:7	overfed, decked out in silk bows of s
Pr	12:23	talkative fools broadcast their s
	13:16	fools litter the country with s
	26:11	so fools recycle s
Mt	7:6	Banter and s give no honor to God
Ro	1:21	trivialized themselves into s
1Co	1:18	Christ on the Cross seems like sheer s
	2:14	They seem like so much s
1Ti	1:4	family trees that digress into s

Silly

Ex	20:7	in curses or s banter
Dt	5:11	in curses or s banter
Ps	9:20	Show them how s they look
	31:6	I hate all this s religion
Ecc	10:17	don't drink themselves s
Isa	3:12	S girls bully them around
	30:15	stop your s efforts to save yourselves
	44:25	and their latest knowledge look s
Jer	2:8	empty god-dreams and s god-schemes
	2:11	empty god-dreams and s god-schemes
	8:19	their s, imported no-gods
	23:13	saw prophets acting like s fools
	23:28	go ahead and tell your s dreams
Mal	1:10	this s, empty-headed worship
Mt	23:24	Do you have any idea how s you look
	25:2	Five were s and five were smart
	25:3	The s virgins took lamps
	25:8	The s virgins said to the smart ones
	25:11	the other virgins, the s ones
Lk	13:17	left looking quite s and red-faced
Ac	14:15	abandon these s god-superstitions
	25:27	s to send a prisoner all that way
Ro	14:10	leaves you looking pretty s
Eph	5:4	Don't talk dirty or s
1Ti	4:7	s stories … dressed up as religion

S

Simple

2Ki	5:13	why not this s 'wash and be clean
Pr	13:7	a plain and s life is a full life
	15:16	A s life in the Fear-of-God
	26:5	Answer a fool in s terms
Isa	28:13	God will start over with the s basics
	33:15	The answer's s: Live right
	66:2	a person s and plain
Jer	13:22	The answer's s: You're guilty
Da	1:12	a s diet of vegetables and water
	10:3	I ate only plain and s food
Mic	6:8	It's quite s: Do what is fair
Zec	8:17	Keep your lives s and honest
Mal	2:14	why? S. Because God was there
Mt	3:2	His message was s and austere
	5:22	The s moral fact is that words kill
	7:12	a s, rule-of-thumb guide for behavior
	8:10	this kind of s trust in Israel
	17:20	The s truth is that if you had
	18:4	Whoever becomes s and elemental again
	18:6	taking advantage of their s trust
	18:14	lose even one of these s believers
Mk	6:8	special appeals for funds. Keep it s
	9:42	one of these s, childlike believers
Lk	6:31	a s rule of thumb for behavior
	7:9	kind of s trust anywhere in Israel
	9:4	Keep it s; you are the equipment
Jn	10:6	Jesus told this s story
	11:38	It was a s cave in the hillside
Ac	16:4	presented the s guidelines
	21:39	I have a s request
Ro	1:14	mannered or rude, smart or s
1Co	2:2	deliberately kept it plain and s
	5:8	s, genuine, unpretentious
	7:29	Keep it s — in marriage
	12:9	s trust healing the sick
	14:15	The answer is s enough. Do both
	14:20	a s no is all that's needed
2Co	11:3	s purity of your love for Christ
	11:5	why can't you put up with s me
Gal	4:3	ordered around by s instructions
Col	1:27	sharing in God's glory. It's that s
	2:6	counsel . . . is s and straightforward
1Ti	2:7	it works by s faith and plain truth
2Ti	2:15	laying out the truth plain and s
	4:2	Don't ever quit. Just keep it s
Jas	1:21	In s humility, let our gardener, God
1Jn	3:10	A s test

Sin

Ge	4:7	s is lying in wait for you
	15:16	s is still a thriving business
	18:20	the s of those cities is immense
	39:9	violate his trust and s against God
	50:17	Forgive your brothers' s
Ex	10:17	Overlook my s one more time
	16:1	the Wilderness of S
	17:1	from the Wilderness of S
	20:20	awe within you so that you won't s
	23:33	get you to s by worshiping their gods

	32:21	you involved them in this huge s
	32:30	You have sinned an enormous s!
	32:31	it's an enormous s!
	32:32	if you will only forgive their s
	32:33	erase from my book those who s
	34:7	forgiving iniquity, rebellion, and s
	34:7	Still, he doesn't ignore s
	34:9	Forgive our iniquity and s
Lev	4:14	When they do become aware of the s
	4:23	When he becomes aware of the s
	4:26	atonement . . . on account of his s
	4:28	When he is made aware of his s
	4:35	atonement for . . . his s
	5:1	If you s by not . . . offering
	5:5	immediately confess the s
	5:6	your penalty to God for the s
	5:7	your penalty to God for the s
	5:10	priest will make atonement for your s
	5:16	additional compensation for the s
	19:22	the ram of compensation for the s
	26:41	make amends for their s
Nu	5:6	When a man or woman commits any s
	5:7	must confess the s
	9:13	That man will pay for his s
	12:11	for this foolish and thoughtless s
	14:18	forgiving iniquity and rebellion and s
	14:18	Still, never just whitewashing s
	15:25	The s was not deliberate
	18:22	they'll be penalized for their s
	33:11	camped in the Wilderness of S
	33:12	left the Wilderness of S
Dt	9:21	s-thing that you made, that calf-god
	9:27	this people, their evil and their s
	19:15	cannot convict anyone of a crime or s
	23:22	there's no s
	24:4	defile the land with s
	24:15	you'll have s on your books
	24:16	shall be put to death for his own s
Jos	22:20	wasn't the only one to die for his s
1Sa	2:17	horrible s these young servants were
	2:25	If you s against another person
	12:23	That would be a s against God
	14:34	don't s against God by eating meat
	14:38	Some s has been committed this day
	14:41	If the s is in me or Jonathan
	15:25	Oh, absolve me of my s!
1Ki	8:34	forgive the s of your people
	8:46	When they s against you
	12:30	This was blatant s
	13:34	the root s of Jeroboam's government
	14:22	They set new records in s
	15:3	continued to s just like his father
	15:26	who both sinned and made Israel s
	15:30	punishment for . . . making Israel s
	15:34	who both sinned and made Israel s
	16:2	s and making me seethe over their s
	21:22	angry by making Israel s
	22:52	who led Israel into a life of s
2Ki	8:18	continuing the Ahab line of s
	8:27	same evil-in-God's-sight line of s
	13:2	led Israel into a life of s
	14:24	from all the s of Jeroboam

S

	15:9	who led Israel into a life of s
	15:18	S for s, he repeated the sins
	15:24	stuck to the old s tracks of Jeroboam
	15:28	who led Israel into a life of s
	17:7	The exile came about because of s
	17:21	led them into a life of total s
	21:11	eclipsing the s-performance of
	21:17	his sorry record of s
	23:15	who had led Israel into a life of s
2Ch	6:25	forgive the s of your people Israel
	6:36	When they s against you
	22:4	related by both marriage and s
	24:18	and Jerusalem because of this s
	28:10	this is a terrible s against your God
	29:24	atone for the s of all Israel
Ne	4:5	don't wipe away their s
	13:26	Didn't Solomon the king of Israel s
Job	1:22	Not once through all this did Job s
	2:10	Not once through all this did Job s
	11:14	If you scrub your hands of s
	15:5	s that taught you to talk this way
	15:35	have sex with s and give birth to evil
	20:27	strip them of their s-soaked clothes
	31:7	messed around with s
	31:33	Did I hide my s the way Adam did
	34:23	their s is an open-and-shut case
	34:31	Say, 'I sinned, but I'll s no more
	34:37	You've compounded your original s
	35:6	If you s, what difference could that
Ps	1:1	don't hang out at S Saloon
	7:14	sex with s, he's pregnant with evil
	25:18	Then lift this ton of s
	32:5	my guilt dissolved, my s disappeared
	34:14	Turn your back on s; do something good
	36:1	all ears, eager to s
	38:3	brittle as dry sticks because of my s
	38:18	I'm no longer smug in my s
	39:11	to purge us from our s
	69:5	God, you know every s I've committed
	78:17	All they did was s even more
	78:38	Compassionate! Forgave the s!
	84:10	honored as a guest in the palace of s
	85:3	took back your s-provoked threats
	107:17	bodies feeling the effects of your s
	109:7	let his prayer turn to s
	109:14	memorial to the s of his father
	119:11	so I won't s myself bankrupt
	130:8	buy back Israel from captivity to s
	141:5	Don't let s anoint my head
Pr	5:11	regrets, nothing but s and bones
	5:22	shadow of your s will overtake you
	10:16	evil person ends up with nothing but s
	12:28	s's detours take you straight to hell
	13:6	s dumps the wicked in the ditch
	17:19	who courts s, marries trouble
	21:4	the wicked — are just plain s
	22:8	Whoever sows s reaps weeds
	24:9	Fools incubate s
Isa	5:18	who haul s to market
	27:9	evidence that his s is removed
	30:1	You pile s on s, one s on top
	32:7	inventive in s and scandal

	40:2	her s is taken care of
	53:10	give himself as an offering for s
	53:12	took on his own shoulders the s
	59:4	pregnant . . . and have s-babies
	64:6	We're all s-infected, s-contaminated
	66:3	Your acts of worship are acts of s
Jer	2:13	My people have committed a compound s
	2:23	you tell me, 'I'm not stained by s
	2:33	You founded schools of s
	2:36	try out another s-project
	4:1	rid of your stinking s paraphernalia
	8:14	damned because of our s against him
	15:17	Their s had me seething
	17:1	s is engraved with a steel chisel
	18:23	don't overlook a single s
	25:12	whole nation of Babylon for their s
	31:30	each person will pay for his own s
	32:35	whole country into one huge act of s
	36:3	let me forgive their perversity and s
	36:31	government for their blatant s
	50:20	a trace of Judah's s — nothing
	51:5	s against Israel's most Holy God
La	2:14	didn't face you with your s
	3:39	complain when punished for s
	4:6	worse than the s of Sodom
Eze	2:4	hardened in their s
	3:7	a hard case, hardened in their s
	3:21	warn these righteous people not to s
	4:4	place the s of the family of Israel
	4:5	The number of days you bear their s
	4:6	bear the s of the family of Judah
	4:17	This is what s does
	7:19	tripped on money and fell into s
	11:2	men who draw up blueprints for s
	16:49	The s of your sister Sodom
	16:51	Samaria didn't s half as much as you
	18:4	You die for your own s, not another's
	18:21	turns his back on that life of s
	18:30	so that s won't drag you down
	21:24	your s is now out in the open
	28:18	By s after s after s
	29:16	a reminder of old s
	33:14	and he repents of his s
	33:18	plunge into s, they'll die for it
	39:24	as their . . . s-sated lives deserved
	40:39	burnt offerings, s offerings
	42:13	grain offerings, s offerings
	43:19	For a s offering, give a bull
	43:21	take the bull for the s offerings
	43:22	without blemish for a s offering
	43:25	a goat for a s offering daily
	44:27	first offer a s offering for himself
	44:29	grain offerings, the s offerings
	45:17	S offerings, grain offerings
	45:19	take blood from the s offerings
	45:22	a bull as a s offering for himself
	45:25	same materials for s offerings
	46:20	cook the guilt offering and s offering
Da	8:12	As judgment against their s
	8:13	this devastating judgment against s
	9:8	deservedly so, because of our s
	9:11	the wages of our s against you

S

	9:24	stop **s**, wipe out crime
Hos	4:7	The more priests, the more **s**
	4:15	don't go to that **s** city Bethel
	5:8	Signal the invasion of **S** City
	7:2	head to toe with the residue of **s**
	9:10	took to **s** like a pig to filth
	10:2	They're guilty as **s**
	10:8	**s** centers will all be torn down
	10:9	You got your start in **s** at Gibeah
	12:8	not a hint of fraud, not a sign of **s**
	13:2	back in the **s** business again
	13:12	Ephraim's **s** documented and stored
	14:2	Take away our **s**, accept our confession
Am	1:5	crime king who lives in **S** Valley
	3:14	pay for the **s**-altars of worship
	4:4	Come along to Bethel and **s**!
	4:4	then to Gilgal and **s** some more!
	8:7	keeping track of their every last **s**
	8:14	oaths at the Samaria **S**-and-Sex Center
	9:8	have my eye on the Kingdom of **S**
	9:9	shaking out all the **s**
Mic	1:5	All this because of Jacob's **s**
	3:8	confront Jacob's crime and Israel's **s**
	6:7	to cancel my **s**
Hab	1:11	Brazen in **s**, they call strength
Zep	1:3	Anything and everything that causes **s**
	1:18	I care about **s** with fiery passion
Zec	3:4	I've stripped you of your **s**
	5:6	It holds the **s** of everyone
Mal	2:17	God loves sinners and **s** alike
Mk	2:17	I'm here inviting the **s**
Jn	8:11	Go on your way. From now on, don't **s**
	8:34	who chooses a life of **s** is trapped
	16:8	error of the godless world's view of **s**
	16:9	refusal to believe in me is . . . **s**
Ac	7:60	don't blame them for this **s**
Ro	2:12	If you **s** without knowing
	3:20	our complicity in everyone else's **s**
	3:25	to clear that world of **s**
	5:12	first **s**, then death
	5:13	**s** disturbed relations with God
	5:14	who didn't **s** precisely as Adam did
	5:15	parallel to the death-dealing **s**
	5:15	If one man's **s** put crowds of people
	5:16	comparison between that . . . **s**
	5:18	all this trouble with **s** and death
	5:20	All that passing laws against **s** did
	5:21	All **s** can do is threaten us with death
	6:2	left the country where **s** is sovereign
	6:3	left the old country of **s** behind
	6:6	decisive end to that **s**-miserable life
	6:8	in Christ's **s**-conquering death
	6:10	When Jesus died, he took **s** down
	6:11	**S** speaks a dead language
	6:12	you must not give **s** a vote
	6:14	**S** can't tell you how to live
	6:16	Offer yourselves to **s**
	6:22	don't have to listen to **s** tell you
	6:23	Work hard for **s** your whole life
	7:5	**s** was calling most of the shots
	7:6	shackled to that domineering mate of **s**
	7:7	no better than **s** itself

	7:8	**s** found a way to pervert the command
	7:9	once **s** got its hands on the law code
	7:11	So **s** was plenty alive
	7:13	**S** simply did what is so famous for
	7:14	I've spent a long time in **s**'s prison
	7:17	power of **s** within me keeps sabotaging
	7:21	**s** is there to trip me up
	7:25	pulled by the influence of **s**
	8:2	brutal tyranny at the hands of **s**
	8:3	used as a Band-Aid on **s**
	8:10	experience all the limitations of **s**
1Co	7:28	certainly no **s** in getting married
	15:56	was **s** that made death so frightening
2Co	11:29	When someone is duped into **s**
Gal	6.1	If someone falls into **s**, forgivingly
Eph	2:1	mired in that old stagnant life of **s**
	2:5	took our **s**-dead lives and made us
Col	2:11	destroying the power of **s**
	2:13	stuck in your old **s**-dead life
1Ti	2:6	everyone held captive by **s**
	2:14	deceived first — our pioneer in **s**
	5:20	If anyone falls into **s**, call that
Tit	3:3	stupid and stubborn, dupes of **s**
Heb	3:13	so **s** doesn't slow down your reflexes
	4:15	experienced it all — all but the **s**
	7:26	completely holy, uncompromised by **s**
	9:26	himself, the final solution of **s**
	10:3	instead of removing awareness of **s**
	10:4	goat blood can't get rid of **s**
	10:11	never makes a dent in the **s** problem
	11:25	soft life of **s** with the oppressors
	12:4	In this all-out match against **s**
	13:11	to the altar as a sacrifice for **s**
Jas	1:15	Lust gets pregnant, and has a baby: **s**
	1:15	**S** grows up to adulthood, and becomes
	4:8	Quit dabbling in **s**.
2Pe	2:14	with adultery, compulsive in **s**
	2:20	they've escaped from the slum of **s**
1Jn	1:7	Jesus, God's Son, purges all our **s**
	1:8	If we claim that we're free of **s**
	2:1	out of **s**. But if anyone does **s**
	2:2	he solved the **s** problem for good
	3:5	Christ showed up . . . to get rid of **s**
	3:5	There is no **s** in him, and **s** is not
	3:6	deeply in Christ makes a practice of **s**
	3:6	None of those who do practice **s**
	3:8	Those who make a practice of **s**
	3:9	don't make a practice of **s**
	5:17	Everything we do wrong is **s**
	5:17	but not all **s** is fatal
	5:18	makes a practice of **s** — fatal **s**
Jude	1:23	not soft on **s**. The **s**

Sincere

2Ch	22:9	famous as a **s** seeker after God
Job	16:17	never hurt a soul and my prayers are **s**
Pr	2:7	bodyguard to the candid and **s**
Php	1:10	your love is **s** and intelligent

Sincerely

1Ki	8:23	loves them as they s live in obedience
2Ch	6:14	they s live in obedience to your way
	30:19	everyone who s desires God

Sinful

2Ki	3:3	hung on to the s practices
Pr	11:6	crooks get trapped in their s lust
Isa	31:7	the no-gods your s hands made
Eze	37:23	out of all their old s haunts
Jn	8:46	a single s act
1Co	7:23	once held hostage in a s society
Gal	3:19	s people in the way of salvation
	5:17	a root of s self-interest in us
1Pe	4:1	weaning from that old s habit
2Pe	1:9	your old s life has been wiped
1Jn	3:4	All who indulge in a s life

Sing

Ex	15:21	Miriam led them in singing, S to God
Nu	21:17	Erupt, Well! S the Song of the Well
	21:27	That is why the folk singers s
Dt	31:19	to s it by heart
Jdg	5:3	I'll s, Make music to God
	5:11	listen to them s
	5:12	Wake up, wake up, s a song
1Sa	21:11	the one they s of at their dances
2Sa	22:4	I s to God the Praise-Lofty
1Ch	15:16	assign their relatives to s in the choir
	16:9	S to him! Play songs for him
	16:23	S to God, everyone and everything
Job	33:27	You'll s God's praises to everyone
Ps	6:5	can't s in your choir if I'm buried
	9:11	S your songs to Zion-dwelling God
	18:3	I s to God, the Praise-Lofty
	30:4	you saints! S your hearts out to God
	32:11	Celebrate God. S together — everyone
	40:3	taught me how to s the latest God-song
	40:16	let them s and be happy
	42:8	s songs all through the night
	43:4	S my thanks with a harp
	47:6	S songs to God, s out!
	47:6	S to our King, s praise
	47:7	s your best songs to God
	51:14	I'll s anthems to your life-giving
	57:7	Ready to s, ready to raise a tune
	61:8	and live what I s
	65:13	let them s
	66:2	S songs to the tune of his glory
	68:3	they'll s, they'll laugh and s for joy
	68:4	S hymns to God; all heaven, s out
	68:32	S, O kings of the earth! S praises
	70:4	Let those on the hunt for you s
	84:2	where I could s for joy to God-alive
	84:4	blessed they are to live and s there
	85:6	your people will laugh and s
	89:1	Your love, God, is my song, and I'll s
	89:5	angels s anthems to your faithful ways
	89:12	mountains Tabor and Hermon s duets

	92:1	to s an anthem to you, the High God
	92:2	s your faithful presence all through
	96:1	S God a brand-new song!
	96:2	S to God — worship God!
	97:8	Daughters of Zion, s your hearts out
	98:1	S to God a brand-new song
	98:4	Let loose and s!
	100:2	s yourselves into his presence
	104:33	s to God all my life long, s hymns
	105:2	S him songs
	107:22	tell the world what he's done — s it
	108:1	Ready to s . . . to raise a God-song
	119:54	set your instructions to music and s
	124:1	all together now, Israel, s out
	132:9	prompt your worshipers to s this
	132:16	holy people will s their hearts out
	135:3	s anthems to his beautiful name
	137:3	mocking: "S us a happy Zion song
	137:4	how could we ever s God's song
	138:1	Angels listen as I s my thanks
	138:5	They'll s of what you've done
	144:9	O God, let me s a new song to you
	147:1	a good thing to s praise to our God
	147:7	S to God a thanksgiving hymn
	149:1	S to God a brand-new song
	149:5	s out from wherever
Pr	23:16	My heart will dance and s
SS	1:4	We'll celebrate, we'll s
Isa	5:1	I'll s a ballad to the one I love
	12:5	S praise-songs to God
	12:6	S your hearts out, O Zion!
	23:16	S your old songs
	25:9	s the joys of his salvation
	26:19	you dead and buried, wake up! S!
	27:2	There's something to s about
	30:29	s, s through an all-night holy feast
	35:1	desert will s joyously
	35:10	They'll s as they make their way home
	38:18	choirs don't s praises from the morgue
	38:20	We'll s, oh we'll s, s, for the rest
	42:10	S to God a brand-new song, s
	44:23	High heavens, s! God has done it
	54:1	S, barren woman
	61:10	I will s for joy in God
Jer	20:13	S to God! All praise to God!
	31:7	Raise cheers! S praises
Eze	19:1	S the blues over the princes of Israel
	32:2	s a funeral lament over Pharaoh
Am	8:10	make every song you s a dirge
Mic	2:4	you yourselves will s the blues
Zep	3:14	So s, Daughter Zion!
Ro	5:11	We s and shout our praises to God
	15:9	in a hymn-s; I'll s to your name
1Co	14:15	s with my spirit, and s with my mind
	14:26	S a hymn, teach a lesson
Eph	5:19	S hymns instead of drinking songs
	5:19	S songs from your heart to Christ
	5:20	S praises over everything
Col	3:16	And s, s
Jas	5:13	Do you feel great? S

Singing

Ex	15:1	I'm s my heart out to God
	15:21	Miriam led them in s
Dt	31:21	this song; they'll be s it
1Sa	18:6	villages of Israel s and dancing
	29:5	David they celebrate ..., s
2Sa	6:5	s at the top of their lungs
	22:50	I'm s songs that rhyme your name
1Ki	1:40	band playing and the people s
	1:45	parade is headed up this way s
1Ch	6:31	persons David appointed to lead the s
	25:6	in charge of leading the s
2Ch	5:13	s and playing praise to God
	7:6	Levites that David had provided for s
	20:21	to march ahead of the troops, s
	29:27	the sacred choir began s
Ne	12:46	choir directors for s songs of praise
Job	21:12	have good times s and dancing
Ps	7:17	I'm s the fame of heaven-high God
	8:8	whales s in the ocean deeps
	9:2	I'm s your song, High God
	13:6	I'm s at the top of my lungs
	18:49	I'm s songs that rhyme your name
	21:13	We are out s the good news
	26:7	S God-songs at the top of my lungs
	27:6	Already I'm s God-songs
	28:7	shouting and s my thanks to him
	31:7	s in the circle of your love
	35:10	s, "God, there's no one like you
	42:4	Shouting praises, s thanksgiving
	57:9	s your praises in town and country
	59:16	I'm s your prowess
	75:9	s the praises of Jacob's God
	84:3	s their songs in the place
	95:2	march into his presence s praises
	101:1	I'm s it right to you, God
	104:34	I'm so pleased to be s to God
	105:43	led his people out s for joy
	108:3	s your praises in town and country
	109:30	I'm s his hallelujahs
	146:2	I'll praise God, s songs to my God
Pr	25:20	S light songs to the heavyhearted
SS	2:12	The whole world's a choir — and s
Isa	24:16	the s: "All praise to the Righteous
	66:10	join in the happy s
Jer	25:10	banish every sound of joy — s
	31:4	You'll resume your s
Da	4:37	why I'm s — I, Nebuchadnezzar — s
Joel	1:16	joy and s from God's Sanctuary
Hab	3:18	I'm s joyful praise to God
Lk	2:13	huge angelic choir s God's praises
Ac	16:25	s a robust hymn to God
Ro	15:6	our very lives s in harmony
1Pe	1:8	you trust him — with laughter and s
Rev	5:13	all voices in all places, s
	7:10	heartily s: Salvation to our God
	7:12	s: Oh, Yes! The blessing and glory
	14:3	harpists s a new song
	19:1	like massed choirs in Heaven s
	19:3	Then, more s: Hallelujah!

Sinned

Ex	9:27	I've s for sure this time
	10:16	s against your God and against you
	32:30	You have s an enormous sin!
	32:31	This people has s
Nu	14:40	We s, but now we're ready
	15:28	the person who accidentally s
	16:38	men who have s and are now dead
	21:7	We s when we spoke out against God
	22:34	Balaam said to God's angel, "I have s
Dt	1:41	We've s against God
Jos	7:11	has s: They've broken the covenant
	7:20	It's true. I s against God
Jdg	10:10	We've s against you! We left our God
	10:15	We've s. Do to us whatever you
1Sa	7:6	We have s against God
	12:10	We've s! We've gone off and left God
	14:39	whoever s will die
	15:24	Saul gave in and confessed, "I've s
	15:30	Saul tried again, "I have s
	24:11	I'm no rebel. I haven't s against you
	26:21	Saul confessed, "I've s!
2Sa	12:13	David confessed to Nathan, "I've s
	19:20	I know I s, but look at me now
	24:10	David prayed to God, "I have s badly
	24:17	he prayed, "Please! I'm the one who s
1Ki	8:33	because they've s against you
	8:35	no rain because your people have s
	8:47	We've s; we've done wrong
	8:50	Forgive your people who have s
	15:26	father who both s and made Israel sin
	15:34	who both s and made Israel sin
	16:26	who not only s but dragged Israel
2Ki	17:7	The children of Israel s against God
1Ch	21:8	Then David prayed, "I have s badly
	21:17	I'm the one who s; I'm the one
2Ch	6:24	s against you, but then turn to you
	6:26	no rain because your people have s
	6:37	We've s; we've done wrong
	6:39	Forgive your people who have s
	28:13	We've already s against God
Ne	1:6	among those who have s against you
Job	1:5	s by defying God inwardly
	7:20	Even suppose I'd s
	8:4	your children s against him
	34:31	I s, but I'll sin no more
	35:3	difference whether I've s or not
Ps	106:6	We've s a lot, both we and our parents
Isa	42:24	this God against whom we've s
	64:5	We've s and kept at it so long!
Jer	3:25	All because we s against our God
	14:7	we've s against you
	14:20	We've s, they've s, we've all s
	31:34	I'll forget they ever s!
	40:3	because you all s against God
	44:23	and you s against God
	50:14	She's s — oh, how she's s
La	5:7	Our parents s and are no more
	5:16	Would that we'd never s
Eze	28:16	you turned violent, you s
Da	9:5	we have s in every way imaginable

S

	9:15	We confess that we have **s**
Mic	7:9	I deserve it — I **s**
Zep	1:17	They've **s** against God
Mt	27:4	I've **s**. I've betrayed an innocent man
Lk	15:18	Father, I've **s** against God, I've **s**
	15:21	Father, I've **s** against God, I've **s**
Jn	9:2	who **s**: this man or his parents
Jas	5:15	if you've **s**, you'll be forgiven
1Jn	1:10	If we claim that we've never **s**

Sinner

Job	40:8	Are you calling me a **s**
Ecc	5:6	Don't let your mouth make a total **s**
Eze	33:6	the bloodshed of any unwarned **s**
Mt	5:47	Any run-of-the-mill **s** does that
Lk	5:8	I'm a **s** and can't handle this holiness
	15:7	over one **s**'s rescued life
	18:13	God, give mercy. Forgive me, a **s**
Ro	3:15	race for the honor of **s**-of-the-year
1Ti	1:15	I'm proof — Public **S** Number One
1Jn	5:16	life to the **s** whose sin is not fatal

Sinners

Ge	13:13	evil — flagrant **s** against God
Nu	32:14	just one more mob of **s**
1Sa	15:18	Go and put those **s**, the Amalekites
2Ki	21:11	to debase Judah into a nation of **s**
	21:16	turned them into a nation of **s**
Job	24:19	**s** disappear in the grave
Ps	104:35	But clear the ground of **s**
Pr	13:21	Disaster entraps **s**
	21:26	**S** are always wanting what they don't
Ecc	2:26	**s** are assigned a life of hard labor
Isa	13:9	clean out all the **s**
	33:14	The **s** in Zion are rightly terrified
Am	9:9	shaking out all the sin, all the **s**
	9:10	all the **s** will be sifted out
Mal	2:17	God loves **s** and sin alike
Mt	26:45	handed over to the hands of **s**
Mk	14:41	betrayed into the hands of **s**
Lk	5:30	drinking with crooks and '**s**
	6:32	Run-of-the-mill **s** do that
	6:33	Garden-variety **s** do that
	13:2	worse **s** than all other Galileans
	15:2	He takes in **s** and eats meals with them
	24:7	he had to be handed over to **s**
Jn	9:31	God isn't at the beck and call of **s**
Ro	3:9	we all start out as **s**
	3:19	we're **s**, every one of us
	3:23	long and sorry record as **s**
Gal	2:15	advantage of birth over "non-Jewish **s**
1Ti	1:15	Christ came into the world to save **s**
Jude	1:23	Be tender with **s**, but not soft on sin

Sinning

Ge	20:6	I kept you from **s** against me
Ex	9:34	kept right on **s**, stubborn as ever
Nu	32:23	you will be **s** against God
Dt	9:16	**s** against God, your God

	9:18	all your sins, **s** against God
	20:18	you end up **s** against God
Jos	24:19	put up with your fooling around and **s**
1Sa	14:33	soldiers are **s** against God
	19:5	think of **s** against an innocent person
1Ki	16:19	**s** and then dragging Israel into
Ps	78:32	they kept right on **s**
Isa	1:14	while you go right on **s**
	43:27	original ancestor started the **s**
Jer	3:5	Meanwhile you keep **s** nonstop
Eze	3:19	they keep right on **s** anyway
	18:24	starts **s**, plunging into the same vile
	18:26	away from his good life and takes up **s**
Da	9:13	We kept at our **s**
Hos	8:11	uses them for **s**. ...Altars for **s**
	10:9	war to end all the **s**
Jn	5:14	Don't return to a **s** life
Ro	6:1	Keep on **s** so God can keep on forgiving
2Co	12:21	crowd that keeps **s** over and over
	13:2	that bunch that keeps **s** over and over
1Jn	5:16	if we see a Christian believer **s**

Sins

Ge	50:17	Will you forgive the **s** of the servants
Ex	20:5	any **s** their parents pass on to them
	32:34	their **s** will certainly be part
	34:7	grandsons responsible for a father's **s**
Lev	4:2	When a person **s** unintentionally
	4:3	if it's the anointed priest who **s**
	4:13	whole congregation **s** unintentionally
	4:22	When a ruler **s** unintentionally
	4:27	**s** unintentionally
	5:13	make atonement for . . . any of these **s**
	5:15	betrays his trust and unknowingly **s**
	5:17	**s** by breaking any of the commandments
	6:2	**s** by betraying trust with God
	6:3	falsely regarding any of these **s**
	6:4	when he **s** and is found guilty
	16:16	rebellion, and all their other **s**
	16:21	their acts of rebellion, all their **s**
	16:21	will put all the **s** on the goat
	16:30	you will be made clean of all your **s**
	16:34	atonement is to be made for all the **s**
	26:18	seven times over for your **s**
	26:21	seven times more than your **s**
	26:24	punish you for your **s** seven times over
	26:28	punishing you for your **s** seven times
	26:39	because of their **s**, their **s** compounded
	26:40	if they confess their **s** and the **s**
	26:43	They'll pay for their **s**
Nu	14:18	fallout of parents' **s** to children
	14:34	sentence to serve for your **s**
	15:27	just one person who **s** by mistake
	15:29	for everyone who **s** by mistake
	15:30	the person . . . who **s** defiantly
	16:22	when one man **s** are you going to take
	16:26	carried off on the flood of their **s**
	18:1	**s** having to do with the Sanctuary
	27:3	He died for his own **s**
Dt	5:9	parents responsible for any **s** they pass on
	9:18	because of you, all your **s**

1Sa	12:19	On top of all our other s
1Ki	8:35	quitting their s because
	8:36	forgive the s of your servants
	14:16	because of Jeroboam's s
	15:30	punishment for Jeroboam's s
	16:13	wages for the s of Baasha
	16:19	It was a fit end for his s
	16:26	dragged Israel into his s
	16:31	copy the s of Jeroboam
	17:18	a holy man barging in, exposing my s
2Ki	10:29	s of Jeroboam son of Nebat, the s
	10:31	from the s of Jeroboam
	13:6	didn't turn away from the Jeroboam-s
	13:11	the s of Jeroboam
	15:18	repeated the s of Jeroboam
	17:22	went along with all the s
	21:11	committed these outrageous s
	21:16	s in which he involved his people
	24:3	the enormity of the s of Manasseh
2Ch	6:26	quit their s because you have scourged
	6:27	forgive the s of your servants
	7:14	I'll . . . forgive their s
	30:7	Don't repeat the s of your ancestors
	33:19	a list of all his s
Ezr	9:7	kings and priests, because of our s
Ne	1:6	confessing the s of the People
	9:2	stood up, and confessed their s
	9:37	kings you put over us because of our s
Job	7:21	Why don't you just forgive my s
	13:23	How many s have been charged
	13:26	accountable for the s of my youth
	14:17	My s will be stuffed in a sack
	19:29	Worry about your own s
	22:5	there's no end to your s
Ps	19:13	Keep me from stupid s
	40:12	a mob of s past counting
	41:4	my s have torn me to pieces
	51:2	soak out my s in your laundry
	51:3	my s are staring me down
	65:3	Our s too much for us
	79:8	blame us for the s of our parents
	79:9	forgive us our s
	85:2	you put their s far out of sight
	90:8	You keep track of all our s
	99:8	But you were never soft on their s
	103:3	He forgives your s — every one
	103:10	doesn't treat us as our s deserve
	103:12	he has separated us from our s
	106:43	finally their s destroyed them
	109:15	Their s recorded forever before God
Pr	28:13	You can't whitewash your s
Ecc	8:12	though a person s and gets by with it
Isa	1:18	If your s are blood-red
	3:9	flout their s like degenerate Sodom
	6:7	Gone your guilt, your s wiped out
	24:20	Its piled-up s are too much for it
	38:17	my s you let go of
	43:24	you haven't been stingy with your s
	43:25	I, am the one who takes care of your s
	44:22	There's nothing left of your s
	50:1	It's your s that put you here
	53:5	it was our s that did that to him

	53:6	God has piled all our s . . . on him
	53:8	beaten bloody for the s of my people
	53:11	carries the burden of their s
	57:17	angry, because of Israel's s
	58:1	face my family Jacob with their s
	58:9	quit gossiping about other people's s
	59:2	Your s got between you
	59:12	our s stand up and accuse us
	59:20	those in Jacob who leave their s
	64:7	left us to stew in our s
	65:6	Their s are all written out
	65:7	their s. And for the s of their
Jer	5:6	the people's s are piled sky-high
	5:25	s keep my blessings at a distance
	11:10	reenact the s of their ancestors
	14:10	note their guilt and punish their s
	15:13	punishment for your s, I'm giving away
	16:17	neither them nor their s
	17:3	reparations for your s
	30:14	the endless list of your s
	30:15	the endless list of your s
	32:18	fallout from their parents' s
	51:6	I pay her back for her s
La	1:14	wove my s into a rope and harnessed me
	1:22	what you gave me for my s
	4:13	Because of the s of her prophets
	4:22	put all your s on display
Eze	3:20	they'll die because of their s
	7:13	country is bankrupt because of its s
	7:16	Each one moaning for his own s
	14:13	s against me by living faithlessly
	18:14	sees all the s done by his parent
	18:18	for what the parent did, for the s of
	18:20	The soul that s is the soul that dies
	24:23	your s will eat away at you
	33:8	wicked will die unwarned in their s
	33:9	they'll die in their s well-warned
	33:10	rebellions and s are weighing us down
	33:12	A good person who s can't expect
	33:16	None of his s will be kept on
	39:23	because of their s that Israel went
	45:20	for anyone who s without knowing it
Da	4:27	Make a clean break with your s
	9:16	because of our s and our parents' s
	9:20	baring my s and the s of my people
Hos	4:8	They pig out on my people's s
	7:1	soon filled the slate with new s
	8:13	punish their s and send them back
	9:9	He'll make them pay for their s
Joel	2:12	fasting and weeping, sorry for your s
	3:21	The s I haven't already forgiven
Am	1:3	three great s of Damascus
	1:6	three great s of Gaza — make that four
	1:9	three great s of Tyre — make that four
	1:11	three great s of Edom — make that four
	1:13	three great s of Ammon
	2:1	three great s of Moab — make that four
	2:4	three great s of Judah
	2:6	three great s of Israel
	3:2	holding you responsible for all your s
	3:14	The day I make Israel pay for its s
	5:12	the enormity of your s

S

Mic	1:13	s in Israel also got their start
	6:13	You'll pay for your s
	7:18	blind eye, a deaf ear, to the past s
	7:19	You'll sink our s to the bottom
Zec	13:1	for washing away their s
Mt	1:21	he will save his people from their s
	3:6	those who came to confess their s
	9:2	Cheer up, son. I forgive your s
	9:5	I forgive your s
	26:28	for the forgiveness of s
Mk	1:4	change that leads to forgiveness of s
	1:5	confessed their s, were baptized
	2:5	paraplegic, "Son, I forgive your s
	2:7	God and only God can forgive s
	2:9	I forgive your s
	11:25	wipe your slate clean of s
Lk	1:77	the forgiveness of their s
	3:3	change leading to forgiveness of s
	5:20	Friend, I forgive your s
	5:21	God and only God can forgive s
	5:23	I forgive your s
	7:47	She was forgiven many, many s
	7:48	I forgive your s
	7:49	Who does he think he is, forgiving s
	24:47	change through the forgiveness of s
Jn	1:30	He forgives the s of the world
	1:31	scrubbing s from your life
	8:24	you're at the dead end of s
	20:23	If you forgive someone's s
Ac	2:38	so your s are forgiven
	3:19	so he can wipe away your s
	5:31	gift of a changed life and s forgiven
	10:43	he is the means to forgiveness of s
	13:38	forgiveness of your s can be promised
	22:16	scrubbed clean of those s
	26:18	present my offer of s forgiven
Ro	3:25	the s he had so patiently endured
	4:7	whose s are wiped clean from the slate
	5:16	verdict on the many s that followed
	8:35	even the worst s listed in Scripture
	11:27	to my people: removal of their s
1Co	6:18	sexual s are different from all others
	13:5	Doesn't keep score of the s of others
	15:3	the Messiah died for our s
2Co	5:19	offering forgiveness of s
Gal	1:4	himself as a sacrifice for our s
Col	1:14	the s we were doomed to keep repeating
	2:13	Think of it! All s forgiven
1Ti	5:22	involved in some serious s
	5:24	The s of some people are blatant
Heb	2:17	priest to get rid of the people's s
	5:1	offer sacrifices for their s
	5:3	for his own s as well as the people's s
	7:27	sacrifices for his own s every day
	8:12	slate of their s forever wiped clean
	9:7	own s and the people's accumulated s
	9:16	old obligations and accompanying s
	9:22	regarding forgiveness of s
	9:24	as the sacrifice for our s
	9:28	sacrifice that took care of s forever
	10:2	no longer dragged down by their s
	10:12	Christ made a single sacrifice for s

	10:17	wipe the slate clean of their s
	10:18	Once s are taken care of for good
	12:1	No extra spiritual fat, no parasitic s
Jas	5:16	Confess your s to each other
1Pe	2:24	used his servant body to carry our s
	3:18	suffered because of others' s
1Jn	1:9	if we admit our s
	2:2	he served as a sacrifice for our s
	2:12	Your s are forgiven in Jesus' name
	4:10	as a sacrifice to clear away our s
Rev	1:5	blood-washed our s from our lives
	11:10	impossible for them to enjoy their s
	18:4	don't get mixed up in her s
	18:5	Her s stink to high Heaven

Skeptic

| Pr | 30:1 | The s swore, "There is no God! |
| 1Co | 15:35 | Some s is sure to ask, "Show me |

Skeptical

Mk	2:8	Why are you so s
Lk	11:16	Others were s, waiting
Ro	4:20	asking cautiously s questions

Skeptics

Pr	3:34	He gives proud s a cold shoulder
Lk	1:17	devout understanding among hardened s
2Pe	3:7	destruction of the desecrating s

Skill

Ex	31:3	with the Spirit of God, giving him s
	35:31	with the Spirit of God, with s
	36:1	everyone whom God has given the s
Ps	25:21	Use all your s to put me together
	136:5	The God whose s formed the cosmos
Da	1:17	knowledge and s in both books and life
Php	3:21	whole with the same powerful s

Skilled

Ge	21:20	became a s archer
Ex	26:1	A s craftsman should do it
	26:31	woven into it by a s craftsman
	28:3	Consult with the s craftsmen
	28:6	fine twisted linen by a s craftsman
	28:15	using s craftsmen, the same as
	35:25	All the women s at weaving
	35:33	working in every kind of s craft
	36:8	all the s artisans on The Dwelling
1Ch	5:18	fit and s in handling shield
	9:13	s and seasoned servants in the work
2Ch	34:12	they were all s musicians
Pr	9:10	S living gets its start in
	15:33	Fear-of-God is a school in s living
	22:29	s workers are always in demand
	31:19	She's s in the crafts of home
Jer	24:1	craftsmen, and the s laborers
	29:2	all the s laborers and craftsmen

Eze	21:31	give you to vicious men s in torture
Am	2:15	S archers won't make it
Eph	4:12	train Christians in s servant work
Jas	3:4	ship in the hands of a s captain

Skills

Ex	31:6	given the s to make all the things
	35:10	Come — all of you who have s

Slain

Dt	32:42	Feasting on s and captive alike
Eze	32:25	section set aside for the s in battle
	32:26	section set aside for the s
	32:28	section sct aside for the s
	37:9	Breathe on these s bodies
Rev	5:9	S! Paying in blood, you bought men
	5:12	The s Lab is worthy!

Slander

Ps	55:3	stockpile angry s
	109:4	I loved them and now they s me
Pr	10:18	fools openly spread s
	11:12	Mean-spirited s is heartless
	24:28	no s or gossip, please
Mt	12:25	Jesus confronted their s
Mk	3:23	Jesus confronted their s with a story
	7:22	mean looks, s, arrogance
Ro	3:8	That's pure s
2Pe	2:11	trying to s others before God

Slandered

Ps	119:161	s unmercifully by the politicians
2Co	6:8	when we're blamed; s, and honored

Slanders

Ps	41:7	whisper s all over town
Mt	12:31	persist in your s against God's Spirit
Mk	3:29	persist in your s against God

Sloppy

Jdg	5:7	Warriors became fat and s
Pr	18:9	Slack habits and s work are as bad
Isa	28:1	Tipsy, s-fat, beer-bellied
Jer	48:10	S work in God's name is cursed
Mal	1:6	By your shoddy, s, defiling worship
1Co	9:26	No s living for me
1Pe	1:17	won't let you get by with s living

Slut

Dt	22:14	calling her a s
1Sa	20:30	You son of a s!
Isa	57:3	Sons of a s, daughters of a whore
Jer	18:13	Virgin Israel has become a s
Na	3:6	on a pedestal: 'S on Exhibit

Sluttish

Eze	16:24	exposed your s sex
	16:27	were shocked at your s life
	16:43	obscenities with all your s ways
	23:27	I'll put a stop to your s sex
	23:29	Your s lust
	23:35	pay for your s sex and whoring life
	23:48	I'll put an end to s sex

Sly

2Ki	17:9	did all kinds of things on the s
Job	31:27	worshiped them on the s
Ac	16:37	get us out of the way on the s
2Co	2:11	not oblivious to his s ways

Smart

Job	22:2	or s enough to give him advice
	37:19	If you're so s, give us a lesson
	39:17	She wasn't created very s
Ps	1:1	don't go to S-Mouth College
	75:4	I say to the s alecks
	94:8	how long before you get s
Pr	10:5	hay while the sun shines — that's s
	16:14	s to stay clear of someone like that
	16:27	their words s and burn
	17:28	keep their mouths shut, they're s
	19:11	S people know how to hold their tongue
	25:27	It's not s to stuff yourself
	26:12	See that man who thinks he's so s
Ecc	2:12	look at what's s and what's stupid
	2:13	it's better to be s than stupid
	2:14	the s ones see where they're going
	2:16	The s and the stupid both disappear
	8:17	No matter how s you are, you won't get
	9:11	Nor riches to the s
Isa	5:21	Doom to you who think you're so s
	29:14	s people who thought they knew
Jer	7:8	Get s! Your leaders are handing you
	31:34	the s and the slow
Mt	7:24	you are like a s carpenter
	25:2	Five were silly and five were s
	25:4	The s virgins took jars of oil
	25:8	The silly virgins said to the s ones
Lk	6:48	like a s carpenter who dug deep
	16:9	want you to be s in the same way
Ro	1:14	mannered or rude, s or simple
	11:34	who can explain God? Anyone s enough
	16:19	want you also to be s
1Co	3:19	world calls s, God calls stupid
Gal	3:3	If you weren't s enough
1Th	5.6	keep our eyes open and be s

Smile

Nu	6:25	God s on you and gift you
Dt	33:16	the s of the Burning-Bush Dweller
Job	9:27	force a s
	10:20	let me s just once
	33:26	You'll see God's s and celebrate

S

Ps	21:6	you make him glad when you s
	31:16	Warm me, your servant, with a s
	34:5	give him your warmest s
	42:5	He puts a s on my face
	42:11	He puts a s on my face
	43:5	He puts a s on my face
	67:1	mark us with grace and blessing! S
	77:7	Will he never s again
	80:3	God, come back! S your blessing s
	80:7	come back! S your blessing s
	80:19	S your blessing s
	119:58	s, be gracious to me
	119:135	S on me, your servant; teach me
	120:2	They s so sweetly but lie
Pr	14:3	Frivolous talk provokes a derisive s
	15:13	A cheerful heart brings a s
	31:25	always faces tomorrow with a s
SS	4:2	Your s is generous and full
	6:6	Your s is generous and full
Isa	60:5	When you see them coming you'll s
Jer	9:8	Neighbor greets neighbor with a s
Mic	2:11	a good s and glib tongue
Mt	7:15	Be wary of false preachers who s a lot
Ro	12:8	Keep a s on your face
Eph	6:7	work with a s on your face
Heb	10:34	you let them go with a s

Smiled

Job	29:24	When I s at them
Ps	85:1	God, you s on your good earth

Smiles

Isa	60:5	you'll smile — big s
Jer	7:34	I'll empty both s and laughter
	16:9	I'm about to banish s and laughter
Hos	10:2	Their sweet s are sheer lies
Na	3:17	full of s and promises

Smiling

Ge	33:10	it was as the face of God s on me
Ps	44:3	You gave it, s as you gave it
Jer	12:6	especially when they're s

Sneer

Joel	2:17	pagans take over and rule them and s
Mt	7:3	oblivious to the ugly s on your own
	7:5	Wipe that ugly s off your own face
Lk	6:41	oblivious to the ugly s on your own
	6:42	Wipe that ugly s off your own face
Jude	1:10	s at anything they can't understand

Sneered

1Sa	17:42	took one look down on him and s
1Ti	4:4	Nothing is to be s at and thrown out

Sneering

1Sa	26:19	s, 'Out of here! Go get a job

Isa	57:4	taunting, s, and sticking out

Sneers

Ps	79:10	their s: "Where's your God?

Sober

1Sa	1:14	S up, woman
Pr	23:35	When I'm s enough to manage it
Isa	28:22	S up, friends, and don't scoff
Joel	1:5	S up, you drunks!
Jn	3:11	I'm speaking s truth to you
	6:47	the most solemn and s truth
1Th	5:8	Walk out into the daylight s
2Ti	2:25	God might s them up
1Jn	1:2	telling you in most s prose

Sobered

1Sa	25:37	after Nabal had s up, she told him
Mt	14:9	That s the king up fast
Mk	6:26	That s the king up fast

Solitary

Jos	17:14	just one allotment, one s share
2Sa	18:10	A s soldier saw him
	18:24	He saw a s runner
Ecc	4:8	s person, completely alone
Isa	51:2	One s man when I called him
Jn	5:30	I can't do a s thing on my own

Sorcery

Lev	19:26	Don't practice divination or s
Nu	24:1	he didn't work in any s as he had
Dt	18:10	Don't practice divination, s
2Ki	17:17	all the black arts of magic and s
Isa	47:15	That's the fate of your friends in s

Sorrow

Ge	41:52	prospered me in the land of my s
	48:7	Rachel, to my deep s, died
Est	9:22	month in which their s turned to joy
Job	14:22	a lifetime of pain, a lifetime of s
Ps	89:47	Remember my s and how short life is
Hos	13:14	abolishing regret, banishing s
Mic	7:1	I'm overwhelmed with s!
Mt	26:37	plunged into an agonizing s
	26:38	This s is crushing my life out
Ro	9:1	I carry with me at all times a huge s
Heb	5:7	Jesus cried out in pain and wept in s

Sorrows

Isa	3:26	brought to her knees by her s
	35:10	all s and sighs scurry into the night
Zep	3:18	s of your exile will dissipate

S

Sovereign

1Ki	4:21	Solomon was s over all
	4:24	Solomon was s over everything
2Ki	19:15	the one and only God, s over all
Job	12:9	all know and agree that God is s
	23:13	But he is singular and s
	25:2	God is s, God is fearsome
Ps	47:8	God is Lord of godless nations — s
	66:7	Ever s in his high tower
	68:18	sit there in state, God, s God
	84:11	All sunshine and s is God
	102:12	God, are s still, always and ever s
	149:2	celebrate their S Creator
La	5:19	God, you're s still
Da	4:3	his s rule goes on forever
	4:22	your s rule stretches to the four
	4:34	His s rule lasts and lasts
Am	9:12	everyone else under my s judgment
Hag	2:23	sign of my s presence and authority
Ac	19:20	the Word of the Master was now s
Ro	5:17	recovery life makes, s life
	6:2	left the country where sin is s
	6:5	going in our new grace-s country
Rev	1:8	I'm the S-Strong
	4:8	God our Master, S-Strong
	11:17	We thank you, O God, S-Strong
	15:3	O God, the S-Strong
	16:7	Yes, O God, the S-Strong
	16:14	the Great Day of God, the S-Strong
	19:6	our God, the S-Strong
	19:15	raging wrath of God, the S-Strong
	21:22	for the Lord God — the S-Strong

Sow

Ex	23:10	S your land for six years and gather
Lev	25:3	S your fields, prune your vineyards
	25:4	you will not s your fields or prune
	25:11	Don't s; don't reap what volunteers
2Ki	19:29	the third year you'll s and harvest
Job	4:8	those who plow evil and s trouble
Isa	30:23	will provide rain for the seeds you s
Hos	10:12	S righteousness, reap love
	13:8	like a s grizzly robbed of her cubs
Lk	8:5	A farmer went out to s his seed

Sowed

Jdg	9:45	then s it with salt
Ps	25:7	Forget that I s wild oats
	107:37	They s the fields
Mt	13:25	his enemy s thistles all through

Sower

Jn	4:36	S is arm in arm with the Harvester

Sowing

Isa	37:30	back to normal, with regular s
Hos	6:11	You've been s wild oats

Zec	8:12	S and harvesting will resume
Ac	14:2	s mistrust and suspicion in the minds

Sown

Dt	22:9	you will forfeit what you've s
Ps	17:14	famine food, The weeds they've s
1Co	15:44	The seed s is natural

Speech

Ge	11:7	we'll go down and garble their s
	42:20	confirming the truth of your s
Ex	23:8	twist the s of good people
Nu	22:28	God gave s to the donkey
	24:16	of the man who hears godly s
1Sa	17:16	took his stand and made his s
2Ki	18:37	reported . . . the s of the Rabshakeh
	19:4	blasphemous s of the Rabshakeh
2Ch	13:4	gave this s: "Listen, Jeroboam
Job	41:3	flatter you with flowery s
Ps	55:21	All my life I've been charmed by his s
Pr	1:20	At the town center she makes her s
	7:21	bewitched by her honeyed s
	10:20	s of a good person is worth waiting
	10:32	The s of a good person clears the air
	12:6	the s of the upright saves
	14:3	wise s evokes nothing but respect
	16:13	Good leaders cultivate honest s
	16:24	Gracious s is like clover honey
	18:17	The first s in a court case
	22:18	give it bold expression in your s
	23:33	with your s all slurred
	25:15	gentle s breaks down rigid defenses
Isa	29:4	Your s will whisper from the dust
	49:2	He gave me s that would cut
Eze	11:5	That's a fine public s, Israel
	33:22	restored my s
Mt	5:34	making your s sound more religious
Mk	7:35	hearing was clear and his s plain
	7:37	s to the speechless
Lk	15:21	The son started his s
Jn	8:20	He gave this s in the Treasury
	16:25	I've used figures of s in telling you
	16:29	plain talk — no more figures of s
Ac	24:4	tire you out with a long s
1Co	1:5	it's beyond s, beyond knowledge
	13:8	Inspired s will be over some day
	14:3	proclaim his truth in everyday s
Col	4:6	Be gracious in your s
2Th	2:17	invigorate your work, enliven your s
Jas	3:2	someone whose s was perfectly true
	3:6	By our s we can ruin the world

Speechless

Ge	45:3	They were s
Job	40:4	I'm s, in awe
Ps	107:42	bad people are s
	112:10	Blusters away but ends up s
	119:120	decisions leave me s with reverence
Jer	19:8	shocked s by the savage brutality

S

Eze	16:63	it will leave you s
Mic	7:16	their arrogance, s and clueless
Mt	9:32	struck s by an evil spirit
	22:12	The man was s
	22:22	The Pharisees were s
Mk	7:37	hearing to the deaf, speech to the s
	9:17	my mute son, made s by a demon
	12:17	Their mouths hung open, s
Lk	1:22	He continued s and had to use sign
	2:33	Jesus' father and mother were s
	9:36	They were s. And they continued s
	11:14	a demon that had kept him s
	20:26	caught them off guard and left them s

Spirit

Ge	1:2	God's S brooded like a bird
	5:3	his very s and image
	41:38	anyone else who has God's s in him
	45:27	their father Jacob's s revived
Ex	6:9	beaten down in s by the harsh
	31:3	I've filled him with the S of God
	35:21	whose s was freely responsive
	35:31	He's filled him with the S of God
Nu	11:17	take some of the S that is on you
	11:25	took some of the S that was on him
	11:26	the S also rested on them
	11:29	God would put his S on all of them
	14:24	He has a different s
	24:2	The S of God came on him
	27:18	Josua . . . the S is in him
Dt	2:30	God, your God, turned his s mean
	20:8	his timidity and cowardly s
	34:9	was filled with the s of wisdom
Jos	7:5	all s knocked out of them
Jdg	3:9	The S of God came on him
	6:34	God's S came over Gideon
	11:29	God's S came upon Jephthah
	13:25	The S of God began working in him
	14:6	the S of God came on him powerfully
	14:19	the S of God came powerfully on him
	15:14	the S of God came on him
	15:19	Samson drank. His s revived
1Sa	10:6	the S of God will come on you
	10:10	the S of God came on Saul
	11:6	The S of God came on Saul
	16:13	The S of God entered David
	16:14	the S of God left Saul
	19:20	the S of God was on them, too
	19:23	the S of God was on him, too
	28:13	a s ascending from the underground
2Sa	23:2	God's S spoke through me
1Ki	18:12	the S of God will whisk you away
	22:24	Since when did the S of God leave me
2Ki	2:15	The s of Elijah lives in Elisha
	2:16	Maybe God's s has swept him off
	5:26	I was with you in s
	23:24	trashed s-mediums, sorcerers
1Ch	5:26	stirred up the s of Pul king
	12:18	chief of the Thirty, moved by God's S
	28:12	everything that God's S had brought
	29:18	keep this generous s alive forever

2Ch	15:1	moved by the S of God
	18:23	Since when did the S of God leave me
	20:14	was moved by the S of God to speak
	24:20	the S of God moved Zechariah
	31:21	did well in a s of prayerful worship
Ne	9:20	gave them your good S to teach them
	9:30	warned them by your s
Job	4:15	A s glided right in front of me
	17:1	My s is broken
	32:8	it's God's S in a person
	33:4	The S of God made me what I am
Ps	69:32	The poor in s see and are glad
	104:29	Take back your S and they die
	104:30	Send out your S and they spring
	112:8	S firm, unperturbed, Ever blessed
	139:7	anyplace I can go to avoid your S
	142:3	sink in despair, my s ebbing away
	143:4	in despair, my s draining away
	143:10	Lead me by your blessed S
Pr	1:23	ready to pour out my s on you
	15:18	a calm, cool s keeps the peace
	18:14	A healthy s conquers adversity
	22:1	a gracious s is better than money
Ecc	3:21	that the human s rises to heaven
	12:7	The s returns to God
Isa	8:19	Why not tap into the s-world
	11:2	S of God will hover over him, the S
	26:9	my s reaches out to you
	30:1	You make deals, but not in my S
	31:3	their horses are flesh, not S
	32:15	grieve until the S is poured down
	34:16	His S set it in motion
	38:16	my s is still alive
	42:1	I've bathed him with my S, my life
	44:3	I will pour my S into your descendants
	48:16	the Master, God, sends me and his S
	57:15	with the low-spirited, the s-crushed
	59:21	My S that I've placed upon you
	61:1	The S of God, the Master, is on me
	61:3	praising heart instead of a languid s
	63:10	they grieved his Holy S
	63:11	the One who set his Holy S within them
	63:14	the S of God gave them rest
Eze	1:12	Wherever the s went, they went
	1:20	Wherever the s went, they went
	1:21	the s of the living creatures was in
	2:2	I heard the voice, the S entered me
	3:12	Then the S picked me up
	3:14	The S lifted me and took me away
	3:24	the S entered me and put me on my feet
	8:3	The S swept me high in the air
	10:17	the s of the living creatures
	11:1	the S picked me up
	11:5	the S of God came upon me
	11:19	I'll put a new s in you
	11:24	the vision given me by the S of God
	11:24	the S took me and carried
	18:31	Get a new heart! Get a new s!
	36:26	put a new s in you
	36:27	I'll put my S in you
	37:1	God grabbed me. God's S took me
	39:29	After I've poured my S on Israel

S

	43:5	The S put me on my feet and led me
Da	4:8	a man full of the divine Holy S
	4:9	a man full of the divine Holy S
	4:18	You're full of the divine Holy S
	5:11	who is full of the divine Holy S
	5:14	you're full of the Holy S
	5:20	developed a big head and a hard s
	6:3	brimming with s and intelligence
Hos	9:4	souls polluted by the s-dirty air
	9:7	The 'man of the S' is nuts!"
Joel	2:28	I will pour out my S on every kind
	2:29	even pour out my S on the servants
Mic	3:8	filled with God's S of justice
Zep	3:12	you who are poor in s
Zec	4:6	They only come about through my S
	6:8	conveying a sense of my S, screne
	7:12	the S-filled sermons preached
	12:10	I'll pour out a s of grace and prayer
Mal	2:15	His S inhabits even the smallest
Mt	1:18	It was by the Holy S
	1:20	Mary's pregnancy is S-conceived
	1:20	God's Holy S has made
	3:11	the Holy S within you
	3:16	skies opened up and he saw God's S
	3:17	along with the S, a voice
	4:1	into the wild by the S for the Test
	7:2	critical s has a way of boomeranging
	9:14	discipline body and s by fasting
	9:32	struck speechless by an evil s
	9:33	Jesus threw the evil tormenting s out
	10:20	the S of your Father will supply
	12:18	I've placed my S on him
	12:31	your slanders against God's S
	12:32	the Holy S can forgive you
	12:43	defiling evil s is expelled
	15:22	cruelly afflicted by an evil s
	28:19	name: Father, Son, and Holy S
Mk	1:8	a holy baptism by the Holy S
	1:10	sky split open and God's S
	1:11	Along with the S, a voice
	1:12	this same S pushed Jesus out
	1:26	The afflicting s threw the man
	3:29	your slanders against God's Holy S
	5:8	commanded the tormenting evil s
	9:25	gave the vile s its marching orders
	12:36	David, inspired by the Holy S, said
	13:11	the Holy S will make his witness
Lk	1:15	He'll be filled with the Holy S
	1:35	The Holy S will come upon you
	1:41	She was filled with the Holy S
	1:67	Zachariah was filled with the Holy S
	2:25	And the Holy S was on him
	2:26	the Holy S had shown him
	2:27	Led by the S, he entered the Temple
	2:40	grew strong in body and wise in s
	2:52	growing up in both body and s
	3:16	a fire, the Holy S within you
	3:22	the Holy S, like a dove descending
	4:1	Now Jesus, full of the Holy S
	4:14	returned to Galilee powerful in the S
	4:18	God's S is on me; he's chosen me
	4:35	demonic s threw the man down

	8:29	order the unclean s out of him
	9:39	Often a s seizes him
	9:42	ordered the vile s gone
	9:48	s, not your size, makes the difference
	10:21	exuberant in the Holy S
	11:13	will give the Holy S when you ask
	11:24	When a corrupting s is expelled
	12:10	taking aim at the Holy S
	12:12	Holy S will give you the right words
Jn	1:32	I watched the S, like a dove
	1:33	One on whom you see the S come down
	3:6	can't see and touch — the S
	3:8	the wind of God, the S of God
	3:34	don't think he rations out the S
	4:23	Your worship must engage your s
	4:24	God is sheer being itself — S
	6:63	The S can make life
	7:39	He said this in regard to the S
	14:17	This Friend is the S of Truth
	14:26	the Holy S whom the Father will send
	15:26	the S of Truth issuing from the Father
	16:13	the S of the Truth, he will take you
	19:30	Bowing his head, he offered up his s
	20:22	"Receive the Holy S," he said
Ac	1:2	chosen through the Holy S
	1:5	you will be baptized in the Holy S
	1:8	What you'll get is the Holy S
	1:8	And when the Holy S comes on you
	1:16	the Holy S spoke through David
	2:3	the Holy S spread through their ranks
	2:4	different languages as the S prompted
	2:17	I will pour out my S on every kind
	2:18	pour out my S On those who serve me
	2:33	receiving the promise of the Holy S
	2:38	Receive the gift of the Holy S
	4:8	Peter, full of the Holy S, let loose
	4:25	By the Holy S you spoke
	4:31	were all filled with the Holy S
	5:3	did Satan get you to lie to the Holy S
	5:9	conspire against the S of the Master
	5:32	Holy S, whom God gives
	6:3	men full of the Holy S and good sense
	6:5	men full of faith and the Holy S
	6:10	no match for his wisdom and s
	7:51	Deliberately ignoring the Holy S
	7:55	Stephen, full of the Holy S
	8:15	pray for them to receive the Holy S
	8:16	the Holy S hadn't yet fallen on them
	8:17	they did receive the Holy S
	8:18	laying on hands conferred the S
	8:29	The S told Philip, "Climb into
	8:39	the S of God suddenly took Philip
	9:17	be filled with the Holy S
	9:31	The Holy S was with them
	10:19	so the S whispered to him
	10:38	anointed by God with the Holy S
	10:44	the Holy S came on the listeners
	10:45	the gift of the Holy S was poured out
	10:47	received the Holy S exactly as we did
	11:12	The S told me to go with them
	11:15	the Holy S fell on them
	11:16	will be baptized with the Holy S

S

	11:24	confident in the Holy S's ways		3:14	able to receive God's life, his S
	11:28	prompted by the S, warned		4:6	sent the S of his Son into our lives
	13:2	the Holy S spoke: "Take Barnabas		4:29	child who came — empowered by the S
	13:4	new assignment by the Holy S		5:5	satisfying relationship with the S
	13:9	Saul (or Paul), full of the Holy S		5:16	animated and motivated by God's S
	13:52	brimming with joy and the Holy S		5:17	at odds with a free s
	15:8	gave them the Holy S exactly as		5:17	just as the free s is
	15:28	It seemed to the Holy S and to us be		5:18	choose to be led by the S
	16:6	the Holy S blocked that route		5:25	we have chosen, the life of the S
	16:7	the S of Jesus wouldn't let them go		6:8	letting God's S do the growth work
	16:18	commanded the s that possessed her	Eph	1:13	delivered by the Holy S
	19:2	receive the Holy S when you believed		2:18	we both share the same S
	19:6	the Holy S entered them		3:5	been made clear by God's S
	19:15	when the evil s talked back		3:16	I ask him to strengthen you by his S
	20:23	the Holy S has let me know repeatedly		3:20	his S deeply and gently within us
	20:28	The Holy S has put you in charge		4:30	Holy S, moving and breathing in you
	21:4	Paul, from insight given by the S		5:18	Drink the S of God
	21:11	This is what the Holy S says	Php	1:19	response of the S of Jesus Christ
	23:8	a resurrection or angels or even a s		2:1	being in a community of the S
	23:9	what if a s has spoken to him		3:3	the ones the S of God leads to work
	28:25	The Holy S sure knew what he was	Col	1:8	worked into your lives by the S
Ro	1:4	Son of God was shown by the S		1:28	teach in a s of profound common sense
	5:5	into our lives through the Holy S		2:8	empty superstitions of s beings
	8:2	The S of life in Christ	1Th	1:5	Holy S put steel in your convictions
	8:4	embrace what the S is doing in us		1:6	take great joy from the Holy S
	8:5	find that God's S is in them		4:8	making you a gift of his Holy S
	8:9	clearly present God, the S of Christ		5:19	Don't suppress the S
	8:11	With his S living in you		5:23	put you together — s, soul, and body
	8:14	God's S beckons	2Th	2:7	the s of anarchy is not now at work
	8:16	God's S touches our spirits		2:14	the life of the S he invited you to
	8:22	The S of God is arousing us within	1Ti	3:16	was proved right by the invisible S
	8:26	God's S is right alongside		4:1	The S makes it clear that as
	9:2	Christ and the Holy S are my witnesses	2Ti	1:14	placed in your custody by the Holy S
	9:6	Israelites of the s	Tit	3:5	washed inside and out by the Holy S
	15:13	life-giving energy of the Holy S	Heb	2:4	with gifts through the Holy S
	15:30	Jesus, through the love of the S		3:7	That's why the Holy S says
	15:31	accepted in the s in which it is given		6:4	part of the work of the Holy S
1Co	2:4	God's S and God's power did it		9:8	the Holy S's way of showing
	2:10	God by his S has brought it all		9:15	Through the S, Christ offered himself
	2:16	anyone around who knows God's S		10:15	The Holy S confirms this
	5:4	I'll be present in s with you		10:29	insult this most gracious S
	6:11	by our God present in us, the S	Jas	2:16	Be filled with the Holy S!
	6:19	the place of the Holy S		2:26	moment you separate body and s
	12:1	God's S gets worked into our lives	1Pe	1:2	determined by the work of the S
	12:3	the S of God would never prompt		1:11	The Messiah's S let them in
	12:4	they all originate in God's S		1:12	through the Holy S — the Message
	12:5	they all originate in God's S		4:14	It's the S of God and his glory
	12:7	things are handed out by the S	2Pe	1:21	resulted when the Holy S prompted
	12:11	by the one S of God	1Jn	3:24	by the S he gave us
	12:13	By means of his one S, we all		4:2	how you test for the genuine S of God
	14:14	If I pray in tongues, my s prays		4:3	This is the s of antichrist
	15:45	the Last Adam is a life-giving S		4:4	the S in you is far stronger
2Co	1:22	By his S he has stamped us		4:6	the S of Truth from the s of deception
	3:3	not with ink, but with God's living S		4:13	from his life, from his very own S
	3:6	your s. It's written with S on s		5:6	the S is confirming the truth
	3:8	the Government of Living S		5:8	the S, the Baptism, the Crucifixion
	3:17	God is personally present, a living S	Jude	1:19	nothing to them, no sign of the S
	5:5	The S of God whets our appetite		1:20	praying in the Holy S
	10:1	the gentle but firm s of Christ	Rev	1:10	I was in the S, praying
	11:4	different s, different message		2:7	the S blowing through the churches
	13:14	intimate friendship of the Holy S		2:11	the S blowing through the churches
Gal	3:5	with his own presence, his Holy S		2:17	the S blowing through the churches

S

	2:29	the S blowing through the churches
	3:6	the S blowing through the churches
	3:13	the S blowing through the churches
	3:22	the S blowing through the churches
	4:5	these are the Sevenfold S of God
	11:11	the Living S of God will enter them
	14:13	"Yes," says the S, "and blessed rest
	17:3	In the S he carried me out
	19:10	witness of Jesus is the s of prophecy
	21:10	He took me away in the S
	22:17	"Come!" say the S and the Bride

Spirits

Ex	35:22	all the willing s among them
Nu	27:16	the God of the s of everyone living
1Sa	25:36	He was in high s
	28:7	Find me someone who can call up s
2Ki	21:6	He . . . consulted s from the underworld
2Ch	33:6	He . . . consulted s from the underworld
Job	7:13	A little nap will lift my s
Isa	65:14	wail from crushed s
Zec	10:3	He'll revive their s, make them proud
Mt	8:31	The evil s begged Jesus
	10:1	power to kick out the evil s
	12:28	I am sending the evil s packing
	12:45	rounds up seven other s more evil
Mk	1:27	shuts up defiling, demonic s
	1:34	cured their . . . tormented s
	3:11	Evil s, when they recognized him
	6:13	healing their s
Lk	4:36	orders demonic s to get out
	6:18	Those disturbed by evil s were healed
	7:21	from diseases, distress, and evil s
	11:26	seven other s dirtier than itself
Jn	4:24	their s, their true selves
Ac	8:7	The evil s protested loudly
	19:13	over victims of evil s
	20:2	lifting their s and charging them
Rn	8:16	God's Spirit touches our s
1Co	2:14	God's Spirit and our s
	12:10	distinguishing between s tongues
2Co	13:11	Keep your s up
Eph	6:18	Keep each other's s up
Col	1:9	minds and s attuned to his will
	3:21	children or you'll crush their s
Rev	1:4	from the Seven S assembled
	3:1	One holding the Seven S of God
	5:6	the Seven S of God sent into all
	16:14	These are demon s performing signs
	18:2	A garrison of carrion s
	22:6	Master of the s of the prophets

Spiritual

2Sa	24:11	Gad the prophet, David's s advisor
2Ki	21:2	all the moral rot and s corruption
2Ch	33:2	all the moral rot and s corruption
Job	15:4	turn s conversation into empty gossip
Ps	105:27	worked marvels in that s wasteland
Isa	30:10	They tell their s leaders
Da	5:11	intellectual brilliance and s wisdom

Mk	3:22	tricks to impress them with s power
Ro	7:14	all God's commands are s, but I'm not
	15:16	serving the s needs
	15:27	got in on all the s gifts
1Co	1:9	got you started in this s adventure
	2:6	get your feet on firm s ground
	5:10	with s phonies
	6:8	the people of your own s family
	6:16	Sex is as much s mystery as physical
	6:19	belonging to the s part of you
	7:14	included in the s purposes of God
	9:11	we have planted s seed among you
	11:34	It is a s meal — a love feast
	15:44	raised up in s immortality
	15:46	Physical life comes first, then s
Col	2:15	stripped all the s tyrants
1Ti	4:7	no s flabbiness, please
2Ti	4:3	fill up on s junk food
Heb	6:19	It's an unbreakable s lifeline
	12:1	No extra s fat, no parasitic sins
1Pe	2:17	Love your s family. Revere God
	4:13	This is a s refining process
2Pe	1:5	good character, s understanding

Spiritualists

Isa	8:19	Consult the s
Jer	27:9	your prophets and s and fortunetellers

Spirituality

1Co	10:27	both bad manners and bad s

Spiritually

Mk	2:17	inviting the sin-sick, not the s-fit
1Co	2:15	S alive, we have access to everything
	6:12	doesn't mean that it's s appropriate
	6:17	want to become s one with the Master
	7:38	Marriage is s and morally right
	14:15	be s free and expressive as I pray
2Co	4:9	we've been s terrorized
Rev	11:8	the Great City s called Sodom

Spiritually-fit

Mk	2:17	inviting the sin-sick, not the s

Spiteful

Pr	31:12	Never s, she treats him generously
Eze	25:12	in s revenge

Spoiled

1Ki	1:6	His father had s him rotten
Ps	78:19	They whined like s children
Pr	29:15	s adolescents embarrass their parents
SS	7:5	I'm s for anyone else
Hos	13:6	You were s
Mt	11:16	The people have been like s children
Lk	7:32	They're like s children complaining

S

1Co	4:14	want you to grow up well, not s
Jas	1:21	throw all s virtue and cancerous evil
	4:3	You're s children, each wanting

Spoiling

Jdg	12:3	Are you s for a fight with me
2Ch	35:22	Josiah was s for a fight
Ps	55:10	Day and night s for a fight
	68:30	s for a fight
Pr	3:30	always s for a fight
Heb	12:9	for training and not s us

Spoils

2Sa	2:21	be content with those s
Isa	33:4	picking the field clean of the enemy s
Heb	7:2	gave him a tenth of the s

Spouse

Pr	18:22	Find a good s, you find a good life
	19:13	a nagging s is a leaky faucet
	19:14	a congenial s comes straight from God
	21:9	than share a mansion with a nagging s
	21:19	than with a cross and petulant s
	25:24	than share a mansion with a nagging s
	27:15	A nagging s is like the drip
Ecc	9:9	Relish life with the s you love
Isa	47:9	S and children gone
Eze	18:6	doesn't seduce a neighbor's s
	18:11	seduces his neighbor's s
	18:15	doesn't seduce his neighbor's s
Mic	7:5	Watch your words, even with your s
Mal	2:15	Don't cheat on your s
Mt	5:27	Don't go to bed with another's s
	19:9	where the s has committed adultery
Lk	14:26	refuses to let go of father, mother, s
	18:29	No one who has sacrificed home, s
Ro	13:9	don't sleep with another person's s
1Co	7:15	if the unbelieving s walks out
	7:33	and in wanting to please your s

Spouses

1Ti	3:12	be committed to their s

Spurn

Dt	23:7	But don't s an Edomite
2Ti	2:19	S evil, all you who name God as God

Spurned

1Ki	12:13	He s the counsel of the elders
2Ch	10:13	He s the counsel of the elders
Ne	9:29	flouted your commands, s your rules
Ps	78:40	often in the desert they had s him
Da	11:21	a reject, a man s and passed over

Spy

Jos	2:2	men arrived tonight to s out the land
	2:3	come to s out the whole country
	6:25	whom Josua sent to s out Jericho
	7:2	Go up and s out the land
	14:7	sent me . . . to s out the land
2Sa	3:25	He was here to s on you
2Ki	6:11	Who is the s in our ranks

Spying

Ge	42:11	we'd never think of s

Squabble

Mt	12:25	family that's in a constant s
	12:41	you s about 'proofs
Lk	11:31	you s about 'proofs
Ac	18:15	sounds to me like one more Jewish s
	23:29	turned out to be a s turned vicious
1Co	11:34	or a family s

Squabbling

2Sa	22:44	You rescued me from a s people
Ps	18:43	You rescued me from a s people
Mk	3:24	A constantly s family disintegrates
Lk	11:17	A constantly s family falls to pieces

Squander

Pr	5:9	don't want to s your wonderful life
	8:33	don't s your precious life
Ro	13:13	not s these precious daylight hours
2Co	6:1	don't s one bit of this marvelous life

Squandered

Hos	10:1	The more money they got, the more they s
Ac	7:53	gift-wrapped! — and you s it
Gal	5:2	Christ's hard-won gift of freedom is s

Squandering

1Co	6:19	s what God paid such a high price for

Stability

1Ki	7:21	the pillar to the north S (Boaz
2Ch	3:17	the left pillar he named Boaz (S
Pr	29:4	A leader of good judgment gives s
Isa	39:8	enjoy peace and s as long as I live

Stable

Ps	119:161	but my awe at your words keeps me s
Isa	33:6	God keeps your days s and secure
	33:16	A safe and s way to live

Stagnant

Pr	10:31	a foul mouth is a s swamp
Isa	19:6	The canals will become s and stink
Eze	47:8	the sea of s waters
Eph	2:1	mired in that old s life of sin
Rev	3:16	You're stale. You're s

Stalking

Jdg	14:19	S out, smoking with anger
Jer	3:2	camped out like hunters s deer
Hos	2:13	s her lovers
	13:7	like a leopard s in the brush

Starve

Ge	42:2	survive and not s to death
	43:8	all going to s to death
	47:19	s to death right in front of you
Ex	16:3	into this wilderness to s us to death
Pr	10:3	God won't s an honest soul
	12:9	act important and s in the process
Isa	5:13	Their "big men" will s to death
	14:30	those who don't s, God will kill
Jer	15:2	If assigned to s, go s
	18:21	Let their children s
	27:13	get killed or s to death
	38:2	will be killed or s to death
	38:9	leaving him there to s
	42:17	be killed, s, or get sick and die
	42:22	You'll be killed, you'll s to death
	44:12	either be killed or s to death
La	4:9	than to slowly s to death

Starved

Ge	25:29	Esau came in from the field, s
	25:30	some of that red stew — I'm s
Dt	11:17	In no time at all you're s out
2Sa	17:29	the army must be s and exhausted
Job	30:3	Half-s, scavenging the back alleys
Ps	6:2	I'm so s for affection
	107:5	Half-s and parched with thirst
	107:9	the s and hungry got plenty
	119:20	My soul is s and hungry
Pr	27:7	when you're s, you could eat a horse
Isa	9:20	But still they s
Jer	16:4	all the killed and s corpses
	21:7	died from disease, been killed, or s
Eze	34:29	no more living half-s
Hos	9:4	You'll be s for God
Jas	2:15	old friend dressed in rags and half-s

Starving

Ge	25:32	Esau said, "I'm s!
	42:33	take food for your s families
2Ki	7:12	They knew that we were s
Ne	5:3	get enough grain to keep from s
Job	5:20	In famine, he'll keep you from s
Jer	14:18	shocked by the sight of s bodies

La	2:19	your children who are s to death
Eze	6:12	whoever's left in the city s to death
Lk	1:53	The s poor sat down to a banquet
	15:17	here I am s to death

Steadily

Ge	5:22	Enoch walked s with God
	5:24	Enoch walked s with God
	12:9	kept moving, s making his way south
2Ch	24:13	workers kept at their jobs s
Ps	89:21	And I'll keep my hand s on him
	119:1	walking s on the road revealed by God
Isa	42:3	he'll s and firmly set things right
Ro	9:11	flowing s from his initiative
1Co	13:13	Trust s in God
Eph	4:2	not in fits and starts, but s
1Jn	4:13	living s and deeply in him

Steady

Ge	49:24	But he held s under fire
Ex	17:12	his hands remained s
Jos	23:6	Now, stay strong and s
Ru	2:7	She's been at it s ever since
2Ki	20:3	My heart's been true and s
2Ch	27:6	s and determined life of obedience
Ne	9:8	found his heart to be s and true
Ps	3:5	rested, tall and s
	61:7	post S Love and Good Faith as lookouts
	63:8	you hold me s as a post
	119:5	Oh, that my steps might be s
	119:83	keep a s gaze on the instructions
	119:133	S my steps with your Word of promise
	119:173	Put your hand out and s me
Pr	13:11	s diligence pays off
Isa	26:3	completely whole, S on their feet
	41:10	I'll hold you s
	50:6	held s while they pulled out my beard
Jer	7:25	supplied a s stream of my servants
	25:4	sent a s stream of prophets to you
Hab	2:4	through loyal and s believing
Mt	4:4	a s stream of words from God's mouth
Lk	13:22	keeping on a s course
Ac	23:1	with a s gaze
Ro	15:4	his s, constant calling
	15:5	dependably s and warmly personal God
1Co	1:8	to keep you s and on track
2Co	6:6	pure heart, clear head, s hand
Gal	2:14	not maintaining a s, straight course
Php	4:1	Stay on track, s in God
Col	1:4	your s faith in Christ, our Jesus
	1:23	grounded and s in that bond of trust
2Th	1:4	s and determined in your faith
2Ti	1:10	life vindicated in a s blaze of light
Jas	5:8	Stay s and strong
1Jn	2:14	God's word is so s in you
Rev	7:1	standing s with a firm grip

Steal

Ge	31:30	why did you s my household gods

S

	44:8	s it back from your master
Lev	19:11	Don't s. "Don't lie. "Don't deceive
2Ki	19:29	whatever you can beg, borrow, or s
Pr	6:30	Hunger is no excuse for a thief to s
	9:17	S off with me
	30:9	If I'm poor, I might s
Jer	49:29	S their camels
Eze	18:7	doesn't pile up bad debts, doesn't s
	18:16	doesn't s, doesn't refuse food
	23:26	clothes and s your jewelry
	26:12	The invaders will s and loot
Hos	7:1	they s you blind, pick you clean
Mt	19:18	don't s, don't lie
	27:64	disciples will come and s the corpse
Mk	10:19	don't s, don't lie, don't cheat
Jn	10:10	A thief is only there to s and kill
	10:28	No one can s them from out of my hand
Ro	2:21	While preaching "Don't s!"
2Co	11:20	rip you off, s you blind

Stealing

Ex	20:15	No s
Dt	5:19	No s
2Sa	16:8	and for s his kingdom
Job	24:2	s and lying and cheating
Hab	2:6	getting rich by s and extortion
Lk	18:20	no killing, no s, no lying
Eph	4:28	used to make ends meet by s

Steals

Ex	22:1	If someone s an ox or a lamb sells
Job	9:12	If he s you blind, who can stop him
Eze	18:12	s, piles up bad debts
Zec	5:3	disposes of everyone who s
Rev	3:11	distracts you and s your crown

Sterile

Isa	34:9	the soil s, poisoned with waste
Jer	51:43	the land empty and bare and s
Joel	1:10	The fields are s
Zep	2:9	the other a s salt flat
Ro	8:23	These s and barren bodies of ours

Stern

Mt	9:30	Jesus became very s
Mk	4:38	Jesus was in the s
Heb	12:26	from top to bottom, stem to s

Steward

Ge	43:16	he told his house s
	43:17	The s did what Joseph had said
	43:19	went up to Joseph's house s
	43:23	The s said, "Everything's in order
	44:1	Joseph ordered his house s
	44:4	Joseph said to his house s
	44:10	The s said, "Very well then
	44:12	The s searched their bags

2Sa	16:1	Mephibosheth's s Ziba
	19:17	Ziba, Saul's s
2Ch	28:7	Azrikam the palace s
Isa	22:15	Go to this s, Shebna
Da	1:11	Daniel appealed to a s
	1:14	The s agreed to do it
	1:16	the s continued to exempt them

Stewards

1Ch	28:1	s in charge of the property
	29:6	s of the king's affairs
2Ch	8:15	priests and Levites and financial s

Stillborn

Nu	12:12	don't make her like a s baby
Job	3:16	Why wasn't I s and buried
	10:19	I wish I'd never lived — a s
Ecc	6:3	a s baby gets the better deal

Stingy

Ex	22:29	Don't be s as your wine vats fill up
Dt	15:10	Don't have a s heart
2Sa	12:4	He was too s to take an animal
Ps	37:22	S is cut off at the pass
Pr	11:24	world of the s gets smaller
	23:7	He'll be as s with you
Isa	43:24	so s with me, so closefisted
Zec	11:13	This s wage was all they thought
Mt	20:15	Are you going to get s
2Co	9:6	A s planter gets a s crop

Stole

Ge	30:33	you will know that I s it
	31:19	Rachel s her father's household gods
Lev	6:4	must return what he s or extorted
Jdg	17:2	I have the money; I s it
2Sa	15:6	s the hearts of everyone in Israel
Job	1:15	They s the animals
Ps	69:4	What I never s Must I now give back
Mt	28:13	came in the night and s the body

Stolen

Ge	31:32	Rachel had s the gods
Ex	22:3	make full restitution for what is s
	22:4	caught red-handed with the s goods
	22:7	things for safekeeping and they are s
	22:9	In all cases of s goods
	22:12	if it turns out it was s
Dt	28:31	donkey will be s from in front of you
Jos	7:11	s and then covered up the theft
1Sa	12:3	Have I ever s so much as an ox
Job	29:17	made them give back what they'd s
Pr	20:17	S bread tastes sweet
Isa	3:14	what you've s from the poor
Eze	33:15	restoring what he had s
Da	5:2	Nebuchadnezzar had s from God's Temple
Mt	6:19	s by burglars

S

Stories

Ex	10:2	tell them the **s** of the signs
Jdg	16:10	playing with me, making up **s**
1Sa	2:24	reports I'm getting, **s** spreading
2Ki	8:4	Tell me some **s** of the great things
Job	12:8	fish . . . will tell you their **s**
	13:7	to make up **s** 'to get him off the hook
	21:29	Have you not listened to their **s**
Ps	9:11	tell his **s** to everyone you meet
	26:7	at the top of my lungs, telling God-**s**
	30:9	my songs and **s** of you won't sell
	44:1	the **s** their fathers told them
	69:26	Made up **s** about anyone wounded by God
	78:3	**S** we heard from our fathers
	78:6	Know the truth and tell the **s**
	145:4	each one tells **s** of your mighty acts
Isa	40:21	heard these **s** all your life
	41:6	making up **s** in the dark
	60:18	no more **s** of crime in your land
Eze	20:49	He just makes up **s**
	42:3	rooms rose level by level for three **s**
Da	2:9	cook up some fancy **s** and confuse
Hos	12:10	Using prophets, I tell revealing **s**
Mic	6:5	Remember all those **s** about Shittim
Mt	13:3	addressed his congregation, telling **s**
	13:10	asked, "Why do you tell **s**
	13:13	That's why I tell **s**
	13:34	All Jesus did that day was tell **s**
	13:35	I will open my mouth and tell **s**
	13:53	When Jesus finished telling these **s**
	22:1	responded by telling still more **s**
Mk	4:2	He taught by using **s**, many **s**
	4:10	asked about the **s**
	4:11	everything comes in **s**
	4:13	All my **s** work this way
	4:33	With many **s** like these, he presented
	12:1	Then Jesus started telling them **s**
Lk	8:10	There are others who need **s**
	8:10	But even with **s** some of them
Ac	20:11	went on telling **s** of the faith
2Co	9:7	protect you against sob **s**
Gal	1:18	to compare **s** with Peter
1Ti	1:4	have been introducing fantasy **s**
	4:7	**s** that get dressed up as religion
Heb	11:37	We have **s** of those who were stoned

Story

Ge	2:4	This is the **s** of how it all started
	6:9	This is the **s** of Noah
	11:10	This is the **s** of Shem
	11:27	This is the **s** of Terah
	19:29	the **s**: When God destroyed the Cities
	20:8	told them the whole **s**
	24:33	I won't eat until I tell my **s**
	24:66	told Isaaac the whole **s** of the trip
	29:13	Jacob told Laban the **s** of everything
	32:30	and lived to tell the **s**
	37:2	the **s** of Jacob. The **s** continues
	39:17	She told him the same **s**
	39:19	his master heard his wife's **s**

	41:39	God has given you the inside **s**
	45:16	The **s** was reported in Pharaoh's palace
Ex	18:8	the **s** of all that God had done
Nu	4:49	that's the **s** of their numbering
	13:27	they told the **s** of their trip
	14:24	this is a different **s**
Dt	4:33	and lived to tell the **s**
	5:26	and lived to tell the **s**
1Sa	2:23	**s** after **s** of your corrupt and evil
	14:35	**s** behind Saul's building an altar
	25:37	she told him the whole **s**
2Sa	13:21	King David heard the whole **s**
1Ki	1:14	I'll come in and corroborate your **s**
	9:8	What's the **s** behind these ruins
	13:11	the **s** of what the holy man had done
2Ki	4:7	told the **s** to the man of God
	6:28	king continued, "Tell me your **s**."
	6:30	When the king heard the woman's **s**
	7:11	giving them the whole **s**
	8:5	**s** of the dead person brought back
	8:6	so she told him the **s**
	10:28	the **s** of Jehu's wasting of Baal
1Ch	21:28	the **s** of what happened when David saw
2Ch	7:21	What's the **s** behind these ruins
	24:27	The **s** of his sons
	35:27	The whole **s** . . . is written
Ezr	4:19	rebellion is an old **s** there
Est	1:1	This is the **s** of something
	4:5	get the full **s** of what was happening
	6:2	They came across the **s** there
Job	36:6	it's a different **s**
	41:8	you won't live to tell the **s**
Ps	22:22	Here's the **s** I'll tell my friends
	38:9	my groans an old **s** to you
	38:18	I'm ready to tell my **s** of failure
	40:10	let the congregation know the whole **s**
	48:13	detail by detail the **s** of God
	75:9	telling the **s** of God Eternal
	89:2	never quit telling the **s** of your love
	102:21	Write it so the **s** can be told in Zion
	119:26	When I told my **s**, you responded
Pr	11:7	the **s**'s over, end of hope
Ecc	1:10	it's the same old **s**
	10:3	The way they walk tells the **s**
Jer	9:12	Anyone who has the inside **s** from God
	44:22	a death valley, a horror **s**
Eze	5:15	turned into a horror **s** circulating
	17:2	Tell them a **s**
	24:3	Tell this company of rebels a **s**
Da	11:27	There's more to this **s**
	11:40	the final wrap-up of this **s**
	12:6	How long is this astonishing **s**
	12:7	the **s** would be complete
Hos	1:7	Judah's another **s**
	3:5	the End of the **s** of his love
	3:7	telling his prophets the whole **s**
Am	3:19	When the **s** of your fate gets out
Na	10:9	keep the **s** alive in their children
Zec	9:23	the gossips looking for a **s**
Mt	13:18	Study this **s** of the farmer planting
	13:24	He told another **s**
	13:31	Another **s**. "God's kingdom

S

	13:33	Another s. "God's kingdom
	13:36	Explain to us that s of the thistles
	21:4	This is the full s of what
	21:28	Tell me what you think of this s
	21:33	Here's another s. Listen closely
	21:45	religious leaders heard this s
	23:24	writing a life s that's wrong
	28:15	That s, cooked up
Mk	3:23	confronted their slander with a s
	4:13	Do you see how this s works?
	4:30	What kind of s can we use
	4:34	He was never without a s when he spoke
	5:14	told their s in town and country
	5:19	Tell them your s—what the Master did
	5:33	gave him the whole s
	5:38	the gossips looking for a s
	12:12	They knew the s was about them
	14:15	a spacious second-s room
Lk	1:1	a s of the wonderful harvest
	1:3	starting from the s's beginning
	8:4	He addressed them, using this s
	8:9	Why did you tell this s
	8:11	This s is about some of those people
	8:34	told their s in town and country
	8:47	she blurted out her s
	10:30	Jesus answered by telling a s
	12:16	Then he told them this s
	12:41	are you telling this s just for us
	13:6	Then he told them a s
	13:18	What kind of s can I use
	14:7	He went on to tell a s to the guests
	15:3	Their grumbling triggered this s
	18:1	Jesus told them a s showing
	18:9	He told his next s to some
	19:11	he told this s
	20:9	Jesus told another s to the people
	20:19	They knew the s was about them
	21:29	He told them a s. "Look at a fig tree
	22:12	a spacious second-s room
	24:23	the s that they had seen a vision
Jn	4:25	When he arrives, we'll get the whole s
	10:6	Jesus told this simple s
Ac	2:14	get this s straight
	10:37	the s of what happened in Judea
	12:15	She stuck by her s, insisting
	15:14	Simeon has told us the s
	16:32	in detail the s of the Master
	18:26	told him the rest of the s
	20:9	toppled out the third-s window
	21:19	Paul told the s, detail by detail
	21:20	They had a s to tell, too
	25:22	like to see this man and hear his s
	26:1	Paul took the stand and told his s
Ro	2:12	that's a different s entirely
	4:2	the s we're given is a God-s
	4:16	that's reading the s backwards
	5:12	the s of how Adam landed us
	10:6	right living in us is a different s
1Co	8:5	don't add up to anything but a tall s
	14:26	teach a lesson, tell a s
2Co	7:15	the s of your prompt obedience
Gal	1:13	heard the s of my earlier life

Eph	3:3	inside s on this from God himself
Heb	7:15	s provides a perfect analogy
	12:3	go over that s again
Jude	1:6	the s of the angels who didn't

Strangle

Job	7:15	I'd rather s in the bedclothes than
Mt	13:22	s what was heard, and nothing comes

Strangled

Mt	13:7	it was s by the weeds
Mk	4:7	it was s among the weeds
Lk	8:7	weeds grew with it and s it

Strategic

Pr	24:6	S planning is the key to warfare

Strategically

1Sa	11:11	Saul had s placed his army
2Sa	2:25	deployed s on a hill
Isa	30:4	officials s established in Zoan

Strategy

Jdg	20:38	The s for the main body of the ambush
1Sa	23:9	David got wind of Saul's s to destroy
2Sa	17:4	Absalom thought it was an excellent s
	20:22	The woman presented her s
1Ki	18:29	every religious trick and s they knew
	20:24	Here's the s: Remove each sheik
2Ki	18:20	substitute for military s and troops
	24:2	The s was to destroy Judah
2Ch	23:1	worked out a s with certain
	32:2	Sennacherib's s was to take Jerusalem

Stray

2Sa	9:8	pay attention to a s dog like me
1Ki	14:11	will be eaten by s dogs
	16:11	rid of them all like so many s dogs
	21:24	will be eaten by s dogs
Job	24:5	The poor, like s dogs and cats
	30:2	good for nothing, s, mangy animals
Isa	14:19	unburied, like a s dog or cat
	23:13	refuge for wild dogs and s cats
Jer	9:11	fit for nothing but s cats and dogs
	10:22	left to all the s dogs and cats
	33:12	unfit for even a s dog
	34:20	carrion food for vultures and s dogs
	51:37	rubble, scavenged by s dogs and cats
Eze	28:10	You'll die like a s dog
Hos	2:12	feeding grounds for s dogs and cats

Straying

Lev	4:2	by s from any of God's commands
	4:13	s from one of the commandments of God
	4:22	s from one of the commands of his God

S

	4:27	s from one of the commandments of God
	5:15	unknowingly sins by s against any
Nu	20:17	s neither right nor left
1Sa	6:12	s neither right nor left

Strength

Ge	49:3	my s, first proof of my manhood
Ex	15:2	God is my s, God is my song
	18:23	s to carry out whatever God commands
	32:11	demonstration of power and s
Nu	14:13	a great show of s
Dt	3:28	Give him courage. Give him s
	5:15	a powerful show of s
	8:18	the s to produce all this wealth
	9:26	using your enormous s to get them out
	11:8	so that you'll have the s to invade
	33:25	your s like iron as long as you live
Jos	1:6	S! Courage! You are going to lead
	1:9	S! Courage! Don't be timid
	1:18	S! Courage
Jdg	6:14	Go in this s that is yours
	9:51	The Tower-of-S stood in the middle
	16:5	Discover what's behind his great s
	16:6	the secret of your great s
	16:9	The secret of his s was still
	16:15	tell me the secret of your great s
	16:17	If I were shaved, my s would leave me
	16:19	His s drained from him
	16:28	please, give s yet once more
1Sa	2:4	the weak are infused with fresh s
	2:10	he'll give s to his king
	28:20	wasn't an ounce of s left in him
	28:22	It will give you s
2Ki	19:3	No s to birth them
	23:25	obedience to God, heart and mind and s
1Ch	16:11	Study God and his s
	16:27	s and joy fill his place
	16:28	in awe of the S
	29:12	You hold s and power in the palm
2Ch	26:16	the s and success went to his head
	27:6	Jotham's s was rooted in his
Ne	6:9	I prayed, "Give me s
	8:10	The joy of God is your s
Job	6:11	Where's the s to keep my hopes up
	12:16	S and success belong to God
	31:21	used my s . . . to take advantage
	40:16	look at the s of his back
Ps	21:1	Your s, God, is the king's s
	21:13	Show your s, God, so no one can miss
	28:8	God is all s for his people
	33:16	no warrior wins by brute s
	62:7	God — granite-s and safe-harbor-God
	62:11	S comes Straight from God
	63:2	drinking in your s and glory
	68:34	His splendor and s rise huge
	86:16	give your servant the s to go on
	93:1	God is robed and surging with s
	110:14	God's my s, he's also my song
	121:1	does my s come from mountains
	121:2	No, my s comes from God
	138:3	you made my life large with s
	147:5	Our Lord is great, with limitless s

	147:11	they can depend on his s
Ecc	7:19	Wisdom puts more s in one wise person
Isa	11:2	gives direction and builds s
	12:2	God . . . is my s and song
	28:6	s and prowess to those who guard
	30:15	Your s will come from settling
	30:18	He's gathering s to show mercy to you
	37:3	without even the s to have a baby
	40:29	gives fresh s to dropouts
	40:31	those who wait upon God get fresh s
	41:1	Recover your s. Gather around me
	41:10	I'm your God. I'll give you s
	45:24	Salvation and s are in God!
	49:5	That God should be my s
	57:10	always found s for the latest fad
Jer	16:19	God, my s, my stronghold
	49:4	Why do you brag of your once-famous s
Eze	17:9	won't take much s or many hands to pull
	20:33	a mighty show of s
	20:34	a mighty show of s
	30:6	her proud s will collapse
Da	2:37	rule, power, s, and glory
	2:40	a fourth kingdom, iron-like in s
	10:18	touched me again and gave me s
Joel	2:11	And the s of those who obey him
Am	2:14	The s of the strong won't count
Mic	3:8	God's Spirit of justice and s
	5:4	his shepherd-rule by God's s
Hab	1:11	Brazen in sin, they call s their god
	3:19	I take heart and gain s
Lk	1:17	in the style and s of Elijah
	1:51	bared his arm and showed his s
	3:18	words that gave s to the people
	21:36	the s and wits to make it through
Jn	2:14	loan sharks were also there in full s
Ac	27:34	You'll need s for the rescue ahead
Ro	15:1	S is for service, not status
1Co	1:25	Human s can't begin to compete
	14:4	whole church into growth and s
2Co	1:9	trusting in our own s or wits
	12:9	My s comes into its own
	13:9	celebrate every s, every triumph
Eph	1:19	endless energy, boundless s
Col	1:11	We pray that you'll have the s
	3:12	humility, quiet s, discipline
1Th	3:13	May you be infused with s and purity
1Jn	2:14	such vitality and s! God's word
Jude	1:25	be glory, majesty, s, and rule
Rev	1:5	Glory and s to Christ
	3:8	You don't have much s, I know that
	5:12	the wealth, the wisdom, the s
	5:13	the honor, the glory, the s
	7:12	The honor and power and s

Strengthen

Dt	33:7	S his grip, be his helper
Jdg	19:5	S yourself with a hearty breakfast
2Sa	2:7	S your resolve and do what must be
1Ch	29:12	build up and s all
Isa	35:3	s the rubbery knees
Eph	3:16	I ask him to s you by his Spirit

S

Strengthened

1Sa	30:6	David s himself with trust in his God
2Sa	16:21	everyone on your side will be s
1Ki	18:46	God s Elijah mightily
Ps	37:40	God-s, we're delivered from evil
Lk	22:30	be s as you take up responsibilities
Ac	15:32	s their new friends with many words
2Co	13:4	we'll be alive in Christ, s by God

Strengthening

1Ch	15:26	God helped the Levites, s them
Lk	22:43	an angel . . . was at his side, s him
Ac	9:31	The Holy Spirit was with them, s them

Stress

Mk	4:19	The s strangles what they heard
1Co	7:28	you marry, you take on additional s

Stressful

1Co	7:28	additional stress in an already s time

Strict

1Sa	21:2	The king . . . gave s orders
1Ki	13:17	I'm under s orders from God
	13:21	didn't keep the s orders your God gave
	13:26	holy man who disobeyed God's s orders
Da	3:10	You gave s orders, O king
Mk	1:43	Jesus dismissed him with s orders
	5:43	s orders that no one was to know
Ac	5:28	s orders not to teach in Jesus' name
	26:5	I lived as a s Pharisee
1Co	8:7	In s logic, then, nothing happened
Php	3:5	a s and devout adherent to God's law
Heb	13:17	work under the s supervision of God

Strong

Ge	17:1	I am The S God
	18:18	become a large and s nation
	28:3	may The S God bless you
	34:3	he felt a s attraction to Dinah
	35:11	God continued, I am The S God
	43:14	may The S God give you grace
	48:3	The S God appeared to me at Luz
	49:25	S God . . . give you his blessings
Ex	1:20	a very s people
	6:1	With a s hand he'll send them out
	6:3	as The S God, but by my name God
	15:6	Your s right hand, God
Lev	10:9	don't drink wine or s drink
	26:19	I'll break your s pride
Nu	13:18	the people: Are they s or weak
	24:4	who sees what The S God shows him
	24:16	Who sees what The S God reveals
	28:7	quart of s beer with each lamb
Dt	4:34	putting his s hand in
	26:8	took us out of Egypt with his s hand

	31:6	Be s. Take courage
	31:7	Be s. Take courage
	31:23	Be s. Take courage
Jos	4:24	recognize how s God's rescuing hand is
	10:25	Don't be timid. Be s! Be confident
	14:11	as s as I was the day Moses sent
	17:17	you are very s
	23:6	Now, stay s and steady
Jdg	5:21	stomp on the necks of the s
	14:14	From the s came something sweet
Ru	1:20	The S One has dealt me a bitter blow
	1:21	The S One ruined me
1Sa	2:4	weapons of the s are smashed
	14:23	army was . . . ten thousand s
	14:52	Saul conscripted every s and brave man
2Sa	15:3	you've got a s case
1Ki	2:2	be s; show what you're made of
	11:28	stood out . . . as s and able
2Ki	18:17	with a s military force
1Ch	26:8	all of them outstanding and s
	28:7	s-minded in doing what I command
2Ch	11:12	making them very s
	12:1	secured his kingdom and was s again
	15:7	Be s. Take heart
	17:10	a s sense of the fear of God
	25:8	you go by yourself and be s
	26:13	a s royal defense against any attack
	32:7	Be s! Take courage!
	32:13	single god anywhere s enough to stand
Ezr	4:20	their share of s kings
Ne	9:25	They took s cities and fertile fields
Job	12:21	disarms the s and mighty
	18:7	Their s strides weaken, falter
	22:2	any of us s enough to give God a hand
	22:8	s and honored by everyone
	38:10	a s playpen so it couldn't run loose
	39:11	He's hugely s
Ps	18:1	I love you, God — you make me s
	29:11	God makes his people s
	31:24	Be brave. Be s. Don't give up
	37:17	the righteous are God-s
	59:9	S God, I'm watching you do it
	59:17	S God, I'm watching you do it
	68:35	It's Israel's s God!
	71:18	news Of your s right arm to this world
	78:26	gave a s push to South Wind
	81:1	A song to our s God
	92:10	made me s as a charging bison
	99:4	S King, lover of justice
	103:11	s is his love to those who fear him
	110:2	You were forged a s scepter by God
	118:7	God's my s champion
	124:8	God's s name is our help
	132:2	made a vow to the S God of Jacob
	132:5	a house for the S God of Jacob
	140:7	God, my Lord, S Savior, protect me
Pr	14:4	good harvest requires a s ox
	14:34	God-devotion makes a country s
	24:5	It's better to be wise than s
	31:1	the s advice his mother gave him
Ecc	7:19	one wise person Than ten s men give
	9:11	Nor the battle to the s

S

	9:14	A s king came and mounted an attack
SS	4:2	expressive and s and clean
	5:15	like a cedar, s and deep-rooted
	6:6	expressive and s and clean
Isa	1:24	God-of-the-Angel-Armies, the S One
	9:6	Amazing Counselor, S God
	10:21	will come back to the S God
	13:6	avalanche crashing down from the S God
	23:1	your s seaports all in ruins
	23:14	your s seaports all in ruins
	25:2	the s city to a pile of stones
	26:1	We have a s city, Salvation City
	28:2	someone tough and s to flatten them
	33:23	free for all — for weak and s
	37:26	using you to devastate s cities
	44:14	lets it grow s in the forest
	51:17	the s drink of his anger
	51:20	the s drink of God's anger
	58:11	firm muscles, s bones
	60:22	the weakling become a s nation
Jer	17:5	Cursed is the s one who depends
	50:34	Rescuer is s: God-of-the-Angel-Armies
Eze	1:24	like the voice of The S God
	10:5	voice was like The S God in thunder
	19:5	made him a s young lion
	30:24	make the arms of the king of Babylon s
	30:25	make the arms of the king of Babylon s
	34:16	oversee the s ones
Da	2:23	You made me wise and s
	2:44	standing s and eternal
	3:20	ordered some s men from the army
	4:11	the tree grew huge and s
	4:22	You have grown great and s
	9:27	will forge many and s alliances
	10:19	Take courage. Be s
	11:5	king of the south will grow s
	11:32	loyal to their God will take a s stand
Hos	10:11	seeing her s, sleek neck
Joel	1:15	The S God has arrived
Am	2:14	The strength of the s won't count
	4:10	stink of rot . . . was so s
	9:11	David's people will be s again
Mic	4:7	a s nation out of the long lost
Na	3:9	s friends, were ready to step in
Zep	1:14	even s men screaming for help
	3:5	he's still at it, s as ever
	3:17	God is present among you, a s Warrior
Zec	10:12	I'll make them s, God-s
	12:2	turn Jerusalem into a cup of s drink
	12:5	our leaders are s and able through God
Mk	5:4	No one was s enough to tame him
Lk	2:40	child grew s in body and wise
	5:38	get s, clean bottles
	11:21	a s man . . . stands guard
	16:3	I'm not s enough for a laboring job
Jn	21:6	weren't s enough to pull it in
Ac	2:2	a sound like a s wind
	4:24	S God, you made heaven and earth
	11:24	grew large and s in the Master
	14:21	establishing a s core of disciples
Ro	4:20	came up s, ready for God
	8:2	Spirit of life in Christ, like a s

	14:1	s on opinions but weak in the faith
	15:1	who are s and able in the faith
	16:25	the One who is s enough to make you s
1Co	7:2	Sexual drives are s
	7:2	but marriage is s enough
	14:3	so that they can grow and be s
2Co	1:19	Wasn't it a clean, s Yes
	11:21	stomachs aren't s enough to tolerate
Gal	3:3	you weren't smart enough or s enough
Eph	6:10	God is s, and he wants you s
Php	4:10	showing such s concern for me
Col	1:12	Father who makes us s enough
2Th	1:6	. blaze of fire with his s angels
Jas	5:8	Stay steady and s
1Pe	5:6	God's s hand is on you
Rev	1:8	I'm the Sovereign-S
	4:8	God our Master, Sovereign-S
	6:10	How long, S God, Holy and True
	6:15	princes, generals, rich and s
	11:12	heard a s voice out of Heaven calling
	11:17	We thank you, O God, Sovereign-S
	12:10	heard a s voice out of Heaven
	15:3	marvelous, O God, the Sovereign-S
	16:7	God, the Sovereign-S
	16:14	Great Day of God, the Sovereign-S
	18:8	God, the S God who judges her
	18:10	City of Babylon, s city
	18:21	A s Angel reached for a boulder
	19:6	the sound of s thunder
	19:15	raging wrath of God, the Sovereign-S
	20:8	will gather a huge army, millions s
	21:22	the Lord God — the Sovereign-S

Stronger

Nu	13:31	they're way s than we are
	14:12	a nation bigger and s than they
Dt	1:28	bigger and s than we are
	4:38	displace bigger and s and older
	7:1	all bigger and s than you are
	9:1	much bigger and s than you are
	11:23	nations much bigger and s than you
Jos	17:13	when the Israelites got s
Jdg	1:28	When Israel became s they put
	14:18	What is s than a lion
2Sa	1:23	s than proud lions
	3:1	the s David became
	13:14	much s than she, he raped her
1Ki	16:22	Omri side proved s than the Tibni side
	20:25	we're sure to prove s than they are
2Ch	17:12	Jehoshaphat became s by the day
Job	9:19	a question of who's s, he wins
	17:9	clean, pure hands will get s and s
Ps	93.4	S than wild sea storms
Da	11:5	one of his princes will grow s
Joel	2:20	The bigger the enemy, the s the stench
Lk	11:22	But what if a s man comes along?
Ac	16:5	congregations became s in faith
Ro	1:11	watch you grow s right before my eyes
2Co	12:10	the weaker I get, the s I become
Col	1:6	Message . . . gets larger and s
1Jn	4:4	Spirit in you is far s than anything

S

Strongest

2Sa	10:7	with his s fighters in full force
1Ch	5:2	Judah became the s of his brothers
	19:8	with his s fighters in full force
Job	9:30	wash myself with the s soap
Ecc	7:7	destroys the s heart
Jer	2:22	Scrub, using the s soaps
	46:6	the s soldiers won't escape
Mal	3:2	He'll be like the s lye soap
Jas	3:4	a course in the face of the s winds

Struggle

Job	7:1	Human life is a s, isn't it
Ecc	8:15	compensation for the s for survival
2Co	11:26	s with friends, s with foes
Php	1:30	same kind of s you saw me go through
1Ti	1:18	do this well, fearless in your s

Struggling

Mk	6:48	could see his men s with the oars
Ro	8:3	the disordered mess of s humanity
1Co	8:10	someone still s over this issue

Stubborn

Ex	4:21	make him s so that he will refuse
	7:13	Pharaoh was as s as ever
	7:14	Pharaoh is a s man
	7:22	Still Pharaoh remained s
	8:15	he got s again and wouldn't listen
	8:19	Pharaoh was s and wouldn't listen
	8:32	Pharaoh became s once again
	9:7	But Pharaoh stayed s
	9:34	he kept right on sinning, s as ever
	10:1	Go to Pharaoh. I've made him s
	10:20	God made Pharaoh s as ever
	10:27	God kept Pharaoh s as ever
	11:10	God turned Pharaoh more s than ever
	14:4	I'll make Pharaoh's heart s again
	14:8	God made Pharaoh king of Egypt s
	14:17	the Egyptians keep up their s chase
	32:9	what a s, hard-headed people
	33:3	you're such a s, hard-headed people
Dt	9:6	You're s as mules
	21:18	When a man has a s son, a real rebel
	21:20	This son of ours is a s rebel
	31:27	how s and willful you can be
Jdg	2:19	S as mules, they didn't drop a single
1Sa	6:6	Why be s like the Egyptians
2Ki	17:14	more bullheaded than their s ancestors
2Ch	36:13	He became set in his own s ways
Ne	9:17	They turned s
Pr	29:1	hate discipline and only get more s
Isa	1:20	if you're willful and s, you'll die
	57:17	he kept at his s, willful ways
	63:17	Why did you make us cold and s
Jer	7:26	S as mules and worse than

	13:17	Weep because of your s arrogance
Hos	4:16	Israel is s as a mule
Mk	16:14	severely for their s unbelief
Ac	21:12	begged Paul not to be s and persist
Tit	3:3	we ourselves were stupid and s

Student

1Ch	25:8	young or old, teacher or s
Pr	11:27	the s of evil becomes evil
Mt	10:24	s doesn't get a better desk than
	13:52	every s well-trained in God's kingdom

Students

Pr	15:20	lazy s embarrass their parents
Mt	10:25	my s, my harvest hands, get the same
	22:16	don't pander to your s
Mk	12:14	don't pander to your s

Studies

Mt	7:26	if you just use my words in Bible s
Lk	6:49	if you just use my words in Bible s

Study

Ex	25:40	S the design you were given
Dt	17:19	he is to s it every day
1Ch	16:11	S God and his strength
	28:8	s every last one of the commandments
2Ch	13:22	s written by Iddo the prophet
Job	8:8	s what they learned
Ps	27:4	I'll s at his feet
	111:2	worth A lifetime of s
Ecc	12:12	constant s wears you out
Isa	8:20	we're going to s the Scriptures
Jer	31:21	S the road conditions
La	5:1	S our plight
Hos	6:3	We're ready to s God
Mt	13:18	S this story of the farmer planting
Col	1:21	You yourselves are a case s
1Ti	2:12	They should s to be quiet and obedient
Heb	12:2	S how he did it

Studying

Ezr	7:10	committed himself to s the Revelation
Ecc	7:25	s and exploring and seeking wisdom
Isa	58:2	love s all about me
Col	2:7	quit s the subject and start living it

Stumble

1Sa	2:9	leaves the wicked to s in the dark
Job	18:7	they s into their own traps
Ps	38:16	won't smugly strut off when I s
	91:12	If you s, they'll catch you
	121:3	He won't let you s, your Guardian God
Pr	29:18	they s all over themselves
Isa	40:30	young folk in their prime s and fall

S

	59:9	but **s** through the night
Jer	46:6	they'll stagger, **s**, and fall
Eze	44:12	my people Israel **s** and fall
Hos	4:5	You **s** around in broad daylight
Na	2:5	they stagger and **s**
Jn	11:9	who walks in daylight doesn't **s**
	11:10	might very well **s** because he can't see
1Jn	1:6	continue to **s** around in the dark

Stumbled

2Sa	6:6	the oxen **s**
1Ch	13:9	the oxen **s**
Ps	9:3	they **s** on you and fell on their faces
	105:37	not one among his tribes even **s**
Hab	3:16	I staggered and **s**
Ac	13:11	a shadowy mist and **s** around
Ro	9:32	they **s** into him and went sprawling

Stumbles

Ps	37:24	If he **s**, he's not down for long
Isa	5:27	None drag their feet, no one **s**
Mt	21:44	Whoever **s** on this Stone gets shattered
Jn	8:12	No one who follows me **s** around
1Jn	2:11	whoever hates . . . **s** around in the dark

Stumbling

Lev	19:14	don't put a **s** block in front of
Job	4:4	have put **s** people on their feet
Ps	107:5	parched with thirst, staggering and **s**
	112:6	No shuffling or **s** around for this one
	116:8	you, Foot, were kept from **s**
	119:165	no **s** around in the dark for them
Pr	5:22	find yourself **s** all over yourself
Hos	14:9	are always tripping and **s**
Eph	5:8	So no more **s** around

Stupid

Ge	31:28	It was a **s** thing for you to do
Nu	24:22	you Kenites will look **s**
2Sa	24:10	I've been really **s**
1Ki	16:13	angry with their **s** idols
1Ch	21:8	forgive my sin — I've been really **s**
2Ch	32:11	Don't be **s** — Hezekiah has fed you
Job	17:4	You know firsthand how **s** they can be
Ps	14:2	He's looking for someone not **s**
	19:13	Keep me from **s** sins
	53:2	He's looking for someone not **s**
	73:13	I've been **s** to play by the rules
Pr	3:35	**s** living gets the booby prize
	10:1	**s** son, sad mother
	10:5	go fishing during harvest — that's **s**
	11:29	it's a **s** way to live
	14:9	The **s** ridicule right and wrong
	17:18	**s** to try to get something for nothing
	17:25	**s** child is sheer pain to a father
	18:13	Answering before listening is both **s**
	19:13	parent is worn . . . by a **s** child
Ecc	2:12	look at what's smart and what's **s**

	2:13	it's better to be smart than **s**
	2:14	the **s** ones grope in the dark
	2:16	The smart and the **s** both disappear
	10:2	**S** thinking leads to wrong living
Isa	19:11	the advisors of Pharaoh **s**
	30:5	Anyone **s** enough to trust them
	44:18	Pretty **s**, wouldn't you say
Jer	10:21	It's because our leaders are **s**
Hos	4:14	a **s** people, ruined by whores
	10:6	disgraces Israel with his **s** idols
	13:13	too **s** to come out of the womb
Zec	11:15	Dress up like a **s** shepherd
Mt	5:22	Thoughtlessly yell '**s**!' at a sister
	7:26	a **s** carpenter who built his house
	15:16	Are you being willfully **s**
	23:26	**S** Pharisee! Scour the insides
Mk	7:18	Are you being willfully **s**
Lk	11:40	**S** Pharisees! Didn't the One
Ac	2:40	get out of this sick and **s** culture
Ro	1:31	**S**, slimy, cruel, cold-blooded
	10:19	people you think are religiously **s**
1Co	3:19	world calls smart, God calls **s**
Tit	3:3	we ourselves were **s** and stubborn

Stupidity

Ps	94:11	knows your **s**, sees your shallowness
Pr	14:29	quick-tempered person stockpiles **s**
	19:3	People ruin their lives by their own **s**
	26:4	Don't respond to the **s** of a fool
Ecc	7:25	wanted to identify evil and **s**
Mt	23:16	You're hopeless! What arrogant **s**!
1Co	6:5	the **s** of what you're doing

Stupidly

Ps	31:17	leave them **s** shaking their heads
Jer	8:6	They just kept at it, blindly and **s**
	10:8	**S**, they line them up

Stupor

Pr	23:21	in a **s** and dressed in rags
Isa	5:11	drinking themselves into a **s**
Jer	51:8	senseless in a drunken **s**
Hos	4:11	leave my people in a **s**
Zec	12:2	staggering in a drunken **s**

Stutter

Ex	4:10	I **s** and stammer
	6:12	And besides, I **s**
	6:30	Look at me. I **s**

Stuttered

| Hab | 3:16 | I stammered and **s** |

Stutters

| Lk | 21:15 | your accusers to stammers and **s** |

S

Stymied

Job	19:8	a barricade across my path — I'm s
	32:1	s because Job wouldn't budge
1Th	2:18	Satan s us each time

Subdue

| 1Ch | 22:18 | s the land to God and his people |
| Rev | 19:15 | so he can s the nations |

Subdued

| Jdg | 3:30 | Moab was s under the hand of Israel |
| | 4:23 | On that day God s Jabin king of Canaan |

Subduing

| Jdg | 1:8 | captured Jerusalem, s the city |

Subjection

| Jer | 25:11 | countries will be in s to the king |

Submit

Jer	27:8	any nation or kingdom that won't s
	27:14	telling you not to s to the king
	27:17	Don't listen to them. S to the king
Mt	16:21	s to an ordeal of suffering
1Co	11:7	s their "heads" to the Head: God
Gal	6:15	s to circumcision, reject circumcision

Submits

Jn	3:5	s to this original creation
Gal	5:2	anyone of you s to circumcision
Eph	5:24	just as the church s to Christ

Submitted

Dt	29:26	s to gods they'd never heard of
2Sa	22:45	moment they got wind of me they s
Ac	6:7	many priests s themselves to the faith

Substance

Nu	11:7	Manna was a seedlike s
Dt	27:26	give s to the words of this Revelation
Isa	30:5	All show, no s
	30:7	Egypt is all show, no s
Am	5:5	all show, no s
Col	1:27	That is the s of our Message
	2:5	the solid s of your faith in Christ
	2:17	the s is Christ

Substitute

Ge	30:3	Let her s for me so I can have a child
Lev	27:10	must not exchange or s a good one
	27:33	both animals, the original and the s
2Ki	18:20	words are any s for military strategy

| Isa | 5:20 | Who s bitter for sweet |
| Eze | 13:8 | prophets who s illusions for visions |

Succeed

Lev	6:22	Aaron's son who is anointed to s him
	16:32	ordained to s his father
Jos	1:8	then you'll s
1Sa	26:25	s in all you attempt
2Sa	7:12	your own flesh and blood, to s you
1Ki	5:5	whom I will provide to s you as king
	19:16	to s you as prophet
2Ki	3:27	firstborn who would s him as king
	14:21	to s his father Amaziah as king
1Ch	17:11	raise up your child to s you
Ne	2:20	God-of-Heaven will make sure we s
Job	21:8	They get to see their children s
Ps	37:1	wish you could s like the wicked
	106:5	I want to see your chosen s
Pr	15:22	take good counsel and watch them s
	24:19	wish you could s like the wicked
Da	11:17	the plot will fizzle. It won't s
Jn	3:27	It's not possible for a person to s
Ro	11:7	self-interest, she didn't s

Succeeded

Dt	10:6	His son Eleazar s him as priest
2Sa	10:1	Hanun, his son, s him as king
1Ki	8:20	I have s David my father
2Ki	8:24	His son Ahaziah s him as king
	13:9	His son Jehoash s him as king
	23:30	was anointed and s his father as king
1Ch	19:1	his son s him as king
	27:7	his son Zebadiah s him
2Ch	6:10	I have s David my father
	32:30	Hezekiah s in everything he did
Jer	22:11	who s his father as king
Da	5:31	Darius the Mede s him as king
Mt	2:22	Archelaus had s his father, Herod

Succeeding

| 1Ki | 1:35 | takes his place on my throne, s me |

Succeeds

| Ex | 29:30 | The son who s him as priest |
| Ps | 33:16 | No king s with a big army alone |

Success

Ge	24:21	Had God made his trip a s
Jdg	18:5	whether our mission will be a s
1Sa	30:21	As he came near he called out, "S
2Ch	7:11	Everything was done — s! Satisfaction
	26:16	the strength and s went to his head
	31:21	He was a great s
Job	12:16	Strength and s belong to God
Mt	10:23	It is not s you are after
Jn	3:27	I'm talking about eternal s
Gal	6:13	boast of their s in recruiting you

Successful

1Sa	18:15	As Saul saw David becoming more s
1Ch	22:13	That's what will make you s
Ne	1:11	make me s today
Isa	48:15	I've brought him here. He'll be s
Mt	7:13	formulas for a s life

Suffer

Pr	13:13	Ignore the Word and s
Mk	9:12	who will . . . s terribly
Lk	17:25	it's necessary that he s many things
	19:21	don't s fools gladly
	19:22	I don't s fools gladly
	24:26	the Messiah had to s
2Co	1:6	When we s for Jesus, it works out
1Pe	3:14	Even if you s for it, you're still
	3:17	better to s for doing good
Rev	2:10	the things you're about to s
	14:10	s torment from fire and brimstone

Suffered

1Sa	6:4	all of you . . . s the same plague
Ezr	9:13	on top of all we've already s
Isa	53:3	a man who s, who knew pain firsthand
Eze	36:21	I s much pain over my holy reputation
Na	3:19	Everyone has felt it and s
Mk	5:25	had s a condition of hemorrhaging
Heb	5:8	learned . . . by what he s
	12:4	others have s far worse than you
1Pe	2:21	He s everything that came his way
	2:23	He s in silence
	3:18	s because of others' sins
Rev	18:20	wrong you s from her has been judged

Suffering

Ge	16:5	your fault that I'm s this abuse
Dt	28:53	the s from the siege gets extreme
	28:55	s of the siege that your enemy mounts
	28:57	s of the siege that your enemy mounts
Job	2:13	how deeply he was s
	30:16	s seizes and grips me hard
	30:27	Each day confronts me with more s
	33:19	throwing them on a bed of s
	36:8	when affliction and s descend
	36:15	their s, God delivers from their s
	36:21	that's what's behind your s
Jer	11:4	out of the iron furnace of s
	40:3	now you're all s the consequences
Mt	16:21	submit to an ordeal of s
	16:24	Don't run from s; embrace it
Mk	8:31	Son of Man proceed to an ordeal of s
	8:34	Don't run from s; embrace it
Lk	6:25	There's s to be met
	9:22	Son of Man proceed to an ordeal of s
	9:23	Don't run from s; embrace it
	22:15	before I enter my time of s
Ac	9:16	the hard s that goes with this job
Gal	6:12	faith that shares Christ's s and death

Superior

Jdg	8:2	s to the vintage of Abiezer
2Ch	16:8	come against you with s forces
Da	1:19	far s to all the other young men
Na	3:8	Do you think you're s to Egyptian
Mal	1:13	You act so s
Lk	11:22	man comes along with s weapons
Ro	11:23	don't get to feeling s to those
Heb	9:11	the s things of this new covenant

Superiors

2Co	10:12	those who boast that they're our s
2Pe	2:11	Even angels, their s in every way

Php	1:29	There's also s for him. And the s is
	3:10	be a partner in his s
Col	1:24	a lot of s to be entered into
	1:25	experienced this s as a sheer gift
2Th	1:5	fit for the kingdom. You're s now
2Ti	1:8	Take your share of s for the Message
	3:11	s along with me in all the grief
Heb	2:10	Salvation Pioneer perfect through s
	11:26	valued s in the Messiah's camp
1Pe	1:7	genuine faith put through this s
	1:11	the Messiah would experience s
	5:10	The s won't last forever

Sufferings

2Ti	3:11	troubles, s — suffering along with me
1Pe	4:1	Think of your s as a weaning
	5:1	Christ's s as well as the coming glory

Suffers

Mt	17:15	goes out of his mind and s terribly
Lk	24:46	it is written that the Messiah s

Suicide

Ps	34:21	The wicked commit slow s
Ecc	4:5	His sloth is slow s

Sulk

Ge	4:5	lost his temper and went into a s
1Ki	20:43	The king of Israel went home in a s
Ps	68:16	All you mountains not chosen, s now
Pr	3:11	don't s under his loving correction
Jnh	4:5	sat down in a s
	4:6	get him out of his angry s
Lk	15:28	stalked off in an angry s

Sulking

Ge	4:6	Why this tantrum? Why the s
1Ki	21:4	Ahab went home in a black mood, s

S

343

Supernatural

1Sa	6:2	experts on the s for consultation
Ac	8:10	They all thought he had s powers
1Co	15:44	the seed grown is s

Superstitions

Zep	1:9	punish all who import pagan s
Ac	14:15	abandon these silly god-s and embrace
Gal	4:10	all the traditions, taboos, and s
Col	2:8	the empty s of spirit beings

Supervise

Nu	4:28	the priest is to s their work
2Ki	23:5	s the local sex-and-religion shrines
2Ch	2:7	he will s the trained craftsmen
Ne	10:38	priest descended from Aaron will s

Supervised

Nu	3:32	s the leaders of the Levites
	8:22	Aaron and his sons s them
1Ch	25:2	they were s by Asaph
	25:3	they were s by their father Jeduthun
	26:12	security guards, s by their leaders
	26:22	They s the finances of the sanctuary
	27:25	king's storage facilities were s by
2Ch	34:13	s the workers as they went from job

Supervision

Nu	4:27	to be done under the s of Aaron
	4:33	under the s of Ithamar son of Aaron
	19:5	under Eleazar's s burn the cow
Dt	17:18	under the s of the Levitical priests
1Ch	25:6	Under their father's s they were
Ac	27:1	placed under the s of a centurion
Heb	13:17	work under the strict s of God

Surprise

Jos	10:9	took them by total s
	11:7	took them by s
Jdg	3:24	they saw with s that the doors
Ru	3:8	suddenly startled and sat up. S!
2Sa	17:2	take him by complete s
1Ki	19:6	He looked around and, to his s
2Ki	6:15	S! Horses and chariots surrounding
	7:5	s! Not a man in the camp
	7:10	s! — the place was deserted
	24:13	This should have been no s
2Ch	13:13	take them by s from the rear
Ps	17:3	s me in the middle of the night
	35:8	S them with your ambush
	56:6	through the alleys To take me by s
	90:14	S us with love at daybreak
Pr	25:22	Your generosity will s him
Isa	29:5	Because, s, as if out of nowhere
Jer	13:21	You didn't expect this? S!
	18:22	as you s them with war parties

	50:28	And here's a s: Runaways
Da	10:5	to my s saw a man dressed in linen
	11:21	He'll s everyone
Zec	3:2	I rebuke you and choose Jerusalem. S
	5:1	and saw — s! — a book on the wing
	5:9	to my s saw two women flying
Lk	1:30	God has a s for you
	1:63	That took everyone by s
	1:64	S followed s
	2:33	speechless with s at these words
	11:14	taking the crowd by complete s
	16:8	Now here's a s: The master
	21:34	going to take you by complete s
Ac	3:12	take you by such complete s
Ro	6:22	listening to God telling you, what a s
	12:20	Your generosity will s him
2Co	11:15	So it shouldn't s us when
Gal	2:17	No great s, right?
Eph	3:7	a sheer gift to me, a real s
1Th	3:3	troubles should come as any s to you
Rev	17:7	The Angel said, "Does this s you?

Surprised

1Sa	10:11	the prophets, they were totally s
2Sa	22:20	I stood there saved — s to be loved
Ps	18:19	I stood there saved — s to be loved
Pr	30:33	Don't be s if someone bloodies
Da	8:3	I was s to see a ram also standing
	10:16	s by something like a human hand
Ob	1:8	don't be s" — it's God's sure Word
Zec	1:18	was s by another vision: four horns
	2:1	s to see a man holding a tape measure
Mk	1:22	They were s at his teaching
Lk	4:22	s at how well he spoke
	4:32	They were s and impressed
Jn	3:7	So don't be so s when I tell you
	5:28	Don't act so s at all this
	8:33	S, they said, "But we're descendants
Ac	23:5	Paul acted s. "How was I to know
2Th	2:16	s you with gifts of unending help
1Jn	3:13	don't be s . . . when the world hates

Surprises

Job	5:9	there's no end to his s
	9:10	his miracle-s can't be counted
Pr	3:25	No need to panic over alarms or s
	19:23	full life, and serene — no nasty s
	31:14	brings back exotic s
Mt	26:24	marked by the Scriptures — no s here
Mk	14:21	marked by the Scriptures — no s here
Lk	22:22	a path already marked out — no s

Surprising

Isa	9:4	a deliverance as s and sudden as
Da	4:3	his wonders are s
2Co	8:1	the s and generous ways in which God

Surrender

Jdg	15:13	We will tie you up and s you to them
	20:13	S the men right here and now

Surrendered

2Ki	24:12	advisors, and government leaders, s
Jer	39:9	along with those who had s to him

Surrenders

Jer	21:9	goes out and s to the Chaldeans

Survival

Ge	7:3	to insure their s on Earth
	47:19	all we ask is seed for s
Job	24:6	eke out s on handouts
Ecc	8:15	compensation for the struggle for s
Zec	11:6	It's dog-eat-dog, s of the fittest
Mt	10:23	in such times but s. Be survivors
Lk	16:9	stimulate you to creative s

Survive

Ge	42:2	so that we can s and not starve
Nu	31:23	anything else that can s fire
Dt	4:27	a few of you will s here and there
Ne	5:2	we need food just to s
Job	27:18	houses that won't s a single winter
	31:12	expect anything I count dear to s it
Ps	147:17	who can s his winter
Pr	27:4	who can s jealousy
Isa	6:13	even if some should s
	33:14	Who among us can s this firestorm
Jer	48:6	S by your wits in the wild
	48:8	Not a city will s
Da	11:6	will weaken and her child will not s
Joel	2:11	Who can possibly s this
Zec	13:8	will be devastated and one-third s
Mal	3:2	Who can s his appearance
1Co	3:15	you won't be torn out; you'll s
2Co	10:11	Such talk won't s scrutiny
Heb	10:39	We'll stay with it and s

Survived

Ex	14:28	Not one of them s
Jdg	2:7	the leaders who s him
2Ch	30:6	who have s the predations of the kings
Ne	1:2	who had s the exile
Jer	31:2	these people who s the killing

Survives

Ex	21:21	if the slave s a day or two
Pr	12:26	A good person s misfortune
Zec	11:9	Whoever s can eat what's left

Surviving

Lev	10:12	spoke to Aaron and his s sons
Job	20:28	nothing s God's wrath
Zec	8:11	taking the side of my core of s people
	13:9	deliver the s third to the refinery
Lk	16:8	looking for angles, s by their wits

Survivor

Nu	21:35	there was not a single s
Dt	7:20	until every s-in-hiding is dead
Jos	8:22	a real massacre. And not a single s
Jdg	9:5	managed to hide, the only s
2Sa	17:12	there won't be a single s
2Ch	36:20	Any s was taken prisoner into exile
Ps	106:11	there wasn't a single s
Eze	24:26	on that very day a s will arrive
	24:27	talking to the s
	33:21	a s from Jerusalem came to me
	33:22	The evening before the s arrived
Am	6:10	discovers a s huddled in a closet

Survivors

Dt	2:34	men, women, and children. No s
	3:3	utterly crushed them. Again, no s
Jos	10:28	carried out the holy curse. No s
	10:30	massacred the lot. No s
	10:33	nothing left of them. No s
	10:37	its villages, and their people. No s
	10:39	everything under the holy curse. No s
	10:40	including all kings. He left no s
	11:8	Mizpah on the east. No s
	13:12	one of the last s of the Rephaim
Jdg	21:17	alive for the Benjaminite s
1Sa	2:36	S from your family will come
1Ki	9:21	s of the holy wars, were rounded up
	20:30	fall on 27,000 of the s
2Ki	10:14	Forty-two of them — no s
	10:25	Enter and kill! No s!
	19:31	the s from Mount Zion
2Ch	8:8	s of the holy wars, were rounded up
Ne	1:3	exile s who are left there
Pr	28:26	real s learn wisdom from others
Isa	1:9	left us a few s
	4:2	give Israel's s something to be proud
	7:21	when s will count themselves lucky
	10:20	the ragtag s of Jacob
	14:22	strip Babylon of name and s
	37:32	Mount Zion s will take hold again
	66:19	I'll send the s of judgment all over
Jer	21:7	any s left in the city
	24:8	along with the s here
	40:11	had left a few s in Judah
	42:17	No s, not one!
Eze	7:16	S run for the hills
	14:22	there'll be s
Joel	2:32	the s are those that God calls
Ob	1:14	turned in helpless s
Mic	2:12	want everyone back — all the s
Hab	2:8	All the s are out to plunder you

S

Zep	2:5	slated for destruction — no s
Zec	8:6	rebuilding by just a few s
	9:7	will be all God's — a core of s
	14:16	All the s from the godless nations
	14:17	If any of these s fail to make
Mt	10:23	in such times but survival. Be s

Suspect

Ac	2:15	aren't drunk as some of you s
Ro	2:21	Who would s you
Gal	5:4	I s you would never intend this

Suspected

Mk	3:21	They s he was getting carried away
Lk	17:27	They s nothing until the flood hit

Suspecting

Lk	11:44	never s the rot and corruption
2Co	8:20	anyone s us of taking one penny

Suspects

Nu	5:14	he s that his wife is impure
	5:30	jealousy because he s his wife

Suspicion

Ge	20:16	clears you of even a shadow of s
Nu	35:23	no s that there was bad blood
Ac	14:2	sowing mistrust and s in the minds
Eph	2:15	centuries of animosity and s

Suspicions

Nu	5:14	his jealousy and s are groundless
Ac	9:22	their s didn't slow Saul down

Suspicious

1Sa	29:3	I've found nothing to be s of
Lk	22:23	immediately became s of each other
1Ti	6:4	controversy, bad-mouthing, s rumors

Swear

Ge	14:22	I s to God, The High God
	21:23	s to me that you won't do anything
	21:24	Abraham said, "I s it
	22:16	I s — God's sure word!
	24:3	s by God — God of Heaven, God of Earth
	25:33	Jacob said, "First, s to me."
	50:5	My father made me s
Ex	13:19	made the Israelites solemnly s
Lev	5:4	if you impulsively s to do something
	19:12	Don't s falsely using my name
Jos	2:17	to keep this oath you made us s
	2:20	the oath you made us s is canceled
	23:7	the names of their gods or s by them
Jdg	15:7	I s I'll get even with you

2Sa	19:7	I s to God that if you don't go
1Ki	17:12	I s, as surely as your God lives
	18:10	s that you were not to be found
2Ch	36:13	earlier had made him s in God's name
Ezr	10:5	all Israel solemnly s to do
Ne	13:25	I made them s to God
Ps	16:4	I s I'll never treat god-names like
Jer	22:5	then I s — God's Decree!
	22:6	I s I'll turn you into a wasteland
	44:26	I s by my great name
	49:13	I s by all that I am
Eze	17:13	making him s his loyalty
Da	12:7	heard him . . . s by the Eternal One
Mt	26:72	I s, I never laid eyes on the man
Mk	5:7	I s to God, don't give me a hard time
	6:23	I s, I'll split my kingdom with you
Jas	5:12	Don't add words like "I s to God"

Swears

Lev	6:3	s falsely regarding any of these sins
Am	8:7	God s against the arrogance of Jacob
Mt	23:16	if he s with his hand on the Bible

Swore

Ge	21:31	two of them s a covenant oath there
	26:3	the oath that I s to your father
Lev	6:5	anything else about which he s falsely
Nu	32:10	did he get angry! He s
Dt	1:34	he exploded in anger. He s
	4:21	He s that I'd never cross the Jordan
	4:31	covenant . . . which he s to them
Jos	6:26	Joshua s a solemn oath at that time
	9:15	leaders of the congregation s to it
1Sa	28:10	Saul s solemnly, "As God lives
2Sa	3:35	David solemnly s, "I'll not so much as
	21:17	Then David's men s to him
1Ki	2:23	Then King Solomon s under God
2Ki	11:4	s them to secrecy
1Ch	16:16	the very one he s to Isaaac
Ps	50:5	who s on the Bible their loyalty
	66:14	What I solemnly s I'd do
	105:9	the same oath he s to Isaaac
	106:26	God s that he'd lay them low
Pr	30:1	The skeptic s, "There is no God!
Jer	38:16	Zedekiah s to Jeremiah right there
Eze	20:23	s that I would scatter them all over
	47:14	I s in a solemn oath to give it
Mt	16:20	He s the disciples to secrecy
	17:9	Jesus s them to secrecy
	26:74	nervous and s. "I don't know the man!"
Mk	9:9	Jesus s them to secrecy
	14:71	s, "I never laid eyes on this man
Lk	1:73	What he s to our father Abraham
Heb	3:18	when he s that they'd never get
Rev	10:6	s by the One Living Forever and Ever

Sworn

Ge	24:8	free from this oath you've s to me
Dt	2:14	as God had s they would

	29:12	into the solemnly s Covenant
Jdg	2:15	just as he had s he would do
	21:7	We have s by God not to give any
Jer	9:3	the s enemies of truth
	51:14	God-of-the-Angel-Armies has solemnly s
Eze	21:23	leaders, who themselves have s oaths
	36:7	s that the nations around you are next
Am	4:2	I, God, have s by my holiness
	6:8	God, the Master, has s
Ac	2:30	God had solemnly s that a descendant

Symbol

Ex	13:16	a s on the middle of your forehead
Ps	74:9	not a sign or s of God in sight
Zec	6:14	in the Temple of God as a s of royalty

Symbols

2Ki	17:10	set up their sex-and-religion s
Job	36:31	s of his sovereignty, his generosity

T

Tainted

1Ki	21:24	Anyone t by Ahab who dies in the city
Pr	13:14	no more drinking from death-t wells
Isa	6:5	Every word I've ever spoken is t
1Co	8:13	never go to these idol-t meals
1Th	5:22	Throw out anything t with evil

Talents

1Ch	19:7	a cost of a thousand t of silver
	22:14	100,000 t . . . of gold, a million t
	29:4	3,000 t (about 113 tons) of gold
	29:7	They gave 5,000 t (188 tons)
2Ch	3:8	It was veneered with 600 t
Ezr	7:22	up to a hundred t of silver

Tangle

Ps	10:2	t them up in their fine-tuned plots
Jer	2:21	a t of rancid growth
	18:15	underbrush in a t of roots and vines
Ro	8:33	who would dare t with God

Tangled

Lev	21:10	not let his hair go wild and t
Job	18:8	all t up in their own red tape
Ps	9:15	feet all t in the net they spread
Isa	8:15	Get t up in that barbed wire
Jer	3:25	t up in the dirty sheets of dishonor
Jnh	2:5	My head was all t in seaweed

Tangles

Pr	21:8	Mixed motives twist life into t
Mk	4:34	sorting out the t, untying the knots

Tantrums

2Ki	19:27	your temper t against me
Job	38:11	wild t are confined to this place
Isa	37:28	the t you throw against me
	51:13	before the t of a tyrant
Ro	10:19	you'll throw temper t

Target

2Sa	5:8	one must t the water system
Job	16:12	He set me up as his t
	40:11	T the arrogant and lay them flat
	40:12	T the arrogant and bring them
Ps	119:137	God; your decisions are right on t
Zec	6:10	T Heldai, Tobiah, and Jedaiah

Targeted

Jer	44:27	I've t each one of you for doom
	48:16	disaster t and launched
Ac	2:39	promise is t to you and your children
	13:26	message . . . has been precisely t

Taste

Dt	8:16	to give you a t of the hard life
1Sa	14:26	put his finger in the honey to t it
2Sa	3:35	not so much as t a piece of bread
	19:35	Can't t food; can't hear music
Job	12:11	as common as the sense of t
	20:23	God gives them a t of his anger
	21:25	never getting a t of happiness
	34:3	as common as the sense of t
Ps	18:25	The good people t your goodness
	18:26	The true people t your truth
	34:8	Open your mouth and t
	57:4	wild for a t of human flesh
	68:23	your dogs t of your enemies
	70:3	Give them a t of their own medicine
	109:17	he had no t for blessing
	109:25	a joke in poor t to those who see me
Pr	5:2	you'll acquire a t for good sense
	8:7	I can't stand the t of evil
	13:2	acquire a t for helpful conversation
	16:24	good t to the soul
SS	2:3	to t and savor his delicious love
Jer	4:18	The bitter t is from your evil life
	23:17	congregations with no t for God
	48:26	falling-down drunk, a joke in bad t
La	3:19	the utter lostness, the t of ashes
Eze	13:18	head scarves to suit every t
	16:38	I'll give you a t of my wrath
Hos	5:11	a t of his own medicine
	13:2	Religion customized to t
Hab	2:8	you'll get a t of your own medicine
Zep	1:13	plant vineyards and never t the wine
Mt	5:13	how will people t godliness
Jn	8:52	never have to face death, not even a t
Ac	13:46	no t or inclination for eternal life
	20:33	never . . . had any t for wealth
2Co	5:5	giving us a t of what's ahead

T

Eph	5:4	some tongues just love the t of gossip
Col	2:21	Don't touch this! Don't t that!
Heb	6:4	gotten a t of heaven
1Pe	2:2	You've had a t of God
Rev	10:9	It will t sweet like honey
	11:18	nations now get a t of your anger

Tasted

Ex	16:31	it t like a cracker with honey
Nu	11:8	It t like a delicacy cooked in
Eze	3:3	It t so good — just like honey
Mt	27:34	when he t it he wouldn't drink it
Lk	5:39	no one who has ever t fine aged wine
Jn	2:9	t the water that had become wine
Ac	10:14	never . . . t food that was not kosher
	11:8	never . . . t food that wasn't kosher

Tasteless

Jer	10:15	deadwood gods, t jokes
	51:17	deadwood gods, t jokes
Mic	6:16	life will be laughed at, a t joke

Taught

Lev	19:5	do it as you've been t
Dt	31:22	t it to the People of Israel
	31:30	Moses t them the words of this song
2Ki	12:2	T and trained by Jehoiada the priest
	17:28	t them how to honor and worship God
2Ch	22:5	He did what they t him
	24:2	T and trained by Jehoiada the priest
Job	15:5	your sin that t you to talk this way
	15:18	what wise men and women have always t
Ps	40:3	t me how to sing the latest God-song
	71:17	t me everything I know
	119:75	your testing has t me what's true
	119:171	you've t me the truth about life
Pr	3:1	don't forget all I've t you
Ecc	12:9	the Quester also t others' knowledge
Isa	40:13	told God what to do or t him
	40:14	What god . . . might have t him
	50:4	God, has given me a well-t tongue
Jer	2:33	t graduate courses in evil
	5:4	were never t anything about God
	12:16	t my people to pray to that god Baal
	32:33	refused to listen, refused to be t
Mal	2:6	He t the truth and did not lie
Mt	4:23	t people the truth of God
	5:2	and t his climbing companions
	9:35	He t in their meeting places
Mk	2:13	a crowd came to him, and he t them
	4:2	He t by using stories, many stories
	6:30	all that they had done and t
	10:1	he, as he so often did, t them
	11:17	then he t them, quoting this text
Lk	1:4	the reliability of what you were t
	4:15	He t in their meeting places
	5:3	boat for a pulpit, he t the crowd
	6:6	he went to the meeting place and t
	11:1	pray just as John t his disciples

Jn	19:47	he t each day in the Temple
	6:45	they will all be personally t by God
	8:2	He sat down and t them
	8:28	speaking only what the Father t me
	18:20	I've t regularly in meeting places
Ac	18:25	everything he t about Jesus
	20:20	I t you out in public and I t you
Ro	2:9	what your parents t you
1Co	2:13	t us person-to-person through Jesus
Gal	1:12	I wasn't t it in some school
Col	2:7	Now do what you've been t
1Th	4:9	You're God-t in these matters
2Th	2:15	Keep a tight grip on what you were t
	3:6	refuse to work the way we t you
1Ti	1:20	wander off to Satan to be t a lesson
1Jn	2:27	Live deeply in what you were t

Taunt

Job	19:18	when I come out, they t and jeer
Ps	102:8	All day long my enemies t me
Isa	14:4	this satire, a t against the king
	66:5	They t you, 'Let us see God's glory

Taunted

Jdg	8:15	my worn-out men; you t us
1Sa	1:6	her rival wife t her cruelly
	1:7	she could expect to be t
2Ki	2:23	little kids came out . . . and t him
Jer	51:51	we've been humiliated, t and abused
Eze	23:32	You'll be shunned and t
	34:29	no longer t by outsiders
Lk	22:64	They put a blindfold on him and t

Taunting

1Sa	17:26	t the armies of God-Alive
	17:36	t the troops of God-Alive
1Ki	18:27	started making fun of them, t
Job	30:9	mistreating me, t and mocking
Ps	42:10	T day after day, "Where is this God
	89:51	The t jokes of your enemies, God
Isa	57:4	What business do you have t, sneering
Mic	7:10	This enemy who kept t
Hab	2:6	Soon the whole world will be t them
Lk	23:11	soldiers joined in, t and jeering
	23:35	ringleaders made faces, t

Taunts

Ps	69:20	I'm broken by their t
	74:18	remember, God, all the enemy t
	79:12	let their God-t boomerang
Isa	47:3	on public display, exposed to vulgar t
Eze	21:28	and against their cruel t
	36:15	never again let the t of outsiders
Zep	2:8	I've heard the crude t of Moab
	2:10	bloated pride, their t and mockeries

T

Teach

Ex	4:12	right there to **t** you what to say
	18:16	**t** them God's laws and instructions
	18:20	Your job is to **t** them the rules
Lev	10:11	**T** the People of Israel all the decrees
Dt	4:9	**T** what you've seen and heard
	4:10	**t** these same words to their children
	4:14	God commanded me at that time to **t** you
	5:31	regulations that you must **t** them
	6:1	God, your God, commanded me to **t** you
	11:19	**T** them to your children
	20:18	won't be any of them left to **t** you
	31:19	**t** the People of Israel to sing it
	33:10	Let him **t** your rules to Jacob
Jdg	13:8	come to us again and **t** us how to
1Sa	23:2	these Philistines and **t** them a lesson
Ne	9:20	gave them your good Spirit to **t** them
Job	8:10	why not let the ancients **t** you
	12:7	let them **t** you; let the birds tell
	33:33	going to **t** you the basics of wisdom
	34:32	**T** me to see what I still don't see
	35:11	using birds and beasts to **t** wisdom
	38:39	**t** the lioness to stalk her prey
	39:27	command the eagle's flight, and **t** her
Ps	78:5	commanded our parents to **t** it
	90:12	**T** us to live well! **T** us to live
	119:33	God, **t** me lessons for living
	119:108	**t** me your holy rules
	119:124	**t** me from your textbook on life
	119:135	**t** me the right way to live
	132:12	learn to live the way I **t** them
	143:10	**T** me how to live to please you
Pr	1:4	To **t** the inexperienced the ropes
	6:6	let it **t** you a thing or two
	22:17	take to heart what I can **t** you
Isn	28:9	who do you think you are to **t** us
	51:16	I **t** you how to talk, word by word
Jer	9:20	**T** your daughters songs for the dead
	16:21	going to **t** these wrongheaded people
	18:18	have the priests to **t** us the law
	31:34	schools to **t** each other about God
	32:33	took great pains to **t** them how to live
Eze	44:23	Their job is to **t** my people
Da	11:33	will **t** the crowds right from wrong
Hos	7:12	I'll **t** them to mind me
	10:10	I'll come to **t** them a lesson
Mic	4:2	He will **t** us how to live
Hab	2:19	Can they **t** you anything about anything
Mal	2:7	the job of priests to **t** the truth
	2:9	you don't **t** my revelation truly
Mt	11:1	he went on to **t** and preach
	22:16	we know you have integrity, **t**
Mk	9:31	he wanted to **t** his disciples
Lk	11:1	Master, **t** us to pray just as John
Jn	7:16	What I **t** comes from the One
	7:35	to **t** the Jews
Ac	1:1	thing that Jesus began to do and **t**
	4:18	to speak or **t** in the name of Jesus
	5:28	strict orders not to **t** in Jesus' name
Ro	12:7	if you **t**, stick to your teaching
1Co	14:26	Sing a hymn, **t** a lesson

Col	1:28	**t** in a spirit of profound common sense
1Ti	4:11	Get the word out. **T** all these things
	4:12	**T** believers with your life
	6:3	leaders there who **t** otherwise
2Ti	2:2	leaders who are competent to **t** others

Teacher

Ex	35:34	And he's also made him a **t**
1Ch	25:8	Nobody, whether . . . **t** or student
2Ch	15:3	the help of priest or **t** or book
	26:5	his pastor and **t** Zechariah
Job	36:22	Have you ever heard of a **t** like him
Ps	94:10	the **t** of Adam doesn't know
Isa	28:26	Their God is their **t**
	30:20	he'll keep your **t** alive and present
	54:13	children will have God for their **t**
Joel	2:23	He's giving you a **t** to train you
Mt	9:11	example is this from your **T**
	10:24	doesn't get a better desk than her **t**
	12:38	**T**, we want to see your credentials
	17:24	Does your **t** pay taxes
	19:16	**T**, what good thing must I do to get
	22:16	**T**, we know you have integrity
	22:24	**T**, Moses said that if a man dies
	22:36	**T**, which command in God's Law is
	23:8	You all have a single **T**
	26:18	The **T** says, My time is near
Mk	4:38	They roused him, saying, "**T**, is it
	5:35	Why bother the **T** any more
	9:17	**T**, I brought my mute son
	9:38	**T**, we saw a man using your name
	10:17	Good **T**, what must I do to get
	10:20	**T**, I have — from my youth — kept them
	10:35	**T**, we have something we want you to do
	12:14	**T**, we know you have integrity
	12:19	**T**, Moses wrote that if a man dies
	12:32	scholar said, "A wonderful answer, **T**
	13:1	**T**, look at that stonework!
	14:14	**T** wants to know, Where is my . . . room
Lk	3:12	**T**, what should we do
	6:40	be careful who you follow as your **t**
	8:49	No need now to bother the **T**
	9:38	please, **T**, take a look at my son
	10:25	a question to test Jesus. "**T**, what do
	11:45	**T**, do you realize that in saying
	12:13	**T**, order my brother to give me
	18:18	Good **T**, what must I do to deserve
	19:39	**T**, get your disciples under control
	20:21	**T**, we know that you're honest
	20:28	**T**, Moses wrote us that if a man dies
	20:39	said, "**T**, that's a great answer
	21:7	**T**, when is this going to happen?
	22:11	The **T** wants to know
Jn	1:38	said, "Rabbi" (which means "**T**")
	3:2	know you're a **t** straight from God
	3:10	You're a respected **t** of Israel
	8:4	**T**, this woman was caught red-handed
	11:28	The **T** is here and is asking for you
	13:13	You address me as '**T**' and 'Master,'
	13:14	I, the Master and **T**, washed your feet
	20:16	"Rabboni!" meaning "**T**

Ac	5:34	Gamaliel, a t of God's Law
Eph	4:11	prophet, evangelist, and pastor-t
2Ti	1:11	as preacher, emissary, and t
	2:24	gentle listener and a t who keeps cool
Jas	3:1	Don't be in any rush to become a t

Teachers

Ezr	8:16	for the t Joiarib and Elnathan
Ps	119:99	I've even become smarter than my t
Pr	5:13	take my t seriously
Isa	3:2	judges and courts, pastors and t
Mt	7:29	quite a contrast to their religion t
	16:17	get that answer out of books or from t
	23:2	competent t in God's Law
Lk	2:46	in the Temple seated among the t
	2:47	The t were all quite taken with him
	5:17	Pharisees and religion t were sitting
Ac	13:1	a number of prophet-preachers and t
	15:35	a number of t and preachers
1Co	12:28	apostles prophets t miracle workers
Gal	4:17	Those heretical t go to great lengths
2Ti	3:14	sure of the integrity of your t
Heb	5:12	you ought to be t yourselves
Jas	3:1	T are held to the strictest standards
2Pe	2:1	will be lying religious t among you
	2:10	against these "t" who live by lust
	3:17	lawless and loose-talking t
1Jn	4:4	a big victory over those false t

Teaching

Ex	4:15	as he speaks, t you step by step
	13:9	and the t of God in your mouth
	16:4	see if they'll live according to my T
Dt	4:1	rules and regulations that I am t you
	4:5	I'm t you the rules and regulations
	32:2	My t, let it fall like a gentle rain
	32:11	t them to fly
	33:3	sit at your feet, honoring your t
1Sa	12:23	t you the good and right way to live
2Ch	17:7	on a t mission to the cities
	17:9	t the people and using the Book
	35:3	Levites who were in charge of t
Ezr	7:10	t Israel to live its truths and ways
	7:12	scholar of the T of the God-of-Heaven
	7:14	in relation to the T of your God
	7:21	scholar of the T of the God-of-Heaven
	7:25	who live by the T of your God
	7:26	who does not obey the T of your God
Ne	8:9	the Levites who were t the people
	9:13	true t, sound rules and commands
Ps	51:13	Give me a job t rebels your ways
Pr	6:23	good t is a light
	7:2	My t is as precious as your eyesight
	13:14	t of the wise is a fountain of life
Isa	8:16	preserve the t for my followers
	42:4	islands wait expectantly for his t
	51:7	you who hold my t inside you
Jer	6:19	had nothing but contempt for my t
	9:13	Because they abandoned my plain t
	26:4	refuse to . . . live by my t

Da	9:10	you told us how to live, the clear t
Joel	2:23	how to live right — T, like rain
Mic	3:11	priests mass-market their t
	4:2	True t will issue from Zion
Mal	2:8	Your t has messed up many lives
Mt	7:28	They had never heard t like this
	7:29	the best t they had ever heard
	15:9	t whatever suits their fancy
	16:12	wasn't concerned about eating, but t
	21:23	Then he was back in the Temple, t
	26:55	I have been sitting in the Temple t
Mk	1:21	He spent the day there t
	1:22	They were surprised at his t
	1:27	A new t that does what it says?
	2:2	He was t the Word
	4:1	He went back to t by the sea
	6:6	a circuit of the other villages, t
	6:34	He went right to work t them
	7:7	t whatever suits their fancy
	11:18	crowd was carried away by his t
	12:35	While he was t in the Temple
	12:38	He continued t
	14:49	I've been sitting in the Temple t
Lk	4:31	He was t the people on the Sabbath
	4:32	his t was so forthright, so confident
	5:4	When he finished t, he said
	5:17	One day as he was t
	13:10	He was t in one of the meeting places
	13:22	He went on t from town to village
	20:1	he was t the people in the Temple
	21:37	He spent his days in the Temple t
	23:5	with his t, disturbing the peace
Jn	6:59	He said these things while t
	6:60	This is tough t, too tough to swallow
	7:14	Jesus showed up in the Temple, t
	7:17	test this t and know whether it's
	7:28	Jesus, who was t in the Temple
	8:20	while t in the Temple
	18:19	regarding his disciples and his t
Ac	2:42	committed themselves to the t
	5:21	went on with their t
	5:25	back in the Temple t the people
	5:28	you have filled Jerusalem with your t
	5:42	t and preaching Christ Jesus
	6:2	responsibilities for preaching and t
	11:26	t a lot of people
	15:35	t and preaching the Word of God
	18:5	give all his time to preaching and t
	18:11	faithfully t the Word of God
Ro	12:7	if you teach, stick to your t
	16:17	who take bits and pieces of the t
1Co	14:6	truth or proclamation or t
1Ti	1:3	so that the t stays on track
	4:6	have followed sound t
	4:13	reading Scripture, giving counsel, t
	4:16	both your character and your t
	5:17	work hard at preaching and t
	6:1	don't blame God and our t
2Ti	3:10	a part of my t, my manner of life
	4:3	will have no stomach for solid t
Tit	1:11	disrupting . . . families with their t
	2:7	incorruptible in your t
	2:10	adding luster to the t of our Savior

Jas	3:1	**T** is highly responsible work
1Jn	2:27	don't need any of their so-called **t**
2Jn	1:9	he walks out on the **t** of Christ
	1:10	who doesn't hold to this **t**

Teachings

Ge	26:5	my commands, my guidelines, my **t**
Ex	24:12	**t** and commandments that I've written
Pr	6:20	don't wander off from your mother's **t**
Mt	19:1	When Jesus had completed these **t**
	23:3	won't go wrong in following their **t**
Jn	18:21	My **t** have all been aboveboard

Team

2Ki	5:17	as much as a **t** of donkeys can carry
2Ch	35:5	a **t** of Levites for every grouping
2Co	0:5	recruited ... as an advance **t**

Teams

1Ch	26:1	The **t** of security guards
	26:12	These **t** of security guards
	26:19	These are the **t** of security guards
Job	1:3	five hundred **t** of oxen
	42:12	one thousand **t** of oxen
Lk	14:19	I just bought five **t** of oxen

Tearful

Jer	9:18	make **t** music of our crying
Ac	21:1	with the **t** good-byes behind us
2Ti	1:4	remember that last **t** good-bye

Tears

Ge	29:11	he kissed Rachel and broke into **t**
	43:30	his brother and about to burst into **t**
Dt	33:20	roams like a lion, **t** off an arm
Jdg	14:16	Samson's bride turned on the **t**
	14:17	turned on the **t** all the seven days
1Sa	1:7	Hannah was reduced to **t**
	2:33	a hard life, with many **t**
2Sa	13:36	loud weeping, many **t**
2Ki	20:5	I've observed your **t**
2Ch	21:20	no **t** shed when he died
Est	8:3	begging with **t** to counter the evil
Job	12:14	If he **t** something down, it's down
	16:9	Your anger **t** at me
	31:38	furrows fill with **t** from my abuse
Ps	6:6	the flood of my **t**
	39:12	just look at these **t** of mine
	42:3	diet of **t** — **t** for breakfast, **t** for
	42:9	Why am I walking around in **t**
	80:5	You put us on a diet of **t**
	80:5	bucket after bucket of salty **t**
	88:9	blinded by **t** of pain and frustration
	102:9	I draw drink from a barrel of my **t**
	116:8	Eye, you've been rescued from **t**
	119:136	I cry rivers of **t**
Pr	14:1	Sir Fool comes along and **t** it down

Ecc	4:1	the **t** of the victims
Isa	15:3	Everyone in **t**, everyone in grief
	16:9	I'll mingle my **t** with your **t**
	22:12	Called for a day of repentant **t**
	23:6	cry buckets of **t**
	25:8	God will wipe the **t** from every face
	30:19	your time of **t** is over
	32:12	Shed honest **t** for the lost harvest
	32:13	Cry **t**, real **t**, for the happy homes
	33:7	Peacemaking diplomats are in bitter **t**
	38:3	wept as he prayed — painful **t**
	38:5	I have seen your **t**
	66:10	all you who have shed **t** over her
Jer	9:1	my eyes fountains of **t**
	9:18	Help us get our **t** flowing
	9:19	Listen to that torrent of **t**
	13:17	bitter **t**, Rivers of **t** from my eyes
	14:17	pour out **t**. Day and night, the **t**
	15:5	Who do you think will waste **t** on you
	20:18	Life's been nothing but trouble and **t**
	22:10	Don't waste your **t**
	22:18	Nobody will shed **t** over him
	25:33	No **t** will be shed and no burials
	31:16	hold back your **t**
	49:3	Dress in mourning, weep buckets of **t**
La	1:2	each night, **t** soaking her pillow
	1:16	I weep, weep buckets of **t**
	2:11	My eyes are blind with **t**
	2:18	Let the **t** roll like a river
	3:48	Rivers of **t** pour from my eyes
	3:49	The **t** stream from my eyes
	3:50	look and see my **t**
	5:17	we can't see through the **t**
Eze	23:33	**t** will flow as you drink from that cup
	24:16	But, please, no **t**
	24:23	go about your work. No **t**
Joel	2:17	God's servants, weep **t** of repentance
Am	8:8	dissolve the whole world into **t**
Mic	1:10	Don't waste your **t**
Mk	14:72	He collapsed in **t**
Lk	6:21	You're blessed when the **t** flow freely
	7:38	weeping, raining **t** on his feet
	7:44	she rained **t** on my feet
Ac	20:37	And then a river of **t**
Ro	12:15	share **t** when they're down
1Co	5:2	bring you to your knees in **t**
2Co	2:4	more **t** than ink on the parchment
	6:10	immersed in **t**, yet always filled
	12:21	**t** over that crowd that keeps sinning
Heb	12:17	it was too late, **t** or no **t**
Jas	5:1	need buckets for the **t**
Rev	18:7	to torment and **t**
	21:4	Death is gone for good — **t** gone

Temper

Ge	4:5	Cain lost his **t** and went into a sulk
	49:6	They kill men in fits of **t**
Ex	16:20	Moses lost his **t** with them
	32:11	Why, God, would you lose your **t**
Nu	16:15	Moses' **t** blazed white-hot
	22:27	Balaam lost his **t**; he beat the donkey

T

	24:10	Balak lost his t with Balaam
1Sa	17:28	lost his t: "What are you doing here
2Sa	3:8	Abner lost his t with Isah-Bosheth
2Ki	5:11	Naaman lost his t. He turned on his heel
	19:27	your t tantrums against me
	19:28	your t, your blasphemous foul t
1Ch	13:11	David lost his t, angry
2Ch	16:10	At that, Asa lost his t. Angry
	26:19	lost his t; angry words were exchanged
Est	1:12	The king lost his t
Job	5:2	hot t of a fool eventually kills him
	32:2	Then Elihu lost his t
Ps	78:21	he lost his t with Israel
	89:38	lost your t with the one you anointed
	106:33	Moses exploded and lost his t
Pr	15:1	a sharp tongue kindles a t-fire
	21:14	a heartfelt present cools a hot t
	22:25	Bad t is contagious
Ecc	10:4	If a ruler loses his t against you
Isa	48:9	tight rein on my anger and hold my t
Jer	10:24	Don't lose your t
La	3:43	You lost your t with us
Da	2:12	That set the king off. He lost his t
Jnh	4:1	Jonah was furious. He lost his t
Mic	2:7	Does God lose his t?
Na	1:3	But God doesn't lose his t
Mt	26:65	Chief Priest lost his t
Mk	14:63	The Chief Priest lost his t
Ro	10:19	you'll throw t tantrums
Gal	5:20	a brutal t; an impotence to love
Eph	2:3	It's a wonder God didn't lose his t
Col	3:8	bad t, irritability, meanness

Tempered

Jdg	18:25	fierce, hot-t men to attack you
Pr	14:29	a quick-t person stockpiles stupidity
	16:15	Good-t leaders invigorate lives
	19:12	Mean-t leaders are like mad dogs
	20:2	Quick-t leaders are like mad dogs
Ro	5:4	forges the t steel of virtue
Col	3:13	Be even-t, content with second
Tit	1:7	not pushy, not short-t

Tempers

Pr	15:18	Hot t start fights
Mt	20:24	lost their t, thoroughly disgusted
Mk	10:41	lost their t with James and John
Ac	15:39	T flared, and they ended up
2Co	12:20	quarrels, jealousy, flaring t

Tempt

Pr	1:10	if bad companions t you, don't go
Lk	4:12	Don't you dare t the Lord your God
Ro	7:13	using the good as a cover to t me

Temptation

Mt	26:41	so you don't wander into t
Lk	22:40	Pray that you don't give in to t

	22:46	Pray so you won't give in to t
Ro	7:8	to pervert the command into a t
1Co	10:5	most of them were defeated by t
	10:13	No test or t that comes your way
Jas	1:14	The t to give in to evil comes from us

Temptress

Pr	2:16	will rescue you from the T
	6:24	from the seductive talk of some t
	7:5	be with you to fend off the T

Tender

Ps	71:21	turn to me, be t to me
	86:15	you, O God, are both t and kind
SS	1:7	outside the orbit of your t care
Isa	60:10	It's my desire now to be t
Jude	1:23	Be t with sinners, but not soft on sin

Tenderly

Job	15:11	spoken so gently and t
Ps	73:24	You wisely and t lead me
	80:15	Care for what you once t planted
Isa	40:2	Speak softly and t to Jerusalem
	49:13	his people. He has t nursed
	54:8	love that I'm t caring for you
Jer	12:15	relent and take them t to my heart
	31:20	Softly and t I wait for him
La	3:32	If he works severely, he also works t
Eze	16:5	one thing to care for you t
Mt	10:1	to t care for the bruised
	11:27	talking to the people, but now t
1Pe	5:3	but t showing them the way

Terrified

Ge	28:17	He was t. He whispered in awe
	42:21	how t he was when he was begging
Dt	1:29	Don't be t of them
	2:4	They are t of you
	2:25	people around here are thoroughly t
	9:19	I was t of God's furious anger
	28:66	constant jeopardy, t of every shadow
Jos	9:24	We were t because of you
1Sa	16:14	settled on him. He was t
	17:11	they were t and lost all hope
	28:20	t by Samuel's words
	31:4	wouldn't do it. He was t
2Ki	10:4	absolutely t at the letter
1Ch	13:12	David was t of God that day
	21:30	David, t by the angel's sword
Isa	33:14	sinners in Zion are rightly t
Da	4:19	came swarming into his mind t him
	7:1	saw as he slept in his bed t him
	8:17	I became t and fell facedown
Jnh	1:5	The sailors were t
	1:16	no longer t by the sea
Hab	3:7	adversaries . . . were t
Mt	2:3	Herod, he was t
Lk	2:9	glory blazed around them. They were t

T

Heb	12:19	words and soul-shaking message t them
	12:21	Even Moses was t

Terror

Ex	14:10	They cried out in t to God
	15:16	Dread and t sent them reeling
	23:27	I'll send my T on ahead of you
	32:25	t in the houses
Dt		
Jdg	13:6	angel of God — t laced with glory
1Sa	11:7	The t of God seized the people
2Sa	24:16	God felt the pain of the t
2Ch	23:21	no more Athaliah t
Est	7:6	Haman was t-stricken before the king
Job	4:14	Dread stared me in the face, and T
	9:34	free me from this t so I could breathe
	13:21	the t is too much for me
	15:24	They live in constant t
	22:10	Now you're the one trapped in t
	39:20	strike t with his royal snorts
Ps	10:18	The reign of t is over
Isa	2:10	hide in the caves From the t of God
	2:19	Hide from the t of God
	2:21	hide from the t of God
	14:30	The needy will escape the t
	17:14	At bedtime, t fills the air
	19:17	Judah will strike t in Egyptians
	21:1	out of the desert, that t filled place
	24:17	T and pits and booby traps
	24:18	If you run from the t
	28:19	disaster will send you cowering in t
	54:14	nothing to fear! far from t
Jer	6:1	Doom pours out . . . massive t
	6:24	T has a death grip on our throats
	6:26	The T is on us
	8:15	for healing — and t showed up
	47:2	Men and women will scream in t
	48:43	T and pit and trap are what you have
	48:44	man running in t will fall into a trap
	49:5	I'll face you with t from all sides
	49:29	T! Death! Doom! Danger
	49:32	I'll bring t from every direction
	49:37	live in constant fear and t
	50:43	T-stricken, he doubles up in pain
	51:29	The very land trembles in t
Eze	12:19	drink your water in t
	23:33	drink from that cup titanic with t
	23:46	Let a mob loose on them: T
	26:16	wrap themselves in sheer t
	27:35	Everyone on shore looks on in t
	30:4	T will paralyze Ethiopia
	32:27	heroes who spread t through the land
	32:30	t they spread with their brute power
	32:32	used him to spread t in the land
Da	10:16	saw you, master, I was t-stricken
Joel	2:6	people panic, faces white with t
	3:16	Earth and sky quake in t
Am	3:9	a snake pit of brutality and t
Zep	1:10	Cries of t from the city
	2:11	truly terrible — a Holy T
Zec	14:13	killing each other — holy t
Mt	14:26	they said, crying out in t

Ac	9:13	his reign of t against your people
	26:11	a one-man t obsessed

Terrorized

Nu	22:3	They were t
Dt	28:60	malady that once t you
	28:67	Afraid, t at what's coming next
Isa	10:24	don't be t by the Assyrians
	14:16	the one Who t earth and its kingdoms
	31:9	T, that rock-solid people will fall
Jer	51:29	t by my plans against Babylon
Eze	19:7	t by the roars of the lion
	30:9	easygoing Ethiopians. They'll be t
	32:23	people who t the land of the living
	32:24	people who t the land of the living
	32:25	They once t the land of the living
Mt	8:28	had t the region for so long
2Co	4:9	we've been spiritually t

Terrors

Job	18:11	T come at them from all sides
	24:17	the t of darkness their companions
	27:20	T pour in on them like flash floods
	30:15	T assault me — my dignity in shreds
Ecc	12:5	Even a stroll down the road has its t
SS	8:6	Passion laughs at the t of hell
Isa	33:18	you'll go over the old t
Eze	26:21	introduce you to the t of death

Test

Ge	42:15	This is how I'll t you
Ex	16:4	I'm going to t them to see if
	20:20	God has come to t you
Dt	8:16	taste of the hard life, to t you
Jdg	2:22	I'll use them to t Israel
	3:1	using them to t the Israelites
	3:4	They were there to t Israel
1Ki	10:1	put his reputation to the t
2Ch	9:1	put his reputation to the t
	32:31	he wanted to t his heart
Job	23:10	I'll pass the t with honors
Ps	11:6	Fail the t and you're out
	95:8	As on the day of the Wilderness T
	95:9	turned and put me to the t
	139:23	Cross-examine and t me
Zec	13:9	t them for purity as gold is tested
Mal	3:10	T me in this and see if I don't
Mt	4:1	into the wild by the Spirit for the T
	4:2	Jesus prepared for the T by fasting
	4:3	Devil took advantage of in the first t
	4:5	For the second t the Devil took him
	4:7	Don't you dare t the Lord your God
	4:8	For the third t, the Devil took him
	4:11	The T was over. The Devil left
	22:41	off balance with his own t question
Lk	4:3	gave the first t
	4:5	For the second t he led him up
	4:9	For the third t the Devil took him
	10:25	with a question to t Jesus

T

Jn	7:17	can t this teaching and know
	7:24	to t what is authentically right
1Co	10:13	No t or temptation that comes your way
	10:25	don't have to run an "idolatry t"
	11:28	Examine your motives, t your heart
2Co	13:5	T yourselves to make sure
	13:6	t won't show that we have failed
	13:7	rather the t showed our failure
Eph	3:18	T its length! Plumb the depths
Php	1:9	use your head and t your feelings
1Jn	3:10	A simple t
	4:2	t for the genuine Spirit of God
	4:6	t for telling the Spirit of Truth from
	5:2	reality t on whether or not we love
Rev	3:10	safe in the time of ting

Tested

Ge	22:1	After all this, God t Abraham
Nu	14:22	who have t me over and over
Dt	33:8	loyal saint; The one you t at Massah
2Sa	22:31	Every God-direction is road-t
	24:1	He t David by telling him
Job	28:27	sure it was all set and t and ready
Ps	18:30	Every God-direction is road-t
	66:12	Road-t us inside and out
	118:18	God t me, he pushed me hard
	119:140	Your promise has been t
Pr	22:20	t guidelines to live by
	23:12	open your ears to t knowledge
	27:21	purity of . . . gold is t by . . . fire
Ecc	7:23	I t everything in my search for wisdom
Isa	48:10	I've t you like silver in the furnace
Zec	13:9	test them for purity as gold is t
Mk	1:13	he was t by Satan
Lk	4:2	he was t by the Devil
Ac	26:7	held on to this t and tried hope
1Th	2:3	God t us thoroughly to make sure

Testify

Lk	21:13	on the witness stand, called to t
Ac	6:13	forward their bribed witnesses to t
Rev	22:16	I, Jesus, sent my Angel to t

Testimony

Ex	16:34	before The T to preserve it
	23:1	wicked person and give corrupt t
	23:2	don't fudge your t in a case
	25:16	Place The T that I give you in
	25:21	place in the Chest The T
	26:33	bring the Chest of The T in
	26:34	lid on the Chest of The T
	27:21	curtain that veils The T
	30:6	curtain that hides the Chest of The T
	30:26	the Chest of The T
	30:36	place some of it before The T
	31:7	the Chest of The T and its
	31:18	he gave Moses two tablets of T
	32:15	carrying the two tablets of The T
	34:29	carrying the two Tablets of The T

	38:21	The Dwelling that housed The T
	39:35	Chest of The T with its poles
	40:3	Place the Chest of The T in it
	40:5	Incense before the Chest of The T
	40:20	He placed The T in the Chest
	40:21	screening off the Chest of The T
Lev	16:13	Atonement-Cover which is over The T
	24:3	curtain that screens The T
Nu	1:50	in charge of The Dwelling of The T
	1:53	around The Dwelling of The T
	4:5	cover the Chest of The T with it
	7:89	Cover on the Chest of The T
	9:15	covered The Dwelling of the Tent of T
	10:11	over The Dwelling of The T
	17:4	in front of The T where I keep
	17:7	before God in the Tent of T
	17:8	Moses walked into the Tent of T
	17:10	to the front of The T. Keep it there
	18:2	your duties in the Tent of T
	35:30	executed only on the t of eyewitnesses
Dt	17:6	on the t of two or three witnesses
Jos	4:16	priests carrying the Chest of the T
Isa	8:16	Gather up the t, preserve the teaching
Jn	5:33	gave expert and reliable t about me
	5:34	not to appeal to mere human t
	8:17	count on the t of two witnesses
Heb	11:5	know on the basis of reliable t
1Jn	5:7	A triple t
	5:9	If we take human t at face value
	5:10	Son of God inwardly confirms God's t
	5:11	This is the t in essence

Testing

Ex	15:26	that's where he started t them
	17:2	Why are you t God
	17:7	He named the place Massah (T-Place)
Dt	6:16	that day at Massah, the T-Place
	8:2	pushing you to your limits, t you
	9:22	there was . . . Massah (T-Place)
	13:3	God, your God, is t you to find out
Ps	119:75	your t has taught me what's true
Ecc	3:18	God's t the lot of us
Eze	21:13	T comes
Da	11:33	be put to severe t for a season
	11:34	When the t is intense
	11:35	The t will refine, cleanse, and purify
Lk	4:13	That completed the t
	22:32	you have come through the time of t
1Co	11:19	the t process will bring truth
Heb	2:18	all the pain, all the t
	3:8	that time of wilderness t
	4:15	He's been through weakness and t
	11:17	By faith, Abraham, at the time of t
Jas	1:12	meets a t challenge head-on
Rev	2:10	in jail for a time of t — ten days
	3:10	keep you safe in the time of t

Tests

Ps	11:5	He t the good and the bad alike
	26:2	order your battery of t

T

1Th	2:4	put through that battery of t
Jas	1:2	when t and challenges come at you

Thank

Dt	29:19	live just the way I please, t you
1Sa	16:22	**T** you. David will stay here
2Sa	16:4	Ziba said, "How can I ever t you?
1Ki	2:38	answered the king, "Oh, t you!
	2:42	didn't you say, 'Oh, t you
2Ki	5:20	without so much as a t-you
1Ch	16:8	**T** God! Call out his Name!
2Ch	29:31	bring your sacrifices and **T**-Offerings
	33:16	Peace-Offerings and **T**-Offerings
Ps	30:4	God! **T** him to his face
	30:12	God, my God, I can't t you enough
	44:8	we t you by name over and over
	52:9	I t you always
	54:6	I t you, God — you're so good
	67:3	God! Let people t and enjoy you
	67:3	Let all people t
	67:5	God! Let people t and enjoy you
	67:5	Let all people t
	71:22	I'll take up the lute and t you
	75:1	We t you, God, we t you
	79:13	will t you over and over
	86:12	I t you, dear Lord
	100:4	Enter with the password: "T you!"
	105:1	Hallelujah! **T** God!
	106:1	Hallelujah! **T** God!
	107:1	Oh, t God — he's so good!
	107:8	So t God for his marvelous love
	107:15	So t God for his marvelous love
	107:21	So t God for his marvelous love
	107:31	So t God for his marvelous love
	118:1	**T** God because he's good
	118:19	walk right through and t God
	118:21	**T** you for responding to me
	118:28	You're my God, and I t you
	118:29	**T** God — he's so good
	119:7	I t you for speaking straight
	119:62	in the middle of the night to t you
	136:1	**T** God! He deserves your thanks
	136:2	**T** the God of all gods
	136:3	**T** the Lord of all lords
	136:4	**T** the miracle-working God
	136:26	**T** God, who did it all!
	138:1	**T** you! Everything in me says "T you
	138:2	**T** you!" **T** you for your love, t
	138:4	all earth's kings will say "T you
	139:14	I t you, High God
	140:13	the righteous personally t you
	142:7	so I can t you in public
Pr	30:15	That's enough, t you
Isa	12:1	will say in that day, "I t you, God
	38:18	The dead don't t you
	38:19	live men, live women — who t you
	43:20	Wild animals will say 'T you!'
Jer	33:11	**T** God-of-the-Angel-Armies
Am	4:5	Burn pure sacrifices — t offerings
Mt	11:25	Jesus broke into prayer: "T you
Lk	10:21	I t you, Father, Master of heaven

	17:16	He couldn't t him enough
	18:11	God, I t you that I am not like other
Ro	1:8	I t God through Jesus
	6:17	But t God you've started listening
	7:25	answer, t God, is that Jesus Christ
	14:6	and t God for prime rib
1Co	1:4	I t God for your lives of free
	15:57	gift of . . . Jesus Christ. **T** God
2Co	2:14	And I got it, t God!
	8:16	I t God for giving Tit
	9:15	**T** God for this gift, his gift
Eph	1:17	But I do more than t. I ask
1Th	1:2	we t God for you
	2:13	look back on all this and t God
	5:18	t God no matter what happens
2Ti	1:3	all the time — I t God for you
Phm	1:4	I say, "Oh, t you, God
Rev	11:17	sang, We t you, O God

Thank-offerings

2Ch	29:31	bring your sacrifices and **T**
	33:16	sacrificing Peace-Offerings and **T**

Thanks

2Sa	3:8	Is this the t I get
	18:22	You'll get no t for it
1Ch	16:4	to intercede, give t, and praise
	16:34	Give t to God — he is good
	16:35	So we can give t to your holy Name
	16:41	Give t to God, for his love
	25:3	responsible for leading the t
	29:13	O God, our God, giving t to you
2Ch	5:13	one voice of praise and t to God
	20:21	Give t to God
	24:22	That's the t King Joash showed
	31:2	sure that t and praise took place
Ps	28:7	shouting and singing my t to him
	43:4	Sing my t with a harp
	69:30	tell his greatness in a prayer of t
	92:1	What a beautiful thing, God, to give t
	97:12	Give t to our Holy God
	106:47	So we can give t to your holy name
	111:1	Hallelujah! I give t to God
	122:4	To give t to the name of God
	136:1	Thank God! He deserves your t
	138:1	Angels listen as I sing my t
Isa	12:4	Give t to God. Call out his name
Jer	17:26	grains, incense, expressions of t
Da	2:23	God of all my ancestors, all t!
Mt	8:4	appropriate expressions of t to God
	15:36	After giving t, he divided it up
Mk	8:6	After giving t, he took the seven
Lk	17:9	Does the servant get special t
Jn	6:11	took the bread and, having given t
Ac	27:35	He broke the bread, gave t to God
1Co	11:24	Having given t, he broke it
Eph	1:16	I'd think of you and give t
Php	1:3	break out in exclamations of t to God
1Th	2:13	thank God, an artesian well of t
2Th	1:3	it's only right that we give t

T

1Ti	4:4	to be received with t
Rev	4:9	Animals gave glory and honor and t

Thanksgiving

Lev	7:12	offer t, then along with the T
	7:13	Along with the Peace-Offering of t
	7:15	meat from the Peace-Offering of t
	22:29	sacrifice a T-Offering to God
Ezr	3:11	praise and t to God
Ne	11:17	director who led in t and prayer
	12:27	t hymns, songs, cymbals
	12:46	songs of praise and t to God
Ps	42:4	Shouting praises, singing t
	100:1	A t psalm On your feet now
	107:22	Offer t sacrifices
	116:17	offer the t sacrifice and pray
	147:7	Sing to God a t hymn
Jnh	2:9	worshiping you, God, calling out in t
Ac	28:15	led us in prayers of t
Eph	5:4	T is our dialect
Col	2:7	let your living spill over into t
1Th	3:9	What would be an adequate t to offer
1Ti	4:3	created to be eaten . . . with t
Rev	7:12	glory and wisdom and t

Thanksgiving-offering

Lev	7:12	with the T present unraised loaves
	22:29	When you sacrifice a T to God

Thanksgivings

Jer	30:19	T will pour out of the windows
2Co	9:12	abundant and bountiful t to God
Col	1:3	always spilling over into t

Theft

Jos	7:11	stolen and then covered up the t
1Ki	21:19	First murder, then t?
Hos	4:2	lying and killing, t and loose sex

Thefts

Mt	15:19	fornications, t, lies
Mk	7:21	lusts, t, murders

Thief

Ge	31:27	Why .. run off like a t in the night
Ex	22:1	the t must pay five cattle
	22:2	If the t is caught while breaking in
	22:3	A t must make full restitution
	22:4	the t pays double
	22:7	the t, if caught, must pay back double
	22:8	If the t is not caught
Ps	50:18	If you find a t, you make him
Pr	6:30	Hunger is no excuse for a t to steal
Jer	2:26	a t is chagrined, but only when caught
Zec	5:4	will fly into the house of every t
Jn	10:10	A t is only there to steal

	10:29	greater than the Destroyer and T
	12:6	but because he was a t
2Pe	3:10	it will be unannounced, like a t
Rev	3:3	break into your life like a t
	16:15	I come unannounced, like a t

Thievery

Isa	61:8	I, God, . . . hate t and crime
Tit	2:10	no petty t

Thieves

Job	29:17	I grabbed street t
Pr	23:28	she's worse than a pack of t
Hos	5:10	Israel's rulers are crooks and t
Ob	1:5	If t crept up on you, they'd rob you
Zec	5:3	the verdict . . . against t and liars
Mt	21:13	You have made it a hangout for t
Mk	11:17	You've turned it into a hangout for t
Lk	23:12	Herod and Pilate became thick as t

Thieving

Ex	22:3	unable to pay is to be sold for his t
Rev	9:21	occult, promiscuous, and t ways

Thirst

Ge	24:19	When he had satisfied his t she said
Ne	9:15	sent water from the rock for their t
Job	6:18	waterless gulch and die of t
Ps	63:1	worked up such hunger and t for God
	104:11	wild donkeys quench their t
	107:5	Half-starved and parched with t
Isa	5:13	the common people die of t
	32:6	those dying of t in the streets
	44:12	works away, fatigued with hunger and t
Joel	1:20	Wild animals, dying of t
Am	4:8	and never quenching their t
	8:13	young girls will faint of Word-t
Jn	4:14	drinks the water I give will never t
Rev	7:16	no more hunger, no more t

Thirsts

Jn	6:35	hungers no more and t no more
	7:37	If anyone t, let him come to me

Thirsty

Ex	17:3	But the people were t for water
Jdg	4:19	Please, a little water. I'm t
	15:18	Now he was suddenly very t
Ru	2:9	When you get t, feel free to . . . drink
2Sa	17:29	must be starved and exhausted and t
Job	22:7	so much as give a drink to the t
Ps	5:6	Blood-T and Truth-Bender disgust you
	42:2	I'm t for God-alive
	73:10	Like t puppies, they lap up
	143:6	as t for you as a desert t for rain
Pr	25:21	if he's t, bring him a drink

T

Isa	21:14	Haul water to the t
	29:8	Like a t woman dreaming she's drinking
	34:6	God has a sword, t for blood
	35:7	t ground a splashing fountain
	41:17	God of Israel, will not leave them t
	44:3	I will pour water on the t ground
	48:21	They weren't t when he led them
	49:10	Nobody hungry, nobody t
	55:1	All who are t, come to the water
	65:13	servants will drink, and you'll go t
La	2:12	I'm hungry! I'm t!
Am	4:8	you never got t for me
Hag	1:6	but you're always t
Mt	10:42	water to someone who is t
	25:35	I was t and you gave me a drink
	25:37	t and give you a drink
	25:42	I was t and you gave me no drink
	25:44	When did we ever see you hungry or t
Jn	4:13	who drinks this water will get t again
	4:15	water so I won't ever get t
	19:28	then said, "I'm t
Ro	12:20	if he's t, get him a drink
Rev	21:6	Water-of-Life Well I give . . . to the t
	22:17	Is anyone t? Come!

Thought

Ge	6:5	People t evil, imagined evil
	8:21	God smelled the sweet fragrance and t
	26:9	I t I might get killed
	31:31	I t you would take your daughters away
	32:8	He t, "If Esau comes
	32:20	He t, "I will soften him up
	39:8	doesn't give a second t to anything
	40:23	never gave Joseph another t
	48:17	he t he had made a mistake
Ex	7:23	never giving it a second t
	13:17	God t, "If the people encounter war
Dt	1:41	you t it would be so easy
	31:6	Don't give them a second t
Jos	10:8	Don't give them a second t
Jdg	20:39	t they were on their way to victory
Ru	4:4	I t you ought to know about it
1Sa	16:6	t, "Here he is! God's anointed
	23:7	t immediately, "Good! God has
	27:1	David t to himself
	27:12	came to trust David completely. He t
2Sa	6:12	So David t, "I'll get that blessing
	17:4	t it was an excellent strategy
	18:3	enemy won't give it a second t
1Ki	12:26	then Jeroboam t, "It won't be long
	20:5	On second t, I want it all
2Ki	5:11	I t he'd personally come out
	18:21	You t Egypt would, but
2Ch	28:23	he t, "If I worship the gods
	32:3	they t it was a good idea
	36:13	he never gave God a t
Ne	6:9	They t, "They'll give up
Est	6:6	Haman t to himself, "He must
Job	29:18	I t, 'I'll die peacefully
	33:2	has been carefully t out
	34:27	no longer even t about him or his ways

	35:10	never give God a t when things go well
Ps	35:21	t you'd get away with it?
	50:21	you t I went along with your game
	57:6	I t I was dead and done for
	90:6	cut down without a second t
	107:18	you t you'd be better off dead
Pr	2:17	never gave a second t to her promises
	17:28	dunces who keep quiet are t to be wise
Ecc	9:1	took all this in and t it through
Isa	1:29	that you t was the latest thing
	20:6	we t they were our best hope
	25:1	miracle-wonders, well-t-out plans
	28:15	We've t of everything
	29:14	people who t they knew everything
	47:7	never gave tomorrow a t
	47:10	You t you knew so much
	53:1	Who would have t God's saving power
	53:3	looked down on him, t he was scum
	53:4	We t he brought it on himself
	53:8	died without a t for his own welfare
	57:1	people die and no one gives them a t
	66:18	everything they've ever done or t
Jer	2:8	priests never t to ask, 'Where's God?'
	2:32	they never give me a t
	3:21	never once giving her God a t
	9:14	Baal gods, who they t would give them
	14:10	never giving a t to where
	16:6	no one will give them a second t
	22:23	t you were so important, t you were
	23:14	never giving it a second t
	30:14	without giving you a second t
	48:13	calf-gods that t were so great
La	2:2	The Master, without a second t
	2:7	you'd have t it was a feast day
Eze	20:9	Then I t better of it
	20:14	But I t better of it
	20:22	But I t better of it
Da	9:13	never giving you a second t
Hos	2:13	And not a t for me
	10:13	You t you could do it all on your own
	13:6	You t you didn't need me
	13:10	trusty king you t would save you
Ob	1:3	You t you were so great
Hab	2:6	Don't give people like this a second t
	2:16	t you were having the time
Zep	1:6	no longer giving him a t
	3:7	I t, 'Surely she'll honor me now
	11:13	stingy wage was all they t of me
Mt	19:12	never give marriage a t
	21:29	Later on he t better of it
	21:37	he t, 'they will respect my son
Mk	6:35	t this had gone on long enough
	6:49	they t it was a ghost
Lk	7:39	If this man was the prophet I t he was
	18:2	who never gave God a t
	24:11	t they were making it all up
	24:37	They t they were seeing a ghost
Jn	11:13	disciples t he was talking about
	13:29	t that since Judas was their treasurer
Ac	2:23	deliberate and well-t-out plan of God
	6:5	congregation t this was a great idea
	7:25	He t his brothers would be glad

T

	8:10	They all t he had supernatural powers
	10:19	Peter, lost in t, didn't hear them
	12:9	he t he was dreaming
	20:28	God himself t they were worth dying
	21:38	I t you were the Egyptian
	26:9	t it was my duty to oppose this Jesus
Ro	11:21	He wouldn't give it a second t
1Co	4:10	You might be well-t-of by others
	6:12	whatever I t I could get by with
	11:29	If you give no t (or worse, don't care
2Co	5:12	We just t it would make you feel good
	7:14	how great I t you were
	10:5	every loose t and emotion and impulse
	11:26	betrayed by those I t were my brothers
Eph	1:8	He t of everything
Php	2:5	the way Christ Jesus t of himself
	3:8	things I once t were so important
1Ti	3:2	A leader must be well-t-of
Tit	1:6	Is this man well-t-of?
	1:15	dirty fingerprints on every t and act
Phm	1:8	command this if I t it necessary
Jas	1:6	believingly, without a second t
	5:3	You t you were piling up wealth
1Pe	3:14	Don't give the opposition a second t
	4:16	don't give it a second t
1Jn	4:3	here it is, sooner than we t

Thoughtful

Pr	14:22	the t win love and trust
	15:24	Life ascends to the heights for the t
	18:2	Fools care nothing for t discourse
Ro	1:20	t look at what God has created
1Co	14:15	should also be t and mindful as I pray
Gal	3:18	a t addition to the original covenant

Thoughts

Est	2:1	having second t about what Vashti
Ps	39:3	My t boiled over
	40:5	God-wonders and God-t
	92:5	your work, God! How profound your t
	139:17	Your t — how rare, how beautiful!
Ecc	9:10	neither work to do nor t to think
SS	6:12	carried away by lofty t
Da	2:29	t you regarding what is coming
	4:19	t that came swarming into his mind
Hos	11:8	can't bear to even think such t
Ac	15:8	always knows a person's t
Col	1:21	thinking rebellious t of him

Threadbare

Jos	9:5	t sandals on their feet
Job	24:10	They go about patched and t
Ps	77:8	Is his love worn t?
	102:26	t and discarded like an old suit
Isa	50:9	accusers are a clothes bin of t socks
1Co	4:11	we wear patched and t clothes
Heb	1:11	they become t like an old coat
Rev	3:17	pitiful, blind beggar, t and homeless

Threat

1Ki	19:2	sent a messenger to Elijah with her t
2Ki	24:7	The t from Egypt was now over
Isa	7:16	the t of war will be over
Eze	6:10	judgment against them was no empty t
Da	3:16	Your t means nothing to us
	11:44	he'll rush to stamp out the t
Lk	21:26	by the t of doom
Ro	13:3	authorities are only a t if you're

Threaten

Ps	46:6	kings and kingdoms t
Isa	10:24	with clubs and t you with rods
Ro	5:21	All sin can do is t us with death

Threatened

Ex	32:14	the evil he had t against his people
1Sa	5:11	We're t with mass death!
	19:17	Michal said, "He t me
Est	8:11	killing anyone who t them
Jer	26:13	reconsider the disaster he has t
	26:19	call off the disaster he had t
	27:13	what God has t to any nation

Threatening

Lev	6:2	by robbing or cheating or t him
Isa	35:9	Nothing and no one dangerous or t
Jer	16:10	Why is God talking this way, t us
Mk	4:37	into the boat, t to sink it

Threats

Ps	27:12	filling the air with their t
	58:5	Deaf to t, deaf to charm
	76:5	to show for their swagger and t
	85:3	took back your sin-provoked t
Pr	13:8	but the poor are free of such t
Hos	13:14	Who cares about your t, Tomb?
Mt	10:28	bluffed into silence by the t
Lk	12:4	the t of religious bullies
Ac	4:17	let's silence them with t
	4:21	religious leaders renewed their t
	4:29	Take care of their t
Ro	8:35	not bullying t, not backstabbing
Eph	6:9	No abuse, please, and no t

Thrive

Pr	13:19	Souls who follow their hearts t
Jer	29:6	have children so that you'll t
	30:19	They'll t, they'll flourish
Eze	17:9	God, the Master, says, Will it t
	17:10	Even if it's transplanted, will it t
Hag	1:11	not animal or crop — is going to t

Thugs

| Ps | 22:16 | t gang up on me |

T

	26:4	I don't pal around with t
	35:4	those t try to knife me in the back
	86:14	A gang of t is after me
Isa	16:8	Foreign t have crushed and torn
	42:24	turned Jacob over to the t
La	1:15	called in t to break their fine
Zec	10:5	undeterred by the world's t
Mt	22:7	sent his soldiers to destroy those t
Ac	21:38	with his four thousand t

Timid

Jos	1:9	Courage! Don't be t
	8:1	God said to Josua, "Don't be t
	10:25	Don't hold back. Don't be t
1Ch	22:13	Courage! Take charge! Don't be t
Isa	7:13	your pious, t hypocrisies
	40:9	Speak loud and clear. Don't be t
Hag	2:5	Don't be t. Don't hold back
Ro	8:15	not a t, grave-tending life

Timidity

Lev	26:36	I'll give them over to fearful t
Dt	20:8	doesn't infect his fellows with his t

Tire

Job	19:22	Don't you ever t of abusing me
Pr	3:23	you'll neither t nor trip
Isa	40:30	even young people t and drop out
	42:4	He won't t out and quit
	57:16	These souls I created would t out
Mal	2:17	all your talk. "How do we t
Ac	24:4	I'm not going to t you out

Tired

Ex	17:12	But Moses' hands got t
Dt	9:28	God couldn't do it; he got t
	25:18	he attacked you when you were t
Jdg	8:4	bone-t but still pressing the pursuit
1Sa	30:21	who had been too t to continue
2Sa	5:8	he was so sick and t of it
	17:2	I'll come on him when he's bone t
Job	22:15	persist in that t old line
	35:14	you're t of waiting to be heard
Ps	6:6	I'm t of all this — so t
	12:4	I'm t of hearing
Pr	17:22	gloom and doom leave you bone-t
SS	5:6	My loved one had t of waiting
Isa	7:13	make people t with your pious, timid
	40:28	He doesn't get t out, doesn't pause
	40:29	He energizes those who get t
	40:31	They run and don't get t
	43:22	You so quickly t of me, Israel
	50:4	I know how to encourage t people
	57:10	never got t of trying new religions
Jer	15:6	I'm t of letting you off the hook
	31:25	refresh t bodies; I'll restore t souls
Eze	23:22	lovers you got t of and left
Mic	6:12	I'm t of the violent rich bullying

Zec	11:8	I got t of putting up with them
	11:9	then I got t of the sheep
Mal	2:17	You make God t with all your talk
Mt	11:17	you were always too t
	11:28	Are you t? Worn out?
Lk	7:32	you were always too t
Ro	8:26	the moment we get t in the waiting
2Co	5:2	and we're t of it
1Ti	5:10	helping out . . . t Christians

Tithe

Nu	18:26	get the t from the People of Israel
Dt	12:17	eat there the t of your grain
	14:22	an offering of ten percent, a t
	14:23	there eat the t from your grain
	14:24	you can't carry your t that far
	14:25	exchange your t for money
	14:28	gather the t from all your produce
	26:12	Every third year, the year of the t
2Ch	31:5	turning over a t of everything
	31:6	They also brought in a t
Ne	13:12	bringing in the t of grain
Am	4:4	Every third day bring your t
Mal	3:8	The t and the offering
	3:10	Bring your full t to the Temple
Lk	18:12	and t on all my income

Tithes

Nu	18:21	giving the Levites all the t of Israel
	18:24	turn over to them the t
	18:28	making offerings to God from all the t
Dt	12:0	your t and Tribute-Offerings
	12:11	t and Tribute-Offerings
2Ch	31:12	brought in all the offerings of t
Ne	10:37	bring the t from our fields
	10:38	the Levites as they collect the t
	12:44	the firstfruits, and the t
	13:5	the t of grain, wine, and oil
Heb	7:5	commanded by law to collect t
	7:6	collected t from Abraham
	7:8	We pay our t to priests who die
	7:9	Abraham, who paid t to Melchizedek
	7:10	pay t to the priestly tribe of Levi

Tithing

Mt	23:23	t on every nickel and dime you get
Lk	11:42	t on every nickel and dime you get

Tongue

Dt	30:14	as near as the t in your mouth
Jos	15:2	the Salt Sea south of The T
Jdg	7:5	Everyone who laps with his t
2Sa	23:2	his words took shape on my t
Ne	13:24	language of Ashdod or some other t
Job	13:13	So hold your t while I have my say
Ps	22:15	dry as a bone, my t black and swollen
	34:13	Guard your t from profanity
	37:30	rolls virtue around on his t

T

	39:1	determined to watch steps and t
	52:2	your t cuts razor-sharp
	66:17	my t shaped the sounds of music
	119:172	let your promises ring from my t
	137:6	Let my t swell and turn black
Pr	6:17	a t that lies
	11:9	t of the godless spreads destruction
	15:1	a sharp t kindles a temper-fire
	19:11	Smart people know how to hold their t
	21:23	Watch your words and hold your t
	25:23	and a gossipy t stormy looks
SS	7:9	your t and lips like the best wine
Isa	23:2	Hold your t, you who live on
	32:4	the t-tied will speak with eloquence
	42:14	I've held back, biting my t
	50:4	God, has given me a well-taught t
	57:4	sneering, and sticking out your t
	59:3	t swollen from muttering obscenities
	62:1	I can't hold my t
Eze	3:26	your t stick to the roof of your mouth
	3:27	I'll free your t and you'll say
Mic	2:11	a good smile and glib t and told lies
Mk	7:33	some spit on the man's t
Lk	1:64	mouth was now open, his t loose
	16:24	in water to cool my t
Ro	6:11	God speaks your mother t
	10:8	as near as the t in your mouth
	14:11	Every t will tell the honest truth
Jas	1:19	follow up with your t
	3:8	you can't tame a t . . . The t runs
Rev	14:6	every t and people

Tongues

Dt	33:2	t of fire streaming from his right
Jdg	7:6	lapped with their t from
2Sa	22:9	T of fire darted in and out
Job	20:12	roll it around on their t
Ps	5:9	their t slick as mudslides
	10:7	their t spit venom like adders
	12:2	They doubletalk with forked t
	12:3	Pull The braggart t from their mouths
	18:8	T of fire dart in and out
	55:9	Come down hard, Lord—slit their t
	57:4	their t are sharp daggers
	58:4	poison, drips from their forked t
	64:3	Using their t as weapons
	70:3	gossips off clucking their t
	109:2	Their lying t are like a pack of dogs
Isa	41:17	t parched and no water to be found
Jer	9:3	Their t shoot out lies
	9:5	They've trained their t to tell lies
	9:8	Their t are poison arrows!
La	4:4	t stick to the roofs of their mouths
Eze	1:13	T of fire shot back and forth
Zec	14:12	will rot . . . their t in their mouths
Mk	16:17	in my name, they will speak in new t
Ac	2:6	their own mother t being spoken
	2:8	talk in our various mother t
	10:46	they heard them speaking in t
	19:6	they were praising God in t
Ro	3:13	their t slick as mud slides

1Co	12:10	spirits t interpretation of t
	12:28	those who pray in t
	12:30	Prayer in T, not all Interpreter of T
	13:8	praying in t will end
	14:2	in the private language of t
	14:14	If I pray in t, my spirit prays
	14:18	the gift of praying in t
	14:21	In strange t and from the mouths
	14:22	this speaking in t no one understands
	14:23	as you're all praying in t
	14:27	If prayers are offered in t
	14:39	praying in t that you don't understand
Eph	5:4	some t just love the taste of gossip
Heb	1:7	the servants are t of fire
Jas	3:9	With our t we bless God our Father
Rev	13:7	all tribes and peoples, t and races
	16:10	men and women bit and chewed their t

Torment

Job	24:12	dying right and left, groaning in t
	26:5	All the buried dead are in t
Isa	29:7	all who trouble and hassle and t her
Mk	7:30	the t gone for good
Lk	16:23	In hell and in t, he looked up
	16:28	won't end up here in this place of t
2Pe	2:8	righteous man was in constant t
Rev	14:10	suffer t from fire and brimstone
	14:11	Smoke from their t will rise
	16:11	cursed the God of Heaven for their t
	18:7	Bring her . . . ways to t and tears
	20:10	the three in t around the clock

Tormented

Nu	5:30	husband is t with feelings of jealousy
1Sa	16:23	depression from God t Saul
Mt	8:16	He relieved the inwardly t
Mk	1:34	cured their sick bodies and t spirits
Lk	16:25	Here he's consoled and you're t

Tormentors

Ps	31:7	saw my pain, you disarmed my t
	42:10	these t with their obscenities
	119:84	you haul my t into court

Torture

Ps	44:19	Do we deserve t in a den of jackals
	72:14	He frees them from tyranny and t
Isa	14:6	a violent rule of anger rife with t
Eze	21:31	give you to vicious men skilled in t
Mt	20:19	over to the Romans for mockery and t
Ac	22:24	interrogate Paul under t
	22:29	of putting him under t
2Co	4:10	trial and t, mockery and murder
Heb	11:35	those who, under t, refused to give in
Rev	9:5	ordered to t but not kill, t them
	9:6	are going to prefer death to t
	9:10	ordered to t the human race

T

Tortured

Isa	53:7	He was beaten, he was **t**
1Co	7:9	preferable by far to a sexually **t** life

Tradition

Ezr	3:10	praise God in the **t** of David
Est	9:23	What started then became a **t**
	9:27	It became a **t** for them
	9:32	Esther's word confirmed the **t** of Purim
Isa	16:5	established in the venerable David **t**
	22:23	He'll secure the Davidic **t**
Ac	7:52	you've kept up the family **t**
2Ti	1:3	worship . . . in the **t** of my ancestors
Heb	9:22	is used so much in our **t**

Traditions

1Ch	4:22	These records are from very old **t**
	26:12	keeping up the **t** of their ancestors
Jer	44:17	keeping up the **t** set by our ancestors
Mt	5:33	This counsel is embedded deep in our **t**
Ac	21:21	or keep up the old **t**
	22:3	instructed in our religious **t**
Ro	4:16	those who keep the religious **t**
Gal	1:12	didn't receive it through the **t**
	1:14	enthusiastic about the **t**
	4:10	scrupulously observing all the **t**
Col	2:8	the empty **t** of human beings

Train

Ge	18:19	the one to **t** his children
Jdg	3:2	did it to **t** the descendants of Israel
1Ki	10:13	with her **t** of servants
2Ki	23:2	bringing everyone in his **t**
2Ch	6:27	**t** them to live right and well
	9:12	with her **t** of servants
	34:30	bringing everyone in his **t**
Ps	48:10	name . . . evokes a **t** of Hallelujahs
	86:11	**T** me, God, to walk straight
	94:12	How blessed the man you **t**, God
	105:22	and **t** his advisors in wisdom
	119:12	**t** me in your ways of wise living
	119:26	**t** me well in your deep wisdom
	119:64	**T** me to live by your counsel
	119:66	**T** me in good common sense
	119:68	**t** me in your goodness
Pr	1:30	brushed aside all my offers to **t** you
Isa	6:1	the **t** of his robes filled the Temple
Jer	2:30	trying to **t** your children
Joel	2:23	a teacher to **t** you how to live right
Mt	28:19	Go out and **t** everyone you meet
1Co	9:25	All good athletes **t** hard
Eph	4:12	**t** Christians in skilled servant work

Trained

2Ki	12:2	Taught and **t** by Jehoiada the priest
1Ch	5:18	Manasseh had 44,760 men **t** for war
	25:7	They were well-**t** in the sacred music

2Ch	2:7	will supervise the **t** craftsmen
	24:2	Taught and **t** by Jehoiada the priest
	26:5	well **t** by his pastor and teacher
Ps	66:10	He **t** us first
SS	3:8	armed to the teeth, **t** for battle
Jer	9:5	They've **t** their tongues to tell lies
	31:18	You **t** me well
	31:19	After you **t** me to obedience
Hos	10:11	a **t** heifer that loved to thresh
Mt	13:52	every student well-**t** in God's kingdom
Ro	3:1	who has been **t** in God's ways
Gal	6:6	**t** to a self-sufficient maturity
Heb	12:11	the well-**t** who find themselves mature

Traitor

Dt	13:10	tried to turn you **t** against God
2Ki	25.25	killed Gedaliah, the **t** Jews
Mt	26:24	turns **t** to the Son of Man
	26:25	Then Judas, already turned **t**
Mk	14:21	turns **t** to the Son of Man
Lk	22:22	turns **t** to the Son of Man
Gal	1:6	how easily you have turned **t**

Traitors

Ps	25:3	It's the **t** who should be humiliated
	55:23	Cut the lifespan of assassins and **t**
	78:57	**t** — crooked as a corkscrew
Isa	1:28	it's curtains for rebels and God-**t**
Eze	20:38	I'll cull out the rebels and **t**
Ac	7:52	family tradition — **t** and murderers
	17:7	**t** and turncoats who say Jesus is king

Translated

Ezr	4:7	letter was written in Aramaic and **t**
	4:18	letter that you sent has been **t**
Ne	8:8	**t** the Book of The Revelation of God

Trap

Dt	7:16	they'll **t** you for sure
Jdg	2:3	their gods will become a **t**
1Sa	28:9	Why are you trying to **t** me
2Ki	9:23	It's a **t**, Ahaziah
Ps	7:15	digging, then concealing, his man-**t**
	35:7	they set a **t** to catch me
	35:8	catch them in the very **t** they set
	69:22	bait in a **t** that snaps shut
	106:36	caught in the **t** of idols
Pr	5:23	your foolish decisions **t** you
	20:25	An impulsive vow is a **t**
Ecc	9:12	caught in a cruel net or birds in a **t**
	10:8	The **t** you set might catch you
Isa	24:18	you'll get caught in the **t**
Jer	48:43	and **t** are what you have facing you
	48:44	running in terror will fall into a **t**
	50:24	I set out a **t** and you were caught
Eze	13:18	devices to **t** souls
	19:4	He was caught in a **t**
Am	3:5	Does a **t** spring shut if nothing

T

Mt	22:15	t him into saying something damaging
	22:18	Why are you trying to t me
Lk	11:54	plotting how they could t him
	20:26	couldn't t him into saying
	21:34	spring on you suddenly like a t
Jn	8:6	t him into saying something
1Ti	3:7	a way to lure him into his t
2Ti	2:26	enabling them to escape the Devil's t

Traps

2Sa	22:6	death t barred every exit
Job	18:7	they stumble into their own t
Ps	18:5	death t barred every exit
	31:4	Free me from hidden t
	64:5	lists of the t they've secretly set
	91:3	he rescues you from hidden t
	124:7	free of their t, free as a bird
	140:5	These crooks invent t to catch me
	142:3	the t hidden in my path
Pr	29:6	Evil people fall into their own t
Isa	24:17	pits and booby t are everywhere
Jer	5:26	They set t for the unsuspecting
La	1:13	then he set t all around
	4:20	anointed of God, was caught in their t
Eze	19:8	set out their t and caught him

Trash

Ge	49:7	I'll throw them out with the t
2Sa	23:6	thorns culled and piled as t
Job	2:8	then went and sat on a t heap
	5:13	intrigue swept out with the t
Ps	2:9	throw them out with tomorrow's t
	31:12	discard me like a broken dish in the t
	37:8	Bridle your anger, t your wrath
	51:11	Don't throw me out with the t
	55:10	t piled in the streets
	113:7	thrown out with the t
Isa	30:14	swept up and thrown in the t
	30:22	throw them in the t as so much garbage
	37:19	thrown their gods into the t
Jer	49:17	end up t. Stinking, despicable t
La	4:5	pick through the t for something
Hos	8:5	Throw that gold calf-god on the t heap
Mic	7:10	my enemy disgraced, t in the gutter
Na	1:14	Your gods and goddesses go in the t
Mt	3:12	put out with the t to be burned
	5:29	be dumped on a moral t pile
	13:42	pitch them in the t, and be done
Lk	3:17	put out with the t to be burned
Php	3:7	throwing out with the t
	3:8	dumped it all in the t

Treachery

Hos	7:1	the t of Samaria written out in bold
	12:12	made it big through t and deceit
Mt	26:24	Son of Man is entering into a way of t
Mk	14:21	Son of Man is entering into a way of t

Treasure

Ex	19:5	you'll be my special t
Dt	7:6	for himself as a cherished, personal t
	14:2	as his cherished personal t
	26:18	reaffirmed that you are dearly held t
Job	22:25	God Almighty will be your t
Ps	19:11	directs us to hidden t
Pr	2:4	like an adventurer on a t hunt
	7:1	t my careful instructions
	10:14	accumulate knowledge — a true t
	22:17	You'll t its sweetness
Isa	33:6	best of all, Zion's t, Fear-of-God
Mt	6:19	Don't hoard t down here
	6:20	Stockpile t in heaven
	6:21	The place where your t is
	13:44	God's kingdom is like a t hidden
Lk	9:44	T and ponder each of these next words
	12:34	The place where your t is
1Ti	6:20	guard the t you were given
Heb	7:4	gave him a tenth of the captured t
	10:34	couldn't touch your real t

Treasured

1Sa	19:1	But because Jonathan t David
Job	23:12	not just obeyed his advice—I've t it
Isa	10:14	took all that they t as easily
Eze	7:22	as my t place and people are violated

Treasures

Dt	33:19	gleaned t from the beaches
1Ki	14:26	the royal palace of their t
Isa	39:2	proudly showing them all his t
	45:3	I'll lead you to buried t
Zec	14:14	T from all the nations will be piled
Col	2:3	the richest t of wisdom and knowledge

Treasuries

1Ki	15:18	left in the t of The Temple of God
2Ki	16:8	Ahaz robbed the t of the palace
	18:15	and in the palace t
	24:13	Nebuchadnezzar emptied the t
2Ch	8:15	no innovations — including the t
	16:2	took silver and gold from the t
	32:27	He built t for all his silver
	36:18	the t of The Temple of God, the t
Da	11:43	confiscate the t of Egyptian gold

Treaty

Dt	7:2	Don't make a t with them
Jdg	18:7	had no t with the Arameans
	18:28	had no t with the Arameans
1Sa	11:1	Make a t with us and we'll serve you
	11:2	make a t with you on one condition
2Sa	3:21	They'll make a t with you
	5:3	the king made a t with them
	21:2	protected by a t with Israel
1Ki	5:12	formalized by a t

T

	15:19	a t like the one between our fathers
2Ch	16:3	a t like the one between our fathers
Isa	33:8	The peace t is broken
Da	11:17	He'll cook up a peace t and even give
	11:27	Nothing will come of the t
Hos	2:18	a peace t between you and wild animals
Am	1:9	breaking the t she had with her kin

Tree-of-knowledge-of-good-and-evil

Ge	2:9	the middle of the garden, also the **T**
	2:17	except from the **T**. Don't eat from it

Tree-of-life

Ge	2:9	The **T** was in the middle of the garden
	3:22	take fruit from the **T** and eat
	3:24	guarding the path to the **T**
Rev	2:7	I'm spreading a banquet of **T** fruit

Tremble

Ge	27:33	Isaaac started to t, shaking violently
Ps	114:7	T, Earth!
Isa	32:11	t, you indolent women
Eze	32:10	On the day you crash, they'll t
	38:20	every human being will t and shake
Hab	3:6	Nations t
Mt	24:29	cosmic powers t
Mk	13:25	cosmic powers t

Trembled

Ex	15:14	Philistines writhed and t
Ps	68:8	Even Sinai t at the sight of God
	77:16	saw you and t with fear
Isa	5:25	The mountains t as their dead bodies
	6:4	foundations t at the sound
Ac	4:31	place where they were meeting t

Trembles

Ps	97:4	Earth, wide-eyed, t in fear
Isa	10:29	Ramah t with fright
	15:4	The soul of Moab t
Jer	51:29	The very land t in terror
Am	9:5	touches the earth . . . and it t

Trembling

Dt	11:25	God-sent fear and t will precede you
2Sa	22:46	they came t from their hideouts
Ezr	9:4	Many were in fear and t
Ps	2:11	Celebrate in t awe
Jer	4:24	the mountains—they were t
Eze	12:18	drink your water t with fear
Mic	7:17	Fill them with holy fear and t
Mk	5:33	stepped up in fear and t
Lk	8:47	she knelt t before him

Trespass

Nu	20:17	We won't t through your fields
	21:22	We won't t into your fields
Dt	2:27	I won't t right or left
Isa	8:14	preventing t to the citizens

Trespasser

Mt	13:44	accidentally found by a t

Trial

Jos	20:6	stay in that city until he has stood t
	20:9	a fair t before the congregation
Job	34:5	but God won't give me a fair t
Ps	50:7	I'm about ready to bring you to t
Jer	25:31	He's about to put the human race on t
Eze	17:20	have him brought to t because of
Joel	3:2	put them all on t, and judge them
Jn	16:11	this godless world is brought to t
Ac	4:9	brought to t today for helping
	8:33	never got a fair t
	22:25	Roman citizen without a fair t
	24:1	along with Tertullus, a t lawyer
	25:9	let me conduct your t there
	25:25	He requested a t before Caesar
	25:27	send a prisoner all that way for a t
	26:7	They should be the ones standing t
	27:21	avoided all this trouble and t
2Co	4:10	t and torture, mockery and murder
	8:2	The t exposed their true colors
Php	1:7	I was thrown in jail, put on t
Rev	1:9	I, John, with you all the way in the t

Trials

Dt	4:34	using t, miracles, and war
	29:3	t to which you were eyewitnesses
1Ki	11:39	but the t won't last forever
Hab	2:9	above it all, above t and troubles
Lk	17:1	t and temptations are bound to come
2Pe	2:9	rescue the godly from evil t

Tribute

Dt	12:6	your tithes and **T**-Offerings
	12:11	tithes and **T**-Offerings
	12:17	Freewill-Offerings and **T**-Offerings
Jdg	3:15	Israel sent t by him
	3:17	presented the t to Eglon
	3:18	After Ehud finished presenting the t
2Sa	3:33	king sang this t to Abner
	8:2	were forced to bring t
	8:6	were forced to bring t
1Ki	4:21	They brought t and were vassals
	10:14	tons of gold in t annually
2Ki	17:3	regularly sent him t
	17:4	behind on his annual payments of t
	18:14	I'll pay whatever t you set
	23:33	He demanded that Judah pay t
1Ch	18:2	paid regular t

T

	18:6	were forced to bring t
2Ch	26:8	The Ammonites also paid t
Ezr	4:13	will no longer pay a penny of t
	4:20	exacted taxes, t, and duty
	7:24	no one is permitted to impose t
Ps	98:9	A t to God when he comes
Pr	14:19	Eventually, evil will pay t to good
Isa	18:7	t will be brought to God

Triumph

Dt	33:29	the Sword who brings t
Jdg	15:14	came to meet him, shouting in t
Ps	118:15	t songs in the camp of the saved
Pr	11:21	God's loyal people will t
Mic	5:9	arms raised in t over your foes
Mt	12:20	his justice will t
	21:21	also t over huge obstacles
Lk	10:20	t is not in your authority over evil
2Co	13:9	every t of the truth in you

Triumphant

Lk	10:17	The seventy came back t
Jn	4:36	arm in arm with the Harvester, t
1Co	15:54	Death swallowed by t Life
Rev	15:2	t over the Beast, its image

Trouble

Ge	16:12	Always stirring up t
	35:3	God who answered me when I was in t
	42:21	now we're the ones in t
Ex	18:8	all the t they had experienced
Lev	26:16	I'll step in and pour on the t
Nu	20:14	You are familiar with all the t
	33:55	They'll give you endless t
Dt	15:7	When you happen on someone who's in t
	15:11	give to your neighbors in t
	26:7	he saw our destitution, our t
Jos	6:18	making t for everyone
	7:24	off to the Valley of Achor (T Valley
	7:25	God will now t you
	7:26	the place came to be called T Valley
	15:7	ascended to Debir from T Valley
	23:13	They'll be nothing but t to you
Jdg	9:31	stirring up t against you
	11:7	coming to me now? Because you are in t
	19:19	We wouldn't be any t
1Sa	13:6	outnumbered and in deep t
	25:17	big t is ahead for our master
	26:24	rescue me from all t
	28:10	you won't get in any t for this
	28:15	Because I'm in deep t," said Saul
	30:6	suddenly David was in even worse t
2Sa	4:9	the One who got me out of every t
	11:25	Don't t yourself over this
	12:11	make t for you out of your own family
	16:12	maybe God will see the t I'm in
1Ki	1:29	delivered me from every kind of t
	11:39	pain and t on David's descendants
	12:28	It's too much t for you to go

	18:18	not I who has caused t in Israel
	20:7	He's just looking for t
2Ki	6:33	This t is directly from God
	14:26	God was fully aware of the t in Israel
	21:15	They've been nothing but t to me
	23:18	Josiah said, "Don't t his bones."
1Ch	21:3	risk getting Israel into t with God
	22:14	gone to a lot of t to stockpile
2Ch	15:4	when they were in t and got serious
	15:6	God let loose every kind of t
	16:9	Now you're in t
	20:9	pray out our pain and t
	21:16	The t started with an invasion
	33:12	Now that he was in t
Ne	4:8	create as much t as they could
	9:32	Don't treat lightly the t
	9:37	We're in deep t
Job	2:11	Job's friends heard of all the t
	3:10	into a life with so much t
	3:17	Where the wicked no longer t anyone
	4:5	But now you're the one in t
	4:8	plow evil and sow t reap evil and t
	5:6	t doesn't come from nowhere
	5:7	Mortals are born and bred for t
	15:20	can expect nothing but t
	19:28	see that his t is all his own fault
	29:12	I was known for helping people in t
	35:12	until, of course, they're in t
	36:9	how their pride has caused their t
	37:20	Wouldn't that just be asking for t
	38:23	I keep in readiness for times of t
	42:11	consoled him for all the t God had
Ps	4:1	Now I'm in t again
	13:2	Long enough I've carried this ton of t
	22:11	t moved in next-door
	25:16	I'm all alone and in big t
	25:20	watch over me and keep me out of t
	31:9	I'm in deep, deep t again
	32:10	God-defiers are always in t
	34:19	Disciples so often get into t
	39:1	so they won't land me in t
	50:15	call for help when you're in t
	66:14	that day when I was in so much t
	69:17	I'm in t. Answer right now
	71:20	You, who made me stare t in the face
	77:2	I found myself in t
	77:15	out of the worst kind of t
	86:7	Every time I'm in t I call on you
	88:2	take notes on the t I'm in
	88:3	I've had my fill of t
	90:10	what do we have to show for it? T
	90:10	Toil and t and a marker
	91:14	I'll get you out of any t
	106:44	God saw the t they were in
	107:39	abuse and evil and t declined
	119:153	look at my t, and help me
	120:1	I'm in t. I cry to God
	138:7	When I walk into the thick of t
	143:11	In your justice, get me out of this t
Pr	4:16	restless unless they're making t
	5:2	what I tell you will keep you out of t
	6:14	always stirring up t

	10:10	An evasive eye is a sign of t ahead
	10:26	will give you nothing but t
	11:8	A good person is saved from much t
	12:13	gossip of bad people gets them in t
	16:30	a clenched jaw signals t ahead
	17:11	out looking for nothing but t
	17:17	stick together in all kinds of t
	17:19	person who courts sin, marries t
	17:20	double-talk brings you double t
	21:10	Wicked souls love to make t
	22:3	A prudent person sees t coming
	23:27	loose woman can get you in deep t fast
	24:2	all they talk about is making t
	25:19	a double-crosser when you're in t
	26:6	You're only asking for t when
	27:12	A prudent person sees t coming
	28:25	A grasping person stirs up t
	29:9	gets only scorn and sarcasm for his t
	29:22	the intemperate stir up t
Ecc	1:18	Much learning earns you much t
Isa	5:30	you'll see nothing but darkness and t
	9:1	no darkness for those who were in t
	14:3	time to recover from the abuse and t
	14:32	Those in need and in t find refuge
	25:4	take care of poor people in t
	26:16	for help when they were in t
	29:7	all who t and hassle and torment her
	38:14	Master, I'm in t! Get me out of this
	45:18	didn't go to all that t to just leave
	50:11	if all you're after is making t
	51:19	hit with a double dose of t
	54:14	far from any t—nothing to fear
	61:7	you got a double dose of t
Jer	6:8	You're in deep t, Jerusalem
	9:17	Look over the t we're in
	14:8	Israel's last chance in this t
	16:19	my safe retreat when t descends
	17:16	I never wanted t
	20:18	Life's been nothing but t and tears
	23:33	you're the t, and I'm getting rid
	30:7	A time of deep t for Jacob
	35:14	a lot of t to get your attention
	48:11	never faced any t
La	1:20	O God, look at the t I'm in!
	1:21	enemies heard of the t you gave me
	3:19	never forget the t
	3:30	Don't run from t
Da	12:1	a time of t, the worst t
Hos	7:13	Now they're really in t!
	9:7	your great guilt, you're in big t
Jnh	1:6	Maybe your god will see we're in t
	2:2	In t, deep t, I prayed to God
Na	1:8	No matter how desperate the t
Hab	1:3	stare t in the face day after day
Zep	3:7	a way of escape from the t she's in
Zec	6:8	No more t from that direction
Mal	1:9	You priests have gotten everyone in t
Mt	5:12	always gotten into this kind of t
	8:8	don't want to put you to all that t
	24:21	going to be t on a scale beyond
	24:22	If these days of t were left to run
Mk	13:20	If he let the days of t run

Lk	6:24	t ahead if you think you have it made
	6:25	it's t ahead if you're satisfied
	6:26	t ahead when you live only for
	7:6	don't have to go to all this t
	8:13	the moment there's t it's gone
	20:20	get him in t with the law
	22:36	This is different. Get ready for t
Jn	3:17	all the t of sending his Son
Ac	21:22	There's bound to be t
	22:30	determined to get to the root of the t
	24:19	who started all this t
	27:21	could have avoided all this t
	28:19	get our people in t with Rome
Ro	5:18	got us in all this t with sin
	7:1	shouldn't have any t understanding
	8:35	Not t, not hard times, not hatred
	10:21	nothing for my t but cold shoulders
	11:24	isn't going to have any t grafting
	16:17	then use them to make t
2Co	12:19	all the t of supporting ourselves
Eph	3:13	my present t on your behalf
Col	1:21	giving him t every chance you got
1Th	1:6	Although great t accompanied the Word
	3:4	clear that there was t ahead
	3:7	middle of our t and hard times here
2Th	1:5	All this t is a clear sign
1Ti	6:10	brings t and nothing but t
2Ti	1:12	the cause of all this t I'm in
	3:12	for Christ is in for a lot of t
	4:15	he caused no end of t
Tit	1:6	Do they respect him and stay out of t
Heb	2:16	didn't go to all this t for angels
	12:7	This t you're in isn't punishment
Rev	20:3	No more t out of him

Troubled

Jos	7:25	Josua said, "Why have you t us?
Isa	38:15	I'm that upset, that t
	63:9	In all their troubles, he was t, too
Zec	10:11	They'll sail through t seas
Mt	27:19	t night because of a dream about him
Ro	15:3	I took on the troubles of the t
1Ti	5:10	tired Christians, the hurt and t

Troubles

Dt	1:12	how can I carry, all by myself, your t
	4:30	When t come and all these awful things
Jdg	10:16	God took Israel's t to heart
1Sa	10:19	has a history of getting you out of t
2Ch	14:7	he has given us rest from all t
	36:13	compounded his t by rebelling
Ne	9:27	called out for help in their t
Est	7:4	our t wouldn't have been worth
Job	9:28	All these t would still be like grit
	11:16	You'll forget your t
	14:1	too few days, too many t
	19:5	using my t as a stick to beat me
	29:24	their t took wing
	36:13	always blaming others for their t
	36:20	when people sleep off their t

T

Ps	31:10	My t have worn me out
	40:12	t ganged up on me, a mob of sins
	55:22	Pile your t on God's shoulders
	60:3	gave us cheap wine to drown our t
	119:71	My t turned out all for the best
	119:143	t came down on me hard
	132:1	remember David, remember all his t
	142:2	spell out my t in detail
Pr	1:26	joke about your t
Isa	38:17	good for me to go through all those t
	63:9	In all their t, he was troubled
	65:16	earlier t are gone and forgotten
	65:17	All the earlier t, chaos, and pain
Jer	12:5	going to happen when t break loose
	17:17	Don't add to my t
Ob	1:13	not have been amused by their t
Hab	2:9	above trials and t
Mk	10:30	but also in t
Ac	7:10	rescued him from all his t
Ro	5:3	even when we're hemmed in with t
	5:3	because we know how t can
	15:3	by avoiding people's t
2Co	4:8	surrounded and battered by t
	7:4	overwhelmed with joy despite all our t
	8:2	Fierce t came down on the people
Php	4:14	you came alongside me in my t
1Th	3:3	Not that the t should come as any
2Ti	3:11	t, sufferings

Truce

1Ki	20:31	carry a white flag of t
Ps	25:17	Call a t to this civil war
Lk	14:32	send an emissary and work out a t

Trust

Ge	39:9	violate his t and sin against God
	42:37	T me with Benjamin
Ex	4:1	Moses objected, "They won't t me
	4:5	they will t that God appeared to you
	4:8	if they don't t you
	4:9	after these two signs they don't t you
	19:9	can listen in and t you completely
Lev	5:15	When a person betrays his t
	6:2	anyone sins by betraying t with God
Nu	5:6	the person has broken t with God
	14:11	How long refuse to t me
	20:12	Because you didn't t me
Dt	1:32	now that you're here, you won't t God
	9:23	your God. Refused to t him
Jdg	11:20	But Sihon didn't t Israel
	16:15	when you won't even t me
1Sa	27:12	Achish came to t David completely
	30:6	strengthened himself with t in his God
2Sa	24:10	replacing t with statistics
2Ki	3:12	said, "Good! A man we can t!"
	4:23	I need to go right now. T me
	18:5	put his whole t in the God of Israel
	25:24	T me, everything is going to be
1Ch	12:19	We can't t them with our lives
	21:8	substituting statistics for t

2Ch	14:11	we t in you and who you are
	32:15	don't t him. No god of any country
Ezr	10:10	You've broken t. You've married
Job	4:18	God doesn't even t his own servants
	6:30	Don't you t me to discern good
	15:15	God can't even t his holy angels
	36:4	T me, I'm giving you undiluted truth
	39:11	but could you t him
Ps	31:6	but you, God, I t
	44:6	I don't t in weapons
	55:23	And I t in you
	56:3	I come to you in t
	56:4	fearless now, I t in God
	56:11	Fearless now, I t in God
	62:8	So t him absolutely, people
	78:7	t in God, Never forget
	91:2	God, you're my refuge. I t in you
	91:14	if you'll only get to know and t me
	115:8	become just like the gods they t
	115:9	put your t in God! — t your Helper! t
	115:10	t in God!
	115:10	t your Helper! t your Ruler
	115:11	You who fear God, t in God!
	115:11	t your Helper! t your Ruler
	118:8	better to take refuge in God than t
	118:9	better to take refuge in God than t
	125:1	Those who t in God are like Zion
	135:18	Those who make and t them become
Pr	3:5	T God from the bottom of your heart
	14:22	the thoughtful win love and t
	16:20	things work out when you t in God
	19:1	than a rich person no one can t
	21:31	then t God to bring victory
	22:19	make sure your foundation is t in God
	25:10	and no one will t you
	26:28	flatterers sabotage t
	28:25	t in God brings a sense of well-being
	29:3	you'll destroy their t if you run
Isa	12:2	God is my salvation. I t
	19:11	dare tell Pharaoh, "T me: I'm wise
	30:5	Anyone stupid enough to t them
	32:17	quiet lives and endless t
	43:10	you'll come to know and t me
	50:10	T in God. Lean on your God
	59:4	They t in illusion
Jer	9:4	Don't even t your grandmother
	12:6	Don't t them
	27:16	prophets who keep telling you, 'T us
	46:25	Pharaoh and those who t in him
	51:47	T me, the time is coming
	51:52	but t me: The time is coming
Eze	33:13	if they t in their good deeds
	44:7	you've broken t with me
Mic	7:5	Don't t your neighbor
Zep	3:2	Wouldn't t God
	3:4	opportunists — you can't t them
Mal	2:11	a sickening violation of t
Mt	8:10	this kind of simple t in Israel
	18:6	taking advantage of their simple t
	19:26	if you t God to do it
Mk	5:36	Don't listen to them; just t me
	9:42	taking advantage of their simple t

Lk	7:9	simple t anywhere in Israel
	8:25	disciples, "Why can't you t me?"
	8:50	Don't be upset. Just t me
	18:27	if you t God to do it
Jn	3:18	Anyone who ts in him is acquitted
	5:30	You can t my decision
	12:37	still wouldn't t him
	14:1	You t God, don't you? **T** me
	16:27	committed . . . to love and t in me
Ac	5:14	those who put their t in the Master
	9:21	not at all sure they could t him
	9:26	They didn't t him one bit
	9:42	many put their t in the Master
	13:48	put their t in God
	15:26	We picked men we knew you could t
	16:31	Put your entire t in the Master Jesus
	16:34	had put their t in God
	18:8	put his t in the Master
	20.21	equally radical t in our Master Jesus
Ro	1:5	entering into obedient t in Jesus
	4:5	something only God can do, and you t
	4:14	eliminates personal t completely
	4:17	t God to do what only God could do
	7:13	mean I can't even t what is good
	8:5	Those who t God's action in them
	10:4	everything right for those who t him
	10:14	if they don't know who to t
	10:14	And how can they know who to t
	10:17	Before you t, you have to listen
1Co	1:21	bring those who t him into the way
	7:25	you can t my counsel
	12:9	simple t healing the sick
	13:13	**T** steadily in God, hope unswervingly
2Co	1:2	Timothy, someone you know and t
	5:7	It's what we t in but don't yet see
	6:15	Do t and mistrust hold hands
	7:2	**T** us. We've never hurt a soul
	8:7	you t God, you're articulate
Gal	3:5	because you t him to do them
	3:7	persons who put their t in Christ
Eph	1:15	the solid t you have in the Master
	1:19	his work in us who t him
	2:8	t him enough to let him do it
	3:12	When we t in him, we're free
Php	1:27	for people's t in the Message
Col	1:23	steady in that bond of t
2Th	2:12	they refuse to t truth
Tit	3:8	those who have put their t in God
Heb	2:13	Even I live by placing my t in God
	6:1	turning in t toward God
	10:38	right with me thrives on loyal t
	11:1	this t in God, this faith
	11:31	those who refused to t God
1Pe	1:8	You still don't see him, yet you t him
	1:21	that you t God, that you know
	2:7	To you who t him, he's a Stone
	4:19	take it in stride. **T** him

Trusted

Ex	4:31	the people t and listened believingly
	14:31	t in God and his servant Moses

Jdg	9:26	The leaders of Shechem t him
1Ch	5:20	answered . . . because they t him
2Ch	13:18	won hands down because they t God
Job	12:20	He forces t sages to keep silence
Ps	22:5	they t and lived a good life
	52:7	t in big money
	52:8	I t in the generous mercy of God
	119:42	I t your Word
Pr	11:13	gossip can't be t with a secret
	20:9	can be t to be always diligent
	21:22	their t defenses fell to pieces
Jer	2:37	I, God, have blacklisted those you t
	39:18	safe and sound because you t me
	48:7	You t in thick walls and big money
Da	3:28	rescued his servants who t in him
	6:23	He had t his God
Hos	11:12	Not a word of Israel can be t
Jnh	3:5	listened, and t God
Ac	15:9	as they t and believed him
Ro	4:3	He t God to set him right
	7:16	So if I can't be t to figure out
	10:14	heard of the One who can be t
1Co	15:12	believers because you t
2Co	8:22	we're sending another t friend along
Col	4:7	a t minister and companion
	4:9	become such a t and dear brother
1Th	2:3	qualified to be t with this Message
2Ti	1:12	I've t in can take care of what he's t
Jas	2:4	you are judges who can't be t

Trusting

2Ki	18:30	give you that line about t in God
Ps	78:22	had no intention of t in his help
	112:7	Heart ready, t in God
	143:8	I'll go to sleep each night t in you
Pr	3:29	sitting there t and unsuspecting
	25:19	**T** a double-crosser
	29:25	t in God protects you
Isa	28:16	a t life won't topple
La	4:13	exploited good and t people
Mic	1:13	t not God but chariots
Lk	8:48	Daughter, you took a risk t me
Jn	3:15	everyone who looks up to him, t
	16:33	t me, you will be unshakable
Ac	16:14	the Master gave her a t heart
Ro	1:17	right standing before God by t him
	4:5	t-him-to-do-it is what gets you set
	4:16	promise depends entirely on t God
	4:22	declared fit before God by t God
	9:32	instead of t God, they took over
	10:6	t God to shape the right living
	10:9	calling out to God, t him to do it
2Co	1:9	Instead of t in our own strength
Gal	2:16	right before God by t in the Messiah
Php	1:25	joy in this life of t God continues
	1:29	more to this life than t in Christ
	3:9	kind that comes from t Christ
1Ti	1:12	out on a limb . . . in t me
	1:16	right on the edge of t him forever
Heb	5:8	God's Son, he learned t-obedience
	10:39	survive, t all the way

Truth

Ge	20:12	the t is that she is my half sister
	42:16	see if you're telling the t or not
	42:20	confirming the t of your speech
Dt	18:17	They're right; they've spoken the t
Jdg	16:18	this time he's told me the t
1Sa	14:41	Show me the t. If the sin is in me
2Sa	15:20	God's grace and t go with you
1Ki	22:16	tell me the t and nothing but the t
2Ch	18:15	tell me the t and nothing but the t
Job	6:24	Confront me with the t
	16:19	who knows the t about me
	32:21	the t, the whole t, and nothing but
	36:4	I'm giving you undiluted t
Ps	5:6	Blood-Thirsty and T-Bender disgust you
	15:2	Walk straight, act right, tell the t
	18:26	The true people taste your t
	19:4	unspoken t is spoken everywhere
	25:5	Lead me down the path of t
	40:10	didn't hold back pieces of love and t
	40:11	Your love and t are all that keeps me
	45:4	Ride on the side of t!
	51:6	What you're after is t from the inside
	78:1	Listen, dear friends, to God's t
	78:6	Know the t and tell the stories
	85:10	Love and T meet in the street
	85:11	T sprouts green from the ground
	89:14	Love and T are its fruits
	111:7	He manufactures truth and justice
	119:43	Don't ever deprive me of t
	119:45	I look for your t and your wisdom
	119:72	T from your mouth means more
	119:90	Your t never goes out of fashion
	119:91	Your Word and t are dependable as ever
	119:142	your revelation is the only t
	119:150	farther from the t you reveal
	119:160	Your words all add up to . . . T
	119:171	you've taught me the t about life
Pr	8:7	mouth chews and savors and relishes t
	8:9	t-ready minds will see it at once
	10:19	The more talk, the less t
	12:19	T lasts
	15:14	always eager to take in more t
	16:6	Guilt is banished through love and t
	16:13	love advisors who tell them the t
	20:28	Love and t form a good leader
	21:28	a person who speaks t is respected
	23:16	sing to the tuneful t you'll speak
	23:23	Buy t—don't sell it
Ecc	12:10	right words and write the plain t
Isa	33:15	Live right, speak the t
	59:14	T staggers down the street
Jer	5:3	God, you have an eye for t
	6:13	twist words and doctor t
	7:28	T has disappeared
	8:10	twist words and doctor t
	9:3	liars, the sworn enemies of t
	9:5	never telling the t
	38:15	If I told you the whole t, you'd kill
Da	8:12	The horn cast God's T aside
	11:2	tell you the t of how things stand

Hos	5:9	the unvarnished t
Am	5:10	Raw t is never popular
Na	3:5	get their fill of the ugly t
Zec	8:3	Jerusalem's new names will be T City
	8:16	Tell the t, the whole t
	8:19	Embrace t! Love peace
Mal	2:6	He taught the t and did not lie
	2:7	It's the job of priests to teach the t
Mt	4:23	taught people the t of God
	5:11	the t is too close for comfort
	17:20	The simple t is that if you had
	24:2	The t of the matter is
	25:40	I'm telling the solemn t
	25:45	I'm telling the solemn t
Mk	12:43	The t is that this poor widow gave
	13:9	placed there as sentinels to t
Lk	6:22	the t is too close for comfort
	6:26	Popularity contests are not t contests
	6:27	To you who are ready for the t
	19:21	To tell you the t, I was
	21:3	The plain t is that this widow
Jn	1:20	He told the plain t: "I am not
	3:11	I'm speaking sober t to you
	3:21	anyone working and living in t
	3:33	God himself is the t
	4:18	You spoke the t there
	4:23	engage your spirit in the pursuit of t
	4:37	That's the t of the saying
	6:47	the most solemn and sober t
	8:32	experience for yourselves the t
	8:32	and the t will free you
	8:33	How can you say, 'The t will free you
	8:40	the t he got straight from God
	8:44	He couldn't stand the t because
	8:44	because there wasn't a shred of t
	8:45	tell you the plain t
	8:46	telling the t, why don't you believe
	13:38	t is that before the rooster crows
	14:6	I am the Road, also the T
	14:17	This Friend is the Spirit of T
	15:25	verified the t of their own Scriptures
	15:26	Spirit of T issuing from the Father
	16:7	let me say it again, this t
	16:13	the Friend comes, the Spirit of the T
	17:17	Make them holy . . . with the t
	17:19	be t-consecrated in their mission
	18:23	But if I've spoken the plain t
	18:37	so that I could witness to the t
	18:38	Pilate said, "What is t?"
	19:35	saw it himself and is telling the t
	21:18	I'm telling you the very t now
Ac	10:34	God's own t, nothing could be plainer
	20:20	Every t and encouragement that could
Ro	1:18	try to put a shroud over t
	2:14	confirm its t by their obedience
	3:7	my lies serve to show off God's t
	9:29	had looked ahead and spoken the t
	14:11	the honest t that I and only I am God
	16:26	can now know the t
1Co	2:3	if you want the t of it
	11:19	will bring t into the open
	13:6	pleasure in the flowering of t

	13:9	We know only a portion of the t
	14:1	Most of all, try to proclaim his t
	14:3	proclaim his t in everyday speech
	14:4	proclaiming God's t to the church
	14:5	proclaim his clear t to others
	14:6	some insight or t or proclamation
	14:22	Plain t-speaking
	14:24	where people are speaking out God's t
	14:39	When you speak forth God's t
	15:11	We spoke God's t
	15:20	t is that Christ has been raised up
2Co	1:13	writing plain, unembellished t
	4:2	the whole t on display
	4:4	bother believing a T they can't see
	6:7	when we're telling the t
	10:5	barriers erected against the t of God
	12:6	still be speaking plain t all the way
	13:8	We're rooting for the t to win out
	13:9	every triumph of the t in you
Gal	1:20	I'm telling you the absolute t
	2:5	preserve the t of the Message for you
	4:16	simply by telling you the t
Eph	1:13	once you heard the t and believed it
	4:15	know the whole t and tell it in love
	4:21	the t precisely as we have it in Jesus
	4:25	Tell your neighbor the t
	6:14	T, righteousness
Col	1:6	heard and recognized the t
	1:25	laying out the whole t
2Th	2:10	who hate the t that could save them
	2:12	Since they refuse to trust t
	2:13	the bond of faith in the living t
1Ti	1:10	sex, t, whatever
	2:4	get to know the t we've learned
	2:7	it works by simple faith and plain t
	3:15	this God-alive church, bastion of t
	4:2	lost their capacity for t
	6:5	t is but a distant memory
2Ti	2:15	laying out the t plain and simple
	2:18	believers off stride and missing the t
	2:25	change of heart and a turning to the t
	3:6	religious fad that calls itself "t
	3:8	defying t itself
	3:16	showing us t, exposing our rebellion
	4:4	turn their backs on t
Tit	1:3	he went public with his t
	1:9	knowing how to use the t
	1:13	He certainly spoke the t
Heb	10:26	all the t we now know, we repudiate
Jas	3:14	Twisting the t to make yourselves
	5:19	wandered off from God's t
1Pe	1:22	your lives by following the t
	5:12	This is God's generous t
2Pe	1:12	up-to-date on all this t and practice
	2:2	give the way of t a bad name
1Jn	2:21	to confirm the t you do know
	2:27	Christ's anointing teaches you the t
	3:7	don't let anyone divert you from the t
	4:6	test for telling the Spirit of T
	5:6	while the Spirit is confirming the t
	5:20	recognize and understand the t of God
2Jn	1:1	I, your pastor, love you in very t

	1:3	mercy, and peace be with us in t
	1:4	living out the T, exactly as commanded
3Jn	1:3	persist in following the way of T
	1:4	continue diligently in the way of T
	1:8	companions in spreading the T
	1:12	the T itself stands up for Demetrius
Rev	2:25	Hold on to the t you have

Turmoil

1Sa	14:16	confusion and t raging in the camp
Ps	138:7	keep me alive in the angry t
Isa	23:11	threw the sea kingdoms into t

Tyrannize

Lev	25:43	Don't t them; fear your God
	25:46	you must not t your brother
	25:53	sure that his owner does not t him

Tyrannized

Ps	106:42	they were t under that rule
1Pe	4:2	instead of being t by what you want

Tyranny

Jdg	8:22	You have saved us from Midian's t
	8:28	Midian's t was broken
	9:17	rescued you from Midian's t
Ps	72:14	He frees them from t and torture
Isa	14:4	The tyrant is gone! The t is over
Ro	6:14	not living under that old t any longer
	6:15	out from under the old t
	8:2	brutal t at the hands of sin and death

Tyrant

Isa	14:4	The t is gone! The tyranny is over
	16:4	the t toppled, The killing at an end
	19:4	turn . . . over to a t most cruel
	49:24	prisoners of war gotten back from a t
	49:25	a t holds my people prisoner
	51:13	the tantrums of a t who thinks he can

Tyrants

Jos	13:3	there were five Philistine t
Jdg	3:3	He left the five Philistine t
	16:5	The Philistine t approached her
	16:8	t brought her seven bowstrings
	16:18	she sent for the Philistine t
	16:23	Philistine t got together to offer
	16:27	including all the Philistine t
	16:30	building crashed on the t
Job	21:28	the castles of t fall to pieces
Ps	72:4	come down hard on the cruel t
Isa	9:4	abuse of oppressors and cruelty of t
	13:11	trip strutting t, leave them flat
	29:5	the mob of t who will be blown away
	52:5	T on the warpath, whooping it up
Lk	1:52	He knocked t off their high horses
Col	2:15	stripped all the spiritual t

T

U

Ugly

Ge	41:20	seven skinny, **u** cows ate up the first
	41:21	were just as skinny and **u** as before
	41:27	sick and **u** cows that followed them
1Sa	17:26	rid of this **u** blot on Israel's honor
	18:10	**u** mood was sent by God to afflict Saul
Ps	35:21	They open their mouths in **u** grins
Na	3:5	the **u** truth of who you really are
Mt	7:3	oblivious to the **u** sneer on your own
	7:5	Wipe that **u** sneer off your own face
Lk	6:41	oblivious to the **u** sneer on your own
	6:42	Wipe that **u** sneer off your own face
Ac	13:45	making an **u** scene
	17:5	soon had an **u** mob terrorizing the city
1Co	6:7	These court cases are an **u** blot
	11:6	she dishonors herself — an **u** sight
Gal	5:21	**u** parodies of community
Php	4:8	the beautiful, not the **u**

Ulterior

| Job | 33:3 | I have no **u** motives in this |
| Gal | 2:4 | Their **u** motive was to reduce us |

Ultimate

Ge	49:10	Until the **u** ruler comes
1Co	1:24	Christ is God's **u** miracle and wisdom
Col	3:24	the **u** Master you're serving is Christ

Ultimately

| Jn | 11:26 | lives believing in me does not **u** die |
| Heb | 7:9 | **U** you could even say that since Levi |

Unbelief

Isa	45:24	disgraced by their **u**
Mk	16:14	severely for their stubborn **u**
Eph	2:2	filled your lungs with polluted **u**
Heb	3:12	sure there's no evil **u** lying around

Unbelievers

Mt	10:5	some far-off place to convert **u**
	12:21	signal hope, even among far-off **u**
Ac	21:11	hand him over to godless **u**
	28:25	When the **u** got cantankerous
Ro	15:31	delivered from the lions' den of **u**
1Co	14:22	it only gives **u** something to gawk at
Tit	1:15	nothing is clean to dirty-minded **u**
3Jn	1:7	get no help from **u**

Unbelieving

| 1Ch | 9:1 | were exiled . . . because of their **u** |
| Jn | 20:27 | Don't be **u**. Believe |

Ac	14:2	**u** Jews worked up a whispering campaign
1Co	7:14	The **u** husband shares to an extent
	7:15	if the **u** spouse walks out
	14:23	some **u** outsiders walk in on you
	14:24	if some **u** outsiders walk in on
Heb	11:7	between the evil of the **u** world

Unchangeable

| Nu | 18:19 | eternal and **u** before God |
| Heb | 6:18 | the promise is likewise **u** |

Unchanged

| Lev | 13:37 | if he sees that the itch is **u** |
| Jer | 6:29 | but the ore stays a lump, **u** |

Uncircumcised

Ge	17:14	**u** male, one who has not had
	34:14	to a man who was **u**
Ex	12:48	no **u** person can eat it
Jdg	14:3	a wife from the **u** Philistines
	15:18	fall into the hands of the **u**
1Sa	14:6	let's go across to these **u** pagans
	17:26	this **u** Philistine, taunting
Eze	31:18	among the other **u** who are dead
	32:26	a cemetery in **u** ground
	44:7	outsiders, **u** in heart and flesh
	44:9	aliens, **u** in heart or flesh
Ro	2:26	**u** who keep God's ways are as good
	2:27	Better to keep God's law **u** than
	4:12	unidentified as God's, in an "**u**

Unclean

Ge	7:2	one pair of every **u** animal
	7:8	Clean and **u** animals
Lev	5:2	if you touch anything ritually **u**
	5:2	like the carcass of an **u** animal
	7:19	has touched anything ritually **u**
	7:21	if you touch anything ritually **u**
	10:10	between the ritually clean and **u**
	11:4	doesn't have a split hoof, so it's **u**
	11:5	split hoof and so it's **u**
	11:6	doesn't have a split hoof so is **u**
	11:7	doesn't chew the cud and so is **u**
	11:8	they are **u** to you
	11:24	will make yourselves ritually **u**
	11:25	you'll be **u** until evening
	11:26	doesn't chew the cud is **u** for you
	11:27	that goes on its paws is **u** for you
	11:28	you . . . are **u** until evening
	11:28	They are **u** for you
	11:29	the following are **u** for you
	11:31	these are **u** for you
	11:32	becomes **u** no matter what it's used for
	11:33	everything in the pot is **u**
	11:34	water on it from such a pot is **u**
	11:35	one of these carcasses falls on is **u**
	11:36	you're ritually **u**

11:38	falls on it, you must treat it as **u**	
11:39	is ritually **u** until evening	
11:40	you are **u** until evening	
11:43	Don't make yourselves **u** or be defiled	
11:44	Don't make yourselves ritually **u**	
11:47	between the ritually **u** and the clean	
12:2	birth to a boy is ritually **u**	
12:5	birth to a girl, she is **u**	
13:3	he will pronounce the person **u**	
13:8	priest will pronounce him **u**	
13:11	The priest will pronounce him **u**	
13:14	are open, running sores, he is **u**	
13:15	pronounce him **u**. The open sores are **u**	
13:20	priest will pronounce him **u**	
13:22	priest will diagnose him as **u**	
13:25	priest will pronounce him **u**	
13:27	priest will diagnose him as **u**	
13:30	will pronounce the person ritually **u**	
13:36	yellow hair, for instance; he is **u**	
13:44	has a serious skin disease and is **u**	
13:45	and cry out, 'U! U	
13:46	continues to be ritually **u**	
13:51	and the material is **u**	
13:55	though it hasn't spread, it is still **u**	
13:59	for pronouncing them clean or **u**	
14:36	nothing in the house is declared **u**	
14:44	a malignant fungus. The house is **u**	
14:46	while it is closed up is **u**	
14:57	to determine when it is **u**	
15:2	from his genitals, the discharge is **u**	
15:3	seepage or an obstruction he is **u**	
15:3	He is **u** all the days his body	
15:4	bed on which he lies is ritually **u**	
15:4	everything on which he sits is **u**	
15:5	he remains **u** until evening	
15:8	he remains **u** until evening	
15:9	man with the discharge rides is **u**	
15:10	that has been under him becomes **u**	
15:11	he remains **u** until evening	
15:16	he remains **u** until evening	
15:17	it remains **u** until evening	
15:18	they remain **u** until evening	
15:19	who touches her is **u** until evening	
15:20	lies or sits during her period is **u**	
15:21	he remains **u** until evening	
15:24	menstrual blood gets on him, he is **u**	
15:25	she is **u** the same as during the time	
15:26	everything on which she sits becomes **u**	
15:27	who touches these things becomes **u**	
15:30	the discharge that made her **u**	
15:31	that which makes them ritually **u**	
15:31	lest they die in their **u**	
15:32	emission of semen that makes him **u**	
15:33	who sleeps with a woman who is **u**	
17:15	he remains **u** until evening	
18:19	her menstrual period when she is **u**	
20:25	clean and **u** animals and birds	
21:3	he may make himself ritually **u**	
22:6	will be ritually **u** until evening	
27:11	what he vowed is a ritually **u** animal	
27:27	If it's one of the ritually **u** animals	
Nu	5:2	**u** from contact with a dead body

	9:6	ritually **u** on account of a corpse
	9:7	ritually **u** because of a corpse
	9:10	ritually **u** because of a corpse
	19:7	he remains ritually **u** until evening
	19:8	He also is **u** until evening
	19:10	he is ritually **u** until evening
	19:11	touches a dead body is ritually **u**
	19:13	he remains ritually **u**
	19:14	already in the tent is ritually **u**
	19:15	open container without a lid is **u**
	19:16	bone or a grave is **u** for seven days
	19:17	For this **u** person, take some ashes
	19:19	sprinkle the **u** person on the third
	19:20	if an **u** person does not go through
	19:21	is also ritually **u** until evening
	19:22	ritually **u** man touches becomes **u**
Dt	12:15	Both the ritually clean and **u** may eat
	12:22	ritually **u** and clean may eat
	14:7	that makes them ritually **u**
	14:8	cud, which makes them ritually **u**
	14:10	may not eat it. It's ritually **u**
	14:19	Winged insects are ritually **u**
	15:22	ritually clean and **u** may eat it
	23:10	**u** because of a nocturnal emission
	24:4	She has made herself ritually **u**
	26:14	removed any of it while ritually **u**
Jdg	13:4	eat nothing ritually **u**
	13:7	eat nothing ritually **u**
	13:14	eat no ritually **u** foods
1Sa	20:26	made him **u**. . . . he's probably **u**
Ezr	2:62	from priestly work as ritually **u**
Ne	7:64	from priestly work as ritually **u**
Eze	44:23	how to discern between **u** and clean
Lk	8:29	order the **u** spirit out of him

Uncompromised

2Co	1:12	God who kept us focused on him, **u**
Heb	7:26	completely holy, **u** by sin

Unconvicted

Jos	21:13	the asylum-city for the **u** killers
	21:21	the asylum-city for the **u** killer
	21:27	an asylum-city for the **u** killer
	21:32	an asylum-city for the **u** killer
	21:38	an asylum-city for the **u** killer

Underhanded

Ge	21:23	that you won't do anything **u** to me
Pr	30:10	They'll accuse you of being **u**
Isa	32:7	**U** sneaks they are, inventive in sin

Undisciplined

Pr	5:23	Death is the reward of an **u** life
	15:32	An **u**, self-willed life is puny
Lk	15:13	There, **u** and dissipated, he wasted

U

Unfair

Job	31:13	Have I ever been **u** to my employees
Isa	58:9	get rid of **u** practices
Zec	8:17	plans to take **u** advantage of others
Mt	5:41	if someone takes **u** advantage of you
	20:13	Friend, I haven't been **u**
Lk	6:30	If someone takes **u** advantage of you
Ro	9:14	grounds for complaining that God is **u**

Unfaithful

Nu	5:12	wife . . . is **u** to him
	5:27	in being **u** to her husband
1Ki	11:4	he became **u** — he didn't stay true
2Ch	12:2	he and the people were **u** to God
	26:18	you are **u** and a disgrace
Eze	16:32	Wives who are **u** to their husbands
Hos	1:2	become a whorehouse, **u** to me, God

Unfaithfulness

Nu	14:33	fallout of your whoring **u**
Jer	23:10	Their **u** is turning the country

Unfit

Ps	1:5	**u** company for innocent people
Jer	33:12	desolation, **u** for even a stray dog
Eze	44:31	**u** for ordinary human consumption
Hos	9:12	I'd declare them **u** parents
Mt	13:48	those **u** to eat are thrown away

Unhappy

1Sa	1:16	I'm so desperately **u** and in such pain
Jer	3:21	the **u** sound of Israel's crying
	15:10	**u** job of indicting the whole country

Unholy

Ex	30:9	don't burn on this Altar any **u** incense
Isa	66:17	initiation in those **u** rituals
Hos	2:11	her wild weekends and **u** holidays
Am	7:9	Israel's **u** shrines will be knocked
Rev	2:14	throwing **u** parties

Unified

Jn	17:22	they'll be as **u** and together as we are
1Co	10:17	Rather, we become **u** in him

Unique

2Sa	7:23	Israel, a nation **u** in the earth
1Ch	17:21	Israel, a nation **u** on earth
Mt	11:27	This is a **u** Father-Son operation
Jn	10:36	the **u** One the Father consecrated
Ro	1:4	his **u** identity as Son of God

United

Jos	9:19	leaders were **u** in their response
Jdg	20:11	gathered against the city, totally **u**
1Ch	12:38	**u** and determined to make David king
	14:8	made king over a **u** Israel
2Ch	20:4	Judah **u** in seeking God's help
Ps	48:4	kings got together, they **u** and came
Isa	11:14	Blood brothers **u**
Jer	23:5	make sure of justice and keep people **u**
Zep	3:9	in worship and, **u**, to serve me
Ac	4:32	congregation of believers was **u** as one
2Co	5:17	anyone **u** with the Messiah gets
Php	1:27	Stand **u**, singular in vision

Unleash

Dt	7:20	God will **u** the Hornet on them
Job	3:8	**U** the sea beast, Leviathan
	40:11	**U** your outrage. Target the arrogant
Jer	25:16	killing that I'm going to **u** among them
Eze	38:16	I'll **u** you against my land

Unloved

Ge	29:31	When God realized that Leah was **u**
	29:33	"God heard," she said, "that I was **u**
Ro	9:25	I'll call the **u** and make them beloved

Unlucky

1Ch	7:23	named him Beriah (**U**)
Ps	10:10	the **u** victim is brutally axed
Pr	14:20	An **u** loser is shunned by all
Ecc	10:16	**U** the land whose king is a young pup
Jer	8:3	**u** enough to still be alive
	15:10	**U** mother — that you had me as a son

Unmarried

Lev	21:3	an **u** sister who is dependent on him
Eze	44:25	brother or **u** sister
1Co	7:8	tell the **u** and widows that singleness
	7:27	Are you **u**? Don't get married
	7:32	When you're **u**, you're free
	7:34	**u** can spend in becoming whole and holy

Unmercifully

Ne	5:15	underlings bullied the people **u**
Ps	119:161	slandered **u** by the politicians
Ac	27:20	waves were battering us **u**

Unruly

Ps	11:4	examining Adam's **u** brood
	89:9	calm its waves when they turn **u**
Pr	17:2	servant takes charge of an **u** child
Jer	31:19	ashamed of my past, my wild, **u** past

Unshakable

Jn	16:33	trusting me, you will be **u** and assured
Heb	12:27	so that the **u** essentials stand clear
	12:28	what we've got? An **u** kingdom!

Unspeakable

Isa	13:21	**u** night hags will haunt it
Jer	5:30	**U**! Sickening! What's happened
Hos	9:9	that ancient and **u** crime at Gibeah
	10:9	that ancient, **u**, shocking sin
2Co	12:3	There he heard the **u** spoken

Unspiritual

1Co	2:14	The **u** self, just as it is by nature
	2:15	can't be judged by **u** critics
	3:1	frustrated by your **u** dealings

Unthinkable

Job	37:23	It's **u** that he'd treat anyone unfairly
Isa	14:21	**U** that they should own a square foot
	52:15	what was **u** they'll have
Ac	8:20	that's **u** — trying to buy God's gift
Ro	8:39	high or low, thinkable or **u**

Untouchables

Mt	10:8	Raise the dead. Touch the **u**

Untouched

Ps	32:6	we'll be on high ground, **u**
	91:8	You'll stand **u**, watch it all
Zep	3:5	righteous in her midst, **u** by the evil

Upright

Ge	31:45	a stone and set it **u** as a pillar
1Sa	7:12	took a single rock and set it **u**
Job	4:7	Do genuinely **u** people ever lose out
	8:6	If you're as innocent and **u** as you say
Ps	92:15	Such witnesses to **u** God
	112:2	the homes of the **u** — how blessed
Pr	12:6	the speech of the **u** saves
Ecc	7:29	God made men and women true and **u**
Jer	10:4	use hammer and nails to keep it **u**
Eze	4:3	place it **u** between you and the city
	18:9	person who lives **u** and well
	18:20	If you live **u** and well, you get
	18:24	who turns his back on an **u** life
	20:21	my laws for living **u** and well
Jn	6:39	put together, **u** and whole
Ac	4:14	seeing him standing there so **u**
Rev	1:17	His right hand pulled me **u**

Upstart

Ex	15:7	you smash your **u** enemies
Ps	2:10	**U**-judges, learn your lesson

Isa	43:12	long before these **u** gods appeared
Mic	5:2	He'll be no **u**, no pretender
Ac	4:2	these **u** apostles were instructing

Upstarts

2Sa	22:40	you smashed the **u**
	22:49	You pulled me from the grip of **u**
Ps	18:39	you smashed the **u**
	18:48	he pulled me from the grip of **u**
	36:12	Send the **u** sprawling flat
Pr	16:5	he'll put those **u** in their place
Ecc	10:7	seen unproven **u** riding in style

V

Vain

Dt	32:42	the proud and **v** enemy corpses
Job	11:11	He sees through **v** pretensions
Ps	69:20	looked in **v** for one friendly face
	78:63	their young women waited in **v**
Hos	4:15	taking God's name in **v**
Mic	1:12	wait in **v** for sweet peace

Vengeance

Ge	27:42	Esau is plotting **v** against you
Nu	31:3	to exact God's **v** on Midian
Dt	32:35	I'm in charge of **v** and payback
	32:41	I take **v** on my enemies
	32:43	Pays back his enemies with **v**
1Sa	14:24	before I've wreaked **v** on my enemies
	18:24	evidence of your **v**
2Sa	4:8	God has given **v** to my master
Ps	149:7	**v** on the God-defying nations
Isa	34:8	It's God's scheduled time for **v**
	47:3	It's **v** time, and I'm taking **v**
	63:4	I was set on **v**
Jer	46:10	when Sword exacts **v**
	49:30	to go after you with a **v**
	50:15	Operation God's **V**. Pile on the **v**
	50:28	God's **v**, taking **v** for my own Temple
	51:6	linger and lose your lives to my **v**
	51:9	a skyscraper-memorial of **v**
Eze	24:8	provoke my wrath, to trigger my **v**
	25:14	bring my **v** down on Edom
	25:17	Huge acts of **v**, massive punishments
Lk	21:22	This is **V** Day
Heb	10:30	**V** is mine, and I won't overlook
	12:24	a homicide that cried out for **v**

Vicious

Ge	37:20	say that a **v** animal ate him up
Job	5:21	protected from **v** gossip
Ps	140:1	protect me from these **v** people
	140:4	protect me from these **v** people
Isa	25:5	**v** foreigners like high noon
Jer	6:23	Armed to the teeth, **v** and pitiless
La	3:61	You heard, God, their **v** gossip
Eze	21:31	give you to **v** men skilled in torture

V

	28:7	the most **v** of all nations
Da	11:26	honeycombed with **v** plots
Ac	12:11	from Herod's **v** little production
	20:29	**v** wolves are going to show up and rip
	23:29	a squabble turned **v**
Ro	1:29	**v** backstabbing
2Co	12:20	angry words, **v** rumors
Gal	5:21	**v** habit of depersonalizing everyone
3Jn	1:10	spreading **v** rumors about us

Victim

2Sa	3:34	you fell as a **v** in a street brawl
	3:38	a prince and hero fell **v** of foul play
Ps	10:10	the unlucky **v** is brutally axed
	10:17	The **v**'s faint pulse picks up
Mic	5:1	prepare for the worst, **v** daughter
Lk	8:27	he was a **v** of demons

Victims

Ge	18:20	cries of the **v** in Sodom and Gomorrah
	19:13	outcries of **v** here to God
Jos	7:7	To make us **v** of the Amorites
2Sa	1:12	**v** in a failed battle
	3:29	forever be **v** of crippling diseases
2Ki	21:16	the innocent blood of his **v**
	24:4	the innocent blood of his **v**
Job	36:6	champions the rights of their **v**
Ps	10:8	then pounce on their **v**
	14:5	God takes the side of **v**
	74:21	Don't leave the **v** to rot
	103:6	he puts **v** back on their feet
	140:12	you, God, are on the side of **v**
Pr	7:26	Countless **v** come under her spell
	26:28	Liars hate their **v**
	29:24	When the **v** cry out
Ecc	4:1	the tears of the **v**
Isa	5:7	and heard only the moans of **v**
	10:1	who make laws that make **v**
	42:22	**V** licking their wounds
	51:14	The **v** will be released
	58:9	quit blaming **v**
Jer	2:34	stained with the blood of your **v**
	5:26	Their **v** are innocent men and women
	6:7	**V**, bleeding and moaning, lie all over
	14:16	**v** of war and starvation
	21:12	Rescue **v** from their exploiters
	22:3	Rescue **v** from their exploiters
	22:17	bulldozing your way, bullying **v**
La	3:35	Refusing justice to **v** in the court
Eze	32:21	Join the ranks of the **v** of war
Da	7:7	It crunched and swallowed its **v**
Am	2:8	wine they've conned from their **v**
Mic	2:9	You make **v** of the children
Hab	1:9	collect **v** like squirrels gathering
	2:7	how long before your **v** wake up
Zec	11:16	a shepherd indifferent to **v**
Mt	8:28	two madmen, **v** of demons
Lk	1:52	pulled **v** out of the mud
Ac	19:13	Master Jesus over **v** of evil spirits
Heb	13:3	Look on **v** of abuse as if what happened

Rev	20:8	searching out **v** in every nook

Victory

Ex	15:1	singing my heart out to God — what a **v**
	15:21	Sing to God — what a **v**
	32:18	Those aren't songs of **v**
Dt	21:10	your God, gives you **v**
	23:14	give you **v** over your enemies
Jos	10:10	a major **v** at Gibeon
Jdg	4:14	God has given you **v** over Sisera
	11:30	give me a clear **v** over the Ammonites
	15:18	given your servant this great **v**
	20:28	Tomorrow I'll give you **v**
	20:39	thought they were on their way to **v**
1Sa	14:45	this stunning salvation **v** for Israel
	14:47	he came up with a **v**
	15:12	set up a **v** monument in his own honor
	19:5	What a great **v** God gave Israel
2Sa	8:6	God gave **v** to David
	8:13	David built a **v** monument
	8:14	God gave David **v** wherever he marched
	18:31	God has given **v** today over all
	19:2	**v** turned into a day of mourning
	23:12	Another great **v** for God
1Ki	22:12	An easy **v**! God's gift to the king
	22:15	An easy **v**. God's gift to the king
2Ki	5:1	by him that God had given **v** to Aram
1Ch	10:9	reporting the **v** news to their idols
	11:14	God helping them — a huge **v**
	14:10	Will you give me the **v**?
	18:6	God gave **v** to David
	18:13	God gave David **v** wherever he marched
	29:11	the glory, the **v**, the majesty
2Ch	13:16	God gave them the **v**
	13:19	followed up his **v** by pursuing
	16:7	you've lost a **v** over the army
	16:8	God for help and he gave you the **v**
	18:11	An easy **v**! God's gift to the king
	18:14	an easy **v**! God's gift to the king
	20:9	you will listen and give **v**
Ps	41:11	no **v** shouts yet from the enemy camp
	96:2	worship God! Shout the news of his **v**
	118:16	The hand of God is raised in **v**!
Pr	21:31	trust God to bring **v**
SS	6:13	dance her **v** dances of love and peace
Isa	9:4	Gideon's old **v** over Midian
	49:8	When **v**'s due, I help you
Jer	51:14	like locusts chanting **v** songs over you
	51:48	throw a **v** party over Babylon
Da	11:7	win a resounding **v**
	11:12	But his **v** won't last long
2Co	2:14	one perpetual **v** parade
Php	1:28	defeat for them, **v** for you
1Pe	1:7	on display as evidence of his **v**
1Jn	2:13	won a big **v** over the Evil One
	2:14	God enables you to gain a **v**
	4:4	won a big **v** over those false teachers
Rev	3:5	will march in the **v** parade
	6:2	Its rider ... was given a **v** garland

Vigil

1Sa	4:13	beside the road keeping **v**
Mt	26:38	Stay here and keep **v** with me
	28:1	other Mary came to keep **v** at the tomb
Mk	14:34	Stay here and keep **v** with me
Lk	23:49	a respectful distance and kept **v**

Vigilant

Ex	34:12	Stay **v**. Don't let down your guard
Dt	4:9	Stay **v** as long as you live
	11:16	be **v**, lest you be seduced away up
	11:32	Be **v**. Observe all the regulations
	12:28	Be **v**, listen obediently to these words
Jos	22:5	Be **v** in keeping the Commandment
Pr	4:23	Keep **v** watch over your heart
	30:28	they sneak past **v** palace guards
Mt	24:44	Be **v** just like that
2Co	5:11	That keeps us **v**

Vigor

1Sa	14:27	his eyes lit up with renewed **v**
Job	21:10	Their bulls breed with great **v**
Ps	110:3	join you with all the **v** of youth
Pr	20:29	Youth may be admired for **v**
Ecc	11:9	Relish your youthful **v**
	12:1	years take their toll and your **v** wanes
Rev	3:1	You have a reputation for **v** and zest

Vile

Ge	19:7	Brothers, please, don't be **v**
Dt	9:5	the **v** wickedness of these nations
Jdg	19:24	don't do anything so senselessly **v**
	20:6	This **v** and outrageous crime
	20:10	this outrageous and **v** evil
Ps	74:22	all the **v** obscenities
Eze	7:20	deck out their **v** and vulgar no-gods
	16:58	shame of your obscene and **v** life
	18:24	plunging into the same **v** obscenities
	20:7	Get rid of all the **v** things
	20:8	None got rid of the **v** things
	20:30	repeating their **v** practices
	35:12	I, God, have overheard all the **v** abuse
	37:23	all those **v** obscenities
	43:8	their obscene and **v** worship
	44:6	No more of these **v** obscenities
	44:7	With all your **v** obscenities
	44:13	shame of their **v** and obscene lives
Zec	9:7	abandon his **v** ways
Mk	9:25	gave the **v** spirit its marching orders
Lk	9:42	ordered the **v** spirit gone

Vindicated

Ge	20:16	before the eyes of the world. You're **v**
	30:6	God took my side and **v** me
2Ti	1:10	death defeated, life **v**

Violate

Ge	39:9	How could I **v** his trust
Lev	18:7	Don't **v** your father
	18:10	That would **v** your own body
	18:14	Don't **v** your father's brother
	18:16	that would **v** your brother
	18:20	neighbor's wife and **v** yourself
	18:23	sex with an animal and **v** yourself
	19:29	Don't **v** your daughter
Dt	22:30	that would **v** his father's rights
	31:16	abandon me and **v** my Covenant
Job	30:14	They **v** my broken body
Ps	125:3	wicked will never **v** What is due
Pr	11:13	won't **v** a confidence
Isa	5:23	you **v** the rights of the innocent
Mic	4:11	Kick her when she's down! V her
1Co	6:18	**v** the sacredness of our own bodies
Rev	17:16	they'll hate her, **v** her

Violated

Lev	19:8	he has **v** what is holy to God
	20:11	he has **v** his father
	20:17	He has **v** his sister
Nu	15:31	he has **v** God's command
Dt	27:20	**v** the woman who belongs to his father
Jos	7:1	the People of Israel **v** the holy curse
	22:20	Achan son of Zerah **v** the holy curse
2Sa	13:32	Amnon **v** his sister Tamar
1Ch	2:7	doom on Israel when he **v** a holy ban
Ps	51:4	You're the One I've **v**
	74:7	**v** the place of worship
	79:1	**v** your holy temple
Ecc	5:8	justice and right **v** all over
Isa	24:5	**v** the sacred and eternal covenant
	33:8	treaty is broken, its conditions **v**
Jer	34:18	Everyone who **v** my covenant
Eze	4:14	found dead or **v** by wild animals
	7:22	my treasured place and people are **v**
	22:26	Your priests **v** my law
Hos	5:7	devastate their **v** land
Am	2:1	She **v** the corpse of Edom's king
Lk	18:3	My rights are being **v**

Violates

Lev	18:8	That **v** your father
	20:19	That **v** a close relative
Ezr	6:11	who **v** this order is to be impaled
Mic	5:5	invades and **v** our land
	5:6	anyone who invades or **v** our land

Violation

Jos	22:16	this **v** against the God of Israel
2Ki	21:7	**v** of God's well-known statement
2Ch	33:7	**v** of God's well-known command
Mal	2:11	a sickening **v** of trust in Israel

V

Violence

Ge	6:11	there was **v** everywhere
	6:13	The **v** is everywhere
	32:11	Save me . . . from the **v** of my brother
Jdg	9:24	**V** boomeranged: The murderous **v**
2Sa	3:29	crippling diseases, **v**, and famine
Ps	7:16	mischief backfires; **v** boomerangs
	73:6	wear the latest fashions in **v**
	125:3	provoking wrongful **v**
Pr	4:17	**v** their drug of choice
	11:16	men of rough **v** grab for loot
Ecc	4:1	outrageous **v** that takes place
Isa	4:4	scrub the bloodstained city of its **v**
	33:15	reject **v**, avoid evil amusements
	59:6	They weave wickedness, they hatch **v**
Jer	6:6	full of brutality, bursting with **v**
	6:7	streets echo the cries: 'V'! Rape
	51:46	rumors of **v**, rumors of war
Eze	7:11	**V** strutting, brandishing the evil
	7:23	crime and **v** fill the city
	8:17	fill the country with **v**
	36:5	an orgy of **v** and shameless insolence
Am	3:10	They stockpile **v** and blight
Mic	2:9	leave them vulnerable to **v** and vice
Na	3:1	bursting with loot, addicted to **v**
Hab	1:3	Anarchy and **v** break out
	2:17	hung over from Lebanon **v**
Ac	22:24	provoked this outraged **v**
Jas	4:2	risk **v** to get your hands on it

Violent

Ge	45:2	his sobbing was so **v**
Nu	19:16	whether dead from **v** or natural causes
Dt	21:5	settling legal disputes and **v** crimes
Job	27:14	Their children . . . will die **v** deaths
	38:1	answered Job from the eye of a **v** storm
Ps	63:10	They'll die **v** deaths
	74:20	city is in darkness, the countryside **v**
	124:3	swallowed alive by their **v** anger
Pr	11:30	a **v** life destroys souls
Isa	14:6	Established a **v** rule of anger
	37:7	he'll die there. Killed — a **v** death
Eze	7:22	**v** strangers walk in and desecrate
	18:10	if this person has a child who turns **v**
	23:20	more virile, vulgar, and **v** lovers
	28:16	you turned **v**, you sinned
Jnh	3:8	evil life and the **v** ways that stain
Mic	6:12	tired of the **v** rich bullying
Mal	2:16	I hate the **v** dismembering
Ac	21:35	the mob became so **v**
	23:10	quarrel flamed up and became so **v**

Virtue

Ps	37:30	rolls **v** around on his tongue
Pr	8:14	I am both Insight and the **V** to live
Mt	5:28	don't think you've preserved your **v**
Ro	5:4	forges the tempered steel of **v**
	7:7	covetousness up to look like a **v**
Jas	1:21	throw all spoiled **v** and cancerous evil

1Pe	2:20	no particular **v** in accepting

Virtuous

Gal	2:17	aren't perfectly **v**
Tit	2:5	be **v** and pure, keep a good house

Vision

Ge	15:1	word of God came to Abram in a **v**
	46:2	God spoke to Israel in a **v** that night
Nu	24:3	decree of a man with 20/20 **v**
	24:15	decree of the man with **v**
1Sa	3:15	dreaded having to tell the **v** to Eli
2Sa	7:17	everything he heard and saw in the **v**
1Ch	17:15	everything he heard and saw in the **v**
2Ch	32:32	written in the **v** of the prophet Isaiah
Job	33:15	In a dream . . . a **v** at night
Ps	89:19	A long time ago you spoke in a **v**
Ecc	12:2	Before your **v** dims and the world blurs
Isa	1:1	The **v** that Isaiah son of Amoz saw
	21:2	A hard **v** is given me
	22:1	A Message concerning the Valley of **V**
	22:5	stampeding in the Valley of **V**
Eze	8:4	like the **v** I had seen out on the plain
	11:24	still in the **v** given me by the Spirit
	40:2	brought me in divine **v** to the land
Da	2:19	was given to Daniel in a **v**
	2:28	the **v** that filled your mind
	8:1	another **v** came to me, Daniel
	8:2	In the **v**, I saw myself in Susa
	8:16	Explain the **v** to him
	8:17	**v** has to do with the time of the end
	8:26	This **v** of the 2,300 sacrifices
	8:27	I continued to be upset by the **v**
	9:21	one I had seen in an earlier **v**
	10:14	The **v** has to do with what's ahead
Am	7:1	God, my Master, showed me this **v**
	7:4	God showed me this **v**
	7:7	God showed me this **v**
	8:1	My Master God showed me this **v**
Hab	2:3	This **v**-message is a witness
Zec	1:18	was surprised by another **v**
	1:20	God expanded the **v** to include
	4:10	back to the **v**, the Messenger-Angel
Mt	18:9	**v** from inside the fire of hell
Mk	9:48	**v** from inside the fire of hell
Lk	1:22	they knew he had seen a **v**
	24:23	they had seen a **v** of angels
Ac	9:10	The Master spoke to him in a **v**
	10:3	he had a **v**. An angel of God
	11:5	I fell into a trance and saw a **v**
	26:19	couldn't just walk away from a **v**
Php	1:27	Stand united, singular in **v**
	3:15	God will clear your blurred **v**
Rev	4:1	trumpet-voice, the first voice in my **v**
	9:17	both horses and riders in my **v**

Visionary

Dt	13:1	prophet or **v** gets up in your community
	13:3	what that prophet or **v** says
	13:5	that prophet or **v** must be put to death

Visions

Nu	12:6	I make myself known to him in **v**
2Ch	9:29	in the **v** of Iddo the seer
SS	6:4	the ravishing **v** of my ecstasy
Eze	1:1	the sky opened up and I saw **v** of God
	8:3	carried me in **v** of God to Jerusalem
	13:8	who substitute illusions for **v**
	13:16	all their **v** telling us things
	22:28	pretending to have received **v**
Da	1:17	gifted in understanding all sorts of **v**
	7:15	All these dream-**v** had me agitated
Joel	2:28	your young men will see **v**
Am	1:1	It came to him in **v** during the time
Zec	13:4	never swindled people with their '**v**.'
Ac	2:17	Your young men will see **v**
2Co	12:1	**v** and revelations that God gave me
Col	2:18	you seek out **v**

Voracious

Pr	27:20	Hell has a **v** appetite
Isa	56:11	they do know how to eat, **v** dogs
Eze	6:9	their betrayals, by their **v** lust

Vulnerable

Ne	4:13	guards at the most **v** places
Pr	30:26	**v** as they are, manage to arrange
SS	8:9	She's a virgin and **v**
Jer	49:20	the **v** — mere lambs and kids
	50:45	the **v** — mere lambs and kids
Eze	16:7	naked and **v**, fragile and exposed
	34:6	exposed and **v** across mountains
Mic	2:9	leave them **v** to violence and vice
1Co	8:9	still **v** to those old associations
2Pe	2:14	seducing every **v** soul they come upon

W

Wanderer

Ge	4:12	You'll be a homeless **w** on Earth
	4:14	I'm a homeless **w** on Earth
	20:13	God sent me out as a **w**

Weak

Ge	42:9	You've come to look for our **w** spots
	42:12	You've come to look for our **w** spots
Nu	13:18	the people: Are they strong or **w**
Jdg	16:7	I would become **w**, just like anyone
	16:19	Immediately he began to grow **w**
1Sa	2:4	the **w** are infused with fresh strength
2Ch	28:15	put the **w** ones on donkeys
	36:17	the elderly and **w**
Job	24:4	bully the **w** so that they fear
Ps	109:24	**w** from hunger and can hardly stand
Pr	14:34	God-avoidance leaves people **w**
	22:22	don't use your position to crush the **w**
	24:12	Someone not impressed with **w** excuses
Isa	22:9	found the **w** places in the city walls

	33:23	free for all — for **w** and strong
Jer	20:13	All praise to God! He saves the **w**
	22:17	Taking advantage of the **w**
Eze	17:14	make sure that this kingdom stayed **w**
	18:12	bullies the **w**, steals
	18:18	oppressing the **w**, robbing brothers
	34:4	You don't build up the **w** ones
	34:16	I'll build up the **w** ones
Da	10:8	I went **w** in the knees
Joel	3:10	Let the **w** one throw out his chest
Am	6:13	beating up on the **w** and crowing
	8:4	you who walk all over the **w**
Mk	12:40	exploiting the **w** and helpless
Lk	20:47	exploiting the **w** and helpless
Ac	20:35	work on behalf of the **w**
Ro	5:6	we were far too **w** and rebellious
	14:1	strong on opinions but **w** in the faith
1Co	8:12	at the cost of even one of these "**w**
	15:43	in the ground **w**, it comes up powerful

Wealth

Ge	31:1	Jacob has used our father's **w**
	31:16	Any **w** that God has seen fit to return
	46:6	the **w** they had accumulated
Dt	8:18	strength to produce all this **w**
Jos	22:8	Share the **w** with your friends
1Sa	2:7	God brings poverty and God brings **w**
1Ki	3:13	I'm giving you both the **w** and glory
1Ch	29:28	full of days, **w**, and glory
2Ch	1:11	didn't grasp for money, **w**, fame
	1:12	a bonus — money, **w**, and fame
Est	1:4	on exhibit the huge **w** of his empire
Job	22:8	surrounded by immense **w**
	22:25	Almighty will be your treasure, more **w**
	31:25	Did I boast about my **w**, show off
Ps	72:10	resplendent will turn over their **w**
	105:44	helped them seize the **w** of the nations
	112:3	houses brim with **w** And a generosity
Pr	3:15	value exceeds all the trappings of **w**
	8:11	better than all the trappings of **w**
	8:18	**W** and Glory accompany me
	10:4	diligence brings **w**
	10:15	The **w** of the rich is their bastion
	13:22	ill-gotten **w** ends up with good people
	18:11	The rich think their **w** protects them
	19:4	**W** attracts friends as honey
	23:5	**w** sprouts wings and flies off
Ecc	4:9	Share the work, share the **w**
	5:10	Nor the one who loves **w**
	5:13	hoards far more **w** than is good for him
	7:12	Double protection: wisdom and **w**
Isa	2:7	world rolling in **w**
	8:4	plundered the **w** of Damascus
	60:11	Receiving deliveries of **w** from all
Eze	26:12	all that **w**, all that stuff
	27:12	because of your great **w**
	29:19	He'll haul away its **w**
	30:4	killed, their **w** hauled off
Da	11:2	powerful enough as a result of his **w**
Mic	4:13	their **w** to the Master of the earth
	6:10	expect me to overlook obscene **w**

W

Hab	2:5	more hungry for w than the grave is
Hag	2:7	They'll bring bushels of w
Zec	9:4	dump all that w into the ocean
Mt	19:21	All your w will then be in heaven
Mk	10:21	All your w will then be heavenly w
Ac	20:33	any taste for w or fashion
1Ti	6:6	A devout life does bring w
	6:17	those rich in this world's w to quit
Heb	11:26	far greater than Egyptian w
Jas	5:3	You thought you were piling up w
Rev	2:9	but I also see your w
	5:12	Take the power, the w, the wisdom
	18:17	in one hour such w wiped out

Weep

1Sa	2:32	but you'll see it and w
2Sa	1:24	Women of Israel, w for Saul
2Ki	8:12	Hazael said, "Why does my master w?"
Ne	8:9	day is holy to God . . . . Don't w
Ps	102:14	w with compassion over its dust
Isa	15:5	Up the slopes of Luhith they w
	16:9	I'll w right along with Jazer, w
	32:13	W for my people's gardens and farms
	32:15	w and grieve until the Spirit
	33:7	Tough men w openly
Jer	4:8	Dress in funeral black. W and wail
	6:26	W most bitterly, as for an only child
	8:21	I w, seized by grief
	9:1	could w day and night for casualties
	13:17	w over you, W because of your stubborn
	22:10	Don't w over dead King Josiah
	22:20	climb a Lebanon peak and w
	48:5	Up the ascent of Luhith climbers w
	48:17	W for Moab, friends and neighbors
	48:20	Wail and w your eyes out!
	48:31	But I will w for Moab
	48:32	I'll w for the grapevines of Sibmah
	49:3	Dress in mourning, w buckets of tears
La	1:4	Zion's roads w, empty of pilgrims
	1:16	For all this I w, w buckets of tears
Joel	1:5	Get in touch with reality — and w
	1:8	W like a young virgin dressed in black
	2:17	priests . . . w tears of repentance
Am	5:16	W loudly, 'Not me! Not us, Not now!'
Zec	11:2	W, great pine trees! Mourn, you sister
	12:10	they'll w — oh, how they'll w!
	12:12	Everyone will w and grieve
Jn	11:31	on her way to the tomb to w there
	20:13	said to her, "Woman, why do you w?"
	20:15	Woman, why do you w?
Rev	5:5	One of the Elders said, "Don't w

Whim

Ge	49:6	slash oxen on a w
Dt	17:20	changing the commands at w
Job	9:5	flips them on their heads on a w
Isa	57:5	find some shade and fornicate at w
Jer	7:24	indulged any and every evil w
	20:4	kill them at w
Da	5:19	killed or spared people on w

Mt	5:32	as a cover for selfishness and w
Mk	7:13	God's Word and scrawl a w in its place
Jn	6:38	from heaven not to follow my own w

Whimper

| Ps | 9:12 | registers every w and moan |
| | 64:1 | I'm reduced to a whine And a w |

Whims

Pr	12:11	the witless chase w and fancies
1Co	6:12	I'd be a slave to my w
Jude	1:18	make a religion of their own w

Whine

Ex	5:17	Lazy! That's why you w
Ps	64:1	I'm reduced to a w And a whimper
Isa	40:27	or, w, Israel, saying, "God has

Whined

| Ps | 78:19 | They w like spoiled children |

Whiners

| Isa | 29:24 | complainers and w learn gratitude |

Whining

Ex	5:9	That'll cure them of their w
Nu	11:4	they had the People of Israel w
	11:10	heard the w, all those families w
	11:13	meat for all these people who are w
	11:18	You've been w to God, 'We want meat
	11:20	right here among you, w to his face
Jer	15:19	Don't stoop to cheap w
Eze	18:29	Israel keeps on w, 'That's not fair
Am	6:7	They'll leave the country w
Mal	2:13	fill the place of worship with your w
Mt	11:16	spoiled children w to their parents
Ac	7:40	w to Aaron, 'Make us gods we can see

Whisper

Jos	6:10	not so much as a w until you hear
1Ki	18:26	not so much as a w of breeze
	18:29	not so much as a w
	19:12	after the fire a gentle and quiet w
2Ki	6:12	even what you w in your bedroom
Job	4:12	a mere w of a word, but I heard it
	26:14	a mere w of his rule
Ps	41:7	who hate me w slanders all over
	55:2	Come close and w your answer
	81:5	hear this most gentle w from One
	107:29	He quieted the wind down to a w
Isa	21:7	note every w, every rumor
	26:16	so heavy they could barely w a prayer
	29:4	Your speech will w from the dust
Jer	8:6	but heard not so much as a w
Hos	2:17	so much as a w of those names again
Lk	10:24	but never got so much as a w
	12:3	You can't w one thing in private

Whispered

Ge	28:17	He was terrified. He w in awe
1Sa	24:4	David's men w to him
	26:6	Abishai w, "I'll go with you
Ps	27:8	When my heart w, "Seek God,"
Isa	22:14	God-of-the-Angel-Armies w to me
Mt	9:3	Some religion scholars w
	21:25	pulled back into a huddle and w
Mk	11:31	pulled back into a huddle and w
Lk	20:5	pulled back into a huddle and w
Jn	11:28	went to her sister Mary and w
Ac	10:19	so the Spirit w to him

Whispering

1Sa	22:8	conspiring against me, w behind my
2Sa	12:19	servants were w behind his back
Jer	20:10	I hear w behind my back
Mt	9:4	and said, "Why this gossipy w
Mk	2:6	started w among themselves
Lk	4:36	set everyone back . . . w and wondering
	5:22	said, "Why all this gossipy w
Ac	14:2	worked up a w campaign
1Th	2:12	holding your hand, w encouragement

Whispers

Dt	13:6	comes to you in secret and w
Mt	16:7	discussed in w what to do
	16:8	said, "Why all these worried w
Lk	12:3	those w will be repeated all over town
Jn	7:13	This kind of talk went on in guarded w

Whitewash

Pr	28:13	can't w your sins and get by with it
Jer	18:23	Don't w their crimes
Eze	13:10	right behind them slapping on w
	13:11	Tell those who are slapping on the w
	13:12	what's the good of the w
	13:14	wall you've slapped with w collapse
	13:15	those who plastered it with w

Whitewashed

Da	5:5	the lamp-illumined, w wall

Whitewashes

Pr	24:24	Whoever w the wicked gets a black mark

Whitewashing

Nu	14:18	never just w sin
Pr	17:15	W bad people and throwing mud on good
Eze	13:15	those who did such a good job of w it

Wholehearted

Ne	5:13	Everyone gave a w "Yes, we'll do it!"

Wholeheartedly

2Ch	15:12	seek God, the God of their fathers, w
	25:2	wasn't w devoted to God
Ro	6:13	Throw yourselves w and full-time

Wholeness

Ps	37:37	There's a future in strenuous w
Isa	9:6	Eternal Father, Prince of W
	9:7	no limits to the w he brings
Hag	2:9	I will hand out w and holiness
Php	4:7	a sense of God's w

Whore

Ge	34:31	treat our sister like a w and get
	38:24	the w — and now she's a pregnant w
Lev	19:29	your daughter by making her a w
Dt	22:21	lived like a w while still
	23:18	don't bring the fee of a sacred w
Jdg	11:1	He was the son of a w
1Ki	11:5	Ashtoreth, the w goddess
	15:13	memorial to the w goddess Asherah
	16:33	shrine to the sacred w Asherah
	18:19	prophets of the w goddess Asherah
2Ki	17:16	for the w goddess Asherah
Pr	5:20	for cheap thrills with a w
	6:26	You can buy an hour with a w
	9:13	this other woman, Madame W
	22:14	The mouth of a w is a bottomless pit
	23:27	A w is a bottomless pit
	30:23	when a w is voted "woman of the year
Isa	1:21	The chaste city has become a w!
	23:15	the comeback of a worn-out w
	23:16	circle the city, unremembered w
	57:3	Sons of a slut, daughters of a w
Jer	2:20	on the way, like a common w
	3:2	Like a streetwalking w chasing
	3:6	as a w at large
	3:8	took up a w's life also
Eze	16:15	you became a common w
	16:20	bad enough that you had become a w
	16:30	the champion w
	16:35	w, listen to God's Message
	20:29	It's still called "W Hills
	23:7	She was a w to the Assyrian elite
	23:19	just starting out as a w
	23:29	your w's body exposed
	23:44	as men do when they're after a w
Hos	1:2	Find a w and marry her. Make this w
	2:2	to quit dressing like a w
	2:5	Your mother's been a w
	5:4	Every breath they take is a w's breath
	9:1	like a w sell yourself promiscuously
Joel	3:3	would trade a boy for a w
Am	2:7	sleeps with the 'sacred w'
	7:17	Your wife will become a w in town
Mic	1:7	earnings from her life as a w
Na	3:4	W City, Fatally seductive
	3:5	I'm your enemy, W Nineveh
Rev	17:1	the great W who sits enthroned

W

	17:2	W with whom the kings of the earth
	17:15	on which the W was enthroned
	17:16	the Beast, will turn on the W
	19:2	great W who corrupted the earth

Whored

Jer	3:1	'w' your way with god after god
Eze	23:30	because you w with pagan nations

Whoredom

Eze	16:34	You even pervert w

Whorehouse

Hos	1:2	This whole country has become a w
	2:4	children, born one and all in a w
	6:10	worshiping in a religious w
1Co	6:15	take the Master's body off to a w

Whorehouses

Eze	16:19	served them as delicacies in your w
	16:31	opened up your w in every neighborhood
Hos	4:14	men who worship at the holy w

Whores

1Ki	22:38	where the town w bathed
Ps	106:39	they lived like w
Pr	29:3	destroy their trust if you run with w
Isa	57:8	climbed into bed with the 'sacred' w
Jer	3:3	Brazen as w, you carry on
	5:7	went off with the 'sacred' w
Eze	16:31	different from regular w
	16:33	men commonly pay their w
	16:34	the regular w who get paid for sex
	20:28	trees where the sacred w practiced
	20:30	you've become w yourselves
	23:3	became w in Egypt, w from a young
	23:44	used . . . the worn-out w
Hos	4:10	for a life of rutting with w
	4:13	your daughters are w and
	4:14	who pick up the w that I'm after
	7:14	whoop it up in bed with their w
Na	3:4	And w! W without end! Whore City
Mt	21:31	crooks and w are going to precede you
	21:32	crooks and w believed him
Lk	15:30	thrown away your money on w
Rev	17:5	mother of w and abominations

Whoring

Nu	14:33	the fallout of your w unfaithfulness
Dt	31:16	w after the foreign gods
2Ki	9:22	w and sorceries of your mother Jezebel
Isa	23:17	She'll go back to her old w trade
Eze	16:25	went international with your w
	16:41	have put a full stop to your w life
	23:5	started w while she was still mine
	23:8	The w she began while young in Egypt

	23:11	worse than her sister in lust and w
	23:19	went at her w harder than ever
	23:27	the w life you began in Egypt
	23:35	pay for your sluttish sex and w life
	43:7	holy name through the mud with their w
	43:9	get rid of their w ways
Hos	2:12	bragged, 'W paid for all this!'
	3:3	No more w, no more sleeping around
	4:14	not going after your w daughters
	8:10	their w life among the pagans
Rev	2:23	bastard offspring of their idol-w
	14:8	nations drunk on the wine of her w
	17:2	kings of the earth have gone w
	18:3	drank the wild wine of her w
	18:3	kings of the earth went w

Wicked

Ex	23:1	Don't link up with a w person
	23:7	I don't let the w off the hook
Lev	18:17	her close relatives. That is w
	20:14	both a woman and her mother, that's w
1Sa	2:9	leaves the w to stumble in the dark
1Ki	8:47	we've done wrong; we've been most w
	14:22	Judah was openly w before God
2Ch	6:37	we've done wrong; we've been most w
	7:14	turning their backs on their w lives
	24:7	w Queen Athaliah and her sons
Job	3:17	Where the w no longer trouble anyone
	9:24	the w take over running the world
	10:3	blessing the plots of the w
	11:20	the w will see none of this
	16:11	lets w people do what they want
	18:5	The light of the w is put out
	20:5	good times of the w are short-lived
	20:29	That's God's blueprint for the w
	21:7	Why do the w have it so good
	21:17	often does it happen that the w fail
	21:28	achievements of the w collapse
	22:15	line that w men . . . have always used
	27:7	Let my enemy be exposed as w
	27:13	This is how God treats the w
	31:3	Isn't calamity reserved for the w
	34:12	impossible for God to do anything w
	34:20	Don't w rulers tumble to their doom
	34:26	punishes the w for their wickedness
	36:6	For the w . . . it's a different story
	36:17	laden with the guilt of the w
	38:13	shake out the w like cockroaches
	38:15	cover . . . is snatched from the w
	40:12	Stop the w in their tracks
Ps	1:4	the w, who are mere windblown dust
	5:4	don't socialize with W, or invite
	9:16	cunning machinery made by the w
	9:17	The w bought a one-way ticket to hell
	10:2	the w are hot on the trail of the poor
	10:3	The w are windbags
	10:4	The w snub God
	10:13	wonder why the w scorn God
	10:15	Break the w right arms
	11:2	the w arrows Aimed to shoot
	12:7	From the w who stalk us with lies
	12:8	From the w who collect honors

W

	17:9	From the w who are out to get me	12:21	the w have their hands full of it
	31:17	Embarrass the w	12:26	a w life invites disaster
	34:21	The w commit slow suicide	13:6	sin dumps the w in the ditch
	37:1	wish you could succeed like the w	13:9	lives of the w are dark alleys
	37:10	the w will have had it	13:25	the belly of the w always wants more
	37:16	One righteous will outclass fifty w	14:19	the w will respect God-loyal people
	37:17	the w are moral weaklings	15:28	the w are sewers of abuse
	37:21	W borrows and never returns	15:29	God keeps his distance from the w
	37:32	W sets a watch for Righteous	16:4	even the w are included
	37:33	W won't hurt a hair of his head	17:23	The w take bribes under the table
	37:34	while you watch the w lose it	19:28	the mouths of the w spew malice
	37:35	saw W bloated like a toad	21:4	distinguishing marks in the w
	39:1	as long as W is in the room	21:7	The w get buried alive by their loot
	50:16	Next, God calls up the w	21:10	W souls love to make trouble
	58:3	The w crawl from the wrong side	21:12	will see right through the w
	58:10	see the w get their reward	21:27	Religious performance by the w stinks
	68:2	one look at God and the w vanish	24:16	the w end up flat on their faces
	71:4	My God, free me from the grip of W	24:19	wish you could succeed like the w
	73:4	envying the w who have it made	24:24	Whoever whitewashes the w gets a black
	73:12	The w get by with everything	24:25	whoever exposes the w will be thanked
	75:8	Earth's w ones drink it all	25:5	Remove the w from leadership
	75:10	The fists of the w are bloody stumps	28:1	The w are edgy with guilt
	82:2	let the w get away with murder	28:3	The w who oppress the poor
	91:8	watch the w turn into corpses	28:15	the w lord it over the poor
	92:7	the w popped up like weeds	29:27	the w can't stand the sight of well-chosen
	94:3	God, the w get away with murder	Ecc 3:17	God will judge righteous and w
	94:13	a jail is being built for the w	8:10	saw w men given a solemn burial
	94:16	Who stood up for me against the w	8:14	Good people get what's coming to the w
	97:10	Snatches them from the grip of the w	9:2	fate for everybody — righteous and w
	101:7	rounded up all the w like cattle	Isa 3:11	But doom to the w! Disaster!
	112:10	Someone w takes one look and rages	9:18	Their w lives raged
	119:53	I see the w ignore your directions	11:4	will topple the w
	119:61	The w hemmed me in	13:11	terminate the dark acts of the w
	119:95	The w lie in ambush to destroy me	14:5	God has broken the rule of the w
	119:110	The w do their best to throw me off	14:21	slaughter the sons of the w
	119:119	reject earth's w as so much rubbish	26:10	If the w are shown grace
	119:155	Salvation" is only gibberish to the w	48:22	no peace," says God, "for the w
	125:3	The fist of the w will never violate	53:9	They buried him with the w
	140:4	out of the clutch of these w ones	55:7	Let the w abandon their way of life
	140:8	Don't let the w have their way, God	57:20	But the w are storm-battered seas
	141:10	Let the w fall flat on their faces	57:21	no peace," God says, "for the w
	146:9	makes short work of the w	Jer 4:4	Your w ways are fuel for the fire
	147:6	pushes the w into the ditch	5:26	My people are infiltrated by w men
Pr	3:33	God's curse blights the house of the w	9:7	can I do with a people this w
	4:14	Don't take W Bypass	12:4	because of wickedness, these w lives
	6:18	feet that race down a w track	13:10	w bunch of people who won't obey me
	10:3	frustrates the appetites of the w	15:21	deliver you from the grip of the w
	10:6	mouth of the w is a dark cave of abuse	18:8	if they repent of their w lives
	10:7	a w life leaves a rotten stench	20:13	saves the weak from the grip of the w
	10:11	mouth of the w is a dark cave of abuse	23:19	Spinning the heads of the w like tops
	10:20	blabber of the w is worthless	25:31	For the w the verdict is clear-cut
	10:24	The nightmares of the w come true	30:23	Spinning the heads of the w
	10:25	there's nothing left of the w	32:32	the w lives of the people of Israel
	10:27	a w life is a puny life	Eze 3:18	say to the w, 'You are going to die
	10:30	the w are here today, gone tomorrow	3:19	warn the w and they keep right on
	10:32	the words of the w pollute	18:20	if you live a w life, you're guilty
	11:7	When the w die, that's it	18:21	w person who turns his back on that
	11:21	The w won't get off scot-free	18:23	pleasure in the death of w men
	11:23	w ambition ends in angry frustration	18:24	obscenities that the w person
	12:6	The words of the w kill	21:3	killing both the w and the righteous
	12:7	W people fall to pieces	33:8	If I say to the w, 'W man, w woman
	12:12	What the w construct finally falls	33:9	warn the w to change their ways

W

	33:11	no pleasure from the death of the w
	33:11	I want the w to change their ways
	33:14	a w person, "You'll die for your w
	33:19	w person turns away from his w life
Da	4:27	Quit your w life
	12:10	w will just keep on being w
Hos	10:13	instead you plowed w ways
Hab	1:4	The w have the righteous hamstrung
	3:13	beat the stuffing out of King W
Zec	5:8	He said, "This is Miss W."
Mal	4:3	you'll tromp on the w
2Pe	2:9	hold the feet of the w to the fire

Wickedness

Lev	20:14	purging the w from the community
Dt	9:5	because of the vile w of these nations
Job	21:30	who never had to pay for their w
	34:26	punishes the wicked for their w
Ps	50:21	laying your w out in plain sight
	139:19	do away with w for good
Pr	18:3	When w arrives, shame's not far behind
Isa	59:6	They weave w, they hatch violence
Jer	6:7	she supplies w nonstop
	12:4	all because of w, these wicked lives
	23:14	Subsidizing a culture of w
Eze	5:6	ranged around her —sheer w
	14:3	embraced the w that will ruin them
	14:4	embrace the w that will ruin them
	14:7	install the w that will ruin them

Widow

Ge	38:8	sleep with your brother's w
	38:9	he slept with his brother's w
	38:11	Live as a w at home with your father
	38:14	She took off her w's clothes
	38:19	put her w's clothes back on
Lev	21:14	not a w, not a divorcee
Nu	30:9	Any vow or pledge taken by a w
Dt	14:29	the orphan, and the w who live
	16:11	the orphan and w among you
	24:17	cloak of a w as security for a loan
	24:19	the orphan, and the w so that God
	24:20	the foreigner, the orphan, and the w
	24:21	the foreigner, the orphan, and the w
	25:5	w of the dead brother shall not marry
	26:12	the foreigner, the orphan, and the w
	26:13	foreigner, orphan, and w
	27:19	due the foreigner, orphan, or w
Ru	4:3	being sold by his w Naomi
	4:5	Ruth ..., the w of our dead relative
	4:10	Ruth the foreigner, the w of Mahlon
1Sa	27:3	Abigail, w of Nabal of Carmel
	30:5	Abigail w of Nabal of Carmel
2Sa	2:2	Abigail the w of Nabal of Carmel
	3:3	Abigail of Carmel, Nabal's w
	14:5	"I'm a w," she said
1Ki	7:14	Hiram's mother was a w
	11:26	his mother a w named Zeruah
	17:9	instructed . . . a w, to feed you
	17:10	met a woman, a w, gathering firewood

	17:20	this w who has opened her home to me
Ps	109:9	dress his wife in w's weeds
Isa	47:8	I'll never be a w
	54:4	indignities of being a w will fade
La	1:1	A w, this city, once in the front rank
Mt	22:24	brother is obligated to marry his w
Mk	12:19	brother is obligated to marry the w
	12:42	One poor w . . . put in two small coins
	12:43	this poor w gave more
Lk	2:37	and a w for eighty-four
	4:26	the only w to whom Elijah was sent
	7:12	the mother was a w
	18:3	A w in that city kept after him
	18:5	this w won't quit badgering me
	20:28	brother is obligated to take the w
	21:2	saw a poor w put in two pennies
	21:3	this w has given by far the largest
1Ti	5:4	If a w has family members to take
	5:5	tell a legitimate w by the way
	5:6	a w who exploits people's emotions
Rev	18:7	I'm queen over all, and no w

Widowed

Lev	22:13	if the priest's daughter is w
Jer	18:21	Let their wives be childless and w
	51:5	Israel and Judah are not w after all

Widows

Ex	22:22	Don't mistreat w or orphans
	22:24	your wives will end up w
Dt	10:18	orphans and w are treated fairly
	16:14	w who live in your neighborhood
2Sa	20:3	w as long as they lived
Job	22:9	turned poor w away from your door
	27:15	none of the w will shed a tear
Ps	68:5	Father of orphans, champion of w
	78:64	their w never shed a tear
	146:9	takes the side of orphans and w
Isa	9:17	no feeling for their orphans and w
	10:2	Exploiting defenseless w
Jer	7:6	street people and orphans and w
	15:8	I created more w among you
	22:3	the homeless, the orphans, the w
	49:11	Your w can depend on me
La	5:3	our mothers no better than w
Eze	22:7	oppressive against orphans and w
	22:25	leaving w in their wake
	44:22	Priests are not to marry w
Zec	7:10	Don't take advantage of w
Mal	3:5	who take advantage of w and orphans
Lk	4:25	there were many w in Israel
Ac	6:1	w were being discriminated against
	9:39	Her old friends, most of them w
	9:40	Peter put the w all out of the room
	9:41	he called in the believers and w
1Co	7:8	the unmarried and w that singleness
1Ti	5:3	Take care of w who are destitute
	5:9	Sign some w up for the special
	5:11	Don't put young w on this list
	5:14	I'd rather the young w . . . get married
	5:16	woman who has w in her family

Willful

Dt	31:27	how stubborn and **w** you can be
1Ki	15:5	**w** defiance of God's clear directions
Ps	37:38	the **w** will soon be discarded
Isa	1:20	if you're **w** and stubborn, you'll die
	8:14	Rock standing in the **w** way of both
	57:17	kept at his stubborn, **w** ways
La	3:42	We've been contrary and **w**
Eze	5:7	been more headstrong and **w** than any
Jas	4:6	God goes against the **w** proud

Willfully

Dt	10:16	stop being so **w** hardheaded
	30:17	refuse to listen obediently, and **w** go
Isa	42:19	blind as a bat — **w** blind
Mt	15:16	Are you being **w** stupid
Mk	7:10	Are you being **w** stupid?
Jn	12:48	is **w** choosing rejection

Windbag

Job	15:2	so much like a **w**, belching hot air
	16:3	Is there no end to your **w** speeches
Isa	5:15	**W** boasters crumpled, flaccid
Jer	2:5	Took up with Sir **W** and turned

Windbags

Nu	24:17	the skulls of all the noisy **w**
Ps	10:3	The wicked are **w**
Jer	2:5	turned into **w** themselves
	5:13	The prophets are all **w**
Ro	1:30	Bullies, swaggerers, insufferable **w**
1Ti	6:4	ignorant **w** who infect the air
2Ti	3:4	treacherous, ruthless, bloated **w**

Wisdom

Ge	41:39	qualified as you in experience and **w**
Dt	34:9	filled with the spirit of **w**
1Ki	3:28	was God's **w** that enabled him to judge
	4:29	God gave Solomon **w**
	4:30	Solomon's **w** outclassed the vaunted **w**
	4:34	to listen to the **w** of Solomon
	5:12	God, for his part, gave Solomon **w**
	10:4	experienced for herself Solomon's **w**
	10:6	reputation for accomplishment and **w**
	10:7	Such **w** and elegance
	10:24	drink in the **w** God had given him
	11:41	life and rule, his work and his **w**
2Ch	1:10	give me **w** and knowledge
	1:11	You asked for **w** and knowledge
	1:12	what you asked for — **w** and knowledge
	9:3	experienced for herself Solomon's **w**
	9:5	reputation for accomplishment and **w**
	9:6	Such **w** and elegance
	9:23	get in on the **w** God had given him
Ezr	7:25	exercising the **w** of God that you have
Job	9:4	God's **w** is so deep
	11:6	how **w** looks . . . , for true **w**

	12:12	think the elderly have a corner on **w**
	12:13	True **w** and real power belong to God
	12:20	deprives . . . of their good sense and **w**
	13:5	silence is your only claim to **w**
	13:12	Your wise sayings are knickknack **w**
	17:10	haven't come across one scrap of **w**
	26:12	by his **w** he tames sea monsters
	28:12	where, oh where, will they find **W**
	28:18	None of this is . . . **W**
	28:19	can't hold a candle to **W**
	28:20	So where does **W** come from
	28:23	God alone knows the way to **W**
	28:27	focused on **W**, made sure it was all set
	28:28	Fear-of-the-Lord — that's **W**
	32:9	The experts have no corner on **w**
	33:33	going to teach you the basics of **w**
	35:11	using birds and beasts to teach **w**
	38:36	gave weather **w** to the ibis
Ps	5:10	Let their so-called **w** wreck them
	37:30	Righteous chews on **w** like a dog
	49:3	I set plainspoken **w** before you
	104:24	with **W** at your side
	105:22	and train his advisors in **w**
	119:15	I ponder every morsel of **w** from you
	119:26	train me well in your deep **w**
	119:36	Give me a bent for your words of **w**
	119:45	I look for your truth and your **w**
	119:73	now breathe your **w** over me
	119:94	look high and low for your words of **w**
Pr	1:6	Fresh **w** to probe and penetrate
	1:7	fools thumb their noses at such **w**
	1:20	**W** goes out in the street and shouts
	2:2	Tune your ears to the world of **W**
	2:6	God gives out **W** free
	2:10	Lady **W** will be your close friend
	3:13	You're blessed when you meet Lady **W**
	3:19	With Lady **W**, God formed Earth
	4:5	Sell everything and buy **W**!
	4:6	Never walk away from **W** — she guards
	4:7	do this: Get **W**!
	4:11	clear directions to **W** Way
	5:1	pay close attention to this, my **w**
	7:4	Talk to **W** as to a sister
	8:1	Do you hear Lady **W** calling?
	8:11	**W** is better than all the trappings
	8:12	I am Lady **W**, and I live next to Sanity
	9:1	**W** has built and furnished her home
	9:3	Lady **W** goes to town
	9:11	through me, Lady **W**, that your life
	9:12	Live wisely and **w** will permeate
	10:13	**w** on the lips of a person of insight
	10:23	a mindful person relishes **w**
	10:31	mouth is a clear fountain of **w**
	14:1	Lady **W** builds a lovely home
	14:6	Cynics look high and low for **w**
	14:8	**w** of the wise keeps life on track
	14:24	The wise accumulate **w**
	14:33	**W** is at home in an understanding heart
	16:16	Get **w** — it's worth more than money
	17:16	Fools out shopping for **w**!
	17:24	find **w** in their own front yard
	18:4	deep **w** flows up from artesian springs

W

	22:17	Listen carefully to my w
	23:23	buy w, buy education, buy insight
	24:3	It takes w to build a house
	24:14	knowledge, and w for your soul
	28:7	get a reputation for w
	28:26	survivors learn w from others
	29:3	love w, you'll delight your parents
	29:15	Wise discipline imparts w
	30:3	I flunked 'w.' I see no evidence
Ecc	1:16	I've stockpiled w and knowledge
	1:17	so-called w and knowledge are mindless
	2:3	all the w I could muster
	2:26	God may give w and knowledge
	4:13	A poor youngster with some w
	7:11	W is better . . . with money
	7:12	w and wealth! Plus this bonus: W
	7:19	W puts more strength in one wise
	7:23	tested everything in my search for w
	7:25	seeking w—the meaning of life
	7:28	the w I've looked for I haven't found
	8:1	W puts light in the eyes
	8:16	determined to load up on w
	9:13	observing how w fares on this earth
	9:15	whose w saved the town
	9:16	w is better than muscle
	9:18	W is better than warheads
	10:1	a little foolishness decomposes much w
Isa	11:2	Spirit that brings w and understanding
	19:11	descended from the old w of Egypt
	33:6	salvation, w, and knowledge
Jer	3:15	rule you with intelligence and w
	9:23	Don't let the wise brag of their w
	10:12	whose w gave shape to the world
	49:7	Has their w gone wormy and rotten
	51:15	His w gave shape to the world
Eze	28:17	corrupted w by using it to get
Da	5:11	brilliance and spiritual w
Mt	12:42	W far greater than Solomon's
Lk	11:32	W far greater than Solomon's
	11:49	That accounts for God's W saying
	21:15	I'll give you the words and w
Ac	6:10	were no match for his w
	15:21	This is basic w from Moses
Ro	11:33	generosity of God, this deep, deep w
1Co	1:19	I'll turn conventional w on its head
	1:21	the world in all its fancy w never
	1:22	Greeks go in for philosophical w
	1:24	Christ is God's ultimate miracle and w
	1:25	Human w is so tinny, so impotent
	2:6	plenty of w to pass on to you
	2:7	God's w is something mysterious
	3:19	that's the path to true w
Col	2:3	All the richest treasures of w
Tit	2:2	lives of temperance, dignity, and w
Jas	3:13	to build a reputation for w
	3:14	Mean-spirited ambition isn't w
	3:15	It's the furthest thing from w
	3:17	Real w, God's w, begins with
2Pe	3:15	Paul, who was given much w
Rev	5:12	Take the power, the wealth, the w
	7:12	glory and w and thanksgiving

Wise

Ge	41:33	look for a w and experienced man
Ex	7:11	Pharaoh called in his w men
	8:26	Moses said, "That would not be w
Dt	1:13	select some w, understanding . . . men
	1:15	top men of your tribes, w and seasoned
	4:6	You'll become w and understanding
	16:19	a bribe blinds even a w person
2Sa	14:2	he sent to Tekoa for a w woman
	14:20	my master is as w as God's angels
1Ki	2:9	You're w, you know how to handle
	3:12	I'm giving you a w and mature heart
	4:30	vaunted wisdom of w men of the East
	5:7	w son to rule this flourishing people
	10:8	hear your w words firsthand
1Ch	27:32	a w and literate counselor
2Ch	2:12	who gave King David a son so w
	9:7	hear your w words firsthand
Ezr	8:18	brought back to us a w man
	8:21	pray for w guidance for our journey
Job	11:12	Hollow men, hollow women, will w up
	13:12	Your w sayings are knickknack wisdom
	15:2	If you were truly w, would you sound
	15:18	what w men and women have . . . taught
	32:8	makes w human insight possible
	34:34	the w who have listened to me concur
	37:24	If you're w, you'll . . . worship him
Ps	16:7	w counsel God gives when I'm awake
	49:4	tuned my ear to the sayings of the w
	72:1	Give the gift of w rule to the king
	107:43	If you are really w, you'll think
	119:12	train me in your ways of w living
	119:23	absorbed in pondering your w counsel
	119:79	evidence of your w guidance
	119:93	saved my life with those w words
	119:100	become wiser than the w old sages
Pr	1:1	These are the w sayings of Solomon
	1:6	reasons of w men and women
	2:16	W friends will rescue you
	3:35	W living gets rewarded with honor
	9:9	Save your breath for the w
	10:1	W son, glad father
	10:8	A w heart takes orders
	10:14	The w accumulate knowledge
	10:19	the w measure their words
	11:14	more w counsel you follow, the better
	12:15	w people take advice
	12:18	healing in the words of the w
	13:10	w men and women listen to each other
	13:14	The teaching of the w is a fountain
	13:20	Become w by walking with the w
	14:3	w speech evokes nothing but respect
	14:8	wisdom of the w keeps life on track
	14:16	The w watch their steps and avoid evil
	14:18	w realists plant their feet
	14:24	The w accumulate wisdom
	15:2	flows like spring water from the w
	15:12	avoid the company of w men and women
	15:31	honored guest among w men and women
	16:21	A w person gets known for insight
	16:23	make a lot of sense, these w folks

W

	17:2	A w servant takes charge of
	17:28	who keep quiet are thought to be w
	18:15	W men and women are always learning
	19:8	Grow a w heart
	20:5	a w person draws from the well within
	20:26	w leader makes a clean sweep of rebels
	21:11	the w learn by listening
	21:20	safe in a w person's home
	23:15	Dear child, if you become w
	23:19	dear child — become w
	23:24	w children become proud parents
	24:5	It's better to be w than strong
	24:7	W conversation is way over the head
	25:12	a w friend's timely reprimand is
	27:11	Become w, dear child
	29:15	W discipline imparts wisdom
	30:24	creatures, wisest of the w they are
Ecc	2:15	So why bother being w?
	7:7	Brutality stupefies even the w
	7:10	W folks don't ask questions like that
	7:16	don't go overboard being w
	7:19	more strength in one w person
	7:23	set out to be w, but it was beyond me
	8:1	nothing better than being w
	8:5	the w person obeys promptly
	9:1	good, the w, and all that they do
	9:11	Nor satisfaction to the w
	9:15	a poor but w man in that town
	9:16	w poor man was treated with contempt
	9:17	words of the w are more effective
	10:2	W thinking leads to right living
	10:12	words of a w person are gracious
	12:9	Besides being w himself, the Quester
	12:11	words of the w prod us to live well
Isa	1:26	set honest judges and w counselors
	19:11	Trust me: I'm w
	19:12	There's not a w man or woman left
	29:14	The w ones who had it all figured out
	31:2	a most w God who knows what he's doing
Jer	9:23	Don't let the w brag of their wisdom
	18:18	w counselors to give us advice
	49:7	nobody w left in famous Teman
	50:35	war against people, leaders, and the w
La	5:14	The city gate is empty of w elders
Da	2:12	company of Babylonian w men killed
	2:18	whole company of Babylonian w men
	2:23	You made me w and strong
	2:27	no w man, enchanter, magician
	2:48	in charge of all the Babylonian w men
	4:6	sent for all the w men of Babylon
	4:18	None of the w men of Babylon could
	5:14	that you are incredibly w
	5:15	The w men and enchanters were brought
Ob	1:8	its famous w men
Mt	12:42	to listen to w Solomon
	13:54	How did he get so w
	23:34	I send prophets and w guides
Mk	6:2	How did he get so w all of a sudden
Lk	2:40	grew strong in body and w in spirit
	11:32	to listen to w Solomon
Ac	24:2	your w and gentle rule
Ro	16:27	this incomparably w God

1Co	1:20	where can you find someone truly w
	3:18	Don't think that you can be w merely
	12:8	w counsel clear understanding
Col	1:9	asking God to give you w minds
Tit	1:8	be helpful, w, fair, reverent
Jas	3:13	Do you want to be counted w
	3:14	Boasting that you are w isn't wisdom

Wisely

Dt	29:9	live well and w in every detail
Ne	9:20	good Spirit to teach them to live w
Ps	73:24	You w and tenderly lead me
	78:72	guided the people w and well
	90:12	Teach us to live w and well
Pr	8:33	Mark a life of discipline and live w
	9:12	Live w and wisdom will permeate
	19:20	the way to live w and well
Da	2:14	Daniel w took him aside
	12:3	who have lived w and well
	12:10	Those who live w and well
Gal	5:23	direct our energies w
Jas	3:13	Live well, live w, live humbly

Wiser

1Ki	4:31	He was w than anyone
	4:31	w than Ethan the Ezrahite, w than
	10:23	King Solomon was w and richer
2Ch	9:22	King Solomon was richer and w
Job	4:21	are never the w for having lived
	32:7	The longer you live, the w you become
Ps	119:100	I've become w than the wise old sages
Pr	9:9	they'll be w for it
Ecc	1:10	I'm w than anyone before me

Wisest

Jdg	5:29	w of her ladies-in-waiting answers
Pr	30:24	creatures, w of the wise they are

Wish

Ge	20:15	live wherever you w
Nu	20:3	We w we'd died when the rest
Dt	12:8	each of us doing as we w
	28:67	you'll say, "I w it were evening."
1Ki	5:8	your w is my command
Est	9:12	Your w is my command
Job	9:33	How I w we had an arbitrator
	10:18	I w no one had ever laid eyes on me
	10:19	I w I'd never lived—a stillborn
	11:5	I w God would give you a piece
	11:6	I w he'd show you how wisdom looks
	13:5	I w you'd shut your mouths
Ps	37:1	w you could succeed like the wicked
Pr	3:15	nothing you could w for holds
	8:11	nothing you could w for holds
	19:7	your best friends w you'd get lost
	20:25	you'll w you could get out of it
	24:19	w you could succeed like the wicked
SS	8:1	I w you'd been my twin brother

Jer	2:3	would soon w he hadn't
	8:3	will w they were dead
	9:1	I w my head were a well of water
	9:2	I w I had a wilderness hut
	40:4	Go and live wherever you w
Da	4:19	I w this dream were about your enemies
Mic	4:5	other people live however they w
Zec	13:4	they'll w they'd never swindled people
Mt	18:6	you'll soon w you hadn't
Mk	6:26	let her have her w
	9:42	you'll soon w you hadn't
Lk	4:6	turn them over to whomever I w
	12:49	how I w it were blazing right now
1Co	7:7	Sometimes I w everyone were single

Wished

2Sa	3:34	free to go and do as you w
Jn	21:18	went wherever you w
Ac	5:4	money was yours to do with as you w

Wishes

Dt	21:14	let her go and live wherever she w
	23:16	Let him live wherever he w
Ps	20:5	May all your w come true
Da	4:17	arranges kingdom affairs however he w
	4:32	puts whomever he w in charge

Wishing

Ps	41:5	My enemies are w the worst for me
1Co	7:17	don't be w you were someplace else
Gal	4:20	I keep w that I was with you
2Pe	1:16	We weren't . . . just w on a star

Wishy-washy

2Co	10:1	painted as cringing and w

Witless

Job	12:17	exposes judges as w fools
Pr	12:11	the w chase whims and fancies
Ecc	1:17	wisdom and knowledge are . . . w

Witness

Ge	31:44	God will be the w between us
	31:47	Yegar-sahadutha (W Monument)
	31:48	This monument of stones will be a w
	31:50	God will see you and stand w
	31:51	pillar that I have set up is a w
	31:52	w that I won't cross this line
Ex	22:10	injured or lost and there is no w
Lev	5:1	offering yourself as a w
Nu	5:13	even though there was no w
Dt	19:15	crime or sin on the word of one w
	19:16	If a hostile w stands to accuse
	19:18	if the w turns out to be a false w
	30:19	call Heaven and Earth to w against you
	31:19	have it then as my w against them

	31:21	with them as a w to who they are
	31:26	Keep it there as a w
	32:46	these words to which I give w today
Jos	22:27	built this altar as a w between us
	22:28	It's a w connecting us with you
	22:34	named the altar: A W Between Us
	24:27	This stone is a w against us
Jdg	11:10	God is between us
1Sa	12:5	God is w, and his anointed is w
	12:6	the people said, "He is w."
	20:12	As God, the God of Israel, is my w
2Sa	19:13	As God is my w, I'm making you
1Ki	11:36	maintain a w to my servant David
2Ki	10:16	w my zeal for God
Job	13:10	if he detected a bias in your w
	16:8	a mute w to your treatment of me
Ps	72:3	Let the mountains give exuberant w
	78:5	He planted a w in Jacob
	78:35	gave w that God was their rock
	135:5	I too give w to the greatness of God
Pr	12:17	Truthful w by a good person clears
	14:5	A true w never lies
	14:5	a false w makes a business of it
	14:25	Souls are saved by truthful w
	19:28	unprincipled w desecrates justice
	21:28	A lying w is unconvincing
Isa	8:2	to w the document
	38:18	Those buried . . . don't w to
	55:4	set him up as a w to the nations
Jer	42:5	Let God be our w
	42:5	a true and faithful w against us
Am	3:13	bring w against Jacob's family
	8:14	As the lord god of Da is my w
Mic	1:2	God, takes the w stand against you
Hab	2:3	a w pointing to what's coming
Mal	2:14	God was there as a w when you spoke
Mt	8:4	will bear w to what I have done
	23:18	raise your hand that God is your w
	24:14	a w staked out in every country
Mk	13:11	the Holy Spirit will make his w
Lk	5:14	will bear w to what I have done
	21:13	You'll end up on the w stand
Jn	1:32	John clinched his w with this
	1:40	heard John's w and followed Jesus
	3:11	I give w only to what I have seen
	3:26	The one you authorized with your w
	4:39	because of the woman's w
	5:31	an empty, self-serving w
	5:32	But an independent w confirms me
	5:32	the most reliable W
	5:36	the w that really confirms me
	17:20	Because of them and their w about me
	18:37	so that I could w to the truth
Ac	1:22	as a w to his resurrection
	2:32	every one of us here is a w to it
	4:33	gave powerful w to the resurrection
	8:25	to w and spread the Message of God
	10:42	solemn w that he is in fact the One
	10:43	Our w that he is the means to
	13:31	continue to give w that he is alive
	22:15	You are to be a key w to everyone
	22:20	when your w Stephen was murdered

W

	23:11	You've been a good w for me
	26:16	handpicked you to be a servant and w
2Co	1:23	As God is my w, the only reason
	11:10	With Christ as my w
Rev	1:2	God's Word — the w of Jesus Christ
	1:5	Jesus Christ — Loyal W, Firstborn
	1:9	God's Word, the w of Jesus
	2:13	Antipas, my w who stayed faithful
	3:14	the Faithful and Accurate W
	6:9	held firm in their w to the Word
	11:7	When they've completed their w
	12:11	the bold word of their w
	12:17	hold firm to the w of Jesus
	15:5	the Tent of W in Heaven
	19:10	hold to the w of Jesus. The w of Jesus
	20:4	beheaded because of their w to Jesus

Witnessed

Ge	23:18	town council . . . w the transaction
Dt	28:67	because of the sights you've w
Jer	29:23	I've w it all
Lk	19:37	all the mighty works they had w
Ro	3:21	What Moses and the prophets w to
1Jn	1:2	what we w was

Witnesses

Ge	23:9	price for a burial plot, with you as w
	23:11	With my people as w, I give it to you
Dt	4:26	with Heaven and Earth as w
	17:6	on the testimony of two or three w
	17:7	The w must throw the first stones
	19:15	two or three w to make a case
	31:28	with Heaven and Earth as w
Jos	24:22	You are w against yourselves
Ru	4:9	You are w today that I have bought
	4:10	To all this you are w this very day
	4:11	said, "Yes, we are w
Job	10:17	You line up fresh w against me
Ps	92:15	Such w to upright God!
Isa	43:9	Let them present their expert w
	43:10	But you are my w
	43:12	you're my w, you're the evidence
Jer	6:18	the nations as w: 'Watch, w
	32:10	In the presence of w I wrote
	32:12	the w who had signed the deed
	32:25	make sure there are w
	32:44	sealed documents, proper w
Mt	5:12	My prophets and w have always gotten
	18:16	presence of w will keep things honest
	26:65	Why do we need w to accuse him?
Mk	14:63	After that do we need w
Lk	6:23	my preachers and w have always been
	24:48	You're the w
Jn	8:17	count on the testimony of two w
Ac	1:8	you will be able to be my w
	3:15	from the dead — and we're the w
	5:32	we are w to these things
	6:13	put forward their bribed w to testify
	10:41	W had been carefully handpicked by God
	24:13	backed up with evidence or w

Ro	9:2	Christ and the Holy Spirit are my w
2Co	13:1	after two or three w give evidence
1Ti	5:19	two or three responsible w
	6:12	in the presence of so many w
Rev	11:3	I'll provide my two W

Wits

Jer	4:22	A company of half-w, dopes and
	12:5	if you can't keep your w during times
	46:5	They're scared out of their w
	48:6	Survive by your w in the wild
Da	5:6	white as a ghost, scared out of his w
Mt	14:26	They were scared out of their w
Mk	6:49	screamed, scared out of their w
Lk	16:8	surviving by their w
	21:36	the strength and w to make it through
2Co	1:9	trusting in our own strength or w

Wizard

Ac	8:10	called him "the Great W
	13:6	at Paphos came upon a Jewish w
	13:7	The w's name was Bar-Jesus
	13:8	that's the w's name in plain English

Worker

1Ki	7:14	a master w in bronze
	11:28	observed what a good w he was
Ezr	7:24	any other w connected with The Temple
Mal	1:6	honors his father and a w his master
Lk	10:7	a w deserves three square meals
	16:13	No w can serve two bosses
Ro	4:4	If you're a hard w and do a good job
	16:6	What a w she has turned out to be
	16:12	a dear friend and hard w in Christ
1Co	12:29	not all Prophet, not all Miracle W
Col	1:7	He is one reliable w for Christ
1Ti	5:18	A w deserves his pay

Workers

Ex	5:19	having to go back and tell their w
	9:20	got their w and animals under cover
	9:21	left their w and animals out
	23:12	w may . . . get their needed rest
Lev	25:45	buy the children of foreign w
Ru	2:21	Stick with my w until my harvesting
1Sa	8:16	prize w and best animals he'll take
1Ki	5:15	unskilled w and another
	5:18	Hiram's construction w
2Ki	12:11	pay the carpenters, construction w
	22:5	w who are repairing God's Temple
	22:6	carpenters, construction w, and masons
	22:9	to the foremen to pay The Temple w
1Ch	4:21	the family of linen w at Beth Ashbea
	22:15	w both plentiful and prepared
	27:26	in charge of the field w on the farms
2Ch	2:8	I'll send w to join your crews
	24:13	w kept at their jobs steadily
	34:11	on to the w repairing God's Temple

W

	34:13	supervised the w as they went
	34:17	handed it over to the managers and w
Ezr	3:10	When the w laid the foundation
Job	24:10	even the hard w go hungry
Ps	94:16	Who took my side against evil w
Pr	19:10	any more than w should give orders
	21:15	for the w of evil it's a bad day
	22:29	skilled w are always in demand
	29:12	all the w get infected with evil
	29:19	takes more than talk to keep w in line
	30:10	on your fellow w behind their backs
Isa	19:9	Textile w will be out of work
	24:2	owners and w alike
	45:14	The w of Egypt, the merchants
Jer	22:13	Who cheats his w and won't pay them
	25:30	shouting hurrahs like w in harvest
Eze	48:19	W from all the tribes of Israel
Mal	3:5	those who exploit w
Mt	9:37	How few w
	10:25	what can the w expect
	20:1	to hire w for his vineyard
	20:8	Call the w in and pay them their wages
	20:12	last w put in only one easy hour
	24:45	feed the w on time each day
Ac	19:25	rounded up his w and others
1Co	12:28	teachers miracle w healers
	16:16	w who show us how to do it
2Co	11:13	lying preachers, crooked w
Tit	2:9	Guide slaves into being loyal w
Jas	5:4	the w you've exploited and cheated

Workforce

1Ki	5:13	Solomon raised a w of 30,000 men
	9:23	550 of them in charge of the w
	11:28	in charge of the entire w
	12:18	Adoniram, head of the w
2Ch	2:2	3,600 foremen to manage the w
	8:10	250 in all in charge of the w
	10:18	Adoniram, head of the w
Zec	10:5	They'll be a w to be proud of

Workplace

Pr	16:11	God cares about honesty in the w
Isa	58:6	get rid of exploitation in the w
Heb	13:16	take place in kitchen and w

Workplaces

Dt	28:8	a blessing on your barns and w
Am	5:16	Empty offices, stores, factories, w

Worried

Ge	38:11	w that Shelah would also end up dead
Jdg	3:25	They waited. And then they w
1Sa	4:13	extremely w about the Chest of God
	10:2	is w about you
2Sa	6:22	these maids you're so w about
Ps	127:2	work your w fingers to the bone
Ecc	4:6	better than two fistfuls of w work

Isa	7:16	those two kings that have you so w
Hab	3:7	I saw everyone w, in a panic
Mt	16:8	Why all these w whispers
Mk	16:3	They w out loud to each other
Ac	21:22	We're w about what will happen
2Co	2:13	W about you, I left
1Jn	3:20	God is greater than our w hearts

Worries

Ps	41:2	we're free from enemy w
Isa	8:12	Don't take on their w
	31:4	gnaws and chews and w its prey
Na	1:15	No more w about this enemy
Mk	4:19	are overwhelmed with w
Php	4:6	shape your w into prayers

Worry

Ge	15:4	Don't w, he won't be your heir
	43:23	Everything's in order. Don't w
	45:20	Don't w about having to leave things
Ex	34:24	won't have to w about your land
Dt	31:8	Don't be intimidated. Don't w
Jos	11:6	said to Josua: "Don't w about them
Ru	2:9	don't w about a thing
	3:11	don't you w about a thing
1Sa	9:20	have been found, so don't w about them
	10:16	Saul said, "He told us not to w
1Ki	17:13	Don't w about a thing. Go ahead
2Ki	6:16	Don't w about it — there are more
	8:10	Don't w; you'll live
	8:14	told me, 'Don't w; you'll live
Job	19:29	Start worrying about yourselves. W
Ps	73:5	Who have nothing to w about
Pr	3:24	take afternoon naps without a w
	12:25	W weighs us down
	31:21	She doesn't w about her family
SS	8:8	My brothers used to w about me
Isa	8:13	If you're going to w, w about The Holy
	14:30	The poor won't have to w
	37:33	Don't w, he won't enter this city
	44:8	Don't be afraid, and don't w
Jer	4:10	All is well, don't w
	14:13	there's nothing to w about
	17:8	Never a w through the hottest
	28:9	there's nothing to w about
	45:5	don't w. I'll keep you alive
	46:27	there's no need to w. Look up!
	49:23	they pace back and forth in w
Eze	7:12	Buyer, don't crow; seller, don't w
Mic	5:5	don't w. We'll put him in his place
Mt	6:33	Don't w about missing out
	10:19	don't w about what you'll say
	13:22	weeds of w and illusions
Mk	13:11	don't w about what you'll say
Lk	12:11	don't w about defending yourselves
	21:14	Make up your mind . . . not to w
	23:43	Don't w, I will. Today you will join
Jn	14:30	don't w — he has nothing on me
1Co	10:30	can I w about what someone will say
2Co	7:7	I went from w to tranquility

W

	12:14	But don't w about it
Php	4:6	Don't fret or w
	4:7	what happens when Christ displaces w
2Th	2:8	don't w. The Master Jesus will be
1Ti	5:23	don't w too much about what
Jas	1:6	People who "w their prayers"
1Jn	4:17	free of w on Judgment Day

Worrying

1Sa	9:5	start w about us
Job	19:29	Forget it. Start w about yourselves
Eze	4:16	w where the next meal's coming from
Da	12:13	without fretting or w. Relax
Lk	8:14	go about their lives w about tomorrow
1Co	10:29	w about what small-minded people
	10:31	not w about what others say about you
Php	4:6	Instead of w, pray
1Th	3:5	That's why I couldn't quit w

Worship

Ge	22:5	going over there to w
	24:26	the man bowed in w before God
	24:48	bowed in w to God
	24:52	he bowed in w before God
Ex	3:12	you will w God right here
	3:18	wilderness where we will w God
	5:3	the wilderness we can w our God
	5:8	Give us time off so we can w our God
	5:17	Let us go so we can w God
	7:16	they can w me in the wilderness
	8:1	Release my people so they can w me
	8:8	make their sacrifices and w God
	8:20	Release my people so they can w me
	9:1	Release my people so they can w me
	9:13	Release my people so they can w me
	10:3	Release my people so that they can w
	10:7	Let these people go and w their God
	10:8	Go ahead then. Go w your God
	10:9	this is our w-celebration of God
	10:11	go ahead and w God
	10:24	Go and w God. Leave your flocks
	10:25	sacrifice them in w to our God
	10:26	they are part of the w of our God
	12:31	Go w God on your own terms
	20:24	cause my name to be honored in your w
	23:24	don't w or serve their gods
	24:1	They will w from a distance
	33:10	then bow down in w
	34:14	Don't w any other god
	35:21	furnishing it for w
	36:1	involved in the w of the Sanctuary
Lev	26:1	bow down to in w. I am God
Nu	3:31	articles of the Sanctuary used in w
	3:38	and the rituals of w
	24:4	Who falls on his face in w
	24:16	who bows in w and sees what's real
	25:2	to their sex-and-religion w
	25:3	ended up joining in the w of the Baal
	25:5	who joined in the w of Baal Peor
	28:18	Begin the first day in holy w

	28:25	Conclude the seventh day in holy w
	28:26	gather in holy w
	29:1	in holy w and do no regular work
	29:7	gather in holy w
	29:12	Gather in holy w on the fifteenth
	29:35	Gather in holy w; do no regular work
	33:52	level their w-mounds
Dt	4:28	you can w your homemade gods
	6:13	Serve and w him exclusively
	7:16	don't w their gods
	12:2	driving out w of their gods
	12:4	contaminate the w of God
	13:2	let's w them
	13:6	Let's go and w some other gods
	13:13	Let's go and w other gods
	14:23	at the place he designates for w
	14:24	the place God . . . designates for w
	15:20	the place that God designates for w
	16:6	God, your God, designates for w
	17:3	going off to w other gods
	17:8	place of w that God . . . has designated
	18:6	the place God designates for w
	26:2	God, sets apart for you to w him
	28:36	there you'll w other gods, no-gods
	28:64	You'll w all kinds of other gods
	30:17	go off to serve and w other gods
	33:19	offer sacrifices of right w
Jos	22:27	where we w God in his Sacred Dwelling
	23:7	don't w or pray to them
	23:16	go off and serve and w other gods
	24:14	Fear God. W him in total commitment
	24:15	decide that it's a bad thing to w God
	24:16	We'd never leave God to w other gods
	24:18	We too are going to w God
	24:19	you're not able to w God
	24:20	take up the w of foreign gods
	24:21	No! No! We w God
	24:22	chosen God for yourselves — to w him
	24:24	We will w God. What he says, we'll do
1Sa	1:3	to Shiloh to w and offer a sacrifice
	1:21	annual trip to Shiloh to w God
	2:29	offerings that I commanded for my w
	7:3	ground yourselves firmly in God, w him
	10:3	three men going up to w God
	10:8	I'll come down and join you in w
	12:14	If you fear God, w and obey him
	12:20	don't turn your back on God. W and
	12:24	fear God and w him honestly
	15:12	Saul had just finished an act of w
	15:25	lead me to the altar so I can w God
	15:30	alongside me as I go back to w God
	16:5	lead you in the w of God
	20:6	w with his family
1Ki	3:4	prestigious of the local shrines, to w
	10:5	the elaborate w extravagant with
	12:27	As soon as these people resume w
	12:28	to go to Jerusalem to w
	12:30	all the way to Da to w a calf
	12:32	complete with w offered on the Altar
	12:33	leading the w at the Altar
	14:21	for the w of his Name
	18:39	fell on their faces in awed w

W

	19:10	destroyed the places of **w**		13:10	the Levites to lead us in **w**
	19:14	destroyed your places of **w**		15:11	for a great assembly of **w**
	22:43	continued to pray and **w** at these		19:8	matters that had to do with **w**
2Ki	5:17	never . . . **w** any god other than God		19:11	all cases regarding the **w** of God
	10:24	Then they launched the **w**		20:8	built a holy house of **w** to honor you
	16:12	arranged a service of **w**		20:33	**w** at these idolatrous god shops
	17:12	persistent **w** of gods carved out		24:7	upkeep of the place of **w**
	17:28	taught them how to honor and **w** God		24:14	making sacred vessels for Temple **w**
	17:35	Don't honor other gods: Don't **w** them		28:23	If I **w** the gods who helped Damascus
	17:36	**W** God, the God who delivered you		29:7	canceled all the acts of **w** of the God
	17:37	don't **w** other gods		29:11	serve in conducting and leading **w**
	17:38	don't **w** other gods		29:30	with joy and reverence, kneeling in **w**
	17:39	**W** God, and God only		29:35	**w** in The Temple of God was on a firm
	18:22	You must **w** at the Jerusalem altar		30:8	Come to his Temple of holy **w**
	23:5	round-the-clock **w** of Baal		30:22	led the people in the **w** of God
	25:14	used in the services of Temple **w**		30:24	sheep for the congregation's **w**
1Ch	6:32	ministers of music in the place of **w**		31:2	for conducting the services of **w**
	6:33	by preparing for and directing **w**		31:3	for the morning and evening **w**
	6:48	other work in the place of **w**		31:18	themselves and their gifts to **w**
	9:19	in charge of the services of **w**		31:21	had to do with **w** in God's Temple
	9:23	gates of God's house, the house of **w**		32:12	all the neighborhood **w** shrines
	9:28	the articles used in The Temple **w**		32:23	offerings for the **w** of God
	9:31	the bread for the services of **w**		33:16	restored **w**, sacrificing
	15:2	service in the work of **w**		35:2	in the work of leading **w**
	15:26	they paused to **w** by sacrificing		35:3	guiding Israel in all matters of **w**
	16:2	David had completed the offerings of **w**		35:10	complete for the service of **w**
	16:4	to the Chest of God to lead **w**		35:16	went without a hitch in the **w**
	16:7	inaugurated regular **w** of praise to God		36:23	build him a Temple of **w** at Jerusalem
	16:37	in charge of the work of **w**	Ezr	1:2	build him a Temple of **w** in Jerusalem
	16:40	services of morning and evening **w**		4:2	We **w** your God the same as you
	21:29	set up at the **w** center at Gibeon		6:9	Whatever is required for their **w**
	22:1	this is the site for the **w** of God		7:19	given to you for the services of **w**
	22:19	build the sacred house of **w** to God	Ne	8:6	fell to their knees in **w** of God
	23:4	administering **w** in the sanctuary		9:6	heaven's angels **w** you
	23:24	work groups that took care of the **w**		11:22	singers who led **w** in The Temple of God
	23:26	furniture required for the work of **w**		12:9	opposite them in the services of **w**
	23:28	assist Aaron's sons in the work of **w**		12:45	conducted the **w** of their God
	23:32	companions in the ministry of holy **w**		13:5	incense, **w** vessels, and the tithes
	25:1	David and the **w** leaders selected		13:9	Only then did I put back the **w** vessels
	25:6	musical accompaniment in the work of **w**		13:10	singers who led the services of **w**
	26:27	to the work of the **w** of God		13:14	done for The Temple of God and its **w**
	26:29	affairs outside the work of **w**	Job	31:24	making big money or **w** at the bank
	26:30	matters related to the **w** of God		37:24	If you're wise, you'll . . . **w** him
	26:32	matters related to the **w** of God	Ps	2:11	**W** God in adoring embrace
	28:13	ordering **w** in the house of God		22:22	tell my friends when they come to **w**
	28:14	article used in the services of **w**		22:25	Here in this great gathering for **w**
	28:20	conducting the **w** of God		31:19	piled up for those who **w** you
	29:3	making this place of **w** for my God		34:9	**W** God if you want the best
	29:16	building a house of **w** for you		34:9	**w** opens doors to all his goodness
	29:21	offered in the **w** of Israel to God		34:11	I'll give you a lesson in God **w**
2Ch	1:3	went to the **w** center at Gibeon		35:18	when everyone gathers for **w**
	1:13	Solomon left the **w** center at Gibeon		43:4	To enter the place of **w**
	2:1	begin construction on the house of **w**		50:8	don't find fault with your acts of **w**
	2:4	build a house of **w** in honor of God		51:17	I learned God-**w** when my pride
	5:5	sacred things in the Tent used in **w**		51:19	real **w** from us, acts of **w**
	5:12	dressed in their **w** robes		52:6	Good people will watch and **w**
	7:12	a temple for sacrifice, a house of **w**		54:6	I'm ready now to **w**, so ready
	8:13	schedule of **w** set down by Moses		63:2	here I am in the place of **w**
	8:14	priests carrying out the work of **w**		65:8	take turns calling, "Come and **w**
	9:4	the elaborate **w** extravagant with		72:11	All kings will fall down and **w**
	11:15	priests to preside over the **w** centers		74:4	While your people were at **w**
	11:16	to Jerusalem to **w** there		74:7	violated the place of **w**

W

74:8	burned down all the places of **w**	18:15	have left me to **w** the Big Lie
81:9	don't **w** the latest in gods	26:2	come from all over Judah to **w**
84:3	their songs in the place where we **w**	32:29	the **w** of who knows how many other gods
84:10	your house, this beautiful place of **w**	33:18	the sacrificial **w** in my honor
86:11	undivided, I'll **w** in joyful fear	41:5	on their way to **w** at the Temple
95:6	let us **w**: bow before him	44:3	**w** the latest in gods — no-gods
96:2	Sing to God — **w** God!	52:18	used in the services of Temple **w**
96:9	Then to your knees — everyone **w**	Eze 8:16	bowing in **w** to the sun
97:7	On your knees, all you gods — **w** him	18:6	doesn't **w** the idols so popular
99:5	Honor God, our God; **w** his rule!	18:15	doesn't **w** the popular idols
99:9	God, our God; **w** at his holy mountain	20:32	**w** gods we can make and control
100:4	Thank him. **W** him	20:40	entire people of Israel will **w** me
102:15	see your glory, **w** your name	28:18	defiled your holy places of **w**
102:22	along with their rulers to **w** him	33:25	you **w** no-god idols
116:19	In the place of **w**, in God's house	37:26	my holy place of **w** at the center
122:3	built as a place for **w**	37:28	my holy place of **w** is established
122:4	all God's tribes go up to **w**	43:8	set up their **w** shrines
132:7	Let's **w** at God's own footstool	44:4	I fell on my face in **w**
138:2	kneel in **w** facing your holy temple	44:15	offering the solemn sacrifices of **w**
139:14	I **w** in adoration — what a creation	44:29	Everything . . . offered to God in **w**
147:12	**w** God! Zion, praise your God	44:30	All that is given in **w** to God
150:1	Praise God in his holy house of **w**	45:4	those who lead **w** in the Sanctuary
Ecc 3:14	simply **w** in holy fear	45:5	administer the affairs of **w**
Isa 1:12	commotion in the place provided for **w**	46:3	the people are to **w** before God
1:13	Quit your **w** charades	46:9	come to **w** God at the commanded feasts
2:8	their own gods and **w** what they make	Da 3:5	and **w** the gold statue
19:19	there will be a place of **w** to God	3:6	Anyone who does not kneel and **w**
19:21	**w** him seriously with sacrifices	3:10	and **w** the gold statue
19:23	No longer rivals, they'll **w** together	3:11	whoever did not . . . **w** it
27:13	come and **w** God on the holy mountain	3:12	won't **w** the gold statue you set up
29:23	In holy **w** they'll honor the Holy One	3:14	refuse to **w** the gold statue
33:20	Centering our **w** in festival feasts	3:15	**w** the statue I have made
36:7	gotten rid of all the places of **w**	3:18	wouldn't serve your gods or **w**
36:7	telling you, "You've got to **w** at	3:28	serve or **w** any god but their own
40:16	adequate fuel and offerings for his **w**	7:25	try to get rid of sacred **w**
43:23	bring sheep for offerings in **w**	8:11	it threw out daily **w**
44:17	a handy, convenient no-god to **w**	8:12	same treatment as the daily **w**
46:6	delivers the god, and they kneel and **w**	8:13	the abolishing of daily **w**
52:11	Purify yourselves in the process of **w**	9:21	about the time of evening **w**
56:7	welcome to **w** the same as the 'insiders	9:27	he will banish **w** and prayers
57:6	Your **w** will be your doom	9:27	At the place of **w**, a
57:8	made your bed your place of **w**	11:31	They'll throw out the daily **w**
58:2	They're busy, busy, busy at **w**	12:11	daily **w** is banished from the Temple
60:7	Welcome gifts for **w** at my altar	Hos 2:13	all that sensuous Baal **w**
60:10	kings assist you in the conduct of **w**	4:13	They **w** on the tops of mountains
65:7	practiced their blasphemous **w**	4:14	men who **w** at the holy whorehouses
66:3	Your acts of **w** are acts of sin	4:19	sex-**w** leaves them finally impotent
66:20	offer them in living **w** to God	9:4	you won't have much chance to **w** God
66:23	everyone will come to **w** me	9:5	Will you miss festival **w** of God
Jer 6:20	sacrifices in **w** give me no pleasure	10:1	the more promiscuous the **w**
7:2	who come through these gates to **w** God	10:2	God will smash their **w** shrines
7:9	tell lies nonstop, **w** the local gods	10:5	travel . . . to **w** the golden calf-god
7:10	this Temple, set apart for my **w**	12:11	expose their **w** centers as stinking
7:11	this Temple, set apart for my **w**	13:1	convicted in the lewd sex-**w** of Baal
7:14	this Temple, set aside for my **w**	Joel 1:9	**w** has been brought to a standstill
8:2	like a congregation at **w**	1:13	lead people in **w**, lead them in lament
11:10	go after other gods and **w** them	Am 3:14	pay for the sin-altars of **w**
11:15	And right in the house of **w**!	4:4	Bring your sacrifices for morning **w**
11:17	your continuous **w** and offerings	5:25	Didn't you . . . **w** me faithfully
13:10	all kinds of no-gods and **w** them	Jnh 1:9	He told them, "I'm a Hebrew. I **w** God
16:13	You can **w** your precious no-gods	2:8	Those who **w** hollow gods, god-frauds
17:26	They'll come to **w**, bringing all kinds	Na 1:15	Celebrate! **W** and recommit to God!

W

Zep	1:5	to w the star gods and goddesses
	2:11	will fall to the ground and w him
	3:9	Words to address God in w
	3:10	will come home with offerings for w
Zec	14:16	travel to Jerusalem every year to w
	14:17	annual pilgrimage to Jerusalem to w
	14:18	don't make the pilgrimage and w
	14:21	People who come to w, preparing meals
Mal	1:6	By your shoddy, sloppy, defiling w
	1:7	w of God is no longer a priority
	1:8	worthless animals for sacrifices in w
	1:10	this silly, empty-headed w
	1:11	people who know how to w me all over
	1:12	W is not important
	2:2	me, God-of-the-Angel-Armies, in w
	2:11	women who w alien gods
	2:13	fill the place of w with your whining
Mt	2:2	We're on pilgrimage to w him
	2:8	I'll join you at once in your w
	4:9	go down on your knees and w me
	4:10	W the Lord your God, and only him
	5:23	If you enter your place of w
	6:24	You can't w two gods at once
	6:25	decide for God, living a life of God-w
	23:20	promise inside or outside a house of w
Mk	5:6	ran and bowed in w before him
	15:19	spit on him, and knelt down in mock w
Lk	1:74	So we can w him without a care
	4:7	W me and they're yours, the whole
	4:8	W the Lord your God and only the Lord
	13:1	killed while they were at w
	24:5	awestruck and bowed down in w
Jn	4:21	will w the Father neither here
	4:22	You w guessing in the dark; we Jews w
	4:23	where you go to w will not matter
	4:24	Those who w him must do it out of
	12:20	who had come up to w at the Feast
Ac	2:46	followed a daily discipline of w
	7:7	so they can w me in this place
	7:42	w every new god that came down
	7:44	a tent shrine for true w
	7:46	asked God for a permanent place for w
	17:23	so you can w intelligently
	18:13	acts of w that are illegal
	20:7	to w and celebrate the Master's Supper
	24:14	serve and w the very same God
Ro	1:9	God, whom I so love to w and serve
	1:21	refusing to w him, they trivialized
	9:4	revelation, w, promises
1Co	11:6	women wearing head coverings in w
	11:20	you bring your divisions to w
	14:19	when I'm in a church assembled for w
	14:26	When you gather for w, each one
	14:33	When we w the right way, God doesn't
	14:34	Wives must not disrupt w
	14:35	the time of w for unwarranted speaking
2Co	7:1	lives fit and holy temples for the w
Gal	1:24	response was to recognize and w God
Php	2:10	will bow in w before this Jesus Christ
Col	2:16	details of diet, w services, or holy
2Ti	1:3	God I w with my whole life
Heb	1:6	All angels must w him

	2:12	I'll join them in w and praise to you
	8:2	conducting w in the one true sanctuary
	9:1	plan contained directions for w
	9:21	did the same thing with the place of w
	12:28	brimming with w, deeply reverent
	13:16	particular pleasure in acts of w
Jude	1:12	warts on your love feasts as you w
Rev	4:2	I was caught up at once in deep w
	13:8	will w the Beast
	13:12	everyone in it w the first Beast
	14:7	W the Maker of Heaven and earth
	14:11	No respite for those who w the Beast
	15:4	all nations will come and w you
	19:10	I fell at his feet to w him
	20:4	refused to w either the Beast
	22:8	fell on my face to w at the feet
	22:9	keep the words of this book. W God

Worshiped

Ge	21:33	w God there, praying to the Eternal
	31:54	w, calling in all his family
	46:1	He arrived at Beersheba and w
Ex	4:31	They bowed low and they w
	12:27	The people bowed and w
	32:8	They made a molten calf and w it
	34:8	Moses fell to the ground and w
Nu	25:2	ate together and then w their gods
Dt	14:25	place God . . . has chosen to be w
	16:2	at the place God chooses to be w
	16:11	your God, will set aside to be w
	29:26	they went off and w other gods
Jos	5:14	fell, face to the ground, and w
	24:2	They w other gods
	24:14	Get rid of the gods your ancestors w
	24:15	the gods your ancestors w
Jdg	2:7	The people w God throughout
	2:12	They actually w them!
	2:13	they w god Baal and goddess Astarte
	2:17	to other gods—w them
	3:6	And they w their gods
	3:7	forgot their God and w the Baal gods
	10:6	They w the Baal gods
	10:10	We left our God and w the Baal gods
	10:16	w only God
1Sa	1:19	Up before dawn, they w God
	1:28	Then and there, they w God
	6:15	everyone . . . w God most heartily
	11:15	there they w, sacrificing
	12:10	left God and w the fertility gods
	15:31	went to his knees before God and w
	28:14	fell down, face to the ground, and w
2Sa	6:17	Then and there David w
	12:20	went into the sanctuary and w
	15:32	the hill where God was w
1Ki	1:47	On his death bed the king w God
	3:3	he also w at the local shrines
	3:15	w by sacrificing Whole-Burnt-Offerings
	8:62	king and all Israel with him then w
	9:25	Solomon w at the Altar of God
2Ki	17:16	They w cosmic forces—sky gods
	17:25	they neither honored nor w him

	17:32	**w** God, but not exclusively
	17:33	They honored and **w** God, but
	21:3	He **w** the cosmic powers
1Ch	13:8	David and all Israel **w** exuberantly
	16:1	they **w** by presenting burnt offerings
	29:20	**w** reverently in the presence of God
2Ch	1:6	Solomon **w** God at the Bronze Altar
	7:3	bowed their heads, and **w**
	7:4	all Israel **w**, offering sacrifices
	7:5	King Solomon **w** by sacrificing
	29:28	while the entire congregation **w**
	29:29	knelt to the ground and **w**
	31:2	wherever and whenever God was **w**
	33:3	**w** the cosmic powers
	33:19	idolatrous images that he **w**
	34:4	graves of those who had **w** at them
Ne	9:3	they confessed and **w** their God
Job	1:20	then fell to the ground and **w**
	31:27	seduced by them and **w** them on the sly
Ps	106:19	and **w** the statue they'd made
	106:36	They **w** their idols
	130:4	that's why you're **w**
Isa	2:20	to look like gods and then **w**
	63:17	we no longer **w** you in awe
Jer	10:7	It's your very nature to be **w**!
	16:11	the no-gods, **w** and doted on them
	22:9	took up with other gods and **w** them
Eze	8:10	gods and goddesses — being **w** by Israel
Da	3:7	**w** the gold statue
	6:26	Daniel's God shall be **w** and feared
	11:38	in the place where God is **w**
Hos	11:2	He **w** the popular sex gods
	12:9	old days when you **w** in the wilderness
Jnh	1:16	They **w** God, offered a sacrifice
Mic	1:7	sticks and stones she **w** as gods
Mt	2:11	they kneeled and **w** him
	14:33	**w** Jesus, saying, " . . . You are God
	28:9	embraced his feet, and **w** him
	28:17	The moment they saw him they **w** him
Jn	4:20	Our ancestors **w** God at this mountain
	9:38	I believe," the man said, and **w** him
Ac	24:14	worship the very same God served and **w**
Ro	1:25	a fake god, and **w** the god they made
	15:20	where Jesus was not yet known and **w**
1Co	8:5	these so-called gods are named and **w**
Rev	4:10	They **w** the age-after-age Living One
	5:8	Elders fell down and **w** the Lab
	5:14	The Elders fell to their knees and **w**
	7:11	faces before the Throne and **w** God
	11:16	fell to their knees, **w**
	13:4	They **w** the Dragon
	16:2	the Beast and **w** its image
	19:4	Animals fell to their knees and **w** God
	19:20	mark of the Beast and **w** his image

Worshiper

2Ki	10:21	every **w** of Baal in the country

Worshipers

2Ki	10:19	destroy all the **w** of Baal

	10:23	there are no **w** of God in here
Ps	22:23	Shout Hallelujah, you God-**w**
	22:25	right here in front of the God-**w**
	25:12	What are God-**w** like?
	25:14	God-friendship is for God-**w**
	132:9	prompt your **w** to sing this prayer
Ecc	9:2	the nice and the nasty, **w** and non-**w**
Isa	44:11	Watch all the no-god **w** hide
Jer	10:14	Stick-god **w** looking mighty foolish
	48:46	You **w** of Chemosh will be finished
	51:17	Stick-god **w** look mighty foolish
Hos	6:9	gangs of priests Assaulting **w**
Heb	10:2	**w** would have gone merrily on their way

Worshipful

Isa	25:3	brutal oppressors bow in **w** reverence
Lk	7:16	They were quietly **w**

Worshipfully

Ac	10:2	to live **w** before God
Heb	11:21	as he bowed **w** upon his staff

Worshiping

Ge	4:26	began praying and **w** in the name of God
Ex	23:33	get you to sin by **w** their gods
Dt	4:19	be seduced into **w** and serving them
	7:4	they'd involve you in **w** their gods
	8:19	other gods, serving and **w** them
	11:16	end up serving and **w** other gods
	12:30	was like for them, **w** their gods
	28:14	following and **w** other gods
	31:20	with other gods and **w** them
Jos	22:25	cause our children to quit **w** God
Jdg	2:19	other gods, serving and **w** them
	10:6	walked off and left God, quit **w** him
	10:13	betrayed me, **w** other gods
1Ki	3:2	the people were **w** at local shrines
	8:5	there at the Chest **w** and sacrificing
	9:6	alien gods by serving and **w** them
	9:9	took up with alien gods, **w** and serving
	11:33	went off **w** Ashtoreth goddess
	16:31	serving and **w** the god Baal
	22:53	**W** at the Baal shrines, he made God
2Ki	5:18	with him there, **w** Rimmon
	17:34	still doing it, still **w** any old god
	17:41	putting on a front of **w** God
	19:37	**w** in the temple of his god Nisroch
	21:21	serving and **w** the same foul gods
	23:4	made for **w** Baal and Asherah
1Ch	9:13	servants in the work of **w** God
2Ch	5:6	before the Chest, **w** and sacrificing
	7:19	alien gods by serving and **w** them
	7:22	took up with alien gods, **w** and serving
	20:18	Jerusalem did the same, **w** God
	25:14	installed them as his own gods, **w** them
	28:2	figurines for **w** the pagan Baal gods
	28:25	shrines for **w** any and every god
	34:33	serving and **w** their God
Ps	22:29	power-mongers are before him — **w**

W

	42:4	always at the head of the **w** crowd
Isa	29:13	act like they're **w** me but don't mean
	37:38	was **w** in the sanctuary of his god
Jer	1:16	**w** as gods sticks they'd carved
	19:4	this place strange by **w** strange gods
	19:13	a center for **w** the star gods
	25:6	taking up and **w** these no-gods
Eze	21:10	by **w** every tree-idol
Hos	6:10	Ephraim **w** in a religious whorehouse
Jnh	2:9	But I'm **w** you, God, calling out
Mic	5:13	**w** what you do or make
Zep	1:5	cover their bases by **w** other king-gods
Mt	15:9	They act like they're **w** me
Mk	7:7	They act like they are **w** me
Lk	2:37	**w** night and day with her fastings
	24:52	they were on their knees, **w** him
Ac	7:43	**W** them with all your might
	10:25	then down on his face **w** him
	13:2	**w** God — they were also fasting
	24:11	express purpose of **w** in Jerusalem
1Co	10:28	messages to him about who you are **w**
Heb	10:25	not avoiding **w** together as some do
Rev	9:20	didn't quit **w** demons
	11:1	God's Temple and Altar and everyone **w**
	13:15	anyone not **w** the Beast would be killed
	22:3	will offer God service — **w**

Worships

2Ki	5:18	shrine of Rimmon and **w** there
Ps	40:4	ignore what the world **w**
	66:4	it **w** you, sings to you
Isa	44:15	he makes a god that he **w** — carves it
Eze	46:2	while he **w** there on the porch
Hab	1:16	fishing gear on an altar and **w** it
Ac	19:27	the whole world **w** our Artemis
Rev	14:9	If anyone **w** the Beast and its image

Wound

Ge	3:15	He'll **w** your head, you'll **w** his heel
Ex	21:25	burn for burn, **w** for **w**
Dt	32:39	I **w** and I heal
1Ki	20:35	Hit me; **w** me. Do it for God's sake
	20:37	Hit me; **w** me." That man did it
	22:35	Blood from his **w** pooled in the chariot
Job	5:18	he wounds, but he also dresses the **w**
Ps	77:2	life was an open **w** that wouldn't heal
Pr	5:4	a pain in your gut, a **w** in your heart
	15:4	cutting words **w** and maim
Isa	19:22	God will **w** Egypt
Jer	15:18	this ever worsening **w** and no healing
	51:8	Get anointing balm for her **w**
Na	3:19	Your **w** is fatal

Wounded

Jdg	9:40	turned tail and ran. Many fell **w**
1Sa	17:53	**W** Philistines were strewn along
	31:1	Philistines . . . **w** on Mount Gilboa
	31:3	got his range and **w** him badly
2Sa	1:6	Saul, badly **w** and leaning on his spear

	10:18	he mortally **w** Shobach
1Ki	22:34	Get me out of here — I'm **w**
2Ki	8:28	The archers **w** Joram
	9:27	shot and **w** him in his chariot
1Ch	10:3	Saul—the archers found him and **w** him
2Ch	18:33	Get me out of here—I'm **w**
	22:5	Joram, **w** by the Arameans
	24:25	They left Joash badly **w**
	35:23	Get me out of here — I'm badly **w**
Ps	69:26	Made up stories about anyone **w** by God
Jer	10:19	Hopelessly **w**, I said
	14:17	hopelessly and cruelly **w**
	37:10	a few **w** soldiers in their tents
	51:4	Babylon littered with the **w**
	51:52	all over this land her **w** will groan
Eze	26:15	at the groans of your **w**
	30:24	groan like one who is mortally **w**
Mic	1:9	has been **w** with no healing in sight
Zec	12:10	the One they so grievously **w**

Wounding

| Ge | 4:23 | I killed a man for **w** me |

Wounds

2Ch	22:6	to recover from the **w** he received
Job	5:18	he **w**, but he also dresses the wound
Ps	147:3	heartbroken and bandages their **w**
Pr	25:20	like pouring salt in their **w**
	27:6	The **w** from a lover are worth it
Isa	1:6	**W** and bruises and running sores
	30:26	God heals his people of the **w**
	42:22	Victims licking their **w**
Jer	30:15	all this self-pity, licking your **w**
La	4:9	Better to have died of battle **w**
Mic	1:9	God has inflicted punishing **w**
Lk	10:34	disinfecting and bandaging his **w**
Ac	16:33	feel at home, dressed their **w**
1Pe	2:24	His **w** became your healing

Wrath

Ge	49:7	on their indiscriminate **w**
Nu	1:53	that **w** will not fall on the community
2Ch	12:7	to express my **w** against Jerusalem
	19:10	going to be dealing with God's **w**
	25:15	a fiery blast of God's **w**
Ezr	7:23	risk stirring up his **w**
Ne	13:18	accumulating more **w** on Jerusalem
Job	20:28	nothing surviving God's **w**
	21:20	the full force of God's **w** firsthand
Ps	37:8	Bridle your anger, trash your **w**
	78:38	restrained his considerable **w**
	110:5	crushing kings in his terrible **w**
Isa	10:5	My **w** is a cudgel in his hands
	13:5	God . . . with the weapons of his **w**
	13:9	a day of **w** and anger
	13:13	earth quake to its roots Under the **w**
	26:20	until the punishing **w** is past
	63:6	crushed them under foot in my **w**
Jer	6:11	I'm bursting with the **w** of God

	25:15	this cup filled with the wine of my w
	42:18	away with my anger and w
	44:6	a firestorm of w in the cities
	48:26	drunk on the wine of my w
	49:12	have to drink the cup of God's w
	50:25	I brought out my weapons of w
La	2:22	on the big day of God's w no one
	4:11	He poured out his raging w
	4:21	what it's like to drink God's w
	4:21	Get drunk on God's w and wake up
Eze	7:8	Soon now I'll pour my w on you
	7:12	Judgment w has turned the world
	7:14	My w has them paralyzed
	13:13	let the hurricane of my w loose
	13:15	I'll dump my w on that wall
	16:38	I'll give you a taste of my w
	21:31	I'll empty out my w on you
	22:20	in my w I'll gather you and melt
	22:21	the fire of my w to melt you down
	22:22	I, God, have let my w loose on you
	22:31	So I'll empty out my w on them
	24:8	provoke my w, to trigger my vengeance
	25:14	My w will fuel their action
	30:15	Pour my w on Pelusium
Da	8:19	as the judgment days of w wind down
Ob	1:16	godless nations will drink God's w
Hab	2:16	drinking from the cup of God's w
Zep	1:18	the Day of God's Judgment— my w!
	2:2	Before God's Judgment Day w descends
	3:8	the brunt of my anger, my raging w
Rev	6:16	the w of the Lab
	6:17	The great Day of their w has come
	14:10	drink the wine of God's w
	14:19	the giant winepress of God's w
	15:1	the wrap-up of God's w
	15:7	bowls, brimming with the w of God
	16:1	Pour out the seven bowls of God's w
	19:15	winepress of the raging w of God

Wrathful

Da	11:36	this time of w judgment is completed

Wrongdoing

Ge	50:17	Forgive your brothers . . . all that w
Lev	5:1	cases of w, you'll be held responsible
Nu	14:19	Please forgive the w of this people
	15:31	ostracized, left alone in his w
1Sa	22:15	don't accuse me of any w
Pr	4:19	the road of w gets darker
	14:11	Lives of careless w are tumbledown
	16:12	Good leaders abhor w of all kinds
Isa	64:9	Don't keep a permanent account of w
Mic	7:19	You'll stamp out our w
Ac	28:19	not to accuse them of any w or to get
Ro	1:18	as acts of . . . w and lying accumulate
	3:5	if our w only underlines and confirms
	5:17	upper hand through one man's w
1Jn	1:9	forgive our sins and purge us of all w

Wrongdoings

Ps	130:3	If you, God, kept records on w
Isa	44:22	I've wiped the slate of all your w
	59:12	Our w pile up before you, God

Wronged

Nu	5:7	must be made to whoever was w
	5:8	If the w person has no close relative
Jdg	11:27	No, I haven't w you
1Sa	19:4	He hasn't w you, has he?
Ps	59:4	crossed no one, w no one
	146:7	defends the w, he feeds the hungry
1Co	6:1	When you think you have been w
	6:7	let yourselves be w and forget it
2Co	7:12	who did the wrong or even the one w

Wrongful

Dt	19:13	Clean out the pollution of w murder
Ps	125:3	provoking w violence

Wrongheaded

Isa	59:2	Your w lives caused the split
Jer	16:21	I'm going to teach these w people

Υ

Yell

Dt	22:24	she didn't y out for help in the town
Jdg	18:25	Don't y at us; you just might provoke
1Sa	20:21	If I y after the servant
	20:22	if I y, 'The arrows are farther out
Ps	56:9	turn tail when I y at them
	77:1	I y out to my God
	77:1	I y with all my might
	77:1	I y at the top of
Isa	13:2	Y loud. Get their attention.
	57:11	Because I don't y and make a scene
La	4:15	People y at them, "Get out of here
Eze	6:11	y out, "No, no, no!"
	21:12	Y out and wail, son of man
Hab	1:2	How many times do I have to y, "Help
Mt	5:22	Thoughtlessly y 'stupid!' at a sister
	12:19	he won't y, won't raise his voice
Jn	10:36	why do you y, 'Blasphemer! Blasphemer
Jas	4:7	Y a loud no to the Devil

Yelled

Ge	19:5	They y to Lot, "Where are the men
	38:24	Judah y, "Get her out here.
	39:14	but I y as loud as I could
	39:18	When I y and screamed
Dt	22:27	when the engaged girl y out for help
Jdg	7:21	They y and fled
	19:22	They y for the owner of the house
1Sa	14:12	they y down to Jonathan
	20:37	Jonathan y out, "Isan't the arrow

Y

	20:38	He y again, "Hurry! Quickly!
2Sa	22:42	y for God and got no for an answer
1Ki	22:32	Jehoshaphat y out
2Ch	18:31	Jehoshaphat y out
Ps	18:41	y for God and got no for an answer
	30:2	God, my God, I y for help
	137:7	That day they y out, "Wreck it
Da	5:7	He y out for the enchanters
Jnh	4:2	He y at God
Mt	25:6	someone y out, 'He's here!
	27:23	they y all the louder
Mk	10:48	he y all the louder
	14:63	Ripping his clothes, he y
	15:13	They y, "Nail him to a cross
	15:14	they y all the louder
Lk	18:38	He y, "Jesus! Son of David!
	18:39	he only y all the louder
Jn	1:29	saw Jesus coming toward him and y out
Ro	9:26	they y out, "You're nobody!"
Rev	13:6	It y blasphemies against God

Yelling

Ge	39:15	With all my y and screaming
Jdg	20:39	on their way to victory, y out
1Ki	13:4	grab him, y, "Arrest him!"
2Ki	9:23	fled, y to Ahaziah
	9:27	chased him, y out, "Get him, too!"
Ps	6:1	Please, God, no more y
Jer	26:8	grabbed him, y, "Death!
Mt	26:65	y, "He blasphemed!
Mk	1:23	man who was deeply disturbed and y out
Ac	7:57	Y and hissing, the mob drowned him
	16:17	everyone's attention to us by y
	17:6	y hysterically, "These people
	19:28	ran into the street y
	19:32	Some were y one thing, some another
	21:28	started y at the top of their lungs
	21:34	one y this, another that

Yield

Lev	25:19	The land will y its fruit
	25:21	land will y enough for three years
	26:4	ground will y its crops
Isa	5:2	a vintage y of grapes

Yoke

Dt	21:3	never had a y on it
	28:48	he'll put an iron y on your neck
1Sa	11:7	He grabbed the y of oxen
1Ki	19:21	took his y of oxen and butchered them
Isa	10:27	the y of slavery lifted from your neck
Jer	27:2	Make a harness and a y
	27:8	must take the y of the king of Babylon
	27:11	accepts the y of the king of Babylon
	27:12	the y of the king
	28:2	break the y of the king of Babylon
	28:4	I will break the king of Babylon's y
	28:10	the y from Jeremiah's shoulders
	28:11	smash the y of the king of Babylon

	28:12	smashed the y from off his shoulders
	28:13	y-bars; now you've got iron y-bars
	28:14	an iron y on all these nations
	30:8	I'll break the y from their necks
La	1:14	harnessed me to captivity's y
Na	1:13	I'm taking the y from your neck

Youth

Nu	11:28	Moses' right-hand man since his y
1Sa	12:2	led you faithfully from my y
	17:56	find out the lineage of this raw y
2Ki	8:12	murder their y, smash their babies
Job	13:26	accountable for the sins of my y
Ps	71:17	got me when I was an unformed y, God
	103:5	He renews your y
	109:23	passing away, my y gone
	110:3	join you with all the vigor of y
	127:4	the children of a vigorous y
Pr	20:29	Y may be admired for vigor
Ecc	4:14	I saw a y just like this
	11:9	make the most of your y
	11:10	Y lasts about as long as smoke
Isa	54:4	all about the humiliations of your y
Jer	6:11	Let it loose on the gangs of y
Eze	4:14	Since my y I've never eaten
	23:21	sexual prowess of her y
Am	2:11	set aside your best y for training
	2:12	made the y-in-training break training
Mk	10:20	I have — from my y — kept them all
Ac	26:4	time of my y, my life has been lived

Youthful

Job	15:27	picture of health, trim and fit and y
	20:11	y and vigorous, they'll die
Ecc	11:9	Relish your y vigor
Jer	2:2	I remember your y loyalty

Z

Zeal

2Ki	10:16	witness my z for God
	19:31	The Z of God will make it happen
Pr	19:2	Ignorant z is worthless
Isa	9:7	The z of God-of-the-Angel-Armies
	37:32	The z of God-of-the-Angel-Armies
Zep	3:8	My z is a fire that will purge
Jn	2:17	Z for your house consumes me

Zealot

| Lk | 6:15 | Simon, called the Z |
| Ac | 1:13 | Simon the Z, Judas, son of James |

Zealous

Nu	25:11	was as z for my honor as I myself
	25:13	he was z for his God
Isa	26:11	see your z love for your people
Eze	39:25	I'll be z for my holy name
Zec	8:2	I am z for Zion—I care!
Ac	21:20	more z than ever in observing the laws

Synonyms Used in *The Message*

Synonyms of familiar words used in other translations of the Bible

Other Versions	*The Message*
	A
Abide	Stay, invited, set, spend the night, stick it out, survive, have a good and safe home, be content, abide, live, make yourselves at home
Afflict	Mistreat, detriment, humble, grow weak, afflict, bringing pain and trouble on, treat anyone unfairly, puts them in their place, harass
Adultery	Adultery, to bed with another's spouse, sex and religion games
Anger/Rage	Seethe, furious, anger, flaring tempers, bad temper, blind rage
	B
Beautiful	Attractive, bright-eyed, good-looking, beautiful, breathtaking, Sunday best, wonderfully significant
Blameless	Free, no longer responsible, not held against them, blameless, a clear conscience before God, steady and on track, uncorrupted, fit for, well-thought-of, peace, holy
Believe	Accept, believe, trust
Body	Corpse, body, person, skin, way you conduct your life
Born-again	Born from above, God-begotten
Bread	Bread, food, supper, square meals
	C
Christ	Messiah, Christ
Compassion	Heart went out to, thinking about me, tender and kind, mercy, compassion, take them tenderly to my heart, pity, hurt for, deeply moved, go easy on
Confess	Tell the truth, say out loud, confess, come out in the open
Condemn	Incriminate, condemn, verdict of guilty, dismissed, point an accusing finger, debilitating self-criticism, finding fault
Conversion	Conversion, breakthrough to the Gentile outsiders, Master gave her a trusting heart
Covenant	Covenant, do what he said he'd do, my commitment to my people, plan

Other Versions	*The Message*
Counsel	Direction, talked to, counsel, how to live
Cross	All the way with me, cross

D

Darkness	Inky blackness, darkness, abyss, storm clouds, a dank cellar, out in the cold, private, dead-end alleys, black hole in hell, sudden eclipse
Death	Destruction, death, a real killer, your last free act, Death Valley
Deceive	Spy on, tease, fool, deceive, behind their backs, dupe, get taken in, lies, kid yourselves
Desire	Covet, interest, exactly what he wanted, longings, all I want, desire, desperately homesick, like very much, give yourselves, prefer, decide
Destroy	Get rid of, destroy, making a clean sweep, kill, step on me-squash me like a bug, skinned alive, wreck, smash them to smithereens, take apart
Devil	Evil tormenting spirit, afflicting demon, devil
Discern	Look around, identify, discern, distinguish, tell, know, forecast, see, figure out, use your head
Disciple	Student, harvest hands, true apprentice, disciple, follower
Doubt	Jeopardy, what got into you, shuffling, shilly-shallying, keep us guessing, couldn't make head or tail of any of it, a second thought, doubt, hesitate

E

Election	God's grace and purpose, chosen ones of God, long-range perspective of God's purpose, his hand on you for something special, his choice of you
Envy	Jealous anger, runaway emotions, envy, jealousy, hate-bloated anger, sheer spite, step right into the spotlight, going around with a chip on our shoulder, want what it doesn't have
Eternal Life	Eternal reward, whole and lasting life, eternal life, will live always, real life, a life that goes on and on and on, life without end, infinite Life of God, the unending life
Everlasting	Eternal, forever, permanent, everlasting, ancient, perpetual, guaranteed, always, never quit, kingdom come

Other Versions	The Message
Evil	Terrible thing, bad, vicious, evil, hard, wrong, up to no good, doom, the worst, make things worse

F

Faith	Right standing before God, simple trust, bold belief, faith, what you believe, confident in the Holy Spirit's ways, Jesus-setting-things-right, personal trust, the promises that keep us going, trust in God
Fear	Be afraid of, awe, hesitate, fear, be intimidated, be bluffed, scared, be upset, reverence, worship
Flesh	Life itself, soft spot, skin, flesh, people, everything living, a part of you, a body you can look at and touch, trying to get your own way all the time, our own efforts
Follow	Run after, chase after, follow, are serious, go on the hunt for, come with, go after, live, fool around with, keeping up the traditions
Fool	Bilious and bloated, empty-head, moral dunce, fool, a real clown
Forgiveness	Forgiveness, free of punishments and penalties chalked up by all our misdeeds, got us out of the pit we were in
Forsake	Abandon, give up on, forsake, leave, walk out on, ignoring my guidance and judgments, throw me out, let you down

G

Gift	Offering, appropriate expressions of thanks, gift, handouts
Glory	High position, dignity, ablaze in beauty, glory, splendor, royal, Eden's dawn light, beauty of God, dazzling presence
Gluttony	Lush, gluttony
Gospel	Kingdom news, God is on their side, gospel, the Message, good news, Message of God, Message of God's good news, Message of God's salvation, Message of God's powerful plan
Grace	Approval, treat me so kindly, a firm foothold in his holy place, generous inside and out, pure gift, grace, his arms wide open for you

H

Heal	Restore, treat me nice, pick up the pieces, heal, put me back together again, bring health

Other Versions	The Message
Heart	Your life, your inside world, heart, the place you most want to be, everything about me, passion
Hell	Hell, Sheol, the Pit, the dump, torment
Hope	Aspirations, passionate patience, cheerfully expectant, hope, look forward to

I

Iniquity	Sin, iniquity, exposing how bad we are, evil, anything false
Instruction	Written down, advice, a disciplined life, school, instruction, training, what to do, lead them in the way

J

Joy	Laughter, a glad shout, joy, praise, Hosannas, sheer gift, sounds of pleasure, foot-tapping songs, satisfaction
Judgment	The way he works, judgment, justice, haul me into court, critical spirit, to bring everything into the clear light of day, point your fingers at, jump all over them, the consequences
Justice	GOD's right ways, fair and evenhanded, justice, the right, when everything fits
Justification	Set us right with God, grand setting-everything-right, put many in the right

K

Kingdom of God	God-reality, God-initiative, God-provisions, God's kingdom, kingdom of God
Know	Has proof of, tell, find out everything, know, just so it's clear, familiar with, plan to

L

Law	Teachings, instructions, law, revelation, all I've taught you, rule, the Revelation of God, God's Word, law code, strenuous moral striving
Lord	GOD, Master, Lord, the King of Israel, Teacher, Jesus Christ
Love	Love, loving care, best of care
Lust	Wanting your own way, greed, lust, compulsions of selfishness, sexual obsession

Other Versions	The Message

M

Mercy — Immense favor, reached out in kindness, unswervingly loyal, love, mercy, bighearted, grace, compassion, passion

Messiah — Messiah, Anointed Leader

Miracle — Something good and powerful, something spectacular, miracle, sign

O

Obey — Listen, ponder, meditate, obey, do what you tell me to do, practice, beck and call, doing what I've told you, be responsive to

P

Peace — At ease, friendly, joined up with, come to terms with him, whole living, healing, have it all together, peace, harmony, all's well

Perish — Devastated, die, perish, it will be all over, driven out, obliterate, lost, destroyed, long gone, to hell with

Praise — Make music, punctuate with Hallelujahs, praise, thank and enjoy, approval, bless

Pride — Full of hot air, stuck-up, pride, bloated by arrogance, standing out

R

Redeem — Keep, give your people a break, snatches, get you out, redeem, deliver, free

Rejoice — Celebrate, dancing, be jubilant, rejoice, raise the roof, sing, be glad, laugh

Remember — Observe, don't forget, remember, mark the milestones, read up on, look on me again

Repentance — Life-change, turns us around, space and time to change, change of heart, repentance

Righteousness — Set-Right-with-God, righteousness, what's right, sound inside and out, Right Living, a God-loyal life, the right direction, God-setting-things-right

S

Sacrifice — Worship, offering, sacrifice, doing something for you, religion, give everything of himself

Other Versions	*The Message*
Sanctify	Consecrate, sanctify, set apart, make them holy, cleanse, keep your hearts at attention, make you holy and whole
Sin	God-avoidance, wrong, evil, sin, give a hard time
Soul	Life, prayer, soul, mind
Stranger	Outsiders, immigrant, foreigner, stranger, a bum off the street, homeless

T

Teach	Confront, school me, teach, train, explain, instruct, take over and tell
Thought	Planned, pondered, thought, trying to figure, entire attention, said
Treasure	A bonus, storage, good things, prize possession, treasure, a rich life, precious Message, riches
Trust	Keep on hoping, get insurance with, take refuge in, have no doubts, trust, depend
Truth	Held nothing back, straight-arrow, truth, sound inside and out, a wonderful answer, endless knowing and understanding, in step with you, what's going on here, true course of obedience

U

Understanding	Intelligent, God-listening, the ability to lead and govern well, what to live for, insight, understanding, the way I see it, reputation for wisdom

V

Vanity	Aimlessness, vanity, lie language, puff of air, weeds, smoke, don't amount to a thing, empty-headed, full of hot air
Voice	Voice, sound, counsel, thunder, cries, torrent, the top of his lungs

W

Walk	Get moving, live, follow, walk, stay on course, when the way goes through, striding, travel, keeps us going, stumble around
Witness	Take it as proof, witness, testimony, show the way to, confirm

Other Versions	*The Message*
Wisdom	Skill, ability, know-how, discernment, wisdom, how to live well, Lady Wisdom, philosophy, proof of the pudding, good sense
World	Home sweet home, us earthlings, earth, world, everything you want, the culture

Unique Phrases in *The Message*

Phrases unique to the writing style used in *The Message Bible*

A

Mt 11:28 [Jesus said,] "Are you tired? Worn out? Burned out on religion?"

Pr 31:10 A good woman is hard to find

Ps 111:7 All his products are guaranteed to last

Ecc 7:9 Anger boomerangs

Jn 4:14 Artesian spring within

Ps 109:22 At the end of my rope
Ps 116:6
Ps 143:7
Ro 7:24

B

Col 3:13 Be even-tempered, content with second place

1Co 3:19 Be God's fool — that's the path to true wisdom

1Jn 5:21 Be on guard against all clever facsimiles

Mt 7:26 But if you just use my words in Bible studies and don't work them into your life

C

Joel 2:13 Change your life, not just your clothes

Job 6:24 Confront me with the truth and I'll shut up, show me where I've gone off the track

Ps 72:16 Cornucopias of praise

D

Mt 23:11 Do you want to stand out? Then step down

Lk 11:10 Don't bargain with God
Mt 7:7

Jos 1:9 Don't be timid; don't get discouraged.

| 1Pe 2:11 | Don't indulge your ego at the expense of your soul |

| Mt 7:13 | Don't look for shortcuts to God |

| Mt 7:1 | Don't pick on people |

E

| Gal 5:26 | Each of us is an original |

| Pr 25:16 | Eat too much chocolate and you'll make yourself sick |

| Mk 11:22 | Embrace this God-life |

| Ps 23:4 | Even when the way goes through Death Valley, I'm not afraid |

| Ps 57:10 | Every cloud is a flag to your faithfulness |

| 1Co 15:14 | Everything we've told you is smoke and mirrors |

F

| Ps 90:2 | From "once upon a time" to "kingdom come" You are God |

| Ps 28:3 | Full-time employees of evil |

G

| Lk 6:38
Mk 4:25
Lk 11:28 | Generosity begets generosity |

| Mt 11:28 | Get away with me and you'll recover your life |

| 1Ki 3:9 | Give me a God-listening heart |

| Ps 46:1 | God is a safe place to hide |

| Ro 2:4 | God is kind, but he's not soft |

| Heb 13:6 | God is there, ready to help |

Ps 18:24   God rewrote the text of my life

Php 4:9   God, who makes everything work together, will work you into his most excellent harmonies

Ps 36:5   God's love is meteoric

Ps 19:9   God's reputation is twenty-four carat gold, with a lifetime guarantee

H

Ps 37:34   He'll give you your place in the sun

Gal 3:2   How did your new life begin? Was it by working your heads off to please God?

Eph 5:25   Husbands, go all out in your love for your wives

I

Am 5:21   I can't stand your religious meetings. I'm fed up with your conferences and conventions

Mk 1:17
Mt 4:19   I'll show you how to catch men and women instead of perch and bass

Ps 22:14   I'm a bucket kicked over and spilled

Rev 22:13   I'm A to Z, the First and the Final, Beginning and Conclusion

Php 4:12   I've found the recipe for being happy

Ac 2:26   I've pitched my tent in the land of hope

Mt 5:47   If all you do is love the loveable, do you expect a bonus?

Mt 5:40
Lk 6:29   If someone drags you into court and sues for the shirt off your back, giftwrap your best coat and make a present of it

Mt 5:39   If someone strikes you, stand there and take it

J

Eph 6:20   Jailbird preacher that I am

K

Mt 6:11   Keep us alive with three square meals

L

Ro 12:15   Laugh with your happy friends when they're happy; share tears when they're down

Jas 1:19   Lead with your ears, follow up with your tongue, and let anger straggle along in the rear

Mt 11:29   Learn the unforced rhythms of grace

Mt 5:13   Let me tell you why you are here

Ecc 1:15   Life's a corkscrew that can't be straightened, A minus that won't add up

Isa 53:12   Looked death in the face and didn't flinch

1Sa 16:7   Looks aren't everything.

Jude 1:13   Lost stars in outer space on their way to the black hole

1Co 13:4   Love doesn't strut

1Jn 2:15   Love of the world squeezes out love for the Father

M

Ge 28:3   May The Strong God bless you

Eph 5:1   Mostly what God does is love you

Jn 1:14   Moved into the neighborhood
Rev 21:3

Ps 42:8   My life is God's prayer

Jer 6:14   My people are broken—shattered!—and they put on band-aids

Ps 119:28   My sad life's dilapidated, a falling-down barn

N

Mt 5:42 Lk 6:30	No more tit-for-tat stuff
Ex 20:3	No other gods, only me
1Sa 15:23	Not doing what GOD tells you is far worse than fooling around in the occult
Mt 6:26	Not tied down to a job description, careless in the care of God

O

2Co 2:14	One perpetual victory parade

P

Ps 89:15	Passwords of praise
Mt 7:4	Playing a holier-than-thou part
Ps 6:1	Please God, no more yelling, no more trips to the woodshed

Q

Isa 1:13	Quit your worship charades

R

1Sa 2:8	Rekindles burned-out lives with fresh hope
Gal 3:12	Rule-keeping does not naturally evolve into living by faith

S

Eze 19:14	Sad song, a text for singing the blues
Jas 1:21	Salvation-garden of your life
Col 2:7	School's out; quit studying the subject and start living it!
Mt 16:25 Mk 8:35 Lk 9:24	Self-help is no help at all

Ecc 1:2	Smoke, nothing but smoke
Ru 1:17	So help me GOD — not even death itself is going to come between us!
1Jn 2:2	Solved the sin problem for good — not only ours, but the whole world's
2Co 1:20	Stamped with the Yes of Jesus
Mt 6:33	Steep your life in God-reality, God-initiative, God-provisions
Mt 6:20	Stockpile treasure in heaven
Jn 2:16	Stop turning my Father's house into a shopping mall!
Ro 15:1	Strength is for service, not status
Col 1:11	Strength to stick it out over the long haul

T

Ro 12:1	Take your everyday, ordinary life — your sleeping, eating, going-to-work, and walking-around life — and place it before God
Eph 5:4	Thanksgiving is our dialect
Jas 2:25	That seamless unity of believing and doing
1Pe 1:4	The future starts now
Isa 8:14	The Holy can either be a Hiding Place or a Boulder blocking your way
1Th 4:18	Then there will be one huge family reunion with the Master
2Co 5:17	The old life is gone; a new life burgeons
Mt 5:22	The simple moral fact is that words kill
Rev 4:8	THE WAS, THE IS, THE COMING
Mt 6:7	The world is full of so-called prayer warriors who are prayer-ignorant
1Jn 4:18	There is no room in love for fear

1Co 6:16	There's more to sex than mere skin on skin
Lk 6:26	There's trouble ahead when you live only for the approval of others
Jer 23:17	They preach their 'Everything Will Turn Out Fine' sermon
2Ti 4:3	They will fill up on spiritual junk food — catchy opinions that tickle their fancy
Lk 11:10 Mt 7:7	This is not a cat-and-mouse, hide-and-seek game we're in
Hos 1:2	This whole country has become a whorehouse, unfaithful to me
Jer 2:5	Took up with Sir Windbag
Pr 3:5	Trust God from the bottom of your heart
Ps 51:8	Tune me in to foot-tapping songs, set these once-broken bones to dancing
Ps 62:9	Two times nothing is nothing

W

Heb 12:16	Watch out for the Esau syndrome
Eph 5:1	Watch what God does, and then you do it
Mt 6:31	What I'm trying to do here is get you to relax
Jas 1:9	When down-and-outers get a break, cheer!
Ro 5:20	When its sin versus grace, grace wins hands down
La 3:28	When life is heavy and hard to take, go off by yourself
1Co 13:10	When the Complete arrives, our incompletes will be canceled
Ps 20:5	When you win, we plan to raise the roof
Ps 24:3	Who can climb Mount God? Who can scale the holy north-face?
Mt 7:16	Who preachers are is the main thing, not what they say

Ro 5:2	Wide open spaces of God's grace and glory
Jn 1:14	Word became flesh and blood, and moved into the neighborhood
Mt 5:45	Working out of your true selves, your God-created selves
Col 2:2	Woven into a tapestry of love

Y

Ecc 7:9	You can spot a fool by the lumps on his head
Mt 5:34	You don't make your words true by embellishing them with religious lace
Jer 2:33	You founded schools of sin, taught graduate courses in evil
Jn 5:39	You have your heads in your Bibles
2Sa 22:28	You take the side of the down-and-out, but the stuck–up you take down a peg
Ps 103:5	You're always young in his presence
Mt 5:9	You're blessed when you can show people how to cooperate instead of compete
Mt 5:5	You're blessed when you're content with just who you are
Zec 7:6	You're interested in religion, I'm interested in people
Mt 6:22	Your eyes are windows into your body
1Sa 25:29	Your God-honored life is tightly bound in the bundle of God-protected life
Mt 5:28	Your heart can be corrupted by lust even quicker than your body
Ps 119: 77	Your revelation is the tune I dance to
Lk 6:26	Your task is to be true, not popular
Ps 119:90	Your truth is never out of fashion